Brief Contents

LIFE SPAN DEVELOPMENT
A Topical Approach

LIFE SPAN DEVELOPMENT
A Topical Approach

Robert S. Feldman

University of Massachusetts, Amherst

Boston   Columbus   Indianapolis   New York   San Francisco   Upper Saddle River
Amsterdam   Cape Town   Dubai   London   Madrid   Milan   Munich   Paris   Montreal   Toronto
Delhi   Mexico City   Sao Paulo   Sydney   Hong Kong   Seoul   Singapore   Taipei   Tokyo

To my family

Editorial Director: Craig Campanella
Editor in Chief: Jessica Mosher
Executive Editor: Jeff Marshall
Associate Editor: LeeAnn Doherty
Editorial Assistant: Courtney Elezovic
VP/Director of Marketing: Brandy Dawson
Marketing Manager: Nicole Kunzmann
Managing Editor: Maureen Richardson
Senior Project Manager/Liaison: Harriet Tellem
Senior Operations Specialist: Sherry Lewis
Text Designer: Laura Gardner
Art Director: Jodi Notowitz
Manager, Visual Research: Beth Brenzel

Photo Research: LeeAnn Doherty and Beth Brenzel
Manager, Rights and Permissions: Zina Arabia
Text Research: Lisa Black
Senior Media Editor: Beth Stoner
Supplements Editor: LeeAnn Doherty
Copy Editor: Betty Pessagno
Proofreader: Donna Mulder
Full-Service Project Management: Preparé Inc./Cécile Billioti de Gage
Composition: Preparé, Inc.
Printer/Binder: Courier Kendallville
Text Font: 10/12 Minion

Credits and acknowledgments borrowed from other sources and reproduced, with permission, in this textbook appear on appropriate page within text (or on page 519).

If you purchased this book within the United States or Canada you should be aware that it has been imported without the approval of the Publisher or the Author.

10 9 8 7 6 5 4 3 2 1

Prentice Hall
is an imprint of

PIE ISBN-10:   0-205-84021-3
PIE ISBN-13: 978-0-205-84021-2

Contents

15 Death and Grieving: The End of Life   434

Life Span Development: A Topical Approach is the outgrowth of conversations and survey data drawing on the thinking of literally hundreds of instructors. These instructors voiced two main challenges in teaching life span development, reaching a surprising degree of consensus. First, almost every instructor acknowledged that the breadth of life span development is so vast that it is difficult to cover the entire field within the confines of a traditional college term. Consequently, many instructors saw most life span development texts as too long. Their students were concerned about the length of the texts and had trouble completing the entire book.

Second, many instructors expressed the concern that traditional, chronologically based life span development books were arranged in a way that made it difficult for students to understand the scope of development within particular topical areas (such as social or personality development across the entire life span) without skipping from one chapter to another.

Life Span Development: A Topical Approach addresses both of these concerns. This book, which is based on the chronologically organized, highly popular ***Development Across the Life Span,*** is shorter than traditional life span books, and it is arranged in a way that helps students to see the "big picture" of development across the entre life span within a specific topical area.

Life Span Development: A Topical Approach maintains the student friendliness that has been the hallmark of the original. It is rich in examples and illustrates the applications that can be derived from the research and theory of life span developmentalists. It pays particular attention to the applications that can be drawn from theory and research in the field.

To optimize student learning and to provide instructors with maximum flexibility, the book uses a modular approach. Each chapter is divided into three modules focusing on particular subtopics. Consequently, rather than facing long, potentially daunting chapters, students encounter material that is divided into smaller, more manageable chunks. Of course, presenting material in small chunks represents a structure that research long ago found to be optimum for promoting learning.

The modular approach has another advantage: It allows instructors to customize instruction by assigning only those modules that fit their course. Because the modules are self-contained, instructors can pick and choose which modules best contribute to their course. Because of the flexibility of this structure, instructors who wish to highlight a particular topic can do so easily and—equally important—have the option of not including specific modules.

Overview of *Life Span Development: A Topical Approach*

Life Span Development: A Topical Approach provides a broad overview of the field of human development. It covers major topics such as physical development, cognitive development, and social and personality development. In addition, separate chapters focus on health and wellness, language development, intelligence, development of the self, moral development and aggression, gender and sexuality, relationships, living in a multicultural world, and death and grieving.

The book seeks to accomplish the following four major goals:

- First and foremost, the book is designed to provide a broad, balanced overview of the field of life span development. It introduces readers to the theories, research, and applications that constitute the discipline, examining both the traditional areas of the field and more recent innovations. It pays particular attention to the applications developed by life span development specialists, demonstrating how life span developmentalists use theory, research, and applications to help solve significant social problems.

- The second goal of the text is to explicitly tie development to students' lives. Findings from the study of life span development have a significant degree of relevance to students, and this text illustrates how these findings can be applied in a meaningful, practical sense. Applications are presented in a contemporaneous framework, including current news items, timely world events, and contemporary uses of life span development that draw readers into the field. Numerous descriptive scenarios and vignettes reflect everyday situations in people's lives, explaining how they relate to the field.

- The third goal is to highlight both the commonalities and diversity of today's multicultural society. Consequently, the book incorporates material relevant to diversity in all its forms—racial, ethnic, gender, sexual orientation, religion, and cultural diversity—throughout every chapter. In addition, every chapter has at least one *Developmental Diversity* section. These features explicitly consider how cultural factors relevant to development both unite and diversify our contemporary global society.

- Finally, the fourth goal is one that is implicit in the other three: making the field of life span development engaging, accessible, and interesting to students. Life span development is a joy both to study and teach because so much of it has direct, immediate meaning for our lives. Because all of us are involved in our own developmental paths, we are tied in very personal ways to the content areas covered by the book. *Life Span Development: A Topical Approach,* then, is meant to engage and nurture this interest, planting a seed that will develop and flourish throughout readers' lifetimes.

In accomplishing these goals, the book strives to be user friendly. Written in a direct, conversational voice, it duplicates as much as possible a dialogue between author and student. The text is meant to be understood and mastered on its own by students of every level of interest and motivation. To that end, it includes a variety of pedagogical features that promote mastery of the material and encourage critical thinking.

In short, the book blends and integrates theory, research, and applications, focusing on the breadth of human development. Furthermore, rather than attempting to provide a detailed historical record of the field, it focuses on the here and now, drawing on the past where appropriate, but with a view toward delineating the field as it now stands and the directions toward which it is evolving. Similarly, while providing descriptions of classic studies, the emphasis is on current research findings and trends.

Life Span Development: A Topical Approach is meant to be a book that readers will want to keep in their own personal libraries, one that they will take off the shelf when considering problems related to that most intriguing of questions: How do people come to be the way they are?

Features of *Life Span Development: A Topical Approach*

Finally, in addition to the features described next, *Life Span Development: A Topical Approach* provides complete integration between the book and a huge array of electronic media in *MyVirtualChild* and *MyDevelopmentLab,* comprising online electronic exercises, videos, sample tests, and literally hundreds of activities that extend the text and make concepts come alive. The online material is referenced throughout the book in a way meant to entice students to go online and make use of the electronic materials that will help them understand the material in the book more deeply.

I am very excited about this book. I believe its topical approach, length, modular structure and other features, and media and text integration present the material in a highly effective way and will help students learn it. Just as important, I hope the book will spark and nurture students' interest in the field of life span development, drawing them into its way of looking at the world, building their understanding of developmental issues, and showing them how the field can have a significant impact on their own and others' lives.

In addition to its modular structure, *Life Span Development: A Topical Approach* presents a set of features designed to engage students and help them learn the material effectively. These include:

Prologue
Jesse's Dilemma

The most important game of the football season had ended in disappointment for Jesse and his friends. Their archrival team, the Southridge Wolverines, had trounced them 28 to 3. Now, Jesse and his friends stood before the Wolverines' empty bus, their disappointment turning to anger. Suddenly, a rock smashed one of the bus's windows. A second rock made a large dent just behind the driver's seat. "Wolverines SUCK!" the boys shouted as they lobbed every rock within their reach. Two more windows shattered. The door was bent in its frame.

CHAPTER-OPENING PROLOGUES

Each chapter begins with a short vignette, describing an individual or a situation that is relevant to the basic developmental issues being addressed in the chapter.

LOOKING AHEAD SECTIONS

These opening sections orient readers to the topics to be covered, bridging the opening Prologue with the remainder of the chapter and providing orienting questions.

LOOKING AHEAD
After reading this chapter, you will be able to answer the following questions:

► What is attachment in infancy, and how does it affect a person's future social competence?
► Do infants experience emotions?
► What dangers do adolescents face as they deal with the emotional stresses of adolescence?
► How do people deal with aging?
► What are temperament and personality, and what stages do individuals pass through in their social development?
► Is there continuity in personality development during adulthood?

FROM RESEARCH TO PRACTICE
The Downside of High Self-Esteem

According to many, low self-esteem lies at the heart of a variety of social ills, ranging from teenage pregnancy to gang violence to drug abuse. For example, government officials in California set up a task force to encourage self-esteem, arguing that increased self-esteem might raise the general psychological health of the population and even help the state balance its budget.

But not everyone agrees with this view. According to psychologist Roy Baumeister and colleagues, if high self-esteem is unjustified by actual accomplishment, it can be psychologically damaging. Unwarranted high self-esteem can lead to a variety of social problems, including violence (Baumeister et al., 2003; Baumeister et al., 2005).

may provoke the opposite result. For example, in one study, students who were receiving Ds and Fs in one class were divided into two groups. One group received the message that good grades were caused by a lack of confidence and low self-esteem. The other group received a different message; they were told that it was hard work that produced good grades. At the end of the semester, the group that received the self-esteem message ended up with significantly lower grades than the group that received the hard work message (Forsyth & Kerr, 1999).

Of course, such findings don't mean that high self-esteem is a bad thing. In fact, people with high self-esteem are significantly happier than those with low self-esteem, and they are less likely to be

FROM RESEARCH TO PRACTICE

Each chapter includes a box that describes current developmental research or research issues applied to everyday problems.

DEVELOPMENTAL DIVERSITY

Every chapter incorporates at least one *Developmental Diversity* section into the text. These sections highlight issues relevant to today's multicultural society.

DEVELOPMENTAL DIVERSITY
Is Aggression as American as Apple Pie?

Anyone who reads a daily newspaper is exposed to a constant stream of incidents of murder, rape, mugging, and other violence, often committed by teenagers and sometimes even by younger children. Does this perception of violence match the reality, and is aggression "as American as apple pie," as one expert on aggression put it (Berkowitz, 1993)? Unfortunately, in many ways, the perception matches reality. For example, more men between the ages of 15 and 24 are murdered in the United States than in any other developed country in the world (see Figure 11.4).

On the other hand, aggression is hardly unique to the United States. In some cultures, aggression by children is substantial, while in others it is less pronounced. According to the findings of one classic study, childrearing practices help explain the substantial cross-cultural differences. In the study, researchers examined aggression in Kenya, India, Mexico, Okinawa, the Philippines, and the United States (Lambert, 1971).

BECOMING AN INFORMED CONSUMER OF DEVELOPMENT
Bulking Up the Brain

Research shows that continued intellectual stimulation keeps cognitive abilities sharp; the real threat to older people's cognitive functioning lies in a decline in their opportunities and motivation for cognitive challenges as they pass retirement age. Research provides some suggestions.

- A relatively small investment of time and effort in mental workouts can pay big dividends. Older people don't have to run mental marathons (unless, of course, they want to); they can benefit a great deal from ongoing mental exercise.
- Types of training that have proven effective include memory training, reasoning training, and processing speed training.

- Especially when backed up by booster sessions, the effects of such training appear to be remarkably durable.
- Ongoing mental exercise can result in improved confidence in the ability to perform daily tasks demanding cognition, such as housework, meal preparation, finances, and shopping.
- The self-confidence that may result from mental activities is associated with greater independence, less reliance on health services, and longer life.
- Mental exercise that is performed regularly appears to slow cognitive declines. The key is to perform some form of mental workout consistently and to increase the level of difficulty to sustain a sense of challenge.

BECOMING AN INFORMED CONSUMER OF DEVELOPMENT

These boxes show students how they can make use of the research presented in the text by actively applying the concepts they are learning to real life situations.

NEUROSCIENCE AND DEVELOPMENT

To illustrate the influence of neuroscience throughout the field of life span development, most chapters include a box presenting the latest neuroscientific advances and their impact on our understanding of life span development.

NEUROSCIENCE AND DEVELOPMENT
Memory and the Brain: I Am Stuck on Palmitate, and Palmitate Is Stuck in Me

Fats tend to have a bad reputation—after all, ingesting too much of them leads to obesity and heart attacks—but it turns out that certain kinds of fats are quite helpful in producing long-term memories.

Recently a team of researchers at Johns Hopkins University discovered that *palmitate*, a sticky fatty acid, is involved in activating special brain proteins called NMDA receptors, which are needed in long-term memory and learning. Palmitate helps move NMDA receptors to specific locations in the brain where cell connections are strengthened or weakened to change memory circuits (Hayashi, Thomas, & Huganir, 2009).

Why is the NMDA receptor important? Some scientists believe that the NMDA receptor is related to intelligence because it plays a

significant role in the rapid, intense development of the child's brain. The discovery of the palmitate-NMDA receptor connection is thus important because it offers greater understanding of how synapses are regulated and how memory is formed. In addition, the identification of palmitate may lead to the development of drug therapies that allow for the manipulation or regulation to enhance learning and memory. Ultimately, the control of disease-induced increases or decreases in NMDA receptor activity (which in turn affect memory formation and maintenance) may occur by manipulating palmitate or palmitate-like substances in the brain.

- What ethical questions arise if substances can be identified and produced to help enhance learning and memory beyond what occurs naturally in humans?

REVIEW

▶ Theories are systematically derived explanations of facts or phenomena. Theories suggest hypotheses, which are predictions that can be tested.

▶ Correlational studies examine relationships between factors without demonstrating causality, while experimental research seeks to discover cause-and-effect relationships.

▶ Researchers measure age-related change by longitudinal studies, cross-sectional studies, and sequential studies.

APPLY

▶ Formulate a theory about one aspect of human development and a hypothesis that relates to it.

▶ Egyptian King Psamtik's experiment of removing two children from their mothers would be unheard of today. How could the same experiment be done today following ethical guidelines?

REVIEW AND APPLY SECTIONS

Interspersed throughout each chapter are three short recaps of the chapters' main points, followed by questions designed to provoke critical thinking.

functional play play that involves simple, repetitive activities typical of 3-year-olds.

constructive play play in which children manipulate objects to produce or build something.

parallel play action in which children play with similar toys, in a similar manner, but do not interact with each other.

onlooker play action in which children simply watch others at play but do not actually participate themselves.

RUNNING GLOSSARY

Key terms are defined in the margins of the page on which the term is presented.

Epilogue

In this chapter we considered both moral development and aggression, and explored the development of religious thought and the purpose of spiritual beliefs. First, we looked at a variety of theories about how children develop a sense of right and wrong. We discussed how reasoning about moral dilemmas grows more sophisticated as children move into adolescence. We also explored a range of parenting styles and discussed their implications for shaping children's behavior, both present and future. Then, we considered religion and spirituality, and asked: Why is religion important to many people? We considered how religion helps people to find meaning in their lives and how it helps them cope with disasters. We also discussed the development of religious thought, using both Piaget's approach to cognitive development and James Fowler's stages of faith development. We examined the relationship between religious belief and life satisfaction in late adulthood, and we discussed the special significance religion holds for older adults, especially African Americans. In the final part of the chapter, we examined the sources of aggression and violence, and considered the question: Is nature or nurture more responsible for aggression? We explored ways of

decreasing aggression in children and increasing their moral behaviors. We also considered the factors that predict a lifelong problem with aggression. In conclusion, we examined the epidemic of family violence involving abuse of children, spouses, and elders.

Before moving on to the next chapter, take a moment to reread the Prologue to this chapter about Jesse's dilemma over the destruction of the bus, and answer the following questions:

1. Is Kohlberg's/Piaget's moral reasoning approach helpful in interpreting Jesse's actions in this instance? Why or why not?

2. Does the fact that the other boys throw rocks at the bus prove they think it's morally okay to do so? Why might there be a disconnect between their beliefs and their actions?

3. What evidence, if any, do you see in this story that Jesse has developed a set of core beliefs and values as part of his identity? What might some of those beliefs and values be?

4. Do you think Jesse's actions would have been different if a Wolverines' team member had injured one of Jesse's friends? Why or why not?

END-OF-CHAPTER MATERIAL

Each chapter ends with an Epilogue that refers back to the opening Prologue and a numbered summary. This material is designed to help students study and retain the information in the chapter.

Ancillaries

Life Span Development: A Topical Approach is accompanied by a superb set of teaching and learning materials.

Print and Media Supplements for the Instructor

- **Instructor's Resource Manual (ISBN: 0205777031).** The Instructor's Resource Manual includes learning objectives, key terms and concepts, self-contained lecture suggestions and class activities for each chapter with handouts, supplemental reading suggestions, and an annotated list of additional multimedia resources.

  The Instructor's Resource Manual will be available for download via the Pearson Instructor's Resource Center (www.pearsonhighered.com/irc) or on the MyDevelopmentLab® platform (www.mydevelopmentlab.com).

- **Video Enhanced PowerPoint Slides.** These slides, available on the Instructor's Resource DVD (ISBN 0205820212), bring the Feldman design right into the classroom, drawing students into the lecture and providing wonderful interactive activities, visuals, and videos.

- **PowerPoint Lecture Slides (ISBN: 0205773540).** The lecture slides have been wholly reworked and completely revised by Pauline D. Zeece of the University of Nebraska—Lincoln, and feature prominent figures and tables from the text. The PowerPoint Lecture Slides are available for download via the Pearson Instructor's Resource Center (www.pearsonhighered.com) or on the MyDevelopmentLab® platform (www.mydevelopmentlab.com).

- **Classroom Response System PowerPoint Slides (ISBN: 0205004059).** These slides are intended to be the basis not only for class lectures but also for class discussions. The incorporation of the CRS questions into each chapter slideshow facilitates the use of "clickers"—small hardware devices similar to remote controls, which process student responses to questions, and interpret and display results in real time. CRS questions are a great means to engage students in learning and precipitate contemplation of text concepts. The slides will be available for download via the Pearson Instructor's Resource Center (www.pearsonhighered.com) or on the MyDevelopmentLab® platform (www.mydevelopmentlab.com).

- **Test Item File (ISBN: 0205777023).** Written by Richard Cavasina at the California University of Pennsylvania, each question was accuracy checked to ensure that the correct answer was marked and the page reference was accurate. The test bank contains over 3,000 multiple-choice, true/false, and essay questions, each referenced to the relevant page in the textbook. An additional feature for the test bank is the identification of each question as factual, conceptual, or applied. This allows professors to customize their tests and to ensure a balance of question types. Each chapter of the test item file begins with the Total Assessment Guide: an easy-to-reference grid that makes creating tests easier by organizing the test questions by text section, question type, and whether it is factual, conceptual, or applied.

- **MyTest (ISBN: 0205773532).** The test item file comes with the NEW Pearson MyTest, a powerful assessment generation program that helps instructors easily create and print quizzes and exams. Questions and tests can be authored online, allowing instructors ultimate flexibility and the ability to efficiently manage assessments anytime, anywhere. For more information, go to www.PearsonMyTest.com.

- **My Virtual Child.** *My Virtual Child* is an interactive, Web-based simulation that allows students to act as a parent and raise their own "child." By making decisions about specific scenarios, students can raise their children from birth to age 18 and learn first-hand how their own decisions and other parenting actions affect their child over time. At each age, students are given feedback about the various milestones their child has attained; key stages of the child's development will include personalized feedback. As in real life, certain "unplanned" events may occur randomly. The just released 2.0 version includes a complete redesign, a student personality test at the beginning of the program—the results of which will have an impact on the temperament of their child—*Observations* video throughout the program to help illustrate key concepts, and a wider range of ethnicities for students to select from. Access codes are needed for the Virtual Child, and instructors can obtain a code at no cost via the Pearson website (www.pearsonhighered.com) or at (www.myvirtualchild.com).

- **MyDevelopmentLab (ISBN: 0205604250).** MyDevelopmentLab is a learning and assessment tool that enables instructors to assess student performance and adapt course content—without investing additional time or resources. Students benefit from an easy-to-use site on which they can test themselves on key content, track their progress, and utilize an individually tailored study plan. MyDevelopmentLab is designed with instructor flexibility in mind—you decide the extent of integration into your course—from independent self-assessment for students, to total course management. By transferring faculty members' most time-consuming tasks—content delivery, student assessment, and grading—to automated tools, MyDevelopmentLab enables faculty to spend more quality time with students. In addition to the activities students access through their customized study plans, instructors are provided with extra lecture notes, video clips, and activities that reflect the content areas their class is struggling with. Instructors can bring theses resources to class or easily post them online for students to access. An access code is required and can be obtained at www.mydevelopmentlab.com. To order MyDevelopmentLab at no additional cost with this textbook, please use ISBN: 0205802605 for MyDevelopmentLab or ISBN: 0205018491 for MyDevelopmentLab in Pegasus.

- **MyClassPrep.** This new offering from Pearson makes lecture preparation simpler and less time-consuming! Pearson has collected the very "best of" instructor resources, including art and figures from our leading texts, videos, lecture activities, classroom activities, demonstrations, and much more. Instructors are able to search through this extensive database by content topic (arranged by standard topics within the lifespan developmental curriculum) or by content type (video, audio, simulation, Word documents). MyClassPrep allows instructors to select resources appropriate for lecture, many of which can be downloaded directly. Or instructors may build their own folder of resources and present them from within the MyClassPrep program. Available to instructors from within MyDevelopmentLab.

Video Resources for Instructors

- **Prentice Hall Lecture Launcher Video for Developmental Psychology (ISBN 0205811965).** Adopters can receive this DVD covering all the major topics in developmental psychology.
- **Pearson Teaching Films Life Span Development Video (ISBN: 0205656021)**

Print and Media Supplements for the Student

- **CourseSmart eTextbook (ISBN: 0205773516).** This new Pearson Choice offers students an online subscription to *Life Span Development: A Topical Approach, 1/e* at a 60% savings. With the CourseSmart eTextbook, students can search the text, make notes online, print our reading assignments that incorporate lecture notes, and bookmark important passages. Ask your Pearson sales representative for details or visit www.coursesmart.com.

- **Observations in Developmental Psychology (ISBN: 0136016588).** These videos bring to life more than 30 key concepts discussed in the narrative of the text, indicated by a marginal icon, and offer additional extended videos that coincide with each part in the text to allow students to see real children in action. Students get to view each video twice: once with an introduction to the concept being illustrated and again with commentary describing what is taking place at crucial points in the video. Whether or not your course has an observation component, these videos provide your students the opportunity to see children in action. The videos can be accessed through MyDevelopmentLab (www.mydevelopmentlab.com) or by purchasing the supplementary CD-ROM on www.pearsonhighered.com.

- **MyDevelopmentLab.** With this exciting new tool students are able to self-assess using embedded diagnostic tests and instantly view results along with a customized study plan.

  The customized study plan will focus on the student's strengths and weaknesses, based on the results of the diagnostic testing, and present a list of activities and resources for review and remediation, organized by chapter section. Some study resources intended for use with portable electronic devices are made available exclusively through the MyDevelopmentLab, such as key terms flashcards and optimized *Observations* video clips. Students will be able to quickly and easily analyze their own comprehension level of the course material and study more efficiently, leading to exceptional exam results! An access code is required and can be purchased at www.pearsonhighered.com or at www.mydevelopmentlab.com.

Supplementary Texts

Contact your Prentice Hall representative to package any of these supplementary texts with *Life Span Development: A Topical Approach*.

- *Current Directions in Developmental Psychology* (ISBN: 0205597505). Readings from the American Psychological Society. This new and exciting reader includes over 20 articles that have been carefully selected for the undergraduate audience, and taken from the very accessible *Current Directions in Psychological Science* journal. These timely, cutting-edge articles allow instructors to bring their students a real-world perspective about today's most current and pressing issues in psychology. Discounted when packaged with this text for college adoptions.

- *Twenty Studies That Revolutionized Child Psychology* by Wallace E. Dixon Jr. (ISBN: 0130415723). Presenting the seminal research studies that have shaped modern developmental psychology, this brief text provides an overview of the environment that gave rise to each study, its experimental design, its findings, and its impact on current thinking in the discipline.

- *Human Development in Multicultural Contexts: A Book of Readings* (ISBN: 0130195235). Written by Michele A. Paludi, this compilation of readings highlights cultural influences in developmental psychology.

- *The Psychology Major: Careers and Strategies for Success* (ISBN: 0205684688). Written by Eric Landrum (Idaho State University), Stephen Davis (Emporia State University), and Terri Landrum (Idaho State University), this 160-page paperback provides valuable information on career options available to psychology majors, tips for improving academic performance, and a guide to the APA style of research reporting.

Acknowledgments

I am grateful to the following reviewers who provided a wealth of comments, constructive criticism, and encouragement:

- **Lola Aagaard** Morehead State University
- **Kristine Anthis** Southern Connecticut State University
- **Mitchell Baker** Moraine Valley Community College
- **Jonathan Bates** Hunter College
- **Manolya Bayar** University of Hartford
- **Janine Buckner** Seton Hall University
- **Michael Caruso** University of Toledo
- **Elaine Cassel** Lord Fairfax Community College—Fauquier
- **Jean Choi** Humber College
- **Michelle Clark** James Madison University
- **Jeff Cookston** San Francisco State University
- **Brent Costleigh** Brookdale Community College
- **Lisa End-Berg** Kennesaw State University
- **Carolyn Fallahi** Central Connecticut State
- **Lisa Fozio-Thielk** Waubonsee Community College
- **Jackie Goldstein** Samford University
- **Troianne Grayson** Florida Community College at Jacksonville—Deerwood Center
- **James Guinee** University of Central Arkansas
- **Tomo Imamichi** Borough of Manhattan Community College
- **Marsha Ironsmith** East Carolina University
- **Alisha Janowsky** University of Central Florida
- **Laura Johnson** Davidson County Community College
- **Tara Johnson** Indiana University of Pennsylvania
- **Linda Jones** Blinn College—Bryan Campus
- **Stefanie Keen** University of South Carolina Upstate
- **Franz Klutschkowski** North Central Texas College
- **Jonathan Lang** Borough of Manhattan Community College
- **Ann Lim-Brand** Brookdale Community College
- **Geri Lotze** Virginia Commonwealth University
- **Pei-Wen Ma** William Patterson University
- **Salvador Macias** University of South Carolina at Sumter
- **Nicole Martin** Kennesaw State University
- **Ronnie Naramore** Angelina College
- **Lisa Newell** Indiana University of Pennsylvania
- **Kathleen Rudasill** University of Louisville
- **Lynne Schmelter-Davis** Brookdale Community College
- **Sandy Sego** American International College
- **Jenessa Steele** Radford University
- **Barry Stennett** Athens Technical College & Gainesville State College
- **Timothy Trant** Louisiana State University—Eunice
- **Larry Venuk** Northern Virginia Community College
- **Diane Wille** Indiana University Southeast
- **Christine Ziegler** Kennesaw State University

Many others deserve a great deal of thanks. I am indebted to the numerous people who provided me with a superb education, first at Wesleyan University and later at the University of Wisconsin. Specifically, Karl Scheibe played a pivotal role in my undergraduate education, and the late Vernon Allen acted as mentor and guide through my graduate years. It was in graduate school that I learned about development, being exposed to such experts as Ross Parke, John Balling, Joel Levin, Herb Klausmeier, and many others. My education continued when I became a professor. I am especially grateful to my colleagues at the University of Massachusetts, who make the university such a wonderful place in which to teach and do research.

Several people played central roles in the development of this book. John Bickford and Christopher Poirier provided important research and editorial input, and I am thankful for their help. Most of all, John Graiff was essential in juggling and coordinating the multiple aspects of writing a book, and I am very grateful for the substantial role he played.

I am also grateful to the superb Pearson team that was instrumental in the inception and development of this book. Jeff Marshall, Executive Editor, has brought enthusiasm, creativity, and a wealth of good ideas to this edition. Associate Editor LeeAnn Doherty went way beyond the call of duty to provide direction and support in every respect. I am grateful for their support. On the production end of things, Maureen Richardson, managing editor, and Harriet Tellem, project manager, helped bring all the aspects of the book together and Nancy Wells, Art Director, and Laura Gardner, designer, helped in giving the book its distinctive look. Finally, I'd like to thank (in advance) marketing manager Nicole Kunzmann, on whose skills I'm counting.

I also wish to acknowledge the members of my family, who play such an essential role in my life. My brother, Michael, my sisters-in-law and brother-in-law, my nieces and nephews—all make up an important part of my life. In addition, I am always indebted to the older generation of my family, who led the way in a manner I can only hope to emulate. I will always be obligated to the late Harry Brochstein, Mary Vorwerk, and Ethel Radler. Most of all, the list is headed by my father, the late Saul Feldman, and my mother, Leah Brochstein.

In the end, it is my immediate family who deserve the greatest thanks. My terrific kids, Jonathan and wife Leigh, Joshua and wife Julie, and Sarah not only are nice, smart, and good-looking but also my pride and joy. My grandson Alex has brought immense happiness from the moment of his birth. And ultimately my wife, Katherine Vorwerk, provides the love and grounding that makes everything worthwhile. I thank them, with all my love.

ROBERT S. FELDMAN
University of Massachusetts, Amherst

About the Author

Robert S. Feldman is Professor of Psychology and Dean of the College of Social and Behavioral Sciences at the University of Massachusetts, Amherst. A recipient of the College Distinguished Teacher Award, he teaches psychology classes ranging in size from 15 to nearly 500 students. During the course of more than two decades as a college instructor, he has taught both undergraduate and graduate courses at Mount Holyoke College, Wesleyan University, and Virginia Commonwealth University in addition to the University of Massachusetts.

Professor Feldman, who initiated the Minority Mentoring Program at the University of Massachusetts, also has served as a Hewlett Teaching Fellow and Senior Online Teaching Fellow. He initiated distance learning courses in psychology at the University of Massachusetts.

A Fellow of both the American Psychological Association and the Association for Psychological Science, Professor Feldman received a B.A. with High Honors from Wesleyan University (and from which he received the Distinguished Alumni Award). He has an MS and Ph.D. from the University of Wisconsin-Madison. He is a winner of a Fulbright Senior Research Scholar and Lecturer award, and he has written more than 100 books, book chapters, and scientific articles.

Professor Feldman has edited *Development of Nonverbal Behavior in Children* and *Applications of Nonverbal Behavioral Theory and Research*, and co-edited *Fundamentals of Nonverbal Behavior*. He is also author of *Child Development, Understanding Psychology* and *P.O.W.E.R. Learning: Strategies for Success in College and Life*. His books have been translated into a number of languages, including Spanish, French, Portuguese, Dutch, Chinese, Korean, and Japanese. His research interests include honesty and deception in everyday life, work that he described in *The Liar in Your Life*, a trade book published in 2009. His research has been supported by grants from the National Institute of Mental Health and the National Institute on Disabilities and Rehabilitation Research.

Professor Feldman loves music, is an enthusiastic pianist, and enjoys cooking and traveling. He has three children, a young grandson, and he and his wife, a psychologist, live in western Massachusetts in a home overlooking the Holyoke Mountain Range.

1 An Orientation to Lifespan Development

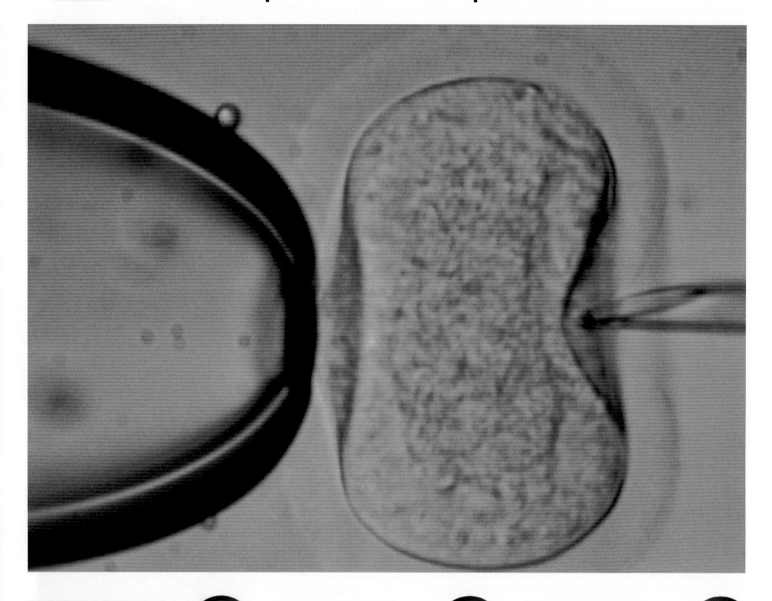

Prologue
New Conceptions

What if for your entire life, the image that others held of you was colored by the way in which you were conceived?

In some ways, that's what it has been like for Louise Brown, who was the world's first "test tube baby," born by in vitro fertilization (IVF), a procedure in which fertilization of a mother's egg by a father's sperm takes place outside the mother's body.

Louise was a preschooler when her parents told her how she was conceived, and throughout her childhood she was bombarded with questions. It became routine to explain to her classmates that she in fact was not born in a laboratory.

As a child, Louise sometimes felt completely alone. But as she grew older, her isolation declined as more and more children were born in the same manner.

Today Louise is hardly isolated. More than 1.5 million babies have been born using the procedure, which has become almost routine. And at the age of 28, Louise became a mother herself, giving birth to a baby boy name Cameron—conceived, by the way, in the old-fashioned way. (Moreton, 2007)

Louise Brown (center front) celebrates with hundreds of other guests, all of whom have been conceived by in vitro fertilization.

Louise Brown's conception may have been novel, but her development since then has followed a predictable pattern. While the specifics of our development vary, the broad strokes set in motion in that test tube 28 years ago are remarkably similar for all of us. Shaquille O'Neal, Donald Trump, the Queen of England—all are traversing the territory known as lifespan development.

In vitro fertilization is just one of the brave new worlds of recent days. Issues that affect human development range from cloning to poverty to the prevention of AIDS. Underlying these concerns are even more fundamental issues: How do we develop physically? How does our understanding of the world change throughout our lives? And how do our personalities and social relationships develop as we move through the life span?

These questions and many others are central to lifespan development. The field encompasses a broad span of time and a wide range of areas. Consider the range of interests that different specialists might focus on when considering Louise Brown:

- Lifespan development researchers who investigate behavior at the biological level might ask if Louise's functioning before birth was affected by her conception outside the womb.
- Specialists in lifespan development who study genetics might examine how the genetic endowment from Louise's parents affects her later behavior.
- Lifespan development specialists who investigate thinking processes might examine how Louise's understanding of the circumstances of her conception changed as she grew older.
- Other researchers in lifespan development, who focus on physical growth, might consider whether her growth rate differed from that of children conceived more traditionally.
- Lifespan development experts who specialize in the social world and social relationships might look at the ways that Louise interacted with others and the kinds of friendships she developed.

PEARSON
mydevelopmentlab
To begin to learn about pregnancy, birth, and newborn children, use **MyVirtualChild** on the Web at **www.mydevelopmentlab.com**.

Although their interests take many forms, these specialists share one concern: understanding the growth and change that occur during life. Taking many different approaches, developmentalists study how both our biological inheritance from our parents and the environment in which we live jointly affect our future behavior, personality, and potential as human beings.

Whether they focus on heredity or environment, all developmental specialists acknowledge that neither one alone can account for the full range of human development. Instead, we must look at the interaction of heredity and environment, attempting to grasp how both underlie human behavior.

In this module, we orient ourselves to the field of lifespan development. We begin with a discussion of the scope of the discipline, illustrating the wide array of topics it covers and the full range of ages it examines. We also survey the key issues and controversies of the field and consider the broad perspectives that developmentalists take. Finally, we discuss the ways developmentalists use research to ask and answer questions. Many of the questions that developmentalists ask are, in essence, the scientist's version of the questions that parents ask about their children and themselves: how the genetic legacy of parents plays out in their children; how children learn; why they make the choices they make; whether personality characteristics are inherited and whether they change or are stable over time; how a stimulating environment affects development; and many others. To pursue their answers, of course, developmentalists use the highly structured, formal scientific method, while parents mostly use the informal strategy of waiting, observing, engaging, and loving their kids.

LOOKING AHEAD

After reading this module, you will be able to answer these questions:

▶ What is lifespan development, and what are some of the basic influences on human development?

▶ What are the key issues in the field of development?

▶ Which theoretical perspectives have guided lifespan development?

▶ What role do theories and hypotheses play in the study of development?

▶ How are developmental research studies conducted?

MODULE 1.1

Determining the Nature—and Nurture—of Lifespan Development

Have you ever wondered at the way an infant tightly grips your finger with tiny, perfectly formed hands? Or marveled at how a preschooler methodically draws a picture? Or at the way an adolescent can make involved decisions about whom to invite to a party or the ethics of downloading music files? Or the way a middle-aged politician can deliver a long, flawless speech from memory? Or what makes a grandfather at 80 so similar to the father he was at 40?

If you've ever wondered about such things, you are asking the kinds of questions that scientists in the field of lifespan development pose. **Lifespan development** is the field of study that examines patterns of growth, change, and stability in behavior that occur throughout the life span.

In its study of growth, change, and stability, lifespan development takes a *scientific* approach. Like members of other scientific disciplines, researchers in lifespan development test their assumptions by applying scientific methods. They develop theories about development and use methodical, scientific techniques to validate the accuracy of their assumptions systematically.

Lifespan development focuses on *human* development. Although there are developmentalists who study nonhuman species, the vast majority study people. Some seek to understand universal principles of development, while others focus on how cultural, racial, and ethnic differences affect development. Still others aim to understand the traits and characteristics that differentiate one person from another. Regardless of approach, however, all developmentalists view development as a continuing process throughout the life span.

lifespan development is the field of study that examines patterns of growth, change, and stability in behavior that occur throughout the entire life span.

As developmental specialists focus on change during the life span, they also consider stability. They ask in which areas, and in what periods, people show change and growth, and when and how their behavior reveals consistency and continuity with prior behavior.

Finally, developmentalists assume that the process of development persists from the moment of conception to the day of death, with people changing in some ways right up to the end of their lives and in other ways exhibiting remarkable stability. They believe that no single period governs all development, but instead that people maintain the capacity for substantial growth and change throughout their lives.

Characterizing Lifespan Development: The Scope of the Field

The definition of lifespan development is broad and the scope of the field extensive. Typically, lifespan development specialists cover several diverse areas, choosing to specialize in both a topical area and an age range.

Topical Areas in Lifespan Development. Some developmentalists focus on **physical development**, examining the ways in which the body's makeup—the brain, nervous system, muscles, and senses, and the need for food, drink, and sleep—helps determine behavior. For example, one specialist in physical development might examine the effects of malnutrition on the pace of growth in children, while another might look at how athletes' physical performance declines during adulthood.

Other developmental specialists examine **cognitive development**, seeking to understand how growth and change in intellectual capabilities influence a person's behavior. Cognitive developmentalists examine learning, memory, problem solving, and intelligence. For example, specialists in cognitive development might want to see how problem-solving skills change over the course of life, or if cultural differences exist in the way people explain their academic successes and failures, or how traumatic events experienced early in life are remembered later in life.

Finally, some developmental specialists focus on personality and social development. **Personality development** is the study of stability and change in the characteristics that differentiate one person from another over the life span. **Social development** is the way in which individuals' interactions and relationships with others grow, change, and remain stable over the course of life. A developmentalist interested in personality development might ask whether there are stable, enduring personality traits throughout the life span, while a specialist in social development might examine the effects of racism or poverty or divorce on development. These four major topic areas—physical, cognitive, social, and personality development—are summarized in Table 1.1 on page 6.

Age Ranges and Individual Differences. In addition to choosing a particular topical area, developmentalists also typically look at a particular age range. The life span is usually divided into broad age ranges: the prenatal period (from conception to birth); infancy and toddlerhood (birth to 3); the preschool period (3 to 6); middle childhood (6 to 12); adolescence (12 to 20); young adulthood (20 to 40); middle adulthood (40 to 60); and late adulthood (60 to death).

It's important to keep in mind that these periods are social constructions. A *social construction* is a shared notion of reality that is widely accepted but is a function of society and culture at a given time. Thus, the age ranges within a period—and even the periods themselves—are in many ways arbitrary and culturally derived. For example, we'll see how the concept of childhood as a special period did not even exist during the seventeenth century, when children were seen simply as miniature adults. Furthermore, while some periods have a clear-cut boundary (infancy begins with birth, the preschool period ends with entry into public school, and adolescence starts with sexual maturity), others do not.

For instance, consider the period of young adulthood, which at least in Western cultures is typically assumed to begin at age 20. That age, however, is notable only because it marks the end of the teenage period. In fact, for many people, such as those enrolled in higher education, the age change from 19 to 20 has little special significance, coming as it does in the middle of college. For them, more substantial changes are likely to occur when they leave college around age 22. Furthermore, in some cultures adulthood starts much earlier, as soon as a child can begin full-time work.

In short, there are substantial *individual differences* in the timing of events in people's lives. In part, this is a biological fact of life: People mature at different rates and reach developmental

physical development   development involving the body's physical makeup, including the brain, nervous system, muscles, and senses, and the need for food, drink, and sleep.

cognitive development   development involving the ways that growth and change in intellectual capabilities influence a person's behavior.

personality development   development involving the ways that the enduring characteristics that differentiate one person from another change over the life span.

social development   the way in which individuals' interactions with others and their social relationships grow, change, and remain stable over the course of life.

TABLE 1.1	Approaches to Lifespan Development	
ORIENTATION	**DEFINING CHARACTERISTICS**	**EXAMPLES OF QUESTION ASKED***
Physical Development	Emphasizes how brain, nervous system, muscles, sensory capabilities, needs for food, drink and sleep affect behavior	· What determines the sex of a child? (2.1) · What are the long-term results of premature birth? (2.3) · What are the benefits of breast milk? (4.3) · What are the consequences of early or late sexual maturation? (3.1) · What leads to obesity in adulthood? (4.2) · How do adults cope with stress? (4.1) · What are the outward signs of aging? (3.1) · What is the relationship between aging and illness? (4.3)
Cognitive Development	Emphasizes intellectual abilities, including learning, memory, problem solving, and intelligence	· What are the earliest memories that can be recalled from infancy? (6.2) · What are the intellectual consequences of watching television? (14.2) · What is intelligence and how has it been measured over the years? (8.1) · Are there benefits to bilingualism? (7.3) · What are the fundamental elements of information processing? (6.1) · Are there ethnic and racial differences in intelligence? (8.2) · What is cognitive development and how did Piaget revolutionize its study? (5.1) · How does creativity relate to intelligence? (8.1)
Personality and Social Development	Emphasizes enduring characteristics that differentiate one person from another, and how interactions with others and social relationships grow and change over the lifetime	· Do newborns respond differently to their mothers than to others? (9.1) · What is the best procedure for disciplining children? (11.1) · When does a sense of gender identity develop? (12.1) · How can we promote cross-race friendships? (13.1) · What are the emotions involved in confronting death? (15.3) · How do we choose a romantic partner? (14) · What sort of relationships are important in late adulthood? (13.3) · What are typical patterns of marriage and divorce in middle adulthood? (12.3) · In what ways are individuals affected by culture and ethnicity? (13.3)

*Numbers in parentheses indicate in which chapter the question is addressed.

milestones at different points. However, environmental factors also play a significant role. For example, the typical age of marriage varies from one culture to another, depending in part on the functions that marriage plays.

The Links Between Topics and Ages. Each of the broad topical areas of lifespan development—physical, cognitive, and social and personality development—plays a role throughout the life span. Consequently, some developmental experts may focus on physical development during the prenatal period, and others during adolescence. Some might specialize in social development during the preschool years, whereas others look at social relationships in late adulthood. And still others might take a broader approach, examining cognitive development through every period of life.

Influences on Lifespan Development

In this book, we take a comprehensive approach to lifespan development, proceeding topically across the life span through physical, cognitive, and social and personality development. Within each developmental area we consider various topics related to that area as a way of presenting an overview of the scope of development through the life span.

One of the first observations that we make is that no one develops alone, without interacting with others who share the same society and the same time period. This universal truth leads not to unity, but to the great diversity that we find in cultures and societies across the world and—on a smaller scale—within a larger culture.

DEVELOPMENTAL DIVERSITY
How Culture, Ethnicity, and Race Influence Development

Mayan mothers in Central America are certain that almost constant contact between themselves and their infant children is necessary for good parenting, and they are physically upset if contact is not possible. They are shocked when they see a North American mother lay her infant down, and they attribute the baby's crying to the poor parenting of the North American (Morelli et al., 1992).

What are we to make of the two views of parenting depicted in this passage? Is one right and the other wrong? Probably not, if we take cultural context into consideration. Different cultures and subcultures have their own views of appropriate and inappropriate childrearing, just as they have different developmental goals for children (Greenfield, 1997; Haight, 2002; Tolchinsky, 2003; Feldman & Masalha, 2007).

To understand development, developmentalists must take account of broad cultural factors, such as an orientation toward individualism or collectivism, as well as finer ethnic, racial, socioeconomic, and gender differences. If they succeed in doing this, not only can they achieve a better understanding of human development, but they may be able to derive more precise applications for improving the human social condition.

Culture, ethnicity, and race have significant effects on development.

To complicate the study of diverse populations, the terms *race* and *ethnic group* are often used inappropriately. *Race* is a biological concept that should refer to classifications based on the physical and structural characteristics of species. In contrast, *ethnic group* and *ethnicity* are broader, referring to cultural background, nationality, religion, and language.

The concept of race has proven especially problematic. It has inappropriately taken on nonbiological meanings ranging from skin color to religion to culture. Moreover, as a concept it is exceedingly imprecise; depending on how it is defined, there are between 3 and 300 races, and no race is genetically distinct. The fact that 99.9 percent of humans' genetic makeup is identical in all humans makes the question of race seem insignificant (Bamshad & Olson, 2003; Helms, Jernigan, & Mascher, 2005; Smedley & Smedley, 2005).

In addition, there is little agreement about which names best reflect different races and ethnic groups. Should the term *African American*—which has geographical and cultural implications—be preferred to *black,* which focuses primarily on race and skin color? Is *Native American* preferable to *Indian*? Is *Hispanic* more appropriate than *Latino*? And how can researchers accurately categorize people with multiracial backgrounds?

To fully understand development, then, we need to consider the complex issues associated with human diversity. It is only by looking for similarities and differences among various ethnic, cultural, and racial groups that developmental researchers can distinguish universal principles of development from culturally determined differences. Lifespan development will continue its transition from a focus on North American and European development to a global focus (Bamshad et al., 2003; Fowers & Davidov, 2006; Matsumoto & Yoo, 2006).

Cohort and Other Influences on Development: Developing with Others in a Social World. Bob, born in 1947, is a baby boomer; he was born soon after the end of World War II, when returning soldiers caused an enormous bulge in the birthrate. He was an adolescent at the height of the civil rights movement and protests against the Vietnam War. His mother, Leah, was born in 1922; her generation passed its childhood and teenage years in the shadow of the Depression. Bob's son, Jon, was born in 1975. Now building a career and starting a family, he is a member of what has been called Generation X. Jon's younger sister, Sarah, who was born in 1982, is part of the next generation, which sociologists have called the Millennial Generation.

These people are in part products of the social times in which they live. Each belongs to a particular **cohort**, a group of people born at around the same time in the same place. Such major social events as wars, economic upturns and depressions, famines, and epidemics (like the one due to the AIDS virus) work similar influences on members of a particular cohort (Mitchell, 2002; Dittmann, 2005).

Cohort effects are an example of *history-graded influences,* biological and environmental influences associated with a particular historical moment. For instance, people who lived in New York City during the 9/11 terrorist attack on the World Trade Center experienced shared biological and environmental challenges due to the attack (Bonanno, Galea, & Bucciarelli, 2006; Laugharne, Janca, & Widiger, 2007). The specter of terrorism is a history-graded influence that is common to people living in the United States today.

In contrast, *age-graded influences* are biological and environmental influences that are similar for individuals in a particular age group, regardless of when or where they are raised. For example, biological events such as puberty and menopause are universal events that occur at about the same time in all societies. Similarly, a sociocultural event such as entry into formal education can be considered an age-graded influence because it occurs in most cultures around age 6.

Development is also affected by *sociocultural-graded influences,* the social and cultural factors present at a particular time for a particular individual, depending on such variables as ethnicity, social class, and subcultural membership. For example, sociocultural-graded influences will be considerably different for white and nonwhite children, especially if one lives in poverty and the other in affluence (Rose et al., 2003; Tyler et al., 2008).

Finally, *non-normative life events* are specific, atypical events that occur in a particular person's life at a time when such events do not happen to most people. For example, a child whose parents die in an automobile accident when she is 6 has experienced a significant non-normative life event.

Key Debates in Lifespan Development

Lifespan development is a decades-long journey through shared milestones, with many individual routes along the way. For developmentalists, the variations in lifespan development raise many questions. What are the best ways to think about the enormous changes that a person undergoes from before birth to death? How important is chronological age? Is there a clear timetable for development? How can one begin to find common threads and patterns?

These questions have been debated since lifespan development became established as a separate field in the late nineteenth and early twentieth centuries, though a fascination with the nature and course of humans' development can be traced back to the ancient Egyptians and Greeks.

Continuous Change Versus Discontinuous Change. One of the primary issues challenging developmentalists is whether development proceeds in a continuous or discontinuous fashion. In **continuous change**, development is gradual, with achievements at one level building on those of previous levels. Continuous change is quantitative; the underlying developmental processes remain the same over the life span. In this view, changes are a matter of degree, not of kind—like changes in a person's height. Some theorists suggest that changes in people's thinking abilities are also continuous, building on gradual improvements rather than developing entirely new processing capabilities.

In contrast, others see development as primarily a matter of **discontinuous change**, occurring in distinct stages. Each stage brings about behavior that is assumed to be qualitatively different from behavior at earlier stages. Consider cognitive development again. Some cognitive developmentalists suggest that our thinking changes in fundamental ways as we develop, not just quantitatively but qualitatively.

Most developmentalists agree that it makes little sense to take an either/or position on this issue. Although many types of developmental change are continuous, others are clearly discontinuous (Flavell, 1994; Heimann, 2003).

Critical and Sensitive Periods: Gauging the Impact of Environmental Events. If a woman comes down with a case of rubella (German measles) in the 11th week of pregnancy, the consequences for the child she is carrying—possible blindness, deafness, and heart defects—can be devastating. However, if she comes down with the same strain of rubella in the 30th week of pregnancy, damage to the child is unlikely.

**FROM AN
EDUCATOR'S
PERSPECTIVE**
How would a student's cohort membership affect his or her readiness for school? For example, what would be the benefits and drawbacks of coming from a cohort in which Internet use was routine, compared with earlier cohorts before the appearance of the Internet?

---

cohort a group of people born at around the same time in the same place.

continuous change gradual development with achievements at one level building on those of previous levels.

discontinuous change development that occurs in distinct steps or stages, with each stage bringing about behavior that is assumed to be qualitatively different from behavior at earlier stages.

The differing outcomes demonstrate the concept of critical periods. A **critical period** is a specific time during development when a particular event has its greatest consequences. Critical periods occur when the presence of certain kinds of environmental stimuli is necessary for development to proceed normally (Uylings, 2006).

Although early specialists in lifespan development placed great emphasis on critical periods, recent thinking suggests that individuals are more malleable, particularly in the domain of personality and social development. For instance, rather than suffering permanent damage from a lack of certain early social experiences, there is increasing evidence that people can use later experiences to help overcome earlier deficits.

Consequently, developmentalists are now more likely to speak of **sensitive periods** rather than critical periods. In a sensitive period, organisms are particularly susceptible to certain kinds of stimuli in their environments. In contrast to a critical period, however, the absence of those stimuli during a sensitive period does not always produce irreversible consequences (Barinaga, 2000; Thompson & Nelson, 2001; Beauchaine, 2003).

Lifespan Approaches Versus a Focus on Particular Periods. Early developmentalists tended to focus their attention on infancy and adolescence, largely to the exclusion of other parts of the life span. Today, however, developmentalists believe the entire life span is important, largely because developmental growth and change continue during every part of life—as we'll discuss throughout this book.

Furthermore, to fully understand the social influences on a person of a given age, we need to understand the person's social environment—the people who in large measure provide those influences. For instance, to understand development in infants, we need to unravel the effects of their parents' ages on their social environments. A 15-year-old first-time mother and an experienced 37-year-old mother will provide parental influences of very different sorts. Consequently, infant development is in part an outgrowth of adult development.

In addition, as lifespan developmentalist Paul Baltes points out, development across the life span involves both gains and losses. With age, certain capabilities become more refined and sophisticated, while others decline. For example, vocabulary tends to grow throughout childhood and continues through most of adulthood, but certain physical abilities, such as reaction time, improve until early and middle adulthood, and then begin to decline (Baltes, 2003; Ebner, Freund, & Baltes, 2006).

People also invest their resources of motivation, energy, and time differently at different points during the life span. Early in life, more of one's personal resources are devoted to activities involving growth, such as studying or learning new skills. Later, especially during late adulthood, more resources are devoted to dealing with loss (Staudinger & Leipold, 2003).

The Relative Influence of Nature and Nurture on Development. One of the enduring questions of development involves how much of people's behavior is due to genetics (nature) and how much to the physical and social environment (nurture) (Wexler, 2006).

Nature refers to traits, abilities, and capacities that are inherited from one's parents. It encompasses any factor that is produced by the predetermined unfolding of genetic information—a process known as **maturation**. These genetic, inherited influences are at work as we move from the one-cell organism created at conception to the billions of cells that make up a fully formed human. Nature influences whether our eyes are blue or brown, whether we have thick hair throughout life or eventually go bald, and how good we are at athletics. Nature allows our brains to develop in such a way that we can read the words on this page.

In contrast, *nurture* refers to the environmental influences that shape behavior. Some influences may be biological, such as the impact of a pregnant mother's use of cocaine on her unborn child or the amount and kind of food available to children. Other influences are more social, such as the ways parents discipline their children and the effects of peer pressure on an adolescent. Finally, some influences are a result of societal factors, such as the socioeconomic circumstances in which people find themselves.

Although developmentalists reject the notion that behavior is the sole result of either nature or nurture, the nature–nurture question can cause heated debate. Take, for instance, intelligence. If intelligence is primarily determined by heredity and is largely fixed at birth, then efforts to improve intellectual performance later in life may be doomed to failure. In contrast, if intelligence is primarily a result of environmental factors, such as the amount and quality of schooling and home stimulation, then an improvement in social conditions could cause intelligence to increase.

critical period   a specific time during development when a particular event has its greatest consequences and the presence of certain kinds of environmental stimuli is necessary for development to proceed normally.

sensitive period   a point in development when organisms are particularly susceptible to certain kinds of stimuli in their environments, but the absence of those stimuli does not always produce irreversible consequences.

maturation   the predetermined unfolding of genetic information.

Clearly, neither nature nor nurture stands alone in most developmental matters. The interaction of genetic and environmental factors is complex, in part because certain genetically determined traits have not only a direct influence on children's behavior, but an indirect influence in shaping children's *environments*. For example, children who cry a great deal—a trait that may be produced by genetic factors—may influence their environment by making their parents rush to comfort them whenever they cry. The parents' responsivity to their children's genetically determined behavior becomes an environmental influence on the children's subsequent development.

Similarly, although our genetic background orients us toward particular behaviors, those behaviors will not necessarily occur without an appropriate environment. People with similar genetic backgrounds (such as identical twins) may behave in very different ways; and people with highly dissimilar genetic backgrounds can sometimes behave quite similarly (Morange, 2002; Harris, 2006).

In sum, the nature–nurture question is challenging. Ultimately, we should consider the two sides of the issue as ends of a continuum, with particular behaviors falling somewhere between the ends. The same can be said of the other controversies that we have considered. For instance, continuous versus discontinuous development is not an either/or proposition; some forms of development fall toward the continuous end of the continuum, whereas others lie closer to the discontinuous end. In short, few statements about development involve either/or absolutes (Rutter, 2006; Deater-Deckard & Cahill, 2007).

REVIEW

▶ Lifespan development, a scientific approach to understanding human growth and change throughout life, encompasses physical, cognitive, and social and personality development.

▶ Membership in a cohort, based on age and place of birth, subjects people to influences based on historical events (history-graded influences). People are also subject to age-graded influences, sociocultural-graded influences, and non-normative life events.

▶ Four important issues in lifespan development are continuity versus discontinuity in development, the importance of sensitive periods, whether to focus on certain periods or on the entire life span, and the nature–nurture controversy.

APPLY

▶ What are some examples of the ways culture (either broad culture or aspects of culture) has affected your development?

▶ How do different age-graded influences and history-graded influences contribute to making you and your parents different?

MODULE 1.2

Theoretical Perspectives on Lifespan Development

Until the seventeenth century in Europe, there was no concept of "childhood." Instead, children were simply thought of as miniature adults. They were assumed to be subject to the same needs and desires as adults, to have the same vices and virtues, and to warrant no more privileges. They were dressed the same as adults, and their work hours were the same. Children also received the same punishments for misdeeds. If they stole, they were hanged; if they did well, they could achieve prosperity, at least so far as their station in life or social class would allow.

This view of childhood seems wrongheaded now, but at the time it was society's understanding of lifespan development. From this perspective, there were no differences due to age; except for size, people were assumed to be virtually unchanging, at least on a psychological level, throughout most of the life span (Aries, 1962; Acocella, 2003; Hutton, 2004; Wines, 2006).

Theories Explaining Developmental Change

It is easy to reject the early perspective on childhood but less clear how to formulate a contemporary substitute. Should our view of development focus on the biological aspects of change, growth, and stability over the life span? The cognitive or social aspects? Or some other factors?

People who study lifespan development approach the field from different perspectives. Each perspective encompasses one or more **theories**, broad, organized explanations and predictions concerning phenomena of interest. A theory provides a framework for understanding the relationships among a seemingly unorganized set of facts or principles.

We all develop theories about development, based on our experience, folklore, and stories in the media. However, theories in lifespan development are different. Whereas our own personal theories are haphazardly built on unverified observations, developmentalists' theories are more formal, based on a systematic integration of prior findings and theorizing. Theories allow developmentalists to summarize and organize prior observations, and they also permit them to move beyond existing observations to form deductions that may not be immediately apparent. In addition, theories are subject to rigorous testing through research. By contrast, the developmental theories of individuals are not subject to testing and may never be questioned at all (Thomas, 2001).

We will consider six major theoretical perspectives used in lifespan development: the psychodynamic, behavioral, cognitive, humanistic, contextual, and evolutionary perspectives. Each emphasizes somewhat different aspects of development and steers developmentalists in particular directions. Furthermore, each perspective continues to evolve, as befits a dynamic discipline.

Sigmund Freud.

The Psychodynamic Perspective: Focusing on the Inner Person

> When Marisol was 6 months old, she was involved in a terrible automobile accident—or so her parents tell her, since she has no recollection of it. Now, however, at age 24, she is having difficulty maintaining relationships, and her therapist is seeking to determine whether her current problems are a result of the earlier accident.

Looking for such a link might seem a bit far-fetched—but not to proponents of the **psychodynamic perspective**. Advocates of this theory believe that much behavior is motivated by inner forces, memories, and conflicts of which a person has little awareness or control. The inner forces, which may stem from childhood, influence behavior throughout life.

Freud's Psychoanalytic Theory.
The psychodynamic perspective is most closely associated with Sigmund Freud. Freud, who lived from 1856 to 1939, was a Viennese physician whose revolutionary ideas had a profound effect not only on psychology and psychiatry, but on Western thought in general throughout the twentieth century (Masling & Bornstein, 1996; Aichhorn, 2008; Tryon, 2008).

Freud's **psychoanalytic theory** suggests that unconscious forces act to determine personality and behavior. To Freud, the *unconscious* is a part of the personality about which a person is unaware. It contains infantile wishes, desires, demands, and needs that, because of their disturbing nature, are hidden from conscious awareness. Freud suggested that the unconscious is responsible for a good part of our everyday behavior.

According to Freud, everyone's personality has three aspects: id, ego, and superego. The *id* is the raw, unorganized, inborn part of personality that is present at birth. It represents primitive drives related to hunger, sex, aggression, and irrational impulses. The id operates according to the *pleasure principle*, in which the goal is to maximize satisfaction and reduce tension.

The *ego* is the part of personality that is rational and reasonable. The ego acts as a buffer between the external world and the primitive id. The ego operates on the *reality principle*, in which instinctual energy is restrained in order to maintain the safety of the individual and help integrate the person into society.

Finally, Freud proposed that the *superego* represents a person's conscience, incorporating distinctions between right and wrong. It begins to develop around age 5 or 6 and is learned from an individual's parents, teachers, and other significant figures.

Freud also addressed personality development during childhood. He argued that **psychosexual development** occurs as children pass through distinct stages in which pleasure, or gratification, is focused on a particular biological function and body part. As illustrated in Table 1.2, he suggested that pleasure shifts from the mouth (the *oral stage*) to the anus (the *anal stage*) and eventually to the genitals (the *phallic stage* and the *genital stage*).

theories explanations and predictions concerning phenomena of interest, providing a framework for understanding the relationships among an organized set of facts or principles.

psychodynamic perspective the approach that states behavior is motivated by inner forces, memories, and conflicts that are generally beyond people's awareness and control.

psychoanalytic theory the theory proposed by Freud that suggests that unconscious forces act to determine personality and behavior.

psychosexual development according to Freud, a series of stages that children pass through in which pleasure, or gratification, is focused on a particular biological function and body part.

TABLE 1.2		Freud's and Erikson's Theories		
APPROXIMATE AGE	FREUD'S STAGES OF PSYCHOSEXUAL DEVELOPMENT	MAJOR CHARACTERISTICS OF FREUD'S STAGES	ERIKSON'S STAGES OF PSYCHOSOCIAL DEVELOPMENT	POSITIVE AND NEGATIVE OUTCOMES OF ERIKSON'S STAGES
Birth to 12–18 months	Oral	Interest in oral gratification from sucking, eating, mouthing, biting	Trust vs. mistrust	*Positive*: Feelings of trust from environmental support *Negative*: Fear and concern regarding others
12–18 months to 3 years	Anal	Gratification from expelling and withholding feces; coming to terms with society's controls relating to toilet training	Autonomy vs. shame and doubt	*Positive*: Self-sufficiency if exploration is encouraged *Negative*: Doubts about self, lack of independence
3 to 5–6 years	Phallic	Interest in the genitals; coming to terms with Oedipal conflict, leading to identification with same sex parent	Initiative vs. guilt	*Positive*: Discovery of ways to initiate actions *Negative*: Guilt from actions and thoughts
5–6 years to adolescence	Latency	Sexual concerns largely unimportant	Industry vs. inferiority	*Positive*: Development of sense of competence *Negative*: Feelings of inferiority, no sense of mastery
Adolescence to adulthood (Freud) Adolescence (Erikson)	Genital	Reemergence of sexual interests and establishment of mature sexual relationships	Identity vs. role diffusion	*Positive*: Awareness of uniqueness of self, knowledge of role to be followed *Negative*: Inability to identify appropriate roles in life
Early adulthood (Erikson)			Intimacy vs. isolation	*Positive*: Development of loving, sexual relationships and close friendships *Negative*: Fear of relationships with others
Middle adulthood (Erikson)			Generativity vs. stagnation	*Positive*: Sense of contribution to continuity of life *Negative*: Trivialization of one's activities
Late adulthood (Erikson)			Ego integrity vs. despair	*Positive*: Sense of unity in life's accomplishments *Negative*: Regret over lost opportunities of life

According to Freud, if children are unable to gratify themselves sufficiently during a particular stage, or if they receive too much gratification, fixation may occur. *Fixation* is behavior reflecting an earlier stage of development due to an unresolved conflict. For instance, fixation at the oral stage might produce an adult unusually absorbed in oral activities—eating, talking, or chewing gum. Freud also argued that fixation is represented through symbolic oral activities, such as the use of "biting" sarcasm.

psychosocial development the approach that encompasses changes in our interactions with and understandings of one another, as well as in our knowledge and understanding of ourselves as members of society.

Erikson's Psychosocial Theory. Psychoanalyst Erik Erikson, who lived from 1902 to 1994, provided an alternative psychodynamic view, emphasizing our social interaction with other people. In Erikson's view, society and culture both challenge and shape us. **Psychosocial development** encompasses changes in our interactions with and understandings of one another as well as in our knowledge and understanding of us as members of society (Erikson, 1963).

Erikson's theory suggests that development proceeds throughout our lives in eight stages (see Table 1.2), which emerge in a fixed pattern and are similar for all people. Each stage presents a crisis or conflict that the individual must resolve. Although no crisis is ever fully resolved, the individual must at least address the crisis of each stage sufficiently to deal with demands made during the next stage of development. Unlike Freud, who regarded development as relatively complete by adolescence, Erikson suggested that growth and change continue throughout the life span (De St. Aubin, McAdams, & Kim, 2004).

Assessing the Psychodynamic Perspective. Freud's insight that unconscious influences affect behavior was a monumental accomplishment, and the fact that it seems at all reasonable to us shows how extensively the idea of the unconscious has pervaded thinking in Western cultures. In fact, work by contemporary researchers studying memory and learning suggests that we unconsciously carry with us memories that have a significant impact on our behavior.

Some of the most basic principles of Freud's psychoanalytic theory have been questioned, however, because they have not been validated by research. In particular, the notion that childhood stages determine adult personalities has little research support. In addition, because much of Freud's theory was based on a limited population of upper-middle-class Austrians living during a strict, puritanical era, its application to broad, multicultural populations is questionable. Finally, because Freud's theory focuses primarily on male development, it has been criticized as sexist and interpreted as devaluing women (Guterl, 2002; Messer & McWilliams, 2003; Chrisler & Smith, 2004).

Erikson's view that development continues throughout the life span is highly important—and has received considerable support. However, the theory also has its drawbacks. Like Freud's theory, it focuses more on men than women. Furthermore, its vagueness makes it difficult to test rigorously. And, as with psychodynamic theories in general, it is difficult to make definitive predictions about a given individual's behavior using the theory (Whitbourne et al., 1992; Zauszniewski & Martin, 1999; De St. Aubin & McAdams, 2004).

The Behavioral Perspective: Focusing on Observable Behavior

When Elissa Sheehan was 3, a large brown dog bit her, and she needed dozens of stitches and several operations. From the time she was bitten, she broke into a sweat whenever she saw a dog, and in fact never enjoyed being around any pet.

To a lifespan development specialist using the behavioral perspective, the explanation for Elissa's behavior is straightforward: She has a learned fear of dogs. Rather than looking inside the organism at unconscious processes, the **behavioral perspective** suggests that the keys to understanding development are observable behavior and environmental stimuli. If we know the stimuli, we can predict the behavior. In this respect, the behavioral perspective reflects the view that nurture is more important to development than nature.

Behavioral theories reject the notion that people universally pass through a series of stages. Instead, people are affected by the environmental stimuli to which they happen to be exposed. Developmental patterns, then, are personal, reflecting a particular set of environmental stimuli, and behavior is the result of continuing exposure to specific factors in the environment. Furthermore, developmental change is viewed in quantitative, rather than qualitative, terms. For instance, behavioral theories hold that advances in problem-solving capabilities as children age are largely a result of greater mental *capacities* rather than changes in the *kind* of thinking that children can bring to bear on a problem.

Classical Conditioning: Stimulus Substitution

Give me a dozen healthy infants, well-formed, and my own specified world to bring them up in and I'll guarantee to take any one at random and train him to become any type of specialist I might select—doctor, lawyer, artist, merchant-chief, and yes, even beggar-man and thief, regardless of his talents, penchants, tendencies, abilities. (Watson, 1925)

With these words, John B. Watson, one of the first American psychologists to advocate a behavioral approach, summed up the behavioral perspective. Watson, who lived from 1878 to 1958, believed strongly that we could gain a full understanding of development by carefully

Erik Erikson.

FROM A
CHILD CARE PROVIDER'S
PERSPECTIVE
How important do you think it is to have an understanding of the behavioral perspective, and how would you apply it to your daily work?

behavioral perspective
the approach that suggests that the keys to understanding development are observable behavior and outside stimuli in the environment.

John B. Watson.

FROM A
SOCIAL WORKER'S
PERSPECTIVE

How do the concepts of social learning and modeling relate to the mass media, and how might exposure to mass media influence a child's family life?

classical conditioning   a type of learning in which an organism responds to a neutral stimulus that normally does not bring about that type of response.

operant conditioning   a form of learning in which a voluntary response is strengthened or weakened by its association with positive or negative consequences.

behavior modification   a formal technique for promoting the frequency of desirable behaviors and decreasing the incidence of unwanted ones.

social-cognitive learning theory learning by observing the behavior of another person, called a model.

studying the stimuli that composed the environment. He argued that by effectively controlling—or *conditioning*—a person's environment, it was possible to produce virtually any behavior.

Classical Conditioning. **Classical conditioning** occurs when an organism learns to respond in a particular way to a neutral stimulus. For instance, if the sound of a bell is paired with the arrival of meat, a dog will learn to react to the bell alone in the same way it reacts to the meat—by salivating and wagging its tail. The behavior is a result of conditioning, a form of learning in which the response associated with one stimulus (food) comes to be connected to another—in this case, the bell.

The same process of classical conditioning explains how we learn emotional responses. In the case of dog bite victim Elissa Sheehan, for instance, Watson would say that one stimulus has been substituted for another: Elissa's unpleasant experience with a particular dog (the initial stimulus) has been transferred to other dogs and to pets in general.

Operant Conditioning. In addition to classical conditioning, the behavioral perspective accounts for other types of learning, especially what behavioralists call operant conditioning. **Operant conditioning** is a form of learning in which a voluntary response is strengthened or weakened by its association with positive or negative consequences. It differs from classical conditioning in that the response being conditioned is voluntary and purposeful rather than automatic (such as salivating). In operant conditioning, formulated and championed by psychologist B. F. Skinner (1904–1990), individuals learn to *operate* on their environments in order to bring about desired consequences (Skinner, 1975).

Whether or not children and adults will seek to repeat a behavior depends on whether it is followed by reinforcement. *Reinforcement* is the process by which a behavior is followed by a stimulus that increases the probability that the behavior will be repeated. Hence, a student is apt to work harder if he or she receives good grades; workers are likely to labor harder if their efforts are tied to pay increases; and people are more apt to buy lottery tickets if they are reinforced by winning occasionally. In addition, *punishment*, the introduction of an unpleasant or painful stimulus or the removal of a desirable stimulus, will decrease the probability that a preceding behavior will occur in the future.

Behavior that is reinforced, then, is more likely to be repeated, while behavior that receives no reinforcement or is punished is likely to be *extinguished*, in the language of operant conditioning. Principles of operant conditioning are used in **behavior modification**, a formal technique for promoting the frequency of desirable behaviors and decreasing the incidence of unwanted ones. Behavior modification has been used in situations ranging from teaching people with severe retardation basic language to helping people with self-control problems stick to diets (Katz, 2001; Christophersen & Mortweet, 2003; Hoek & Gendall, 2006).

Social-Cognitive Learning Theory: Learning Through Imitation. A 5-year-old boy seriously injures his 22-month-old cousin while imitating a violent wrestling move he has seen on television. Although the baby sustained spinal cord injuries, he improved and was discharged 5 weeks after his hospital admission (Reuters Health eLine, 2002). Is this a case of cause and effect? We can't know for sure, but it certainly seems possible, especially to social-cognitive learning theorists. According to developmental psychologist Albert Bandura and colleagues, a significant amount of learning is explained by **social-cognitive learning theory**, an approach that emphasizes learning by observing the behavior of another person, called a *model* (Bandura, 1994, 2002, 2007).

If operant conditioning makes learning a matter of trial and error, social-cognitive learning theory makes learning a product of observation. Social-cognitive learning theory holds that when we see the behavior of a model being rewarded, we are likely to imitate that behavior. For instance, in one classic experiment, children who were afraid of dogs were exposed to a model, nicknamed the "Fearless Peer," who was seen playing happily with a dog (Bandura, Grusec, & Menlove, 1967). After exposure, the children who previously had been afraid were more likely to approach a strange dog than children who had not seen the model.

Assessing the Behavioral Perspective. Research using the behavioral perspective has made significant contributions, ranging from the education of children with severe mental retardation to the development of procedures for curbing aggression. At the same time, the perspective has experienced internal disagreements. For example, although they are part of the same behavioral perspective, classical and operant conditioning and social learning theory disagree in some basic ways. Classical and operant conditioning considers learning in terms of external stimuli and responses, in which the only important factors are the observable features of the environment. People and other organisms are like inanimate "black boxes"; what occurs inside the box is neither understood nor cared about.

To social learning theorists, such an analysis is an oversimplification. They argue that what makes people different from rats and pigeons is mental activity, in the form of thoughts and expectations. We cannot derive a full understanding of people's development without moving beyond external stimuli and responses.

In many ways, social learning theory has won this argument in recent decades. In fact, another perspective that focuses explicitly on internal mental activity has become enormously influential: the cognitive perspective.

The Cognitive Perspective: Examining the Roots of Understanding. When 3-year-old Jake is asked why it sometimes rains, he answers "so the flowers can grow." When his 11-year-old sister Lila is asked the same question, she responds "because of evaporation from the surface of the Earth." And when their cousin Ajima, who is studying meteorology in graduate school, considers the same question, her extended answer includes a discussion of cumulonimbus clouds, the Coriolis Effect, and synoptic charts.

To a developmental theorist using the cognitive perspective, the difference in the sophistication of the answers is evidence of a different degree of knowledge and understanding, or cognition. The **cognitive perspective** focuses on the processes that allow people to know, understand, and think about the world.

The cognitive perspective emphasizes how people internally represent and think about the world. By using this perspective, developmental researchers hope to understand how children and adults process information and how their ways of thinking and understanding affect their behavior. They also seek to learn how cognitive abilities change as people develop, the degree to which cognitive development represents quantitative and qualitative growth in intellectual abilities, and how different cognitive abilities are related to one another.

Piaget's Theory of Cognitive Development. No one has had a greater impact on the study of cognitive development than Jean Piaget, a Swiss psychologist who lived from 1896 to 1980. Piaget proposed that all people pass through a fixed sequence of universal stages of cognitive development—and not only does the *quantity* of information increase in each stage, but the *quality* of knowledge and understanding changes as well. His focus is on the change in cognition that occurs as children move from one stage to the next (Piaget, 1952, 1962, 1983).

Broadly speaking, Piaget suggests that human thinking is arranged into *schemes*, organized mental patterns that represent behaviors and actions. In infants, schemes represent concrete behavior—a scheme for sucking, for reaching, and for each separate behavior. In older children, the schemes become more sophisticated and abstract, such as the skills involved in riding a bike or playing an interactive video game. Schemes are like intellectual computer software that directs and determines how data from the world are looked at and handled.

Piaget suggests that the growth in children's understanding of the world can be explained by two basic principles: assimilation and accommodation. *Assimilation* is the process in which people understand a new experience in terms of their current stage of cognitive development and existing ways of thinking. In contrast, *accommodation* refers to changes in existing ways of thinking in response to encounters with new stimuli or events. Assimilation and accommodation work in tandem to bring about cognitive development.

Assessing Piaget's Theory. Piaget has profoundly influenced our understanding of cognitive development and is one of the towering figures in lifespan development. He provided masterful descriptions of intellectual growth during childhood—descriptions that have stood the test of literally thousands of investigations. Broadly, then, Piaget's view of cognitive development is accurate. However, the specifics of the theory have been questioned. For instance, some cognitive skills clearly emerge earlier than Piaget suggested. Furthermore, the universality of Piaget's stages has been disputed. Growing evidence suggests that particular cognitive skills emerge on a different timetable in non-Western cultures. And in every culture, some people

On the reality show *Survivor*, contestants often must learn new survival skills in order to be successful. What form of learning is at work?

cognitive perspective the approach that focuses on the processes that allow people to know, understand, and think about the world.

information processing approaches
models that seek to identify the ways
individuals take in, use, and store
information.

cognitive neuroscience approaches
approaches that examine cognitive
development through the lens of brain
processes.

never seem to reach Piaget's highest level of cognitive sophistication: formal, logical thought (Rogoff & Chavajay, 1995; McDonald & Stuart-Hamilton, 2003; Genovese, 2006).

Ultimately, the greatest criticism of Piaget's work is that cognitive development is not necessarily as discontinuous as his stage theory suggests. Many developmental researchers argue that growth is considerably more continuous. These critics have suggested an alternative perspective, known as the information processing approach, that focuses on the processes that underlie learning, memory, and thinking throughout the life span.

Information Processing Approaches. Information processing approaches have become an important alternative to Piagetian approaches. **Information processing approaches** to cognitive development seek to identify the ways individuals take in, use, and store information.

Information processing approaches grew out of developments in computers. These approaches assume that even complex behavior such as learning, remembering, categorizing, and thinking can be broken down into a series of individual, specific steps. They contend that children, like computers, have limited capacity for processing information. As children develop, however, they employ increasingly sophisticated strategies that allow them to process information more efficiently.

In stark contrast to Piaget's view, information processing approaches assume that development is marked more by quantitative than qualitative advances. Our capacity to handle information changes with age, as does our processing speed and efficiency. Furthermore, information processing approaches suggest that as we age, we are better able to control the nature of processing and the strategies we choose to process information.

An information processing approach that builds on Piaget's research is known as neo-Piagetian theory. In contrast to Piaget's original work, which viewed cognition as a single system of increasingly sophisticated general cognitive abilities, *neo-Piagetian theory* considers cognition as being made up of different types of individual skills. Using the terminology of information processing approaches, neo-Piagetian theory suggests that cognitive development proceeds quickly in certain areas and more slowly in others. For example, reading ability and the skills needed to recall stories may progress sooner than the abstract computational abilities used in algebra or trigonometry. Furthermore, neo-Piagetian theorists believe that experience plays a greater role in advancing cognitive development than traditional Piagetian approaches (Case, Demetriou, & Platsidou, 2001; Yan & Fischer, 2002; Morra et al., 2008; Johnson, 2009).

Assessing Information Processing Approaches. Information processing approaches have become a central part of our understanding of development, but they do not offer a complete explanation of behavior. For example, they have paid little attention to behavior such as creativity, in which the most profound ideas often are developed in a seemingly nonlogical, nonlinear manner. In addition, they do not take into account the social context in which development takes place—and theories that do this have become increasingly popular.

Cognitive Neuroscience Approaches. Among the most recent additions to the array of approaches are **cognitive neuroscience approaches**, which look at cognitive development at the level of brain processes. Like other cognitive perspectives, cognitive neuroscience approaches consider internal, mental processes, but they focus specifically on the neurological activity that underlies thinking, problem solving, and other cognitive behavior.

Cognitive neuroscientists seek to identify actual locations and functions within the brain that are related to different types of cognitive activity. For example, using sophisticated brain scanning techniques, cognitive neuroscientists have demonstrated that thinking about the meaning of a word activates different areas of the brain than thinking about how the word sounds when spoken.

Cognitive neuroscientists are also providing clues to the cause of *autism*, a major developmental disability that can produce profound language deficits and self-injurious behavior in young children. For example, neuroscientists have found that the brains of children with the disorder show explosive, dramatic growth in the first year of life, making their heads significantly larger than those of children without the disorder (see Figure 1.1). By identifying children with the disorder very early in their lives, health care practitioners can provide crucial early intervention (Courchesne, Carper, & Akshoomoff, 2003; Herbert et al., 2005; Akshoomoff, 2006).

Cognitive neuroscience approaches are also on the forefront of cutting-edge research that has identified genes associated with disorders ranging from physical problems such as breast cancer to psychological disorders such as schizophrenia (DeLisi & Fleischhaker, 2007).

FIGURE 1.1 The Autistic Brain
Neuroscientists have found that the brains of individuals with autism are larger than the brains of those without autism in the first year of life. This finding can help diagnose the disorder early so that proper health care can be provided.
(*Source:* Reprinted with permission from Dr. Eric Courchesne. www.courchesneautismlab.org/mri.html.)

NEUROSCIENCE AND DEVELOPMENT
The Essential Principles of Neuroscience

It is quiet in the computer lab as three students download assignments in preparation for upcoming midterm exams. Jonathan, a business major, reviews an article on how advertising influences buying behavior; Christina, a music and special education major, reads about how music helps motor control in children with cerebral palsy; and Marisha, a criminal justice major, takes notes on an article about variables that influence early release from prison. None of these students is enrolled in a bioscience program, yet they all have one thing in common as they prepare for their tests: neuroscience.

Contemporary neuroscience and its subareas address an array of relevant problems with methods and insights from brain research and encourage translation of this research to the application of new scientific knowledge to every facet of the human condition. In 2007, the Society for Neuroscience (SfN) spearheaded an effort in which hundreds of neuroscientists and educators across the United States developed eight concepts within four overarching concepts that contain fundamental principles (named *Neuroscience Core Concepts*) they believe everyone should know about the brain and the nervous system (Society for Neuroscience (SfN), 2007).

Fill in the blanks or check yes or no in the statements below to learn how much you know about the brain and its workings.

1. **The ___ ___ controls and responds to body functions and directs behavior.**

   ___Yes ___No The brain is the body's most complex organ.

   ___Yes ___No Neurons communicate using both electrical and chemical agents.

2. **Nervous system structure and functions are determined by both ___ and ___throughout life.**

   ___Yes ___No Genetically determined circuits are the foundation of the nervous system.

   ___Yes ___No Life experiences change the nervous system.

3. **The ___ is the foundation of the mind.**

   ___Yes ___No Intelligence arises as the brain reasons, plans, and solves problems.

   ___Yes ___No The brain makes it possible to communicate knowledge through language.

4. **Research leads to understanding that is essential for development of ___ for nervous system disorders.**

   ___Yes ___No The human brain endows us with a natural curiosity to understand how the world works.

   ___Yes ___No Fundamental discoveries promote healthy living and treatment of disease.

How did you do?

10–12 correct: Bravo!

7–9 correct: You are on your way. Keep learning.

4–6 correct: Fire up those neurons to learn more about your brain.

0–3 correct: Don't give up. Learn a new brain fact every day.

For more information, go to the SfN website for additional information (http://www.sfn.org/index.aspx?pagename=brainfacts)

Source: Society for Neuroscience (SfN) (2007). *Brain Facts*. Washington, DC: SfN.

ANSWERS: 1. nervous system; 2. genes; environment; 3. brain; 4. therapies. All subcore concepts answers are "Yes."

Identifying the genes that make one vulnerable to such disorders is the first step in genetic engineering in which gene therapy can reduce or even prevent the disorder from occurring. (See the *Neuroscience and Development* box above.)

The Humanistic Perspective: Concentrating on Uniquely Human Qualities. The unique qualities of humans are the central focus of the humanistic perspective, the fourth of the major theories used by lifespan developmentalists. Rejecting the notion that behavior is largely determined by unconscious processes, the environment, or cognitive processing, the **humanistic perspective** contends that people have a natural capacity to make decisions about their lives and to control their behavior. According to this approach, each individual has the ability and motivation to reach more advanced levels of maturity, and people naturally seek to reach their full potential. The humanistic perspective emphasizes *free will*, the ability of humans to make choices and come to decisions about their lives instead of relying on societal standards.

Carl Rogers, one of the major proponents of the humanistic perspective, suggests that people need positive regard, which results from an underlying wish to be loved and respected. Because positive regard comes from other people, we become dependent on them. Consequently, our view of ourselves and our self-worth is a reflection of how we think others view us (Rogers, 1971; Motschnig & Nykl, 2003; Park & Maner, 2009).

humanistic perspective the theory that contends that people have a natural capacity to make decisions about their lives and control their behavior.

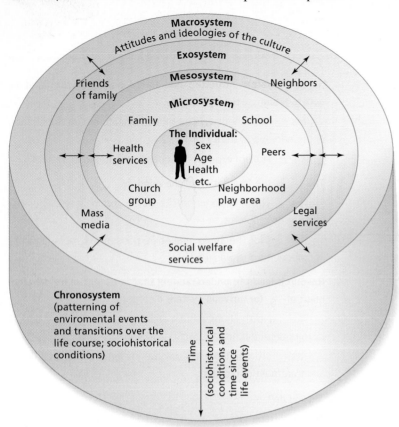

FIGURE 1.2 Bronfenbrenner's Approach to Development
Urie Bronfenbrenner's bioecological approach to development offers five levels of the environment that simultaneously influence individuals: the macrosystem, the exosystem, the mesosystem, the microsystem, and chronosystem.
(*Source:* Bronfenbrenner, 1998.)

Rogers, along with another key figure in the humanistic perspective, Abraham Maslow, suggests that self-actualization is a primary goal in life. *Self-actualization* is a state of self-fulfillment in which people achieve their highest potential in their own unique way (Maslow, 1970; Sheldon, Joiner, & Pettit, 2003; Merry, 2008).

Assessing the Humanistic Perspective. Despite its emphasis on important and unique human qualities, the humanistic perspective has not had a major impact on the field of lifespan development. This is primarily due to its inability to identify any sort of broad developmental change that is the result of increasing age or experience. Still, some of the concepts drawn from the humanistic perspective, such as self-actualization, have helped describe important aspects of human behavior and are widely discussed in areas ranging from health care to business (Neher, 1991; Dorer & Mahoney, 2006; Laas, 2006; Zalenski & Raspa, 2006).

The Contextual Perspective: Taking a Broad Approach to Development. Although lifespan developmentalists often consider development in terms of physical, cognitive, personality, and social factors separately, this categorization has one serious drawback: In the real world, none of these broad influences occurs in isolation from any other. Instead, the different types of influence interact constantly.

The **contextual perspective** considers the relationship between individuals and their physical, cognitive, personality, and social worlds. It suggests that a person's unique development cannot be properly viewed without seeing how that person is enmeshed within a rich social and cultural context. We'll next consider two major theories that fall under this category: Bronfenbrenner's bioecological approach and Vygotsky's sociocultural theory.

The Bioecological Approach to Development. In acknowledging the problem with traditional approaches to lifespan development, psychologist Urie Bronfenbrenner (2000, 2002; Bronfenbrenner & Morris, 2006) has proposed an alternative perspective, the bioecological approach. The **bioecological approach** suggests that five levels of the environment simultaneously influence individuals. Bronfenbrenner suggests that we cannot fully understand development without considering how a person is influenced by each of these levels (illustrated in Figure 1.2).

- The *microsystem* is the everyday, immediate environment of children's daily lives. Homes, caregivers, friends, and teachers all are influences, but children are not just passive recipients. Instead, children actively help construct the microsystem, shaping their immediate world. The microsystem is the level to which most traditional work in child development has been directed.

- The *mesosystem* connects the various aspects of the microsystem. The mesosystem binds children to parents, students to teachers, employees to bosses, friends to friends. It acknowledges the direct and indirect influences that bind us to one another, such as those that affect a mother who has a bad day at the office and then is short-tempered with her son at home.

- The *exosystem* represents broader influences: societal institutions such as local government, the community, schools, places of worship, and the local media. Each of these institutions can have an immediate, and major, impact on personal development, and each affects how the microsystem and mesosystem operate. For example, the quality of a school will affect a child's cognitive development and potentially can have long-term consequences.

- The *macrosystem* represents the larger cultural influences on an individual, including society in general, types of governments, religious and political value systems, and other

contextual perspective the theory that considers the relationship between individuals and their physical, cognitive, personality, and social worlds.

bioecological approach the perspective suggesting that different levels of the environment simultaneously influence individuals.

broad, encompassing factors. For example, the value a culture places on education affects the values of the people who live in that culture. Children are part of both a broader culture (such as Western culture) and members of one or more subcultures (for instance, the Mexican American subculture).

- Finally, the *chronosystem* underlies each of the previous systems. It involves the way the passage of time—including historical events (such as the terrorist attacks in September of 2001) and more gradual historical changes (such as changes in the number of women who work outside the home)—affects children's development.

The bioecological approach emphasizes the *interconnectedness of the influences on development.* Because the various levels are related to one another, a change in one part of the system affects other parts. For instance, a parent's loss of a job (involving the mesosystem) has an impact on a child's microsystem.

Conversely, changes on one environmental level may make little difference if other levels are not also changed. For instance, improving the school environment may have a negligible effect on academic performance if children receive little support for academic success at home. Similarly, the influences among family members are multidirectional. Parents don't just influence their child's behavior—the child also influences the parents' behavior.

Finally, the bioecological approach stresses the importance of broad cultural factors that affect development. Researchers in lifespan development increasingly look at how membership in cultural groups influences behavior.

Consider, for instance, whether you agree that children should be taught that their classmates' assistance is essential to getting good grades in school, or that they should plan to continue their fathers' businesses, or that they should take their parents' advice in choosing a career. If you have been raised in the most widespread North American culture, you would likely disagree with all three statements, since they violate the premises of *individualism,* the dominant Western philosophy that emphasizes personal identity, uniqueness, freedom, and the worth of the individual.

If you were raised in a traditional Asian culture, however, you would much more likely agree with the three statements because the statements reflect the value orientation known as collectivism. *Collectivism* is the notion that the well-being of the group is more important than that of the individual. People raised in collectivistic cultures sometimes emphasize the welfare of the group at the expense of their own personal well-being (Choi, 2002; Sedikides, Gaertner, & Toguchi, 2003; Leung, 2005).

Assessing the Bioecological Approach. Although Bronfenbrenner regards biological influences as an important component of the bioecological approach, ecological influences are central to the theory. Some critics even argue that the perspective pays insufficient attention to biological factors. Still, the bioecological approach is important because it suggests the multiple levels at which the environment affects children's development.

Vygotsky's Sociocultural Theory. To Russian developmentalist Lev Semenovich Vygotsky, a full understanding of development is impossible without taking into account the culture in which people develop. Vygotsky's **sociocultural theory** emphasizes how cognitive development proceeds as a result of social interactions between members of a culture (Vygotsky, 1979, 1926/1997; Beilin, 1996; Winsler, 2003; Edwards, 2005).

Vygotsky, who lived a brief life from 1896 to 1934, argued that children acquire an understanding of the world through their problem-solving interactions with adults and other children. As children play and cooperate with others, they learn what is important in their society and, at the same time, advance cognitively. Consequently, to understand development, we must consider what is meaningful to members of a given culture.

More than most other theories, sociocultural theory emphasizes that development is a *reciprocal transaction* between the people in a child's environment and the child. Vygotsky believed that people and settings influence the child, who in turn influences the people and settings. This pattern continues in an endless loop, with children being both recipients of socialization influences and sources of influence. For example, a child raised with his or her extended family nearby will grow up with a different sense of family life than a child whose relatives live far away. Those relatives, too, are affected by that situation and that child, depending on the closeness and frequency of their contact.

sociocultural theory   the approach that emphasizes how cognitive development proceeds as a result of social interactions between members of a culture.

According to Vygotsky, children can develop cognitively in their understanding of the world, and learn what is important in society, through play and cooperation with others.

evolutionary perspective   the theory that seeks to identify behavior that is a result of our genetic inheritance from our ancestors.

Assessing Vygotsky's Theory. Sociocultural theory has become increasingly influential, despite Vygotsky's death almost eight decades ago. The reason is the growing acknowledgment of the central importance of cultural factors in development. Children do not develop in a cultural vacuum. Instead, their attention is directed by society to certain areas, and as a consequence, they develop particular kinds of skills. Vygotsky was one of the first developmentalists to recognize and acknowledge the importance of the cultural environment, and—as today's society becomes increasingly multicultural—sociocultural theory helps us to understand the rich and varied influences that shape development (Matusov & Hayes, 2000; Reis, Collins, & Berscheid, 2000; Fowers & Davidov, 2006).

Sociocultural theory is not without its critics, however. Some suggest that Vygotsky's strong emphasis on the role of culture and social experience led him to ignore the effects of biological factors on development. In addition, his perspective seems to minimize the role that individuals play in shaping their environment.

The Evolutionary Perspective: Our Ancestors' Contributions to Behavior. One increasingly influential approach is the **evolutionary perspective**, the sixth and final developmental perspective that we will consider. The evolutionary perspective seeks to identify behavior that is the result of our genetic inheritance from our ancestors (Blasi & Bjorklund, 2003; Buss & Kern, 2003; Bjorklund, 2005; Goetz & Shackelford, 2006).

Evolutionary approaches have grown out of the groundbreaking work of Charles Darwin. In 1859, Darwin argued in *On the Origin of Species* that a process of natural selection creates traits in a species that are adaptive to its environment. Using Darwin's arguments, evolutionary approaches contend that our genetic inheritance not only determines such physical traits as skin and eye color, but certain personality traits and social behaviors as well. For instance, some evolutionary developmentalists suggest that behaviors such as shyness and jealousy are produced in part by genetic causes, presumably because they helped in increasing the survival rates of humans' ancient relatives (Buss, 2003; Workman & Reader, 2008).

The evolutionary perspective draws heavily on the field of *ethology*, which examines the ways in which our biological makeup influences our behavior. A primary proponent of ethology was Konrad Lorenz (1903–1989), who discovered that newborn geese are genetically preprogrammed to become attached to the first moving object they see after birth. His work, which demonstrated the importance of biological determinants in influencing behavior patterns, led developmentalists to consider the ways in which human behavior might reflect inborn genetic patterns.

The evolutionary perspective encompasses one of the fastest growing areas within the field of lifespan development: behavioral genetics. *Behavioral genetics* studies the effects of heredity on behavior. Behavioral geneticists seek to understand how we might inherit certain behavioral traits and how the environment influences whether we actually display those traits. It also considers how genetic factors may produce psychological disorders such as schizophrenia (Eley, Lichtenstein, & Moffitt, 2003; Gottlieb, 2003; Li, 2003; Bjorklund, 2005).

Assessing the Evolutionary Perspective. There is little argument among lifespan developmentalists that Darwin's evolutionary theory provides an accurate description of basic genetic processes, and the evolutionary perspective is increasingly visible in the field of lifespan development. However, applications of the evolutionary perspective have been subjected to considerable criticism.

Some developmentalists are concerned that because of its focus on genetic and biological aspects of behavior, the evolutionary perspective pays insufficient attention to the environmental and social factors involved in producing children's and adults' behavior. Other critics argue that there is no good way to experimentally test theories derived from this approach because humans evolved so long ago. For example, it is one thing to say that jealousy helped individuals to survive more effectively and another thing to prove it. Still, the evolutionary approach has stimulated research on how our biological inheritance at least partially influences our traits and behaviors (Buss & Reeve, 2003; Quartz, 2003; Scher & Rauscher, 2003).

Konrad Lorenz, seen here with geese that from their birth have followed him, considered the ways in which behavior reflects inborn genetic patterns.

Why "Which Approach Is Right?" Is the Wrong Question

We have considered the six major perspectives on development—psychodynamic, behavioral, cognitive, humanistic, contextual, and evolutionary—which are summarized in Table 1.3 and applied as an example to a case of a young adult who is overweight. It would be natural to wonder which of the six provides the most accurate account of human development.

For several reasons, this is not an appropriate question. For one thing, each perspective emphasizes different aspects of development. For instance, the psychodynamic approach emphasizes unconscious determinants of behavior, whereas behavioral perspectives emphasize overt behavior. The cognitive and humanistic perspectives look more at what people *think* than at what they do. The contextual perspective examines social and cultural influences on development, and the evolutionary perspective focuses on how inherited biological factors underlie development.

Each perspective is based on its own premises and focuses on different aspects of development—the way different maps of the same geographical area focus on different aspects and features of that area. In the same way, the same developmental phenomenon can be examined from a number of perspectives. Some lifespan developmentalists use an *eclectic* approach, drawing on several perspectives simultaneously.

The various theoretical perspectives provide different ways of looking at development. Considering them together paints a fuller portrait of the many ways humans change and grow over the life span. However, not all theories and claims derived from the various perspectives are accurate. How do we choose among competing explanations? The answer is *research*, which we consider in the final module of this chapter.

TABLE 1.3   Major Perspectives on Lifespan Development

PERSPECTIVE	KEY IDEAS ABOUT HUMAN BEHAVIOR AND DEVELOPMENT	MAJOR PROPONENTS	EXAMPLE
Psychodynamic	Behavior throughout life is motivated by inner, unconscious forces, stemming from childhood, over which we have little control.	Sigmund Freud, Erik, Erikson	This view might suggest that a young adult who is overweight has a fixation in the oral stage of development.
Behavioral	Development can be understood through studying observable behavior and environmental stimuli.	John B. Watson, B. F., Skinner, Albert, Bandura	In this perspective, a young adult who is overweight might be seen as not being rewarded for good nutritional and exercise habits.
Cognitive	Emphasis on how changes or growth in the ways people know, understand, and think about the world affect behavior.	Jean Piaget	This view might suggest that a young adult who is overweight has not learned effective ways to stay at a healthy weight and does not value good nutrition.
Humanistic	Behavior is chosen through free will and motivated by our natural capacity to strive to reach our full potential.	Carl Rogers, Abraham, Maslow	In this view, a young adult who is overweight may eventually choose to seek an optimal weight as part of an overall pattern of individual growth.
Contextual	Development should be viewed in terms of the interrelationship of a person's physical, cognitive, personality, and social worlds.	Urie Bronfenbrenner, Lev Vygotsky	In this perspective, being overweight is caused by a number of interrelated factors in that person's physical, cognitive, personality, and social worlds.
Evolutionary	Behavior is the result of genetic inheritance from our ancestors; traits and behavior that are adaptive for promoting the survival of our species have been inherited through natural selection.	Influenced by early work of Charles Darwin, Konrad Lorenz	This view might suggest that a young adult may have a genetic tendency toward obesity because extra fat helped his or her ancestors to survive in times of famine.

REVIEW

▶ The psychodynamic perspective looks primarily at the influence of internal, unconscious forces on development.

▶ The behavioral perspective focuses on external, observable behaviors as the key to development.

▶ The cognitive perspective focuses on mental activity.

▶ The humanistic perspective maintains that individuals have the ability and motivation to reach advanced levels of maturity and that people naturally seek to reach their full potential.

▶ The contextual perspective focuses on the relationship between individuals and the context in which they lead their lives.

▶ The evolutionary perspective seeks to identify behavior that is a result of our genetic inheritance.

APPLY

▶ Some of the most basic principles of Freud's psychoanalytic theory have been called into question. Can you name some of these principles and explain why they have not been validated by recent research?

▶ What examples of human behavior have you seen that appear to have been inherited from our ancestors because they helped individuals survive and adapt more effectively? Why do you think they are inherited?

MODULE 1.3

Research Methods

The Egyptians had long believed that they were the most ancient race on earth, and Psamtik [king of Egypt in the seventh century B.C.], driven by intellectual curiosity, wanted to prove that flattering belief. Like a good researcher, he began with a hypothesis: If children had no opportunity to learn a language from older people around them, they would spontaneously speak the primal, inborn language of humankind—the natural language of its most ancient people—which, he expected to show, was Egyptian.

To test his hypothesis, Psamtik commandeered two infants of a lower-class mother and turned them over to a herdsman to bring up in a remote area. They were to be kept in a sequestered cottage, properly fed and cared for, but were never to hear anyone speak so much as a word. The Greek historian Herodotus, who tracked the story down and learned what he calls "the real facts" from priests of Hephaestus in Memphis, says that Psamtik's goal "was to know, after the indistinct babblings of infancy were over, what word they would first articulate."

The experiment, he tells us, worked. One day, when the children were two years old, they ran up to the herdsman as he opened the door of their cottage and cried out "Becos!" Since this meant nothing to him, he paid no attention, but when it happened repeatedly, he sent word to Psamtik, who at once ordered the children brought to him. When he too heard them say it, Psamtik made inquiries and learned that becos was the Phrygian word for bread. He concluded that, disappointingly, the Phrygians were an older race than the Egyptians (Hunt, 1993, pp. 1–2).

With the perspective of several thousand years, we can easily see the shortcomings—both scientific and ethical—in Psamtik's approach. Yet his procedure represents an improvement over mere speculation and as such is sometimes regarded as the first developmental experiment in recorded history (Hunt, 1993).

The Scientific Method

Theories and Hypotheses: Posing Developmental Questions. Questions such as those raised by Psamtik drive the study of development to the point that developmentalists are still studying how children learn language. Others are working on such questions as, What are the effects of malnutrition on intellectual performance? How do infants form relationships with their parents, and does day care disrupt such relationships? Why are adolescents particularly susceptible to peer pressure? Can mentally challenging activities reduce the decline in intellectual abilities related to aging? Do any mental faculties improve with age?

To answer such questions, developmentalists, like all psychologists and other scientists, rely on the scientific method. The **scientific method** is the process of posing and answering questions using careful, controlled techniques that include systematic, orderly observation and the collection of data. The scientific method involves three major steps: (1) identifying questions of interest, (2) formulating an explanation, and (3) carrying out research that either lends support to the explanation or refutes it.

The scientific method involves the formulation of **theories**, broad explanations and predictions about phenomena of interest. For instance, the idea that a crucial bonding period takes place between parent and child immediately after birth is a theory.

Developmental researchers use theories to form hypotheses. A **hypothesis** is a prediction stated in a way that permits it to be tested. For instance, someone who subscribes to the general theory that bonding is crucial might derive the hypothesis that effective bonding occurs only if it lasts for a certain length of time.

Choosing a Research Strategy: Answering Questions. Once researchers have formed a hypothesis, they must develop a research strategy to test its validity. There are two major categories of research: correlational research and experimental research. Correlational research seeks to identify whether an association or relationship between two factors exists. As we'll see, **correlational research** cannot determine whether one factor *causes* changes in the other. For instance, correlational research could tell us if an association exists between the number of minutes a mother and her newborn child are together immediately after birth and the quality of the mother–child relationship when the child reaches age 2. Such correlational research indicates whether the two factors are *associated* or *related* to one another, but not whether the initial contact caused the relationship to develop in a particular way (Schutt, 2001; Barry et al., 2008).

In contrast, **experimental research** is designed to discover *causal* relationships between various factors. In experimental research, researchers deliberately introduce a change in a carefully structured situation in order to see the consequences of that change. For instance, a researcher conducting an experiment might vary the number of minutes that mothers and children interact immediately following birth, in an attempt to see whether the different bonding time affects the mother–child relationship.

Because experimental research is able to answer questions of causality, it is fundamental to finding answers to various developmental hypotheses. However, some research questions cannot be answered through experiments for either technical or ethical reasons. (For example, it would be unethical to design an experiment in which a group of infants was offered no chance to bond with a caregiver at all.) A great deal of pioneering developmental research—such as that conducted by Piaget and Vygotsky—employed correlational techniques. Consequently, correlational research remains an important tool for developmental researchers.

Correlational Studies. As we've noted, correlational research examines the relationship between two variables to determine whether they are associated, or *correlated*. For instance, researchers interested in the relationship between televised aggression and subsequent behavior have found that children who watch a good deal of aggression on television—murders, crime shows, shootings, and the like—tend to be more aggressive than those who watch only a little. In other words, viewing aggression and actual aggression are strongly associated, or correlated (Center for Communication & Social Policy, 1998; Singer & Singer, 2000; Murray, 2008; Savage, 2008).

scientific method   the process of posing and answering questions using careful, controlled techniques that include systematic, orderly observation and the collection of data.

theories   broad explanations and predictions about phenomena of interest.

hypothesis   a prediction stated in a way that permits it to be tested.

correlational research   research that seeks to identify whether an association or relationship between two factors exists.

experimental research   research designed to discover causal relationships between various factors.

In experimental research, a researcher uses controlled conditions to attempt to discover causal relationships among various factors.

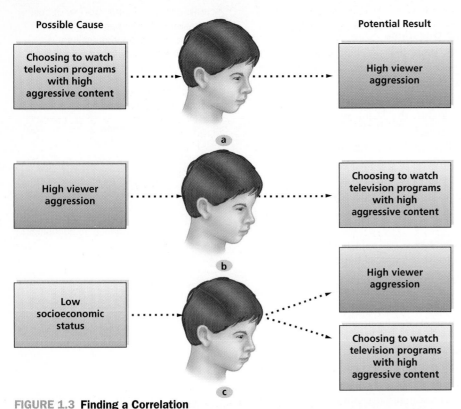

Possible Cause

Choosing to watch television programs with high aggressive content

High viewer aggression

a

High viewer aggression

Choosing to watch television programs with high aggressive content

b

Low socioeconomic status

Potential Result

High viewer aggression

Choosing to watch television programs with high aggressive content

c

FIGURE 1.3 Finding a Correlation
Finding a correlation between two factors does not imply that one factor *causes* the other factor to vary. For instance, suppose a study found that viewing television shows with high levels of aggression is correlated with actual aggression in children. The correlation may reflect at least three possibilities: (a) watching television programs containing high levels of aggression causes aggression in viewers; (b) children who behave aggressively choose to watch TV programs with high levels of aggression; or (c) some third factor, such as a child's socioeconomic status, leads both to high viewer aggression and to choosing to watch television programs with high levels of aggression. What other factors, besides socioeconomic status, might be plausible third factors?

But can we conclude that the viewing of televised aggression *causes* the more aggressive behavior? Not at all. Consider some of the other possibilities: It might be that being aggressive in the first place makes children more likely to choose to watch violent programs. In this case, the aggressive tendency causes the viewing behavior, not the other way around.

Or consider that a *third* factor may be operating on both the viewing and the aggression. Suppose, for example, that children of lower socioeconomic status are more likely to behave aggressively *and* to watch higher levels of aggressive television than those raised in more affluent settings. In this case, the third variable—socioeconomic status—causes *both* the aggressive behavior and the television viewing. (The various possibilities are illustrated in Figure 1.3.)

In short, finding that two variables are correlated proves nothing about causality. Although it is possible that the variables are linked causally, this is not necessarily the case. Still, we have learned a lot from correlational studies. For instance, we have learned that the closer the genetic link between two people, the more highly associated is their intelligence. We have learned, too, that the more parents speak to their young children, the more extensive are the children's vocabularies. And we have learned that the better the nutrition that infants receive, the fewer the cognitive and social problems they experience later (Plomin, 1994b; Hart, 2004; Colom, Lluis-Font, & Andrés-Pueyo, 2005).

The Correlation Coefficient. The strength and direction of a relationship between two factors is represented by a mathematical score, called a *correlation coefficient*, that ranges from +1.0 to −1.0. A *positive* correlation indicates that as the value of one factor increases, it can be predicted that the value of the other will also increase. For instance, if we administer a job satisfaction survey and find that the more money people make in their first job, the higher their job satisfaction, and the less money they make the lower their job satisfaction, we have found a positive correlation. The correlation coefficient would be indicated by a positive number, and the stronger the association between salary and job satisfaction, the closer the number would be to +1.0.

In contrast, a correlation coefficient with a *negative* value informs us that as the value of one factor increases, the value of the other factor declines. For example, suppose we found that the more time adolescents spend texting on their cell phones, the worse their academic performance is. This would produce a negative correlation, a number between 0 and −1. More texting would be associated with lower performance, and less texting with higher performance. The stronger the association between texting and school performance, the closer the correlation coefficient will be to −1.0.

Finally, it may be that two factors are unrelated to one another. For example, it is unlikely that we would find a correlation between school performance and shoe size. In this case, the lack of a relationship would be indicated by a correlation coefficient close to 0.

It is important to repeat that, even if a correlation coefficient is very strong, there is no way we can know whether one factor *causes* the other factor to vary. It simply means that the two factors are associated with one another in a predictable way.

Types of Correlational Studies. There are several types of correlational studies. **Naturalistic observation** is the observation of a naturally occurring behavior without intervention. For instance, an investigator who wishes to learn how often preschool children share toys might ob-

naturalistic observation
a type of correlational study in which some naturally occurring behavior is observed without intervention in the situation.

serve a classroom over a 3-week period, recording how often the preschoolers spontaneously share with one another. The key point is that the investigator observes without interfering (e.g., Beach, 2003; Prezbindowski & Lederberg, 2003).

While naturalistic observation has the advantage of seeing subjects in their "natural habitat," there is an important drawback: Researchers can exert no control over factors of interest. For instance, in some cases researchers might find so few naturally occurring instances of the behavior of interest that they are unable to draw any conclusions at all. In addition, children who know they are being watched may modify their behavior so that it is not representative of how they would behave if they were not being watched.

Ethnography.   Increasingly, naturalistic observation employs *ethnography,* a method borrowed from anthropology and used to investigate cultural questions. In ethnography, the goal is to understand a culture's values and attitudes through careful, extended examination. Typically, researchers act as participant observers, living for a period of weeks, months, or even years in another culture. By carefully observing everyday life and conducting in-depth interviews, researchers can obtain a deep understanding of life within another culture (Fetterman, 1998; Dyson, 2003; Polkinghome, 2005).

Case studies involve extensive, in-depth interviews with a particular individual or small group of individuals. They often are used not just to learn about the individual being interviewed, but to derive broader principles or draw tentative conclusions that might apply to others. For example, case studies have been conducted on children who display unusual genius and on children who have spent their early years in the wild, apparently without human contact. These case studies have provided important information to researchers and have suggested hypotheses for future investigation (Lane, 1976; Goldsmith, 2000; Cohen & Cashon, 2003).

Using *diaries,* participants are asked to keep a record of their behavior on a regular basis. For example, a group of adolescents may be asked to record each time they interact with friends for more than 5 minutes, thereby providing a way to track their social behavior.

Surveys represent another sort of correlational research. In **survey research**, a group of people chosen to represent some larger population are asked questions about their attitudes, behavior, or thinking on a given topic. For instance, surveys have been conducted about parents' use of punishment on their children and on attitudes toward breastfeeding. From the responses, inferences are drawn regarding the larger population represented by the individuals being surveyed.

Psychophysiological Methods.   Some developmental researchers, particularly those using a cognitive neuroscience approach, make use of psychophysiological methods. **Psychophysiological methods** focus on the relationship between physiological processes and behavior. For instance, a researcher might examine the relationship between blood flow in the brain and problem-solving ability. Similarly, some studies use infants' heart rate as a measure of their interest in stimuli to which they are exposed.

Among the most frequently used psychophysiological measures are the following:

- **Electroencephalogram (EEG).** The EEG uses electrodes placed on the skull to record electrical activity in the brain. The brain activity is transformed into a pictorial representation of brain wave patterns, permitting the diagnosis of disorders such as epilepsy and learning disabilities.
- **Computerized axial tomography (CAT) scan.** In a CAT scan, a computer constructs an image of the brain by combining thousands of individual X-rays taken at slightly different angles. Although it does not show brain activity, it does illuminate the structure of the brain.
- **Functional magnetic resonance imaging (fMRI) scan.** An fMRI provides a detailed, three-dimensional computer-generated image of brain activity by aiming a powerful magnetic field at the brain. It offers one of the best ways of learning about the operation of the brain, down to the level of individual nerves.

Experiments: Determining Cause and Effect.   In an **experiment**, an investigator or experimenter typically devises two different conditions (or *treatments*) and then compares how the behavior of the participants exposed to each condition is affected. One group, the *treatment* or *experimental group*, is exposed to the treatment variable being studied; the other, the *control group*, is not.

case studies   studies that involve extensive, in-depth interviews with a particular individual or small group of individuals.

survey research   a type of study in which a group of people chosen to represent some larger population are asked questions about their attitudes, behavior, or thinking on a given topic.

psychophysiological methods   approaches that focus on the relationship between physiological processes and behavior.

experiment   a process in which an investigator, called an experimenter, devises two different experiences for subjects or participants.

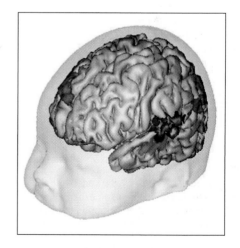

Brain scans permit researchers to understand the structure and functioning of the brain.

For instance, suppose you want to see if exposure to movie violence makes viewers more aggressive. You might show a group of adolescents a series of movies with a great deal of violent imagery. You would then measure their subsequent aggression. This group would constitute the treatment group. For the control group you might show a second group of adolescents movies that contain no aggressive imagery, and measure their subsequent aggression. By comparing the amount of aggression displayed by members of the treatment and control groups, you would be able to determine whether exposure to violent imagery produces aggression in viewers. This procedure describes an experiment conducted at the University of Louvain in Belgium. Psychologist Jacques-Philippe Leyens and colleagues found that the level of aggression rose significantly for the adolescents who had seen the movies containing violence (Leyens et al., 1975).

The central feature of this experiment—and all experiments—is the comparison of the consequences of different treatments. The use of both treatment and control groups allows researchers to rule out the possibility that something other than the experimental manipulation produced the results found in the experiment. For instance, if a control group was not used, experimenters could not be certain that some other factor, such as the time of day the movies were shown or even the mere passage of time, produced the observed changes. By using a control group, experimenters can draw accurate conclusions about causes and effects.

Independent and Dependent Variables. The **independent variable** is the variable that researchers manipulate in the experiment (in our example, it is the type of movie participants saw—violent or nonviolent). In contrast, the **dependent variable** is the variable that researchers measure to see if it changes as a result of the experimental manipulation. In our example, the degree of aggressive behavior shown by the participants after viewing violent or nonviolent films is the dependent variable. (One way to remember the difference is as follows: A hypothesis predicts how a dependent variable *depends* on the manipulation of the independent variable.) Every experiment has an independent and dependent variable.

Experimenters must make sure their studies are not influenced by factors other than those they are manipulating. For this reason, they take great care to make sure that the participants in both the treatment and control groups are not aware of the purpose of the experiment (which could affect their responses or behavior) and that the experimenters do not influence who is chosen for the control and treatment groups. The procedure used for this is known as random assignment. In *random assignment*, participants are assigned to different experimental groups or "conditions" purely on the basis of chance. This way the laws of statistics ensure that personal characteristics that might affect the outcome of the experiment are divided proportionally among the participants in the different groups, making the groups equivalent. Equivalent groups achieved by random assignment allow an experimenter to draw conclusions with confidence (Boruch, 1998; Lesik, 2006).

Given these advantages, why aren't experiments always used? The answer is that there are some situations that a researcher, no matter how ingenious, simply cannot control. And there are some situations in which control would be unethical, even if it were possible. For instance, no researcher would be able to assign different groups of infants to parents of high and low socioeconomic status in order to learn the effects of such status on subsequent development. In situations in which experiments are logistically or ethically impossible, developmentalists employ correlational research.

Furthermore, keep in mind that a single experiment is insufficient to answer a research question definitively. Before complete confidence can be placed in a conclusion, research must be replicated, or repeated, sometimes using other procedures and techniques with other participants. Sometimes developmentalists use a procedure called *meta-analysis*, which permits the combination of results of many studies into one overall conclusion (Peterson & Brown, 2005).

Choosing a Research Setting. Deciding *where* to conduct a study may be as important as determining *what* to do. In the Belgian experiment on the influence of exposure to media aggression, the researchers used a real-world setting—a group home for boys who had been convicted of juvenile delinquency. They chose this **sample**, the group of participants chosen for the experiment, because it was useful to have adolescents whose normal level of aggression was relatively high, and because they could incorporate the films into the everyday life of the home with minimal disruption.

Using a real-world setting (as in the aggression experiment) is the hallmark of a field study. A **field study** is a research investigation carried out in a naturally occurring setting. Field studies capture behavior in real-life settings, where research participants may behave more naturally than in a laboratory.

independent variable the variable that researchers manipulate in an experiment.

dependent variable the variable that researchers measure in an experiment and expect to change as a result of the experimental manipulation.

sample the group of participants chosen for the experiment.

field study a research investigation carried out in a naturally occurring setting.

Field studies may be used in both correlational studies and experiments. They typically employ naturalistic observation, the technique in which researchers observe a naturally occurring behavior without intervening or changing the situation. A researcher might examine behavior in a child-care center, view the groupings of adolescents in high school corridors, or observe elderly adults in a senior center.

Because it is often difficult to control the situation and environment enough to run an experiment in a real-world setting, field studies are more typical of correlational designs than experimental designs. Most developmental research experiments are conducted in laboratory settings. A **laboratory study** is a research investigation conducted in a controlled setting explicitly designed to hold events constant. The laboratory may be a room or building designed for research, as in a university psychology department. Researchers can exert enough control in a laboratory study to learn how their treatments affect participants.

Theoretical and Applied Research: Complementary Approaches. Developmental researchers typically focus on either **theoretical research** or **applied research**. Theoretical research is designed to test some developmental explanation and expand scientific knowledge, whereas applied research is meant to provide practical solutions to immediate problems. For instance, if we were interested in the processes of cognitive change during childhood, we might carry out a study of how many digits children of various ages can remember after one exposure to multidigit numbers—a theoretical approach. Alternatively, we might focus on the more practical question of how teachers can help children to remember information more easily. Such a study would represent applied research because the findings are applied to a particular setting and problem.

> **laboratory study** a research investigation conducted in a controlled setting explicitly designed to hold events constant.
>
> **theoretical research** research designed specifically to test some developmental explanation and expand scientific knowledge.
>
> **applied research** research meant to provide practical solutions to immediate problems.

FROM RESEARCH TO PRACTICE
Using Developmental Research to Improve Public Policy

Is national legislation designed to "leave no child behind" effective in improving the lives of children?

Does research support the legalization of marijuana?

What are the effects of gay marriage on the children of such unions?

Should preschoolers diagnosed with attention-deficit/hyperactivity disorder receive drugs to treat their condition?

Is DARE—the national program designed to curb drug abuse in schoolchildren—effective?

Each of these questions represents a national policy issue that can be answered only by research. By conducting controlled studies, developmental researchers have made important contributions to education, family life, and health. The following are examples of ways that public policy issues have been informed by research findings (Brooks-Gunn, 2003; Maton et al., 2004; Mervis, 2004; Aber et al., 2007):

- ***Research findings can provide policymakers a means of determining what questions to ask in the first place.*** For example, studies of children's caregivers have led policymakers to question whether the benefits of infant day care are outweighed by possible deterioration in parent–child bonds.

- ***The findings and testimony of researchers are often part of the process by which laws are drafted.*** Legislation is often based on findings from developmental researchers. For example, research revealed that children with developmental disabilities benefit from exposure to children without special needs, ultimately leading to passage of national legislation mandating that children with disabilities be placed in regular school classes as much as possible.

- ***Policymakers and other professionals use research findings to determine how best to implement programs.*** Research has shaped programs designed to reduce the incidence of unsafe sex among teenagers, to increase the level of prenatal care for pregnant mothers, to raise class attendance rates in school-age children, and to promote flu shots for older adults. The common thread is that many of the programs are based on research findings.

- ***Research techniques are used to evaluate the effectiveness of existing programs and policies.*** It is often necessary to determine whether an existing program has been successful in accomplishing its goals. To do this, researchers employ formal evaluation techniques, developed from basic research procedures. For instance, careful studies of DARE, a highly popular program meant to reduce children's use of drugs, began to find that it was ineffective. Using the research findings of developmentalists, DARE introduced new techniques, and preliminary findings suggest the revised program is more effective (Rhule, 2005; University of Akron, 2006).

By building on research findings, developmentalists often work hand in hand with policymakers, making a substantial impact on public policies.

- *What are some policy issues affecting children and adolescents that are currently being debated nationally?*

- *Despite the existence of research data that might inform policy about development, politicians rarely discuss such data in their speeches. Why do you think that is the case?*

longitudinal research research in which the behavior of one or more participants in a study is measured as they age.

cross-sectional research research in which people of different ages are compared at the same point in time.

There is not always a clear distinction between theoretical and applied research. For instance, is a study that examines the consequences of ear infections in infancy on later hearing loss theoretical or applied? Because such a study may help illuminate the basic processes involved in hearing, it can be considered theoretical. But if it helps to prevent hearing loss, it may be considered applied (Lerner, Fisher, & Weinberg, 2000; Hunt & Joslyn, 2007).

As we discuss in the preceding *From Research to Practice* box, research of both a theoretical and an applied nature has played a significant role in shaping and resolving a variety of public policy questions.

Measuring Developmental Change

Growth and change are central to the work of all developmental researchers, and one of the thorniest research issues researchers face is the measurement of change and differences over age and time. To measure change, researchers have developed three major research strategies: longitudinal research, cross-sectional research, and sequential research.

Longitudinal Studies: Measuring Individual Change. If you were interested in learning how a child develops morally between 3 and 5, the most direct approach would be to take a group of 3-year-olds and follow them until they were 5, testing them periodically.

This strategy illustrates longitudinal research. In **longitudinal research**, the behavior of one or more study participants is measured as they age. Longitudinal research measures change over time. By following many individuals over time, researchers can understand the general course of change across some period of life.

The granddaddy of longitudinal studies, which has become a classic, is a study of gifted children begun by Lewis Terman about 80 years ago. In the study—which has yet to be concluded—a group of 1,500 children with high IQs were tested about every 5 years. Now in their 80s, the participants—who call themselves "Termites"—have provided information on everything from intellectual accomplishment to personality and longevity (Terman & Oden, 1959; Feldhusen, 2003; McCullough, Tsang, & Brion, 2003).

Longitudinal research has also provided insight into language development. For instance, by tracing how children's vocabularies increase on a day-by-day basis, researchers have been able to understand the processes that underlie the human ability to become competent language users.

Longitudinal studies can provide a wealth of information about change over time, but they have disadvantages. For one thing, they require a tremendous investment of time because researchers must wait for participants to become older. Furthermore, participants often drop out over the course of the research because they lose interest, move away, become ill, or die.

In addition, participants may become "test-wise" and perform better each time they are assessed as they become more familiar with the procedure. Finally, they may be affected by the repeated presence of an experimenter or observer.

Consequently, despite the benefits of longitudinal research, particularly its ability to look at change within individuals, developmental researchers often turn to other methods. The alternative they choose most often is the cross-sectional study.

Cross-Sectional Studies. Suppose again that you want to consider how children's moral development—their sense of right and wrong—changes from ages 3 to 5. Instead of following the same children over several years, we might look simultaneously at three groups of children: 3-year-olds, 4-year-olds, and 5-year-olds, perhaps presenting each group with the same problem and then seeing how they respond to it and explain their choices.

Such an approach typifies cross-sectional research. In **cross-sectional research**, people of different ages are compared at the same point in time. Cross-sectional studies provide information about differences in development between different age groups.

Cross-sectional research takes far less time than longitudinal research: Participants are tested at just one point in time. Terman's study might have been completed 75 years ago if Terman had simply looked at a group of gifted 15-year-olds, 20-year-olds, 25-year-olds, and so forth, up to 80-year-olds. Because the

Cross-sectional research allows researchers to compare representatives of different age groups at the same time.

participants would not be periodically tested, there would be no chance that they would become test-wise, and problems of participant attrition would not occur.

Cross-sectional research, however, brings its own difficulties. Recall that every person belongs to a particular *cohort* of individuals born at around the same time in the same place. If we find that people of different ages vary along some dimension, the differences may be due to differences in cohort membership, not age per se.

Consider a concrete example: If we find in a correlational study that people who are 25 perform better on a test of intelligence than those who are 75, there are several possible explanations other than that intelligence declines in old age. Instead, the finding may be attributable to cohort differences. The 75-year-olds may have had less formal education than the 25-year-olds because members of the older cohort were less likely to finish high school and attend college than members of the younger one. Or perhaps the older group received less adequate nutrition as infants than the younger group. In short, we cannot rule out the possibility that age-related differences in cross-sectional studies are actually cohort differences.

Cross-sectional studies may also suffer from *selective dropout*, in which participants in some age groups are more likely to stop participating than others. For example, suppose a study of cognitive development in preschoolers includes a long test of cognitive abilities, which young preschoolers find more difficult than older preschoolers. If more young children quit than the older preschoolers and if it is the least competent young preschoolers who drop out, then the remaining sample of that age group will consist of the more competent young preschoolers—together with a broader and more representative sample of older preschoolers. The results of such a study would be questionable (Miller, 1998).

Finally, cross-sectional studies have an additional, and more basic, disadvantage: They are unable to inform us about changes in individuals or groups. If longitudinal studies are like videos taken of a person at various ages, cross-sectional studies are like snapshots of entirely different groups. Although we can establish differences related to age, we cannot fully determine whether such differences are related to change over time.

Sequential Studies. Because both longitudinal and cross-sectional studies have disadvantages, researchers have turned to some compromise techniques. Among the most frequently employed techniques are sequential studies, which are essentially a combination of longitudinal and cross-sectional studies.

In **sequential studies**, researchers examine a number of different age groups at several points in time. For instance, an investigator interested in children's moral behavior might begin a sequential study by examining the behavior of three groups of children, who are either 3, 4, or 5 years old at the time the study begins.

The study continues for the next several years, with each participant tested annually. Thus, the 3-year-olds would be tested at ages 3, 4, and 5; the 4-year-olds at ages 4, 5, and 6; and the 5-year-olds at ages 5, 6, and 7. By combining the advantages of longitudinal and cross-sectional research, this approach permits developmental researchers to tease out the consequences of age *change* versus age *difference*. The major research techniques for studying development are summarized in Figure 1.4.

Ethics and Research. In the "study" conducted by Egyptian King Psamtik, two children were removed from their mothers and held in isolation in an effort to learn about the roots of language. If you found yourself thinking this was extraordinarily cruel, you are in good company. Clearly, such an experiment raises blatant ethical concerns, and nothing like it would ever be done today.

But sometimes ethical issues are more subtle. For instance, U.S. government researchers proposed a conference to examine possible genetic roots of aggression. Some researchers had begun to raise the possibility that genetic markers might be found that would identify particularly violence-prone children. If so, it might be possible to track these children and provide interventions to reduce the likelihood of later violence.

Critics objected strenuously, however, arguing that identification might lead to a self-fulfilling prophecy. Children labeled as violence-prone might be treated in a way that would actually *cause* them to be more aggressive. Ultimately, under intense political pressure, the conference was canceled (Wright, 1995).

sequential studies   research in which researchers examine a number of different age groups over several points in time.

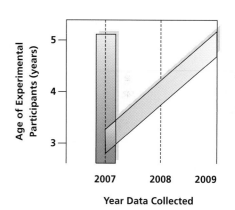

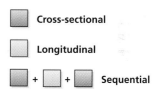

FIGURE 1.4 Research Techniques for Studying Development
In a *cross-sectional study*, 3-, 4-, and 5-year-olds are compared at a similar point in time (in 2011). In *longitudinal research*, a set of participants who are 3 years old in 2011 are studied when they are 4 years old (in 2012) and when they are 5 years old (in 2013). Finally, a *sequential study* combines cross-sectional and longitudinal techniques. Here, a group of 3-year-olds would be compared initially in 2011 with 4- and 5-year-olds, but would also be studied 1 and 2 years later, when they themselves are 4 and 5 years old. Although the graph does not illustrate this, researchers carrying out this sequential study might also choose to retest the children who were 4 and 5 in 2011 for the next 2 years. What advantages do the three kinds of studies offer?

FROM A
HEALTH CARE PROVIDER'S
PERSPECTIVE

Do you think there are some special circumstances involving adolescents, who are not legally adults, that would justify allowing them to participate in a study without obtaining their parents' permission? What might such circumstances involve?

In order to help researchers deal with ethical problems, the major organizations of developmentalists, including the Society for Research in Child Development and the American Psychological Association, have developed ethical guidelines for researchers. Among the principles are those involving freedom from harm, informed consent, the use of deception, and maintenance of participants' privacy (Sales & Folkman, 2000; American Psychological Association, 2002; Fisher, 2003, 2004, 2005):

- **Researchers must protect participants from physical and psychological harm.** Their welfare, interests, and rights come before those of researchers. In research, participants' rights always come first (Sieber, 2000; Fisher, 2004).

- **Researchers must obtain informed consent from participants before their involvement in a study.** If they are over the age of 7, participants must voluntarily agree to be in a study. If under 18, parents or guardians must also provide consent.

  Informed consent can be a sensitive requirement. Suppose, for instance, researchers want to study the psychological effects of abortion on adolescents. To obtain the consent of an adolescent minor who has had an abortion, the researchers would need to get her parents' permission as well. But if the adolescent hasn't told her parents about the abortion, the request for parental permission would violate her privacy—leading to a breach of ethics.

- **The use of deception in research must be justified and cause no harm.** Although deception to disguise the true purpose of an experiment is permissible, any experiment that uses deception must undergo careful scrutiny by an independent panel before it is conducted. Suppose, for example, we want to know the reaction of participants to success and failure. It is ethical to tell participants that they will be playing a game when the true purpose is actually to observe how they respond to doing well or poorly on the task. However, this is ethical only if it causes no harm to participants, has been approved by a review panel, and includes a full explanation for participants when the study is over (Underwood, 2005).

- **Participants' privacy must be maintained.** If participants are videotaped during a study, for example, they must give their permission for the videotapes to be viewed. Furthermore, access to the tapes must be carefully restricted.

REVIEW

▶ Theories are systematically derived explanations of facts or phenomena. Theories suggest hypotheses, which are predictions that can be tested.

▶ Correlational studies examine relationships between factors without demonstrating causality, while experimental research seeks to discover cause-and-effect relationships.

▶ Researchers measure age-related change by longitudinal studies, cross-sectional studies, and sequential studies.

APPLY

▶ Formulate a theory about one aspect of human development and a hypothesis that relates to it.

▶ Egyptian King Psamtik's experiment of removing two children from their mothers would be unheard of today. How could the same experiment be done today following ethical guidelines?

BECOMING AN INFORMED CONSUMER OF DEVELOPMENT
Thinking Critically About "Expert" Advice

*If you immediately comfort crying babies, you'll spoil them.
If you let babies cry without comforting them, they'll be untrusting and clingy as adults.*

***

*Spanking is one of the best ways to discipline your child.
Never hit your child.*

***

*If a marriage is unhappy, children are better off if their parents divorce than if they stay together.
No matter how difficult a marriage is, parents should avoid divorce for the sake of their children.*

There is no lack of advice on the best way to raise a child or, more generally, to lead one's life. From best sellers such as *Chicken Soup for the Soul: On Being a Parent,* to magazine and newspaper columns that provide advice on every imaginable topic, to a myriad of websites and blogs, each of us is exposed to tremendous amounts of information.

Yet not all advice is equally valid. The mere fact that something is in print, on television, or on the Web does not make it legitimate or accurate. Fortunately, some guidelines can help distinguish when recommendations and suggestions are reasonable and when they are not:

- Consider the source of the advice. Information from established, respected organizations such as the American Medical Association, the American Psychological Association, and the American Academy of Pediatrics reflects years of study and is usually accurate. If you don't know the organization, investigate it.
- Evaluate the credentials of the person providing advice. Trustworthy information tends to come from established, acknowledged researchers and experts, not from persons with obscure credentials. Consider where the author is employed and whether he or she has a particular political or personal agenda.

- Understand the difference between anecdotal evidence and scientific evidence. Anecdotal evidence is based on one or two instances of a phenomenon, haphazardly discovered or encountered; scientific evidence is based on careful, systematic procedures. If an aunt tells you that all her children slept through the night by 2 months of age and therefore your child will too, that is quite different from reading a report that 75% of children sleep through the night by 9 months. Of course, even with such a report, it would be a good idea to find out how large the study was or how this number was arrived at.
- If advice is based on research findings, there should be a clear, transparent description of the studies on which the advice is based. Who were the participants? What methods were used? What do the results show? Think critically about the way the findings were obtained before accepting them.
- Don't overlook the cultural context of the information. An assertion may be valid in some contexts, but not in all. For example, it is typically assumed that providing infants the freedom to move about and exercise their limbs facilitates their muscular development and mobility. Yet in some cultures, infants spend most of their time closely bound to their mothers—with no apparent long-term damage (Cole, 2006; Lancy, 2007).

In short, the key to evaluating information relating to human development is to maintain a healthy dose of skepticism. No source of information is invariably, unfailingly accurate. By keeping a critical eye on the statements you encounter, you'll be in a better position to determine the very real contributions made by developmentalists to understanding how humans develop over the course of the life span.

Epilogue

As we've seen, the scope of lifespan development is broad, touching on a wide range of topics that address how people grow and change through the course of life. We've also found that developmentalists use a variety of techniques to answer questions of interest.

Before proceeding to the next chapter, take a few minutes to reconsider the prologue of this chapter—about Louise Brown, the first child to be born through in vitro fertilization. Based on what you now know about lifespan development, answer the following questions:

1. What are some of the potential benefits, and the costs, of the type of conception—in vitro fertilization—that was carried out for Louise's parents?

2. What are some questions that developmentalists who study either physical, cognitive, or personality and social development might ask about the effects on Louise of being conceived via in vitro fertilization?

3. Louise reported feeling lonely and isolated as a child. Why do you think this was so, and what effects might it have on her as an adult?

4. Louise's own son was conceived in the traditional manner. How do you think his development will differ from that of his mother, and why?

Looking Back

What is lifespan development, and what are some of the basic influences on human development?

1. Lifespan development is a scientific approach to questions about growth, change, and stability in the physical, cognitive, and social and personality characteristics at all ages from conception to death.

2. Culture—both broad and narrow—is an important issue in lifespan development. Many aspects of development are influenced not only by broad cultural differences, but by ethnic, racial, and socioeconomic differences within a particular culture.

3. Each individual is subject to normative history-graded influences, normative age-graded influences, normative sociocultural-graded influences, and non-normative life events.

What are the key issues in the field of development?

4. Four key issues in lifespan development are (1) whether developmental change is continuous or discontinuous; (2) whether development is largely governed by critical periods during which certain influences or experiences must occur for development to be normal; (3) whether to focus on certain particularly important periods in human development or on the entire life span; and (4) the nature–nurture controversy, which focuses on the relative importance of genetic versus environmental influences.

Which theoretical perspectives have guided lifespan development?

5. Six major theoretical perspectives currently dominate lifespan development: the psychodynamic perspective (which focuses on inner, largely unconscious forces), the behavioral perspective (which focuses on external, observable actions), the cognitive perspective (which focuses on intellectual, cognitive processes), the humanistic perspective (which focuses on the unique qualities of human beings), the contextual perspective (which focuses on the relationship between individuals and their physical, cog-

nitive, personality, and social worlds), and the evolutionary perspective (which focuses on our genetic inheritance).

6. The psychodynamic perspective is exemplified by the psychoanalytic theory of Freud and the psychosocial theory of Erikson. Freud focused attention on the unconscious and on stages through which children must pass successfully to avoid harmful fixations. Erikson identified eight distinct stages of development, each characterized by a conflict, or crisis, to work out.

7. The behavioral perspective typically concerns stimulus–response learning, exemplified by classical conditioning, the operant conditioning of Skinner, and Bandura's social-cognitive learning theory.

8. Within the cognitive perspective, the most notable theorist is Piaget, who identified the developmental stages through which all children are assumed to pass. Each stage involves qualitative differences in thinking. In contrast, information processing approaches attribute cognitive growth to quantitative changes in mental processes and capacities, and cognitive neuroscience approaches focus on biological brain processes.

9. The humanistic perspective contends that people have a natural capacity to make decisions about their lives and control their behavior. The humanistic perspective emphasizes free will and the natural desire of humans to reach their full potential.

10. The contextual perspective considers the relationship between individuals and their physical, cognitive, personality, and social worlds. The bioecological approach stresses the interrelatedness of developmental areas and the importance of broad cultural factors in human development. Vygotsky's sociocultural theory emphasizes the central influence on cognitive development exerted by social interactions between members of a culture.

11. The evolutionary perspective attributes behavior to genetic inheritance from our ancestors, contending that genes determine not only traits such as skin and eye color, but certain personality traits and social behaviors as well.

What role do theories and hypotheses play in the study of development?

12. Theories are broad explanations of facts or phenomena of interest, based on a systematic integration of prior findings and theories. Hypotheses are theory-based predictions that can be tested. The process of posing and answering questions systematically is called the scientific method.

13. Researchers test hypotheses through correlational research (to determine whether two factors are associated) and experimental research (to discover cause-and-effect relationships).

How are developmental research studies conducted?

14. Correlational studies use naturalistic observation, case studies, and survey research to investigate whether certain characteristics of interest are associated with other characteristics. Correlational studies lead to no direct conclusions about cause and effect.

15. Typically, experimental research studies are conducted on participants in a treatment group who receive the experimental treatment and participants in a control group who do not. Following the treatment, differences between the two groups can help the experimenter to determine the effects of the treatment. Experiments may be conducted in a laboratory or in a real-world setting.

16. To measure change across human ages, researchers use longitudinal studies of the same participants over time, cross-sectional studies of different-age participants conducted at one time, and sequential studies of different-age participants at several points in time.

17. Ethical guidelines for research include the protection of participants from harm, informed consent of participants, limits on the use of deception, and maintenance of privacy.

PEARSON

mydevelopmentlab™

For more review plus MyVirtualChild, practice tests, videos, flashcards, and more, log on to **mydevelopmentlab.com**

2 Genetics, Prenatal Development, and Birth

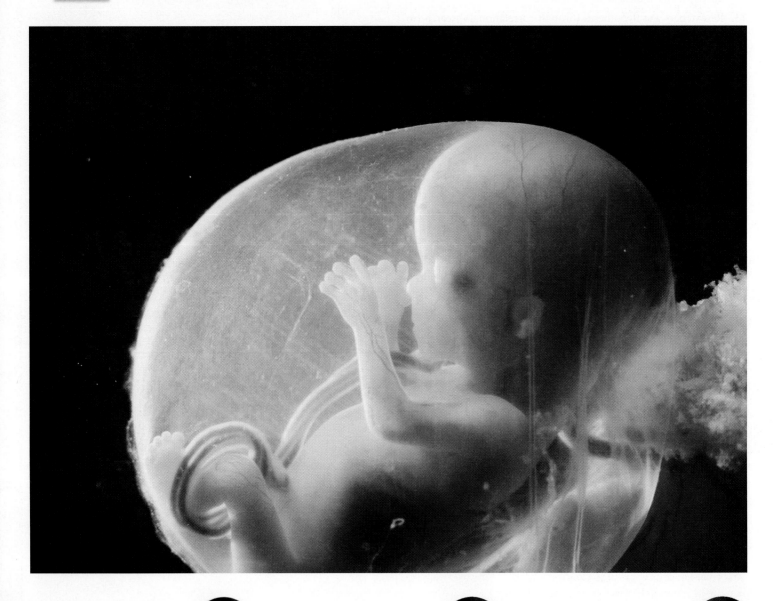

Prologue
The Future Is Now

It came out of the blue: Jana and Tom Monaco's seemingly healthy 3-year-old son Stephen developed a life-threatening stomach virus that led to severe brain damage. His diagnosis: a rare but treatable disease called isovaleric acidemia (IVA), marked by the body's inability to metabolize an amino acid found in dietary protein. Jana and Tom were unknowing carriers of the disease. . . . The Monacos had no warning whatsoever.

Not so when Jana got pregnant again. Her daughter, Caroline, was tested by amniocentesis while still in the womb. Knowing Caroline had the mutation, doctors were able to administer medication the day she was born—and the Monacos were prepared to monitor her diet immediately to keep her healthy. Today Stephen, 9, is unable to walk, talk or feed himself. Caroline, meanwhile, is an active, healthy 4-year-old. Genetic testing, says Jana, "gives Caroline the future that Stephen didn't get to have." (Kalb, 2006, p. 52)

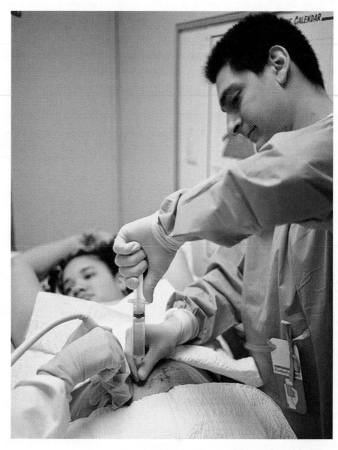

Prenatal tests have become increasingly sophisticated.

The Monacos were able to spare Caroline from Stephen's fate due to truly astounding medical advances based on a rapidly growing understanding of the course of human development prior to birth. In this chapter, we'll examine what developmental researchers and other scientists have learned about ways that heredity and the environment work in tandem to create and shape human beings, and how that knowledge is being used to improve people's lives. We begin with the basics of heredity, the genetic transmission of characteristics from biological parents to their children, by examining how we receive our genetic endowment. We'll consider an area of study, behavioral genetics, which specializes in the consequences of heredity on behavior. We'll also discuss what happens when genetic factors cause development to go off track, and how such problems are dealt with through genetic counseling and gene therapy.

But genes are only one part of the story of prenatal development. We'll also consider the ways in which a child's genetic heritage interacts with the environment in which he or she grows up—how one's family, socioeconomic status, and life events can affect a variety of characteristics, including physical traits, intelligence, and even personality.

Finally, we'll focus on the very first stages of development, tracing prenatal growth and birth. We'll review some of the alternatives available to couples who find it difficult to conceive. We'll also talk about the stages of the prenatal period and how the prenatal environment offers both threats to—and the promise of—future growth. We will then discuss the birth process, including some alternatives to the traditional model of birthing that has dominated American life for decades, and we will finish with a discussion of some of the complications that can cloud the birth process.

PEARSON
mydevelopmentlab

To begin to learn about pregnancy, birth, and newborn children, use **MyVirtualChild** on the Web at **www.mydevelopmentlab.com**.

LOOKING AHEAD

After reading this chapter, you will be able to answer these questions:

▶ What is our basic genetic endowment, and how can human development go off track?

▶ How do the environment and genetics work together to determine human characteristics?

▶ Which human characteristics are significantly influenced by heredity?

▶ What happens during the prenatal stages of development?

▶ What are the threats to the fetal environment, and what can be done about them?

▶ What is the normal process of labor?

▶ What complications can occur at birth, and what are their causes, effects, and treatments?

MODULE 2.1

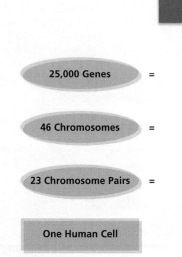

FIGURE 2.1 **The Contents of a Single Human Cell**
At the moment of conception, humans receive about 25,000 genes, contained on 46 chromosomes in 23 pairs.

To watch the process you are reading about here, check **MyDevelopmentLab** for an Observations video on zygote development.

zygote the new cell formed by the process of fertilization.

genes the basic unit of genetic information.

DNA (deoxyribonucleic acid) molecules the substance that genes are composed of that determines the nature of every cell in the body and how it will function.

chromosomes rod-shaped portions of DNA that are organized in 23 pairs.

Earliest Development and the Foundations of Genetics

We humans begin the course of our lives simply.

Like individuals from tens of thousands of other species, we start as a single cell, a tiny speck probably weighing no more than one 20-millionth of an ounce. But from this humble beginning, in a matter of just a few months (if all goes well), a living, breathing individual is born. This first cell is created when a male reproductive cell, a *sperm*, pushes through the membrane of the *ovum*, the female reproductive cell. These *gametes*, as the male and female reproductive cells also are known, each contain huge amounts of genetic information. About an hour or so after the sperm enters the ovum, the two gametes suddenly fuse, becoming one cell, a **zygote.** The resulting combination of their genetic instructions—over 2 billion chemically coded messages—is sufficient to begin creating a whole person.

Genes and Chromosomes: The Code of Life

The blueprints for creating a person are stored and communicated in our **genes**, the basic units of genetic information. The roughly 25,000 human genes are the biological equivalent of "software" that programs the future development of all parts of the body's "hardware."

All genes are composed of specific sequences of **DNA (deoxyribonucleic acid) molecules.** The genes are arranged in specific locations and in a specific order along 46 **chromosomes**, rod-shaped portions of DNA that are organized in 23 pairs. However, sex cells—the ova and the sperm—contain half this number, so that a child's mother and father each provides one of the two chromosomes in each of the 23 pairs. The 46 chromosomes (in 23 pairs) in the new zygote contain the genetic blueprint that will guide cell activity for the rest of the individual's life (Pennisi, 2000; International Human Genome Sequencing Consortium, 2001; see Figure 2.1). Through a process called *mitosis*, which accounts for the replication of most types of cells, nearly all the cells of the body will contain the same 46 chromosomes as the zygote.

Specific genes in precise locations on the chain of chromosomes determine the nature and function of every cell in the body. For instance, genes determine which cells will ultimately become part of the heart and which will become part of the muscles of the leg. Genes also establish how different parts of the body will function: how rapidly the heart will beat or how much strength a muscle will have.

If each parent provides just 23 chromosomes, where does the potential for the vast diversity of human beings come from? The answer resides primarily in the nature of the processes that underlie the cell division of the gametes. When gametes—sperm and ova—are formed in the adult human body in a process called *meiosis*, each gamete receives one of the two chromosomes that make up each of the 23 pairs. Because for each of the 23 pairs it is largely a matter of chance which member of the pair is contributed, there are 2^{23}, or some 8 million, different combinations possible. Furthermore, other processes, such as random transformations of particular genes, add to the variability of the genetic brew. The outcome: tens of *trillions* of possible genetic combinations.

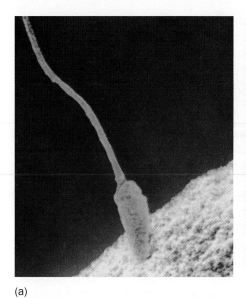
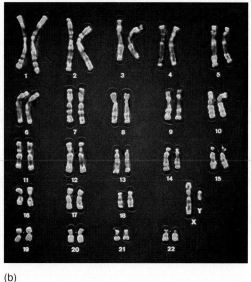
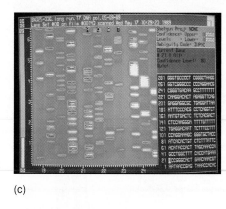

(c)

(a)

(b)

At the moment of conception (a), humans receive 23 pairs of chromosomes (b), half from the mother and half from the father. These chromosomes contain thousands of genes, shown in the computer-generated map (c).

With so many possible genetic mixtures provided by heredity, there is no likelihood that someday you'll bump into a genetic duplicate of yourself—with one exception: an identical twin.

Multiple Births: Two—or More—for the Genetic Price of One. Although it doesn't seem surprising when dogs and cats give birth to several offspring at one time, in humans multiple births are cause for comment. They should be: Less than 3 percent of all pregnancies produce twins, and the odds are even slimmer for three or more children.

Why do multiple births occur? Sometimes a cluster of cells in the ovum splits off within the first 2 weeks after fertilization. The result is two genetically identical zygotes, which, because they come from the same original zygote, are called monozygotic. **Monozygotic twins** are twins who are genetically identical. Any differences in their future development can be attributed only to environmental factors, since genetically they are exactly the same.

There is a second, and actually more common, mechanism that produces multiple births. In these cases, two separate ova are fertilized by two separate sperm at roughly the same time. Twins produced in this fashion are known as **dizygotic twins**. Because they are the result of two separate ovum–sperm combinations, they are no more genetically similar than two siblings born at different times.

Of course, not all multiple births produce only two babies. Triplets, quadruplets, and even more births are produced by either (or both) of the mechanisms that yield twins. Thus, triplets may be some combination of monozygotic, dizygotic, or trizygotic.

Although the chances of having a multiple birth are typically slim, the odds rise considerably when couples use fertility drugs to improve the probability they will conceive a child. For example, 1 in 10 couples using fertility drugs have dizygotic twins, compared to an overall figure of 1 in 86 for all Caucasian couples in the United States. Older women, too, are more likely to have multiple births, and multiple births are also more common in some families than in others. The increased use of fertility drugs and the rising average age of mothers giving birth have meant that multiple births have increased in the last 25 years (see Figure 2.2; Martin et al., 2005).

There are also racial, ethnic, and national differences in the rate of multiple births, probably due to inherited differences in the likelihood that more than one ovum will be released at a time. One out of 70 African American couples have dizygotic births, compared with 1 out of 86 for white American couples (Wood, 1997; Chulada et al., 2006).

Mothers carrying multiple children run a higher-than-average risk of premature delivery and birth complications. Consequently, these mothers must be particularly concerned about their prenatal care.

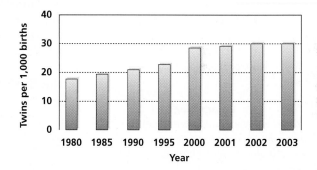

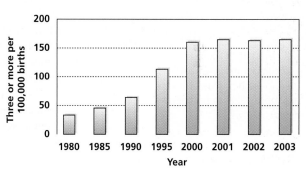

FIGURE 2.2 Rising Multiples
Multiple births have increased significantly over the last 25 years. What are some of the reasons for this phenomenon?
Source: Martin et al., 2005.

monozygotic twins   twins who are genetically identical.

dizygotic twins   twins who are produced when two separate ova are fertilized by two separate sperm at roughly the same time.

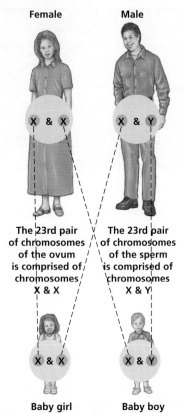

Female   Male

The 23rd pair
of chromosomes
of the ovum
is comprised of
chromosomes
X & X

The 23rd pair
of chromosomes
of the sperm
is comprised of
chromosomes
X & Y

Baby girl   Baby boy

FIGURE 2.3 Determining Sex
When an ovum and sperm meet at the moment of fetilization, the ovum is certain to provide an X chromosome, while the sperm will provide either an X or a Y chromosome. If the sperm contributes its X chromosome, the child will have an XX pairing on the 23rd chromosome and will be a girl. If the sperm contributes a Y chromosome, the result will be an XY pairing—a boy. Does this mean that girls are more likely to be conceived than boys?

**FROM A
HEALTH CARE PROVIDER'S
PERSPECTIVE**
In speaking with young parents expecting their first child, how would you explain which human characteristics are significantly influenced by heredity?

dominant trait the one trait that is expressed when two competing traits are present.

recessive trait a trait within an organism that is present, but is not expressed.

genotype the underlying combination of genetic material present (but not outwardly visible) in an organism.

phenotype an observable trait; the trait that actually is seen.

Boy or Girl? Establishing the Sex of the Child. Recall that there are 23 matched pairs of chromosomes. In 22 of these pairs, each chromosome is similar to the other member of its pair. The one exception is the 23rd pair, which is the one that determines the sex of the child. In females, the 23rd pair consists of two matching, relatively large X-shaped chromosomes, appropriately identified as XX. In males, on the other hand, the members of the pair are dissimilar. One consists of an X-shaped chromosome, but the other is a shorter, smaller Y-shaped chromosome. This pair is identified as XY.

As we discussed earlier, each gamete carries one chromosome from each of the parents' 23 pairs of chromosomes. Since a female's 23rd pair of chromosomes are both Xs, an ovum will always carry an X chromosome, no matter which chromosome of the 23rd pair it gets. A male's 23rd pair is XY, so each sperm could carry either an X or a Y chromosome. If the sperm contributes an X chromosome when it meets an ovum (which, remember, will always contribute an X chromosome), the child will have an XX pairing on the 23rd chromosome—and will be a female. If the sperm contributes a Y chromosome, the result will be an XY pairing—a male (see Figure 2.3).

It is clear from this process that the father's sperm determines the gender of the child. Accordingly, techniques are being developed that will allow parents to increase the chances of specifying the gender of their child. In one new technique, lasers measure the DNA in sperm. By discarding sperm that harbor the unwanted sex chromosome, the chances of having a child of the desired sex increase dramatically (Hayden, 1998; Belkin, 1999; Van Balen, 2005).

Procedures for choosing a child's gender raise ethical and practical issues. For example, in cultures that value one gender over the other, might there be a kind of gender discrimination prior to birth? Furthermore, a shortage of children of the less preferred sex might ultimately emerge. Many questions remain, then, before sex selection can become routine (Liao, 2005).

The Basics of Genetics: The Mixing and Matching of Traits

What determined the color of your hair? Why are you tall or short? What made you susceptible to hay fever? And why do you have so many freckles? To answer these questions, we need to consider the basic mechanisms involved in the way that the genes we inherit from our parents transmit information.

We can start by examining the discoveries of an Austrian monk, Gregor Mendel, in the mid-1800s. In a series of simple yet convincing experiments, Mendel cross-pollinated pea plants that always produced yellow seeds with pea plants that always produced green seeds. The result was not, as one might guess, a plant with a combination of yellow and green seeds. Instead, all of the resulting plants had yellow seeds. At first it appeared that the green-seeded plants had had no influence.

However, Mendel's additional research proved this was not true. He bred together plants from the new, yellow-seeded generation that had resulted from his original crossbreeding of the green-seeded and yellow-seeded plants. The consistent result was a ratio of three-quarters yellow seeds to one-quarter green seeds.

Why did this 2-to-1 ratio of yellow to green seeds appear so consistently? It was Mendel's genius to provide an answer. Based on his experiments with pea plants, he argued that when two competing traits, such as a green or yellow coloring of seeds, were both present, only one could be expressed. The one that was expressed was called a **dominant trait**. Meanwhile, the other trait remained present in the organism, but was unexpressed. This was called a **recessive trait**. In the case of Mendel's original pea plants, the offspring plants received genetic information from both the green-seeded and yellow-seeded parents. However, the yellow trait was dominant, and consequently the recessive green trait did not assert itself.

Keep in mind, however, that genetic material relating to both parent plants is present in the offspring, even though it cannot be seen. The genetic information is known as the organism's genotype. A **genotype** is the underlying combination of genetic material present (but outwardly invisible) in an organism. In contrast, a **phenotype** is the observable trait, the trait that actually is seen.

Although the offspring of the yellow-seeded and green-seeded pea plants all have yellow seeds (i.e., they have a yellow-seeded phenotype), the genotype consists of genetic information relating to both parents.

And what is the nature of the information in the genotype? To answer that question, let's turn from peas to people. The principles are the same not just for plants and humans, but for the majority of species.

Recall that parents transmit genetic information to their offspring via the chromosomes they contribute through the gamete they provide during fertilization. Some of the genes form pairs called *alleles*, genes governing traits that may take alternate forms, such as hair or eye color. For example, brown eye color is a dominant trait (B); blue eyes are recessive (b). A child's allele may contain similar or dissimilar genes from each parent. If the child receives similar genes, he or she is said to be **homozygous** for the trait. On the other hand, if the child receives different forms of the gene from its parents, he or she is said to be **heterozygous**. In the case of heterozygous alleles (Bb), the dominant characteristic, brown eyes, is expressed. However, if the child happens to receive a recessive allele from each of its parents, and therefore lacks a dominant characteristic (bb), it will display the recessive characteristic, such as blue eyes.

Transmission of Genetic Information. We can see this process at work in humans by considering the transmission of *phenylketonuria (PKU)*, an inherited disorder in which a child is unable to make use of phenylalanine, an essential amino acid present in proteins found in milk and other foods. If left untreated, PKU allows phenylalanine to build up to toxic levels, causing brain damage and mental retardation.

PKU is produced by a single allele, or pair of genes. As shown in Figure 2.4, we can label each gene of the pair with a *P* if it carries a dominant gene, which causes the normal production of phenylalanine, or a *p* if it carries the recessive gene that produces PKU. In cases in which neither parent is a PKU carrier, both the mother's and the father's pairs of genes are the dominant form, symbolized as *PP*. Consequently, no matter which member of the pair is contributed by the mother and father, the resulting pair of genes in the child will be *PP*, and the child will not have PKU.

Consider what happens, however, if one of the parents has a recessive *p* gene. In this case, which we can we symbolize as *Pp*, the parent will not have PKU, since the normal *P* gene is dominant. But the recessive gene can be passed down to the child. This is not so bad: If the child has only one recessive gene, it will not suffer from PKU. But what if both parents carry a recessive *p* gene? In this case, although neither parent has the disorder, it is possible for the child to receive a recessive gene from both parents. The child's genotype for PKU then will be *pp*, and he or she will have the disorder.

Remember, though, that even children whose parents both have the recessive gene for PKU have only a 25 percent chance of inheriting the disorder. Due to the laws of probability, 25 percent of children with *Pp* parents will receive the dominant gene from each parent (these children's genotype would be *PP*), and 50 percent will receive the dominant gene from one parent and the recessive gene from the other (their genotypes would be either *Pp* or *pP*). Only the unlucky 25 percent who receive the recessive gene from each parent and end up with the genotype *pp* will suffer from PKU.

Polygenic Traits. The transmission of PKU is a good way to illustrate the basic principles of how genetic information passes from parent to child, although the case of PKU is simpler than most. In reality, relatively few traits are governed by a single pair of genes; instead, most traits are the result of **polygenic inheritance**, through which a combination of multiple gene pairs is responsible for the production of a particular trait.

Furthermore, some genes come in several alternate forms, and still others act to modify the way that particular genetic traits (produced by other alleles) are displayed. Genes also vary in terms of their *reaction range*, the potential degree of variability in the actual expression of a trait

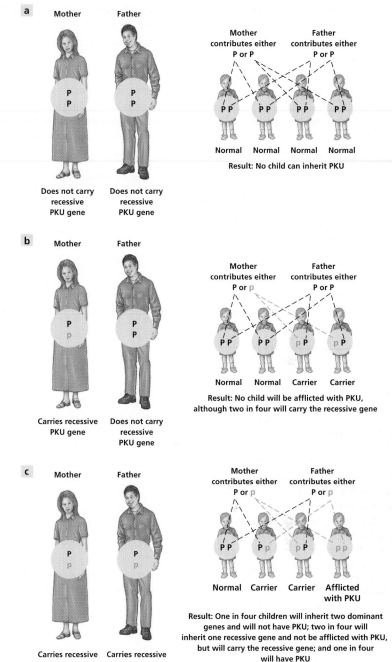

FIGURE 2.4 PKU Probabilities
PKU, a disease that causes brain damage and mental retardation, is produced by a single pair of genes inherited from one's mother and father. If neither parent carries a gene for the disease (a), a child cannot develop PKU. Even if one parent carries the recessive gene, but the other doesn't (b), the child cannot inherit the disease. However, if both parents carry the recessive gene (c), there is a 1 in 4 chance the child will have PKU.

homozygous inheriting from parents similar genes for a given trait.

heterozygous inheriting from parents different forms of a gene for a given trait.

polygenic inheritance inheritance in which a combination of multiple gene pairs is responsible for the production of a particular trait.

X-linked genes genes that are considered recessive and located only on the X chromosome.

behavioral genetics the study of the effects of heredity on behavior.

due to environmental conditions. And some traits, such as blood type, are produced by genes in which neither member of a pair of genes can be classified as purely dominant or recessive. Instead, the trait is expressed in terms of a combination of the two genes—such as type AB blood.

A number of recessive genes, called **X-linked genes**, are located only on the X chromosome. Recall that in females, the 23rd pair of chromosomes is an XX pair, while in males it is an XY pair. One result is that males have a higher risk for a variety of X-linked disorders, since males lack a second X chromosome that can counteract the genetic information that produces the disorder. For example, males are significantly more apt to have red-green color blindness, a disorder produced by a set of genes on the X chromosome. Similarly, *hemophilia*, a blood disorder, is produced by X-linked genes.

The Human Genome and Behavioral Genetics: Cracking the Genetic Code. Mendel's achievements in recognizing the basics of genetic transmission of traits were trailblazing. However, they mark only the beginning of our understanding of the ways those particular sorts of characteristics are passed on from one generation to the next.

The most recent milestone in understanding genetics was reached in early 2001, when molecular geneticists succeeded in mapping the specific sequence of genes on each chromosome. This accomplishment stands as one of the most important moments in the history of genetics and, for that matter, all of biology (International Human Genome Sequencing Consortium, 2001).

Already, the mapping of the gene sequence has provided important advances in our understanding of genetics. For instance, the number of human genes, long thought to be 100,000, has been revised downward to 25,000—not many more than organisms that are far less complex (see Figure 2.5). Furthermore, scientists have discovered that 99.9 percent of the gene sequence is shared by all humans. What this means is that we humans are far more similar to one another than we are different. It also indicates that many of the differences that seemingly separate people—such as race—are, literally, only skin-deep. Mapping of the human genome will also help in the identification of particular disorders to which a given individual is susceptible (International Human Genome Sequencing Consortium, 2001; Human Genome Program, 2003; Gee, 2004; DeLisi & Fleischhaker, 2007; Gupta & State, 2007).

The mapping of the human gene sequence is supporting the field of behavioral genetics. As the name implies, **behavioral genetics** studies the effects of heredity on psychological characteristics. Rather than simply examining stable, unchanging characteristics such as hair or eye color, behavioral genetics takes a broader approach, considering how our personality and behavioral habits are affected by genetic factors (Dick & Rose, 2002; Eley, Lichtenstein, & Moffitt, 2003; Li, 2003). Personality traits such as shyness or sociability, moodiness, and assertiveness are among the areas being studied. Other behavioral geneticists study psychological disorders, such as depression, attention-deficit/hyperactivity disorder, and schizophrenia, looking for possible genetic links (Conklin & Iacono, 2002; Lemery & Doelger, 2005; Keller & Miller, 2006; see Table 2.1).

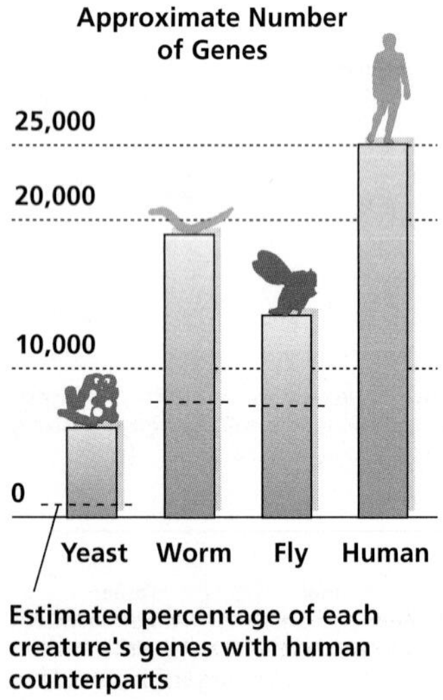

Approximate Number of Genes

FIGURE 2.5 Uniquely Human?
Humans have about 25,000 genes, making them not much more genetically complex than some primitive species.
Source: Celera Genomics: International Human Genome Sequencing Consortium, 2001.

TABLE 2.1	Current Understanding of the Genetic Basis of Selected Behavioral Disorders and Traits
BEHAVIORAL TRAIT	**CURRENT IDEAS OF GENETIC BASIS**
Huntington's disease	Huntington gene identified.
Early-onset (familial) Alzheimer's disease	Three distinct genes have been identified.
Fragile X mental retardation	Two genes have been identified.
Late-onset Alzheimer's disease	One set of genes has been associated with increased risk.
Attention-deficit/hyperactivity disorder	Three locations related to the genetics involved with the neurotransmitter dopamine may contribute.
Dyslexia	Relationships to two locations, on chromosomes 6 and 15, have been suggested.
Schizophrenia	There is no consensus, but links to numerous chromosomes, including 1, 5, 6, 10, 13, 15, and 22, have been reported.

Source: Adapted from McGuffin, Riley, & Plomin, 2001.

The promise of behavioral genetics is substantial. For one thing, researchers working within the field have gained a better understanding of the specifics of the genetic code that underlie human behavior and development.

Even more important, researchers are seeking to identify how genetic defects may be remedied (Plomin & Rutter, 1998; Peltonen & McKusick, 2001; Miller et al., 2008). To understand how that might come about, we need to consider the ways in which genetic factors, which normally cause development to proceed so smoothly, may falter.

Inherited and Genetic Disorders:
When Development Deviates from the Norm

Phenylketonuria (PKU) is just one of several disorders that may be inherited. Like a bomb that is harmless until its fuse is lit, a recessive gene responsible for a disorder may be passed on unknowingly from one generation to the next, revealing itself only when, by chance, it is paired with another recessive gene. It is only when two recessive genes come together like a match and a fuse that the gene will express itself and a child will inherit the genetic disorder.

But there is another way that genes are a source of concern: In some cases, genes become physically damaged. For instance, they may break down due to wear and tear or chance events occurring during the cell division processes of meiosis and mitosis. Sometimes genes, for no known reason, spontaneously change their form, a process called *spontaneous mutation.*

Alternatively, certain environmental factors, such as exposure to X-rays or even highly polluted air, may produce a malformation of genetic material. When such damaged genes are passed on to a child, the results can be disastrous in terms of future physical and cognitive development (Samet, DeMarini, & Malling, 2004).

In addition to PKU, which occurs once in 10,000 to 20,000 births, other inherited and genetic disorders include the following:

- **Down syndrome.** As we noted earlier, most people have 46 chromosomes, arranged in 23 pairs. One exception is individuals with **Down syndrome**, a disorder produced by the presence of an extra chromosome on the 21st pair. Once referred to as mongolism, Down syndrome is the most frequent cause of mental retardation. It occurs in about 1 out of 500 births, although the risk is much greater in mothers who are unusually young or old (Crane & Morris, 2006).

- **Fragile X syndrome.** **Fragile X syndrome** occurs when a particular gene is injured on the X chromosome. The result is mild to moderate mental retardation.

- **Sickle-cell anemia.** Around one-tenth of people of African descent carry genes that produce sickle-cell anemia, and 1 in 400 actually has the disease. **Sickle-cell anemia** is a blood disorder that gets its name from the shape of the red blood cells in those who have it. Symptoms include poor appetite, stunted growth, swollen stomach, and yellowish eyes. People afflicted with the most severe form of the disease rarely live beyond childhood. However, for those with less severe cases, medical advances have produced significant increases in life expectancy.

- **Tay-Sachs disease.** Occurring mainly in Jews of eastern European ancestry and in French Canadians, **Tay-Sachs disease** usually causes death before its victims reach school age. There is no treatment for the disorder, which produces blindness and muscle degeneration prior to death.

- **Klinefelter's syndrome.** One male out of every 400 is born with **Klinefelter's syndrome**, the presence of an extra X chromosome. The resulting XXY complement produces underdeveloped genitals, extreme height, and enlarged breasts. Klinefelter's syndrome is one of a number of genetic abnormalities that result from receiving the improper number of sex chromosomes. For instance, there are disorders produced by an extra Y chromosome (XYY), a missing second chromosome (called *Turner syndrome)* (X0), and three X chromosomes (XXX). Such disorders are typically characterized by problems relating to sexual characteristics and by intellectual deficits (Sorenson, 1992; Sotos, 1997; Wodrich & Tarbox, 2008).

Down syndrome   a disorder produced by the presence of an extra chromosome on the 21st pair; once referred to as mongolism.

fragile X syndrome   a disorder produced by injury to a gene on the X chromosome, producing mild to moderate mental retardation.

sickle-cell anemia   a blood disorder that gets its name from the shape of the red blood cells in those who have it.

Tay-Sachs disease   a disorder that produces blindness and muscle degeneration prior to death; there is no treatment.

Klinefelter's syndrome   a disorder resulting from the presence of an extra X chromosome that produces underdeveloped genitals, extreme height, and enlarged breasts.

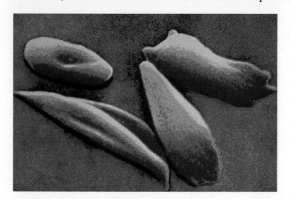

Sickle-cell anemia, named for the presence of misshapen red blood cells, is carried in the genes of 1 in 10 African Americans.

It is important to remember that the mere fact a disorder has genetic roots does not mean that environmental factors do not also play a role (Moldin & Gottesman, 1997; Rolland & Willams, 2006; Finn, 2008). Consider, for instance, sickle-cell anemia, which primarily afflicts people of African descent. Because the disease can be fatal in childhood, we'd expect that those who suffer from it would be unlikely to live long enough to pass it on. And this does seem to be true, at least in the United States: Compared with parts of West Africa, the incidence in the United States is much lower.

But why shouldn't the incidence of sickle-cell anemia also be gradually reduced for people in West Africa? This question proved puzzling for many years, until scientists determined that carrying the sickle-cell gene raises immunity to malaria, which is a common disease in West Africa. This heightened immunity meant that people with the sickle-cell gene had a genetic advantage (in terms of resistance to malaria) that offset, to some degree, the disadvantage of being a carrier of the sickle-cell gene (Mohammed et al., 2006).

The lesson of sickle-cell anemia is that genetic factors are intertwined with environmental considerations and can't be looked at in isolation. Furthermore, we need to remember that although we've been focusing on inherited factors that can go awry, in the vast majority of cases the genetic mechanisms with which we are endowed work quite well. Overall, 95 percent of children born in the United States are healthy and normal. For the 250,000 who are born with some sort of physical or mental disorder, appropriate intervention often can help treat and, in some cases, cure the problem.

Moreover, due to advances in behavioral genetics, genetic difficulties increasingly can be forecast, anticipated, and planned for before a child's birth, enabling parents to take steps before the child is born to reduce the severity of certain genetic conditions. As scientists' knowledge regarding the specific location of particular genes expands, predictions of what the genetic future may hold are becoming increasingly exact, as we discuss next (Plomin & Rutter, 1998; Fransen, Meertens, & Schrander-Stumpel, 2006).

Genetic Counseling: Predicting the Future from the Genes of the Present. If you knew that your mother and grandmother had died of Huntington's disease—a devastating, always fatal inherited disorder marked by tremors and intellectual deterioration—to whom could you turn to learn your own chances of coming down with the disease? The best person to turn to would be a member of a field that, just a few decades ago, was nonexistent: genetic counseling. **Genetic counseling** focuses on helping people deal with issues relating to inherited disorders.

Genetic counselors use a variety of data in their work. For instance, couples contemplating having a child may seek to determine the risks involved in a future pregnancy. In such a case, a counselor will take a thorough family history, seeking any familial incidence of birth defects that might indicate a pattern of recessive or X-linked genes. In addition, the counselor will take into account factors such as the age of the mother and father and any previous abnormalities in other children they may have already had (Fransen, Meertens, & Schrander-Stumpel, 2006; Resta et al., 2006).

Typically, genetic counselors suggest a thorough physical examination. Such an exam may identify physical abnormalities that potential parents may have and not be aware of. In addition, samples of blood, skin, and urine may be used to isolate and examine specific chromosomes. Possible genetic defects, such as the presence of an extra sex chromosome, can be identified by assembling a *karyotype*, a chart containing enlarged photos of each of the chromosomes.

genetic counseling the discipline that focuses on helping people deal with issues relating to inherited disorders.

ultrasound sonography a process in which high-frequency sound waves scan the mother's womb to produce an image of the unborn baby, whose size and shape can then be assessed.

Prenatal Testing. If the woman is already pregnant, a variety of techniques are available to assess the health of her unborn child. The earliest test is a *first-trimester screen,* which combines a blood test and ultrasound sonography in the 11th to 13th week of pregnancy and can identify chromosomal abnormalities and other disorders, such as heart problems. In **ultrasound sonography**, high-frequency sound waves bombard the mother's womb. These waves produce a rather indistinct, but useful, image of the unborn baby, whose size and shape can then be assessed. Repeated use of ultrasound sonography can reveal developmental patterns. Although blood tests and ultrasound are not very accurate in identifying abnormalities early in pregnancy, they become more accurate later in pregnancy as the developing child becomes more differentiated.

A more invasive test, **chorionic villus sampling (CVS)**, can be employed in the 10th to 13th week of the first trimester if blood tests and ultrasound have identified a potential problem or if there is a family history of inherited disorders. CVS involves inserting a thin needle into the fetus and taking small samples of hairlike material that surrounds the embryo. The test can be done between the eighth and eleventh week of pregnancy. However, it produces a risk of miscarriage of 1 in 100 to 1 in 200. Because of the risk, its use is relatively infrequent.

In **amniocentesis**, a small sample of fetal cells is drawn by a tiny needle inserted into the amniotic fluid surrounding the unborn fetus. Carried out 15 to 20 weeks into the pregnancy, amniocentesis allows the analysis of the fetal cells that can identify a variety of genetic defects with nearly 100 percent accuracy. In addition, it can determine the sex of the child. Although there is a danger to the fetus in an invasive procedure such as amniocentesis, it is generally safe.

After the various tests are complete and all possible information is available, the couple will meet with the genetic counselor again. Typically, counselors avoid giving specific recommendations. Instead, they lay out the facts and present various options, ranging from doing nothing to taking more drastic steps, such as terminating the pregnancy through abortion. Ultimately, it is the parents who must decide what course of action to follow.

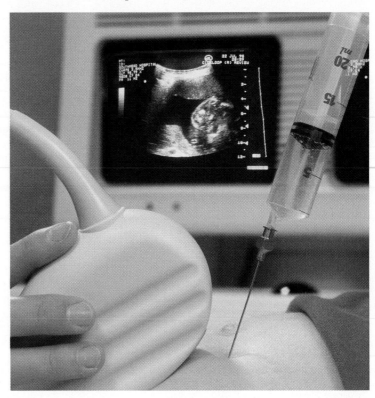

In amniocentisis, a sample of amniotic fluid surrounding the fetus is examined to identify genetic defects.

Screening for Future Problems. The newest role of genetic counselors involves testing people to identify whether they themselves, rather than their children, are susceptible to future disorders because of genetic abnormalities. For instance, Huntington's disease typically does not appear until people reach their 40s. However, genetic testing can identify much earlier whether a person carries the flawed gene that produces Huntington's disease. Presumably, people's knowledge that they carry the gene can help them prepare themselves for the future (van't Spijker & ten Kroode, 1997; Ensenauer, Michels, & Reinke, 2005).

In addition to Huntington's disease, more than a thousand disorders can be predicted on the basis of genetic testing (see Table 2.2 on page 44). Although such testing may bring welcome relief from future worries—if the results are negative—positive results may produce just the opposite effect. In fact, genetic testing raises difficult practical and ethical questions (Johannes, 2003; Human Genome Project, 2006; Twomey, 2006).

Suppose, for instance, a woman who thought she was susceptible to Huntington's disease was tested in her 20s and found that she carried the flawed gene and would therefore get the disease. She might experience depression and distress. Some studies show that 10 percent of people who find they have the flawed gene that leads to Huntington's disease never recover fully on an emotional level (Groopman, 1998; Hamilton, 1998; Myers, 2004; Wahlin, 2007).

Genetic testing is clearly a complicated issue. It rarely provides a simple yes or no answer, instead presenting a range of probabilities. In some cases, the likelihood of actually becoming ill depends on the type of environmental stressors to which a person is exposed. Personal differences also affect a given person's susceptibility to a disorder (Holtzman et al., 1997; Patenaude, Guttmacher, & Collins, 2002; Bonke et al., 2005).

As our understanding of genetics continues to grow, researchers and medical practitioners have moved beyond testing and counseling to actively working to change flawed genes. The possibilities for genetic intervention and manipulation increasingly border on what once was science fiction—as we consider in the accompanying *From Research to Practice* box about preimplantation genetic diagnosis.

chorionic villus sampling (CVS) a test used to find genetic defects that involves taking samples of hairlike material that surrounds the embryo.

amniocentesis the process of identifying genetic defects by examining a small sample of fetal cells drawn by a needle inserted into the amniotic fluid surrounding the unborn fetus.

TABLE 2.2   Some Currently Available DNA-Based Gene Tests

DISEASE	DESCRIPTION
Adult polycystic kidney disease	Kidney failure and liver disease
Alpha-1-antitrypsin deficiency	Emphysema and liver disease
Alzheimer's disease	Late-onset variety of senile dementia
Amyotrophic lateral sclerosis (Lou Gehrig's disease)	Progressive motor function loss leading to paralysis and death
Ataxia telangiectasia	Progressive brain disorder resulting in loss of muscle control and cancers
Breast and ovarian cancer (inherited)	Early-onset tumors of breasts and ovaries
Charcot-Marie-Tooth	Loss of feeling in ends of limbs
Congenital adrenal hyperplasia	Hormone deficiency, ambiguous genitalia and male pseudohermaphroditism
Cystic fibrosis	Thick mucus accumulations in lungs and chronic infections in lungs and pancreas
Duchenne muscular dystrophy (Becker muscular dystrophy)	Severe to mild muscle wasting, deterioration, weakness
Dystonia	Muscle rigidity, repetitive twisting movements
Factor V-Leiden	Blood-clotting disorder
Fanconi anemia, group	Anemia, leukemia, skeletal deformities
Fragile X syndrome	Mental retardation
Gaucher disease	Enlarged liver and spleen, bone degeneration
Hemophilia A and B	Bleeding disorders
Hereditary nonpolyposis colon cancer[a]	Early-onset tumors of colon and sometimes other organs
Huntington's disease	Progressive neurological degeneration, usually beginning in midlife
Myotonic dystrophy	Progressive muscle weakness
Neurofibromatosis, type 1	Multiple benign nervous system tumors that can be disfiguring; cancers
Phenylketonuria	Progressive mental retardation due to missing enzyme; correctable by diet
Prader Willi/Angelman syndromes	Decreased motor skills, cognitive impairment, early death
Sickle-cell disease	Blood cell disorder, chronic pain and infections
Spinal muscular atrophy	Severe, usually lethal, progressive muscle-wasting disorder in children
Spinocerebellar ataxia, type 1	Involuntary muscle movements, reflex disorders, explosive speech
Tay-Sachs disease	Seizures, paralysis, fatal neurological disease of early childhood
Thalassemias	Anemias

[a]These are susceptibility tests that provide only an estimated risk for developing the disorder.

Source: Human Genome Project, 2006, http://www.ornl.gov/sci/techresources/Human_Genome/medicine/genetest.shtml.

FROM RESEARCH TO PRACTICE
Are "Designer Babies" in Our Future?

Adam Nash was born to save his older sister Molly's life—literally. Molly was suffering from a rare disorder called Fanconi anemia, which meant that her bone marrow was failing to produce blood cells. This disease can have devastating effects on young children, including birth defects and certain cancers. Many don't survive to adulthood. Molly's best hope for overcoming this disease was to grow healthy bone marrow by receiving a transplant of immature blood cells from the placenta of a newborn sibling. But not just any sibling would do—it had to be one with compatible cells that would not be rejected by Molly's immune system. So Molly's parents turned to a new and risky technique that had the potential to save Molly by using cells from her unborn brother.

Molly's parents were the first to use a genetic screening technique called *preimplantation genetic diagnosis* (PGD) to ensure that their next child would be free of Fanconi anemia. With PGD, a newly fertilized embryo can be screened for a variety of genetic diseases before it is implanted in the mother's uterus to develop. Doctors fertilized several of Molly's mother's eggs with her husband's sperm in a test tube. They then examined the embryos to ensure that they would implant one that PGD revealed to be both genetically healthy and a match for Molly. When Adam was born 9 months later, Molly got a new lease on life, too: The transplant was a success, and Molly was cured of her disease.

Molly's parents were understandably focused on saving their seriously ill daughter's life, but they and their doctors also opened a controversial new chapter in genetic engineering involving the use of advances in reproductive medicine that give parents a degree of prenatal control over the traits of their children. Another procedure that makes this level of genetic control possible is *germ line therapy,* in which cells are taken from an embryo and then replaced after the defective genes they contain have been repaired.

Although PGD and germ line therapy have important uses in the prevention and treatment of serious genetic disorders, concerns have been raised over whether such scientific advances can lead to the development of "designer babies"—infants that have been genetically manipulated to have traits selected by their parents. The question is whether these procedures can and should be used not only to correct undesirable genetic defects, but also to breed infants for specific purposes or to "improve" future generations on a genetic level.

The ethical concerns are numerous: Is it right to tailor babies to serve a specific purpose, however noble? Does this kind of genetic control pose any dangers to the human gene pool? Would unfair advantages be conferred on the offspring of those who are wealthy or privileged enough to have access to these procedures (Frankel & Chapman, 2000; Sheldon & Wilkinson, 2004)?

Designer babies aren't with us yet; scientists do not yet understand enough about the human genome to identify the genes that control most traits, much less to make genetic modifications to control how those traits will be expressed. Moreover, the term itself is a bit misleading. For one thing, babies aren't being genetically engineered; PGD merely entails selecting an embryo that already has the desired genetic makeup. For another thing, it's a difficult and expensive procedure that does not lend itself to casual use. Still, as Adam Nash's case reveals, we are inching closer to a day when it is possible for parents to decide what genes their children will and will not have.

- *How might the circumstances of Adam's birth affect the relationship between him and Molly as they grow up?*

- *How might Adam feel when he learns that he was selected to be born in order to save his sister?*

- *What if our understanding of the human genome develops to the point that it becomes possible to use PGD to control the future intelligence, attractiveness, or sexuality of one's children? Where should we draw the line on parents' ability to dictate what traits their children will have?*

REVIEW

▶ In humans, the male sex cell (the sperm) and the female sex cell (the ovum) provide the developing baby with 23 chromosomes each.

▶ A genotype is the underlying but invisible combination of genetic material present in an organism; a phenotype is the visible trait, the expression of the genotype.

▶ The field of behavioral genetics, a combination of psychology and genetics, studies the effects of genetics on behavior.

▶ Several inherited and genetic disorders are due to damaged or mutated genes.

▶ Genetic counselors use a variety of data and techniques to advise future parents of possible genetic risks to their unborn children.

APPLY

▶ How can the study of identical twins who were separated at birth help researchers determine the effects of genetic and environmental factors on human development?

▶ If genetic testing revealed that you had what is almost always a fatal disease, what use would the information have for you? Would it change your career goals? Chosen partner? Choice of college?

MODULE 2.2

The Interaction of Heredity and Environment

Like many other parents, Jared's mother, Leesha, and his father, Jamal, tried to figure out which one of them their new baby resembled the most. He seemed to have Leesha's big, wide eyes, and Jamal's generous smile. As he grew, Jared grew to resemble his mother and father even more. His hair grew in with a hairline just like Leesha's, and his teeth, when they came, made his smile resemble Jamal's even more. He also seemed to act like his parents. For example, he was a charming little baby, always ready to smile at people who visited the house—just like his friendly, jovial dad. He seemed to sleep like his mom, which was lucky since Jamal was an extremely light sleeper who could do with as little as 4 hours a night, while Leesha liked a regular 7 or 8 hours.

Were Jared's ready smile and regular sleeping habits something he just luckily inherited from his parents? Or did Jamal and Leesha provide a happy and stable home that encouraged these welcome traits? What causes our behavior? Nature or nurture? Is behavior produced by inherited, genetic influences, or is it triggered by factors in the environment?

The simple answer is: There is no simple answer.

The Role of the Environment in Determining the Expression of Genes: From Genotypes to Phenotypes

As developmental research accumulates, it is becoming increasingly clear that to view behavior as due to *either* genetic *or* environmental factors is inappropriate. A given behavior is not caused just by genetic factors; nor is it caused solely by environmental forces. Instead, as we first discussed in Chapter 1, the behavior is the product of some combination of the two.

For instance, consider **temperament**, patterns of arousal and emotionality that represent consistent and enduring characteristics in an individual. Suppose we found—as increasing evidence suggests is the case—that a small percentage of children are born with temperaments that produce an unusual degree of physiological reactivity. Having a tendency to shrink from anything unusual, such infants react to novel stimuli with a rapid increase in heartbeat and unusual excitability of the limbic system of the brain. Such heightened reactivity to stimuli at the start of life, which seems to be linked to inherited factors, is also likely to cause children, by the time they are 4 or 5, to be considered shy by their parents and teachers. But not always: some of them behave indistinguishably from their peers at the same age (Kagan & Snidman, 1991; McCrae et al., 2000).

What makes the difference? The answer seems to be the environment in which the children are raised. Children whose parents encourage them to be outgoing by arranging new opportunities for them may overcome their shyness. In contrast, children raised in a stressful environment marked by marital discord or a prolonged illness may be more likely to retain their shyness later in life (Kagan, Arcus, & Snidman, 1993; Joseph, 1999; Propper & Moore, 2006). Jared may have been born with an easy temperament, which was easily reinforced by his caring parents.

Interaction of Factors. Such findings illustrate that many traits reflect **multifactorial transmission**, meaning that they are determined by a combination of both genetic and environmental factors. In multifactorial transmission, a genotype provides a particular range within which a phenotype may achieve expression. For instance, people with a genotype that permits them to gain weight easily may never be slim, no matter how much they diet. They may be *relatively* slim, given their genetic heritage, but they may never be able to reach a certain degree of thinness. In many cases, then, it is the environment that determines the way in which a particular genotype will be expressed as a phenotype (Fernandez et al., 2008; Stroebe, 2008; Markward, Markward, & Peterson, 2009).

temperament　patterns of arousal and emotionality that represent consistent and enduring characteristics in an individual.

multifactorial transmission the determination of traits by a combination of both genetic and environmental factors in which a genotype provides a range within which a phenotype may be expressed.

Nature ►►►►►►►►►► ◄◄◄◄◄◄◄◄◄ Nurture

Intelligence is provided entirely by genetic factors; environment plays no role. Even a highly enriched environment and excellent education make no difference.	Although largely inherited, intelligence is affected by an extremely enriched or deprived environment.	Intelligence is affected both by a person's genetic endowment and environment. A person genetically predisposed to low intelligence may perform better if raised in an enriched environment or worse in a deprived environment. Similarly, a person genetically predisposed to higher intelligence may perform worse in a deprived environment or better in an enriched environment.	Although intelligence is largely a result of environment, genetic abnormalities may produce mental retardation.	Intelligence depends entirely on the environment. Genetics plays no role in determining intellectual success.

Possible Causes

FIGURE 2.6 Possible Sources of Intelligence
Intelligence may be explained by a range of differing possible sources, spanning the nature–nurture continuum. Which of these explanations do you find most convincing, given the evidence discussed in the chapter?

On the other hand, certain genotypes are relatively unaffected by environmental factors. In such cases, development follows a preordained pattern, relatively independent of the specific environment in which a person is raised. For instance, research on pregnant women who were severely malnourished during famines caused by World War II found that their children were, on average, unaffected physically or intellectually as adults (Stein et al., 1975). Similarly, no matter how much health food people eat, they are not going to grow beyond certain genetically imposed limitations in height. Little Jared's hairline was probably affected very little by any actions on the part of his parents.

Ultimately, of course, it is the unique interaction of inherited and environmental factors that determines people's patterns of development.

The more appropriate question, then, is *how much* of the behavior is caused by genetic factors, and *how much* by environmental factors? (See, for example, the range of possibilities for the determinants of intelligence, illustrated in Figure 2.6.) At one extreme is the idea that opportunities in the environment are solely responsible for intelligence, and on the other, that intelligence is purely genetic—you either have it or you don't. The usefulness of such extremes seems to be to point us toward the middle—that intelligence results from some combination of natural mental ability and environmental opportunity.

Studying Development: How Much Is Nature, How Much Is Nurture?

Developmental researchers use several strategies to try to resolve the question of the degree to which traits, characteristics, and behavior are produced by genetic or environmental factors. Their studies involve both nonhuman species and humans.

Nonhuman Animal Studies: Controlling Both Genetics and Environment. It is relatively simple to develop breeds of animals that are genetically similar to one another in terms of specific traits. The people who raise Butterball turkeys for Thanksgiving do it all the time, producing turkeys that grow especially rapidly so that they can be brought to market inexpensively. Similarly, strains of laboratory animals can be bred to share similar genetic backgrounds.

By observing animals with similar genetic backgrounds in different environments, scientists can determine, with reasonable precision, the effects of specific kinds of environmental stimulation. For example, to determine the effects of living in different settings, animals can be raised in unusually stimulating environments, with lots of items to climb over or through, or relatively barren

"The title of my science project is 'My Little Brother: Nature or Nurture.'"

Monozygotic and dizygotic twins present opportunities to learn about the relative contributions of heredity and situational factors. What kinds of things can psychologists learn from studying twins?

environments. Conversely, researchers can examine groups of animals that have been bred to have significantly *different* genetic backgrounds on particular traits. Then, by exposing such animals to identical environments, they can determine the role that genetic background plays.

The drawback to using nonhumans as research subjects is that we can't be sure how well the findings we obtain can be generalized to people. Still, animal research offers substantial opportunities.

Contrasting Relatedness and Behavior: Adoption, Twin, and Family Studies. Obviously, researchers can't control either the genetic backgrounds or the environments of humans in the way they can with nonhumans. However, nature conveniently has provided the potential to carry out various kinds of "natural experiments"—in the form of twins. Recall that identical, monozygotic twins are also identical genetically. Because their inherited backgrounds are precisely the same, any variations in their behavior must be due entirely to environmental factors.

It would be rather simple for researchers to make use of identical twins to draw unequivocal conclusions about the roles of nature and nurture. For instance, by separating identical twins at birth and placing them in totally different environments, researchers could assess the impact of environment unambiguously. Of course, ethical considerations make this impossible. What researchers can—and do—study, however, are cases in which identical twins have been put up for adoption at birth and are raised in substantially different environments. Such instances allow us to draw fairly confident conclusions about the relative contributions of genetics and environment (Bouchard & Pederson, 1999; Bailey et al., 2000; Richardson & Norgate, 2007).

The data from such studies of identical twins raised in different environments are not always without bias. Adoption agencies typically take the characteristics (and wishes) of birth mothers into account when they place babies in adoptive homes. For instance, children tend to be placed with families of the same race and religion. Consequently, even when monozygotic twins are placed in different adoptive homes, there are often similarities between the two home environments, making it often impossible to attribute differences in behavior to differences in the environment.

Studies of nonidentical, dizygotic twins also present opportunities to learn about the relative contributions of nature and nurture. Recall that dizygotic twins are genetically no more similar than siblings in a family born at different times. By comparing behavior within pairs of dizygotic twins with that of pairs of monozygotic twins (who are genetically identical), researchers can determine whether monozygotic twins are more similar on a particular trait, on average, than dizygotic twins. If so, they can assume that genetics plays an important role in determining the expression of that trait.

Still another approach is to study people who are totally unrelated to one another and who therefore have dissimilar genetic backgrounds, but who share an environmental background. For instance, a family that adopts, at the same time, two very young unrelated children probably will provide them with quite similar environments throughout their childhood. In this case, similarities in the children's characteristics and behavior can be attributed with some confidence to environmental influences (Segal, 2000; Segal et al., 2007; van den Berg et al., 2008).

Finally, developmental researchers have examined groups of people in light of their degree of genetic similarity. For instance, if on one hand we find a high association on a particular trait between biological parents and their children, but a weaker association between adoptive parents and their children, we have evidence for the importance of genetics in determining the expression of that trait. On the other hand, if there is a stronger association on a trait between adoptive parents and their children than between biological parents and their children, we have evidence for the importance of the environment in determining that trait (Rowe, 1994; Plomin, 2007).

Developmental researchers have used all these approaches, and more, to study the relative impact of genetic and environmental factors. What have they found? Based on decades of research, they have concluded that virtually all traits, characteristics, and behaviors are the joint result of the combination and interaction of nature and nurture. Genetic and environmental factors work in tandem, each affecting and being affected by the other, creating the unique individual that each of us is and will become (Robinson, 2004; Waterland & Jirtle, 2004).

Physical Traits: Family Resemblances. Monozygotic twins are merely the most extreme example of the fact that the more genetically similar two people are, the more likely they are to share physical characteristics. Tall parents tend to have tall children, and short ones tend to have short children. Obesity also has a strong genetic component. For example, in one study pairs of identical twins were put on diets that contained an extra 1,000 calories a day—and ordered not to exercise. Over a 3-month period, the twins gained almost identical amounts of weight. Moreover, different pairs of twins varied substantially in how much weight they gained, with some pairs gaining almost three times as much weight as other pairs (Bouchard et al., 1990).

Other, less obvious physical characteristics also show strong genetic influences. For instance, blood pressure, respiration rates, and even the age at which life ends are more similar in closely related individuals than in those who are less genetically alike (Price & Gottesman, 1991; Finkel et al., 2003).

Intelligence: More Research, More Controversy. No issue involving the relative influence of heredity and environment has generated more research than intelligence. Why? The main reason is that intelligence, generally measured in terms of an IQ score, is a central human characteristic that differentiates humans from other species. In addition, intelligence is strongly related to success in scholastic endeavors and, somewhat less strongly, to other types of achievement.

Genetics plays a significant role in intelligence. In studies of both overall or general intelligence and of specific subcomponents of intelligence (such as spatial skills, verbal skills, and memory), as can be seen in Figure 2.7, the closer the genetic link between two individuals, the greater the correspondence of their overall IQ scores.

Not only is genetics an important influence on intelligence, but the impact increases with age. For instance, as fraternal (i.e., dizygotic) twins move from infancy to adolescence, their IQ scores become less similar. In contrast, the IQ scores of identical (monozygotic) twins become increasingly similar over the course of time. These opposite patterns suggest the intensifying influence of inherited factors with increasing age (McGue et al., 1993; van Leeuwen, van den Berg, & Boomsma, 2008).

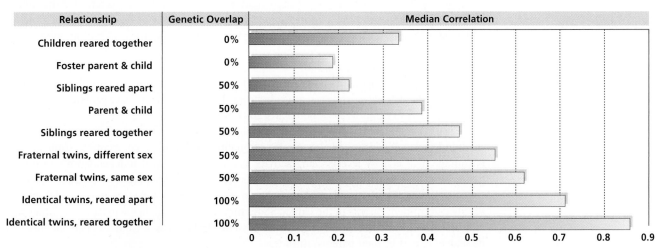

FIGURE 2.7 Genetics and IQ
The closer the genetic link between two individuals, the greater the correspondence between their IQ scores. Why do you think there is a sex difference in the frjternal twins' figures? Might there be other sex differences in other sets of twins or siblings, not shown on this chart?
Source: Bouchard & McGue, 1981.

FROM AN
EDUCATOR'S
PERSPECTIVE
If you had a pair of twins in your classroom, would you teach them any differently than if they were two unrelated students? Why or why not?

Although it is clear that heredity plays an important role in intelligence, investigators are much more divided on the question of the degree to which it is inherited. Perhaps the most extreme view is held by psychologist Arthur Jensen (2003), who argued that as much as 80 percent of intelligence is a result of heredity. Others have suggested more modest figures, ranging from 50 to 70 percent. It is critical to keep in mind that such figures are averages across large groups of people, and any particular individual's degree of inheritance cannot be predicted from these averages (e.g., Herrnstein & Murray, 1994; Devlin, Daniels, & Roeder, 1997).

It is important to keep in mind that although heredity clearly plays an important role in intelligence, environmental factors such as exposure to books, good educational experiences, and intelligent peers are profoundly influential. Even those researchers like Jensen who make the most extreme estimates of the role of genetics still admit that environmental factors play a significant role. In terms of public policy, environmental influences are the focus of efforts geared toward maximizing people's intellectual success. As developmental psychologist Sandra Scarr suggests, we should be asking what can be done to maximize the intellectual development of each individual (Scarr & Carter-Saltzman, 1982; Storfer, 1990; Bouchard, 1997; Garcia et al., 2005).

Genetic and Environmental Influences on Personality: Born to Be Outgoing? Do we inherit our personality?

At least in part. There's increasing research evidence suggesting that some of our most basic personality traits have genetic roots. For example, two of the key "Big Five" personality traits, neuroticism and extroversion, have been linked to genetic factors. *Neuroticism*, as used by personality researchers, is the degree of emotional stability an individual characteristically displays. *Extroversion* is the degree to which a person seeks to be with others, to behave in an outgoing manner, and generally to be sociable. For instance, Jared, the baby described earlier in this chapter, may have inherited a tendency to be outgoing from his extroverted father, Jamal (Plomin & Caspi, 1998; Benjamin, Ebstein, & Belmaker, 2002; Zuckerman, 2003).

How do we know which personality traits reflect genetics? Some evidence comes from direct examination of genes themselves. For instance, it appears that a specific gene is very influential in determining risk-taking behavior. This novelty-seeking gene affects the production of the brain chemical dopamine, making some people more prone than others to seek out novel situations and to take risks (Ebstein et al., 1996; Gillespie et al., 2003).

Other evidence for the role of genetics in determining personality traits comes from studies of twins. For instance, in one major study, researchers looked at the personality traits of hundreds of pairs of twins. Because a good number of the twins were genetically identical but had been raised apart, it was possible to determine with some confidence the influence of genetic factors (Tellegen et al., 1988). The researchers found that certain traits reflected the contribution of genetics considerably more than others. As you can see in Figure 2.8, social potency (the tendency to be a masterful, forceful leader who enjoys being the center of attention) and traditionalism (strict endorsement of rules and authority) are strongly associated with genetic factors (Harris, Vernon, & Jang, 2007).

Even less basic personality traits are linked to genetics. For example, political attitudes, religious interests and values, and even attitudes toward human sexuality have genetic components (Eley, Bolton, & O'Connor, 2003; Bouchard, 2004; Koenig et al., 2005).

Clearly, genetic factors play a role in determining personality. At the same time, the environment in which a child is raised also affects personality development. For example, some parents encourage high activity levels, seeing activity as a manifestation of independence and intelligence. Other parents may encourage lower levels of activity on the part of their children, feeling that more passive children will get along better in society. In part, these parental attitudes are culturally determined: Parents in the United States may encourage higher activity levels, while parents in Asian cultures may encourage greater passivity. In both cases, children's personalities will be shaped in part by their parents' attitudes.

Can Genes Influence the Environment? According to developmental psychologist Sandra Scarr (1993, 1998), the genetic endowment provided to children by their parents not

Trait	%
Social potency	61%

A person high in this trait is masterful, a forceful leader who likes to be the center of attention.

| **Traditionalism** | 60% |

Follows rules and authority, endorses high moral standards and strict discipline.

| **Stress reaction** | 55% |

Feels vulnerable and sensitive and is given to worries and is easily upset.

| **Absorption** | 55% |

Has a vivid imagination readily captured by rich experience; relinquishes sense of reality.

| **Alienation** | 55% |

Feels mistreated and used, that "the world is out to get me."

| **Well-being** | 54% |

Has a cheerful disposition, feels confident and optimistic.

| **Harm avoidance** | 50% |

Shuns the excitement of risk and danger, prefers the safe route even if it is tedious.

| **Aggression** | 48% |

Is physically aggressive and vindictive, has taste for violence and is "out to get the world."

| **Achievement** | 46% |

Works hard, strives for mastery, and puts work and accomplishment ahead of other things.

| **Control** | 43% |

Is cautious and plodding, rational and sensible, likes carefully planned events.

| **Social closeness** | 33% |

Prefers emotional intimacy and close ties, turns to others for comfort and help.

FIGURE 2.8 Inheriting Traits
These traits are among the personality factors that are related most closely to genetic factors. The higher the percentage, the greater the degree to which the trait reflects the influence of heredity. Do these figures mean that "leaders are born, not made"? Why or why not?
Source: Adapted from Tellegen et al., 1988.

only determines their children's genetic characteristics, but also actively influences their environment. Scarr suggests three ways a child's genetic predisposition might influence his or her environment.

First, children tend to actively focus on those aspects of their environment that are most connected with their genetically determined abilities. For example, an active, more aggressive child will gravitate toward sports, while a more reserved child will be more engaged by academics or solitary pursuits like computer games or drawing. They also pay less attention to those aspects of the environment that are less compatible with their genetic endowment. For instance, two girls may be reading the same school bulletin board. One may notice the sign advertising tryouts for Little League baseball, while her less coordinated but more musically endowed friend might be more apt to spot the notice recruiting students for an afterschool chorus. In each case, the child is attending to those aspects of the environment in which her genetically determined abilities can flourish.

Second, in some cases, the gene–environment influence is more passive and less direct. For example, a particularly sports-oriented parent, who has genes that promote good physical coordination, may provide many opportunities for a child to play sports.

Finally, the genetically driven temperament of a child may *evoke* certain environmental influences. For instance, an infant's demanding behavior may cause parents to be more attentive to the infant's needs than they would be if the infant were less demanding. Or a child who is genetically inclined to be well coordinated may play ball with anything in the house so often that her parents notice. They may then decide that she should have some sports equipment.

In sum, determining whether behavior is primarily attributable to nature or to nurture is a bit like shooting at a moving target. Not only are behaviors and traits a joint outcome of genetic and environmental factors, but the relative influence of genes and environment for specific characteristics shifts over the course of people's lives. Although the pool of genes we inherit at birth sets the stage for our future development, the constantly shifting scenery and the other characters in our lives determine just how our development eventually plays out. The environment both influences our experiences and is molded by the choices we are temperamentally inclined to make.

REVIEW

▶ Human characteristics and behavior are a joint outcome of genetic and environmental factors.

▶ Genetic influences have been identified in physical characteristics, intelligence, and personality traits and behaviors.

▶ There is some speculation that entire cultures may be predisposed genetically toward certain types of philosophical viewpoints and attitudes.

APPLY

▶ How might an environment different from the one you experienced have affected the development of personality characteristics that you believe you inherited from one or both of your parents?

▶ Some people have used the proven genetic basis of intelligence to argue against strenuous educational efforts on behalf of individuals with below-average IQs. Does this viewpoint make sense based on what you have learned about heredity and environment? Why or why not?

MODULE ● **2.3**

Prenatal Growth and Birth

Robert accompanied Lisa to her first appointment with the midwife. The midwife checked the results of tests done to confirm the couple's own positive home pregnancy test. "Yep, you're going to have a baby," she confirmed, speaking to Lisa. "You'll need to set up monthly visits for the next 6 months, then more frequently as your due date approaches. You can get this prescription for prenatal vitamins filled at any pharmacy, and here are some guidelines about diet and exercise. You don't smoke, do you? That's good." Then she turned to Robert. "How about you? Do you smoke?" After giving lots of instructions and advice, she left the couple feeling slightly dazed, but ready to do whatever they could to have a healthy baby.

From the moment of conception, development proceeds relentlessly. As we've seen, many aspects are guided by the complex set of genetic guidelines inherited from the parents. Prenatal growth, like all development, is also influenced from the start by environmental factors (Leavitt & Goldson, 1996; Rettew, 2008). As we'll see, both parents, like Lisa and Robert, can take part in providing a good prenatal environment.

Fertilization: The Moment of Conception

When most of us think about the facts of life, we tend to focus on the events that cause a male's sperm cells to begin their journey toward a female's ovum. Yet the act of sex that brings about the potential for conception is both the consequence and the start of a long string of events that precede and follow **fertilization**, or conception: the joining of sperm and ovum to create the single-celled zygote from which each of us began our lives.

Both the male's sperm and the female's ovum come with a history of their own. Females are born with around 400,000 ova located in the two ovaries. However, the ova do not mature until the female reaches puberty. From that point until she reaches menopause, the female will ovulate about every 28 days. During ovulation, an egg is released from one of the ovaries and pushed by minute hair cells through the fallopian tube toward the uterus. If the ovum meets a sperm in the fallopian tube, fertilization takes place (Aitken, 1995; Stella, Verrischi, & Lipay, 2008).

fertilization   the process by which a sperm and an ovum—the male and female gametes, respectively—join to form a single new cell.

Sperm, which look a little like microscopic tadpoles, have a shorter life span. They are created by the testicles at a rapid rate: An adult male typically produces several hundred million sperm a day. Consequently, the sperm ejaculated during sexual intercourse are of considerably more recent origin than the ovum to which they are heading.

When sperm enter the vagina, they begin a winding journey that takes them through the cervix, the opening into the uterus, and into the fallopian tube, where fertilization may take place. However, only a tiny fraction of the 300 million cells that are typically ejaculated during sexual intercourse ultimately survive the arduous journey. That's usually okay, though: It takes only one sperm to fertilize an ovum, and each sperm and ovum contain all the genetic data necessary to produce a new human.

The Stages of the Prenatal Period: The Onset of Development. The prenatal period consists of three phases: the germinal, embryonic, and fetal stages. They are summarized in Table 2.3.

The Germinal Stage: Fertilization to 2 Weeks In the **germinal stage**, the first—and shortest—stage of the prenatal period, the zygote begins to divide and grow in complexity during the first 2 weeks following conception. During the germinal stage, the fertilized egg (now called a *blastocyst*) travels toward the *uterus*, where it becomes implanted in the uterus's wall, which is rich in nutrients. The germinal stage is characterized by methodical cell division, which gets off to a quick start: Three days after fertilization, the organism consists of some 32 cells, and by the next day the number doubles. Within a week, it is made up of 100 to 150 cells, and the number rises with increasing rapidity.

In addition to increasing in number, the cells of the organism become increasingly specialized. For instance, some cells form a protective layer around the mass of cells, while others begin to establish the rudiments of a placenta and umbilical cord. When fully developed, the **placenta** serves as a conduit between the mother and fetus, providing nourishment and oxygen via the *umbilical cord*. In addition, waste materials from the developing child are removed through the umbilical cord.

The Embryonic Stage: 2 Weeks to 8 Weeks. By the end of the germinal period—just 2 weeks after conception—the organism is firmly secured to the wall of the mother's uterus. At this point, the child is called an *embryo*. The **embryonic stage** is the period from 2 to 8 weeks following fertilization. One of the highlights of this stage is the development of the major organs and basic anatomy.

At the beginning of the embryonic stage, the developing child has three distinct layers, each of which will ultimately form a different set of structures as development proceeds. The outer layer of the embryo, the *ectoderm*, will form skin, hair, teeth, sense organs, and the brain and spinal cord. The *endoderm*, the inner layer, produces the digestive system, liver, pancreas, and

germinal stage   the first—and shortest—stage of the prenatal period, which takes place during the first 2 weeks following conception.

placenta   a conduit between the mother and fetus, providing nourishment and oxygen via the umbilical cord.

embryonic stage   the period from 2 to 8 weeks following fertilization during which significant growth occurs in the major organs and body systems.

TABLE 2.3	Stages of the Prenatal Period	
GERMINAL	**EMBRYONIC**	**FETAL**
Fertilization to 2 Weeks	2 Weeks to 8 Weeks	8 Weeks to Birth
The germinal stage is the first and shortest, characterized by methodical cell division and the attachment of the organism to the wall of the uterus. Three days after fertilization, the zygote consists of 32 cells, a number that doubles by the next day. Within a week, the zygote multiplies to 100 to 150 cells. The cells become specialized, with some forming a protective layer around the zygote.	The zygote is now designated an embryo. The embryo develops three layers, which ultimately form a different set of structures as development proceeds. The layers are as follows: Ectoderm: Skin, sense organs, brain, spinal cord Endoderm: Digestive system, liver, respiratory system Mesoderm: Muscles, blood, circulatory system At 8 weeks, the embryo is 1 inch long.	The fetal stage formally starts when the differentiation of the major organs has occurred. Now called a fetus, the individual grows rapidly as length increases 20 times. At 4 months, the fetus weighs an average of 4 ounces; at 7 months, 3 pounds; and at the time of birth, the average child weighs just over 7 pounds.

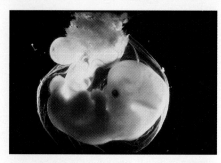

Embryo at 5–6 weeks.

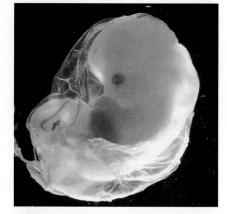

Fetus at 8 weeks.

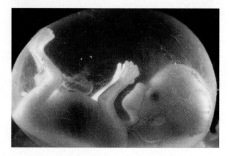

Fetus at 14 weeks.

fetal stage   the stage that begins at about 8 weeks after conception and continues until birth.

fetus   a developing child, from 8 weeks after conception until birth.

infertility   the inability to conceive after 12 to 18 months of trying to become pregnant.

respiratory system. Sandwiched between the ectoderm and endoderm is the *mesoderm*, from which the muscles, bones, blood, and circulatory system are forged. Every part of the body is formed from these three layers.

If you were looking at an embryo at the end of the embryonic stage, you might be hard-pressed to identify it as human. Only an inch long, an 8-week-old embryo has what appear to be gills and a tail-like structure. A closer look, however, reveals several familiar features. Rudimentary eyes, nose, lips, and even teeth can be recognized, and the embryo has stubby bulges that will form arms and legs.

The head and brain undergo rapid growth during the embryonic period. The head begins to represent a significant proportion of the embryo's size, encompassing about 50 percent of its total length. The growth of nerve cells, called *neurons*, is astonishing: As many as 100,000 neurons are produced every minute during the second month of life! The nervous system begins to function around the fifth week, and weak brain waves begin to be produced as the nervous system starts to function (Nelson & Bosquet, 2000; de Graaf-Peters, & Hadders-Algra, 2006).

The Fetal Stage: 8 Weeks to Birth.   It is not until the final period of prenatal development, the fetal stage, that the developing child becomes easily recognizable. The **fetal stage** starts at about 8 weeks after conception and continues until birth. The fetal stage formally starts when the differentiation of the major organs has occurred.

Now called a **fetus**, the developing child undergoes astoundingly rapid change during the fetal stage. For instance, it increases in length some 20 times, and its proportions change dramatically. At 2 months, around half the fetus is what will ultimately be its head; by 5 months, the head accounts for just over a quarter of its total size (see Figure 2.9). The fetus also substantially increases in weight. At 4 months, the fetus weighs an average of about 4 ounces; at 7 months, it weighs about 3 pounds; and at the time of birth the average child weighs just over 7 pounds.

At the same time, the developing child is rapidly becoming more complex. Organs become more differentiated and start to work. By 3 months, for example, the fetus swallows and urinates. In addition, the interconnections between the different parts of the body become more complex and integrated. Arms develop hands; hands develop fingers; fingers develop nails.

As this is happening, the fetus makes itself known to the outside world. In the earliest stages of pregnancy, mothers may be unaware that they are, in fact, pregnant. As the fetus becomes increasingly active, however, most mothers certainly take notice. By 4 months, a mother can feel the movement of her child, and several months later others can feel the baby's kicks through the mother's skin. In addition to the kicks that alert its mother to its presence, the fetus can turn, do somersaults, cry, hiccup, clench its fist, open and close its eyes, and suck its thumb.

The brain becomes increasingly sophisticated during the fetal stage. The two symmetrical left and right halves of the brain, known as *hemispheres*, grow rapidly, and the interconnections between neurons become more complex. The neurons become coated with an insulating material called *myelin*, which helps speed the transmission of messages from the brain to the rest of the body.

By the end of the fetal period, brain waves are produced that indicate the fetus passes through different stages of sleep and wakefulness. The fetus is also able to hear (and feel the vibrations of) sounds to which it is exposed. For instance, researchers Anthony DeCasper and Melanie Spence (1986) asked a group of pregnant mothers to read aloud the Dr. Seuss story *The Cat in the Hat* two times a day during the latter months of pregnancy. Three days after the babies were born, they appeared to recognize the story they had heard, responding more to it than to another story that had a different rhythm.

In weeks 8 to 24 following conception, hormones are released that lead to the increasing differentiation of male and female fetuses. For example, high levels of androgen are produced in males that affect the size of brain cells and the growth of neural connections, which, some scientists speculate, ultimately may lead to differences in male and female brain structure and even later variations in gender-related behavior (Berenbaum & Bailey, 2003; Reiner & Gearhart, 2004; Knickmeyer & Baron-Cohen, 2006).

NEUROSCIENCE AND DEVELOPMENT
Autism and the Toddler Brain

Jeffery arrived in the world with signs of good health. An uneventful pregnancy and birth gave no clue about what Jeffery would be like in only 3 years. By 6 months, the little boy's parents noted he did not smile like other children; by his first birthday he had not yet babbled, pointed, or waved. At age 3, Jeffrey regressed and was withdrawn, even to caring family members. It was at this time that Jeffery was diagnosed with Autism Spectrum Disorder (ASD).

Autism Spectrum Disorder (ASD) is a neurodevelopmental disorder characterized by abnormal brain development and functioning. Although its cause remains unknown, researchers currently hypothesize that ASD is related to problems with the function or structure of the central nervous system, especially the amygdala.

The amygdala is an almond-shaped complex cluster of neurons located deep within the inner side of each temporal lobe of the brain. In the past, scientists theorized that the amygdala, using sensory input from visual, auditory, and somatosensory systems, helps humans to process and respond to many kinds of events, particularly those involving fear and panic. More recent evidence suggests that fluctuations in the amygdala also occur when people are exposed to subtle, biologically relevant emotional and social information, such as facial expressions (Whalen et al., 2009).

Furthermore, new evidence suggests that the development of the amygdala in people with ASD undergoes a specific growth pattern in which the amygdala early in life is larger than typical, but later is smaller compared to people without ASD. To investigate this pattern, a team of researchers used imaging scans to measure amygdala size and collected social and communication function information from 89 toddlers between the ages of 1 and 5 years (Schumann et al., 2009).

Follow-up scanning and testing were completed after 5 years. Toddlers who were later diagnosed with ASD had significantly larger right and left amygdala compared with typically developing toddlers. Amygdala size was also related to the severity of social and communication impairments as measured by standardized tests in boys, but not in girls with ASD.

Early-life amygdala overgrowth may provide an early clue to later diagnosis of ASD. In addition, differential social and communication impairments for boys and girls may potentially be revealed by studying the size of the amygdala.

- *Based on these research findings, do you think all toddlers should be screened early in life for amygdala size? Why or why not?*

Just as no two adults are alike, no two fetuses are the same. Although development during the prenatal period follows the broad patterns outlined here, there are significant differences in the specific nature of individual fetuses' behavior. Some fetuses are exceedingly active, while others are more sedentary. (The more active fetuses will probably be more active after birth.) Some have relatively quick heart rates, while others' heart rates are slower, with the typical range varying between 120 and 160 beats per minute (DiPietro et al., 2002; Niederhofer, 2004; Tongsong et al., 2005).

Such differences in fetal behavior are due in part to genetic characteristics inherited at the moment of fertilization. Other kinds of differences, though, are brought about by the nature of the environment in which the child spends its first 9 months of life. As we will see, there are numerous ways in which the prenatal environment of infants affects their development—in good ways and bad (also see the *Neuroscience and Development* box).

Pregnancy Problems.   For some couples, conception presents a major challenge. Let's consider some of the challenges—both physical and ethical—that relate to pregnancy.

Infertility.   Some 15 percent of couples suffer from **infertility**, the inability to conceive after 12 to 18 months of trying to become pregnant. Fertility is negatively correlated with age: The older the parents, the more likely infertility will occur; see Figure 2.10 on page 56.

In men, infertility is typically a result of producing too few sperm. Use of illicit drugs or cigarettes and previous bouts of sexually transmitted diseases also increase infertility. For women, the most common cause of infertility is failure to

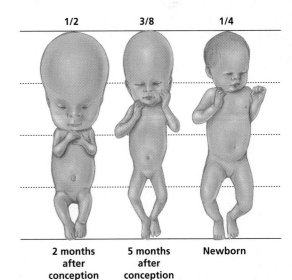

| 1/2 | 3/8 | 1/4 |

| 2 months after conception | 5 months after conception | Newborn |

FIGURE 2.9 Body Proportions
During the fetal period, the proportions of the body change dramatically. At 2 months, the head represents about half the fetus, but by the time of birth, it is one-quarter of the fetus's total size.

FIGURE 2.10 Older Women and Risks of Pregnancy

Not only does the rate of infertility increase as women get older, but the risk of chromosomal abnormality increases as well.

Source: Reproductive Medicine Associates of New Jersey, 2002.

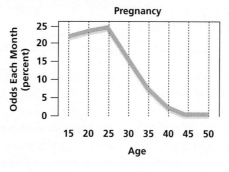

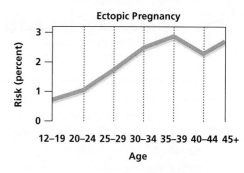

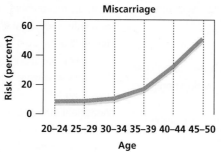

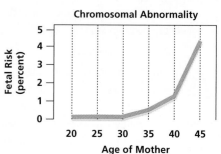

release an egg through ovulation. This may occur because of a hormone imbalance, a damaged fallopian tube or uterus, stress, or abuse of alcohol or drugs (Gibbs, 2002; Pasqualotto et al., 2005; Lewis, Legato, & Fisch, 2006).

Several treatments for infertility exist. Some difficulties can be corrected through the use of drugs or surgery. Another option may be **artificial insemination**, a procedure in which a man's sperm are placed directly into a woman's vagina by a physician. In some situations, the woman's husband provides the sperm, while in others it is an anonymous donor from a sperm bank.

In other cases, fertilization takes place outside of the mother's body. **In vitro fertilization (IVF)** is a procedure in which a woman's ova are removed from her ovaries, and a man's sperm are used to fertilize the ova in a laboratory. The fertilized egg is then implanted in a woman's uterus. Similarly, *gamete intrafallopian transfer (GIFT)* and *zygote intrafallopian transfer (ZIFT)* are procedures in which an egg and sperm or fertilized egg are implanted in a woman's fallopian tubes. In IVF, GIFT, and ZIFT, implantation is done either in the woman who provided the donor eggs or in rarer instances, in a *surrogate mother*, a woman who agrees to carry the child to term. Surrogate mothers may also be used in cases in which the mother is unable to conceive; the surrogate mother is artificially inseminated by the biological father, and she agrees to give up rights to the infant (Frazier et al., 2004; Kolata, 2004).

In vitro fertilization is increasingly successful, with success rates as high as 33 percent for younger women (lower for older women). Furthermore, reproductive technologies are becoming increasingly sophisticated, permitting parents to choose the sex of their baby. One technique is to separate sperm carrying the X and Y chromosome and later to implant the desired type into a woman's uterus. In another technique, eggs are removed from a woman and fertilized with sperm using in vitro fertilization. Three days after fertilization, the embryos are tested to determine their sex. If they are the desired gender, they are then implanted into the mother (Duenwald, 2003, 2004; Kalb, 2004).

Ethical Issues. The use of surrogate mothers, in vitro fertilization, and sex selection techniques presents a web of ethical and legal issues, as well as many emotional concerns. In some cases, surrogate mothers have refused to give up the child after its birth, while in others the surrogate mother has sought to have a role in the child's life. In such cases, the rights of the mother, the father, the surrogate mother, and ultimately the baby are in conflict. Even more troubling are concerns raised by sex selection techniques.

Is it ethical to terminate the life of an embryo based on its sex? Do cultural pressures that may favor boys over girls make it permissible to seek medical intervention to produce male off-

artificial insemination   a process of fertilization in which a man's sperm are placed directly into a woman's vagina by a physician.

in vitro fertilization (IVF)   a procedure in which a woman's ova are removed from her ovaries, and a man's sperm are used to fertilize the ova in a laboratory.

spring? And—even more disturbing—if it is permissible to intervene in the reproductive process to obtain a favored sex, what about other characteristics determined by genetics that it may be possible in the future to preselect for? For instance, assuming the technology advances, would it be ethical to select for a favored eye or hair color, a certain level of intelligence, or a particular kind of personality? That's not feasible now, but it is not out of the realm of possibility in the future.

For the moment, many of these ethical issues remain unresolved. But we can answer one question: How do children conceived using emerging reproductive technologies such as in vitro fertilization fare?

Research shows that they do quite well. Some studies find that the quality of family life for those who have used such techniques may be superior to that in families with naturally conceived children. Furthermore, the later psychological adjustment of children conceived using in vitro fertilization and artificial insemination is no different from that of children conceived using natural techniques (Hahn & DiPietro, 2001; Golumbok et al., 2004; Dipietro, Costigan, & Gurewitsch, 2005; Hjelmstedt, Widstrom, & Collins, 2006).

On the other hand, the increasing use of IVF techniques by older individuals (who might be quite elderly when their children reach adolescence) may change these positive findings. Because widespread use of IVF is only recent, we just don't know yet what will happen with aging parents (Colpin & Soenen, 2002).

"I'm their real child, and you're just a frozen embryo thingy they bought from some laboratory."

Miscarriage and Abortion. A *miscarriage*—known as a spontaneous abortion—occurs when pregnancy ends before the developing child is able to survive outside the mother's womb. The embryo detaches from the wall of the uterus and is expelled.

Some 15 to 20 percent of all pregnancies end in miscarriage, usually in the first several months of pregnancy. Many occur so early that the mother is not even aware she was pregnant and may not even know she has suffered a miscarriage. Typically, miscarriages are attributable to some sort of genetic abnormality.

In *abortion*, a mother voluntarily chooses to terminate pregnancy. Because it involves a complex set of physical, psychological, legal, and ethical issues, abortion is a difficult choice for women. A task force of the American Psychological Association, which looked at the aftereffects of abortion, found that, following an abortion, most women experienced a combination of relief over terminating an unwanted pregnancy and regret and guilt. However, in most cases, the negative psychological aftereffects did not last, except for a small proportion of women who already had serious emotional problems (APA Reproductive Choice Working Group, 2000).

Other research finds that abortion may be associated with an increased risk of future psychological problems. However, the findings are mixed, and there are significant individual differences in how women respond to the experience. What is clear is that in all cases, abortion is a difficult decision (Fergusson, Horwood, & Ridder, 2006).

The Prenatal Environment: Threats to Development. According to the Siriono people of South America, if a pregnant woman eats the meat of certain kinds of animals, she runs the risk of having a child who may act and look like those animals. According to opinions offered on daytime television talk, a pregnant mother should avoid getting angry in order to spare her child from entering the world with anger (Cole, 1992).

Such views are largely the stuff of folklore, although there is some evidence that a mother's anxiety during pregnancy may affect the sleeping patterns of the fetus prior to birth. Certain aspects of a mother's and father's behavior, both before and after conception, can produce lifelong consequences for the child. Some consequences show up immediately, but some are not apparent before birth. Other problems, more insidious, may not appear until years after birth (Groome et al., 1995; Couzin, 2002). Some of the most profound consequences are brought about by teratogenic agents. A **teratogen** is an environmental agent such as a drug, chemical, virus, or other factor that produces a birth defect. Although it is the job of the placenta to keep teratogens from reaching the fetus, the placenta is not entirely successful at this, and probably every fetus is exposed to some teratogens.

teratogen an environmental agent such as a drug, chemical, virus, or other factor that produces a birth defect.

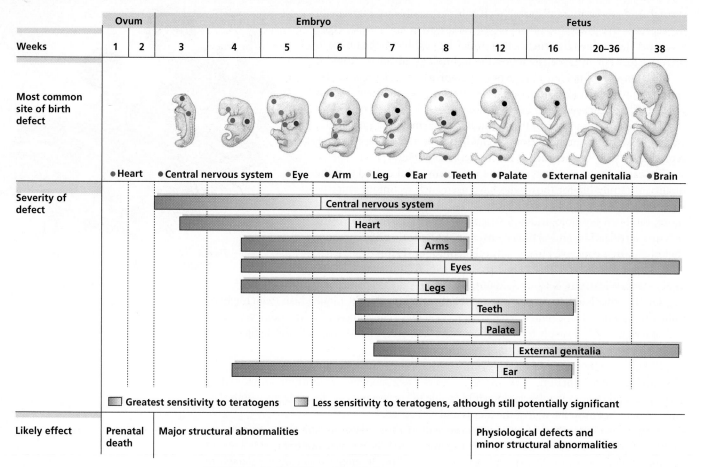

	Ovum	Embryo						Fetus			
Weeks	1 | 2	3	4	5	6	7	8	12	16	20–36	38

Most common site of birth defect

● Heart   ● Central nervous system   ● Eye   ● Arm   ● Leg   ● Ear   ● Teeth   ● Palate   ● External genitalia   ● Brain

Severity of defect

Central nervous system
Heart
Arms
Eyes
Legs
Teeth
Palate
External genitalia
Ear

▭ Greatest sensitivity to teratogens   ▭ Less sensitivity to teratogens, although still potentially significant

Likely effect

Prenatal death	Major structural abnormalities	Physiological defects and minor structural abnormalities

FIGURE 2.11 Teratogen Sensitivity
Depending on their state of development, some parts of the body vary in their sensitivity to teratogens.
Source: Moore, 1974.

The timing and quantity of exposure to a teratogen are crucial. At some phases of prenatal development, a certain teratogen may have only a minimal impact. At other periods, however, the same teratogen may have profound consequences. Generally, teratogens have their largest effects during periods of especially rapid prenatal development. Sensitivity to specific teratogens is also related to racial and cultural background. For example, Native American fetuses are more susceptible to the effects of alcohol than those of European American descent (Kinney et al., 2003; Winger & Woods, 2004).

Furthermore, different organ systems are vulnerable to teratogens at different times during development. For example, the brain is most susceptible 15 to 25 days after conception, while the heart is most vulnerable 20 to 40 days following conception (see Figure 2.11; Needleman & Bellinger, 1994; Bookstein et al., 1996; Pakjrt, 2004).

When considering the findings relating to specific teratogens, as we'll do next, we need to keep in mind the broader social and cultural context in which teratogen exposure occurs. For example, living in poverty increases the chances of exposure to teratogens. Mothers who are poor may not be able to afford adequate diets, and they may not be able to afford adequate medical care, making them more susceptible to illness that can damage a developing fetus. They are more likely to be exposed to pollution. Consequently, it is always important to consider the context of exposure to teratogens.

Mother's Diet. Most of our knowledge of the environmental factors that affect the developing fetus comes from study of the mother. For instance, as the midwife pointed out in the example of Lisa and Robert, a mother's diet clearly plays an important role in bolstering the development of the fetus. A mother who eats a varied diet high in nutrients is apt to have fewer complications during pregnancy, an easier labor, and a generally healthier baby than a mother whose diet is restricted in nutrients (Kaiser & Allen, 2002; Guerrini, Thomson, & Gurling, 2007).

Mother's Age. More women are giving birth later in life than was true just two or three decades ago. The cause for this change is largely due to transformations in society, as more women choose to pursue advanced degrees and to start careers before giving birth to their first child (Gibbs, 2002; Wildberger, 2003; Bornstein et al., 2006).

Consequently, the number of women who give birth in their 30s and 40s has grown considerably. This delay in childbirth has potential consequences for both mothers' and children's health. Women who give birth when over the age of 30 are at greater risk for a variety of pregnancy and birth complications than younger ones. For instance, they are more apt to give birth prematurely, and their children are more likely to have low birth weights. This occurs in part because of a decline in the condition of a woman's eggs. For example, by the time they are 42 years old, 90 percent of a woman's eggs are no longer normal (Cnattingius, Berendes, & Forman, 1993; Gibbs, 2002).

Older mothers are also considerably more likely to give birth to children with Down syndrome, a form of mental retardation. About 1 out of 100 babies born to mothers over 40 has Down syndrome; for mothers over 50, the incidence increases to 25 percent, or 1 in 4 (Gaulden, 1992; Weijerman et al., 2008). On the other hand, some research shows that older mothers are not automatically at risk for more pregnancy problems. For instance, one study found that when women in their 40s who had not experienced health difficulties were considered, they were no more likely to have prenatal problems than those in their 20s (Ales, Druzin, & Santini, 1990; Dildy et al., 1996).

The risks involved in pregnancy are greater not only for older mothers, but for atypically young women as well. Women who become pregnant during adolescence—and such pregnancies actually encompass 10 percent of all pregnancies—are more likely to have premature deliveries. Furthermore, the mortality rate of infants born to adolescent mothers is double that for mothers in their 20s (Kirchengast & Hartmann, 2003).

Mother's Prenatal Support. The higher mortality rate for babies of adolescent mothers reflects more than just physiological problems related to the mothers' youth. Young mothers often face adverse social and economic factors that can affect infant health. Many teenage mothers do not have enough money or social support, a situation that prevents them from getting good prenatal care and parenting support after the baby is born. Poverty or social circumstances, such as a lack of parental involvement or supervision, may even have set the stage for the adolescent to become pregnant in the first place (DePietro, 2004; Huizink, Mulder, & Buitelaar, 2004).

Mother's Health. Depending on when it strikes, an illness in a pregnant woman can have devastating consequences. For instance, the onset of *rubella* (German measles) in the mother prior to the 11th week of pregnancy is likely to cause serious consequences in the baby, including blindness, deafness, heart defects, or brain damage. In later stages of a pregnancy, however, adverse consequences of rubella become increasingly less likely.

Several other diseases may affect a developing fetus, again depending on when the illness is contracted. For instance, *chicken pox* may produce birth defects, while *mumps* may increase the risk of miscarriage. Furthermore, some sexually transmitted infections such as *syphilis* can be transmitted directly to the fetus, who will be born suffering from the disease. In some cases, sexually transmitted diseases such as *gonorrhea* are communicated to the child as it passes through the birth canal to be born. *AIDS (acquired immune deficiency syndrome)*, too, may be passed on to the fetus through the blood that reaches the placenta (Nesheim et al., 2004).

Mothers' Drug Use. Mothers' use of many kinds of drugs—both legal and illegal—poses serious risks to the unborn child. Even over-the-counter remedies for common ailments can have surprisingly injurious consequences. For instance, aspirin taken for a headache can lead to fetal bleeding and growth impairments (Griffith, Azuma, & Chasnoff, 1994; Finnegan & Kandall, 2008).

Some drugs taken by mothers cause difficulties in their children literally decades after they were taken. As recently as the 1970s, the artificial hormone *DES (diethylstilbestrol)* was frequently prescribed to prevent miscarriage. Only later was it found that the daughters of mothers who took DES stood a much higher than normal chance of developing a rare form of vaginal or cervical cancer and had more difficulties during their pregnancies. Sons of the mothers who had taken DES had their own problems, including a higher rate than average of reproductive difficulties (Adams Hillard, 2001; Schecter, Finkelstein, & Koren, 2005).

fetal alcohol syndrome (FAS)
a disorder caused by the pregnant mother consuming substantial quantities of alcohol during pregnancy, potentially resulting in mental retardation and delayed growth in the child.

fetal alcohol effects (FAE) a condition in which children display some, though not all, of the problems of fetal alcohol syndrome due to the mother's consumption of alcohol during pregnancy.

FROM A
HEALTH CARE PROVIDER'S
PERSPECTIVE
In addition to avoiding smoking, what other sorts of things might fathers-to-be do to help their unborn children develop normally in the womb?

Pregnant women who use tobacco place their unborn children at significant risk.

Birth control or fertility pills taken by pregnant women before they are aware of their pregnancy can also cause fetal damage. Such medicines contain sex hormones that affect developing brain structures in the fetus. These hormones, which when produced naturally are related to sexual differentiation in the fetus and gender differences after birth, can cause significant damage (Miller, 1998; Brown, Hines, & Fane, 2002).

Illicit drugs may pose equally great, and sometimes even greater, risks for the environments of prenatal children. For one thing, the purity of drugs purchased illegally varies significantly, so drug users can never be quite sure specifically what they are ingesting. Furthermore, the effects of some commonly used illicit drugs such as marijuana and cocaine can be particularly devastating (Jones, 2006).

Mother's Use of Alcohol and Tobacco. A pregnant woman who reasons that having a drink every once in a while or smoking an occasional cigarette has no appreciable effect on her unborn child is kidding herself: Increasing evidence suggests that even small amounts of alcohol and nicotine can disrupt the development of the fetus.

Mothers' use of alcohol can have profound consequences for the unborn child. The children of alcoholics, who consume substantial quantities of alcohol during pregnancy, are at the greatest risk. Approximately 1 out of every 750 infants is born with **fetal alcohol syndrome (FAS)**, a disorder that may include below-average intelligence and sometimes mental retardation, delayed growth, and facial deformities. FAS is now the primary preventable cause of mental retardation (Steinhausen & Spohr, 1998; Burd et al., 2003; Calhoun & Warren, 2007).

Even mothers who use smaller amounts of alcohol during pregnancy place their child at risk. **Fetal alcohol effects (FAE)** is a condition in which children display some, although not all, of the problems of FAS due to their mother's consumption of alcohol during pregnancy (Streissguth, 1997; Baer, Sampson, & Barr, 2003).

Children who do not have FAE may still be affected by their mothers' use of alcohol. Studies have found that maternal consumption of an average of just two alcoholic drinks a day during pregnancy is associated with lower intelligence in their offspring at age 7. Other research concurs, suggesting that relatively small quantities of alcohol taken during pregnancy can have future adverse effects on children's behavior and psychological functioning. Furthermore, the consequences of alcohol ingestion during pregnancy are long-lasting. For example, one study found that 14-year-olds' success on a test involving spatial and visual reasoning was related to their mothers' alcohol consumption during pregnancy. The more the mothers reported drinking, the less accurately their children responded (Johnson et al., 2001; Lynch et al., 2003; Mattson, Calarco, & Lang, 2006).

Because of the risks associated with alcohol, physicians today counsel pregnant women (and even those who are trying to become pregnant) to avoid drinking any alcoholic beverages. In addition, they caution against another practice proven to have an adverse effect on an unborn child: smoking.

Smoking produces several consequences, none good. For starters, smoking reduces the oxygen content and increases the carbon monoxide of the mother's blood, which quickly reduces the oxygen available to the fetus. In addition, the nicotine and other toxins in cigarettes slow the respiration rate of the fetus and speed up its heart.

The ultimate result is an increased possibility of miscarriage and a higher likelihood of death during infancy. Estimates suggest that smoking by pregnant women leads to more than 100,000 miscarriages and the deaths of 5,600 babies in the United States alone each year (Mills, 1999; Ness et al., 1999; Haslam & Lawrence, 2004).

Smokers are two times as likely as nonsmokers to have babies with an abnormally low birthweight, and smokers' babies are shorter, on average, than those of nonsmokers. Furthermore, women who smoke during pregnancy are 50 percent more likely to have mentally retarded children. Finally, mothers who smoke are more likely to have children who exhibit disruptive behavior during childhood (Fried & Watkinson, 1990; Drews et al., 1996; Dejin-Karlsson et al., 1998; Wakschalg et al., 2006).

Do Fathers Affect the Prenatal Environment? It would be easy to reason that once the father has done his part in the sequence of events leading to conception, he would have no role in the *prenatal* environment of the fetus. Developmental researchers have in the past generally shared this view, and there is relatively little research investigating fathers' influence on the prenatal environment.

BECOMING AN INFORMED CONSUMER OF DEVELOPMENT
Optimizing the Prenatal Environment

If you are contemplating ever having a child, you may be overwhelmed, at this point in the chapter, by the number of things that can go wrong. Don't be. Although both genetics and the environment pose their share of risks, in the vast majority of cases, pregnancy and birth proceed without mishap. Moreover, there are several things that women can do—both before and during pregnancy—to optimize the probability that pregnancy will progress smoothly. Among them are the following:

- Take several precautions if you are planning to become pregnant. First, women should have nonemergency X-rays only during the first 2 weeks after their menstrual periods. Second, they should be vaccinated against rubella (German measles) at least 3, and preferably 6, months before getting pregnant. Finally, they should avoid birth control pills at least 3 months before trying to conceive, because of disruptions to hormonal production caused by the pills.

- Eat well, both before and during (and after, for that matter!) pregnancy. Pregnant mothers are, as the old saying goes, eating for two. This means that it is more essential than ever to eat regular, well-balanced meals. In addition, physicians typically recommend taking prenatal vitamins that include folic acids, which can decrease the likelihood of birth defects (Amitai et al., 2004).

- Don't use alcohol and other drugs. The evidence is clear that many drugs pass directly to the fetus and may cause birth defects. It is also clear that the more one drinks, the greater the risk to the fetus. The best advice, whether you are already pregnant or planning to have a child: Don't use *any* drug unless directed by a physician. If you are planning to get pregnant, encourage your partner to avoid using alcohol or other drugs too (O'Connor & Whaley, 2006).

- Monitor caffeine intake. Although it is still unclear whether caffeine produces birth defects, it is known that the caffeine found in coffee, tea, and chocolate can pass to the fetus, acting as a stimulant. Because of this, you probably should not drink more than a few cups of coffee a day (Wisborg et al., 2003).

- Whether pregnant or not, don't smoke. This holds true for mothers, fathers, and anyone else in the vicinity of the pregnant mother, since research suggests that smoke in the fetal environment can affect birthweight.

- Exercise regularly. In most cases, women can continue to exercise, particularly exercises involving low-impact routines. On the other hand, extreme exercise should be avoided, especially on very hot or very cold days. "No pain, no gain" isn't applicable during pregnancy (O'Toole & Sawicki, 2003; Paisley, Joy, & Price, 2003; Schmidt et al., 2006).

It is becoming increasingly clear, however, that fathers' behavior may well influence the prenatal environment. Consequently, as illustrated by the example of Lisa and Robert's visit to the midwife, earlier in the chapter, health practitioners are applying the research to suggest ways fathers can support healthy prenatal development.

For instance, fathers-to-be should avoid smoking. Secondhand smoke from a father's cigarettes may affect the mother's health, which in turn influences her unborn child. The greater the level of a father's smoking, the lower the birthweight of his children (Tomblin, Hammer, & Zhang, 1998; Delpisheh et al., 2006; da Veiga & Wilder, 2008).

Similarly, a father's use of alcohol and illegal drugs can have significant effects on the fetus. Alcohol and drug use impairs sperm and may lead to chromosomal damage that may affect the fetus at conception. In addition, alcohol and drug use during pregnancy may also affect the prenatal environment by creating stress in the mother and generally producing an unhealthy environment. Environmental toxins in the father's workplace—such as lead or mercury—may bind to sperm and cause birth defects (Wakefield et al., 1998; Choy et al., 2002; Dare et al., 2002).

Finally, fathers who are physically or emotionally abusive to their pregnant wives can damage their unborn children. By increasing the level of maternal stress, or actually causing physical damage, abusive fathers increase the risk of harm to their unborn children. It has been shown that 4 to 8 percent of women face physical abuse during pregnancy (Gilliland & Verny, 1999; Gazmarian et al., 2000; Bacchus, Mezey, & Bewley, 2006; Martin et al., 2006).

The Process of Birth

About 266 days after conception, a protein called *corticotropin-releasing hormone* (CRH) triggers (for some still unknown reason) the release of various hormones, and the process that leads to birth begins. One critical hormone is *oxytocin,* which is released by the mother's pituitary gland. When the concentration of oxytocin becomes high enough, the mother's uterus begins periodic contractions (Smith, 1999; Heterelendy & Zakar, 2004).

episiotomy   an incision sometimes made to increase the size of the opening of the vagina to allow the baby to pass.

During the prenatal period, the uterus, which is composed of muscle tissue, slowly expands as the fetus grows. Although for most of the pregnancy it is inactive, after the fourth month it occasionally contracts in order to ready itself for the eventual delivery. These contractions, called *Braxton-Hicks contractions*, are sometimes called "false labor" because while they can fool eager and anxious expectant parents, they do not signify that the baby will be born soon.

When birth is actually imminent, the uterus begins to contract intermittently. Its increasingly intense contractions act as if it were a vise, opening and closing to force the head of the fetus against the *cervix*, the neck of the uterus that separates it from the vagina. Eventually, the force of the contractions becomes strong enough to propel the fetus slowly down the birth canal until it enters the world as a newborn (Mittendorf et al., 1990). It is this exertion and the narrow birth passageway that often give newborns a battered conehead appearance.

Labor proceeds in three stages (see Figure 2.12). In the *first stage of labor,* the uterine contractions initially occur around every 8 to 10 minutes and last about 30 seconds. As labor proceeds, the contractions occur more frequently and last longer. Toward the end of labor, the contractions may occur every 2 minutes and last almost 2 minutes. During the final part of the first stage of labor, the contractions increase to their greatest intensity, a period known as *transition*. The mother's cervix fully opens, eventually expanding enough (usually to around 10 cm) to allow the baby's head (the widest part of the body) to pass through.

This first stage of labor is the longest. Its duration varies significantly, depending on the mother's age, race, ethnicity, number of prior pregnancies, and a variety of other factors involving both the fetus and the mother. Typically, labor takes 16 to 24 hours for firstborn children, but there are wide variations. Births of subsequent children usually involve shorter periods of labor.

During the *second stage of labor,* which typically lasts around 90 minutes, the baby's head emerges further from the mother with each contraction, increasing the size of the vaginal opening. Because the area between the vagina and rectum must stretch a good deal, an incision called an **episiotomy** is sometimes made to increase the size of the opening of the vagina. However, this practice has been increasingly criticized in recent years as potentially causing more harm than good, and the number of episiotomies has fallen drastically in the last decade (Goldberg et al., 2002; Graham et al, 2005).

The second stage of labor ends when the baby has completely left the mother's body. Finally, the *third stage of labor* occurs when the child's umbilical cord (still attached to the neonate) and the placenta are expelled from the mother. This stage is the quickest and easiest, taking just a few minutes.

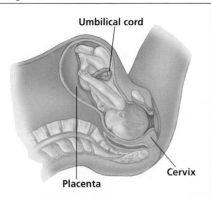

The process of labor produces a range of emotions.

Stage 1

Umbilical cord

Cervix

Placenta

Uterine contractions initially occur every 8 to 10 minutes and last 30 seconds. Toward the end of labor, contractions may occur every 2 minutes and last as long as 2 minutes. As the contractions increase, the cervix, which separates the uterus from the vagina, becomes wider, eventually expanding to allow the baby's head to pass through.

Stage 2

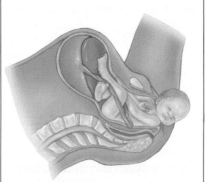

The baby's head starts to move through the cervix and birth canal. Typically lasting around 90 minutes, the second stage ends when the baby has completely left the mother's body.

Stage 3

Uterus

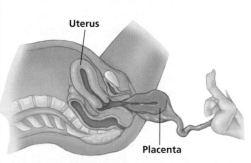

Placenta

The child's umbilical cord (still attached to the neonate) and the placenta are expelled from the mother. This stage is the quickest and easiest, taking just a few minutes.

FIGURE 2.12 The Three Stages of Labor

From Fetus to Neonate. The exact moment of birth occurs when the fetus, having left the uterus through the cervix, passes through the vagina to emerge fully from its mother's body. In most cases, babies automatically make the transition from taking in oxygen via the placenta to using their lungs to breathe air. Consequently, as soon as they are outside the mother's body, most newborns spontaneously cry. This helps them clear their lungs and breathe on their own.

What happens next varies from situation to situation and from culture to culture. In Western cultures, health care workers are almost always on hand to assist with the birth. In the United States, 99 percent of births are attended by professional health care workers, but worldwide only about 50 percent of births have professional health care workers in attendance (United Nations, 1990).

Approaches to Childbirth: Where Medicine and Attitudes Meet.

Ester Iverem knew herself well enough to know that she didn't like the interaction she had with medical doctors. So she opted for a nurse-midwife at Manhattan's Maternity Center where she was free to use a birthing stool and to have her husband, Nick Chiles, by her side. When contractions began, Iverem and Chiles went for a walk, stopping periodically to rock—a motion, she says, "similar to the way children dance when they first learn how, shifting from foot to foot." That helped her work through the really powerful contractions.

"I sat on the birthing chair [a Western version of the traditional African stool, which lies low to the ground and has an opening in the middle for the baby to come through] and Nick was sitting right behind me. When the midwife said 'Push!' the baby's head just went 'pop!,' and out he came." Their son, Mazi (which means "Sir" in Ibo) Iverem Chiles, was placed on Ester's breast while the midwives went to prepare for his routine examination. (Knight, 1994, p. 122)

Parents in the Western world have developed a variety of strategies—and some very strong opinions—to help them deal with something as natural as giving birth, which apparently occurs without much thought throughout the nonhuman animal world. Today parents need to decide, should the birth take place in a hospital or in the home? Should a physician, a nurse, or a midwife assist? Is the father's presence desirable? Should siblings and other family members be on hand to participate in the birth?

Most of these questions cannot be answered definitively, primarily because the choice of childbirth techniques often comes down to a matter of values and opinions. No single procedure will be effective for all mothers and fathers, and no conclusive research evidence has proven that one procedure is significantly more effective than another. As we'll see, a wide variety of different issues and options are involved, and certainly one's culture plays a role in choices of birthing procedures.

The abundance of choices is largely due to a reaction to traditional medical practices that had been common in the United States until the early 1970s. Before that time, the typical birth went something like this: A woman in labor was placed in a room with many other women, all of whom were in various stages of childbirth, and some of whom were screaming in pain. Fathers and other family members were not allowed to be present. Just before delivery, the woman was rolled into a delivery room, where the birth took place. Often she was so drugged that she was not aware of the birth at all.

Physicians argued that such procedures were necessary to ensure the health of the newborn and the mother. However, critics charged that alternatives were available that not only would maximize the medical well-being of the participants in the birth, but would represent an emotional and psychological improvement as well (Pascoe, 1993).

Alternative Birthing Procedures. Not all mothers give birth in hospitals, and not all births follow a traditional course. Among the major alternatives to traditional birthing practices are the following:

- **Lamaze birthing techniques.** The Lamaze method has achieved widespread popularity in the United States. Based on the writings of Dr. Fernand Lamaze, the method makes use of breathing techniques and relaxation training (Lamaze, 1970). Typically, mothers-to-be participate in a series of weekly training sessions in which they learn exercises that help them relax various parts of the body on command. A "coach," most typically the father, is trained along with the future mother. The training allows women to cope with painful contractions by concentrating on their breathing and producing relaxation response, rather than by tensing up, which can make the pain more acute. Women learn to focus on a relaxing stimulus, such as a tranquil scene in a picture. The goal is to learn how to deal positively with pain and to relax at the onset of a contraction.

Does the procedure work? Most mothers, as well as fathers, report that a Lamaze birth is a very positive experience. They enjoy the sense of mastery that they gain over the process of labor, a feeling of being able to exert some control over what can be a formidable experience. On the other hand, we can't be sure that parents who choose the Lamaze method aren't already more highly motivated about the experience of childbirth than parents who do not choose the technique. It is therefore possible that the accolades they express after Lamaze births are due to their initial enthusiasm, and not to the Lamaze procedures themselves (Mackey, 1990; Larsen, 2001).

- **Bradley Method.** The Bradley Method, which is sometimes known as "husband-coached childbirth," is based on the principle that childbirth should be as natural as possible and involve no medication or medical interventions. Women are taught to "tune into" their bodies in order to deal with the pain of childbirth.

  To prepare for childbirth, mothers-to-be are taught muscle relaxation techniques, similar to Lamaze procedures, and good nutrition and exercise during pregnancy are seen as important to prepare for delivery. Parents are urged to take responsibility for childbirth, and the use of physicians is viewed as unnecessary and sometimes even dangerous. As you might expect, the discouragement of traditional medical interventions is quite controversial (McCutcheon-Rosegg, Ingraham, & Bradley, 1996).

- **Hypnobirthing.** Hypnobirthing is a new, but increasingly popular, technique. It involves a form of self-hypnosis during delivery that produces a sense of peace and calm, thereby reducing pain. The basic concept is to produce a state of focused concentration in which a mother relaxes her body while focusing inward. Increasing research evidence shows the technique can be effective in reducing pain (Mongan, 2005; Cyna, Andrew, & McAuliffe, 2006; Olson, 2006).

Childbirth Attendants: Who Delivers? Traditionally, *obstetricians,* physicians who specialize in delivering babies, have been the childbirth attendants of choice. In the last few decades, more mothers have chosen to use a *midwife,* a childbirth attendant who stays with the mother throughout labor and delivery. Midwives—most often nurses specializing in childbirth—are used primarily for pregnancies in which no complications are expected. The use of midwives has increased steadily in the United States—there are now 7,000 of them—and they are employed in 10 percent of births. Midwives help deliver some 80 percent of babies in other parts of the world, often at home. Home birth is common in countries at all levels of economic development. For instance, a third of all births in the Netherlands occur at home (Ayoub, 2005).

Use of Anesthesia and Pain-Reducing Drugs. Among the greatest advances of modern medicine is the ongoing discovery of drugs that reduce pain. However, the use of medication during childbirth is a practice that holds both benefits and pitfalls (Shute, 1997; Williams, Povey, & White, 2008).

About a third of women who receive anesthesia do so in the form of *epidural anesthesia,* which produces numbness from the waist down. Traditional epidurals produce an inability to walk and in some cases prevent women from helping to push the baby out during delivery. However, a newer form of epidural, known as a *walking epidural* or *dual spinal-epidural,* uses smaller needles and a system for administering continuous doses of anesthetic. It permits women to move about more freely during labor and has fewer side effects than traditional epidural anesthesia.

It is clear that drugs hold the promise of greatly reducing, and even eliminating, pain associated with labor, which can be extreme and exhausting. However, pain reduction comes at a cost: Drugs administered during labor reach not just the mother but the fetus as well. The stronger the drug, the greater its effects on the fetus and neonate. Because of the small size of the fetus relative to the mother, drug doses that might have only a minimal effect on the mother can have a magnified effect on the fetus.

Anesthetics may temporarily depress the flow of oxygen to the fetus and slow labor. In addition, newborns whose mothers have been anesthetized are less physiologically responsive, show poorer motor control during the first days of life after birth, cry more, and may have more difficulty in initiating breastfeeding (Walker & O'Brien, 1999; Ransjö-Arvidson, 2001; Torvaldsen et al., 2006).

Most research suggests, however, that drugs, as they are currently employed during labor, produce only minimal risks to the fetus and neonate. Guidelines issued by the American College of Obstetricians and Gynecologists suggest that a woman's request for pain relief at any stage of labor should be honored, and that the proper use of minimal amounts of drugs for pain relief is reasonable and has no significant effect on a child's later well-being (Shute, 1997; ACOG, 2002; Alberst et al., 2007).

Birth Complications

In addition to the usual complimentary baby supplies that most hospitals bestow on new mothers, the maternity nurses at Greater Southeast Hospital have become practiced in handing out "grief baskets."

Inside are items memorializing one of [Washington, D.C.'s] grimmest statistics—an infant mortality rate that's more than twice the national average. The baskets contain a photograph of the dead newborn, a snip of its hair, the tiny cap it wore, and a yellow rose. (Thomas, 1994, p. A14)

The infant mortality rate in Washington, D.C., capital of the richest country in the world, is 12.2 deaths per 1,000 births, exceeding the rate of countries such as Hungary, Cuba, Kuwait, and Costa Rica. Overall, the United States ranks 22nd among industrialized countries, with 6.37 deaths for every 1,000 live births (Singh & Yu, 1995; *Washington Post*, 2007; *The World Factbook*, 2007; see Figure 2.13).

Why is infant survival less likely in the United States than in other, less developed countries? To answer this question, we need to consider the nature of the problems that can occur during labor and delivery.

Preterm Infants: Too Soon, Too Small. Eleven percent of infants are born earlier than normal. **Preterm infants**, or premature infants, are born prior to 38 weeks after conception. Because they have not had time to develop fully as fetuses, preterm infants are at high risk for illness and death (Jeng, Yau, & Teng, 1998; Lucas-Thompson et al., 2008).

The extent of danger faced by preterm babies depends largely on the child's weight at birth, which has great significance as an indicator of the extent of the baby's development. Although the average newborn weighs around 3,400 grams (about 7 1/2 pounds), **low-birthweight infants** weigh less than 2,500 grams (around 5 1/2 pounds). Only 7 percent of all newborns in the United States fall into the low-birthweight category, but they account for the majority of newborn deaths (Gross, Spiker, & Haynes, 1997).

Although most low-birthweight infants are preterm, some are small-for-gestational-age babies. **Small-for-gestational-age infants** are infants who, because of delayed fetal growth, weigh 90 percent (or less) of the average weight of infants of the same gestational age. Small-for-gestational-age infants are sometimes also preterm, but may not be (Meisels & Plunket, 1988; Shiono & Behrman, 1995; Rodrigues & Barros, 2007).

If the degree of prematurity is not too great and weight at birth is not extremely low, the threat to the child's well-being is relatively minor. In such cases, the main treatment may be to keep the baby in the hospital to gain weight. Additional weight is critical because fat layers help prevent chilling in neonates, who are not particularly efficient at regulating body temperature.

Newborns who are born more prematurely and who have birthweights significantly below average face a tougher road. For them, simply staying alive is a major task. For instance, low-birthweight infants are highly vulnerable to infection and because their lungs have not

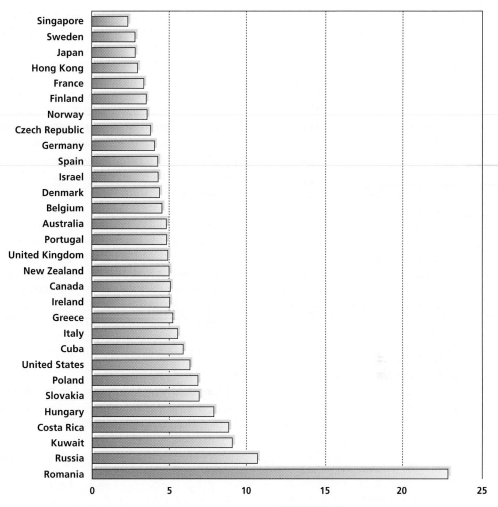

FIGURE 2.13
International Infant Mortality
While the United States has greatly reduced its infant mortality rate in the past 25 years, it ranks only 26th among industrialized countries as of 2007. What are some of the reasons for this?
Source: Child Health USA, 2009.

preterm infants   infants who are born prior to 38 weeks after conception (also known as premature infants).

low-birthweight infants   infants who weigh less than 2,500 grams (around 5 1/2 pounds) at birth.

small-for-gestational-age infants   infants who, because of delayed fetal growth, weigh 90 percent (or less) of the average weight of infants of the same gestational age.

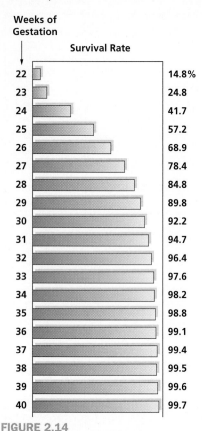

Weeks of Gestation

Survival Rate

Weeks of Gestation	Survival Rate
22	14.8%
23	24.8
24	41.7
25	57.2
26	68.9
27	78.4
28	84.8
29	89.8
30	92.2
31	94.7
32	96.4
33	97.6
34	98.2
35	98.8
36	99.1
37	99.4
38	99.5
39	99.6
40	99.7

FIGURE 2.14

Survival and Gestational Age
Chances of a fetus surviving greatly improve after 28 to 32 weeks. Rates shown are the percentages of babies born in the United States after specified lengths of gestation who survive the first year of life.
Source: National Center for Health Statistics, 1997.

very-low-birthweight infants infants who weigh less than 1,250 grams (around 2.25 pounds) or, regardless of weight, have been in the womb less than 30 weeks.

had sufficient time to develop completely, they have problems taking in sufficient oxygen. As a consequence, they may experience *respiratory distress syndrome (RDS)*, with potentially fatal consequences.

To deal with respiratory distress syndrome, low-birthweight infants are often placed in incubators, enclosures in which temperature and oxygen content are controlled. The exact amount of oxygen is carefully monitored. Too low a concentration of oxygen will not provide relief, and too high a concentration can damage the delicate retinas of the eyes, leading to permanent blindness.

The immature development of preterm neonates makes them unusually sensitive to stimuli in their environment. They can easily be overwhelmed by the sights, sounds, and sensations they experience, and their breathing may be interrupted or their heart rates may slow. They are often unable to move smoothly; their arm and leg movements are uncoordinated, causing them to jerk about and appear startled. Such behavior is quite disconcerting to parents (Doussard-Roosevelt et al., 1997; Miles et al., 2006).

Despite the difficulties they experience at birth, the majority of preterm infants eventually develop normally in the long run. However, the tempo of development often proceeds more slowly for preterm children compared to children born at full term, and more subtle problems sometimes emerge later. For example, by the end of their first year, only 10 percent of prematurely born infants display significant problems, and only 5 percent are seriously disabled. By the age of 6, however, approximately 38 percent have mild problems that call for special educational interventions. For instance, some preterm children show learning disabilities, behavior disorders, or lower-than-average IQ scores. Others have difficulties with physical coordination. Still, around 60 percent of preterm infants are free of even minor problems (Nadeau et al., 2001; Arseneault et al., 2002; Dombrowski, Noonan, & Martin, 2006).

Very-Low-Birthweight Infants: The Smallest of the Small. The story is less positive for the most extreme cases of prematurity—very-low-birthweight infants. **Very-low-birthweight infants** weigh less than 1,250 grams (around 2 1/4 pounds) or, regardless of weight, have been in the womb less than 30 weeks.

Very-low-birthweight infants not only are tiny—some fitting easily in the palm of the hand at birth—they hardly seem to belong to the same species as full-term newborns. Their eyes may be fused shut and their earlobes may look like flaps of skin on the sides of their heads. Their skin is a darkened red color, whatever their race.

Very-low-birthweight babies are in grave danger from the moment they are born, due to the immaturity of their organ systems. Before the mid-1980s, these babies would not have survived outside their mothers' wombs. However, medical advances have led to a higher chance of survival, pushing the *age of viability*, the point at which an infant can survive prematurely, to about 22 weeks—some 4 months earlier than the term of a normal delivery. Of course, the longer the period of development beyond conception, the higher are a newborn's chances of survival. A baby born earlier than 25 weeks has less than a 50–50 chance of survival (see Figure 2.14).

The physical and cognitive problems experienced by low-birthweight and preterm babies are even more pronounced in very-low-birthweight infants, with astonishing financial consequences. A 3-month stay in an incubator in an intensive care unit can run into hundreds of thousands of dollars, and about half of these newborns ultimately die, despite massive medical intervention (Taylor et al., 2000; Doring et al., 2006).

Even if a very-low-birthweight preterm infant survives, the medical costs can continue to mount. For instance, one estimate suggests that the average monthly cost of medical care for such infants during the first 3 years of life may be between 3 and 50 times higher than the medical costs for a full-term child. Such astronomical costs have raised ethical debates about the expenditure of substantial financial and human resources in cases in which a positive outcome may be unlikely (Prince, 2000; Doyle, 2004; Petrou, 2006).

As medical capabilities progress and developmental researchers come up with new strategies for dealing with preterm infants and improving their lives, the age of viability is likely to be pushed even earlier. Emerging evidence suggests that high-quality care can provide protection from some of the risks associated with prematurity, and that in fact by the time they reach adulthood, premature babies may be little different from other adults (Hack, 2002).

Research also shows that preterm infants who receive more responsive, stimulating, and organized care are apt to show more positive outcomes than those children whose care is not as good. Some of these interventions are quite simple. For example, "Kangaroo Care" in which infants are held skin-to-skin against their parents' chests, appears to be effective in helping preterm infants develop. Massaging preterm infants several times a day triggers the release of hormones that promote weight gain, muscle development, and abilities to cope with stress (Field, 2001; Burkhammer, Anderson, & Chiu, 2004; Feldman et al., 2004; Tallandini & Scalembra, 2006).

What Causes Preterm and Low-Birthweight Deliveries?   About half of preterm and low-birthweight births are unexplained, but several known causes account for the remainder. In some cases, premature labor results from difficulties relating to the mother's reproductive system. For instance, mothers carrying twins have unusual stress placed on them, which can lead to early labor. In fact, most multiple births are preterm to some degree (Paneth, 1995; Cooperstock et al., 1998; Tan et al., 2004).

In other cases, preterm and low-birthweight babies are a result of the immaturity of the mother's reproductive system. Young mothers—under the age of 15—are more prone to deliver prematurely than older ones. In addition, a woman who becomes pregnant within 6 months of her previous delivery is more likely to deliver a preterm or low-birthweight infant than a woman whose reproductive system has had a chance to recover from a prior delivery. The father's age matters, too: Wives of older fathers are more likely to have preterm deliveries (Smith et al., 2003; Zhu, 2005; Branum, 2006).

Finally, factors that affect the general health of the mother, such as nutrition, level of medical care, amount of stress in the environment, and economic support, all are related to prematurity and low birthweight. Rates of preterm births differ between racial groups, not because of race per se, but because members of racial minorities have disproportionately lower incomes and higher stress as a result. For instance, the percentage of low-birthweight infants born to African American mothers is double that for Caucasian American mothers (Carlson & Hoem, 1999; Stein, Lu, & Gelberg, 2000; Field, Diego, & Hernandex-Reif, 2006).

Postmature Babies: Too Late, Too Large.   One might imagine that a baby who spends extra time in the womb might have some advantages, given the opportunity to continue growth undisturbed by the outside world. Yet **postmature infants**—those still unborn 2 weeks after the mother's due date—face several risks.

For example, the blood supply from the placenta may become insufficient to nourish the still-growing fetus adequately. Consequently, the blood supply to the brain may be decreased, leading to the potential of brain damage. Similarly, labor becomes riskier (for both the child and the mother) as a fetus who may be equivalent in size to a 1-month-old infant has to make its way through the birth canal (Shea, Wilcox, & Little, 1998; Fok, 2006).

Difficulties involving postmature infants are more easily prevented than those involving preterm babies, since medical practitioners can induce labor artificially if the pregnancy continues too long. Not only can certain drugs bring on labor, but physicians also have the option of performing Cesarean deliveries, a form of delivery we consider next.

Cesarean Delivery: Intervening in the Process of Birth.

As Elena entered her 18th hour of labor, the obstetrician who was monitoring her progress began to look concerned. She told Elena and her husband, Pablo, that the fetal monitor revealed that the fetus's heart rate had begun to repeatedly fall after each contraction. After trying some simple remedies, such as repositioning Elena on her side, the obstetrician came to the conclusion that the fetus was in distress. She told them that the baby should be delivered immediately, and to accomplish that, she would have to carry out a Cesarean delivery.

Elena became one of the more than 1 million mothers in the United States who have a Cesarean delivery each year. In a **Cesarean delivery** (sometimes known as a *c-section*), the baby is surgically removed from the uterus, rather than traveling through the birth canal.

Cesarean deliveries occur most frequently when the fetus shows distress of some sort. For instance, if the fetus appears to be in danger, as indicated by a sudden rise in its heart rate or if blood is seen coming from the mother's vagina during labor, a Cesarean may be performed. In addition, older mothers, over the age of 40, are more likely to have Cesarean deliveries than younger ones (Dulitzki et al., 1998; Gilbert, Nesbitt, & Danielsen, 1999; Tang, Wu, Liu, Lin, & Hsu, 2006).

Cesarean deliveries are also used in some cases of *breech position,* in which the baby is positioned feet first in the birth canal. Breech position births, which occur in about 1 out of 25 births, place the baby at risk because the umbilical cord is more likely to be compressed, depriving the baby of oxygen. Cesarean deliveries are also more likely in *transverse position* births, in which the baby lies crosswise in the uterus, or when the baby's head is so large it has trouble moving through the birth canal.

The routine use of **fetal monitors**, devices that measure the baby's heartbeat during labor, has contributed to the soaring rate of Cesarean deliveries. Some 25 percent of all children in the

Preterm infants stand a much greater chance of survival today than they did even a decade ago.

postmature infants   infants still unborn 2 weeks after the mother's due date.

Cesarean delivery   a birth in which the baby is surgically removed from the uterus, rather than traveling through the birth canal (sometimes known as a *c-section*).

fetal monitor   a device that measures the baby's heartbeat during labor.

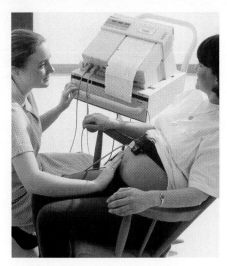

Routine use of fetal monitors has led to an increase in Cesarean deliveries.

United States are born in this way, up some 500 percent from the early 1970s (U.S. Center for Health Statistics, 2003).

Are Cesareans an effective medical intervention? Other countries have substantially lower rates of Cesarean deliveries, and there is no association between successful birth consequences and the rate of Cesarean deliveries. In addition, Cesarean deliveries carry dangers. Cesarean delivery represents major surgery, and the mother's recovery can be relatively lengthy, particularly when compared to a normal delivery. In addition, the risk of maternal infection is higher with Cesarean deliveries (Koroukian, Trisel, & Rimm, 1998; Porter et al., 2007).

Finally, a Cesarean delivery presents some risks for the baby. Because Cesarean babies are spared the stresses of passing though the birth canal, their relatively easy passage into the world may deter the normal release of certain stress-related hormones, such as catecholamines, into the newborn's bloodstream. These hormones help prepare the neonate to deal with the stress of the world outside the womb, and their absence may be detrimental to the newborn child. Research indicates that babies born by Cesarean delivery who have not experienced labor are more likely to experience breathing problems upon birth than those who experience at least some labor prior to being born via a Cesarean delivery. Finally, mothers who deliver by Cesarean are less satisfied with the birth experience, although their dissatisfaction does not influence the quality of mother–child interactions (Hales, Morgan, & Thurnau, 1993; Durik, Hyde, & Clark, 2000).

Because the increase in Cesarean deliveries is, as we have said, connected to the use of fetal monitors, medical authorities now currently recommend that they not be used routinely. There is evidence that outcomes are no better for newborns who have been monitored than for those who have not been monitored. In addition, monitors tend to indicate fetal distress when there is none—false alarms—with disquieting regularity (Levano et al., 1986; Albers & Krulewitch, 1993). Monitors do, however, play a critical role in high-risk pregnancies and in cases of preterm and postmature babies.

Mortality and Stillbirth: The Tragedy of Premature Death. The joy that accompanies the birth of a child is completely reversed when a newborn dies. The relative rarity of their occurrence makes infant deaths even harder for parents to bear.

Sometimes a child does not even live beyond its passage through the birth canal. **Stillbirth**, the delivery of a child who is not alive, occurs in less than 1 delivery out of 100. Sometimes the death is detected before labor begins. In this case, labor is typically induced, or physicians may carry out a Cesarean delivery in order to remove the body from the mother as soon as possible. In other cases of stillbirth, the baby dies during its travels through the birth canal.

The overall rate of **infant mortality** (defined as death within the first year of life) is 7.0 deaths per 1,000 live births. Infant mortality generally has been declining since the 1960s (MacDorman et al., 2005).

Whether the death is a stillbirth or occurs after the child is born, the loss of a baby is tragic, and the impact on parents, enormous. The loss and grief parents feel, and their passage through it, is similar to that experienced when an older loved one dies. The juxtaposition of the first dawning of life and an unnaturally early death may make the death particularly difficult to accept and manage. Depression is common (Murray et al., 2000; Barr & Cacciatore, 2007; Cacciatore & Bushfield, 2007).

DEVELOPMENTAL DIVERSITY
Overcoming Racial and Cultural Differences in Infant Mortality

Even though there has been a general decline in the infant mortality rate in the United States over the past several decades, African American babies are more than twice as likely to die before the age of 1 than white babies. This difference is largely the result of socioeconomic factors: African American women are significantly more likely to be living in poverty than Caucasian women and to receive less prenatal care. As a result, their babies are more likely to be of low birthweight—the factor most closely linked to infant mortality—than infants of mothers of other racial groups (see Figure 2.15; Stolberg, 1999; Duncan & Brooks-Gunn, 2000; Grady, 2006).

But it is not just members of particular racial groups in the United States who suffer from poor mortality rates. As mentioned earlier, the rate of infant mortality in the United States is higher than the rate in many other countries. For example, the mortality rate in the United States is almost double that of Japan.

stillbirth the delivery of a child who is not alive, occurring in less than 1 delivery in 100.

infant mortality death within the first year of life.

Why does the United States fare so poorly in terms of newborn survival? One answer is that the United States has a higher rate of low-birthweight and preterm deliveries than many other countries. When U.S. infants are compared to infants of the same weight who are born in other countries, the differences in mortality rates disappear (Paneth, 1995; Wilcox et al., 1995).

Another reason for the higher U.S. mortality rate relates to economic diversity. The United States has a higher proportion of people living in poverty than many other countries. Because people in lower economic categories are less likely to have adequate medical care and tend to be less healthy, the relatively high proportion of economically deprived individuals in the United States has an impact on the overall mortality rate (Terry, 2000; Bremner & Fogel, 2004; MacDorman et al., 2005).

Many countries do a significantly better job than the United States in providing prenatal care to mothers-to-be. For instance, low-cost and even free care, both before and after delivery, is often available in other countries. Furthermore, paid maternity leave is frequently provided to pregnant women, lasting in some cases as long as 51 weeks. The opportunity to take an extended maternity leave can be important: Mothers who spend more time on maternity leave may have better mental health and higher-quality interactions with their infants (Clark et al., 1997; Waldfogel, 2001; Feldman, Sussman, & Zigler, 2004).

Better health care is only part of the story. In certain European countries, in addition to a comprehensive package of services involving general practitioner, obstetrician, and midwife, pregnant women receive many privileges, such as transportation benefits for visits to health care providers. In Norway, pregnant women may be given living expenses for up to 10 days so they can be close to a hospital when it is time to give birth. And when their babies are born, new mothers receive, for just a small payment, the assistance of trained home helpers (Morice, 1998; DeVries, 2005).

In the United States, the story is very different. The lack of national health care insurance or a national health policy means that prenatal care is often haphazardly provided to the poor. About one out of every six pregnant women has insufficient prenatal care. Some 20 percent of white women and close to 40 percent of African American women receive no prenatal care early in their pregnancies. Five percent of white mothers and 11 percent of African American mothers do not see a health care provider until the last 3 months of pregnancy; some never see a health care provider at all (Johnson, Primas, & Coe, 1994; Mikhail, 2000; Laditka, Laditka, & Probst, 2006).

Ultimately, the lack of prenatal services results in a higher mortality rate. Yet this situation can be changed if greater support is provided. A start would be to ensure that all economically disadvantaged pregnant women have access to free or inexpensive high-quality medical care from the very beginning of pregnancy. Furthermore, barriers that prevent poor women from receiving such care should be reduced. For instance, programs can be developed that help pay for transportation to a health facility or for the care of older children while the mother is making a health care visit. The cost of these programs is likely to be offset by the savings they make possible—healthy babies cost less than infants with chronic problems as a result of poor nutrition and prenatal care (Carnegie Task Force on Meeting the Needs of Young Children, 1994; Fangman et al., 1994; Kronenfeld, 2002).

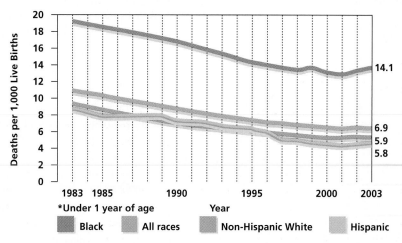

FIGURE 2.15 Race and Infant Mortality
Although infant mortality is dropping for both African American and white children, the death rate is still more than twice as high for African American children. These figures show the number of deaths in the first year of life for every 1,000 live births.
Source: Child Health USA, 2005.

Racial and cultural differences are related to prenatal health care.

REVIEW

▶ Fertilization joins the sperm and ovum to start the journey of prenatal development. Some couples, however, need medical help to conceive. Among the alternate routes to conception are artificial insemination and in vitro fertilization (IVF).

▶ The prenatal period consists of three stages: germinal, embryonic, and fetal.

- The prenatal environment significantly influences the development of the baby. The diet, age, prenatal support, and illnesses of mothers can affect their babies' health and growth.

- Mothers' use of drugs, alcohol, tobacco, and caffeine can adversely affect the health and development of the unborn child. Fathers' and others' behaviors (e.g., smoking) can also affect the health of the unborn child.

- In the first stage of labor, contractions increase in frequency, duration, and intensity until the baby's head is able to pass through the cervix. In the second stage, the baby moves through the cervix and birth canal and leaves the mother's body. In the third stage, the umbilical cord and placenta emerge.

- Immediately after birth, birthing attendants usually examine the neonate using a measurement system such as the Apgar scale.

- Many birthing options are available to parents today. They may weigh the advantages and disadvantages of anesthetic drugs during birth, and they may choose alternatives to traditional hospital birthing, including the Lamaze method, the use of a birthing center, and the use of a midwife.

- Largely because of low birthweight, preterm infants may have substantial difficulties after birth and later in life.

- Very-low-birthweight infants are in special danger because of the immaturity of their organ systems.

- Preterm and low-birthweight deliveries can be caused by health, age, and pregnancy-related factors in the mother. Income (and, because of its relationship with income, race) is also an important factor.

- Cesarean deliveries are performed with postmature babies or when the fetus is in distress, in the wrong position, or unable to progress through the birth canal.

- Infant mortality rates can be affected by the availability of inexpensive health care and good education programs for mothers-to-be.

APPLY

- It has been found that a mother's diet is a crucial part of the development of the fetus. What sorts of environmental and social factors affect development?

- Studies show that "crack babies" who are now entering school have significant difficulty dealing with multiple stimuli and forming close attachments. How might both genetic and environmental influences have combined to produce these results?

Epilogue

In this chapter, we discussed the basics of heredity and genetics, including the way in which the code of life is transmitted across generations through DNA. We have also seen how genetic transmission can go wrong, and we have discussed ways in which genetic disorders can be treated—and perhaps prevented—through new interventions such as genetic counseling and gene therapy.

One important theme in this chapter has been the interaction between hereditary and environmental factors in the determination of a number of human traits. While we have encountered a number of surprising instances in which heredity plays a part—including in the development of personality traits and even personal preferences and tastes—we have also seen that heredity is virtually never the sole factor in any complex trait. Environment nearly always plays an important role.

Finally, we reviewed the main stages of prenatal growth—germinal, embryonic, and fetal—and examined threats to the prenatal environment and ways to optimize that environment for the fetus.

Before moving on, return to the prologue of this chapter—about the Monaco children with IVA—and answer the following questions based on your understanding of genetics and prenatal development.

1. How could Jana and Tom Monaco have passed on a rare genetic disease to their children without knowing that they were carriers of it?

2. From the Monacos' story, would you guess that IVA is an X-linked trait or not?

3. What evidence is there in the story of the Monacos' children that the debilitating effects of IVA are determined by a combination of both genetic and environmental factors?

4. Could the Monacos have learned that they were carriers of IVA before their son Stephen was born? How?

Looking Back

What is our basic genetic endowment, and how can human development go off track?

1. A child receives 23 chromosomes from each parent. These 46 chromosomes provide the genetic blueprint that will guide cell activity for the rest of the individual's life.

2. Gregor Mendel discovered an important genetic mechanism that governs the interactions of dominant and recessive genes and their expression in alleles. Traits such as hair and eye color and the presence of phenylketonuria (PKU) are alleles and follow this pattern.

3. Genes may become physically damaged or may spontaneously mutate. If damaged genes are passed on to the child, the result can be a genetic disorder.

4. Behavioral genetics, which studies the genetic basis of human behavior, focuses on personality characteristics and behaviors. Researchers are now discovering how to remedy certain genetic defects through gene therapy.

5. Genetic counselors use data from tests and other sources to identify potential genetic abnormalities in women and men who plan to have children. Recently, they have begun testing individuals for genetically based disorders that may eventually appear in the individuals themselves.

How do the environment and genetics work together to determine human characteristics?

6. Behavioral characteristics are often determined by a combination of genetics and environment. Genetically based traits represent a potential, called the genotype, which may be affected by the environment and is ultimately expressed in the phenotype.

7. To work out the different influences of heredity and environment, researchers use nonhuman studies and human studies, particularly of twins.

Which human characteristics are significantly influenced by heredity?

8. Virtually all human traits, characteristics, and behaviors are the result of the combination and interaction of nature and nurture. Many physical characteristics show strong genetic influences. Intelligence contains a strong genetic component but can be significantly influenced by environmental factors.

9. Some personality traits, including neuroticism and extroversion, have been linked to genetic factors, and even attitudes, values, and interests have a genetic component. Some personal behaviors may be genetically influenced through the mediation of inherited personality traits.

10. The interaction between genetic and environmental effects has been classified into three types: active genotype–environment influences, passive genotype–environment influences, and evocative genotype–environment influences.

What happens during the prenatal stages of development?

11. The union of a sperm and an ovum at the moment of fertilization, which begins the process of prenatal development, can be difficult for some couples. Infertility, which occurs in some 15 percent of couples, can be treated by drugs, surgery, artificial insemination, and in vitro fertilization.

12. The germinal stage (fertilization to 2 weeks) is marked by rapid cell division and specialization, and the attachment of the zygote to the wall of the uterus. During the embryonic stage (2 to 8 weeks), the ectoderm, the mesoderm, and the endoderm begin to grow and specialize. The fetal stage (8 weeks to birth) is characterized by a rapid increase in complexity and differentiation of the organs. The fetus becomes active and most of its systems become operational.

What are the threats to the fetal environment, and what can be done about them?

13. Factors in the mother that may affect the unborn child include diet, age, illnesses, and drug, alcohol, and tobacco use. The behaviors of fathers and others in the environment may also affect the health and development of the unborn child.

What is the normal process of labor?

14. In the first stage of labor contractions occur about every 8 to 10 minutes, increasing in frequency, duration, and intensity until the mother's cervix expands. In the second stage of labor, which lasts about 90 minutes, the baby begins to move through the cervix and birth canal and ultimately leaves the mother's body. In the third stage of labor, which lasts only a few minutes, the umbilical cord and placenta are expelled from the mother.

15. After it emerges, the newborn, or neonate, is usually inspected for irregularities, cleaned, and returned to its mother and father.

16. Parents-to-be have a variety of choices regarding the setting for the birth, medical attendants, and whether or not to use pain-reducing medication. Sometimes, medical intervention, such as Cesarean birth, becomes necessary.

What complications can occur at birth, and what are their causes, effects, and treatments?

17. Preterm, or premature, infants, born less than 38 weeks following conception, generally have low birthweight, which can cause chilling, vulnerability to infection, respiratory distress syndrome, and hypersensitivity to environmental stimuli. They may even show adverse effects later in life, including slowed development, learning disabilities, behavior disorders, below-average IQ scores, and problems with physical coordination.

18. Very-low-birthweight infants are in special danger because of the immaturity of their organ systems. However, medical advances have pushed the age of viability of the infant back to about 24 weeks following conception.

19. Postmature babies, who spend extra time in their mothers' wombs, are also at risk. However, physicians can artificially induce labor or perform a Cesarean delivery to address this situation. Cesarean deliveries are performed when the fetus is in distress, in the wrong position, or unable to progress through the birth canal.

20. The infant mortality rate in the United States is higher than the rate in many other countries, and higher for low-income families than higher-income families.

3 Physical Growth and Aging Across the Life Span

Prologue
Cycling Through Life

Remarkable. Unbelievable. Inspirational.

Pick your adjective. They all apply to Carol Deland, [who] recently accomplished a feat that would intimidate a buff 20-year-old with bulging muscles, a strong heart and unlimited lung capacity.

But Deland isn't 20. Far from it. She's a divorced 66-year-old retired physical education teacher. . . .

"I go by a wonderful expression," she said. "'If you rest, you rust.'"

Rust won't form on Deland anytime soon. . . . [She] proved that recently when she biked across the country—starting March 8 in San Diego, Calif., and finishing May 4 in St. Augustine, Fla. That's a total of 3,115 miles in just 58 days—an average of more than 50 miles per day. . . .

When it was over, she was greeted at the beach in Florida by her three children and her sister.

"The last day, we had a 47-mile ride going into the ocean. It was a real feeling of accomplishment," Deland said. "My children are all real active, so I really had their support. They thought Mom was pretty cool. And so did Mom." (Heiser, 2007, p. 1)

Gerontologists have found that people in late adulthood can be as vigorous and active as those many years younger.

Carol Deland's physical achievements are truly unusual. Yet her accomplishments, however remarkable, are only some of many that characterize the dramatic physical attainments that occur throughout the course of life.

In this chapter, we focus on physical growth and aging across the life span. We begin by discussing the growth of the body from birth to old age, covering the major body changes along the life span. We also address height and weight change, maturation and puberty in adolescence, and the onset of aging and the physical changes it brings.

The chapter then examines brain growth and motor development, showing how the connections that the brain makes during early life influence development and the reflexes and motor skills that children develop as they age. We look at some surprising cultural differences as well as differences between males and females. Along the way, we discuss toilet training, and we ask why some people prefer their left hand and others their right.

Finally, the chapter turns to perceptual development. We discuss the development and progress of sensory perception early in life and we see how the senses change later in life. We track the relationship of the senses to such school topics as reading, writing, and self-esteem, and, in considering adulthood and old age, we look at the effects on daily life activities of sensory changes and the tendency to slow down.

LOOKING AHEAD

After reading this chapter, you will be able to answer the following questions:

▶ What physical changes are typical of the major periods of human development, and what factors influence their growth?

▶ How does the brain grow, and how do environmental factors affect brain growth?

▶ What reflexes do infants and young children possess, and what function do they serve?

▶ How do gross and fine motor skills change as people grow older?

▶ In what ways do the senses develop across the life span, and what consequences do the changes have?

MODULE 3.1

Physical Growth and Change

We had intimations that his first steps would not be too far in the future. Josh had previously dragged himself up, and, clutching the side of chairs and tables, managed to progress slowly around our living room. For the last few weeks, he'd even been able to stand, unmoving, for several moments without holding on.

But walking? It seemed too early: Josh was only 10 months old, and the books we read told us that most children would not take their first steps on their own until they were a year old. And our older son, Jon, hadn't walked until he was 14 months of age.

So, when Josh suddenly lurched forward, taking one awkward step after another away from the safety of the furniture and moved toward the center of the room, we were astounded. Despite the appearance that he was about to keel over at any second, he moved one, then two, then three steps forward, until our awe at his accomplishment overtook our ability to count each step.

Josh tottered all the way across the room, until he reached the other side. Not quite knowing how to stop, he toppled over, landing in a happy heap. It was moment of pure glory.

mydevelopmentlab

Raise a virtual child in **MyVirtualChild** to experience the changes you are reading about firsthand.

Physical Growth in Infancy

Josh's first steps at 10 months were the beginning of a succession of physical milestones that humans experience following birth. The period of infancy, which starts at birth and continues until the second birthday, is a time of obvious changes in height and weight and less apparent changes in the nervous system. Infants quickly develop increasingly stable patterns in such basic activities as sleeping, eating, and attending to the world.

The average newborn weighs just over 7 pounds, which is less than the weight of the average Thanksgiving turkey. It is about 20 inches long, shorter than a loaf of French bread. It is helpless; if left to fend for itself, it could not survive.

Yet after just a few years, the story is very different. Babies become much larger, they are mobile, and they grow increasingly independent. How does this growth happen? We can answer this question first by describing the changes in weight and height that occur over the first 2 years of life.

Rapid Advances. Infants grow rapidly over their first 2 years (see Figure 3.1). By 5 months, the average infant's birthweight has doubled to around 15 pounds. By the first birthday, the baby's weight has tripled to about 22 pounds. Although the pace of weight gain slows during the second year, it continues to increase. By the end of his or her second year, the average child weighs around four times as much as he or she did at birth. Of course, there is a good deal of variation among infants. Height and weight measurements, which are taken regularly during physicians' visits during a baby's first year, provide a way to spot problems in development.

The weight gains of infancy are matched by increased length. By the end of the first year, the typical baby grows almost a foot and is about 30 inches tall. By the second birthday, children average 3 feet.

Not all parts of an infant's body grow at the same rate. For instance, at birth the head accounts for one-quarter of the newborn's entire body size. During the first 2 years of life, the rest

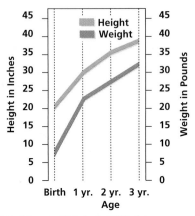

FIGURE 3.1 Height and Weight
Although the greatest increase in height and weight occurs during the first year of life, children continue to grow throughout infancy and toddlerhood.
Source: Craty, 1979.

of the body begins to catch up. By age 2 the baby's head is only one-fifth of body length, and by adulthood it is only one-eighth (see Figure 3.2).

There also are gender and ethnic differences in weight and length. Girls generally are slightly shorter and weigh slightly less than boys, and these differences remain throughout childhood (and, as we will see later, the disparities become considerably greater during adolescence). Furthermore, Asian infants tend to be slightly smaller than North American Caucasian infants, and African American infants tend to be slightly bigger than North American Caucasian infants.

Integrating Body Systems: The Life Cycles of Infancy. If you happen to overhear new parents discussing their newborns, chances are one or several bodily functions will be the subject. In the first days of life, infants' body rhythms—waking, eating, sleeping, and elimination—govern the infant's behavior, often at seemingly random times.

These most basic activities are controlled by a variety of bodily systems. Although each behavioral pattern probably is functioning effectively, it takes some time and effort for infants to integrate the separate behaviors. One of the neonate's major missions is to make its individual behaviors work in harmony, helping it, for example, to sleep through the night (Ingersoll & Thoman, 1999; Waterhouse & DeCoursey, 2004).

Rhythms and States. One of the most important ways that behavior becomes integrated is through the development of various **rhythms**, which are repetitive, cyclical patterns of behavior. Some rhythms are immediately obvious, such as the change from wakefulness to sleep. Others are more subtle, but still easily noticeable, such as breathing and sucking patterns. Still others may require careful observation to be noticed. For instance, newborns may go through periods in which they jerk their legs in a regular pattern every minute or so. Although some of these rhythms are apparent just after birth, others emerge slowly over the first year as the neurons of the nervous system become increasingly integrated (Thelen & Bates, 2003; Harvey, Mullin, & Hinshaw, 2006).

One of the major body rhythms is an infant's **state**, the degree of awareness to both internal and external stimulation. As can be seen in Table 3.1 on page 76, such states include various levels of wakeful behaviors, such as alertness, fussing, and crying, and different levels of sleep as well. Each change in state brings about an alteration in the amount of stimulation required to get the infant's attention (Diambra & Menna-Barreto, 2004).

Sleep: Perchance to Dream? At the beginning of infancy, the major state that occupies a baby's time is sleep—much to the relief of exhausted parents, who often regard sleep as a welcome respite from caregiving responsibilities. On average, newborn infants sleep some 16 to 17 hours a day, with wide variations from 10 to 20 or more (Peirano, Algarin, & Uauy, 2003; Buysse, 2005).

Still, you shouldn't wish to "sleep like a baby." Their sleep comes in spurts of around 2 hours, followed by periods of wakefulness. Because of this, infants—and their sleep-deprived parents—are "out of sync" with the rest of the world, for whom sleep comes at night and wakefulness during the day. Most babies do not sleep through the night for several months (Groome et al., 1997; Burnham et al., 2002; Sadeh, 2007; Best et al., 2009).

Luckily for their parents, infants gradually settle into a more adultlike pattern. After a week, babies sleep a bit more at night and are awake for slightly longer periods during the day. Typically, by the age of 16 weeks infants begin to sleep as much as 6 continuous hours at night, and daytime sleep falls into regular naplike patterns. Most infants sleep through the night by the end of the first year, and the total amount of sleep they need each day is down to about 15 hours (Mao, 2004).

Hidden beneath the supposedly tranquil sleep of infants is another cyclic pattern. During periods of sleep, infants' heart rates increase and become irregular, their blood pressure rises, and they begin to breathe more rapidly (Montgomery-Downs & Thomas, 1998). Sometimes, though not always, their closed eyes begin to move in a back-and-forth pattern, as if they were

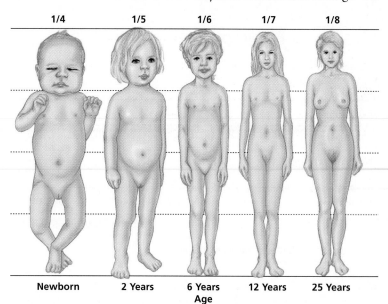

1/4 1/5 1/6 1/7 1/8

Newborn 2 Years 6 Years 12 Years 25 Years
Age

FIGURE 3.2 Decreasing Proportions At birth, the head represents one-quarter of the neonate's body. By adulthood, the head is only one-eighth the size of the body. Why is the neonate's head so large?

rhythms repetitive, cyclical patterns of behavior.

state degree of awareness an infant displays to both internal and external stimulation.

TABLE 3.1   Primary Behavioral States

STATES	CHARACTERISTICS	PERCENTAGE OF TIME WHEN ALONE IN STATE
Awake States		
Alert	Attentive or scanning, the infant's eyes are open, bright, and shining.	6.7
Nonalert waking	Eyes are usually open, but dull and unfocused. Varied, but typically high motor activity.	2.8
Fuss	Fussing is continuous or intermittent, at low levels.	1.8
Cry	Intense vocalizations occurring singly or in succession.	1.7
Transition States Between Sleep and Waking		
Drowse	Infant's eyes are heavy-lidded, but opening and closing slowly. Low level of motor activity.	4.4
Daze	Open, but glassy and immobile eyes. State occurs between episodes of Alert and Drowse. Low level of activity.	1.0
Sleep–wake transition	Behaviors of both wakefulness and sleep are evident. Generalized motor activity; eyes may be closed, or they open and close rapidly. State occurs when baby is awakening.	1.3
Sleep States		
Active sleep	Eyes closed; uneven respiration; intermittent rapid eye movements. Other behaviors: smiles, frowns, grimaces, mouthing, sucking, sighs, and sigh-sobs.	50.3
Quiet sleep	Eyes are closed and respiration is slow and regular. Motor activity limited to occasional startles, sigh-sobs, or rhythmic mouthing.	28.1
Transitional Sleep States		
Active–quiet transition sleep	During this state, which occurs between periods of Active Sleep and Quiet Sleep, the eyes are closed and there is little motor activity. Infant shows mixed behavioral signs of Active Sleep and Quiet Sleep.	1.9

Source: Adapted from Thoman & Whitney, 1990.

viewing an action-packed scene. This period of active sleep is similar, although not identical, to the **rapid eye movement,** or **REM, sleep,** that is found in older children and adults and is associated with dreaming.

At first, this active, REM-like sleep takes up around one-half of an infant's sleep, compared with just 20 percent of an adult's sleep. However, the quantity of active sleep quickly declines, and by the age of 6 months amounts to just one-third of total sleep time (Burnham et al., 2002; Staunton, 2005).

The appearance of active sleep periods that are similar to REM sleep in adults raises the intriguing question of whether infants dream during those periods. No one knows the answer, although it seems unlikely. First of all, young infants do not have much to dream about, given their relatively limited experiences. Furthermore, the brain waves of sleeping infants appear to be qualitatively different from those of adults who are dreaming. It is not until the baby reaches 3 or 4 months of age that the wave patterns become similar to those of dreaming adults (McCall, 1979; Parmelee & Sigman, 1983; Zampi et al., 2002).

What is the function of REM sleep in infants? Some researchers think it provides a means for the brain to stimulate itself—a process called *autostimulation* (Roffwarg, Muzio, & Dement, 1966). Stimulation of the nervous system would be particularly important in infants, who spend so much time sleeping and relatively little in alert states.

Infants' sleep cycles seem largely preprogrammed by genetic factors, but environmental influences also play a part. For instance, among the Kipsigis of Africa, infants sleep with their mothers at

rapid eye movement, or **REM, sleep**
the period of sleep that is found in older children and adults and is associated with dreaming.

night and are allowed to nurse whenever they wake. In the daytime, they accompany their mothers during daily chores, often napping while strapped to their mothers' backs. Because they are often out and on the go, Kipsigis infants do not sleep through the night until much later than babies in Western societies, and for the first 8 months of life, they seldom sleep longer than 3 hours at a stretch. In comparison, 8-month-old infants in the United States may sleep as long as 8 hours at a time (Super & Harkness, 1982; Gerard, Harris, & Thach, 2002; Rothrauff, Middlemiss, & Jacobson, 2004; Owens, 2008).

Physical Growth in the Preschool Years

Infancy presents challenges of its own; but add to these the ability to move about and the preschool years give caregivers a wealth of worries. In addition to worrying about colds and other illnesses and, especially in recent years, about what and how much their child eats, they must insist on quiet time and a bedtime that will afford their child adequate sleep, just at the time when their child becomes most active. If this seems like a long list of worries, remember that the list of delights that the preschool years bring is far longer.

During the preschool years, children experience rapid advances in their physical abilities that are nothing short of astounding. Just how far they develop is apparent when we look at the changes they undergo in their size, shape, and physical abilities.

By age 2, the average child in the United States weighs around 25 to 30 pounds and is close to 36 inches tall. By the time children are 6 years old, they weigh about 46 pounds and stand 46 inches tall (see Figure 3.3).

These averages mask significant individual differences. For instance, 10 percent of 6-year-olds weigh 55 pounds or more, and 10 percent weigh 36 pounds or less. Furthermore, average differences between boys and girls increase during the preschool years. Although at age 2 the differences are relatively small, during the preschool years boys start becoming taller and heavier, on average, than girls.

Changes in Body Shape and Structure. The bodies of a 2-year-old and a 6-year-old vary not only in height and weight, but also in shape. During the preschool years, boys and girls become less round and more slender. Moreover, their arms and legs lengthen, and the size relationship between the head and the rest of the body becomes more adultlike. By the time children reach age 6, their proportions are similar to those of adults.

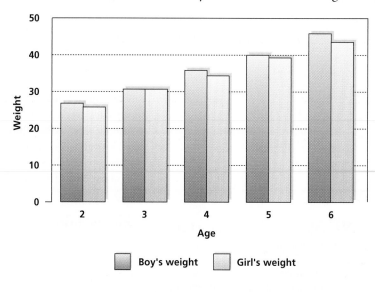

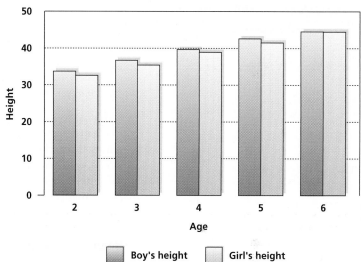

FIGURE 3.3 Gaining Height and Weight
The preschool years are marked by steady increases in height and weight. The figures show the median point for boys and girls at each age, in which 50% of children in each category are above this height or weight level and 50% are below.
Source: National Center for Health Statistics in collaboration with the National Center for Chronic Disease Prevention and Health Promotion, 2000.

Variations of six inches in height between children of the same age are not unusual and well within normal ranges.

Other physical changes occur internally. Muscle size increases, and children grow stronger. Bones become sturdier, and the sense organs continue to develop. For instance, the eustachian tube in the ear changes its orientation so radically that it may cause the earaches that are so typical of the preschool years.

Economic Factors. Economics also affects these averages. The better nutrition and health care typically received by children in developed countries translates into differences in growth. For instance, the average Swedish 4-year-old is as tall as the average 6-year-old in Bangladesh (United Nations, 1991; Leathers & Foster, 2004). Within the United States, children in families with incomes below the poverty level are more likely to be shorter than children raised in more affluent homes (Barrett & Frank, 1987; Ogden et al., 2002; Zhang & Wang, 2004).

To better understand the changes that the preschool period brings—and to get a sense of how parents and caregivers have to adjust to those changes—log onto **My-VirtualChild** through **MyDevelopmentLab**.

Physical Growth in Middle Childhood and Adolescence

Cinderella, dressed in yella,
Went upstairs to kiss her fellah.
But she made a mistake and she kissed a snake.
How many doctors did it take?
One, two, . . .

While the other girls chanted this jump-rope rhyme, Kat proudly displayed her new ability to jump backwards. In second grade, Kat was becoming quite good at jumping rope. In first grade, she simply had not been able to master it. But over the summer, she had spent many hours practicing, and now that practice was paying off.

As Kat is gleefully experiencing, children make great physical strides in middle childhood, mastering many new skills. How does this progress occur? We'll first consider typical physical growth during this period and then turn our attention to exceptional children.

Slow but steady—these words characterize the nature of growth during middle childhood. In contrast to the swift growth from birth to age 5 and the remarkable growth spurt of adolescence, middle childhood is relatively tranquil. The body has not shifted into neutral; physical growth continues but at a more stately pace than in the preschool years.

Height and Weight Changes. In elementary school, children in the United States grow, on average, 2 to 3 inches a year. By age 11, the average height for girls is 4 feet, 10 inches while boys average 4 feet, 9 1/2 inches. This is the only period in life when girls tend to be taller than boys. This pattern reflects the slightly more rapid physical development of girls, who start their adolescent growth spurt around age 10.

Weight gain in middle childhood follows a similar pattern; boys and girls both gain around 5 to 7 pounds a year. Weight is also redistributed. As "baby fat" disappears, children's bodies become more muscular and their strength increases.

Cultural Patterns of Growth. Most children in North America receive sufficient nutrients to grow to their full potential. In other parts of the world, however, inadequate nutrition and disease take their toll, producing children who are shorter and weigh less. The discrepancies can be dramatic: Poor children in cities such as Calcutta, Hong Kong, and Rio de Janeiro are smaller than affluent children in the same cities.

In the United States, most variations in height and weight are the result of people's unique genetic inheritance, including genetic factors relating to racial and ethnic background. Asian and Oceanic Pacific children tend to be shorter than those of northern and central European ancestry. In addition, the rate of growth is generally more rapid for black children than for white (Deurenberg, Deurenberg-Yap & Guricci, 2002; Deurenberg et al., 2003).

Even within racial and ethnic groups, individuals vary significantly. We cannot attribute racial and ethnic differences solely to genetic factors because dietary customs as well as variations in levels of affluence also may contribute to differences. In addition, severe stress—brought on by factors such as parental conflict or alcoholism—can affect the pituitary gland, thereby affecting growth (Powell, Brasel, & Blizzard, 1967; Koska et al., 2002; Dobrova-Krol et al., 2008; Emack et al., 2008).

Changes in Adolescence.

For young males of the Awa tribe, adolescence begins with an elaborate and—to Western eyes—gruesome ceremony to mark the passage from childhood to adulthood. The boys are whipped for two or three days with sticks and prickly branches. Through the whipping, the boys atone for their previous infractions and honor tribesmen who were killed in warfare. This ritual continues for days.

We are no doubt grateful we were spared such physical trials when we entered adolescence. But members of Western cultures have their own rites of passage, admittedly less fearsome, such as bar mitzvahs and bat mitzvahs at age 13 for Jewish boys and girls, and confirmation ceremonies in many Christian denominations (Dunham, Kidwell, & Wilson, 1986; Delaney, 1995; Herdt, 1998; Eccles, Templeton, & Barber, 2003; Hoffman, 2003).

Regardless of their nature, the underlying purpose of these ceremonies tends to be the same across cultures: symbolically celebrating the physical changes that transform a child's body into an adult body capable of reproduction.

The Rapidly Maturing Adolescent.

In only a few months, adolescents can grow several inches as they are transformed, at least physically, from children to young adults. During such a growth spurt—a period of very rapid growth in height and weight—boys, on average, grow 4.1 inches a year and girls 3.5 inches. Some adolescents grow as much as 5 inches in a single year (Tanner, 1972; Caino et al., 2004).

Boys' and girls' growth spurts begin at different ages. As you can see in Figure 3.4, girls' spurts begin around age 10, while boys' start around age 12. During the 2-year period from age 11, girls tend to be taller than boys, but then the situation reverses itself and males, on average, are taller than females for the remainder of the life span.

Puberty.

Puberty, the period when the sexual organs mature, begins when the pituitary gland in the brain signals other glands to begin producing the sex hormones, *androgens* (male hormones) or *estrogens* (female hormones), at adult levels. (Males and females produce both

puberty the period of maturation during which the sexual organs mature.

FROM AN EDUCATOR'S PERSPECTIVE: Why do you think many cultures regard the passage to adolescence as a significant transition that calls for unique ceremonies?

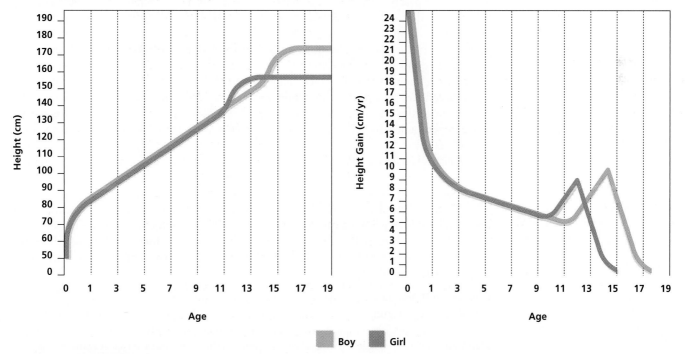

Boy   Girl

FIGURE 3.4 Growth Patterns
Patterns of growth are depicted in two ways. The first figure shows height at a given age, while the second shows the height increase that occurs from birth through the end of adolescence. Notice that girls begin their growth spurt around age 10, while boys begin their growth spurt at about age 12. However, by the age of 13, boys tend to be taller than girls. What are the social consequences of being taller or shorter than average for boys and girls?
Source: Adapted from Cratty, 1986.

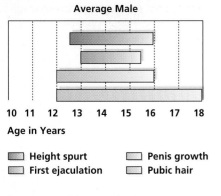

Average Male

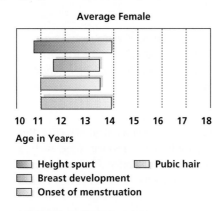

Average Female

Height spurt   **Penis growth**
First ejaculation   **Pubic hair**

Height spurt   **Pubic hair**
Breast development
Onset of menstruation

FIGURE 3.5 Sexual Maturation
The changes in sexual maturation that occur for males and females during early adolescence.
Source: Adapted from Tanner, 1978.

Log onto **MyDevelopmentLab** to watch 12-year-old Kianna, her mother, and her best friend talk about how important body image is in adolescence.

menarche   the onset of menstruation.

primary sex characteristics
characteristics associated with the development of the organs and structures of the body that directly relate to reproduction.

secondary sex characteristics
the visible signs of sexual maturity that do not directly involve the sex organs.

types of sex hormones, but males have higher levels of androgens and females, of estrogens.) The pituitary gland also signals the body to produce more growth hormones. These interact with the sex hormones to cause the growth spurt and puberty. The hormone *leptin*, too, appears to play a role in the onset of puberty.

Like the growth spurt, puberty begins earlier for girls, starting at around age 11 or 12, whereas boys begin at about age 13 or 14. However, this time frame varies widely. Some girls begin puberty as early as 7 or 8 or as late as age 16.

Puberty in Girls. Although it is not clear why puberty begins when it does, environmental and cultural factors play a role. For example, **menarche**, the onset of menstruation and probably the most obvious sign of puberty in girls, varies greatly around the world. In poorer, developing countries, menstruation begins later than in more economically advantaged countries. Even within wealthier countries, more affluent girls begin to menstruate earlier than less affluent girls.

It appears that girls who are better nourished and healthier tend to start menstruation earlier. Some studies have suggested that weight or the proportion of fat to muscle in the body plays a key role in the onset of menarche. For example, in the United States, athletes with a low percentage of body fat may start menstruating later than less active girls. Conversely, obesity—which increases the secretion of leptin, a hormone related to the onset of menstruation—leads to earlier puberty (Richards, 1996; Vizmanos & Marti-Henneberg, 2000; Woelfle, Harz, & Roth, 2007).

Other factors can affect the timing of menarche. For example, environmental stress from parental divorce or intense family conflict can effect an early onset (Hulanicka, 1999; Kim & Smith, 1999; Kaltiala-Heino, Kosunen, & Rimpela, 2003; Ellis, 2004).

Over the past century or so, girls in the United States and other cultures have been entering puberty at earlier ages. In the late nineteenth century, menstruation began, on average, around age 14 or 15, compared with today's 11 or 12. The average age for other indicators of puberty, such as the attaining of adult height and sexual maturity, has also dropped, probably due to reduced disease and improved nutrition.

Menstruation is one of several changes in puberty related to the development of primary and secondary sex characteristics. **Primary sex characteristics** are associated with the development of the organs and body structures related directly to reproduction. **Secondary sex characteristics** are the visible signs of sexual maturity that do not involve the sex organs directly.

In girls, primary sex characteristics pertain to changes in the vagina and uterus. Secondary sex characteristics include the development of breasts and pubic hair. Breasts begin to grow around age 10, and pubic hair appears at about age 11. Underarm hair appears about 2 years later.

For some girls, signs of puberty start unusually early. One out of seven Caucasian girls develops breasts or pubic hair by age 8. For African American girls, the figure is 1 out of 2. The reasons for this earlier onset are unclear, and what defines normal and abnormal onset is a controversy among specialists (Lemonick, 2000; The Endocrine Society, 2001; Ritzen, 2003).

Puberty in Boys. Boys' sexual maturation follows a somewhat different course. Growth of the penis and scrotum accelerates around age 12, reaching adult size about 3 or 4 years later. As boys' penises enlarge, other primary sex characteristics develop. The prostate gland and seminal vesicles, which produce semen (the fluid that carries sperm), enlarge. A boy's first ejaculation, known as *spermarche*, usually occurs around age 13, more than a year after the body begins producing sperm. At first, the semen contains relatively few sperm, but the sperm count increases significantly with age. Secondary sex characteristics are also developing. Pubic hair begins to grow around age 12, followed by the growth of underarm and facial hair. Finally, boys' voices deepen as the vocal cords become longer and the larynx larger. (Figure 3.5 summarizes the changes that occur in sexual maturation during early adolescence.)

Note the changes that have occurred in just a few years in these pre- and post-puberty photos of the same boy.

The surge in hormones that triggers puberty may also lead to rapid mood swings. Boys may have feelings of anger and annoyance associated with higher hormone levels. In girls, higher levels of hormones are associated with depression as well as anger (Buchanan, Eccles, & Becker, 1992; Hyde, Mezulis, & Abramson, 2008; Van den Bergh et al., 2008).

Physical Growth in Adulthood

As Anton ate his lunch one sunny day in Bryant Part, he idly watched two young men playing a high-speed chess game at the next table. One of the players was sitting in a wheelchair. As the game proceeded, with first one player then the other announcing his moves and slamming his timer, Anton found himself hoping that the guy in the wheelchair would win the match.

No such luck. After only a few more moves, the opponent loudly and triumphantly called "Check," and the handicapped player, after surveying the board, tipped his king and conceded defeat. Anton was disappointed: He had hoped that the able-bodied player would go easy on his opponent.

But Anton almost choked on his sandwich when he saw the winner reach for his cane as he rose to shake the hand of the man in the wheelchair. The winner was blind. Both players had a disability, and the one who couldn't even see the board had won the match.

As Anton learned, many people have disabilities, and focusing on what they lack instead of what they have is itself a kind of blindness. It is also a mistake to offer sympathy for the handicap instead of understanding of the individual who has it.

Most people are at their physical peak in early adulthood, which starts at the end of adolescence (around age 20) and continues until roughly the start of middle age (around age 40). For them, the body acts as if it's on automatic pilot: Physical health and fitness are never better. Still, there are others who have mild or severe disabilities, and they too are developing during this period. And often, aside from the area of their disability, they too are at their peak.

The Ups and Downs of Physical Transitions. In most respects, physical development and maturation are complete at early adulthood. Most people have attained their full height, with limbs proportional to their size, rendering the gangliness of adolescence a memory. People in their early 20s tend to be healthy, vigorous, and energetic. Although **senescence**, the natural physical decline brought about by increasing age, has begun, age-related changes are not usually obvious until later in life. At the same time, some growth continues; for example, some people, particularly late maturers, continue to gain height in their early 20s.

senescence the natural physical decline brought about by increasing age.

Negative Change. For many people, early adulthood is the first time—but by no means the last—that they have to deal seriously with the negative consequences of developmental change. As middle adulthood continues, people become aware of the gradual physical changes that aging brings. Some are the result of senescence, or naturally occurring declines; others are related to lifestyle choices, such as diet, exercise, smoking, and alcohol or drug use.

Although physical changes occur throughout life, these changes take on new significance in midlife, particularly in Western cultures that highly value a youthful appearance. The psychological significance of aging may far exceed the relatively minor and gradual changes a person experiences. A woman may have had gray hairs in her 20s, but in her 40s they may multiply to an extent she cannot ignore. She may feel no longer young.

People's emotional reactions to midlife's physical changes depend in part on their self-concepts. When self-image is tied closely to one's physical attributes—as it is for very athletic men and women or those who are physically quite attractive—middle adulthood can be particularly difficult. The changes the mirror reveals signal aging and mortality as well as a loss of physical attractiveness. On the other hand, because most people's self-concepts are not so closely tied to physical attributes, middle-aged adults generally report no less satisfaction with their body images than younger adults (Eitel, 2003; McKinley, 2006).

Late Adulthood.

"Feel the burn." That's what the exercise tape says, and many of the 14 women in the group are doing just that. As the tape continues through its drills, some of the women stretch and reach vigorously, while others mostly just sway to the music. It's not much different from thousands of exercise classes across the United States, and yet there is one surprise: The youngest woman in the group is 66 years old, and the oldest, dressed in sleek Spandex leotards, is 81.

The surprise registered by this observer reflects the stereotype that people over 65 are sedentary, incapable of vigorous exercise. The reality is different. Although their physical capabilities are likely to have changed, many older persons remain agile and fit long into old age (Riebe, Burbank, & Garber, 2002; Dionigi & O'Flynn, 2007). Still, the outer and inner changes that began subtly during middle adulthood become unmistakable during old age.

As we discuss aging, we should take note of the distinction between primary and secondary aging. As we saw earlier, **primary aging**, or *senescence*, involves universal and irreversible changes due to genetic programming. In contrast, **secondary aging** encompasses changes that are due to illness, health habits, and other individual factors, which are not inevitable. Although the physical and cognitive changes of secondary aging are common, they are potentially avoidable and can sometimes be reversed.

Outward Signs of Aging. One of the most obvious indicators of aging is the hair, which usually becomes distinctly gray and eventually white, and may thin out. The face and other parts of the body become wrinkled as the skin loses elasticity and *collagen,* the protein that forms the basic fibers of body tissue (Bowers & Thomas, 1995; Medina, 1996; Lesnoff-Caravaglia, 2007).

People may become shorter by as much as 4 inches, partially due to changes in posture, but mostly because the cartilage in the disks of the backbone becomes thinner. This is particularly true for women, who are more susceptible than men to **osteoporosis**, or thinning of the bones, largely from reduced estrogen production.

As we have seen, osteoporosis, which affects 25 percent of women over 60, is a primary cause of broken bones among older people. It is largely preventable if exercise is adequate and calcium and protein intake is sufficient earlier in life. Osteoporosis can be treated and even prevented with drugs such as Fosamax (alendronate) (Moyad, 2004; Picavet & Hoeymans, 2004).

Although negative stereotypes against appearing old affect both genders, they are particularly potent for women. In Western cultures there is a *double standard* for appearance, by which women are judged more harshly than men. For instance, gray hair in men is often viewed as "distinguished"; in women it is a sign of being "over the hill" (Frerking, 2006).

As a consequence, women feel considerably more pressure than men to hide the signs of aging by dyeing their hair, undergoing cosmetic surgery, and using age-concealing cosmetics. The double standard is diminishing, however, as more men grow interested in looking younger and fall prey to a new wave of male-oriented cosmetic products, such as wrinkle creams (Unger & Crawford, 2003; Clarke & Griffin, 2007).

Log onto **MyDevelopmentLab** to hear a 90-year-old man talk about the difference between what he used to enjoy doing and what he is physically capable of doing now.

primary aging aging that involves universal and irreversible changes that, due to genetic programming, occur as people get older.

secondary aging changes in physical and cognitive functioning that are due to illness, health habits, and other individual differences, but that are not due to increased age itself and are not inevitable.

osteoporosis a condition in which the bones become brittle, fragile, and thin, often brought about by a lack of calcium in the diet.

Internal Aging.   As the outward signs become more apparent, changes also take place in the internal functioning of the organ systems (Whitbourne, 2001; Aldwin & Gilmer, 2004).

The brain becomes smaller and lighter. As it shrinks, it pulls away from the skull, and the space between brain and skull doubles from age 20 to age 70. The brain uses less oxygen and glucose, and blood flow is reduced. The number of neurons, or brain cells, declines in some parts of the brain, although not as much as was once thought. Recent research suggests that the number of cells in the cortex may drop only minimally or not at all. In fact, some evidence suggests that certain types of neuronal growth may continue throughout the life span (Tisserand & Jolles, 2003; Lindsey & Tropepe, 2006; Raz et al., 2007).

The reduced flow of blood in the brain is due in part to the heart's diminished ability to pump blood through hardening and shrinking blood vessels. A 75-year-old man pumps less than three-quarters of the blood that he could pump during early adulthood (Kart, 1990; Yildiz, 2007).

Other bodily systems also work at lower capacity. The respiratory system is less efficient, and the digestive system produces less digestive juice and is less efficient in pushing food through the system—thereby increasing the incidence of constipation. Some hormones are produced at lower levels. Muscle fibers decrease both in size and in amount, and they become less efficient at using oxygen from the bloodstream and storing nutrients (Fiatarone & Garnett, 1997; Lamberts, van den Beld, & van der Lely, 1997; Vecchiet, 2002).

Although these changes are normal, they often occur earlier in people who have less healthy lifestyles. For example, smoking accelerates declines in cardiovascular capacity at any age.

Lifestyle factors can also slow the changes associated with aging. For instance, people whose exercise program includes weightlifting may lose muscle fiber at a slower rate than those who are sedentary. Similarly, physical fitness is related to better performance on mental tests, may prevent a loss of brain tissue, and may even aid in the development of new neurons. Studies suggest that sedentary older adults who begin aerobic fitness training ultimately show cognitive benefits (Colcombe et al., 2006; Elder, DeGasperi, & GamaSosa, 2006; Kramer, Erickson, & Colcombe, 2006; Pereira et al., 2007).

The Myth and Reality of Aging

The astronaut-turned-senator, John Glenn, was 77 years old when he returned to space on a 10-day mission to help NASA study how the elderly adjust to space travel. Although sheer altitude sets Glenn apart from others, many people lead active, vigorous lives during late adulthood, fully engaged with life.

Old age used to be equated with loss: loss of brain cells, intellectual capabilities, energy, sex drive. That view is being displaced as **gerontologists**, specialists who study aging, paint a very different picture. Rather than a period of decline, late adulthood is seen as a stage in which people continue to change—to grow in some areas and, yes, to decline in others.

Even the definition of "old" is changing. Many people in late adulthood, which begins around age 65 and continues to death, are as vigorous and involved with life as people several decades younger. We can no longer define old age by chronological years alone; we also must take into account people's physical and psychological well-being, their *functional ages*. Some researchers divide people into three groups according to functional ages: the *young old* are healthy and active; the *old old* have some health problems and difficulties with daily activities; and the *oldest old* are frail and need care. According to functional age, an active, healthy 100-year-old would be considered young old, while a 65-year-old in the late stages of emphysema would be among the oldest old.

Late adulthood holds a unique distinction among life's stages: Because people are living longer, late adulthood is getting longer. Whether we start counting at 65 or 70, a greater proportion of people are alive in late adulthood today than at any time in world history. Demographers have taken to divide the period using the same terms—but with different meanings—as researchers of functional aging. For demographers, the terms are purely chronological. The *young old* are 65 to 74 years old. The *old old* are between 75 and 84, and the *oldest old* are 85 and older.

The Demographics of Late Adulthood.   One out of every eight Americans is 65 or older, and projections suggest that by 2050 nearly one-quarter of the population will be 65 and above. The number of people over 85 is projected to increase from 4 million to 18 million by 2050 (Schneider, 1999; Administration on Aging, 2003).

gerontologists   specialists who study aging.

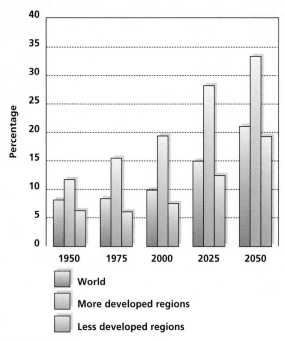

FIGURE 3.6
The Elderly Population Worldwide
Longer life is transforming population profiles worldwide, with the proportion of those over the age of 60 predicted to increase substantially by the year 2050.
Source: United Nations Population Division, 2002.

The fastest growing segment of the population is the oldest old—people 85 or older. In the last two decades, the size of this group has nearly doubled. The population explosion among older people is not limited to the United States. As can be seen in Figure 3.6, the number of elderly is increasing substantially in countries around the globe. By 2050, the number of adults worldwide over 60 will exceed the number of people under 15 for the first time in history (Sandis, 2000; United Nations, 2002).

REVIEW

▶ The pattern of physical development is rapid growth over the first 2 years, a middle childhood of slow and steady growth, a spurt in adolescence, and gradual change over adulthood.

▶ Infants integrate their behavior through the development of various rhythms and states, and within a year they develop the ability to sleep through the night.

▶ The key physical change of adolescence is puberty, which can have powerful effects on adolescents depending on whether they are male or female and late maturing or early maturing.

▶ In general, early adulthood is the first time that people have to deal seriously with negative changes.

APPLY

▶ How might biology and environment combine to affect the physical growth of a child adopted as an infant from a developing country and reared in a more industrialized one?

▶ Projections indicate that the world population will get much older in the future. What sorts of impact will this have on different cultures and the world in general?

MODULE 3.2

Brain Growth and Motor Development

Suzanne McGuire

It is a hot summer day in Atlanta. Adults move slowly through the humid air, but not 8-year-old Suzanne McGuire. A look of triumph crosses her face as she rounds the corner from third base to home plate.

Moments before, she was waiting for the pitcher to throw the ball. Her first two turns at bat, Suzanne had struck out, leaving her unhappy and a bit humiliated.

On her third at bat, though, the pitch looked perfect. She swung at it with confidence and high hope. When the bat connected with the ball, lobbing it well beyond the left fielder for a home run, it created a moment she would never forget.

Suzanne McGuire has come a long way since the preschool years, when quick, coordinated running and batting to the mark were not possible. As a child's motor and brain development proceeds from infancy onward, parents watch in awe as skills emerge that eventually will allow their kids to roll over, take their first step, and pick up a cookie crumb from the floor. And these skills will ultimately form the basis of later, even more complex behaviors as the child develops gross motor skills—like swinging a bat—and fine motor skills—like playing scales on a piano.

The Nervous System and Brain: Making Connections

When their first baby is born, parents marvel at the infant, oohing and aahing at every sneeze and smile and whimper, trying to guess their meaning. Whatever feelings, movements, and thoughts the baby is experiencing, they are all brought about by the same complex network: the infant's nervous system. The nervous system comprises the brain and the nerves that extend throughout the body.

The Growing Brain. The brain grows at a faster rate than any other part of the body. Two-year-olds have brains that are about three-quarters the size and weight of an adult brain. By age 5, children's brains weigh 90 percent of average adult brain weight. In comparison, the average 5-year-old's total body weight is just 30 percent of average adult body weight (Lowrey, 1986; Schuster & Ashburn, 1986; Nihart, 1993).

Why does the brain grow so rapidly? One reason is an increase in the number of interconnections among cells, which supports more complex communication between neurons and permits the rapid growth of cognitive skills. In addition, the amount of protective myelin increases, which speeds the transmission of electrical impulses along brain cells.

Neurons are the basic cells of the nervous system. Figure 3.7 shows the structure of an adult neuron. Like all cells in the body, neurons have a cell body containing a nucleus. But unlike other cells, neurons have a distinctive ability: They can communicate with other cells, using a cluster of fibers called *dendrites* at one end. Dendrites receive messages from other cells. At their opposite end, neurons have a long extension called an *axon,* the part of the neuron that carries messages destined for other neurons. Neurons do not actually touch one another. Rather, they communicate with other neurons by means of chemical messengers, *neurotransmitters,* that travel across the small gaps, known as synapses, between neurons.

Although estimates vary, infants are born with between 100 and 200 billion neurons. In order to reach this number, neurons multiply at an amazing rate prior to birth. At some points in prenatal development, cell division creates some 250,000 additional neurons every minute.

At birth, most neurons in an infant's brain have relatively few connections to other neurons. During the first 2 years of life, however, a baby's brain will establish billions of new connections between neurons. Furthermore, the network of neurons becomes increasingly complex, as illustrated in Figure 3.8. The intricacy of neural connections continues to increase throughout life. In fact, in adulthood a single neuron is likely to have a minimum of 5,000 connections to other neurons or other body parts.

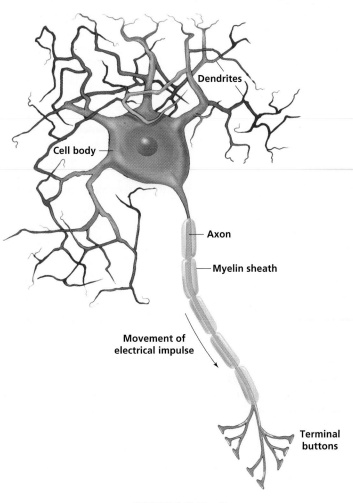

FIGURE 3.7 The Neuron
The basic element of the nervous system, the neuron, has a number of components.
Source: Van de Graaf, 2000.

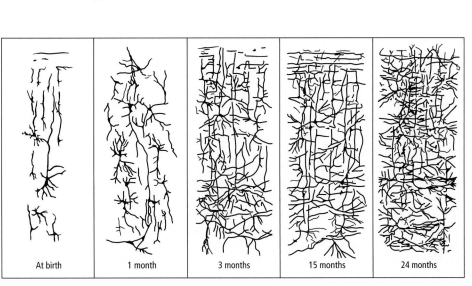

| At birth | 1 month | 3 months | 15 months | 24 months |

FIGURE 3.8 Neuron Networks
Over the first 2 years of life, networks of neurons become increasingly complex and interconnected. Why are these connections important?
Source: Conel, 1939/1975.

Synaptic Pruning. Babies are actually born with many more neurons than they need. In addition, although synapses are formed throughout life based on our changing experiences, the billions of new synapses infants form during the first 2 years are more numerous than necessary. What happens to the extra neurons and synaptic connections?

Like a horticulturalist who, to strengthen the vitality of a fruit tree, prunes away unnecessary branches, brain development enhances certain capabilities in part by "pruning down" unnecessary neurons. Neurons that do not become interconnected with other neurons as the infant's experience of the world increases eventually die out, enhancing the efficiency of the nervous system.

Similarly, if a baby's experiences do not stimulate certain nerve connections, these, like unused neurons, are eliminated—a process called **synaptic pruning**. The result of synaptic pruning is to allow established neurons to build more elaborate communication networks with other neurons. Unlike most other aspects of growth, then, the development of the nervous system proceeds most effectively through the loss of cells (Johnson, 1998; Mimura, Kimoto, & Okada, 2003; Iglesias et al., 2005).

After birth, neurons continue to increase in size. In addition to growth in dendrites, the axons of neurons become coated with **myelin**, a fatty substance that, like the insulation on an electric wire, provides protection and speeds the transmission of nerve impulses. So, even though many neurons are lost, the increasing size and complexity of the remaining ones contribute to impressive brain growth. A baby's brain triples its weight during his or her first 2 years of life, and it reaches more than three-quarters of its adult weight and size by the age of 2.

As they grow, the neurons also reposition themselves, becoming arranged by function. Some move into the **cerebral cortex**, the upper layer of the brain, while others move to *subcortical levels,* which are below the cerebral cortex. The subcortical levels, which regulate such fundamental activities as breathing and heart rate, are the most fully developed at birth. As time passes, however, the cells in the cerebral cortex, which are responsible for higher-order processes such as thinking and reasoning, become more developed and interconnected.

Although the brain is protected by the bones of the skull, it is highly sensitive to some forms of injury. One particularly devastating injury comes from a form of child abuse called *shaken baby syndrome,* in which an infant is shaken by a caretaker, usually out of frustration or anger due to a baby's crying. Shaking can lead the brain to rotate within the skull, causing blood vessels to tear and destroying the intricate connections between neurons, producing severe medical problems, long-term physical and learning disabilities, and often death (Gerber & Coffman, 2007; Jayawant & Parr, 2007).

Environmental Influences on Brain Development. Brain development, much of which unfolds automatically because of genetically predetermined patterns, is also strongly susceptible to environmental influences. The brain's **plasticity**, the degree to which a developing structure or behavior is modifiable due to experience, is relatively great. For instance, as we've seen, an infant's sensory experience affects both the size of individual neurons and the structure of their interconnections. Consequently, compared with those brought up in more enriched environments, infants raised in severely restricted settings are likely to show differences in brain structure and weight (Cicchetti, 2003; Cirulli, Berry, & Alleva, 2003; Couperus & Nelson, 2006).

Furthermore, researchers have found that there are sensitive periods during development. A **sensitive period** is a specific, but limited, time, usually early in an organism's life, during which the organism is particularly susceptible to environmental influences relating to some particular facet of development. A sensitive period may be associated with a behavior—such as the development of vision—or with the development of a structure of the body, such as the configuration of the brain (Uylings, 2006).

The existence of sensitive periods suggests that if deprived of a certain level of early environmental stimulation during a sensitive period, the infant may suffer damage or fail to develop capabilities that can never be fully remedied. If this is true, providing successful later intervention for such children may prove challenging (Gottlieb & Blair, 2004).

The opposite question also arises: Does an unusually high level of stimulation during sensitive periods produce developmental gains beyond what a more commonplace level of stimulation would provide?

synaptic pruning the elimination of neurons as the result of nonuse or lack of stimulation.

myelin protective insulation that surrounds parts of neurons, increasing the speed of transmission of electrical impulses along brain cells.

cerebral cortex the upper layer of the brain.

plasticity the degree to which a developing structure or behavior is modifiable due to experience.

sensitive period a point in development when organisms are particularly susceptible to certain kinds of stimuli in their environments, but the absence of those stimuli does not always produce irreversible consequences.

There is no simple answer. Determining how unusually impoverished or enriched environments affect later development is one of the major questions addressed by developmental researchers as they look for ways to maximize opportunities for developing children. In the meantime, many developmentalists suggest that simple activities can provide a stimulating environment that will encourage healthy brain growth, including cuddling, talking and singing, and playing with babies all help enrich their environment (Lafuente et al., 1997; Garlick, 2003).

Brain Lateralization. By the end of the preschool period, the *corpus callosum,* a bundle of nerve fibers that connects the two hemispheres of the brain, becomes considerably thicker, developing as many as 800 million individual fibers that help coordinate brain functioning between the two hemispheres. At the same time, the two halves of the brain become increasingly differentiated and specialized. **Lateralization**, the process in which certain functions are located more in one hemisphere than the other, becomes more pronounced during the preschool years.

For most people, the left hemisphere is primarily involved with tasks that necessitate verbal competence, such as speaking, reading, thinking, and reasoning. The right hemisphere develops its own strengths, especially in nonverbal areas such as comprehension of spatial relationships, recognition of patterns and drawings, music, and emotional expression (McAuliffe & Knowlton, 2001; Koivisto & Revonsuo, 2003; Pollak, Holt, & Wismer Fries, 2004; see Figure 3.9).

Each hemisphere also begins to process information in a slightly different manner. The left hemisphere processes data sequentially, one piece at a time. The right hemisphere processes information in a more global manner, reflecting on it as a whole (Springer & Deutsch, 1989; Leonard et al., 1996; Geschwind & Iacoboni, 2007).

While there is some specialization, in most respects the two hemispheres act in tandem and are interdependent. In fact, each hemisphere can perform most of the tasks of the other. For example, the right hemisphere does some language processing and plays an important role in language comprehension (Knecht et al., 2000; Corballis, 2003; Hutchinson, Whitman, & Abeare, 2003).

Individual Differences in Lateralization. There are also individual and cultural differences in lateralization. For example, many of the 10 percent of people who are left-handed or ambidextrous (able to use both hands interchangeably) have language centered in the right hemisphere or have no specific language center (Banich & Nicholas, 1998; Compton & Weissman, 2002).

Among the most controversial findings relating to the specialization of the hemispheres of the brain is evidence that lateralization is related to gender and culture. For instance, starting during the first year of life and continuing in the preschool years, boys and girls show some hemispheric differences associated with lower body reflexes and the processing of auditory information. Boys also clearly tend to show greater specialization of language in the left hemisphere; among females, language is more evenly divided between the two hemispheres. Such differences may help explain why girls' language development proceeds at a more rapid pace during the preschool years than boys' language development (Gur et al., 1982; Grattan et al., 1992; Bourne & Todd, 2004).

According to psychologist Simon Baron-Cohen, the differences between male and female brains may help explain the puzzling riddle of *autism*, the profound developmental disability that produces language deficits and great difficulty in interacting with others. Baron-Cohen argues that children with autism (who are predominately male) have what he calls an "extreme male brain." The extreme male brain, though relatively good at systematically sorting out the world, is poor at understanding the emotions of others and experiencing empathy for others' feelings. To Baron-Cohen, individuals with an extreme male brain have traits associated with the normal male brain, but display the traits to such an extent that their behavior is viewed as autistic (Baron-Cohen, 2003, 2005; Ingudomnukul et al., 2007).

Although Baron-Cohen's theory is quite controversial, it is clear that some kind of gender differences exist in lateralization. But we still don't know the extent of the differences and why they occur. One explanation is genetic: Female brains and male brains are predisposed to function in slightly different ways. Such a view is supported by data suggesting the existence of minor structural differences between males' and females' brains. For instance, a section of the corpus callosum is proportionally larger in women than in men. Furthermore, studies conducted among other species, such as primates, rats, and hamsters, have found size and structural differences in the brains of males and females (Hohm et al., 2007; Christova et al., 2008; Colibazzi et al., 2008; Redcay & Courchesne, 2008).

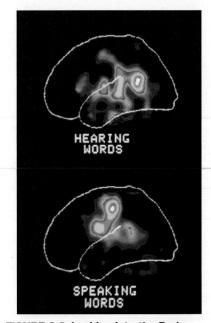

HEARING
WORDS

SPEAKING
WORDS

FIGURE 3.9 Looking into the Brain
This set of PET brain scans illustrates that activity in the right or left hemisphere of the brain differs according to the task in which a person is engaged. How might educators use this finding in their approach to teaching?

**FROM A
SOCIAL WORKER'S
PERSPECTIVE:**
What are some cultural or subcultural influences that might affect parents' childrearing practices?

lateralization the process in which certain cognitive functions are located more in one hemisphere of the brain than in the other.

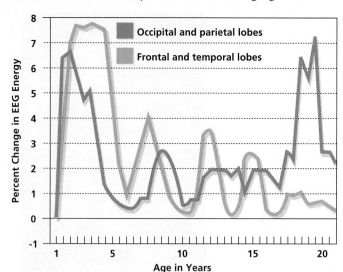

FIGURE 3.10 Brain Growth Spurt
According to one study, electrical activity in the brain has been linked to advances in cognitive abilities at various stages across the life span. In this graph, activity increases dramatically between 1¹⁄₂ and 2 years of age, a period during which language rapidly develops.
Source: Fischer & Rose, 1995.

Before we accept a genetic explanation for the differences between female and male brains, we need to consider an equally plausible alternative: It may be that verbal abilities emerge earlier in girls because girls receive greater encouragement for verbal skills than boys do. For instance, even as infants, girls are spoken to more than boys. Such higher levels of verbal stimulation may produce growth in particular areas of the brain that does not occur in boys. Consequently, environmental factors rather than genetic ones may lead to the gender differences we find in brain lateralization (Beal, 1994; Hohm et al., 2007).

Lateralization by Culture. Not only may there be differences in brain lateralization between boys and girls, but the culture in which they are raised may be related to brain lateralization. For instance, native speakers of Japanese process information related to vowel sounds primarily in the left hemisphere of the brain. In comparison, North and South Americans and Europeans—as well as people of Japanese ancestry who learn Japanese as a second language—process vowel sounds primarily in the brain's right hemisphere.

The explanation for this cultural difference in processing of vowels seems to rest on the nature of the Japanese language. Specifically, the Japanese language allows for the expression of complex concepts using only vowel sounds. Consequently, a specific type of brain lateralization may develop while learning and using Japanese at a relatively early age (Tsunoda, 1985; Hiser & Kobayashi, 2003).

This explanation, which is speculative, does not rule out the possibility that some type of subtle genetic difference may also be at work in determining the difference in lateralization. Once again, then, we find it challenging to tease out the relative impact of heredity and environment.

The Links Between Brain Growth and Cognitive Development. Neuroscientists are just beginning to understand the ways in which brain development is related to cognitive development. For example, it appears that there are periods during childhood in which the brain shows unusual growth spurts, and these periods are linked to advances in cognitive abilities. One study that measured electrical activity in the brain across the life span found unusual spurts at between 1 1/2 and 2 years, a time when language abilities increase rapidly. Other spurts occurred around other ages when cognitive advances are particularly intense (see Figure 3.10; Fischer & Rose, 1995).

Other research has suggested that increases in myelin may be related to preschoolers' growing cognitive capabilities. For example, myelination of the reticular formation, an area of the brain associated with attention and concentration, is completed by the time children are about 5. This may be associated with children's growing attention spans as they approach school age. The improvement in memory that occurs during the preschool years may also be associated with myelination: During the preschool years, myelination is completed in the hippocampus, an area associated with memory (Rolls, 2000; de Bellis et al., 2001).

We do not yet know the direction of causality. (Does brain development produce cognitive advances, or do cognitive accomplishments fuel brain development?) However, it is clear that increases in our understanding of the physiological aspects of the brain will eventually have important implications for parents and teachers.

During the rest of the life span, brain development and cognitive growth are interrelated. Teenagers tend to assert themselves more as they gain greater independence. This independence is, in part, the result of changes in the brain that bring significant advances in cognitive abilities. As the number of neurons continues to grow, and their interconnections become richer and more complex, adolescent thinking becomes more sophisticated (Thompson & Nelson, 2001; Toga & Thompson, 2003).

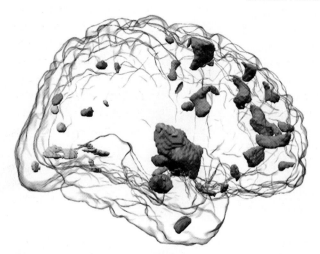

FIGURE 3.11 Pruning Gray Matter
This three-dimensional view of the brain shows areas of gray matter that are pruned from the brain between adolescence and adulthood.
Source: Sowell et al., 1999.

The brain produces an oversupply of gray matter during adolescence, which is later pruned back by 1 to 2 percent each year (see Figure 3.11). Myelination increases, making the transmission of neural messages more efficient. Both pruning and increased myelination contribute to the growing cognitive abilities of adolescents (Sowell et al., 2001; Sowell et al., 2003).

The prefrontal cortex of the brain, which is not fully developed until the early 20s, undergoes considerable development during adolescence. The *prefrontal cortex* allows people to think, evaluate, and make complex judgments in a uniquely human way. It underlies the increasingly complex intellectual achievements that are possible during adolescence.

At this stage, the prefrontal cortex becomes increasingly efficient in communicating with other parts of the brain, creating a communication system that is more distributed and sophisticated, which permits the different areas of the brain to process information more effectively (Scherf, Sweeney, & Luna, 2006). The prefrontal cortex also provides impulse control. An individual with a fully developed prefrontal cortex is able to inhibit the desire to act on such emotions as anger or rage. In adolescence, however, the prefrontal cortex is biologically immature; the ability to inhibit impulses is not fully developed. As discussed in the *From Research to Practice* box, this brain immaturity may lead to the risky and impulsive behaviors that characterize adolescence—and some behaviors that are even more extreme (Weinberger, 2001; Steinberg & Scott, 2003).

Brain development also produces changes in regions involving dopamine sensitivity and production. As a result, adolescents may become less affected by alcohol, requiring more drinks to experience its effects—leading to higher alcohol intake. Changes in dopamine sensitivity also may increase sensitivity to stress, leading to further alcohol use (Spear, 2002).

The prefrontal cortex, the area of the brain responsible for impulse control, is biologically immature during adolescence, leading to some of the risky and impulsive behavior associated with people in this age group.

FROM RESEARCH TO PRACTICE
The Immature Brain Argument: Too Young for the Death Penalty?

Just after 2 a.m. on September 9, 1993, Christopher Simmons, 17, and Charles Benjamin, 15, broke into a trailer south of Fenton, Missouri, just outside of St. Louis. They woke Shirley Ann Crook, a 46-year-old truck driver who was inside, and proceeded to tie her up and cover her eyes and mouth with silver duct tape. They then put her in the back of her minivan, drove her to a railroad bridge and pushed her into the river below, where her body was found the next day. Simmons and Benjamin later confessed to the abduction and murder, which had netted them $6. (Raeburn, 2004, p. 26)

This horrific case sent Benjamin to life in prison, but Simmons was given the death penalty. Simmons's lawyers appealed, and ultimately the U.S. Supreme Court ruled that no one under the age of 18 could be executed, citing their youth. Among the factors affecting the Court's decision was evidence from neuroscientists and child developmentalists that adolescents' brains were still developing in important ways and thus lacked judgment due to brain immaturity. This reasoning says adolescents are not fully capable of making sound decisions because their brains differ from those of adults.

The research that figured in the trial showed continued brain growth and maturation during the teenage years, and beyond. For example, neurons that make up unnecessary gray matter begin to disappear. The volume of white matter begins to increase. This change permits more sophisticated, thoughtful cognitive processing (Beckman, 2004).

When the brain's frontal lobes contain more white matter, they are better at restraining impulsivity. As neuroscientist Ruben Gur puts it, "If you've been insulted, your emotional brain says, 'Kill,' but your frontal lobe says you're in the middle of a cocktail party, 'so let's respond with a cutting remark'" (Beckman, 2004, p. 597). In adolescence, the censoring process is still developing. Teenagers may act impulsively, responding with emotion rather than reason. Their ability to foresee consequences may also be hindered by their less mature brains.

Are adolescents' brains so immature that offenders should receive a lesser punishment for their crimes than adults? The answer to this difficult question may come from students of ethics rather than science.

- *Do you think that the penalty for criminal behavior should be tied to the maturity of a criminal's brain? Why or why not?*

- *Are there other aspects of physical development that should be considered in determining a person's responsibility for criminal activity?*

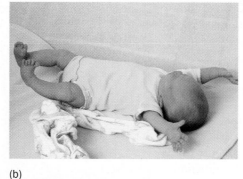

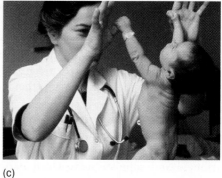

(a)   (b)   (c)

Infants showing (a) the sucking reflex, (b) the grasping reflex, and (c) the Babinski reflex.

Teenagers tend to assert themselves more as they gain greater independence. This independence is, in part, the result of changes in the brain that bring significant advances in cognitive abilities. As the number of neurons (the cells of the nervous system) continues to grow, and their interconnections become richer and more complex, adolescent thinking becomes more sophisticated (Thompson & Nelson, 2001; Toga & Thompson, 2003).

Reflexes: Protective Reactions

When her father pressed 3-day-old Christina Michaelson's palm with his finger, she responded by tightly winding her small fist around his finger and grasping it. When he moved his finger upward, she held on so tightly that it seemed he might be able to lift her completely off her crib floor.

In fact, her father was right: Christina probably could have been lifted in this way. The reason for her resolute grip was activation of one of the dozens of reflexes with which infants are born. Newborns enter the world with a repertoire of reflexive behavioral patterns that help them adapt to their new surroundings and serve to protect them.

The Redesigned Infant. Suppose you were hired by a genetic engineering firm to redesign newborns and were charged with replacing the current version with a new, more mobile one. The first change you'd probably consider in carrying out this (luckily fictitious) job would be in the conformation and composition of the baby's body.

The shape and proportions of newborn babies are simply not conducive to easy mobility. Their heads are so large and heavy that young infants lack the strength to raise them. Because their limbs are short in relation to the rest of the body, their movements are further impeded. Furthermore, their bodies are mainly fat, with a limited amount of muscle; the result is that they lack strength.

Fortunately, it doesn't take too long before infants begin to develop a remarkable amount of mobility. Even at birth they have an extensive repertoire of behavioral possibilities brought about by innate reflexes, and their range of motor skills grows rapidly during the first 2 years of life.

Reflexes: Our Inborn Physical Skills. **Reflexes** are unlearned, organized involuntary responses that occur automatically in the presence of certain stimuli. As we can see from the list of reflexes in Table 3.2, many reflexes clearly represent behavior that has survival value, helping to

During the preschool years, children grow in both gross and fine motor skills.

To watch infants demonstrate the reflexes you are reading about, log onto **MyDevelopmentLab**.

ensure the well-being of the infant. For instance, the *swimming reflex* makes a baby who is lying face down in a body of water paddle and kick in a sort of swimming motion. The obvious consequence of such behavior is to help the baby move from danger and survive until a caregiver can come to its rescue. Similarly, the *eye blink reflex* seems designed to protect the eye from too much direct light, which might damage the retina.

reflexes unlearned, organized involuntary responses that occur automatically in the presence of certain stimuli.

Given the protective value of many reflexes, it might seem beneficial for them to remain with us for our entire lives. In fact, some do: The eye blink reflex remains functional throughout the full life span. Quite a few reflexes, however, such as the swimming reflex, disappear after a few months. Why should this be the case?

Researchers who focus on evolutionary explanations of development attribute the gradual disappearance of reflexes to the increase in voluntary control over behavior that occurs as infants become more able to control their muscles. In addition, it may be that reflexes form the foundation for future, more complex behaviors. As these more intricate behaviors become well learned, they encompass the earlier reflexes. Finally, it is possible that reflexes stimulate parts of the brain responsible for more complex behaviors, helping them develop (Zelazo, 1998; Myklebust & Gottlieb, 1993; Lipsitt, 2003).

Ethnic and Cultural Differences and Similarities in Reflexes. Although reflexes are, by definition, genetically determined and universal throughout all infants, there are actually some cultural variations in the ways they are displayed. For instance, consider the *Moro reflex* (often called the *startle response*), which is activated when support for the neck and head is suddenly removed. The Moro reflex consists of the infant's arms thrusting outward and then appearing to seek to grasp onto something. Most scientists feel that the Moro reflex represents a leftover response that we humans have inherited from our nonhuman ancestors. The Moro reflex is an extremely useful behavior for monkey babies, who travel about by clinging to their mothers' backs. If they lose their grip, they fall down unless they are able to grasp quickly onto their mother's fur—using a Moro-like reflex (Prechtl, 1982; Zafeiriou, 2004).

The Moro reflex is found in all humans, but it appears with significantly different vigor in different children. Some differences reflect cultural and ethnic variations (Freedman, 1979). For instance, Caucasian infants show a pronounced response to situations that produce the Moro

TABLE 3.2	**Some Basic Reflexes in Infants**		
REFLEX	**APPROXIMATE AGE OF DISAPPEARANCE**	**DESCRIPTION**	**POSSIBLE FUNCTION**
Rooting reflex	3 weeks	Neonate's tendency to turn its head toward things that touch its cheek.	Food intake
Stepping reflex	2 months	Movement of legs when held upright with feet touching the floor.	Prepares infants for independent locomotion
Swimming reflex	4–6 months	Infant's tendency to paddle and kick in a sort of swimming motion when lying face down in a body of water.	Avoidance of danger
Moro reflex	6 months	Activated when support for the neck and head is suddenly removed. The arms of the infant are thrust outward and then appear to grasp onto something.	Similar to primates' protection from falling
Babinski reflex	8–12 months	An infant fans out its toes in response to a stroke on the outside of its foot.	Unknown
Startle reflex	Remains in different form	An infant, in response to a sudden noise, flings out its arms, arches its back, and spreads its fingers.	Protection
Eye-blink reflex	Remains	Rapid shutting and opening of eye on exposure to direct light.	Protection of eye from direct light
Sucking reflex	Remains	Infant's tendency to suck at things that touch its lips.	Food intake
Gag reflex	Remains	An infant's reflex to clear its throat.	Prevents choking

reflex. Not only do they fling out their arms, but they also cry and respond in a generally agitated manner. In contrast, Navajo babies react to the same situation much more calmly. Their arms do not flail out as much, and they cry only rarely.

Revving Up the Motor Skills

Anya sat in the sandbox at the park, chatting with the other parents and playing with her two children, 5-year-old Nicholai and 13-month-old Sofia. While she chatted, she kept a close eye on Sofia, who would still put sand in her mouth sometimes if she wasn't stopped. Today, however, Sofia seemed content to run the sand through her hands and try to put it into a bucket. Nicholai, meanwhile, was busy with two other boys, rapidly filling and emptying the other sand buckets to build an elaborate sand city, which they would then destroy with toy trucks.

When children of different ages gather at a playground, it's easy to see that preschool children have come a long way in their motor development since infancy. Both their gross and their fine motor skills have become increasingly fine-tuned. Sofia, for example, is still mastering putting sand into a bucket, while her brother, Nicolai, uses that skill easily as part of his larger goal of building a sand city.

Gross Motor Skills.   Probably no physical changes are more obvious—and more eagerly anticipated—than the increasing array of motor skills that babies acquire during infancy. Most parents can remember their child's first steps with a sense of pride and awe at how quickly she or he changed from a helpless infant, unable even to roll over, into a person who could navigate quite effectively in the world.

Even though the motor skills of newborn infants are not terribly sophisticated, at least compared with attainments that will soon appear, young infants still are able to accomplish some kinds of movement. For instance, when placed on their stomachs they wiggle their arms and legs and may try to lift their heavy heads. As their strength increases, they are able to push hard enough against the surface on which they are resting to propel their bodies in different directions. They often end up moving backwards rather than forwards, but by the age of 6 months they become rather accomplished at moving themselves in particular directions. These initial efforts are the forerunners of crawling, in which babies coordinate the motions of their arms and legs and propel themselves forward. Crawling appears typically between 8 and 10 months. (Figure 3.12 provides a summary of some of the milestones of normal motor development.)

Walking comes later. At around the age of 9 months, most infants are able to walk by supporting themselves on furniture, and half of all infants can walk well by the end of their first year of life.

At the same time infants are learning to move around, they are perfecting the ability to remain in a stationary sitting position. At first, babies cannot remain seated upright without support. But they quickly master this ability, and most are able to sit without support by the age of 6 months.

By the time they are 3 years old, children have mastered a variety of skills: jumping, hopping on one foot, skipping, and running. By ages 4 and 5, their skills have become more refined as they have gained greater control over their muscles. For instance, at age 4 they can throw a ball with enough accuracy that a friend can catch it, and by age 5 they can toss a ring and have it land on a peg 5 feet away. Five-year-olds can learn to ride bikes, climb ladders, and ski downhill—activities that all require considerable coordination (Clark & Humphrey, 1985; Williams & Monsma, 2007). Table 3.3 summarizes major gross motor skills that emerge during the preschool years.

Activity Level.   The advances in gross motor skills are related to brain development and myelination of neurons in areas of the brain related to balance and coordination. Another reason motor skills develop at such a rapid clip during the preschool years is that children spend a great deal of time practicing them. During this period, the general level of activity is extraordinarily high: Preschoolers seem to be perpetually in motion. In fact, the activity level is higher at age 3 than at any other point in the entire life span. In addition, as they age, preschoolers' general physical agility increases (Poest et al., 1990; Planinsec, 2001).

Despite generally high activity levels, there are also significant variations among children. Some differences are related to inherited temperament. Because of temperamental factors, children who are unusually active during infancy tend to continue to be so during the preschool years, whereas those who are relatively docile during infancy generally remain fairly docile dur-

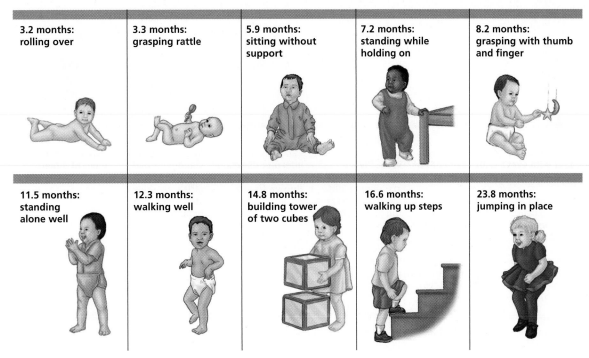

FIGURE 3.12 Milestones of Motor Development
Fifty percent of children are able to perform each skill at the month indicated in the figure. However, the specific timing at which each skill appears varies widely. For example, one-quarter of children are able to walk well at 11.1 months; by 14.9 months, 90% of children are walking well. Is knowledge of such average benchmarks helpful or harmful to parents?
Source: Adapted from Frankenburg et al., 1992.

ing those years. Furthermore, monozygotic (identical) twins tend to show more similar activity levels than do dizygotic twins, a fact that suggests the importance of genetics in determining activity level (Wood et al., 2007).

Of course, genetics is not the sole determinant of preschoolers' activity levels. Environmental factors, such as a parent's style of discipline and, more broadly, a particular culture's view of what is appropriate and inappropriate behavior, also play a role. Some cultures are fairly lenient in allowing preschoolers to play vigorously, whereas others are considerably more restrictive.

Ultimately, a combination of genetic and environmental factors determines just how active a child will be. But the preschool period generally represents the most active time of the child's entire life.

TABLE 3.3   Major Gross Motor Skills in Early Childhood

3-YEAR-OLDS	4-YEAR-OLDS	5-YEAR-OLDS
Cannot turn or stop suddenly or quickly	Have more effective control of stopping, starting, and turning	Start, turn, and stop effectively in games
Jump a distance of 15 to 24 inches	Jump a distance of 24 to 33 inches	Can make a running jump of 28 to 36 inches
Ascend a stairway unaided, alternating the feet	Descend a long stairway alternating the feet, if supported	Descend a long stairway alternating the feet
Can hop, using largely an irregular series of jumps with some variations added	Hop 4 to 6 steps on one foot	Easily hop a distance of 16 feet

Source: Corbin, 1973.

6 Years	7 Years	8 Years	9 Years	10 Years	11 Years	12 Years
Girls superior in accuracy of movement; boys superior in more forceful, less complex acts. Can throw with the proper weight shift and step. Acquire the ability to skip.	Can balance on one foot with eyes closed. Can walk on a 2-inch-wide balance beam without falling off. Can hop and jump accurately into small squares (hopscotch). Can correctly execute a jumping-jack exercise.	Can grip objects with 12 pounds of pressure. Can engage in alternate rhythmical hopping in a 2-2, 2-3, or 3-3 pattern. Girls can throw a small ball 33 feet; boys can throw a small ball 59 feet. The number of games participated in by both sexes is the greatest at this age.	Girls can jump vertically 8.5 inches over their standing height plus reach; boys can jump vertically 10 inches. Boys can run 16.6 feet per second; girls can run 16 feet per second.	Can judge and intercept directions of small balls thrown from a distance. Both girls and boys can run 17 feet per second.	Boys can achieve standing broad jump of 5 feet; girls can achieve standing broad jump of 4.5 feet.	Can achieve high jump of 3 feet.

FIGURE 3.13 Gross Motor Skills Developed Between the Ages of 6 and 12 Years
Why would it be important that a social worker be aware of this period of development?
Source: Adapted from Cratty, 1978, p. 222.

**FROM AN
EDUCATOR'S
PERSPECTIVE:**
How might culture influence activity level in children? What might the long-term effects be on children influenced in this way?

Cultural influences affect the rate of the development of motor skills.

Continued Development of Gross Motor Skills. Later, during the school years, muscle coordination in particular improves. Watching a softball player pitch a ball past a batter to her catcher, a runner reach the finish line in a race, or a jump-roper execute complex movements involving the feet, legs, body, and arms, we are struck by the huge strides that these children have made since the more awkward days of preschool.

During middle childhood, children master many types of skills that earlier they could not perform well. For instance, most school-age children can readily learn to ride a bike, ice skate, swim, and skip rope (Cratty, 1986; see Figure 3.13).

Gender Differences in Gross Motor Skills. Girls and boys differ in several aspects of gross motor coordination. In part, this difference is produced by variations in muscle strength, which is somewhat greater in boys than in girls. For instance, boys can typically throw a ball better and jump higher. Furthermore, boys' overall activity levels are generally greater than girls' (Pelligrini & Smith, 1998; Olds et al., 2009).

Although they are not as strong as boys and have lower overall activity levels, girls generally surpass boys in tasks that involve the coordination of their arms and legs. For instance, at the age of 5, girls are better than boys at performing jumping jacks and balancing on one foot (Cratty, 1979; Pollatou, Karadimou, & Gerodimos, 2005).

The gender differences on some tasks involving gross motor skills are due to a number of factors. In addition to genetically determined differences in strength and activity levels, social factors likely play a role. As we will discuss later, gender increasingly determines the sorts of activities that society views as appropriate for girls and appropriate for boys. For instance, if the games that are considered acceptable for preschool boys tend to involve gross motor skills more than the games deemed appropriate for girls, boys will have more practice than girls in gross motor activities and ultimately be more proficient in them (Golombok & Fivush, 1994; Yee & Brown, 1994; Haines, 2003).

Regardless of their gender, however, children typically show significant improvement in their gross motor skills during the preschool years. Such improvement permits them by the time they are 5 to climb ladders, play follow-the-leader, and snowboard with relative ease. And when

TABLE 3.4	Milestones of Fine Motor Development
AGE (MONTHS)	**SKILL**
3	Opens hand prominently
3	Grasps rattle
8	Grasps with thumb and finger
11	Holds crayon adaptively
16	Places pegs in board
24	Imitates strokes on paper
33	Copies circle

Source: Adapted from Frankenburg et al., 1992.

comparisons are made between boys and girls who regularly take part in similar activities—such as softball—gender variations in gross motor skills are minimal (Hall & Lee, 1984; Jurimae & Saar, 2003).

Why the change? Expectations probably played a role. Society did not expect girls to be highly active physically and told girls that they would do worse than boys in sports, and the girls' performance reflected that message.

Today, however, society's message has changed, at least officially. For instance, the American Academy of Pediatrics suggests that boys and girls should engage in the same sports and games, and that they can do so together in mixed-gender groups. There is no reason to separate the sexes in physical exercise and sports until puberty, when the smaller size of females begins to make them more susceptible to injury in contact sports (Raudsepp & Liblik, 2002; Vilhjalmsson & Kristjansdottir, 2003; American Academy of Pediatrics, 1989, 2004).

Fine Motor Skills.   As infants are perfecting their gross motor skills, such as sitting upright and walking, they are also making advances in their fine motor skills (see Table 3.4). For instance, by the age of 3 months, infants show some ability to coordinate the movements of their limbs.

Furthermore, although infants are born with a rudimentary ability to reach toward an object, this ability is neither very sophisticated nor very accurate, and it disappears around the age of 4 weeks. A different, more precise, form of reaching reappears at 4 months. It takes some time for infants to coordinate successful grasping after they reach out, but in fairly short order they are able to reach out and hold onto an object of interest (Claxton, Keen, & McCarty, 2003).

The sophistication of fine motor skills continues to grow. By the age of 11 months, infants are able to pick up off the ground objects as small as marbles—something caregivers need to be concerned about, since the next place such objects often go is the mouth. By the time they are 2 years old, children can carefully hold a cup, bring it to their lips, and take a drink without spilling a drop.

Grasping, like other motor advances, follows a sequential developmental pattern in which simple skills are combined into more sophisticated ones. For example, infants first begin picking things up with their whole hand. As they get older, they use a *pincer grasp,* where thumb and index finger meet to form a circle. The pincer grasp allows for considerably more precise motor control.

As children move further into the preschool and school years, their ability to use fine motor skills, which involve smaller, more delicate body movements, grows apace. After infancy, fine motor skills encompass such varied activities as using a fork and spoon, cutting with scissors, tying one's shoelaces, typing at a keyboard, writing in cursive, and playing the piano.

The skills involved in fine motor movements require a good deal of practice, as anyone knows who has watched a 4-year-old struggling painstakingly to copy letters of the alphabet. Yet fine motor skills show clear developmental patterns (see Table 3.5 on page 96). At the age of 3, children can undo their clothes when they go to the bathroom, they can put a simple jigsaw puzzle together, and they can fit blocks of different shapes into matching holes. However, they do not show much polish in accomplishing such tasks; for instance, they may try to force puzzle pieces into place.

TABLE 3.5	Fine Motor Skills in Early Chilhood	
3-YEAR-OLDS	**4-YEAR-OLDS**	**5-YEAR-OLDS**
Cuts paper	Folds paper into triangles	Folds paper into halves and quarters
Pastes using finger	Prints name	Draws triangle, rectangle, circle
Builds bridge with three blocks	Strings beads	Uses crayons effectively
Draws ○ and +	Copies X	Creates clay objects
Draws doll	Builds bridge with five blocks	Copies letters
Pours liquid from pitcher without spilling	Pours from various containers	Copies two short words
Completes simple jigsaw puzzle	Opens and positions clothespins	

By the ages of 4, their fine motor skills are considerably better. For example, they can fold paper into triangular designs and print their name with a crayon. And by the time they are 5, most children are able to hold and manipulate a thin pencil properly.

By ages 6 and 7, children are able to tie their shoes and fasten buttons; by age 8, they can use each hand independently; and by 11 and 12, they can manipulate objects with almost as much capability as they will show in adulthood.

One reason for advances in fine motor skills is that the amount of myelin in the brain increases significantly between the ages of 6 and 8 (Lecours, 1982). *Myelin* provides protective insulation that surrounds parts of nerve cells. Because increased levels of myelin raise the speed at which electrical impulses travel between neurons, messages can reach muscles more rapidly and control them better. (Also see the Development Diversity box.)

Developmental Norms: Comparing the Individual to the Group.   Keep in mind that the timing of the milestones in motor development that we have been discussing is based on norms. **Norms** represent the average performance of a large sample of children of a given age. They permit comparisons between a particular child's performance on a particular behavior and the average performance of the children in the norm sample.

For instance, one of the most widely used techniques to determine infants' normative standing is the **Brazelton Neonatal Behavior Assessment Scale (NBAS)**, a measure designed to determine infants' neurological and behavioral responses to their environment.

Taking about 30 minutes to administer, the NBAS includes 27 separate categories of responses that constitute four general aspects of infants' behavior: interactions with others (such as alertness and cuddliness), motor behavior, physiological control (such as the ability to be soothed after being upset), and responses to stress (Brazelton, 1973, 1990; Davis & Emory, 1995; Canals et al., 2003).

Although the norms provided by scales such as the NBAS are useful in making broad generalizations about the timing of various behaviors and skills, they must be interpreted with caution. Because norms are averages, they mask substantial individual differences in the times when children attain various achievements.

Norms are useful only to the extent that they are based on data from a large, heterogeneous, culturally diverse sample of children. Unfortunately, many of the norms on which developmental researchers have traditionally relied have been based on groups of infants who are predominantly Caucasian and from the middle and upper socioeconomic strata (e.g., Gesell, 1946). The reason: Much of the research was conducted on college campuses, using the children of graduate students and faculty.

This limitation would not be critical if no differences existed in the timing of development in children from different cultural, racial, and social groups. But they do. For example, as a group, African American babies show more rapid motor development than Caucasian babies throughout infancy. Moreover, there are significant variations related to cultural factors, as we discuss next (Werner, 1972; Keefer et al., 1991; Gartstein et al., 2003; deOnis et al., 2007).

norms   the average performance of a large sample of children of a given age.

Brazelton Neonatal Behavioral Assessment Scale (NBAS)   a measure designed to determine infants' neurological and behavioral responses to their environment.

DEVELOPMENTAL DIVERSITY
The Cultural Dimensions of Motor Development

Among the Ache people, who live in the rain forest of South America, infants face an early life of physical restriction. Because the Ache lead a nomadic existence, living in a series of tiny camps in the rain forest, open space is at a premium. Consequently, for the first few years of life, infants spend nearly all their time in direct physical contact with their mothers. Even when they are not physically touching their mothers, they are permitted to venture no more than a few feet away.

Infants among the Kipsigis people, who live in a more open environment in rural Kenya, Africa, lead quite a different existence. Their lives are filled with activity and exercise. Parents seek to teach their children to sit up, stand, and walk from the earliest days of infancy. For example, very young infants are placed in shallow holes in the ground designed to keep them in an upright position. Parents begin to teach their children to walk starting at the eighth week of life. The infants are held with their feet touching the ground, and they are pushed forward.

Clearly, the infants in these two societies lead very different lives (Super, 1976; Kaplan & Dove, 1987; Super & Harkness, 1999). But do the relative lack of early motor stimulation for Ache infants and the efforts of the Kipsigis to encourage motor development really make a difference?

The answer is both yes and no. It's yes, in that Ache infants tend to show delayed motor development, relative both to Kipsigis infants and to children raised in Western societies. Although their social abilities are no different, Ache children tend to begin walking at around 23 months, about a year later than the typical child in the United States. In contrast, Kipsigis children, who are encouraged in their motor development, learn to sit up and walk several weeks earlier, on average, than U.S. children.

In the long run, however, the differences between Ache, Kipsigis, and Western children disappear. By late childhood, about age 6, there is no evidence of differences in general, overall motor skills among Ache, Kipsigis, and Western children.

As we see with the Ache and Kipsgis babies, variations in the timing of motor skills seem to depend in part on parental expectations of what is the "appropriate" schedule for the emergence of specific skills. For instance, one study examined the motor skills of infants who lived in a single city in England, but whose mothers varied in ethnic origin. In the research, English, Jamaican, and Indian mothers' expectations were first assessed regarding several markers of their infants' motor skills. The Jamaican mothers expected their infants to sit and walk significantly earlier than the English and Indian mothers, and the actual emergence of these activities was in line with their expectations. The source of the Jamaican infants' earlier mastery seemed to lie in the treatment of the children by their parents. For instance, Jamaican mothers gave their children practice in stepping quite early in infancy (Hopkins & Westra, 1989, 1990).

In sum, cultural factors help determine the time at which specific motor skills appear. Activities that are an intrinsic part of a culture are more apt to be purposely taught to infants in that culture, leading to the potential of their earlier emergence (Nugent, Lester, & Brazelton, 1989; Nixon-Cave, 2001).

Potty Wars. Another aspect of muscular skills—one that parents of toddlers often find most problematic—is bowel and bladder control. The timing and nature of toilet training are controversial issues.

Ann Wright, of University Park, Maryland, woke up on a sweltering night in June at 3 a.m., her head spinning as she reenacted the previous day's parenting trauma: She and her husband, Oliver, had told their 4-year-old daughter, Elizabeth, on Thursday night that it was time for her to stop using her pull-up training pants. For the next 18 $\frac{1}{2}$ hours, the girl had withheld her urine, refusing to use the toilet.

"We had been talking to her for months about saying goodbye to the pull-ups, and she seemed ready," says Wright. "But on the day of the big break she refused to sit on the toilet. Two hours before she finally went, she was crying and constantly moving, clearly uncomfortable."

Eventually the child wet herself. (Gerhardt, 1999, p. Z10)

Few child-care issues raise as much concern among parents as toilet training. And on few issues are there so many opposing opinions from experts and laypersons. Often the various viewpoints are played out in the media and even take on political overtones. On the one hand, for instance, the well-known pediatrician T. Berry Brazelton (1997; Brazelton et al., 1999) suggests a flexible approach to toilet training, advocating that it be put off until the child shows signs of readiness. On the other hand, psychologist John Rosemond, known primarily for his media advocacy of a conservative, traditional stance to childrearing, argues for a more rigid approach, saying that toilet training should be done early and quickly.

What is clear is that the age at which toilet training takes place has been rising over the past few decades. For example, in 1957, fully 92 percent of children were toilet trained by the age of 18 months. In 1999, only 25 percent were toilet trained at that age, and just 60 percent at 36 months. Two percent were still not toilet-trained at the age of 4 (Goode, 1999).

The current guidelines of the American Academy of Pediatrics support Brazelton's position, suggesting that there is no single time to begin toilet training and that training should begin only when children show that they are ready. Children have no bladder or bowel control until the age of 12 months and only slight control for 6 months after that. Although some children show signs of readiness for toilet training between 18 and 24 months, some are not ready until 30 months or older (American Academy of Pediatrics, 1999b; Stadtler, Gorski, & Brazelton, 1999).

Handedness: Separating Righties from Lefties.   How do preschoolers decide which hand to hold the pencil in as they work on their copying and other fine motor skills? For many, their choice was established soon after birth.

By the end of the preschool years, most children show a clear preference for the use of one hand over the other—the development of **handedness**. Actually, some signals of future handedness are seen early in infancy, when infants may show a preference for one side of the body over the other. By the age of 7 months, some infants seem to favor one hand by grabbing more with it than the other. Many children, however, show no preference until the end of the preschool years (Saudino & McManus, 1998; Segalowitz & Rapin, 2003).

By the age of 5, most children display a clear tendency to use one hand over the other, with 90 percent being right-handed and 10 percent left-handed. More boys than girls are left-handed.

Much speculation has been devoted to the meaning of handedness, fueled in part by long-standing myths about the sinister nature of left-handedness. (The word *sinister* itself is derived from a Latin word meaning "on the left.") In Islamic cultures, for instance, the left hand is generally used when going to the toilet, and it is considered uncivilized to serve food with that hand. In Christian art, portrayals of the devil often show him as left-handed.

However, there is no scientific basis for myths that suggest that there is something wrong with being left-handed. In fact, some evidence exists that left-handedness may be associated with certain advantages. For example, a study of 100,000 students who took the Scholastic Assessment Test (SAT) showed that 20 percent in the highest-scoring category were left-handed, double the proportion of left-handed people in the general population. Such gifted individuals as Michelangelo, Leonardo da Vinci, Benjamin Franklin, and Pablo Picasso were left-handed (Bower, 1985).

Although some educators of the past tried to force left-handed children to use the right hand, particularly when learning to write, that attitude has changed. Most teachers now encourage children to use whichever hand they prefer. Still, most left-handed people will agree that the design of desks, scissors, and most other everyday objects favors the right-handed. The world is so "right biased" that it may prove to be a dangerous place for lefties: Left-handed people have more accidents and are at greater risk of dying younger than right-handed people (Ellis & Engh, 2000; Bhushan & Khan, 2006; Dutta & Mandal, 2006).

Art: The Picture of Development.   It is a basic feature of many kitchens: the refrigerator covered with recent art created by the children of the house. Yet the art that children create is far more important than mere kitchen decoration. Developmentalists suggest that art plays an important role in honing fine motor skills, as well as in several other aspects of development (Morra, 2008).

handedness   the preference of using one hand over the other.

At the most basic level, the production of art involves practice with tools such as paint-brushes, crayons, pencils, and markers. As preschoolers learn to manipulate these tools, they gain motor control skills that will help them as they learn to write.

But art also teaches several important lessons. For example, children learn the importance of planning, restraint, and self-correction. When 3-year-olds pick up a brush, they tend to swish it across the page, with little thought of the ultimate product. By the time they are 5, however, children spend more time thinking about and planning the final product. They are more likely to have a goal in mind when they start out, and when they are finished, they examine their creation to see how successful they have been. Older children will also produce the same artwork over and over, seeking to overcome their previous errors and improve the final product.

According to developmental psychologist Howard Gardner, the rough, unformed art of preschoolers represents the equivalent of linguistic babbling in infants. He argues that the random marks that young preschoolers make contain all the building blocks of more sophisticated creations that will be produced later (Gardner, 1989; Golumb, 2002, 2003).

Other researchers suggest that children's art proceeds through a series of stages during the preschool years (Kellogg, 1970; Winner, 2006). The first is the *scribbling* stage, in which the end product appears to be random scrawls across a paper. But this is not the case: Instead, scribbles can be categorized, consisting of 20 distinct types, such as horizontal lines and zigzags.

The *shape* stage, which is reached around the age of 3, is marked by the appearance of shapes such as squares and circles. In this stage, children draw shapes of various sorts, as well as X's and plus signs. After reaching this stage, they soon move into the *design* stage, which is characterized by the ability to combine more than one simple shape into a more complex one. Finally, children enter the *pictorial* stage between the ages of 4 and 5. At this point, drawings begin to approximate recognizable objects.

The depiction of recognizable real-world objects, known as representational art, may appear to be a substantial advance over previous art, and adults often strongly encourage its creation. However, in some respects this change to representational art is regrettable, for it marks a shift in focus away from an interest in form and design. Because form and design are important and in some ways essential, a focus on representation may ultimately have disadvantages. As the great artist Pablo Picasso once remarked, "It has taken me a whole lifetime to learn to draw like children" (Winner, 1989).

REVIEW

▶ Brain growth is very fast during infancy, mostly because of a startling increase in the number of interconnections among neurons and the amount of myelin produced. Billions of connections form immediately after birth, and the brain shows a great deal of plasticity, or susceptibility to environmental influences. Later, the number of neurons and connections decreases as a result of the infant's experiences.

▶ Infants are born with an array of reflexes that protect the baby through involuntary behavior until it can protect itself. In addition, reflexes may form the foundation of future, more complex behaviors.

▶ From newborns with little mobility or strength, children quickly learn to push their bodies up, sit up, crawl, walk, jump, hop, run, and eventually perform sports activities that rely on both the gross and fine motor skills. Motor development and control continue through late into the life span.

APPLY

▶ Do you think that differences in males' and females' motor skills are primarily innate or environmental? Why? Will differences eventually disappear?

▶ By definition reflexes are genetically determined and universal throughout all infants, yet there are actually some cultural variations in the ways they are displayed. What are some examples?

MODULE 3.3

Perceptual Development

Ryan was thrilled to finally reach first grade. On the "Wishing Star" he made for Parents' Night, he had his teacher write his wish for the year: "My #1 wish: I want to read and write."

But reading and writing were proving difficult for Ryan. It was hard for him to decode even simple words, and hand–eye coordination made writing a chore, often resulting in a heavily smudged page.

In most ways, Ryan's physical and cognitive development was right on target for his 7 years. He was an enthusiastic hiker, and he was able to memorize complex stories. Testing showed that Ryan's intelligence was above average, but vision and motor problems were frustrating his attempts to achieve normal developmental goals.

These frustrations affected Ryan's social development, too. As a child who spent several hours each day in the special needs room, who could neither track the path of a soccer ball during a game nor ride a two-wheel bike, his social status was low. Several peers made fun of him, and he responded by withdrawing further into himself.

Ryan's parents and teachers kept in constant contact to discuss how best to support him both academically and socially. He worked with a reading specialist, and the school provided physical therapy services to help Ryan develop his motor skills.

The early intervention worked. It boosted Ryan's grades and his self-esteem. By the end of second grade, he was riding his bike all over the neighborhood, reading at a sixth-grade level, and writing rather than dictating stories about his favorite subject—pirates. In the regular classroom all day now, he made three close friends with whom he played "Star Wars" at recess, a happy, laughing, confident child.

In middle childhood, children enter school eager to learn all they can about the world. Often the regular classroom setting serves them well and contributes to their physical, intellectual, and social development; sometimes, however, children display needs or deficits that require special interventions—such as the reading specialist and physical therapist provided for Ryan—to make the most of their abilities and keep their self-esteem intact.

The Development of the Senses

FIGURE 3.14 Visual Cliff
The "visual cliff" experiment examines the depth perception of infants. Most infants in the age range of 6 to 14 months cannot be coaxed to cross the cliff, apparently responding to the fact that the patterned area drops several feet.

Organizing the Sensory World. William James, one of the founding fathers of psychology, believed that the world of the infant is a "blooming, buzzing confusion" (James, 1890/1950). Was he right?

In this case, James's wisdom failed him. The newborn's sensory world does lack the clarity and stability that we can distinguish as adults, but day by day the world grows increasingly comprehensible as the infant's ability to sense and perceive the environment develops. Babies appear to thrive in an environment enriched by pleasing sensations.

The processes that underlie infants' understanding of the world around them are sensation and perception. **Sensation** is the physical stimulation of the sense organs, and **perception** is the mental process of sorting out, interpreting, analyzing, and integrating stimuli from the sense organs and brain.

The study of infants' capabilities in the realm of sensation and perception challenges the ingenuity of investigators. As we'll see, researchers have developed a number of procedures for understanding sensation and perception in different realms.

Infants' Eyesight. From the time of Lee Eng's birth, everyone who met him felt that he gazed at them intently. His eyes seemed

A neonate's view of the world is limited to 8 to 14 inches. Objects beyond that distance are fuzzy.

A month after birth, newborns' vision has improved, but still lacks clarifying detail.

By 3 months, objects are seen with clarity.

to meet those of visitors. They seemed to bore deeply and knowingly into the faces of people who looked at him.

How good in fact was Lee's vision, and what, precisely, could he make out of his environment? Quite a bit, at least up close. According to some estimates, a newborn's distance vision ranges from 20/200 to 20/600, which means that an infant can only see with accuracy visual material up to 20 feet that an adult with normal vision is able to see with similar accuracy from a distance of between 200 and 600 feet (Haith, 1991).

These figures indicate that infants' distance vision is 1/10th to 1/3rd that of the average adult. This isn't so bad, actually: The vision of newborns provides the same degree of distance acuity as the uncorrected vision of many adults who wear eyeglasses or contact lenses. Furthermore, infants' distance vision grows increasingly acute. By 6 months of age, the average infant's vision is already 20/20—in other words, identical to that of adults (Aslin, 1987; Cavallini et al., 2002).

Depth perception is a particularly useful ability, helping babies acknowledge heights and avoid falls. In a classic study, developmental psychologists Eleanor Gibson and Richard Walk (1960) placed infants on a sheet of heavy glass. A checkered pattern appeared under one-half of the glass sheet, making it seem that the infant was on a stable floor. However, in the middle of the glass sheet, the pattern dropped down several feet, forming an apparent "visual cliff." The question Gibson and Walk asked was whether infants would willingly crawl across the cliff when called by their mothers (see Figure 3.14).

The results were clear: Most of the infants in the study, who ranged in age from 6 to 14 months, could not be coaxed over the apparent cliff. Clearly, most of them had already developed the ability to perceive depth by that age (Gibson & Walk, 1960; Campos, Langer, & Krowitz, 1970).

Infants also show clear visual preferences, preferences that are present from birth. Given a choice, infants reliably prefer to look at stimuli that include patterns than to look at simpler stimuli (see Figure 3.15). How do we know? Developmental psychologist Robert Fantz (1963) created a classic test. He built a chamber in which babies could lie on their backs and see pairs of visual stimuli above them. Fantz could determine which of the stimuli the infants were looking at by observing the reflections of the stimuli in their eyes.

Fantz's work was the impetus for a great deal of research on the preferences of infants, most of which points to a critical conclusion: Infants are genetically preprogrammed to prefer particular kinds of stimuli. For instance, just minutes after birth they show preferences for certain colors, shapes, and configurations of various stimuli. They prefer curved to straight lines, three-dimensional figures to two-dimensional ones, and human faces to nonfaces. Such capabilities may point to the existence of highly specialized cells in the brain that react to stimuli of a particular pattern, orientation, shape, and direction of movement (Rubenstein, Kalakanis, & Langlois, 1999; Hubel & Wiesel, 1979, 2004; Kellman & Arterberry, 2006).

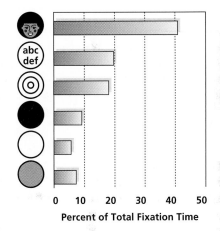

Percent of Total Fixation Time

FIGURE 3.15 Preferring Complexity
In a classic experiment, researcher Robert Fantz found that 2- and 3-month-old infants preferred to look at more complex stimuli than simple ones.
Source: Adapted from Fantz, 1961.

sensation the physical stimulation of the sense organs.

perception the sorting out, interpretation, analysis, and integration of stimuli involving the sense organs and brain.

Genetics is not the sole determinant of infant visual preferences. Just a few hours after birth, infants have already learned to prefer their own mother's face to other faces. Similarly, between the ages of 6 and 9 months, infants become more adept at distinguishing between the faces of humans, while they become less able to distinguish the faces of members of other species. They also distinguish between male and female faces. Such findings provide another clear piece of evidence of how heredity and environmental experiences are woven together to determine an infant's capabilities (Pascalis, deHaan, & Nelson, 2002; Ramsey-Rennels & Langlois, 2006; Turati et al., 2006).

Auditory Perception: Sound in Infancy. What is it about a mother's lullaby that helps soothe a crying baby? Some clues emerge when we look at the capabilities of infants in the realm of auditory sensation and perception.

Infants hear from the time of birth—and even before, as the ability to hear begins prenatally. Even in the womb, the fetus responds to sounds outside of its mother. Furthermore, infants are born with preferences for particular sound combinations (Schellenberg & Trehub, 1996; Trehub, 2003).

Because they have had some practice in hearing before birth, it is not surprising that infants have reasonably good auditory perception after they are born. Infants actually are more sensitive to certain very high and very low frequencies than adults—a sensitivity that seems to increase during the first 2 years of life. However, infants are initially less sensitive than adults to middle-range frequencies, though eventually their capabilities within the middle range improve (Fenwick & Morongiello, 1991; Werner & Marean, 1996; Frenald, 2001).

In addition to the ability to detect sound, infants need several other abilities in order to hear effectively. For instance, *sound localization* permits us to pinpoint the direction from which a sound is emanating. Compared to adults, infants have a slight handicap in this task because effective sound localization requires the use of the slight difference in the times at which a sound reaches our two ears. Sound that we hear first in the right ear tells us that the source of the sound is to our right. Because infants' heads are smaller than those of adults, the difference in timing of the arrival of sound at the two ears is less than it is in adults, so they have difficulty determining from which direction sound is coming.

Despite the potential limitation brought about by their smaller heads, infants' sound localization abilities are fairly good even at birth, and they reach adult levels of success by the age of 1 year. Furthermore, young infants are capable of making the fine discriminations that their future understanding of language will require (Bijeljac-Babic, Bertoncini, & Mehler, 1993; Fenwick, Kimberley, &Morrongiello, 1998; Werner, 2007).

Smell and Taste in Infancy. What do infants do when they smell a rotten egg? Pretty much what adults do—crinkle their noses and generally look unhappy. On the other hand, the scent of bananas and butter evokes a pleasant reaction from infants (Steiner, 1979; Pomares, Schirrer, & Abadie, 2002).

The sense of smell is so well developed, even among very young infants, that at least some 12- to 18-day-old babies can distinguish their mothers on the basis of smell alone. For instance, in one experiment infants were exposed to the smell of gauze pads worn under the arms of adults the previous evening. Infants who were being breast-fed were able to distinguish their mothers' scent from those of other adults. However, not all infants could do this: Those who were being bottle-fed were unable to make the distinction. Moreover, both breast-fed and bottle-fed infants were unable to distinguish their fathers on the basis of odor (Porter, Bologh, & Malkin, 1988; Mizuno & Ueda, 2004).

Infants seem to have an innate sweet tooth (even before they have teeth!), and they show facial expressions of disgust when they taste something bitter. Very young infants smile when a sweet-tasting liquid is placed on their tongues. They also suck harder at a bottle if it is sweetened. Since breast milk has a sweet taste, it is possible that this preference may be part of our evolutionary heritage, retained because it offered a survival advantage (Porges, Lipsitt, & Lewis, 1993; Liem & Mennella, 2002; Silveira et al., 2007).

Infants' Sensitivity to Pain and Touch. Infants are born with the capacity to experience pain. Obviously, no one can be sure if the experience of pain in children is identical to that in adults, any more than we can tell if an adult friend who complains of a headache is experiencing pain that is more or less severe than our own pain when we have a headache.

NEUROSCIENCE AND DEVELOPMENT
Beyond Band-Aids: How Pain in Infancy Affects Pain in Adulthood

Over a decade ago, researchers discovered that newborns exposed to painful stimuli early in life experience changes in their later sensory processing. For example, premature infants exposed to painful medical procedures in the neonatal intensive care unit are less sensitive to pain at 18 months of age (Grunau et al., 1994).

Is this a lasting effect? To help answer this question, neuroscientists Jamie LaPrairie and Anne Murphy administered a drug called naloxone to laboratory rats injured at birth. Naloxone blocks the actions of endogenous opioid peptides, a substance in the brain that is released following an injury and that inhibits pain. These peptides also play an important role in motivation, emotion, and stress responses (LaPrairie & Murphy, 2009).

The birth-injured rats were again tested as adult animals, and their midbrain gray matter was examined to see if the birth trauma had altered the functioning of natural opioid. The researchers found that the level of endogenous opioid peptides in brain-injured rats was two times higher than that in nonbirth-injured rats. Apparently, their painful early-life trauma created a brain response with fewer receptors to permit optimal sensitivity to pain medications later in life.

One critical question is whether these findings can be generalized to humans, particularly to premature infants who may experience dozens of procedures after birth. Since neonatal procedures cause such discomfort, it is conceivable that it may produce a change in the wiring of children's brains in adulthood (Simons et al., 2003; LaPrairie & Murphy, 2009).

- *What advice might you provide to a friend who has just delivered a premature infant?*
- *What questions might you suggest be asked about the infant's care?*

What we do know is that pain produces distress in infants. Their heartbeat increases, they sweat, they show facial expressions of discomfort, and they change the intensity and tone of crying when they are hurt (Simons et al., 2003; Warnock & Sandrin, 2004).

There appears to be a developmental progression in reactions to pain. For example, a newborn infant who has her heel pricked for a blood test responds with distress, but it takes her several seconds to show the response. In contrast, only a few months later, the same procedure brings a much more immediate response. It is possible that the delayed reaction in infants is produced by the relatively slower transmission of information within the newborn's less developed nervous system (Anand & Hickey, 1992; Axia, Bonichini, & Benini, 1995; Puchalsi & Hummel, 2002; also see the *Neuroscience and Development* box above).

Responding to Touch. Touch is one of the most highly developed sensory systems in a newborn. It is also one of the first to develop; there is evidence that by 32 weeks after conception, the entire body is sensitive to touch. Furthermore, several of the basic reflexes present at birth, such as the rooting reflex, require touch sensitivity to operate: An infant must sense a touch near the mouth in order to seek automatically a nipple to suck (Haith, 1986; Byrd, Nelson, & Manthey, 2006).

Infants' abilities in the realm of touch are particularly helpful in their efforts to explore the world. Several theorists have suggested that one of the ways children gain information about the world is through touching. As mentioned earlier, at the age of 6 months, infants are apt to place almost any object in their mouths, apparently taking in data about its configuration from their sensory responses to the feel of it in their mouths (Ruff, 1989; Byrd et al., 2006).

Multimodal Perception: Combining Individual Sensory Inputs. When Eric Pettigrew was 7 months old, his grandparents presented him with a squeaky rubber doll. As soon as he saw it, he reached out for it, grasped it in his hand, and listened as it squeaked. He seemed delighted with the gift.

One way of considering Eric's sensory reaction to the doll is to focus on each of the senses individually: what the doll looked like to Eric, how it felt in his hand, and what it sounded like. This approach has dominated the study of sensation and perception in infancy.

Let's consider another approach, however: We might examine how the various sensory responses are integrated with one another. Instead of looking at each individual sensory response, we could consider how the responses work together and are combined to produce Eric's ultimate reaction. The **multimodal approach to perception** considers how information that is collected by various individual sensory systems is integrated and coordinated.

multimodal approach to perception the approach that considers how information that is collected by various individual sensory systems is integrated and coordinated.

affordances the option that a given situation or stimulus provides.

FROM A
HEALTH CARE WORKER'S
PERSPECTIVE:
Persons who are born without the use of one sense often develop unusual abilities in one or more other senses. What can health care professionals do to help infants who are lacking in a particular sense?

Although the multimodal approach is a relatively recent innovation in the study of how infants understand their sensory world, it raises some fundamental issues about the development of sensation and perception. For instance, some researchers argue that sensations are initially integrated with one another in the infant, while others maintain that the infant's sensory systems are initially separate and that brain development leads to increasing integration (Lickliter & Bahrick, 2000; De Gelder, 2000; Lewkowicz, 2002).

We do not know yet which view is correct. However, it does appear that by an early age infants are able to relate what they have learned about an object through one sensory channel to what they have learned about it through another. For instance, even 1-month-old infants are able to recognize by sight objects that they have previously held in their mouths but never seen. Clearly, some cross-talk between various sensory channels is already possible a month after birth (Steri & Spelke, 1988; Streri, 2003).

Infants' abilities at multimodal perception showcase the sophisticated perceptual abilities of infants, which continue to grow throughout the period of infancy. Such perceptual growth is aided by infants' discovery of **affordances**, the options that a given situation or stimulus provides. For example, infants learn that they might potentially fall when walking down a steep ramp—that is, the ramp *affords* the possibility of falling. Such knowledge is crucial as infants make the transition from crawling to walking. Similarly, infants learn that an object shaped in a certain way can slip out of their hands if not grasped correctly. For example, Eric is learning that his toy has several affordances: He can grab it and squeeze it, listen to it squeak, and even chew comfortably on it if he is teething (McCarty & Ashmead, 1999; Flom & Bahrick, 2007; Wilcox et al., 2007).

Sensory Development in Preschoolers. The increasing development of the brain permits improvements in the senses during the preschool period. For instance, brain maturation leads to better control of eye movements and focusing. Still, preschoolers' eyes are not as capable as they will be in later stages of development. Specifically, preschool-age children are unable to easily and precisely scan groupings of small letters, as is required when reading small print. Consequently, preschoolers who start to read often focus on just the initial letter of a word and guess at the rest—leading, as you might expect, to relatively frequent errors. It is not until they are approximately 6 years of age that children can effectively focus and scan. Even at this point, however, they still don't have the capabilities of adults (Willows, Kruk, & Corcos, 1993; Burgund & Abernathy, 2008).

Preschool-age children also begin a gradual shift in the way they view objects made up of multiple parts. For instance, consider the rather unusual vegetable-fruit-bird combination shown in Figure 3.16. Rather than identifying it as a bird, as most adults do, preschool-age children see the figure in terms of the parts that make it up ("carrots" and "cherries" and "a pear"). Not until they reach middle childhood, about the age of 7 or 8, do they begin to look at the figure in terms of both its overall organization and its parts ("a bird made of fruit").

Preschoolers' judgments of objects may reflect the way in which their eyes move when perceiving figures (Zaporozhets, 1965). Until the age of 3 or 4, preschoolers devote most of their looking to the insides of two-dimensional objects they are scanning, concentrating on the internal details and largely ignoring the perimeter of the figure. In contrast, 4- and 5-year-olds begin to look more at the surrounding boundaries of the figure, and at 6 and 7 years of age, they look at the outside systematically, with far less scanning of the inside. The result is a greater awareness of the overall organization of the figure.

Vision is not the only sense that improves during the preschool period. For instance, *auditory acuity*, or the sharpness of hearing, improves as well. However, because hearing is more fully developed at the start of the preschool period, the improvement is not as significant as with vision.

One area in which preschoolers' auditory acuity does show some deficits is in their ability to isolate specific sounds when many sounds are heard simultaneously (Trehub et al., 1988; Moores & Meadow-Orlans, 1990; McAdams & Drake, 2002). This deficiency may account for why some preschoolers are easily distracted by competing sounds in group situations such as classrooms.

FIGURE 3.16 Sensory Development
Preschool-age children who view this odd vegetable-fruit-bird combination focus on the components that make it up. Not until they reach middle childhood do they begin to look at the figure as a whole in addition to its parts.
Source: Elkind, 1978.

Sensory Difficulties in the School Years:
Visual, Auditory, and Speech Problems

Anyone who has lost his or her eyeglasses or a contact lens knows how difficult even basic, everyday tasks must be for the sensory impaired. To function without adequate vision, hearing, or speech poses a tremendous challenge.

BECOMING AN INFORMED CONSUMER OF DEVELOPMENT
Exercising Your Infant's Body and Senses

Recall how cultural expectations and environments affect the age at which various physical milestones, such as the first step, occur. Although most experts feel that attempts to accelerate physical and sensory-perceptual development yield little advantage, parents should ensure that their infants receive sufficient physical and sensory stimulation. There are several specific ways to accomplish this goal:

- Carry a baby in different positions—in a backpack, in a front-pack, or in a football hold with the infant's head in the palm of your hand and its feet lying on your arm. This lets the infant view the world from several perspectives.

- Let infants explore their environment. Don't contain them too long in a barren environment. Let them crawl or wander around—after first making the environment "childproof" by removing dangerous objects.

- Engage in "rough-and-tumble" play. Wrestling, dancing, and rolling around on the floor—if not violent—are activities that are fun and that stimulate older infants' motor and sensory systems.

- Let babies touch their food and even play with it. Infancy is too early to start teaching table manners.

- Provide toys that stimulate the senses, particularly toys that can stimulate more than one sense at a time. For example, brightly colored, textured toys with movable parts are enjoyable and help sharpen infants' senses.

Visual impairment has both a legal and an educational meaning. Legal impairment is defined precisely: *Blindness* is visual acuity below 20/200 after correction (meaning the inability to see at 20 feet what is typically seen at 200 feet), while *partial sightedness* is visual acuity of less than 20/70 after correction.

Even if a child is not legally blind, visual problems may seriously affect schoolwork. For one thing, the legal criterion pertains solely to distance vision, while most school tasks require close-up vision. The legal definition does not consider abilities in the perception of color, depth, and light either—all of which might influence a student's success. About one student in a thousand requires special education services due to visual impairment.

Most severe visual problems are identified fairly early, but an impairment can go undetected. Visual problems can also emerge gradually as development brings changes in the apparatus of the eye. Parents and teachers need to look out for frequent eye irritation (redness, sties, or infection), continual blinking and facial contortions when reading, holding reading material unusually close to the face, difficulty in writing, and frequent headaches, dizziness, or burning eyes. All are signs of visual problems.

Auditory impairments can cause social as well as academic problems since much peer interaction involves informal conversation. Hearing loss affects 1 to 2 percent of the school-age population (Yoshinaga-Itano, 2003; Smith, Bale, & White, 2005).

In some cases, hearing is impaired at only certain frequencies, or pitches. For example, the loss may be great at pitches in the normal speech range, yet minimal in other frequencies, such as those of very high or low sounds. Different levels of amplification at different frequencies may be required; a hearing aid that amplifies all frequencies equally may be ineffective, amplifying sounds the child can hear to an uncomfortable degree.

How a child adapts depends on when the hearing loss begins. The effects will likely be more severe in a child with little or no exposure to the sound of language, producing an inability to understand or produce speech. For a child who has learned language, hearing loss will not seriously affect subsequent linguistic development.

Severe and early loss of hearing can impair abstract thinking. Concrete concepts can be visually illustrated, but abstract concepts depend on language for meaning. For example, it is difficult to explain the concept of "freedom" or "soul" without use of language (Butler & Silliman, 2002; Marschark, Spencer, & Newsom, 2003).

Auditory difficulties may be accompanied by **speech impairments**, one of the most public types of exceptionality: Speech that deviates from the norm is obvious whenever the child speaks. It also interferes with communication and may produce maladjustment in the speaker. Speech impairments occur in around 3 to 5 percent of the school-age population (Bishop & Leonard, 2001).

Stuttering, the most common speech impairment, produces substantial disruption in the rhythm and fluency of speech. Despite much research, no specific cause has been identified. Occasional stuttering is not unusual in young children—or even normal adults—but chronic

Auditory impairments can produce both academic and social difficulties, and may lead to speech difficulties.

visual impairment a special need that involves significant loss of sight.

auditory impairment a special need that involves the loss of hearing or some aspect of hearing.

speech impairment speech that deviates so much from the speech of others that it calls attention to itself, interferes with communication, or produces maladjustment in the speaker.

stuttering substantial disruption in the rhythm and fluency of speech; the most common speech impairment.

Visual impairments can have profound effects on daily living.

stuttering can be a severe problem. Stuttering hinders communication and can be embarrassing or stressful for children, who may come to fear conversation and speaking aloud in class (Whaley & Parker, 2000; Altholz & Golensky, 2004).

Parents and teachers can help children who stutter by not drawing attention to the issue and by giving them sufficient time to finish what they are saying, no matter how protracted the statement becomes. It does not help stutterers to finish their sentences for them or otherwise correct their speech (Ryan, 2001).

The Senses in Adulthood

Soon after turning 40, Sharon Boker-Tov noticed that it took longer to bounce back from minor illnesses such as colds and the flu. Then she noticed changes in her eyesight: She needed more light to read fine print, and she had to adjust how far she held newspapers from her face in order to read them easily. Finally, she couldn't deny that the gray strands in her hair, which had first appeared in her late 20s, were becoming a virtual forest.

Middle Adulthood. The vision changes Sharon Boker-Tov experienced are so common that reading glasses and bifocals have become a stereotypical emblem of middle age. Like Sharon, most people notice changes in the sensitivity, not only of their eyes, but also of other sense organs. All the organs seem to shift at about the same rate, but the changes are particularly marked in vision and hearing.

Vision. Starting at around age 40, *visual acuity*—the ability to discern fine spatial detail in both close and distant objects—begins to decline. The shape of the eye's lens changes and its elasticity deteriorates, which makes it harder to focus images sharply onto the retina. The lens becomes less transparent, so less light passes through the eye (DiGiovanna, 1994; Uttl, 2006).

A nearly universal change in midlife is the loss of near vision, called **presbyopia**. Even people who have never needed glasses or contact lenses find themselves holding print at an increasing distance in order to bring it into focus. Eventually, they need reading glasses. For those who were already near-sighted, presbyopia may require bifocals or two sets of glasses (Kalsi, Heron, & Charman, 2001; Koopsmans & Kooijman, 2006).

Midlife brings other vision changes. Depth perception, distance perception, and the ability to see in three dimensions all decline. The loss of elasticity in the lens also impairs people's ability to adapt to darkness, making it more difficult to navigate a dark room (Spear, 1993; Stuen & Fischer, 2007).

Although normal aging brings changes in vision, in some cases disease is involved. One of the most frequent eye problems is glaucoma, which may, if left untreated, lead to blindness. **Glaucoma** occurs when pressure in the fluid of the eye increases, either because the fluid cannot drain properly or because too much is produced. Around 1 to 2 percent of people over age 40 are afflicted, and African Americans are particularly susceptible (Wilson, 1989).

Initially, the increased pressure may constrict the neurons involved in peripheral vision and lead to tunnel vision. Ultimately, the pressure can become so high that all nerve cells are constricted, which causes complete blindness. Fortunately, with early detection, glaucoma can be treated. Medication can reduce the pressure, as can surgery to restore normal drainage of eye fluid (Plosker & Keam, 2006).

Hearing. Hearing declines in acuity in midlife, though the changes tend to be less evident than those affecting vision.

Environmental factors cause some of the hearing losses. People who work near loud noises—such as airplane mechanics and construction workers—are more apt to suffer debilitating and permanent hearing loss.

Many changes are simply related to aging. Age brings a loss of *cilia* or *hair cells* in the inner ear, which transmit neural messages to the brain when vibrations bend them. Like the lens of the eye, the eardrum becomes less elastic with age, reducing sensitivity to sound (Wiley et al., 2005).

The ability to hear high-pitched, high-frequency sounds usually degrades first, a problem called **presbycusis**. About 12 percent of people between 45 and 65 suffer from presbycusis. Men are more prone to hearing loss than women, starting at around age 55. People with hearing problems may also have trouble identifying the direction and origin of a sound, a process called *sound localization* (Schneider, 1997; Versa & Mattos, 2007).

presbyopia   a nearly universal change in eyesight during middle adulthood that results in some loss of near vision.

glaucoma   a condition in which pressure in the fluid of the eye increases, either because the fluid cannot drain properly or because too much fluid is produced.

presbycusis   loss of the ability to hear sounds of high frequency.

Slowing down can be slowed down. In many cases, it's "use it or lose it."

Declines in hearing do not markedly affect most people in middle age. Many compensate for any losses relatively easily—by asking people to speak up, turning up the volume of a television set, or paying closer attention to what others are saying.

Reaction Time in Adulthood: Not-So-Slowing Down. One common concern is that people slow down once they reach middle adulthood. Such a worry is not valid in most cases. Reaction time does increase (i.e., it takes longer to react to a stimulus), but usually the increase is mild and hardly noticeable. For instance, reaction time in responding to a loud noise increases by about 20 percent from age 20 to 60. Tasks requiring the coordination of various skills—such as driving a car—show less of an increase. Still, it takes more time to move the foot from the gas pedal to the brake when a driver faces an emergency situation. Changes in the speed at which the nervous system processes nerve impulses increase reaction time (Nobuyuki, 1997; Roggeveen, Prime, & Ward, 2007).

Despite increased reaction time, middle-aged drivers have fewer accidents than younger ones, partly because they tend to be more careful and take fewer risks. Moreover, older drivers' greater experience benefits them. The minor slowing of reaction time is compensated by their expertise (MacDonald, Hultsch, & Dixon, 2003; Marczinski, Milliken, & Nelson, 2003).

Lifestyle choices can retard the slowing down process. An active exercise program counteracts the effects of aging, improving health, muscle strength, and endurance (see Figure 3.17 on page 108). Developmentalists would agree: "Use it or lose it" (Conn et al., 2003).

Late Adulthood. Old age brings declines in the sense organs; this has major psychological consequences because the senses are people's link with the world.

Vision. Changes in the physical apparatus of the eye—the cornea, lens, retina, and optic nerve—diminish visual abilities. The lens becomes less transparent, allowing only a third as much light to reach the retina at 60 as at 20. The optic nerve also becomes less efficient in transmitting nerve impulses (Scheiber, 1992; Gawande, 2007). As a result, vision declines along several dimensions. We see distant objects less well, need more light to see clearly, and take longer to adjust from dark to light and vice versa.

These changes cause everyday problems. Driving, particularly at night, becomes more challenging. Reading requires more light, and eye strain comes more easily. Of course, eyeglasses and contact lenses can correct many of these problems, and the majority of older people see reasonably well (Horowitz, 1994; Ball & Rebok, 1994; Owsley, Stalvey, & Phillips, 2003).

Several eye diseases become more common during late adulthood. For instance, *cataracts*— cloudy or opaque areas on the lens of the eye that interfere with the passage of light—frequently develop. Cataracts bring blurred vision and glare in bright light. If cataracts are left untreated, the lens becomes milky white and blindness results. However, cataracts can be surgically

FIGURE 3.17 The Benefits of Exercise
There are many benefits from maintaining a high level of physical activity throughout life.
Source: DiGiovanna, 1994.

The advantages of exercise include

Muscle System

Slower decline in energy molecules, muscle cell thickness, number of muscle cells, muscle thickness, muscle mass, muscle strength, blood supply, speed of movement, stamina

Slower increase in fat and fibers, reaction time, recovery time, development of muscle soreness

Nervous System

Slower decline in processing impulses by the central nervous system

Slower increase in variations in speed of motor neuron impulses

Circulatory System

Maintenance of lower levels of LDLs and higher HDL/cholesterol and HDL/LDL ratios

Decreased risk of high blood pressure, atherosclerosis, heart attack, stroke

Skeletal System

Slower decline in bone minerals

Decreased risk of fractures and osteoporosis

Psychological Benefits

Enhanced mood

Feelings of well-being

Reduced stress

FIGURE 3.18 The World Through Macular Degeneration
Macular degeneration leads to a gradual deterioration of the center of the retina, leaving only peripheral vision. This is an example of what a person with macular degeneration might see.
Source: AARP, 2005, p. 34.

removed, and eyesight can be restored with eyeglasses, contact lenses, or *intraocular lens implants,* in which a plastic lens is permanently placed in the eye (Walker, Anstey, & Lord, 2006).

Another serious problem among elderly individuals is glaucoma. As we noted earlier, *glaucoma* occurs when pressure in the fluid of the eye increases, either because the fluid cannot drain properly or too much fluid is produced. Glaucoma can be treated by drugs or surgery if it is detected early enough.

The most common cause of blindness in people over 60 is *age-related macular degeneration (AMD),* which affects the *macula,* a yellowish area near the retina at which visual perception is most acute. When a portion of the macula thins and degenerates, the eyesight gradually deteriorates (see Figure 3.18). If diagnosed early, macular degeneration can sometimes be treated with medication or lasers. There is also some evidence that a diet rich in antioxidant vitamins (C, E, and A) can reduce the risk of AMD (Mayo Clinic, 2000; Sun & Nathans, 2001; Rattner & Nathans, 2006; Wiggins & Uwaydat, 2006).

Hearing. Around 30 percent of adults between 65 and 74 have some hearing loss, and the figure rises to 50 percent among people over 75. Overall, more than 10 million elderly people in the United States have hearing impairments of one kind or another (HHL, 1997; Chisolm, Willott, & Lister, 2003).

Aging particularly affects the ability to hear higher frequencies. This makes it hard to hear conversations amid background noise or when several people are speaking simultaneously. Some elderly persons actually find loud noises painful.

Although hearing aids would probably be helpful around 75 percent of the time, only 20 percent of elderly people wear them. One reason is that hearing aids are far from perfect. They amplify background noises as much as conversations, making it difficult for wearers to separate what they want to hear from other sounds. Furthermore, many people feel that hearing aids make them appear even older and encourage others to treat them as if they were disabled (Lesner, 2003; Meister & von Wedel, 2003).

A hearing loss can be deadly to one's social life. Unable to hear conversations fully, some elderly people with hearing problems withdraw from others, unwilling to respond since they are unsure what was said to them. They can easily feel left out and lonely. Hearing loss can also lead to feelings of paranoia as conversational blanks are filled according to fear rather than reality. If someone hears "I hate going to Maude's" instead of "I hate going to the mall," a bland opinion about shopping can be interpreted as an expression of personal animosity (Knutson & Lansing, 1990; Myers, 2000).

Hearing loss may hasten cognitive decline. The struggle to understand what is being said can shunt mental resources away from processing information, causing difficulties in remembering and understanding information (Wingfield, Tun, & McCoy, 2005).

Taste and Smell. Elderly people who have always enjoyed eating may experience a real decline in the quality of life because of changes in sensitivity to taste and smell. Both senses become less discriminating, causing food to be less appetizing than it was earlier (Kaneda et al., 2000; Nordin, Razani, & Markison, 2003). The decrease in taste and smell sensitivity has a physical cause. The tongue loses taste buds over time, making food less tasty. The problem is compounded as the olfactory bulbs in the brain begin to shrivel. Because taste depends on smell, this makes food taste even blander.

The loss of taste and smell sensitivity has an unfortunate side effect: Because food does not taste as good, people eat less and open the door to malnutrition. They may also oversalt their food, thereby increasing their risk of *hypertension,* or high blood pressure, one of the most common health problems of old age (Smith et al., 2006).

Game Over?

Karl winced as the "game over" message came up on his grandsons' video game system. He enjoyed trying out their games, but he just couldn't shoot down those bad guys as quickly as his grandkids could.

As people get older and reach late adulthood, they take longer: longer to put on a tie, longer to reach a ringing phone, longer to press the buttons in a video game. One reason is a lengthening of reaction time, which begins to increase in middle age and by late adulthood may rise significantly (Fozard et al., 1994; Benjuya, Melzer, & Kaplanski, 2004; Der & Deary, 2006).

It is not clear why people slow down. One explanation, known as the **peripheral slowing hypothesis,** suggests that the peripheral nervous system, which encompasses the nerves that branch from the spinal cord and brain to the extremities of the body, becomes less efficient with age. As a result, it takes longer for information from the environment to reach the brain and for commands from the brain to be transmitted to the muscles (Salthouse, 1989, 2006).

According to the **generalized slowing hypothesis,** on the other hand, processing in all parts of the nervous system, including the brain, is less efficient. As a consequence, slowing occurs throughout the body, including the processing of both simple and complex stimuli and the transmission of commands to the muscles (Cerella, 1990).

Although we don't know which explanation is more accurate, it is clear that the slowing of reaction time and general processing results in a higher incidence of accidents for elderly persons. Slowed reaction and processing time means they can't efficiently receive information from the environment that may indicate a dangerous situation. Slowed decision-making processes impair their ability to remove themselves from harm's way. Drivers over 70 have as many fatal accidents per mile driven as teenagers (Whitbourne, Jacobo, & Munoz-Ruiz, 1996).

Although response time slows, the *perception* of time seems to speed up with age. The days and weeks seem to go by more quickly and time seems to rush by faster for older adults, perhaps because of changes in the way the brain coordinates its internal time clock (Mangan, 1997; Coelho et al., 2004).

REVIEW

▶ Infants' sensory abilities are surprisingly well developed at or shortly after birth. Very early, infants can see depth and motion, distinguish colors and patterns, localize and discriminate sounds, and recognize the sound and smell of their mother.

▶ Infants are sensitive to pain, which manifests itself after a slight delay, and touch, which is one of the most highly developed sensory systems in the newborn. Infants largely use touch to explore their world.

peripheral slowing hypothesis the theory that suggests that overall processing speed declines in the peripheral nervous system with increasing age.

generalized slowing hypothesis the theory that processing in all parts of the nervous system, including the brain, is less efficient.

- School-age children experience sensory impairments that may interfere with their learning and academic success.

- Old age brings many changes in sensory perception that can cause social and psychological difficulties for older people, such as hearing impairments that can hamper one's social life and the loss of taste and smell sensitivity that can make food unappealing and lead to malnutrition.

- In old age people slow down, and their reaction time increases. Two explanations generated to explain this phenomenon are the nervous-system-oriented peripheral slowing hypothesis and the whole-body-oriented generalized slowing hypothesis.

APPLY

- If hearing is associated with abstract thinking, how do people who were born deaf think?

- Should older people, who are susceptible to slowing, be subject to strict examinations to renew their drivers' licenses? Should such tests cover more than eyesight (e.g., response time, mental abilities)? What issues should be taken into consideration?

Epilogue

Remember Carol Deland, the 66-year-old retired physical education teacher who completed a cross-country bicycle ride from San Diego, California, to St. Augustine, Florida? It is hard to believe that this mature, capable woman began her life as a small, weak infant incapable of much movement and totally lacking the physical strength and skills to balance on a bicycle, let alone ride one more than 3,000 miles.

Think of the development that Deland has experienced in her brain, motor skills, physical strength, coordination, and perceptions to enable her to climb on a bicycle and pedal her way across America. Also think how she has single-handedly broken the stereotypes associated with 66-year-olds.

As you think of Carol Deland, consider these questions.

1. Does development research suggest that Deland started her life with particular physical skills and abilities that set her apart from others born when she was? Is it more likely that a healthy, strong baby will grow to be an excellent physical specimen like Deland? If not, what accounts for her physical development?

2. If Deland had been born at a different time, how would her gender have affected expectations for her and her likelihood of endeavoring to bicycle across country?

3. If she had been born in a different culture or under different circumstances, how would her expectations and abilities have been affected?

Looking Back

What physical changes are typical of the major periods of human development, and what factors influence their growth?

1. Infants grow very rapidly over their first 2 years. During the middle childhood years, the body grows at a slow but steady pace that is influenced by both genetic and social factors.

2. Adolescence is a period of rapid physical growth, including the major changes associated with puberty.

3. By young adulthood, the body and the senses are at their peak, but growth is still proceeding, particularly in the brain. Old age brings both external and internal changes.

4. During adulthood, people experience gradual declines in physical characteristics and appearance.

How does the brain grow, and how do environmental factors affect brain growth?

5. The development of the nervous system first entails the development of billions of neurons and interconnections among them. Later, the numbers of both neurons and connections decrease in a process called synaptic pruning as a result of the infant's experiences.

6. Brain plasticity, the susceptibility of a developing organism to environmental influences, is relatively high. Researchers have identified sensitive periods during the development of body systems and behaviors—limited periods when the organism is particularly susceptible to environmental influences.

7. Babies integrate their individual behaviors by developing rhythms—repetitive, cyclical patterns of behavior. A major rhythm relates to the infant's state—the awareness it displays to internal and external stimulation.

8. Brain growth is rapid during the preschool years. In addition, the brain develops lateralization, a tendency of the two hemispheres to adopt specialized tasks.

What reflexes do infants and young children possess, and what function do they serve?

9. Babies are born with reflexes—unlearned, organized involuntary responses to particular environmental stimuli. Reflexes include the swimming reflex, the eye blink reflex, and the Moro reflex.

10. The function of reflexes appears to be to protect the infant from sudden threats until a voluntary system of responses develops.

How do gross and fine motor skills change as people grow older?

11. Infants progress from a state of few motor skills to the ability to sit up, crawl, and eventually stand and walk. Both gross and fine motor development is rapid during the first four years.

12. During the school years, muscle coordination improves to the extent that athletic activities become possible. These skills constantly improve through the school years, adolescence, and at least young adulthood.

13. During middle childhood, boys generally surpass girls in muscle strength, while girls' muscle coordination is often more advanced than that of boys.

14. The fine motor skills follow a predetermined pattern of development of steadily increasing ability to use the hands and fingers.

15. As their motor skills develop, children develop handedness and artistic skills.

In what ways do the senses develop across the life span, and what consequences do the changes have?

16. Infants' sensory abilities are reasonably good at birth. For example, they can see depth, motion, color, and patterns, and they can distinguish and locate sounds in their environment. By 6 months eyesight equals that of most adults.

17. Infants can smell and taste, and they are sensitive to touch, which is their main sense for exploring and interpreting the world.

18. Aging brings many changes in the senses, most of which represent deterioration and many of which can cause social isolation. In addition, the decrease in taste and smell sensitivity among older adults can lead to undereating and malnutrition.

19. In middle and late adulthood, reaction time increases as older people simply slow down. However, most people learn ways to compensate for diminished sensation by increased attention and care.

Health and Wellness

Prologue

Rosa Convoy's Crowded Life

It's 5:00 PM. Rosa Convoy, a 25-year-old single mother, has just finished her work as a receptionist at a dentist's office and is on her way home. She has exactly 2 hours to pick up her daughter Zoe from child care, get home, make and eat dinner, pick up and return with a babysitter from down the street, say goodbye to Zoe, and get to her 7 o'clock programming class at a local community college. It's a marathon she runs every Tuesday and Thursday night, and she knows she doesn't have a second to spare if she wants to reach the class on time.

The multiple demands of single motherhood produce stress.

Threats to wellness do not simply end with adulthood; threats of different kinds pursue the individual throughout life. Still, it is increasingly possible to live the majority of one's life without running into serious problems.

In this chapter, we focus on the physical aspects of health and wellness. We begin by considering stress, a potential barrier to wellness. We discuss the origins and consequences of stress, as well as proven techniques for coping with it. We take a look at ways stress now affects even school-age children.

We turn from stress to illness and its opposite, well-being. We consider malnutrition, which is mainly a problem in developing countries, and we examine obesity, which is very much an issue in the United States. We see the effects of obesity, including the eating disorders that are sometimes used as a way to avoid it. We then turn to a discussion of the major threats to wellness and health, including the threats that face children and their parents, and threats that plague adolescents in particular: substance abuse and sexually transmitted infections.

We take a look at fitness and health in childhood and adulthood—particularly the lack of exercise—and continue with a consideration of physical and psychological disorders, including the influence of personality type and cultural factors on such health issues as coronary heart disease and cancer, which rank at the top of people's fears as they age. We end the module with a discussion of Alzheimer's disease.

The final module of the chapter covers ways to promote health and wellness. We examine the effects of a good diet and exercise, with suggestions for promoting exercise among children so that it becomes a lifelong activity. We also discuss typical changes in men's and women's sexuality and the physical effects of menopause, as well as recent research on the use of hormone therapy to control the unpleasant aspects of menopause.

PEARSON mydevelopmentlab

Young adults experience many kinds of stress and cope in different ways. Log onto **MyDevelomentLab** to hear two young adults, Amanda and Gary, talk about the stress in their lives.

LOOKING AHEAD

After reading this chapter, you will be able to answer the following questions:

▶ What are the main causes and consequences of stress, and how do people cope?
▶ What are the consequences of malnutrition, obesity, and eating disorders?
▶ What threats to their health do children and young adults face as they age?
▶ What are the major threats to good health across the life span? How do cultural factors affect wellness and health?
▶ How do diet and exercise contribute to health and wellness across the life span?
▶ What changes do people encounter in their sex lives as they age?

MODULE 4.1

Stress and Coping

Because of her crowded life, Rosa Convoy, whom we met in the chapter opening prologue, feels stress, the physical and emotional response to events that threaten or challenge us. Our lives are crowded with events and circumstances, known as stressors, that threaten our equilibrium. Stressors need not be unpleasant events: Even the happiest events—starting a long-sought job, planning a wedding—can produce stress (Crowley, Hayslip, & Hobdy, 2003; Shimizu & Pelham, 2004). How well people cope with this state depends on a complex interplay of physical and psychological factors (Hetherington & Blechman, 1996).

The Origins of Stress

Experienced job interviewers, college counselors, and owners of bridal shops all know that not everyone reacts the same way to a potentially stressful event. What makes the difference? According to psychologists Arnold Lazarus and Susan Folkman, people move through a series of stages that determine whether they will experience stress (Lazarus & Folkman, 1984; Lazarus, 1968, 1991).

Primary appraisal is the first step—the individual's assessment of an event to determine whether its implications are positive, negative, or neutral. If a person sees the event as primarily negative, he or she appraises it in terms of the harm that it has caused in the past, how threatening it is likely to be, and how likely it is that the challenge can be resisted successfully. For example, you are likely to feel differently about an upcoming French test if you passed the last one with flying colors than you would if you did poorly.

Secondary appraisal follows. **Secondary appraisal** is the person's answer to the question, "Can I handle it?," an assessment of whether the coping abilities and resources on hand are adequate. If resources are lacking and the threat is great, the person will feel stress. A traffic ticket is always upsetting, but if you can't afford the fine, the stress is greater.

Stress varies with the person's appraisal, and that appraisal varies with the person's temperament and circumstances. Some general principles help predict when an event will be appraised as stressful. Psychologist Shelley Taylor (1991; Taylor & Stanton, 2007) suggests the following characteristics of events that have a high likelihood of producing stress:

- Events and circumstances that produce negative emotions—for example, dealing with the illness of a loved one produces more stress than planning for the adoption of a new baby.
- Situations that are uncontrollable or unpredictable—for example, professors who give surprise quizzes produce more stress than those who schedule them in advance.
- Events and circumstances that are ambiguous and confusing—for example, a new job that does not have a clear job description is likely to produce more stress than a well-defined position.
- Having to simultaneously accomplish many tasks that strain a person's capabilities—for example, a graduate student who is expecting her first child the same month she is scheduled to submit her dissertation is likely to feel more stress than a student with less on her agenda.

The Consequences of Stress

Brian and Tiffany Aske of Oakland, Calif., desperately want their daughter, Ashlyn, to succeed in first grade.... When they started Ashlyn in kindergarten last year, they had no reason to worry. A bright child with twinkling eyes, Ashlyn was eager to learn, and the neighborhood school had a great reputation. But by November, Ashlyn, then 5, wasn't measuring up. No matter how many times she was tested, she couldn't read the 130-word list her teacher gave her: words like "our," "house" and "there." She became so exhausted and distraught over homework—including a weekly essay on "my favorite animal" or "my family vacation"—that she would put her head down on the dining-room table and sob. "She would tell me, 'I can't write a story, Mama. I just can't do it,'" said Tiffany. (Tyre, 2006, p. 34)

Researchers in the new field of **psychoneuroimmunology (PNI)**—the study of the relationship among the brain, the immune system, and psychological factors—have examined the outcomes

FROM A

HEALTH CARE PROVIDER'S
PERSPECTIVE:

Are there periods of life that are relatively stress-free, or do people of all ages experience stress? Do stressors differ from age to age?

primary appraisal   an individual's assessment of an event to determine whether its implications are positive, negative or neutral.

secondary appraisal   a person's answer to the question, "Can I handle it?," an assessment of whether the coping abilities and resources on hand are adequate.

psychoneuroimmunology (PNI)   the study of the relationship among the brain, the immune system, and psychological factors.

of stress. The most immediate is a biological reaction, as hormones secreted by the adrenal glands cause a rise in heart rate, blood pressure, respiration rate, and sweating. In some situations, these immediate effects are beneficial because the "emergency reaction" they produce in the sympathetic nervous system enables people to defend themselves from a sudden, threatening situation (Parkes, 1997; Ray, 2004).

On the other hand, long-term, continuous exposure to stressors may reduce the body's ability to deal with stress. As stress-related hormones are constantly secreted, the heart, blood vessels, and other body tissues may deteriorate. As a consequence, people become more susceptible to diseases as their ability to fight off germs declines (Cohen, Tyrrell, & Smith, 1997; Lundberg, 2006).

Ultimately, the Askes found their own solution to the pressure that Ashylyn was facing: They moved to a different state where Ashlyn could attend a less intense public school that offered more flexibility and less pressure. But this option is not open to everyone, and most kids have to cope as well as they can with the pressure cookers that schools have become.

The Pressure to Make the Grade. *The No Child Left Behind Act of 2002* aimed to ensure that all children would be able to read by the time they reached the third grade. The law requires school principals to meet this goal or risk losing their jobs and their school funding. Although the intentions of this law may have been good, in some cases there has been an unforeseen outcome: so much focus is placed on reading that other important topics such as social studies and music and activities such as recess have been excluded from the school day. Worse, some schools' reading programs have become so intense that some children are simply burning out (Abril & Gault, 2006; Paige, 2006).

Whereas once kindergarten was a time for finger painting, story time, and free play, children are increasingly beginning reading lessons at that level. Frequent testing to ensure that children are meeting short-term and long-term literacy goals has become more commonplace. The experience of failure—and of competitive pressure to be at the top of the class—is hitting children at younger ages than before.

All Work and No Play. One trend that has many parents and educators concerned is an increase in the amount of homework assigned. A study conducted by the Institute for Social Research at the University of Michigan determined that children are spending a lot more time on academics today than they did 20 years ago. The time spent in school for children ages 6 to 8 has increased from about 5 hours to about 7 hours per weekday. Time spent studying and reading has increased over that time period, while play time, sports, and other outdoor activities have decreased (Juster, Ono, & Stafford, 2004).

But is the extra homework worth the cost? While time spent on homework is associated with greater academic achievement in secondary school, the relationship gets less strong for the lower grades; below grade 5, the relationship disappears. Experts explain this finding in terms of younger children's inability to tune out distractions as well as their yet undeveloped study skills. Moreover, research with older children shows that more homework is not necessarily better. In fact, the benefits of homework may reach a plateau beyond which additional time spent on homework produces no further benefits (Cooper & Valentine, 2001; Trautwein et al., 2006).

Some educational experts fear that the social and emotional development of children is taking a back seat to literacy education, and that the pressure, the testing, the accelerated programs, and the time spent in school—as well as in after-school programs and on homework—may be robbing kids of opportunities to just be kids. Some parents, such as the Askes whom we encountered in the module opener, are worried that their children are simply becoming frustrated and discouraged with learning (Kohn, 2006).

Adolescents: Late to Bed, Early to Rise. In view of the increasing academic and social demands, children—and especially adolescents—go to bed later and get up earlier, leaving them sleep-deprived. This deprivation coincides in adolescence with a shift in their internal clocks. Older adolescents have a need to go to bed later and to sleep later in the morning, requiring 9 hours of sleep to feel rested. In the conflict between late nights and early morning classes, however, they get far less sleep than their bodies crave (National Sleep Foundation, 2002; Dorofaeff & Denny, 2006; Fuligni & Hardway, 2006). Sleep-deprived teens have lower grades, are more depressed, and have greater difficulty controlling their moods. They are also at great risk for auto accidents (Fredriksen et al., 2004; also see the *Neuroscience and Development* box on the genetic underpinnings of sleep).

Over the long run, the constant wear and tear of fighting off stress can have formidable costs. Headaches, backaches, skin rashes, indigestion, chronic fatigue, and even the common cold are stress-related illnesses (Cohen, Tyrrell, & Smith, 1993, 1997; Suinn, 2001; McGrady, 2007).

For younger children, homework may not have the benefits it has for older children.

FROM AN
EDUCATOR'S
PERSPECTIVE:
Do you accept the view that children in U.S. society are "pushed" academically to the extent that they feel too much stress and pressure at a young age? Why?

NEUROSCIENCE AND DEVELOPMENT
Sleep Deprivation and Your Genes: Do You Have the Snooze Blues?

It's eight o'clock in the morning and your professor just distributed midterm exams. With a total of 4 hours sleep in the last 24, do you tackle the exam feeling wide awake and ready, or is it all you can do to stay awake as you fight your extreme feelings of fatigue?

The answer to this question might have to do with your genetic endowment, for there seems to be a genetic difference in PERIOD3 (*PER3*)—one of the genes involved in regulating the body's internal clock. *PER3* comes in a longer and shorter form. It turns out that people with an intense preference for early mornings are more likely to have a long version of *PER3* and those with an intense preference for evenings are more likely to have the shorter version (Mu et al., 2004).

In a recent brain scan imaging study, participants were selected according to their PER3 gene variants. As part of the experiment, they completed a working memory task that required both cognition and attention. The length of the *PER3* gene variants and differences in vulnerability to sleep deprivation were studied to examine the relationship between genetic differences in brain activity and cognitive performance and fatigue (Maquet & Derk-Jan Dijk, 2009).

People with the short *PER3* variant showed expanded brain activity, were resilient to sleep loss, and performed well on cognitive tasks after sleep deprivation. They seemed to use extra brain structures (in frontal, temporal, and subcortical areas) to deter the effects of a sleepless night. In contrast, those with the long *PER3* variant showed reduced brain activity and deficits in cognitive performance after sleep deprivation. Some reduction in task effectiveness was also seen in the evening, even when these participants had not been sleep deprived.

- *Think about your performance on an early morning exam or other cognitive tasks that demand competence after you have had little sleep. Would you guess you have the long or short version of the* PER3 *gene?*

Stress and Eating Disorders. As we will see when we discuss eating disorders, some experts suggest that adolescent eating disorders are a result of such stressful situations as perfectionistic, overdemanding parents or other family difficulties. Culture also seems to play a role. Cultural demands regarding body type that particularly affect adolescents can take their toll. Anorexia nervosa, for instance, is found only in cultures that idealize slender female bodies. Because in most places such a standard does not hold, anorexia is not prevalent outside the United States (Haines & Neumark-Sztainer, 2006; Harrison & Hefner, 2006).

The Stresses of Adulthood. Stress continues to have a significant impact on health during middle adulthood, as it did in young adulthood, although the nature of what is stressful may have changed. For example, parents may experience stress over their adolescent children's potential drug use rather than worry about whether their toddler is ready to give up his pacifier.

In later adulthood, the challenges continue. If it isn't declining strength and energy, it's worries about the frequent loss of memory and a feared decrease in intelligence or sexual passion. Sometimes the worry becomes intense and affects significant relationships with others: with parents and children, siblings and friends, supervisors and coworkers.

Consequences of Stress. No matter what events trigger stress, the results are similar. According to *psychoneuroimmunologist* —scientists who study the relationship between the brain, the

FIGURE 4.1 The Consequences of Stress
Stress produces three major consequences: direct physiological effects, harmful behaviors, and indirect health-related behaviors.
Source: Adapted from Baum, 1994.

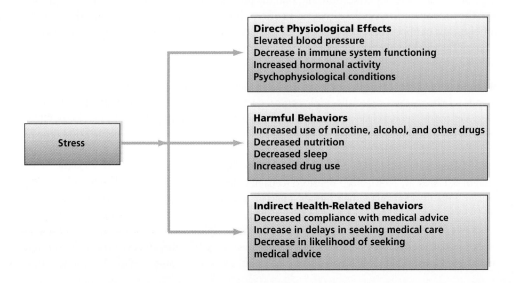

immune system, and psychological factors—stress produces three main consequences, summarized in Figure 4.1. First, stress has direct physiological outcomes, ranging from increased blood pressure and hormonal activity to decreased immune system response. Second, stress also leads people to engage in unhealthy behaviors, such as cutting back on sleep, smoking, drinking, or taking other drugs. Finally, stress has indirect effects on health-related behavior. People under a lot of stress may be less likely to seek out good medical care, to exercise, or to comply with medical advice (Suinn, 2001; Suls & Wallston, 2003; Zellner et al., 2006). All of these failures can lead to or affect serious health conditions, including such major problems as heart disease, which we will discuss in greater detail in the next module.

In addition, the immune system—the organs, glands, and cells that are the body's line of defense against disease—may be damaged by stress. Stress can interfere with the immune system's ability to stop germs from reproducing or cancer cells from spreading. In addition, stress may overstimulate the immune system into attacking the body itself and damaging healthy tissue (Ader, Felten, & Cohen, 2001; Miller & Cohen, 2001; Cohen et al., 2002; Caserta et al., 2008; Connor, 2008).

Stress may also lead to **psychosomatic disorders**, medical problems caused by the interaction of psychological, emotional, and physical difficulties. For instance, ulcers, asthma, arthritis, and high blood pressure may sometimes be produced by stress (Lepore, Palsane, & Evans, 1991; Jones & Bright, 2007).

To get a sense of how much stress you have in your own life, complete the questionnaire in Table 4.1.

psychosomatic disorders medical problems caused by the interaction of psychological, emotional, and physical difficulties.

TABLE 4.1   How Stressed Are You?

Test your level of stress by answering these questions, and adding the score from each box. Questions apply to the last month only. A key below will help you determine the extent of your stress.

1. How often have you been upset because of something that happened unexpectedly?

☐ 0 = never, 1 = almost never, 2 = sometimes, 3 = fairly often, 4 = very often

2. How often have you felt that you were unable to control the important things in your life?

☐ 0 = never, 1 = almost never, 2 = sometimes, 3 = fairly often, 4 = very often

3. How often have you felt nervous and "stressed"?

☐ 0 = never, 1 = almost never, 2 = sometimes, 3 = fairly often, 4 = very often

4. How often have you felt confident about your ability to handle your personal problems?

☐ 4 = never, 3 = almost never, 2 = sometimes, 1 = fairly often, 0 = very often

5. How often have you felt that things were going your way?

☐ 4 = never, 3 = almost never, 2 = sometimes, 1 = fairly often, 0 = very often

6. How often have you been able to control irritations in your life?

☐ 4 = never, 3 = almost never, 2 = sometimes, 1 = fairly often, 0 = very often

7. How often have you found that you could not cope with all the things that you had to do?

☐ 0 = never, 1 = almost never, 2 = sometimes, 3 = fairly often, 4 = very often

8. How often have you felt that you were on top of things?

☐ 4 = never, 3 = almost never, 2 = sometimes, 1 = fairly often, 0 = very often

9. How often have you been angered because of things that were outside your control?

☐ 0 = never, 1 = almost never, 2 = sometimes, 3 = fairly often, 4 = very often

10. How often have you felt difficulties were piling up so high that you could not overcome them?

☐ 0 = never, 1 = almost never, 2 = sometimes, 3 = fairly often, 4 = very often

HOW YOU MEASURE UP
Stress levels vary among individuals—compare your total score to the averages below:

Age		Gender	
18–29	14.2	Men	12.1
30–44	13.0	Women	13.7
45–54	12.6		
55–64	11.9		
65 & over	12.0		

Marital Status

Widowed	12.6
Married or living with	12.4
Single or never wed	14.1
Divorced	14.7
Separated	16.6

Source: Sheldon Cohen et al., 1983. Dept. of Psychology, Carnegie Mellon University.

defensive coping unconscious strategies that distort or deny the true nature of a situation.

hardiness a personality characteristic associated with a lower rate of stress-related illness.

Coping with Stress

Ally McKennon, 17, never seems to catch up. She works dawn till dusk at her schoolwork and has a part-time job as a waitress on weekends. She has her heart set on a small eastern liberal arts college, and though she knows it is listed as "highly competitive," she thinks she has the grades and the standardized test scores to get in, and she chose four courses that would impress college admissions officers. If she can only manage to stay up a few hours longer each night to study and can avoid entanglements with boys....

Todd Comins, also 17 and a student at the same school as Ally, always seems rested, fed, and happy. He works a part-time job at the same restaurant as Ally but always seems cheerful and has lots of friends of both sexes. He has a list of highly challenging colleges that he would be happy to attend, along with a couple of "safety schools," any one of which would suit him fine. He never seems overworked and doesn't much care about his test scores or grades. Paradoxically, he gets A's in his courses and scored high on his standardized tests.

Ally knows that Todd is no brighter than she, but his approach to life seems different. She can't seem to be relaxed; he can't seem to get anxious. What gives?

How to Cope. Stress is a normal part of every life. But some people are better than others at coping—the effort to control, reduce, or learn to tolerate the threats that lead to stress. What's the secret to coping? It turns out that people use a variety of strategies.

Some people use *problem-focused coping*—managing a threatening situation by directly changing it to make it less stressful. For example, a man having difficulties on the job may ask his boss to change his responsibilities, or he may look for another job.

Other people employ *emotion-focused coping*—the conscious regulation of emotion. For instance, a mother having trouble finding appropriate care for her child while she is at work may tell herself that she should look at the bright side: At least she has a job in a difficult economy (Folkman & Lazarus, 1988; 1990; Greenberg, 2008).

Sometimes people acknowledge that they are in a stressful situation that cannot be changed, but they cope by managing their reactions. For example, they may take up meditation or exercise to reduce their physical reactions.

Coping is also aided by the presence of *social support*—assistance and comfort supplied by others. Turning to others can provide both emotional support (in the form of a shoulder to cry on) and practical, tangible support (such as a temporary loan) (Spiegel, 1993; Giacobbi, Lynn, & Wetherington, 2004; Jackson, 2006).

Finally, even if people do not consciously cope with stress, some psychologists suggest that they may unconsciously use defensive coping mechanisms. **Defensive coping** involves unconscious strategies that distort or deny the true nature of a situation. For instance, people may trivialize a life-threatening illness or tell themselves that failing a major test is unimportant.

Another type of defensive coping is *emotional insulation*, through which people unconsciously try to block emotions and thereby avoid pain. But if defensive coping becomes a habitual response to stress, its reliance on avoidance can stand in the way of dealing with the reality of the situation (Ormont, 2001).

In some cases, people use drugs or alcohol to escape from stressful situations. Like defensive coping, drinking and drug use do not help address the situation causing the stress, and they can increase a person's difficulties. For example, people may become addicted to the substances that initially provided them with a pleasurable sense of escape.

Hardiness, Resilience, and Coping. The success with which people deal with stress depends in part on their *coping style,* their general tendency to deal with stress in a particular way. For example, people with a "hardy" coping style are especially successful. **Hardiness** is a personality characteristic associated with a lower rate of stress-related illness.

Hardy individuals are take-charge people who revel in life's challenges. People who are high in hardiness are more resistant to stress-related illness than those with less hardiness. Hardy people react to stressors with optimism, convinced that they can respond effectively. By turning threats into challenges, they are less apt to experience high levels of stress (Horner, 1998; Maddi, 2006; Maddi et al., 2006).

Assistance and comfort by others in times of stress can provide both emotional and practical support.

BECOMING AN INFORMED CONSUMER OF DEVELOPMENT
Coping with Stress

General guidelines that can help people cope with stress include the following (Kaplan, Sallis, & Patterson, 1993; Sacks, 1993; Bionna, 2006).

- Seek control over the situation. Taking charge of a situation that is producing stress can take you a long way toward coping with it. For example, if you are feeling stress about a test, do something about it—such as forming a study group or starting to study more intensively.

- Redefine "threat" as "challenge." Changing the definition can make a situation seem less threatening. "Look for the silver lining" is not bad advice. For example, if you're fired, look at it as an opportunity to get a new and better job.

- Find social support. Almost any difficulty can be faced more easily with the help of others. Friends, family members, and even telephone hot lines staffed by trained counselors can provide significant support. (For help in identifying appropriate hot

lines, the U.S. Public Health Service maintains a "master" toll-free number that can provide phone numbers and addresses of many national groups. Call 800-336-4794.)

- Use relaxation techniques. Reducing the physiological arousal brought about by stress can be effective in coping with stress. Techniques that produce relaxation, such as transcendental meditation, Zen and yoga, progressive muscle relaxation, and even hypnosis, have been shown to be effective. One that works particularly well was devised by physician Herbert Benson and is illustrated in Table 4.2 on page 120 (Benson, 1993).

- Maintain a healthy lifestyle that will reinforce your body's natural coping mechanisms. Exercise, eat nutritiously, get enough sleep, and avoid or reduce use of alcohol, tobacco, or other drugs.

- If all else fails, keep in mind that a life without stress would be dull. Stress is natural, and successfully coping with it can be gratifying.

For people who face the most profound difficulties—such as the unexpected death of a loved one—a key factor in their reactions is their level of resilience. *Resilience* is the ability to withstand, overcome, and even thrive after profound adversity (Bonanno, 2004; Norlander et al., 2005; Werner, 2005; Kim-Cohen, 2007).

Resilient people tend to be easygoing and good-natured, with good social and communication skills. They are independent, feeling that they can shape their own fate and are not dependent on others or luck. They work with what they have and make the best of any situation (Humphreys, 2003; Spencer, 2003; Deshields et al., 2005; Friborg et al., 2005).

REVIEW

▶ Not everyone responds to stress the same way. People move through stages—primary appraisal and secondary appraisal—to determine whether they will experience stress.

▶ Stress may appear at any time of life, from schooling to old age. Some educational initiatives, for example, have caused students and teachers to experience stress.

▶ Long-term exposure to stressors may cause deterioration in the heart, blood vessels, and other body tissues. Stress is linked to many common ailments.

▶ Students are subject to stress because they get too much homework to enjoy sleep, sports, and other activities—possibly endangering their social and emotional development.

▶ Strategies for coping with stress include problem-focused coping, emotion-focused coping, the use of social support, and defensive coping.

▶ People who react effectively to stress have a positive coping style, which may involve hardiness and/or resilience. Less successful strategies include resorting to drugs or drink.

APPLY

▶ In what circumstances can stress be an adaptive, helpful response? In what circumstances is it maladaptive?

▶ Why might it be the case that students who spend a lot of time doing homework tend not to have better academic success than students who spend a moderate amount of time?

TABLE 4.2	**How to Elicit the Relaxation Response**

Some general advice on regular practice of the relaxation response:

- Try to find 10 to 20 minutes in your daily routine; before breakfast is a good time.

- Sit comfortably.

- For the period you will practice, try to arrange your life so you won't have distractions. Put on the answering machine, and ask someone else to watch the kids.

- Time yourself by glancing periodically at a clock or watch (but don't set an alarm). Commit yourself to a specific length of practice, and try to stick to it.

There are several approaches to eliciting the relaxation response. Here is one standard set of instructions:

Step 1. Pick a focus word or short phrase that's firmly rooted in your personal belief system. For example, a nonreligious individual might choose a neutral word like *one* or *peace* or *love*. A Christian person desiring to use a prayer could pick the opening words of Psalm 23, *The Lord is my shepherd*; a Jewish person could choose *Shalom*.

Step 2. Sit quietly in a comfortable position.

Step 3. Close your eyes.

Step 4. Relax your muscles.

Step 5. Breathe slowly and naturally, repeating your focus word or phrase silently as you exhale.

Step 6. Throughout, assume a passive attitude. Don't worry about how well you're doing. When other thoughts come to mind, simply say to yourself, "Oh, well," and gently return to the repetition.

Step 7. Continue for 10 to 20 minutes. You may open your eyes to check the time, but do not use an alarm. When you finish, sit quietly for a minute or so, at first with your eyes closed and later with your eyes open. Then do not stand for one or two minutes.

Step 8. Practice the technique once or twice a day.

Source: Benson, 1993.

MODULE 4.2

Illness and Well-Being

Malnutrition, Obesity, and Eating Disorders

Although height can be of concern to both children and parents, weight is an even greater worry for some. Weight concerns can border on obsession, particularly in girls. Many 6-year-old girls worry about becoming "fat," and some 40 percent of girls ages 9 to 10 are trying to lose weight. Their concern with weight often reflects the U.S. preoccupation with slimness, which permeates the entire society (Schreiber et al., 1996; Greenwood & Pietromonaco, 2004).

Malnutrition. *Malnutrition,* the condition of having an improper amount and balance of nutrients, produces several results, none good. For instance, malnutrition is more common among children living in many developing countries than among children who live in more industrialized, affluent countries. Malnourished children in these countries begin to show a slower growth rate by the age of 6 months. By the time they reach the age of 2 years, their height and weight are only 95 percent the height and weight of children in more industrialized countries.

Children who have been chronically malnourished during infancy later score lower on IQ tests and tend to do less well in school. These effects may linger even after the children's diet has improved substantially (Grantham-McGregor, Ani, & Fernald, 2001; Ratanachu-Ek, 2003).

The problem of malnutrition is greatest in underdeveloped countries, where overall 10 percent of infants are severely malnourished. In some countries the problem is especially severe. For example, 60 percent of North Korean children aged 6 months to 7 years are suffering moderate to severe malnutrition (World Food Programme, 2004; see Figure 4.2). Problems of malnourishment are not restricted to developing countries, however. In the United States, some 12 million children live in poverty, which puts them at risk for malnutrition. Although overall poverty rates are no worse than they were 20 years ago, the poverty rate for children under the age of 3 has *increased*. Some one-quarter of families who have children 2 years old and younger live in poverty. And, as we can see in Figure 4.3, the rates are even higher for African American and Hispanic families as well as for single-parent families (Einbinder, 1992; Carnegie Task Force on Meeting the Needs of Young Children, 1994; Duncan & Brooks-Gunn, 2000).

Social service programs mean that these children rarely become severely malnourished, but such children remain susceptible to *undernutrition*, in which there is some deficiency in diet. Some surveys find that as many as a quarter of 1- to 5-year-old children in the United States have diets that fall below the minimum caloric intake recommended by nutritional experts. Although the consequences are not as severe as those of malnutrition, undernutrition also has long-term costs. For instance, cognitive development later in childhood is affected by even mild to moderate undernutrition (Pollitt et al., 1996; Tanner & Finn-Stevenson, 2002; Arija et al., 2006).

Severe malnutrition during infancy may lead to several disorders. Malnutrition during the first year can produce *marasmus*, a disease in which infants stop growing. Marasmus, attributable to a severe deficiency in proteins and calories, causes the body to waste away and ultimately results in death. Older children are susceptible to *kwashiorkor*, a disease in which a child's stomach, limbs, and face swell with water. To a casual observer, it appears that a child with kwashiorkor is actually chubby. However, this is an illusion: The child's body is in fact struggling to make use of the few nutrients that are available.

In some cases, infants who receive sufficient nutrition act as though they have been deprived of food. Looking as though they suffer from marasmus, they are underdeveloped, listless, and apathetic. The real cause, though, is emotional: They lack sufficient love and emotional support. In such cases, known as **nonorganic failure to thrive**, children stop growing not for biological reasons but owing to a lack of stimulation and attention from their parents. Usually occurring by the age of 18 months, nonorganic failure to thrive can be reversed through intensive parent training or by placing children in a foster home where they can receive emotional support.

Obesity.

At 20 pounds and 27 inches long, Zachary Miller was a happy and healthy, but not especially active, baby. "The pediatrician told me, 'The big ones don't like to move,'" says Zach's mom, Ellie. "She told me to put him on the floor and on his tummy as often as possible. He hates that. But it does get him to push up on his arms and roll over."

At 7 months, Zach was already overweight. (Sachs, 2006, p. 112)

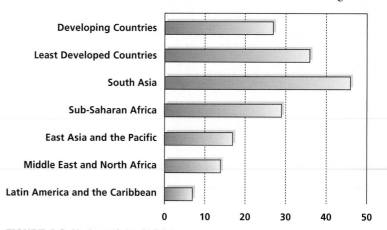

FIGURE 4.2 Underweight Children
The percentage of children under 5 years who are moderately or severely underweight.
Source: UNICEF, The State of the World's Children, 2005.

FROM AN
EDUCATOR'S
PERSPECTIVE:
What might be some of the reasons that malnourishment, which slows physical growth, also harms IQ scores and school performance? How might malnourishment affect education in Third World countries?

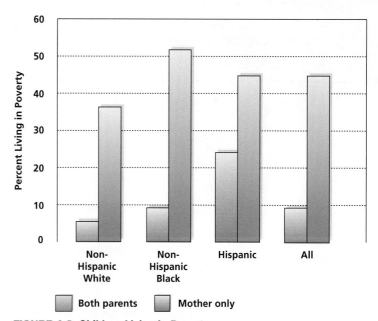

FIGURE 4.3 Children Living in Poverty
The incidence of poverty among children under the age of 3 is particularly high in minority and single-parent households. (Figures are shown only for single mothers, and not fathers, because 97% of all children under 3 who live with a single parent live with their mothers; only 3% live with their fathers.)
Source: National Center for Children in Poverty at the Joseph L. Mailman School of Public Health of Columbia University, 2007.

nonorganic failure to thrive   a disorder in which infants stop growing due to a lack of stimulation and attention as the result of inadequate parenting.

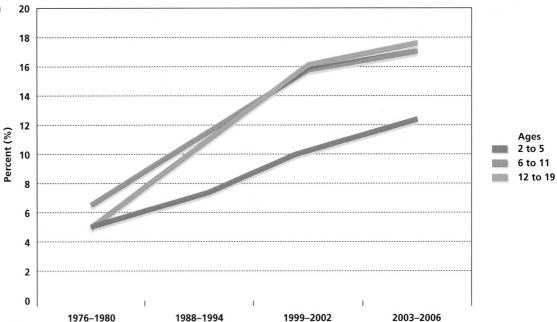

FIGURE 4.4 Obesity in Children
Obesity in children ages 6 to 12 has risen dramatically over the past four decades by more than threefold.
Source: Centers for Disease Control and Prevention. *NHANES Surveys (1976–1980 and 2003–2006)* Retrieved November 17, 2009 from World Wide Web (http://www.cdc.gov/obesity/childhood/prevalence.html)

Ages
2 to 5
6 to 11
12 to 19

Note: Sex- and age-specific BMI ≥ 95th percentile based on the CDC growth charts.

Malnourishment at an early age can lower IQ scores, even if diet improves later. How might this deficit be overcome?

FROM A
HEALTH CARE WORKER'S
PERSPECTIVE:
How might biology and environment combine to affect the nutritional habits of a child adopted as an infant from a developing country and reared in a more industrialized one?

obesity weight greater than 20 percent above average for a given age and height.

Despite the prevalent view that thinness is a virtue, childhood **obesity**—defined as weight greater than 20 percent above average for a given age and height—is rising. Fifteen percent of U.S. children are obese—a figure that has tripled since the 1960s (see Figure 4.4; Brownlee, 2002; Dietz, 2004; Mann, 2005).

It is clear that malnourishment has potentially disastrous consequences for an infant. Less clear, however, are the effects of obesity. Although there is no demonstrable correlation between obesity during infancy and obesity at the age of 16 years, some research suggests that overfeeding during infancy may lead to the creation of an excess of fat cells, which remain in the body throughout life and may predispose a person to be overweight. Weight gains during infancy are associated with weight at age 6. Other research shows an association between obesity after the age of 6 and adult obesity, suggesting that obesity in babies ultimately may be found to be associated with adult weight problems. A clear link between overweight babies and overweight adults, however, has not yet been found (Gunnarsdottir & Thorsdottir, 2003; Toschke et al., 2004; Dennison, Edmunds, Stratton, & Pruzek, 2006).

Although the evidence linking infant obesity to adult obesity is inconclusive, it's plain that the old view that "a fat baby is a healthy baby" may well be incorrect. Parents should concentrate less on their baby's weight and more on providing appropriate nutrition.

Adolescence. Obesity remains the most common nutritional concern in adolescence and adulthood. One in 5 adolescents is overweight, and 1 in 20 can be classified as obese (more than 20 percent above average body weight). Furthermore, the proportion of females who are classified as obese increases over the course of adolescence (Brook & Tepper, 1997; Critser, 2003; Kimm et al., 2003).

Adolescents are obese for the same reasons as younger children, but special concerns with body image may have severe psychological consequences at this age. The potential health consequences of obesity during adolescence are also problematic. Obesity taxes the circulatory system, increasing the risk of high blood pressure and diabetes. Obese adolescents also have an 80 percent chance of becoming obese adults (Blaine, Rodman, & Newman, 2007).

Adulthood. The adult population of the United States is growing—in more ways than one. As in childhood, obesity is on the rise. In the 1-year period from 1998 to 1999, obesity increased 6 percent. Some 12 percent of those age 18 to 29 are obese, and the numbers edge up throughout adulthood (Centers for Disease Control and Prevention, 2000).

Poor diets contribute to obesity not just in childhood, but in adolescence and adulthood as well. During childhood, many parents provide their children with too few fruits and vegetables and more fats and sweets than recommended. School lunch programs may contribute to the problem, failing to provide nutritious options. Adults continue the trend when they grow up.

The Cost of Obesity.   People pay the costs of childhood obesity throughout their lives. Obese children are more likely to be overweight as adults and have a greater risk of heart disease, diabetes, and other diseases. Some scientists believe an epidemic of obesity may be leading to a decline in life span in the United States (Freedman et al., 2004; Olshansky et al., 2005; Krishnamoorthy, Hart, & Jelalian, 2006).

Genetic and social characteristics as well as diet influence obesity. Particular inherited genes predispose certain children to be overweight. For example, adopted children's weights tend to reflect those of their birth parents rather than their adoptive parents (Zhang et al., 1994; Whitaker et al., 1997; Hebebrand & Hinney, 2009).

Childhood obesity is on the rise, and as the story of Zachary Miller, whom we met in the opening of this module, suggests, the problem sometimes begins very early. Children of overweight parents are particularly at risk of becoming overweight themselves, but heredity seems to be only part of the explanation. At issue is what children are eating in their first years of life—or rather, what their parents are feeding them (Breen, Plomin, & Wardle, 2006; Flegal et al., 2006; Mennella, Kennedy, & Beauchamp, 2006).

Food Preferences.   Research shows that children's food preferences are determined early on. One study that tracked children's eating habits over a period of 6 years found that the strongest predictor of preferred foods at age 8 was the preferred foods at age 4, and moreover that children were more likely to accept new foods before age 4 than after that time. In other words, children develop their taste for certain foods at an early age and then tend to stick with those foods as they get older (Skinner et al., 2002).

But the real issue is what children are developing a taste for. The same study also found that children tended to like foods that their mothers liked, which is unsurprising—the mothers tended not to offer foods that they themselves did not like (Skinner et al., 2002; Cooke, 2007).

So what kinds of foods are parents feeding their young children? Another study examined the foods actually eaten over the course of a day by 3,000 infants and toddlers aged 4 to 24 months. Some of the findings were startling: infants as young as 7 months were being fed adult diets. About a quarter of infants and toddlers between 7 and 24 months were eating no vegetables, and about the same proportion were eating no fruits. Even among the children who were eating vegetables, French fries topped the list for toddlers over 18 months—and it was in the top three vegetables for infants between 9 and 12 months. By 8 months, nearly half of infants were already consuming desserts or sweetened drinks. By 24 months, a majority of toddlers were eating pastries and nearly half were drinking sweetened drinks (Fox et al., 2004).

These findings reveal a problem with how we are feeding our children in the critical early years, when they are developing food preferences and eating habits that will likely remain with them through adulthood. Convenience foods that are high in sugar and fat but low in nutrients may be a significant component of parents' diets, but if parents provide these same foods to their young children, they may be paving the way to a lifetime of unhealthful dietary habits. Experts recommend that such foods be offered to infants and toddlers sparingly, if at all. Better options include fruits, vegetables, or grains in place of snack foods and water, milk, or pure fruit juices in place of sweetened drinks. Providing these foods may take extra planning and effort on the part of parents—especially when they are foods that parents don't particularly like themselves—but experts agree that doing so is essential to stem the growing problem of childhood obesity (Fox et al., 2004; Linsday et al., 2006; O'Dea & Wilson, 2006).

Social Influences.   Social factors affect children's weight problems. Children need to control their own eating. Parents who are controlling and directive about their children's eating may produce children who lack internal controls to regulate their own food intake (Johnson & Birch, 1994; Faith, Johnson, & Allison, 1997; Wardle, Guthrie, & Sanderson, 2001; van Strien & Bazelier, 2007).

In many cases, students up to the age of adolescence are unaware of the future consequences of the typical American junk-food-and-fat diet because their bodies are engaged in vigorous growth, which masks the effects of poor diet.

Obesity has become the most common nutritional concern during adolescence. In addition to issues of health, what are some psychological concerns about obesity in adolescence?

This young woman suffers from anorexia nervosa, a severe eating disorder in which people refuse to eat, while denying that their behavior and appearance are out of the ordinary.

While some young people seem uncaring about an intake of food that is harmful and excessive, others have the opposite problem. These people—mostly adolescents—have serious eating problems that cause them to be overconcerned about fat to the point of self-harm. These young people suffer from eating disorders, a topic that we examine next.

Eating Disorders.

A rice cake in the afternoon, an apple for dinner. That was Heather Rhodes's typical diet her freshman year at St. Joseph's College in Rensselaer, Indiana, when she began to nurture a fear (exacerbated, she says, by the sudden death of a friend) that she was gaining weight. But when Rhodes, now 20, returned home to Joliet, Illinois, for summer vacation a year and a half ago, her family thought she was melting away.... Her 5'7" frame held a mere 85 pounds—down 22 pounds from her senior year in high school.... "[But] when I looked in the mirror," she says, "I thought my stomach was still huge and my face was fat." (Sandler, 1994, p. 56)

Heather's problem: a severe eating disorder, anorexia nervosa. As we know, the cultural ideal of slim and fit favors late-developing girls. But when development does occur, how do girls (and increasingly, boys) cope with an image in the mirror that deviates from the popular media ideal?

Concerns about weight are especially troubling among older children and adolescents, amounting to a dangerous disorder. The prevalence of serious eating disorders has increased significantly over the last 20 years.

A dramatic increase in food consumption fuels the rapid physical growth of adolescence. During the growth spurt, the average girl requires some 2,200 calories a day, and the average boy 2,800. Of course, not just any calories nourish this growth. Several nutrients are essential, particularly calcium and iron. Milk provides calcium for bone growth, and calcium may prevent the osteoporosis—the thinning of bones—that affects 25 percent of women in later life. Iron is also necessary, as iron-deficiency anemia is not uncommon among teenagers.

For most adolescents, the major issue is eating a sufficient balance of nutritious foods. However, two extremes of nutrition can create real threats to health for a substantial minority: obesity and eating disorders like the one afflicting Heather Rhodes.

Anorexia Nervosa. Fear of fat and of growing obese can create its own problem. Heather Rhodes suffered from **anorexia nervosa,** a severe eating disorder in which individuals refuse to eat. A troubled body image leads some adolescents to deny that their behavior and appearance, which may become skeletal, are out of the ordinary.

Anorexia is a dangerous psychological disorder; some 15 to 20 percent of its victims starve themselves to death. It primarily afflicts women between the ages of 12 and 40; intelligent, successful, and attractive white adolescent girls from affluent homes are the most susceptible. Anorexia is also becoming a problem for boys; about 10 percent of victims are male. This percentage is rising and is associated with the use of steroids (Robb & Dadson, 2002; Jacobi et al., 2004; Ricciardelli & McCabe, 2004; Crisp et al., 2006).

Though they eat little, anorexics tend to focus on food. They may shop often, collect cookbooks, talk about food, or cook huge meals for others. They may be incredibly thin, but their body images are so distorted that they see themselves as disgustingly fat and try to lose more weight. Even when they grow skeletal, they cannot see what they have become.

Bulimia, another eating disorder, is characterized by *binge eating,* consuming large amounts of food, followed by *purging* through vomiting or the use of laxatives. Bulimics may eat an entire gallon of ice cream or a whole package of tortilla chips, but then feel such powerful guilt and depression that they intentionally rid themselves of the food. The disorder poses real risks. Though a bulimia sufferer's weight remains fairly normal, the constant vomiting and diarrhea of the binge-and-purge cycles may produce a chemical imbalance that triggers heart failure.

Why eating disorders occur is not clear, but several factors are implicated. Dieting often precedes the onset of eating disorders, as society exhorts even normal-weight individuals to be ever thinner. Losing weight may lead to feelings of control and success that encourage more dieting. Girls who mature early and have a higher level of body fat are more susceptible to eating disorders in later adolescence as they try to trim their mature bodies to fit the cultural ideal of a thin,

anorexia nervosa a severe eating disorder in which individuals refuse to eat, while denying that their behavior and appearance, which may become skeletal, are out of the ordinary.

bulimia an eating disorder characterized by binges on large quantities of food, followed by purges of the food through vomiting or the use of laxatives.

boyish physique. Clinically depressed adolescents are also prone to develop eating disorders later (Pratt, Phillips, & Greydanus, 2003; Walcott, Pratt, & Patel, 2003; Giordana, 2005).

A biological cause may underlie both anorexia nervosa and bulimia. Twin studies suggest that genetic components are involved. In addition, hormonal imbalances sometimes occur in sufferers (Condit, 1990; Irwin, 1993; Treasure & Tiller, 1993; Kaye et al., 2004).

Other explanations emphasize psychological and social factors. Some experts suggest that perfectionist, overdemanding parents or other family difficulties lead to the disorders. Culture also plays a role. For example, anorexia nervosa is found only in cultures that idealize slender female bodies. Because this standard is not widespread, anorexia is not prevalent outside the United States (Haines & Neumark-Sztainer, 2006; Harrison & Hefner, 2006). For example, it is nonexistent in Asia, with two exceptions: the upper classes of Japan and Hong Kong, where Western influence is greatest.

Anorexia nervosa was not seen in the seventeenth and eighteenth centuries, when the ideal female body was plump. The increasing number of boys with anorexia in the United States may reflect a male ideal that emphasizes muscles and spurns body fat (Keel, Leon, & Fulkerson, 2001; Mangweth, Hausmann, & Walch, 2004; Makino et al., 2006; Greenberg, Cwikel, & Mirsky, 2007).

Because anorexia nervosa and bulimia have both biological and environmental causes, treatment typically requires a mix of approaches, for example, both psychological therapy and dietary modifications. In more extreme cases, hospitalization may be necessary (Porzelius, Dinsmore, & Staffelbach, 2001; Stice & Shaw, 2004; Robergeau, Joseph, & Silber, 2006).

Adulthood: Facing Reality. As people leave adolescence, they gradually learn that they can't simply extend their living habits indefinitely. One particularly painful area of change is diet.

Most young adults know which foods are nutritionally sound and how to maintain a balanced diet; they just don't bother to follow the rules—even though the rules are not that hard to follow. According to the U.S. Department of Agriculture, people can achieve good nutrition by eating foods that are low in fat and salt. Such foods—whole grain foods and cereal products, vegetables (including dried beans and peas), and fruit—also help people in their intake of complex carbohydrates and fiber. Milk and other sources of calcium are also needed to prevent osteoporosis (USDA, 1992).

Adolescents don't suffer too much from a diet high in junk foods and fat because they are undergoing tremendous growth. The body is less forgiving to young adults, who must reduce their caloric intake to maintain their health (Insel & Roth, 1991; Mattison et al., 2005).

Weight control is a difficult, and often losing, battle for many young adults. Most diets fail, producing nothing more than a seesaw cycle of gain and loss. Some obesity experts argue that the rate of dieting failure is so great that people should avoid dieting altogether and instead eat the foods they like, but in moderation (Polivy & Herman, 2002; Lowe, 2004; Putterman & Linden, 2004; Quatromoni et al., 2006; Annunziato & Lowe, 2007). With the failure of many programmed weight loss diets, a significant trend toward individualized treatment plans has emerged.

Threats to Wellness and Health

The majority of children in the United States are reasonably healthy. For example, the average preschooler experiences seven to ten colds and other minor respiratory illnesses in each of the years from age 3 to 5 (Denny & Clyde, 1983; Kalb, 1997). A runny nose due to the common cold is the most frequent—and happily, the most severe—health problem during the preschool years. Although the sniffles and coughs that are the symptoms of such illnesses are certainly distressing to children, the unpleasantness is usually not too severe and the illnesses usually last only a few days.

The danger of injuries during the preschool years is in part a result of children's high levels of physical activity. It is important to take protective measures to reduce the hazards.

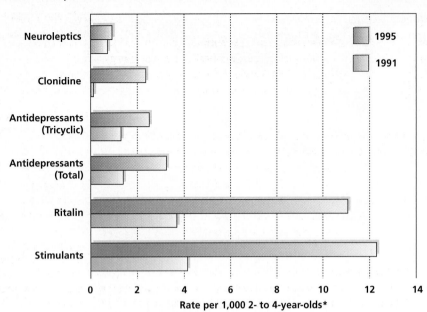

FIGURE 4.5 Numbers of Preschool Children Taking Medication for Behavioral Problems

Although there is no clear explanation as to why the use of stimulants and antidepressants has increased among children, some experts believe that medication is a quick-fix solution for behavior problems that may in fact represent normal difficulties.
Source: Zito et al., 2000.

Behavioral Problems. Although physical illness is typically a minor problem during the preschool and school years, an increasing number of children are being treated with drugs for emotional disorders such as depression. In fact, the use of drugs such as antidepressants and stimulants has grown significantly (see Figure 4.5). Although it is not clear why the increase has occurred, some experts believe that parents and teachers may be seeking a quick fix for behavior problems that may, in fact, represent normal difficulties (Pear, 2000; Zito et al., 2000; Colino, 2002; Zito, 2002).

Accidents. The greatest risk that children face comes from neither illness nor mental health problems but from accidents: Before age 10, children are twice as likely to die from an injury as from an illness. U.S. children have a 1 in 3 chance every year of receiving an injury that requires medical attention (National Safety Council, 1989; Field & Behrman, 2003).

The danger of injuries is in part a result of high levels of physical activity. Combine the physical activity, curiosity, and lack of judgment that characterize this age group, and it is no wonder that preschoolers are accident-prone.

Furthermore, some children are more apt than others to take risks and consequently to be injured. Boys, who are more active than girls and tend to take more risks, have a higher rate of injuries. Economic factors also play a role. Children raised under conditions of poverty in urban areas, whose inner-city neighborhoods may contain more hazards than more affluent areas, are two times more likely to die of injuries than children living in affluence (Morrongiello, Midgett, & Stanton, 2000; Morrongiello & Hogg, 2004).

Safeguarding the Childhood Environment. Many threats to children can be prevented entirely, or at least limited and lessened. For instance, parents and caregivers can take precautions to prevent injuries, starting by "child-proofing" homes and classrooms with electrical outlet covers and child locks on cabinets. Car seats and bike helmets can help prevent injuries from accidents. Parents and teachers also need to be aware of the dangers from long-term hazards.

For example, lead poisoning is a significant danger for many children. Some 14 million children are at risk for lead poisoning due to exposure to lead, according to the Centers for Disease Control and Prevention. Despite stringent legal restrictions on the amount of lead in paint and gasoline, lead is still found on painted walls and window frames—particularly in older homes—and in gasoline, ceramics, lead-soldered pipes, automobile and truck exhaust, and even dust and water. The U.S. Department of Health and Human Services has called lead poisoning the most severe health threat to children under age 6 (Duncan & Brooks-Gunn, 2000; Ripple & Zigler, 2003; Hubbs-Tait et al., 2005).

Lead can permanently harm children. Exposure to lead has been linked to lower intelligence, problems in verbal and auditory processing, hyperactivity, and distractibility. High lead levels have also been linked to antisocial behavior, including aggression and delinquency in school-age children. At yet higher levels of exposure, lead poisoning results in illness and death (Morgan, Garavan, & Smith, 2001; Canfield, Kreher, & Cornwell, 2003; Coscia, Ris, & Succop, 2003; Wasserman, Factor-Litvak, & Liu, 2003).

SIDS: An Ill-Understood Killer. There is one other instance of accidental death—this one affecting the very young. For a tiny percentage of infants, the normal rhythms of sleep are tragically interrupted by a mysterious disorder known as sudden infant death syndrome, or SIDS. **Sudden infant death syndrome (SIDS)** is a disorder in which seemingly healthy infants die in their sleep. Put to bed for a nap or for the night, the infant simply never wakes up.

SIDS strikes about 1 in 1,000 infants in the United States each year. Although it seems to occur when normal breathing patterns during sleep are interrupted, scientists have been unable

sudden infant death syndrome (SIDS) a disorder in which seemingly healthy infants die in their sleep.

to discover why. It is clear that infants don't smother or choke; they die a peaceful death, simply ceasing to breathe.

Although no reliable way to prevent the syndrome has been found, the American Academy of Pediatrics now suggests that babies sleep on their backs rather than on their sides or stomachs—called the back-to-sleep guideline. In addition, they suggest that parents consider giving their babies a pacifier during naps and bedtime (Task Force on Sudden Infant Death Syndrome, 2005).

The number of deaths from SIDS has decreased significantly since these guidelines were developed (see Figure 4.6). Still, SIDS is the leading cause of death in children under the age of 1 year (Eastman, 2003; Daley, 2004).

Threats to Adolescents.

Substance Use and Abuse. The use of drugs, alcohol, and tobacco, and the incidence of sexually transmitted infections may sometimes threaten health during adolescence, usually one of the healthiest periods of life. While the extent of risky behavior is difficult to gauge, preventable problems can be serious problems for adolescents' health and well-being.

Illegal Drugs. How common is illegal drug use during adolescence? Very. For instance, the most recent annual survey of nearly 50,000 U.S. students shows that almost 50 percent of high school seniors and almost 20 percent of eighth graders report having used marijuana within the past year. Although marijuana use (as well as use of other drugs) has declined over the last few years, the data on drug use still reveal substantial adolescent involvement (;Nanda & Konnur, 2008; Johnston, Bachman, & O'Malley, 2009; see Figure 4.7 and the *Neuroscience and Development* box on page 128).

Adolescents have a variety of reasons for using drugs. Some use them for the pleasurable experience they supposedly provide. Others use them to try to escape from the pressures of everyday life, however temporarily. Some adolescents try drugs simply for the thrill of doing something illegal. The drug use of well-known role models, such as film star Robert Downey Jr., may also contribute. Finally, peer pressure plays a role: Adolescents are particularly susceptible to the perceived standards of their peer groups (Urberg, Luo, & Pilgrim, 2003; Nation & Heflinger, 2006; Young et al., 2006).

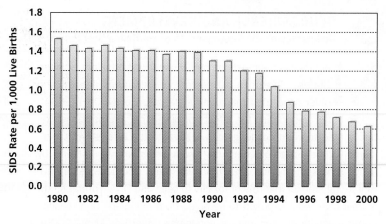

FIGURE 4.6 Declining Rates of SIDS
In the United States, SIDS rates have dropped dramatically as parents have become more informed and now put babies to sleep on their backs instead of their stomachs.
Source: American SIDS Institute, based on data from the Centers for Disease Control and Prevention and the National Center for Health Statistics, 2004.

How would you deal with adolescent drug use by your child, student, or patient? Log onto **MyVirtualChild** through **MyDevelopmentLab** to start making these decisions.

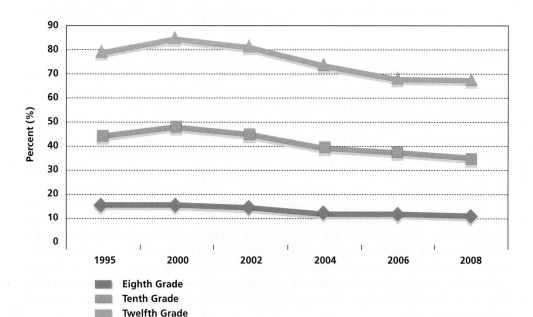

Eighth Grade
Tenth Grade
Twelfth Grade

FIGURE 4.7 Downward Trend in Marijuana Use
According to an annual survey, the proportion of students reporting marijuana use over the past 12 months has decreased since 1999. What might account for the decline in drug use?
Source: Johnston, L. D., et al., 2009.

NEUROSCIENCE AND DEVELOPMENT
Understanding the Consequences of Marijuana Use: Pot—or Not?

Marijuana is the most commonly used illicit drug in the United States. More than 40 percent of individuals age 12 and older have tried marijuana at least once (NSDUH, 2004).

To better understand the effects of marijuana, neuroscientist Rebecca Maertens and colleagues investigated the effects from marijuana versus tobacco, comparing *mainstream smoke* (inhaled by active smokers) and *sidestream smoke* (major components of environmental smoke) in terms of toxicity to cells and DNA. For the study, animal cells were exposed to samples from marijuana and tobacco under a variety of experimental conditions (Maertens et al., 2009).

The results showed that tobacco and marijuana smoke differed substantially in terms of their toxicity to cells, their ability to induce or increase cell mutation, and their ability to induce chromosomal damage. Specifically, marijuana smoke was more damaging to cells and DNA than tobacco smoke. However, tobacco smoke caused chromosomal damage, while marijuana smoke did not.

In short, both marijuana and tobacco smoke was damaging, though in different ways. Furthermore, the findings do not speak to the fact that smoke of any kind is dangerous in terms of increasing the risks of lung cancer.

- *Based on these results, what advice would you give an adolescent regarding the use of tobacco and marijuana?*

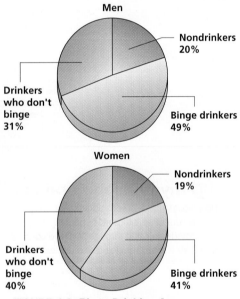

FIGURE 4.8 Binge Drinking Among College Students
For men, binge drinking was defined as consuming five or more drinks in one sitting; for women, the total was four or more. Why is binge drinking popular?
Source: Wechsler et al., 2002.

The use of illegal drugs is dangerous in several respects. For instance, some drugs are addictive. **Addictive drugs** are drugs that produce a biological or psychological dependence in users, leading to increasingly powerful cravings for them.

When drugs produce a biological addiction, their presence in the body becomes so common that the body is unable to function in their absence. Furthermore, addiction causes actual physical—and potentially lingering—changes in the nervous system. In such cases, drug intake no longer may provide a "high," but may be necessary simply to maintain the perception of everyday normalcy (Cami & Farré, 2003; Munzar, Cami, & Farré, 2003).

In addition to physical addiction, drugs also can produce psychological addiction. In such cases, people grow to depend on drugs to cope with the everyday stress of life. If drugs are used as an escape, they may prevent adolescents from confronting—and potentially solving—the problems that led them to drug use in the first place. Finally, drugs may be dangerous because even casual use of less hazardous drugs can escalate to more dangerous forms of substance abuse (Toch, 1995; Segal & Stewart, 1996).

Alcohol: Use and Abuse. More than 75 percent of college students have something in common: They've consumed at least one alcoholic drink during the last 30 days. More than 40 percent say they've had 5 or more drinks within the past 2 weeks, and some 16 percent have 16 or more drinks per week. High school students, too, are drinkers: Some 76 percent of high school seniors report having had an alcoholic drink in the last year, and in some groups—such as male athletes—the proportion of drinkers is even higher (Carmody, 1990; NIAAA, 1990; Center on Addiction and Substance Abuse, 1994; Carr, Kennedy, & Dimick, 1996).

Binge drinking is a particular problem on college campuses. For men, it is defined as drinking five or more drinks in one sitting; for women, who tend to weigh less and whose bodies absorb alcohol less efficiently, binge drinking is defined as four drinks in one sitting. Surveys find that almost half of male college students and over 40 percent of female college students say they participated in binge drinking during the previous 2 weeks (see Figure 4.8).

Binge drinking affects even those who don't drink or drink very little. Two-thirds of lighter drinkers reported that they had been disturbed by drunken students while sleeping or studying. Around a third had been insulted or humiliated by a drunken student, and 25 percent of women said they had been the target of an unwanted sexual advance by a drunk classmate (Wechsler et al., 2000, 2002, 2003).

Why do adolescents start to drink? There are many reasons. For some—especially male athletes, whose rate of drinking tends to be higher than that of the adolescent general population—drinking is seen as a way of proving they can drink as much as anybody. Others drink for the same reason that some use drugs: It releases inhibitions and tension and reduces stress. Many begin because the conspicuous examples of drunkenness strewn around campus cause them to assume that everyone is drinking heavily, a phenomenon known as the *false consensus effect* (Pavis, Cunningham-Burley, & Amos, 1997; Nelson & Wechsler, 2003; Weitzman, Nelson, & Wechsler, 2003).

addictive drugs drugs that produce a biological or psychological dependence in users, leading to increasingly powerful cravings for them.

For some adolescents, alcohol use becomes a habit that cannot be controlled. **Alcoholics**, those with alcohol problems, learn to depend on alcohol and are unable to control their drinking. They also become increasingly able to tolerate alcohol and therefore need to drink ever-larger amounts of liquor in order to bring about the positive effects they crave. Some drink throughout the day, while others go on binges in which they consume huge quantities of alcohol (NIAAA, 1990; Morse & Flavin, 1992).

The reasons that some adolescents–or anyone—become alcoholics are not fully understood. Genetics plays a role: Alcoholism runs in families. Yet not all alcoholics have family members with alcohol problems. For those adolescents, alcoholism may be triggered by efforts to deal with the stress that having an alcoholic parent or family member can cause (Bushman, 1993; Boyd, Howard, & Zucker, 1995; Berenson, 2005).

Tobacco: The Dangers of Smoking.   Most adolescents are well aware of the dangers of smoking, but many still indulge in it. Recent figures show that, overall, a smaller proportion of adolescents smoke than in prior decades, but the numbers remain substantial; and within certain groups they are increasing. Smoking is on the rise among girls, and in several countries, including Austria, Norway, and Sweden, the proportion of girls who smoke is higher than the proportion of boys. There are racial differences as well: White children and children in lower socioeconomic status households are more likely to experiment with cigarettes and to start smoking earlier than African American children and children living in higher socioeconomic status households. Also, significantly more white males of high school age smoke than do African American males in high school, although the differences have narrowed in recent years (Harrell et al., 1998; Stolberg, 1998; Baker, Brandon, & Chassin, 2004; Fergusson et al., 2007).

Smoking is becoming a habit that is harder and harder to maintain. There are growing social sanctions against it. And as more places, including schools and places of business, have become "smoke-free," it's becoming more difficult to find a comfortable place to smoke. Even so, a good number of adolescents still smoke, despite knowing the dangers of smoking and of secondhand smoke.

Why do adolescents begin to smoke and maintain the habit? For one thing, adolescents are influenced by advertisements for cigarettes in the media, even if the ads aren't targeting their age group. In addition, the number of images of attractive, popular actors smoking in films viewed by adolescents is increasing. As a result, among at least some adolescents, smoking is viewed as a "cool" activity (Aloise-Young, Slater, & Cruickshank, 2006; Weiss et al., 2006; Golmier, Chebat, & Gelinas-Chebat, 2007; Sargent, Tanski, & Gibson, 2007).

Cigarettes are also very addicting. Nicotine, the active chemical ingredient of cigarettes, can produce biological and psychological dependency very quickly. Although one or two cigarettes generally do not usually produce a lifetime smoker, it takes only a little more to start the habit. People who smoke as few as 10 cigarettes early in their lives stand an 80 percent chance of becoming habitual smokers (Bowen et al., 1991; Stacy et al., 1992; Haberstick et al., 2007).

Smoking produces a pleasant emotional state that smokers seek to maintain. Seeing parents and peers smoking increases the chances that an adolescent will take up the habit. Finally, smoking is sometimes seen as an adolescent rite of passage, a sign of growing up (Botvin et al., 1994; Webster, Hunter, & Keats, 1994; Kodl & Mermelstein, 2004).

Sexually Transmitted Infections.

Krista Blake was 18 and looking forward to her first year at Youngstown State University in Ohio. She and her boyfriend were talking about getting married. Her life was, she says, "basic, white-bread America." Then she went to the doctor, complaining about a backache, and found out she had the AIDS virus.

Blake had been infected with HIV, the virus that causes AIDS, two years earlier by an older boy, a hemophiliac. "He knew that he was infected, and he didn't tell me," she says. "And he didn't do anything to keep me from getting infected, either." (Becahy, 1992, p. 49)

AIDS.   Krista Blake, who later died from the disorder, was not alone: *Acquired immunodeficiency syndrome,* or *AIDS,* is one of the leading causes of death among young people. AIDS has no cure and ultimately brings death to those who are infected with the HIV virus that produces the disease.

Because AIDS is spread primarily through sexual contact, it is classified as a **sexually transmitted infection (STI)**. Although it began as a problem that primarily affected homosexuals,

Alcoholism is a serious problem for some adolescents.

alcoholics   persons with alcohol problems who have learned to depend on alcohol and are unable to control their drinking.

sexually transmitted infection (STI)   a disease that is spread through sexual contact.

FIGURE 4.9 Sexually Transmitted Infections (STIS) Among Adolescents
Why are adolescents in particular danger of contracting an STI?
Source: Alan Guttmacher Institute, 1993a; Weinstock, Berman, & Cates, 2004.

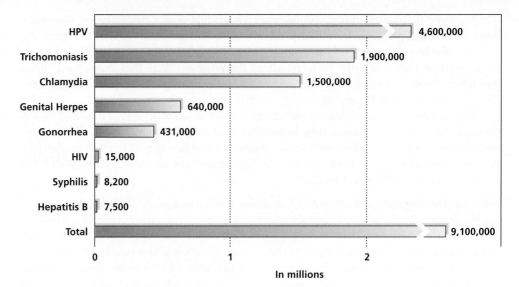

In millions

it has spread to other populations, including heterosexuals and intravenous drug users. Minorities have been particularly hard hit. For example, African Americans account for 49 percent of new diagnoses of the AIDS virus, and 19 percent of those with the disease are Hispanic American. Already, 20 million people have died due to AIDS, and the number of people living with the disease numbers almost 40 million worldwide (Centers for Disease Control and Prevention, 2006; UNAIDS & World Health Organization, 2006).

Other Sexually Transmitted Infections. Although AIDS is the deadliest of sexually transmitted infections, there are a number of other STIs that are far more common (see Figure 4.9). In fact, one out of four adolescents contracts an STI before graduating from high school. Overall, around 2.5 million teenagers contract an STI, such as the ones listed in the figure (Leary, 1996; Weinstock, Berman, & Cates, 2004).

The most common STI is *human papilloma virus (HPV)*. HPV can be transmitted through genital contact without intercourse. Most infections do not have symptoms, but HPV can produce genital warts and in some cases lead to cervical cancer. A vaccine that protects against some kinds of HPV is now available. The U.S. Centers for Disease Control and Prevention recommends it be routinely administered to girls 11 to 12 years of age—a recommendation that has provoked considerable political reaction (Friedman et al., 2006; Kahn, 2007).

Another common STI is *trichomoniasis,* an infection in the vagina or penis, which is caused by a parasite. Initially without symptoms, it can eventually cause a painful discharge. *Chlamydia,* a bacterial infection, initially has few symptoms, but later it causes burning urination and a discharge from the penis or vagina. It can lead to pelvic inflammation and even to sterility. Chlamydial infections can be treated successfully with antibiotics (Nockels & Oakshott, 1999; Favers et al., 2003).

Genital herpes is a virus not unlike the cold sores that sometimes appear around the mouth. The first symptoms of herpes are often small blisters or sores around the genitals, which may break open and become quite painful. Although the sores may heal after a few weeks, the infection often recurs after an interval, and the cycle repeats itself. When the sores reappear, the infection, for which there is no cure, is contagious.

Gonorrhea and *syphilis* are the STIs that have been recognized for the longest time; cases were recorded by ancient historians. Until the advent of antibiotics, both infections were deadly. However, today both can be treated quite effectively.

Contracting an STI is not only an immediate problem during adolescence, but could become a problem later in life, too. Some infections increase the chances of future infertility and cancer.

Avoiding STIs. Short of abstinence, there is no certain way to avoid STIs. Even when adolescents have been exposed to substantial sex education, the use of safer sex practices is far from universal because teens are prone to feel invulnerable and are therefore more likely to engage in risky behavior. This is particularly true when adolescents perceive that their partner is "safe"—

someone they know well and with whom they are involved in a relatively long-term relationship (Freiberg, 1998; Lefkowitz, Sigman, & Kit-fong Au, 2000; Tinsley, Lees, & Sumartojo, 2004).

Unfortunately, unless an individual knows the complete sexual history and STI status of a partner, unprotected sex remains a risky business. And learning a partner's complete sexual history is difficult. Not only is it embarrassing to ask, but partners may not be accurate reporters, whether from ignorance of their own exposure, embarrassment, a sense of privacy, or simply forgetfulness. As a result, STIs remain a significant problem.

Fitness and Health: Staying Well.   Obesity remains a concern right up through adolescence and into adulthood largely because an unhealthy diet is often accompanied by a low level of exercise.

"Remember when we used to have to fatten the kids up first?"

One survey found that by the end of the teenage years, few females get much exercise outside of school physical education classes; the older they get, the less they exercise. This is especially true for older black female adolescents, more than half of whom report *no* physical exercise outside of school, compared with about a third of white adolescents (Burke et al., 2006; Deforche, De Bourdeaudhuij, & Tanghe, 2006; Delva, O'Malley, & Johnston, 2006).

Given how energetic children can be, it is surprising that a major factor in childhood obesity is a lack of exercise. School-age children tend to engage in relatively little exercise and are not particularly fit. Around 40 percent of boys 6 to 12 are unable to do more than one pull-up, and a quarter can't do any.

Furthermore, children have shown little or no improvement in the amount of exercise they get, despite national efforts to increase the fitness of school-age children, in part because many schools have reduced the time available for recess and gym classes. From 6 to 18, boys decrease their physical activity by 24 percent and girls by 36 percent (Lipton, 2003; Moore, Gao, & Bradlee, 2003; Sallis & Glanz, 2006; Weiss & Raz, 2006).

For school-age girls, the lack of exercise may reflect a lack of organized sports or good athletic facilities for women. It may be the result of lingering cultural norms that suggest athletic participation is more the realm of boys than girls. Whatever the reason, lack of exercise feeds the increase in obesity.

Another possible answer is that many kids are watching television and playing computer games. Such sedentary activities not only prevent exercise, but children often snack while viewing TV or surfing the Web (Tartamella, Herscher, & Woolston, 2005; Anderson & Butcher, 2006; Taveras et al., 2006).

Adulthood: An Unforgiving World.   The situation only gets worse in adulthood. If you are a professional athlete, you are generally considered over the hill by the end of your 20s. Although there are notable exceptions, even athletes who train constantly tend to lose their physical edge once they reach their 30s. In some sports, the peak passes even sooner. Swimmers are at their best in their late teens, and gymnasts even younger (Schultz & Curnow, 1988).

The fitness of adulthood doesn't come naturally or to everyone. To reach their physical potential, people must exercise and maintain a proper diet.

Height and Weight.   Most people reach their maximum height in their 20s and remain close to that height until around 55. People then begin a "settling" process in which the bones attached to the spinal column become less dense. Although the loss of height is very slow, women average a 2-inch decline and men a 1-inch decline over the rest of the life span (Rossman, 1977).

Women are more prone to this decline because they are at greater risk of osteoporosis. **Osteoporosis**, a condition in which the bones become brittle, fragile, and thin, is often caused by a lack of calcium in the diet. Although it has a genetic component, osteoporosis is one aspect of aging that can be affected by lifestyle choices. Women—and men—can reduce the risk of osteoporosis by eating a calcium-rich diet (calcium is found in milk, yogurt, cheese, and other dairy products) and by exercising regularly (Prince et al., 1991; Alvaret-Leon, Roman-Vinas, & Serra-Majem, 2006; Schoenmaker et al., 2006).

osteoporosis   a condition in which the bones become brittle, fragile, and thin, often brought about by a lack of calcium in the diet.

Body fat tends to increase in middle adulthood. Even those who have always been slim may begin to gain weight. Because height is not increasing, and actually may be declining, these gains increase the incidence of obesity.

This weight gain can often be avoided. Lifestyle choices play a major role. People who exercise regularly tend to avoid obesity, as do those who live in cultures where life is more active than it is in many Western cultures.

Declines in strength accompany height and weight changes. Strength gradually decreases, particularly in the back and leg muscles. By age 60, people average a 10 percent loss of their maximum strength. Still, such a loss is relatively minor, and most people are easily able to compensate (Spence, 1989). Lifestyle choices matter. Regular exercise tends to make people feel stronger and more able to compensate for any losses.

Only a small time commitment is enough to yield significant health benefits. According to the American College of Sports Medicine and the Centers for Disease Control and Prevention, people should accumulate at least 30 minutes of moderate physical activity at least 5 days a week. Exercise time can be continuous or in bouts of at least 10 minutes, as long as the daily total reaches 30 minutes. Moderate activity includes walking briskly at 3 to 4 mph, biking at speeds up to 10 mph, golfing while carrying or pulling clubs, fishing by casting from shore, playing Ping-Pong, or canoeing at 2 to 4 mph. Even common household chores, such as weeding, vacuuming, and mowing with a power mower, provide moderate exercise (American College of Sports Medicine, 1997).

The advantages of exercise are many. It increases cardiovascular fitness, meaning that the heart and circulatory system operate more efficiently. Furthermore, lung capacity increases, raising endurance. Muscles become stronger, and the body is more flexible and maneuverable. The range of movement is greater, and the muscles, tendons, and ligaments are more elastic. Moreover, exercise during this period helps reduce *osteoporosis,* the thinning of the bones, in later life.

Exercise also may optimize the immune response of the body, helping it fight off disease. It may even decrease stress and anxiety and reduce depression. It can provide a sense of control over the body and a feeling of accomplishment (Mutrie, 1997; Faulkner & Biddle, 2004; Harris, Cronkite, & Moos, 2006; Wise et al., 2006). The kicker is its ultimate reward: It is associated with increased longevity (see Figure 4.10; Stevens et al., 2002).

Health.   Health risks in general increase only slightly immediately after childhood. People are less susceptible to colds and other minor illnesses than they were as children, and they recover quickly from those that they do come down with.

Not all adults fare equally well. Lifestyle decisions, such as the use—or abuse—of alcohol, tobacco, or drugs or engaging in unprotected sex, can hasten *secondary aging,* physical declines brought about by environmental factors or behavioral choices. These substances can also increase the risk from the causes mentioned earlier.

FROM AN
EDUCATOR'S
PERSPECTIVE:
Can people be taught the lifelong advantages of regular exercise? Should school-based physical education programs be changed to foster a lifelong commitment to exercise?

FIGURE 4.10 The Result of Fitness: Longevity
The greater the fitness level, the lower the death rate tends to be for both men and women.
Source: Blair et al., 1989, pp. 2395–2401.

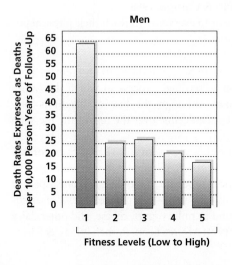

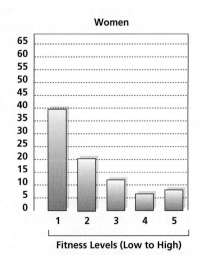

Adults in their 20s and 30s stand a higher risk of dying from accidents, primarily car accidents, than from most other causes. But there are other killers: Among the leading sources of death for people 25 to 34 are AIDS, cancer, heart disease, and suicide. Amid the grim statistics of mortality, the age 35 represents a significant milestone. It is at that point that illness and disease overtake accidents as the leading cause of death—the first time this is true since infancy.

Midlife Transitions. Middle adulthood is a time of significant transitions. Grown children leave home. People change the way they view their career. Sometimes they change careers entirely. Marriages undergo reevaluation. Often, couples find this a period of strengthened ties as the "empty nest" leaves them free for uninterrupted intimacy. But sometimes they divorce. Middle age is also a period of deepening roots. Family and friends ascend in importance as career ambitions begin to take a backseat. And there is more time for leisure activities.

Health concerns become increasingly important to people in middle age. Surveys Surveys show that not only are adults worried about specific health issues (such as obesity and cancer), but are even more concerned about access to health care and its cost (Jones, 2008; see Figure 4.11).

For most people, however, midlife is a period of health. According to census figures, the vast majority of middle-aged adults report no chronic health difficulties and face no limitations on their activities.

In some ways health is better in middle adulthood than in earlier periods of life. People ages 45 to 65 are less likely than younger adults to experience infections, allergies, respiratory diseases, and digestive problems. They may contract fewer of these diseases now because they have already experienced them and built up immunities (Sterns, Barrett, & Alexander, 1985).

Certain chronic diseases do begin to appear in middle adulthood. Arthritis typically begins after age 40, and diabetes is most likely to occur between ages 50 and 60, particularly in those who are overweight. Hypertension (high blood pressure) is one of the most frequent chronic disorders. Often called the "silent killer" because it is symptomless, hypertension, if left untreated, greatly increases the risk of strokes and heart disease. For such reasons, many preventive and diagnostic medical tests are routinely recommended for midlife adults (see Table 4.3 on page 134).

The onset of chronic diseases in middle age boosts the death rate above that of earlier periods. Still, death remains rare: Only three out of every hundred 40-year-olds are expected to die before age 50, and eight out of every hundred 50-year-olds are expected to die before age 60. And the death rate for people between 40 and 60 has declined dramatically over the past 50 years. It now stands at just half of what it was in the 1940s. There also are cultural variations in health, as we consider next (Smedley & Syme, 2000).

Cultural Factors.   Overall figures for the health of middle-aged adults mask vast individual differences. While most people are healthy, some are beset by a variety of ailments. Genetics plays a role. For instance, hypertension often runs in families.

SES.   Socioeconomic status (SES) is a significant factor. For whites and African Americans of the same SES level, the death rate for African Americans is actually lower than for whites. Members of lower-income families, however, are more likely to experience a disabling illness. There are many reasons for this. People in lower SES households are more apt to work in dangerous occupations, such as mining or construction work. Lower-income people also often have inferior or no health care coverage. The crime rates and environmental pollutants are generally higher in lower-income neighborhoods. A higher incidence of accidents and health hazards, and thus a higher death rate, are linked to lower levels of income (U.S. Bureau of the Census, 1990b; Fingerhut & Makuc, 1992; Dahl & Birkelund, 1997).

Gender.   Gender also makes a difference. Men in midlife are more apt to die than women of the same age (e.g., in automobile accidents), a trend that holds true from birth.

Still, the incidence of illness among women is higher than among men. Women are more susceptible to minor, short-term illness and chronic, but non-life-threatening diseases such as

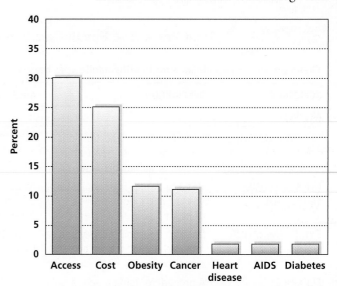

FIGURE 4.11 Health Worries of Adulthood
During adulthood, healthcare cost and access are significant concerns—even greater than specific health problems such as obesity and cancer.
Source: Jones, J. (2008, December 1). Healthcare access, cost are top health concerns. Gallup Poll, reported at http://www.gallup.com/poll/112516/healthcare-access-cost-top-health-concerns.aspx)

TABLE 4.3   Adult Preventive Health Care Screening Recommendations

These are general guidelines for healthy adults who have no symptoms of disease.

SCREENING	DESCRIPTION	AGES 40–49	AGES 50–59	AGE 60+
All Adults				
BLOOD PRESSURE	Used to detect hypertension, which can lead to heart attack, stroke, or kidney disease	Every 2 years	Every 2 years	Every 2 years. Every year if family history of hypertension
CHOLESTEROL—TOTAL/HDL	Used to detect high cholesterol levels, which increase risk of heart disease	All adults should receive total cholesterol screening, HDL cholesterol, LDL cholesterol, and triglycerides AT LEAST ONCE. Cardiac risk factors and lipoprotein results will determine frequency of follow-up by your health care provider		
EYE EXAMINATION	Used to determine if glasses required and check for eye disease	Every 2–4 years Diabetics—Every year	Every 2–4 years Diabetics—Every year	Every 2–4 years. At age 65 and over, every 1–2 years. Diabetics—Every year
FLEXIBLE SIGMOIDOSCOPY OR DOUBLE CONTRAST BARIUM ENEMA OR COLONOSCOPY	A procedure using a scope or X-ray to detect cancer of the colon and rectum		Baseline at age 50. Every 3–5 years after initial test	Every 3–5 years. Age to stop depends on health. Follow up normal colonoscopy in 8–10 years
FECAL OCCULT BLOOD SCREENING	Detects unseen blood in stool, which is early warning sign for colon cancer		Every year	Every year
RECTAL EXAM (DIGITAL)	Examination of prostate or ovaries to detect cancer		Every year	Every year
URINALYSIS SCREENING	Examination to detect presence of excess of protein in urine	Every 5 years	Every 5 years	Every 3–5 years
IMMUNIZATIONS (SHOTS): Tetanus	Protection against infection after injury	Every 10 years	Every 10 years	Every 10 years
INFLUENZA (FLU)	Protection against the influenza virus	Any person with chronic medical conditions such as heart, lung, kidney disease, diabetes	Annually, age 50 and over	Annually, age 65 and over
PNEUMOCOCCAL	Protection against pneumonia			At age 65, then every 6 years
Additional Guidelines for Women				
BREAST SELF-EXAM/BREAST EXAM BY PROVIDER	Examination to detect changes in breast that may indicate cancer	Every month/Every year	Every month/Every year	Every month/Every year
MAMMOGRAM	Low-dose X-ray used to locate tumors for early detection of breast cancer	Every year	Every year	Every year
PAP SMEAR	Test that takes small sample of cells to detect cervical cancer or precancer cells	After 3 normal tests in a row, screen every 2–3 years unless at special risk	After 3 normal tests in a row, screen every 2–3 years unless at special risk	Women 70 and older with 3 normal tests in a row and no abnormal tests in the 10 years prior to age 70 may cease having Pap test
PELVIC EXAM	Examination to detect pelvic abnormality	Every year (if ovaries remain after hysterectomy)	Every year (if ovaries remain after hysterectomy)	Every year (if ovaries remain after hysterectomy)
Additional Guidelines for Men				
PROSTATE SPECIFIC ANTIGEN	Blood test used to detect cancer of the prostate gland	Positive family history cancer—Every year (African Americans: Every year)	Every year upon doctor's advice	Until age 75, every year upon doctor's advice
TESTICULAR SELF-EXAM	Examination to detect changes in testicles that may indicate cancer	Every month	Every month	Every month

Source: Adapted from Ochsner Clinic Foundation, 2003.

The murder rate in the United States is significantly higher than in any other developed country.

migraine headaches, while men are more susceptible to serious illnesses such as heart disease. Fewer women smoke than men, which reduces their risk for cancer and heart disease; women drink less alcohol than men, which lowers the incidence of cirrhosis of the liver and auto accidents; and they work at less dangerous jobs (McDonald, 1999).

Another reason for the higher rate of illness in women may be that more medical research targets men and the disorders they suffer. The vast majority of medical research money goes to preventing life-threatening diseases faced mostly by men, rather than to chronic conditions such as heart disease that may cause disability and suffering, but not necessarily death. Typically, research on diseases that strike both men and women focuses on men as subjects rather than women. This bias is now being addressed in initiatives by the U.S. National Institutes of Health, but the historical pattern has been one of gender discrimination by a male-dominated research community (Vidaver, 2000).

Race and Violence. Another major cause of death is violence. The murder rate is significantly higher in the United States than in any other developed country (see Figure 4.12). The U.S. murder rate of 4.5 per 100,000 men is more than nine times greater than that of Japan. Statistics like this can justify the conclusion that violence is "as American as apple pie" (Berkowitz, 1993; Smith-Rosenberg, 2010).

Murder rates also depend significantly on racial factors. African Americans have twice the death rate of Caucasians, and minorities in general have a higher likelihood of dying through homicide than the Caucasian majority.

Murder—the fifth most frequent cause of death for young adult white Americans—is the most likely cause of death for African Americans, and it is a significant factor for Hispanic Americans. In some areas of the country, a young black male has a higher probability of dying violently than a soldier in the Iraq War had. Overall, an African American male has a 1 in 21 chance of being murdered during his lifetime, compared with the 1 in 131 chance for white males (Centers for Disease Control, 1991; Berkowitz, 1993; Triandis, 1994).

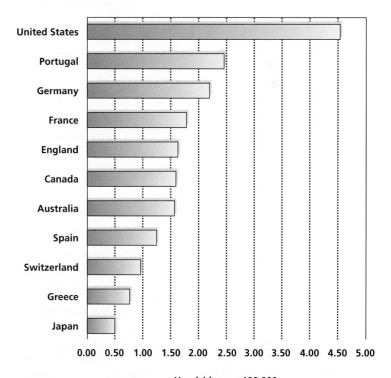

Homicides per 100,000

FIGURE 4.12 Tracking Murder
The murder rate (per 100,000 men) is far higher in the United States than in any other developed country. What features of U.S. society contribute to this state of affairs?
Source: United Nations Survey on Crime Trends, 2000.

Cultural factors also influence younger adults' lifestyles and health-related behavior, as we examine next.

DEVELOPMENTAL DIVERSITY
How Cultural Beliefs Influence Health and Health Care

Manolita recently suffered a heart attack. She was advised by her doctor to change her eating and activity habits or face the risk of another life-threatening heart attack. During the period that followed, Manolita dramatically changed her eating and activity habits. She also began going to church and praying extensively. After a recent check-up, Manolita is in the best shape of her life. What are some of the reasons for Manolita's amazing recovery? (Murguia, Peterson, & Zea, 1997, p. 16)

After reading this passage, would you conclude that Manolita recovered her health because (a) she changed her eating and activity habits; (b) she became a better person; (c) God was testing her faith; or (d) her doctor prescribed the correct changes?

When asked this question in a survey, more than two-thirds of Latino immigrants from Central America, South America, or the Caribbean believed that "God was testing her faith" had a moderate or great effect on her recovery, although most also agreed that a change in eating and activity habits was important (Murguia, Peterson, & Zea, 1997).

According to psychologists Alejandro Murguia, Rolf Peterson, and Maria Zea (1997), cultural health beliefs, along with demographic and psychological barriers, can affect the use of physicians and medical care. They suggest that Latinos are more likely than non-Hispanic whites to believe in supernatural causes of illness, which may explain why Latinos are the least likely of any Western ethnic group to seek the help of a physician when they are ill.

Health care providers need to take cultural beliefs into account when treating members of different cultural groups. For example, if a patient believes that the source of his or her illness is a spell cast by a jealous romantic rival, the patient may not comply with medical regimens that ignore that perceived source. To provide effective health care, then, health care providers must be sensitive to such cultural health beliefs.

Risks Across the Life Span

It was a normal exercise session for Jerome Yanger. Up at 5:30 AM, he climbed onto his exercise bike and began vigorously peddling, hoping to meet, and exceed, his average speed of 14 miles per hour. Stationed in front of the television, he used the remote control to tune to the morning business news. Occasionally glancing up at the television, he began reading a report he had begun the night before, silently cursing at some of the poor sales figures he was seeing. By the time his half-hour of exercise was over, he had finished the report, signed a few letters his administrative assistant had typed for him, and left two voice-mail messages for some colleagues.

Most of us would be ready for a nap after such a packed half-hour. For Jerome Yanger, however, it was routine: He always tried to multitask, thinking it more efficient. Developmentalists might see it as symptomatic of a behavior style that puts Jerome at risk for coronary heart disease.

Physical and Psychological Disorders. Despite common misconceptions, most people are healthy in adulthood, and most of the illnesses and diseases found in late adulthood are not peculiar to old age; people of all ages suffer from cancer and heart disease, for instance. However, the incidence of these and many other diseases rises with age, raising the odds that an elderly person will be ill during the period. Moreover, while younger people can readily rebound from a variety of health problems, older persons bounce back more slowly from illnesses. And ultimately, the illness may get the best of an older person, preventing a full recovery.

Common Physical Disorders. The leading causes of death in elderly people are heart disease, cancer, and stroke. Close to three-quarters of people in late adulthood die from these problems. Because aging is associated with a weakening of the body's immune system, older adults are also more susceptible to infectious diseases (Feinberg, 2000). In addition to their risk of fatal diseases and conditions, most older people have at least one chronic, long-term condition (AARP, 1990). For instance, *arthritis,* an inflammation of one or more joints, afflicts roughly half of older people. Arthritis can cause painful swelling in various parts of the body, and it can be disabling. Sufferers can find themselves unable to carry out the simplest of everyday activities, such as unscrewing the cap of a jar of food or turning a key in a lock. Although aspirin and other drugs can relieve some of the swelling and reduce the pain, the condition cannot be cured (Burt & Harris, 1994).

Around one-third of older people have *hypertension,* or high blood pressure. Many people who have high blood pressure are unaware of their condition because it does not have any symptoms, which makes it more dangerous. Over time, higher tension within the circulatory system can result in deterioration of the blood vessels and heart, and can raise the risk of cerebrovascular disease, or stroke, if it is not treated (Wiggins & Uwaydat, 2006).

Coronary Heart Disease. More men die in middle age from heart and circulatory system diseases than from any other cause. Women are less vulnerable, but they are not immune. Each year such diseases kill around 200,000 people under the age of 65, and they are responsible for more loss of work and disability days due to hospitalization than any other cause.

Risk Factors for Heart Disease. Although heart and circulatory diseases are a major problem, some people have a much lower risk than others. The death rate in some countries, such as Japan, is only a quarter the rate in the United States. A few other countries have a considerably higher death rate. Why?

The answer is both genetics and environment. Some people seem genetically predisposed to heart disease. If a person's parents suffered from it, the likelihood is greater that she or he will too. Similarly, sex and age are risk factors: Men are more likely to suffer from heart disease, and the risk rises as people age.

Environment and lifestyle choices are also important. Cigarette smoking, a diet high in fats and cholesterol, and a lack of physical exercise all increase the risk of heart disease. Such factors may explain country-to-country variations in the rate of heart disease. For example, the death rate from heart disease in Japan is relatively low and may be due to differences in diet: The typical Japanese diet is much lower in fat than it is in the United States (Zhou et al., 2003; Wilcox et al., 2006; De Meersman & Stein, 2007).

Diet is not the only factor. Psychological factors—particularly how stress is perceived and experienced—appear to be related to heart disease. For instance, a set of personality characteristics, known as Type A behavior, appears to be a factor in the development of coronary heart disease.

The **Type A behavior pattern** is characterized by competitiveness, impatience, and a tendency toward frustration and hostility. Type A people are extremely ambitious and they engage in *polyphasic activities*—multiple activities carried out simultaneously. They are the true multitaskers whom you see talking on their phones while working on their laptop computers while riding the commuter train—and eating breakfast. Easily angered, they become both verbally and nonverbally hostile if prevented from reaching their goals.

In contrast, many people have virtually the opposite characteristics in what is known as the Type B behavior pattern. The **Type B behavior pattern** is characterized by noncompetitiveness, patience, and a lack of aggression. In contrast to Type A's, Type B's experience little sense of time urgency, and they are rarely hostile.

Most people are not purely Type A's or Type B's. In fact, these types represent the ends of a continuum, with most people falling somewhere in between. Still, the majority come close to one or the other of the two categories. These categories become important in midlife because research suggests that the distinction is related to the risk of coronary heart disease. Type A men have twice the rate of coronary heart disease, a greater number of fatal heart attacks, and five times as many heart problems as Type B men (Rosenman, 1990; Strube, 1990; Wielgosz & Nolan, 2000).

The Threat of Cancer. Few diseases are as frightening as cancer, and many middle-aged adults view a cancer diagnosis as a death sentence. Although the reality is different—many forms of cancer respond well to medical treatment, and 40 percent of those diagnosed are still alive 5 years later—the disease raises many fears. And there is no denying that cancer is the second-leading cause of death in the United States (Smedley & Syme, 2000).

Type A behavior pattern behavior characterized by competitiveness, impatience, and a tendency toward frustration and hostility.

Type B behavior pattern behavior characterized by noncompetitiveness, patience, and a lack of aggression.

The precise trigger for cancer is still not known, but the process by which it spreads is clear. Certain cells in the body begin to multiply rapidly and uncontrollably. As they increase in number, these cells form tumors. Unimpeded, they draw nutrients from healthy cells and body tissue. Eventually, they destroy the body's ability to function.

Like heart disease, cancer is associated with a variety of genetic and environmental risk factors. Some cancers have clear genetic components. For example, a family history of breast cancer—the most common cause of cancer death among women—raises the risk for a woman.

Several environmental and behavioral factors are also related to the risk of cancer. Poor nutrition, smoking, alcohol use, exposure to sunlight, exposure to radiation, and particular occupational hazards (such as exposure to certain chemicals or asbestos) are all known to increase the chances of developing cancer.

After a diagnosis, several forms of treatment are possible, depending on the type of cancer. One treatment is *radiation therapy,* in which radiation targets the tumor in an attempt to destroy it. Patients undergoing *chemotherapy* ingest controlled doses of toxic substances meant to poison the tumor. Finally, surgery is used to remove the tumor (and often the surrounding tissue). The form of treatment is determined by how far the cancer has spread when it is first identified.

Because early detection improves a patient's chances, diagnostic techniques that help identify the first signs of cancer are of great importance. This is especially true in middle adulthood, when the risk of certain cancers increases.

Physicians urge that women do routine breast exams and men regularly check their testicles for signs of cancer. Cancer of the prostate gland, the most common type of cancer in men, can be detected by routine rectal exams and by a blood test that identifies prostate-specific antigen (PSA).

Mammograms provide internal scans of women's breasts to help identify early-stage cancer. However, at what age women should begin to routinely have the procedure has been controversial, as we see in the *From Research to Practice* box.

Psychological and Mental Disorders. Some 15 to 25 percent of those over age 65 are thought to show some symptoms of psychological disorder, although this represents a lower prevalence rate than in younger adults. The behavioral symptoms related to these disorders are sometimes different in those over 65 than those displayed by younger adults (Haight, 1991; Whitbourne, 2001).

FROM RESEARCH TO PRACTICE
When to Begin Routine Mammograms

I found the lump in February.... Buried deep in my left breast, it was rock-hard, the size of a BB, and it hurt. I wondered if it might be cancer. Like blue eyes and a sense of humor, the disease runs in my family. But not breast cancer. And not me. I was too young. OK. I had recently turned 40, but I was healthy. I worked out three times a week and I was almost a vegetarian. My next physical was only a month away. I'd have it checked then. (Driedger, 1994, p. 46)

For Sharon Driedger, feeling healthy, exercising, and eating a good diet was not enough: She did have cancer. But she was also lucky. After aggressive treatment with radiation therapy, she stands a good chance of a full recovery.

Her good luck is partly a result of early identification. Statistically, the earlier breast cancer is diagnosed, the better the chances for survival. But how to go about early identification has caused some contention in the medical field. The controversy surrounds the age at which *mammograms,* a kind of weak X-ray used to examine breast tissue, should be routinely administered to women.

Mammograms are among the best means for early detection of breast cancer. The technique allows tumors to be identified while they are still very small. Patients can be treated before the tumor grows and spreads. Mammograms save many lives, and nearly all medical professionals suggest that women routinely obtain them at some point in midlife. When, is the question. The risk of breast cancer begins to grow at around the age of 30 and then increases. Ninety-five percent of new cases occur in women aged 40 and above (SEER, 2005).

The current consensus among medical care providers is that age 40 is the most reasonable age to begin annual mammograms. The debate is not over, but the American Cancer Society, American Medical Association, and the National Cancer Institute all recommend annual mammograms for women aged 40 and above (Rimer et al., 2001).

- *If the likelihood of detecting cancer from a mammogram is statistically small, would you personally feel comfortable not having one?*

One of the more prevalent problems is major depression, which is characterized by feelings of intense sadness, pessimism, and hopelessness. One obvious reason older people may become depressed is their experience of cumulative losses with the death of spouses and friends. Their own declining health and physical capabilities, which may make them feel less independent and in control, may also contribute to the prevalence of depression (Penninx et al., 1998; Kahn, Hessling, & Russell, 2003).

These explanations make sense, but it is not yet entirely clear that depression is a significantly worse problem in late adulthood than it is earlier in life. Some studies suggest that the rate of depression actually may be lower during late adulthood. One reason for this contradictory finding is that there may be two kinds of depression in older adulthood: depression that continues from earlier stages of life and depression that occurs as a result of aging (Gatz, 1997).

It is not unusual for some elderly people to suffer from drug-induced psychological disorders brought about by combinations of drugs they may be taking for various medical conditions. Because of changes in metabolism, a dose of a particular drug that would be appropriate for a 25-year-old might be much too large for a person of 75. The effects of drug interactions can be subtle, and they can manifest themselves in a variety of psychological symptoms, such as drug intoxication or anxiety. Because of these possibilities, older people who take medications must be careful to inform their physicians and pharmacists of every drug they take. They should also avoid medicating themselves with over-the-counter drugs because a combination of nonprescription and prescription drugs may be dangerous, or even deadly.

The most common mental disorder of elderly people is **dementia**, a broad category of serious memory loss accompanied by declines in other mental functioning, which encompasses a number of diseases. Although dementia has many causes, the symptoms are similar: declining memory, lessened intellectual abilities, and impaired judgment. The chances of experiencing dementia increase with age. Less than 2 percent of people between 60 and 65 years are diagnosed with dementia, but the percentages double for every 5-year period past 65. Consequently, almost one-third of people over the age of 85 suffer from some sort of dementia. There are some ethnic differences, too, with African Americans and Hispanics showing higher levels of dementia than Caucasians (National Research Council, 1997).

The most common form of dementia is Alzheimer's disease. Alzheimer's represents one of the most serious mental health problems faced by the aging population.

Alzheimer's Disease.

For an actor, there is no greater loss than the loss of his audience. I can part the Red Sea, but I can't part with you, which is why I won't exclude you from this stage in my life.

For now, I'm not changing anything. I'll insist on work when I can; the doctors will insist on rest when I must.

If you see a little less spring to my step, if your name fails to leap to my lips, you'll know why. And if I tell you a funny story for the second time, please laugh anyway. (Heston, 2002)

With these words, actor Charlton Heston announced that he had joined the 4.5 million Americans who suffer from **Alzheimer's disease**, a progressive brain disorder that produces loss of memory and confusion. In some ways, Alzheimer's disease—which led to the death of former president Ronald Reagan in 2004—symbolizes our view of elderly people, who, according to popular stereotypes, are more apt to be ill than healthy.

However, the reality is different: Most elderly people are in relatively good health for most of old age. According to surveys conducted in the United States, almost three-quarters of people 65 years old and above rate their health as good, very good, or excellent (USDHHS, 1990; Kahn & Rowe, 1999).

On the other hand, to be old is to be susceptible to a host of diseases. We now consider some of the major physical and psychological problems that beset older people.

Alzheimer's disease is a debilitating condition that saps both the physical and mental powers of its victims. This progressive brain disorder produces loss of memory and confusion, and leads to the deaths of 100,000 people in the United States each year. Nineteen percent of people 75 to 84 have Alzheimer's, and nearly half of people over the age of 85 are affected by the disease. Unless a cure is found, some 14 million people will be victims of Alzheimer's by 2050—more than three times the current number (Cowley, 2000).

dementia the most common mental disorder of the elderly, covering several diseases, each of which includes serious memory loss accompanied by declines in other mental functioning.

Alzheimer's disease a progressive brain disorder that produces loss of memory and confusion.

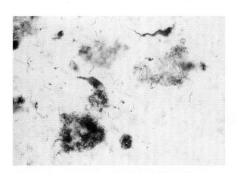

Brain scans of a patient with Alzheimer's disease show twisted clumps of nerve cells that are characteristic of the disease.

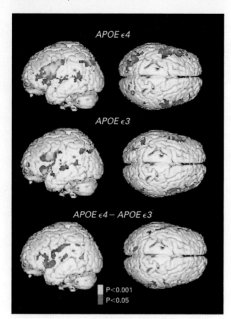

FIGURE 4.13 A Different Brain?
Brain scans during memory recall tasks show differences between the brains of people who have an inherited tendency toward Alzheimer's disease and those who do not. The brains at the top are a composite of those at risk; the brains in the middle are a composite of normal brains. The bottom row indicates areas of difference between the first two rows.
Source: Bookheimer et al., 2000.

The symptoms of Alzheimer's disease develop gradually. Generally, the first sign is unusual forgetfulness. A person may stop at a grocery store several times during the week, forgetting that he or she has already done the shopping. People may also have trouble recalling particular words during conversations. At first, recent memories are affected, and then older memories fade. Eventually, people with the disease are totally confused, unable to speak intelligibly or to recognize even their closest family and friends. In the final stages of the disease, they lose voluntary control of their muscles and are bedridden. Because victims of the disorder are initially aware that their memories are failing and often understand quite well the future course of the disease, they may suffer from anxiety, fear, and depression—emotions not difficult to understand, given the grim prognosis.

Biologically, Alzheimer's occurs when production of the protein *beta amyloid precursor protein*—a protein that normally helps the production and growth of neurons—goes awry, producing large clumps of cells that trigger inflammation and deterioration of nerve cells. The brain shrinks, and several areas of the hippocampus and frontal and temporal lobes show deterioration. Furthermore, certain neurons die, which leads to a shortage of various neurotransmitters, such as acetylcholine (Lanctot, Herrmann, & Mazzotta, 2001; Blennow & Vanmechelen, 2003; Wolfe, 2006; Medeiros et al., 2007).

Although the physical changes in the brain that produce the symptoms of Alzheimer's are clear, what is not known is what triggers the problem in the first place. Several explanations have been advanced. For instance, as we saw in Chapter 2, genetics clearly plays a role, with some families showing a much higher incidence of Alzheimer's than others. In certain families, half the children appear to inherit the disease from their parents. Furthermore, years before the actual symptoms of Alzheimer's emerge, people who are genetically at high risk for the disease show differences in brain functioning when they are trying to recall information, as illustrated in the brain scans in Figure 4.13 (Bookheimer et al., 2000; Coon et al., 2007; Nelson et al., 2007; Thomas & Fenech, 2007).

Most evidence suggests that Alzheimer's is an inherited disorder, but nongenetic factors such as high blood pressure or diet may increase susceptibility to the disease. In one cross-cultural study, poor black residents in a Nigerian town were less likely to develop Alzheimer's than a comparable sample of African Americans living in the United States. The researchers speculate that variations in diet between the two groups—the residents of Nigeria ate mainly vegetables— might account for the differences in the Alzheimer's rates (Hendrie et al., 2001; Friedland, 2003; Wu, Zhou, & Chen, 2003; Lahiri et al., 2007).

Other explanations for the disease have also been investigated. For example, scientists are studying certain kinds of viruses, dysfunctions of the immune system, and hormonal imbalances that may produce the disease. Other studies have found that lower levels of linguistic ability in the early 20s are associated with declines in cognitive capabilities due to Alzheimer's much later in life (Small et al., 1995; Snowdon et al., 1996; Alisky, 2007).

At the present time, there is no cure for Alzheimer's disease; treatment deals only with the symptoms. While understanding of the causes of Alzheimer's is incomplete, several drug treatments for Alzheimer's appear promising, although none is effective in the long term. The most promising drugs are related to the loss of the neurotransmitter acetylcholine (Ach) that occurs in some forms of Alzheimer's disease. Donepezil (Aricept), galantamine (Razadyne), rivastigmine (Exelon), and tacrine (Cognex) are among the most common drugs prescribed, and they alleviate some of the symptoms of the disease. Still, they are effective in only half of Alzheimer's patients, and only temporarily (Corliss, 1996; de Jesus Moreno Moreno, 2003).

Other drugs being studied include anti-inflammatory drugs, which may reduce the brain inflammation that occurs in Alzheimer's. In addition, the chemicals in vitamins C and E are being tested, since some evidence suggests that people who take such vitamins are at lower risk for developing the disorder. Still, at this point, it is clear that no drug treatment is truly effective (Alzheimer's Association, 2004).

As victims lose the ability to feed and clothe themselves, or even to control bladder and bowel functions, they must be cared for 24 hours a day. Because such care is typically impossible for even the most dedicated families, most Alzheimer's victims end their lives in nursing homes. Patients with Alzheimer's make up some two-thirds of residents in nursing homes (Prigerson, 2003).

People who care for the victims of Alzheimer's often become secondary victims of the disease. It is easy to become frustrated, angry, and exhausted by the demands of Alzheimer's patients, whose needs may be overpowering. In addition to the physical chore of providing total

BECOMING AN INFORMED CONSUMER OF DEVELOPMENT
Caring for People with Alzheimer's Disease

Alzheimer's disease is one of the most difficult illnesses to deal with, as a friend or loved one progressively deteriorates both mentally and physically. However, several steps can be taken to help both patient and caregiver deal with Alzheimer's.

- Make patients feel secure in their home environments by keeping them occupied in the everyday tasks of living as long as possible.

- Provide labels for everyday objects, furnish calendars and detailed but simple lists, and give oral reminders of time and place.

- Keep clothing simple: Provide clothes with few zippers and buttons, and lay them out in the order in which they should be put on.

- Put bathing on a schedule. People with Alzheimer's may be afraid of falling and of hot water, and may therefore avoid needed bathing.

- Prevent people with the disease from driving. Although patients often want to continue driving, their accident rate is high—some 20 times higher than average.

- Monitor the use of the telephone. Alzheimer patients who answer the phone have been victimized by agreeing to requests of telephone salespeople and investment counselors.

- Provide opportunities for exercise, such as a daily walk. This prevents muscle deterioration and stiffness.

- Caregivers should remember to take time off. Although caring for an Alzheimer's patient can be a full-time chore, caregivers need to lead their own lives. Seek out support from community service organizations.

- Call or write the Alzheimer's Association, which can provide support and information. The association can be reached at 225 N. Michigan Ave. Fl. 17 Chicago, IL 60601-7633; Tel. 1-800-272-3900; http://www.alz.org.

care, caregivers face the loss of a loved one, who not only is visibly deteriorating but can act emotionally unstable and even fly into rages. The burdens of caring for a person with Alzheimer's can be overwhelming (Schulz, 2000; Ferrario, Vitaliano, & Zotti, 2003; Danhauer, McCann, & Gilley, 2004; Kosmala & Kloszewska, 2004; Thomas et al., 2006).

REVIEW

▶ Adequate nutrition is important for physical, social, and cognitive development. Malnutrition can slow growth, affect intellectual performance, and cause diseases.

▶ Adolescents are particularly susceptible to eating disorders, especially anorexia nervosa and bulimia.

▶ Adolescents are also susceptible to unhealthy, addictive habits (e.g., use of drugs, alcohol, or tobacco) and sexually transmitted infections.

▶ Young adults are generally as fit and healthy as they will ever be. Accidents present the greatest risk of death, and violence is a significant risk, particularly for nonwhite males.

▶ Heart disease is a risk for middle-aged adults. Both genetic and environmental factors contribute to heart disease, including the Type A behavior pattern.

▶ The incidence of cancer begins to be significant in middle adulthood. Therapies such as radiation therapy, chemotherapy, and surgery can successfully treat cancer.

▶ Although most older people are healthy, the incidence of some serious diseases rises in old age, and most people have at least one chronic ailment, such as depression, before they die. The most prevalent and damaging brain disorder among older people is Alzheimer's disease.

▶ Proper diet, exercise, and avoidance of health risks can lead to prolonged wellness during old age.

APPLY

▶ How can societal and environmental influences contribute to the emergence of an eating disorder?

▶ What social policies might be developed to lower the incidence of disabling illness among members of lower socioeconomic groups?

MODULE 4.3

Promoting Health and Wellness

Juana Sandino sighed as she sat down to nurse the baby—again. She had fed 4-week-old Juan about every hour today, and he still seemed hungry. Some days, it seemed like all she did was breast-feed her baby. "Well, he must be going through a growth spurt," she decided, as she settled into her favorite rocking chair and put the baby to her nipple.

Good Diet: The Foundation of Wellness

As we saw in the previous module, malnutrition has serious and long-lasting consequences. The opposite can also be true: The habits formed in infancy support to a surprising extent the robust physical growth that occurs during infancy and continues—now rapidly, now slowly—through the life span.

Without proper nutrition, infants cannot reach their physical potential, and they may suffer cognitive and social consequences as well (Tanner & Finn-Stevenson, 2002; Costello et al., 2003; Gregory, 2005). Although there are vast individual differences in what constitutes appropriate nutrition—infants differ in terms of growth rates, body composition, metabolism, and activity levels—some broad guidelines do hold. In general, infants should consume about 50 calories per day for each pound they weigh—an allotment that is twice the suggested caloric intake for adults (Dietz & Stern, 1999; Skinner et al., 2004).

Typically, though, it's not necessary to count calories for infants. Most infants regulate their caloric intake quite effectively on their own. If they are allowed to consume as much as they seem to want and are not pressured to eat more, they will do fine.

Breast or Bottle? Fifty years ago, if a mother asked her pediatrician whether breastfeeding or bottle-feeding was better, she would have received a simple and clear-cut answer: Bottle-feeding was the preferred method. Starting around the 1940s, the general belief among child-care experts was that breastfeeding was an obsolete method that put children unnecessarily at risk.

With bottle-feeding, the argument went, parents could keep track of the amount of milk their baby was receiving and could thereby ensure that the child was taking in sufficient nutrients. In contrast, mothers who breast-fed their babies could never be certain just how much milk their infants were getting. Use of the bottle was also supposed to help mothers keep their feedings to a rigid schedule of one bottle every 4 hours, the recommended procedure at that time.

Today a mother would get a very different answer to the same question. Child-care authorities agree: for the first 12 months of life, there is no better food for an infant than breast milk. Breast milk not only contains all the nutrients necessary for growth, but it also seems to offer some degree of immunity to a variety of childhood diseases, such as respiratory illnesses, ear infections, diarrhea, and allergies. Breast milk is more easily digested than cow's milk or formula, and it is sterile, warm, and convenient for the mother to dispense. There is even some evidence that breast milk may enhance cognitive growth, leading to high adult intelligence (Feldman & Eidelman, 2003; American Academy of Pediatrics, 2005; Der, Batty, & Deary, 2006).

Breastfeeding is not a cure-all for infant nutrition and health, and the millions of individuals who have been raised on formula should not be concerned that they have suffered irreparable harm. But it does continue to be clear that the popular slogan used by groups advocating the use of breastfeeding is right on target: "Breast Is Best" (Birch et al., 2000; Austad et al., 2003; Rabin, 2006).

Solid Foods: When and What? Although pediatricians agree that breast milk is the ideal initial food, at some point infants require more nutrients than breast milk alone can provide. The American Academy of Pediatrics and the American Academy of Family Physicians suggest that babies can start solids at around 6 months, although they aren't needed until 9 to 12 months of age (American Academy of Family Physicians, 1997; American Academy of Pediatrics, 1997).

Solid foods are introduced into an infant's diet gradually, one at a time, in order to permit monitoring of preferences and allergies. Most often cereal comes first, followed by strained fruits. Vegetables and other foods typically are introduced next, although the order varies significantly from one infant to another.

Breast or bottle? Although infants receive adequate nourishment from breast- or bottle-feeding, most authorities agree "breast is best."

mydevelopmentlab

Would you choose to breast feed or bottle feed your child? To make this and other important decisions about raising a child log on to **MyVirtualChild** through **MyDevelopmentLab**.

The timing of *weaning*, the gradual cessation of breast or bottle-feeding, varies greatly. In developed countries such as the United States, weaning frequently occurs as early as 3 or 4 months. Some mothers, however, continue breastfeeding for 2 or 3 years. The American Academy of Pediatrics recommends that infants be fed breast milk for the first 12 months (American Academy of Pediatrics, 1997).

Because the rate of growth is slower than during infancy, preschoolers need less food, which may cause parents to worry. However, children tend to be adept at eating enough if they are provided with nutritious meals. In fact, anxiously encouraging children to eat more than they want may lead to obesity. The prevalence of obesity among children—even older preschoolers—has increased significantly over the last 20 years.

Effects of Diet.   In general, popular wisdom holds that the more a baby eats, the stronger and healthier it will become. Although there is a relationship between size and nutrition, it is not all positive. Diet has many effects, and size isn't the only area affected. For instance, diet is related to social and emotional functioning at school age. Children who receive more nutrients are more involved with their peers, show more positive emotion, and have less anxiety than children with less adequate nutrition.

Diet is also linked to cognitive performance. For example, in one study, children in Kenya who were well nourished performed better on a test of verbal abilities and other cognitive measures than those who had mild to moderate undernutrition. Malnutrition may influence cognitive development by dampening children's curiosity, responsiveness, and motivation to learn (McDonald et al., 1994; Brown & Pollitt, 1996; Wachs, 2002; Grigorenko, 2003).

Eating the Right Foods.   Ultimately, some children's food consumption can become so high as to lead to obesity. The prevalence of obesity among older preschoolers has increased significantly over the last 20 years. (We discussed obesity in greater depth in the preceding module.)

How do parents ensure that their children have good nutrition without turning mealtimes into a tense, adversarial situation? In most cases, the best strategy is to make sure that a variety of foods, low in fat and high in nutritional content, is available. Because of the danger of iron deficiency anemia, foods that have a relatively high iron content are particularly important. Iron deficiency anemia is one of the most prevalent nutritional problems in developed countries such as the United States. High-iron foods include dark green vegetables (such as broccoli), whole grains, and some kinds of meat such as lean hamburger (Ranade, 1993).

Because preschool children, like adults, will not find all foods equally appealing, children should be given the opportunity to develop their own natural preferences. As long as their overall diet is adequate, no single food is indispensable. Exposing children to a wide variety of foods by encouraging them to take just one bite of new foods is a relatively low-stress way of expanding children's diets (Shapiro, 1997).

Health and Illness.   The average preschooler has seven to ten colds and other minor respiratory illnesses in each of the years from age 3 to 5. The majority of children in the United States are reasonably healthy during this period (Denny & Clyde, 1983; Kalb, 1997).

Actually, such minor illnesses may offer some unexpected benefits: not only may they help children build up immunity to more severe illnesses to which they may be exposed in the future, but they also may provide some emotional benefits. Specifically, some researchers argue that minor illness permits children to understand their bodies better. It also may permit them to learn coping skills that will help them deal more effectively with future, more severe diseases. Furthermore, it gives them the ability to understand better what others who are sick are going through. This ability to put oneself in another's shoes, known as empathy, may teach children to be more sympathetic and better caretakers (Notaro, Gelman, & Zimmerman, 2002; Raman & Winer, 2002; Williams & Binnie, 2002).

Sexuality

At age 51, Elaine was really looking forward to her postmenopausal life. Her youngest child had just left home to study art, and she had recently reduced her work schedule to a comfortable 30 hours a week. She envisioned the year to come as an opportunity for a "second honeymoon" with her husband, Greg, with no need for contraceptives or fears of becoming pregnant.

Her imagined honeymoon quickly evaporated in a heat wave of hot flashes and night sweats. Though Elaine recognized these as normal symptoms of menopause, she was having

BECOMING AN INFORMED CONSUMER OF DEVELOPMENT
Keeping Children Fit

Here is a brief portrait of a contemporary American: Sam works all week at a desk and gets no regular physical exercise. On weekends he spends many hours sitting in front of the TV, often snacking on sodas and sweets. Both at home and at restaurants, his meals feature high-calorie, fat-saturated foods. (Segal & Segal, 1992, p. 235)

Although this sketch fits many adults, Sam is just 6. Many Americans, like Sam, get little or no regular exercise and consequently are physically unfit and at risk for obesity and other health problems.

To encourage physical activity among children, try applying the following principles (Tyre & Scelfo, 2003; Okie, 2005):

· *Make exercise fun.* Children repeat what they enjoy. Overly competitive activities or those that sideline children with inferior skills, though, may create a lifelong distaste for exercise.

· *Be an exercise role model.* Children who see their parents, teachers, or adult friends exercising regularly may view fitness as a regular part of their lives, too.

· *Gear activities to the child's physical level and motor skills.* Use child-size equipment to make children feel successful.

· *Encourage the child to find a partner.* Roller skating, hiking, and many other activities are more fun when shared with a friend, a sibling, or a parent.

· *Start slowly.* Ease sedentary children into regular physical activity. Try 5 minutes of exercise daily. Over 10 weeks, aim for 30 minutes three to five times a week.

· *Urge participation in organized sports activities, but do not push too hard.* Not every child is athletically inclined. Make participation and enjoyment—not winning—the goal.

· *Don't use physical activity as a punishment.* Encourage children to join organized activities they enjoy.

· *Provide a healthy diet.* Good nutrition gives children energy; soda and sugary, fatty snack foods do not.

---

to change her clothing three or more times a day. And she was having more headaches. Her doctor prescribed hormone therapy to replace the estrogen she was losing through menopause. As she was not a likely candidate for any of the drug's negative side effects, she took her doctor's recommendation. The hormone therapy eased her symptoms and revitalized her spirits. Four months later, she and Greg booked a month's romantic getaway in Greece.

Although interest in sex remains fairly high for many people throughout the life span, as Elaine's story illustrates, the physical changes associated with aging, such as menopause for women, can throw a curve ball at romance. We will look at some of the factors that affect men's and women's sexuality in midlife, and the roles both attitude and prescription drugs can play in alleviating some of the problems commonly associated with this life stage.

Ongoing Sexuality. For those who can—or choose to—enjoy it, sex contributes to wellness across the life span, a fact that applies to old age as well as to younger periods of life. Of course, there are some changes in sexual functioning related to age.

Testosterone, the male hormone, declines during adulthood, with some research finding a decrease of approximately 30 to 40 percent from the late 40s to the early 70s. It takes a longer time, and more stimulation, for men to get a full erection. The refractory period—the time following an orgasm during which men are unable to become aroused again—may last as long as a day or even several days.

Women's vaginas become thin and inelastic, and they produce less natural lubrication, making intercourse more difficult (Frishman, 1996; Seidman, 2003). For most women, though, the changes do not reduce sexual pleasure. Those women who do find intercourse less enjoyable can seek help from an increasing array of drugs, such as topical creams and testosterone patches, designed to increase sexual pleasure (Laumann, Paik, & Rosen, 1999; Freedman & Ellison, 2004).

The need to engage in responsible sex applies even to the elderly. Older adults—like younger ones—are susceptible to sexually transmitted diseases. In fact, 10 percent of people diagnosed with AIDS are over the age of 50 (National Institute of Aging, 2004).

female climacteric the period that marks the transition from being able to bear children to being unable to do so.

menopause the cessation of menstruation.

The Climacteric and Menopause. Women enter a period, around age 45, known as the climacteric, which lasts for 15 to 20 years. The **female climacteric** marks the transition that ends the childbearing years.

The most notable sign of this transition is menopause. **Menopause** is the cessation of menstruation. Menstrual periods begin to occur irregularly and less frequently during a 2-year period starting at around age 47 or 48, although this may begin as early as age 40 or as late as age 60. Menopause is completed when a woman passes a year without a menstrual period.

Menopause is important because it marks the end of a woman's natural fertility (although eggs implanted in a postmenopausal woman can produce a pregnancy). In addition, estrogen and progesterone levels—the female sex hormones—begin to drop (Schwenkhagen, 2007).

These changes in hormone production may produce a variety of symptoms, although they vary significantly for individuals. One of the most prevalent symptoms is "hot flashes," in which women experience a surge of heat above the waist. A woman may get red and begin to sweat when a hot flash occurs. Afterward, she may feel chilled. Some women have hot flashes several times a day; others, not at all.

During menopause, headaches, feelings of dizziness, heart palpitations, and aching joints are relatively common, though not universal. In one survey, only half of the women reported having hot flashes, and only about one-tenth of all women experienced severe distress during menopause. Many women—perhaps as many as half—have no significant symptoms at all (Hyde & DeLamater, 2003; Grady, 2006).

For many women, menopause symptoms may begin a decade before menopause actually occurs. *Perimenopause* describes this period prior to menopause when hormone production begins to change. It is marked by sometimes radical fluctuations in hormone levels, resulting in some of the same symptoms found in menopause (Winterich, 2003; Shea, 2006).

For some women, the symptoms of perimenopause and menopause are considerable. Treating these problems can be challenging, as we consider in the *From Research to Practice* box on page 146.

While women in some cultures anticipate menopause with dread, Mayan women have no notion of hot flashes, and they generally look forward to the end of their childbearing years.

The Psychological Consequences of Menopause. Traditionally, many people, including experts, believed that menopause was linked directly to depression, anxiety, crying spells, lack of concentration, and irritability. Some researchers estimated that as many as 10 percent of menopausal women suffered severe depression. It was assumed that the physiological changes of menopause caused such problems (Schmidt & Rubinow, 1991).

Today, most researchers take a different view, regarding menopause as a normal part of aging that does not, by itself, produce psychological symptoms. Some women do experience psychological difficulties, but they do so at other times in life as well (Dell & Stewart, 2000; Matthews et al., 2000; Freeman, Sammel, & Liu, 2004; Somerset et al., 2006).

Research shows that a woman's expectations can significantly affect her experience of menopause. Women who expect to have difficulties are more likely to attribute every physical symptom and emotional swing to menopause, while those with more positive attitudes are less apt to do so. A woman's attribution of physical symptoms, then, may affect her perception of menopause—and thus her actual experience of the period (Dell & Stewart, 2000; Breheny & Stephens, 2003).

The Male Climacteric. Do men experience the equivalent of menopause? Not really. Lacking anything akin to menstruation, they cannot experience its discontinuation. But men do experience changes in midlife that are referred to as the male climacteric. The **male climacteric** is the period of physical and psychological change in the reproductive system that occurs late in midlife, typically in a man's 50s.

Because the changes are gradual, it is hard to pinpoint the exact period of the male climacteric. For instance, despite declines in testosterone levels and sperm count, men are able to father children throughout middle age. And it is no easier for men than women to attribute psychological symptoms to subtle physiological changes.

One physical change that occurs frequently is enlargement of the *prostate gland.* By age 40, about 10 percent of men have enlarged prostates, and the percentage increases to half of all men by the age of 80. Enlargement of the prostate produces problems with urination, including difficulty starting urination or a need to urinate frequently at night.

Sexual problems also increase as men age. In particular, *erectile dysfunction,* in which men are unable to achieve or maintain an erection, becomes more common. Drugs such as Viagra, Levitra, and Cialis, as well as patches that deliver doses of testosterone, often prove an effective treatment (Noonan, 2003; Kim & Park, 2006).

Men, like women, undergo psychological development in middle adulthood, but the extent to which psychological changes are related to reproductive or other physical changes remains an open question.

FROM A
HEALTH CARE
PROFESSIONAL'S
PERSPECTIVE:
What cultural factors in the United States might contribute to a woman's negative experience of menopause? How?

male climacteric   the period of physical and psychological change relating to the male reproductive system that occurs during late middle age.

FROM RESEARCH TO PRACTICE
The Dilemma of Hormone Therapy: No Easy Answer

Not long ago, a forty-something friend of ours stopped at a convenience store to pick up a sports drink for her 13-year-old son. As she was about to pay, she felt a sensation of intense heat throughout her body and became nauseated and dizzy. The alarmed cashier asked if she needed help. Our friend shook her head and quickly made her way outside. But when she and her son got back in the car, she panicked and told him to call 911 on her cell phone because she was sure she was having a heart attack. Within minutes, she heard sirens coming closer. It was only then, as the heat dissipated and she began to sweat, that our friend realized what all these symptoms meant. She'd had her first hot flash! (Wingert & Kantrowitz, 2007, p. 38)

A few years ago, physicians would have prescribed regular doses of a hormone replacement drug for hot flashes and other uncomfortable symptoms caused by the onset of menopause.

For millions of women who experienced such difficulties, it was a solution that worked. In *hormone therapy* (HT), estrogen and progesterone are administered to alleviate the worst menopause symptoms. HT reduces a variety of problems, such as hot flashes and loss of skin elasticity. HT may also reduce coronary heart disease by changing the ratio of "good" cholesterol to "bad" cholesterol. And HT decreases the thinning of the bones related to osteoporosis, which poses a problem for many people in late adulthood (Palan et al., 2005; McCauley, 2007; Birkhäuser et al., 2008).

Some studies also show that HT reduces the risks of stroke and colon cancer. Estrogen may even slow the mental deterioration in Alzheimer's patients, and some research shows that it improves memory and cognitive performance in healthy women. Finally, increased estrogen may lead to a greater sex drive (Sarrel, 2000; O'Hara et al., 2005; Stephens et al., 2006; Schwenkhagen, 2007).

Although hormone therapy may sound like a cure-all, in fact after it became popular in the early 1990s, its risks became better known.

For instance, it seemed to increase the risk of breast cancer and blood clots. Still, though, it was thought that the benefits outweighed the risks.

All that changed after 2002, when a large study conducted by the Women's Health Initiative determined that the long-term risks of HT outweighed the benefits. Women taking a combination of estrogen and progestin were found to be at higher risk for breast cancer, stroke, pulmonary embolism, and heart disease. Increased risk of stroke and pulmonary embolism were later found to be associated with estrogen-alone therapy (Parker-Pope, 2003).

These results led to a profound rethinking of the benefits of HT, calling into question the wisdom that HT could protect against chronic disease. Many women stopped taking hormone replacement drugs, choosing instead to use alternative herbal and dietary therapies for menopausal symptoms. Unfortunately, the most popular of such remedies have proven ineffective (Ness, Aronow, & Beck, 2006; Newton et al., 2006).

The sharp decline in HT use is probably an overreaction. The most recent thinking among medical experts is that some women are simply better candidates for HT than others. Whereas HT seems to be less appropriate for older, postmenopausal women (such as the participants in the Women's Health Initiative study) because of the increased risk of coronary heart disease and other health complications, younger women at the onset of menopause, who are experiencing severe symptoms, might still benefit from the therapy, at least on a short-term basis (Plonczynski & Plonczynski, 2007; Rossouw et al., 2007; Birkhäuser et al., 2008).

HT remains a gamble. Women nearing menopause need to read literature on the topic, consult their physicians, and make an informed decision.

• *If you were a physician, what would you tell your patients?*

Wellness: The Relationship Between Aging and Illness

Is getting sick an inevitable part of growing old? Not necessarily. Whether an older person is ill or well depends less on age than on a variety of factors, including genetic predisposition, past and present environmental factors, and psychological factors.

Certain diseases, such as cancer and heart disease, have a clear genetic component. Some families have a higher incidence of breast cancer, for instance, than others. At the same time, however, a genetic predisposition does not automatically mean that a person will get a particular illness. People's lifestyles—whether or not they smoke, the nature of their diet, their exposure to cancer-causing agents such as sunlight or asbestos—may raise or lower their chances of coming down with such a disease.

Furthermore, economic well-being also plays a role. For instance, as at all stages of life, living in poverty restricts access to medical care. Even relatively well-off people may have difficulties finding affordable health care. In 2002, for example, older individuals averaged $3,600 in out-of-pocket health care expenditures, an increase of 45 percent in 10 years. Furthermore, older people spend almost 13 percent of their total expenditures on health care, over twice as much as younger individuals.

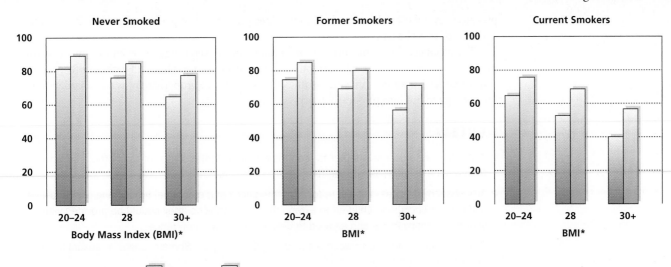

Percent Chance that an [Inactive] or [Active] Man Will Reach Age 65 Free of Coronary Artery Disease, Stroke, or Diabetes

FIGURE 4.14 **Benefits of Exercise and a Healthy Diet**
A study of more than 7,000 men, aged 40 to 59, found that not smoking, keeping weight down, and exercising regularly can greatly reduce the risk of coronary heart disease, stroke, and diabetes. Although the study included only men, a healthy lifestyle can benefit women too. *To find your body mass index (BMI) multiply your weight in pounds by 705. Divide the result by your height in inches; then divide by your height again.
Source: Adapted from Wannamethee et al., 1998.

Because the United States has until recently lacked a health care insurance system that provides for universal medical coverage, many elderly individuals have faced financial burdens in obtaining affordable health care. As a result, many have received inadequate care. They are less likely to have regular checkups, and when they finally go for treatment, their illnesses may be more advanced (Administration on Aging, 2003; Leonhardt, 2010).

Finally, psychological factors play an important role in determining people's susceptibility to illness—and ultimately the likelihood of death. For example, having a sense of control over one's environment, even over choices involving everyday matters, leads to a better psychological state and superior health outcomes (Taylor, 1991; Levy et al., 2002; Montpetit & Bergeman, 2007).

Promoting Good Health. People can do specific things to enhance their physical well-being—as well as their longevity—during old age. It is probably no surprise that the right things to do are no different from what people should do during the rest of the life span: eat a proper diet, exercise, and avoid obvious threats to health, such as smoking (see Figure 4.14). Medical and social service providers who work with elderly people have begun to emphasize the importance of these lifestyle choices. The goal of many such professionals has become not just to ward off illness and death, but to extend people's *active life spans,* the amount of time they remain healthy and able to enjoy their lives (Burns, 2000; Resnick, 2000; Sawatzky & Naimark, 2002; Gavin & Myers,2003; Katz & Marshall, 2003).

Sometimes, however, older people experience difficulties that prevent them from following even these simple guidelines. For instance, varying estimates suggest that between 15 and 50 percent of elderly people do not have adequate nutrition, and several million experience hunger every day (Burt & Harris, 1994; McCarthy, 1994; deCastro, 2002; Donini, Savina, & Cannella, 2003).

The reasons for such malnutrition and hunger are varied. Some elderly people are too poor to purchase adequate food, and some are too frail to shop or cook for themselves. Others feel little motivation to prepare and eat proper meals, particularly if they live alone or are depressed. For those who have experienced significant declines in taste and smell sensitivity, eating well-prepared food may no longer be enjoyable. And some older people may never have eaten well-balanced meals in earlier periods of life (Horwath, 1991; Wolfe, Olson, & Kendall, 1998).

Obtaining sufficient exercise may also prove problematic for older persons. Physical activity increases muscle strength and flexibility, reduces blood pressure and the risk of heart attack, and produces several other benefits, but many older people do not get sufficient exercise to experience any of these benefits.

For instance, illness may prevent older adults from exercising, and even inclement weather during the winter may restrict a person's ability to get out of the house. Furthermore, problems can combine: A poor person with insufficient money to eat properly may as a consequence have little energy to put into physical activity.

REVIEW

▶ Parents have to decide whether to feed their infants via the breast or the bottle, and when to introduce solid foods into the diet.

▶ An unhealthy diet has negative effects on the social and emotional functioning of school-age children. To encourage children to extend their food choices, they should be provided with a variety of healthy foods and allowed to develop their own preferences.

▶ Sexuality can contribute to wellness all along the life span. Some changes in sexual functioning occur as people age.

▶ Menopause, the cessation of menstruation, may last quite a long time and may be accompanied by physically uncomfortable symptoms. In some cases the symptoms are so severe that women and their physicians may consider hormone therapy, but despite its effectiveness, this treatment bears decided risks.

▶ Men also experience a climacteric, typically in the 50s. The prostate gland may become enlarged, and some men may experience erectile dysfunction.

▶ Wellness and illness in old age depend on many factors, such as genetic predisposition, environmental factors, and psychological factors. Economic well-being also plays a role.

APPLY

▶ How might the frequently changing opinions of medical experts regarding hormone therapy affect women's decisions about what course of action to follow?

▶ Can wellness and sexuality be maintained in old age?

Epilogue

We have surveyed a significant landscape of health, illness, and stress in this chapter, considering their causes and looking into ways to deal with many of them. We have covered stress, nutrition, several serious diseases, and Alzheimer's, a grievous psychological disease. We have looked at the upside and downside of nutrition and sexuality throughout the life span, and we have discovered that well-being and good health depend to a large extent on a good diet and ongoing exercise.

Think back to Rosa Convoy, the single mom who began this chapter, and consider these questions about her busy, stressful life.

1. Does Rosa's busy lifestyle suggest that she may be more or less prone to a serious physical ailment in later life? What factors might determine your answer?

2. What might be the effects of Rosa's lifestyle on the future life of her daughter Zoe? What sorts of things is Zoe learning from her mother—about lifestyle, food choices, lifelong learning, hard work, and other things?

3. What strategies do you think Rosa might be using to cope with her stress? Does she give evidence of hardiness? Resilience? Reliance on social supports? Defensive coping?

Looking Back

What are the main causes and consequences of stress, and how do people cope?

1. People move through stages—primary appraisal and secondary appraisal—to determine whether what they face will be stressful.

2. Long-term exposure to stressors may cause deterioration in the heart, blood vessels, and other body tissues. Stress is linked to many common ailments.

3. Strategies for coping with stress include problem-focused coping, emotion-focused coping, the use of social support, and defensive coping.

4. People who react effectively to stress have a positive coping style, which may involve hardiness and/or resilience.

What are the consequences of malnutrition, obesity, and eating disorders?

5. Adequate nutrition is important for physical, social, and cognitive development. Malnutrition can slow growth, affect intellectual performance, and cause diseases.

6. The high incidence of obesity in the United States is unhealthy because obesity taxes the circulatory system and increases the risk of high blood pressure and diabetes.

7. Obese children are more likely to be overweight as adults. Some evidence suggests that infant obesity is linked to adult obesity, but the evidence is not entirely clear.

8. Weight and body image can be virtual obsessions in adolescence, particularly for girls, making them susceptible to eating disorders such as anorexia nervosa and bulimia.

9. Anorexia leads its victims to cut out food so radically that they become skeletal. Some 15 to 20 percent of anorexics starve themselves to death.

10. People with bulimia undergo cycles of binging and purging, which may cause heart failure.

What threats to their health do children and young adults face as they age?

11. Children face their greatest risk from accidents, leading parents and caregivers to take special pains to childproof their environments.

12. Sudden Infant Death Syndrome is ill-understood, but since experts began recommending that babies sleep on their backs, the incidence is down.

13. Adolescents' risky behavior can lead them to take up an unhealthy, addictive habit (e.g., use of drugs, alcohol, or tobacco) or contract a sexually transmitted infection.

14. AIDS is the deadliest sexually transmitted infection, but not as common as human papilloma virus, trichomoniasis, chlamydia, genital herpes, gonorrhea, or syphilis.

What are the major threats to good health across the life span? How do cultural factors affect wellness and health?

15. Young adults are generally as fit and healthy as they will ever be, but for some an unhealthy diet and a low level of exercise combine to cause obesity.

16. Women are susceptible to osteoporosis, in which the bones become brittle, fragile, and thin. A calcium-rich diet can combat osteoporosis.

17. The health of adults is partly determined by genetics. Socioeconomic status is a significant contributor to health because lower SES households are likelier to work in hazardous occupations and to have inadequate health care.

18. Americans are more likely to die from violence than are residents of any other developed country, and African Americans have twice the death rate of Caucasians.

19. Heart disease is a risk for middle-aged adults. Both genetic and environmental factors contribute to heart disease, including the Type A behavior pattern.

20. The incidence of cancer begins to be significant in middle adulthood. Therapies such as radiation therapy, chemotherapy, and surgery can successfully treat cancer.

21. Although most older people are healthy, the incidence of some serious diseases rises in old age, and most people have at least one chronic ailment, such as depression, before they die. The most prevalent and damaging brain disorder among older people is Alzheimer's disease.

How do diet and exercise contribute to health and wellness across the life span?

22. Proper diet, exercise, and avoidance of health risks can lead to prolonged wellness during old age.

23. An unhealthy diet has negative effects on the social and emotional functioning of school-age children. To encourage children to extend their food choices, they should be provided with a variety of healthy foods and allowed to develop their own preferences.

What changes do people encounter in their sex lives as they age?

24. Sexuality can contribute to wellness all along the life span. Some changes in sexual functioning occur as people age.

25. Menopause, the cessation of menstruation, may last quite a long time and may be accompanied by physically uncomfortable symptoms. In some cases, the symptoms are so severe that women and their physicians may consider hormone therapy, but despite its effectiveness, this treatment bears decided risks.

26. Men also experience a climacteric, typically in their 50s. The prostate gland often becomes enlarged, and some men may experience erectile dysfunction. Several effective drug treatments have been developed to deal with erectile dysfunction.

27. Wellness and illness in old age depend on genetic, environmental, psychological, and economic factors.

Cognitive Growth:
Piaget and Vygotsky

Prologue
Jared

Jared, who is 7 months old, watches as his dad picks up his toy bell, one of his favorite playthings. Jared reaches for it, but his father slides it under the covers in his crib. Without any further sign of interest, Jared turns away. His father pulls out the bell from under the covers and rings it. Jared turns back and reaches for it, but once again his father hides it from view. Jared's reaction, or rather lack of reaction, is the same as before: As soon as the bell is hidden from view, he loses interest. Jared's father repeats the sequence several times, finding that each time the bell is hidden from sight, Jared acts as if it never existed.

It's now 4 years later. Jared's parents are delighted when he comes home from kindergarten one day and explains that he has learned why the sky is blue. He talks about the earth's atmosphere—although he doesn't pronounce the word correctly—and how tiny bits of moisture in the air reflect the sunlight. Although his explanation has rough edges (he can't quite grasp what the "atmosphere" is), he still has the general idea. That, his parents feel, is quite an achievement for their 5-year-old.

Fast-forward 6 years. Jared, now 11, has already spent an hour laboring over his evening's homework. After completing a two-page worksheet on multiplying and dividing fractions, he begins work on his U.S. Constitution project. He is taking notes for his report, which will explain what political factions had been involved in the writing of the document and how the Constitution had been amended since its creation.

Children experience cognitive advances that develop at breathtaking speed throughout childhood.

Jared, of course, is not alone in making the vast intellectual progress that these situations exemplify. Quite universally, children experience cognitive advances that develop at breathtaking speed throughout childhood, becoming increasingly able to understand and master complex skills.

In this chapter we consider cognitive development during childhood and adolescence in general, and from two important theoretical perspectives. After reviewing the basics of cognitive development, we examine in detail the work of Swiss psychologist Jean Piaget, whose stage theory of development has served as a highly influential impetus for a considerable amount of work on cognitive development. We'll look at the foundations of Piaget's theory in the use of schemes and in the processes of assimilation and accommodation, and we will trace cognitive development through the four stages that Piaget identified and defined through his observations of children and adolescents.

Next we will evaluate Piaget's theory, considering both its enormous contributions to developmental research and the many criticisms of his approach that have been voiced by researchers in the field.

Finally, we will conclude the chapter with a discussion of the work of Lev Vygotsky, a Russian psychologist. Vygotsky's views on the importance of culture to cognitive development have become increasingly influential, particularly in his focus on the social and cultural aspects of development and learning. Our discussions of Piaget and Vygotsky pave the way for consideration of the information processing approaches to cognitive development to which we turn in the next chapter.

LOOKING AHEAD

After reading this chapter, you will be able to answer the following questions:

▶ What is cognitive development, and how did Piaget revolutionize its study?

▶ What theoretical elements underlie Piaget's theory?

▶ What are the key features—and criticisms—of Piaget's theory?

▶ What are some alternate approaches to Piaget's view of cognitive development?

▶ What are the key features—and criticisms—of Vygotsky's theory?

MODULE **5.1**

Piaget's Approach to Cognitive Development

Piaget: The Master Observer of Children

Action = Knowledge.

Swiss psychologist Jean Piaget.

If a simple equation could summarize a comprehensive theory of cognitive development, this one might encapsulate the ideas of Swiss psychologist Jean Piaget (1896–1980) about how we begin to understand the world. Unlike previous theorists, Piaget argued that infants do not acquire knowledge from facts communicated by others, nor through sensation and perception. Instead, Piaget suggested that knowledge is the product of direct motor behavior. Although many of his basic explanations and propositions have been challenged by subsequent research, as we'll discuss later, the view that in significant ways infants learn by doing remains unquestioned (Piaget, 1952, 1962, 1983; Bullinger, 1997).

Piaget's background and training influenced both the development of his theory and the methods he used to investigate it. Piaget was educated as a biologist and philosopher, and he received a Ph.D. in zoology. His initial work was aimed at producing an account of how knowledge was related to biology, which ultimately led to a theory of how children's understanding of the world develops. In doing research, Piaget relied on methods that are common among investigations of nonhuman species. For instance, his studies would often intensively focus on only a few children, including his own offspring. Furthermore, he frequently would observe children in their "natural habitat," such as while they were playing games. His goal was to understand *how* children think, rather than characterizing whether their thinking was right or wrong at a given age.

Key Elements of Piaget's Theory. As we first noted in Chapter 1, Piaget's theory is based on a stage approach to development. He assumed that all children pass through a series of four universal stages in a fixed order from birth through adolescence: sensorimotor, preoperational, concrete operational, and formal operational. He also suggested that movement from one stage to the next occurs when a child reaches an appropriate level of physical maturation and is exposed to relevant experiences. Without such experience, Piaget assumed that children were incapable of reaching their cognitive potential. Some approaches to cognition focus on changes in the content of children's knowledge about the world, but Piaget argued that it was critical to also consider the changes in the quality of children's knowledge and understanding as they move from one stage to another.

For instance, as they develop cognitively, infants experience changes in their understanding about what can and cannot occur in the world. Consider a baby who participates in an experiment during which she is exposed to three identical versions of her mother all at the same time, thanks to some well-placed mirrors. A 3-month-old infant will interact happily with each of these images of mother. However, by 5 months of age, the child becomes quite agitated at the sight of multiple mothers. Apparently by this time the child has figured out that she has but one mother, and viewing three at a time is thoroughly alarming (Bower, 1977). To Piaget, such reactions indicate that a baby is beginning to master principles regarding the way the world operates, indicating that she has begun to construct a mental sense of the world that she didn't have 2 months earlier.

According to Piaget, a baby will use a sensorimotor scheme, such as mouthing or banging, to understand a new object.

Piaget believed that the basic building blocks of the way we understand the world are mental structures called **schemes**, organized patterns of functioning, that adapt and change with mental development. At first, schemes are related to physical, or sensorimotor, activity, such as picking up or reaching for toys. As children develop, their schemes move to a mental level, reflecting thought. Schemes are similar to computer software: They direct and determine how data from the world, such as new events or objects, are considered and dealt with (Achenbach, 1992; Rakison & Oakes, 2003).

If you give a baby a new cloth book, for example, he or she will touch it, mouth it, perhaps try to tear it or bang it on the floor. To Piaget, each of these actions represents a scheme, and they are the infant's way of gaining knowledge and understanding of this new object.

Piaget suggested that two principles underlie the growth in children's schemes: assimilation and accommodation. **Assimilation** is the process by which people understand an experience in terms of their current stage of cognitive development and way of thinking. Assimilation occurs, then, when a stimulus or an event is acted upon, perceived, and understood in accordance with existing patterns of thought. For example, an infant who tries to suck on any toy in the same way is assimilating the objects to her existing sucking scheme. Similarly, a child who encounters a flying squirrel at a zoo and calls it a "bird" is assimilating the squirrel to his existing scheme of bird.

In contrast, **accommodation** refers to changes in existing ways of thinking, understanding, or behaving in response to encounters with new stimuli or events. For instance, when a child sees a flying squirrel and calls it "a bird with a tail," he is beginning to accommodate new knowledge, modifying his scheme of bird.

Piaget believed that the earliest schemes are primarily limited to the reflexes with which we are all born, such as sucking and rooting. Infants start to modify these simple early schemes almost immediately, through the processes of assimilation and accommodation, in response to their exploration of the environment. Schemes quickly become more sophisticated as infants become more advanced in their motor capabilities—to Piaget, a signal of the potential for more advanced cognitive development.

Cognitive Development in Infancy

Olivia's dad is wiping up the mess around the base of her high chair—for the third time today! It seems to him that 14-month-old Olivia takes great delight in dropping food from the high chair. She also drops toys, spoons, anything it seems, just to watch how it hits the floor. She almost appears to be experimenting to see what kind of noise or what size of splatter is created by each different thing she drops.

Piaget probably would have said that Olivia's dad is right in theorizing that Olivia is conducting her own series of experiments to learn more about the workings of her world. As we noted at the beginning of this module, Piaget's views of the ways infants learn can be summed up in a simple equation: Action = Knowledge.

Piaget argued that infants acquire knowledge through direct motor behavior. Although many of his basic explanations and propositions have been challenged by subsequent research, the view that in significant ways infants learn by doing remains unquestioned (Piaget, 1952, 1962, 1983; Bullinger, 1997).

Piaget's theory, as noted earlier, is based on a stage approach to development, with children and adolescents passing through four universal stages in a predetermined sequence: sensorimotor, preoperational, concrete operational, and formal operational.

The Sensorimotor Period: The Earliest Stage of Cognitive Growth (Birth to 2 Years).
Piaget suggests that the **sensorimotor stage**, the initial major stage of cognitive development, can be broken down into six substages. These are summarized in Table 5.1 on page 154. It is important to keep in mind that although the specific substages of the sensorimotor period may at first appear to unfold with great regularity, as though infants reach a particular age and smoothly proceed into the next substage, the reality of cognitive development is somewhat different. First, the ages at which infants actually reach a particular stage vary a good deal among different children. The exact timing of a stage reflects an interaction between the infant's level of physical maturation and the nature of the social environment in which the child is being raised.

Piaget viewed development as a more gradual process than the notion of different stages might seem to imply. Infants do not go to sleep one night in one substage and wake up the next

scheme an organized pattern of sensorimotor functioning.

assimilation the process in which people understand an experience in terms of their current stage of cognitive development and way of thinking.

accommodation changes in existing ways of thinking that occur in response to encounters with new stimuli or events.

sensorimotor stage (of cognitive development) Piaget's initial major stage of cognitive development, which can be broken down into six substages.

TABLE 5.1   Piaget's Six Substages of the Sensorimotor Stage

SUBSTAGE	AGE	DESCRIPTION	EXAMPLE
Substage 1: Simple reflexes	First month of life	During this period, the various reflexes that determine the infant's interactions with the world are at the center of the infant's cognitive life.	The sucking reflex causes the infant to suck at anything placed in his lips.
Substage 2: First habits and primary circular reactions	From 1 to 4 months	At this age infants begin to coordinate what were separate actions into single, integrated activities.	An infant might combine grasping an object with sucking on it, or staring at something with touching it.
Substage 3: Secondary circular reactions	From 4 to 8 months	During this period, infants take major strides in shifting their cognitive horizons beyond themselves and begin to act on the outside world.	A child who repeatedly picks up a rattle in her crib and shakes it in different ways to see how the sound changes is demonstrating her ability to modify her cognitive scheme about shaking rattles.
Substage 4: Coordination of secondary circular reactions	From 8 to 12 months	In this stage infants begin to use more calculated approaches to producing events, coordinating several schemes to generate a single act. They achieve object performance during this stage.	An infant will push one toy out of the way to reach another toy that is lying, partially exposed, under it.
Substage 5: Tertiary circular reactions	From 12 to 18 months	At this age infants develop what Piaget regards as the deliberate variation of actions that bring desirable consequences. Rather than just repeating enjoyable activities, infants appear to carry out miniature experiments to observe the consequences.	A child will drop a toy repeatedly, varying the position from which he drops it, carefully observing each time to see where it falls.
Substage 6: Beginnings of thought	From 18 months to 2 years	The major achievement of Substage 6 is the capacity for mental representation or symbolic thought. Piaget argued that only at this stage can infants imagine where objects that they cannot see might be.	Children can even plot in their heads unseen trajectories of objects, so that if a ball rolls under a piece of furniture, they can figure out where it is likely to emerge on the other side.

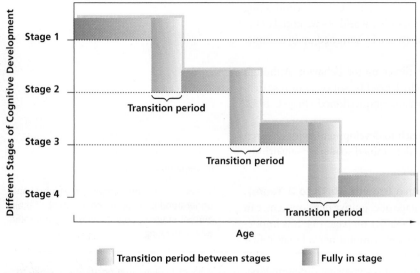

FIGURE 5.1 Transitions

Infants do not suddenly shift from one stage of cognitive development to the next. Instead, Piaget argues that there is a period of transition in which some behavior reflects one stage, while another behavior reflects the more advanced stage. Does this gradualism argue against Piaget's interpretation of stages?

morning in the next one. Instead, there is a rather steady shifting of behavior as a child moves toward the next stage of cognitive development. Infants also pass through periods of transition, in which some aspects of their behavior reflect the next higher stage, while other aspects indicate their current stage (see Figure 5.1).

Substage 1: Simple Reflexes (First Month). The first substage of the sensorimotor period is Substage 1: Simple reflexes, encompassing the first month of life. During this time, various inborn reflexes are at the center of infants' physical and cognitive lives, determining the nature of their interactions with the world. At the same time, some of the reflexes begin to accommodate the infant's experience with the nature of the world. For instance, an infant who is being breast-fed, but who also receives supplemental bottles, may start to change the way he or she sucks, depending on whether a nipple is on a breast or a bottle.

Substage 2: First Habits and Primary Circular Reactions (1 to 4 Months). Substage 2: First habits and primary circular reactions occurs from 1 to 4 months of age. In this period, infants begin to coordinate what were separate actions into single, integrated activities. For instance, an infant might combine grasping an object with sucking on it, or staring at something while touching it.

If an activity engages a baby's interests, he or she may repeat it over and over, simply for the sake of continuing to experience it. This repetition of a chance motor event helps the baby start building cognitive schemes through a process known as a circular reaction. Primary circular reactions are schemes reflecting an infant's repetition of interesting or enjoyable actions, just for the enjoyment of doing them, which focus on the infant's own body.

Substage 3: Secondary Circular Reactions (4 to 8 Months).

Substage 3: Secondary circular reactions are more purposeful. According to Piaget, this third stage of cognitive development in infancy occurs from 4 to 8 months of age. During this period, a child begins to act upon the outside world. For instance, infants now seek to repeat enjoyable events in their environments if they happen to produce them through chance activities. A child who repeatedly picks up a rattle in her crib and shakes it in different ways to see how the sound changes is demonstrating her ability to modify her cognitive scheme about shaking rattles. She is engaging in what Piaget calls secondary circular reactions, which are schemes regarding repeated actions that bring about a desirable consequence.

Substage 4: Coordination of Secondary Circular Reactions (8 to 12 Months).

Some major leaps forward occur in Substage 4: Coordination of secondary circular reactions, which lasts from around 8 months to 12 months. In Substage 4, infants begin to employ **goal-directed behavior**, in which several schemes are combined and coordinated to generate a single act to solve a problem. For instance, they will push one toy out of the way to reach another toy that is lying, partially exposed, under it.

Infants' newfound purposefulness, their ability to use means to attain particular ends, and their skill in anticipating future circumstances owe their appearance in part to the developmental achievement of object permanence that emerges in Substage 4. **Object permanence** is the realization that people and objects exist even when they cannot be seen. It is a simple principle, but its mastery has profound consequences.

Consider, for instance, 7-month-old Chu, who has yet to learn the idea of object permanence. Chu's mother shakes a rattle in front of him, then takes the rattle and places it under a blanket. To Chu, who has not mastered the concept of object permanence, the rattle no longer exists. He will make no effort to look for it.

Several months later, when he reaches Substage 4, the story is quite different (see Figure 5.2). This time, as soon as his mother places the rattle under the blanket, Chu tries to toss the cover

Infants in Substage 4 can coordinate their secondary circular reactions, displaying an ability to plan or calculate how to produce a desired outcome.

To see a video of an infant demonstrating the principle of object permanence that you have been reading about, log on to **MyDevelopmentLab**.

goal-directed behavior   behavior in which several schemes are combined and coordinated to generate a single act to solve a problem.

object permanence   the realization that people and objects exist even when they cannot be seen.

Before Object Permanence

After Object Permanence

FIGURE 5.2 Object Permanence
Before an infant has understood the idea of object permanence, he will not search for an object that has been hidden right before his eyes. But several months later, he will search for it, illustrating that he has attained object permanence. Why would the concept of object permanence be important to a caregiver?

mental representation   an internal image of a past event or object.

deferred imitation   an act in which a person who is no longer present is imitated by children who have witnessed a similar act.

aside, eagerly searching for the rattle. Chu clearly has learned that the object continues to exist even when it cannot be seen. For the infant who achieves an understanding of object permanence, then, out of sight is decidedly not out of mind.

The attainment of object permanence extends not only to inanimate objects, but to people, too. It gives Chu the security that his father and mother still exist even when they have left the room.

Substage 5: Tertiary Circular Reactions (12 to 18 Months).   Substage 5: Tertiary circular reactions is reached at around the age of 12 months and extends to 18 months. As the name of the stage indicates, during this period infants develop these reactions, which are schemes regarding the deliberate variation of actions that bring desirable consequences. Rather than just repeating enjoyable activities, as they do with secondary circular reactions, infants appear to carry out miniature experiments to observe the consequences.

For example, Piaget observed his son Laurent dropping a toy swan repeatedly, varying the position from which he dropped it, carefully observing each time to see where it fell. Instead of just repeating the action each time, Laurent made modifications in the situation to learn about their consequences. As you may recall from our discussion of research methods in Chapter 1, this behavior represents the essence of the scientific method: An experimenter varies a situation in a laboratory to learn the effects of the variation.

What is most striking about infants' behavior during Substage 5 is their interest in the unexpected. Unanticipated events are treated not only as interesting, but also as something to be explained and understood. Infants' discoveries can lead to newfound skills, some of which may cause a certain amount of chaos. For instance, an infant may pull at a tablecloth in order to reach a plate of cookies or throw a water toy into the tub with increasing vigor to see how high the water splashes.

Substage 6: Beginnings of Thought (18 Months to 2 Years).   The final stage of the sensorimotor period is Substage 6: Beginnings of thought, which lasts from around 18 months to 2 years. The major achievement of Substage 6 is the capacity for mental representation, or symbolic thought. A **mental representation** is an internal image of a past event or object. Piaget argued that by this stage infants can imagine where objects might be that they cannot see. They can even plot in their heads unseen trajectories of objects, so if a ball rolls under a piece of furniture, they can figure out where it is likely to emerge on the other side.

Because of children's new abilities to create internal representations of objects, their understanding of causality also becomes more sophisticated. For instance, consider Piaget's description of his son Laurent's efforts to open a garden gate:

> *Laurent tries to open a garden gate but cannot push it forward because it is held back by a piece of furniture. He cannot account either visually or by any sound for the cause that prevents the gate from opening, but after having tried to force it he suddenly seems to understand; he goes around the wall, arrives at the other side of the gate, moves the armchair which holds it firm, and opens it with a triumphant expression.(Piaget, 1954, p. 296)*

The attainment of mental representation also permits another important development: the ability to pretend. Using the skill of what Piaget refers to as **deferred imitation**, in which a person who is no longer present is imitated later, children are able to pretend that they are driving a car, feeding a doll, or cooking dinner long after they have witnessed such scenes played out in reality.

FROM A
CAREGIVER'S
PERSPECTIVE
What are some implications for childrearing practices of Piaget's observations about the ways children gain an understanding of the world? Would you use the same approaches in childrearing for a child growing up in a non-Western culture?

Cognitive Development in the Preschool Years

Three-year-old Sam was talking to himself in two very different voices. "Find your shoes," he said in a low voice. "Not today. I'm not going. I hate the shoes," he said in a higher-pitched voice. The lower voice answered, "You are a bad boy. Find the shoes, bad boy." The higher-voiced response was "No, no, no."

Sam's parents realized that he was playing a game with his imaginary friend, Gill—a bad boy who often disobeyed his mother. In fact, according to Sam's musings, Gill often was guilty of the very same misdeeds for which his parents blamed Sam.

Infants begin to use goal-directed behavior in Substage 4 of the sensorimotor stage.

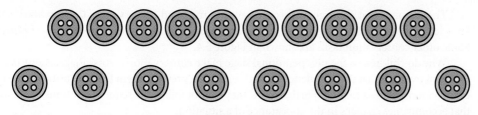

Piaget saw the preschool years as a time of both stability and change. He placed the preschool years into a single stage of cognitive development—the preoperational stage—which lasts from 2 until around 7.

Piaget's Stage of Preoperational Thinking (Ages 2 to 7). During the **preoperational stage**, children's use of symbolic thinking grows, mental reasoning emerges, and the use of concepts increases. Seeing Mom's car keys may prompt a question, "Go to store?" as the child comes to see the keys as a symbol of a car ride. In this way, children become better at representing events internally and less dependent on sensorimotor activity to understand the world around them. Yet they are still not capable of **operations**: organized, formal, logical mental processes.

According to Piaget, a key aspect of preoperational thought is **symbolic function**, the ability to use a mental symbol, a word, or an object to stand for or represent something that is not physically present. For example, preschoolers can use a mental symbol for a car (the word "car"), and they understand that a small toy car is representative of the real thing. They have no need to get behind the wheel of an actual car to understand its basic purpose and use.

The Relation Between Language and Thought. Symbolic function is at the heart of one of the major advances of the preoperational period: the increasingly sophisticated use of language. Piaget suggests that the advances in language during the preschool years reflect improvements over the type of thinking that is possible during the earlier sensorimotor period. Instead of slow sensorimotor-based thinking, symbolic thought, which relies on improved linguistic ability, allows preschoolers to represent actions virtually, at much greater speed.

Even more important, language allows children to think beyond the present to the future. Rather than being grounded in the here-and-now, preschoolers can imagine future possibilities through language in the form of fantasies and daydreams.

Centration: What You See Is What You Think. Place a dog mask on a cat and what do you get? According to 3- and 4-year-old preschoolers, a dog. To them, a cat with a dog mask ought to bark like a dog, wag its tail like a dog, and eat dog food. In every respect, the cat has been transformed into a dog (deVries, 1969).

To Piaget, the root of this belief is **centration**, a key element, and limitation, of thinking in the preoperational period. Centration is the process of concentrating on one limited aspect of a stimulus—typically its superficial elements—and ignoring others. These elements come to dominate preschoolers' thinking, leading to inaccuracy.

Centration is the cause of the error illustrated in Figure 5.3. Asked which row contains more buttons, children who are 4 or 5 usually choose the row that looks longer rather than the one that actually contains more buttons. This occurs even though children of this age know quite well that 10 is more than 8. Rather than taking into account their understanding of quantity, they focus on appearance.

Preschoolers' focus on appearances might be related to another aspect of preoperational thought, the lack of conservation.

Conservation: Learning That Appearances Are Deceiving. Consider the following scenario:

Four-year-old Jaime is shown two drinking glasses. One is short and broad; the other, tall and thin. A teacher half-fills the short, broad glass with apple juice. The teacher then pours the juice into the tall, thin glass. The juice fills the tall glass almost to the brim. The teacher asks Jaime a question: Is there more juice in the second glass than there was in the first?

If you view this as an easy task, so do children like Jaime. The problem is that they almost always get it wrong.

Most 4-year-olds say that there is more apple juice in the tall, thin glass than there was in the short, broad one. In fact, if the juice is poured back into the shorter glass, they are quick to say that there is now less juice than there was in the taller.

FIGURE 5.3 Which Row Contains More Buttons?
When preschoolers are shown these two rows and asked which row has more buttons, they usually respond that the lower row of buttons contains more because it looks longer. They answer in this way even though they know quite well that 10 is greater than 8. Do you think preschoolers can be *taught* to answer correctly?

To see a reenactment of the scenario you are reading about, log onto **MyDevelopmentLab** and check out the video clip "Conservation."

preoperational stage   according to Piaget, the stage from approximately age 2 to age 7 in which children's use of symbolic thinking grows, mental reasoning emerges, and the use of concepts increases.

operations   organized, formal, logical mental processes.

symbolic function   the ability to use a mental symbol, a word, or an object to stand for or represent something that is not physically present.

centration   the process of concentrating on one limited aspect of a stimulus and ignoring other aspects.

(a)

(b)

FIGURE 5.4 Which Glass Contains More?
Most 4-year-old children believe that
the amount of liquid in the two glasses
in **(a)** differs because of the differences
in the containers' shapes, even though
they may have seen equal amounts
of liquid being poured into each **(b)**.

To watch an experiment that demonstrates egocentrism in preschoolers,
check out the video clip "Egocentrism"
on **MyDevelopmentLab**.

conservation   the knowledge that quantity
is unrelated to the arrangement and
physical appearance of objects.

transformation   the process in which one
state is changed into another.

egocentric thought   thinking that does
not take into account the viewpoints of
others.

intuitive thought   thinking that reflects
preschoolers' use of primitive reasoning
and their avid acquisition of knowledge
about the world.

The reason is that children of this age have not mastered conservation. **Conservation** is the
knowledge that quantity is unrelated to the arrangement and physical appearance of objects.
Some other conservation tasks are shown in Figure 5.4.

Why do children in the preoperational stage make conservation errors? Piaget suggests that
the main reason is that their tendency toward centration prevents them from focusing on the relevant features of the situation. Furthermore, they cannot follow the sequence of transformations
that accompanies changes in the appearance of a situation.

Incomplete Understanding of Transformation.   A preoperational, preschool child who sees
several worms during a walk in the woods may believe that they are all the same worm. The reason: She views each sighting in isolation, unable to understand that a transformation would be
necessary for a worm to move quickly from one location to the next.

As Piaget used the term, **transformation** is the process in which one state is changed into another. For instance, adults know that if a pencil that is held upright is allowed to fall down, it
passes through a series of successive stages until it reaches its final, horizontal resting spot. In
contrast, children in the preoperational period are unable to envision or recall the successive
transformations that the pencil followed in moving from the upright to the horizontal position.

Egocentrism: The Inability to Take Others' Perspectives.   Another hallmark of the preoperational period is egocentric thinking. **Egocentric thought** is thinking that does not take into account the viewpoints of others. Preschoolers do not understand that others have different
perspectives. Egocentric thought takes two forms: lack of awareness that others see things from a
different physical perspective and failure to realize that others may hold thoughts, feelings, and
points of view that differ from theirs. (Note that egocentric thought does not imply intentional
selfishness or a lack of consideration.)

Egocentric thinking lies behind children's lack of concern over their nonverbal behavior and
the impact it has on others. For instance, a 4-year-old who receives a gift of socks may frown as
he opens the package, unaware that his face can be seen by others and reveals his true feelings
(Feldman, 1992; Nilsen & Graham, 2009).

Egocentrism largely explains why many preschoolers talk to themselves, even in the presence of others, and often ignore what others are telling them. This behavior illustrates the egocentric nature of preoperational children's thinking: the lack of awareness that their behavior
acts as a trigger to others' reactions and responses. Consequently, much of preschoolers' verbal
behavior has no social motivation but is meant purely for their own consumption.

Egocentrism can also be seen in hiding games. In hide-and-seek, 3-year-olds may "hide" by
covering their faces with a pillow—even though they remain in plain view. Their reasoning: If
they cannot see others, others cannot see them. They assume that everyone else shares their view.

The Emergence of Intuitive Thought.   Because Piaget labeled this the "preoperational period" and focused on cognitive deficiencies, it is easy to assume that preschoolers are marking
time, but the period is far from idle. Cognitive development proceeds steadily, and new abilities
emerge, including intuitive thought.

Intuitive thought refers to preschoolers' use of primitive reasoning and their avid acquisition of
world knowledge. From about age 4 through 7, curiosity blossoms. Children ask "Why?" questions
about nearly everything. At the same time, they may act as if they are authorities on particular topics, certain that they have the final word on an issue. Their intuitive thought leads them to believe
that they know answers to all kinds of questions, with little or no logical basis for this confidence.

In the late stages of the preoperational period, children's intuitive thinking prepares them
for more sophisticated reasoning. For instance, preschoolers come to understand that pushing
harder on the pedals makes a bicycle move faster, or that pressing a button on a remote control
makes the television change channels. By the end of the preoperational stage, preschoolers
begin to grasp functionality, the idea that actions, events, and outcomes are related to one another in fixed patterns. They also become aware of identity, the understanding that certain
things stay the same, regardless of changes in shape, size, and appearance—for instance, that a
lump of clay contains the same amount of clay whether it is clumped into a ball or stretched out
like a snake. Comprehension of identity is necessary for children to develop an understanding
of conservation (the understanding, as we discussed earlier, that quantity is not related to physical appearances). For suggestions on promoting cognitive development in preschooler, see the
Becoming an Informed Consumer of Development box.

BECOMING AN INFORMED CONSUMER OF DEVELOPMENT
Promoting Cognitive Development in Preschoolers: From Theory to the Classroom

Piaget's theory has had enormous influence on educational practice, particularly during the preschool years. Among the suggestions for parents and preschool teachers that arise out of the Piagetian approach are the following:

- Both parents and teachers should be aware of the general stage of cognitive development, with its capabilities and limitations, that each individual child has reached. Unless they are aware of a child's current level of development, it will be impossible to provide appropriate materials and experiences.

- Instruction should be at a level that reflects—but is just slightly higher than—each student's current level of cognitive development. For instance, Piaget suggests that cognitive growth is more likely to occur when information and material are of moderate novelty. With too little novelty, children will be bored; with too much, they will be confused.

- Instruction should be individualized as much as possible. Because children of the same age may hover around different levels of cognitive development, curriculum materials that are prepared individually stand a better chance of success.

- Students should be kept actively engaged in learning, and they should be allowed to pace themselves as they move through new material.

- Opportunities for social interaction—both with other students and with adults—should be provided. By receiving feedback from others and observing how others react in given situations, children learn new approaches and ways of thinking about the world.

- Students should be allowed to make mistakes. Cognitive growth often flows from confronting errors.

- Because cognitive development can occur only when children have achieved the appropriate level of maturation, children should not be pushed too far ahead of their current state of cognitive development. For instance, although it may be possible through intensive training to get preoperational children to recite, in a rote manner, the correct response to a conservation problem, this does not mean that they will have true comprehension of what they are verbalizing.

Cognitive Development in the School Years and Adolescence

As we have seen, from Piaget's perspective preschoolers think preoperationally. They are largely egocentric and lack the ability to use *operations*—organized, formal, logical mental processes.

The Rise of Concrete Operational Thought (Ages 7 to 12). All this changes during the school years in what Piaget calls the concrete operational stage. Occurring between ages 7 and 12, this stage is characterized by the active, and appropriate, use of logic. Concrete operational thought applies logical operations to concrete problems. For instance, when children in this stage confront a conservation problem (such as determining whether the amount of liquid poured from one container to another of a different shape stays the same), they use cognitive and logical processes to answer, no longer judging solely by appearance. They are able to reason correctly that since none of the liquid has been lost, the amount stays the same. Being less egocentric, they can consider multiple aspects of a situation, an ability known as decentering. Jared, the sixth-grader described in the chapter Prologue, used decentering to consider the views of the various factions behind the U.S. Constitution.

The shift from preoperational to concrete operational thought takes time. Children shift between these modes of thought before concrete operations take a firm hold, able to answer conservation problems but unable to explain why. When asked for their reasoning, they may simply respond, "Because."

Once concrete operations take hold, however, children make several cognitive leaps, such as the concept of reversibility—the notion that transformations to a stimulus can be reversed. Grasping this notion, children realize that a ball of clay squeezed into a long, thin rope can become a ball again. More abstractly, this concept allows children to understand that if 3 + 5 equals 8, then 5 + 3 also equals 8—and, later, that 8 − 3 equals 5.

Concrete operational thinking also permits children to grasp such concepts as the relationship between time and speed. For instance, consider the problem in which two cars traveling different-length routes start and finish at the same points in the same amount of time. Children entering the concrete operational period reason that the cars' speed is the same. However, between ages 8 and 10, children begin to understand that for both cars to arrive simultaneously at the finish point, the car traveling the longer route must be moving faster.

Despite these advances, children still have one critical thinking limitation. They remain tied to concrete, physical reality. Furthermore, they cannot understand truly abstract or hypothetical questions, or questions involving formal logic, such as the concept of free will or determinism.

The ability to think beyond the concrete, current situation to what might or could be distinguishes adolescents' thinking from that of younger children. Adolescents are able to consider a variety of abstract possibilities; they can see issues in relative, as opposed to absolute, terms. When problems arise, they can perceive shadings beyond the black-and-white solutions of younger days (Keating, 1980, 1990; Lehalle, 2006).

Mrs. Kirby smiled as she read a highly creative paper. As part of her eighth-grade American Government class, she asked students to write about what their lives would be like if America had not won its war for independence from Britain. She had tried a similar task with her sixth-graders, but many of them were unable to imagine anything other than what they knew. Her eighth-graders, however, were inventing some very interesting scenarios. One boy imagined himself as Lord Lucas; a girl imagined that she would serve a rich landowner; another that she would plot to overthrow the government.

There are several explanations for adolescents' cognitive development. According to Piaget, with adolescence comes the formal operational stage.

Piaget's Formal Operational Stage (Ages 12 to 15). Leigh, age 14, is asked to solve the problem: What determines the speed at which a pendulum moves back and forth? Leigh is given a weight hanging from a string and told that she can vary several things: the length of the string, the weight of the object, the amount of force used to push the string, and the height to which the weight is raised in an arc before it is released.

Leigh doesn't remember, but she was asked to solve the same problem at age 8 as part of a longitudinal research study. She was then in the concrete operational period, and her efforts were not very successful. Her haphazard approach showed no systematic plan of action. For instance, she simultaneously tried to push the pendulum harder and shorten the length of the string and increase the weight on the string. Because she varied so many factors at once, when the pendulum's speed changed, she had no way of knowing what had made the difference.

Now, Leigh is more systematic. Rather than immediately pushing and pulling at the pendulum, she stops to think about which factors to consider. She ponders how she might test which factor is important, forming a hypothesis. Then, as a scientist conducts an experiment, she varies only one factor at a time. By examining each variable separately and systematically, she comes to the correct solution: The length of the string determines the speed of the pendulum.

Like scientists who form hypotheses, adolescents in the formal operational stage use systematic reasoning. They start with a general theory about what produces a particular outcome and then deduce explanations for specific situations in which they see that particular outcome.

Using Formal Operations to Solve Problems. Leigh's approach to the pendulum question, a problem devised by Piaget, shows she has moved into the formal operational period of cognitive development (Piaget & Inhelder, 1958). In the formal operational stage, people develop the ability to think abstractly. Piaget suggested that people reach it at the start of adolescence, around age 12.

Adolescents can consider problems in abstract rather than concrete terms by using formal principles of logic. They can test their understanding by systematically conducting rudimentary experiments and observing the results. Thus, the adolescent Leigh could think about the pendulum problem abstractly, and she understood how to test her hypotheses.

Adolescents are able to use formal reasoning, starting with a general theory about what causes a certain outcome, and then deducing explanations for the situations in which that outcome occurs. Like the scientists who form hypotheses, discussed in Chapter 1, they can test their theories. What distinguishes this kind of thinking from earlier stages is the ability to start with the abstract and move to the concrete; in previous stages, children are tied to the concrete present. At age 8, Leigh just moved things around to see what would happen in the pendulum problem, a concrete approach. At age 12, she began with the abstract idea that each variable should be tested separately.

Adolescents also can use propositional thought during this stage. Propositional thought is reasoning that uses abstract logic in the absence of concrete examples. Such thinking allows adolescents to understand that if certain premises are true, then a conclusion must also be true. For example:

All men are mortal. [*premise*]

Socrates is a man. [*premise*]

Therefore, Socrates is mortal. [*conclusion*]

Adolescents understand that if both premises are true, then so is the conclusion. They are capable of using similar reasoning when premises and conclusions are stated more abstractly, as follows:

All As are B. [*premise*]

C is an A. [*premise*]

Therefore, C is a B. [*conclusion*]

Although Piaget proposed that the formal operational stage begins at the onset of adolescence, he also hypothesized that—as with all the stages—full cognitive capabilities emerge gradually through a combination of physical maturation and environmental experiences. It is not until around age 15, Piaget says, that adolescents fully settle into the formal operational stage.

In fact, evidence suggests that many people hone these skills at a later age, and some never fully employ them at all. Most studies show that only 40 to 60 percent of college students and adults achieve formal operational thinking completely, with some estimates as low as 25 percent. But many adults who do not use formal operational thought in every domain are fully competent in some aspects (Keating & Clark, 1980; Sugarman, 1988; Commons & Richards, 2003).

The culture in which they are raised affects how adolescents use formal operations. People with little formal education, who live in isolated, technologically unsophisticated societies, are less likely to use formal operations than formally educated persons in more sophisticated societies (Jahoda, 1980; Segall et al., 1990; Oesterdiekhoff, 2007).

It is not that adolescents (and adults) from cultures using few formal operations are incapable of attaining them. It is more likely that what characterizes formal operations—scientific reasoning—is not equally valued in all societies. If everyday life does not require or promote a certain type of reasoning, it is not likely that people will use such reasoning when confronting a problem (Greenfield, 1976; Shea, 1985; Gauvain, 1998; Smorti, 2008).

Adolescents' ability to reason abstractly leads them to question accepted rules and explanations.

The Consequences of Adolescents' Use of Formal Operations.

The ability to reason abstractly, to use formal operations, changes adolescents' everyday behavior. Whereas earlier they may have blindly accepted rules and explanations, their increased abstract reasoning abilities may lead to strenuous questioning of their parents and other authority figures.

In general, adolescents become more argumentative. They enjoy using abstract reasoning to poke holes in others' explanations, and their increased critical thinking abilities zero in on parents' and teachers' perceived shortcomings. For instance, they may see their parents' arguments against using drugs as inconsistent if their parents used drugs in adolescence without consequence. But adolescents can be indecisive, too, as they are able to see the merits of multiple sides to issues (Elkind, 1996; Kuhn & Franklin, 2006).

Coping with these new critical abilities can be challenging for parents, teachers, and other adults who deal with adolescents. But it makes adolescents more interesting, as they actively seek to understand the values and justifications they encounter.

REVIEW

▶ Cognitive developmentalists study both continuity and change linked to changes in a person's intellectual abilities.

▶ Jean Piaget argued that infants acquire knowledge directly through motor behavior, organizing their world into mental structures called schemes and subsequently either assimilating experiences into their current level of understanding or accommodating their ways of thinking to include the new experience.

▶ Piaget's theory is based on a stage approach to development in which children pass through a series of stages in a fixed order from birth through adolescence: sensorimotor, preoperational, concrete operational, and formal operational.

▶ The key way in which Piaget differs from many theorists who preceded him is in his observation that children experience *qualitative* changes in knowledge and understanding as they move from stage to stage, not just *quantitative* changes.

▶ Piaget's theory of human cognitive development involves a succession of stages through which children progress from birth to adolescence. As people move from one stage to another, the way they understand the world changes.

▶ The sensorimotor stage, from birth to about 2 years, involves a gradual progression through simple reflexes, single coordinated activities, interest in the outside world, purposeful combinations of activities, manipulation of actions to produce desired outcomes, and symbolic thought. The sensorimotor stage has six substages.

▶ According to Piaget, children in the preoperational stage develop symbolic function, a change in their thinking that is the foundation of further cognitive advances, but they are hampered by a tendency toward egocentric thought.

▶ Individuals in middle childhood are in the concrete operational stage of cognitive development, characterized by the application of logical processes to concrete problems and by "decentering," the ability to take multiple aspects of a situation into account.

▶ As they enter Piaget's formal operational stage, adolescents begin to think abstractly, use logic, and perform systematic experiments to answer questions.

APPLY

▶ Think of a common young children's toy with which you are familiar. How might its use be affected by the principles of assimilation and accommodation?

▶ Do you think it is possible to break a preschooler's habit of egocentric thought by directly teaching him to take another person's point of view? Would showing him a picture of himself "hidden" behind a chair change his thinking? Why?

MODULE 5.2

Appraising Piaget: Support, Challenges, and Alternatives

Most developmental researchers would probably agree that in many significant ways, Piaget's descriptions of how cognitive development proceeds are largely accurate. Yet, there is substantial disagreement over the validity of the theory and many of its specific predictions (Marcovitch, Zelazo, & Schmuckler, 2003; Demetriou & Raftopoulos, 2004).

Let's start with what is clearly correct about the Piagetian approach. Piaget was a virtuoso observer and masterly reporter of children's behavior, and his descriptions of growth remain a monument to his powers of observation. His many books contain brilliant, careful observations of children at work and play.

Furthermore, literally thousands of studies have supported Piaget's view that children learn much about the world by acting on objects in their environment. Finally, the broad outlines sketched out by Piaget of the sequence of cognitive development and the increasing cognitive accomplishments that occur during infancy and the preschool years, in particular, are generally accurate (Gratch & Schatz, 1987; Kail, 2004). His theories have had powerful educational implications, and many schools use his principles to guide instruction (Flavell, 1996; Siegler & Ellis, 1996; Brainerd, 2003).

The Critics Weigh In

Despite the powerful influence of Piaget's work, specific aspects of his theory have come under increasing scrutiny—and criticism—in the decades since he carried out his pioneering work. For example, some researchers question the concept of stages that forms the basis of Piaget's theory. Although even Piaget acknowledged that children's transitions between stages are gradual, critics, particularly those who favor the information processing approach, contend that development proceeds in a much more continuous fashion. Rather than showing major leaps of competence at the end of one stage and the beginning of the next, improvement comes in more gradual increments, growing step by step in a skill-by-skill manner (Siegler, 2003; Lavelli & Fogel, 2005).

Regarding infants in particular, some critics dispute Piaget's notion that cognitive development is grounded in motor activities. They charge that Piaget overlooked the importance of the sensory and perceptual systems that are present from a very early age in infancy—systems about which Piaget knew little, since so much of the research illustrating how sophisticated they are even in infancy was done relatively recently (Butterworth, 1994; Johnson, 2009).

- **Timing of Mastery of Object Permanence.** Piaget's critics also point to more recent studies that cast doubt on Piaget's view that infants are incapable of mastering the concept of object permanence until they are close to a year old. For instance, some work suggests that younger infants did not appear to understand object permanence because the techniques used to test their abilities were not sensitive enough to their true capabilities (Aguiar & Baillargeon, 2002; Baillargeon, 2004; Krojgaard, 2005).

  It may be that a 4-month-old doesn't search for a rattle hidden under a blanket because she hasn't learned the motor skills necessary to do the searching—not because she doesn't understand that the rattle still exists. Similarly, the apparent inability of young infants to comprehend object permanence may reflect more about their memory deficits than their lack of understanding of the concept: The memories of young infants may be poor enough that they simply do not recall the earlier concealment of the toy. In fact, when more age-appropriate tasks are employed, some researchers have found indications of object permanence in children as young as 3 $\frac{1}{2}$ months (Aguiar & Baillargeon, 2002; Wang, Baillargeon, & Paterson, 2005; Ruffman, Slade, & Redman, 2006).

  Many researchers contend that Piaget underestimated children's capabilities generally, in part due to the limitations of the mini-experiments he conducted. Subjected to a broader array of experimental tasks, children show less consistency within stages than Piaget predicted. Increasing evidence suggests that children's cognitive abilities emerge earlier than supposed; for example, some children demonstrate concrete operational thinking before age 7, when Piaget suggested these abilities first appear (Bjorklund, 1997b; Dawson-Tunik, Fischer, & Stein, 2004).

- **Children's Understanding of Numbers.** Piaget may also have erred in asserting that preschoolers have little understanding of numbers, as shown by their inability to grasp conservation and reversibility (the understanding that a transformation can be reversed to return something to its original state). Recent experimental work calls that assertion into question. For instance, developmental psychologist Rochel Gelman has found that children as young as 3 can easily tell the difference between rows of two and three toy animals, regardless of the animals' spacing. Older children are able to identify which of two numbers is larger and show a rudimentary understanding of addition and subtraction (Wynn, 1992; Sophian, Garyantes, & Chang, 1997; Vilette, 2002).

  Gelman concludes that children have an innate ability to count, akin to the ability to use language that some theorists see as universal and genetically determined. This is clearly at odds with Piagetian notions, which suggest that children's numerical abilities do not blossom until after the preoperational period (i.e., after about age 7).

Appraising Piaget: Research on babies in non-Western cultures suggests that Piaget's stages are not universal, but are to some degree culturally derived.

- **Conservation.** There are further difficulties with Piaget's contention that conservation does not emerge until the end of the preoperational period. This contention has not stood up to experimental scrutiny. Children can learn to answer conservation tasks correctly if they are given certain training and experiences. The fact that one can improve children's performance argues against the Piagetian view that children in the preoperational period have not reached a level of cognitive maturity to understand conservation (Siegal, 2003; Halford & Andrews, 2006).

- **Cultural Issues.** Piaget's work also seems to describe children from developed, Western countries better than those in non-Western cultures. For instance, some evidence suggests that cognitive skills emerge on a different timetable for children in non-Western cultures than for children living in Europe and the United States. Infants raised in the Ivory Coast of Africa, for example, reach the various substages of the sensorimotor period at an earlier age than infants reared in France (Dasen et al., 1978; Rogoff & Chavajay, 1995; Mistry & Saraswathi, 2003).

Despite these criticisms—which research has shown to be valid—we cannot dismiss Piaget. Although some early cross-cultural research implied that children in certain cultures remain preoperational, failing to master conservation and develop concrete operations, more recent research suggests otherwise. For instance, with proper training in conservation, children in non-Western cultures who do not conserve learn to do so. In one study, urban Australian children—who develop concrete operations on Piaget's timetable—were compared to rural Aborigine children, who typically do not conserve at the age of 14 (Dasen, Ngini, & Lavallee, 1979; Maynard & Greenfield, 2003). With training, the rural Aborigine children showed conservation skills similar to those of their urban counterparts, although about 3 years later (see Figure 5.5).

When children are interviewed by researchers from their own culture, who share their language and customs, and whose reasoning tasks relate to important cultural domains, the children are much more likely to display concrete operational thinking. Such research suggests that Piaget was right in arguing that concrete operations are universally achieved during middle childhood. Performance differences between Western and some non-Western children on Piagetian measures of conservation and concrete operations probably reflect a difference in experiences. The progress of cognitive development cannot be understood without considering a child's culture (Jahoda, 1983; Mishra, 2001; Lau, Lee, & Chiu, 2004).

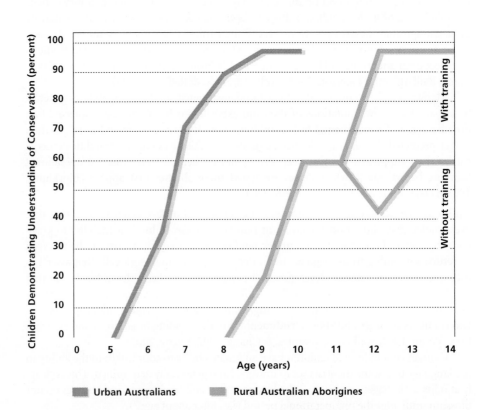

FIGURE 5.5 Conservation Training
Rural Australian Aborigine children trail their urban counterparts in the development of their understanding of conservation; with training, they later catch up. Without training, around half of 14-year-old Aborigines do not have an understanding of conservation. What can be concluded from the fact that training influences the understanding of conservation?

A Final Summation. Even Piaget's most passionate critics concede that he has provided us with an ingenious description of the broad outlines of cognitive development during infancy. His failings seem to be in underestimating the capabilities of younger infants and in his claims that sensorimotor skills develop in a consistent, fixed pattern.

Still, his influence has been enormous. Piaget's theories have inspired countless studies on the development of thinking capacities and processes, and they have spurred much classroom reform. His bold statements about the nature of cognitive development sparked opposition that brought forth new approaches, such as the information processing perspective we examine next. Piaget remains a towering, pioneering figure in the field of development (Zigler & Gilman, 1998; Roth, Slone, & Dar, 2000; Kail, 2004; Taylor, 2005).

Beyond Piaget

As we've seen, Piaget, for all his brilliance and influence, has drawn his share of criticism. Let's look at several contemporary approaches that differ from Piaget's on the question of when cognitive development comes to an end. The developmentalists who espouse these approaches all agree on one thing: that Piaget underestimated the portion of the life span during which cognitive development occurs.

Consider the following scenario drawn from research by Adams and Labouvie-Vief (1986).

> *Ben is known to be a heavy drinker, especially when he goes to parties. Tyra, Ben's wife, warns him that if he comes home drunk one more time, she will leave him and take the children. Tonight Ben is out late at an office party. He comes home drunk. Does Tyra leave Ben?*

To the typical adolescent this case is open-and-shut: Tyra leaves Ben. But in early adulthood, the answer is less clear. People become less concerned with sheer logic and instead take into account real-life concerns that may influence and temper behavior.

To Piaget, the first stage of development is the sensorimotor stage, achieved in infancy, and the final stage is the formal operations stage, reached in adolescence. If we subscribed to the traditional Piagetian view of cognitive development, we would expect to find little intellectual growth in early adulthood.

Piaget argued that by the time people left adolescence, their thinking, at least qualitatively, had largely become what it would be for the rest of their lives. They might gather more information, but the ways in which they thought about it would not change. But this view of development seems overly limited. Does development really stop in adolescence?

Labouve-Vief and Postformal Thought.   Gisela Labouvie-Vief and several other modern developmentalists have begun to conclude that the answer is No. They have found that cognitive development continues beyond adolescence because people are faced with dealing with the complexities of life throughout adulthood.

Labouvie-Vief suggests that the nature of thinking changes during early adulthood. She asserts that thinking based solely on formal operations is insufficient to meet the demands placed on young adults. The complexity of society, which requires specialization, and the challenge of finding one's way through that complexity require thought that transcends logic to include practical experience, moral judgments, and values (Labouvie-Vief, 1990, 2006).

For example, imagine a young, single woman in her first job. Her boss, a married man whom she respects greatly and who is in a position to help her career, invites her to go with him to make an important presentation to a client. When the presentation, which has gone very well, is over, he suggests they go out to dinner and celebrate. Later that evening, after sharing a bottle of wine, he attempts to accompany her to her hotel room. What should she do?

Logic alone doesn't answer such questions. Labouvie-Vief suggests that young adults' thinking must develop to handle ambiguous situations like these. She suggests that young adults learn to use analogies and metaphors to make comparisons, confront society's paradoxes, and become comfortable with a more subjective understanding. This requires weighing all aspects of a situation according to one's values and beliefs. It allows for interpretive processes and reflects the fact that the reasons behind events in the real world are painted in shades of gray rather than black and white (Labouvie-Vief, 1990; Sinnott, 1998; Thornton, 2004).

To demonstrate how this sort of thinking develops, Labouvie-Vief presented experimental subjects, ranging in age from 10 to 40, with scenarios similar to the Ben and Tyra scenario above. Each story had a clear, logical conclusion, but it could be interpreted differently if real-world demands and pressures were taken into account.

The nature of thought changes qualitatively during early adulthood.

postformal thought thinking that acknowledges that adult predicaments must sometimes be solved in relativistic terms.

In responding to the scenarios, adolescents relied heavily on the logic of formal operations. They tended to predict that Tyra would immediately pack up her bags and leave with the children when Ben came home drunk. After all, that's what she said she would do. In contrast, young adults were more apt to consider various real-life possibilities: Would Ben be apologetic and beg Tyra not to leave? Did Tyra really mean it when she said she would leave? Does Tyra have some place to go?

Young adults exhibited what Labouvie-Vief calls postformal thinking. **Postformal thought** is thinking that goes beyond Piaget's formal operations. Rather than being based on purely logical processes, with absolutely right and wrong answers to problems, postformal thought acknowledges that adult predicaments must sometimes be solved in relativistic terms.

Postformal thought also encompasses dialectical thinking, an interest in and appreciation for argument, counterargument, and debate (Basseches, 1984; Sinnott, 2003). Dialectical thinking accepts that issues are not always clear-cut and that answers to questions must sometimes be negotiated. According to psychologist Jan Sinnott (1998), postformal thinkers shift back and forth between an abstract, ideal solution and real-world constraints that might prevent implementation of that solution. Postformal thinkers understand that just as there can be multiple causes of a situation, there can be multiple solutions.

Perry's Approach to Postformal Thinking. To psychologist William Perry (1970, 1981), the developmental growth of early adulthood involves mastering new ways of understanding the world. To examine intellectual and moral growth during college, Perry interviewed students at Harvard University. He found that students entering college tended to use *dualistic thinking* in their views of the world: Something was either right or wrong; people were either good or bad; others were either for them or against them.

However, as these students encountered new ideas and points of view from other students and their professors, their dualistic thinking declined. Consistent with postformal thinking, they understood that it is possible to hold multiple perspectives on an issue. Their attitude toward authorities also changed: Instead of assuming that experts had all the answers, they began to realize that their own thinking had validity if their position was well thought out and rational.

In fact, according to Perry, they had reached a stage in which knowledge and values were regarded as relativistic. Rather than seeing the world as having absolute standards and values, they argued that different societies, cultures, and individuals could have different standards and values, and all of them could be equally valid.

It's important to keep in mind that Perry's theory is based on a sample of interviews conducted with well-educated students attending an elite college. His findings may not apply as well to people who have never learned how to examine multiple points of view.

Schaie's Stages of Cognitive Development. Developmental psychologist K. Warner Schaie offers another perspective on postformal thought. Taking up where Piaget left off, Schaie suggests that adults' thinking follows a set pattern of stages (illustrated in Figure 5.6). But Schaie

FROM AN EDUCATOR'S PERSPECTIVE

Do you think it is possible for adolescent students to learn postformal thinking (e.g., by direct instruction on breaking the habit of dualistic thinking)? Why or why not?

FIGURE 5.6
Schaie's Stages of Adult Development
Source: Schaie, 1977–1978.

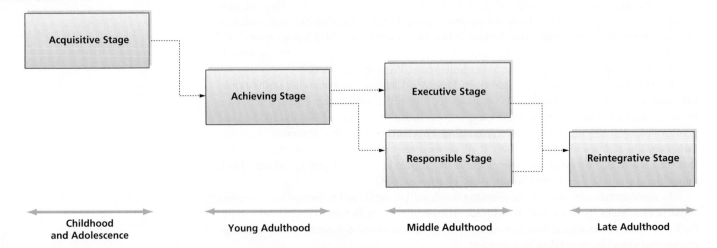

focuses on the ways in which information is used during adulthood, rather than on changes in the acquisition and understanding of new information, as in Piaget's approach (Schaie & Willis, 1993; Schaie & Zanjani, 2006).

Schaie suggests that before adulthood, the main cognitive developmental task is acquisition of information. Consequently, he labels the first stage of cognitive development, which encompasses all of childhood and adolescence, the **acquisitive stage**. Information gathered before we grow up is largely squirreled away for future use. Much of the rationale for education during childhood and adolescence, then, is to prepare people for future activities.

The situation changes considerably in early adulthood when the focus shifts from the future to the here-and-now. According to Schaie, young adults are in the **achieving stage**, applying their intelligence to attain long-term goals regarding their careers, family, and contributions to society. During the achieving stage, young adults must confront and resolve several major issues, and the decisions they make—such as what job to take and whom to marry—have implications for the rest of their lives.

During the late stages of early adulthood and in middle adulthood, people move into the responsible and executive stages. In the **responsible stage**, middle-aged adults are mainly concerned with protecting and nourishing their spouses, families, and careers.

Sometime later, further into middle adulthood, many people (but not all) enter the **executive stage** in which they take a broader perspective, becoming more concerned about the larger world. People in the executive stage put energy into nourishing and sustaining societal institutions. They may become involved in town government, religious congregations, service clubs, charitable groups, factory unions—organizations that have a larger purpose in society (Sinnott, 1997, 2003).

Finally, the **reintegrative stage** is the period of late adulthood during which people focus on tasks that have personal meaning. They no longer focus on acquiring knowledge to solve potential problems that they may encounter. Instead, they acquire information about issues that specifically interest them. Furthermore, they have less interest in—and patience for—things that they do not see as having some immediate application to their lives.

acquisitive stage according to Schaie, the first stage of cognitive development, encompassing all of childhood and adolescence, in which the main developmental task is to acquire information.

achieving stage the point reached by young adults in which intelligence is applied to specific situations involving the attainment of long-term goals regarding careers, family, and societal contributions.

responsible stage the stage where the major concerns of middle-aged adults relate to their personal situations, including protecting and nourishing their spouses, families, and careers.

executive stage the period in middle adulthood when people take a broader perspective than earlier, including concerns about the world.

reintegrative stage the period of late adulthood during which the focus is on tasks that have personal meaning.

REVIEW

▶ Recent developmentalists, while acknowledging Piaget's acute observational ability and his pioneering contributions to cognitive development, have questioned many of his conclusions, including the boundaries between his stages, the severe limits he attached to preschoolers' abilities, the universality of cognitive development across cultures, and his judgment that cognitive development is essentially complete by the end of adolescence.

▶ In contrast to Piaget, Gisela Labouvie-Vief maintains that adults engage in postformal thought, in which predicaments must sometimes be solved in relativistic terms, rather than as absolute rights and wrongs.

▶ William Perry suggests that people move from dualistic thinking to relativistic thought during early adulthood.

▶ K. Warner Schaie argues that adults pass through five stages in the way they use information: acquisitive, achieving, responsible, executive, and reintegrative.

According to Schaie, children in the acquisitive stage gather information that helps prepare them for future activities. How might the girl in the photo use her current play in the future?

APPLY

▶ Do adults use schemes to organize their environment? Do the principles of assimilation and accommodation apply to adult learning as well as children's learning? How?

▶ When faced with complex problems, do adults routinely use formal operations? What aspects of a culture might encourage or discourage the use and application of formal operational approaches?

Vygotsky's View of Cognitive Development: Taking Culture into Account

As her daughter watches, a member of the Chilcotin Indian tribe prepares a salmon for dinner. When the daughter asks a question about a small detail of the process, the mother takes out another salmon and repeats the entire process. According to the tribal view of learning, understanding and comprehension can come only from grasping the total procedure, and not from learning about the individual subcomponents of the task. (Tharp, 1989)

The Chilcotin view of how children learn about the world contrasts with the prevalent view of Western society, which assumes that only by mastering the separate parts of a problem can one fully comprehend it. Do differences in the ways particular cultures and societies approach problems influence cognitive development? According to Russian developmental psychologist Lev Vygotsky, who lived from 1896 to 1934, the answer is a clear Yes.

Vygotsky viewed cognitive development as the product of social interactions. Instead of concentrating on individual performance, Vygotsky's increasingly influential view focuses on the social aspects of development and learning.

Vygotsky sees children as apprentices, learning cognitive strategies and other skills from adult and peer mentors who not only present new ways of doing things, but also provide assistance, instruction, and motivation. Consequently, he focuses on the child's social and cultural world as the source of cognitive development. According to Vygotsky, children gradually grow intellectually and begin to function on their own because of the assistance that adult and peer partners provide (Vygotsky, 1979, 1926/1997; Tudge & Scrimsher, 2003).

Vygotsky contends that culture and society establish the institutions, such as preschools and play groups, that promote development by providing opportunities for cognitive growth. Furthermore, by emphasizing particular tasks, culture and society shape the nature of specific cognitive advances. Unless we look at what is important and meaningful to members of a given society, we may seriously underestimate the nature and level of cognitive abilities that ultimately will be attained (Tappan, 1997; Schaller & Crandall, 2004). For example, children's toys reflect what is important and meaningful in a particular society. In Western societies, preschoolers commonly play with toy wagons, automobiles, and other vehicles, in part reflecting the mobile nature of the culture. In this way, a society subtly communicates to children a great deal about its expectations and characteristics.

In much the same way, societal expectations about gender play a role in how children come to understand the world. For example, one study conducted at a science museum found that parents provided more detailed scientific explanations to boys than to girls at museum displays. Such differences in level of explanation may lead to more sophisticated understanding of science in boys and ultimately may produce later gender differences in science learning (Crowley et al., 2001).

Vygotsky's approach is therefore quite different from Piaget's. Where Piaget looked at children and saw junior scientists, working by themselves to develop an independent understanding of the world, Vygotsky saw cognitive apprentices, learning from master teachers the skills valued in the child's culture (Kitchener, 1996; Fernyhough, 1997; Halford, 2005; Karpov, 2006).

The Zone of Proximal Development

Vygotsky proposed that children's cognitive abilities increase through exposure to information that is new enough to be intriguing, but not too difficult to contend with. He called this the **zone of proximal development,** or **ZPD,** the level at which a child can almost, but not fully, perform a task independently, but can do so with the assistance of someone more competent. For cognitive

zone of proximal development or **ZPD** according to Vygotsky, the level at which a child can *almost,* but not fully, perform a task independently, but can do so with the assistance of someone more competent.

scaffolding the support for learning and problem solving that encourages independence and growth.

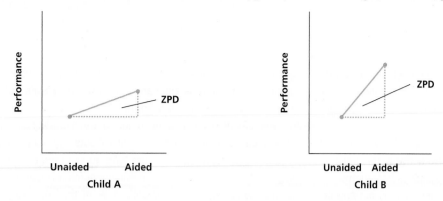

FIGURE 5.7 Sample Zones of Proximal Development (ZPD) for Two Children Although the performance of the two children is similar when working at a task without aid, the second child benefits more from aid and therefore has a larger ZPD. Is there any way to measure a child's ZPD? Can it be enlarged?

development to occur, new information must be presented—by parents, teachers, or more skilled peers—within the zone of proximal development. For example, a preschooler might not be able to figure out by herself how to stick a handle on the clay pot she's making, but she can do it with advice from her child-care teacher (Blank & White, 1999; Chaiklin, 2003; Kozulin, 2004).

The concept of the zone of proximal development suggests that even though two children might be able to achieve the same amount without help, if one child receives aid, he or she may improve substantially more than the other. The greater the improvement that comes with help, the larger the zone of proximal development (see Figure 5.7).

The assistance or structuring provided by others has been termed **scaffolding**, after the temporary scaffolds that aid in building construction. Scaffolding is the support for learning and problem solving that encourages independence and growth (Puntambekar & Hübscher, 2005). As in construction, the scaffolding that older people provide, which facilitates the completion of identified tasks, is removed once children can solve a problem on their own (Rogoff, 1995; Warwick & Maloch, 2003).

To Vygotsky, scaffolding not only helps children solve specific problems, it also aids in the development of their overall cognitive abilities. In education, scaffolding involves, first of all, helping children think about and frame a task appropriately. In addition, a parent or teacher is likely to provide clues to task completion that fit the child's level of development and to model behavior that can lead to task completion.

To illustrate how scaffolding operates, consider the following conversation between mother and son:

Mother: Do you remember how you helped me make the cookies before?
Child: No.
Mother: We made the dough and put it in the oven. Do you remember that?
Child: When Grandma came?
Mother: Yes, that's right. Would you help me shape the dough into cookies?
Child: OK.
Mother: Can you remember how big we made the cookies when Grandma was here?
Child: Big.
Mother: Right. Can you show me how big?
Child: We used the big wooden spoon.
Mother: Good boy, that's right. We used the wooden spoon, and we made big cookies. But let's try something different today by using the ice cream scoop to form the cookies.

Although this conversation may not appear to be a particularly sophisticated specimen of teaching and learning, it illustrates the practice of scaffolding. The mother is supporting her son's efforts, and she gets him to respond conversationally. In the process, she not only expands her son's abilities by using a different tool (the scoop instead of the spoon), she models how conversations proceed.

In some societies parental support for learning differs by gender. In one study, Mexican mothers were found to provide more scaffolding than fathers. A possible explanation is that mothers may be more aware of their children's cognitive abilities than are fathers (Tenenbaum & Leaper, 1998; Tamis-LeMonda & Cabrera, 2002; also see the *From Research to Practice* box on page 170).

mydevelopmentlab

Log onto **MyDevelopmentLab** and watch several videos of the zone of proximal development principle displayed in preschoolers. Also check out the video "Scaffolding" to watch a teacher using the scaffolding technique with preschoolers.

FROM AN EDUCATOR'S PERSPECTIVE
How might a teacher use Vygotsky's approach to teach 10-year-olds about colonial America?

Students working in cooperative groups benefit from the insights of others.

FROM RESEARCH TO PRACTICE
Vygotsky in the Classroom

Educators have seized on Vygotsky's notion that cognitive advances occur through exposure to information within a child's zone of proximal development, or ZPD. In the ZPD, a child can almost, but not quite, understand or perform a task.

Vygotsky's approach has particularly encouraged the development of classroom practices that promote children's active participation in their learning (e.g., Holzman, 1997). Consequently, classrooms are seen as places where children should experiment and try out new activities (Vygotsky, 1926/1997).

According to Vygotsky, education should focus on activities that involve interaction with others. Both child–adult and child–child interactions can promote cognitive growth. The interactions must be carefully structured to fall within each child's zone of proximal development.

Vygotsky's work has influenced several current and noteworthy innovations. For example, *cooperative learning,* where children work in groups to achieve a common goal, uses several aspects of Vygotsky's theory. Students working in cooperative groups benefit from the insights of others. A wrong turn by one child may be corrected by others in the group. On the other hand, not every group member is equally helpful: As Vygotsky's approach would imply, individual

children benefit most when some of the group members are more competent at the task and can act as experts (Slavin, 1995; Karpov & Haywood, 1998; Gillies & Boyle, 2006).

Reciprocal teaching, a technique to teach reading comprehension strategies, is another practice that reflects Vygotsky's approach to cognitive development. Students learn to skim the content of a passage, ask questions about its meaning, summarize, and predict what will happen next. The reciprocal nature of this technique gives students a chance to adopt the role of teacher. Teachers initially lead students through the comprehension strategies. Gradually, students progress through their zones of proximal development, taking increasing control of the strategies, until they assume the teaching role. The method has impressively raised comprehension levels, particularly for students with reading difficulties (Palincsar, Brown, & Campione, 1993; Greenway, 2002; Takala, 2006).

- *How do Vygotsky's approaches to teaching differ from those of Piaget?*
- *Given Vygotsky's emphasis on culture, how would educational practice differ according to the culture in which education was being carried out?*

Cultural Tools

One key aspect of the aid that more accomplished individuals provide to learners comes in the form of cultural tools. Cultural tools are actual, physical items (e.g., pencils, paper, calculators, computers, and so forth), as well as an intellectual and conceptual framework for solving problems. The framework includes the language that is used within a culture, its alphabetical and numbering schemes, its mathematical and scientific systems, and even its religious systems. These cultural tools provide a structure that can be used to help children define and solve specific problems, as well as an intellectual point of view that encourages cognitive development.

For an example of the pervasive influence of culture on thinking and action, consider the *Developmental Diversity* feature.

Evaluating Vygotsky's Contributions

Vygotsky's view has become increasingly influential, which is surprising given that he died over 70 years ago at the age of 37 (Van Der Veer & Valsiner, 1993, 1994; Winsler, 2003). His influence has grown because his writings are only now becoming widely disseminated in the United States due to the growing availability of good English translations. For most of the 20th century Vygotsky was not widely known even within his native land. His work was banned for some time, and it was not until the breakup of the Soviet Union in the 1990s that it became freely available in the formerly Soviet countries. Thus, Vygotsky, long hidden from his fellow developmentalists, didn't emerge onto the scene until long after his death.

Even more important, though, is the quality of Vygotsky's ideas. They represent a consistent theoretical system and help explain a growing body of research on the importance of social interaction in promoting cognitive development. The idea that children's comprehension of the world flows from their interactions with their parents, peers, and other members of society is increasingly well supported. It is also consistent with a growing body of multicultural and cross-cultural research, which finds evidence that cognitive development is shaped, in part, by cultural factors (Daniels, 1996; Scrimsher & Tudge, 2003).

Of course, not every aspect of Vygotsky's theorizing has been supported, and he can be criticized for a lack of precision in his conceptualization of cognitive growth. For instance, such

DEVELOPMENTAL DIVERSITY
A Walk Through a Cultural Landscape

"Dad, how far is it to school?"

"It's about three blocks past the supermarket."

"School is about a 20-minute ride downtown on the subway that stops across the street from our apartment."

"If you walk to the public well, and then walk that distance again, and then again, you will reach the school."

"You know how the boys and girls all race to that tall tree in the grove by the river? The school is maybe two of those races from our house, in the direction of the morning sun."

Our culture is all around us, as invisible and as much taken for granted as water is to fish. No matter what we do or think about, we are expressing ourselves in terms of our culture.

Consider the cultural differences in how people talk about distance. In cities, distance is usually measured in blocks ("the store is about 15 blocks away"). To a child from a rural background, more culturally meaningful terms are needed, such as yards or miles, such practical rules of thumb as "a stone's throw," or references to known distances and landmarks ("about half the distance to town"). To make matters more complicated, "how far" questions are sometimes answered in terms not of distance, but of time ("it's about 15 minutes to the store"), which will be understood variously to refer to walking or riding time, depending on context—and, if riding time, to different forms of riding—by ox cart, bicycle, bus, canoe, or automobile, again depending on cultural context.

In short, not only is the nature of the tools available to children to solve problems and perform tasks highly dependent on the culture in which they live, but also the ways they think about problems and questions, and the ways they use those tools.

broad concepts as the zone of proximal development are not terribly precise, and they do not always lend themselves to experimental tests (Wertsch, 1999).

Furthermore, aside from his observations about the social function that children's private speech serves and his approach to the development of intelligence, both of which we will discuss in a later chapter, Vygotsky was largely silent on how basic cognitive processes such as attention and memory develop and how children's natural cognitive capabilities unfold. Because of his emphasis on broad cultural influences, he did not focus on how individual bits of information are processed and synthesized. These processes, essential to a complete understanding of cognitive development, are more directly addressed by information processing theories.

Still, Vygotsky's melding of the cognitive and social worlds of children has marked an important advance in our understanding of cognitive development.

REVIEW

▶ Lev Vygotsky proposed that the nature and progress of children's cognitive development are dependent on the children's social and cultural context.

▶ According to Vygotsky, culture and society determine how people engage in thought and set the agenda for education and the cognitive abilities that their members are expected to attain.

▶ Vygotsky's theory features the concepts of the zone of proximal development and scaffolding.

▶ Vygotsky suggests that schoolchildren should have the opportunity to experiment and participate actively with their peers in their learning.

▶ Vygotsky's ideas have influenced educational practices in the United States and other nations. In particular, the practice of cooperative learning and the technique of reciprocal teaching owe their development to his insights about how teachers can best help students learn.

▶ Despite a lack of precision about basic cognitive processes, Vygotsky has become in the years since his death an influential figure in the study of cognitive development and the practice of education.

▶ If children's cognitive development is dependent on interactions with others, what obligations does society have regarding such social settings as preschools and neighborhoods?

▶ In what ways have educators and others begun to apply Vygotsky's ideas in schools and communities? Should governments take an active role in this endeavor?

Epilogue

We have examined the work of two major cognitive development researchers, Jean Piaget and Lev Vygotsky, as well as several critics of their approaches. We have seen the weighty influence of Piaget's work on subsequent theoretical approaches and experimental work, and we have marveled at the posthumous ability of a Russian psychologist to construct a structure of theory and thought that has recently gained a strong footing in American education.

Think back to Jared, the child whom we looked in on at ages from 7 months to 11 years, and who began this chapter. Jared shows a pace and range of cognitive development that are on the one hand

ordinary for children of all cultures, and on the other hand, quite breathtaking. Consider these questions about Jared.

1. With what Piagetian stages do Jared's actions at 7 months, 5 years, and 11 years most closely align? What are some characteristics in Jared's behavior that suggest which stage he has reached?

2. What would be Vygotsky's approach to instruction if he were a teacher in Jared's kindergarten or sixth grade? How might the U.S. Constitution project be handled differently by a teacher steeped in the zone of proximal development and scaffolding?

Looking Back

What is cognitive development and how did Piaget revolutionize its study?

1. Cognitive development focuses on changes in behavior that correspond to changes in an individual's intellectual abilities, with special attention to intelligence, language, and similar topics.

2. Piaget differed from earlier psychologists in arguing that infants learn by doing, not by listening to the teaching of adults or through sensation and perception.

3. Piaget's background as a biologist led him to use observational techniques to study children one or two at a time in their "natural habitat."

What theoretical elements underlie Piaget's theory?

4. Piaget theorized that the foundations of the way we understand the world are mental structures called schemes, organized patterns of functioning, that adapt and change with mental development.

5. Two underlying principles explain how children's schemes grow. Assimilation consists of fitting stimuli or events into existing patterns of thought, while accommodation consists of expanding existing patterns of thought to fit stimuli or events.

6. Piaget has been criticized for neglecting any consideration of development beyond the end of adolescence. Several cognitive researchers extend the stage approach to adulthood.

What are the key features—and criticisms—of Piaget's theory?

7. Piaget's theory is based on a stage approach to development, with children and adolescents passing through four universal stages in a predetermined sequence: sensorimotor, preoperational, concrete operational, and formal operational.

8. In the six substages of the sensorimotor period, simple reflexes at first determine behaviors, then the infant's earliest habits become circular reactions, which eventually become goal-oriented problem-solving activities. In the next substage, infants deliberately vary their actions as if conducting experiments, and in the final substage, they begin to produce mental representations of events or objects.

9. The preoperational stage occurs during the preschool years, as children's use of symbolic thinking, reasoning, and concepts increases. The preoperational stage has several limitations, including centration, a failure to conserve, an incomplete understanding of transformation, and egocentrism.

10. Concrete operational thought develops during the early adolescent years. This stage is characterized by the active and appropriate use of logic. However, individuals in this stage are still limited to concrete reality and unable to deal with abstract or hypothetical questions.

11. Piaget's final stage, the formal operational period, occurs in later adolescence as people develop the ability to think abstractly.

What are some alternate approaches to Piaget's view of cognitive development?

12. Despite Piaget's great influence on the field, specific aspects of his theory have been criticized, including the concept of stages that forms the basis of his theory and what many critics perceive as his persistent underestimation of children's abilities. We have also noted the criticism that his theory neglects ongoing cognitive development in adulthood.

13. Gisela Labouvie-Vief maintains that postformal thought develops in young adulthood. Postformal thinking surpasses logic to encompass interpretive and subjective thinking.

14. William Perry suggests that people move from dualistic thinking to relativistic thought during early adulthood, and K. Warner Schaie argues that adults pass through the acquisitive, achieving, responsible, executive, and reintegrative stages in the way they use information.

What are the key features—and criticisms—of Vygotsky's theory?

15. In Vygotsky's view, cognitive development is the product of culture and of social interactions.

16. Vygotsky notes that children learn best by participating in active learning through child–adult and child–child interactions that fall within each child's zone of proximal development.

17. He also observes that learners need support—a process called scaffolding—to encourage their learning and problem solving until they achieve independence and growth.

18. Vygotsky's views are respected because they represent a consistent theoretical system and are consistent with modern research on learning and cognitive development.

19. Critics contend that Vygotsky's theories lack precision and lend themselves only with difficulty to experimental tests. Furthermore, Vygotsky never addressed some of the major topics in cognitive development, such as attention and memory, and dealt only slightly with intelligence.

6 Cognitive Growth: Information Processing Approaches

Prologue
Forgotten Memories

Like thousands of other Romanian orphans, Simona Young spent her infancy with little human contact. She was left alone in a crib, often for 20 hours a day. Milk bottles, propped up in her crib, were left for nourishment, and she would rock back and forth, alone in a desolate world. When she cried, no one would comfort her.

Unlike many other orphans who suffered in Romanian orphanages, Simona was rescued. A Canadian couple adopted her when she was 2 years old, and 4 years later she appears to be a normal, happy preschooler. She has friends and playmates and is part of a loving family. At the age of 6, she remembers virtually nothing of her horrendous early years. It's as if the memories have been totally blanked out of her mind (Blakeslee, 1995; Rose, 2009).

While we remember some information from infancy, it is still not clear when and how our earliest memories are formed.

Did Simona really forget the first 2 years of her life, or do her memories still exist, hidden behind more current—and pleasant—recollections? Will she ever recall her past? Will any memories of her infancy be accurate?

Such questions go the heart of the nature of memory. Clearly, we remember *some* information from infancy because without memory we would be unable to speak, recognize others, or, more generally, show the enormous advances in cognitive development that routinely occur throughout childhood. Yet it is still not entirely clear how accurate are our earliest recollections, and when—and how—our earliest memories are formed.

We address these and related questions as we continue our consideration of cognitive development. In this chapter we diverge from the roads that Piaget and Vygotsky laid out for us. Rather than seeking to identify the universal milestones in cognitive development, as Piaget tried to do, or to recognize the contribution of the social world to thinking, as Vygotsky attempted, we now take a different approach based on *information processing*. According to the information processing approach, we can best understand cognitive development by considering the processes by which individuals acquire and use the information to which they are exposed. We need, then, to focus less on the qualitative changes in infants' mental lives and to consider more closely their quantitative capabilities.

Information processing approaches to cognitive development seek to identify the way that individuals take in, use, and store information. According to this approach, the quantitative changes in infants' abilities to organize and manipulate information represent the hallmarks of cognitive development.

According to this perspective, cognitive growth is characterized by increasing sophistication in information processing, similar to the way a computer program becomes more sophisticated and useful as the programmer modifies it and as the capacity of the computer's memory and its computational sophistication increase. Information processing approaches, then, focus on the types of "mental programs" that people use when they seek to solve problems.

In this chapter, we'll first consider the foundations of information processing in three elementary functions, encoding, storage, and retrieval, that are involved in any processing of information, whether by humans or computers. We'll also consider the topic of attention, discussing the functions and development of attention in children, the use of planning and control strategies to focus attention, and the ways that attention affects our ability to accomplish our goals and complete our tasks. We will also discuss an increasingly prevalent attention disorder that affects learning and normal life functioning.

information processing approaches approaches to cognitive development that seek to identify the ways that individuals take in, use, and store information.

175

Next we'll consider memory, discussing first the development of basic memory capabilities in infancy and the surprising retention of information even at very young ages. We will discuss how infants' memories become lost or corrupted, and we will examine the reliability of children's memories of their own experiences. We'll then consider how and why memory improves as children age, and we'll discuss strategies that people use to control and improve cognitive processing. We'll also discuss whether culture affects the quality of memory—and the difficulty of conducting sound studies of memory across cultures.

Finally, we conclude the chapter with a look at some practical applications of information processing theory in the courtroom, the classroom, and the home. We also offer a general appraisal of the information processing perspective and its contributions to our understanding of human cognition.

LOOKING AHEAD

After reading this chapter, you will be able to answer these questions:

▶ What are the fundamental elements of information processing?

▶ What explanations have been proposed for the way information is processed in the brain?

▶ What is attention, how does it develop, and what are the consequences of an attention deficit?

▶ What memory capabilities—and limitations—do people have, and how does memory develop as we age?

▶ What practical insights have been gained from the information processing perspective?

MODULE 6.1

The Basics of Information Processing

"Who is the president of the United States?" "When is your birthday?" "Where did you leave your gloves?"

They're not very hard questions for an adult, or even for a 5-year-old. But whether someone is able to answer them depends on a series of processing steps that are hardly simple.

Encoding, Storage, and Retrieval: The Foundations of Information Processing

Whether someone is able to answer the questions posed at the start of this module depends on several basic processes of information processing (see Figure 6.1). For instance, it is necessary for the information to be encoded in memory. *Encoding* is the process by which information is initially recorded in a form usable to memory. All of us are exposed to a massive amount of information; if we tried to process it all, we would be overwhelmed. Consequently, people encode selectively, picking and choosing the information to which they will pay attention. The ability to answer questions such as the preceding, then, depends first on whether someone has been exposed to the information in the first place and subsequently on whether he or she has encoded it in a meaningful way.

Even if an individual has been exposed to the information initially, and has encoded it in an appropriate way, there is still no guarantee that he or she will be able to answer questions about it correctly. Information must also have been stored in memory adequately. *Storage* refers to the

FIGURE 6.1

Information Processing

The process by which information is encoded, stored, and retrieved.

| Encoding (initial recording of information) | Storage (information saved for future use) | Retrieval (recovery of stored information) |

maintenance of material saved in memory. If , for example, we have not adequately stored information about the name of the U.S. president, we will be unable to recall it later.

Finally, the success of an individual in answering informational questions will depend on retrieval processes. *Retrieval* is the process by which material in memory storage is located, brought into awareness, and used. Success in responding to the questions posed earlier, then, is a result of how well the material can be retrieved from storage.

Information processing approaches suggest that the processes of encoding, storage, and retrieval are analogous to different parts of a computer. Encoding can be thought of as a computer's keyboard, through which one inputs information; storage is the computer's hard drive, where information is stored; and retrieval is analogous to a computer's screen, where information is displayed. Only when all three processes are operating—encoding, storage, and retrieval—can information be processed.

Automatization. In some cases, encoding, storage, and retrieval are relatively automatic, whereas in other cases they are deliberate. *Automatization* is the degree to which an activity requires attention. Processes that require relatively little attention are automatic; processes that require relatively large amounts of attention are controlled.

Automatic processes help us in our initial encounters with the world by "automatically" priming us to process information in particular ways. For instance, by the age of 5, children automatically encode information in terms of frequency. They automatically become aware of how often they have encountered various people, permitting them to differentiate familiar from unfamiliar people (McCrink & Wynn, 2007).

Furthermore, without intending to and without being aware of it, they develop a sense of how often different stimuli are found together simultaneously. This permits them to develop an understanding of *concepts*, categorizations of objects, events, or people that share common properties. For example, by encoding the information that four legs, a wagging tail, and barking are often found together, children are able to acquire the concept of "dog." Children—as well as adults—are rarely aware of how they learn such concepts, and they are often not able to articulate the features that distinguish one concept (such as a dog) from another (such as cat). Instead, learning tends to occur automatically.

Automatization also provides the benefit of permitting more efficient information processing, allowing children to concentrate on other mental problems. At the same time, automatization can backfire: In some situations a nonautomatic response is required, but an automatic response, which occurs readily, is employed instead. For instance, a young child who encounters a cat for the first time, but who automatically categorizes it as a dog because it has four legs and a tail, is a victim of automaticity.

Cognitive Architecture: The Three-System Approach

Although the ability to encode, store, and retrieve material is central to information processing, these processes are not the whole story. In fact, they don't provide an explanation of how information actually moves through the cognitive architecture. *Cognitive architecture* refers to the basic, enduring structures and features of information processing that are relatively constant over the course of development.

Cognitive architecture determines the specific steps through which material is processed as it travels through the human mind. Information processing theorists assume that the basic architecture of information processing systems is constant over the course of development, although the speed and capacity of the system are thought to grow. In short, developmental change is reflected not in changes in cognitive architecture, but in the efficiency and capacity of information processing over time (Siegler, 1998).

The *three-system approach* is the oldest—and most influential—of the approaches to information processes. According to cognitive psychologists Richard Atkinson and Richard Shiffrin (1968), there are several steps in the overall process that permit a person to encode, store, and retain information. Atkinson and Shiffrin describe the process in much the same way that we illustrated information processing by comparing it to a computer that passes information through a sequential series of steps. The three-system model consists of a sensory store, short-term memory, and long-term memory (see Figure 6.2 on page 178).

Before we consider the three-system model, keep this idea in mind: Although the three-part description of memory may seem to imply the existence of separate memory storage areas in the

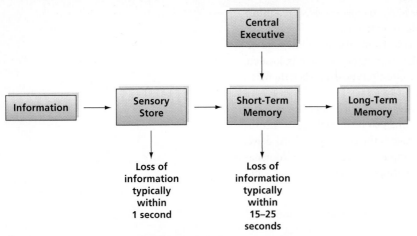

FIGURE 6.2 An Information Processing Model
According to the Atkinson and Shiffrin model, there are several steps in the process that permit the encoding, storage, and retention of information, similar to a computer that passes information through a sequential series of steps. The three-system model consists of a sensory store, short-term memory, and long-term memory.
Source: Adapted from Atkinson & Shiffrin, 1968.

brain where each system is located, in fact this view is oversimplified and largely erroneous. Instead, the three types of memory represent abstract systems that describe distinct components or functions of memory as opposed to actual physical locations.

The Sensory Store. According to the Atkinson–Shiffrin three-system model, information first encounters what is called a sensory story. The **sensory store** is the initial, momentary storage of information, lasting only an instant. Sensory memories are simply a cognitive representation of some stimulus, unfiltered and unevaluated. Because they are a raw representation of the stimulus, they are not analyzed in terms of their meaning.

There are actually several types of sensory stores. Information can be initially registered as a visual image, a sound, a smell, or even a twinge of pain. However, unless the information is processed and passed to the next stage, it is lost almost immediately and forever. Still, despite its rapid decay, the sensory store is highly accurate, representing an almost identical replica of every stimulus to which it is exposed. It is as if we take a sequential series of snapshots of the world around us. However, only a few of the snapshots are preserved, while the rest are destroyed by the arrival of each new one. The few snapshots that are maintained are preserved only because they are transferred to the next information way station: short-term memory.

Short-Term Memory. **Short-Term memory** is the short-duration, limited-capacity memory component in which selected input from the memory store is worked on. It is in short-term memory that thoughtful, deliberate information processing first takes place, giving meaning to the raw, nonmeaningful information from the sensory store. It is not clear how the transfer from the sensory store to short-term memory takes place. Some researchers suggest that the sensory information is first translated into images or graphical representations, while others argue that the transfer takes place when sensory stimuli are changed into words (Baddeley & Wilson, 1985). Whatever the exact process, short-term memory begins the process of storing information in terms of meaning.

Storage in short-term memory, though longer than in the sensory store, is still relatively short, lasting from 15 to 25 seconds. In addition, the capacity of short-term memory is limited. In adults, short-term memory can hold up to seven items, or "chunks," of information, with variations of plus or minus two chunks. A *chunk* is a meaningful group of stimuli that can be stored as a unit in short-term memory. A chunk might be a letter or number, a word, or even a well-known maxim ("two's company, three's a crowd"). The important point about the definition of a chunk is that it relates less to physical size than to meaningfulness. Consequently, a group of seven maxims may be held in short-term memory as effectively as seven unrelated letters.

The capacity of short-term memory increases with age. For instance, in one frequently used experimental task, lists of stimuli such as the numbers from 0 through 9 are presented in a random order, typically at a pace of one per second. Experimental participants of different ages are then asked to repeat the numbers. Results of such research clearly show that short-term memory capacity increases with age. Whereas 2- and 3-year-old children can remember only around two numbers, 7-year-old children can recall around five. But with increasing age, the increase in the quantity of numbers that can be recalled slows down. For instance, there is only a one-number increase between 12 years of age (where, on average, six numbers can be recalled) to adulthood, when the quantity of numbers that can be recalled reaches seven (see Figure 6.3; Dempster, 1981).

Performance of other memory tasks also improves with age. For instance, children are increasingly able to listen to a string of digits ("1-5-6-3-4") and then repeat the string in reverse order ("4-3-6-5-1"). At the start of the preschool period, they can remember and reverse only about two digits; by the beginning of adolescence they can perform the task with as many as six digits (Bjorklund et al., 1994; Halford et al., 1994; Klibanoff et al., 2006).

sensory store the initial, momentary storage of information, lasting only an instant.

short-term memory the short-duration, limited-capacity memory component in which selected input from the memory store is worked on.

The capacity of short-term memory is also affected by the nature of the material being remembered. For example, lists of single numbers are usually remembered slightly better than lists of single letters. Recall that the capacity of short-term memory is not based on the physical size of the material being encoded, but on whether it forms meaningful chunks of information. Thus, a list of five random letters (c, s, h, t, c) will be considered five chunks, while a list of five words (cat, son, hand, tree, car) are also stored as five chunks. Clearly, the words contain more physical information and yet are just as easily memorized. The specific nature of what constitutes a chunk depends on an individual's prior experience (Miller, 1956).

Why does memory capacity (which in short-term memory is also called *memory span*) increase? One important reason is that with increasing age we are able to rehearse material in short-term memory more rapidly, and the shorter the time lag between repetitions of a stimulus, the less likely it is to be forgotten. This simple fact explains why older children, who are able to pronounce words more quickly, are also able to remember more: Their greater pronunciation speed permits them to rehearse words more quickly than younger children. According to some research, when speed of repetition is taken into account, the memory span of 6-year-olds is as great as that of young adults (Case, Kurland, & Goldberg, 1982; Hitch & Towse, 1995).

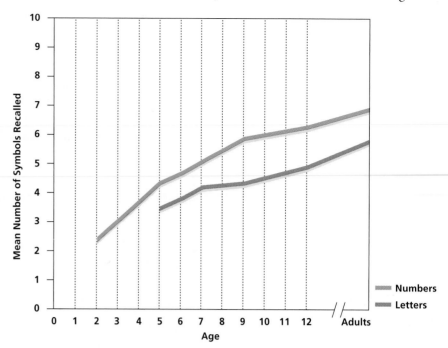

FIGURE 6.3 Increases in Memory Span
Memory span increases with age both for numbers and letters.
Source: Adapted from Dempster, 1981.

Although capacity and speed of processing change with age, the process used to handle material in short-term memory—rehearsal—is assumed to be constant. *Rehearsal* is the repetition of information that has entered short-term memory. As long as information in short-term memory is rehearsed, it is kept alive and is not lost. Even more important, rehearsal permits the transfer of material into long-term memory.

Working Memory. Contemporary researchers view short-term memory as an information processing system that is highly active. In this perspective, short-term memory is referred to as **working memory**, a set of memory stores that actively manipulate and rehearse information (Bayliss et al., 2005a, 2005b; Unsworth & Engle, 2005).

According to the working memory view, the way in which we process information in working memory is determined by a "central executive." The *central executive* controls the functions of short-term memory, coordinating the processing of material, determining problem-solving strategies, directing attention, and selecting strategies for remembering in short-term memory (Baddeley, 1993, 1996).

Long-Term Memory. If sufficiently processed in short-term memory, information passes into the third and final information processing unit, long-term memory. **Long-term memory** is the memory component in which information is stored on a relatively permanent basis. In a process similar to the one that attends the arrival of a new book at a library, information arriving in long-term memory is filed and cataloged so that—at least in theory—it can be retrieved when it is needed.

Long-term memory is a repository that is nearly limitless in capacity. Even when they are young, children can remember a huge amount of information about the world. When they are older, the capacity is even greater. For instance, if you're like the average college student, your vocabulary consists of some 50,000 words, you know thousands of facts, and you have little trouble recalling sights, sounds, and even smells from your childhood.

If long-term memory is so large, why don't we remember everything that is stored there? The reason is that we suffer from retrieval problems. *Retrieval* is the process of locating and bringing information stored in memory into awareness. We are able to recall information through the use of *retrieval cues*, stimuli that permit people to recall information. Retrieval cues are like a library's catalog; they guide people to the location of a specific memory.

**FROM AN
EDUCATOR'S
PERSPECTIVE**
What are some educational implications of the short attention spans of young children?

working memory a set of temporary memory stores that actively manipulate and rehearse information.

long-term memory the memory component in which information is stored on a relatively permanent basis.

Retrieval cues may take the form of a word, an image, a smell, or a sound. When triggered by a retrieval cue, a memory comes to mind. For example, the smell of freshly baked chocolate chip cookies may trigger memories of one's childhood, including the emotions that are attached to specific recollections.

Long-Term Memory Modules. In the same way that short-term memory can be viewed as working memory, contemporary researchers view long-term memory as having different components called *memory modules* representing different memory systems in the brain.

For example, researchers distinguish between *declarative memory,* memory for factual information such as names, dates, and facts, and *procedural memories*, memories relating to skills and habits, such as how to ice skate or ride a bike. We remember information about *things* in declarative memory, while we remember information about *how to do things* in procedural memory (Schacter, Wagner, & Buckner, 2000; Eichenbaum, 2004; Feldhusen, 2006).

Comparing Information Processing Approaches to Alternative Theories of Cognitive Development

It should be clear that information processing approaches differ significantly from the theories of cognitive development that we considered in the last chapter, particularly that of Piaget. You'll recall, of course, that Piaget's theory ties cognitive development to particular stages. At each stage, children are presumed to have developed a particular set of cognitive structures that determines the quality of their thinking. When children move to another stage, according to Piaget, the quality of their thinking changes significantly. Developmental changes, then, are largely qualitative.

In contrast, information processing approaches attribute cognitive development to gradual, continuous improvements in the ways children perceive, understand, and remember information. With age and practice, children process information more efficiently and with greater sophistication, and they are able to handle increasingly complex problems. Although some information processing theories do propose that cognitive development proceeds in a stagelike fashion, the stages to which they refer apply to specific subtypes of cognitive skills and are far narrower than Piaget's broad stages (Case, 1991, 1992; Case & Okamoto, 1996). For the proponents of information processing approaches, then, it is quantitative advances in information-processing skills—and not the qualitative changes suggested by Piaget—that constitute cognitive development. In the remainder of this chapter, we'll consider the specific nature of some of these changes.

REVIEW

▶ The fundamental elements of information processing are encoding, storage, and retrieval. Automatization refers to the degree to which these processes require attention.

▶ The three-system model proposes that information processing involves the sensory store, short-term memory, and long-term memory. The sensory store is the initial, momentary storage of nonmeaningful information. Selected information is passed to short-term memory, in which deliberate information processing first takes place and meaning is added.

▶ Contemporary approaches consider short-term memory as working memory, in which a central executive processor coordinates the processing of information.

▶ Information that has been sufficiently processed in short-term memory is passed to long-term memory, where it is stored on a relatively permanent basis for later retrieval.

▶ Long-term memories can be considered as memory modules, each of which is related to separate memory systems.

▶ Information processing models assume that development is quantitative in nature, rather than qualitative, as Piaget assumes.

APPLY

▶ It has been said that poets and artists process information differently than other people. Do you agree? Why? If you agree, in which of the three basic processes—encoding, storage, or retrieval—do you think the difference mostly lies?

▶ Automatization in information processing can backfire, producing an automatic response when a nonautomatic response is required. Can you think of instances when this happens? Can anything be done about it?

MODULE 6.2

Attention and Memory

Two-month-old Meredith lies in her crib. Her gaze shifts from the mobile that is slowly moving above her head, repeatedly playing "Mary Had a Little Lamb," to her father, who is singing along with the tune. At the same time, her father strokes the wisps of hair on her head, as her older brother calls out from the next room, "Dad, where are you?"

Consider the multiple sources of information in Meredith's environment: the sights of the mobile and her father, the sound of the mobile and her father's and brother's voices, and the touch of her father's hand on her head. To which of these stimuli does she pay attention?

Attention

The choices Meredith makes are determined by **attention**, information processing involving the ability to strategically choose among and sort out different stimuli in the environment. Attention is the first step in information processing. If a child doesn't attend to a stimulus, or is unaware of it in the first place, that material cannot be processed further. Furthermore, if children are constantly distracted by incoming stimuli, they will be unable to sustain focus on their current activity.

From the time of birth, infants pay more attention to some objects and less to others. What they attend to and how long they attend to it are largely a result of the nature of the stimuli in the environment and the alternatives that are available. Some stimuli act as *attention-getting* stimuli due to their physical characteristics. Other stimuli are *attention-holding*; it is their meaningfulness that sustains attention (Cohen, 1972).

The properties that make a stimulus attention-getting are fairly constant throughout the life span. For instance, a loud noise or sudden movement is apt to evoke attention in both an infant and an adult. However, attention-holding stimuli vary across the life span according to an individual's age and experience. Thus, a toy truck is more of an attention-holding stimulus to a 4-year-old than it would be to a 12-year-old, while a book is obviously of greater interest to an older reader than to a child who has not yet learned to read.

Are differences in attention due to younger children's lack of sensory capabilities? Although it seems plausible that the less well-developed sensory store of young children would render them incapable of initially taking in as much information as older individuals, in fact this does not seem to be the case. Experiments have found that initial encoding of information in the sensory store is little different between 5-year-olds and adults. On the other hand, when 5-year-olds are asked to recall what they have been exposed to, they remember significantly less than older children and adults (Sheingold, 1973; Morrison, Holmes, & Haith, 1974).

In short, children and adults seem to initially record information in the sensory store in the same way. Failures of information processing, then, are more likely due to the inability to draw out information from the sensory store and to processing deficiencies in short-term memory. Several attentional factors determine whether and how effectively information is processed, including the control and planning of attention.

Control of Attention.   When we watch children of different ages react to their environments, it seems obvious that as they get older their attention becomes more concentrated and lasting. A 2-year-old is more apt to leap from one activity to another than a 6-year-old. Older children are better able to concentrate on a particular activity for a longer period of time, ignoring extraneous distractions. Yet even 5- and 6-year-olds don't have long attention spans, averaging only 7 minutes on a single activity during preschool play periods (Stodolsky, 1974; Ruff & Lawson, 1990).

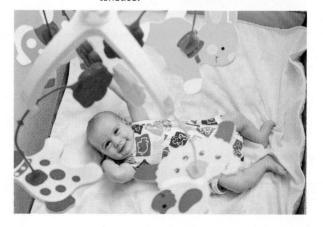

Brightly-colored objects act as *attention-getting* stimuli due to their physical characteristics.

planning the ability to allocate attentional resources on the basis of goals that one wishes to achieve.

attention-deficit/hyperactivity disorder (ADHD) a disorder marked by inattention, impulsiveness, a low tolerance for frustration, and a great deal of inappropriate activity.

Infants have the ability to plan or calculate how to produce a desired outcome.

FIGURE 6.4 Planning
When comparing whether houses such as these were different from one another, preschoolers' eye movements showed that they did not systematically compare the features of the two houses in order to make their determination. In contrast, school-age children's eye movements showed that they systematically compared the features of the houses on a window-by-window basis, and they were considerably more accurate than the younger children.
Source: Vurpillot, 1968.

The increasing ability to tune into certain stimuli, while tuning out of others, is an indication of increasing cognitive *control* of attention. With age, children become increasingly aware of their sensory and memory limitations, and they develop strategies for responding to stimuli of interest (Miller, Woody-Ramsey, & Alise, 1991; Miller & Seier, 1994).

With age, children become more effective not only at controlling what they are attending to, but also at excluding irrelevant or extraneous stimuli. For instance, children who are completing a task become better at focusing on what is central to the task and ignoring elements of the situation that will not further its completion. Thus, a preschool child might focus on the brightly colored pin worn by an individual who is giving directions on how to complete at task, rather than on the directions themselves, as would an older child (Lane & Pearson, 1982).

Planning. With increasing age, people don't only learn to control their attention in the face of irrelevant stimuli. They also become more proficient at mapping out and devising strategies for using their attention effectively; that is, they become better at planning. **Planning** is the ability to allocate attentional resources on the basis of goals that one wishes to achieve (Haith, 1993, 1994).

Even infants show their ability to plan. They are able to anticipate when routine child-care procedures are going to take place, beginning to shift attention according to what they expect to happen (Canfield & Haith, 1991; Benson & Haith, 1995).

Despite early indication of "planfulness," young children are not highly proficient at planning, and the ability to plan effectively develops throughout the course of childhood and adolescence. For example, young children are unable to take into account all the steps that will be involved in solving complex problems. They are also less systematic than older children. In one experiment, children were asked to compare whether complex stimuli consisting of two houses were different (as in the top row of Figure 6.4) or the same (as in the bottom row of Figure 6.4). Examination of the eye movements of preschoolers comparing the two houses showed that they did not systematically compare the features of the two houses. Instead, their eyes moved back and forth in a disorderly fashion, missing key features of the houses. As a result, they frequently said two different houses were the same. In contrast, school-age children used a more systematic strategy, comparing window-to-window, and they were much more accurate in determining whether the two were the same or different (Vurpillot, 1968).

According to Shari Ellis and Robert Siegler (1997), several reasons explain why younger children are deficient in planning, even when they may know that planning will help them reach a goal. For one thing, planning requires considering not only what one must do, but also what one must *not* do. However, the ability to refrain from acting develops relatively slowly throughout childhood (Dempster, 1993).

In addition, children frequently are more optimistic about their ability to reach their goal than is warranted. Their overoptimism leaves them unmotivated to engage in planning. Furthermore, planning may require coordination with others, and young children may not have the skills to cooperate effectively with others (Stipek, 1984; Baker-Sennet, Matusov, & Rogoff, 1992).

Still, children's ability to determine how they will allocate their attentional resources, as well as their general ability to control attention, grow significantly over the course of development. By the time they reach adolescence, they are more adept at effectively dividing their attention across more than one stimulus at a time—such as simultaneously studying for a biology test and listening to a Black Eyed Peas CD.

The improvements that occur in the control of attention and planning related to attention are likely produced by increases in maturation of the brain, as well as by the increasing educational demands placed on children.

For some children, however, the course of attentional development is not so smooth. As we consider in the accompanying *From Research to Practice* box, attentional disorders are at the heart of a problem that strikes 3 to 5 percent of the school-age population: attention-deficit/hyperactivity disorder.

Memory

Think back to the story of Simona, the Romanian orphan, described at the beginning of the chapter. How likely is it that Simona truly remembers nothing of her infancy? And if she ever does recall her first 2 years of life, how accurate will her memories be? To answer these questions, we need to consider the qualities of memory during infancy and beyond.

FROM RESEARCH TO PRACTICE
Attention-Deficit/Hyperactivity Disorder: A Failure in Attention

Dusty Nash, an angelic-looking blond child of 7, awoke at 5 one recent morning in his Chicago home and proceeded to throw a fit. He wailed. He kicked. Every muscle in his 50-pound body flew in furious motion. Finally, after about 30 minutes, Dusty pulled himself together sufficiently to head downstairs for breakfast. While his mother bustled about the kitchen, the hyperkinetic child pulled a box of Kix cereal from the cupboard and sat on a chair.

But sitting still was not in the cards this morning. After grabbing some cereal with his hands, he began kicking the box, scattering little round corn puffs across the room. Next he turned his attention to the TV set, or rather, the table supporting it. The table was covered with checkerboard Con-Tact paper, and Dusty began peeling it off. Then he became intrigued with the spilled cereal and started stomping it to bits. At this point his mother interceded. In a firm but calm voice she told her son to get the stand-up dustpan and broom and clean up the mess. Dusty got out the dustpan but forgot the rest of the order. Within seconds he was dismantling the plastic dustpan, piece by piece. His next project: grabbing three rolls of toilet paper from the bathroom and unraveling them around the house. (Wallis, 1994, p. 43)

Seven-year-old Dusty Nash's high energy and low attention span are due to attention-deficit/hyperactivity disorder, which occurs in 3 to 5 percent of the school-age population.

It was only 7:30 AM.

Dusty suffers from attention-deficit/hyperactivity disorder. **Attention-deficit/hyperactivity disorder,** or **ADHD**, is marked by inattention, impulsiveness, a low tolerance for frustration, and generally a great deal of inappropriate activity. All children show such traits some of the time, but for those diagnosed with ADHD, such behavior is common and interferes with their home and school functioning (American Academy of Pediatrics, 2000a; Nigg, 2001; Whalen et al., 2002).

What are the most common signs of ADHD? It is often difficult to distinguish between children who simply have a high level of activity

and those with ADHD. Some of the most common symptoms include the following:

- Persistent difficulty in finishing tasks, following instructions, and organizing work.
- Inability to watch an entire television program.
- Frequent interruption of others or excessive talking.
- A tendency to jump into a task before hearing all the instructions.
- Difficulty in waiting or remaining seated.
- Fidgeting, squirming.

Because there is no simple test to identify whether a child has ADHD, it is hard to know for sure how many children have the disorder. Most estimates put the number between 3 and 7 percent of those under the age of 18. Only a trained clinician can make an accurate diagnosis, following an extensive evaluation of the child and interviews with parents and teachers.

The treatment of children with ADHD has been a source of considerable controversy. Because it has been found that doses of Ritalin or Dexadrine (which, paradoxically, are stimulants) reduce activity levels in hyperactive children, many physicians routinely prescribe drug treatment (Volkow et al., 2001; Kaplan et al., 2004; HMHL, 2005; Schachar et al., 2008).

Although in many cases such drugs are effective in increasing attention span and compliance, in other cases the side effects (such as irritability, reduced appetite, and depression) are considerable, and the long-term health consequences of this treatment are unclear. It is also true that although the drugs often help scholastic performance in the short run, the long-term evidence for continuing improvement is mixed. Some studies suggest that after a few years children treated with drugs do not perform academically any better than untreated children with ADHD. Nonetheless the drugs are being prescribed with increasing frequency (Marshall, 2000; Zernike & Petersen, 2001; Mayes & Rafalovich, 2007; Rose, 2008).

In addition to drugs, behavior therapy is often employed for treating ADHD. With behavior therapy, parents and teachers are trained in techniques for improving behavior, primarily involving the use of rewards (such as verbal praise) for desired behavior. In addition, teachers can increase the structure of classroom activities and use other class management techniques to help children with ADHD, who have great difficulty with unstructured tasks. (Parents and teachers can receive support from the Children and Adults with Attention-Deficit/Hyperactivity Disorder organization at www.chadd.org.)

- *Why is ADHD sometimes overdiagnosed by educators and medical practitioners?*
- *Why are some parents reluctant to treat the symptoms of ADHD with drugs?*

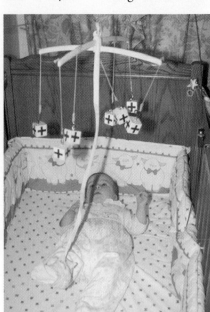

FIGURE 6.5 Early Signs of Memory
Infants who had learned the association between a moving mobile and kicking showed surprising recall ability if they were exposed to a reminder of the early memory.

The Development of Basic Memory Capabilities. The ability of infants to distinguish new stimuli from old implies that some memory of the old must be present. Unless the infants had some memory of an original stimulus, it would be impossible for them to recognize that a new stimulus differed from the earlier one.

Other evidence confirms the ability of infants to remember. In one study, a string was tied to infants' ankles so that when they kicked that leg, an enticing mobile above their crib moved and made noise (see Figure 6.5). It took only a few days for 2-month-old infants to forget their training, but 6-month-old infants still remembered for as long as 3 weeks (Rovee-Collier, 1984, 1993; Bearce & Rovee-Collier, 2006).

Furthermore, infants who were later prompted to recall the association between kicking and moving the mobile showed evidence that the memory continued to exist even longer. Infants who had received just two training sessions lasting 9 minutes each still recalled about a week later, as illustrated by the fact that they began to kick when placed in the crib with the mobile. Two weeks later, however, they made no effort to kick, suggesting that they had forgotten entirely.

But they hadn't: When the babies saw a reminder—a moving mobile—their memories were apparently reactivated. In fact, the infants could remember the association, following prompting, for as long as an additional month. Other evidence confirms these results, suggesting that hints can reactivate memories that at first seem lost and that the older the infant, the more effective such prompting is (Hildreth, Sweeney, & Rovee-Collier, 2003; Bearce & Rovee-Collier, 2006; Kraebel & Gerhardstein, 2006).

Is infant memory qualitatively different from that in older children and adults? Researchers generally believe that information is processed similarly throughout the life span, even though the kind of information being processed changes and different parts of the brain may be used. According to memory expert Carolyn Rovee-Collier, people, regardless of their age, gradually lose memories, although, just like babies, they may regain them if reminders are provided. Moreover, the more times a memory is retrieved, the more enduring the memory becomes (Rovee-Collier, 1999; Barr, Marrott, & Rovee-Collier, 2003; Barr et al., 2007).

The Duration of Memories

Although the processes that underlie memory retention and recall seem similar throughout the life span, the quantity of information stored and recalled does differ markedly as infants develop. Older infants can retrieve information more rapidly, and they can remember it longer. But just how long? Can memories from infancy be recalled, for example, after babies grow up?

Researchers disagree on the age from which memories can be retrieved. Although early research supported the notion of **infantile amnesia**—the lack of memory for experiences occurring prior to 3 years of age—more recent research shows that infants do retain memories. For example, Nancy Myers and her colleagues exposed a group of 6-month-old children to an unusual series of events in a laboratory, such as intermittent periods of light and dark and unusual sounds. When the children were later tested at the age of $1\frac{1}{2}$ years or $2\frac{1}{2}$ years, they demonstrated clear evidence that they had some memory of their participation in the earlier experience. Other research shows that infants show memory for behavior and situations that they have seen only once (Myers, Clifton, & Clarkson, 1987; Howe, Courage, & Edison, 2004; Neisser, 2004).

Such findings are consistent with evidence that the physical trace of a memory in the brain appears to be relatively permanent; this suggests that memories, even from infancy, may be enduring. However, memories may not be easily, or accurately, retrieved. For example, memories are susceptible to interference from other, newer information, which may displace or block out the older information, thereby preventing its recall.

One reason why infants appear to remember less may be because language plays a key role in determining the way memories from early in life can be recalled: Older children and adults may be able to report memories using only the vocabulary that they had available at the time of the initial event, when the memories were stored. Because their vocabulary at the time of initial storage may have been quite limited, they are unable to describe the event later in life, even though it is actually in their memories (Bauer et al., 2000; Simcock & Hayne, 2002; Heimann et al., 2006).

The question of how well memories formed during infancy are retained in adulthood remains not fully answered. Although infants' memories may be highly detailed and can be enduring if the infants experience repeated reminders, it is still not clear how accurate those memories remain over the course of the life span. Early memories are susceptible to incorrect recollection if people are exposed to related, and contradictory, information following the initial formation of the memory.

infantile amnesia the lack of memory for experiences that occurred prior to 3 years of age.

Not only does such new information potentially impair recall of the original material, but the new material may be inadvertently incorporated into the original memory, thereby corrupting its accuracy (Bauer, 1996; Dubreuil, Garry, & Loftus, 1998; Cordon et al., 2004).

In sum, the data suggest that although it is at least theoretically possible for memories to remain intact from a very young age—if subsequent experiences do not interfere with their recollection—in most cases memories of personal experiences in infancy do not last into adulthood. Current findings suggest that memories of personal experience do not seem to become accurate before age 18 to 24 months (Howe, 2003; Howe, Courage, & Edison, 2004; also see the accompanying *Neuroscience and Development* box).

Autobiographical Memory. Think back to your own earliest memory. If you are like most people, the memory probably is of an event that occurred after the age of 3. **Autobiographical memory**, memory of particular events from one's own life, doesn't achieve much accuracy until after 3 years of age (Sutton, 2002; Ross & Wilson, 2003; De Roten, Favez, & Drapeau, 2004; Nelson & Fivush, 2004).

Preschool children's recollections of events that happened to them are sometimes, but not always, accurate. For instance, 3-year-olds can remember fairly well the central features of routine occurrences, such as the sequence of events involved in eating at a restaurant. In addition, preschoolers are typically accurate in their responses to open-ended questions, such as "What rides did you like best at the amusement park?" (Price & Goodman, 1990; Wang, 2006).

The accuracy of preschoolers' memories is partly determined by how soon the memories are assessed. Unless an event is particularly vivid or meaningful, it is not likely to be remembered at all. Moreover, not all autobiographical memories last into later life. For instance, a child may remember the first day of kindergarten 6 months or a year later, but later in life might not remember that day at all.

Memories are also affected by cultural factors. For example, Chinese college students' memories of early childhood are more likely to be unemotional and reflect activities involving social roles, such as working in their family's store, whereas U.S. college students' earliest memories are more emotionally elaborate and focus on specific events such as the birth of a sibling (Wang, 2001, 2004, 2006).

Preschoolers' autobiographical memories not only fade, but what is remembered may not be wholly accurate. For example, if an event happens often, such as a trip to a grocery store, it may be hard to remember one specific time it happened (Fivush, Kuebli, & Clubb, 1992; Sutherland, Pipe, & Schick, 2003).

Adults, too, show errors in their autobiographical memories. For example, they forget information about their past that conflicts with their view of themselves in the present. If they feel well adjusted as adults, they view themselves as well-adjusted children—even if the reality was that they suffered from emotional problems as children. Similarly, college students are much

This preschooler may recall this ride in 6 months, but by the time he is 12, it will probably be forgotten. Can you explain why?

autobiographical memory memory of particular events from one's own life.

NEUROSCIENCE AND DEVELOPMENT
Memory and the Brain: I Am Stuck on Palmitate, and Palmitate Is Stuck in Me

Fats tend to have a bad reputation—after all, ingesting too much of them leads to obesity and heart attacks—but it turns out that certain kinds of fats are quite helpful in producing long-term memories.

Recently a team of researchers at Johns Hopkins University discovered that *palmitate*, a sticky fatty acid, is involved in activating special brain proteins called NMDA receptors, which are needed in long-term memory and learning. Palmitate helps move NMDA receptors to specific locations in the brain where cell connections are strengthened or weakened to change memory circuits (Hayashi, Thomas, & Huganir, 2009).

Why is the NMDA receptor important? Some scientists believe that the NMDA receptor is related to intelligence because it plays a

significant role in the rapid, intense development of the child's brain. The discovery of the palmitate–NMDA receptor connection is thus important because it offers greater understanding of how synapses are regulated and how memory is formed. In addition, the identification of palmitate may lead to the development of drug therapies that allow for manipulation or regulation to enhance learning and memory. Ultimately, the control of disease-induced increases or decreases in NMDA receptor activity (which in turn affects memory formation and maintenance) may occur by manipulating palmitate or palmitate-like substances in the brain.

- *What ethical questions arise if substances can be identified and produced to help enhance learning and memory beyond what occurs naturally in humans?*

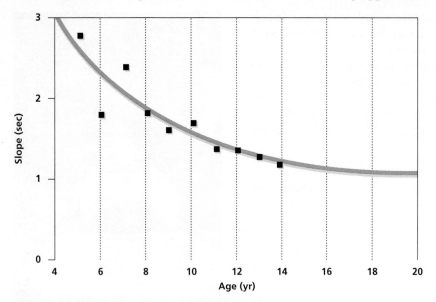

FIGURE 6.6 Information Processing and Age

As this figure, which represents a summary of many studies, indicates, people are increasingly able to process the same quantity of information in less time with increasing age. For example, it takes 5-year-olds about 3 seconds to process the information that a 16-year-old processes in just over 1 second.
Source: Kail, 1991.

more apt to accurately remember their good grades, while inaccurately remembering their bad ones (Bahrick et al., 1996; Walker, Skowronski, & Whompson, 2003; Kemps & Tiggemann, 2007).

Explaining Improvements in Memory. Despite the occasional failures of autobiographical memory, it is clear that memory improves throughout the course of childhood and adolescence. But why? First, there are improvements in the basic processes and capacities related to memory. Although there is little evidence to suggest that the capacity of either sensory memory or long-term memory changes during childhood, it does appear that short-term, or working, memory does improve with age. To explain this improvement, developmental psychologist Robbie Case (1985, 1992; Case & Okamoto, 1996), who is known as a *neo-Piagetian* theorist, has blended information processing and Piagetian approaches.

Case suggests that cognitive development proceeds because of increases in working memory capabilities. As we mentioned earlier, the number of chunks of information that can be held in working memory increases throughout childhood, suggesting an increase in its capacity. But increased capacity does not necessarily imply increased size. Case suggests that observed improvements in working memory are due to increases in the operating efficiency of working memory.

According to the *operating efficiency hypothesis*, people are able to remember material better with age because they process information more quickly and use more effective, suitable strategies. Memory improvements are *not* due to increases in the size of working memory. Yet, even though the storage capacity of short-term memory is not expanding with age, less effort is needed to process information, and more cognitive resources are available to store information. The ultimate result is that, with age, more information can be processed in working memory (Case & Okamoto, 1996).

The greater efficiency of processing is indicated by increases in speed of processing with age. As individuals become older, they are able to process the same material with greater speed (see Figure 6.6). One important reason is that increases in brain maturation permit the faster manipulation of letters and numbers (Kail, 1991).

But improvements in the efficiency of processing are not the full story of memory improvement. As we see next, increases in the use of memory control strategies and the growth of metamemory and general knowledge also lead to improvements in memory.

Memory Control Strategies. Children's understanding of memory becomes more sophisticated as they grow older and increasingly engage in *control strategies*—conscious, intentionally used tactics to improve cognitive processing. For instance, school-age children are aware that rehearsal, the repetition of information, is a useful strategy for improving memory, and they increasingly employ it over the course of middle childhood.

Similarly, children progressively make more effort to organize material into coherent patterns, a strategy that permits them to recall it better. For instance, when faced with remembering a list including cups, knives, forks, and plates, older school-age children are more likely to group the items into coherent patterns—cups and plates, forks and knives—than children just entering the school-age years (Howe & O'Sullivan, 1990; Weed, Ryan, & Day, 1990; Pressley & Van Meter, 1993).

Children also begin to use strategies that are explicitly taught. For instance, a technique called the keyword strategy can help students learn the vocabulary of a foreign language, the capitals of the states, or other information in which two sets of words or labels are paired. In the *keyword strategy,* one word is paired with another that sounds like it.

For example, in learning foreign language vocabulary, a foreign word is paired with a common English word that has a similar sound. The English word is the keyword. Thus, to learn the

Spanish word for duck (*pato,* pronounced *pot-o*), the keyword might be "pot"; for the Spanish word for horse (*caballo,* pronounced *cob-eye-yo*), the keyword might be "eye." Once the keyword is chosen, children then form a mental image of the two words interacting with one another. For instance, a student might use an image of a duck taking a bath in a pot to remember the word *pato,* or a horse with bulging eyes to remember the word *caballo* (Pressley & Levin, 1983; Pressley, 1987).

In addition to increasingly using explicit strategies as they get older, children also begin to recall memories more frequently in terms of **scripts**, general representations in memory of a sequence or series of events. For instance, when preschoolers experience the same activity or event repeatedly—such as being driven to preschool five days a week—the activity becomes remembered in terms of a general script. Subsequently, unless something unusual occurs, such as seeing an accident, it is difficult to recall anything specific about any particular ride to school because it is remembered in terms of the general script (Pressley & Schneider, 1997).

The Growth of Metamemory and Content Knowledge. The more you know, the better you're able to remember. At least that's the theory—largely supported by research—behind work on metamemory, as well as on the role of increasing general knowledge in memory capabilities.

Metamemory is the understanding and knowledge that children and adults have about memory and the processes that underlie it. The simple fact that people forget is almost universally realized by the age of 6. Before then, though, many children deny that they ever forget anything! By the time they enter first grade, children have a general notion of what memory is. Furthermore, they know that some people have "good" memories and others "bad" memories (Flavell, Friedriches, & Hoyt, 1970; Schneider & Pressley, 1989; Lewis & Mitchell, 1994).

Development of metamemory skills helps children know how much time is needed to study material in order to remember it accurately. The amount of time that children say they need to understand material increases from the age of 4 up until adolescence. Presumably, children come to realize their memory limitations and that these limitations can be overcome by spending more time examining and studying the material (Dufresne & Kobasigawa, 1989).

Teaching metamemory skills to children has produced positive results. For example, teaching children to monitor how well they are comprehending material as they are studying helps them to understand the material better (Palincsar & Brown, 1984; Pressley, 1995).

It's not just knowledge of how memory operates that leads to improvements in memory. The increasing knowledge of children in all domains also leads to increases in how much they recall as well as what they remember. As the amount of material on a given topic stored in memory grows, it becomes easier to learn new, but related, material. The process of memorizing becomes more efficient, as prior memories provide a context for new information. Furthermore, when children are familiar with information that is being remembered, they are more likely to employ control strategies effectively. In short, the greater content knowledge that older children possess helps them to recall information better than younger children, who have less overall content knowledge (Rabinowitz & Chi, 1987; Harris, Durso, Mergler, & Jones, 1990).

Perspectives on Memory Development. We've seen that memory improves throughout the course of childhood and adolescence. Several processes account for this improvement (Brown & DeLoache, 1978; Siegler, 1998). First, the amount of information that can be remembered in working memory increases with age, primarily because the processing of information becomes more efficient. At the same time, the use of control strategies improves as people get older. Older individuals know more strategies, and they can apply them more effectively and efficiently.

Finally, memory improvement occurs through growth in metamemory, understanding and knowledge about how memory works, as well as knowledge in general. As children come to understand more about memory, they begin to choose appropriate control strategies. Furthermore, older children simply know more than younger children, and this increased knowledge permits them to learn new but related material more efficiently. As we have noted, the more children know about a given topic, the better they can remember it and the faster they can learn new material that relates to it.

In short, memory improvements come about through several types of developmental change, summarized in Table 6.1 on page 189. It is important to remember that these underlying processes do not all produce memory improvements at the same time, but take on varying levels of importance across different periods of childhood. Together, however, they result in

scripts general representations in memory of a sequence or series of events.

metamemory an understanding about the processes that underlie memory, which emerges and improves during middle childhood.

DEVELOPMENTAL DIVERSITY
Memory and Culture

When psychologist Michael Cole and colleagues presented rural Liberian children who did not attend school with a group of objects, one at a time, and asked them to recall as many as they could, they found a clear—and puzzling—result: Unlike children in Western, industrialized countries, the Liberian children showed no improvement in memory during middle childhood (Cole et al., 1971).

At first glance, it might appear that the Liberian children had deficient memories compared to Western children. Fortunately, however, Cole and his colleagues also tried the same task with a group of children who did go to school in Liberia, and the results were quite different. In this case, there was little difference between the educated Liberian children and children who were raised in the United States. The schooled Liberian children showed the same increases in memory over the middle school years as were typically found in Western cultures.

Despite substantial differences in upbringing, children's basic memory capabilities are similar across cultures.

The findings of this study are consistent with other research: When appropriate comparisons are made between members of different cultures, generally few memory differences arise. What are appropriate comparisons? Notably, the populations must be comparable in terms of educational level; the information people are seeking to recall must be equally meaningful to children in both cultures; and children must be similarly motivated to perform well on the task. When these criteria are met, differences in memory are generally not found.

Most memory experts conclude that there are both similarities and differences in memory across cultures. Basic memory processes are universal, regardless of the culture in which children are raised. In contrast, cultural factors affect what information is attended to, learned, rehearsed, and retrieved from memory. Consequently, there are *apparent* differences in memory, relating to the experiences that children have been presented within their own cultural context (Wagner, 1981; Rubin, 1995; Cole, 1996).

astonishing improvements in the amount and kind of information that children are able to remember (Pressley & Schneider, 1997; Schneider & Pressley, 1997).

Memory in Adulthood: You Must Remember This. Whenever Mary Donovan can't find her car keys, she mutters to herself that she is "losing her memory." Mary probably believes that memory loss is pretty common in middle age and later adulthood.

During early adulthood, most adults' memory abilities are at their peak. Both sensory memory and short-term memory show virtually no weakening during middle adulthood. The story is a bit different for long-term memory, which declines with age for some people. It appears, how-

TABLE 6.1	Contributions of Three Aspects of Memory During Several Periods of Development		
Source of Development	**AGE**		
	0–5	**5–10**	**10–Adulthood**
Basic capacities	Many capacities present: association, generalization, recognition, etc. By age 5, if not earlier, absolute capacity of sensory memory at adult-like levels.	Speed of processing increases.	Speed of processing continues to increase.
Strategies	A few rudimentary strategies such as naming, pointing, and selective attention.	Acquisition and increasing use of many strategies: rehearsal, organization, etc.	Continuing improvement in quality of all strategies.
Metamemory and content knowledge	Little factual knowledge about memory. Some monitoring of ongoing performance. Steadily increasing content knowledge helps memory in areas in which the knowledge exists.	Increasing factual knowledge about memory. Improved monitoring of ongoing performance. Steadily increasing content knowledge helps memory in areas in which the knowledge exists. Also helps in learning of new strategies.	Continued improvements in knowledge.

Source: Adapted from Siegler, 1998.

ever, that the reason for the decline is not a fading or a complete loss of memory, but rather that with age, people register and store information less efficiently. In addition, age makes people less efficient in retrieving information that is stored in memory. In other words, even if the information was adequately stored in long-term memory, it may become more difficult to locate or isolate it (Schieber et al., 1992; Salthouse, 1994b).

Memory declines in middle age are relatively minor, and most can be compensated for by various cognitive strategies. As mentioned earlier, paying greater attention to material when it is first encountered can aid in its later recall. Your lost car keys may have relatively little to do with memory declines but may instead reflect your inattentiveness when you put them down.

Still, at least in middle adulthood, most people show only minimal memory losses and many exhibit none at all. Furthermore, because of societal stereotypes about aging, people in middle adulthood may be prone to attribute their absentmindedness to aging, even though they have been absentminded throughout their lives. Consequently, it is the *meaning* they give to their forgetfulness that changes, rather than their actual ability to remember (Erber, Rothberg, & Szuchman, 1991; Phillips & Henry, 2008).

Furthermore, adults whose memory ability begins to show actual signs of decline often develop or exercise strategies for remaining at the peak of competence for many years. We will look at this compensatory ability when we turn to practical intelligence—the kind of intelligence that IQ tests don't measure. It is possible for older people to remain competent because they have developed particular kinds of expertise and particular competencies. These competencies do not mask a loss of memory; they compensate for it.

Expertise develops as people become more experienced in a particular domain and are able to be flexible with procedures and rules.

Differentiating Information Processing Approaches from Piaget's Perspective on Cognitive Development

The information processing perspective on memory—and cognitive development in general—is very different from Piaget's. Rather than focusing on broad explanations of the *qualitative* changes that occur in children's capabilities, as Piaget does, information processing looks at

BECOMING AN INFORMED CONSUMER OF DEVELOPMENT
Effective Strategies for Remembering

All of us are forgetful at one time or another. However, certain techniques can help us remember more effectively and make it less likely that we will forget things we want to remember. **Mnemonics** (pronounced "nee-MON-iks") are formal strategies for organizing material in ways that make it more likely to be remembered. Among the mnemonics that work not only in middle adulthood, but at other points of the life span, are the following (Bellezza, Six, & Phillips, 1992; Guttman, 1997; Bloom & Lamkin, 2006; Morris & Fritz, 2006).

· *Get organized.* For people who have trouble keeping track of where they left their keys or remembering appointments, the simplest approach is for them to become more organized. Using an appointment book, hanging one's keys on a hook, or using Post-It notes can help jog one's memory.

· *Pay attention.* You can improve your recall by initially paying attention when you are exposed to new information and by purposefully thinking that you wish to recall it in the future. If you are particularly concerned about remembering something, such as where you parked your car, pay particular attention at

the moment you park the car and remind yourself that you really want to remember.

· *Use the encoding specificity phenomenon.* According to the encoding specificity phenomenon, people are most likely to recall information in environments that are similar to those in which they initially learned ("encoded") it (Tulving & Thompson, 1973). For instance, people are best able to recall information on a test if the test is held in the room in which they studied.

· *Visualize.* Making mental images of ideas can help you recall them later. For example, if you want to remember that global warming may lead to a rise in the sea level, think of yourself on a beach on a hot day, with the waves coming closer and closer to where you've set out your beach blanket.

· *Rehearse.* In the realm of memory, practice makes perfect, or if not perfect, at least better. Adults of all ages can improve their memories if they expend more effort in rehearsing what they want to remember. By practicing what they wish to recall, people can substantially improve their recall of the material.

---

quantitative change. Piaget sees cognitive growth occurring in fairly sudden spurts; information processing sees more gradual, step-by-step growth. (Think of the difference between a track and field runner leaping hurdles versus a slow but steady marathon racer.)

Because information processing researchers consider cognitive development in terms of a collection of individual skills, they are often able to use more precise measures of cognitive ability, such as processing speed and memory recall, than proponents of Piaget's approach. Still, the very precision of these individual measures makes it harder to get an overall sense of the nature of cognitive development, something at which Piaget was a master. It's as if information processing approaches focus more on the individual pieces of the puzzle of cognitive development, while Piagetian approaches focus more on the whole puzzle.

Ultimately, both Piagetian and information processing approaches are critical in providing an account of cognitive development. Coupled with advances in the biochemistry of the brain and theories that consider the effects of social factors on learning and cognition, the two help us paint a full picture of cognitive development.

REVIEW

▶ Attention, which involves being aware of and interested in stimuli, is responsible for differences in information processing between young children and adults. Some failures of information processing appear to relate to the control and planning of attention.

▶ As they age, children become increasingly aware of their sensory and memory limitations and develop strategies to control their attention to stimuli of interest and exclude extraneous stimuli.

▶ With age, children also become more adept at planning the use of attention, allocating attentional resources to meet their goals.

▶ Attention-deficit/hyperactivity disorder (ADHD) is a disorder related to attention in which the inability to complete tasks and work toward goals leads to impulsiveness and inappropriate activity.

▶ Infants have memory capabilities from the earliest ages, but the parts of the brain involved in memory may change as they age and their ability to store and retrieve memories efficiently will increase.

mnemonics   formal strategies for organizing material in ways that make it more likely to be remembered.

▶ The phenomenon of infantile amnesia is probably not as absolute as once supposed, but the accuracy of infants' and young children's memories is questionable. Autobiographical memory does not achieve much accuracy until after the age of 3.

▶ Short-term memory increases in capacity during childhood, largely because of increases in operating efficiency that result in greater availability of resources to store information. In addition, memory functioning improves as children use more sophisticated control strategies to improve cognitive processing. The use of scripts to store and recall information also conserves memory resources.

▶ Metamemory, the understanding of memory and its functioning, permits children to plan and monitor memory use to meet goals. Furthermore, children's increasing knowledge of the world permits them to memorize and recall information more efficiently and effectively.

APPLY

▶ Are there practical applications of knowledge about attention in such areas as advertising and politics? Do these fields use attention-getting and attention-holding strategies? Do the strategies vary with intended audience?

▶ Recently, there has been interest in reviving memories from early childhood and even infancy through hypnosis or other treatments. What dangers do you see in such practices? Can the accuracy of revived memories be verified?

MODULE 6.3

Applying Information Processing Approaches

I was looking and then I didn't see what I was doing and it got in there somehow. . . . The mousetrap was in our house because there's a mouse in our house. . . . The mousetrap is down in the basement, next to the firewood. . . . I was playing a game called "Operation" and then I went downstairs and said to Dad, "I want to eat lunch," and then it got stuck in the mousetrap. . . . My daddy was down in the basement collecting firewood. . . . [My brother] pushed me [into the mousetrap]. . . . It happened yesterday. The mouse was in my house yesterday. I caught my finger in it yesterday. I went to the hospital yesterday. (Ceci, 1993, p. A23)

Despite the detailed account by this 4-year-old boy of his encounter with a mousetrap and subsequent trip to the hospital, there's a problem: The incident never happened, and the memory is entirely false.

We turn now to two important applied areas that rely on research inspired by the information processing perspective: the courtroom and the classroom.

Children's Eyewitness Testimony: Memory on Trial

The 4-year-old's explicit recounting of a mousetrap incident that had not actually occurred was the product of a study on children's memory. Each week for 11 weeks, the 4-year-old boy was told, "You went to the hospital because your finger got caught in a mousetrap. Did this ever happen to you?"

The first week, the child quite accurately said, "No. I've never been to the hospital." But by the second week, the answer changed to, "Yes, I cried." In the third week, the boy said, "Yes. My mom went to the hospital with me." By the eleventh week, the answer had expanded to the quote presented earlier (Ceci, 1993).

The embellishment of a completely false incident is characteristic of the fragility and inaccuracy of memory in young children. Young children may recall things quite mistakenly, but with great conviction, contending that events occurred that never really happened and forgetting events that did occur.

Furthermore, children's memories are susceptible to the suggestions of adults asking them questions. This is particularly true of preschoolers, who are considerably more vulnerable to suggestion than either adults or school-age children. Preschoolers are also more prone to make inaccurate inferences about the reasons behind others' behavior and are less able to draw appropriate conclusions based on their knowledge of a situation (Ceci & Bruck, 1993, 1998; Ceci, Loftus, Leichtman, & Bruck, 1994; Ceci & Huffman, 1997).

Of course, preschoolers recall many things accurately; as we discussed earlier in the chapter, children as young as 3 recall some events in their lives without distortion. However, not all recollections are accurate, and some events that are seemingly recalled with accuracy never occurred.

The error rate for children is further heightened when the same question is asked repeatedly (Cassel, Roebers, & Bjorklund, 1996). Furthermore, false memories—of the type reported by the 4-year-old who "remembered" going to the hospital after his finger was caught in a mousetrap—actually may be more persistent than their actual memories (Brainerd, Reyna, & Brandse, 1995).

In addition, when questions are highly suggestive (that is, when questioners attempt to lead a person to particular conclusions), children are more apt to make mistakes in recall (Ceci & Huffman, 1997). For instance, consider the following excerpt, which presents an extreme example of a child being questioned. It comes from an actual case involving a teacher, Kelly Michaels, who was accused of sexually molesting children in a preschool:

> *Social worker:* Don't be so unfriendly. I thought we were buddies last time.
> *Child:* Nope, not any more.
> *Social worker:* We have gotten a lot of other kids to help us since I last saw you . . . did we tell you that Kelly is in jail?
> *Child:* Yes. My mother already told me.
> *Social worker:* Did I tell you that this is the guy (pointing to the detective) that arrested her? . . . Well, we can get out of here real quick if you just tell me what you told me the last time, when we met.
> *Child:* I forgot.
> *Social worker:* No you didn't. I know you didn't.
> *Child:* I did! I did!
> *Social worker:* I thought we were friends last time.
> *Child:* I'm not your friend any more!
> *Social worker:* How come?
> *Child:* Because I hate you!
> *Social worker:* You have no reason to hate me. We were buddies when you left.
> *Child:* I hate you now!
> *Social worker:* Oh, you do not, you secretly like me, I can tell.
> *Child:* I hate you.
> *Social worker:* Oh, come on. We talked to a few more of your buddies. And everyone told me about the nap room, and the bathroom stuff, and the music room stuff, and the choir stuff, and the peanut butter stuff, and everything. . . . All your buddies [talked]. . . . Come on, do you want to help us out? Do you want to keep her in jail? I'll let you hear your voice and play with the tape recorder; I need your help again. Come on. . . . Real quick, will you just tell me what happened with the wooden spoon? Let's go.
> *Child:* I forgot.
> *Detective:* Now listen you have to behave.
> *Social worker:* Do you want me to tell him to behave? Are you going to be good boy, huh? While you are here, did he [the detective] show you his badge and his handcuffs? (Ceci & Bruck, 1993, pp. 422–423)

Clearly, the interview is filled with leading questions, not to mention social pressure to conform ("all your buddies talked"), bribery ("I'll let you hear your voice and play with the tape recorder"), and even implicit threats ("did the detective show you his badge and handcuffs?").

FROM A LAWYER'S PERSPECTIVE

In what ways might children's tendency to make inaccurate inferences about the reasons behind people's behavior make them unreliable witnesses?

It is easy to influence children's recollections of events, depending on the questions that are posed to them.

How can children be questioned to produce the most accurate recollections? One way is to question them as soon as possible after an event has occurred. The longer the time between the actual event and questioning, the less firm are children's recollections. Furthermore, more specific questions are answered more accurately than more vague questioning. Asking the questions outside of a courtroom is also preferable, as the courtroom setting can be intimidating and frightening (Saywitz & Nathanson, 1993; Ceci & Bruck, 1995; Landstrom, Granhag & Hartwig, 2007).

Although some experts have advocated the use of anatomically correct dolls, on which children can point out where they have may have experienced sexual contact, in fact careful research has not been supportive of the technique. In some instances, children make claims, using anatomically correct dolls, that they have touched another person in particular places that are wholly implausible—such as when a child claims to have touched a female's penis (Wolfner, Faust, & Dawes, 1993; Bruck et al., 1995; Everson & Boat, 2002; Hungerford, 2005).

Ultimately, no foolproof way exists to test the accuracy of children's recollections. Testimony needs to be evaluated on a case-by-case basis, and judges must ensure that children are questioned in a low-key, nonthreatening manner by impartial questioners.

It's not only children's memories that are easily influenced and subject to bias. Adults, too, are prone to significant error when they try to remember details of crimes they have witnessed. Even when people are highly confident, their memories can be remarkably wrong (Miller, 2000; Thompson, 2000; Wells, Olson, & Charman, 2002; Zaragoza, Belli, & Payment, 2007).

As in the case of children, the specific wording of questions can affect adult eyewitness testimony. For example, in one classic experiment (Loftus & Palmer, 1974), participants watched a film of two cars crashing into each other. Those viewers who were later asked how fast the cars were going when they *smashed* into each other responded, on average, with a speed of 41 miles per hour. In contrast, viewers asked how fast they were traveling when they *contacted* each other estimated the speed at only 32 miles per hour on average.

Information Processing Contributions to the Classroom

Some of the most significant applications of information processing approaches have been made in the classroom. Not only has instruction in fundamental academic subjects been influenced by research in information processing, but efforts to teach children to think critically have also received a significant boost from researchers employing the information processing perspective.

How Should We Teach Reading?   Educators have long been engaged in an ongoing debate regarding the most effective means of teaching reading. At the heart of this debate is a disagreement about the nature of the mechanisms by which information is processed during reading. According to proponents of *code-based approaches to reading*, reading should be taught by presenting the basic skills that underlie reading. Code-based approaches emphasize the components of reading, such as the sounds of letters and their combinations—phonics—and how letters and sounds are combined to make words. They suggest that reading consists of processing the individual components of words, combining them into words, and then using the words to derive the meaning of written sentences and passages (Vellutino, 1991; Jimenez & Guzman, 2003; Rego, 2006).

In contrast, some educators argue that reading is taught most successfully by using a whole-language approach. In *whole-language approaches to reading*, reading is viewed as a natural process, similar to the acquisition of oral language. According to this view, children should learn to read through exposure to complete writing—sentences, stories, poems, lists, charts, and other examples of actual uses of writing. Instead of being taught to sound out words, children are encouraged to make guesses about the meaning of words based on the context in which they appear. Through such a trial-and-error approach, children come to learn whole words and phrases at a time, gradually becoming proficient readers (Shaw, 2003; Sousa, 2005; Donat, 2006).

A growing body of data, based on careful research, suggests that code-based approaches are superior to whole-language approaches. For example, one study found that a group of children tutored in phonics for a year not only improved substantially in their reading, compared to a group of good readers, but that the neural pathways involved in reading became closer to those of good readers (see Figure 6.7; Shaywitz et al., 2004).

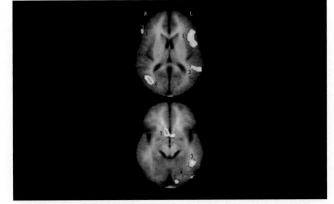

FIGURE 6.7 Improved Reading Proficiency
Students with reading difficulties who were tutored in phonics showed improved reading proficiency and increased activity in brain areas related to skilled reading.
Source: Shaywitz et al., 2004.

Based on research such as the Shaywitz study, the National Reading Panel and National Research Council now support reading instruction using code-based approaches. Their position may signal an end to the debate over which approach to teaching reading is more effective (Rayner et al., 2002).

Teaching Critical Thinking. "There's no cereal that has more vitamins than Wheaties." "Using Crest toothpaste is the best way to fight cavities." "Be the first to buy Barbie's new playhouse."

The way that children evaluate such statements, which are typical of arguments made in commercials targeted to children, is dependent on their critical thinking skills. **Critical thinking** is thinking that makes use of cognitive skills and strategies that increase the likelihood of solving problems, forming inferences, and making decisions appropriately and successfully (Halpern, 1996). It involves not jumping to conclusions on the basis of limited facts, but considering information, weighing the alternatives, and coming to a reasoned decision. Critical thinkers scrutinize the assumptions that underlie their decisions, beliefs, and actions, and they pay attention to the contexts in which ideas are implemented.

Although all of us naturally use thinking, it is often not *critical* thinking. We jump to conclusions on the basis of limited facts and make mistakes in logic. Children, especially, are more willing to take statements, such as those made in commercials, at face value. They respond to complex questions with simple answers. Even older children and adolescents often do not take all relevant information into account, and sometimes they are unaware what significant information is missing from a problem in order to come to a reasonable conclusion.

Although educators acknowledge the importance of critical thinking, in fact the critical thinking skills of students are not terribly high. For instance, one study found that less than 40 percent of 17-year-olds can find, summarize, and explain information. Another study comparing Japanese and U.S. students on mathematical problem solving found that the best students from the United States scored lower than the worst Japanese students. The differences can best be attributed to a lack of critical thinking skills in the U.S. students (Neubert & Binko, 1992; Izawa & Hayden, 1993).

What are the ingredients of critical thinking? Four primary principles must be used in order for thinking to be appropriately critical. First, thinkers must identify and challenge the assumptions underlying a statement or contention. Second, they must check for factual accuracy and logical consistency among statements. Third, they need to take into account the context of a situation. Finally, they need to imagine and explore alternatives (Coats, Feldman, & Schwartzberg, 1994).

Although many children and adults could not be characterized as critical thinkers, such skills can be taught. In fact, teaching critical thinking is becoming a recommended part of the curriculum in many schools, beginning at the elementary level and running all the way up to the college level (Baron & Sternberg, 1987; Halpern, 1996).

Reconsidering the Information Processing Perspective

Throughout this chapter we've considered the information processing perspective on cognitive development. The fact that we've devoted a full chapter to it is one indication of its status within the field of child development. For many child developmentalists, information processing approaches represent the dominant, most comprehensive, and ultimately the most accurate explanation of how children develop cognitively.

According to information processing approaches, cognitive development consists of gradual improvements in the ways people perceive, understand, and remember information. With age and practice, preschoolers process information more efficiently and with greater sophistication, and they are able to handle increasingly complex problems. In the eyes of proponents of information processing approaches, it is these quantitative advances in information processing—and not the qualitative changes suggested by Piaget—that constitute cognitive development (Case & Okamoto, 1996; Goswami, 1998; Zhe & Siegler, 2000).

For supporters of information processing approaches, the reliance on well-defined processes that can be tested by research studies with relative precision is one of the perspective's most important features. Rather than relying on concepts that are relatively vague, such as Piaget's notions of assimilation and accommodation or Vygotsky's ideas on the zone of proximal devel-

critical thinking thinking that makes use of cognitive skills and strategies that increase the likelihood of solving problems, forming inferences, and making decisions appropriately and successfully.

opment and scaffolding, information processing approaches provide a comprehensive, logical set of concepts, focusing on the processes that underlie children's thinking.

Proponents of information processing theory have also been successful in focusing on important cognitive processes to which alternative approaches traditionally have paid little attention. For example, Piaget wrote relatively little about memory, and Vygotsky paid scant attention to the way information is processed mentally. In contrast, information processing comes to a different solution to some of Piaget's observations.

For instance, as preschoolers grow older, they have longer attention spans, can monitor and plan what they are attending to more effectively, and become increasingly aware of their cognitive limitations. These advances may be due to brain development. Such increasing attentional abilities place some of Piaget's findings in a different light. For instance, as we have seen, increased attention allows older children to attend to both the height *and* the width of tall and short glasses into which liquid is poured. This permits them to understand that the amount of liquid in the glasses stays the same when it is poured back and forth. Preschoolers, in contrast, are unable to attend to both dimensions simultaneously and thus are less able to conserve (Miller & Seier, 1994; Hudson, Sosa, & Shapiro, 1997; Stock, Desoete, & Roeyers, 2007).

Proponents of information processing approaches have also been successful in focusing on important cognitive processes to which alternative approaches traditionally have paid little attention, such as the contribution of mental skills like memory and attention to children's thinking. They suggest that information processing provides a clear, logical, and full account of cognitive development.

Yet information processing approaches have their detractors, who raise significant points. For one thing, the focus on a series of single, individual cognitive processes leaves out of consideration some important factors that appear to influence cognition. For instance, information processing theorists pay relatively little attention to social and cultural factors—a deficiency that Vygotsky's approach attempts to remedy.

An even more important criticism is that information processing approaches "lose the forest for the trees." In other words, information processing approaches pay so much attention to the detailed, individual sequence of processes that compose cognitive processing and development that they never adequately paint a whole, comprehensive picture of cognitive development—which Piaget did uniquely well.

Information processing theories have also been criticized as providing too sterile an account of what goes on in children's minds. Where, for instance, are the hopes, the dreams, the aspirations, that inform so much of people's thinking? Because of their use of computer analogies, information processing proponents have been accused of forgetting about the qualities of thinking that set humans apart from other animals and focusing excessively on people as cold processing machines.

Of course, developmentalists using information processing approaches have responded to such criticisms. They contend that their model of cognitive development has the advantage of being precisely stated and capable of leading to testable hypotheses. They also argue that far more research supports their approach than alternative theories of cognitive development. In short, they suggest that their approach provides a more accurate account than any other.

Are they right? While it is tempting to try to answer the question "Which theory is best?" it is also premature to ask such a question, at least at this point in our understanding of cognitive development. Information processing theories remain just that—theories. It is too early to say if the approach will provide a better description of cognitive development than the alternatives.

What is clear is that information processing approaches have been highly influential over the past two decades. They have been the impetus for a tremendous amount of research that has given us a better understanding of how children develop cognitively. Furthermore, it is clear that the information processing perspective will continue to be an important guide as we seek to understand how people make such remarkable cognitive strides as they move from infancy through childhood into adulthood.

In the meantime, we end with a consideration of what steps parents, educators, and other adults can take in order to reach a goal that is inherent in all theories of cognitive development: ensuring that children reach their full cognitive potential.

▶ Because young children's memories are highly subject to suggestion and distortion, they can be unreliable witnesses in emotionally charged law cases.

▶ In the classroom, information processing approaches have supported approaches to reading instruction that are based on children's progression from low-level cognitive skills to higher-level skills. Information processing has been used to support both code-based and whole-language approaches to reading, and the best approach is probably a combination of the two.

▶ Information processing approaches have also been used to develop critical thinking instruction, which focuses on the use of cognitive skills and strategies to analyze assumptions, evaluate arguments, solve problems, and make decisions.

▶ The information processing perspective has proven fruitful in offering explanations of cognitive phenomena and suggesting additional research through its generation of testable hypotheses. It is less successful in accounting for social and cultural factors that affect cognitive processes and in producing a rich, comprehensive picture of cognitive development.

APPLY

▶ How do children's critical thinking limitations affect their understanding and interpretation of television commercials and written advertisements?

▶ Based on your knowledge about children's critical thinking skills, do you think advertising directed to children should be closely regulated or even prohibited? Why?

Epilogue

We have taken a look at information processing approaches to the study of cognitive development, discussing the basics of information processing compared with Piaget's and Vygotsky's theories. We have seen how information processing's practical, experimental methods have illuminated our understanding of memory and enlightened us as we considered some of the important issues of the day, including the reliability of children's testimony in court and the usefulness of its insights and findings for education.

Think back to the case of Simona Young, the Romanian infant who spent the first years of her life in a harsh orphanage. Consider these questions:

1. To what extent do you think that Simona will remember her first years when she reaches adulthood?

2. If she does recall those early years, how likely is it that her memories will be accurate?

3. Does the research on children's and adults' eyewitness testimony make you think that through appropriate questioning she could accurately recall her early years? Why?

4. Even if Simona does not remember her early years, do you think her experiences will affect her development as an adult? How?

Looking Back

What are the fundamental elements of information processing?

1. The three elements of information processing are encoding, storage, and retrieval. Encoding is the process by which information is initially recorded in a form usable to memory. Storage refers to the maintenance of material saved in memory. Retrieval is the process by which stored material is located, brought to awareness, and used.

2. Automatization refers to the degree to which the processes of encoding, storage, and retrieval require attention. Processes that require little attention are automatic; those that require relatively large amounts of attention are controlled.

What explanations have been proposed for the way information is processed in the brain?

3. Cognitive architecture refers to the basic, enduring mental structures and features that determine the steps through which information is processed.

4. According to the three-system model, information processing involves the sensory store, short-term memory, and long-term memory. The sensory store is where information is momentarily stored without meaning. Short-term memory receives selected information from the sensory store and begins processing it, adding meaning. Sufficiently processed information then is

passed to long-term memory, where it is stored on a relatively permanent basis for later retrieval.

5. The three-system model assumes that both the size of the processing system and the type of processing it engages in develop over time. It holds that development involves quantitative changes in cognitive processes, rather than qualitative changes in the nature of thinking, as Piaget assumes.

What is attention, how does it develop, and what are the consequences of an attention deficit?

6. Attention—awareness of and interest in stimuli—is the first step in information processing. Although the ability to take in information through the senses is constant from childhood to adulthood, the ability to control and plan attention improves with age.

7. As they age, people become increasingly aware of their sensory and memory limitations and develop strategies to control attention. They also become better at planning and allocating attentional resources to meet their goals.

8. Attention-deficit/hyperactivity disorder (ADHD) is a disorder characterized by inattention, impulsiveness, a low tolerance for frustration, and a great deal of inappropriate activity. ADHD is a serious disorder that interferes with normal life and learning.

What memory capabilities—and limitations—do infants and young children have, and how does memory develop as we age?

9. Infants have memory capabilities from the earliest ages, but it is possible that infantile memory depends on the hippocampus rather than additional brain structures that will be involved as the child develops. The gradual loss of information, and its return in response to appropriate stimuli, operate similarly throughout life.

10. Infantile amnesia generally makes it unlikely that events that occurred before the age of 3 will be recalled. The phenomenon is probably not as absolute as was once supposed, but memories from infancy and early childhood, including autobiographical memories, are highly unreliable until after the age of 3.

11. Memory improvements in childhood appear to be largely attributable to increased capabilities within short-term memory. According to the operating efficiency hypothesis, memory improves because children are able to process information more quickly and use more appropriate strategies. The use of scripts to store and recall information also conserves memory resources.

12. Metamemory, the understanding of memory and its underlying processes, helps children understand the need to plan and monitor memory use to meet goals. In addition, the increasing knowledge of the world that children acquire permits them to learn and remember information more efficiently and effectively.

What practical insights have been gained from the information processing perspective?

13. Reliance on the memories of young children in the courtroom has been shown to be risky because they are highly subject to suggestion and distortion. Recall of events is most reliable if it is obtained soon after the events. Specific questions asked in a nonthreatening setting elicit the most trustworthy results, but even so, the memories of young children must be carefully evaluated before being used.

14. The information processing approach has provided insight into the way children learn to read, which has influenced the nature of reading instruction. Children progress from low-level cognitive skills to higher-level skills. The debate between code-based and whole-language approaches to reading is not decided by information processing research, and the best approach is probably a combination of the two.

15. Critical thinking is an important skill that information processing approaches have illuminated. As children grow, they become increasingly able to think critically, using cognitive skills and strategies to analyze assumptions, evaluate arguments, solve problems, and make decisions. However, the development of critical thinking skills is not automatic or universal; explicit instruction appears to be necessary.

16. The information processing perspective has contributed significantly to our understanding of cognitive phenomena and development. It provides a coherent, logical, relatively complete account of cognitive processes in terms that permit scientific testing. The perspective has been criticized for failing to address social and cultural factors that affect cognitive processes and for yielding an overly mechanistic, atomistic view of cognition.

PEARSON

mydevelopmentlab™

For more review plus **MyVirtualChild**, practice tests, videos, flashcards, and more, log on to **mydevelopmentlab.com**

7 Language Development

Prologue
The First Word Spoken

Vicki and Dominic were engaged in a friendly competition over whose name would be the first word their baby, Maura, said. "Say 'mama,'" Vicki would coo, before handing Maura over to Dominic for a diaper change. Grinning, he would take her and coax, "No, say 'daddy.'" Both parents ended up losing—and winning—when Maura's first word sounded more like "baba," and seemed to refer to her bottle.

Although we tend to think of language in terms of the production of words and then groups of words, infants can begin to communicate linguistically well before they say their first word.

Mama. No. Cookie. Dad. Jo. Most parents can remember their baby's first word, and no wonder. It's an exciting moment, this emergence of a skill that is, arguably, unique to human beings.

But those initial words are just the first and most obvious expression of language. Many months earlier, infants began to understand the language used by others to make sense of the world around them. How does this linguistic ability develop? For that matter, what is language and what are its characteristics? What is the pattern and sequence of language development? And how does the use of language transform the cognitive world of infants and their parents?

In this chapter, we address these questions as we trace the ways that language develops. We begin by considering the route of language development, examining how the use of language changes as children grow older. We consider children's first words and how children rapidly build up a vocabulary and move from phrases to complex sentences and, ultimately, to an understanding of grammar and the pragmatic aspects of language use in social situations.

We then consider the roots of language. We present several different perspectives, and we also consider the relationship between language and thought.

Finally, we conclude the chapter with a look at the ways in which adults speak to children and the influences that these adult speech patterns may have on children's later development. We also examine some social issues in language development, including the relationship between poverty and language, bilingualism, and a controversy concerning the use of nonstandard English in the classroom.

LOOKING AHEAD

After reading this chapter, you will be able to answer the following questions:

▶ What is the process of language development during the childhood years?

▶ What are various perspectives on the origins of language development, and what evidence supports each one?

▶ How are language and thought related?

▶ In what ways does the language adults use with children affect language development?

▶ How do social issues influence language development?

MODULE 7.1

The Course of Language Development

When an infant utters his or her first word, no matter what it is, it marks the start of a dramatic transformation from an entity seemingly not so different from animals of many other species to an entity with skills that are, arguably, unique to human beings.

But those initial words are just the first and most obvious manifestations of language. Many months earlier, infants have been using language to comprehend the world around them. How does this linguistic ability develop? What are the pattern and sequence of language development? And how does the use of language mark a transformation in the cognitive world of children and their parents? We'll consider these questions, and others, as we address the development of language through the course of childhood.

The Fundamentals of Language: From Sounds to Symbols

Language, the systematic, meaningful arrangement of symbols, provides the basis for communication. But it does more than that: It closely relates to the way infants think and understand the world. It enables them to reflect on people and objects, and to convey their thoughts to others.

Language has several formal characteristics that children must master as they develop linguistic competence. They include:

- **Phonology.** Phonology refers to the basic sounds of language, called *phonemes*, that can be combined to produce words and sentences. For instance, the "a" in "mat" and the "a" in "mate" represent two different phonemes in English. Although English employs just 40 phonemes to create every word in the language, other languages have as many as 85 phonemes—and some as few as 15 (Akmajian, Demers, & Harnish, 1984; Mishra & Stainthorp, 2007).

- **Morphemes.** Morphemes are the smallest language unit that has meaning. Some morphemes encompass complete words, while others add information necessary for interpreting a word, such as the endings "-s" for plural or "-ed" for past tense.

- **Semantics.** Semantics are the rules that govern the meaning of words and sentences. As their knowledge of semantics develops, children are able to understand the distinction between "Ellie was hit by a car" (an answer to the question of why Ellie has not been in school for the last week) and "A car hit Ellie" (used to announce an emergency situation).

In considering the development of language, we also need to distinguish between linguistic *comprehension,* the understanding of speech, and linguistic *production,* the use of language to communicate. One principle underlies the relationship between the two: Comprehension precedes production. An 18-month-old girl may be able to understand a complex series of directions ("pick up your coat from the floor and put it on the chair by the fireplace") but may not yet have strung more than two words together herself.

Comprehension, then, begins earlier than production, and throughout infancy comprehension increases at a faster rate than production. For instance, during infancy comprehension of words expands at a rate of 22 new words a month, while production of words increases at a rate of about 9 new words a month (Benedict, 1979; Werker & Fennell, 2009). Other forms of language ability show the same pattern, with comprehension consistently preceding production (see Figure 7.1).

Let's turn now to the course that language development typically follows.

Prelinguistic Communication. Consider the following "dialogue" between a mother and her 3-month-old child (Snow, 1977):

Mother	Infant
	[Smiles]
Oh, what a nice little smile!	
Yes, isn't that pretty?	
There now.	
There's a nice little smile.	
	[Burps]
What a nice wind as well!	
Yes, that's better, isn't it?	
Yes.	
Yes.	
	[Vocalizes]
Yes!	
There's a nice noise.	

language the systematic, meaningful arrangement of symbols, which provides the basis for communication.

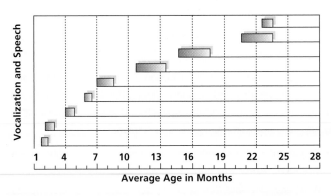

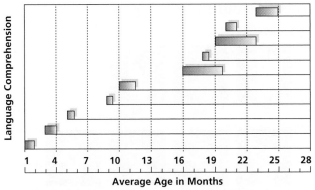

FIGURE 7.1 Comprehension Precedes Production
Throughout infancy, the comprehension of speech precedes the production of speech.
Source: Adapted from Bornstein & Lamb, 1992.

Although we tend to think of language in terms of the production first of words and then of groups of words, infants actually begin to communicate linguistically well before they say their first word. Spend 24 hours with even a very young infant and you will hear a variety of sounds: cooing, crying, gurgling, murmuring, and various types of other noises. These sounds, though not meaningful in themselves, play an important role in linguistic development, paving the way for true language (Bloom, 1993; Swingley, 2008).

Prelinguistic communication is communication through sounds, facial expressions, gestures, imitation, and other nonlinguistic means. When a father responds to his daughter's "ah" with an "ah" of his own, and then the daughter repeats the sound, and the father responds once again, they are engaged in prelinguistic communication. Clearly, the "ah" sound has no particular meaning. However, its repetition, which mimics the give-and-take of conversation, teaches the infant something about turn-taking (Drom, 1993; Tomasello, Carpenter, & Liszkowski, 2007).

The most obvious manifestation of prelinguistic communication is babbling. **Babbling**, making speechlike but meaningless sounds, starts at the age of 2 or 3 months and continues until around the age of 1 year. When they babble, infants repeat the same vowel sound over and over, changing the pitch from high to low (as in "ee-ee-ee," repeated at different pitches). After the age of 5 months, the sounds of babbling begin to expand, reflecting the addition of consonants (such as "bee-bee-bee-bee").

Babbling is a universal phenomenon, accomplished in the same way throughout all cultures. While they are babbling, infants spontaneously produce all of the sounds found in every language, not just the language they hear people around them speaking. In fact, as we discuss in the *From Research to Practice* box on page 202, even deaf children display their own form of babbling.

The form of babbling follows a progression from sounds that are the simplest to make to more complex sounds. Furthermore, although at first exposure to a particular language does not seem to influence babbling, experience eventually does make a difference. By the age of 6 months, babbling differs according to the language to which infants are exposed. The difference is so noticeable that even untrained listeners can distinguish between babbling infants who have been raised in cultures in which French, Arabic, or Cantonese languages are spoken (Vihman, 1991; Blake & Boysson-Bardies, 1992; Midaeva & Lyubimova, 2008).

Babbling may be the most obviously language-like achievement of early infancy, but there are other indications of prelinguistic speech. For instance, consider 5-month-old Marta, who

prelinguistic communication
communication through sounds, facial expressions, gestures, imitation, and other nonlinguistic means.

babbling making speechlike but meaningless sounds.

FROM RESEARCH TO PRACTICE
Talking with Our Hands: How Gestures Relate to Language

Is the ability to hear the spoken language of others necessary to learn language?

An increasing body of research suggests the answer to the question is "no." Researchers who study American Sign Language, as well as other kinds of sign languages, have found that sign language is just as complicated as the spoken word, and that it is acquired in much the same way that spoken language is acquired. Consequently, children who are unable to hear the spoken word learn sign language in much the same way, and on the same developmental schedule, as children who have hearing.

For example, infants who are profoundly deaf from birth and who are exposed to sign language show their own form of babbling. However, rather than babbling verbally, they use their hands instead of their voices. Furthermore, deaf infants and hearing children reach the same language acquisition milestones at roughly the same time. And infants who have the ability to hear and who are learning sign language babble silently using their hands when exposed to the sign language of adults (Petitto & Marentette, 1991; Petitto, 2000; Petitto et al., 2004).

There's also evidence that if deaf children are raised in an environment in which sign language is not used, they will spontaneously use gestures that are similar in form and structure to those used in formal sign languages. Even adults who are not deaf use gestures that show linguistic qualities if they are prevented from speaking. According to research by psychologist Susan Goldin-Meadow, when hearing adults typically use gestures when they are speaking, the gestures support the speech but do not show formal linguistic properties. But if hearing adults are told to use gestures only to describe an event, without speaking, the gestures they use begin to show formal linguistic properties that are similar to those found in deaf children (Goldin-Meadow, 2006, 2009).

In short, language acquisition appears to develop in an analogous manner in hearing and deaf individuals. Humans' sophisticated linguistic abilities appear in both speech and gestures, providing a highly sophisticated communication mechanism.

- *Do you think that children who are not deaf also babble using gestures? Why or why not?*
- *What does the fact that deaf children babble with their hands suggest about the origins of language development?*

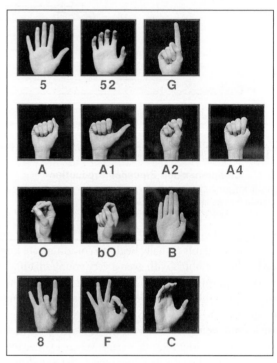

Deaf infants who are exposed to sign language do their own type of babbling, related to the use of signs.

spies her red ball just beyond her reach. After reaching for it and finding that she is unable to get to it, she makes a cry of anger that alerts her parents that something is amiss, and her mother hands it to her. Communication, albeit prelinguistic, has occurred.

Four months later, when Marta faces the same situation, she no longer bothers to reach for the ball and doesn't respond in anger. Instead, she holds out her arm in the direction of the ball, but now, with great purpose, seeks to catch her mother's eye. When her mother sees the behavior, she knows just what Marta wants. Clearly, Marta's communicative skills—though still prelinguistic—have taken a leap forward.

Even these prelinguistic skills are supplanted in just a few months, when the gesture gives way to a new communication skill: producing an actual word. Marta's parents clearly hear her say "ball."

First Words. When a mother and father first hear their child say "Mama" or "Dada," or even "baba," as in the case of Maura, the baby described in the chapter prologue, it is hard to be anything but delighted. But their initial enthusiasm may be dampened a bit when they find that the same sound is used to ask for a cookie, a doll, and a ratty old blanket.

First words generally are spoken somewhere around the age of 10 to 14 months but may occur as early as 9 months. Once an infant starts to produce words, vocabulary increases at a rapid rate. By the age of 15 months, the average child has a vocabulary of 10 words and methodically expands his or her repertoire until the one-word stage of language development ends at around 18 months. Once that happens, a sudden spurt in vocabulary occurs. In just a short period—a few weeks somewhere between 16 and 24 months of age—there is an explosion of language, in which a child's vocabulary typically increases from 50 to 400 words (Gleitman & Landau, 1994; Fernald et al., 1998; Nazzi & Bertoncini, 2003).

The first words in children's early vocabularies typically regard objects and things, both animate and inanimate. Most often they refer to people or objects who constantly appear and disappear ("Mama"), to animals ("kitty"), or to temporary states ("wet"). These first words are often **holophrases**, one-word utterances that stand for a whole phrase, whose meaning depends on the particular context in which they are used. For instance, a youngster may use the phrase "ma" to mean, depending on the context, "I want to be picked up by Mom" or "I want something to eat, Mom" or "Where's Mom?" (Dromi, 1987; O'Grady & Aitchison, 2005).

Culture has an effect on the type of first words spoken. For example, unlike North American English-speaking infants, who are more apt to use nouns initially, Chinese Mandarin-speaking infants use more verbs than nouns. On the other hand, by the age of 20 months, there are remarkable cross-cultural similarities in the types of words spoken. For example, a comparison of 20-month-olds in Argentina, Belgium, France, Israel, Italy, and the Republic of Korea found that children's vocabularies in every culture contained greater proportions of nouns than other classes of words (Tardif, 1996; Bornstein et al., 2004).

By the age of 2, most children use two-word phrases, such as "ball play."

First Sentences. When Aaron was 19 months old, he heard his mother coming up the back steps, as she did every day just before dinner. Aaron turned to his father and distinctly said, "Ma come." In stringing those two words together, Aaron took a giant step in his language development.

The increase in vocabulary that comes at around 18 months is accompanied by another accomplishment: the linking together of individual words into sentences that convey a single thought. Although there is a good deal of variability in the time at which children first create two-word phrases, it is generally around 8 to 12 months after they say their first word.

The linguistic advance represented by two-word combinations is important because the linkage not only provides labels for things in the world but also indicates the relations between them. For instance, the combination may declare something about possession ("Mama key") or recurrent events ("Dog bark"). Interestingly, most early sentences don't represent demands or even necessarily require a response. Instead, they are often merely comments and observations about events occurring in the child's world (Halliday, 1975; O'Grady & Aitchison, 2005).

Two-year-olds using two-word combinations tend to employ particular sequences that are similar to the ways in which adult sentences are constructed. For instance, sentences in English typically follow a pattern in which the subject of the sentence comes first, followed by the verb, and then the object ("Josh threw the ball"). Children's speech most often uses a similar order, although not all the words are initially included. Consequently, a child might say "Josh threw" or "Josh ball" to indicate the same thought. What is significant is that the order is typically not "threw Josh" or "ball Josh," but rather the usual order of English, which makes the utterance much easier for an English speaker to comprehend (Brown, 1973; Hirsh-Pasek & Michnick-Golinkoff, 1995; Masataka, 2003).

Linguistic Inaccuracies. Although the creation of two-word sentences represents an advance, the language used by children still is by no means adultlike. As we've just seen, 2-year-olds tend to leave out words that aren't critical to the message, in the same way we might write a telegram for which we were paying by the word. For that reason, their talk is often called **telegraphic speech.** Rather than saying, "I showed you the book," a child using telegraphic speech might say, "I show book." "I am drawing a dog" might become "Drawing dog" (see Table 7.1 on page 204).

Early language has other characteristics that differentiate it from the language used by adults. For instance, consider Sarah, who refers to the blanket she sleeps with as "blankie." When her Aunt Ethel gives her a new blanket, Sarah refuses to call the new one a "blankie," restricting the word to her original blanket.

Sarah's inability to generalize the label of "blankie" to blankets in general is an example of *underextension,* using words too restrictively, which is common among children just mastering spoken language. Underextension occurs when language novices think that a word refers to a specific instance of a concept, instead of to all examples of the concept (Caplan & Barr, 1989; Masataka, 2003).

holophrases   one-word utterances that depend on the particular context in which they are used to determine meaning.

telegraphic speech   speech in which words not critical to the message are left out.

TABLE 7.1   Children's Imitation of Sentences Showing Decline of Telegraphic Speech

	Eve, 25.5 Months	Adam, 28.5 Months	Helen, 30 Months	Ian, 31.5 Months	Jimmy, 32 Months	June, 35.5 Months
I showed you the book.	I show book.	(I show) book.	C	I show you the book.	C	Show you the book.
I am very tall.	(My) tall.	I (very) tall.	I very tall.	I'm very tall.	Very tall.	I very tall.
It goes in a big box.	Big box.	Big box.	In big box.	It goes in the box.	C	C
I am drawing a dog.	Drawing dog.	I draw dog.	I drawing dog.	Dog.	C	C
I will read the book.	Read book.	I will read book.	I read the book.	I read the book.	C	C
I can see a cow.	See cow.	I want see cow.	C	Cow.	C	C
I will do that again.	Do-again.	I will that again.	I do that.	I again.	C	C

C = correct imitation.

Source: Adapted from R. Brown & Fraser, 1963.

As infants like Sarah grow more adept with language, the opposite phenomenon sometimes occurs. In *overextension*, words are used too broadly, overgeneralizing their meaning. For example, when Sarah refers to buses, trucks, and tractors as "cars," she is guilty of overextension, making the assumption that any object with wheels must be a car. Although overextension reflects speech errors, it also shows that advances are occurring in the child's thought processes: The child is beginning to develop general mental categories and concepts (Johnson & Eilers, 1998; McDonough, 2002; Stahl & Nagy, 2006).

Language Advances During the Preschool Years

I tried it out and it was very great!
This is a picture of when I was running through the water with Mommy.
Where you are going when I go to the fireworks with Mommy and Daddy?
I didn't know creatures went on floats in pools.
We can always pretend we have another one.
And the teacher put it up on the counter so no one could reach it.
I really want to keep it while we're at the park.
You need to get your own ball if you want to play "hit the tree."
When I grow up and I'm a baseball player, I'll have my baseball hat, and I'll put it on, and I'll play baseball. (Schatz, 1994, p. 179)

Listen to Ricky, at the age of 3. In addition to recognizing most letters of the alphabet, printing the first letter of his name, and writing the word *HI*, he is readily capable of producing the complex sentences quoted here.

During the preschool years, children's language skills reach new heights of sophistication. They begin the period with reasonable linguistic capabilities, though with significant gaps in both comprehension and production. In fact, no one would mistake the language used by a 3-year-old for that of an adult. However, by the end of the preschool years, they can hold their own with adults, both comprehending and producing language that has many of the qualities of adults' language. How does this transformation occur?

The two-word utterances of the 2-year-old soon increase in both number of words and scope. Language blooms so rapidly between the late 2s and the mid-3s that researchers have yet to understand the exact pattern. What is clear is that sentence length increases steadily, and the number of ways children combine words and phrases to form sentences—known as **syntax**—doubles each month. By the time a preschooler is 3, the various combinations reach into the thousands (see Table 7.2 for an example of one child's growth in the use of language; Wheeldon, 1999; Pinker, 2005).

syntax   the combining of words and phrases to form sentences.

TABLE 7.2	Growing Speech Capabilities

Over the course of just a year, the sophistication of the language of a boy named Adam increased amazingly, as these speech samples show.

AGE	SENTENCES PRODUCED
2 years, 3 months	Play checkers. Big drum. I got horn. A bunny-rabbit walk.
2 years, 4 months	See marching bear go? Screw part machine. That busy bulldozer truck.
2 years, 5 months	Now put boots on. Where wrench go? Mommy talking 'bout lady. What that paper clip doing?
2 years, 6 months	Write a piece of paper. What that egg doing? I lost a shoe. No, I don't want to sit seat.
2 years, 7 months	Where piece a paper go? Ursula has a boot on. Going to see kitten. Put the cigarette down. Dropped a rubber band. Shadow has hat just like that. Rin Tin Tin don't fly, Mommy.
2 years, 8 months	Let me get down with the boots on. Don't be afraid a horses. How tiger be so healthy and fly like kite? Joshua throw like a penguin.
2 years, 9 months	Where Mommy keep her pocketbook? Show you something funny. Just like turtie make mud pie.
2 years, 10 months	Look at that train Ursula brought. I simply don't want put in chair. You don't have paper. Do you want little bit, Cromer? I can't wear it tomorrow.
2 years, 11 months	That birdie hopping by Missouri in bag. Do want some pie on your face? Why you mixing baby chocolate? I finish drinking all up down my throat. I said why not you coming in? Look at that piece of paper and tell it. Do you want me tie that round? We going turn light on so you can't see.
3 years, 0 months	I going come in fourteen minutes. I going wear that to wedding. I see what happens. I have to save them now. Those are not strong mens. They are going sleep in wintertime. You dress me up like a baby elephant.
3 years, 1 month	I like to play with something else. You know how to put it back together. I gon' make it like a rocket to blast off with. I put another one on the floor. You went to Boston University? You want to give me some carrots and some beans? Press the button and catch it, sir. I want some other peanuts. Why you put the pacifier in his mouth? Doggies like to climb up.
3 years, 2 months	So it can't be cleaned? I broke my racing car. Do you know the light wents off? What happened to the bridge? When it's got a flat tire it's need a go to the station. I dream sometimes. I'm going to mail this so the letter can't come off. I want to have some espresso. The sun is not too bright. Can I have some sugar? Can I put my head in the mailbox so the mailman can know where I are and put me in the mailbox? Can I keep the screwdriver just like a carpenter keep the screwdriver?

Source: Pinker, 1994.

There are also enormous leaps in the number of words children use. By age 6, the average child has a vocabulary of around 14,000 words, acquired at a rate of nearly one new word every 2 hours, 24 hours a day. They manage this feat through a process known as **fast mapping**, in which new words are associated with their meaning after only a brief encounter (Clark, 1983; Fenson et al., 1994; Kan & Kohnert, 2008).

By the age of 3, preschoolers routinely use plurals and possessive forms of nouns (such as "boys" and "boy's"), the past tense (adding "-ed" at the end of words), and articles ("the" and "a"). They can ask, and answer, complex questions ("Where did you say my book is?" and "Those are trucks, aren't they?").

Preschoolers' skills extend to the appropriate formation of words that they have never before encountered. For example, in one classic experiment, preschool children were shown cards with drawings of a cartoon-like bird, such as those shown in Figure 7.2 on page 206 (Berko, 1958). The experimenter told the children that the figure was a "wug," and then showed them a card with two of the cartoon figures. "Now there are two of them," the children were told, and they were then asked to supply the missing word in the sentence, "There are two _____" (the answer to which, of course, is "wugs").

FROM A
PRESCHOOL TEACHER'S
PERSPECTIVE
How would you go about teaching new words to preschoolers knowing how they develop language?

fast mapping   the process in which new words are associated with their meaning after only a brief encounter.

This is a wug.

Now there is another one.
There are two of them.
There are two _____ .

FIGURE 7.2 Forming Plurals
Even though preschoolers—like the rest of us—are unlikely to have ever before encountered a wug, they are able to produce the appropriate word to fill in the blank (which, for the record, is *wugs*).
Source: Adapted from Berko, 1958.

grammar the system of rules that determine how our thoughts can be expressed.

pragmatics the aspect of language relating to communicating effectively and appropriately with others.

private speech spoken language that is not intended for others, commonly used by children during the preschool years.

social speech speech directed toward another person and meant to be understood by that person.

Not only did children show that they knew the rules about forming plural nouns, but that they understood the possessive forms of nouns and the third-person singular and past-tense forms of verbs—all for words they had never encountered before, since they were nonsense words with no real meaning (O'Grady & Aitchison, 2005).

Preschoolers also learn what *cannot* be said as they acquire the principles of grammar. **Grammar** is the system of rules that determine how our thoughts can be expressed. For instance, preschoolers come to learn that "I am sitting" is correct, while the similarly structured "I am knowing [that]" is incorrect. Although they still make frequent mistakes of one sort or another, 3-year-olds follow the principles of grammar most of the time. Some errors are very noticeable—such as the use of "mens" and "catched"—but these errors (called, as we saw, *overextension)* are actually quite rare. Actually, young preschoolers are correct in their grammatical constructions more than 90 percent of the time (deVilliers & deVilliers, 1992; Pinker, 1994; Guasti, 2002; Musolino & Lidz, 2006).

Finally, preschoolers' pragmatic abilities grow. **Pragmatics** is the aspect of language relating to communicating effectively and appropriately with others. The development of pragmatic abilities permits children to understand the basics of conversations—turn-taking, sticking to a topic, and what should and should not be said, according to the conventions of society. When children are taught that the appropriate response to receiving a gift is "thank you," they are learning the pragmatics of language.

Private Speech and Social Speech. Over the course of the preschool years, children's use of **private speech**, spoken language that is not intended for others, is common. As much as 20 to 60 percent of what children say is private speech, and such speech is a normal practice during even later stages of childhood. Some research suggests that its use grows over the preschool years, peaking between the ages of 4 and 7. On the other hand, private speech becomes more secretive as children grow older and realize that society discourages talking to oneself. Consequently, older children tend to whisper private speech or silently move their lips, rather than speaking out loud (Quay & Blanau, 1992; Berk & Landau, 1993; Manfra & Winsler, 2006).

Some developmentalists suggest that private speech performs an important function. For instance, as we discussed in Chapter 5, developmental psychologist Lev Vygotsky suggests that private speech facilitates children's thinking and helps them control their behavior. (Have you ever said to yourself, "Take it easy" or "Calm down" when trying to control your anger over some situation?) In Vygotsky's view, then, private speech ultimately serves an important social function, allowing children to solve problems and reflect on difficulties they encounter. Vygotsky also suggests that private speech is a forerunner to the internal dialogues that we use when we reason with ourselves during thinking. As we have seen, Vygotsky's views are at odds with those of Piaget, who suggests that private speech is egocentric and a sign of immature thought—and ultimately a failure to communicate effectively (Vygotsky, 1962, 1986).

The preschool years also mark the growth of social speech. **Social speech** is speech directed toward another person and meant to be understood by that person. Before the age of 3, children may seem to be speaking only for their own entertainment, apparently not caring whether anyone else can understand. However, during the preschool years, children begin to direct their speech to others, wanting others to listen and becoming frustrated when they cannot make themselves understood. As a result, they begin to adapt their speech to others. Recall that Piaget contended that most speech during the preoperational period was egocentric: Preschoolers were seen as taking little account of the effect their speech was having on others. However, more recent experimental evidence suggests that children are somewhat more adept in taking others into account than Piaget initially suggested.

Language Development During Middle Childhood: Mastering Language

Listen to a pair of school-age children conversing with one another. Their speech, at least at first hearing, probably doesn't sound too different from that of adults.

In reality, however, the apparent similarity is deceiving. The linguistic sophistication of children—particularly at the start of the school-age period—still requires refinement to reach adult levels of expertise.

For instance, vocabulary continues to grow during the school years. Although children know thousands of words, they continue to add new words to their vocabularies, and at a fairly rapid clip. The average 6-year-old has a vocabulary of from 8,000 to 14,000 words, whereas the vocabulary grows by another 5,000 words between the ages of 9 and 11.

Furthermore, school-age children's mastery of grammar improves. For instance, the use of the passive voice is rare during the early school-age years (as in "The dog was walked by Lee," compared with the active-voice "Lee walked the dog"). Six- and 7-year-olds only infrequently use conditional sentences, such as "If Sarah will set the table, I will wash the dishes." However, over the course of middle childhood, the use of both passive voice and conditional sentences increases. In addition, children's understanding of *syntax,* the rules that indicate how words and phrases can be combined to form sentences, grows during middle childhood.

By the time they reach first grade, most children pronounce words quite accurately. However, certain *phonemes,* units of sound, remain troublesome. For instance, the ability to pronounce *j, v, th,* and *zh* sounds develops later than the ability to pronounce other phonemes.

School-age children also may have difficulty decoding sentences when the meaning depends on *intonation,* or tone of voice. For example, consider the sentence, "George gave a book to Roberto and he gave one to Bill." If the word "he" is emphasized, the meaning is "George gave a book to Roberto and Roberto gave a different book to Bill." But if the intonation emphasizes the word "and," then the meaning changes to "George gave a book to Roberto and George also gave a book to Bill." Such subtleties are not easily sorted out by school-age children (Moshman, Glover, & Bruning, 1987; Woolfolk, 1993; Meng & Jijia, 2006).

Children also become more competent during the school years in their use of *pragmatics,* the rules governing the use of language to communicate in a social context. Pragmatics concern children's ability to use appropriate and effective language in a given social setting.

For example, although children are aware of the rules of conversational turn-taking at the start of the early childhood period, their use of these rules is sometimes primitive. Consider the following conversation between 6-year-olds Yonnie and Ali:

Yonnie: My dad drives a Fedex truck.
Ali: My sister's name is Molly.
Yonnie: He gets up really early in the morning.
Ali: She wet her bed last night.

Later, however, conversations show more give-and-take, with the second child actually responding to the comments of the first. For instance, this conversation between 11-year-olds Mia and Yan reflects a more sophisticated mastery of pragmatics:

Mia: I don't know what to get Claire for her birthday.
Yan: I'm getting her earrings.
Mia: She already has a lot of jewelry.
Yan: I don't think she has that much.

Metalinguistic Awareness: Learning Self-Control. One of the most significant developments in middle childhood is the increasing metalinguistic awareness of children. **Metalinguistic awareness** is an understanding of one's own use of language. By the time they are 5 or 6, children understand that language is governed by a set of rules. Whereas in the early years these rules are learned and comprehended implicitly, during middle childhood children come to understand them more explicitly (Kemper & Vernooy, 1993; Merriman & Lipko, 2008).

Metalinguistic awareness helps children achieve comprehension when information is fuzzy or incomplete. For instance, when preschoolers are given ambiguous or unclear information, they rarely ask for clarification, and they tend to blame themselves if they do not understand. By the time they reach the age of 7 or 8, children realize that miscommunication may be due to factors attributable not only to themselves, but to the person communicating with them as well. Consequently, school-age children are more likely to ask for clarification of information that is unclear to them (Kemper & Vernooy, 1993; Zipke, 2007; Merriman & Lipko, 2008).

The growing sophistication of their language also helps school-age children control their behavior. For instance, in one experiment, children were told that they could have one marshmallow treat if they chose to eat one immediately, but two treats if they waited. Most of the children, who ranged in age from 4 to 8, chose to wait, but the strategies they used while waiting differed significantly.

The 4-year-olds often chose to look at the marshmallows while waiting, a strategy that was not terribly effective. In contrast, 6- and 8-year-olds used language to help them overcome temptation, though in different ways. The 6-year-olds spoke and sang to themselves, reminding themselves that if they waited they would get more treats in the end. The 8-year-olds focused on aspects of the marshmallows that were not related to taste, such as their appearance, which helped them to wait.

metalinguistic awareness
an understanding of one's own use of language.

BECOMING AN INFORMED CONSUMER OF DEVELOPMENT
Assessing Early Language Development

Given the critical role that language plays in cognitive development, parents often are concerned about whether their child's language development is proceeding on schedule. Although there are no hard-and-fast rules, given the wide variability in the timing of children's first words and the ways their vocabularies develop, there are several guidelines that indicate whether language development is normal. An infant who shows the following abilities is probably developing normally, according to psycholinguist Anne Dunlea (Fowler, 1990; Yarrow, 1990):

- **Understanding at least some things that are heard.** This means that, at the minimum, the child has some receptive language and can hear. For instance, most children can discriminate between friendly and angry speech by the age of 6 months.
- **Producing sounds, such as a raspberry noise, at around 6 or 7 months of age.** Children who are deaf may cease producing

prelinguistic speech at this point, even if they produced it earlier, because they cannot hear themselves speaking.

- **Using gestures to communicate.** Pointing and reaching are often forerunners of language. By the age of 9 months, most children look toward an object that an adult is pointing to, and most use pointing themselves before the end of their first year.
- **Pretending to use language.** Even if the words make no sense, children may pretend to use language before they actually begin to speak, indicating that they at least know how language functions.

What if you cannot observe any of these indicators? It would be reasonable to have a pediatrician evaluate your child. Keep in mind, however, the wide range of variations in language development among different children, and the fact that the vast number of children develop quite normally.

REVIEW

▶ Before they *produce* their first word, infants *comprehend* many adult utterances and engage in several forms of prelinguistic communication, including the use of facial expressions, gestures, and babbling.

▶ Children typically produce their first words between 10 and 14 months, and rapidly increase their vocabularies from that point on. Language development proceeds through a pattern of holophrases, two-word combinations, and telegraphic speech, and reflects a growing sense of the relations between objects in the world, and the acquisition of general mental categories and concepts.

▶ In the preschool years, linguistic ability increases rapidly, including advances in sentence length, vocabulary, and syntax. Children also develop a strong sense of the grammar of their language, knowing which forms and utterances are permissible and which are not, and improve their use of pragmatics, the appropriate use of language in social situations.

▶ Another linguistic development is a gradual shift from private to social speech. Piaget regards private speech as a sign of immaturity and egocentrism; Vygotsky views it as a useful cognitive mechanism that ultimately serves a social function.

▶ Language development in middle childhood is characterized by improvements in vocabulary, syntax, and pragmatics; by the use of language as a self-control device; and by the growth of metalinguistic awareness.

APPLY

▶ We have noted that deaf children babble with their hands. What other similarities and differences do you think there might be between the development of language—spoken and signed—in hearing and nonhearing children?

▶ This module discusses some rules of pragmatics that govern the social uses of language, such as turn-taking and addressing the same topic. Can you think of other rules of pragmatics?

MODULE 7.2

The Origins of Language Development

The immense strides in language development during childhood raise a fundamental question: How does proficiency in language come about? Linguists are deeply divided on how to answer this question. They've considered two major aspects of the question, asking how language is acquired and what relationship exists between language and thought.

Language Acquisition

Three major approaches have guided thinking on language acquisition. One is based on learning theory, the second centers on innate and genetically determined capabilities, and the third represents a combination of the first two approaches.

Learning Theory Approaches: Language as a Learned Skill.   One view of language development emphasizes the basic principles of learning. According to the **learning theory approach**, language acquisition follows the fundamental laws of reinforcement and conditioning discussed in the first chapter (Skinner, 1957). For instance, a child who articulates the word "da" may be hugged and praised by her father, who jumps to the conclusion that she is referring to him. This reaction reinforces the child, who is more likely to repeat the word. In sum, the learning theory perspective on language acquisition suggests that children learn to speak by being rewarded for making sounds that approximate speech. Through the process of *shaping*, language becomes more and more similar to adult speech.

There's a problem, though, with the learning theory approach. It doesn't seem to adequately explain how children acquire the rules of language as readily as they do. For instance, young children are reinforced when they make errors. Parents are apt to be just as responsive if their child says, *Why the dog won't eat?* as they are if the child phrases the question more conventionally *(Why won't the dog eat?)*. Both forms of the question are understood correctly, and both elicit the same response; reinforcement is provided for both correct and incorrect language usage. Under such circumstances, learning theory falls short of explaining satisfactorily how children learn to speak properly.

Children are also able to move beyond specific utterances they have heard and produce novel phrases, sentences, and constructions, an ability that also cannot be explained by learning theory. Furthermore, children can apply linguistic rules to nonsense words. In one study, 4-year-old children heard the nonsense verb "to pilk" in the sentence "the bear is pilking the horse." Later, when asked what was happening to the horse, they responded by placing the nonsense verb in the correct tense and voice: "He's getting pilked by the bear."

Nativist Approaches: Language as an Innate Skill.   Such conceptual difficulties with the learning theory approach have led to the development of an alternative, championed by the linguist Noam Chomsky and known as the nativist approach (1968, 1978, 1991, 1999, 2005). The **nativist approach** argues that there is a genetically determined, innate mechanism that directs the development of language. According to Chomsky, people are born with an innate capacity to use language, which emerges, more or less automatically, through maturation.

Chomsky's analysis of different languages suggests that all the world's languages share a similar underlying structure, which he calls **universal grammar**. In this view, the human brain is wired with a neural system called the **language-acquisition device (LAD)**, or, that both permits the understanding of language structure and provides a set of strategies and techniques for learning the particular characteristics of the language to which a child is exposed. In this view, language is uniquely human, made possible by a genetic predisposition to both comprehend and produce words and sentences (Nowak, Komarova, & Niyogi, 2001, 2002; Hauser, Chomsky, & Fitch, 2002; Lidz & Gleitman, 2004).

Support for Chomsky's nativist approach comes from recent findings identifying a specific gene related to speech production. Further support comes from research showing that language processing in infants involves brain structures similar to those in adult speech processing, suggesting an evolutionary basis to language (see Figure 7.3; Wade, 2001; Monaco, 2005; Dehaene-Lambertz, Hertz-Pannier, & Dubois, 2006).

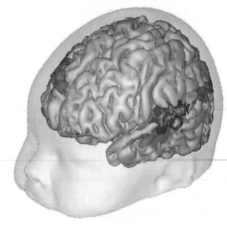

FIGURE 7.3 Infant's Speech Processing This fMRI scan of a 3-month-old infant shows speech processing activity similar to that of an adult, suggesting there may be an evolutionary basis to language. *Source:* Dehaene-Lambertz, Hertz-Pannier, & Dubois, 2006.

learning theory approach   the theory that language acquisition follows the basic laws of reinforcement and conditioning.

nativist approach   the theory that a genetically determined, innate mechanism directs the development of language.

universal grammar   a similar underlying structure shared by all the world's languages, according to linguist Noam Chomsky.

language-acquisition device (LAD) a neural system of the brain hypothesized to permit understanding of language structure and provide strategies for learning the particular characteristics of a language.

The view that language is an innate ability unique to humans also has its critics. For instance, some researchers argue that certain primates are able to learn at least the basics of language, an ability that calls into question the uniqueness of the human linguistic capacity. Others point out that although humans may be genetically primed to use language, its use still requires significant social experience in order for it to be used effectively (MacWhinney, 1991; Savage-Rumbaugh et al., 1993; Goldberg, 2004).

The Interactionist Perspective on Language Development. Neither the learning theory nor the nativist perspective fully explains language acquisition. As a result, some theorists have turned to a theory that combines both schools of thought. The *interactionist perspective* suggests that language development is produced through a combination of genetically determined predispositions and environmental circumstances that help teach language.

The interactionist perspective accepts that innate factors shape the broad outlines of language development. However, interactionists also argue that the specific course of language development is determined by the language to which children are exposed and the reinforcement they receive for using language in particular ways. Social factors are considered to be key to development, since the motivation provided by one's membership in a society and culture and one's interactions with others leads to the use of language and the growth of language skills (Dixon, 2004; Yang, 2006).

Just as there is support for some aspects of learning theory and nativist positions, the interactionist perspective has also received some support. We don't know, at the moment, which of these positions will ultimately provide the best explanation. More likely, different factors play different roles at different times during childhood.

How Are Language and Thought Related?

It seems reasonable that Eskimo children, whose experience with freezing precipitation is far more extensive than that of children growing up in warmer climates, would have many words in their vocabulary to describe "snow." At least that was the thinking of linguist Benjamin Lee Whorf in the early 1900s. He argued that because snow was so much a part of Eskimo lives, Eskimos had a richer snow-related vocabulary than, for example, English speakers. Whorf's account seemed to be supported by data, and at least one expert contended that there were no fewer than 400 snow-related words in the Eskimo vocabulary—far more than in English.

Not so fast. Contemporary research has found that Whorf's claims regarding the Eskimo vocabulary were greatly exaggerated. Eskimos have no more words for "snow" than do English speakers. In fact, English contains many words of its own relating to snow: Sleet, slush, blizzard, dusting, powder, and avalanche are just a few examples (Martin & Pullum, 1991; Pinker, 1994; Chiu, Leung, & Kwan, 2007).

The early contention that the Eskimo language was particularly rich in snow-related words was used to support an influential proposition called the linguistic-relativity hypothesis. The **linguistic-relativity hypothesis** states that language shapes and may even determine the way people of a particular culture perceive and understand the world (Whorf, 1956; Lucy, 1992; Casasanto, 2008). The hypothesis suggests that language provides categories that help children construct their perceptions of people and events in their surroundings. In short, the notion is that language shapes and produces thinking.

The view that language shapes and produces thought is not the only plausible sequence, however. Consider an alternative: that instead of language being the *cause* of thought, the relationship works in the opposite direction, with language being the *result* of thinking about the world in particular ways and undergoing certain experiences. In this view, thought *produces* language.

The view that thinking shapes language is consistent with Piaget's views of the development of language. As we considered in Chapter 5, Piaget argued that the emergence of symbolic function (the ability to use mental symbols, words, and objects to represent something that is not physically present) during the preoperational period is a key aspect of the development of language skill. In short, advances in the sophistication of thinking permit language development.

FROM A
SPEECH PATHOLOGIST'S
PERSPECTIVE
How important is it to understand the origin of language? Would it be the same across cultures? Why or why not?

linguistic-relativity hypothesis
the theory that language shapes and may determine the way people of a given culture perceive and understand the world.

Some developmentalists reject both the view that language shapes thought *and* the view that thought shapes language. Instead, they support an intermediate position: that language and thought are intertwined and influence one another. For instance, Vygotsky (1962) argues that although in the early stages of life language and thinking develop independently, by the age of 2 they become interdependent. From that point, each influences the other. More precise thought permits language to become increasingly sophisticated, and more refined language capabilities allow more advanced thought.

We now have three views about the relationship between language and thought: Language shapes thought (the linguistic-relativity hypothesis); thought shapes language; and thought and language influence one another. Research supports all three views. Although most linguists would reject the notion that language is the *predominant* influence on thought, there is evidence that language does shape at least some kinds of thinking. For instance, the way in which information is stored and retrieved in memory is related to language, and the way that people evaluate others is influenced by the linguistic categories they have available to them (Gleitman & Papafragou, 2005; Casasanto, 2008).

On the other hand, there is also experimental support for the opposite position, that thinking shapes language. For instance, the experiences that children have shape their first words, which are usually about people, animals, and foods in their environment, regardless of the language they speak. Furthermore, cross-cultural research shows that even if there is no word for particular colors in a given language, people speaking that language can still distinguish the different colors, suggesting that language is not a prerequisite for thought (Rosch, 1974; Zhang, He, & Zhang, 2007).

The existence of evidence supporting both the language-shapes-thought and thought-shapes-language sequences suggests that the third position—that thought and language jointly influence one another—may ultimately prove to be the most accurate. Such a position seems plausible and is supported by direct experimental evidence (Kuczaj, Borys, & Jones, 1989; Riley, 2008). Most developmentalists, then, suggest that although initially language and thought may develop more or less independently, by the time children are 2 years of age, language and thinking work in tandem, as Vygotsky suggested.

REVIEW

▶ The way language develops is a complex and controversial question. Several theoretical perspectives have been adopted to explain the phenomenon, including the learning theory, the nativist approach, and the interactionist approach.

▶ According to the learning theory, language acquisition is little different from learning of any sort, with children's language reinforced and shaped by adults. The emergence of a sense of grammar is not well explained by this approach.

▶ The nativist approach, developed by Noam Chomsky, claims that humans have an innate language capacity that naturally facilitates language development. The existence of sensitive periods for learning language, the lack of language among nonhuman species, and the existence of areas of the brain associated with language support the nativist approach, while the failure to specify a truly universal grammar weakens it.

▶ A compromise position is held by the interactionists, who argue that language development, though innate, is determined by social factors, such as children's linguistic environment and the reinforcement they receive from others.

▶ The linguistic-relativity hypothesis, advanced by Benjamin Lee Whorf, holds that language shapes thought. However, the opposite view, that thought shapes language, as Piaget believed, is also a prevalent view, and the truth is probably that language and thought influence one another.

APPLY

▶ If humans have a language-acquisition device, why do children raised in isolation not develop language naturally? Why do adults have such difficulty learning a new language?

▶ Do you think language influences thought more than thought influences language? Why?

MODULE 7.3

Children's Conversations: Speaking to and with Children

Say the following sentence aloud: Do you like the apple dumpling?

Now pretend that you are going to ask the same question of an infant, and speak it as you would for the child's ears.

Chances are that several things happened when you translated the phrase for the infant. First of all, the wording probably changed, and you may have said something like, "Does baby like the apple dumpling?" At the same time, the pitch of your voice probably rose, your general intonation most likely had a singsong quality, and you probably separated your words carefully.

The change in your language illustrates just one facet of the nature of conversations involving children. We turn now to several aspects of language involving children's conversations, beginning with speech directed at infants.

The Language of Infant-Directed Speech

When talking to an infant, the shift in your language was due to your use of **infant-directed speech**, a style of speech that characterizes much of the verbal communication directed toward infants. This type of speech pattern used to be called *motherese*, because it was assumed that it applied only to mothers. However, that assumption was wrong, and the gender-neutral term *infant-directed speech* is now used more frequently.

Infant-directed speech is characterized by short, simple sentences. Pitch becomes higher, the range of frequencies increases, and intonation is more varied. There is also repetition of words, and topics are restricted to items that are assumed to be comprehensible to infants, such as concrete objects in the baby's environment.

Sometimes infant-directed speech includes amusing sounds that are not even words, imitating the prelinguistic speech of infants. In other cases, it has little formal structure, but is similar to the kind of telegraphic speech that infants use as they develop their own language skills.

Infant-directed speech changes as children become older. Around the end of the first year, infant-directed speech takes on more adultlike qualities. Sentences become longer and more complex, although individual words are still spoken slowly and deliberately. Pitch is also used to focus attention on particularly important words.

Infant-directed speech plays an important role in infants' acquisition of language. As discussed next, infant-directed speech occurs all over the world, though there are cultural variations. New-

infant-directed speech a type of speech directed toward infants that is characterized by short, simple sentences.

 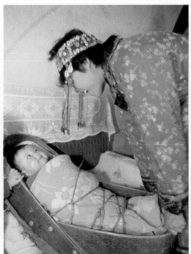 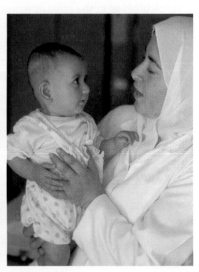

Motherese, or, more precisely, infant-directed speech, includes the use of short, simple sentences and is said in a pitch that is higher than that used with older children and adults.

borns prefer such speech to regular language, which suggests that they may be particularly receptive to it. Furthermore, some research indicates that babies who are exposed to a great deal of infant-directed speech early in life seem to begin to use words and exhibit other forms of linguistic competence earlier (Englund & Behne, 2006; Soderstrom, 2007; Werker et al., 2007). For a discussion of infant-directed speech across cultures see the *Developmental Diversity* Box.

DEVELOPMENTAL DIVERSITY
Is Infant-Directed Speech Similar in All Cultures?

Do mothers in the United States, Sweden, and Russia speak the same way to their infants?

In some respects, they clearly do. Although the words themselves differ across languages, the way the words are spoken to infants is quite similar. According to a growing body of research, infant-directed speech is basically similar across cultures (Papousek & Papousek, 1991; Rabain-Jamin & Sabeau-Jouannet, 1997; Werker et al., 2007).

Even deaf mothers use a form of infant-directed speech: When communicating with their infants, deaf mothers use sign language at a significantly slower tempo than when communicating with adults, and they frequently repeat the signs (Swanson, Leonard, & Gandour, 1992; Masataka, 1996, 1998, 2000).

The cross-cultural similarities in infant-directed speech are so great, in fact, that they appear in some facets of language specific to particular types of interactions. For instance, evidence comparing American English, German, and Mandarin Chinese speakers shows that in each of the languages, pitch rises when a mother is attempting to get an infant's attention or produce a response, while pitch falls when she is trying to calm an infant (Papousek & Papousek, 1991).

Why do we find such similarities across very different languages? One hypothesis is that the characteristics of infant-directed speech activate innate responses in infants. As we have noted, infants seem to prefer infant-directed speech over adult-directed speech, suggesting that their perceptual systems may be more responsive to such characteristics. Another explanation is that infant-directed speech facilitates language development, providing cues as to the meaning of speech before infants have developed the capacity to understand the meaning of words (Kuhl et al., 1997; Trainor & Desjardins, 2002; Falk, 2004).

Despite the similarities in the style of infant-directed speech across diverse cultures, there are some important cultural differences in the *quantity* of speech that infants hear from their parents. For example, although the Gusii of Kenya care for their infants in an extremely close, physical way, they speak to them less than American parents do (LeVine, 1994).

More precise comparisons, across a broader range of languages, reveal other similarities. For instance, Table 7.3 on page 214 shows the remarkable similarities in speech pitch among speakers of different languages when they are directing speech to infants, as opposed to adults (Fernald et al., 1989). It is particularly interesting that in every case mothers raise their pitch more than fathers when speaking to infants. Furthermore, speakers of American English show the greatest differences between speech to an infant and speech to an adult.

In addition, the language parents employ with their children differs depending on the child's sex. By the age of 32 months, girls hear twice as many diminutives (words such as "kitty" or "dolly" instead of "cat" or "doll") as boys hear. Although the use of diminutives declines with increasing age, their use consistently remains higher in speech directed at girls than in that directed at boys (see Figure 7.4; Gleason et al., 1994; Gleason & Ely, 2002).

Parents also are more apt to respond differently to children's requests depending on the child's gender. For instance, when turning down a child's request, mothers are likely to respond with a firm "no" to a male child, but to soften the blow to a female child by providing a diversionary response ("Why don't you do this instead?") or by somehow making the refusal less direct. Consequently, boys tend to hear firmer, clearer language, while girls are exposed to warmer phrases, often referring to inner emotional states (Perlmann & Gleason, 1990).

(continued)

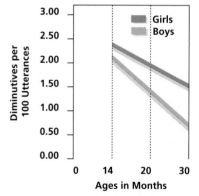

FIGURE 7.4 Gender Differences in Language: Diminishing Diminutives
Although the use of diminutives toward both male and female infants declines with age, they are consistently used more often in speech directed at females. What do you think is the cultural significance of this?
Source: Gleason et al., 1991.

TABLE 7.3	The Most Common Features of Infant-Directed Speech

ENGLISH	SPANISH
1. Exaggerated intonation	1. Exaggerated intonation
2. Breathiness	2. Repetition
3. High pitch	3. High pitch
4. Repetition	4. Instructional
5. Lowered volume	5. Attentionals
6. Lengthened vowel	6. Lowered volume
7. Creaky voice	7. Raised volume
8. Instructional	8. Lengthened vowel
9. Tenseness	9. Fast tempo
10. Falsetto	10. Personal pronoun substitution

Source: Adapted from Blount, 1982

Do such differences in language directed at boys and girls during infancy affect their behavior as adults? There is no direct evidence that plainly supports such an association, but men and women do use different sorts of language as adults. For instance, as adults, women tend to use more tentative, less assertive language, such as "Maybe we should try to go to a movie," than men ("I know, let's go to a movie!"). Though we don't know if these differences are a reflection of early linguistic experiences, such findings are certainly intriguing (Tenenbaum & Leaper, 2003; Hartshorne & Ullman, 2006; Plante et al., 2006).

Of course, gender is not the only factor that influences children's use of language. Increasing evidence suggests that the sheer quantity of speech that occurs in a household influences children's language development, and that quantity is associated with the economic well-being of the family environment, as we see next.

The Links Between Language Development and Poverty

Although it has long been assumed that the language that preschoolers hear at home has profound implications for their future cognitive success, it is only recently that research has addressed the issue in actual home settings. In a landmark study, psychologists Betty Hart and Todd Risley (1995) studied the language used over a 2-year period by a group of parents of varying levels of affluence as they interacted with their children. Coding some 1,300 hours of everyday interactions between parents and children produced several major findings:

- The rate at which language was addressed to children varied significantly according to the economic level of the family. As can be seen in Figure 7.5, the greater the affluence of the parents, the more they spoke to their children.
- In a typical hour, parents classified as professionals spent almost twice as much time interacting with their children as parents who received welfare assistance.
- By the age of 4, children in families that received welfare assistance were likely to have been exposed to some 13 million fewer words than those in families classified as professionals.
- There were differences in the kind of language used in the home by the various types of families. Children in families that received welfare assistance were apt to hear prohibitions ("no" or "stop," for example) twice as frequently as those in families classified as professionals.

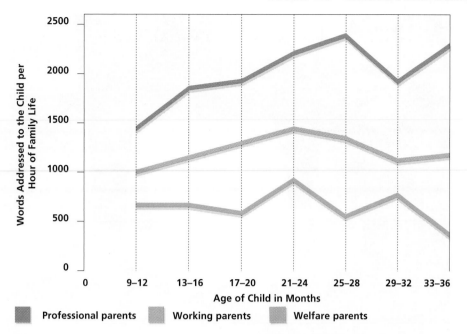

FIGURE 7.5 Different Language Exposure
Parents at differing levels of economic affluence provide different language experiences. Professional parents and working parents address more words to their children on average than parents on welfare. Why do you think this is so?
Source: B. Hart & Risley, 1995.

Ultimately, the study found that the type of language to which children were exposed was associated with their performance on tests of intelligence. The greater the number and variety of words children heard, for instance, the better their performance at age 3 on a variety of measures of intellectual achievement (Hart & Risley, 1995; Fowler et al., 2006).

Several factors may explain why children raised in more affluent homes are spoken to more frequently than children in more financially impoverished households. For instance, more affluent parents may have the luxury of spending more time with their children, as well as more flexible hours. Furthermore, there may be less household stress, thereby permitting more freewheeling interactions and fewer situations in which parents are simply exhausted.

Although the findings are correlational, and thus cannot be interpreted in terms of cause and effect, they suggest the importance of early exposure to language, in terms of both quantity and variety. They also suggest that intervention programs that teach parents to speak to their children more often and to use more varied language may help alleviate some of the potentially damaging consequences of poverty.

The research is also consistent with an increasing body of evidence that family income and poverty have powerful consequences for children's general cognitive development and behavior. By the age of 5, children raised in poverty tend to have lower IQ scores and perform less well on other measures of cognitive development than children raised in affluence. Furthermore, the longer children live in poverty, the more severe are the consequences. Poverty not only reduces the educational resources available to children, but it also has such negative effects on *parents* that it limits the psychological support they can provide their families. In short, the consequences of poverty are severe, and they linger (Duncan, Brooks-Gunn, & Klebanov, 1994; Bolger et al., 1995; Farah et al., 2006).

FROM A
SOCIAL WORKER'S
PERSPECTIVE
What do you think are the underlying reasons for differences between poorer and more affluent households in the use of language, and how do such language differences affect a family's social interactions?

English Language Learners: Bilingual Education vs. Immersion

Children who enter school with little or no English proficiency must learn both the standard curriculum and the language in which that curriculum is taught. Known as *English language learners (ELLs)*, these students face special challenges. Their lack of English language skills may significantly slow their academic progress and isolate them from other children. In addition, their specific cultural background may lead ELLs to understand the educational process differently. For example, in some cultures it is considered disrespectful to ask teachers questions about material they are presenting (Klingner & Artiles, 2006; Stipek & Hakuta, 2007).

In contrast to immersion programs, in which students receive instruction only in English, in bilingual education, children are initially taught in their own language, while also learning English.

Bilingual Education. One approach to educating students whose first language is not English is *bilingual education*, in which students are initially taught in their native language, while at the same time learning English. With bilingual instruction, students are able to develop a strong foundation in basic subject areas using their native language. The ultimate goal of most bilingual education programs is to gradually shift instruction into English.

An alternative approach is to immerse students in English, teaching solely in that language. According to proponents of this approach, initially teaching students in a language other than English hinders students' efforts to learn English and slows their integration into society.

The two quite different approaches have been highly politicized, with some politicians arguing in favor of "English-only" laws and others urging school systems to respect the challenges faced by students who do not speak English by offering some instruction in their native language. Still, the psychological research clearly suggests that knowing more than one language offers several cognitive advantages. Because they have a wider range of linguistic possibilities to choose from as they assess a situation, speakers of two languages show greater cognitive flexibility. They can solve problems with increased creativity and versatility. Furthermore, learning in one's native tongue is associated with higher self-esteem in minority students (Romaine, 1994; Wright & Taylor, 1995; Barker, Giles, & Noels, 2001; Zehr, 2006).

Bilingual students often have greater metalinguistic awareness, understanding the rules of language more explicitly than students who speak only one language. Bilingual students even may score higher on tests of intelligence, according to some research. For example, one survey of French- and English-speaking students in Canada found that bilingual students scored significantly higher on both verbal and nonverbal tests of intelligence than those who spoke only one language (Lambert & Peal, 1972; Bochner, 1996; Crutchley, 2003; Swanson, Saez, & Gerber, 2004).

Finally, because many linguists contend that universal processes underlie language acquisition, instruction in a native language may enhance instruction in a second language. Most educators believe that second-language learning should be a regular part of schooling for *all* adolescents (Perozzi & Sanchez, 1992; Yelland, Pollard, & Mercuri, 1993; Kecskes & Papp, 2000; Bialystok, McBride-Chang, & Luk, 2005).

The Ebonics Controversy: Is Black English a Separate Language from Standard English?

Although the word "Ebonics" had been in use since the 1970s, few people had heard of it before the Oakland, California, school board declared it a distinctive language in the late 1990s. Their decision affirmed that Ebonics—a word derived from a combination of the words "ebony" and "phonics"—

was a separate language from English. According to the school board's declaration, Ebonics was a distinct language with roots in Africa, one spoken by many African Americans in inner cities. The school board ordered that students who spoke Ebonics should receive their initial classroom instruction using Ebonics, and not standard English (Applebome, 1997; Rickford, 2006).

The school board's decision provoked a national controversy, and within a month the board had reversed itself. Members of the board said that they had never meant for students to learn anything other than standard English, and that they had merely wanted recognition for the fact that many African American students needed instruction to make the leap from the Ebonics they spoke at home to standard English.

The controversy raised several issues, none of which has had definitive resolutions. For instance, linguists vary in their views of the legitimacy of Ebonics. According to linguist Dennis Baron, most linguists consider what they call African American Vernacular English, or sometimes Black English, to be a dialect or variety of standard English. Although it has some characteristics that are derived from African languages, it can be understood fairly well by speakers of standard English. Furthermore, certain features of Ebonics, such as the use of different conjugations of the verb "to be" (as in "I be going") are evidence that it is not a separate language, but a dialect of English (Baron, 1997; Sanchez, 1997; Delpit, 2006; Rickford, 2006).

Yet, it is also clear that nonstandard English operates according to a set of consistent rules and conventions. Although in the past African American Vernacular English has been treated as a form of speech disability—one that required the intervention of speech pathologists or special education teachers—today educators have become more accepting. Probably most educators would argue that nonstandard English is not an *inferior* form of language, but one that is *different*—an important distinction. Furthermore, they point out that many words that have their origins in Black English have entered the mainstream of standard English, including "hip," "cool," "chill out," "slick," and "rip-off" (Sanchez, 1997; Rickford, 2006).

Still, the issues revolving around Ebonics or Black English or African American Vernacular English—or whatever else it may be called—are not likely to go away soon. The controversy raises not only important linguistic issues, but many social ones as well.

REVIEW

▶ When talking to infants, adults of all cultures tend to use infant-directed speech. This type of speech seems to appeal to infants and to facilitate their linguistic development.

▶ According to some research, adults tend to speak more indirectly to girls and more directly to boys, which may contribute to behavioral differences later in life.

▶ Economic factors in the home have a significant influence on language development. Children raised in affluence hear a greater quantity and variety of language from their parents than do children of poverty, with positive effects on later measures of intellectual achievement.

▶ Bilingual students who speak more than one language show greater cognitive flexibility, metalinguistic awareness, and even intelligence test performance, but immersion in the language of the dominant culture can be problematic for children of other cultures.

▶ The Ebonics controversy raised issues regarding the stature of nonstandard language that demonstrate the close relationship between linguistic issues and social issues.

APPLY

▶ What are some implications of differences in the ways adults speak to boys and girls? How might such speech differences contribute to later differences not only in speech but also in attitudes?

▶ If parents living in poverty are given instruction in using a greater quantity and variety of language in the home, do you think their children will achieve equality with more affluent children in linguistic and cognitive areas? Why or why not?

Epilogue

We have examined the development of speech in children, observing how they progress from inaccurate users of language to accomplished speakers. The process by which children reach competence in language is complex but seems to come naturally to them. Their capabilities are so apparent that they can easily learn two or more languages if they hear them frequently and naturally—an ability envied by any school-age student or adult who has struggled with *Beginning French* or *Mandarin Made Easy*.

In the chapter prologue, we encountered Vicki and Dominic, who engaged in a friendly competition over whether their daughter Maura would first say the word "mama" or the word "daddy." The quest to encourage Maura and to hear her first word was intense, keeping them occupied for months. When she at last uttered her first word, both parents were delighted—even though Maura's first word referred to neither of her parents, but to her bottle.

1. Why do you think Vicki and Dominic were so fascinated by the emergence of Maura's first word? Is it the same thrill they probably got from Maura's first steps, first solid food, first day at preschool, first sentence read, first words written? How are these experiences similar, and how are they different? Why?

2. What aspects of language are taught, and which ones develop naturally?

3. Nonhuman animals vocalize constantly. Can their oral production be called language? Why or why not? Do you think animal parents are as excited by the first meaningful sounds emitted by their offspring as Vicki and Dominic are about Maura's first word?

4. In what ways do you think the language of nonhuman primates shares the formal characteristics of human speech (phonology, morphology, and semantics)? Do animal sounds display pragmatics?

Looking Back

What is the process of language development during the childhood years?

1. Infants engage in prelinguistic communication, the use of sounds, gestures, facial expressions, imitation, and other non-linguistic means to express thoughts and states. Babbling is a form of prelinguistic communication, which proceeds through regular stages and, with other forms of prelinguistic communication, prepares the infant for speech.

2. Infants typically produce their first words between the ages of 10 and 14 months. Thereafter, vocabulary increases rapidly, especially during a spurt at around 18 months. At about the same time, children typically begin to link words together into primitive sentences that express single thoughts.

3. Beginning speech is characterized by the use of holophrases, in which a single word conveys more complex meaning based on its context; telegraphic speech, in which only essential sentence components are used; underextension, in which an overly restrictive meaning is assigned to a word; and overextension, in which an overly generalized meaning is assigned to a word.

4. Features of the child's native language begin to emerge as early as the babbling stage, when sounds other than those of the home language gradually disappear. In addition, the structure of the home language begins to be reflected even in telegraphic speech, when word order mirrors that used by mature speakers of the home language.

5. The burst in language ability that occurs during the preschool years is dramatic. Children rapidly progress from two-word utterances to longer, more sophisticated expressions that reflect their growing vocabularies, sense of syntax, and emerging grasp of grammar. They also proceed along a continuum from private speech to more social speech.

6. Similarly, the language development of children in the school years is substantial, with improvements in vocabulary, syntax, and pragmatics. Despite these advances, school-age children's language is still not as proficient as it will become in adulthood, and some pronunciation and comprehension difficulties are normal.

7. Improvements in language help children control their behavior through linguistic strategies. Moreover, their growing metalinguistic awareness permits them to realize that language use is rule-governed and is subject to breakdowns for which they are not solely responsible, and which can be remedied by seeking clarification.

What are various perspectives on the origins of language development, and what evidence supports each one?

8. One theory of how humans develop language is the learning theory, which assumes that adults and children use basic behavioral processes—such as conditioning, reinforcement, and shaping—in language learning. The fact that people spontaneously develop a natural grammatical sense argues against this perspective.

9. A radically different approach—the nativist approach—is proposed by Chomsky, who holds that humans are genetically endowed with a language-acquisition device, which permits them to detect and use the principles of universal grammar that underlie all languages. Support for this view is derived from the existence of sensitive periods for learning language, the lack of language among nonhuman species, and the existence of areas of the brain associated with language, while the failure to specify a truly universal grammar weakens it.

10. An intermediate approach—the interactionist perspective—holds that children have innate linguistic capabilities that are

shaped by social factors such as the language to which children are exposed and the interactions that they have with others in their environment.

How are language and thought related?

11. According to Benjamin Lee Whorf's linguistic-relativity hypothesis, the language that people speak influences the ways they perceive and understand the world. This view—that language shapes thought—is controversial; the opposite view—that thought shapes language—which is held by developmentalists such as Jean Piaget, is more mainstream, but also controversial. An intermediate position—that thought and language jointly influence one another—is growing in acceptance and appears to be most accurate.

In what ways does the language adults use with children affect language development?

12. Infant-directed speech takes on characteristics, surprisingly invariant across cultures, that make it appealing to infants and that probably facilitate language development. There is some evidence that infants are especially—and perhaps innately—attuned to the characteristics of infant-directed speech.

13. Adult language also exhibits differences based on the gender of the child to whom it is directed. For example, some research indicates that adult speech addressed to boys is more direct than that addressed to girls. It is possible that gender differences in the language heard during infancy may have effects that emerge later in life.

How do social issues influence language development?

14. Language development and economic circumstances are significantly linked. Preschool children of poverty tend to hear a smaller quantity and variety of language from their parents and caregivers than children of affluence. This linguistic difference in turn is linked to later differential performance on a variety of measures of intellectual achievement.

15. Bilingualism is an increasingly prevalent phenomenon in the school years. There is evidence that many children who are taught all subjects in the first language, with simultaneous instruction in English, experience few deficits and several linguistic and cognitive advantages.

16. Immersion programs work well when majority children are immersed during the school day in a minority language, but do not work as well the other way around: when minority children are immersed in the language of the majority.

17. The controversy over the use of Ebonics (or African American Vernacular English) in schools revealed that linguistic issues are related to issues of power and status, and illuminated the close link between linguistic issues and social ones.

PEARSON
mydevelopmentlab™

For more review plus **MyVirtualChild**, practice tests, videos, flashcards, and more, log on to **mydevelopmentlab.com**

Prologue

The Exceptional Daniel Skandera

"Hey, hey, hey. Fact Track!" The 11-year-old speaker chose one of his favorite programs from the table next to the computer in his parents' dining room. He inserted the floppy disc, booted the system, and waited for the program to load.

"What is your name?" appeared on the monitor.

"Daniel Skandera," he typed. A menu scrolled up listing the program's possibilities. Daniel chose multiplication facts, Level 1.

"How many problems do you want to do?" the computer asked.

"20."

"Do you want to set a goal for yourself, Daniel?"

"Yes, 80 sec."

"Get ready!". . .

Randomly generated multiplication facts flashed on the screen: "4 × 6," "2 × 9," "3 × 3," "7 × 6." Daniel responded, deftly punching in his answers on the computer's numeric key-pad. Twice he recognized errors and corrected them before inputting his answers. . . .

The computer tallied the results. "You completed 20 problems in 66 seconds. You beat your goal. Problems correct = 20. Congratulations, Daniel!" And with that the 11-year-old retreated hastily to the TV room. The Lakers and 76ers were about to tip off for an NBA championship game, and Daniel wanted to see the first half before bedtime. (Heward & Orlansky, 1988, p. 100)

Understanding precisely what is meant by the concept of intelligence has proven to be a major challenge for researchers.

This hardly seems out of the ordinary. But now consider an additional fact: Daniel was born with *Down syndrome,* a genetically produced disorder that causes mental retardation.

Daniel's capabilities raise a number of issues, addressed in this chapter, about the nature of intelligence. How can we define intelligent behavior? What makes one person more, or less, intelligent than others? Ultimately, does intelligence matter?

To answer these questions, we first consider the ways that have been developed to differentiate children on the basis of intelligence. We discuss traditional measures of intelligence—IQ tests—and examine newer alternatives such as those suggested by Lev Vygotsky and information processing approaches to intelligence.

We then explore some of the controversial issues in the realm of intelligence. We consider how to measure intelligence in infancy and the meaning of racial differences in IQ scores. We also look at the contested topic of intelligence among adults and examine whether the picture of declining cognitive competence is an empty stereotype or has some truth in it. We then suggest ways that adults can maintain their cognitive functioning.

The chapter ends with an examination of the two groups that show the extremes of intelligence: people with mental retardation and gifted people. We consider the nature of the exceptionality of each of these populations and focus on the question of how exceptional children should best be integrated into society.

LOOKING AHEAD

After reading this chapter, you will be able to answer the following questions:

▶ What is intelligence, and how has it been measured over the years?

▶ What are newer conceptions of intelligence, and how are they measured?

▶ How is the intelligence of infants measured, and does infant intelligence predict adult intelligence?

▶ Why do some groups perform better than others on IQ tests, and what do such group differences mean?

▶ Does intelligence decline in adulthood and old age? What is the difference between IQ and cognitive competence?

▶ What sorts of mental exceptionalities do people have, and what assistance do they need and receive?

MODULE 8.1

Intelligence: Determining Individual Strengths

"Why should you tell the truth?" "How far is Los Angeles from New York?" "A table is made of wood; a window of ____."

As 10-year-old Hyacinth sat hunched over her desk, trying to answer a long series of questions like these, she tried to guess the point of the test she was taking in her fifth-grade classroom. Clearly, the test didn't cover material that her teacher, Ms. White-Johnston, had talked about in class.

"What number comes next in this series: 1, 3, 7, 15, 31, ____?"

As she continued to work her way through the questions, she gave up trying to guess the rationale for the test. She'd leave that to her teacher, she sighed to herself. Rather than attempting to figure out what it all meant, she simply tried to do her best on the individual test items.

Hyacinth might be surprised to learn that she was not alone in questioning the meaning and import of the items on the test she was taking. For although the test items were painstakingly developed, many developmentalists would admit to harboring their own doubts as to whether questions such as these are appropriate to the task of assessing what they are designed to measure: intelligence.

Understanding precisely what is meant by the concept of intelligence has proven to be a major challenge for researchers interested in delineating what separates intelligent from unintelligent behavior. Although nonexperts have their own conceptions of intelligence (one survey found, for instance, that laypersons believe that intelligence consists of three components: problem-solving ability, verbal ability, and social competence), it has been more difficult for experts to concur (Sternberg et al., 1981; Weinberg, 1989; Davidson, 1990). Still, a general definition of intelligence is possible: **Intelligence** is the capacity to understand the world, think with rationality, and use resources effectively when faced with challenges.

Part of the difficulty in defining intelligence stems from the many—and sometimes unsatisfactory—paths that have been followed over the years in the quest to distinguish more intelligent people from less intelligent ones. To understand how researchers have approached the task of devising batteries of assessments called intelligence tests, we need to consider some of the historical milestones in the area of intelligence.

Intelligence Benchmarks: Differentiating the Intelligent from the Unintelligent

The Paris school system was faced with a problem at the turn of the twentieth century: A significant number of children were not benefiting from regular instruction. Unfortunately, these children—many of whom we would now say had mental retardation—were generally not

intelligence the capacity to understand the world, think with rationality, and use resources effectively when faced with challenges.

identified early enough to shift them to special classes. The French minister of instruction approached psychologist Alfred Binet with the problem of devising a technique for the early identification of students who might benefit from instruction outside the regular classroom.

Binet tackled his task in a thoroughly practical manner. His years of observing school-aged children suggested to him that previous efforts to distinguish intelligent from unintelligent students—some of which were based on reaction time or keenness of sight—were off the mark. Instead, he launched a trial-and-error process in which items and tasks were administered to students who had been previously identified by teachers as being either "bright" or "dull." Tasks that the bright students completed correctly and the dull students failed to complete correctly were retained for the test. Tasks that did not discriminate between the two groups were discarded. The end result of this process was a test that reliably distinguished students who had previously been identified as fast or slow learners.

The Wechsler Intelligence Scale for Children-Fourth Edition (WISC-IV) is widely used as an intelligence test that measures verbal and performance (nonverbal) skills.

Binet's pioneering efforts in intelligence testing left three important legacies. The first was his pragmatic approach to the construction of intelligence tests. Binet did not have theoretical preconceptions about what intelligence was. Instead, he used a trial-and-error approach to psychological measurement that continues to serve as the predominant approach to test construction today. His definition of intelligence as that which his test measured has been adopted by many modern researchers, and it is especially popular among test developers who respect the widespread utility of intelligence tests but wish to avoid arguments about the underlying nature of intelligence.

Our second inheritance from Binet stems from his focus on linking intelligence and school success. Binet's reliance on teachers as the backbone for his procedure for constructing an intelligence test ensured that intelligence—defined as performance on the test—and school success—predicted by teachers—would be virtually one and the same. Binet's intelligence test and its current successors, then, have become reasonable indicators of the degree to which students possess attributes that contribute to successful school performance. Unfortunately, they do not provide particularly useful information regarding a vast number of other attributes that are largely unrelated to academic proficiency.

Finally, Binet developed a procedure of assigning each intelligence test score to a mental age, the age of the children taking the test who, on average, achieved that score. For example, if a 6-year-old girl received a score of 30 on the test, and this was the average score received by 10-year-olds, her mental age would be considered 10 years. Similarly, a 15-year-old boy who scored a 90 on the test—thereby matching the mean score for 15-year-olds—would be assigned a mental age of 15 years.

Although assigning a mental age to students indicates whether or not they are performing at the same level as their peers, it does not permit adequate comparisons between students of different chronological (or physical) ages. By using mental age alone, for instance, one might assume that a 15-year-old responding with a mental age of 17 years would be as bright as a 6-year-old responding with a mental age of 8 years, when actually the 6-year-old would be showing a much greater relative degree of brightness.

A solution to this problem comes in the form of the **intelligence quotient,** or **IQ**, a score that takes into account a student's mental and chronological age. The traditional method of calculating an IQ score uses the following formula, in which MA stands for mental age and CA for chronological age:

$$\text{IQ Score} = \frac{\text{MA} \times 100}{\text{CA}}$$

As a bit of trial-and-error with this formula demonstrates, people whose mental age (MA) is equal to their chronological age (CA) will always have an IQ of 100. Furthermore, if the chronological age exceeds the mental age—implying below-average intelligence—the score will be below 100; and if the chronological age is lower than the mental age—suggesting above-average intelligence—the score will be above 100.

Using this formula, we can return to our earlier example of a 15-year-old who scores at a 17-year-old mental age. This student's IQ is 17/15 × 100, or 113. In comparison, the IQ of a 6-year-old scoring at a mental age of 8 is 8/6 × 100, or 133—a higher IQ score than the 15-year-old's.

intelligence quotient, or **IQ** a score that takes into account a student's mental and chronological age.

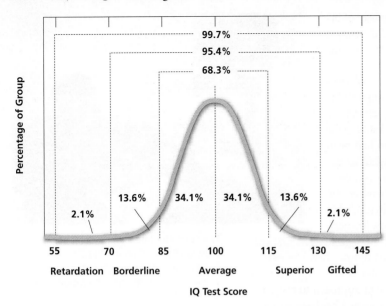

FIGURE 8.1 IQ Scores
The most common and average IQ score is 100, with 68.3 percent of all people falling within 15 points of 100. About 95 percent of the population has scores that are within 30 points above or below 100; fewer than 3 percent score below 55 or above 145.

Stanford-Binet Intelligence Scale A test that consists of a series of items that vary according to the age of the person being tested.

Wechsler Intelligence Scale for Children-IV (WISC-IV) A test for children that provides separate measures of verbal and performance (nonverbal) skills, as well as a total score.

Wechsler Adult Intelligence Scale-IV (WAIS-IV) A test for adults that provides separate measures of verbal and performance (nonverbal) skills, as well as a total score.

Kaufman Assessment Battery for Children (KABC-II) A children's intelligence test permitting unusual flexibility in its administration.

Although the basic principles behind the calculation of an IQ score still hold, scores today are calculated in a more mathematically sophisticated manner and are known as deviation IQ scores. Rather than comparing performance to children who are younger and older, deviation IQ scores are computed by comparing other children of the same age. The average deviation IQ score remains set at 100, and tests are now statistically constructed so that approximately two-thirds of children of a given age fall within 15 points of the average score of 100, achieving scores between 85 and 115. As scores rise or fall beyond this range, the percentage of children in the same score category drops significantly (see Figure 8.1).

Measuring IQ: Present-Day Approaches to Intelligence

Although tests of intelligence have become increasingly sophisticated since the time of Binet in terms of the accuracy with which they measure IQ, most of them can still trace their roots to his original work in one way or another. For example, one of the most widely used tests—the **Stanford-Binet Intelligence Scale**—began as an American revision of Binet's original test. The test consists of a series of items that vary according to the age of the person being tested. For instance, young children are asked to answer questions about everyday activities or to copy complex figures. Older people are asked to explain proverbs, solve analogies, and describe similarities between groups of words. The test is administered orally, and test-takers are given progressively more difficult problems until they are unable to proceed.

The **Wechsler Intelligence Scale for Children–IV (WISC–IV)** and its adult version, the **Wechsler Adult Intelligence Scale–IV (WAIS–IV)**, are two other widely used intelligence tests. The tests provide separate measures of verbal and performance (or nonverbal) skills, as well as a total score. As you can see from the items similar to those actually on the test in Figure 8.2, the verbal tasks are traditional word problems testing skills such as understanding a passage, while typical nonverbal tasks are copying a complex design, arranging pictures in a logical order, and assembling objects. The separate portions of the test allow for easier identification of any specific problems a test-taker may have. For example, significantly higher scores on the performance part of the test than on the verbal part may indicate difficulties in linguistic development.

The **Kaufman Assessment Battery for Children (KABC-II)** takes a different approach than the Stanford-Binet, WISC-IV, and WAIS-IV. In the KABC-II, children are tested on their ability to integrate different kinds of stimuli simultaneously and to use step-by-step thinking. A special virtue of the KABC-II is its flexibility. It allows the person giving the test to use alternative wording or gestures, or even to pose questions in a different language, in order to maximize a test-taker's performance. This makes testing more valid and equitable for children to whom English is a second language (Kaufman et al., 2005).

In addition to individualized IQ tests, there are also several tests designed to be administered to groups of children. Such group IQ tests require written answers to a series of written questions. Their great advantage over other types of IQ tests is the ease with which they can be administered.

Group IQ tests have several disadvantages, however. For one thing, the questions asked on group tests tend to be more restricted than those administered individually. In addition, children are often more motivated when they are asked questions individually by a test administrator than when they are responding in a group. Finally, outside factors, such as being distracted by other students, having their pencils break, or not paying attention to instructions, may interfere with children's performance. Ultimately, group-administered IQ tests may provide a far less accurate assessment of IQ than individually administered tests.

Some IQ tests have been specifically designed to overcome the potential for cultural bias. As we'll discuss later in the chapter, IQ tests have been criticized for discriminating against members of minority racial, ethnic, and cultural groups. In order to overcome this bias, *culture-fair IQ tests* are designed to be independent of the cultural background of test-takers. For example, the *Raven*

Name	Goal of Item	Example
Verbal Scale		
Information	Assess general information	How many nickels make a dime?
Comprehension	Assess understanding and evaluation of social norms and past experience	What is the advantage of keeping money in the bank?
Arithmetic	Assess math reasoning through verbal problems	If two buttons cost 15 cents, what will be the cost of a dozen buttons?
Similarities	Test understanding of how objects or concepts are alike, tapping abstract reasoning	In what way are an hour and a week alike?
Performance Scale		
Digit symbol	Assess speed of learning	Match symbols to numbers using key. 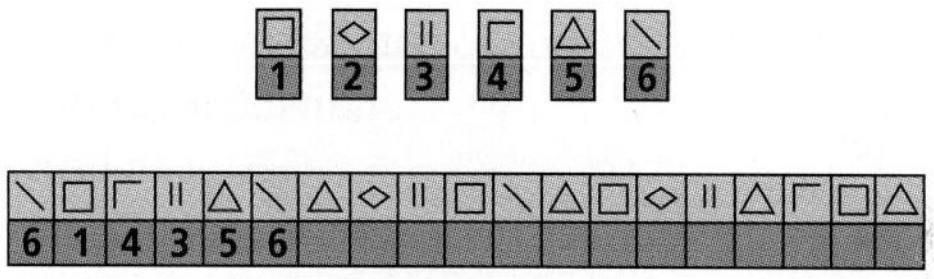
Picture completion	Visual memory and attention	Identify what is missing. 
Object assembly	Test understanding of relationship of parts to wholes	Put pieces together to form a whole. 

FIGURE 8.2 Measuring Intelligence
The Wecshler Intelligence Scales for Children (WISC-IV) includes items such as these. What do such items cover? What do they miss?

FIGURE 8.3 The Raven Progressive Matrices Test

In the Raven Progressive Matrices Test, examinees are shown an abstract figure with a missing piece. They are asked to choose from several possibilities which piece would complete the figure. The Raven is designed to be free of cultural bias because it is assumed that no group is more or less familiar with the task.

Source: NCS Pearson, Inc., 1998.

mydevelopmentlab

How is your virtual child doing in school? Do you think standardized testing should be used to assess his or her performance? Log onto **MyVirtualChild** through **MyDevelopmentLab** to answer questions like these.

reliability   a quality of tests that measure consistently what they are trying to measure.

validity   a quality of tests that actually measure what they are supposed to measure.

learning disabilities   difficulties in the acquisition and use of listening, speaking, reading, writing, reasoning, or mathematical abilities.

Progressive Matrices Test asks test-takers to examine abstract designs that have a missing piece and choose the missing piece from several possibilities (see Figure 8.3).

The assumption behind culture-fair IQ tests is that no particular cultural group will be more or less acquainted with the test content, and consequently the test results will be free from cultural bias. Unfortunately, the culture-fair tests have not been very successful, and the disparities based on minority group membership still occur. A true culture-fair IQ test has yet to be developed (Sattler, 1992; Anastasi, 1997; Ostrosky-Solis & Oberg, 2006).

Reliability and Validity.   Every time we measure our weight on a bathroom scale, we assume that any changes we find are due to fluctuations in our actual weight, and not produced by inaccuracies in the scale. In the same fashion, testing experts who produce IQ tests construct them to have reliability. **Reliability** exists when a test measures consistently what it is trying to measure. If we assume that IQ is a stable characteristic, then a test that has reliability will produce the same score each time it is administered to a particular person. If one time a test produced a score of 105, but the next time it produced a score of 130, then it is not reliable. On the other hand, if each time the test is administered to the same individual it yielded a score of 105, then the test is reliable.

Even if a test is reliable, however, it is not necessarily valid. A test has **validity** when it actually measures what it is supposed to measure. For instance, just as a valid bathroom scale should measure a person's weight correctly and unambiguously, a valid IQ test should measure an individual's underlying intelligence correctly and unambiguously.

Tests can be reliable without being valid. For example, we could devise a completely reliable test for intelligence if we made the assumption that skull circumference was related to intelligence. Because measuring skull size precisely is fairly easy, we would then have a very reliable measure. But would such a test of intelligence be valid? Hardly, because it seems far-fetched that skull size would have much to do with anyone's intelligence. (Well, not far-fetched to everyone: There have been serious efforts in the past to match skull configuration to psychological attributes such as intelligence, although such attempts have, not surprisingly, proved unsuccessful; Gould, 1996; Deary et al., 2007.)

To assess intelligence accurately, IQ tests must be both reliable *and* valid. Although there is wide agreement that well-established IQ tests meet the formal requirements of reliability, their validity, as we will see, is far more controversial.

IQ and School Achievement.   What do IQ scores mean? For most children, they are reasonable predictors of school performance. That's not surprising, given that intelligence tests were developed to identify students who were having difficulties (Sternberg & Grigorenko, 2002).

But the story differs for performance outside of school. Although people with higher scores tend to finish more years of schooling, once this is statistically controlled for, IQ scores do not closely relate to income and later success in life. Two people with different scores may both earn bachelor's degrees at the same college, but the person with a lower IQ might have a higher income and a more successful career. These difficulties with traditional IQ scores have led researchers to consider alternative approaches (McClelland, 1993; Zagorsky, 2007).

Recall what the scores derived from IQ tests mean. For most children, IQ scores are reasonably good predictors of school performance. That's not surprising, given that the initial impetus for the development of intelligence tests was to identify children who were having difficulties in school.

But even within the academic sphere, IQ scores aren't always accurate predictors of school performance. For instance, 2.6 million school-age children in the United States are officially labeled as having learning disabilities. **Learning disabilities** are defined as difficulties in the acquisition and use of listening, speaking, reading, writing, reasoning, or mathematical abilities. A somewhat ill-defined, grab-bag category, learning disabilities are diagnosed when a discrepancy exists between children's actual academic performance and their apparent potential to learn as based on IQ scores and other ability measures (Lyon, 1996; Wong, 1996; Kozey & Siegel, 2008).

Several types of learning disabilities have been identified. The most common is *attention-deficit/hyperactivity disorder (ADHD)*. Children with ADHD are inattentive and impulsive, with a low tolerance for frustration and generally a great deal of inappropriate activity. Yet their IQ scores are either normal or above. Other children with learning disabilities suffer from *dyslexia*, a reading disability that can result in the misperception of letters during reading and writing, unusual difficulty in sounding out letters, confusion between left and right, and difficulties in spelling. Thus, normal IQ scores can fail to detect abnormal learning (Barkely, 1997; Byrne, Shankweiler & Hine, 2008; Nicolson & Fawcett, 2008).

The utility of IQ scores becomes even less clear when we consider performance outside of academic spheres. For instance, although people with higher IQ scores are apt to finish more years of schooling, once this is statistically controlled for, IQ scores are only moderately related to income and later success in life. Furthermore, IQ scores are frequently inaccurate when it comes to predicting a particular individual's future success. For instance, some minimal level of intelligence obviously is needed based on the demands of a specific profession. However, once a person enters a profession, IQ plays only a modest role in determining how successful a particular individual will be. Factors such as motivation, luck, and social skills account for a large part of occupational success (Sternberg, 1997; Wagner, 1997; Zagorsky, 2008).

In short, despite the frequent measurement and use of IQ scores, their relevance to nonscholastic domains is not clear. Because of these difficulties with traditional IQ scores, researchers have turned to alternative approaches to intelligence (McClelland, 1993; Pascual-Leone & Johnson, 2005). (Also see the accompanying *From Research to Practice* box.)

Bodily kinesthetic intelligence, as displayed by dancers, ballplayers and gymnasts is one of Gardner's eight intelligences. What are some examples of other Gardner intelligences?

What IQ Tests Don't Tell: Alternative Conceptions of Intelligence.   The intelligence tests schools use most today regard intelligence as a single factor, a unitary mental ability. This attribute is commonly called *g* (Spearman, 1927; Lubinski, 2004). Assumed to underlie performance on every aspect of intelligence, the *g* factor is what IQ tests presumably measure.

However, many theorists disagree that intelligence is unidimensional. As we will see in the next module, some developmentalists suggest that two kinds of intelligence exist: fluid and crystallized (Cattell, 1987, 2004). **Fluid intelligence** reflects information processing capabilities, reasoning, and memory; for example, a student asked to group a series of letters according to some criterion or to remember a set of numbers would be using fluid intelligence. In contrast,

fluid intelligence   is intelligence that reflects information processing capabilities, reasoning, and memory.

FROM RESEARCH TO PRACTICE
Take-at-Home IQ Tests: Should Parents Test Their Children's IQ?

One of the newest additions to the choices that parents may make in raising their children is the availability of take-at-home IQ tests. The take-at-home IQ test is designed to provide an IQ score for children as young as 6 months of age. (Martin, 2004)

The manufacturer claims that it is responding to parents' concerns over their children's educational achievement. The reasoning goes that by learning their children's IQ scores, parents put themselves in a better position to provide either remedial help (if the IQ is low) or enrichment (if it turns out to be exceptionally high).

Although the take-at-home test seems popular—20,000 units were sold in the first few months of distribution—its availability raises several issues. First is the question of validity. Although traditional IQ tests are standardized with thousands of children before they are published, the degree of development that went into this take-at-home test is unclear. Furthermore, even if the basic material is valid, it is not obvious that parents will be able to administer the test correctly, or that the computer program that presents the test is sufficiently sophisticated to ensure correct administration. This makes the possibility of mislabeling children all too real.

But even if the IQ score a child receives is accurate, it is not apparent how knowing such information will benefit the child. Children who receive a relatively low IQ score may be seen as disappointments to their parents, and parental expectations may be

lowered for such children. It is possible that such lowered expectations may result in fewer opportunities being offered to the child, who could be seen as not worth the investment. Even holding high expectations for a child who scores well on the IQ test may not be so beneficial; such children may be seen as so "naturally" bright that they don't really need enrichment provided by extra opportunities.

It is too early to know if at-home IQ testing will become a routine part of parenting. Certainly it is unlikely that children living in families with restricted incomes will be tested, given that the IQ tests cost money and in-home computers required for the test remain comparatively rarer for families living in poverty than for affluent families. Furthermore, some experts are skeptical of the value of the tests. For instance, psychologist Dianne Brown, director of testing and assessment at the American Psychological Association, says, "I don't like this notion of take this home and put a label on your child. [IQ] tests are criticized horribly even when being used appropriately in the school system" (Kelly, 1997, p. B7). The very real arguments against the use of take-at-home IQ tests may well impede their widespread use.

- *Why would parents choose to learn their child's IQ at an early age?*

- *What might be the drawbacks to knowing that a 6-month-old had a particularly low (or high) IQ?*

crystallized intelligence the store of information, skills, and strategies that people have acquired through education and prior experiences and through their previous use of fluid intelligence.

crystallized intelligence is the cumulative information, skills, and strategies people have learned and can apply in solving problems. A student would likely use crystallized intelligence to solve a puzzle or find the solution to a mystery (Alfonso, Flanagan, & Radwan, 2005; McGrew, 2005).

Other theorists divide intelligence into even more parts. Psychologist Howard Gardner suggests that we have at least eight distinct intelligences, each of them relatively independent of the other (see Figure 8.4). Gardner suggests that, for example, some people may be particularly skilled in linguistic intelligence, while others may be particularly skilled in musical intelligence.

1. *Musical intelligence* (skills in tasks involving music). Case example:
When he was 3, Yehudi Menuhin was smuggled into the San Francisco Orchestra concerts by his parents. The sound of Louis Persinger's violin so entranced the youngster that he insisted on a violin for his birthday and Louis Persinger as his teacher. He got both. By the time he was 10 years old, Menuhin was an international performer.

2. *Bodily kinesthetic intelligence* (skills in using the whole body or various portions of it in the solution of problems or in the construction of products or displays, exemplified by dancers, athletes, actors, and surgeons). Case example:
Fifteen-year-old Babe Ruth played third base. During one game, his team's pitcher was doing poorly and Babe loudly criticized him from third base. Brother Mathias, the coach, called out, "Ruth, if you know so much about it, *you* pitch!" Babe was surprised and embarrassed because he had never pitched before, but Brother Mathias insisted. Ruth said later that at the very moment he took the pitcher's mound, he *knew* he was supposed to be a pitcher.

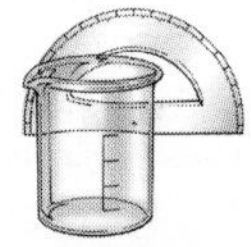

3. *Logical mathematical intelligence* (skills in problem solving and scientific thinking). Case example:
Barbara McClintock won the Nobel Prize in medicine for her work in microbiology. She describes one of her breakthroughs, which came after thinking about a problem for half an hour...: "Suddenly I jumped and ran back to the [corn] field. At the top of the field [the others were still at the bottom] I shouted, 'Eureka, I have it!'"

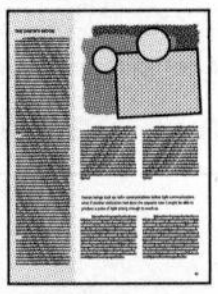

4. *Linguistic intelligence* (skills involved in the production and use of language). Case example:
At the age of 10, T.S. Elliot created a magazine called *Fireside*, to which he was the sole contributor. In a 3-day period during his winter vacation, he created eight complete issues.

5. *Spatial intelligence* (skills involving spatial configurations, such as those used by artists and architects). Case example:
Navigation around the Caroline Islands...is accomplished without instruments....During the actual trip, the navigator must envision mentally a reference island as it passes under a particular star and from that he computes the number of segments completed, the proportion of the trip remaining, and any corrections in heading.

6. *Interpersonal intelligence* (skills in interacting with others, such as sensitivity to the moods, temperaments, motivations, and intentions of others). Case example:
When Anne Sullivan began instructing the deaf and blind Helen Keller, her task was one that had eluded others for years. Yet, just 2 weeks after beginning her work with Keller, Sullivan achieved a great success. In her words, "My heart is singing with joy this morning. A miracle has happened! The wild little creature of 2 weeks ago has been transformed into a gentle child."

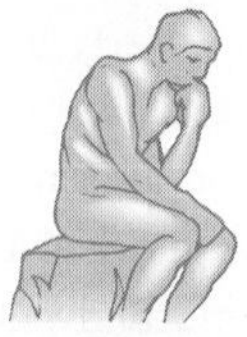

7. *Intrapersonal intelligence* (knowledge of the internal aspects of oneself; access to one's own feelings and emotions). Case example:
In her essay "A Sketch of the Past," Virginia Woolf displays deep insight into her own inner life through these lines, describing her reaction to several specific memories from her childhood that still, in adulthood, shock her: "Though I still have the peculiarity that I receive these sudden shocks, they are now always welcome; after the first surprise, I always feel instantly that they are particularly valuable. And so I go on to suppose that the shock-receiving capacity is what makes me a writer."

8. *Naturalist intelligence* (ability to identify and classify patterns in nature). Case example:
In prehistoric periods, hunter-gatherers required naturalist intelligence in order to identify what types of plants were edible.

FIGURE 8.4 Gardner's Eight Intelligences
Howard Gardner has theorized that there are eight distinct intelligences, each relatively independent of one another. How do you fit into this categorization?
Source: Adapted from Walters & Gardner, 1986.

NEUROSCIENCE AND DEVELOPMENT
When Song Is Silent: Why Amusia Sufferers Can't Hear a Tune

As a preschooler, Alexa put her hands over her ears when her caregiver sang or played music. In third grade her teacher reported that Alexa was disruptive in music class—oftentimes singing the same note louder rather than following the melody of a song. It was not until she participated in a college psychology experiment that Alexa was diagnosed as one of 5 percent of the population with amusia, or tone deafness.

Some people cannot carry a tune, but they still process musical tones normally. In contrast, people with *amusia*, like Alexa, are unable to differentiate pitch and often are unaware when they are singing out of tune. They also may have difficulty recognizing familiar melodies without the assistance of lyrics (Peretz et al., 2009).

New brain imaging research provides insight into the brain's role in amusia. In a recent study, researchers investigated tone deafness and its association with one of the brain's neural highways and major fiber bundles called the arcuate fasciculus (AF). The AF is a white-matter, neural fiber tract that connects the right temporal lobe (where basic sound processing occurs) and frontal brain regions (where higher thinking occurs). It plays a major role in linking music and language perception with vocal production.

In the study, brain scans showed that people with amusia had less neural connectivity in the AF compared to 10 musically normal-functioning people. White matter of the people with amusia was smaller in size and possessed fewer fibers, suggesting a weaker connection. In addition, abnormal AF branching occurred, indicating that dendrites bringing information to the AF cells and axons taking information away from AF cells were less effective in processing music-related information (Loui, Alsop, & Schlaug, 2009).

This study represents the first investigation into the structural and neural correlates of tone deafness. So the next time you hear terrible singing in a karaoke bar, forgive the singer: He or she may be suffering from amusia.

- *Based on these findings, do you think amusia can be corrected? Why or why not?*
- *What suggestions might you give to teachers working with children who are required to take music classes as part of their curriculum?*

Others, in contrast, may show the opposite pattern (Gardner, 2000, 2003; Chen & Gardner, 2005; Gardner & Moran, 2006; also see the *Neuroscience and Development* box.)

The Russian psychologist Lev Vygotsky, whose cognitive development approach we discussed earlier, took a very different approach to intelligence. He suggested that we should assess intelligence by looking not only at fully developed cognitive processes, but at processes in development as well. To do this, he contended that assessment tasks should involve cooperative interaction between the assessed individual and the assessor—a process called *dynamic assessment*. In short, intelligence is reflected both in how children perform on their own and how they perform when helped by adults (Vygotsky, 1927/1976; Brown & Ferrara, 1999; Lohman, 2005).

Psychologist Robert Sternberg (2003a), taking another approach, suggests that intelligence is best viewed as information processing. In this view, how people store material in memory and later use it to solve intellectual tasks provides the most precise concept of intelligence. Rather than focusing on the subcomponents that make up the *structure* of intelligence, information processing approaches examine the *processes* underlying intelligent behavior.

Studies of the nature and speed of problem-solving processes show that people with higher intelligence levels differ from others in the number of problems they solve and the methods they use. People with high IQ scores spend more time on the initial stages of problem solving, retrieving relevant information from memory. In contrast, those who score lower tend to skip ahead and make less informed guesses. The processes used in solving problems may reflect important differences in intelligence (Sternberg, 1982, 1990; Sternberg, Kaufman, & Grigorenko, 2008).

Sternberg's work on information processing approaches led him to develop the triarchic theory of intelligence, which we will look at next.

Smart Thinking: The Triarchic Theory of Intelligence

Your year on the job has been generally favorable. Performance ratings for your department are at least as good as they were before you took over, and perhaps even a little better. You have two assistants. One is quite capable. The other just seems to go through the motions and is of little real help. Even though you are well liked, you believe that there is little that would distinguish you in the eyes of your superiors from the nine other managers at a comparable level in the company. Your goal is rapid promotion to an executive position.

How do you meet your goal? (Based on Wagner & Sternberg, 1985, p. 447)

FROM AN EDUCATOR'S PERSPECTIVE

Does Howard Gardner's theory of multiple intelligences suggest that classroom instruction should be modified from an emphasis on the traditional 3R's of reading, writing, and arithmetic?

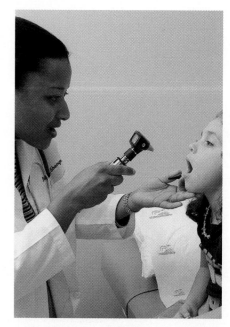

According to Robert Sternberg's triarchic theory of intelligence, practical intelligence is as important as traditional academic intelligence in determining success.

The way adults answer this question may affect their future success. The question is one of a series that psychologist Robert Sternberg designed to assess a particular type of intelligence that may have more of an impact on future success than the IQ measured by traditional tests.

In his **triarchic theory of intelligence**, Sternberg suggests that intelligence is made up of three major components: componential, experiential, and contextual. The *componential aspect* involves the mental components used to solve problems (e.g., selecting and using formulas, choosing problem-solving strategies, and in general making use of what has been learned in the past). The *experiential component* refers to the relationship between intelligence, prior experience, and the ability to cope with new situations. This is the insightful aspect of intelligence, which allows people to relate what they already know to a new situation and facts never before encountered. Finally, the *contextual component* of intelligence takes account of the demands of everyday, real-world environments. For instance, the contextual component is involved in adapting to on-the-job professional demands (Sternberg, 2005).

Traditional IQ tests tend to focus on the componential aspect. Yet increasing evidence suggests that a more useful measure, particularly when comparing and predicting adult success, is the contextual component—the aspect of intelligence that has come to be called practical intelligence.

Practical and Emotional Intelligence. According to Sternberg, traditional IQ scores relate quite well to academic success but not to other types of achievement, such as career success. Although it is clear that success in business requires some level of the IQ sort of intelligence, the rate of career advancement and the ultimate success of business executives is only marginally related to IQ scores (Ree & Carretta, 2002; Cianciolo et al., 2006; Sternberg, 2006).

Sternberg contends that success in a career necessitates practical intelligence (Sternberg et al., 1997). While academic success is based on knowledge obtained largely from reading and listening, **practical intelligence** is learned primarily by observing others and modeling their behavior. People with practical intelligence have good "social radar." They understand and handle even new situations effectively, reading people and circumstances insightfully based on their previous experiences (see Figure 8.5 for sample items from a test of practical intelligence).

There is another related type of intelligence. **Emotional intelligence** is the set of skills that underlies the accurate assessment, evaluation, expression, and regulation of emotions. Emotional intelligence is what enables people to get along well with others, to understand what they are feeling and experiencing, and to respond appropriately to their needs. Emotional intelligence is of obvious value to career and personal success as a young adult (Mayer, Salovey, & Caruso, 2004; Zeidner, Matthews, & Roberts, 2004; Carmeli & Josman, 2006; Sy, Tram, & O'Hara, 2006).

Creativity: Novel Thought. The hundreds of musical compositions of Wolfgang Amadeus Mozart, who died at the age of 35, were largely written during early adulthood. This pattern— major works produced during early adulthood—is true of many other creative individuals (Dennis, 1966a; see Figure 8.6 on page 232).

One reason for the productivity of early adulthood may be that after this period creativity can be stifled by a phenomenon that psychologist Sarnoff Mednick (1963) called "familiarity breeds rigidity." By this he meant that the more people know about a subject, the less likely they are to be creative. Early adulthood may be the peak of creativity because many problems encountered professionally are novel.

On the other hand, many people do not reach their pinnacle of creativity until much later in life. For instance, Buckminster Fuller did not devise the geodesic dome until he was in his 50s. Frank Lloyd Wright designed the Guggenheim Museum in New York at age 70. Charles Darwin and Jean Piaget were still writing influential works well into their 70s, and Picasso was painting in his 90s. Furthermore, overall productivity, as opposed to the period of a person's most important output, remains fairly steady throughout adulthood, particularly in the humanities (Simonton, 1989; Feist & Barron, 2003).

Overall, the study of creativity reveals few consistent developmental patterns. One reason is the difficulty of determining just what constitutes creativity, which is defined as combining

**FROM AN
EDUCATOR'S
PERSPECTIVE**
Do you think educators can teach people to be more intelligent? Are there components or varieties of intelligence that might be more "teachable" than others? If so, which ones: componential, experiential, contextual, practical, or emotional?

triarchic theory of intelligence the belief that intelligence consists of three aspects of information processing: the componential element, the experiential element, and the contextual element.

practical intelligence according to Sternberg, intelligence that is learned primarily by observing others and modeling their behavior.

emotional intelligence the set of skills that underlies the accurate assessment, evaluation, expression, and regulation of emotions.

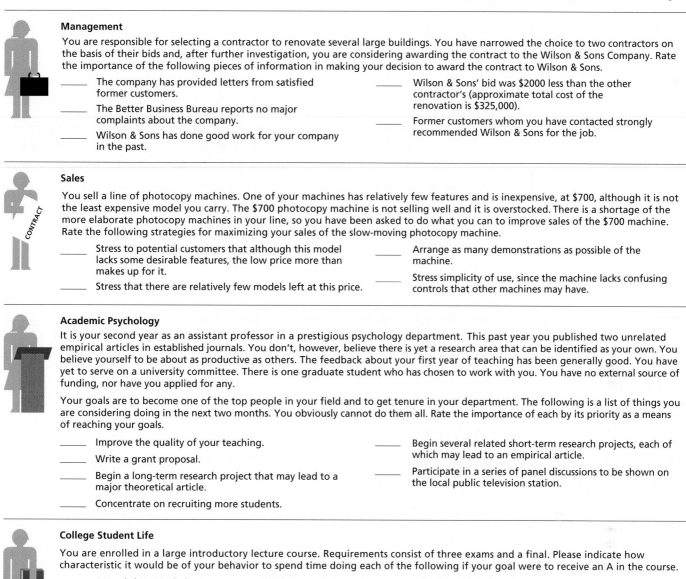

Management

You are responsible for selecting a contractor to renovate several large buildings. You have narrowed the choice to two contractors on the basis of their bids and, after further investigation, you are considering awarding the contract to the Wilson & Sons Company. Rate the importance of the following pieces of information in making your decision to award the contract to Wilson & Sons.

_____ The company has provided letters from satisfied former customers.

_____ The Better Business Bureau reports no major complaints about the company.

_____ Wilson & Sons has done good work for your company in the past.

_____ Wilson & Sons' bid was $2000 less than the other contractor's (approximate total cost of the renovation is $325,000).

_____ Former customers whom you have contacted strongly recommended Wilson & Sons for the job.

Sales

You sell a line of photocopy machines. One of your machines has relatively few features and is inexpensive, at $700, although it is not the least expensive model you carry. The $700 photocopy machine is not selling well and it is overstocked. There is a shortage of the more elaborate photocopy machines in your line, so you have been asked to do what you can to improve sales of the $700 machine. Rate the following strategies for maximizing your sales of the slow-moving photocopy machine.

_____ Stress to potential customers that although this model lacks some desirable features, the low price more than makes up for it.

_____ Stress that there are relatively few models left at this price.

_____ Arrange as many demonstrations as possible of the machine.

_____ Stress simplicity of use, since the machine lacks confusing controls that other machines may have.

Academic Psychology

It is your second year as an assistant professor in a prestigious psychology department. This past year you published two unrelated empirical articles in established journals. You don't, however, believe there is yet a research area that can be identified as your own. You believe yourself to be about as productive as others. The feedback about your first year of teaching has been generally good. You have yet to serve on a university committee. There is one graduate student who has chosen to work with you. You have no external source of funding, nor have you applied for any.

Your goals are to become one of the top people in your field and to get tenure in your department. The following is a list of things you are considering doing in the next two months. You obviously cannot do them all. Rate the importance of each by its priority as a means of reaching your goals.

_____ Improve the quality of your teaching.

_____ Write a grant proposal.

_____ Begin a long-term research project that may lead to a major theoretical article.

_____ Concentrate on recruiting more students.

_____ Begin several related short-term research projects, each of which may lead to an empirical article.

_____ Participate in a series of panel discussions to be shown on the local public television station.

College Student Life

You are enrolled in a large introductory lecture course. Requirements consist of three exams and a final. Please indicate how characteristic it would be of your behavior to spend time doing each of the following if your goal were to receive an A in the course.

_____ Attend class regularly.

_____ Attend optional weekly review sections with the teaching fellow.

_____ Read assigned text chapters thoroughly.

_____ Take comprehensive class notes.

_____ Speak with the professor after class and during office hours.

FIGURE 8.5 Sample Items from a Test That Taps Four Domains of Practical Intelligence
Source: Sternberg & Wagner, 1993.

responses or ideas in novel ways. Because definitions of what is "novel" may vary from one person to the next, it is hard to identify a particular behavior unambiguously as creative (Sasser-Coen, 1993; Kaufman & Sternberg, 2006).

This hasn't stopped psychologists from trying. One suggested component of creativity is a person's willingness to take risks that may yield high payoffs. Creative people are like successful stock market investors who follow the "buy low, sell high" rule. Creative people develop and endorse ideas that are unfashionable or regarded as wrong ("buying low"), assuming that eventually others will see their value and embrace them ("selling high"). According to this theory, creative adults take a fresh look at ideas that were initially discarded, particularly if the problem is a familiar one. They are flexible enough to move away from tried and true ways of doing things and to consider new approaches (Sternberg & Lubart, 1992; Sternberg, Kaufman, & Peretz, 2002).

FIGURE 8.6 Creativity and Age
The period of maximum creativity differs depending on the particular field. The percentages refer to the percent of total lifetime major works produced during the particular age period. Why do poets peak earlier than novelists?
Source: Journal of Gerontology by W. Dennis. Copyright 1966 by The Gerontological Society of America. Reproduced with the permission of The Gerontological Society of America in the format Textbook via Copyright Clearance Center.

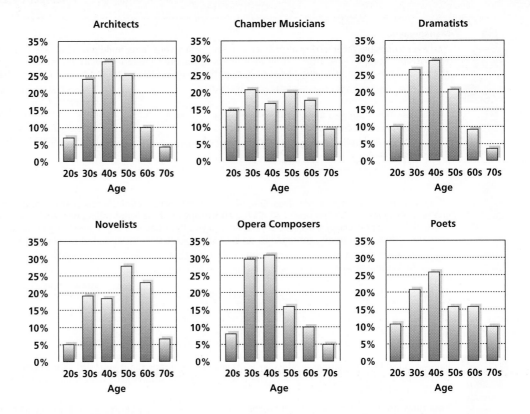

REVIEW

▶ Pinning down the meaning of intelligence and measuring it accurately have proven to be challenging tasks that have occupied psychologists for many years.

▶ The measurement of intelligence began in the twentieth century with the work of Alfred Binet, who took a trial-and-error approach to the question. His work is reflected in the most widely used IQ tests of today.

▶ To Binet we owe three legacies: his pragmatic, nontheoretical approach to intelligence testing; his linkage of intelligence to school success; and his derivation of a mathematical means of classifying children as more or less intelligent according to IQ scores.

▶ Measurements must have both reliability (defined as consistency across persons and over time) and validity (defined as measuring what they claim to measure).

▶ Learning disabilities are defined as difficulties in the acquisition and use of listening, speaking, reading, writing, reasoning, or mathematical abilities.

▶ While they are reasonably predictive of school success, IQ scores fall short in other realms. As a result, a number of alternative conceptions of intelligence have emerged that differentiate different kinds of intelligence.

▶ One of the most successful alternative conceptions is Robert Sternberg's *triarchic theory of intelligence,* which breaks the factor down into componential, experiential, and contextual components.

▶ Creativity is often, though not exclusively, a characteristic of young adults. This appears to be so because young adults' minds are flexible enough to explore novel approaches to problem solving.

APPLY

▶ If a perfectly valid and reliable measure of intelligence were developed, how would it best be used? What uses would be inappropriate?

▶ Do you think that practical and emotional intelligence is distributed equally along gender lines, or do women have more or less of one type than men do? What would be the consequences if the opposite of your answer were true?

MODULE 8.2

Controversies Involving Intelligence

Maddy Rodriguez is a bundle of curiosity and energy. At 6 months of age, she cries heartily if she can't reach a toy, and when she sees a reflection of herself in a mirror, she gurgles and seems, in general, to find the situation quite amusing.

***

Jared Lynch, at 6 months, is a good deal more inhibited than Maddy. He doesn't seem to care much when a ball rolls out of his reach, losing interest in it rapidly. And, unlike Maddy, when he sees himself in a mirror, he pretty much ignores the reflection.

As anyone who has spent any time at all observing more than one baby can tell you, not all infants are alike. Some are full of energy and life, apparently displaying a natural-born curiosity, while others seem, by comparison, somewhat less interested in the world around them. Does this mean that such infants differ in intelligence? This turns out to be a highly controversial subject with potentially devastating effects on children judged less intelligent. Let's see what the data tell us about this and several other issues that illustrate the difficulty in classifying children on the basis of intelligence.

Answering questions about how and to what degree infants vary in their underlying intelligence is not easy. Although it is clear that different infants show significant variations in their behavior, the issue of just what types of behavior may be related to cognitive ability is complicated. Interestingly, the examination of individual differences between infants was the initial approach taken by developmental specialists to understand cognitive development, and such issues still represent an important focus within the field.

What Is Infant Intelligence?

Given the difficulties we discussed earlier in defining intelligence in older children and adults, whose linguistic abilities allow a wide range of measurement techniques, the problem of defining intelligence in infants is even greater. Is infant intelligence the speed with which infants learn a new task through classical or operant conditioning? The rapidity of habituation to stimuli? The age at which an infant learns to crawl or walk? Furthermore, even if we are able to identify particular behaviors that seem validly to differentiate one infant from another in terms of intelligence during infancy, we need to address a further, and probably more important, issue: How well do measures of infant intelligence relate to eventual adult intelligence?

Such questions are not simple, and no simple answers have been found. However, developmental specialists have devised several approaches (summarized in Table 8.1) to illuminate the nature of individual differences in intelligence during infancy.

What is intelligence? Is it doing well on standardized tests or the ability to navigate the sea without modern equipment?

TABLE 8.1	Approaches Used to Detect Differences in Intelligence During Infancy
Developmental quotient	Formulated by Arnold Gesell, the developmental quotient is an overall developmental score that relates to performance in four domains: motor skills (balance and sitting), language use, adaptive behavior (alertness and exploration), and personal–social behavior.
Bayley Scales of Infant Development	Developed by Nancy Bayley, the Bayley Scales of Infant Development evaluate an infant's development from 2 to 42 months. The Bayley Scales focus on two areas: mental (senses, perception, memory, learning, problem solving, and language) and motor abilities (fine and gross motor skills).
Visual-recognition memory measurement	Measures of visual-recognition memory (the memory of and recognition of a stimulus that has been previously seen) also relate to intelligence. The more quickly an infant can retrieve a representation of a stimulus from memory, the more efficient, presumably, is that infant's information processing.

developmental quotient an overall developmental score that relates to performance in four domains: motor skills, language use, adaptive behavior, and personal and social skills.

Bayley Scales of Infant Development a measure that evaluates an infant's development from 2 to 42 months.

Developmental Scales. Developmental psychologist Arnold Gesell formulated the earliest measure of infant development, which was designed to differentiate normally developing babies from those with atypical development (Gesell, 1946). Gesell based his scale on examinations of hundreds of babies. He compared their performance at different ages to learn what behaviors were most common at particular ages. If an infant varied significantly from the norms of a given age, he or she was considered to be developmentally either delayed or advanced.

Gesell's primary motivation in developing his norms was to screen out abnormally developing infants for purposes of adoption. Following the lead of researchers who sought to quantify intelligence through a specific score (an intelligence quotient, or IQ, score), Gesell developed a developmental quotient, or DQ, score. The **developmental quotient** is an overall developmental score that relates to performance in four domains: motor skills (for example, balance and sitting), language use, adaptive behavior (such as alertness and exploration), and personal–social (for example, feeding and dressing). Designed for infants age 2 to 30 months, the DQ provides a summary of an infant's overall competence in comparison to others of a similar age.

Later researchers were motivated by different goals. For instance, Nancy Bayley developed one of the most widely used measures for infants. Like Gesell's DQ, the **Bayley Scales of Infant Development** evaluate an infant's development from 2 to 30 months (Bayley, 1969). The Bayley Scales concentrate on two areas: mental and motor abilities. The mental scale focuses on the senses, perception, memory, learning, problem solving, and language, while the motor scale evaluates fine and gross motor skills (see Table 8.2). Like Gesell's approach, Bayley's yields a developmental quotient (DQ). A child who scores at an average level—meaning average performance for other children at the same age—receives a score of 100.

The virtue of approaches such as those taken by Gesell and Bayley is that they provide a good snapshot of an infant's current developmental level. Using these scales, we can tell in an objective manner whether a particular infant falls behind or is ahead of his or her same-age peers. The scales are particularly useful in identifying infants who are substantially behind their peers and who therefore need immediate special attention (Culbertson & Gyurke, 1990; Blaga et al., 2009).

Except in extreme cases, such scales are not very good at all in predicting a child's future course of intellectual development. An individual whose development at the age of 1 year is relatively slow, as identified by these measures, does not necessarily display slow development at age 5, or 12, or 25. The association between most measures of behavior during infancy and adult intelligence is in fact minimal (DiLalla et al., 1990; Goswami, 2008).

TABLE 8.2	Sample Items from the Bayley Scales of Infant Development	
AGE	**MENTAL SCALE**	**MOTOR SCALE**
2 months	Turns head to sound Reacts to disappearance of face	Holds head erect/steady for 15 seconds Sits with support
6 months	Lifts cup by handle Looks at pictures in book	Sits alone for 30 seconds Grasps foot with hands
12 months	Builds tower of 2 cubes Turns pages of book	Walks with help Grasps pencil in middle
17–19 months	Imitates crayon stroke Identifies objects in photo	Stands alone on right foot Walks up stairs with help
23–25 months	Matches pictures Imitates a 2-word sentence	Laces 3 beads Jumps distance of 4 inches
38–42 months	Names 4 colors Uses past tense Identifies gender	Copies circle Hops twice on 1 foot Walks down stairs, alternating feet

Source: Bayley, N. 7 1993. *Bayley Scales of Infant Development* [BSID-II] 2nd ed., San Antonio, TX: The Psychological Corporation.

Because of the difficulties inherent in using these global measures to obtain measures of infant intelligence that are related to later intelligence, investigators have turned more recently to other techniques that may help assess intelligence in a meaningful way. Some have proven to be quite useful.

Information Processing Approaches to Infant Intelligence. When we speak of intelligence in everyday parlance, we often differentiate between "quick" and "slow" individuals. According to research on the speed of infants' information processing, such terms hold some truth. Contemporary approaches to infant intelligence suggest that the speed with which infants process information may correlate most strongly with later intelligence, as measured by IQ tests administered during adulthood (Rose & Feldman, 1997; Rose, Feldman, & Jankowski, 2004).

For instance, infants who process information efficiently ought to be able to learn about stimuli more quickly. Consequently, we would expect them to turn their attention away from a given stimulus more rapidly than those who are less efficient at information processing. This seems to be the case: Measures of how quickly infants lose interest in stimuli that they have previously seen, as well as their responsiveness to new stimuli, correlate moderately well with later measures of intelligence (Tamis-Lemonda & Bornstein, 1993; Kavšek, 2004).

Similarly, measures of *visual-recognition memory,* the memory of and recognition of a stimulus that has been previously seen, also relate to later IQ. The more quickly an infant can retrieve a representation of a stimulus from memory, the more efficient, presumably, is that infant's information processing. In general, then, infants who are more efficient information processors during the 6 months following birth tend to have higher intelligence scores between 2 and 12 years of age, as well as higher scores on other measures of cognitive competence (Thompson, Fagen, & Fulker, 1991; Rose, Feldman, & Wallace, 1992; Perleth, Lenwald, & Browder, 1993; Rolfe, 1994; Rose & Feldman, 1995; Slater, 1995; Sigman et al., in press).

Other research suggests that abilities related to the *multimodal approach to perception* may offer clues about later intelligence. For instance, the information processing skill of cross-modal transference is associated with intelligence. **Cross-modal transference** is the ability to identify a stimulus that has previously been experienced through only one sense by using another sense. For instance, a baby who is able to recognize by sight a screwdriver that she has previously touched, but not seen, is displaying cross-modal transference. Research has found that the degree of cross-modal transference displayed by an infant at age 1—which requires a high level of abstract thinking—is associated with intelligence scores several years later (Rose et al., 1991, 2004).

Although information processing efficiency and cross-modal transference abilities during infancy relate moderately well to later IQ scores, we need to keep in mind two qualifications. First, even though there is an association between early information processing capabilities and later measures of IQ, the correlation is only moderate in strength. Other factors, such as the degree of environmental stimulation, also play a crucial role in helping to determine adult intelligence. Consequently, we should not assume that intelligence is somehow permanently fixed in infancy.

Second, and perhaps even more important, intelligence measured by traditional IQ tests relates to a particular type of intelligence, one that emphasizes abilities that lead to academic, and certainly not artistic or professional, success. Consequently, predicting that a child may do well on IQ tests later in life is not the same as predicting that the child will be successful later in life.

Still, the findings that an association exists between efficiency of information processing and later IQ scores have changed how we view the consistency of cognitive development across the life span. Whereas the earlier reliance on scales such as the Bayley led to the misconception that little continuity existed, the more recent information processing approaches suggest that cognitive development unfolds in a more orderly, continuous manner from infancy to the later stages of life.

Achievement and Aptitude Tests: How Do They Differ from Intelligence Tests?

IQ tests are not the only tests that children encounter during the course of their schooling. They also take achievement tests and aptitude tests, which are meant to assess characteristics that are somewhat different, though related, to IQ. An **achievement test** is a test intended to determine an individual's level of knowledge in a given subject area. Unlike intelligence tests, which are designed to measure overall, general ability, achievement tests are more targeted to specific areas. For instance, some achievement tests focus on mathematical progress, whereas others look at gains in knowledge of history.

cross-modal transference the ability to identify, using another sense, a stimulus that has previously been experienced only through one sense.

achievement test a test designed to determine a person's level of knowledge in a given subject area.

The issue of whether racial differences in IQ exist is highly controversial and ultimately relates to questions of the genetic and environmental determinants of intelligence.

Aptitude tests are designed to predict ability in a particular subject area or line of work. The emphasis in an aptitude test is on future performance; rather than looking at what children already know, an aptitude test is meant to identify how accomplished they are likely to be in the future. For instance, an aptitude test might be used to identify children who are particularly likely to excel in writing, and based on that information place them in special programs.

Almost all of us had to take one of the two best-known aptitude tests, the *Scholastic Assessment Test (SAT)* or the *American College Test (ACT)*, before entering college. These tests are supposed to predict college-level performance, although the extent to which they predict future success as opposed to past achievement is controversial. The Educational Testing Service, which constructs the SAT, acknowledged the problem several years ago by changing the name of the test from "Scholastic *Aptitude* Test" to the current "Scholastic *Assessment* Test."

Despite the change in name, the controversy continues over whether the SAT is really an aptitude test, predicting future college performance, or, in reality, an achievement test, measuring past performance. In short, the distinction between achievement, aptitude, and intelligence tests is often clearer in theory than in practice.

Group Differences in IQ

A "jontry" is an example of a

    (a) rulpow

    (b) flink

    (c) spudge

    (d) bakwoe

If you found an item composed of nonsense words such as this on an intelligence test, you would likely complain. What sort of intelligence test uses items that incorporate meaningless terms?

Yet for some people, the items used on traditional intelligence tests might appear nonsensical. As a hypothetical example, suppose rural children were asked details about subways, while urban students were asked about the mating practices of sheep. In both cases, we would expect the test-takers' prior experiences to substantially affect their ability to answer the questions. On an IQ test, such questions could rightly be seen as a measure of prior experience rather than of intelligence.

Although traditional IQ tests are not so obviously dependent on test-takers' prior experiences, cultural background and experience can affect test scores. In fact, many educators feel that traditional measures of intelligence subtly favor white, upper- and middle-class students over other cultural groups (Ortiz & Dynda, 2005).

Explaining Racial Differences in IQ. How cultural background and experience affect IQ test scores has led to much debate among researchers, fueled by the finding that certain racial groups' IQ scores are consistently lower, on average, than those of other groups. For example, the mean score of African Americans tends to be about 15 points below the mean score of whites—although the measured difference varies a great deal depending on the IQ test employed (Fish, 2001; Maller, 2003).

The question that emerges from such differences is whether they reflect differences in intelligence or biases in intelligence tests. For example, if whites outperform African Americans on an IQ test because they are more familiar with the language of the test items, the test can hardly be adjudged a fair measure of African Americans' intelligence. Similarly, a test that solely used African American Vernacular English would not be an impartial measure of intelligence for whites.

How to interpret differences between the IQ test scores of different cultural groups is a major controversy in child development: To what degree is intelligence determined by heredity, to what degree by environment? The social implications make this issue important. If intelligence is mostly hereditary and therefore largely fixed at birth, attempts to alter cognitive abilities, such as schooling, will have limited success. If intelligence is largely environmentally determined, modifying social and educational conditions is a more promising strategy to increase cognitive functioning (Weiss, 2003).

aptitude test a test designed to predict a person's ability in a particular area or line of work.

***The Bell Curve* Controversy.** Although the relative contributions of heredity and environment to intelligence have been investigated for decades, the smoldering debate became a raging fire in the 1990s with the publication of a book by Richard J. Herrnstein and Charles Murray (1994), titled *The Bell Curve*. Herrnstein and Murray argue that the average 15-point IQ difference between whites and African Americans is due primarily to heredity. They also argue that this difference accounts for the higher rates of poverty, lower employment, and higher use of welfare among minority groups.

These conclusions met with outrage, and many researchers who examined the data used in the book came to quite different conclusions. Most developmentalists and psychologists argued that racial differences in measured IQ can be explained by environmental differences. In fact, mean IQ scores of black and white children are quite similar when a variety of economic and social factors are statistically taken into account simultaneously. For instance, children from similar middle-class backgrounds, whether African American or white, tend to have similar IQ scores (Brooks-Gunn, Klebanov, & Duncan, 1996; Alderfer, 2003).

Critics also maintained that there is little evidence that lower IQ causes poverty and other social ills. Some critics suggested, as mentioned earlier, that IQ scores were unrelated to later success in life (e.g., McClelland, 1993; Nisbett, 1994; Sternberg, 1995, 1997; Reifman, 2000).

Finally, members of cultural and social minority groups may score lower than those in the majority group due to the biases of the tests. Traditional IQ tests may discriminate against minority groups who lack exposure to the environment majority group members have experienced.

Most traditional IQ tests are constructed using white, English-speaking, middle-class populations as their test subjects. Thus, children from different backgrounds may perform poorly on them—not because they are less intelligent, but because the questions are culturally biased in favor of the majority group. A classic study found that in one California school district, Mexican American students were 10 times more likely than whites to be placed in special education classes (Mercer, 1973). More recent findings show that nationally twice as many African American students as white students are classified as mildly retarded, a difference attributed primarily to cultural bias and poverty (Reschly, 1996; Terman et al., 1996; Ebersole & Kapp, 2007). Although certain IQ tests (such as the System of Multicultural Pluralistic Assessment, or SOMPA) are designed to be valid regardless of cultural background, no test can be completely unbiased (Sandoval et al., 1998).

Most experts were not convinced by *The Bell Curve* contention that genetic factors largely determine differences in group IQ scores. Still, we cannot put the issue to rest because it is impossible to design a definitive experiment to determine the cause of these differences. (One cannot ethically assign children to different living conditions to find the effects of environment, nor genetically control or alter intelligence levels in unborn children.)

Today, IQ is seen as the product of both nature and nurture interacting in a complex manner. Genes are seen to affect experiences, and experiences are viewed as influencing the expression of genes. Psychologist Eric Turkheimer found evidence that while environmental factors play a larger role in the IQ of poor children, genes are more influential for affluent children (Turkheimer et al., 2003).

Ultimately, determining the absolute degree to which intelligence is influenced by genetic and environmental factors may be less important than improving children's living conditions and educational experiences. Enriching the quality of children's environments will better permit all children to reach their full potential and to maximize their contributions to society (Wachs, 1996; Wickelgren, 1999; Posthuma & de Geus, 2006).

Performance on traditional IQ tests is dependent in part on test-takers' prior experiences and cultural background.

Cognitive Functioning in Adulthood

It began innocently enough. Forty-five-year-old Bina Clingman couldn't remember whether she had mailed the letter that her husband had given her, and she wondered, briefly, whether this was a sign of aging. The next day, the question recurred when she spent 20 minutes looking for a phone number she knew she had written down on a piece of paper—somewhere. By the time she found it, she was surprised and even a little anxious. "Am I losing my memory?" she asked herself, feeling both annoyance and a degree of concern.

Many people in their 40s feel more absentminded than they did 20 years earlier, and they have some concern about becoming less mentally able as they age. Common wisdom suggests that

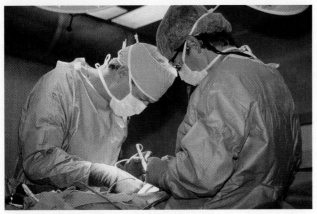

It is difficult to evaluate cognitive abilities in middle adulthood. While some types of mental abilities may begin to decline, crystallized intelligence holds steady and actually may increase.

people lose some mental sharpness in midlife. But how accurate is this notion, and how much of it is a stereotypical view of a much-maligned and much-dreaded age by those who secretly know they will one day soon achieve it—if they're lucky?

The status of intelligence and, more generally, of cognitive functioning as a whole during and beyond middle age remains a controversial topic—nowhere more than in the minds of people who write sitcoms, produce TV commercials, make up jokes, and produce movies. In those environs, people in their middle years are lampooned mercilessly. Among developmentalists, on the other hand, the main controversy revolves around how people in middle age adapt to the changes in their cognitive processing and present themselves as the best representatives of their time.

Does Intelligence Decline in Adulthood? For years, experts provided an unwavering response when asked whether intelligence declined in adulthood: Intelligence peaks at age 18, stays fairly steady until the mid-20s, and then gradually declines until the end of life.

Today, developmentalists view questions about changes in intelligence across the life span as more complicated than that—and they have come to different, and more complex, conclusions.

Cross-Sectional Research. The conclusion that intelligence starts to diminish in the mid-20s was based on extensive research. Cross-sectional studies—which test people of different ages at the same point in time—showed that older subjects were less likely to score well than younger subjects on traditional intelligence tests, of the sort we discussed earlier.

But consider the drawbacks of cross-sectional research in this context—in particular, the possibility that it may suffer from cohort effects. Recall from Chapter 1 that cohort effects are influences associated with growing up at a particular historical time that affect persons of a particular age. For instance, suppose that compared to younger subjects, the older people in a cross-sectional study had had a less adequate education or less stimulating jobs, or were less healthy. In that case, the lower IQ scores of the older group could not be attributed solely, or perhaps even partially, to differences in intelligence based on age. Because they do not control for cohort effects, cross-sectional studies may well underestimate intelligence in older subjects.

Longitudinal Research. To overcome the cohort problems of cross-sectional studies, developmentalists began to use longitudinal studies in which the same people are studied periodically over a span of time. These studies revealed a different developmental pattern for intelligence: Adults tended to show stable and even increasing intelligence test scores until their mid-30s, and in some cases up to their 50s. Then the scores began to decline (Bayley & Oden, 1955).

But let's consider the drawbacks of longitudinal studies, too. People taking an intelligence test repeatedly may perform better because they become familiar—and comfortable—with the testing situation. Similarly, through repeated exposure to the same test, they may begin to remember some of the test items. Consequently, practice effects may account for the superior performance of people on longitudinal measures of intelligence as opposed to cross-sectional measures.

It is also difficult for researchers using longitudinal studies to keep their samples intact. Participants may move away, decide they no longer want to participate, or become ill and die. Over time, the participants who remain may represent a healthier, more stable, and more psychologically positive group of people than those who are no longer part of the sample. If this is the case, longitudinal studies may overestimate intelligence in older subjects.

Crystallized and Fluid Intelligence. Drawing conclusions about age-related changes in intelligence is complicated by the nature of cognitive measures. For instance, many IQ tests include sections based on physical performance, such as arranging a group of blocks. These sections are timed and scored on the basis of how quickly an item is completed. If older people take longer on physical tasks—and as we saw, reaction time slows with age—then their poorer performance on IQ tests may result from physical rather than cognitive changes (Schaie, 1991; Nettelbeck & Rabbit, 1992).

To complicate the issue further, many researchers believe there are age-related changes in the two kinds of intelligence we discussed earlier: fluid intelligence and crystallized intelligence. As we noted earlier, fluid intelligence reflects information processing capabilities, reasoning, and memory. To arrange a series of letters according to some rule or to memorize a set of numbers uses fluid intelligence. In contrast, crystallized intelligence is the information, skills, and strategies that people have accumulated through experience and that they can apply to solve problems. Someone who is solving a crossword puzzle or attempting to identify the murderer in a mystery story is using crystallized intelligence, relying on past experience as a resource.

Researchers once believed that fluid intelligence was largely determined by genetic factors, and crystallized intelligence by experiential, environmental factors. They later abandoned this distinction when they found that crystallized intelligence is determined in part by fluid intelligence. For instance, a person's ability to solve a crossword puzzle (which involves crystallized intelligence) relies on that person's proficiency with letters and patterns (a manifestation of fluid intelligence).

When developmentalists examined the two kinds of intelligence separately, they discovered there are two answers to the question of whether intelligence declines with age: Yes and No. Yes, because fluid intelligence does decline with age; No, because crystallized intelligence holds steady and can actually improve (Ryan, Sattler, & Lopez, 2000; Salthouse, Atkinson, & Berish, 2003; Bugg et al., 2006; see Figure 8.7).

Recent Conclusions About Adult Intelligence. More recent research attempts to address these drawbacks. If we look at more specific types of intelligence, the true nature of age-related differences and developments begins to emerge.

According to developmental psychologist K. Warner Schaie, who has conducted extensive longitudinal research on adult intellectual development, we should consider many types of ability, such as spatial orientation, numeric ability, verbal ability, and so on, rather than the broad divisions of crystallized and fluid intelligence (Schaie, Willis, & Pennak, 2005).

In an ambitious study of intelligence in older people, Schaie used sequential methods, which combine cross-sectional and longitudinal methods by examining several different age groups at a number of points in time.

In Schaie's massive study, carried out in Seattle, Washington, 500 randomly chosen individuals took a battery of tests of cognitive ability. The people belonged to different age groups, starting at age 20 and extending at 5-year intervals to age 70. The participants were tested, and continue to be tested, every 7 years, and more people are recruited every year. At this point, more than 5,000 participants have been tested (Schaie, Willis, & Pennak, 2005).

The study, along with other research, supports several generalizations (Craik & Salthouse, 1999, 2006):

- Some abilities gradually decline starting at around age 25, while others stay relatively steady (see Figure 8.8). There is no uniform pattern of age-related intellectual changes. For example, fluid intelligence (the ability to deal with new problems and situations) declines with age, while crystallized intelligence (the store of information, skills, and strategies that people have acquired) remains steady and in some cases improves (Schaie, 1993).

- On average, some cognitive declines are found in all abilities by age 67, but they are minimal until the 80s. Even at age 81, less than half of the people tested showed consistent declines over the previous 7 years.

- There are also significant individual differences. Some people begin to show declines in their 30s, while others show no declines until their 70s. In fact, around a third of people in their 70s score higher than the average young adult.

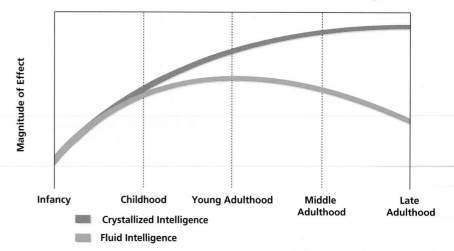

FIGURE 8.7 Changes in Crystallized and Fluid Intelligence
Although crystallized intelligence increases with age, fluid intelligence begins to decline in middle age. What are the implications for general competence in middle adulthood?
Source: From K. W. Schaie, "Longitudinal Studies of Adult Psychological Development," 1985. Copyright © Guilford Press. Reprinted with permission.

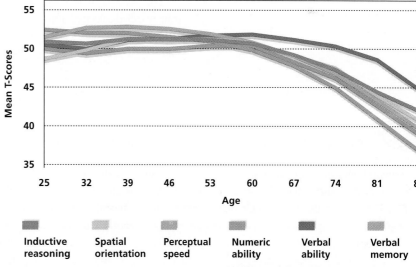

FIGURE 8.8 Changes in Intellectual Functioning
Although some intellectual abilities decline across adulthood, others stay relatively steady.
Source: Changes in Intellectual Functioning from Schaie, K. W. (1994.) "The course of adult intellectual development." P. 307, *American Psychologist,* 49, 403–313. Copyright © 1994 by the American Psychological Association. Reproduced by permission.

• Environmental and cultural factors play a role. People with no chronic disease, higher socioeconomic status (SES), involvement in an intellectually stimulating environment, a flexible personality style, a bright spouse, good perceptual processing speed, and satisfaction with one's accomplishments in midlife or early old age showed less decline.

One reason these changes occur is that brain functioning begins to change in middle adulthood. Researchers have found that 20 genes that are vital to learning, memory, and mental flexibility begin to function less efficiently as early as age 40 (Lu et al., 2004). For tips on keeping your brain sharp, see the *Becoming an Informed Consumer of Development* box.

Reframing the Issue: Focusing on Competence, Not Cognitive Abilities. It is during midlife that people come to hold some of the most important and powerful positions in society, despite gradual declines in certain cognitive abilities. How do we explain such continuing, even growing, competence?

Psychologist Timothy Salthouse (1994a, 2006) suggests that this discrepancy between cognition and competence exists for four reasons. First, it is possible that typical measures of cognitive skills tap a different type of cognition than is required for success in certain occupations. Recall the earlier discussion of practical intelligence, in which we found that traditional IQ tests fail to measure cognitive abilities that are related to occupational success. Perhaps we would find no discrepancy between intelligence and cognitive abilities in midlife if we used measures of practical intelligence rather than traditional IQ tests to assess intelligence.

A second factor also relates to the measurement of IQ and occupational success. It is possible that the most successful middle-aged adults are not representative of midlife adults in general. It may be that only a small proportion of people are highly successful, and the rest, who experience only moderate or little success, have changed occupations, retired, or become sick and died. Highly successful people, then, may be an unrepresentative sample.

Third, the degree of cognitive ability required for professional success may simply not be that high. According to this argument, people can succeed professionally and still be on the decline in certain cognitive abilities. In other words, they have brains to spare.

Finally, perhaps older people are successful because they have developed specific kinds of expertise and particular competencies. Whereas IQ tests measure reactions to novel situations, occupational success may be influenced by very specific, well-practiced abilities. Consequently, middle-aged individuals may maintain and even expand the distinctive talents they need for professional accomplishment, despite a decline in overall intellectual skills.

For example, developmental psychologists Paul Baltes and Margaret Baltes have studied a strategy called selective optimization. *Selective optimization* is the process people use in concentrating on particular skill areas to compensate for losses in other areas. Baltes suggests that cognitive development during middle and later adulthood is a mixture of growth and decline. As

FROM AN
EDUCATOR'S
PERSPECTIVE
How do you think the apparent discrepancy between declining IQ scores and continuing cognitive competence in middle adulthood would affect the learning ability of middle-aged adults who return to school?

BECOMING AN INFORMED CONSUMER OF DEVELOPMENT
Bulking Up the Brain

Research shows that continued intellectual stimulation keeps cognitive abilities sharp; the real threat to older people's cognitive functioning lies in a decline in their opportunities and motivation for cognitive challenges as they pass retirement age. Research provides some suggestions.

• A relatively small investment of time and effort in mental workouts can pay big dividends. Older people don't have to run mental marathons (unless, of course, they want to); they can benefit a great deal from ongoing mental exercise.

• Types of training that have proven effective include memory training, reasoning training, and processing speed training.

• Especially when backed up by booster sessions, the effects of such training appear to be remarkably durable.

• Ongoing mental exercise can result in improved confidence in the ability to perform daily tasks demanding cognition, such as housework, meal preparation, finances, and shopping.

• The self-confidence that may result from mental activities is associated with greater independence, less reliance on health services, and longer life.

• Mental exercise that is performed regularly appears to slow cognitive declines. The key is to perform some form of mental workout consistently and to increase the level of difficulty to sustain a sense of challenge.

people begin to lose certain abilities, they advance in other areas by strengthening skills in those areas. In so doing, they avoid showing any practical deterioration. Overall cognitive competence, then, remains stable and may even improve (Baltes & Carstensen, 2003; Baltes & Freund, 2003; Ebner, Freund, & Baltes, 2006).

REVIEW

▶ Defining infant intelligence is especially challenging, and measuring it even more so. Approaches include developmental scales, which provide good snapshots of an infant's current level of development but are unable to predict future intellectual development.

▶ Information processing approaches—which have a quantitative rather than a qualitative orientation—differentiate more and less intelligent infants by observing the speed at which they process information and learn about stimuli. Visual-recognition memory and cross-modal transference are also regarded as factors in infant intelligence.

▶ A major controversy in the study of intelligence is the role of cultural background in determining IQ. If intelligence levels are determined by nature, academic interventions are of little use. This is the essence of the controversy over the book *The Bell Curve*. However, most developmentalists regard cultural background as unimportant when compared with economic and social background.

▶ The nature and extent of intellectual declines in adulthood and old age are another topic of heated discussion. Some areas of intellectual functioning show marked declines in adulthood, while others are less subject to decline.

▶ Cross-sectional and longitudinal studies are used to address the question of intellectual decline, but both have significant drawbacks. A complicating factor is the fact that intelligence consists of crystallized and fluid components, which show different rates of decline.

▶ The most comprehensive study of the issue ever undertaken—a longitudinal study by developmental psychologist K. Warner Schaie—concludes that certain abilities begin to decline from age 25, while numeric ability increases until the mid-40s and verbal ability rises until about 40 and then holds steady.

APPLY

▶ Why is it important to measure intelligence in infants? What can we find out? What can we do with what we find out?

▶ Can you think of any examples of selective optimization (developing one skill to compensate for losses in another) in areas such as sports, academic study, or the performing arts?

MODULE 8.3

Intellectual Deficits and the Intellectually Gifted

Although Connie kept pace with her peers in kindergarten, by first grade, she was academically the slowest in almost every subject. She tried hard but it took her longer than the others to absorb new material, and she regularly required special attention to keep up with the class.

In some areas, though, she excelled: When asked to draw or produce something with her hands, her performance exceeded her classmates'. She produced beautiful work that was much admired. The other students in the class felt that there was something different about Connie, but they couldn't identify the source of the difference and spent little time pondering the issue.

This boy with mental retardation is mainstreamed into this fifth-grade class.

FROM AN
EDUCATOR'S
PERSPECTIVE
What are some of the challenges of teaching a class that has been mainstreamed? What are some of the advantages?

least restrictive environment the setting most similar to that of children without special needs.

mainstreaming an educational approach in which exceptional children are integrated as much as possible into the traditional educational system and are provided with a broad range of educational alternatives.

full inclusion the integration of all students, even those with the most severe disabilities, into regular classes and all other aspects of school and community life.

mental retardation (or intellectual disability) a state characterized by significant limitations in intellectual functioning and in adaptive behavior involving conceptual, social, and practical skills.

Down syndrome a genetically produced disorder that causes mental retardation.

Connie's parents and teacher knew what made her special. Extensive testing in kindergarten had shown that Connie's intelligence was well below normal, and she was officially classified as a special needs student.

The Least Restrictive Environment

If Connie had been attending school before 1975, she would most likely have been placed in a special needs classroom as soon as her low IQ was identified. Such classes, consisting of students with a range of afflictions, including emotional difficulties, severe reading problems, and physical disabilities such as multiple sclerosis, as well those with lower IQs, were usually kept separate from the regular educational process.

All that changed in 1975 when Congress passed Public Law 94-142, the Education for All Handicapped Children Act. The intent of the law—an intent largely realized—was to ensure that special needs children were educated in the **least restrictive environment**, that is, the setting most similar to that of children without special needs (Yell, 1995).

In practice, the law has integrated children with special needs into regular classrooms and activities to the greatest extent possible, as long as doing so is educationally beneficial. Children are to be removed from the regular classroom only for those subjects specifically affected by their exceptionality; for all other subjects, they are to be taught in regular classrooms. Of course, some children with severe handicaps still need a mostly or entirely separate education. But the law integrates exceptional children and typical children to the fullest extent possible.

This approach to special education, designed to minimize the segregation of exceptional students, is called **mainstreaming**. In mainstreaming, exceptional children are integrated as much as possible into the regular education system and provided with a broad range of alternatives (Hocutt, 1996; Belkin, 2004).

Some professionals promote an alternative model known as **full inclusion**. Full inclusion is the integration of all students, even the most severely disabled, into regular classes, thereby eliminating separate special education programs. Full inclusion is controversial, and it remains to be seen how widespread it will become (Kavale & Forness, 2000; Kavale, 2002; Brehm, 2003; Gersten & Dimino, 2006).

Regardless of whether they are educated using mainstreaming or full inclusion, children whose intelligence is significantly beyond the typical range represent a challenge for educators. We will consider both those who are below and those above the norms.

Below the Norm: Mental Retardation (Intellectual Disability)

Approximately 1 to 3 percent of the school-age population is considered to have mental retardation. **Mental retardation—or intellectual disability**, as it is increasingly being called—is characterized by significant limitations in intellectual functioning and in adaptive behavior involving conceptual, social, and practical skills (AAMR, 2002). (Although experts are increasingly using the term *intellectual disabilities* instead of "mental retardation," our discussion will use the original term because it continues to be more widespread.)

Most cases of mental retardation are classified as *familial retardation*, in which no cause is apparent beyond a history of retardation in the family. In other cases, there is a clear biological cause. The most common such causes are *fetal alcohol syndrome*, resulting from the mother's use of alcohol while pregnant, and **Down syndrome** caused by the presence of an extra chromosome. Birth complications, such as a temporary lack of oxygen, may also produce retardation (Burd, 2003; Plomin, 2005; West & Blake, 2005; Manning & Hoyme, 2007).

Although cognitive limitations can be measured using standard IQ tests, it is more difficult to gauge limitations in other areas. This leads to imprecision in the ways the label "mental retardation" is applied. It also means significant variation exists in the abilities of people categorized as mentally retarded, ranging from those who can be taught to work and function with little special attention to those who are virtually untrainable and who never develop speech or such basic motor skills as crawling or walking.

Some 90 percent of the mentally retarded have relatively low deficit levels. Classified with **mild retardation**, they score in the range of 50 or 55 to 70 on IQ tests. Their retardation may not be identified before they reach school, although their early development is often slower than average. Once they enter school, their retardation and need for special attention usually become apparent, as they did with Connie, the first-grader profiled at the beginning of the module. With appropriate training, these students can reach a third- to sixth-grade level. Although they cannot do complex intellectual tasks, they can hold jobs and function independently and successfully.

Intellectual and adaptive limitations become more apparent at higher levels of mental retardation. People with IQ scores of 35 or 40 to 50 or 55 are classified with **moderate retardation**. The moderately retarded—5 to 10 percent of the mentally retarded population—behave distinctively early in their lives (e.g., they are slow to develop language and motor skills). Regular schooling is seldom effective in teaching academic skills to the moderately retarded because they generally cannot progress beyond a second-grade level. Still, they can learn occupational and social skills, and they can learn to travel independently to familiar places. Typically, they require moderate levels of supervision.

For those classified as **severely retarded** (IQs ranging from 20 or 25 to 35 or 40) and **profoundly retarded** (IQs below 20 or 25), functioning is severely limited. Usually, such people have little or no speech, poor motor control, and may need 24-hour nursing care. At the same time, some people with severe retardation are capable of learning basic self-care skills, such as dressing and eating, and they may become partially independent as adults. Still, they require relatively high levels of care throughout life, and most severely and profoundly retarded people are institutionalized for the majority of their lives.

Above the Norm: The Gifted and Talented

Before her second birthday, Audrey Walker recognized sequences of five colors. When she was 6, her father, Michael, overheard her telling a little boy: "No, no, no, Hunter, you don't understand. What you were seeing was a flashback."

At school, Audrey quickly grew bored as the teacher drilled letters and syllables until her classmates caught on. She flourished, instead, in a once-a-week class for gifted and talented children where she could learn as fast as her nimble brain could take her. (Schemo, 2004, p. A18)

It sometimes surprises people that the gifted and talented are considered to have a form of exceptionality. Yet the 3 to 5 percent of such children present special challenges of their own.

There is no formal definition of gifted and talented students. However, the federal government considers the term *gifted* to include "children who give evidence of high performance capability in areas such as intellectual, creative, artistic, leadership capacity, or specific academic fields, and who require services or activities not ordinarily provided by the school in order to fully develop such capabilities" (Sec 582, P.L. 97-35). In addition to intellectual exceptionality, unusual potential in nonacademic areas is also included in the concept. Gifted and talented children, no less than students with low IQs, warrant special concern—although programs for them are often the first to be dropped when schools face budgetary problems (Robinson, Zigler, & Gallagher, 2000; Schemo, 2004; Mendoza, 2006).

Unsociable Brainiacs or Intelligent, Well-Adjusted People? Despite the stereotype that the gifted are "unsociable," "poorly adjusted," and "neurotic," research suggests that highly intelligent people tend to be outgoing, well adjusted, and popular (Howe, 2004; Bracken & Brown, 2006; Shaunessy et al., 2006).

For instance, one landmark, long-term study of 1,500 gifted students, which began in the 1920s, found that the gifted were healthier, better coordinated, and psychologically better adjusted than their less intelligent classmates. Furthermore, they received more awards and distinctions, earned more money, and made many more contributions in art and literature than the average person. By the time they had reached age 40, they had collectively produced more than 90 books, 375 plays and short stories, and 2,000 articles, and they had registered more than 200 patents. Perhaps not surprisingly, they reported greater satisfaction with their lives than the nongifted (Terman & Oden, 1959; Sears, 1977; Shurkin, 1992; Reis & Renzulli, 2004).

Yet being gifted and talented is no guarantee of school success. The verbal abilities that allow the expression of ideas and feelings can equally voice glib and persuasive statements that happen

mild retardation retardation with IQ scores in the range of 50 or 55 to 70.

moderate retardation retardation with IQ scores from around 35 or 40 to 50 or 55.

severe retardation retardation with IQ scores that range from around 20 or 25 to 35 or 40.

profound retardation retardation with IQ scores below 20 or 25.

acceleration the provision of special programs that allow gifted students to move ahead at their own pace, even if this means skipping to higher grade levels.

enrichment an approach whereby gifted students are kept at grade level but are enrolled in special programs and given individual activities to allow greater depth of study.

to be inaccurate. Furthermore, teachers sometimes misinterpret the humor, novelty, and creativity of unusually gifted children and regard their intellectual fervor as disruptive or inappropriate. And peers may be unsympathetic: Some very bright children try to hide their intelligence in an effort to fit in (Swiatek, 2002).

Educating the Gifted and Talented. Educators have devised two approaches to teaching the gifted and talented: acceleration and enrichment. **Acceleration** allows gifted students to move ahead at their own pace, even if this means skipping grade levels. The materials in acceleration programs are not always different; they may simply be provided at a faster pace than for the average student.

An alternative approach is **enrichment**, through which students are kept at grade level but are enrolled in special programs and given individual activities to allow greater depth of study. In enrichment, the material differs not only in the timing of its presentation, but in its sophistication as well. Thus, enrichment materials are designed to provide an intellectual challenge to the gifted student, encouraging higher-order thinking (Worrell, Szarko, & Gabelko, 2001).

REVIEW

▶ Students with various kinds of exceptionalities receive by federal mandate an education in the least restrictive environment.

▶ Two main ways of providing special education without unduly segregating special needs students are mainstreaming and full inclusion.

▶ IQ scores are also used to classify children with mental retardation. This approach is more useful in measuring cognitive limitations than other limitations. Individuals with mental retardation vary widely across a range of performance and independence levels.

▶ A small but significant sector of students fit into the realm of the gifted and talented. To realize their potential in the school setting, they need special attention and programs, such as acceleration and enrichment programs.

▶ Contrary to stereotypes, gifted and talented individuals tend to be well adjusted and satisfied with their lives.

APPLY

▶ What are some advantages and disadvantages of mainstreaming versus full inclusion? Be sure to address multiple points of view (i.e., the student's, the teacher's, other students', the parents').

▶ Should teacher time and educational resources—both of which are severely limited—be expended on gifted children? What are the ethical issues underlying your response?

Epilogue

We opened the chapter with the question of what intelligence consists of and how it can be defined. We saw some of the ways in which intelligence has been measured, and we considered controversial topics such as group performance differences on IQ tests and the nature of cognitive decline that accompanies aging. Our discussion of intelligence concluded with a look at two groups with intellectual exceptionalities at opposite ends of the intelligence scale: people with mental retardation and people who are gifted or talented. Daniel illustrates how persons with exceptionalities fit (and don't fit) into their worlds.

Think back to the case of 11-year-old Daniel Skandera, who is competent with math games on his computer and yet has Down Syndrome. Daniel illustrates how persons with exceptionalities fit (and don't fit) into their worlds.

1. Does Daniel's love of and skill with computer games tell us anything about his intelligence? How do you think he would do on a traditional IQ test? Why?

2. Is there a fair way to measure Daniel's intelligence? Would Sternberg's triarchic theory work?

3. Is Daniel unique in being comparatively slow in some areas and competent in others? Based on the evidence in the Prologue, does Daniel seem to be a suitable candidate for mainstreaming? For full inclusion?

Looking Back

What is intelligence, and how has it been measured over the years?

1. It is difficult for developmental psychologists to define and measure intelligence. Alfred Binet is responsible for most twentieth-century approaches to the study of intelligence.

2. Binet left three major contributions to the field of intelligence measurement: using a practical, nontheoretical approach; linking intelligence to academic success; and using IQ scores to quantify intelligence.

3. Measurements must be consistent (i.e., have reliability) and measure what they are expected to measure (i.e., have validity).

What are newer conceptions of intelligence, and how are they measured?

4. Alternative conceptions of intelligence have sprung up to explain different kinds of intelligence, including Robert Sternberg's triarchic theory of intelligence, which claims that intelligence is composed of componential, experiential, and contextual components.

5. Creativity is often a young adult trait because young adults' minds are not set in habitual ways of solving problems.

How is the intelligence of infants measured, and does infant intelligence predict adult intelligence?

6. It is particularly difficult to define and measure infant intelligence. Approaches include developmental scales, which provide good cognitive snapshots, and information processing approaches, which focus on the speed at which infants process information and learn about stimuli.

Why do some groups perform better than others on IQ tests, and what do such group differences mean?

7. A major controversy in the study of intelligence is the role of nature versus nurture in IQ. Most developmentalists regard nature as less important than nurture, especially economic and social background.

Does intelligence decline in adulthood and old age? What is the difference between IQ and cognitive competence?

8. Cross-sectional and longitudinal studies, which are used to study intellectual decline, both have disadvantages. Developmental psychologist K. Warner Schaie used longitudinal methods to study intelligence declines comprehensively.

9. Some areas of intellectual function decline in adulthood, but others are less subject to decline. A complicating factor is that the crystallized and fluid components of intelligence decline at different rates.

10. Older people use selective optimization—the practice of concentrating on certain skills to compensate for areas of loss—to maintain high performance.

What sorts of mental exceptionalities do people have, and what assistance do they need and receive?

11. To comply with Public Law 94-142, schools are required to provide students with exceptionalities an education in the least restrictive environment, which may mean mainstreaming or full inclusion.

12. IQ scores focus primarily on academic skills and ignore other aspects of students' abilities.

13. Individuals with mental retardation vary widely across a range of performance and independence levels.

14. A few students may be categorized as gifted or talented and can benefit from special programs such as acceleration and enrichment programs.

15. Contrary to stereotypes, gifted and talented people are usually well adjusted and satisfied with their lives.

Social and Emotional Development

Prologue
The Velcro Chronicles

It was during the windy days of March that the problem in the child-care center first arose. Its source: 10-month-old Russell Ruud. Otherwise a model of decorum, Russell had somehow learned how to unzip the Velcro chin strap to his winter hat. He would remove the hat whenever he got the urge, seemingly oblivious to the potential health problems that might follow.

But that was just the start of the real difficulty. To the chagrin of the teachers in the child-care center, not to speak of the children's parents, soon other children were following his lead, removing their own caps at will. Russell's mother, made aware of the anarchy at the child-care center—and the other parents' distress over Russell's behavior—pleaded innocent. "I never showed Russell how to unzip the Velcro," claimed his mother, Judith Ruud, an economist with the Congressional Budget Office in Washington, D.C. "He learned by trial and error, and the other kids saw him do it one day when they were getting dressed for an outing." (Goleman, 1993, C10)

By then, though, it was too late for excuses: Russell, it seems, was an excellent teacher. Keeping the children's hats on their heads proved to be no easy task. Even more ominous was the thought that if the infants could master the Velcro straps on their hats, would they soon be unfastening the Velcro straps on their shoes and removing them?

Human beings are sociable from a very early age.

As babies like Russell show us, human beings are sociable from a very early age. This anecdote also demonstrates one of the side benefits of even very young children's participation in child care, and something research has begun to suggest: the acquisition of new skills and abilities from more "expert" peers. Children, as we will see, have an amazing capacity to learn from other children, and their interactions with others can play a central role in their developing social and emotional worlds.

In this chapter we consider the foundations of social relationships and how personality develops across the life span. We begin by examining the roots of children's earliest social relationships. We look at how bonds of attachment are forged in infancy and the ways in which children increasingly interact with peers. We also consider what makes a child popular or unpopular and how children can be helped to develop social competence.

We then examine emotional development across the life span, beginning with the emotions infants feel and how well they can decode others' emotions. We look at how children use others to determine how to react, and the development of their ability to express emotions. Next, we discuss the nature and function of emotions in adolescence and see how adolescents learn to regulate their emotions. We also focus on the emotional difficulties adolescents may face, resulting in depression or even suicide, and how suicide can be prevented. We then turn to the relationship between fulfilling psychological needs and happiness in adulthood, and consider what constitutes successful aging.

Finally, we consider personality and the stages of human psychosocial development. We look at the differences among infants, and evaluate the pros and cons of day care for young children. We then examine a variety of theories on how personality develops in adolescence. In closing we review the popular notion of midlife crisis—fact or fiction—and look at the stability of personality in adulthood.

LOOKING AHEAD

After reading this chapter, you will be able to answer the following questions:

▶ What is attachment in infancy, and how does it affect a person's future social competence?

▶ Do infants experience emotions?

▶ What dangers do adolescents face as they deal with the emotional stresses of adolescence?

▶ How do people deal with aging?

▶ What are temperament and personality, and what stages do individuals pass through in their social development?

▶ Is there continuity in personality development during adulthood?

MODULE 9.1

Forging Early Social Relationships

The process of social development begins early and provides the foundation for social relationships throughout a lifetime.

Louis Moore became the center of attention on the way home [from the hospital]. His father brought Martha, aged 5, and Tom, aged 3, to the hospital with him when Louis and his mother were discharged. Martha rushed to see "her" new baby and ignored her mother. Tom clung to his mother's knees in the reception hall of the hospital.

A hospital nurse carried Louis to the car. . . . The two older children immediately climbed over the seat and swamped mother and baby with their attention. Both children stuck their faces into his, smacked at him, and talked to him. They soon began to fight over him with loud voices. The loud argument and the jostling of his mother upset Louis, and he started to cry. He let out a wail that came like a shotgun blast into the noisy car. The children quieted immediately and looked with awe at this new infant. His insistent wails drowned out their bickering. He had already asserted himself in their eyes. (Brazelton, 1983, p. 48)

The arrival of a newborn brings a dramatic change to a family's dynamics. No matter how welcome a baby's birth, it causes a fundamental shift in the roles that people play within the family. Mothers and fathers must start to build a relationship with their infant, and older children must adjust to the presence of a new member of the family and build their own alliance with their infant brother or sister.

Although the process of social development during infancy is neither simple nor automatic, it is crucial: The bonds that grow between infants and their parents, siblings, family, and others provide the foundation for a lifetime's worth of social relationships.

Attachment: Forming Social Bonds

The most important aspect of social development that takes place during infancy is the formation of attachment. **Attachment** is the positive emotional bond that develops between a child and a particular, special individual. When children experience attachment to a given person, they feel pleasure when they are with them and feel comforted by their presence in times of distress. As we'll see in a later chapter, the nature of our attachment during infancy affects how we relate to others throughout the rest of our lives (Fraley, 2002; Grossmann & Waters, 2005; Hofer, 2006).

To understand attachment, the earliest researchers turned to the bonds that form between parents and children in the nonhuman animal kingdom. For instance, ethologist Konrad Lorenz (1965) observed newborn goslings, which have an innate tendency to follow their mother, the first moving object to which they typically are exposed after birth. Lorenz found that goslings whose eggs were raised in an incubator and who viewed him just after hatching would follow his every movement, as if he were their mother. He labeled this process *imprinting:* behavior that takes place during a critical period and involves attachment to the first moving object that is observed.

attachment the positive emotional bond that develops between a child and a particular individual.

Ainsworth Strange Situation a sequence of staged episodes that illustrate the strength of attachment between a child and (typically) his or her mother.

secure attachment pattern a style of attachment in which children use the mother as a kind of home base and are at ease when she is present; when she leaves, they become upset, and they go to her as soon as she returns.

Lorenz's findings suggested that attachment was based on biologically determined factors, and other theorists agreed. For instance, Freud suggested that attachment grew out of a mother's ability to satisfy a child's oral needs.

It turns out, however, that the ability to provide food and other physiological needs may not be as crucial as Freud and other theorists first thought. In a classic study, psychologist Harry Harlow gave infant monkeys the choice of cuddling a wire "monkey" that provided food or a soft, terry cloth monkey that was warm but did not provide food (see Figure 9.1). Their preference was clear: Baby monkeys spent most of their time clinging to the cloth monkey, although they made occasional expeditions to the wire monkey to nurse. Harlow suggested that the preference for the warm cloth monkey provided *contact comfort* (Harlow & Zimmerman, 1959; Blum, 2002).

Harlow's work illustrates that food alone is not the basis for attachment. Given that the monkeys' preference for the soft cloth "mothers" developed some time after birth, these findings are consistent with the research we discussed earlier, showing little support for the existence of a critical period for bonding between human mothers and infants immediately following birth.

The earliest work on human attachment, which is still highly influential, was carried out by British psychiatrist John Bowlby (1951). In Bowlby's view, attachment is based primarily on infants' needs for safety and security—their genetically determined motivation to avoid predators. As they develop, infants come to learn that their safety is best provided by a particular individual. This realization ultimately leads to the development of a special relationship with that individual, who is typically the mother. Bowlby suggested that this single relationship with the primary caregiver is qualitatively different from the bonds formed with others, including the father—a suggestion that, as we'll see later, has been a source of some disagreement.

According to Bowlby, attachment provides a type of home base. As children become more independent, they can progressively roam further away from their secure base.

FIGURE 9.1 Monkey Mothers Matter
Harlow's research showed that monkeys preferred the terry-cloth, soft "mother" over the wire "monkey" that provided food.

The Ainsworth Strange Situation and Patterns of Attachment. Developmental psychologist Mary Ainsworth built on Bowlby's theorizing to develop a widely used experimental technique to measure attachment (Ainsworth et al., 1978; Ainsworth, 1993). The **Ainsworth Strange Situation** consists of a sequence of staged episodes that illustrate the strength of attachment between a child and (typically) his or her mother. The "strange situation" follows this general eight-step pattern: (1) The mother and baby enter an unfamiliar room; (2) the mother sits down, leaving the baby free to explore; (3) an adult stranger enters the room and converses first with the mother and then with the baby; (4) the mother exits the room, leaving the baby alone with the stranger; (5) the mother returns, greeting and comforting the baby, and the stranger leaves; (6) the mother departs again, leaving the baby alone; (7) the stranger returns; and (8) the mother returns and the stranger leaves (Ainsworth et al., 1978; Ainsworth, 1993).

Infants' reactions to the various aspects of the Strange Situation vary considerably, depending on the nature of their attachment to their mothers. One-year-olds typically show one of four major patterns—avoidant, secure, ambivalent, and disorganized-disoriented (summarized in Table 9.1). Children who have a **secure attachment pattern** use the mother as the type of home base that Bowlby described. These children seem at ease in the Strange Situation as long as their mothers are present. They explore independently, returning to her occasionally. Although they

Mary Ainsworth, who devised the Strange Situation to measure infant attachment.

TABLE 9.1	Classification of Infant Attachment			
	CLASSIFICATION CRITERIA			
Label	**Seeking Proximity with Caregiver**	**Maintaining Contact with Caregiver**	**Avoiding Proximity with Caregiver**	**Resisting Contact with Caregiver**
Avoidant	Low	Low	High	Low
Secure	High	High (if distressed)	Low	Low
Ambivalent	High	High (often pre-separation)	Low	High
Disorganized-disoriented	Inconsistent	Inconsistent	Inconsistent	Inconsistent

avoidant attachment pattern a style of attachment in which children do not seek proximity to the mother; after the mother has left, they seem to avoid her when she returns, as if angered by her behavior.

ambivalent attachment pattern a style of attachment in which children display a combination of positive and negative reactions to their mothers; they show great distress when the mother leaves, but upon her return, they may simultaneously seek close contact but also hit and kick her.

disorganized-disoriented attachment pattern a style of attachment in which children show inconsistent, often contradictory behavior, such as approaching the mother when she returns but not looking at her.

may or may not appear upset when she leaves, securely attached children immediately go to her when she returns and seek contact. Most North American children—about two-thirds—fall into the securely attached category.

In contrast, children with an **avoidant attachment pattern** do not seek proximity to the mother, and after she has left, they typically do not seem distressed. Furthermore, they seem to avoid her when she returns. It is as if they are indifferent to her behavior. Some 20 percent of 1-year-old children are in the avoidant category.

Children with an **ambivalent attachment pattern** display a combination of positive and negative reactions to their mothers. Initially, ambivalent children are in such close contact with the mother that they hardly explore their environment. They appear anxious even before the mother leaves, and when she does leave, they show great distress. But upon her return, they show ambivalent reactions, seeking to be close to her but also hitting and kicking, apparently in anger. About 10 to 15 percent of 1-year-olds fall into the ambivalent classification (Cassidy & Berlin, 1994).

Although Ainsworth identified only three categories, a more recent expansion of her work finds that there is a fourth category: disorganized-disoriented. Children who have a **disorganized-disoriented attachment pattern** show inconsistent, contradictory, and confused behavior. They may run to the mother when she returns but not look at her, or seem initially calm and then suddenly break into angry weeping. Their confusion suggests that they may be the least securely attached children of all. About 5 to 10 percent of all children fall into this category (Mayseless, 1996; Cole, 2005).

A child's attachment style would be of only minor importance were it not for the fact that the quality of attachment between infants and their mothers has significant consequences for relationships at later stages of life. For example, boys who are securely attached at the age of 1 year show fewer psychological difficulties at older ages than do avoidant or ambivalent children. Similarly, children who securely attached as infants tend to be more socially and emotionally competent later, and others view them more positively. Adult romantic relationships are associated with the kind of attachment style developed during infancy (Waters et al., 2000; Schneider, Atkinson, & Tardif, 2001; Aviezer, Sagi, & Resnick, 2002; Mikulincer & Shaver, 2005; Simpson et al., 2007).

At the same time, we cannot say that children who do not have a secure attachment style during infancy invariably experience difficulties later in life, nor can we state that those with a secure attachment at age 1 always have good adjustment later on. Some evidence suggests that children with avoidant and ambivalent attachment—as measured by the Strange Situation—do quite well (Lewis, Feiring, & Rosenthal, 2000; Weinfield, Sroufe, & Egeland, 2000; Fraley & Spieker, 2003).

In cases in which the development of attachment has been severely disrupted, children may suffer from *reactive attachment disorder*, a psychological problem characterized by extreme problems in forming attachments to others. In young children, it can be displayed in feeding difficulties, unresponsiveness to social overtures from others, and a general failure to thrive. Reactive attachment disorder is rare and typically the result of abuse or neglect (Hanson & Spratt, 2000; Hardy, 2007).

Producing Attachment: The Roles of the Mother and Father.

As 5-month-old Annie cries passionately, her mother comes into the room and gently lifts her from her crib. After just a few moments, as her mother rocks Annie and speaks softly, Annie's cries cease, and she cuddles in her mother's arms. But the moment her mother places her back in the crib, Annie begins to wail, leading her mother to pick her up once again.

The pattern is familiar to most parents. The infant cries, the parent reacts, and the child responds in turn. Such seemingly insignificant sequences as these, repeatedly occurring in the lives of infants and parents, help pave the way for the development of relationships between children, their parents, and the rest of the social world. We'll consider how each of the major caregivers and the infant play a role in the development of attachment.

In this illustration of the Strange Situation, the infant first explores the playroom on his own, as long as his mother is present. But when she leaves, he begins to cry. On her return, however, he is immediately comforted and stops crying. The conclusion: He is securely attached.

Mothers and Attachment. Sensitivity to their infants' needs and desires is the hallmark of mothers of securely attached infants. Such a mother tends to be aware of her child's moods, and she takes into account her child's feelings as they interact. She is also responsive during face-to-face interactions, provides feeding "on demand," and is warm and affectionate to her infant (Ainsworth, 1993; Thompson, Easterbrooks, & Padilla-Walker, 2003; McElwain & Booth-LaForce, 2006).

It is not only a matter of responding in *any* fashion to their infants' signals that separates mothers of securely attached and insecurely attached children. Mothers of secure infants tend to provide the appropriate level of response. In fact, overly responsive mothers are just as likely to have insecurely attached children as under-responsive mothers. In contrast, mothers whose communication involves *interactional synchrony,* in which caregivers respond to infants appropriately and both caregiver and child match emotional states, are more likely to produce secure attachment (Belsky, Rovine, & Taylor, 1984; Kochanskya, 1998; Hane, Feldstein, & Dernetz, 2003).

Fathers and Attachment. Up to now, we've barely touched on one of the key players involved in the upbringing of a child: the father. If you were to look at the early theorizing and research on attachment, you'd find little mention of the father and his potential contributions to the life of the infant (Tamis-LeMonda & Cabrera, 1999; Tamis-LeMonda, 2004).

However, it has become increasingly clear that—despite societal norms that sometimes relegate fathers to secondary childrearing roles—infants can form their primary initial relationship with their fathers For example, fathers' expressions of nurturance, warmth, affection, support, and concern are extremely important to their children's emotional and social well-being. Furthermore, some psychological disorders, such as substance abuse and depression, have been found to be related more to fathers' than mothers' behavior (Veneziano, 2003; Parke, 2004; Roelofs et al., 2006).

A growing body of research highlights the importance of a father's demonstration of love for his children. In fact, certain disorders such as depression and substance abuse have been found to be more related to fathers' than to mothers' behavior.

DEVELOPMENTAL DIVERSITY
Does Attachment Differ Across Cultures?

John Bowlby's observations of the biologically motivated efforts of the young of other species to seek safety and security were the basis for his views on attachment. His observations also led him to suggest that seeking attachment was a biologically universal tendency that we should find not only in other species, but among humans of all cultures as well.

However, research has shown that human attachment is not as culturally universal as Bowlby predicted. Certain attachment patterns seem more likely among infants of particular cultures. For example, one study of German infants showed that most subjects fell into the avoidant category. Other studies, conducted in Israel and Japan, have found a smaller proportion of infants who were securely attached than in the United States. Finally, comparisons of Chinese and Canadian children show that Chinese children are more inhibited than Canadians in the Strange Situation (Rothbaum et al., 2000; Ijzendoorn, Bakermans-Kranenburg, & Sagi-Schwartz, 2006).

Do such findings suggest that we should abandon the notion that attachment is a universal biological tendency? Not necessarily. Most of the data on attachment have been obtained by using the Ainsworth Strange Situation, which may not be the most appropriate measure in non-Western cultures. For example, Japanese parents seek to avoid separation and stress during infancy, and they don't strive to foster independence to the same degree as parents in many Western societies. Because of their relative lack of prior experience in separation, then, infants placed in the Strange Situation may experience unusual stress—producing the appearance of less secure attachment in Japanese children. If a different measure of attachment were used, one that might be administered later in infancy, more Japanese infants could likely be classified as secure. In short, attachment is affected by cultural norms and expectations (Nakagawa, Lamb, & Miyaki, 1992; Vereijken et al., 1997; Dennis, Cole, & Zahn-Waxler, 2002).

Japanese parents seek to avoid separation and stress during infancy and do not foster independence. As a result, Japanese children often have the appearance of being less securely attached according to the Strange Situation, but using other measurement techniques they may well score higher in attachment.

Infants' Sociability with Their Peers: Infant–Infant Interaction

How sociable are infants with other children? Although it is clear that they do not form "friendships" in the traditional sense, babies do react positively to the presence of peers from early in life, and they engage in rudimentary forms of social interaction.

Infants' sociability is expressed in several ways. From the earliest months of life, they smile, laugh, and vocalize while looking at their peers. They show more interest in peers than in inanimate objects and pay greater attention to other infants than they do to a mirror image of themselves. They also begin to show preferences for peers with whom they are familiar compared with those they do not know. For example, studies of identical twins show that twins exhibit a higher level of social behavior toward each other than toward an unfamiliar infant (Legerstee, Anderson, & Schaffer, 1998; Sanefuji, Ohgami, & Hashiya, 2006).

Infants' level of sociability rises with age. For instance, 9- to 12-month-olds mutually present and accept toys, particularly if they know each other. They also play social games, such as peek-a-boo or crawl-and-chase. Such behavior is important, as it serves as a foundation for future social exchanges in which children will try to elicit responses from others and then offer reactions to those responses. These kinds of exchanges are important to learn because they continue even into adulthood. For example, someone who says, "Hi, what's up?" may be trying to elicit a response to which he or she can then reply (Endo, 1992; Eckerman & Peterman, 2001).

Finally, as infants age, they begin to imitate each other. For instance, 14-month-old infants who are familiar with one another sometimes reproduce each other's behavior. Such imitation serves a social function and can also be a powerful teaching tool (Jones, 2007; Buttelmann et al., 2008; Hamlin, Hallinan, & Woodward, 2008).

To some developmentalists, the capacity of young children to engage in imitation suggests that imitation may be inborn. In support of this view, research has identified a class of neurons in the brain that seems related to an innate ability to imitate. *Mirror neurons* are neurons that fire not only when an individual enacts a particular behavior, but also when the individual simply observes *another* organism carrying out the same behavior (Falck-Ytter, 2006).

For example, research on brain functioning shows activation of the inferior frontal gyrus both when an individual carries out a particular task and also when observing another individual carrying out the same task. Mirror neurons may help infants to understand others' actions and to develop a *theory of mind*, their understanding and beliefs of how the mind operates. Dysfunction of mirror neurons may be related to the development of disorders involving children's theory of mind (a concept we'll discuss later) as well as autism, a psychological disorder involving significant emotional and linguistic problems (Dapretto et al., 2006; Kilner, Friston, & Frith, 2007).

REVIEW

▶ Attachment, the positive emotional bond between an infant and a significant individual, affects a person's later social competence as an adult.

▶ Infants and the persons with whom they interact engage in reciprocal socialization as they mutually adjust to one another's interactions.

APPLY

▶ In what sort of society might an avoidant attachment style be encouraged by cultural attitudes toward childrearing? In such a society, would characterizing the infant's consistent avoidance of its mother as anger be an accurate interpretation?

MODULE 9.2

Emotional Development

Germaine smiles when he catches a glimpse of his mother. Tawanda looks angry when her mother takes away the spoon that she is playing with. Sydney scowls when a loud plane flies overhead.

A smile. A look of anger. A scowl. The emotions of infancy are written all over a baby's face. Yet do infants experience emotions in the same way that adults do? When do they become capable of understanding what others are experiencing emotionally? And how do they use others' emotional states to make sense of their environment? We consider some of these questions as we seek to understand how infants develop emotionally and socially.

Emotions in Infancy: Do Infants Experience Emotional Highs and Lows?

Anyone who spends any time at all around infants knows they display facial expressions that seem indicative of their emotional states. In situations in which we expect them to be happy, they seem to smile; when we might assume they are frustrated, they show anger; and when we might expect them to be unhappy, they look sad.

These basic facial expressions are remarkably similar across the most diverse cultures. Whether we look at babies in India, the United States, or the jungles of New Guinea, the expression of basic emotions is the same (see Figure 9.2). Furthermore, the nonverbal expression of emotion, called *nonverbal encoding,* is fairly consistent among people of all ages. These consistencies have led researchers to conclude that we are born with the capacity to display basic emotions (Scharfe, 2000; Sullivan & Lewis, 2003; Ackerman & Izard, 2004).

Infants display a fairly wide range of emotional expressions. Almost all mothers report that by the age of 1 month their babies nonverbally have expressed interest and joy. Careful coding of infants' nonverbal expressions shows that interest, distress, and disgust are present at birth, and that other emotions emerge over the next few months. Such findings are consistent with the work of the famous naturalist Charles Darwin, whose 1872 book *The Expression of the Emotions in Man and Animals* argued that humans and primates have an inborn, universal set of emotional expressions—a view consistent with today's evolutionary approach to development (Izard, 1982; Sroufe, 1996; Benson, 2003).

Although infants display similar *kinds* of emotions, the *degree* of emotional expressivity varies among infants. Children in different cultures show reliable differences in emotional expressiveness, even during infancy. For example, by the age of 11 months, Chinese infants are generally less expressive than European, American, and Japanese infants (Camras, Meng, & Ujiie, 2002; Izard et al., 2003; Buss & Kiel, 2004).

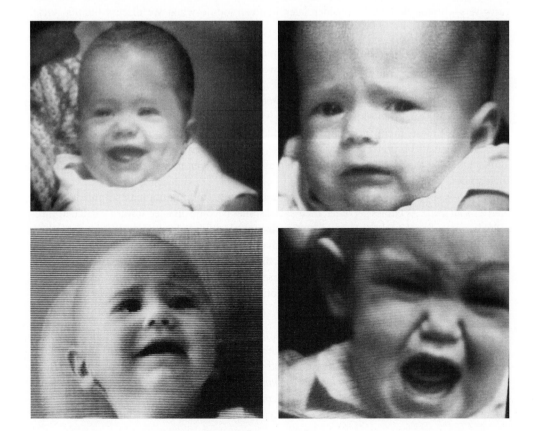

FIGURE 9.2 Universals in Facial Expressions
Across every culture, infants show similar facial expressions relating to basic emotions. Do you think such expressions are similar in nonhuman animals?

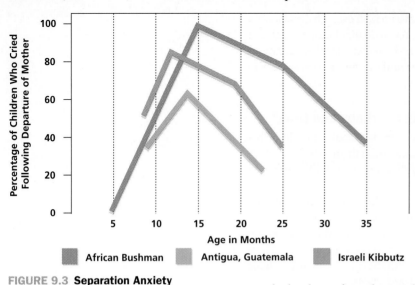

FIGURE 9.3 **Separation Anxiety**
Separation anxiety, the distress displayed by infants when their usual care provider leaves their presence, is a universal phenomenon beginning at around the age of 7 or 8 months. It peaks at around the age of 14 months and then begins to decline. Does separation anxiety have survival value for humans?
Source: Kagan, Kearsley, & Zelazo, 1978.

Has your virtual child shown any stranger anxiety? How are you addressing it? To see a child display stranger anxiety, watch the video in **MyDevelopmentLab**.

stranger anxiety the caution and wariness displayed by infants when encountering an unfamiliar person.

separation anxiety the distress displayed by infants when a customary care provider departs.

Stranger Anxiety and Separation Anxiety. "She used to be such a friendly baby," thought Erika's mother. "No matter who she encountered, she had a big smile. But almost the day she turned 7 months old, she began to react to strangers as if she were seeing a ghost. Her face crinkles up with a frown, and she either turns away or stares at them with suspicion. It's as if she has undergone a personality transplant."

What happened to Erika is, in fact, quite typical. By the end of the first year, infants often develop both stranger anxiety and separation anxiety. **Stranger anxiety** is the caution and wariness displayed by infants when encountering an unfamiliar person. Such anxiety typically appears in the second half of the first year.

What brings on stranger anxiety? Brain development, and the increased cognitive abilities of infants, play a role. As infants' memory develops, they are able to separate the people they know from the people they don't. The same cognitive advances that allow them to respond so positively to those people with whom they are familiar also give them the ability to recognize people who are unfamiliar. Furthermore, between 6 and 9 months, infants begin trying to make sense of their world, trying to anticipate and predict events. When something happens that they don't expect—such as the appearance of an unknown person—they experience fear (Ainsworth, 1973; Kagan, Kearsley, & Zelazo, 1978).

Separation anxiety is the distress displayed by infants when a customary care provider departs. Separation anxiety, which is also universal across cultures, usually begins at about 7 or 8 months (see Figure 9.3). It peaks around 14 months and then decreases. Separation anxiety is largely attributable to the same reasons as stranger anxiety. Infants' growing cognitive skills allow them to ask reasonable questions, but they may be questions that they are too young to understand the answer to: "Why is my mother leaving?" "Where is she going?" and "Will she come back?"

Stranger anxiety and separation anxiety represent important social progress. They reflect both cognitive advances and the growing emotional and social bonds between infants and their caregivers—bonds that we'll consider later in the module when we discuss infants' social relationships.

Smiling. As Luz lay sleeping in her crib, her mother and father caught a glimpse of the most beautiful smile crossing her face. Her parents were sure that Luz was having a pleasant dream. Were they right?

Probably not. The earliest smiles expressed during sleep probably have little meaning, although no one can be absolutely sure. By 6 to 9 weeks babies begin to smile reliably at the sight of stimuli that please them, including toys, mobiles, and—to the delight of parents—people. The first smiles tend to be relatively indiscriminate, as infants first begin to smile at the sight of almost anything they find amusing. However, as they get older, they become more selective in their smiles.

A baby's smile in response to another person, rather than to nonhuman stimuli, is considered a *social smile*. As babies get older, their social smiles become directed toward particular individuals, not just anyone. By the age of 18 months, social smiling, directed more toward mothers and other caregivers, becomes more frequent than smiling directed toward nonhuman objects. Moreover, if an adult is unresponsive to a child, the amount of smiling decreases. In short, by the end of the second year children are quite purposefully using smiling to communicate their positive emotions, and they are sensitive to the emotional expressions of others (Bigelow & Rochat, 2006; Fogel et al., 2006).

Decoding Others' Facial Expressions. Earlier, we discussed the possibility that neonates can imitate adults' facial expressions even minutes after birth. Although their imitative abilities certainly do not imply that they can understand the meaning of others' facial expressions, such imitation does pave the way for *nonverbal decoding* abilities, which begin to emerge fairly soon. Using these abilities, infants can interpret others' facial and vocal expressions that carry emotional meaning. For example, they can tell when a caregiver is happy to see them and pick up on worry or fear in the faces of others (Bornstein & Arterberry, 2003; Hernandez-Reif et al., 2006; Striano & Vaish, 2006).

In the first 6 to 8 weeks, infants' visual precision is sufficiently limited that they cannot pay much attention to others' facial expressions. But they soon begin to discriminate among different facial expressions of emotion and even seem to be able to respond to differences in emotional intensity conveyed by facial expressions. By the time they reach the age of 4 months, infants already have begun to understand the emotions that lie behind the facial and vocal expressions of others (Nelson, 1987; Adamson & Frick, 2003; Bertin & Striano, 2006).

In sum, infants learn early both to produce and to decode emotions, and they begin to learn the effect of their own emotions on others. Such abilities play an important role not only in helping them experience their own emotions, but—as we see next—in using others' emotions to understand the meaning of ambiguous social situations (Buss & Kiel, 2004).

Social Referencing: Feeling What Others Feel

Twenty-three-month-old Stephania watches as her older brother Eric and his friend Chen argue loudly with each other and begin to wrestle. Uncertain of what is happening, Stephania glances at her mother. Her mother, though, wears a smile, knowing that Eric and Chen are just playing. On seeing her mother's reaction, Stephania smiles too, mimicking her mother's facial expression.

Like Stephania, most of us have been in situations in which we feel uncertain. In such cases, we sometimes turn to others to see how they are reacting. This reliance on others, known as social referencing, helps us decide what an appropriate response ought to be.

Social referencing is the intentional search for information about others' feelings to help explain the meaning of uncertain circumstances and events. Like Stephania, we use social referencing to clarify the meaning of a situation and so to reduce our uncertainty about what is occurring.

Social referencing first occurs around the age of 8 or 9 months. It is a fairly sophisticated social ability: Infants need it not only to understand the significance of others' behavior, by using such cues as their facial expressions, but also understand the meaning of those behaviors within the context of a specific situation (Mumme & Fernald, 2003; de Rosnay, Cooper, Tsigaras, & Murray, 2006; Carver & Vaccaro, 2007).

Theory of Mind: Understanding What Others Are Thinking. As the brain matures and myelination within the frontal lobes becomes more pronounced, children develop more emotional capacity involving self-awareness. In addition, hormonal changes seem to be related to emotions that are more evaluative in nature (Davidson, 2003; Schore, 2003).

As they develop, children become more insightful regarding the motives and reasons behind people's behavior. They begin to understand that their mother is angry because she was late for an appointment, even if they themselves haven't seen her be late. Furthermore, by the age of 4, preschool-age children's understanding that people can be fooled and mistaken by physical reality (such as magic tricks involving sleight of hand) becomes surprisingly sophisticated. This increase in understanding helps children become more socially skilled as they gain insight into what others are thinking (Fitzgerald & White, 2002; Eisbach, 2004).

There are limits, however, to 3-year-olds' theory of mind. Although they understand the concept of "pretend" by the age of 3, their understanding of "belief" is still not complete. The difficulty experienced by 3-year-olds in comprehending "belief" is illustrated by their performance on the *false belief* task. In the false belief task, preschoolers are shown a doll named Maxi who places chocolate in a cabinet and then leaves. After Maxi is gone, though, his mother moves the chocolate somewhere else.

After viewing these events, a preschooler is asked where Maxi will look for the chocolate when he returns. Three-year-olds answer (erroneously) that Maxi will look for it in the new location. In contrast, 4-year-olds correctly realize that Maxi has the erroneous false belief that the chocolate is still in the cabinet, and that's where he will look for it (Ziv & Frye, 2003; Flynn, O'Malley, & Wood, 2004; Amsterlaw & Wellman, 2006; Brown & Bull, 2007).

By the end of the preschool years, most children easily solve false belief problems. One group, however, has considerable difficulties throughout their lifetimes: children with autism. *Autism* is a psychological disorder that produces significant language and emotional difficulties.

When infants smile at a person, rather than a nonhuman stimulus, they are displaying a social smile.

After reading about social referencing, watch how it operates in the video in **MyDevelopmentLab**.

FROM A
SOCIAL WORKER'S
PERSPECTIVE

In what situations do adults rely on social referencing to work out appropriate responses? How might social referencing be used to influence parents' behavior toward their children?

Watch a child display separation anxiety in the video in **MyDevelopmentLab**. Has your virtual child experienced separation anxiety? How will you handle outside child care?

social referencing the intentional search for information about others' feelings to help make sense of uncertain circumstances and events.

Children with autism find it particularly difficult to relate to others, in part because they cannot understand what others are thinking. Occurring in about 4 in 10,000 people, particularly males, autism is characterized by a lack of connection to other people, even parents, and an avoidance of interpersonal situations. Individuals with autism are bewildered by false belief problems no matter how old they are (Begeer et al., 2003: Heerey, Keltner, & Capps, 2003; Ropar, Mitchell, & Ackroyd, 2003).

Emotional Development in Middle Childhood

During middle childhood, children's control of their emotions grows. They begin to understand their emotions better, and they are more successful in coping with their emotional highs and lows (Eisenberg, Spinrad, & Sadovsky, 2006; Rothbart, Posner, & Kieras, 2006).

In addition, children become more adept at hiding their emotions from others. Rather than showing their displeasure over a disappointing gift, they learn to hide it in a socially acceptable way. Similarly, they learn to hide their anger with a teacher who is treating them unfairly (Ruihe & Guoliang, 2006; Feldman, 2009).

Children also develop empathy, in which they genuinely experience the emotions of others. Because their cognitive abilities are growing, they are able to take the perspective of other children and understand how events are affecting them. For example, a 10-year-old boy may be able to understand the sadness experienced by a classmate whose father has died, and feel that sadness himself (Eisenberg & Fabes, 2006; Oguz & Akyol, 2008).

Emotional Development in Adolescence

Sometimes I have to stop and ask myself what kind of mood I'm in. Am I happy? sad? contemplative? usually contemplative, if I'm bothering to contemplate what kind of mood I'm in. I'm kind of sad because Kyle can't come tonight. . . , but kind of worried because he's sick. I'm kind of depressed feeling, too. It finally started sinking in a while ago that he's not coming back, that he has finally dropped out of my life as I feared he would.

Happy. . . sad. . . contemplative. . . worried. . . depressed. . . afraid. The feelings experienced by adolescents range from the positive to the negative, as this blog comment illustrates. Traditionally, the adolescent period is viewed as among the most emotionally volatile of the entire life span.

How accurate is this view? To answer the question, we first need to consider the role that emotions play during adolescence. For example, consider an adolescent girl who is experiencing sadness. As the definition suggests, sadness produces a feeling that can be differentiated from other emotions. She likely experiences physiological reactions, too, such as an increase in heart rate or sweating, that are part of her emotional reaction. In addition, the sadness has a cognitive element, in which her understanding and evaluation of the meaning of what is happening to her prompt her feelings of sadness.

It's also possible, however, to experience an emotion without the presence of cognitive elements. For example, adolescents may feel the sadness of depression without knowing why they are feeling that way. In the same way, they may react with fear to an unusual or a novel situation without having an awareness or understanding of what is so frightening.

The Instability of Emotions in Adolescence. Are adolescent emotions more volatile than emotions at other stages of life? That's certainly the stereotype. Adolescence has traditionally been seen as a period in which emotions run high and are easily triggered.

The stereotype does have some truth to it. Although not as extreme as the outmoded "storm and stress" view of adolescence would have us believe, emotions do tend to be more volatile during early adolescence. Younger adolescents experience emotional highs and lows, often in rapid succession. In addition, as they enter adolescence, teenagers report that they are less happy than in prior years. They are also more likely to experience mildly negative emotions as they move into adolescence (Larson & Lampman-Petraitis, 1989; Roenbaum & Lewis, 2003; Ackerman & Izard, 2004).

Not only are the emotions more negative than they were in middle childhood, but adolescents' emotional responses are often more extreme than one would expect from the nature of the situation. For example, an adolescent may react with fury to a parent's suggestion that he might consider wearing a jacket to school because it is chilly. Even seemingly innocuous suggestions may be viewed as critical and arouse extremes of emotion.

If there is a positive side to the more explosive nature of adolescents' emotions, it is that even though they may be extreme, they don't necessarily last very long. Partly because adolescents' moods change so frequently, any given emotional response is apt to be replaced by another before much time passes (Rosenbaum & Lewis, 2003).

Why are emotions so unstable during adolescence? One answer comes from work on the neurological underpinnings of emotion, which we discuss next.

The Neurological Basis of Emotion.   Emotions produce activation of specific parts of the brain. For instance, the *amygdala*, located in the brain's temporal lobe, is central to the experience of emotions. It provides a link between the perception of an emotion-producing stimulus and later memory of that stimulus. For example, someone who was once frightened by a vicious dog is likely to respond with fear when he later sees the dog. Because of neural pathways connecting the amygdala, visual cortex, and the *hippocampus* (a part of the brain that is involved in the storage of memories), the emotion of fear is experienced almost instantly. The response occurs so quickly that rational thought may not be involved at first—the fear response is literally a kind of "gut reaction" produced by the brain. It is only later that the response will be evaluated more thoroughly using rational thought processes (Adolphs, 2002; Dolan, 2002; Monk et al., 2003).

Studies of brain activity help explain the greater volatility of emotions in adolescence than later in life. For example, in one study, adolescents and adults repeatedly viewed faces showing different emotions. Although both age groups showed engagement of the *left ventrolateral prefrontal cortex*, adolescents showed more activity in certain other areas of the brain when viewing familiar faces, depending on the kind of emotion being displayed (see Figure 9.4). These differences suggest that emotional responses may be especially pronounced during adolescence and affect the rationality of adolescents' evaluation of the challenges they encounter and their responses to them (Nelson et al., 2003; also see the *Neuroscience and Development* box).

On the other hand, the physiological reactivity of emotions is not the full story of emotional responses during adolescence. As we'll see next, adolescents have considerable (and increasing) control over their emotions.

Emotional Self-Regulation.   Throughout adolescence, both boys and girls become more adept at controlling their emotions. **Emotional self-regulation** is the ability to adjust emotions to a desired state and level of intensity. When adolescents seek to "keep cool," they are relying on emotional self-regulation.

It's not easy for any of us to regulate our emotions. For example, people asked to hide their responses to the observation of gruesome photos of accident victims show high levels of

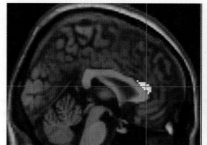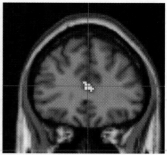

FIGURE 9.4
Brain Activity and Emotions
Although both adolescents and adults viewing pictures of faces displaying different emotions showed activation of the left ventrolateral prefrontal cortex, compared with adults, adolescents showed more activity thsn aduts in other areas of the brain.
Source: Nelson et al., 2003. *Journal of Child Psychology and Psychiatry* 44, 1020, bottom of Figure 2.

emotional self-regulation   the capability to adjust one's emotions to a desired state and level of intensity.

NEUROSCIENCE AND DEVELOPMENT
Aging and Emotional Regulation: It's All in Your Brain

If they are healthy, your grandparents may well be happier than you are. Or at least, that's how they remember the past. Specifically, people show a shift toward memory for positive materials in late adulthood, and the ability to regulate emotions often improves across the adult life span (Schulz & Janowsky, 2004; Neiss et al., 2009).

But what underlying neural networks contribute to more positive recollections as people age? To answer this question, neuroscientist Peggy St. Jacques and colleagues showed emotional pictures to younger and older adults while monitoring their brain activity using fMRI scanning. They found that both younger and older groups could accurately evaluate the negative pictures, but the older adults' evaluations were less negative. Furthermore, older adults

experienced increased functional connectivity between those parts of the brain that contribute to emotional detection (like the amygdala) and emotional control (like some prefrontal cortex regions, including the hippocampus), possibly reflecting increased emotional regulation. At the same time, older adults showed decreased functional connectivity with other brain regions involved with perceptual functions, illustrating the age-related differences in the use of regulatory processes that inhibit emotional responses (St. Jacques, Dolcos, & Cabeza, 2009).

• *How might the findings on the development of greater emotional regulation be of relevance to treating depression in older people?*

physiological reactivity as a result of their efforts to suppress their actual emotion. They also have difficulty later in recalling what they viewed. In short, emotional regulation takes both cognitive and physical effort (Richards & Gross, 2000; Richards, Butler, & Gross, 2003; Osher & Gross, 2005).

During childhood, emotional regulation skills improve considerably, and that trend continues throughout adolescence. The demands and challenges that adolescents face lead to improvements in emotion management (Zahn-Waxler et al., 2000; Eisenberg, Sprinrad, & Smith, 2004; Graber, 2004).

Adolescents use several strategies to regulate their emotional responses. One is to try to cognitively reappraise events that produce emotional responses. Specifically, they may try to change the way they think about something they have encountered, making it seem less bothersome. For example, an adolescent might try to convince himself that his girlfriend's decision to break up is really a good thing because he didn't like being tied down. If he is able to convince himself of this rationale, his initial sadness or anger might be replaced with more positive (or at least neutral) emotions.

Another emotion-regulating strategy that adolescents can use is to suppress troubling emotions. Using such a strategy involves inhibiting outward signs of inner emotional states, despite experiencing particular emotions internally. Although such a strategy may not make the individuals who are suppressing the emotion feel better about negative emotions they might be experiencing, it can be effective in making others feel better. Learning to "put on" a face appropriate to a particular social situation is an important advance in emotional self-regulation that occurs during adolescence.

Emotional Difficulties in Adolescence: Depression and Suicide.

> Brianne Camilleri had it all: Two involved parents, a caring older brother and a comfortable home near Boston. But that didn't stop the overwhelming sense of hopelessness that enveloped her in ninth grade. "It was like a cloud that followed me everywhere," she says. "I couldn't get away from it."
>
> Brianne started drinking and experimenting with drugs. One Sunday she was caught shoplifting at a local store and her mother, Linda, drove her home in what Brianne describes as a "piercing silence." With the clouds in her head so dark she believed she would never see light again, Brianne went straight for the bathroom and swallowed every Tylenol and Advil she could—a total of 74 pills. She was only 14, and she wanted to die. (Wingert & Kantrowitz, 2002, p. 54)

Although the vast majority of teenagers weather the search for identity—as well as other challenges of the age—without major difficulties, some find adolescence very stressful, and some develop severe emotional problems. Two of the most serious problems are depression and suicide.

Between 25 and 40 percent of girls, and 20 to 35 percent of boys, experience occasional episodes of depression during adolescence, although the incidence of major depression is far lower.

Adolescent Depression. No one, including adolescents, is immune to sadness and bad moods. The end of a relationship, failure at an important task, the death of a loved one—all may produce profound feelings of sadness, loss, and grief. In such situations, depression is a typical reaction.

More than a quarter of adolescents report feeling so sad or hopeless for two or more weeks in a row that they stop doing their normal activities. Almost two-thirds of teenagers say they have experienced such feelings at some point. In contrast, only a small minority of adolescents—some 3 percent—experience *major depression*, a full-blown psychological disorder, which is severe and lingers for long periods (Cicchetti & Toth, 1998; Grunbaum, 2001; Galambos, Leadbeater, & Barker, 2004).

Gender, ethnic, and racial differences also affect depression rates. As is true for adults, adolescent girls experience depression more often than boys. Some studies show African American adolescents having a higher rate of depression than white adolescents, though not all research supports this conclusion. Native Americans, too, have higher rates of depression (Stice, Presnell, & Bearman, 2001; Jacques & Mash, 2004; Hightower, 2005; Li, DiGiuseppe, & Froh, 2006).

In cases of severe, long-term depression, biological factors are often involved. Some adolescents do seem genetically predisposed to experience depression, but environmental and social factors related to the extraordinary changes in their social lives also have impact. An adolescent who loses a loved one to death, for example, or who grows up with an alcoholic or a depressed parent, is at a higher risk of depression. Being unpopular, having few close friends, and rejection are also associated with adolescent depression (Lau & Kwok, 2000; Goldsmith et al., 2002; Eley, Liang, & Plomin, 2004; Zalsman et al., 2006).

Why the depression rate is higher for girls than boys is puzzling. There is little evidence of a link to hormone differences or a particular gene. Some psychologists speculate that stress is greater for girls in adolescence due to the many, often conflicting demands of the traditional female role. Such conflict may make them feel helpless. Add to this the fact that traditional gender roles still give higher status to men than to women (Nolen-Hoeksema, 2003; Gilbert, 2004).

The rate of adolescent suicide has tripled over the last 30 years. These girls console one another following the suicide of a classmate.

Girls' higher levels of depression in adolescence may reflect gender differences in coping with stress rather than differences in mood. Girls may be more likely to react to stress by turning inward, resulting in a sense of helplessness and hopelessness. In contrast, boys more often externalize the stress and act more impulsively or aggressively, or turn to drugs and alcohol (Hankin & Abramson, 2001; Winstead & Sanchez, 2005).

Adolescent Suicide. Adolescent suicide in the United States has tripled in the last 30 years. One teenage suicide occurs every 90 minutes, for an annual rate of 12.2 suicides per 100,000 adolescents. The reported rate may actually understate the true number; parents and medical personnel often prefer to report a death as an accident rather than suicide. Even so, suicide is the third most common cause of death for 15- to 24-year-olds, after accidents and homicide. Despite this rise in suicide—more than for other age groups—the highest rate is still found in late adulthood (Healy, 2001; Grunbaum et al., 2002; Joe & Marcus, 2003; Conner & Goldston, 2007). For a discussion of adolescent suicide prevention, see the *Becoming an Informed Consumer of Development* box.

BECOMING AN INFORMED CONSUMER OF DEVELOPMENT
Preventing Adolescent Suicide

If you suspect an adolescent, or anyone else, is contemplating suicide, act! Here are several suggestions:

- Talk to the person. Listen with understanding and without judging.

- Talk specifically about suicidal thoughts; ask questions such as: Do you have a plan? Have you bought a gun? Where is it? Have you stockpiled pills? Where are they? The Public Health Service notes that, "contrary to popular belief, such candor will not give a person dangerous ideas or encourage a suicidal act."

- Try to distinguish between general upset and more serious danger, as when suicide plans *have* been made. If the crisis is acute, *do not leave the person alone.*

- Be supportive, let the person know you care, and try to break down his or her feelings of isolation.

- Take charge of finding help. Do not fear invading the person's privacy. Do not try to handle the problem alone. Get professional help immediately.

- Make the environment safe, removing (not just hiding) weapons such as guns, razors, scissors, medication, and other potentially dangerous items.

- Do not keep suicide talk or threats secret; these are calls for help and call for immediate action.

- Do not challenge, dare, or use verbal shock treatment on the person to correct his or her thinking.

- Make a contract with the person, getting a promise or commitment, preferably in writing, not to attempt suicide until you have talked further.

- Don't be overly reassured by a sudden improvement of mood. Such quick "recoveries" may be merely the relief of deciding to commit suicide or the temporary release of talking to someone; most likely, the underlying problems have not been resolved.

For immediate help with a suicide-related problem, call the National Suicide Prevention Lifeline (800) 784-2433 or the National Runaway Switchboard (800) 621-4000, national hotlines staffed with trained counselors.

The rate of adolescent suicide is higher for boys, although girls *attempt* suicide more frequently. Attempts among males are more likely to be fatal because boys tend to use more violent means, such as guns, while girls usually resort to less violent means, such as drug overdose. Some estimates suggest there are as many as 200 attempted suicides by both sexes for every successful one (Gelman, 1994; Joseph, Reznik, & Mester, 2003; Dervic et al., 2006).

The reasons for the increase in adolescent suicide are unclear. The most obvious explanation is that adolescent stress has increased (Elkind, 1984). But why should stress have increased only for teenagers? The suicide rate for other age groups has remained fairly stable over the same period. Though we are not yet sure why adolescent suicide has increased, certain factors raise the risk. Depression is one. Depressed teenagers who feel profound hopelessness are at greater risk for suicide (although most depressed individuals do not commit suicide). Social inhibition, perfectionism, and high levels of stress and anxiety are also related to an increased risk. The easy availability of guns—more prevalent in the United States than in other industrialized nations—contributes to the suicide rate, too (Huff, 1999; Goldston, 2003).

Some suicide cases are associated with family conflicts and with relationship or school difficulties. Some stem from a history of abuse and neglect. The rate of suicide among drug and alcohol abusers is also relatively high. As shown in Figure 9.5 on page 259, teens who called a hotline because they were considering suicide mentioned other factors as well (Lyon et al., 2000; Bergen, Martin, & Richardson, 2003; Wilcox, Conner, & Caine, 2004).

Emotions in Adulthood: Fufilling Psychological Needs

Think back over the last 7 days of your life. What made you happiest?

According to research on young adults, it probably wasn't money or material objects. It was more likely the product of feelings of independence, competence, self-esteem, or relating well to other people (Sheldon et al., 2001).

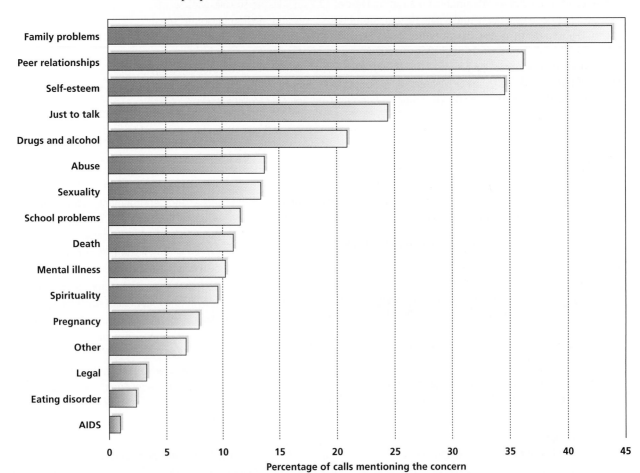

FIGURE 9.5 Adolescent Difficulties
Family, peer relationships, and self-esteem problems were most often mentioned by adolescents contemplating suicide, according to a review of phone calls to a telephone help line.
Source: Boehm & Campbell, 1995.

The Role of Psychological Needs in Determining Happiness. Asked to recall a time when they were happy, young adults are most likely to mention an experience or a moment when their psychological needs rather than material needs were satisfied. Typical answers include being chosen for a new job, developing a deep relationship, or moving into an apartment or a home of their own. Conversely, when they remember times when they were least satisfied, they mention incidents in which basic psychological needs were left unfulfilled.

Culture apparently influences which psychological needs are considered most important to happiness. For example, young adults in Korea more often associate satisfaction with experiences involving other people, whereas young adults in the United States associate satisfaction with experiences relating to the self and self-esteem (Diener, Oishi, & Lucas, 2003; Sedikides, Gaertner, & Toguchi, 2003; Jongudomkarn & Camfield, 2006).

The Stability of Happiness Across the Life Span. Suppose you hit it big on *Jeopardy*. Would you be a happier person? For most people, the answer would be no. A growing body of research shows that adults' *subjective well-being* or general happiness remains stable over their lives. Even winning the lottery increases subjective well-being only temporarily; one year later, people's happiness tends to return to pre-lottery levels (Diener, 2000; Dunn & Laham, 2006).

The stability of subjective well-being suggests that most people have a "set point" for happiness—a level that is consistent despite the ups and downs of life. Specific events may temporarily elevate or depress a person's mood (for example, an outstanding job evaluation or being laid off from work), but people eventually return to their general level of happiness.

Most people's happiness set points seem to be fairly high. Some 30 percent of people in the United States rate themselves as "very happy," while only 10 percent rate themselves as "not too happy." Most people say they are "pretty happy." These findings are similar across different social groups. Men and women rate themselves as equally happy, and African Americans rate themselves as "very happy" at only slightly lower rates than whites. Regardless of their economic situation, residents of countries across the world have similar levels of happiness (Schkade & Kahneman, 1998; Diener, 2000; Diener, Oishi, & Lucas, 2003; Kahneman et al., 2006). The conclusion: Money doesn't buy happiness.

Of course, happiness depends in part on successfully navigating the changing circumstances of our lives. For example, as we'll discuss in the next module, some people experience a period of intense emotional upheaval in middle adulthood—a *midlife crisis*—when they may reassess virtually every aspect of their lives. In late adulthood, people reach another critical juncture as they confront the inevitability of their own death.

Happiness in Late Adulthood: What Is the Secret? At age 77, Elinor Reynolds spends most of her time at home, leading a quiet, routine existence. Never married, Elinor receives visits from her two sisters every few weeks, and some of her nieces and nephews stop by on occasion. But for the most part, she keeps to herself. When asked, she says she is quite happy.

In contrast, Carrie Masterson, also 77, is involved in something different almost every day. If she is not visiting the senior center and participating in some activity, she is out shopping. Her daughter complains that Carrie is "never home" when she tries to reach her by phone, and Carrie replies that she has never been busier—or happier.

While disengagement theory suggests that people in late adulthood begin to gradually withdraw from the world, activity theory argues that successful aging occurs when people maintain their involvement with others.

Clearly, there is no single way to attain happiness during late adulthood. How people age depends on personality factors and people's circumstances. Some people become progressively less involved with the day-to-day, while others maintain active ties to people and their personal interests. Three major approaches provide explanations: disengagement theory, activity theory, and continuity theory.

Disengagement Theory: Gradual Retreat.   According to **disengagement theory**, late adulthood often involves a gradual withdrawal from the world on physical, psychological, and social levels. On a physical level, elderly people have lower energy levels and slow down progressively. Psychologically, they begin to withdraw, showing less interest in the world around them and spending more time looking inward. Finally, on a social level, they engage in fewer interactions—both day-to-day, face-to-face encounters and participation in society as a whole. Older adults also become less involved and invested in the lives of others (Cummings & Henry, 1961; Bishop, 2008; Nair, 2008).

Disengagement theory suggests that withdrawal is a mutual process. Because of norms and expectations about aging, society begins to disengage from those in late adulthood. For example, mandatory retirement ages compel elderly people to withdraw from work, which accelerates disengagement.

Such withdrawal is not necessarily negative. In fact, most theorists who subscribe to the theory maintain that the outcomes of disengagement are largely positive. As people withdraw, they become more reflective about their lives and less constrained by social roles. Furthermore, they can become more discerning in their social relationships, focusing on those who best meet their needs. Thus, disengagement can be liberating (Settersten, 2002; Wrosch, Bauer, & Scheier, 2005).

Similarly, decreased emotional investment in others can be beneficial. By investing less emotional energy in others, people in late adulthood are better able to adjust to serious illness and death among their peers.

Evidence for disengagement comes from a study examining close to 300 people aged 50 to 90, which found that specific events, such as retirement or the death of a spouse, were accompanied by a gradual disengagement in which the level of social interaction with others plummeted (Cummings & Henry, 1961). According to these results, disengagement was related to successful aging.

Activity Theory: Continued Involvement.   Although early findings were consistent with disengagement theory, later research was not so supportive. For example, a follow-up study found that although some of the subjects were happily disengaged, others, who had remained involved and active, were as happy as—and sometimes happier than—than those who disengaged. Furthermore, people in many non-Western cultures remain engaged, active, and busy throughout old age, and are expected to do so. Clearly, disengagement is not a universal process (Havighurst, 1973; Bergstrom & Holmes, 2000; Crosnoe & Elder, 2002).

The lack of support for disengagement theory led to an alternative. **Activity theory** suggests that successful aging occurs when people maintain the interests and activities of middle age and the amount and type of their social interactions. According to this perspective, happiness and satisfaction with life spring from involvement with the world (Charles, Reynolds, & Gatz, 2001; Consedine, Magai, & King, 2004; Hutchinson & Wexler, 2007).

Activity theory suggests that continuation of activities is important. Even when continuation is no longer possible—such as continuing work after retirement—activity theory argues that successful aging occurs when replacement activities are found.

But activity theory, like disengagement theory, is not the full story. For one thing, activity theory makes little distinction among activities. Not every activity will have an equal impact on a person's satisfaction with life; in fact, the nature and quality of the activities are likely to be more critical than mere quantity or frequency (Burrus-Bammel & Bammel, 1985; Adams, 2004).

A more significant concern is that for some people in late adulthood, the principle of "less is more" holds: Less activity brings greater enjoyment because they can slow down and do only the things that bring them the greatest satisfaction (Ward, 1984; Stone, 2003). Some people view the ability to moderate their pace as one of the bounties of late adulthood. For them, a relatively inactive, and perhaps even solitary, existence is welcome (Hansson & Carpenter, 1994; Hansson & Stroebe, 2007).

Continuity Theory: A Compromise Position.   Neither disengagement theory nor activity theory provides a complete picture of successful aging (Johnson & Barer, 1992; Rapkin &

FROM A
SOCIAL WORKER'S
PERSPECTIVE
How might cultural factors affect an older person's likelihood of pursuing either the disengagement strategy or the activity strategy?

disengagement theory   the period in late adulthood that marks a gradual withdrawal from the world on physical, psychological, and social levels.

activity theory   the theory suggesting that successful aging occurs when people maintain the interests, activities, and social interactions with which they were involved during middle age.

Fischer, 1992; Ouwehand, de Ridder, & Bensing, 2007). A compromise view is needed. **Continuity theory** suggests that people simply need to maintain their desired level of involvement in society in order to maximize their sense of well-being and self-esteem (Whitbourne, 2001; Atchley, 2003).

According to continuity theory, those who were highly active and social will be happiest if they largely remain so. Those who enjoy solitude and solitary interests, such as reading or walks in the woods, will be happiest pursuing that level of sociability (Maddox & Campbell, 1985; Holahan & Chapman, 2002).

It is also clear that most older adults experience positive emotions as frequently as younger individuals. Furthermore, they become more skilled at regulating their emotions.

Other factors enhance happiness during late adulthood. The importance of physical and mental health cannot be overestimated, and having enough financial security to provide for basic needs is critical. In addition, a sense of autonomy, independence, and personal control over one's life is a significant advantage (Lawton, 2001; Morris, 2001; Charles, Mather, & Carstensen, 2003).

continuity theory   the theory suggesting that people need to maintain their desired level of involvement in society in order to maximize their sense of well-being and self-esteem.

REVIEW

▶ Infants appear to express and to experience emotions, and their emotions broaden in range to reflect increasingly complex emotional states.

▶ The ability to decode the nonverbal facial and vocal expressions of others develops early in infants.

▶ During middle childhood, children gain increasing control over their emotions, as well as showing greater empathy.

▶ Emotions in adolescence tend to be more changeable and more extreme than in other periods of life.

▶ One of the dangers that adolescents face is depression, which affects girls more than boys.

▶ Most people appear to have a "set point" for happiness—a level that is consistent throughout adulthood despite the temporary ups and downs they experience.

▶ Disengagement theory suggests that older people gradually withdraw from the world, while activity theory suggests that the happiest people continue to be engaged with the world. A compromise theory—continuity theory—may be the most useful approach to successful aging.

APPLY

▶ Why would the sad or flat emotional expressiveness of a depressed parent be hard on an infant? How might it be counteracted?

▶ What are some advantages and disadvantages of emotional self-regulation? Are there dangers in too much self-regulation?

MODULE 9.3

Personality Development Across the Life Span

Lincoln was a difficult baby, his parents both agreed. For one thing, it seemed like they could never get him to sleep at night. He cried at the slightest noise, a problem since his crib was near the windows facing a busy street. Worse yet, once he started crying, it seemed to take forever to calm him down again. One day his mother, Aisha, was telling her mother-in-law, Mary, about the challenges of being Lincoln's mom. Mary recalled that her own son, Lincoln's father Malcom, had been much the same way. "He was my first child, and I thought this was how all babies acted. So, we just kept trying different ways until we

personality the sum total of the enduring characteristics that differentiate one individual from another.

temperament patterns of arousal and emotionality that are consistent and enduring characteristics of an individual.

found out how he worked. I remember, we put his crib all over the apartment until we finally found out where he could sleep, and it ended up being in the hallway for a long time. Then his sister, Maleah, came along, and she was so quiet and easy, I didn't know what to do with my extra time!"

As the story of Lincoln's family shows, babies are not all alike, and neither are their families. As we'll see, some of the differences among people seem to be present from birth. To understand how one individual differs from another, we need to consider the origins of **personality**, the sum total of the enduring characteristics that differentiate one person from another. From birth onward, children begin to show unique, stable traits and behaviors that ultimately lead to their development as distinct, special individuals.

Temperament: Stabilities in Infant Behavior

Sarah's parents thought there must be something wrong. Unlike her older brother Josh, who had been perpetually in motion as an infant, Sarah was much more placid. She took long naps and was easily soothed on those rare occasions when she became agitated. What could be producing her extreme calmness?

The most likely answer: The difference between Sarah and Josh reflected differences in temperament. **Temperament** encompasses patterns of arousal and emotionality that are consistent and enduring characteristics of an individual (Rothbart, Ahadi, & Evans, 2000; Kochanska, 2004).

Temperament refers to *how* children behave, as opposed to *what* they do or *why* they do it. Infants show temperamental differences in general disposition from the time of birth, largely due initially to genetic factors, and temperament tends to be fairly stable well into adolescence. On the other hand, temperament is not fixed and unchangeable: Childrearing practices can modify temperament significantly. In fact, some children show little consistency in temperament from one age to another (McCrae et al., 2000; Rothbart, Derryberry, & Hershey, 2000; Rothbart & Derryberry, 2002).

Temperament is reflected in several dimensions of behavior. One central dimension is *activity level*, which reflects the degree of overall movement. Some babies (like Sarah and Maleah, in the earlier examples) are relatively placid, and their movements are slow and almost leisurely. In contrast, the activity level of other infants (like Josh) is quite high, with strong, restless movements of the arms and legs.

Another important dimension of temperament is the nature and quality of an infant's mood, and in particular a child's *irritability*. Irritable infants fuss a great deal, and they are easily upset. They are also difficult to soothe when they do begin to cry. (Other aspects of temperament are listed in Table 9.2.)

TABLE 9.2 Dimensions of Temperament

DIMENSION	DEFINITION
Activity level	Proportion of active time periods to inactive time periods
Approach-withdrawal	The response to a new person or object, based on whether the child accepts the new situation or withdraws from it
Adaptability	How easily the child is able to adapt to changes in his or her environment
Quality of mood	The contrast of the amount of friendly, joyful, and pleasant behavior with unpleasant, unfriendly behavior
Attention span and persistence	The amount of time the child devotes to an activity and the effect of distraction on that activity
Distractibility	The degree to which stimuli in the environment alter behavior
Rhythmlclty (regularity)	The regularity of basic functions such as hunger, excretion, sleep, and wakefulness
Intensity of reaction	The energy level or reaction of the child's response
Threshold of responsiveness	The intensity of stimulation needed to elicit a response

Source: Thomas, Chess, & Birch, 1968.

Categorizing Temperament: Easy, Difficult, and Slow-to-Warm Babies. Because temperament can be viewed along so many dimensions, some researchers have asked whether broader categories can be used to describe children's overall behavior. According to Alexander Thomas and Stella Chess, who carried out a large-scale study of a group of infants that has come to be known as the *New York Longitudinal Study* (Thomas & Chess, 1980), babies can be described according to one of several profiles:

- **Easy babies** have a positive disposition. Their body functions operate regularly, and they are adaptable. They show curiosity about new situations, and their emotions are moderate or low in intensity. This category applies to about 40 percent (the largest number) of infants.

- **Difficult babies** have more negative moods and are slow to adapt to new situations. When confronted with a new situation, they tend to withdraw. About 10 percent of infants belong in this category.

- **Slow-to-warm babies** are inactive, showing relatively calm reactions to their environment. Their moods are generally negative, and they withdraw from new situations, adapting slowly. Approximately 15 percent of infants are slow to warm.

The remaining 35 percent cannot be consistently categorized. These children show a variety of combinations of characteristics. For instance, one infant may have relatively sunny moods but react negatively to new situations, or another may show little stability of any sort in terms of general temperament.

The Consequences of Temperament: Does Temperament Matter? One obvious question to emerge from the findings of the relative stability of temperament is whether a particular kind of temperament is beneficial. The answer seems to be that no single type of temperament is invariably good or bad. Instead, children's long-term adjustment depends on the **goodness of fit** of their particular temperament and the nature and demands of the environment in which they find themselves. For instance, children with a low activity level and low irritability may do particularly well in an environment in which they are left to explore on their own and are allowed largely to direct their own behavior. In contrast, high-activity-level, highly irritable children may do best with greater direction, which permits them to channel their energy in particular directions (Thomas & Chess, 1977, 1980; Strelau, 1998; Schoppe-Sullivan et al., 2007). Mary, the grandmother in the earlier example, found ways to adjust the environment for her son, Malcom. Malcom and Aisha may need to do the same for their own son, Lincoln.

Some research does suggest that certain temperaments are more adaptive than others. Difficult children, in general, are more likely to show behavior problems by school age than those classified in infancy as easy children. But not all difficult children experience problems. The key determinant seems to be the way parents react to their infant's difficult behavior. If they react by showing anger and inconsistency—responses that their child's difficult, demanding behavior readily evokes—then the child is more likely to experience behavior problems. On the other hand, parents who display more warmth and consistency in their responses are more likely to have children who avoid later problems (Thomas, Chess, & Birch, 1968; Teerikangas et al., 1998; Pauli-Pott, Mertesacker, & Bade, 2003).

Erikson's Theory of Psychosocial Development

As we first discussed in Chapter 1, psychoanalyst Erik Erikson argued that personality starts in infancy and continues across the entire life span. **Erikson's theory of psychosocial development** considers how individuals come to understand themselves and the meaning of others'—and their own—behavior (Erikson, 1963). Building on the *psychodynamic perspective*, which suggests that unconscious influences affect behavior, Erikson's theory suggests that developmental change occurs throughout people's lives in eight distinct stages, starting in infancy.

According to Erikson, infants' early experiences are responsible for shaping one of the key aspects of their personalities: whether they will be basically trusting or mistrustful. The theory suggests that during the first 18 months of life, we pass through the **trust-versus-mistrust stage**, developing a sense of trust or mistrust, largely depending on how well our caretakers meet our needs.

Mary's attention to Malcom's needs, in the example at the beginning of the module, probably helped him develop a basic sense of trust in the world. Erikson suggests that if infants are able to develop trust, they experience a sense of hope, which permits them to feel they can fulfill their

easy babies   babies who have a positive disposition; their body functions operate regularly, and they are adaptable.

difficult babies   babies who have negative moods and are slow to adapt to new situations; when confronted with a new situation, they tend to withdraw.

slow-to-warm babies   babies who are inactive, showing relatively calm reactions to their environment; their moods are generally negative, and they withdraw from new situations, adapting slowly.

goodness of fit   the notion that development is dependent on the degree of match between children's temperament and the nature and demands of the environment in which they are being raised.

Erikson's theory of psychosocial development   the theory that considers how individuals come to understand themselves and the meaning of others'—and their own—behavior.

trust-versus-mistrust stage   according to Erikson, the period during which infants develop a sense of trust or mistrust, largely depending on how well their needs are met by their caregivers.

needs successfully. On the other hand, feelings of mistrust lead infants to see the world as harsh and unfriendly, and they may have later difficulties in forming close bonds with others.

During the end of infancy, children enter the **autonomy-versus-shame-and-doubt stage**, which lasts from around 18 months to 3 years. In this period, children develop independence and autonomy if parents encourage exploration and freedom within safe boundaries. However, if children are restricted and overly protected, they feel shame, self-doubt, and unhappiness.

In the early part of the preschool period, children are ending the autonomy-versus-shame-and-doubt stage and entering what Erikson called the **initiative-versus-guilt stage**, which lasts from around age 3 to age 6. It is during this period that children's views of themselves undergo major change as preschoolers face conflicts between the desire to act independently of their parents and the guilt that comes from the unintended consequences of their actions. In essence, preschoolers come to realize that they are persons in their own right, and they begin to make decisions and to shape the kind of persons that they will become.

Parents who react positively to this transformation toward independence can help their children resolve the opposing forces of initiative and guilt that characterize this period. By providing their children with opportunities to act with self-reliance, while still giving them direction and guidance, parents can support and encourage their children's initiative. On the other hand, parents who discourage their children's efforts to seek independence may contribute to a sense of guilt that persists throughout their lives.

Psychosocial Development During Middle Childhood and Adolescence. Middle childhood encompasses the **industry-versus-inferiority stage**. Lasting from roughly age 6 to age 12, this stage is characterized by a focus on efforts to attain competence in meeting the challenges presented by parents, peers, school, clubs and groups to which they belong, and the other complexities of the modern world.

As they move through middle childhood, children direct their energies not only to mastering what they are presented in school—an enormous body of information—but to making a place for themselves in their social worlds. Success in these efforts brings with it feelings of mastery and proficiency and a growing sense of competence.

On the other hand, difficulties in this stage lead to feelings of failure and inadequacy. Children may come to feel unskilled and incapable. As a result, they may withdraw both from academic pursuits, showing less interest and motivation to excel, and from interactions with peers.

Developing industriousness during the middle childhood years has lasting consequences. For example, one study examined how childhood industriousness and hard work were related to adult behavior by following a group of 450 men over a 35-year period, starting in early childhood. The men who were most industrious and hardworking during childhood were most successful as adults, both in occupational attainment and in their personal lives. Childhood industriousness was more closely associated with adult success than was intelligence or family background (Vaillant & Vaillant, 1981).

During adolescence, teenagers enter the **identity-versus-identity-confusion stage**. In this period, adolescents attempt to determine what is unique and distinctive about themselves and the roles they will play in their future lives. As we'll consider more fully in Chapter 10, they may explore different roles, narrowing their choices and ideally finding out who they really are.

Adolescents with difficulties in resolving this stage may find it difficult to form and maintain close relationships. Alternatively, they may adopt socially inappropriate roles and fail to forge an acceptable identity.

Psychosocial Development During Early Adulthood. Erikson regarded young adulthood as the time of the **intimacy-versus-isolation stage**, which spans the period of postadolescence into the early 30s. During this period, the focus is on developing close, intimate relationships with others.

To Erikson intimacy comprises several aspects. One is selflessness, the sacrifice of one's own needs to those of another. Another is sexuality, the experience of joint pleasure from focusing not just on one's own gratification but also on that of one's partner. Finally, there is deep devotion, marked by efforts to fuse one's identity with the identity of a partner.

According to Erikson, those who experience difficulties during this stage are often lonely, isolated, and fearful of relationships. Their difficulties may stem from an earlier failure to develop a strong identity. In contrast, young adults who are able to form intimate relationships

autonomy-versus-shame-and-doubt stage the period during which, according to Erikson, toddlers (aged 18 months to 3 years) develop independence and autonomy if they are allowed the freedom to explore, or shame and self-doubt if they are restricted and overprotected.

initiative-versus-guilt stage according to Erikson, the period during which children aged 3 to 6 years experience conflict between independence of action and the sometimes negative results of that action.

industry-versus-inferiority stage the period from age 6 to 12 characterized by a focus on efforts to attain competence in meeting the challenges presented by parents, peers, school, and the other complexities of the modern world.

identity-versus-identity-confusion stage the period during which teenagers seek to determine what is unique and distinctive about themselves.

intimacy-versus-isolation stage according to Erikson, the period of postadolescence into the early 30s that focuses on developing close relationships with others.

on a physical, intellectual, and emotional level successfully resolve the crisis of this stage of development.

Erikson's approach has been influential, but it is troubling today because he limited healthy intimacy to heterosexuality. Same-sex partnerships, couples childless by choice, and other relationships different from Erikson's ideal were regarded as less than satisfactory. Furthermore, Erikson focused more on men than on women and did not consider racial and ethnic identity, greatly limiting the applicability of his theory (Yip, Seaton, & Sellers, 2006).

Psychosocial Development During Midlife: Erikson's Stage of Generativity Versus Stagnation.

Psychoanalyst Erik Erikson characterized midlife as a period of **generativity-versus-stagnation stage**, the seventh of his eight stages of psychosocial development. One's middle adulthood, according to Erikson, is either spent in generativity—making a contribution to family, community, work, and society—or in stagnation. Generative people strive to guide and encourage future generations. Often, people find generativity through parenting, but other roles can fill this need, such as working directly with young people, acting as mentors. Or the need for generativity may be satisfied through creative and artistic output, seeking to leave a lasting contribution. The focus of generativity, then, is beyond the self, as one looks toward the continuation of one's own life through others (Pratt et al., 2001; McAdams & Logan, 2004; An & Cooney, 2006; Peterson, 2006).

A lack of psychological growth in this period results in stagnation. Focusing on their own trivial activities, people may feel they have contributed little to the world, that their presence has counted for little. Some people find themselves floundering, still seeking new, potentially more fulfilling careers. Others become frustrated and bored.

Ego Integrity Versus Despair: Erikson's Final Stage.

Psychoanalyst Erik Erikson characterizes late adulthood as the time when people move into the last of life's eight stages of psychosocial development. Labeled the **ego-integrity-versus-despair stage**, this period is characterized by a process of looking back over one's life, evaluating it, and coming to terms with it.

People who are successful in this stage of development experience satisfaction and accomplishment, which Erikson terms "integrity." When people achieve integrity, they feel they have fulfilled the possibilities that have come their way in life, and they have few regrets. Other people look back on their lives with dissatisfaction. They may feel that they have missed important opportunities and have not accomplished what they wished. Such individuals may be unhappy, depressed, angry, or despondent over what they have done, or failed to do, with their lives—in short, they despair.

Erikson's Approach in Perspective.

Erikson's approach has been enormously influential. His theory is comprehensive, covering the entire life span. It has received general support from subsequent research (Whitbourne et al., 1992; McAdams et al., 1997).

Yet, like any theory, it has its weaknesses. Not everyone passes through the stages in the sequence that Erikson has laid out. Furthermore, contemporary research has taken a more refined approach and has provided some alternatives. We'll discuss several alternative views of development, focusing on particular periods of life.

Moving Beyond Erikson: Personality Development During Adulthood

Some theorists have paid particular attention to personality development and change during adulthood, building and moving beyond Erikson's psychosocial theory. We'll look at several approaches.

Developmentalist George Vaillant (1977) argues that an important period, which he calls *keeping the meaning versus rigidity*, takes place between the ages of about 45 and 55. During that period, adults seek to extract the meaning from their lives and to "keep the meaning" by developing an acceptance of the strengths and weaknesses of others. Although they recognize the world is not perfect and has many shortcomings, they strive to safeguard their world, and they are relatively content. People who are not able to keep the meaning in their lives risk becoming rigid and increasingly isolated from others.

Psychiatrist Roger Gould (1978, 1980) offered an alternative to Vaillant's views. While he agrees that people move through a series of stages and potential crises, he suggests that

generativity-versus-stagnation stage
according to Erikson, the stage during middle adulthood in which people consider their contributions to family and society.

ego-integrity-versus-despair stage
Erikson's final stage of life, characterized by a process of looking back over one's life, evaluating it, and coming to terms with it.

TABLE 9.3		Gould's Transformations in Adult Development
STAGE	**APPROXIMATE AGE**	**DEVELOPMENT(S)**
1	16 to 18	Desire to escape parental control
2	18 to 22	Leaving the family; peer group orientation
3	22 to 28	Developing independence; commitment to a career and to children
4	29 to 34	Questioning self; role confusion; marriage and career vulnerable to dissatisfaction
5	35 to 43	Period of urgency to attain life's goals; awareness of time limitation; realignment of life's goals
6	43 to 53	Settling down; acceptance of one's life
7	53 to 60	More tolerance; acceptance of past; less negativism; general mellowing

Source: From *Transformations*, by R. L. Gould & M. D. Gould, 1978, New York: Simon & Schuster.

In spite of there being no strong evidence that people universally experience "midlife crisis," the belief that it is commonplace remains. Why is this belief so prevalent?

adults pass through a series of seven stages associated with specific age periods (see Table 9.3). According to Gould, people in their late 30s and early 40s begin to feel a sense of urgency in terms of attaining life's goals as they realize that their time is limited. Coming to grips with the reality that life is finite can propel people toward adult maturity.

Gould based his model of adult development on a relatively small sample and relied heavily on his own clinical judgments. In fact, little research has supported his description of the various stages, which was heavily influenced by the psychoanalytic perspective.

Another alternative to Erikson's work is psychologist Daniel Levinson's *seasons of life* theory. According to Levinson (1986, 1992), who intensively interviewed a group of men, the early 40s are a period of transition and crisis. Levinson suggests that adult men experience a series of stages beginning with their entry into early adulthood at around age 20 and continuing into middle adulthood. The beginning stages have to do with leaving one's family and entering the adult world.

At around age 40 or 45, however, people move into a period that Levinson calls the midlife transition. The *midlife transition* is a time of questioning. People begin to focus on the finite nature of life, and they question some of their everyday, fundamental assumptions. They experience the first signs of aging, and they confront the knowledge that they will be unable to accomplish all their aims before they die.

In Levinson's view, this period of assessment may lead to a **midlife crisis**, a stage of uncertainty and indecision brought about by the realization that life is finite. Facing signs of physical aging, men may also discover that even the accomplishments of which they are proudest have brought them less satisfaction than they expected. Looking toward the past, they may seek to define what went wrong and look for ways to correct their past mistakes. The midlife crisis, then, is a painful and tumultuous period of questioning.

Levinson's view is that most people are susceptible to a fairly profound midlife crisis. But before accepting his perspective, we need to consider some critical drawbacks in his research. First, his initial theorizing was based on a group of only 40 men, and his work with women was carried out years later and once again on only a small sample. Furthermore, Levinson overstated the consistency and generality of the patterns he found in the samples he used to derive his

midlife crisis   a stage of uncertainty and indecision brought about by the realization that life is finite.

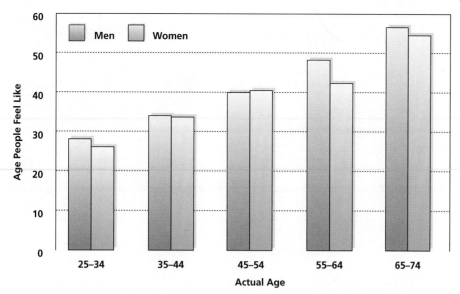

FIGURE 9.6 What Age Do You Feel Most of the Time?
Throughout adulthood, most people say they feel younger than they actually are.
Source: The John D. and Catherine T. MacArthur Foundation Research Network on Successful Midlife Development, 1999.

theory. As we consider next, the notion of a universal midlife crisis has come under considerable criticism (McCrae & Costa, 1990; Stewart & Ostrove, 1998).

The Midlife Crisis: Reality or Myth? Central to Levinson's model of the seasons of life is the concept of midlife crisis, a period in the early 40s presumed to be marked by intense psychological turmoil. The notion has taken on a life of its own: There is a general expectation in U.S. society that the age of 40 represents an important psychological juncture.

There's a problem, though, with such a view: The evidence for a widespread midlife crisis is simply lacking. In fact, most research suggests that for most people, the passage into middle age is relatively tranquil. The majority of people regard midlife as a particularly rewarding time. If they are parents, for example, their children often have passed the period when childrearing is physically demanding, and in some cases children have left the home altogether, allowing parents the opportunity to rekindle an intimacy that they may have lost. Many middle-aged people find that their careers have blossomed—as we discuss later in this chapter—and far from being in crisis, they may feel quite content with their lot in life. Rather than looking toward the future, they focus on the present, seeking to maximize their ongoing involvement with family, friends, and other social groups. Those who feel regret over the course of their lives may be motivated to change the direction of their lives, and those who do change their lives end up better off psychologically (Stewart & Vandewater, 1999).

Furthermore, by the time they approach and enter middle adulthood, most people feel younger than they actually are, as can be seen in Figure 9.6 (Miller, Hemesath, & Nelson, 1997; Wethington, Cooper, & Holmes, 1997).

In short, the evidence for a midlife crisis experienced by most people is no more compelling than the evidence for a stormy adolescence. Yet, like that notion, the idea that the midlife crisis is nearly universal seems unusually well entrenched in "common wisdom." Why is this the case?

One reason may be that people who do experience turmoil during middle age tend to be relatively obvious and easily remembered by observers. For instance, a 40-year-old man who divorces his wife, replaces his sedate Ford station wagon with a red Saab convertible, and marries a much younger woman is likely to be more conspicuous than a happily married man who remains with his spouse (and Ford) throughout middle adulthood. As a consequence, we are more likely to notice and recall marital difficulties more readily than the lack of them. In this way the myth of a blustery and universal midlife crisis is perpetuated. The reality, though, is quite different: For most people, a midlife crisis is more the stuff of fiction than of reality.

Personality in Late Adulthood. Although Erikson's approach provides a picture of the broad possibilities of later adulthood, other theorists offer a more differentiated view of the final stage of life. Psychologist Robert Peck (1968) suggests that personality development in elderly people is occupied by three major developmental tasks.

In Peck's view—part of a comprehensive description of change across adulthood—the first task in old age is to redefine oneself in ways that do not relate to work roles or occupations. He labels this stage the **redefinition-of-self-versus-preoccupation-with-work-role**. As we will see, the changes that occur when people stop working can trigger a difficult adjustment in how they view themselves. Peck suggests that people must adjust their values to place less emphasis on themselves as workers or professionals and more on attributes that don't involve work, such as being a grandparent or a gardener.

The second major developmental task in late adulthood, according to Peck, is **body-transcendence-versus-body-preoccupation**. Elderly individuals can undergo significant changes in their physical abilities as a result of aging. In the body-transcendence-versus-body-preoccupation stage, people must learn to cope with and move beyond those physical changes (transcendence). If they don't, they become preoccupied with their physical deterioration, to the detriment of their personality development.

The third developmental task in old age is **ego transcendence versus ego preoccupation**, in which elderly people must come to grips with their coming death. They need to understand that, although death is inevitable and probably not too far off, they have made contributions to society. If they see these contributions, which can take the form of children or work and civic activities, as lasting beyond their own lives, they will experience ego transcendence. If not, they may become preoccupied with asking whether their lives had value and worth to society.

redefinition-of-self-versus-preoccupation-with-work-role the theory that those in old age must redefine themselves in ways that do not relate to their work roles or occupations.

body-transcendence-versus-body-preoccupation a period in which people must learn to cope with and move beyond changes in physical capabilities as a result of aging.

ego transcendence versus ego preoccupation the period in which elderly people must come to grips with their coming death.

Although genetic factors clearly play a significant role in the development of intelligence, the level of environmental enrichment is also crucial.

Levinson's Final Season: The Winter of Life. Daniel Levinson's theory of adult development does not focus as much on the challenges that aging adults must overcome. Instead, he looks at the processes that can lead to personality change as we grow old. According to Levinson, people enter late adulthood by passing through a transition stage that typically occurs around 60 to 65 (Levinson, 1986, 1992). During this stage, people come to view themselves as entering late adulthood—or, ultimately, as being "old." Knowing full well society's negative stereotypes about elderly individuals, they struggle with the notion that they are now in this category.

According to Levinson, people come to realize that they are no longer on the center stage but are playing bit parts. This loss of power, respect, and authority may be difficult for individuals accustomed to having control in their lives.

On the other hand, people in late adulthood can serve as resources to younger individuals, and they may find that they are viewed as "venerated elders" whose advice is sought and relied upon. Furthermore, old age can bring a new freedom to do things simply for enjoyment and pleasure, rather than as obligations.

Life Review and Reminiscence: The Common Theme of Adult Personality Development.
Life review, in which people examine and evaluate their lives, is a major thread running through the work of Erikson, Peck, and Levinson and a common theme among personality theorists who focus on late adulthood.

According to gerontologist Robert Butler (2002), life review is triggered by the increasingly obvious prospect of death. People look back on their lives, remembering and reconsidering what has happened to them. Far from being a harmful process of reliving the past, wallowing in past problems, and reviving old wounds, life review usually leads to a better understanding of the past. People may resolve lingering problems and conflicts with others, such as an estrangement from a child, and they may feel they can face their current lives with greater serenity (Bohlmeijer, Smit, & Cuijpers, 2003; Arkoff, Meredith, & Dubanoski, 2004; McKee et al., 2005).

Life review offers other benefits, including a sense of mutuality, a feeling of interconnectedness with others. Moreover, it can be a source of social interaction, as older adults share their experiences with others (Sherman, 1991; Parks, Sanna, & Posey, 2003).

Reminiscence may even have cognitive benefits, improving memory. By reflecting on the past, people activate a variety of memories, which may trigger other memories and bring back sights, sounds, and even smells of the past (Thorsheim & Roberts, 1990; Kartman, 1991).

On the other hand, life review can sometimes produce declines in psychological functioning. If people become obsessive about the past, reliving old insults and mistakes that cannot be rectified, they may end up feeling guilt, depression, and anger against acquaintances who may not even still be alive (DeGenova, 1993).

Overall, however, the process of life review and reminiscence can play an important role by providing continuity between past and present and increasing awareness of the contemporary world. It also can lead to new insights into the past and into others, allowing people to continue

**FROM A
SOCIAL WORKER'S
PERSPECTIVE**
What approaches might a nursing home develop to meet the needs of elders with differing personalities?

personality growth and to function more effectively in the present (Stevens-Ratchford, 1993; Turner & Helms, 1994; Webster & Haight, 2002; Coleman, 2005; Haber, 2006).

Trait Approaches to Personality

Roberto is moody, and it makes him hard to get along with.
Jake is a happy-go-lucky, cheerful kind of guy who has a lot of friends.
Rebecca is hardworking and conscientious, a very serious person, and that's why she's at the top of her high school class.

Moody. . . happy-go-lucky. . . cheerful. . . hard working. . . conscientious. When we describe adolescents and seek to understand the reasons behind their behavior, we typically use specific traits to describe them. Furthermore, we usually assume that if someone is happy-go-lucky and cheerful in one situation, he or she is happy-go-lucky and cheerful in other situations (Gilbert et al., 1992; Gilbert, Miller, & Ross, 1998; Mischel, 2004).

But people have many traits. How do we decide which of the traits are the most important ones, the ones that are central to their personality? To answer the question, developmentalists have developed a perspective of personality known as *trait theory*. **Traits** are enduring dimensions of personality characteristics along which people differ.

Trait approaches—which offer an alternative to Erikson's stage theory and psychodynamic approach—do not assume that some people have a trait and others do not. Instead, they suggest that all individuals have certain traits, but to a greater or lesser degree. For example, all people might be assumed to have a "trustworthiness" trait, except that some are relatively trustworthy while others are relatively untrustworthy. In this case, the trustworthy people would be said to have the trait to a large degree, while others have it to a lesser extent.

The Big Five Personality Traits: Mapping Personality.

Using a variety of sophisticated statistical techniques, personality research specialists have identified a set of five broad trait factors that describe basic personality. Known as the *Big Five personality traits* (which you can remember more easily by using the acronym OCEAN for the first letters of each trait), these traits are:

- openness, a person's level of curiosity and interest in new experiences
- conscientiousness, a person's tendencies to be organized and responsible
- extraversion, how outgoing or shy a person is
- agreeableness, how easygoing and helpful a person tends to be
- neuroticism, the degree to which a person is moody, anxious, and self-critical

The Big Five have been found to reflect the basic core traits not only in adolescents but in a variety of populations, including children, older adults, and non-English speakers. Furthermore, cross-cultural studies have found them in a variety of cultures ranging from across the Americas and Europe to the Middle East to Africa (Paunonen, 2003; McCrae et al., 2005; Rossier, Dahourou, & McCrae, 2005).

Although most work examining the Big Five has involved adults, research involving children and adolescents has been highly supportive of the trait approach. For example, the Big Five trait of conscientiousness was associated with more decisiveness about career choices in adolescents in middle and high school. In addition, Big Five traits are related to deviant behavior in adolescents. For instance, one study found that low agreeableness is associated with impulsivity, instability, and social deviance in 13- and 16-year-old boys (Lounsbury, Hutchens, & Loveland, 2005; Lynman et al., 2005).

The Stability of Personality.

It's clear that the Big Five approach to personality, and trait approaches more broadly, provide a good description of personality. But an important question remains: How stable are personality traits across the life span? The answer is that although personality traits are somewhat less stable in childhood and adolescence than in the later stages of life, they are relatively consistent. The personality traits that children and adolescents hold may manifest themselves in different ways over the life span, but the particular constellation of traits that describes an individual is fairly consistent (Costa, McCrae, & Siegler, 1999; Whitbourne, 2001).

traits enduring dimensions of personality characteristics along which people differ.

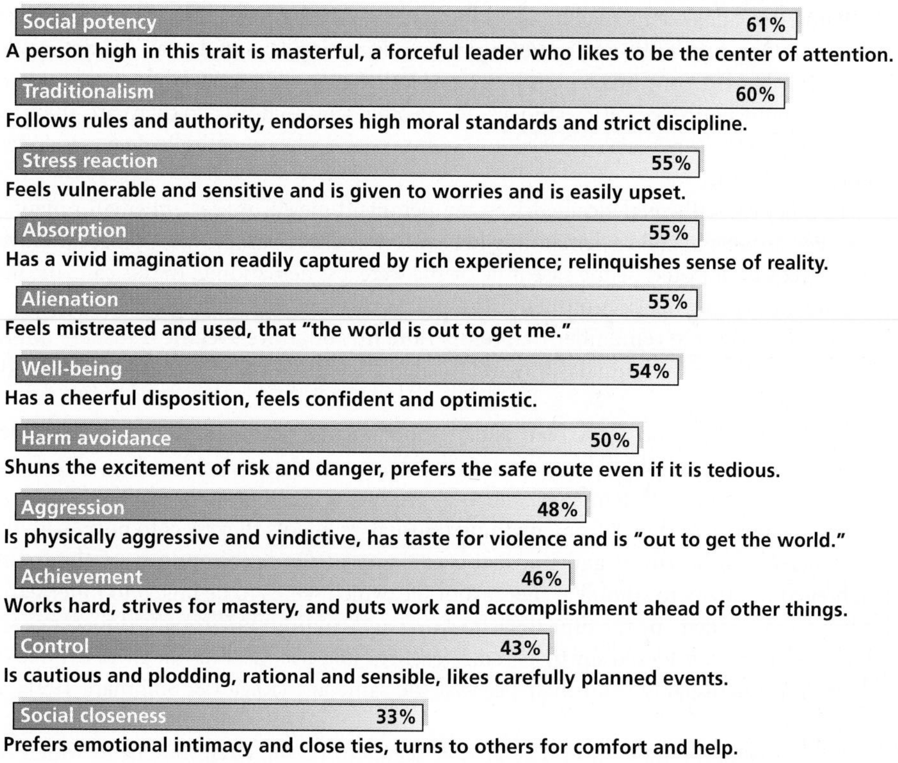

Social potency	61%

A person high in this trait is masterful, a forceful leader who likes to be the center of attention.

Traditionalism	60%

Follows rules and authority, endorses high moral standards and strict discipline.

Stress reaction	55%

Feels vulnerable and sensitive and is given to worries and is easily upset.

Absorption	55%

Has a vivid imagination readily captured by rich experience; relinquishes sense of reality.

Alienation	55%

Feels mistreated and used, that "the world is out to get me."

Well-being	54%

Has a cheerful disposition, feels confident and optimistic.

Harm avoidance	50%

Shuns the excitement of risk and danger, prefers the safe route even if it is tedious.

Aggression	48%

Is physically aggressive and vindictive, has taste for violence and is "out to get the world."

Achievement	46%

Works hard, strives for mastery, and puts work and accomplishment ahead of other things.

Control	43%

Is cautious and plodding, rational and sensible, likes carefully planned events.

Social closeness	33%

Prefers emotional intimacy and close ties, turns to others for comfort and help.

FIGURE 9.7 Heredity and Personality
The influence of the degree of heredity of these 11 personality characteristics is indicated by the percentages noted. *Source:* Tellegen et al., 1988.

For example, an adolescent who is high on the Big Five trait of conscientiousness as an adolescent may be a highly organized student who takes pains to meet deadlines and carefully completes assignments. When he was in kindergarten, he may have carefully arranged his toys, neatly placing each of his action figures on shelves over his bed. As an older adult, he may demonstrate his high conscientiousness by precisely arranging the tools in his garage.

In the same way, we find that adolescents who are well adjusted tend to have been well adjusted during middle childhood—and are more likely to be well adjusted in later adulthood. Similarly, infants and toddlers who are easily frustrated and angered and who show more negative emotions as infants are more likely to evolve into adolescents who are easily frustrated and angered and behave more aggressively (Hart, Hofman, & Edelstein, 1998; Leve, Kim, & Pears, 2005).

Personality and the Interaction of Genetics and the Environment. Traits related to temperament are not the only personality characteristics affected by heredity. The importance of genetics in shaping personality is highlighted by the work of behavioral geneticists and evolutionary psychologists. These scientists believe that personality is determined largely by combinations of inherited genes, similar to the way in which our height and eye color are largely an outcome of genetic contributions from our ancestors. The evolutionary approach argues that personality traits that were beneficial to the survival and reproductive success of our ancestors are more likely to be maintained and passed on to subsequent generations.

Studies of personality traits in genetically identical twins illustrate the importance of heredity in personality development (Tellegen et al., 1988). Identical twins who were raised apart from one another have similar personalities on a number of major dimensions, even when they were separated at an early age and experienced dissimilar upbringings. For example, the traits of social potency (the degree to which a person assumes mastery and leadership roles in social situations) and traditionalism (the tendency to follow authority) have particularly strong genetic components. In contrast, other traits, such as achievement and social closeness, have relatively weak genetic components (see Figure 9.7).

Although it is clear that genetics plays an important role in determining personality, environmental influences also have a significant effect in making these traits consistent throughout the life span. In fact, the environment tends to reinforce inherited traits. For example, a child who is active and aggressive might gravitate toward sports, whereas a more reserved child may be more engaged by academics or solitary pursuits such as computer games or drawing. At the same time, both children may pay less attention to those aspects of the environment that are less compatible with their genetic endowments.

Thus, two adolescents may be checking out school announcements on their high school's Web page. One may notice an announcement advertising tryouts for an intramural baseball team, while her less coordinated but more musically endowed friend might be more apt to pay attention to the notice recruiting students for an after-school chorus. In each case, the adolescent is attending to those aspects of the environment in which her genetically determined temperament can flourish.

In other cases, the genetically driven temperament may *evoke* certain environmental influences. For instance, a child's demanding behavior may cause parents to be more attentive to the child's needs than would be the case if he or she were less demanding. In this case, the inherited traits are influencing the environment.

It is important to remember that temperament, and more specific traits, are not destiny. For instance, some individuals show relatively little consistency in temperament from one age to another.

Childrearing practices, too, can alter temperamental predispositions. An example is the temperamental trait of physiological reactivity, which we discussed earlier. A small percentage of individuals are born with temperaments that produce a high degree of physiological reactivity. Having a tendency to shrink from anything unusual, as infants they react to novel stimuli with a rapid increase in heartbeat and unusual excitability of the limbic system of the brain. Such heightened reactivity to stimuli at the start of life, which seems to be linked to inherited factors, is likely to cause them, by the time they are 4 or 5 and continuing through adolescence and later adulthood, to be considered shy by parents, teachers, and friends. But not always: Some of them behave indistinguishably from their peers at the same age (Kagan & Snidman, 1991; McCrae et al., 2000).

What makes the difference? The answer seems to be the environment in which they are raised. Those whose parents encourage them to be outgoing by arranging new opportunities for them may overcome their shyness by the time they reach adolescence. In contrast, children raised in a stressful environment marked by marital discord or a prolonged illness may retain their shyness into adolescence and later adulthood (Kagan, Arcus, & Snidman, 1993; Pedlow et al., 1993; Joseph, 1999).

The issue of environmental influence on personality development raises a significant concern for parents who want to create the optimal environment for their children. One such concern relates to the question of what long-term effects child care outside the home has on a child's development. We examine the evidence to date in the *From Research to Practice* box.

FROM RESEARCH TO PRACTICE
How Does Infant Child Care Affect Later Development?

For most of the years my two kids were in child care, I worried about it. Did that weird day-care home where my daughter stayed briefly as a toddler do irreparable harm? Was my son irretrievably damaged by that child-care center he disliked? (Shellenbarger, 2003, p. D1)

Every day, parents ask themselves questions like these. The issue of how infant child care affects later development is a pressing one for many parents, who, because of economic, family, or career demands, leave their children to the care of others for a portion of the day. Almost two-thirds of all children between 4 months and 3 years of age spend time in nonparental child care. Overall, more than 80 percent of infants are cared for by people other than their mothers at some point during their first year of life. The majority of these infants begin child care outside the home before the age of 4 months and are enrolled for almost 30 hours per week (Federal Interagency Forum on Child and Family Statistics, 2003; NICHD, 2006; also see Figure 9.8). What effects do such arrangements have on later development?

High-quality infant child care seems to produce only minor differences from home care in most respects and some aspects of development may even be enhanced. What aspects of development might be enhanced by participation in infant child care outside the home?

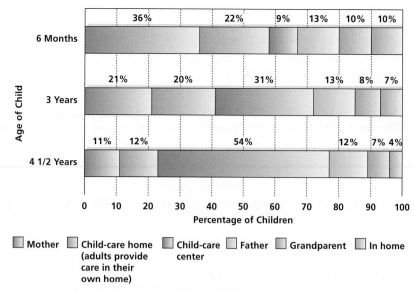

Mother | Child-care home (adults provide care in their own home) | Child-care center | Father | Grandparent | In home

FIGURE 9.8 Where Are Children Cared For?
According to a major study by the National Institute of Child Health and Human Development, children spend more time in some kind of child care outside the home or family as they get older.
Source: NICHD, 2006.

Although the answer is largely reassuring, the newest research to come from the massive, long-term Study of Early Child Care and Youth Development, the longest-running examination of child care ever conducted, suggests that long-term participation in day care may have unanticipated consequences.

First the good news. According to most of the evidence, high-quality child care outside the home produces only minor differences from home care in most respects and may even enhance certain aspects of development. For example, research finds little or no difference in the strength or nature of parental attachment bonds of infants who have been in high-quality child care compared with infants raised solely by their parents (NICHD Early Child Care Research Network, 1997, 1999, 2001; Vandell et al., 2005).

In addition to the direct benefits from involvement in child care outside the home, there are indirect benefits. For example, children in lower-income households and those whose mothers are single may benefit from the educational and social experiences in child care, as well as from the higher income produced by parental employment (Harvey, 1999; Love et al., 2003; NICHD Early Child Care Research Network, 2003a).

Furthermore, children who participate in Early Head Start—a program that serves at-risk infants and toddlers in high-quality child-care centers—can solve problems better, pay greater attention to others, and use language more effectively than poor children who do not participate in the program. In addition, their parents (who are also involved in the program) benefit from their participation. Participating parents talk and read more to their children, and they are less likely to spank them. Likewise, children who receive good, responsive child care were more likely to play well with other children (NICHD Early Child Care Research Network, 2001; Maccoby & Lewis, 2003; Loeb et al., 2004).

Some of the findings on participation in child care outside the home are less positive, however. Infants may be somewhat less secure when they are placed in low-quality child care, if they are placed in multiple child-care arrangements, or if their mothers are relatively insensitive and unresponsive. In addition, children who spend long hours in outside-the-home child-care situations have a lower ability to work independently and have less effective time management skills (Vandell et al., 2005).

The newest research, which focused on preschoolers, finds that children who spend 10 or more hours a week in group child care for a year or more have an increased probability of being disruptive in class, and that the effect continues through the sixth grade. Although the increase in the likelihood of acting disruptive is not substantial—every year spent in a child-care center resulted in a 1 percent higher score on a standardized measure of problem behavior completed by teachers—the results were quite reliable (Belsky et al., 2007).

In sum, the ballooning body of research finds that the effects of participation in group child care are neither unambiguously positive nor unambiguously negative. What is clear, though, is that the *quality* of child care is critical (Marshall, 2004; NICHD Early Child Care Research Network, 2005; Belsky, 2006; deSchipper et al., 2006).

- *Even if they could care for their infants at home, some parents believe that placing their children in child care outside the home is beneficial. Do you agree or disagree, and why?*

- *What are the characteristics of high-quality child care, and how can you ensure that a child-care center is of high quality?*

REVIEW

▶ Personality is the sum total of the enduring characteristics that differentiate one individual from another.

▶ Temperament encompasses enduring levels of arousal and emotionality that are characteristic of an individual.

▶ According to Erik Erikson, people move through eight stages between birth and late adulthood, with the necessity of resolving an important conflict characteristic of each stage.

▶ In general, personality traits are fairly stable throughout life, with only slightly more volatility during adolescence than in other periods.

► In what ways are trait theories of personality more "scientific" than the psychodynamic approach of Freud? Can you devise an experiment to examine the relative influences of the id, ego, and superego on personality? Why or why not?

► What are the educational implications of the finding that some personality traits are inherited and remain consistent over time? Is it wiser for schools to try to change personalities or accommodate to them? Why?

Epilogue

The road people travel as they develop as social individuals is a long and winding one. We began this chapter with an examination of the roots of children's earliest social relationships. We saw how bonds of attachment are forged in infancy, and the ways in which children increasingly interact with peers as they move through the preschool years and into middle childhood. We considered, too, how emotional development proceeds, beginning with the decoding and encoding of emotions by infants, and the role social referencing plays in understanding what others may be feeling. We discussed the nature and function of emotions in adolescence and examined the ways in which adolescents learn to regulate their emotions. We then looked at the emotional difficulties this age group may face, resulting in depression or even suicide. We explored the importance of fulfilling psychological needs to attaining happiness in adulthood, and we considered what constitutes successful aging. In conclusion, we examined personality and Erik Erikson's theory of psychosocial development. We discussed temperament and evaluated the pros

and cons of day care for young children. We looked at a variety of theories on how personality develops in adolescence. We also considered the evidence for and against the popular notion of "midlife crisis," and discussed the stability of personality in adulthood.

Return to the Prologue of this chapter and Russell Ruud's Velcro discovery, and answer the following questions.

1. How closely do Russell's actions in this episode fit in with Erikson's theory of psychosocial development? What do his actions perhaps reveal about the nature of developmental stages?

2. What role do you think social referencing might have played in this scenario? If Russell's care providers had reacted negatively, would this have stopped the other children from imitating Russell?

3. How does this story relate to the sociability of infants?

4. Can we form any opinion about Russell's personality based on this event? Why or why not?

Looking Back

What is attachment in infancy, and how does it relate to the future social competence of individuals?

1. Attachment, a strong, positive emotional bond that forms between an infant and one or more significant persons, is a crucial factor in enabling individuals to develop social relationships. Early studies of attachment, particularly those by ethologist Konrad Lorenz, suggested that attachment was based on biological needs, such as food and safety. To these factors, psychologist Harry Harlow's experiments on attachment among monkeys added contact comfort.

2. The earliest work on human attachment was conducted by John Bowlby, who concluded that safety was the primary motivation behind attachment. According to Bowlby, attachment permits children to explore their world and gradually to become independent.

3. The Ainsworth Strange Situation is an experimental technique used to classify children's attachment styles. The styles identified through this method and a more recent expansion of it are securely attached, avoidant, ambivalent, and disorganized-disoriented.

4. Attachment styles during early childhood have significant effects on the types of relationships that people are able to form later in life. However, attachment styles are not entirely universal and biologically determined; they are susceptible to strong cultural influences.

Do infants experience emotions?

5. Infants display a variety of facial expressions, which are similar across cultures and appear to reflect basic emotional states.

6. By the end of the first year, infants often develop both stranger anxiety, wariness around an unknown person, and separation anxiety, distress displayed when a customary care provider departs.

7. Early in life, infants develop the capability of nonverbal decoding: determining the emotional states of others based on their facial and vocal expressions.

8. Through social referencing, infants from the age of 8 or 9 months use the expressions of others to clarify ambiguous situations and learn appropriate reactions to them.

What dangers do adolescents face as they deal with the stresses of adolescence?

9. Many adolescents have feelings of sadness and hopelessness, and some experience major depression. Biological, environmental, and social factors contribute to depression, and there are gender, ethnic, and racial differences in its occurrence.

10. The rate of adolescent suicide is rising, with suicide now the third most common cause of death in the 15- to 24-year-old bracket.

How do people deal with aging?

11. Disengagement theory and activity theory present opposite views of ways to deal successfully with aging. People's choices depend partly on their prior habits and personalities.

What are temperament and personality, and what stages do individuals pass through in their social development?

12. Temperament encompasses enduring levels of arousal and emotionality that are characteristic of an individual. Several dimensions, such as activity level and irritability, reflect temperament. Temperamental differences are reflected in the broad classification of infants into easy, difficult, and slow-to-warm categories.

13. No single type of temperament is invariably bad or good. Long-term adjustment depends on the goodness of fit between a child's temperament and the environment in which she or he is raised.

14. The origins of personality, the sum total of the enduring characteristics that differentiate one individual from another, are found during infancy. According to Erik Erikson's theory of psychosocial development, developmental change occurs throughout people's lives as they pass through eight stages in which they must confront and resolve characteristic crises.

15. During infancy, children encounter the trust-versus-mistrust stage and the autonomy-versus-shame-and-doubt stage. Then, during early childhood, they pass through the initiative-versus-guilt stage, followed by the industry-versus-inferiority stage, which brings them to adolescence. In adolescence, they enter the identity-versus-identity-confusion stage. Early adulthood is characterized by the intimacy-versus-isolation stage, while middle adulthood is characterized by the generativity-versus-stagnation stage. The final stage of human psychosocial development, the ego-transcendence-versus-ego-preoccupation stage, occurs in late adulthood.

Is there continuity in personality development during middle adulthood?

16. It appears that, in general, the broad personality may be relatively stable over time, with particular aspects changing in response to life changes.

For more review plus MyVirtualChild, practice tests, videos, flashcards, and more, log on to **mydevelopmentlab.com**

10

Development of the Self

Prologue

Who Is Karl Haglund?

Nine-year-old Karl Haglund is perched in his eagle's nest, a treehouse built high in the willow that grows in his backyard. Sometimes he sits there alone among the tree's spreading branches, his face turned toward the sky, a boy clearly enjoying his solitude. Sometimes he's with his friend, engrossed in the kind of talk that boys find fascinating.

This morning Karl is busy sawing and hammering. "It's fun to build," he says. "I started the house when I was 4 years old. Then when I was about 7, my dad built me this platform. 'Cause all my places were falling apart and they were crawling with carpenter ants. So we destroyed them and then built me a deck. And I built on top of it. It's stronger now. You can have privacy here, but it's a bad place to go when it's windy 'cause you almost get blown off. . . .

"I like to draw. I like to play soccer. The favorite position I have is goalie. I like to collect shells when I go to the beach. I like to build clubhouses. I like to play with my chemistry set. And I like to ride skate boards and bikes and stuff." This list of what he likes to do is what Karl offers when asked to describe himself. It takes some coaxing to get him to acknowledge that he's good at carpentry, soccer, and video games, that he has a talent for drawing, and that he's a member of the safety patrol. . . .

Sitting in his treehouse, Karl thinks that someday it might be nice to have a job building things, like his dad does. "Dad's an architect and that means, like, he does buildings for the city and for other people on his own. We know this one person, Dad designed his house in Washington. He designed some of my friends' houses. Mom's a social worker, and she talks to the parents and she goes to meetings. But I don't want to be a social worker. 'Cause I would have to be in important meetings. It's a pretty hard job. But I might be an architect, probably. Or maybe a carpenter." (Kotre & Hall, 1990, pp. 116–119)

During childhood, we develop a sense of self—who we are, and what capabilities we have.

Karl Haglund knows who Karl Haglund is. He is, as he describes himself, someone who likes to draw, play soccer, and work with wood, and he envisions himself as perhaps an architect or a carpenter.

But is this the way Karl will see himself in a few years, or, for that matter, the way he saw himself a few years earlier? Probably not, for our view of who we are shifts considerably throughout the course of childhood. Even in adulthood, a sense of self continues to evolve.

In this chapter we consider the nature of the *self,* examining how we see and evaluate ourselves throughout our life span, and how we go about choosing our life's work. We start by tracing the first evidence that we have that infants are aware of their own existence. We consider how they come to understand that they are individuals distinct from the world around them. We examine how self-concept develops in preschool and middle childhood, and how children develop racial and ethnic awareness. We also consider how adolescents form their views of themselves in their search for identity.

We then turn to the ways that children and adolescents develop a positive—or negative—view of themselves. We discuss how social comparison provides a useful tool for self-evaluation by measuring one's abilities objectively within an appropriate context. We also consider how adolescents' ability to differentiate various aspects of the self leads them to evaluate those aspects in different ways.

Next, we turn to a discussion of how people make decisions about their future work—an important source of identity and self-esteem in adulthood. We see how people, who begin with vague and often unrealistic thoughts during childhood, begin to refine their options and make realistic choices regarding who they wish to be on a professional level. We consider the reasons people work—not only to earn money—and techniques for choosing a career. Finally, we examine the changing role of work in people's lives and some of the difficulties associated with work, such as burnout and unemployment.

LOOKING AHEAD

After reading this chapter, you will be able to answer the following questions:

▶ What sort of mental lives do infants have?

▶ In what ways do children's views of themselves change during the middle childhood years?

▶ What is self-esteem, and what are some factors in and consequences of high and low self-esteem?

▶ How does the development of self-concept and identity proceed during adolescence?

▶ Why is choosing a career such an important issue for young adults, and what factors influence the choice of a career?

▶ What are the characteristics of work and career in middle adulthood?

MODULE 10.1

The Development of the Self

Elysa, 8 months old, crawls past the full-length mirror that hangs on a door in her parents' bedroom. She barely pays any attention to her reflection as she moves by. On the other hand, her cousin Brianna, who is almost 2 years old, stares at herself in the mirror as she passes and laughs as she notices, and then rubs off, a smear of jelly on her forehead.

Perhaps you have had the experience of catching a glimpse of yourself in a mirror and noticing a hair out of place. You probably reacted by attempting to push the unruly hair back into place. Your reaction shows more than that you care about how you look. It implies that you have a sense of yourself, the awareness and knowledge that you are an independent social entity to which others react, and which you attempt to present to the world in ways that reflect favorably on you.

The Roots of Self-Awareness

We are not born with the knowledge that we exist independently from others and the larger world. Very young infants do not have a sense of themselves as individuals; they do not recognize themselves in photos or mirrors. However, the roots of **self-awareness**, knowledge of oneself, begin to grow at around the age of 12 months.

We know this from a simple but ingenious experimental technique in which an infant's nose is secretly colored with a dab of red powder. Then the infant is seated in front of a mirror. If infants touch their noses or attempt to wipe off the rouge, we have evidence that they have at least some knowledge of their physical characteristics. For them, this awareness is one step in developing an understanding of themselves as independent objects. For instance, Brianna, in the example at the beginning of this section, showed her awareness of her independence when she tried to rub the jelly off her forehead (Gallup, 1977; Asendorpf, Warkentin, & Baudonniere, 1996; Rochat, 2004).

Although some infants as young as 12 months seem startled on seeing the rouge spot, for most a reaction does not occur until between 17 and 24 months of age. It is also around this age that children begin to show awareness of their own capabilities. For instance, infants who partic-

self-awareness knowledge of oneself.

ipate in experiments when they are between the ages of 23 and 25 months sometimes begin to cry if the experimenter asks them to imitate a complicated sequence of behaviors involving toys, although they readily accomplish simpler sequences. Their reaction suggests that they are conscious that they lack the ability to carry out difficult tasks and are unhappy about it—a reaction that provides a clear indication of self-awareness (Kagan, 1981; Legerstee, 1998; Asendorpf, 2002; Gergely, 2007).

Children's cultural upbringing also impacts the development of self-recognition. For instance, Greek children—who experience parenting practices that emphasize autonomy and separation—show self-recognition at an earlier age than children from Cameroon in Africa. In the Cameroonian culture, parenting practices emphasize body contact and warmth, leading to more interdependence between infants and parents, and ultimately later development of self-recognition (Keller et al., 2004; Keller, Voelker, & Yovsi, 2005).

In general, by the age of 18 to 24 months, infants in Western cultures have developed at least an awareness of their own physical characteristics and capabilities, and they understand that their appearance is stable over time. Although it is not clear how far this awareness extends, it is becoming increasingly evident that, as we discuss next, infants have not only a basic understanding of themselves, but also the beginnings of an understanding of how the mind operates (Forrester, 2001; Fogel, de Koeyer, & Bellagamba, 2002; Nielsen, Dissanayake, & Kashima, 2003; Lewis & Ramsay, 2004).

Research suggests this young child is exhibiting a sense of self.

Theory of Mind: Infants' Perspectives on the Mental Lives of Others—and Themselves.

What are infants' thoughts about thinking? Infants begin to understand certain things about their own and others' mental processes at quite an early age, developing a *theory of mind*, their knowledge and beliefs about how the mind works and how it influences behavior. As we discussed in the last chapter, theories of mind are the explanations that children use to explain how others think.

For instance, the cognitive advances during infancy that we discussed earlier permit older infants to see people in a very different way from other objects. They learn to see other people as *compliant agents,* beings similar to themselves who behave under their own power and who have the capacity to respond to infants' requests (Poulin-Dubois, 1999; Rochat, 1999, 2004).

In addition, children's capacity to understand intentionality and causality grows during infancy. They begin to understand that others' behaviors have some meaning and that the behaviors they see people enacting are designed to accomplish particular goals, in contrast to the "behaviors" of inanimate objects. For example, a child comes to understand that his father has a specific goal when he is in the kitchen making sandwiches. In contrast, his father's car is simply parked in the driveway, having no mental life or goal (Golinkoff, 1993; Ahn, Gelman, & Amsterlaw, 2000; Tomasello et al., 2005).

Another piece of evidence for infants' growing sense of mental activity is that by the age of 2, infants begin to demonstrate the rudiments of empathy. *Empathy*, as we discussed in Chapter 9, is an emotional response that corresponds to the feelings of another person. At 24 months of age, infants sometimes comfort others or show concern for them. In order to do this, they need to be aware of the emotional states of others. For example, 1-year-olds are able to pick up emotional cues by observing the behavior of an actress on television (Gauthier, 2003; Mumm & Fernald, 2003).

To see the theory of mind at work, watch the video in **MyDevelopmentLab**.

Self-Concept in the Preschool Years: Thinking About the Self.

Although the question "Who am I?" is not explicitly posed by most preschool-age children, it underlies a considerable amount of development during the preschool years. During this period, children wonder about the nature of the self, and the way they answer the "Who am I?" question may affect them for the rest of their lives.

If you ask preschool-age children to specify what makes them different from other kids, they readily respond with answers like, "I'm a good runner" or "I like to color" or "I'm a big girl." Such answers relate to **self-concept**—their identity, or their set of beliefs about what they are like as individuals (Brown, 1998; Tessor, Felson, & Suls, 2000; Marsh, Ellis, & Craven, 2002; Grace, David, & Ryan, 2008).

The statements that describe children's self-concepts are not necessarily accurate. In fact, preschool children typically overestimate their skills and knowledge across all domains of expertise. Consequently, their view of the future is quite rosy: They expect to win the next game they play, to beat all opponents in an upcoming race, to write great stories when they grow up. Even when they have just experienced failure at a task, they are likely to expect to do well in the future.

self-concept a person's identity, or set of beliefs about what one is like as an individual.

This optimistic view is held, in part, because they have not yet started to compare themselves and their performance against others. Their inaccuracy is also helpful, freeing them to take chances and try new activities (Dweck, 2002; Wang, 2004).

Culture and Self-Concept. Preschool-age children's view of themselves also reflects the way their particular culture considers the self. For example, many Asian societies tend to have a **collectivistic orientation**, promoting the notion of interdependence. People in such cultures tend to regard themselves as parts of a larger social network in which they are interconnected with and responsible to others. In contrast, children in Western cultures are more likely to develop a view of the self reflecting an **individualistic orientation** that emphasizes personal identity and the uniqueness of the individual. They are more apt to see themselves as self-contained and autonomous, in competition with others for scarce resources. Consequently, children in Western cultures are more likely to focus on what sets them apart from others—what makes them special.

Such views pervade a culture, sometimes in subtle ways. For instance, one well-known saying in Western cultures states that "the squeaky wheel gets the grease." Preschoolers who are exposed to this perspective are encouraged to gain the attention of others by standing out and making their needs known. On the other hand, children in Asian cultures are exposed to a different perspective; they are told that "the nail that stands out gets pounded down." This perspective suggests to preschoolers that they should attempt to blend in and refrain from making themselves distinctive (Markus & Kitayama, 1991; Dennis et al., 2002; Lehman, Chiu, & Schaller, 2004; Wang, 2004, 2006).

Self-Concept and Attitudes Toward Gender, Race, and Ethnicity. Gender, the sense of being male or female, is well established by the time children reach the preschool years, and this, too, affects their self-concept.

Preschoolers' developing self-concepts can also be affected by their culture's attitudes toward various racial and ethnic groups. For most preschool-age children, racial awareness comes relatively early. Certainly, even infants are able to distinguish different skin colors; their perceptual abilities allow for such color distinctions quite early in life. However, it is only later that children begin to attribute meaning to different racial characteristics, a meaning that is subtly influenced by the attitudes of the people, schools, and other cultural institutions with which they come into contact in their community.

By the time they are 3 or 4 years of age, preschool-age children notice differences among people based on skin color, and they begin to identify themselves as a member of a particular group such as "Hispanic" or "black." Although early in the preschool years they do not realize that ethnicity and race are enduring features of who they are, later they begin to develop an understanding of the significance that society places on ethnic and racial membership (Bernal & Knight, 1993; Sheets & Hollins, 1999; Hall & Rowan, 2003).

Some preschoolers have mixed feelings about their racial and ethnic identity. Some experience **race dissonance**, the phenomenon in which minority children indicate preferences for majority values or people. For instance, some studies find that as many as 90 percent of African American children, when asked about their reactions to drawings of black and white children, react more negatively to the drawings of black children than to those of white children. However, these negative reactions did not translate into lower self-esteem for the African American subjects. Instead, their preferences appear to be a result of the powerful influence of the dominant white culture, rather than a disparagement of their own racial characteristics (Holland, 1994; Margie et al., 2005).

Ethnic identity emerges somewhat later than racial identity because it is usually less conspicuous than race. For instance, in one study of Mexican American ethnic awareness, preschoolers displayed only a limited knowledge of their ethnic identity. However, as they became older, they grew more aware of the significance of their ethnicity. Preschoolers who were bilingual, speaking both Spanish and English, were most apt to be aware of their ethnic identity (Bernal, 1994; Shi & Lu, 2007).

Understanding One's Self in Middle Childhood and Adolescence

Eight-year-old Sonia carefully removes her muddy garden clogs and proudly plops an armload of carrots in the kitchen sink to be rinsed and scrubbed. This year, she has taken over the care for a portion of the family's vegetable garden. Having worked beside her mother since she was 6 she was able to plant and tend the carrots, zucchini, and broccoli on her own this year. Sonia smiles as she washes the vegetables, thinking about how her family depends on her, too, now.

collectivistic orientation a philosophy that promotes the notion of interdependence.

individualistic orientation a philosophy that emphasizes personal identity and the uniqueness of the individual.

race dissonance the phenomenon in which minority children indicate preferences for majority values or people.

In the opening to this chapter, we saw how Karl's growing sense of competence is reflected in his description of building a treehouse with his father. Sonia, too, is coming to see herself as capable and reliable—someone her family can depend on. Conveying what psychologist Erik Erikson calls "industriousness," Karl's and Sonia's quiet pride in their accomplishments illustrates one way children's views of themselves evolve.

During middle childhood, children actively seek to answer the question "Who am I?" Although the question will assume greater urgency in adolescence, elementary-age children still try to find their place in the world.

The Shift in Self-Understanding from the Physical to the Psychological.

The cognitive advances discussed earlier aid children in their quest for self-understanding. They begin to view themselves less in terms of external, physical attributes and more in terms of psychological traits (Marsh & Ayotte, 2003; Sotiriou & Zafiropoulou, 2003; Lerner, Theokas, & Jelicic, 2005).

For instance, 6-year-old Carey describes herself as "a fast runner and good at drawing"—characteristics dependent on motor skills in external activities. In contrast, 11-year-old Meiping characterizes herself as "pretty smart, friendly, and helpful to my friends." Because of her increasing cognitive skills, Meiping's view of herself is based on psychological characteristics, inner traits that are more abstract.

Children's views of who they are also become more complex. As we discussed in Chapter 9, Erikson characterized psychosocial development in middle childhood as the industry-versus-inferiority stage. Children are seeking endeavors in which they can be successfully industrious. As they get older, children discover their strengths and weaknesses. Ten-year-old Ginny, for instance, comes to understand she is good at arithmetic but not very good at spelling; 11-year-old Alberto decides he is good at softball but lacks the stamina to play soccer well.

Children's self-concepts become divided into personal and academic spheres. They evaluate themselves in four major areas, each of which can be broken down further; for example, the nonacademic self-concept includes physical appearance, peer relations, and physical ability, while the academic self-concept is similarly divided. Research on students' self-concepts in English, mathematics, and nonacademic realms shows that the separate realms do not always correlate, although overlap exists. For example, a child who sees herself as a star math student will not necessarily feel she is great at English (Burnett & Proctor, 2003; Marsh & Ayotte, 2003; Marsh & Hau, 2004).

Adolescence: The Search for Identity.

Thirteen is a hard age, very hard. A lot of people say you have it easy, you're a kid, but there's a lot of pressure being 13—to be respected by people in your school, to be liked, always feeling like you have to be good. There's pressure to do drugs, too, so you try not to succumb to that. But you don't want to be made fun of, so you have to look cool. You gotta wear the right shoes, the right clothes. —Carlos Quintana (1998, p. 66)

The thoughts of 13-year-old Carlos Quintana demonstrate a clear awareness—and self-consciousness—regarding his new place in society. During adolescence, questions like "Who am I?" and "Where do I belong in the world?" begin to take a front seat.

One reason issues of identity become so important is that adolescents' intellectual capacities become more adultlike. They see how they stack up to others and realize they are individuals, separate from everyone else. The dramatic physical changes of puberty make adolescents acutely aware of their own bodies and aware that others are reacting to them in new ways. Whatever the cause, adolescence brings major changes in teenagers' self-concepts and self-esteem—in sum, their views of their own identity.

Self-Concept: What Am I Like? Valerie describes herself this way: "Others look at me as laidback, relaxed, and not worrying too much. But really, I'm often nervous and emotional."

The fact that Valerie distinguishes others' views from her own represents a developmental advance. In childhood, she would have characterized herself by traits that would not differentiate her view from the views of others. However, when adolescents describe who they are, they take into account both their own and others' perspectives (Harter, 1990a; Cole et al., 2001; Updegraff et al., 2004).

This broader view of themselves is one aspect of adolescents' increasing sense of identity. They can see various aspects of the self simultaneously, and this view becomes more organized and coherent. They look at the self from a psychological perspective, viewing traits not as concrete entities but as abstractions (Adams, Montemayor, & Gullotta, 1996; Yip, 2008). For

Adolescents' sense of who they are takes their own and others' views into account.

During the identity-versus-identity-confusion stage, teenagers seek to understand who they are by narrowing and making choices about their personal, occupational, sexual, and political commitments. Can this stage be applied to teenagers in other cultures? Why or why not?

example, teenagers are more likely than younger children to define themselves by their ideology (e.g., "I'm an environmentalist") than by physical characteristics (e.g., "I'm the fastest runner in my class").

This broader, multifaceted self-concept, however, can be a mixed blessing, especially during early adolescence. At that time, they may be troubled by the complexity of their personalities. Younger adolescents may want to view themselves in a certain way ("I'm a sociable person and love to be with people"), and they may become concerned when their behavior contradicts that view ("Even though I want to be sociable, sometimes I can't stand being around my friends and just want to be alone"). By the end of adolescence, however, teenagers find it easier to accept that behaviors and feelings change with the situation (Harter, 1990b; Pyryt & Mendaglio, 1994; Trzesniewski, Donnellan, & Robins, 2003; Hitlin, Brown, & Elder, 2006).

Identity Formation: Change or Crisis? According to Erik Erikson, whose theory we discussed earlier, the search for identity inevitably leads some adolescents to an identity crisis involving substantial psychological turmoil (Erikson, 1963). Erikson's theory of this stage (the identity-versus-identity-confusion stage) suggests that teenagers try to figure out what is unique and distinctive about themselves—a task they manage with increasing sophistication due to the cognitive gains of adolescence.

Erikson argues that adolescents strive to discover their strengths and weaknesses and the roles that best suit their future lives. This often involves "trying on" different roles or choices to see if they fit their capabilities and views about themselves. In this process, adolescents seek to understand who they are by narrowing and making choices about their personal, occupational, sexual, and political commitments.

In Erikson's view, adolescents who do not find a suitable identity may go off course in several ways. They may adopt socially unacceptable roles to express what they do *not* want to be. Forming and maintaining lasting close relationships may elude them. In general, their sense of self becomes "diffuse," failing to organize around a unified core identity.

In contrast, those who forge an appropriate identity set a foundation for future psychosocial development. They learn their unique capabilities and believe in them, and they develop an accurate sense of self. They are prepared to take full advantage of their unique strengths (Blustein, & Palladino, 1991; Archer & Waterman, 1994; Allison & Schultz, 2001; Merrell, 2008).

Societal Pressures and Reliance on Friends and Peers. Societal pressures are also high during the identity-versus-identity-confusion stage. Adolescents feel pressure from parents and friends to decide whether their post-high-school plans include work or college and, if the decision is work, which occupation to follow. Up to this point, their educational lives have followed a universal track, laid out by U.S. society. However, the track ends at high school, leaving adolescents with difficult choices about which path to follow (Kidwell et al., 1995; Sampson & Chason, 2008).

During this period, friends and peers are increasingly sought as sources of information. Dependence on adults declines. As we discuss later, this increasing dependence on peers enables adolescents to forge close relationships. Comparing themselves to others helps to clarify their own identities.

Psychological Moratorium. Because of the pressures of the identity-versus-identity-confusion period, Erikson suggested that many adolescents pursue a *psychological moratorium*, a period during which they take time off from the upcoming responsibilities of adulthood to explore various roles and possibilities. For example, many college students take a semester or year off to travel, work, or find another way to examine their priorities.

Many adolescents, for practical reasons, cannot pursue a psychological moratorium to leisurely explore various identities. For economic reasons, some must work part-time after school and then take jobs immediately after high school, leaving them little time to experiment. Such adolescents need by no means be psychologically damaged. Successfully holding a part-time job while attending school may offer a psychological reward that outweighs the lack of opportunity to try out various roles.

Marcia's Approach to Identity Development: Updating Erikson. Using Erikson's theory as a springboard, psychologist James Marcia suggests that identity can be seen in terms of which of two characteristics—crisis or commitment—is present or absent. *Crisis* is a period in which an adolescent consciously chooses between various alternatives and makes decisions.

Commitment is psychological investment in a course of action or an ideology. One adolescent might career from one activity to another, nothing lasting beyond a few weeks, while another becomes totally absorbed in volunteering at a homeless shelter (Marcia, 1980; Peterson, Marcia, & Carpendale, 2004).

After conducting lengthy interviews with adolescents, Marcia proposed four categories of identity (see Table 10.1).

1. **Identity achievement**. Teenagers in this category have successfully explored and thought through who they are and what they want to do. Following a period of crisis during which they considered various alternatives, these adolescents have committed to a particular identity. Teens who have reached this identity status tend to be psychologically healthier, higher in achievement motivation and moral reasoning, than adolescents of any other status.

2. **Identity foreclosure**. These are adolescents who have committed to an identity without passing through a period of crisis in which they explored alternatives. Instead, they accepted others' decisions about what was best for them. Typical of this category is a son who enters the family business because it is expected, or a daughter who becomes a physician because her mother is one. Foreclosers are not necessarily unhappy, but they tend to have something called "rigid strength": Happy and self-satisfied, they have a high need for social approval and tend to be authoritarian.

3. **Moratorium**. Adolescents in this category have explored some alternatives but have made no commitments. As a result, Marcia suggests, they show relatively high anxiety and experience psychological conflict, though they are often lively and appealing, seeking intimacy with others. Such adolescents typically settle on an identity, but only after a struggle.

4. **Identity diffusion**. These adolescents neither explore nor commit to various alternatives. They tend to shift from one thing to the next. While appearing carefree, according to Marcia, their lack of commitment impairs their ability to form close relationships. They are often socially withdrawn.

Some adolescents shift among the four categories, for example, moving between moratorium and identity achievement in what is called a MAMA cycle (**m**oratorium—**i**dentity **a**chievement—**m**oratorium—identity **a**chievement). Or a forecloser who selected a career path without much thought in early adolescence may reassess and make a more active choice later. For some individuals, identity formation takes place beyond adolescence. However, for most people, identity gels in the late teens and early 20s (Kroger, 2000; Meeus, 1996, 2003).

According to Marcia's approach, psychologically healthy identity development can be seen in adolescents who choose to commit to a course of action or ideology.

FROM A
SOCIAL WORKER'S
PERSPECTIVE
Do you believe that all four of Marcia's identity statuses can lead to reassessment and different choices later in life? Are there stages in Marcia's theory that may be difficult to achieve for adolescents who live in poverty? Why?

TABLE 10.1   Marcia's Four Categories of Adolescent Development

		COMMITMENT	
		Present	**Absent**
CRISIS/EXPLORATION	**PRESENT**	**Identity achievement** "I love animals; I'm going to become a vet."	**Moratorium** "I'm going to work at the mall while I figure out what to do next."
	ABSENT	**Identity foreclosure** "I am going into law, just like Mom."	**Identity diffusion** "I don't have a clue."

Source: From Marcia, J. E. (1980). "Identity in Adolescence" in J. Adelson (ed.) HANDBOOK OF ADOLESCENT PSYCHOLOGY. Reprinted with permission from John Wiley & Sons, Inc.

identity achievement the status of adolescents who commit to a particular identity following a period of crisis during which they consider various alternatives.

identity foreclosure the status of adolescents who prematurely commit to an identity without adequately exploring alternatives.

moratorium the status of adolescents who may have explored various identity alternatives to some degree, but have not yet committed themselves.

identity diffusion the status of adolescents who consider various identity alternatives, but never commit to one or never even consider identity options in any conscious way.

social clock the culturally determined psychological timepiece providing a sense of whether we have reached the major benchmarks of life at the appropriate time in comparison to our peers.

Identity, Race, and Ethnicity. Forming an identity is often difficult for adolescents, but it is especially challenging for members of racial and ethnic groups that face discrimination. Society's contradictory values tell adolescents that society should be color-blind, that race and ethnic background should not affect opportunities and achievement, and that if they do achieve, society will accept them. Based on a traditional *cultural assimilation model,* this view says individual cultural identities should be assimilated into a unified culture in the United States—the melting pot model.

In contrast, the *pluralistic society model* suggests that U.S. society is made up of diverse, coequal cultural groups that should preserve their individual features. This model grew from the belief that cultural assimilation denigrates the heritage of minorities and lowers their self-esteem. According to the pluralistic view, racial and ethnic factors form a central part of identity and are not submerged in an attempt to assimilate.

The middle ground says minority group members can form a *bicultural identity*, drawing from their own culture while integrating themselves into the dominant culture. This view suggests that an individual can hold two cultural identities, without having to prefer one over the other (Garcia, 1988; LaFromboise, Coleman, & Gerton, 1993; Phinney, 2006, 2008). Choosing a bicultural identity is increasingly common. According to the 2000 U.S. Census, a considerable number of individuals see themselves as belonging to more than one race (Schmitt, 2001).

The process of identity formation is always complex and may be doubly so for minority group members. Racial and ethnic identity takes time to form. For some, it may require a prolonged period, but the result can be a rich, multifaceted identity (Roberts et al., 1999; Grantham & Ford, 2003; Nadal, 2004; Umana-Taylor & Fine, 2004).

Adulthood: Defining the Self Through Life Events

At 21, Nadine defined herself, largely, as a college senior majoring in political science. At 23, her self-concept centered on the intelligence and persistence she brought to her work as an assistant in an ACLU office. A year later, Nadine added "wife" to her resume, and two years after that, "parent" trumped her former identity as a bright, young professional.

Having children. Receiving a promotion. Getting divorced. Changing jobs. Each of these events marks a moment on what has been called the social clock of life. As Nadine's story illustrates, these life events also shape and reshape identity in early adulthood.

The Social Clocks of Adulthood. The **social clock** is a term used to describe the psychological timepiece that records the major milestones in people's lives. A personal social clock tells each of us whether we have reached the major benchmarks of life early, late, or right on time in comparison to our peers. Our social clocks are culturally determined, reflecting the expectations of the society in which we live.

Until the mid-20th century, the social clocks of adulthood were fairly uniform—at least for upper-class and middle-class people in Western societies. The typical man completed his education by his early 20s, started a career, married in his mid-20s, and was providing for a growing family by his 30s. Women also followed a set pattern, which focused on getting married and raising children—but not, in most cases, entering a profession and developing a career.

Today, there is considerably more heterogeneity in the social clocks of both men and women. The timing of major life events has changed, and women's social clocks have changed dramatically as a result of social and cultural changes.

Women's Social Clocks. Developmental psychologist Ravenna Helson and colleagues suggest that people choose from several social clocks, and the selection they make has implications for personality development during middle adulthood. Focusing on a sample of women who graduated from college during the early 1960s, Helson's longitudinal research has examined women whose social clocks were focused either on their families, on careers, or on a more individualistic target (Helson & Moane, 1987; Helson & Soto, 2005; Helson, Soto, & Cate, 2006).

Helson found that, over the course of the study, which assessed participants at the ages of 21, 27, and 43, the women generally became more self-disciplined and committed to their duties. They also felt greater independence and confidence and could cope with stress and adversity more effectively.

Finding a spouse and embarking on motherhood meant that many women exhibited what Helson called traditional feminine behavior from about age 21 to 27. But as children grew up and maternal duties diminished, women took on less traditional roles.

Always culturally determined, women's social clocks have changed over the years.

The study also found some intriguing similarities in women who chose to focus on family compared with those who focused on career. Both groups showed generally positive changes. In contrast, women who had no strong focus on either family or career tended to show either little change or more negative shifts in personality development, such as becoming less satisfied over time.

Helson's conclusion is that the critical factor in personality development is not which social clock a woman chooses, but the *process* of choosing a social clock, whether it involves motherhood or career. Whether the woman chooses a career first and then motherhood, or the opposite pattern, or an entirely different path is less important than investing in and focusing on a particular trajectory.

It is important to keep in mind that social clocks are culturally determined. The timing of motherhood and the course of a woman's career are both influenced by the social, economic, and cultural worlds in which the woman lives (Helson, Stewart, & Ostrove, 1995; Stewart & Ostrove, 1998; Helson & Soto, 2005; Helson et al., 2006).

The Role of Work in Shaping Identity During Adulthood. According to psychiatrist George Vaillant, the stage of development that young adults reach is called career consolidation. During **career consolidation**, which begins between 20 and 40, young adults become centered on their careers. Vaillant based his conclusion on a comprehensive longitudinal study of male graduates of Harvard, begun when they were freshmen in the 1930s (Vaillant, 1977; Vaillant & Vaillant, 1990; Vaillant, 2003).

In their early 20s, the men tended to be influenced by their parents' authority. But in their late 20s and early 30s, they started to act with greater autonomy. They married, had children, and began to focus on their careers—the period of career consolidation.

Vaillant draws a relatively uninspiring portrait of people in this stage. His participants worked very hard as they climbed the corporate ladder. They tended to be rule-followers conforming to the norms of their professions. Rather than showing the independence and questioning that they had displayed in college, they threw themselves unquestioningly into their work.

Vaillant argues that work plays such an important role that the career consolidation stage should be seen as an addition to Erikson's intimacy-versus-isolation stage of psychosocial identity. In Vaillant's view, career concerns supplant the focus on intimacy, and the career consolidation stage marks a bridge between intimacy-versus-isolation and generativity-versus-stagnation. (Generativity refers to an individual's contribution to society, as we discussed earlier.)

The reaction to Vaillant's viewpoint has been mixed. Critics point out that Vaillant's sample, though relatively large, comprised a highly restricted, unusually bright group of men. Furthermore, societal norms have changed considerably since the 1930s, and people's views of the importance of work may have shifted. Finally, the lack of women in the sample and the fact that there have been major changes in the role of work in *women's* lives make Vaillant's conclusions even less generalizable.

Still, it is hard to dispute the importance of work in most people's lives, and research suggests that it makes up a significant part of both men's and women's identity—if for no other reason than that it occupies so much of their time (Deaux et al., 1995; Thatcher & Greer, 2008). Later in this chapter, we consider how people decide what careers to follow—and the implications of that decision.

REVIEW

▶ Infants develop self-awareness, the knowledge that they exist separately from the rest of the world, after about 12 months of age, and by the age of 2, children have developed the rudiments of a theory of mind.

▶ During the preschool years, children develop their self-concepts, beliefs about themselves that they derive from their own perceptions, their parents' behaviors, and society.

▶ Racial, ethnic, and gender awareness begin to form in the preschool years.

▶ In the middle childhood years, children begin to base their self-concept on psychological rather than physical characteristics.

▶ Self-concept during adolescence grows more differentiated as the view of the self becomes more organized, broader, and more abstract, and takes account of the views of others.

career consolidation a stage that is entered between the ages of 20 and 40, when young adults become centered on their careers.

▶ Marcia's four identity statuses focus on the adolescent's struggle to determine an identity and a role in society.

▶ Choosing a career is an important step in early adulthood, so important that developmental psychologist George Vaillant considers career consolidation a developmental stage on a par with Erikson's intimacy-versus-isolation stage.

APPLY

▶ How might a child's developing sense of empathy be fostered by parents and other caregivers?

▶ Do you believe that there is an optimal time that the period of psychological moratorium should last, and at what point do you think an individual should have completed the process of identity formation? Why? Has the rapid pace of change in today's world, fueled by technological advances, had implications for the timing of identity formation?

MODULE 10.2

Evaluating the Self

Kieran had been given the part of "Frog" in the second-grade class play based on the popular Frog & Toad *stories. Somewhat shy, he was a bit nervous about this, his biggest challenge to date. His older sister helped him learn his lines, and his aunt made a frog costume. With so much support, Kieran's fear ebbed. He started to enjoy the rehearsals and when he took his bow at the close of the performance, he received more applause than anyone else. Meeting his family backstage, he beamed. "I like doing plays. Everyone thought I was great!"*

Self-Esteem: Developing a Positive—or Negative—View of Oneself

Although an awareness of *self* takes root in infancy, and preschoolers are able to form a self-concept, it is not until early middle childhood that children begin to evaluate themselves.

Children don't dispassionately view themselves just in terms of an itemization of physical and psychological characteristics. Instead, they make judgments about themselves as being good or bad in particular ways, as Kieran did. **Self-esteem** is an individual's overall and specific positive and negative self-evaluation. Whereas self-concept reflects beliefs and cognitions about the self (*I am good at trumpet; I am not so good at social studies*), self-esteem is more emotionally oriented (*Everybody thinks I'm a nerd*) (Baumeister, 1993; Davis-Kean & Sandler, 2001; Bracken & Lamprecht, 2003).

Self-esteem develops in important ways during middle childhood. As we'll discuss shortly, children increasingly compare themselves to others, and as they do, they assess how well they measure up to society's standards. In addition, they increasingly develop their own internal standards of success, and they can see how well they compare to those.

One of the advances that occur during middle childhood is that, like self-concept, self-esteem becomes increasingly differentiated. At the age of 7, most children have self-esteem that reflects a global, fairly simple view of themselves. If their overall self-esteem is positive, they believe that they are relatively good at all things. Conversely, if their overall self-esteem is negative, they feel that they are inadequate at most things (Harter, 1990b; Lerner, Theokas, & Jelicic, 2005).

As children progress into the middle childhood years, however, their self-esteem is higher for some areas and lower in others. For example, a boy's overall self-esteem may be composed of positive self-esteem in some areas (such as the positive feelings he gets from his artistic ability) and more negative self-esteem in others (such as the unhappiness he feels over his athletic skills).

Self-Esteem in Adolescence: How Do I Like Myself? *Knowing* who you are and *liking* who you are two different things. As children move into adolescence, they become increasingly accurate in understanding who they are (their self-concept). This knowledge, however, does

self-esteem an individual's overall and specific positive and negative self-evaluation.

not guarantee that they like themselves (their self-esteem) any better. In fact, their increasing accuracy in understanding themselves permits them to see themselves fully—warts and all. It's what they do with these perceptions that leads them to develop a sense of their self-esteem.

The same cognitive sophistication that allows adolescents to differentiate various aspects of the self also leads them to evaluate those aspects in different ways (Chan, 1997; Cohen, 1999; Bos et al., 2006). For instance, an adolescent may have high self-esteem in terms of academic performance, but lower self-esteem in terms of relationships with others. Or it may be just the opposite, as articulated by this adolescent:

> *How much do I like the kind of person I am? Well, I like some things about me, but I don't like others. I'm glad that I'm popular since it's really important to me to have friends. But in school I don't do as well as the really smart kids. That's OK, because if you're too smart you'll lose your friends. So being smart is just not that important. Except to my parents. I feel like I'm letting them down when I don't do as well as they want. (Harter, 1990b, p. 364)*

In pioneering research conducted several decades ago, African American girls' preference for white dolls was viewed as an indication of low self-esteem. More recent evidence, however, suggests that white and African American children show little difference in self-esteem.

Beyond Adolescence: Self-Esteem in Adulthood. Although discussions about identity and self-esteem often focus on middle childhood and adolescence, how we view and judge ourselves continues to be a central part of our development throughout our lives. Moving from being a child in our parents' home to being an adult in our own home (and perhaps a parent, too) dramatically alters our self-concept. How we feel we manage this transition can affect our self-esteem. Choosing our life's work and establishing a career, as we will discuss in the next module, also impact both our identity and self-esteem. Even in late adulthood, as we saw in the last chapter, self-esteem continues to play a large role in how we experience our lives, as elderly people evaluate who they have been and how well they have managed their lives as they prepare for death.

Race and Self-Esteem. If you were a member of a racial group whose members routinely experienced prejudice and discrimination, it seems reasonable to predict that your self-esteem would be affected. Early research confirmed that hypothesis and found that African Americans had lower self-esteem than whites. For example, as noted earlier, a set of pioneering studies a generation ago found that African American children shown black and white dolls preferred the white dolls over the black ones (Clark & Clark, 1947). The interpretation that was drawn from the study: The self-esteem of the African American children was low.

More recent research, however, has shown these early assumptions to be overstated. The picture is more complex regarding relative levels of self-esteem between members of different racial and ethnic groups. For example, although white children initially show higher self-esteem than black children, black children begin to show slightly higher self-esteem than white children around the age of 11. This shift occurs as African American children become more closely identified with their racial group, develop more complex views of racial identity, and increasingly view the positive aspects of their group membership (Gray-Little & Hafdahl, 2000; Oyserman et al., 2003; Tatum, 2007).

Hispanic children also show an increase in self-esteem toward the end of middle childhood, although even in adolescence their self-esteem still trails that of whites. In contrast, Asian American children show the opposite pattern: Their self-esteem in elementary school is higher than that of whites and blacks, but by the end of childhood, their self-esteem is lower than that of whites (Twenge & Crocker, 2002; Umana et al., 2002; Tropp & Wright, 2003).

Social Identity Theory. One explanation for the complex relationship between self-esteem and minority group status comes from *social identity theory*. According to the theory, members of a minority group are likely to accept the negative views held by a majority group only if they perceive that there is little realistic possibility of changing the power and status differences between the groups. If minority group members feel that prejudice and discrimination can be reduced, and they blame society for the prejudice and not themselves, self-esteem should not differ between majority and minority groups (Tajfel, 1982; Turner & Onorato, 1999; Hogg, 2003; Outten et al., 2009).

As group pride and ethnic awareness among minority group members have grown, differences in self-esteem between members of different ethnic groups have narrowed. This trend has further been supported by an increased sensitivity to the importance of multiculturalism (Goodstein & Ponerotto, 1997; Negy, Shreve, & Jensen, 2003; Lee, 2005; Tatum, 2007).

A strong sense of racial identity during adolescence is tied to higher levels of self-esteem.

Another reason for the overall similarity in self-esteem levels found between adolescents of different racial groups is that teenagers in general focus their preferences and priorities on those aspects of their lives at which they excel. Consequently, African American youths may concentrate on the things that they find most satisfying and gain self-esteem from being successful at them (Gray-Little & Hafdahl, 2000; Yang & Blodgett, 2000; Phinney, 2005).

Finally, self-esteem may be influenced not by race alone, but by a complex combination of factors. For instance, some developmentalists have considered race and gender simultaneously, coining the term *ethgender* to refer to the joint influence of race and gender. One study that simultaneously took both race and gender into account found that African American and Hispanic males had the highest levels of self-esteem, while Asian and Native American females had the lowest levels (Dukes & Martinez, 1994; King, 2003; Romero & Roberts, 2003; Saunders, Davis, & Williams, 2004; Biro et al., 2006).

Gender Differences in Self-Esteem. Gender is another factor that affects self-esteem. Particularly during early adolescence, girls' self-esteem tends to be lower and more vulnerable than that of boys (Watkins, Dong, & Xia, 1997; Byrne, 2000; Miyamoto et al., 2000; Ah-Kion, 2006).

One reason for the difference is that, compared to boys, girls tend to be more concerned about physical appearance and social success—in addition to academic achievement. Although boys are also concerned about these things, their attitudes are often more casual. In addition, societal messages suggesting that female academic achievement is a roadblock to social success can put girls in a difficult bind: If they do well academically, they jeopardize their social success. No wonder that the self-esteem of adolescent girls is more fragile than that of boys (Unger, 2001; Ricciardelli & McCabe, 2003).

Although generally self-esteem is higher in adolescent boys than girls, boys do have vulnerabilities of their own. For example, society's stereotypical gender expectations may lead boys to feel that they should be confident, tough, and fearless all the time. Boys facing difficulties, such as not making a sports team or rejection from a girl they wanted to date, are likely to feel not only miserable about the defeat they face, but also incompetent, since they don't measure up to the stereotype (Pollack, 1999; Pollack, Shuster, & Trelease, 2001; Pollack, 2006).

Socioeconomic Status and Self-Esteem. Socioeconomic status (SES) also influences self-esteem. Adolescents of higher SES generally have higher self-esteem than those of lower SES, particularly during middle and later adolescence. It may be that the social status factors that especially enhance one's standing and self-esteem—such as having more expensive clothes or a car—become more conspicuous in the later periods of adolescence (Savin-Williams & Demo, 1983; Van Tassel-Baska, Olszewski, Kubilius, & Kulieke, 1994; Beaudoin & Lachance, 2006).

As we shall see in the next module, socioeconomic status continues to play a role in how we view ourselves throughout our lives. For example, adults who hold jobs with a high status tend to be more satisfied with their work than those in low-status jobs. Since work is a major component of identity for adults, the status of a job may greatly influence an individual's self-esteem.

Social Comparison. If someone were to ask you how good you are at math, how would you respond? Most of us would compare our performance to that of others who are roughly of the same age and educational level. It is unlikely that we'd answer the question by comparing ourselves either to Albert Einstein or to a kindergartner just learning about numbers.

Elementary-school-age children begin to follow the same sort of reasoning when they seek to understand how able they are. When they were younger, they tended to consider their abilities in terms of some hypothetical standard, making a judgment that they are good or bad in an absolute sense. Now they begin to use social comparison processes, comparing themselves to others, to determine their levels of accomplishment during middle childhood (Weiss, Ebbeck, & Horn, 1997; Malmberg, Wanner, & Little, 2008).

The success of many immigrant children can be attributed to the fact that they are often highly motivated to succeed and place great value on education.

DEVELOPMENTAL DIVERSITY
Are Children of Immigrant Families Well Adjusted?

Immigration to the United States has risen significantly in the last 30 years. More than 13 million children in the United States are either foreign born or the children of immigrants—some one-fifth of the total population of children.

How well are these children of immigrants faring? Quite well. In fact, in some ways they are better off than their nonimmigrant peers. For example, they tend to have equal or better grades in school than children whose parents were born in the United States. Psychologically, they also do quite well, showing similar levels of self-esteem to nonimmigrant children, although they do report feeling less popular and less in control of their lives (Kao & Tienda, 1995; Harris, 2000; Kao, 2000; Portes, 2005).

Why is the adjustment of immigrant children to U.S. culture so generally positive? One answer is that often their socioeconomic status is relatively higher. In spite of stereotypes that immigrant families come from lower social classes, many in fact are well educated and come to the United States seeking greater opportunities.

But socioeconomic status is only part of the story. Even the immigrant children who are not financially well off are often more highly motivated to succeed and place greater value on education than do children in nonimmigrant families. In addition, many immigrant children come from societies that emphasize collectivism, and consequently they may feel more obligation and duty toward their family to succeed. Finally, their country of origin may give some immigrant children a strong enough cultural identity to prevent them from adopting undesirable "American" behaviors—such as materialism or selfishness (Fuligini, Tseng, & Lam, 1999; Fuligni & Yoshikawa, 2003).

During the middle childhood years, it thus appears that children in immigrant families typically do quite well in the United States. The story is less clear, however, when children of immigrants reach adolescence and adulthood. Research is just beginning to clarify how effectively immigrants cope over the course of the life span (Fuligini, 1998; Portes & Rumbaut, 2001; Wiley, Perkins, & Deaux, 2008).

Social comparison is the desire to evaluate one's own behavior, abilities, expertise, and opinions by comparing them to those of others. According to a theory first suggested by psychologist Leon Festinger (1954), when concrete, objective measures of ability are lacking, people turn to *social reality* to evaluate themselves. Social reality refers to understanding that is derived from how others act, think, feel, and view the world.

But who provides the most adequate comparison? When they cannot objectively evaluate their ability, children during middle childhood increasingly look to others who are similar to themselves (Suls & Wills, 1991; Summers, Schallert, & Ritter, 2003).

Downward Social Comparison. Although children typically compare themselves to similar others, in some cases—particularly when their self-esteem is at stake—they choose to make *downward social comparisons* with others who are obviously less competent or successful (Aspinwall & Taylor, 1993; Vohs & Heatherton, 2004).

Downward social comparison protects children's self-esteem. By comparing themselves to those who are less able, children ensure that they will come out on top and thereby preserve an image of themselves as successful.

Downward social comparison helps explain why some students in elementary schools with generally low achievement levels are found to have stronger academic self-esteem than very capable students in schools with high achievement levels. The reason seems to be that students in the low-achievement schools observe others who are not doing terribly well academically, and they feel relatively good by comparison. In contrast, students in the high-achievement schools may find themselves competing with a more academically proficient group of students, and their perception of their performance may suffer in comparison. At least in terms of self-esteem, then, it is better to be a big fish in a small pond than a small fish in a big one (Borland & Howsen, 2003; Marsh & Hau, 2003).

Social Comparison in Adolescence: The Importance of Peer Groups. Teenagers' seemingly compulsive need to communicate with friends, exemplified by *Facebook* and cell texting, demonstrates the role that peers play in adolescence. Continuing the trend that began in middle childhood, adolescents spend increasing amounts of time with their peers, and the importance of peer relationships grows as well. There is probably no period of life in which peer relationships are as important as they are in adolescence (Arnon, Shamai, & Ilatov, 2008; Shook et al., 2008).

Peers become more important in adolescence for a number of reasons. For one thing, they provide each other with the opportunity to compare and evaluate opinions, abilities, and even physical changes, extending the process of social comparison begun in middle childhood. Because physical and cognitive changes of adolescence are so unique to this age group and so pronounced, especially during the early stages of puberty, adolescents turn increasingly to others who share, and consequently can shed light on, their own experiences (Paxton et al., 1999; Schutz, Paxton, & Wertheim, 2002; Rankin, Lane, & Gibbons, 2004).

Parents are unable to provide social comparison. Not only are they well beyond the changes that adolescents undergo, but adolescents' questioning of adult authority and their motivation to become more autonomous make parents, other family members, and adults in general inadequate and invalid sources of knowledge. Who is left to provide such information? Peers.

Reference Groups. As we have said, adolescence is a time of experimentation, of trying out new identities, roles, and conduct. Peers provide information about what roles and behavior are most acceptable by serving as a reference group. **Reference groups** are groups of people with whom one compares oneself. Just as a professional ballplayer is likely to compare his performance against that of other professional players, so do teenagers compare themselves to those who are similar to them.

Reference groups present a set of *norms,* or standards, against which adolescents can judge their abilities and social success. An adolescent need not even belong to a group for it to serve as a reference group. For instance, unpopular adolescents may find themselves belittled and rejected by members of a popular group, yet use that more popular group as a reference group (Berndt, 1999; Blanton & Burkley, 2008).

The Consequences of Self-Esteem. Although everyone occasionally goes through periods of low self-esteem, such as after an undeniable failure, some children have chronically low self-esteem. Children with low self-esteem face a tough road, in part because their self-esteem becomes enmeshed in a cycle of failure that grows increasingly difficult to break. Assume, for instance, that

social comparison the desire to evaluate one's own behavior, abilities, expertise, and opinions by comparing them to those of others.

reference groups groups of people with whom one compares oneself.

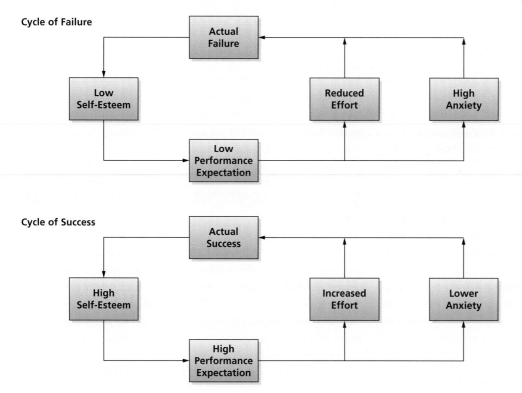

Cycle of Failure

Cycle of Success

FIGURE 10.1 **Cycles of Self-Esteem**
Because children with low self-esteem may expect to do poorly on a test, they may experience high anxiety and not work as hard as those with higher self-esteem. As a result, they actually do perform badly on the test, which in turn confirms their negative view of themselves. In contrast, those with high self-esteem have more positive expectations, which lead to lower anxiety and higher motivation. As a consequence, they perform better, reinforcing their positive self-image. How would a teacher help students with low self-esteem break out of their negative cycle?

Harry, a student with chronically low self-esteem, is facing an important test. Because of his low self-esteem, he expects to do poorly. As a consequence, he is quite anxious—so anxious that he is unable to concentrate well and study effectively. Furthermore, he may decide not to study much because he figures that if he's going to do badly anyway, why bother studying?

Ultimately, of course, Harry's high anxiety and lack of effort bring about the result he expected: He does poorly on the test. This failure, which confirms Harry's expectation, reinforces his low self-esteem, and the cycle of failure continues (see Figure 10.1).

If a child continues to be chronically low in self-esteem in adolescence, life can be very painful. For instance, adolescents with low self-esteem respond more negatively to failure than those with high self-esteem, in part because those with low self-esteem focus on their shortcomings after experiencing failure. Like Harry, whose low expectations for his own performance led him to prepare poorly for a test—and thus fail it—adolescents with low self-esteem can become trapped in a cycle of failure. In addition, low self-esteem is related to higher levels of aggression, antisocial behavior, and delinquency in adolescence (Baumeister, 1993; Dodgson & Wood, 1998; Donnellan et al., 2005).

In contrast, students with high self-esteem travel a more positive path, falling into a cycle of success. Adolescents with high self-esteem focus on their strengths following failure. They hold more positive expectations about their future performance. Having higher expectations leads to increased effort and lower anxiety, increasing the probability of success. In turn, this helps affirm their higher self-esteem that began the cycle.

Clearly, positive self-esteem is associated with desirable consequences, and lower self-esteem is related to negative results. However, this doesn't mean that we should seek to boost the self-esteem of adolescents at any cost. For example, although higher self-esteem is associated with positive outcomes such as academic achievement, the relationship between the two factors is merely correlational. The association simply means that people with higher self-esteem are more likely to have better academic performance, and those with lower self-esteem are more likely to have poorer academic performance.

There are several possible explanations for the relationship between self-esteem and academic performance. On one hand, it may mean that higher self-esteem indeed causes better academic performance. On the other hand, it may be the reverse: that doing well academically causes higher self-esteem. Or, finally, there may be some third factor (intelligence seems to be a reasonable possibility) that produces *both* higher self-esteem and better academic performance (Crocker & Knight, 2005).

FROM RESEARCH TO PRACTICE
The Downside of High Self-Esteem

According to many, low self-esteem lies at the heart of a variety of social ills, ranging from teenage pregnancy to gang violence to drug abuse. For example, government officials in California set up a task force to encourage self-esteem, arguing that increased self-esteem might raise the general psychological health of the population and even help the state balance its budget.

But not everyone agrees with this view. According to psychologist Roy Baumeister and colleagues, if high self-esteem is unjustified by actual accomplishment, it can be psychologically damaging. Unwarranted high self-esteem can lead to a variety of social problems, including violence (Baumeister et al., 2003; Baumeister et al., 2005).

Consider, for example, adolescents who have high, but unjustified, self-esteem—a personality type called *narcissism*. When their unwarranted positive view of themselves is disputed, they may view the challenge as so threatening that they lash out at others, behaving in a violent manner. Consequently, efforts to reduce the violence of bullies (who are typically viewed as low in self-esteem) by raising their self-esteem may backfire, unless there are actual accomplishments to accompany their raised self-esteem (Baumeister, Bushman, & Campbell, 2000; Diamantopoulou, Rydell, & Henricsson, 2008).

Similarly, efforts to boost the self-esteem of students who are facing academic difficulties in order to improve their performance may provoke the opposite result. For example, in one study, students who were receiving Ds and Fs in one class were divided into two groups. One group received the message that good grades were caused by a lack of confidence and low self-esteem. The other group received a different message; they were told that it was hard work that produced good grades. At the end of the semester, the group that received the self-esteem message ended up with significantly lower grades than the group that received the hard work message (Forsyth & Kerr, 1999).

Of course, such findings don't mean that high self-esteem is a bad thing. In fact, people with high self-esteem are significantly happier than those with low self-esteem, and they are less likely to be depressed. Still, the research has relevance to programs that seek to raise self-esteem in everyone. Feel-good messages ("we're all special" and "we applaud ourselves") may be off base, leading adolescents to develop unwarranted self-esteem. Instead, schools and parents should help adolescents *earn* high self-esteem through actual accomplishments (Begley, 1998; Crocker & Park, 2004).

- *Under what circumstances should a school or a society seek to raise the academic self-esteem of adolescents? Is the situation different if the adolescents have high self-esteem in other areas, such as athletics or artistic accomplishments?*

In short, high self-esteem does not necessarily lead to positive outcomes. In fact, it may well be that high self-esteem can have a significant downside, as we see in the *From Research to Practice* box.

REVIEW

▶ During the middle childhood years, self-esteem is based on comparisons with others and internal standards of success; if self-esteem is low, the result can be a cycle of failure.

▶ In adolescence, girls' self-esteem tends to be lower than boys' self-esteem, in part because girls are likely to be more concerned about physical appearance and social success—in addition to academic achievement.

▶ Self-esteem grows increasingly differentiated in adolescence as teens develop the ability to place different values on different aspects of the self.

▶ Peer social groups serve as reference groups in adolescence and offer a ready means of social comparison.

▶ Chronic low self-esteem can lead to physical illness, psychological problems, and the inability to cope with stress. Low self-esteem is also related to aggression, antisocial behavior, and delinquency in adolescence.

APPLY

▶ How would you go about designing a program for elementary students who are academic underachievers to prevent them from falling into a "cycle of failure?"

Picking an Occupation: Choosing Life's Work

Why did I decide that I wanted to be a lawyer? The answer is a bit embarrassing. When I got to my senior year of college, I began to worry about what I was going to do when I graduated. My parents were asking, with increasing frequency, what kind of work I was thinking about, and I felt the pressure rising with each phone call from home. So I began to think seriously about the problem. At the time, the O. J. Simpson trial was in the news all the time, and it got me to thinking about what it might be like to be an attorney. I had always been fascinated by L.A. Law when it had been on television, and I could envision myself in one of those big corner offices with a view of the city. For these reasons, and just about none other, I decided to take the law boards and apply to law school.

For almost all of us, early adulthood is a period of decisions with lifelong implications. One of the most critical is choosing a career path. The choice we make goes well beyond determining how much money we will earn; it also relates to our status, our sense of self-worth, and the contribution that we will make in life. In sum, decisions about work go to the very core of a young adult's identity.

Embarking on a Career

Some people know from childhood that they want to be physicians or firefighters or to go into business, and they follow invariant paths toward their goals. For others, the choice of a career is very much a matter of chance, of turning to the want ads and seeing what's available. Many of us fall somewhere between these two extremes.

Ginzberg's Career Choice Theory. According to Eli Ginzberg (1972), people typically move through a series of stages in choosing a career. The first stage is the **fantasy period**, which lasts until a person is around 11. During the fantasy period, career choices are made and discarded, without regard to skills, abilities, or available job opportunities. Instead, choices are made solely on the basis of what sounds appealing. Thus, a child may decide he wants to be a rock star —despite the fact that she cannot carry a tune.

People begin to take practical considerations into account during the tentative period, which spans adolescence. They begin to think more practically about the requirements of various jobs and how their own abilities and interests might fit with them. They also consider their personal values and goals, exploring how well a particular occupation might satisfy them.

Finally, in early adulthood, people enter the realistic period. In the **realistic period**, young adults explore specific career options either through actual experience on the job or through training for a profession. After initially exploring what they might do, people begin to narrow their choices to a few alternative careers and eventually make a commitment to a particular one.

Although Ginzberg's theory makes sense, critics have charged that it oversimplifies the process of choosing a career. Because Ginzberg's research was based on subjects from middle socioeconomic levels, it may overstate the choices and options available to people in lower socioeconomic levels. Furthermore, the ages associated with the various stages may be too rigid. For instance, a person who does not attend college but begins to work immediately after high school graduation is likely to be making serious career decisions at a much earlier point than a person who attends college. In addition, economic shifts have caused many people to change careers at different points in their adult lives.

Holland's Personality Type Theory. Other theories of career choice emphasize how an individual's personality affects decisions about a career. According to John Holland, for instance, certain personality types match particularly well with certain careers. If the correspondence between personality and career is good, people will enjoy their careers more and be more likely to stay in them; but if the match is poor, they will be unhappy and more likely to shift into other careers (Gottfredson & Holland, 1990; Holland, 1987, 1999).

According to one theory, people move through a series of life stages in choosing a career. The first stage is the fantasy period, which lasts until a person is around 11 years old.

fantasy period according to Ginzberg, the period, lasting until about age 11, when career choices are made, and discarded, without regard to skills, abilities, or available job opportunities.

realistic period the third stage of Ginzberg's theory, which occurs in early adulthood, when people begin to explore specific career options, either through actual experience on the job or through training for a profession, and then narrow their choices and make a commitment.

According to John Holland's personality type theory, the greater the correspondence between career choices and personality traits, the happier people will be in their career choice.

According to Holland, six personality types are important in career choice:

- **Realistic.** These people are down-to-earth, practical problem-solvers, and physically strong, but their social skills are mediocre. They make good farmers, laborers, and truck drivers.

- **Intellectual.** Intellectual types are oriented toward the theoretical and abstract. Although not particularly good with people, they are well suited to careers in math and science.

- **Social.** The traits associated with the social personality type are related to verbal skills and interpersonal relations. Social types are good at working with people, and consequently make good salespersons, teachers, and counselors.

- **Conventional.** Conventional individuals prefer highly structured tasks. They make good clerks, secretaries, and bank tellers.

- **Enterprising.** These individuals are risk-takers and take-charge types. They are good leaders and may be particularly effective as managers or politicians.

- **Artistic.** Artistic types use art to express themselves, and they often prefer the world of art to interactions with people. They are best suited to occupations involving art.

Although Holland's enumeration of personality types is sensible, it suffers from a central flaw: Not everyone fits neatly into particular personality types. Furthermore, there are certainly exceptions to the typology, with jobs being held by people who don't have the particular personality that Holland would predict. Still, the basic notions of the theory have been validated, and they form the foundation of several of the "job quizzes" that people can take to see what occupations they might especially enjoy (Randahl, 1991; Deng, Armstrong, & Rounds, 2007).

Gender and Career Choices: Women's Work.

WANTED: Full-time employee for small family firm. DUTIES: Including but not limited to general cleaning, cooking, gardening, laundry, ironing and mending, purchasing, bookkeeping and money management. Child care may also be required. HOURS: Avg. 55/wk but standby duty required 24 hours/day, 7 days/wk. Extra workload on holidays. SALARY AND BENEFITS: No salary, but food, clothing, and shelter provided at employer's discretion; job security and benefits depend on continued good will of employer. No vacation. No

BECOMING AN INFORMED CONSUMER OF DEVELOPMENT
Choosing a Career

One of the greatest challenges people face in early adulthood is making a decision that will have lifelong implications: the choice of a career. Although there is no single correct choice—most people can be happy in any of several different jobs—the options can be daunting. Here are some guidelines for at least starting to come to grips with the question of what occupational path to follow.

- Systematically evaluate a variety of choices. Libraries contain a wealth of information about potential career paths, and most colleges and universities have career centers that can provide occupational data and guidance.

- Know yourself. Evaluate your strengths and weaknesses, perhaps by completing a questionnaire at a college career center that can provide insight into your interests, skills, and values.

- Create a "balance sheet," listing the potential gains and losses that you will incur from a particular profession. First list the gains and losses that you will experience directly, and then list gains and losses for others, such as family members. Next, write down your projected self-approval or self-disapproval from

the potential career. Finally, write down the projected social approval or disapproval you are likely to receive from others. By systematically evaluating a set of potential careers according to each of these criteria, you will be in a better position to compare different possibilities.

- "Try out" different careers through paid or unpaid internships. By seeing a job firsthand, interns are able to get a better sense of what an occupation is truly like.

- Remember that if you make a mistake, you can change careers. People today increasingly change careers in early adulthood and even beyond. No one should feel locked into a decision made earlier in life. As we have seen throughout this book, people develop substantially over the course of their lives.

- It is reasonable to expect that shifting values, interests, abilities, and life circumstances might make a different career more appropriate later in life than the one chosen during early adulthood.

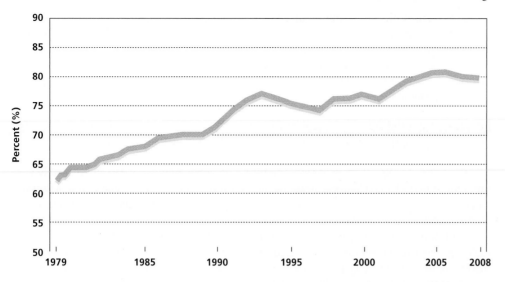

FIGURE 10.2 The Gender Wage Gap
Women's weekly earnings as a percentage of men's have increased since 1979, but still are only a bit more than 75 percent and have remained steady over the past several years.
Source: : U.S. Bureau of Labor Statistics (2009). Highlights of women's earnings in 2008. Washington, DC: U.S. Department of Labor

retirement plan. No opportunities for advancement. REQUIREMENTS: No previous experience necessary, can learn on the job. Only women need apply. (Unger & Crawford, 1992, p. 446)

A generation ago, many women entering early adulthood assumed that this admittedly exaggerated job description matched the work for which they were best suited and to which they aspired: housewife. Even those women who sought work outside the home were relegated to certain professions. For instance, until the 1960s, employment ads in newspapers throughout the United States were almost always divided into two sections: "Help Wanted: Male" and "Help Wanted: Female." The men's job listings encompassed such professions as police officer, construction worker, and legal counsel; the women's listings were for secretaries, teachers, cashiers, and librarians.

The breakdown of jobs deemed appropriate for men and women reflected society's traditional view of what the two genders were best suited for. Traditionally, women were considered most appropriate for **communal professions**, occupations associated with relationships, like nursing. In contrast, men were perceived as best suited for **agentic professions**. Agentic professions are associated with getting things accomplished, like carpentry. It is probably no coincidence that communal professions typically have lower status and pay than agentic professions (Hattery, 2000; Johannesen-Schmidt & Eagly, 2002).

Although discrimination based on gender is far less blatant today than it was several decades ago—it is now illegal, for instance, to advertise a position specifically for a man or a woman—remnants of traditional gender-role prejudice persist. Women are less likely to be found in traditionally male-dominated professions such as engineering and computer programming. As shown in Figure 10.2, although significant progress in closing the gender wage gap was made in the last 30 years, women's weekly earnings still lag behind those of men. In fact, women in many professions earn significantly less than men in identical jobs (Frome et al., 2006; U.S. Bureau of the Census, 2006).

More women are working outside the home than ever before despite status and pay that are often lower than men's. Between 1950 and 2003, the percentage of the female population (aged 16 and over) in the U.S. labor force increased from around 35 percent to over 60 percent, and women today make up around 55 percent of the labor force, a figure comparable to their presence in the general population. Almost all women expect to earn a living, and almost all do at some point in their lives. Furthermore, in about one-half of U.S. households, women earn about as much as their husbands (Lewin, 1995; Bureau of Labor Statistics, 2003).

Opportunities for women are considerably greater than they were in earlier years. Women are more likely to be physicians, lawyers, insurance agents, and bus drivers than they were in the past. However, as noted earlier, within specific job categories, there are still notable gender differences. For example, female bus drivers are more apt to have part-time school bus routes, whereas men hold better-paying full-time routes in cities. Similarly, female pharmacists are more likely to work in hospitals, while men work in higher-paying jobs in retail stores (Unger & Crawford, 2003).

communal professions   occupations that are associated with relationships.

agentic professions   occupations that are associated with getting things accomplished.

Mankekolo Mahlangu-Ngcobo, who fled Botswana, is now a lecturer and minister in the United States.

In the same way, women (and minorities, too) in high-status, visible professional roles may hit what has come to be called the glass ceiling. The glass ceiling is an invisible barrier within an organization that, because of discrimination, prevents individuals from being promoted beyond a certain level. It operates subtly, and often the people responsible for keeping the glass ceiling in place are unaware of how their actions perpetuate discrimination against women and minorities (Goodman, Fields, & Blum, 2004; Stockdale, Crosby, & Malden, 2004).

Immigrants on the Job: Making It in America. We saw earlier in the chapter that children of immigrants do quite well educationally and socially. But what about their parents? How are they doing?

If we were to rely solely on at least one thread of public opinion, we would probably view immigrants to the United States as straining the educational, health-care, welfare, and prison systems while contributing little to U.S. society. But the assumptions that underlie anti-immigrant sentiment are in fact quite wrong.

With the number of immigrants entering the United States hovering around 1.2 million each year, residents born outside the country now represent 10 percent of the population, more than twice the percentage in 1970. First- and second-generation immigrants comprise almost a quarter of the population of the United States (see Figure 10.3; Deaux, 2006).

Today's immigrants are somewhat different from the earlier waves at the beginning of the twentieth century. Only a third are white, compared with almost 90 percent of immigrants who arrived before 1960. Critics argue that many new immigrants lack the skills that will allow them to make a contribution to the high-tech economy of the twenty-first century.

The critics are wrong in many fundamental respects, however. For instance, consider the following data (Topolnicki, 1995; Camarota, 2001):

- **Most legal *and* illegal immigrants ultimately succeed financially.** For example, although they initially experience higher rates of poverty than native-born Americans, immigrants who arrived in the United States prior to 1980 and have had a chance to establish themselves actually have a higher family income than native-born Americans. Immigrants have the same rate of entrepreneurship as nonimmigrants, with one in nine owning their own business.

- **Only a few immigrants come to the United States to get on welfare.** Instead, most say they come because of opportunities to work and prosper in the United States. Nonrefugee immigrants who are old enough to work are less likely to be on welfare than native-born U.S. citizens.

- **Given time, immigrants contribute more to the economy than they take away.** Although initially costly to the government, often because they hold low-paying jobs and therefore pay no income taxes, immigrants become more productive as they get older. Ultimately, immigrants pay $25 billion to $30 billion a year more in taxes than they use in government services.

FIGURE 10.3

Immigrants in the United States

Since 1970 the number of immigrants in the United states has steadily climbed and is approaching a historic high, especially if the estimated 12 million undocumented immigrants are included.

Source: Data for 1900-2000 from Dicennial Census. For 2007, data from the March Current Population Survey. As cited in Camarota, S. A. (2007). Immigrants in the United States — 2007: A profile of America's foreign-born population. Washington, DC: Center for Immigration Studies.

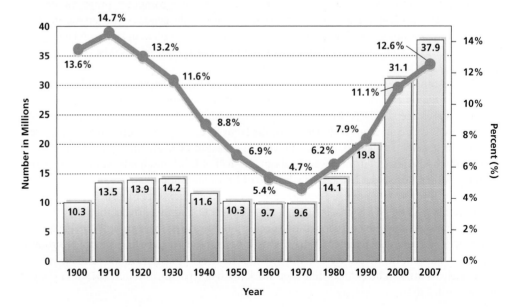

Why are immigrants often ultimately financially successful? One explanation is that immigrants who voluntarily choose to leave their native countries are particularly motivated and driven to be successful, whereas those who choose *not* to immigrate may be relatively less motivated.

In short, the reality is that the majority of immigrants ultimately become contributing members of U.S. society. For instance, they may alleviate labor shortages, and the money they send to relatives who remain at home may invigorate the world economy (World Bank, 2003).

Why Do People Work? It's More than Earning a Living

Why do people work? This may seem an easy question to answer: People work to earn a living. Yet the reality is different, for young adults express many reasons for seeking a job, and middle-aged adults increasingly embark on new careers.

Intrinsic and Extrinsic Motivation. Certainly, people work in order to obtain various concrete rewards, or out of extrinsic motivation. **Extrinsic motivation** drives people to obtain tangible rewards, such as money and prestige (Singer, Stacey, & Lange, 1993; Vansteenkiste et al., 2007).

People also work for their own enjoyment, for personal rewards, not just for the financial rewards a job may bring. This is known as **intrinsic motivation**. People in many Western societies tend to subscribe to the Puritan work ethic, the notion that work is important in and of itself. According to this view, working is a meaningful act that brings psychological and (at least in the traditional view) even spiritual well-being and satisfaction.

Work also brings a sense of personal identity. Consider, for instance, what people say about themselves when they first meet someone. After mentioning their names and where they live, they very typically tell what they do for a living. What people do is a large part of who they are.

Work also may be a central element in people's social lives. Because so much time is spent in work settings, work can be a source of adults' friends and social activities. Social relationships forged at work may spill over into other parts of people's lives. In addition, there are often social obligations—dinner with the boss, or the annual seasonal party in December—that are related to work.

Finally, the kind of work that people do is a factor in determining status. **Status** is the evaluation by society of the role a person plays. Various jobs are associated with a certain status, as indicated in Table 10.2 on page 300. For instance, physicians and college teachers are near the top of the status hierarchy, while ushers and shoe shiners fall to the bottom.

Satisfaction on the Job. The status associated with particular jobs affects people's satisfaction with their work. As might be expected, the higher the status of the job, the more satisfied people tend to be. Furthermore, the status of the job of the major wage-earner can affect the status of the other members of the family (Green, 1995; Schieman, McBrier, & van Gundy, 2003).

Status isn't everything, of course: Worker satisfaction depends on a number of factors, not the least of which is the nature of the job itself. For example, consider the plight of Patricia Alford, who worked at the Equitable Life Assurance Company. Her job consisted of entering data into a computer 9 hours each day except for two 15-minute breaks and an hour off for lunch. She never knew how much she was earning because her salary depended on how many insurance claims she entered into the computer each day. The pay standards were so complicated that her pay varied from $217 to $400 a week, providing her with a weekly surprise at paycheck time (Booth, 1987; Ting, 1997; Hertel & Wittchen, 2008).

Other people who work at computers are monitored on a minute-by-minute basis; supervisors can consistently see how many keystrokes they are entering. In some firms in which workers use the telephone for sales or to take customer orders, their conversations are monitored by supervisors. Workers' Internet use and e-mail are also monitored or restricted by a large number of employers. Not surprisingly, such forms of job stress produce worker dissatisfaction (MacDonald, 2003).

Job satisfaction is higher when workers have input into the nature of their jobs and feel their ideas and opinions are valued. They also prefer jobs that offer variety, requiring many different types of skills, over those that require only a few. Finally, the more influence employees have over others, either directly as supervisors or more informally, the greater their job satisfaction (Steers & Porter, 1991; Peterson & Wilson, 2004; Thompson & Prottas, 2006).

Extrinsic motivation drives people as a way of obtaining tangible rewards, such as money, prestige, or an expensive automobile. How might extrinsic motivation be illustrated in a less developed, non-Western culture?

FROM A
SOCIAL WORKER'S
PERSPECTIVE
Why do you think immigrants' ambition and achievements are widely underestimated?

extrinsic motivation   motivation that drives people to obtain tangible rewards, such as money and prestige.

intrinsic motivation   motivation that causes people to work for their own enjoyment, not for the rewards work may bring.

status   the evaluation of a role or person by other relevant members of a group or society.

TABLE 10.2   Status Hierarchy of Various Professions

OCCUPATION	SCORE	OCCUPATION	SCORE
Physicians and surgeons	100	Court/municipal clerks	53
Lawyers	99	Heavy vehicle mechanics	52
Computer software engineers	94	Sheet metal workers	50
Psychologists	93	Massage therapists	48
Architects	92	Utility meter readers	46
College professors	86	Home appliance repairers	45
High school teachers	86	Animal control workers	44
Health services managers	85	Tax preparers	44
Human resources managers	82	Medical assistants	42
Special education teachers	80	Paper hangers	41
Editors	79	Telephone operators	39
Social workers	77	Chefs	39
Firefighters	77	Tellers	36
Writers/authors	76	Carpenters	35
Funeral directors	75	Dancers/choreographers	32
Clergy	75	Barbers	31
Dental hygienists	74	Motion picture projectionists	27
Private detectives	72	Nonfarm animal caretakers	25
Aircraft mechanics	72	Child-care workers	21
Real estate brokers	70	Telemarketers	20
Postal service clerks	69	Personal/home care aides	19
EMTs and paramedics	65	Crossing guards	11
Correctional officers	60	Maids and housekeeping personnel	7
Electricians	58	Food prep workers	3
Physical therapists	56	Counter attendants	1
Actors	55	Dishwashers	1

Source: Nam & Boyd, 2004.

A Change in Perspective: How Adults View Work at Midlife. For many, middle age is the time of greatest productivity, success, and earning power. It is also a time when occupational success may become considerably less alluring than it once was. This is particularly the case for those who may not have achieved the occupational success they had hoped for when they began their careers. In such cases, work becomes less valued, while family and other off-the-job interests become more important (Howard, 1992; Simonton, 1997; Grzywacz, Butler, & Almeida, 2008).

The factors that make a job satisfying change during middle age. Younger adults are interested in abstract and future-oriented concerns, such as the opportunity for advancement or the possibility of recognition and approval. Middle-aged employees care more about the here-and-now qualities of work. For instance, they are more concerned with pay, working conditions, and specific policies, such as the way vacation time is calculated. Furthermore, as at earlier stages of life, changes in overall job quality are associated with changes in stress levels for both men and women (Hattery, 2000; Peterson & Wilson, 2004; Cohrs, Abele, & Dette, 2006).

In general, though, the relationship between age and work seems to be positive: The older workers are, the more overall job satisfaction they experience. This pattern is not altogether surprising, since younger adults who are dissatisfied with their positions will quit them and find new positions that they like better. Furthermore, older workers have fewer opportunities to change positions. Consequently, they may learn to live with what they have, and accept that the position they have is the best they are likely to get. Such acceptance may ultimately be translated into satisfaction (Tangri, Thomas, & Mednick, 2003).

Yet, as we shall see next, an increasing number of adults do embrace new careers in midlife.

Switching—and Starting—Careers at Midlife. When Perry Nicholas—a former boxer who also worked in construction—hit 50, he decided to go for a lifelong goal of becoming a full-time teacher. The once-amateur middleweight contender knocks 'em out with his poetry, having been nominated for a 2007 Pushcart [Poetry] Prize (Continelli, 2006, p. B3).

One of the remarkable characteristics of middle age is its variety, as the paths that different people travel continue to diverge. The twists and turns in Perry Nicholas's life path are not unusual: Few lives follow a set, predictable pattern through middle adulthood.

People who change careers in midlife do so for several reasons. It may be that their jobs offer little challenge; they have achieved mastery, and what was once difficult is now routine. Other people change because their jobs have changed in ways they do not like, or they may have lost their job. They may be asked to accomplish more with fewer resources, or technological advances may have made such drastic changes in their day-to-day activities that they no longer enjoy what they do.

Still others are unhappy with the status they have achieved and wish to make a fresh start. Some are burned out or feel that they are on a treadmill. In addition, some people simply do not like to think of themselves doing the same thing for the rest of their lives. For them, middle age is seen as the last point at which they can make a meaningful occupational change (Steers & Porter, 1991; Grzywacz et al., 2008).

Finally, a significant number of people, almost all of them women, return to the job market after having taken time off to raise children. Some may need to find paying work after a divorce. Since the mid-1980s, the number of women in the workforce who are in their 50s has grown significantly. Around half of women between the ages of 55 and 64—and an even larger percentage of those who graduated from college—are now in the workforce (see Figure 10.4).

People may enter new professions with unrealistically high expectations and be disappointed by the realities of the situation. Furthermore, middle-aged people who start new careers may find themselves in entry-level positions. As a consequence, their peers on the job may be considerably younger than they are (Sharf, 1992; Barnett & Hyde, 2001). But in the long run, taking on a new career in middle adulthood can be invigorating. Those who switch or start new careers may be especially valued employees (Adelmann, Antonucci, & Crohan, 1990; Connor, 1992; Bromberger & Matthews, 1994; Juntunen, Wegner, & Matthews, 2002).

Some forecasters suggest that career changes may become the rule rather than the exception. According to this point of view, technological advances will occur so rapidly that people will be forced periodically to change what they do to earn a living, often dramatically. In such a scenario, people will have not one, but several, careers during their lifetime.

Challenges of Work: Burnout, Unemployment, and Age Discrimination

Mary Gehrig can't tolerate the thought of another "crisis" deadline in her job as an advertising exec. Twenty years ago, the panic in the office over a client's visit felt like excitement. Now it's just stressful, and Mary, age 42, is tired of missing her children's recitals, plays, and hockey games.

Bill Martin is still recovering from the shock he received last summer when the paper mill he had worked for since high school suddenly closed down. With two kids on the brink of college, Martin, 48, doesn't know where he'll find the money for their educations—or for that matter, where he'll find another job.

Arturo Albanez has worked since he was 15 in a variety of occupations. As none of his jobs provided for a pension, Albanez, 63, knows he will have to continue working the remainder of his life. But the opportunities are thinning out. "They want the young guys," he says.

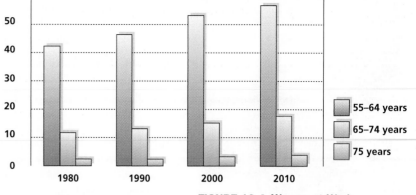

FIGURE 10.4 Women at Work
The percentage of women aged 55 to 64 who are in the labor force has steadily increased since 1980 and is slated to continue to grow over the current decade.
Source: Monthly Labor Review, 2001.

Burnout occurs when a worker experiences dissatisfaction, disillusionment, frustration, or weariness from his or her job. Those who experience it grow increasingly cynical or indifferent toward their work.

The loss of employment during midlife can be a shattering experience leading to pessimism, cynicism, and despondency.

Middle and late adulthood brings a variety of challenges for workers. A job that once held satisfactions becomes stressful or boring. Companies downsize or close, throwing people out of work overnight, uncertain of where they'll land next. Advancing age narrows opportunities for finding new work. These challenges can pose threats to a worker's identity and self-esteem.

Burnout. Job satisfaction is not universal in middle adulthood. For some people, work becomes increasingly stressful as dissatisfaction with working conditions or with the nature of the job mounts. In some cases, conditions become so bad that the result is burnout or a decision to change jobs.

For 44-year-old Peggy Augarten, early-morning shifts in the intensive care unit of the suburban hospital where she worked were becoming increasingly difficult. Although it had always been hard to lose a patient, recently she found herself breaking into tears over her patients at the strangest moments: while she was doing the laundry, washing the dishes, or watching TV. When she began to dread going to work in the morning, she knew that her feelings about her job were undergoing a fundamental change.

Augarten's response can probably be traced to the phenomenon of burnout. **Burnout** occurs when workers experience dissatisfaction, disillusionment, frustration, and weariness from their jobs. It occurs most often in jobs that involve helping others, and it often strikes those who initially were the most idealistic and driven. In some ways, such workers may be overcommitted to their jobs, and the realization that they can make only minor dents in huge societal problems such as poverty and medical care can be disappointing and demoralizing (Demir, Ulusoy, & Ulusoy, 2003; Taris, van Horn, & Schaufeli, 2004; Bakker & Heuven, 2006).

One of the consequences of burnout is a growing cynicism about one's work. For instance, an employee might say to himself, "What am I working so hard on this for? No one is even going to notice that I've come in on budget for the last two years." In addition, workers may feel indifference and lack of concern about how well they do their job. The idealism with which a worker may have entered a profession is replaced by pessimism and the attitude that it is impossible to provide any kind of meaningful solution to a problem (Lock, 1992; Schaufeli & Salanova, 2007).

People can combat burnout, even those in professions with high demands and seemingly insurmountable burdens. For example, the nurse who despairs of not having enough time for every patient can be helped to realize that a more feasible goal—such as giving patients a quick backrub—can be equally important. Jobs can also be structured so that workers (and their supervisors) pay attention to small victories in their daily work, such as the pleasure of a client's gratitude, even though the "big picture" of disease, poverty, racism, and an inadequate educational system may look gloomy.

Unemployment. For many workers, unemployment is a hard reality of life, and the implications of not being able to find work are as much psychological as they are economic. For those who have been fired, laid off by corporate downsizing, or forced out of jobs by technological advances, being out of work can be psychologically and even physically devastating (Sharf, 1992; Winefield, 2002; Galic, 2007).

Unemployment can leave people feeling anxious, depressed, and irritable. Their self-confidence may plummet, and they may be unable to concentrate. According to one analysis, every time the unemployment rate goes up 1 percent, there is a 4 percent rise in suicide, and admissions to psychiatric facilities go up by some 4 percent for men and 2 percent for women (Kates, Grieff, & Hagen, 1990; Connor, 1992; Inoue et al., 2006).

Even aspects of unemployment that might at first seem positive, such as having more time, can produce disagreeable consequences. Perhaps because of feelings of depression and having too much time on their hands, unemployed people are less apt to participate in community activities, use libraries, and read than employed people. They are more likely to be late for appointments and even for meals (Ball & Orford, 2002; Tyre & McGinn, 2003).

And these problems may linger. Middle-aged adults who lose their jobs tend to stay unemployed longer than younger workers and have fewer opportunities for gratifying work as they age. As we shall see next, employers may discriminate against older job applicants and make it more difficult to obtain new employment. Ironically, such discrimination is not only illegal but also is based on misguided assumptions: Research finds that older workers show less absenteeism than younger ones, hold their jobs longer, are more reliable, and are more willing to learn new skills (Allan, 1990; Birsner, 1991; Connor, 1992; Menkens, 2005; Ng & Feldman, 2008).

burnout a situation that occurs when workers experience dissatisfaction, disillusionment, frustration, and weariness from their jobs.

In sum, midlife unemployment is a shattering experience. And for some people, especially those who never find meaningful work again, it taints their entire view of the world. For people forced into such involuntary—and premature—retirement, the loss of a job can lead to pessimism, cynicism, and despondency. Overcoming such feelings often takes time and a good deal of psychological adjustment to come to terms with the situation. There are challenges for those who *do* find a new career, too (Trippet, 1991; Waters & Moore, 2002; Galic, 2007).

Older Workers: Combating Age Discrimination. Many other people continue to work, either full- or part-time, for some part of late adulthood. That they can do so is largely because of legislation that was passed in the late 1970s, in which mandatory retirement ages were made illegal in almost every profession. Part of broader legislation that makes age discrimination illegal, these laws gave most workers the opportunity either to remain in jobs they held previously or to begin working in entirely different fields (Lindemann & Kadue, 2003).

Whether older adults continue to work because they enjoy the intellectual and social rewards that work provides or because they need to work for financial reasons, many encounter age discrimination. Age discrimination remains a reality despite laws making it illegal. Some employers encourage older workers to leave their jobs in order to replace them with younger employees whose salaries will be considerably lower. Furthermore, some employers believe that older workers are not up to the demands of the job or are less willing to adapt to a changing workplace—stereotypes about the elderly that are enduring, despite legislative changes (Moss, 1997; Menkens, 2005).

There is little evidence to support the idea that older workers' ability to perform their jobs declines. In many fields, such as art, literature, science, politics, or even entertainment, it is easy to find examples of people who have made some of their greatest contributions during late adulthood. Even in those few professions that were specifically exempted from laws prohibiting mandatory retirement ages—those involving public safety—the evidence does not support the notion that workers should be retired at an arbitrary age.

For instance, one large-scale, careful study of older police officers, firefighters, and prison guards came to the conclusion that age was not a good predictor of whether a worker was likely to be incapacitated on the job, or the level of his or her general work performance. Instead, a case-by-case analysis of individual workers' performance was a more accurate predictor (Landy & Conte, 2004).

Although age discrimination remains a problem, market forces may help reduce its severity. As baby boomers retire and the workforce drastically shrinks, companies may begin to offer incentives to older adults to either remain in the workforce or to return to it after they have retired. Although retirement remains the norm for most older adults, not everyone wants to—or can afford to—stop working.

REVIEW

▶ According to Eli Ginzberg, people pass through three stages in considering careers: the fantasy period, the tentative period, and the realistic period.

▶ Gender stereotypes are changing, but women still experience subtle prejudice in career choices, roles, and wages.

▶ People work because of both extrinsic and intrinsic motivation factors.

▶ Given the time to establish themselves, most legal *and* illegal immigrants succeed financially, contributing more in taxes paid than they use in government services.

▶ Midlife career changes are becoming more prevalent, motivated usually by dissatisfaction, the need for more challenge or status, or the desire to return to the workforce after childrearing.

▶ Unemployment in midlife can have negative economic, psychological, and physical effects.

APPLY

▶ How would you go about designing a course for high school or college students to assist them in choosing a career?

▶ What might be the effects of a longer life span on career choice? What challenges do people over 60 face if they wish to or need to continue working?

Epilogue

"Who am I?" and "How do I feel about myself?" are two key questions in an individual's ever-evolving sense of self across the life span. In this chapter, we considered the development of the self, examining how we understand and evaluate ourselves, and how we go about choosing our life's work. We began by tracing the evidence we have that infants are aware of their own existence—how they come to understand that they are individuals distinct from the world around them. We then focused on how self-concept develops in the years from preschool to early adulthood, and how children develop racial and ethnic awareness. From there, we looked at self-esteem and discussed the ways that children and adolescents develop a positive—or negative—view of themselves. We saw how social comparison provides a useful tool for evaluating one's abilities in light of the abilities of one's peers. We also considered how adolescents are able to differentiate various aspects of the self, which leads them to evaluate those aspects in different ways. Finally, we examined the stages people go through in choosing their careers, and the reasons they work, both extrinsic and intrinsic. We concluded with a look at the changing role of work in people's lives, and the difficulties brought about by job burnout, unemployment, and age discrimination.

Return to the Prologue—about Karl Haglund—and answer the following questions.

1. Where does Karl's description of himself place him in the shift of self-understanding that occurs in middle childhood? How would you expect his self-concept to change over the next few years?

2. How do Karl's comments demonstrate his use of social comparison to evaluate himself?

3. How does Karl's view of his future fit or not fit with Eli Ginzberg's theory about the stages people pass through in choosing a career? Do you think that working so closely with his dad over the years has affected the way Karl views his future? How so?

4. What educated guesses can you make about Karl's self-esteem based on the information in the Prologue?

Looking Back

What sort of mental lives do infants have?

1. Infants begin to develop self-awareness at about the age of 12 months.

2. They also begin to develop a theory of mind at this time: knowledge and beliefs about how they and others think.

In what ways do children's views of themselves change during the middle childhood years?

3. According to Erikson, children in the middle childhood years are in the industry-versus-inferiority stage, focusing on achieving competence and responding to a wide range of personal challenges.

4. Children in the middle childhood years begin to view themselves in terms of psychological characteristics and to differentiate their self-concepts into separate areas. They use social comparison to evaluate their behavior, abilities, expertise, and opinions.

What is self-esteem, and what are some factors in and consequences of high and low self-esteem?

5. Self-esteem is the emotional side of the self-concept, involving the self-evaluative feelings that people have about various aspects of themselves.

6. In general, adolescents with higher self-esteem hold more positive expectations about their abilities and performance, and adolescents with lower self-esteem hold more negative expectations.

7. Adolescent self-esteem changes over time, with boys and girls experiencing increases and decreases at different times. Males and females also differ in the aspects of themselves that they consider to be particularly important for self-esteem.

8. Socioeconomic status, race, and ethnicity also affect self-esteem, with African American and white adolescents generally having higher self-esteem than other groups.

9. Broad, unfocused efforts at increasing self-esteem are less successful than focused efforts aimed at improving self-esteem.

How does the development of self-concept and identity proceed during adolescence?

10. During adolescence, self-concept differentiates to encompass others' views as well as one's own and to include multiple aspects simultaneously. Differentiation of self-concept can cause confusion as behaviors reflect a complex definition of the self.

11. According to Erik Erikson, adolescents are in the identity-versus-identity-confusion stage, seeking to discover their individuality and identity. They may become confused and exhibit dysfunctional reactions, and they may rely for help and information more on friends and peers than on adults.

12. James Marcia identifies four identity statuses that individuals may experience in adolescence and in later life: identity achievement, identity foreclosure, identity diffusion, and moratorium.

13. The formation of an identity is challenging for members of racial and ethnic minority groups, many of whom appear to be embracing a bicultural identity approach.

Why is choosing a career such an important issue for young adults, and what factors influence the choice of a career?

14. According to Vaillant, career consolidation is a developmental stage in which young adults are involved in defining their careers and themselves.

15. A model developed by Ginzberg suggests that people typically move through three stages in choosing a career: the fantasy period of youth, the tentative period of adolescence, and the realistic period of young adulthood.

16. Other approaches, such as that of Holland, attempt to match people's personality types with suitable careers. This sort of research underlies most career-related inventories and measures used in career counseling.

17. Gender-role prejudice and stereotyping remain a problem in the workplace and in preparing for and selecting careers. Women tend to be pressured into certain occupations and out of others, and they earn less money for the same work.

What are the characteristics of work and career in middle adulthood?

18. For most persons, midlife is a time of job satisfaction. Career ambition becomes less of a force in the lives of middle-aged workers, and outside interests begin to be more valued.

19. Job dissatisfaction can result from disappointment with one's achievements and position in life or from the feeling that one has failed to make a difference in the insurmountable problems of the job. This latter phenomenon, termed *burnout*, often affects those in the helping professions.

20. Some people in middle adulthood must face unexpected unemployment, which brings economic, psychological, and physical consequences.

21. A growing number of people voluntarily change careers in midlife, some to increase job challenge, satisfaction, and status, and others to return to a workforce they left years earlier to rear children.

PEARSON
mydevelopmentlab™

"What decisions would you make while raising a child? What would the consequences of those decisions be?" Find out by accessing **MyVirtualChild** at **www.mydevelopmentlab.com** and raising your own virtual child from birth to age 18.

11

Moral Development and Aggression

Prologue

Jesse's Dilemma

The most important game of the football season had ended in disappointment for Jesse and his friends. Their archrival team, the Southridge Wolverines, had trounced them 28 to 3. Now, Jesse and his friends stood before the Wolverines' empty bus, their disappointment turning to anger. Suddenly, a rock smashed one of the bus's windows. A second rock made a large dent just behind the driver's seat. "Wolverines SUCK!" the boys shouted as they lobbed every rock within their reach. Two more windows shattered. The door was bent in its frame.

Evaluating what is the right course of action becomes increasingly complicated as our ability to reason matures.

Jesse stood rooted to the spot, heart pounding. He couldn't believe his friends were taking things this far. He hated the fact that his team had lost, especially to the Wolverines—rich kids from an affluent community who looked down their noses at working-class boys like Jesse—but he knew it was wrong to smash up the bus. It wouldn't solve any problems.

Glancing nervously at his friends, he confirmed his fear: he was the only one not participating in the spree of destruction. Slowly, he knelt and patted the ground in the darkness until he found a suitable rock. He stood, hefting the rock's weight, raising his arm, then lowering it.

"Cops!" one of the boys shouted. "Run!"

Jesse took careful aim and heaved his rock with his best fast ball pitch. It hit its intended target—the empty space five feet in front of the bus. Jesse turned and ran with the others into the safety of the black night.

As Jesse's story illustrates, morality is a complex issue. Evaluating what is the right course of action becomes increasingly complicated as our ability to reason matures. We must take into account all the specifics of a given situation and often weigh one imperfect course of action against another. And we must find ways to manage our more violent emotions.

In this chapter we examine two key aspects of social behavior: moral development and aggression. We also discuss the role of religion and spirituality in people's lives. We begin by considering how children develop a sense of society's rights and wrongs, and how that development can lead them to be helpful to others. We look at a variety of perspectives, ranging from Piaget's arguments about the changes in children's understanding of morality to approaches that emphasize how children learn to behave morally by imitating the moral acts of others. We see how reasoning about moral dilemmas changes in adolescence, and how the expression of moral and helping behavior develops. We look at a range of parenting styles and discuss how parents and other authority figures use discipline to shape children's behavior.

Next, we focus on religion and spirituality. We examine why religion is important to many people. We consider the comfort it provides in times of trouble and how it helps people make sense of their lives. We discuss how Piaget's approach to cognitive development offers ways to think about the development of religious thought, and we look at the stages of faith development outlined by James Fowler. We examine the role religion plays in developing an identity in adolescence. We also consider the relationship between religious belief and life satisfaction in late adulthood, and religion's special significance for older African Americans.

We then turn to aggression and violence, considering both its sources and consequences. We ask whether aggression is an innate, genetically determined behavior and/or a response a child learns from the environment while growing up. We look, too, at ways of decreasing aggression in children and increasing their moral behaviors. Finally, we consider violence and abuse directed toward children, spouses, and elders by family members. We discuss ways of dealing with spousal abuse and look at the cultural roots of domestic violence.

LOOKING AHEAD

After reading this chapter, you will be able to answer the following questions:

► How do children develop a moral sense?

► How does children's sense of right and wrong change as they age?

► As adolescents become more sophisticated morally, how does their behavior change?

► What sorts of disciplinary styles do parents employ, and what effects do they have?

► What purposes do spirituality and religion serve for many adults?

► How does religious thought develop across the life span?

► How does aggression develop in preschool-age children?

► What are the causes and characteristics of family violence in the United States?

MODULE 11.1

Developing Morality: Following Society's Rights and Wrongs

Preschoolers believe in immanent justice. This child may worry that she will be punished even if no one sees her carrying out the misdeed.

During snack time at preschool, playmates Jan and Meg inspected the goodies in their lunch boxes. Jan found two appetizing cream-filled cookies. Meg's snack offered less tempting carrot and celery sticks. As Jan began to munch on one of her cookies, Meg looked at the cut-up vegetables and burst into tears. Jan responded to Meg's distress by offering her companion one of her cookies, which Meg gladly accepted. Jan was able to put herself in Meg's place, understand Meg's thoughts and feelings, and act compassionately. (Katz, 1989, p. 213)

In this short scenario we see many of the key elements of morality as it is played out among preschool-age children. Changes in children's views of what is ethically right and what is the right way to behave involve a growing awareness of others and are an important element of growth during the preschool years and beyond.

Moral Development

Moral development refers to changes in people's sense of justice and of what is right and wrong, and in their behavior related to moral issues. Developmentalists have considered moral development in terms of children's reasoning about morality, their attitudes toward moral lapses, and their behavior when faced with moral issues. In the process of studying moral development, several approaches have evolved (Langford, 1995; Grusec & Kuczynski, 1997; Hallpike, 2008; Sinnott-Armstrong, 2008).

Piaget's View of Moral Development. Child psychologist Jean Piaget was one of the first to study questions of moral development. He suggested that moral development, like cognitive development, proceeds in stages (Piaget, 1932). The earliest stage is a broad form of moral thinking he called **heteronomous morality**, in which rules are seen as invariant and unchangeable. During this stage, which lasts from about age 4 through age 7, children play games rigidly, assuming that there is one, and only one, way to play and that every other way is wrong. At the same time, though, preschool-age children may not even fully grasp game rules. Consequently, a group of children may be playing together, with each child playing according to a slightly

moral development   the changes in people's sense of justice and of what is right and wrong, and in their behavior related to moral issues.

heteronomous morality   the earliest stage in Piaget's theory of moral development in which rules are seen as invariant and unchangeable.

different set of rules. Nevertheless, they enjoy playing with others. Piaget suggests that every child may "win" such a game because winning is equated with having a good time, as opposed to truly competing with others.

This rigid heteronomous morality is ultimately replaced by two later stages of morality: incipient cooperation and autonomous cooperation. As its name implies, in the **incipient cooperation stage**, which lasts from around age 7 to age 10, children's games become more clearly social. Children learn the actual formal rules of games, and they play according to this shared knowledge. Consequently, rules are still seen as largely unchangeable. There is a "right" way to play the game, and children in the incipient cooperation stage play according to these formal rules.

It is not until the **autonomous cooperation stage**, which begins at about age 10, that children become fully aware that formal game rules can be modified if the people who play them agree. The later transition into more sophisticated forms of moral development—which we will consider further on—also is reflected in school-age children's understanding that rules of law are created by people and are subject to change according to the will of people.

Until these later stages are reached, however, children's reasoning about rules and issues of justice is bounded in the concrete. For instance, consider the following two stories:

> *A little boy who is called John is in his room. He is called to dinner. He goes into the dining room. But behind the door there was a chair, and on the chair there was a tray with fifteen cups on it. John couldn't have known there was all this behind the door. He goes in, the door knocks against the tray, bang go the fifteen cups, and they all get broken!*

* * *

> *Once there was a little boy whose name was Marcello. One day when his mother was out he tried to get some jam out of the cupboard. He climbed up on to a chair and stretched out his arm. But the jam was too high up and he couldn't reach it and have any. But while he was trying to get it he knocked over a cup. The cup fell down and broke. (Piaget, 1932, p. 122)*

Piaget found that a preschool child in the heteronomous morality stage judges the child who broke the 15 cups worse than the one who broke just one. In contrast, children who have moved beyond the heteronomous morality stage consider the child who broke the one cup naughtier. The reason: Children in the heteronomous morality stage do not take *intention* into account. Children who have moved beyond the heteronomous morality stage have come to understand that one must make judgments about the severity of a transgression based on whether the person intended to do something wrong.

Children in the heteronomous stage of moral development also believe in immanent justice. **Immanent justice** is the notion that rules that are broken earn immediate punishment. Preschool children believe that if they do something wrong, they will be punished instantly—even if no one sees them carrying out their misdeeds. In contrast, older children understand that punishments for misdeeds are determined and meted out by people.

Evaluating Piaget's Approach to Moral Development. Recent research suggests that although Piaget was on the right track in his description of how moral development proceeds, his approach suffers from the same problem we encountered in his theory of cognitive development. Specifically, Piaget underestimated the age at which children's moral skills are honed.

It is now clear that preschool-age children understand the notion of intentionality by about age 3, and this allows them to make judgments based on intent at an earlier age than Piaget supposed. Specifically, when provided with moral questions that emphasize intent, preschool children judge someone who is intentionally bad as more "naughty" than someone who is unintentionally bad, but who creates more objective damage. Moreover, by the age of 4, they judge intentional lying wrong (Yuill & Perner, 1988; Bussey, 1992; Leslie, Knobe, & Cohen, 2006).

Social Learning Approaches to Morality. Social learning approaches to moral development stand in stark contrast to those of Piaget, Kohlberg, and Gilligan (we will discuss Kohlberg's and Gilligan's approaches in a moment). Instead of focusing on how an individual's level of cognitive development leads to particular forms of moral *reasoning*, social learning approaches focus more on how the environment in which the individual operates produces moral *behavior* (Eisenberg et al., 1999; Eisenberg, 2004).

incipient cooperation stage   Piaget's stage of moral development that lasts from around ages 7 to 10 in which children learn the actual formal rules of games and they play according to this shared knowledge.

autonomous cooperation stage   Piaget's stage of moral development that begins at about age 10 in which children become fully aware that formal game rules can be modified if the people who play them agree.

immanent justice   the notion that rules that are broken earn immediate punishment.

Social learning approaches build upon the behavioral approaches that we discussed earlier. They acknowledge that some instances of an individual's **prosocial behavior** (helping behavior that benefits others) stem from situations in which they have received positive reinforcement for acting in a morally appropriate way. For instance, when Mia's mother tells her she has been "terrific" for helping her younger brother complete a difficult homework assignment, her mother has reinforced that helping behavior. As a consequence, Mia is more likely to engage in such prosocial behavior in the future.

Social learning approaches go a step further, arguing that not all prosocial behavior has to be directly performed and subsequently reinforced for learning to occur. According to social learning approaches, we also learn moral behavior more indirectly by observing the behavior of others, called *models*. Children and adolescents imitate models who receive reinforcement for their behavior, and ultimately they learn to perform the behavior themselves. For example, when Mia's boyfriend David watches Mia help her brother with the assignment and be praised for it, David is more likely to engage in prosocial behavior himself at some later point (Bandura, 1977, 2004).

Quite a few studies illustrate the power of models and of social learning more generally in producing prosocial behavior in preschool-age children. For example, experiments have shown that children who view someone behaving generously or unselfishly are apt to follow the model's example, subsequently behaving in a generous or an unselfish manner themselves when put in a similar situation. The opposite also holds true: If a model behaves selfishly, children who observe such behavior tend to behave more selfishly themselves (Kim & Stevens, 1987; Nielsen, 2006; Schönpflug & Bilz, 2009).

Not all models are equally effective in producing prosocial responses. For instance, preschoolers are more apt to model the behavior of warm, responsive adults than of adults who appear colder. Furthermore, models viewed as highly competent or high in prestige are more effective than others (Bandura, 1977; Ellis & Zarbatany, 2007).

Children do more than simply mimic unthinkingly behavior that they see rewarded in others. By observing moral conduct, they are reminded of society's norms about the importance of moral behavior as conveyed by parents, teachers, and other powerful authority figures. They notice the connections between particular situations and certain kinds of behavior. This increases the likelihood that similar situations will elicit similar behavior in the observer.

Consequently, modeling paves the way for the development of more general rules and principles in a process called **abstract modeling**. Rather than always modeling the particular behavior of others, children begin to develop generalized principles that underlie the behavior they observe. After observing repeated instances in which a model is rewarded for acting in a morally desirable way, children begin the process of inferring and learning the general principles of moral conduct (Bandura, 1991; Zimmerman & Schunk, 2003).

Empathy and Moral Behavior. According to some developmentalists, **empathy**—the understanding of what another individual feels—lies at the heart of some kinds of moral behavior. The roots of empathy grow early. One-year-old infants cry when they hear other infants crying. By 2 and 3, toddlers will offer gifts and spontaneously share toys with other children and adults, even if they are strangers (Zahn-Wexler & Radke-Yarrow, 1990; Vaish, Carpenter, & Tomasello, 2009).

During the preschool years, empathy continues to grow as children's ability to monitor and regulate their emotional and cognitive responses increases. Some theorists believe that increasing empathy—as well as other positive emotions, such as sympathy and admiration—leads children to behave in a more moral fashion. In addition, some negative emotions—such as anger at an unfair situation or shame over previous transgressions—also may promote moral behavior (Miller & Jansen op de Haar, 1997; Valiente, Eisenberg, & Fabes, 2004; Decety & Jackson, 2006).

The notion that negative emotions may promote moral development is one that Freud first suggested in his theory of psychoanalytic personality development. Recall from our earlier discussion that Freud argued that a child's *superego*, the part of the personality that represents societal do's and don'ts, is developed through resolution of the *Oedipal conflict*. Children come to identify with their same-sex parent, incorporating that parent's standards of morality in order to avoid unconscious guilt raised by the Oedipal conflict.

Whether or not we accept Freud's account of the Oedipal conflict and the guilt it produces, his theory is consistent with more recent findings. These suggest that preschoolers' attempts to avoid experiencing negative emotions sometimes lead them to act in more moral,

prosocial behavior helping behavior that benefits others.

abstract modeling the process in which modeling paves the way for the development of more general rules and principles.

empathy the understanding of what another individual feels.

helpful ways. For instance, one reason children help others is to avoid the feelings of personal distress that they experience when they are confronted with another person's unhappiness or misfortune (Eisenberg, Valiente, & Champion, 2004; Valiente, Eisenberg, & Fabes, 2004).

Around the start of adolescence, more sophisticated kinds of empathy begin to emerge. Adolescents experience empathy not only in specific situations, but empathy for collective groups, such as people living in poverty or victims of racism (Hoffman, 1991, 2001; Eisenberg, Fabes, & Spinread, 2006).

For example, in early adolescence, a teenager may experience empathy when she learns a friend is ill. Understanding the emotions that the friend is experiencing—concerns about missing classes, fear about falling behind, and so forth—may lead the teenager to offer help to her classmate. On the other hand, when hearing about victims of an outbreak of bird flu in China, the same girl may be emotionally unmoved.

Studies have shown that children who view someone behaving generously are apt to follow the model's example.

Later in adolescence, however, as her cognitive abilities increase and she can reason on more abstract levels, the same girl may feel empathy for collective groups. Not only may she feel emotionally involved over victims of specific situations (such as people who lost their homes as a consequence of Hurricane Katrina), but she may experience deep emotional responses toward abstract groups such as the homeless, whose experiences may be completely unfamiliar to her.

Moral Reasoning and Prosocial Behavior

Your wife is near death from an unusual kind of cancer. One drug exists that the physicians think might save her—a form of radium that a scientist in a nearby city has recently developed. The drug, though, is expensive to manufacture, and the scientist is charging ten times what the drug costs him to make. He pays $1,000 for the radium and charges $10,000 for a small dose. You have gone to everyone you know to borrow money, but you can get together only $2,500—one-quarter of what you need. You've told the scientist that your wife is dying and asked him to sell it more cheaply or let you pay later. But the scientist has said, "No, I discovered the drug and I'm going to make money from it." In desperation, you consider breaking into the scientist's laboratory to steal the drug for your wife. Should you do it?

According to developmental psychologist Lawrence Kohlberg and his colleagues, the answer that individuals give to this question reveals central aspects of their sense of morality and justice. He suggests that individuals' responses to moral dilemmas such as this one reveal the stage of moral development they have attained—as well as yield information about their general level of cognitive development (Kohlberg, 1984; Colby & Kohlberg, 1987).

Kohlberg contends that people pass through a series of stages as their sense of justice evolves and in the kind of reasoning they use to make moral judgments. Primarily due to cognitive characteristics that we discussed earlier, younger school-age children tend to think either in terms of concrete, unvarying rules ("It is always wrong to steal" or "I'll be punished if I steal") or in terms of the rules of society ("Good people don't steal" or "What if everyone stole?").

By the time they reach adolescence, however, individuals are able to reason on a higher plane, typically having reached Piaget's stage of formal operations. They are capable of comprehending abstract, formal principles of morality, and they consider cases such as the one presented above in terms of broader issues of morality and of right and wrong ("Stealing may be acceptable if you are following your own conscience and doing the right thing").

Kohlberg suggests that moral development emerges in a three-level sequence, which is further subdivided into six stages (see Table 11.1 on page 312). At the lowest level, **preconventional morality** (Stages 1 and 2), people follow rigid rules based on punishments or rewards. For example, a student at the preconventional level might evaluate the moral dilemma posed in the story by saying that it was not worth stealing the drug because if you were caught, you would go to jail.

In the next level, that of **conventional morality** (Stages 3 and 4), people approach moral problems in terms of their own position as good, responsible members of society. Some at this

preconventional morality Kohlberg's first level of moral reasoning in which the concrete interests of the individual are considered in terms of rewards and punishments.

conventional morality Kohlberg's second level of moral reasoning in which people approach moral problems as members of society.

TABLE 11.1 **Kohlberg's Sequence of Moral Reasoning**

LEVEL	STAGE	SAMPLE MORAL REASONING	
		IN FAVOR OF STEALING	AGAINST STEALING
Level 1 **Preconventional morality:** At this level, the concrete interests of the individual are considered in terms of rewards and punishments.	**Stage 1** Obedience and punishment orientation: At this stage, people stick to rules in order to avoid punishment, and obedience occurs for its own sake.	"If you let your wife die, you will get in trouble. You'll be blamed for not spending the money to save her, and there'll be an investigation of you and the druggist for your wife's death."	"You shouldn't steal the drug because you'll get caught and sent to jail if you do. If you do get away, your conscience will bother you thinking how the police will catch up with you at any minute."
	Stage 2 Reward orientation: At this stage, rules are followed only for a person's own benefit. Obedience occurs because of rewards that are received.	"If you do happen to get caught, you could give the drug back and you wouldn't get much of a sentence. It wouldn't bother you much to serve a little jail term, if you have your wife when you get out."	"You may not get much of a jail term if you steal the drug, but your wife will probably die before you get out, so it won't do much good. If your wife dies, you shouldn't blame yourself; it isn't your fault; she has cancer."
Level 2 **Conventional morality:** At this level, people approach moral problems as members of society. They are interested in pleasing others by acting as good members of society.	**Stage 3** "Good boy" morality: Individuals at this stage show an interest in maintaining the respect of others and doing what is expected of them.	"No one will think you're bad if you steal the drug, but your family will think you're an inhuman husband if you don't. If you let your wife die, you'll never be able to look anybody in the face again."	"It isn't just the druggist who will think you're a criminal; everyone else will, too. After you steal the drug, you'll feel bad thinking how you've brought dishonor on your family and yourself; you won't be able to face anyone again."
	Stage 4 Authority and social-order-maintaining morality: People at this stage conform to society's rules and consider that "right" is what society defines as right.	"If you have any sense of honor, you won't let your wife die just because you're afraid to do the only thing that will save her. You'll always feel guilty that you caused her death if you don't do your duty to her."	"You're desperate and you may not know you're doing wrong when you steal the drug. But you'll know you did wrong after you're sent to jail. You'll always feel guilty for your dishonesty and law-breaking."
Level 3 **Postconventional morality:** At this level, people use moral principles, which are seen as broader than those of any particular society.	**Stage 5** Morality of contract, individual rights, and democratically accepted law: People at this stage do what is right because of a sense of obligation to laws that are agreed upon within society. They perceive that laws can be modified as part of changes in an implicit social contract.	"You'll lose other people's respect, not gain it, if you don't steal. If you let your wife die, it will be out of fear, not out of reasoning. So you'll just lose self-respect and probably the respect of others, too."	"You'll lose your standing and respect in the community and violate the law. You'll lose respect for yourself if you're carried away by emotion and forget the long-range point of view."
	Stage 6 Morality of individual principles and conscience: At this final stage, a person follows laws because they are based on universal ethical principles. Laws that violate the principles are disobeyed.	"If you don't steal the drug, and if you let your wife die, you'll always condemn yourself for it afterward. You won't be blamed and you'll have lived up to the outside rule of the law, but you won't have lived up to your own standards of conscience."	"If you steal the drug, you won't be blamed by other people, but you'll condemn yourself because you won't have lived up to your own conscience and standards of honesty."

Source: Adapted from Kohlberg, 1969.

level would decide *against* stealing the drug because they think they would feel guilty or dishonest for violating social norms. Others would decide *in favor* of stealing the drug because if they did nothing in this situation, they would be unable to face others. All of these people would be reasoning at the conventional level of morality.

Finally, individuals using **postconventional morality** (Level 3; Stages 5 and 6) invoke universal moral principles that are considered broader than the rules of the particular society in which they live. People who feel that they would condemn themselves if they did not steal the drug because they would not be living up to their own moral principles would be reasoning at the postconventional level.

Kohlberg's theory proposes that people move through the periods of moral development in a fixed order and that they are unable to reach the highest stage until adolescence, due to deficits in cognitive development that are not overcome until then. However, not everyone is presumed to reach the highest stages: Kohlberg found that postconventional reasoning is relatively rare (Kurtines & Gewirtz, 1987; Lapsley, 2006).

Lawrence Kohlberg and Carol Gilligan present contrasting explanations for children's moral development, with Gilligan focusing on gender differences in how males and females view morality.

Although Kohlberg's theory provides a good account of the development of moral *judgments,* the links with moral *behavior* are less strong. Still, students at higher levels of moral reasoning are less likely to engage in antisocial behavior at school (such as breaking school rules) and in the community (engaging in juvenile delinquency; Langford, 1995; Carpendale, 2000).

Furthermore, one experiment found that 15 percent of students who reasoned at the postconventional level of morality—the highest category—cheated when given the opportunity, although they were not as likely to cheat as those at lower levels, where more than half of the students cheated. Clearly, though, knowing what is morally right does not always mean acting that way (Killen & Hart, 1995; Hart, Burock, & London, 2003; Semerci, 2006).

Kohlberg's theory has also been criticized because it is based solely on observations of members of Western cultures. In fact, cross-cultural research finds that members of more industrialized, technologically advanced cultures move through the stages more rapidly than members of nonindustrialized countries. Why? One explanation is that Kohlberg's higher stages are based on moral reasoning involving governmental and societal institutions like the police and court system. In less industrialized areas, morality may be based more on relationships between people in a particular village. In short, the nature of morality may differ in diverse cultures, and Kohlberg's theory is more suited for Western cultures (Fu et al., 2007).

An aspect of Kohlberg's theory that has proved even more problematic is the difficulty it has explaining *girls'* moral judgments. Because the theory initially was based largely on data from males, some researchers have argued that it does a better job describing boys' moral development than girls' moral development. This would explain the surprising finding that women typically score at a lower level than men on tests of moral judgments using Kohlberg's stage sequence. This result has led to an alternative account of moral development for girls.

Log onto **MyDevelopmentLab** and watch the video on moral development. In the interviews, children display Kohlberg's theories that you have just been reading about.

Gilligan's Account of Moral Development in Girls. Psychologist Carol Gilligan (1982, 1987) has suggested that differences in the ways boys and girls are raised in our society lead to basic distinctions in how men and women view moral behavior. According to her, boys view morality primarily in terms of broad principles such as justice or fairness, while girls see it in terms of responsibility toward individuals and willingness to sacrifice themselves to help specific individuals within the context of particular relationships. Compassion for individuals, then, is a more prominent factor in moral behavior for women than it is for men (Gilligan, Ward, & Taylor, 1988; Gilligan, Lyons, & Hammer, 1990; Gump, Baker, & Roll, 2000).

Gilligan views morality as developing among females in a three-stage process (summarized in Table 11.2 on page 314). In the first stage, called "orientation toward individual survival," females first concentrate on what is practical and best for them, gradually making a transition from selfishness to responsibility, in which they think about what would be best for others. In the second stage, termed "goodness as self-sacrifice," females begin to think that they must sacrifice their own wishes to what other people want.

postconventional morality   Kohlberg's third level of moral reasoning in which people use moral principles that are seen as broader than those of any particular society.

TABLE 11.2	Gilligan's Three Stages of Moral Development for Women	
STAGE	**CHARACTERISTICS**	**EXAMPLE**
Stage 1		
Orientation toward individual survival	Initial concentration is on what is practical and best for self. Gradual transition from selfishness to responsibility, which includes thinking about what would be best for others.	A first grader may insist on playing only games of her own choosing when playing with a friend.
Stage 2		
Goodness as self-sacrifice	Initial view is that a woman must sacrifice her own wishes to what other people want. Gradual transition from "goodness" to "truth," which takes into account needs of both self and others.	Now older, the same girl may believe that to be a good friend, she must play the games her friend chooses, even if she herself doesn't like them.
Stage 3		
Morality of nonviolence	A moral equivalence is established between self and others. Hurting anyone—including one's self—is seen as immoral. Most sophisticated form of reasoning, according to Gilligan.	The same girl may realize that both friends must enjoy their time together and look for activities that both she and her friend can enjoy.

Ideally, women make a transition from "goodness" to "truth," in which they take into account their own needs plus those of others. This transition leads to the third stage, "morality of nonviolence," in which women come to see that hurting anyone is immoral—including hurting themselves. This realization establishes a moral equivalence between themselves and others and represents, according to Gilligan, the most sophisticated level of moral reasoning.

It is obvious that Gilligan's sequence of stages is quite different from Kohlberg's, and some developmentalists have suggested that her rejection of Kohlberg's work is too sweeping and that gender differences are not as pronounced as first thought. For instance, some researchers argue that both males and females use similar "justice" and "care" orientations in making moral judgments. Clearly, the question of how boys and girls differ in their moral orientations, as well as the nature of moral development in general, is far from settled (Tangney & Dearing, 2002; Jorgensen, 2006; Tappan, 2006; Donleavy, 2008).

The lingering questions about the nature of moral reasoning have not deterred people from applying what has been learned about morality to everyday life.

Moral Behavior and Moral Reasoning: Why the Disconnect? Except for social learning perspectives, most of the approaches to moral development (such as those of Kohlberg and Gilligan) focus on moral reasoning. Why has the research spotlight shone more brightly on reasoning about moral behavior, as opposed to examining actual behavior?

One reason is that the researchers have assumed that moral reasoning lies at the heart of moral behavior. If people don't have a clear internal moral compass, it seems unreasonable to expect that they will behave in a moral way. Unfortunately, though, there has been a persistent disconnect between prosocial *reasoning* and prosocial *behavior*. Obviously, we'd expect moral reasoning and judgments to be closely associated, but that doesn't seem to be the case. Why?

One reason is that in the real world there are often circumstances that override our internal moral compass. Although we may know and truly believe that it is wrong to break the law by not fully stopping at a stop sign, we may feel that because no one is around, we don't have to come to a complete stop. Or perhaps we're driving someone to a hospital emergency department, and our internal principles about aiding someone in distress are more salient at that moment than our principles about obeying traffic laws. Unlike when they are measured in experiments, moral principles in the real world occur in a particular context that brings its own situational pressures.

In addition, moral judgments are made in a variety of contexts, and it may be an oversimplification to expect that morality will be displayed in similar ways across different domains and situations. According to the **social domain approach**, moral reasoning needs to be considered in the context in which judgments are being made at a given time. Major contexts include the *moral domain* (contexts that focus on concerns about justice), the *social-conventional domain* (contexts

FROM AN EDUCATOR'S PERSPECTIVE
Should moral development be taught in public schools?

social domain approach
the concept that moral reasoning needs to be considered in the context in which judgments are being made at a given time.

involving the need for social groups to function well), and the *personal domain* (contexts involving matters of personal choice). The particular moral judgments are likely to vary according to the domain (Smetana & Turiel, 2003; Turiel, 2006).

Finally, people sometimes look at situations through the lens of personal choices and freedom, rather than in terms of ethical dilemmas. For example, consider the decision to engage in premarital sex. For some people, premarital sex is always ethically wrong, and to engage in it is, by definition, an immoral act. But to others, premarital sex is a choice to be decided upon by the individuals who are involved. Similarly, alcohol use—while illegal for adolescents younger than a certain age—may be viewed in terms of a fairly rational, cost-benefit analysis (drinking provides certain benefits, but also accrues certain costs), rather than in terms of morality. The view that such activities as taking drugs, engaging in sex, and drinking are personal, not moral, choices helps explain the lack of relationship between risk-taking and moral reasoning (Kuther, 2000; Kuther & Higgins-D'Alessandro, 2000, 2003; Eisenberg & Morris, 2004).

Prosocial Reasoning and Prosocial Behavior: The Other Side of the Coin. We've been focusing on situations in which people are faced with situations involving some form of wrongdoing—breaking a rule, violating a moral principle, disobeying a law. But what about the other side of the coin: doing positive, unselfish, or altruistic deeds that benefit others, sometimes at the expense of oneself?

Although there is considerably less research in this area, emerging work suggests that people generally become more sophisticated in their thinking about prosocial behavior. For example, their growing cognitive abilities allow them to distinguish between prosocial behavior that is self-serving (done to gain something, such as looking better in others' eyes) or truly *altruistic* (done to help others and requiring clear self-sacrifice).

Individuals who are unusually helpful to others tend to show more sophisticated moral reasoning than people who are less prosocially active. Furthermore, people who show more sophisticated levels of prosocial reasoning are generally more sympathetic. There's a persistent sex difference, too: Females tend to demonstrate higher levels of prosocial reasoning than males (Eisenberg & Morris, 2004).

On the other hand, it's harder to make generalizations about prosocial *behavior*. Although some people become increasingly helpful as they get older, others do not. In a way, the difficulty in finding a relationship between prosocial behavior and personal characteristics is not surprising, given the difficulty that researchers have had in finding any particular personality characteristics related to helpfulness. Most research suggests that people are not invariably helpful or, for that matter, unhelpful. Instead, whether particular individuals act in a prosocial manner depends on their personality *and* the specifics of the situation. Furthermore, no single pattern of specific, individual personality traits determines prosocial behavior. Rather, the way that specific personality factors fit together, as well as the demands of the particular situation, determines whether a person will help (Knight et al., 1994; Eisenberg & Morris, 2004).

Gender and Cultural Differences in Prosocial Behavior. Both gender and culture are related to prosocial behavior. For example, quite consistently, girls are more helpful than boys. They are more caring about others, and they act in a more prosocial manner. By the way, not only are males less likely to provide help, they are less willing to ask for help than females—something we might call the males-hating-to-ask-for-directions-even-when-they-are-lost phenomenon (Wills & DePaulo, 1991; Eisenberg & Morris, 2004).

On the other hand, males don't always act less helpfully than females. If the situation is one in which their behavior is public and visible to others, and the person needing help is female, males are more likely to be helpful. Having the opportunity to act like a "knight in shining armor" and come to the rescue of a damsel in distress elevates the level of male helpfulness beyond its typically more modest level (Hyde & Grabe, 2008).

The typically higher levels of prosocial behavior displayed by females reflect their tendency to hold a *communal* orientation, centering on an interest in relationships and community. In contrast, males are more likely to have an *agentic* orientation, which focuses on individuality and getting things done. Communal orientations lead to greater prosocial behavior (Mosher & Danoff-Burg, 2005; Salmivalli et al., 2005).

Culture, too, affects the extent to which people behave prosocially. For instance, individuals living on Israeli kibbutzim, or collective farms, tend to show greater helpfulness and even different reasoning about morality than members of the dominant culture in the United States. Similarly,

Children with authoritative parents tend to be well adjusted, in part because the parents are supportive and take the time to explain things. What are the consequences of parents who are too permissive? Too authoritarian? Too uninvolved?

people raised in the United States use more rights-based reasoning about morality than people in other societies. In *rights-based reasoning,* certain rights (such as freedom of speech) are assumed; they don't have to be earned, but are the birthright of every citizen. In contrast, people in India are more likely to use *duty-based reasoning,* in which people are expected to behave in a certain way because it is their responsibility (Shweder, Much, & Mahapatra, 1997; Verma, 2004).

Parents' childrearing practices, which we will discuss shortly, produce different forms of helping behavior, which emerge during childhood. For example, the level of helping behavior that children display while playing varies substantially in different cultures. Children raised in cultures in which children are taught to cooperate with other family members to do chores or to help in the upbringing of younger children (such as in Kenya, Mexico, and the Philippines) show relatively high levels of prosocial behavior. In contrast, cultures that promote competition—such as the United States—produce lower levels of prosocial behavior (Whiting & Edwards, 1988; Carlo, 1999; Yablo & Field, 2007).

Furthermore, the degree to which people view helping in the context of reciprocity—the view that we should help because we expect to receive help from others in the future—is related to cultural factors. For example, Hindu Indians see reciprocity as a moral obligation, whereas college students in the United States consider reciprocity as more of a personal choice (Miller & Bersoff, 1994; Miller, 1997; Chadha & Misra, 2004).

Effective Parenting: Teaching Desired Behavior

While she thinks no one is looking, Maria goes into her brother Alejandro's bedroom, where he has been saving the last of his Halloween candy. Just as she takes his last Reese's Peanut Butter Cup, the children's mother walks into the room and immediately takes in the situation.

If you were Maria's mother, which of the following reactions seems most reasonable?

1. Tell Maria that she must go to her room and stay there for the rest of the day, and that she is going to lose access to her favorite blanket, the one she sleeps with every night and during naps.

2. Mildly tell Maria that what she did was not such a good idea, and she shouldn't do it in the future.

3. Explain why her brother Alejandro was going to be upset, and tell her that she must go to her room for an hour as punishment.

4. Forget about it, and let the children sort it out themselves.

Each of these four alternative responses represents one of the major parenting styles identified by Diana Baumrind (1971, 1980) and updated by Eleanor Maccoby and colleagues (Baumrind, 1971, 1980; Maccoby & Martin, 1983).

Authoritarian parents respond as in the first alternative. They are controlling, punitive, rigid, cold. Their word is law, and they value strict, unquestioning obedience from their children. They also do not tolerate expressions of disagreement.

Permissive parents, in contrast, provide lax and inconsistent feedback, as in the second alternative. They require little of their children, and they don't see themselves as holding much responsibility for how their children turn out. They place little or no limits or control on their children's behavior.

Authoritative parents are firm, setting clear and consistent limits. Although they tend to be relatively strict, like authoritarian parents, they are loving and emotionally supportive. They also try to reason with their children, giving explanations for why they should behave in a particular way ("Alejandro is going to be upset"), and communicating the rationale for any punishment they may impose. Authoritative parents encourage their children to be independent.

Finally, **uninvolved parents** show virtually no interest in their children, displaying indifferent, rejecting behavior. They are detached emotionally and see their role as no more than feeding, clothing, and providing shelter for their child. In its most extreme form, uninvolved parenting results in **neglect**, a form of child abuse. (The four patterns are summarized in Table 11.3.)

Does the particular style of discipline that parents use result in differences in children's behavior? The answer is very much yes—although, as you might expect, there are many exceptions (Collett, Gimpel, & Greenson, 2001; Snyder et al., 2005; Arredondo et al., 2006; Simons & Conger, 2007):

authoritarian parents parents who are controlling, punitive, rigid, and cold, and whose word is law. They value strict, unquestioning obedience from their children and do not tolerate expressions of disagreement.

permissive parents parents who provide lax and inconsistent feedback and require little of their children.

authoritative parents parents who are firm, setting clear and consistent limits, but who try to reason with their children, giving explanations for why they should behave in a particular way.

uninvolved parents parents who show almost no interest in their children and indifferent, rejecting behavior.

neglect a form of child abuse.

- Children of authoritarian parents tend to be withdrawn, showing relatively little sociability. They are not very friendly, often behaving uneasily around their peers. Girls who are raised by authoritarian parents are especially dependent on their parents, whereas boys are unusually hostile.

- Permissive parents have children who, in many ways, share the undesirable characteristics of children of authoritarian parents. Children with permissive parents tend to be dependent and moody, and they are low in social skills and self-control.

- Children of authoritative parents fare best. They generally are independent, friendly with their peers, self-assertive, and cooperative. They have strong motivation to achieve, and they are typically successful and likable. They regulate their own behavior effectively, both in terms of their relationships with others and emotional self-regulation.

  Some authoritative parents also display several characteristics that have come to be called *supportive parenting*, including parental warmth, proactive teaching, calm discussion during disciplinary episodes, and interest and involvement in children's peer activities. Children whose parents engage in such supportive parenting show better adjustment and are better protected from the consequences of later adversity they may encounter (Pettit, Bates, & Dodge, 1997; Belluck, 2000; Kaufmann et al., 2000).

- Children whose parents show uninvolved parenting styles are the worst off. Their parents' lack of involvement disrupts their emotional development considerably, leading them to feel unloved and emotionally detached, and impedes their physical and cognitive development as well.

While such classification systems are useful ways of categorizing and describing parents' behavior, they are not a recipe for success. Parenting and growing up are more complicated than that! For instance, in a significant number of cases the children of authoritarian and permissive parents develop quite successfully.

Furthermore, most parents are not entirely consistent: Although the authoritarian, permissive, authoritative, and uninvolved patterns describe general styles, sometimes parents switch from their dominant mode to one of the others. For instance, when a child darts into the street,

TABLE 11.3   Parenting Styles

HOW DEMANDING PARENTS ARE OF CHILDREN ▶	DEMANDING	UNDEMANDING
How Responsive Parents Are to a Child ▼	**Authoritative**	**Permissive**
	Characteristics: firm, setting clear and consistent limits	**Characteristics:** lax and inconsistent feedback
Highly Responsive	**Relationship with Children:** Although they tend to be relatively strict, like authoritarian parents, they are loving and emotionally supportive and encourage their children to be independent. They also try to reason with their children, giving explanations for why they should behave in a particular way, and communicate the rationale for any punishment they may impose.	**Relationship with Children:** They require little of their children, and they don't see themselves as holding much responsibility for how their children turn out. They place little or no limits or control on their children's behavior.
	Authoritarian	**Uninvolved**
	Characteristics: controlling, punitive, rigid, cold	**Characteristics:** displaying indifferent, rejecting behavior
Low Responsive	**Relationship with Children:** Their word is law, and they value strict, unquestioning obedience from their children. They also do not tolerate expressions of disagreement.	**Relationship with Children:** They are detached emotionally and see their role as only providing food, clothing, and shelter. In its extreme form, this parenting style results in neglect, a form of child abuse.

Source: Based on Baumrind, 1971; Maccoby & Martin, 1983.

The style of parenting that is most effective depends on what parents in a particular culture are taught regarding appropriate childbearing practices.

even the most laid-back and permissive parent is likely to react in a harsh, authoritarian manner, laying down strict demands about safety. In such cases, authoritarian styles may be most effective (Janssens & Dekovic, 1997; Holden & Miller, 1999; Eisenberg & Valiente, 2002; Gershoff, 2002).

Cultural Differences in Childrearing Practices. It's important to keep in mind that the findings regarding childrearing styles we have been discussing are chiefly applicable to Western societies. The style of parenting that is most successful may depend quite heavily on the norms of a particular culture—and what parents in a particular culture are taught regarding appropriate childrearing practices (Giles-Sims & Lockhart, 2005; Dwairy et al., 2006; Hulei, Zevenbergen, & Jacobs, 2006).

For example, the Chinese concept of *chiao shun* suggests that parents should be strict, firm, and in tight control of their children's behavior. Parents are seen to have a duty to train their children to adhere to socially and culturally desirable standards of behavior, particularly those manifested in good school performance. Children's acceptance of such an approach to discipline is seen as a sign of parental respect (Chao, 1994; Wu, Robinson, & Yang, 2002).

Parents in China are typically highly directive with their children, pushing them to excel and controlling their behavior to a considerably higher degree than parents typically do in Western countries. And it works: Children of Asian parents tend to be quite successful, particularly academically (Steinberg, Dornbusch, & Brown, 1992; Nelson et al., 2006).

In contrast, U.S. parents are generally advised to use authoritative methods and explicitly to avoid authoritarian measures. Interestingly, it wasn't always this way. Until World War II, the point of view that dominated the advice literature was authoritarian, apparently founded on Puritan religious influences that suggested that children had "original sin" or that they needed to have their wills broken (Smuts & Hagen, 1985).

In short, the childrearing practices that parents are urged to follow reflect cultural perspectives about the nature of children as well as about the appropriate role of parents and their support system (see the *From Research to Practice* box). No single parenting pattern or style, then,

FROM RESEARCH TO PRACTICE
Parenting Coaches: Teaching Parents to Teach Their Children

What tripped Lisa D'Annolfo Levey's maternal tolerance meter on a recent Tuesday afternoon was not just the toy football her 7-year-old son, Skylar, zinged across the living room, nearly toppling her teacup. Or the karate kick sprung by her 4-year-old, Forrest, which Ms. Levey ducked, barely.

The clincher was the full-throttle duel with foam swords, her boys whooping and squealing, flailing their weapons at the blue leather couch, the yellow kidney-shaped rug, and, ultimately, their mother.

"Forrest, how about you come up and hug Skylar instead of whacking him in the head?" Ms. Levey implored. "This is stressing me out, guys." (Belluck, 2005, p. A1)

And then she called her personal parent coach to find out how to deal with the situation.

Personal parent coach? In a new and growing phenomenon, parents are turning to members of a profession that didn't exist only a few years ago called *parent coaching* to help them navigate the trials of parenthood.

Less expensive than formal therapy, but more systematic than the advice one might receive from one's next-door neighbor, parent coaching provides a combination of advice and support. Some parent coaches offer specific childrearing strategies, while others teach parents the basics of child development so that they put their child's behavior in perspective (Marchant, Young, & West, 2004).

For some parents, parent coaching is a lifeline. It provides a way for parents who might not have access to the advice of other, more experienced parents to learn how to deal with the challenges of children. It also provides a relationship with another adult who can offer social support (Smith, 2005).

Although many parents swear by the value of parent coaches, the effectiveness of parent coaching has not been established by much scientific research. In part, the lack of data is a reflection of the newness of the field. In addition, there is great heterogeneity in the qualifications of parent coaches. While some have had formal training in child development, the only qualifications of other coaches is having raised a child themselves (Leonard, 2005).

Because there is no licensing of parent coaches, parents should adopt a buyer-beware attitude. Anyone can call themselves a parent coach, and parents should examine the credentials of prospectrive coaches carefully. Until the field becomes more regulated—and the value of parent coaches has been formally established—parents should be cautious.

- *If you were conducting an interview with a potential parent coach, what kind of questions would you ask?*
- *Do you think parent coaches should be licensed by the government? Why or why not? What kind of qualifications would you require to get a license?*

is likely to be universally appropriate or invariably to produce successful children (Harwood et al., 1996; Hart et al., 1998; Wang & Tamis-LeMonda, 2003).

Similarly, it is important to keep in mind that childrearing practices are not the sole influence on children's development. For example, sibling and peer influences play a significant role in children's development. Furthermore, children's behavior is in part produced by their unique genetic endowment, and their behavior can in turn shape parental behavior. In sum, parents' childrearing practices are just one of a rich array of environmental and genetic influences that influence children (Reiss et al., 2000; Boivin et al., 2005; Loehlin, Neiderhiser, & Reiss, 2005).

REVIEW

▶ Piaget believed that preschoolers are in the heteronomous morality stage of moral development, in which rules are seen as invariant and unchangeable.

▶ Social learning approaches to moral development emphasize the importance of reinforcement for moral actions and the observation of models of moral conduct. Psychoanalytical and other theories focus on children's empathy with others and their wish to help others so they can avoid unpleasant feelings of guilt themselves.

▶ According to Kohlberg, moral development proceeds from a concern with rewards and punishments, through a focus on social conventions and rules, toward a sense of universal moral principles. Gilligan has suggested, however, that girls may follow a somewhat different progression of moral development.

▶ As people become more cognitively sophisticated, they are better able to consider and evaluate prosocial behavior. The likelihood that a person will act prosocially depends on both the individual and the situation rather than on personality traits alone.

▶ There are clear gender and cultural differences in both empathy and prosocial behavior.

▶ There are several distinct childrearing styles, including authoritarian, permissive, authoritative, and uninvolved.

▶ Childrearing styles show strong cultural influences.

APPLY

▶ If high-prestige models of behavior are particularly effective in influencing moral attitudes and actions, are there implications for individuals in such industries as sports, advertising, and entertainment?

▶ How might a rights-based orientation, such as is found in the United States, tend to decrease prosocial behavior, while a duty-based orientation encourages prosocial behavior? Can government policies that encourage volunteerism bring about a change in U.S. attitudes?

MODULE 11.2

Values, Religion, and Spirituality: Focusing on the Meaning of Life

The spirituality of old age is lovely. It takes one places that one needs to go to get ready to die which is one of the biggest challenges which we, as human beings, face. I have found that my Unitarian Universalist [religion] helps me with this task in very satisfying ways. The idea that we are not a self but just a small part of an interdependent web of existence is a profound insight that contributes to a sense that death is not extinguishment but a transformation and that in some sense we all are eternal.

Reading this excerpt from the blog of a 63-year-old man makes it obvious that the search for meaning in life is something that has continued throughout his life. Indeed, the quest to understand who we are and our place in the universe is something that most people consider and often grapple with.

FIGURE 11.1 Changes in values
"Being very well off financially" is
a value that has been of increasing
importance to college students over
the last 40 years, while "developing a
meaningful philosophy of life" has been
on the decline. Why do you think these
trends have occurred?
Source: Pryor et al., 2007.

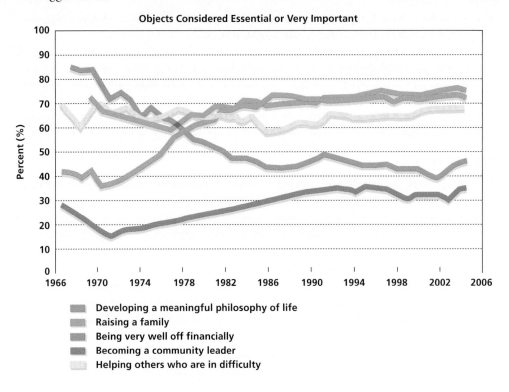

Objects Considered Essential or Very Important

Percent (%)

- Developing a meaningful philosophy of life
- Raising a family
- Being very well off financially
- Becoming a community leader
- Helping others who are in difficulty

values the qualities people see as most
desirable and important, affecting people's
thinking and behavior.

It's in relatively recent years that developmentalists have focused on such questions. They
have sought first to understand how **values**, the qualities people see as most desirable and
important, affect people's thinking and behavior. They have also begun to look at how religion
and spirituality develop across the life span.

Values are part of each person's life, and they affect behavior in significant ways. They help
determine how we feel about school, work, money, religion—just about every aspect of life.
Values determine what goals we choose to pursue and what we see as important at every stage of
our lives.

Surveys of college students show that the goal that they hold most important is raising a
family (held by 77 percent of those surveyed). This was followed by "being very well off financially" (74 percent) and "helping others who are in difficulty" (70 percent). There also have been
marked shifts in the values of college students over the last several decades. For example, finding
a meaningful philosophy of life has declined in importance while being financially well off has
increased significantly (see Figure 11.1; Pryor et al., 2006; Pryor et al., 2007).

Religion often plays a central role in determining people's values. Only 16 percent of
Americans do not have a religious affiliation, with the rest reporting a wide variety of different affiliations. However, religious affiliation is not fixed: Over a quarter of Americans report that they
have left the religious faith in which they were raised and have become affiliated with another religion (Pew Forum on Religion & Public Life, 2008).

Religion is important to many people because it offers a formal
means of satisfying spirituality needs. *Spirituality* is a sense of attachment
to some higher power such as God, nature, or a sacred entity. Although
spirituality needs are typically tied to religious beliefs, they may be
independent. Many people who consider themselves to be spiritual individuals do not participate in formal religious practices or are not tied to
any particular religion.

Often playing a central role in determining
people's values, religion also offers a
formal means at satisfying spiritual needs.

Religion and Spirituality in Childhood and Adolescence

Piaget's approach to cognitive development offers a way of organizing
how religious thinking develops through childhood and adolescence.
Based on children's responses to Bible stories and pictures, children pass
through three stages (Goldman, 1964):

- **Preoperational intuitive religious thought (up to age 7 or 8).** Children in this stage show religious thinking that is unsystematic. They don't understand religious stories very well, or they misinterpret their meaning altogether.

- **Concrete operational religious thought (ages 7 or 8 to 13 or 14).** Children focus on particular concrete details of the stories and pictures rather than the abstract lessons of the stories.

- **Formal operational religious thought (ages 13 or 14 and older).** In this stage, children are able to think more abstractly. They are able to understand the meaning of the stories and pictures, and draw inferences about them.

As teenagers grapple with questions of identity during adolescence, religious identity may be questioned. After having accepted their religious identity in an unquestioning manner during childhood, they may view it more critically and seek to distance themselves from formal religion. In other cases, they may be drawn to their religious affiliation because it offers answers to such abstract questions as "Why am I here on this earth?" and "What is the meaning of life?" (Kiang, Yip, & Fuligni, 2008).

Spirituality During the College Years

Although it is rarely part of the formal college curriculum, surveys of college students show that many students seek discussions and information regarding spirituality, broadly defined. For example, surveys show that three-quarters of students report seeking meaning and purpose in life, and they think that college should help them in this quest. More than two-thirds say that it is "essential" or "very important" for their college experience to enhance their self-understanding (Higher Education Research Institute, 2005; Lindholm, 2006).

College students wanting greater coverage of spirituality are apt to be disappointed. Although 80 percent of faculty identify themselves as spiritual individuals, and more than two-thirds seek out opportunities to develop their own spirituality, they are unlikely to bring talk of spirituality and the meaning of life into the classroom. More than half of students say that their professors never offer opportunities to discuss topics related to spirituality.

There are probably several reasons for this lack of discussion of spirituality. Instructors at public, state-supported schools may feel that talk of spirituality may veer into discussion of religious beliefs, something that instructors may feel violates the neutrality of their classes. In other cases, instructors may feel ill equipped to discuss spirituality and the meaning of life, believing such talk should be left to philosophy and religion classes (Pingree, 2008).

Religion and Spirituality in Adulthood

Religion plays a significant role in many adults' lives. For example, if you've ever suffered a death of a close relative or friend, you might have felt particularly motivated to attend religious services for a time after the death because of the comfort you derived from them.

Similarly, religion can help people make sense of catastrophes and disasters of all sorts. Just after the 9/11 terrorist attacks on the United States, attendance at religious services soared. Christian, Muslim, and Jewish clergy conducted interfaith services to try to help people make sense of the attacks. They urged for calm and called on attendees not to retaliate against others who appeared to be different from mainstream Americans. However, a year after the attacks, attendance at religious services dipped back to their typical levels (Moore, 2002).

Religion helps people make sense of events that otherwise appear to be senseless. It can offer an explanation of why things have happened and give people a sense of shared experience that can be comforting. It also provides perspective, showing people that their personal misfortunes can be viewed in a long-term, historical context (Cox, 2007).

Furthermore, religion may explain misfortunes as being due to some unseen, unknowable plan or simply as being "God's will." Even though people may not understand the "plan" that is unfolding, such a view may be more comforting than simply seeing events as random and without meaning (Marshall & Sutherland, 2008).

Finally, religion can provide direct social support to others. Traditionally, churches, synagogues, and mosques have provided both tangible and emotional help to members in time of need. Even if it is only providing meals to members who are experiencing illness, such social support can be both helpful and emotionally meaningful (Krause, 2008).

Our understanding and practice of faith and spirituality proceeds through a series of stages that extend throughout the lifetime.

FROM AN
EDUCATOR'S
PERSPECTIVE
Given that teenagers are grappling with question of identity and values during adolescence, should schools seek to teach values? And what values are most appropriately taught?

Fowler's Stages of Faith Development. According to James Fowler, our understanding and practice of faith and spirituality proceeds through a series of stages that extend throughout the lifetime. During childhood, individuals hold a fairly literal view of God and biblical figures. For example, children may think of God as living at the top of the earth and being able to see what everyone is doing (Fowler & Dell, 2006).

In adolescence, the view of spirituality becomes more abstract. As they build their identity, adolescents typically develop a core set of beliefs and values. In many cases, however, they have not considered their views either in depth or systematically.

During early and middle adulthood, adults are in what Fowler calls the *individuative-reflective stage* of faith. During this time, people reflect on their beliefs and values. They understand that their views are one of many and that multiple views of God are possible. They do not simply accept the views of their religion, but seek to form a personal belief system that speaks to them.

Finally, in late adulthood, people may move into a final stage of faith development: the conjunctive stage. In the *conjunctive stage* of faith development, elderly individuals develop a broad, inclusive view of religion and all humanity. They see humanity as a whole, and they may work to promote a common good. In this stage, they may move beyond formal religion and hold a unified view of people across the globe.

It's important to note that Fowler does not believe that everyone attains each of these stages. Some people remain "stuck" at an earlier stage, depending on their degree of reflection and their exposure to religious and spiritual thinking.

Religion in the Final Stages of Life

For many people in late adulthood, stronger religious beliefs are related to greater life satisfaction. For instance, one study found that older adults who found a sense of meaning in life from their religion also were more satisfied with their lives, had greater self-esteem, and were more optimistic (Krause, 2003a).

There are also some racial differences in the role that religion plays in people's lives during late adulthood. Older African American adults are more likely to find meaning in religion than older Caucasians. Furthermore, the relationship between religious meaning and life satisfaction, self-esteem, and optimism is stronger for African Americans than for Caucasians. The findings suggest that religious meaning may be an important source of resilience for older black adults (Krause, 2003a).

Prayer itself may produce positive benefits in older adults. For example, the negative effects of financial difficulties on health in older people are reduced in those who pray for others often. Furthermore, higher rates of prayer are associated with reports of greater happiness. However, the question of whether prayer actually extends life remains unanswered. Although some studies show a link between attendance at religious service and a healthier lifestyle, there is no evidence that religious involvement actually extends life (Krause, 2003b; Breslin & Lewis, 2008; Gonnerman et al., 2008; Robbins et al., 2008).

REVIEW

▶ Surveys show that the goals of college students have undergone a shift in recent years. Finding a meaningful philosophy of life has decreased in importance, while being financially well off has increased.

▶ Spirituality needs are frequently tied to religious beliefs, but many people who identify themselves as spiritual individuals do not participate in formal religious practices or have any particular religious affiliation.

▶ Although most Americans report having some religious affiliation, this affiliation is not fixed. One-fourth of Americans say they now have a different religious affiliation than the one with which they were raised.

▶ In adolescence, the question of religion and spiritual beliefs becomes part of the larger quest for an identity as teens seek to develop a core set of beliefs and values.

▶ Religion can offer an explanation of why things happen, and give people a long-term, historical perspective in which to view their personal problems and society's disasters.

▶ Although strong religious beliefs have been linked to greater life satisfaction in older adults, there is no evidence that a strong religious belief or a high rate of prayer is related to a longer life.

APPLY

▶ If formal religion provides people with a set of moral guidelines to live by, how might people not affiliated with any religion develop a moral framework and a set of core values?

▶ How might schools and universities better address students' desire to discuss life's meaning and purpose while still respecting religious diversity and the separation of church and state?

aggression intentional injury or harm to another person.

emotional self-regulation the capability to adjust emotions to a desired state and level of intensity.

instrumental aggression aggression motivated by the desire to obtain a concrete goal, such as playing with a desirable toy that another child is playing with.

MODULE 11.3

Aggression and Violence

Four-year-old Duane could not contain his anger and frustration anymore. Although he usually was mild-mannered, when Eshu began to tease him about the split in his pants and kept it up for several minutes, Duane finally snapped. Rushing over to Eshu, Duane pushed him to the ground and began to hit him with his small, closed fists. Because he was so distraught, Duane's punches were not terribly effective, but they were severe enough to hurt Eshu and bring him to tears before the preschool teachers could intervene.

Log onto **MyDevelopmentLab** and watch the video clips "Relational Aggression" and "Reactive Aggression" to get a better understanding of the types of aggression and what they look like in children.

Aggression among preschoolers is quite common, though attacks such as this are not. The potential for verbal hostility, shoving matches, kicking, and other forms of aggression is present throughout the preschool period, although the degree to which aggression is acted out changes as children become older.

Aggression and Violence in Children: Sources and Consequences

Eshu's taunting was also a form of aggression. **Aggression** is intentional injury or harm to another person. Infants don't act aggressively; it is hard to contend that their behavior is *intended* to hurt others, even if they inadvertently manage to do so. In contrast, by the time they reach preschool age, children demonstrate true aggression.

During the early preschool years, some of the aggression is addressed at attaining a desired goal, such as getting a toy away from another person or using a particular space occupied by another person. Consequently, in some ways the aggression is inadvertent, and minor scuffles may in fact be a typical part of early preschool life. It is the rare child who does not demonstrate at least an occasional act of aggression.

On the other hand, extreme and sustained aggression is a cause of concern. In most children, the amount of aggression declines as they move through the preschool years, as does the frequency and average length of episodes of aggressive behavior (Cummings, Iannotti, & Zahn-Waxler, 1989; Persson, 2005).

The child's personality and social development contribute to this decline in aggression. Throughout the preschool years, children become better at controlling the emotions that they are experiencing. **Emotional self-regulation**, as we discussed earlier, is the capability to adjust emotions to a desired state and level of intensity. Starting at age 2, children are able to talk about their feelings, and they engage in strategies to regulate them. As they get older, they develop more effective strategies, learning to better cope with negative emotions. In addition to their increasing self-control, children are also, as we've seen, developing sophisticated social skills. Most learn to use language to express their wishes, and they become increasingly able to negotiate with others (Eisenberg & Zhou, 2000; Philippot & Feldman, 2005; Zeman et al., 2006).

Despite these typical declines in aggression, some children remain aggressive throughout the preschool period. Furthermore, aggression is a relatively stable characteristic: The most aggressive preschoolers tend to be the most aggressive children during the school-age years, and the least aggressive preschoolers tend to be the least aggressive school-age children (Rosen, 1998; Tremblay, 2001; Schaeffer, Petras, & Ialongo, 2003).

Boys typically show higher levels of physical, instrumental aggression than girls. **Instrumental aggression** is aggression motivated by the desire to obtain a concrete goal, such as playing with a desirable toy that another child is playing with.

Aggression, both physical and verbal, is present throughout the preschool period.

relational aggression nonphysical aggression that is intended to hurt another person's feelings.

Although girls show lower levels of instrumental aggression, they may be just as aggressive, but in different ways from boys. Girls are more likely to practice **relational aggression**, which is nonphysical aggression intended to hurt another person's feelings. Such aggression may be demonstrated through name-calling, withholding friendship, or simply saying mean, hurtful things that make the recipient feel bad (Underwood, 2003; Werner & Crick, 2004; Murray-Close, Ostrov, & Crick, 2006).

The Roots of Aggression

How can we explain the aggression of preschoolers? Some theoreticians suggest that to behave aggressively is an instinct, part and parcel of the human condition. For instance, Freud's psychoanalytic theory suggests that we all are motivated by sexual and aggressive instincts (Freud, 1920). According to ethologist Konrad Lorenz, an expert in animal behavior, animals—including humans—share a fighting instinct that stems from primitive urges to preserve territory, maintain a steady supply of food, and weed out weaker animals (Lorenz, 1966, 1974).

Similar arguments are made by evolutionary theorists and *sociobiologists*, scientists who consider the biological roots of social behavior. They argue that aggression leads to increased opportunities to mate, improving the likelihood that one's genes will be passed on to future generations. In addition, aggression may help to strengthen the species and its gene pool as a whole because the strongest survive. Ultimately, then, aggressive instincts promote the survival of one's genes to pass on to future generations (Reiss, 1984; Pellegrini, 2007).

Although instinctual explanations of aggression are logical, most developmentalists believe they are not the whole story. Not only do instinctual explanations fail to take into account the increasingly sophisticated cognitive abilities that humans develop as they get older, but they also have relatively little experimental support. Moreover, they provide little guidance in determining when and how children, as well as adults, will behave aggressively, other than noting that aggression is an inevitable part of the human condition. Consequently, developmentalists have turned to other approaches to explain aggression and violence.

Social Learning Approaches to Aggression.   The day after Duane lashed out at Eshu, Lynn, who had watched the entire scene, got into an argument with Ilya. They verbally bickered for a while, and suddenly Lynn balled her hand into a fist and tried to punch Ilya. The preschool teachers were stunned: It was rare for Lynn to get upset, and she had never displayed aggression before.

Is there a connection between the two events? Most of us would answer yes, particularly if we subscribed to the view, suggested by social learning approaches, that aggression is largely a learned behavior. Social learning approaches to aggression contend that aggression is based on observation and prior learning. To understand the causes of aggressive behavior, then, we should look at the system of rewards and punishments that exists in a child's environment.

Social learning approaches to aggression emphasize how social and environmental conditions teach individuals to be aggressive. These ideas grow out of behavioral perspectives, which suggest that aggressive behavior is learned through direct reinforcement. For instance, preschool-age children may learn that they can continue to play with the most desirable toys by aggressively refusing their classmates' requests for sharing. In the parlance of traditional learning theory, they have been reinforced for acting aggressively (by continued use of the toy), and they are more likely to behave aggressively in the future.

But social learning approaches suggest that reinforcement also comes in less direct ways. A good deal of research suggests that exposure to aggressive models leads to increased aggression, particularly if the observers are themselves angered, insulted, or frustrated. For example, Albert Bandura and his colleagues illustrated the power of models in a classic study of preschool-age children (Bandura, Ross, & Ross, 1963). One group of children watched a film of an adult playing aggressively and violently with a Bobo doll (a large, inflated plastic clown designed as a punching bag for children that always returns to an upright position after being pushed down). In comparison, children in another condition watched a film of an adult playing sedately with a set of Tinkertoys (see Figure 11.2). Later, the preschool-age children were allowed to play with a number of toys, which included both the Bobo doll and the Tinkertoys. But first, the children were led to feel frustration by being refused the opportunity to play with a favorite toy.

As predicted by social learning approaches, the preschool-age children modeled the behavior of the adult. Those who had seen the aggressive model playing with the Bobo doll were considerably more aggressive than those who had watched the calm, unaggressive model playing with the Tinkertoys.

FIGURE 11.2 **Modeling Aggression** This series of photos is from Albert Bandura's classic Bobo doll experiment, designed to illustrate the social learning of aggression. The photos clearly show how the adult model's aggressive behavior (in the first row) is imitated by children who had viewed the aggressive behavior (second and third rows.)

Later research has supported this early study, and it is clear that exposure to aggressive models increases the likelihood that aggression on the part of observers will follow. These findings have profound consequences, particularly for children who live in communities in which violence is prevalent. For instance, one survey conducted in a city public hospital found that 1 in 10 children under the age of 6 said they had witnessed a shooting or stabbing. Other research indicates that one-third of the children in some urban neighborhoods have seen a homicide and that two-thirds have seen a serious assault. Such frequent exposure to violence certainly increases the probability that observers will behave aggressively themselves (Farver et al., 1997; Evans, 2004).

Viewing Violence on TV: Does It Matter? Even the majority of preschool-age children who are not witnesses to real-life violence are typically exposed to aggression via the medium of television. Children's television programs actually contain higher levels of violence (69 percent) than other types of programs (57 percent). In an average hour, children's programs contain more than twice as many violent incidents than other types of programs (see Figure 11.3 on page 326; Wilson, 2002).

This high level of televised violence, coupled with Bandura and others' research findings on modeling violence, raises a significant question: Does viewing aggression increase the likelihood that children (and later adults) will enact actual—and ultimately deadly—aggression? It is hard to answer the question definitively. Although it is clear that laboratory observation of aggression on television leads to higher levels of aggression, evidence showing that real-world viewing of aggression is associated with subsequent aggressive behavior is correlational. (Think, for a moment, of what would be required to conduct a true experiment involving children's viewing habits. It would require that we control children's viewing of television in their homes for extended periods, exposing some to a steady diet of violent shows and others to nonviolent ones—something that most parents would not agree to.)

Despite the fact, then, that the results are primarily correlational, the overwhelming weight of research evidence is clear in suggesting that observation of televised aggression does lead to subsequent aggression. Longitudinal studies have found that children's preferences for violent television shows at age 8 are related to the seriousness of criminal convictions by age 30. Other evidence supports the notion that observation of media violence can lead to a greater

Social learning explanations of aggression suggest that playing violent video games can prompt children to act aggressively.

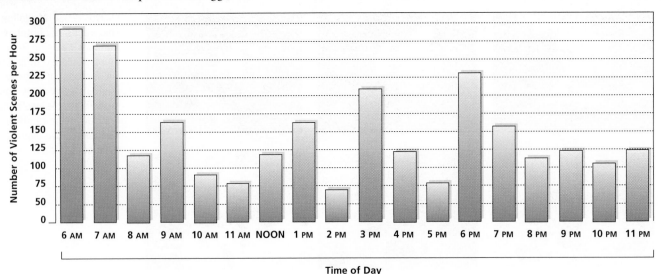

FIGURE 11.3 Televised Acts of Violence
A survey of the violence shown on the major TV networks and several cable channels in Washington, D.C., on one particular weekday found acts of violence during every time period. Do you think depictions of violence on TV should be regulated? Why or why not?
Source: Center for Media and Public Affairs, 1995.

readiness to act aggressively, to bullying, and to an insensitivity to the suffering of victims of violence (Anderson et al., 2003; Slater, Henry, & Swaim, 2003; Ostrov, Gentile, & Crick, 2006).

Television is not the only source of media violence. Many video games contain a significant amount of aggressive behavior, and children are playing such games at high rates. For example, 14 percent of children 3 years of age and younger and around 50 percent of those 4 to 6 play video games. Because research conducted with adults shows that playing violent video games is associated with behaving aggressively, children who play video games containing violence may be at higher risk for behaving aggressively (Funk, Buchman, & Jenks, 2003; Rideout, Vandewater, & Wartella, 2003; Anderson et al., 2004).

Fortunately, social learning principles that lead preschoolers to learn aggression from television and video games suggest ways to reduce the negative influence of the medium. For instance, children can be explicitly taught to view violence with a more skeptical, critical eye. Being taught that violence is not representative of the real world, that the viewing of violence can affect them negatively, and that they should refrain from imitating the behavior they have seen on television can help children interpret the violent programs differently and be less influenced by them (Persson & Musher-Eizenman, 2003; Donnerstein, 2005).

Furthermore, just as exposure to aggressive models leads to aggression, observation of *non*aggressive models can *reduce* aggression. Preschoolers don't just learn from others how to be aggressive; they can also learn how to avoid confrontation and to control their aggression, as we'll discuss later.

Cognitive Approaches to Aggression: The Thoughts Behind Violence. Two children, waiting for their turn in a game of kickball, inadvertently knock into one another. One child's reaction is to apologize; the other's is to shove, saying angrily, "Cut it out."

Despite the fact that each child bears the same responsibility for the minor event, very different reactions result. The first child interprets the event as an accident, while the second sees it as a provocation and reacts with aggression.

The cognitive approach to aggression suggests that the key to understanding moral development is to examine preschoolers' interpretations of others' behavior and of the environmental context in which a behavior occurs. According to developmental psychologist Kenneth Dodge and his colleagues, some children are more prone than others to assume that actions are aggressively motivated. They are unable to pay attention to the appropriate cues in a situation and unable to interpret the behaviors in a given situation accurately. Instead, they assume—often erroneously—that what is happening is related to others' hostility. Subsequently, in deciding how to respond, they base their behavior on their inaccurate interpretation of behavior. In sum, they may behave aggressively in response to a situation that never in fact existed (Dodge & Coie, 1987; Dodge & Crick, 1990; Petit & Dodge, 2003).

For example, consider Jake, who is drawing at a table with Gary. Jake reaches over and takes a red crayon that Gary had just decided he was going to use next. Gary is instantly certain that Jake "knew" that he was going to use the red crayon and that Jake is taking it just to be mean. With this interpretation in mind, Gary hits Jake for "stealing" his crayon. Although the cognitive approach to aggression provides a description of the process that leads some children to behave aggressively, it is less successful in explaining how certain children come to be inaccurate perceivers of situations in the first place. Furthermore, it fails to explain why such inaccurate perceivers so readily respond with aggression, and why they assume that aggression is an appropriate and even desirable response.

On the other hand, cognitive approaches to aggression are useful in pointing out a means to reduce aggression: By teaching preschool-age children to be more accurate interpreters of a situation, we can induce them to be less prone to view others' behavior as motivated by hostility, and consequently less likely to respond with aggression themselves.

DEVELOPMENTAL DIVERSITY
Is Aggression as American as Apple Pie?

Anyone who reads a daily newspaper is exposed to a constant stream of incidents of murder, rape, mugging, and other violence, often committed by teenagers and sometimes even by younger children. Does this perception of violence match the reality, and is aggression "as American as apple pie," as one expert on aggression put it (Berkowitz, 1993)? Unfortunately, in many ways, the perception matches reality. For example, more men between the ages of 15 and 24 are murdered in the United States than in any other developed country in the world (see Figure 11.4).

On the other hand, aggression is hardly unique to the United States. In some cultures, aggression by children is substantial, while in others it is less pronounced. According to the findings of one classic study, childrearing practices help explain the substantial cross-cultural differences. In the study, researchers examined aggression in Kenya, India, Mexico, Okinawa, the Philippines, and the United States (Lambert, 1971).

The study first examined the reactions of mothers (who were the primary caregivers in each of the cultures) to their own children's aggression. The results showed that Mexican parents were the strictest, whereas U.S. mothers showed the greatest tolerance for aggressive behavior

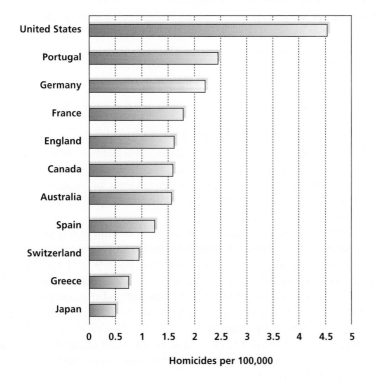

Homicides per 100,000

FIGURE 11.4 Comparative Homicide Rates

This chart, which illustrates the number of killings per 100,000 men between the ages of 15 and 24, shows that the homicide rate is much higher in the United States than in other industrialized nations.
Source: United Nations Surveys on Crime Trends and the Operations of Criminal Justice Systems (CTS), 2000.

(continued)

in their children. In contrast, for aggression against an adult, children living in Kenya, the Philippines, and Mexico received the greatest punishment, whereas children in India received the least punishment. Children living in the United States and Okinawa received a moderate degree of punishment.

As expected, mothers' reactions to aggression were related to their children's overall aggression levels, although the findings were complex. One important finding was that children with the highest activity levels learned the social values of their culture regarding aggression most effectively. Hence, active children in Mexico were less aggressive because their mothers reacted strongly to their aggression. In contrast, the more active children in the United States were more aggressive, a lesson they learned from their mother's lack of strong reactions to their aggression. In contrast, relatively inactive children, who had fewer opportunities to acquire the social values of their society, showed differing patterns of aggression from those of their more active counterparts.

Of course, the results don't show us why, in the first place, mothers in some cultures reacted more to their children's aggression than mothers in other cultures. Still, it is clear that cultures produce a particular set of childrearing practices that is associated with different patterns of aggression in their children.

Although there are substantial cultural differences in level of aggression, in some way patterns of aggression are similar across cultures. The most significant similarity is a gender difference: In every known culture, boys are more aggressive than girls, a pattern that is mirrored in adult behavior (Knight, Fabes, & Higgins, 1996; LaFreniere et al., 2002; Verrity, 2007).

Why should boys be more aggressive than girls? Although it is tempting to look to biological or evolutionary explanations and suggest that boys are genetically preprogrammed to be aggressive, there are other possibilities. As we'll discuss in Chapter 12, parents and society in general hold different expectations about aggression for boys and girls, and in many cultures boys are explicitly encouraged to behave aggressively. In contrast, aggression in girls is typically discouraged (Bettencourt & Miller, 1996; Zahn-Waxler & Polanichka, 2004; Letendre, 2007).

It is also possible that boys may behave aggressively in an effort to distinguish themselves from their female caregivers, given that males in almost all societies are reared primarily by women. Behaving aggressively may make boys believe that they are adopting a behavior that is similar to that of adults (Whiting, 1965).

Although such explanations are plausible, they remain theories, and there is no definitive explanation for the higher levels of male aggression found in every culture. In any case, we should not assume that the general pervasiveness of aggressive behavior is a necessary part of children's behavior.

School Violence. Columbine. . . Jonesboro. . . West Paducah. You may remember the names of these places where school violence occurred, and you may conclude—like many Americans—that schools are particularly dangerous places.

The reality of school violence is different, however. Despite the public perception that school violence is on the upswing, there has in fact been an overall decline in violence. Even in the year of the Columbine shooting, the number of deaths in school-related incidents dropped 40 percent from the previous year. School is actually one of the safest places for adolescents (Spencer, 2001; Jimerson et al., 2006; Newsome & Kelly, 2006).

The likelihood of injury from a school shooting is tiny (a child has about a one in a million chance of being killed in school). Nonetheless, parents and their children still worry about safety issues. Is it possible to identify beforehand students who pose a threat? It turns out that there are students who are prone to violence; for instance, the FBI has identified several characteristics of individuals who are at risk for carrying out violence in schools. They include a low tolerance for frustration, poor coping skills, a lack of resiliency, failed love relationships, resentment over perceived injustices, depression, self-centeredness, and alienation (O'Toole, 2000; Chrisholm & Ward, 2005; Eisenbraun, 2007).

In spite of the public perception that school violence is on the rise, the reality is that there has been an overall decline in violence.

Furthermore, school shootings are rarely spontaneous. Attackers typically make plans, plotting out beforehand whom they wish to harm. Not only do they usually tell someone about their plans, they often are encouraged by others. In almost half the cases of school shootings, attackers were influenced or encouraged to act by friends or fellow students. They also have easy access to guns. In around two-thirds of school shootings, the attackers used guns from their own home or that of a relative (U.S. Secret Service, 2002).

According to psychologist Elliot Aronson, students who carry out violence in schools frequently were the targets of bullying or have been rejected in some way. He notes that there are tremendous status differences in schools, and students who have been taunted and humiliated by students of higher status (or by their parents or other adults) may lash out in frustration (Aronson, 2000, 2004).

To respond to the potential of violence, many schools have instituted programs designed to prevent aggression among students. One of the most prominent programs is *Second Step,* which is designed to teach children to recognize and understand their feelings, experience empathy for others, make effective choices, and keep anger from escalating into violence. Carefully conducted studies have supported the program, finding improvements in students' social skills and a reduction in aggressive acts (Van Schoiack-Edstrom, Frey, & Beland, 2002; McMahon & Washburn, 2003).

Other school programs that involve cooperative learning, peer mediation, and communication skills training appear to be helpful. In addition, teaching students, parents, and educators to take threats seriously is important; many students who become violent threaten to commit violence before they actually engage in violent acts. Ultimately, schools need to be places where students feel comfortable discussing their feelings and problems, rather than sources of alienation and rejection (Aronson, 2000; Spencer, 2001; Aronson, 2004; Eisenbraun, 2007).

Parents who abuse their own spouses and children were often victims of abuse themselves as children, reflecting a cycle of violence.

Family Violence: The Hidden Epidemic

After finding an unidentified earring, the wife accused her husband of being unfaithful. His reaction was to throw her against the wall of their apartment, and then to toss her clothes out the window. In another incident, the husband became angry. Screaming at his wife, he threw her against a wall, and then picked her up and literally threw her out of the house. Another time, the wife called 911, begging for the police to protect her. When the police came, the woman, with a black eye, a cut lip, and swollen cheeks, hysterically screamed, "He's going to kill me."

If nothing else was clear about what was called the murder trial of the century, there is ample evidence that the spousal abuse described in these scenarios was an ingredient in the lives of O.J. Simpson and Nicole Brown Simpson. The allegations of abuse that came out during the trial were both chilling and yet all too familiar.

The Prevalence of Spousal Abuse. Domestic violence is one of the ugly truths about marriage in the United States, occurring at epidemic levels. Some form of violence happens in one-fourth of all marriages, and more than half the women who were murdered in one recent 10-year period were murdered by a partner. Between 21 and 34 percent of women will be slapped, kicked, beaten, choked, or threatened or attacked with a weapon at least once by an intimate partner. Close to 15 percent of all marriages in the United States are characterized by continuing, severe violence. Furthermore, domestic violence is a worldwide problem. Estimates suggest that one in three women throughout the globe experience some form of violent victimization during their lives (Browne, 1993; Walker, 1999; Garcia-Moreno et al., 2005).

In the United States, no segment of society is immune from spousal abuse. Violence occurs across social strata, races, ethnic groups, and religions. Both gay and straight partnerships can be abusive. It also occurs across genders: Although in the vast majority of cases of abuse a husband batters a wife, in about 8 percent of the cases wives physically abuse their husbands (Emery & Laumann-Billings, 1998; de Anda & Becerra, 2000; Harway, 2000; Cameron, 2003; Dixon & Browne, 2003).

Certain factors increase the likelihood of abuse. For instance, spousal abuse is more likely to occur in large families in which there is continuing economic concern and a high level of verbal aggression than in families in which such factors are not present. Those husbands and wives who grew up in families where violence was present are more likely to be violent themselves (Straus & Yodanis, 1996; Ehrensaft, Cohen, & Brown, 2003; Lackey, 2003).

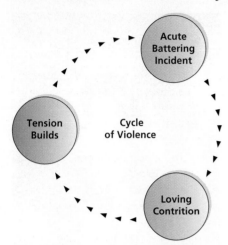

FIGURE 11.5 The Stages of Violence
Source: Adapted from Walker, 1979, 1984; Gondolf, 1985.

Stages of Marital Aggression. Marital aggression by a husband typically occurs in three stages (Walker, 1989; see Figure 11.5). The first is the **tension-building** stage in which a batterer becomes upset and shows dissatisfaction initially through verbal abuse. He may also show some preliminary physical aggression in the form of shoving or grabbing. The wife may desperately try to avoid the impending violence, attempting to calm her spouse or withdraw from the situation. Such behavior may serve only to enrage the husband, who senses his wife's vulnerability, and her efforts to escape may lead to an escalation of his anger.

The next stage consists of an **acute battering incident**, when the physical abuse actually occurs. It may last from several minutes to hours. Wives may be shoved against walls, choked, slapped, punched, kicked, and stepped on. Their arms may be twisted or broken, they may be shaken severely, thrown down a flight of stairs, or burned with cigarettes or scalding liquids. About a quarter of wives are forced to engage in sexual activities during this period, which takes the form of aggressive sexual acts and rape.

Finally, in some—but not all—cases, the episode moves into the **loving contrition stage**. At this point, the husband feels remorse and apologizes for his actions. He may minister to his wife, providing first aid and sympathy, and assuring her that he will never act violently again. Because wives may feel that in some way they were partly at fault in triggering the aggression, they may be motivated to accept the apology and forgive their husbands. They want to believe that the aggression will never occur again.

The loving contrition stage helps explain why many wives remain with abusive husbands and are the continuing victims of abuse. Wishing desperately to keep their marriages intact, and believing that they have no good alternatives, some wives remain out of a vague sense that they are responsible for the abuse. Others remain out of fear: They are afraid their husbands may come after them if they leave.

The Cycle of Violence. Still other wives stay with batterers because they, like their husbands, have learned a seemingly unforgettable lesson from childhood: that violence is an acceptable means of settling disputes.

Individuals who abuse their spouses and children were often as children the victims of abuse themselves. According to the **cycle of violence hypothesis**, abuse and neglect of children lead them to be predisposed to abusiveness as adults. In line with social learning theory, the cycle of violence hypothesis suggests that family aggression is perpetuated from one generation to another as family members follow the lead of the previous generation. It is a fact that individuals who abuse their wives often have been raised in households in which they have witnessed spousal abuse, just as parents who abuse their children frequently have been the victims of abuse themselves as children (McCloskey & Bailey, 2000; Serbin & Karp, 2004; Renner & Slack, 2006).

Growing up in a home where abuse occurs does not invariably lead to abusiveness as an adult. Only about one-third of people who were abused or neglected as children abuse their own children as adults, and two-thirds of abusers were not themselves abused as children. The cycle of violence, then, does not tell the full story of abuse (Jacobson & Gottman, 1998; Hauser, Allen, & Golden, 2006).

Whatever the causes of abuse, there are ways to deal with it, as we consider next.

The Cultural Roots of Domestic Violence. Although the tendency often is to see marital violence and aggression as a particularly North American phenomenon, in fact other cultures have traditions in which violence is regarded as acceptable (Rao, 1997; Abrahams et al., 2006; Wilson-Williams et al., 2008). For instance, wife battering is particularly prevalent in cultures in which women are viewed as inferior to men and treated as property.

In Western societies too, wife beating was acceptable at one time. According to English common law, which formed the foundation of the legal system in the United States, husbands were allowed to beat their wives. In the 1800s this law was modified to permit only certain kinds of beating. Specifically, a husband could not beat his wife with a stick or rod that was thicker than his thumb—the origin of the phrase "rule of thumb." It was not until the late nineteenth century that this law was removed from the books in the United States (Davidson, 1977).

Some experts on abuse suggest that the traditional power structure under which women and men function is a root cause of abuse. They argue that the more a society differentiates between men and women in terms of status, the more likely it is that abuse will occur (Dutton, 1994; Vandello & Cohen, 2003; Vandello et al., 2009).

tension building the first stage of marital aggression in which a batterer becomes upset and shows dissatisfaction initially through verbal abuse.

acute battering incident the second stage of marital aggression in which physical abuse actually occurs.

loving contrition stage the third stage of marital aggression, which occurs in some but not all cases, in which the batterer feels remorse and apologizes for his actions.

cycle of violence hypothesis the theory that the abuse and neglect that children suffer predispose them as adults to abuse and neglect their own children.

BECOMING AN INFORMED CONSUMER OF DEVELOPMENT
Dealing with Spousal Abuse

Despite the fact that spousal abuse occurs in one-quarter of all marriages, efforts to deal with victims of abuse are underfunded and inadequate to meet current needs. Some psychologists argue that the same factors that led society to underestimate the magnitude of the problem for many years now hinder the development of effective interventions. Still, there are several measures available to help the victims of spousal abuse (Dutton, 1992; Browne, 1993; Koss et al., 1993; Hamberger & Holtzworth-Munroe, 2007).

- **Teach both wives and husbands a basic premise:** Physical violence is *never,* under *any* circumstances, an acceptable means of resolving disagreements.

- **Call the police.** It is against the law to assault another person, including a spouse. Although it may be difficult to involve law enforcement officers, this is a realistic way of dealing with domestic abuse. Judges can also issue restraining orders requiring abusive husbands to stay away from their wives.

- **Understand that the remorse shown by a spouse, no matter how heartfelt, may have no bearing on the possibility of future violence.** Even if a husband shows loving regret after a battering session and vows that he will never be violent again, such a promise is no guarantee against future abuse.

- **If you are the victim of abuse, seek a safe haven.** Many communities have shelters for the victims of domestic violence that can house women and their children. Because addresses of shelters are kept confidential, an abusive spouse will not be able to find you. Telephone numbers are listed in the yellow or blue pages of phone books, and local police should also have the numbers.

- **If you feel in danger from an abusive partner, seek a restraining order** from a judge in court. Under a restraining order a spouse is forbidden to come near you, under penalty of law.

- **Call the National Domestic Violence Hotline at 1-800-799-7233** for immediate advice.

Child Abuse. The figures are gloomy and disheartening: At least five children are killed by their parents or caretakers every day, and 140,000 others are physically injured every year. Around 3 million children are abused or neglected in the United States each year.

Child abuse can occur in any household, regardless of economic well-being or the social status of the parents. It is most frequent in families living in stressful environments. Poverty, single-parenthood, and higher-than-average levels of marital conflict help create such environments. Stepfathers are more likely to commit abuse against stepchildren than genetic fathers are against their own offspring. Child abuse is also more likely when there is a history of violence between spouses (Kitzmann, Gaylord, & Holt, 2003; Litrownik, Newton, & Hunter, 2003; Osofsky, 2003; Evans, 2004). (Table 11.4 on page 332 lists some of the warning signs of abuse.)

Abused children are more likely to be fussy, resistant to control, and not readily adaptable to new situations. They have more headaches and stomachaches, experience more bedwetting, are generally more anxious, and may show developmental delays. Children in certain age groups are also more likely to be the targets of abuse: Three- and 4-year-olds and 15- to 17-year-olds are somewhat more likely to be abused by their parents than children of other ages (Straus & Gelles, 1990; Ammerman & Patz, 1996; Haugaard, 2000).

As you consider this information about the characteristics of abused children, keep in mind that labeling children as being at higher risk for receiving abuse does not make them responsible for their abuse; the family members who carry out the abuse are at fault. Statistical findings simply suggest that children with such characteristics are more at risk of being the recipients of family violence.

Reasons for Physical Abuse. Why does physical abuse occur? Most parents certainly do not intend to hurt their children. In fact, most parents who abuse their children later express bewilderment and regret about their own behavior.

One reason for child abuse is the vague demarcation between permissible and impermissible forms of physical violence. Societal folklore in the United States says that spanking is not merely acceptable, but often necessary and desirable. Almost half of mothers with children less than 4 years of age have spanked their child in the previous week, and close to 20 percent of mothers believe it is appropriate to spank a child less than 1 year of age. In some other cultures, physical discipline is even more common (Straus, Gelles, & Steinmetz, 2003; Lansford et al., 2005; Deb & Adak, 2006; Shor, 2006).

FROM A
HEALTH CARE PROVIDER'S
PERSPECTIVE
What can be done to end the cycle of violence, in which people who were abused as children grow up to be abusers of others?

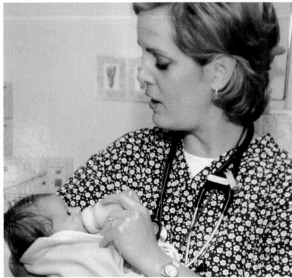

This nine-day-old infant, named Baby Vinnie, was found after being abandoned on the steps behind a church. He later was adopted by a foster family.

TABLE 11.4 What Are the Warning Signs of Child Abuse?

Because child abuse is typically a secret crime, identifying the victims of abuse is particularly difficult. Still, there are several signs in a child that indicate that he or she is the victim of violence (Robbins, 1990):

- Visible, serious injuries that have no reasonable explanation
- Bite or choke marks
- Burns from cigarettes or immersion in hot water
- Feelings of pain for no apparent reason
- Fear of adults or care providers
- Inappropriate attire in warm weather (long sleeves, long pants, high-necked garments)—possibly to conceal injuries to the neck, arms, and legs
- Extreme behavior—highly aggressive, extremely passive, extremely withdrawn
- Fear of physical contact

If you suspect a child is a victim of aggression, it is your responsibility to act. Call your local police or the department of social services in your city or state, or call *Childhelp U.S.A.* at 1-800-422-4453. Talk to a teacher or a member of the clergy. Remember, by acting decisively you can literally save someone's life.

Unfortunately, the line between "spanking" and "beating" is not clear, and spankings begun in anger can escalate into abuse. In fact, there is increasing scientific evidence that spanking should be avoided entirely. Although physical punishment may produce immediate compliance—children typically stop the behavior spanking is meant to end—there are a number of serious long-term side effects. For example, spanking is associated with lower quality parent–child relationships, poorer mental health for both child and parent, higher levels of delinquency, and more antisocial behavior. Spanking also teaches children that violence is an acceptable solution to problems by serving as a model of violent, aggressive behavior. Consequently, according to the American Academy of Pediatrics, the use of physical punishment of any sort is *not* recommended (American Academy of Pediatrics, 1998; Gershoff, 2002; Kazdin & Benjet, 2003; Afifi et al., 2006).

Another factor that leads to high rates of abuse is the privacy in which child care is conducted in Western societies. In many other cultures childrearing is seen as the joint responsibility of several people and even society as a whole. In most Western cultures—and particularly the United States—children are raised in private, isolated households. Because child care is seen as the sole responsibility of the parent, other people are typically not available to help out when a parent's patience is tested (Chaffin, 2006; Elliott & Urquiza, 2006).

Sometimes abuse is the result of an adult's unrealistically high expectations regarding children's abilities to be quiet and compliant at a particular age. Children's failure to meet these unrealistic expectations may provoke abuse (Peterson, 1994).

Elder Abuse: Relationships Gone Wrong. It would be easy to assume that abuse of elderly people by family members is even more rare than child abuse. The truth of the matter, however, is that such cases are considerably more common than we would like to believe. According to some estimates, **elder abuse**, the physical or psychological mistreatment or neglect of elderly individuals, may affect as many as 2 million people above the age of 60 each year. Even these estimates may be too low, since people who are abused are often too embarrassed or humiliated to report their plight. And as the number of elderly people increases, experts believe that the number of cases of elder abuse will also rise (Brubaker, 1991; Jayawardena & Liao, 2006).

Elder abuse is most frequently directed at family members and particularly at elderly parents. Those most at risk are likely to be less healthy and more isolated than the average person in late adulthood, and they are more likely to be living in a caregiver's home. Although there is no single cause for elder abuse, it often is the result of a combination of economic, psychological, and social pressures on caregivers who must provide high levels of care 24 hours a day. Thus, people with Alzheimer's disease or other sorts of dementia are particularly likely to be targets of abuse (Dyer et al., 2000; Arai, 2006; Jayawardena & Liao, 2006; Nahmiash, 2006; Tauriac & Scruggs, 2006; Baker, 2007).

elder abuse the physical or psychological mistreatment or neglect of elderly individuals.

The best approach to dealing with elder abuse is to prevent it from occurring in the first place. Family members caring for an older adult should take occasional breaks. Social support agencies can be contacted; they can provide both advice and concrete support. For instance, the National Family Caregivers Association (800-896-3650) maintains a caregivers' network and publishes a newsletter. Anyone suspecting that an elderly person is being abused should contact local authorities, such as their state's Adult Protective Services or Elder Protective Services.

REVIEW

▶ Aggression typically declines in frequency and duration as children become more able to regulate their emotions and to use language to negotiate disputes.

▶ Ethologists and sociobiologists regard aggression as an innate human characteristic, while proponents of social learning and cognitive approaches focus on learned aspects of aggression.

▶ School violence receives a lot of attention from the media, but a school is in fact a safer environment for adolescents than any other.

▶ Marital violence tends to pass through three stages: tension building, an acute battering incident, and loving contrition.

▶ The incidence of family violence is highest in families of lower socioeconomic status. A "cycle of violence" affords a partial explanation. Cultural norms may also play a role.

▶ Elder abuse typically involves a socially isolated elderly parent in poor health and a caregiver who feels burdened by the parent.

APPLY

▶ What sort of research study would you conduct to confirm or disprove the cycle of violence hypothesis? Would such a study clearly prove either that there is or isn't a cycle of violence?

▶ How might a preschool teacher or parent help children notice the violence in the programs they watch and protect them from its effects?

Epilogue

In this chapter we considered both moral development and aggression, and explored the development of religious thought and the purpose of spiritual beliefs. First, we looked at a variety of theories about how children develop a sense of right and wrong. We discussed how reasoning about moral dilemmas grows more sophisticated as children move into adolescence. We also explored a range of parenting styles and discussed their implications for shaping children's behavior, both present and future. Then, we considered religion and spirituality, and asked: Why is religion important to many people? We considered how religion helps people to find meaning in their lives and how it helps them cope with disasters. We also discussed the development of religious thought, using both Piaget's approach to cognitive development and James Fowler's stages of faith development. We examined the relationship between religious belief and life satisfaction in late adulthood, and we discussed the special significance religion holds for older adults, especially African Americans. In the final part of the chapter, we examined the sources of aggression and violence, and considered the question: Is nature or nurture more responsible for aggression? We explored ways of decreasing aggression in children and increasing their moral behaviors. We also considered the factors that predict a lifelong problem with aggression. In conclusion, we examined the epidemic of family violence involving abuse of children, spouses, and elders.

Before moving on to the next chapter, take a moment to reread the Prologue to this chapter about Jesse's dilemma over the destruction of the bus, and answer the following questions:

1. Is Kohlberg's/Piaget's moral reasoning approach helpful in interpreting Jesse's actions in this instance? Why or why not?

2. Does the fact that the other boys throw rocks at the bus prove they think it's morally okay to do so? Why might there be a disconnect between their beliefs and their actions?

3. What evidence, if any, do you see in this story that Jesse has developed a set of core beliefs and values as part of his identity? What might some of those beliefs and values be?

4. Do you think Jesse's actions would have been different if a Wolverines' team member had injured one of Jesse's friends? Why or why not?

Looking Back

How do children develop a moral sense?

1. Piaget believed that preschool-age children are in the heteronomous morality stage of moral development, characterized by a belief in external, unchangeable rules of conduct and sure, immediate punishment for all misdeeds.

2. In contrast, social learning approaches to morality emphasize interactions between environment and behavior in moral development in which models of behavior play an important role in development.

3. Some developmentalists believe that moral behavior is rooted in a child's development of empathy. Other emotions, including the negative emotions of anger and shame, may also promote moral behavior.

How does children's sense of right and wrong change as children age?

4. According to Kohlberg, people pass from preconventional morality (motivated by rewards and punishments), through conventional morality (motivated by social reference), to postconventional morality (motivated by a sense of universal moral principles). Gilligan has sketched out an alternative progression for girls, from an orientation toward individual survival, through goodness as self-sacrifice, to the morality of nonviolence.

As adolescents become more sophisticated morally, how does their behavior change?

5. Moral reasoning is not the same as moral behavior, as researchers with a social learning orientation have noted. Adolescents who understand moral issues do not invariably behave in a moral manner.

6. Adolescents understand prosocial behavior and can evaluate the motivations behind it, which may be altruistic or self-serving.

7. There are gender and cultural differences in empathy and prosocial behavior.

8. Adolescents have a sophisticated understanding of the motivations behind lying and cheating, but their sophistication does not produce notable gains in honesty.

What kinds of disciplinary styles do parents employ, and what effects do they have?

9. Disciplinary styles differ both individually and culturally. In the United States and other Western societies, parents' styles tend to be mostly authoritarian, permissive, uninvolved, and authoritative, the last regarded as the most effective.

10. Children of authoritarian and permissive parents may develop dependency, hostility, and low self-control, whereas children of uninvolved parents may feel unloved and emotionally detached. Children of authoritative parents tend to be more independent, friendly, self-assertive, and cooperative.

What purposes do spirituality and religion serve for many adults?

11. Religion helps people to grapple with who they are and what their purpose in life may be—one of the major challenges facing every individual.

12. Many people turn to their religion or spiritual beliefs to provide comfort at the death of a loved one. They may look to their religion to make sense of disasters and other seemingly random events.

13. Belonging to a religious group serves to give people a sense that they are part of a formal community. Religious groups often provide direct social support to their members in times of need.

How does religious thought develop across the life span?

14. Using Piaget's theory of cognitive development, religious thinking can be seen to pass through three stages during childhood and adolescence: preoperational intuitive religious thought, in which children's religious thinking is unsystematic and the meanings of religious stories are often misinterpreted; concrete operational religious thought, during which school-age children focus more on the concrete details of religious stories rather than their abstract meanings; and formal operational religious thought, in which adolescents are able to understand the abstract meanings of stories and draw inferences from them.

15. According to James Fowler, religious understanding and thought proceed in a series of stages throughout the life span, though not everyone attains the higher stages. In Fowler's view, children hold literal views of God and biblical figures. In adolescence, spiritual views become more abstract. Most adolescents develop a core set of beliefs and values, but their thinking lacks depth and is usually not systematic. In early and middle adulthood, people reflect on their beliefs and values, and seek to form a personal belief system that makes sense to them. Fowler calls this the individuative-reflective stage of faith. In the conjunctive stage of faith development, older adults come to see humanity as a whole and develop a broad inclusive view of religion. They may move beyond formal religion as they seek to promote a common good for all peoples.

How does aggression develop in preschool-age children?

16. Aggression, which involves intentional harm to another person, begins to emerge in the preschool years. As children age and improve their language skills, acts of aggression typically decline in frequency and duration.

17. Some ethologists, such as Konrad Lorenz, believe that aggression is simply a biological fact of human life, a belief held also by many sociobiologists, who focus on competition within species to pass genes on to the next generation.

18. Social learning theorists focus on the role of the environment, including the influence of models and social reinforcement as factors influencing aggressive behavior.

19. The cognitive approach to aggression emphasizes the role of interpretations of the behaviors of others in determining aggressive or nonaggressive responses.

What are the causes and characteristics of family violence in the United States?

20. Family violence in the United States has reached epidemic proportions, with some form of violence occurring in a quarter of all marriages. The likelihood of violence is highest in families that are subject to economic or emotional stresses. In addition, people who were abused as children have a higher likelihood of becoming abusers as adults—a phenomenon termed the cycle of violence.

21. Marital aggression typically proceeds through three stages: a tension-building stage, an acute battering incident, and a loving contrition stage. Despite contrition, abusers tend to remain abusers unless they get effective help.

PEARSON
mydevelopmentlab™

"What decisions would you make while raising a child? What would the consequences of those decisions be?" Find out by accessing **MyVirtualChild** at www.mydevelopmentlab.com and raising your own virtual child from birth to age 18.

12 Gender and Sexuality

Prologue

Late Love

Photos of their late spouses gaze over the bed of Geraldine Mooers, 76, and Dick Thomas, 73. "They helped us become who we are. We're honoring them, just as we honor each other," Mooers said. . . .

They met at a singles picnic five years ago. He was a staunch Republican and she a liberal Democrat. He was an overweight retired cook, she a retired dietitian who loved to exercise. They belonged to different churches. Both were widowed and had children and grandchildren.

"What an unlikely pair," Thomas said. "But I'll tell you, I love this woman. We can talk, we can disagree and we don't go to bed mad, ever."

Gradually, he moved into her condo but kept his, now rented out as an investment. They were married in church, but not with a wedding license. "Her accountant and my lawyer advised us not to complicate the inheritance issues, and we agreed," Thomas said. "In our eyes, we're married. . . ."

In recent years Thomas has had a pacemaker for his heart, stomach-stapling surgery to lose weight and last year a penile implant "because I wanted to have intercourse with Gerry. It was worth it."

As they age, "with any luck, we'll have a lot of good years to travel, do stuff with others, take classes and just be together," Mooers said. "We've each lost a spouse, and we know one of us will go through that again. All we have is now. And for now we're the best of friends and the best of lovers."

(Wolfe, 2007, p. 1E)

Love and sexuality can occur throughout the life span.

The warmth and affection between Geraldine and Dick are unmistakable. Their mutual love and admiration reach the heights of human interconnectedness. The relationship they share now, however, began in early childhood as they developed a sense of their femaleness or maleness and what that means in our society. It continued as they reached puberty and began to think about and experience their sexuality. It matured still further in their first marriages where, as Geraldine says, their spouses "helped us become who we are."

In this chapter, we focus on gender, sexuality, and relationships. We begin by looking at gender, the sense of being male or female, and how children are both treated differently and behave differently on the basis of whether they are boys or girls. We also consider the various approaches that seek to explain gender differences.

We then turn to sexuality and its behavioral and psychological components. We consider how sexual maturation is tied up with body image, and we note that the timing of puberty has significant consequences for adolescents' psychological well-being. We also look at the nature of sexual relationships and sexual orientation, as well as considering the consequences of teen pregnancy. Then we explore the nature of sexuality in middle and late adulthood.

Finally, we consider the development and course of intimate relationships. We look at the role dating plays in adolescents' lives and the differences between liking and loving. We examine the different types of love and discuss how people choose partners. Then we consider the choice of whether to marry and the factors that influence the course and success of marriage throughout adulthood. We also look at some of the challenges of marriage such as divorce and caring for an ill or dying spouse in late adulthood.

After reading this chapter, you will be able to answer the following questions:

▶ What differences are there between boys and girls in terms of behavior and treatment, and how does a sense of gender develop?

▶ How does sexuality develop in the adolescent years?

▶ Why are there different sexual orientations, and what determines one's orientation?

▶ What are the functions and characteristics of dating during adolescence?

▶ How do young adults form loving relationships, and how does love change over time?

▶ How do people choose spouses, and what makes relationships work and cease working?

▶ What are typical patterns of marriage and divorce in middle adulthood?

▶ How do marriages in late adulthood fare?

MODULE 12.1

Gender: Why Do Boys Wear Blue and Girls Wear Pink?

"It's a boy." "It's a girl."

One of these two statements, or some variant, is probably the first announcement made after the birth of a child. From the moment of birth, girls and boys are treated differently. Their parents send out different kinds of birth announcements. They are dressed in different clothes and wrapped in different-colored blankets. They are given different toys (Bridges, 1993; Coltrane & Adams, 1997; Serbin, Poulin-Dubois, & Colburne, 2001; Basow, 2006).

Parents play with boy and girl babies differently: From birth on, fathers tend to interact more with sons than daughters, while mothers interact more with daughters. Because mothers and fathers play in different ways (with fathers typically engaging in more physical, rough-and-tumble activities and mothers in traditional games such as peek-a-boo), male and female infants are clearly exposed to different styles of activity and interaction from their parents (Parke, 1996; Laflamme, Pomerleau, & Malcuit, 2002; Clearfield & Nelson, 2006).

Parents of girls who play with toys related to activities associated with boys are apt to be less concerned than parents of boys who play with toys associated with girls.

The behavior exhibited by girls and boys is interpreted in very different ways by adults. For instance, when researchers showed adults a video of an infant whose name was given as either "John" or "Mary," adults perceived "John" as adventurous and inquisitive, while "Mary" was fearful and anxious, although it was the same baby performing a single set of behaviors (Condry & Condry, 1976). Clearly, adults view the behavior of children through the lens of gender. **Gender** refers to our sense of being male or female. The term *gender* is often used to mean the same thing as *sex*, but they are not actually the same. **Sex** typically refers to sexual anatomy and sexual behavior, while gender refers to the social perceptions of maleness or femaleness. All cultures prescribe *gender roles* for males and females, but these roles differ greatly from one culture to another.

Gender Differences

There is a considerable amount of disagreement over both the extent and causes of gender differences, even though most agree that boys and girls do experience at least partially different worlds based on gender. Some gender differences are fairly clear from the time of birth. For example, male infants tend to be more active and fussier than female infants. Boys' sleep tends to be more disturbed than that of girls. Boys grimace more, although no gender difference exists in the overall amount of crying. There is also some evidence that male newborns are more irritable than female newborns, although the findings are inconsistent (Eaton & Enns, 1986; Boatella-Costa et al., 2007; Bornstein et al., 2008).

gender the sense of being male or female.

sex typically refers to sexual anatomy and sexual behavior.

Differences between male and female infants, however, are generally minor. In most ways infants seem so similar that usually adults cannot discern whether a baby is a boy or girl, as the "John" and "Mary" video research shows. Furthermore, it is important to keep in mind that there are much larger differences among individual boys and among individual girls than there are, on average, between boys and girls (Crawford & Unger, 2004).

Gender Roles.   Gender differences emerge more clearly as children age—and become increasingly influenced by the gender roles that society sets out for them. For instance, by the age of 1 year, infants are able to distinguish between males and females. Girls at this age prefer to play with dolls or stuffed animals, while boys seek out blocks and trucks. Often, of course, these are the only options available to them, due to the choices their parents and other adults have made in the toys they provide (Caldera & Sciaraffa, 1998; Serbin et al., 2001; Cherney, Kelly-Vance, & Glover, 2003).

Children's preferences for certain kinds of toys are reinforced by their parents. In general, however, parents of boys are more apt to be concerned about their child's choices than are parents of girls. Boys receive more reinforcement for playing with toys that society deems appropriate for boys, and this reinforcement increases with age. On the other hand, a girl playing with a truck is viewed with considerably less concern than a boy playing with a doll might be. Girls who play with toys seen by society as "masculine" are less discouraged for their behavior than boys who play with toys seen as "feminine" (Leaper, 2002; Martin, Ruble, & Szkrybalo, 2002; Schmalz & Kerstetter, 2006; Hill & Flom, 2007).

By the time they reach the age of 2, boys behave more independently and less compliantly than girls. Much of this behavior can be traced to parental reactions to earlier behavior. For instance, when a child takes his or her first steps, parents tend to react differently, depending on the child's gender: Boys are encouraged more to go off and explore the world, while girls are hugged and kept close. It is hardly surprising, then, that by the age of 2, girls tend to show less independence and greater compliance (Kuczynski & Kochanska, 1990; Poulin-Dubois, Serbin, & Eichstedt, 2002).

Societal encouragement and reinforcement do not, however, completely explain differences in behavior between boys and girls. For example, one study examined girls who were exposed before birth to abnormally high levels of *androgen*, a male hormone, because their mothers unwittingly took a drug containing the hormone while pregnant. Later, these girls were more likely to play with toys stereotypically preferred by boys (such as cars) and less likely to play with toys stereotypically associated with girls (such as dolls). Although there are many alternative explanations for these results—you can probably think of several yourself—one possibility is that exposure to male hormones affected the brain development of the girls, leading them to favor toys that involve certain kinds of preferred skills (Levine et al., 1999; Mealey, 2000; Servin et al., 2003).

In sum, differences in behavior between boys and girls begin in infancy and continue throughout our lives. Although gender differences have complex causes, representing some combination of innate, biologically related factors and environmental factors, they play a profound role in the social and emotional development of infants.

During the preschool period, differences in play according to gender become more pronounced. In addition, boys tend to play with boys, and girls with girls.

Gender Identity: Developing Femaleness and Maleness

Boys' awards: Very Best Thinker, Most Eager Learner, Most Imaginative, Most Enthusiastic, Most Scientific, Best Friend, Mr. Personality, Hardest Worker, Best Sense of Humor.

Girls' awards: All-Around Sweetheart, Sweetest Personality, Cutest Personality, Best Sharer, Best Artist, Biggest Heart, Best Manners, Best Helper, Most Creative.

FROM A
PRESCHOOL TEACHER'S
PERSPECTIVE
How important is it to understand gender development in a multicultural class. Why?

What's wrong with this picture? To one parent, whose daughter received one of the girls' awards during a kindergarten graduation ceremony, quite a bit. While the girls were getting pats on the back for their pleasing personalities, the boys were receiving awards for their intellectual and analytic skills (Deveny, 1994).

Such a situation is not rare: Girls and boys often live in very different worlds. As we've discussed, differences in the ways males and females are treated begin at birth, continue during the preschool years, and extend into adolescence and beyond (Coltrane & Adams, 1997; Maccoby, 1999; Martin & Ruble, 2004).

Gender, the sense of being male or female, is well established by the time children reach the preschool years. By the age of 2, children consistently label themselves and those around them as male or female (Poulin-Dubois et al., 1994; Raag, 2003; Campbell, Shirley, & Candy, 2004).

One way gender shows up is in play. Preschool boys spend more time than girls in rough-and-tumble play, while preschool girls spend more time than boys in organized games and role-playing. During this time boys begin to play more with boys and girls play more with girls, a trend that increases during middle childhood. Girls begin to prefer same-sex playmates a little earlier than boys. They first have a clear preference for interacting with other girls at age 2, while boys don't show much preference for same-sex playmates until age 3 (Boyatzis, Mallis, & Leon, 1999; Martin & Fabes, 2001; Raag, 2003).

Such same-sex preferences appear in many cultures. For instance, studies of kindergartners in mainland China show no examples of mixed-gender play. Similarly, gender "outweighs" ethnic variables when it comes to play: A Hispanic boy would rather play with a white boy than with a Hispanic girl (Whiting & Edwards, 1988; Martin, 1993; Aydt & Corsaro, 2003).

Preschool-age children often have very strict ideas about how boys and girls are supposed to act. Their expectations about gender-appropriate behavior are even more gender-stereotyped than those of adults and may be less flexible during the preschool years than at any other point in the life span. Beliefs in gender stereotypes become increasingly pronounced up to age 5, and although they become somewhat less rigid by age 7, they do not disappear. In fact, the gender stereotypes held by preschoolers resemble those held by traditional adults in society (Eichstedt, Serbin, & Poulin-Dubois, 2002; Serbin, Poulin-Dubois, & Eichstedt, 2002; Lam & Leman, 2003).

And what is the nature of preschoolers' gender expectations? Like adults, preschoolers expect that males are more apt to have traits involving competence, independence, forcefulness, and competitiveness. In contrast, females are viewed as more likely to have traits such as warmth, expressiveness, nurturance, and submissiveness. Although these are *expectations*, and say nothing about the way that men and women actually behave, such expectations provide the lens through which preschool-age children view the world and affect their behavior as well as the way they interact with peers and adults (Durkin & Nugent, 1998; Blakemore, 2003; Gelman, Taylor, & Nguyen, 2004).

Explaining Gender Differences

The prevalence and strength of preschoolers' gender expectations, and differences in behavior between boys and girls, have proven puzzling. Why should gender play such a powerful role during the preschool years (as well as during the rest of the life span)? Developmentalists have proposed several explanations.

Biological Perspectives on Gender. Since gender relates to the sense of being male or female, and sex refers to the physical characteristics that differentiate males and females, it would hardly be surprising to find that the biological characteristics associated with sex might themselves lead to gender differences. This has been shown to be true.

Hormones are one sex-related biological characteristic that have been found to affect gender-based behaviors. Girls exposed to unusually high levels of **androgens** (male hormones) prenatally are more likely to display behaviors associated with male stereotypes than are their sisters who were not exposed to androgens (Money & Ehrhardt, 1972; Hines, Golombok, & Rust, 2002; Servin, Nordenstroem, & Larsson, 2003).

androgens male hormones.

According to social learning approaches, children learn gender-related behavior and expectations from their observations of others.

Androgen-exposed girls preferred boys as playmates and spent more time than other girls playing with toys associated with the male role, such as cars and trucks. Similarly, boys exposed prenatally to atypically high levels of female hormones are apt to display more behaviors that are stereotypically female than is usual (Berenbaum & Hines, 1992; Hines & Kaufman, 1994; Servin et al., 2003; Knickmeyer & Baron-Cohen, 2006).

Moreover, as we noted earlier, some research suggests that biological differences exist in the structure of female and male brains. For instance, part of the **corpus callosum**, the bundle of nerves that connects the hemispheres of the brain, is proportionally larger in women than in men. To some theoreticians, this evidence suggests that gender differences may be produced by biological factors such as hormones (Benbow, Lubinski, & Hyde, 1997; Westerhausen, 2004).

Before accepting such contentions, however, it is important to note that alternative explanations abound. For example, the *corpus callosum* may be proportionally larger in women because of certain kinds of experiences that influence brain growth in particular ways. We know that girls are spoken to more than boys as infants, which might produce certain kinds of brain development. If this is true, environmental experience produces biological change—and not the other way around.

Other developmentalists see gender differences as serving the biological goal of survival of the species through reproduction. Basing their work on an evolutionary approach, these theorists suggest that our male ancestors who showed more stereotypically masculine qualities, such as forcefulness and competitiveness, may have been able to attract females who were able to provide them with hardy offspring. Females who excelled at stereotypically feminine tasks, such as nurturing, may have been valuable partners because they could increase the likelihood that children would survive the dangers of childhood (Geary, 1998; Browne, 2006; Ellis, 2006).

As in other domains that involve the interaction of inherited biological characteristics and environmental influences, it is difficult to attribute behavioral characteristics unambiguously to biological factors. Because of this problem, we must consider other explanations for gender differences.

Psychoanalytic Perspectives. You may recall from earlier discussions that Freud's psychoanalytic theory suggests that we move through a series of stages related to biological urges. To Freud, the preschool years encompass the *phallic stage,* in which the focus of a child's pleasure relates to genital sexuality.

Freud argued that the end of the phallic stage is marked by an important turning point in development: the Oedipal conflict. According to Freud, the *Oedipal conflict* occurs at around the age of 5, when the anatomical differences between males and females become particularly evident. Boys begin to develop sexual interests in their mothers, viewing their fathers as rivals. As a consequence, boys conceive a desire to kill their fathers—just as Oedipus did in the ancient Greek tragedy. However, because they view their fathers as all-powerful, boys develop a fear of retaliation, which takes the form of *castration anxiety.* In order to overcome this fear, boys repress their desires for their mothers and instead begin to identify with their fathers, attempting to be as similar to them as possible. *Identification* is the process in which children attempt to be similar to their same-sex parent, incorporating the parent's attitudes and values.

Girls, according to Freud, go through a different process. They begin to feel sexual attraction toward their fathers and experience *penis envy*—a view that not unexpectedly has led to

corpus callosum the bundle of nerves that connects the hemispheres of the brain.

accusations that Freud viewed women as inferior to men. In order to resolve their penis envy, girls ultimately identify with their mothers, attempting to be as similar to them as possible.

In the cases of both boys and girls, the ultimate result of identifying with the same-sex parent is that the children adopt their parents' gender attitudes and values. In this way, says Freud, society's expectations about the ways females and males "ought" to behave are perpetuated into new generations.

You may find it difficult to accept Freud's elaborate explanation of gender differences. So do most developmentalists, who believe that gender development is best explained by other mechanisms. In part, they base their criticisms of Freud on the lack of scientific support for his theories. For example, children learn gender stereotypes much earlier than the age of 5. Furthermore, this learning occurs even in single-parent households. However, some aspects of psychoanalytic theory have been supported, such as findings indicating that preschool-age children whose same-sex parents support sex-stereotyped behavior tend to demonstrate that behavior also. Still, far simpler processes can account for this phenomenon, and many developmentalists have searched for explanations of gender differences other than Freud's (Martin & Ruble, 2004).

Social Learning Approaches. As their name implies, social learning approaches see children as learning gender-related behavior and expectations by observing others. Children watch the behavior of their parents, teachers, siblings, and even peers. A little boy sees the glory of a major league baseball player and becomes interested in sports. A little girl watches her high school neighbor practicing cheerleading moves and begins to try them herself. The observation of the rewards that these others attain for acting in a gender-appropriate manner leads children to conform to such behavior themselves (Rust et al., 2000).

Books and the media, and in particular television and video games, also play a role in perpetuating traditional views of gender-related behavior from which preschoolers may learn. Analyses of the most popular television shows, for example, find that male characters outnumber female characters by 2 to 1. Furthermore, females are more apt to appear with males, whereas female–female relationships are relatively uncommon (Calvert, Kotler, & Zehnder, 2003).

Television also presents men and women in traditional gender roles. Television shows typically define female characters in terms of their relationships with males. Females are more likely to appear as victims than males (Wright et al., 1995; Turner-Bowker, 1996). They are less likely to be presented as productive or as decision makers, and more likely to be portrayed as characters interested in romance, their homes, and their families. Such models, according to social learning theory, are apt to have a powerful influence on preschoolers' definitions of appropriate behavior (Browne, 1998; Nathanson, Wilson, & McGee, 2002; Scharrer et al., 2006).

In some cases, the learning of social roles does not involve models, but occurs more directly. For example, most of us have heard preschool-age children being told by their parents to act like a "little girl" or "little man." What this generally means is that girls should behave politely and courteously, and boys should be tough and stoic—traits associated with society's traditional stereotypes of men and women. Such direct training sends a clear message about the behavior expected of a preschool-age child (Witt, 1997; Leaper, 2002).

Cognitive Approaches. In the view of some theorists, one aspect of the desire to form a clear sense of identity is the desire to establish a **gender identity**, a perception of oneself as male or female. To do this, we develop a **gender schema**, a cognitive framework that organizes information relevant to gender (Martin, 2000; Barbera, 2003; Martin & Ruble, 2004).

Gender schemas are developed early in life and serve as a lens through which preschoolers view the world. For instance, preschoolers use their increasing cognitive abilities to develop "rules" about what is right and what is inappropriate for males and females. Thus, some girls decide that wearing pants is inappropriate for a female and apply the rule so rigidly that they refuse to wear anything but dresses. Or a preschool boy may reason that since makeup is typically worn by females, it is inappropriate for him to wear makeup even when he is in a preschool play and all the other boys and girls are wearing it.

According to a cognitive-developmental theory proposed by Lawrence Kohlberg, this rigidity is in part a reflection of preschoolers' understanding of gender (Kohlberg, 1966). Rigid gender schemas are influenced by the preschooler's erroneous beliefs about sex differences. Specifically, young preschoolers believe that sex differences are based not on biological factors but on differences in appearance or behavior. Employing this view of the world, a girl may reason that she can be a father when she grows up, or a boy may think he could turn into a girl if

gender identity the perception of oneself as male or female.

gender schema a cognitive framework that organizes information relevant to gender.

TABLE 12.1   Four Approaches to Gender Development

PERSPECTIVE	KEY CONCEPTS	APPLYING THE CONCEPTS TO PRESCHOOL CHILDREN
Biological	Our ancestors who behaved in ways that are now stereotypically feminine or masculine may have been more successful in reproducing. Brain differences may lead to gender differences.	Girls may be genetically "programmed" by evolution to be more expressive and nurturing, while boys are "programmed" to be more competitive and forceful. Abnormal hormone exposure before birth has been linked to both boys and girls behaving in ways typically expected of the other gender.
Psychoanalytic	Gender development is the result of identification with the same-sex parent, achieved by moving through a series of stages related to biological urges.	Girls and boys whose parents of the same sex behave in stereotypically masculine or feminine ways are likely to do so, too, perhaps because they identify with those parents.
Social learning	Children learn gender-related behavior and expectations from their observation of others' behavior.	Children notice that other children and adults are rewarded for behaving in ways that conform to standard gender stereotypes—and sometimes punished for violating those stereotypes.
Cognitive	Through the use of gender schemas, developed early in life, preschoolers form a lens through which they view the world. They use their increasing cognitive abilities to develop "rules" about what is appropriate for males and females.	Preschoolers are more rigid in their rules about proper gender behavior than people at other ages, perhaps because they have just developed gender schemas that don't yet permit much variation from stereotypical expectations.

he put on a dress and tied his hair in a ponytail. However, by the time they reach the age of 4 or 5, children develop an understanding of **gender constancy**, the awareness that people are permanently males or females, depending on fixed, unchangeable biological factors.

Interestingly, children's growing understanding of gender constancy during the preschool period has no particular effect on gender-related behavior. In fact, the appearance of gender schemas occurs well before children understand gender constancy. Even young preschool-age children assume that certain behaviors are appropriate—and others are not—on the basis of stereotypic views of gender (Warin, 2000; Martin, Ruble, & Szkrybalo, 2002; Martin & Ruble, 2004).

Like the other approaches to gender development (summarized in Table 12.1), the cognitive perspective does not imply that differences between the two sexes are in any way improper or inappropriate. Instead, it suggests that preschoolers should be taught to treat others as individuals. Furthermore, preschoolers need to learn the importance of fulfilling their own talents, acting as individuals and not as representatives of a particular gender.

REVIEW

▶ Mothers and fathers interact with their babies differently, with mothers interacting more with their daughters and fathers interacting more with their sons. The types of interactions they engage in also differ.

▶ Some gender differences do exist in early infancy, but they are relatively minor. Gender differences become more pronounced as infants age.

▶ Gender awareness develops in the preschool years. Explanations of this phenomenon include biological, psychoanalytical, learning, and cognitive approaches.

▶ Preference for same-sex playmates begins to appear in the preschool years. Such a preference occurs in many cultures.

▶ The books, television, movies, and video games young children see all play a role in perpetuating traditional stereotypes of gender-related behavior.

APPLY

▶ What sorts of activities might you encourage a preschool boy to undertake to encourage him to adopt a less stereotypical gender schema?

Watch the video clip "Gender Constancy" on **MyDevelopmentLab** to see how preschoolers react to questions about gender.

gender constancy   the belief that people are permanently males or females, depending on fixed, unchangeable biological factors.

MODULE 12.2

Sexual Maturation and Sexuality

"I started having periods when I was just nine," Sharon Brewster, 16, recalls. By the time she entered seventh grade, Sharon was fully developed. She looked more like a mature woman in her 20s than a middle school student who struggled with French homework and what to say to boys. "Other girls envied me my very curvy figure, but I hated it," she says. "Guys—older guys, men really—followed me everywhere, and I knew it had nothing to do with who I was. It creeped me out."

Boys who mature early tend to be more successful in athletics and have a more positive self-concept. Why might there also be a downside to early maturation?

mydevelopmentlab

Log onto **MyDevelopmentLab** to watch 12-year-old Kianna, her mother, and her best friend talk about how important body image is in adolescence.

Psychological Aspects of Sexual Maturation

In our discussion of puberty in Chapter 3, we have already considered the profound physical changes that occur in children as they sexually mature. However, the nature and timing of these physical changes produce equally significant—and different—psychological consequences for boys and girls.

Body Image: Reactions to Physical Changes in Adolescence. Unlike infants, who also undergo extraordinarily rapid growth, adolescents are well aware of what is happening to their bodies, and they may react with horror or joy, spending long periods in front of mirrors. Few, though, are neutral about the changes they are witnessing (Mehran, 1997).

Some of the changes of adolescence do not show up in physical changes, but carry psychological weight. In the past, girls tended to react to menarche with anxiety because Western society tended to emphasize the more negative aspects of menstruation, such as the potential of cramps and messiness. Today, however, society's view of menstruation tends to be more positive, in part because menstruation has been demystified and discussed more openly. (For instance, television commercials for tampons are commonplace.) As a consequence, menarche is typically accompanied by an increase in self-esteem, a rise in status, and greater self-awareness, as adolescent girls see themselves as becoming adults (Brooks-Gunn & Reiter, 1990; Johnson, Roberts, & Worell, 1999; Matlin, 2003).

A boy's first ejaculation is roughly equivalent to menarche in a girl. However, while girls generally tell their mothers about the onset of menstruation, boys rarely mention their first ejaculation to their parents or even their friends (Stein & Reiser, 1994; Frankel, 2002). Why? One reason is that girls require tampons or sanitary napkins, and mothers provide them. It also may be that boys see the first ejaculation as an indication of their budding sexuality, an area about which they are quite uncertain and therefore reluctant to discuss with others.

Menstruation and ejaculations occur privately, but changes in body shape and size are quite public. Consequently, teenagers entering puberty frequently are embarrassed by the changes that are occurring. Girls, in particular, are often unhappy with their new bodies. Ideals of beauty in many Western countries call for an unrealistic thinness that is quite different from the actual shape of most women. Puberty brings a considerable increase in the amount of fatty tissue, as well as enlargement of the hips and buttocks—a far cry from the slenderness that society seems to demand (Attie & Brooks-Gunn, 1989; Unger & Crawford, 2004). As we discussed earlier, intense concern about body image can also contribute to eating disorders.

How children react to the onset of puberty depends in part on when it happens. As we shall see next, girls and boys who mature either much earlier or later than most of their peers are especially affected by the timing of puberty.

The Timing of Puberty: The Consequences of Early and Late Maturation. Why does it matter when a boy or girl reaches puberty? There are social consequences of early or late maturation. And as we shall see, social consequences are very important to adolescents.

Early Maturation.   For boys, early maturation is largely a plus. Early-maturing boys tend to be more successful at athletics, presumably because of their larger size. They also tend to be more popular and to have a more positive self-concept.

Early maturation in boys does have a downside, however. Boys who mature early are more apt to have difficulties in school, and they are more likely to become involved in delinquency and substance abuse. The reason: Their larger size makes it more likely that they will seek out the company of older boys who may involve them in activities that are inappropriate for their age. Furthermore, although early-maturers are more responsible and cooperative in later life, they are also more conforming and lacking in humor. Overall, though, the pluses seem to outweigh the minuses for early-maturing boys (Weichold, Silbereisen, & Schmitt-Rodermund, 2003; Taga, Markey, & Friedman, 2006; Costello et al., 2007; Lynne et al., 2007).

The story is a bit different for early-maturing girls. For them, the obvious changes in their bodies—such as the development of breasts—may lead them to feel uncomfortable and different from their peers. Moreover, because girls, in general, mature earlier than boys, early maturation tends to come at a very young age in the girl's life. Early-maturing girls may have to endure ridicule from their less mature classmates (Williams & Currie, 2000; Franko & Striegel-Moore, 2002; Olivardia & Pope, 2002).

On the other hand, early maturation is not a completely negative experience for girls. Girls who mature earlier tend to be sought after more as potential dates, and their popularity may enhance their self-concepts. This attention has a price, however. They may not be socially ready to participate in the kind of one-on-one dating situations that most girls deal with at a later age, and such situations may be psychologically challenging for early-maturing girls. Moreover, the conspicuousness of their deviance from their later-maturing classmates may have a negative effect, producing anxiety, unhappiness, and depression (Kaltiala-Heino, Kosunen, & Rimpela, 2003).

Cultural norms and standards regarding how women should look play a big role in how girls experience early maturation. For instance, in the United States, the notion of female sexuality is looked upon with a degree of ambivalence, being promoted in the media yet frowned upon socially. Girls who appear "sexy," like Sharon Brewster, attract both positive and negative attention. Consequently, unless a young girl who has developed secondary sex characteristics early can handle the disapproval she may encounter when she conspicuously displays her growing sexuality, the outcome of early maturation may be negative. In countries in which attitudes about sexuality are more liberal, the results of early maturation may be more positive. For example, in Germany, which has a more open view of sex, early-maturing girls have higher self-esteem than such girls in the United States. Furthermore, the consequences of early maturation vary even within the United States, depending on the views of girls' peer groups and on prevailing community standards regarding sex (Richards et al., 1990; Petersen, 2000; Dick & Mustanski, 2006).

Late Maturation.   As with early maturation, the situation with late maturation is mixed, although in this case boys fare worse than girls. For instance, boys who are smaller and lighter than their more physically mature peers tend to be viewed as less attractive. Because of their smaller size, they are at a disadvantage when it comes to sports activities. Furthermore, boys are expected to be bigger than their dates, so the social lives of late-maturing boys may suffer. Ultimately, if these difficulties lead to a decline in self-concept, the disadvantages of late maturation for boys could extend well into adulthood. More positively, coping with the challenges of late maturation may actually help males in some ways. Late-maturing boys grow up to have several positive qualities such as assertiveness and insightfulness, and they are more creatively playful than early-maturers (Livson & Peskin, 1980; Kaltiala-Heino, Kosunen, & Rimpela, 2003).

The picture for late-maturing girls is actually quite positive. In the short term, girls who mature later may be overlooked in dating and other mixed-sex activities during junior high school and middle school, and they may have relatively low social status (Clarke-Stewart & Friedman, 1987; Friedlander et al., 2007). However, by the time they are in the tenth grade and have begun to mature visibly, late-maturing-girls' satisfaction with themselves and their bodies may be greater than that of early-maturers. Late-maturing girls may end up with fewer emotional problems. The reason? Late-maturing girls are even more apt to fit the societal ideal of a slender, "leggy" body type than early-maturers, who tend to look heavier in comparison (Simmons & Blythe, 1987; Peterson, 1988; Moore & Rosenthal, 2006).

In sum, the reactions to early and late maturation present a complex picture. As we have seen repeatedly, we need to take into consideration the complete constellation of factors affecting individuals in order to understand their development. Some developmentalists suggest that other factors, such as changes in peer groups, family dynamics, and particularly schools and other societal institutions, may be more pertinent in determining an adolescent's behavior than early and later maturation, and the effects of puberty in general (Paikoff & Brooks-Gunn, 1990; Dorn, Susman, & Ponirakis, 2003; Stice, 2003).

Becoming Sexual

When I started "tuning out," teachers thought I was sick—physically sick that is. They kept sending me to the school nurse to have my temperature taken. If I'd told them I was carrying on with Beyoncé in their classes, while supposedly learning my Caesar and my Latin vocabulary, they'd have thought I was—well, delirious. I was! I'd even think of Beyoncé while jogging; I'd have to stop because it'd hurt down there! You can't run and have sex—or can you. (Based on Coles & Stokes, 1985, pp. 18–19)

Not every adolescent's sexual fantasies are as consuming as those of this teenage boy. But the hormonal changes of puberty not only trigger the maturation of the sexual organs, but also produce a new range of feelings in the form of sexuality. Sexual behavior and thoughts are among the central concerns of adolescents. Almost all adolescents think about sex, and many think about it a good deal of the time (Kelly, 2001; Ponton, 2001; Allen, Seitz, & Apfel, 2007).

Adolescence is not the first time individuals think about sex. You probably know this from your own experiences. Perhaps you "played doctor" as a preschooler. Or maybe you had an erection as a child. Or perhaps you were curious about the pubic hair a sibling was growing.

Even infants and preschoolers experience some sort of sexuality because it is clear that they do take pleasure from touching their genitals and apparently enjoy the stimulation it produces. Later, preadolescents report experiencing sexual pleasure from kissing and touching themselves and others, and some even report going through the motions of sexual intercourse during middle childhood. But it is not until adolescence, and the onset of puberty, that sexuality becomes a central aspect of everyday life.

Masturbation. The first type of sex in which adolescents engage is typically **masturbation**, sexual self-stimulation. By the age of 15, some 80 percent of teenage boys and 20 percent of teenage girls report that they have masturbated. The frequency of masturbation in males occurs more in the early teens and then begins to decline, while in females, the frequency is lower initially and increases throughout adolescence. In addition, patterns of masturbation frequency show differences according to race. For example, African American men and women masturbate less than whites (Oliver & Hyde, 1993; Schwartz, 1999; Hyde & DeLamater, 2003).

Although masturbation is widespread, it still may produce feelings of shame and guilt. There are several reasons for this. One is that adolescents may believe that masturbation signifies the inability to find a sexual partner—an erroneous assumption, since statistics show that three-quarters of married men and 68 percent of married women report masturbating between 10 and 24 times a year (Hunt, 1974; Davidson, Darling, & Norton, 1995).

For some there is also a sense of shame about masturbation, the result of a lingering legacy of misguided views of masturbation. For instance, nineteenth-century physicians and laypersons warned of the horrible effects of masturbation, including "dyspepsia, spinal disease, headache, epilepsy, various kinds of fits. . . impaired eyesight, palpitation of the heart, pain in the side and bleeding at the lungs, spasm of the heart, and sometimes sudden death" (Gregory, 1856). Suggested remedies included bandaging the genitals, covering them with a cage, tying the hands, male circumcision without anesthesia (so that it might better be remembered), and for girls, the administration of carbolic acid to the clitoris. One physician, J. W. Kellogg, believed that certain grains would be less likely to provoke sexual excitation—leading to his invention of corn flakes (Hunt, 1974; Michael et al., 1994).

The reality of masturbation is different. Today, experts on sexual behavior view it as a normal, healthy, and harmless activity. Some suggest that it provides a useful way to learn about one's own sexuality (Hyde & DeLamater, 2007).

Sexual Intercourse. Although it may be preceded by many different types of sexual intimacy, including deep kissing, massaging, petting, and oral sex, sexual intercourse remains a major

masturbation sexual self-stimulation.

milestone in the perceptions of most adolescents. Consequently, the main focus of researchers investigating sexual behavior has been on the act of heterosexual intercourse.

The average age at which people first have sexual intercourse has been steadily declining over the last 50 years, until today when about one in five adolescents has had sex before the age of 15. Overall, around half of adolescents begin having intercourse between the ages of 15 and 18, and at least 80 percent have had sex before the age of 20 (see Figure 12.1). At the same time, many teenagers are postponing sex, and the number of adolescents who say they have never had sexual intercourse increased by nearly 10 percent from 1991 to 2001, largely as a response to the threat of infection by the virus that causes AIDS (Seidman & Reider, 1994; Centers for Disease Control & Prevention, 1998; NCPYP, 2003).

It is impossible to consider sexual activities without also looking at the societal norms governing sexual conduct. The prevailing norm several decades ago was the **double standard** in which premarital sex was considered permissible for males but not for females. Women were told by society that "nice girls don't," while men heard that premarital sex was permissible—although they should be sure to marry virgins.

Today, however, the double standard has begun to give way to a new norm, called **permissiveness with affection**. According to this standard, premarital intercourse is viewed as permissible for both men and women if it occurs in the context of a long-term, committed, or loving relationship (Hyde & Delamater, 2007).

The demise of the double standard is far from complete, however. Attitudes toward sexual conduct are still typically more lenient for males than for females, even in relatively socially liberal cultures. And in some cultures, the standards for men and women are quite distinct. For example, in North Africa, the Middle East, and the majority of Asian countries, most women conform to societal norms suggesting that they abstain from sexual intercourse until they are married. In Mexico, where there are strict standards against premarital sex, males are also considerably more likely than females to have premarital sex. In contrast, in Sub-Saharan Africa, women are more likely to have sexual intercourse prior to marriage, and intercourse is common among unmarried teenage women (Liskin, 1985; Johnson et al., 1992; Spira et al., 1992; Peltzer & Pengpid, 2006).

Sexual Orientation: Heterosexuality, Homosexuality, and Bisexuality. When we consider adolescents' sexual development, the most frequent pattern is *heterosexuality,* sexual attraction and behavior directed to the other sex. Yet some teenagers are *homosexual,* in which their sexual attraction and behavior are oriented to members of their own sex. (Many male homosexuals prefer the term *gay* and female homosexuals the label *lesbian,* because they refer to a broader array of attitudes and lifestyle than the term *homosexual,* which focuses on the sexual act.) Other people find they are *bisexual,* sexually attracted to people of both sexes.

Many teens experiment with homosexuality. At one time or another, around 20 to 25 percent of adolescent boys and 10 percent of adolescent girls have at least one same-sex sexual encounter. In fact, homosexuality and heterosexuality are not completely distinct sexual orientations. Alfred Kinsey, a pioneer sex researcher, argued that sexual orientation should be viewed as a continuum in which "exclusively homosexual" is at one end and "exclusively heterosexual" at the other (Kinsey, Pomeroy, & Martin, 1948). In between are people who show both homosexual and heterosexual behavior. Although accurate figures are difficult to obtain, most experts believe that between 4 and 10 percent of both men and women are exclusively homosexual during extended periods of their lives (Kinsey, Pomeroy, & Martin, 1948; McWhirter, Sanders, & Reinisch, 1990; Michael et al., 1994; Diamond, 2003a, 2003b; Russell & Consolacion, 2003).

The determination of sexual orientation is further complicated by distinctions between sexual orientation and gender identity. While sexual orientation relates to the object of one's sexual interests, *gender identity* is the gender a person believes he or she is psychologically. Sexual orientation and gender identity are not necessarily related to one another: A man who has a strong masculine gender identity may be attracted to other men. Consequently, the extent to which men and women enact traditional "masculine" or "feminine" behavior is not necessarily related to their sexual orientation or gender identity (Hunter & Mallon, 2000).

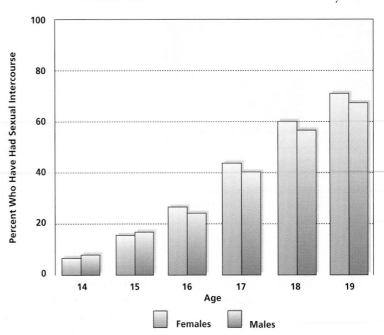

FIGURE 12.1

Adolescents and Sexual Activity
The age at which adolescents have sexual intercourse for the first time is declining, and 80 percent have had sex before the age of 20.
Source: Guttmacher, 2010.

double standard   the standard in which premarital sex is considered permissible for males but not for females.

permissiveness with affection   the standard in which premarital intercourse is viewed as permissible for both men and women if it occurs in the context of a long-term, committed, or loving relationship.

The stresses of adolescence are magnified for homosexuals, who often face societal prejudice. Eventually, most adolescents come to grips and embrace their sexual orientation.

Some people feel they have been born the wrong physical sex, believing, for example, that they are women trapped in men's bodies. These *transgendered* individuals may pursue sexual reassignment surgery, a prolonged course of treatment in which they receive hormones and reconstructive surgery so that they can take on the physical characteristics of the other sex.

What Determines Sexual Orientation? The factors that induce people to develop as heterosexual, homosexual, or bisexual are not well understood. Evidence suggests that genetic and biological factors may play an important role. Studies of twins show that identical twins are more likely to both be homosexual than pairs of siblings who don't share their genetic makeup. Other research finds that various structures of the brain are different in homosexuals and heterosexuals, and hormone production also seems to be linked to sexual orientation (Meyer-Bahlburg et al., 1995; Lippa, 2003; Rahman & Wilson, 2003; Kraemer et al., 2006).

Other researchers have suggested that family or peer environmental factors play a role. For example, Freud argued that homosexuality was the result of inappropriate identification with the opposite-sex parent (Freud, 1922/1959). The difficulty with Freud's theoretical perspective and other similar perspectives that followed is that there simply is no evidence to suggest that any particular family dynamic or childrearing practice is consistently related to sexual orientation. Similarly, explanations based on learning theory, which suggest that homosexuality arises because of rewarding, pleasant homosexual experiences and unsatisfying heterosexual ones, do not appear to be plausible (Golombok & Tasker, 1996; Saravi, 2007).

In short, there is no accepted explanation of why some adolescents develop a heterosexual orientation and others a homosexual orientation. Most experts believe that sexual orientation develops out of a complex interplay of genetic, physiological, and environmental factors (LeVay & Valente, 2003, 2006).

What is clear is that adolescents who find themselves attracted to members of the same sex may face a more difficult time than other teens. U.S. society still harbors great ignorance and prejudice regarding homosexuality, persisting in the belief that people have a choice in the matter—which they do not. Gay and lesbian teens may be rejected by their family or peers, or even harassed and assaulted if they are open about their orientation. As a result, adolescents who find themselves to be homosexual are at greater risk for depression, and suicide rates are significantly higher for homosexual adolescents than heterosexual adolescents (Ryan & Rivers, 2003; Harris, 2004; Murdoch & Bolch, 2005; Koh & Ross, 2006; Lester, 2006).

Ultimately, however, most people are able to come to grips with their sexual orientation and become comfortable with it. Although lesbian, gay, and bisexuals may experience mental health difficulties as a result of the stress, prejudice, and discrimination they face, homosexuality is not considered a psychological disorder by any of the major psychological or medical associations. All of them endorse efforts to reduce discrimination against homosexuals (Stone, 2003; van Wormer & McKinney, 2003; Davison, 2005).

Disclosing Same-Sex Attraction to Parents. As you might imagine, the decision to disclose to one's parents that one is attracted to persons of the same sex is not an easy one. For sexual minority adolescents, such disclosure is an important event in their sexual development. It's also an event that is fraught with anxiety; adolescents typically fear that their parents will react negatively to their coming out, possibly even by throwing them out of the house. Yet many sexual minority adolescents do tell at least one of their parents of their same-sex attraction, although the how, when, why, and to whom of disclosure vary from person to person (Savin-Williams, 1998; Rotheram-Borus & Langabeer, 2001; Hunter, 2007).

While adolescents fear parental rejection in disclosing their sexual orientation, in the overwhelming majority of cases parent-child relations stay the same or even improve over time.

According to the results of research on the issue, gender turns out to be an important factor in the disclosure of sexual orientation. Adolescents are more likely to disclose a same-sex attraction to their mothers than to their fathers, and if they disclose to both parents, they usually disclose to their mothers first. Most often this disclosure comes in a face-to-face meeting. Fathers, on the other hand, are most likely to learn of their adolescent's same-sex attraction by accident or through someone else. Adolescents of both sexes disclose to their mothers because they share a closer relationship with them—in fact, in most cases, the mothers simply asked them whether they were gay. Their reasons for disclosing to their fathers differed, however; male adolescents most frequently did so to seek support, while female adolescents most often simply wanted to get it over with (Savin-Williams & Ream, 2003).

Adolescents' reasons for choosing *not* to come out to their parents differ for mothers versus fathers. Mothers are most often kept in the dark because adolescents perceive that the time is not yet right or because they fear damaging their relationship with their mother. Fathers, on the other hand, are most frequently not told of their children's same-sex attractions because they are less important in their sons' or daughters' lives.

Are adolescents' fears of parental rejection well founded? Usually, no. Parental reactions typically are similar for male and female adolescents and for mothers and fathers, and both parents tend to be either supportive or slightly negative (a frequent reaction is to express disbelief). Moreover, in the overwhelming majority of cases, parent–child relations stay the same or even improve over time. In only about 5 percent of cases do adolescents report a decrease in relationship quality (Savin-Williams & Ream, 2003).

Teenage Pregnancies. Feedings at 3:00 AM, diaper changes, and visits to the pediatrician are not part of most people's vision of adolescence. Yet, every year, tens of thousands of adolescents in the United States give birth.

The good news, though, is the number of teenage pregnancies is declining. In the last 10 years, the teenage birthrate has dropped 30 percent. Births to African American teenagers have shown the steepest decline, with births down by more than 40 percent in a decade. Overall the pregnancy rate of teenagers is 43 births per 1,000, a historic low (see Figure 12.2; Centers for Disease Control and Prevention, 2003; Colen, Geronimus, & Phipps, 2006).

Several factors explain the drop in teenage pregnancies:

- New initiatives have raised awareness among teenagers of the risks of unprotected sex. For example, about two-thirds of high schools in the United States have established comprehensive sex education programs (Villarosa, 2003; Corcoran & Pillai, 2007).

- The rate of sexual intercourse among teenagers has declined. The percent of teenage girls who have ever had sexual intercourse dropped from 51 percent to 43 percent from 1991 to 2001.

- The use of condoms and other forms of contraception has increased. For example, 57 percent of sexually active high school students reported using condoms.

- Substitutes for sexual intercourse may be more prevalent. For example, data from the 1995 National Survey of Adolescent Males found that about half of 15- to 19-year-old boys reported having received oral sex, an increase of 44 percent since the late 1980s. It is possible that oral sex, which many teenagers do not even consider "sex," may increasingly be viewed as an alternative to sexual intercourse (Bernstein, 2004).

One thing that apparently hasn't led to a reduction in teenage pregnancies is asking adolescents to take a virginity pledge. Public pledges to refrain from premarital sex—a centerpiece of some forms of sex education—apparently are ineffective. For example, in one study of 12,000 teenagers, 88 percent reported eventually having sexual intercourse. However, pledges did delay the start of sex an average of 18 months (Bearman et al., 2004).

Even with the decline in the birthrate for U.S. teenagers, the rate of teenage pregnancy in the United States is two to ten times higher compared to that of other industrialized countries. The results of an unintended pregnancy can be devastating to both mother and child. In comparison to earlier times, teenage mothers today are much less likely to be married. In a high percentage of cases, mothers care for their children without the help of the father. Without financial or emotional support, a mother may have to abandon her own education, and consequently she may be relegated to unskilled, poorly paying jobs for the rest of her life. In other cases, she may develop long-term dependency on welfare. An adolescent mother's physical and mental health may suffer as she faces unrelenting stress due to continual demands on her time (Manlove et al., 2004; Gillmore et al., 2006; Oxford et al., 2006).

This 16-year-old mother and her child are representative of a major social problem: teenage pregnancy. Why is teenage pregnancy a greater problem in the United States than in other countries?

FROM A
MEDICAL CARE PROVIDER'S
PERSPECTIVE
A parent asks you how to prevent her 14-year-old son from engaging in sexual activity until he is older. What would you tell her?

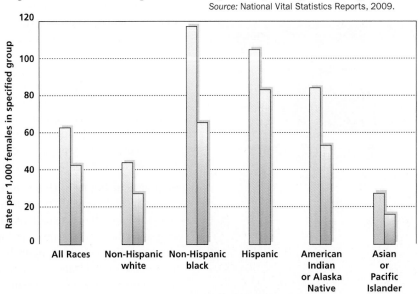

FIGURE 12.2 Teenage Pregnancy Rates
Until recently, the rate of teenage pregnancy in the United States had declined significantly among all ethnic groups.
Source: National Vital Statistics Reports, 2009.

Rate per 1,000 females in specified group

Race and Hispanic origin

All Races | Non-Hispanic white | Non-Hispanic black | Hispanic | American Indian or Alaska Native | Asian or Pacific Islander

1991 | 2006

BECOMING AN INFORMED CONSUMER OF DEVELOPMENT
Preventing Unwanted Pregnancy

If you're concerned about the possibility of an unwanted pregnancy and its harmful consequences, your first line of defense is to educate yourself on prevention methods. A number of birth control options are available that are appropriate for adolescents, each with its own advantages and disadvantages. A physician can help choose the method that is best for each individual. Following are some effective recommendations (Food and Drug Administration, 2003; Knowles, 2005).

- **Abstinence.** Abstaining from sex is the only birth control method that is guaranteed to be 100 percent effective. Abstinence requires no special equipment or medical supervision, costs nothing, and prevents sexually transmitted disease as well as unwanted pregnancy. The downside of abstinence is that some people find it difficult to refrain from sex, and if they have not explored alternative methods of birth control, they may not be prepared to protect themselves from unwanted pregnancy when they do become sexually active.

- **Outercourse.** *Outercourse* is sexual activity that does not involve vaginal intercourse. It may include kissing, masturbation, massage, or oral sex. Outercourse is 100 percent effective against pregnancy as long as no semen comes in contact with the vaginal area.

- **Condoms.** A condom, a sheath that covers the penis during intercourse, provides a barrier against the transmission of semen. Condoms are 85 to 98 percent effective against

pregnancy, depending in part on how they are used (the addition of a spermicidal lubricant enhances their effectiveness). Condoms also provide protection against sexually transmitted diseases, and they are widely available and generally inexpensive. Relying on condoms to prevent unwanted pregnancy means that a condom must be used every time sexual intercourse occurs.

- **Birth control pills.** Birth control pills contain hormones that prevent pregnancy by interfering with egg fertilization. They are 92 to 99 percent effective against pregnancy, but they must be prescribed by a physician. Birth control pills have the advantage of providing continuous protection against unwanted pregnancy—you don't have to remember to do anything special at the time of intercourse. Their main disadvantage is that they must be taken daily, whether or not one is having sex.

- **Prescription barriers.** A prescription barrier, such as a diaphragm, is treated with spermicide and then inserted into the vagina before intercourse, where it blocks the transmission of semen. Prescription barriers are an alternative to daily hormone use for women who have intercourse only occasionally. They are available through a physician, and they are 84 to 94 percent effective against pregnancy. However, barriers can be difficult to use correctly, and like condoms, must be used every time one has intercourse.

The Ongoing Sexuality of Adulthood

Despite a youth-oriented media, where most portrayals of romance occur between young, fit, unwrinkled men and women, interest in sexual activity does not belong exclusively to the under-25 crowd. Indeed, it extends throughout the life span.

For example, sexuality remains an important part of life for many, if not most, middle-aged people. The frequency of sexual intercourse declines with age (see Figure 12.3), but sexual pleasure remains a vital part of most middle-aged adults' lives. About half of men and women age 45 to 59 report having sexual intercourse about once a week or more. Similarly, sex remains an important activity for gay and lesbian couples during middle adulthood (Cain, Johannes, & Avis, 2003; Kimmel & Sang, 2003; Duplassie & Daniluk, 2007).

For many, middle adulthood brings a kind of sexual enjoyment and freedom that was missing during their earlier lives. With their children grown and away from home, middle-aged married couples have more time to engage in uninterrupted sexual activities. Women who have passed through menopause, which we discussed earlier, are liberated from the fear of pregnancy and no longer need to employ birth control techniques (Sherwin, 1991; Lamont, 1997; Norman, 2008).

Sexuality in Old Age: Use It or Lose It. Do your grandparents have sex?

Quite possibly, yes. Although the answer may surprise you, increasing evidence suggests that people are sexually active well into their 80s and 90s. This happens in spite of societal stereotypes suggesting that it is somehow improper for two 75-year-olds to have sexual intercourse, and even worse for a 75-year-old to masturbate. Such negative attitudes are a function of societal expectations in the United States. In many other cultures, elderly people are expected to remain sexually active, and in some societies, people are expected to become less inhibited as they age (Winn & Newton, 1982; Hyde, 1994; Hillman, 2000; Guan, 2004).

Two major factors determine whether an elderly person will engage in sexual activity (Masters, Johnson, & Kolodny, 1982; Papaharitou et al., 2008). One is good physical and mental

Sexuality continues to be a vital part of most couples' lives in middle adulthood.

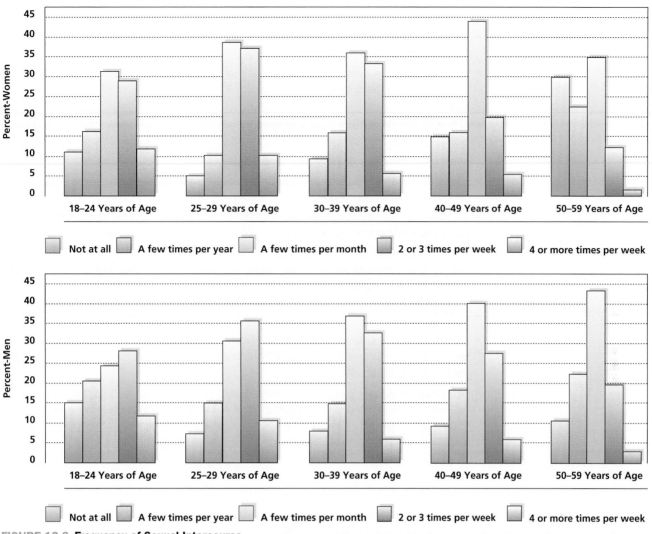

FIGURE 12.3 **Frequency of Sexual Intercourse**
As people age, the frequency of sexual intercourse declines.
Source: Adapted from Michael et al., 1994.

health. People need to be physically healthy and to hold generally positive attitudes about sexual activity in order for sex to take place. The other determinant of sexual activity during old age is previous regular sexual activity. The longer elderly men and women have gone without sexual activity, the less likely is future sexual activity. "Use it or lose it" seems an accurate description of sexual functioning in older people. Sexual activity can and often does continue throughout the life span. Furthermore, there's some intriguing evidence that having sex may have some unexpected side benefits: One study found that having sex regularly is associated with a lower risk of death (Purdy, 1995; Davey, Frankel, & Yarnell, 1997; Gelfand, 2000; Kellett, 2000; Henry & McNab, 2003)!

One survey found that 43 percent of men and 33 percent of women over the age of 70 masturbated. The average frequency for those who masturbated was once per week. Around two-thirds of married men and women had sex with their spouses, again averaging around once per week. In addition, the percentage of people who view their sexual partners as physically attractive actually increases with age (see Figure 12.4; Brecher et al., 1984; Budd, 1999).

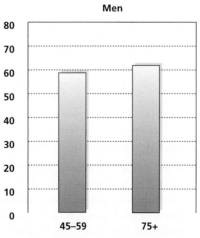
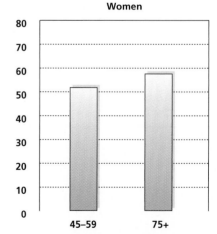

FIGURE 12.4 **Attractiveness over Time**
More than 50 percent of Americans over age 45 find their partners attractive, and as time goes on, more attractive.
Source: AARP/Modern Maturity Sexuality Study, 1999.

REVIEW

▶ Early or late maturation can bring advantages and disadvantages, depending on gender as well as emotional and psychological maturity.

▶ Masturbation, once viewed very negatively, is now generally regarded as a normal and harmless practice that continues into adulthood.

▶ Sexual intercourse is a major milestone that most people reach during adolescence. The age of first intercourse reflects cultural differences and has been declining over the last 50 years.

▶ Sexual orientation, which is most accurately viewed as a continuum rather than categorically, develops as the result of a complex combination of factors.

▶ Teenage pregnancy is a problem in the United States, with negative consequences for adolescent mothers and their children.

▶ Sexuality in middle adulthood changes slightly, but middle-aged couples, freed from concerns about children, can often progress to a new level of intimacy and enjoyment.

▶ Being in good physical and mental health and having a history of regular sexual activity are the key determinants of sexual activity during old age. In healthy adults sexuality can continue throughout the life span.

APPLY

▶ Do you think the double standard, which approved male sexual activity but condemned female sexual activity, has entirely disappeared? Does popular culture work to eliminate or perpetuate the double standard?

▶ Why do you think many people in the United States find it difficult to believe that people in late adulthood can still be sexually active? How do you think our expectations for the behavior of older adults differ from those of other cultures where it is expected that people in late adulthood will continue to be sexual?

MODULE 12.3

Relationships

It took him almost a month, but Sylvester Chiu finally got up the courage to ask Jackie Durbin to go to the movies. It was hardly a surprise to Jackie, though. Sylvester had first told his friend Erik about his resolve to ask Jackie out, and Erik had told Jackie's friend Cynthia about Sylvester's plans. Cynthia, in turn, had told Jackie, who was primed to say "yes" when Sylvester finally did call.

Welcome to the complex world of dating, an important and changing ritual of adolescence.

Getting to Know You: Dating and Falling in Love in the Twenty-First Century

When and how adolescents begin to date is determined by cultural factors that change from one generation to another. Until fairly recently, exclusively dating a single individual was seen as something of a cultural ideal, viewed in the context of romance. In fact, society often encouraged dating in adolescence, in part as a way for adolescents to explore relationships that might eventually lead to marriage. Today, some adolescents believe that the concept of dating is outmoded and limiting, and in some places the practice of "hooking up"—a vague term that covers everything from kissing to sexual intercourse—is viewed as more appropriate. Despite changing cultural norms, dating remains the dominant form of social interaction that leads to intimacy among adolescents (Larson, Clore, & Wood, 1999; Denizet-Lewis, 2004; Manning, Giordano, & Longmore, 2006).

The Functions of Dating. Although on the surface dating is part of a pattern of courtship that can potentially lead to marriage, it actually serves other functions as well, especially early on. Dating is a way to learn how to establish intimacy with another individual. It can provide entertainment and, depending on the status of the person one is dating, prestige. It even can be used to develop a sense of one's own identity (Savin-Williams & Berndt, 1990; Sanderson & Cantor, 1995; Vangelisti, 2006).

Just how well dating serves such functions, particularly the development of psychological intimacy, is an open question. What specialists in adolescence do know, however, is surprising: Dating in early and middle adolescence is not terribly successful at facilitating intimacy. On the contrary, dating is often a superficial activity in which the participants so rarely let down their guards that they never become truly close and never expose themselves emotionally to each other. Psychological intimacy may be lacking even when sexual activity is part of the relationship (Savin-Williams & Berndt, 1990; Collins, 2003; Furman & Shaffer, 2003).

True intimacy becomes more common during later adolescence. At that point, the dating relationship may be taken more seriously by both participants, and it may be seen as a way to select a mate and as a potential prelude to marriage.

For homosexual adolescents, dating presents special challenges. In some cases, blatant homophobic prejudice expressed by classmates may lead gays and lesbians to date members of the other sex in efforts to fit in. If they do seek relationships with other gays and lesbians, they may find it difficult to find partners, who may not openly express their sexual orientation. Homosexual couples who do openly date face possible harassment, making the development of a relationship all the more difficult (Savin-Williams, 2003).

Dating, Race, and Ethnicity. Culture influences dating patterns among adolescents of different racial and ethnic groups, particularly those whose parents have immigrated to the United States from other countries. Parents may try to control their children's dating behavior in an effort to preserve their culture's traditional values or ensure that their child dates within his or her racial or ethnic group.

For example, Asian parents may be especially conservative in their attitudes and values, in part because they themselves may have had no experience of dating. (In many cases, the parents' marriage was arranged by others, and the entire concept of dating is unfamiliar.) They may insist that dating be conducted with chaperones or not at all. As a consequence, they may find themselves involved in substantial conflict with their children (Kibria, 2003; Hamon & Ingoldsby, 2003; Hoelter, Axinn, & Ghimire, 2004).

Forging Relationships: Intimacy, Liking, and Loving During Early Adulthood

Asia Kaia Linn, whose parents chose her name while looking through a world atlas, met Chris Applebaum about 6 years ago at Hampshire College in Massachusetts and fell in love with him one Saturday night while they were dancing.

Although many women might swoon over a guy with perfect hair and fluid dance steps, it was his silly haircut and overall lack of coordination that delighted her. "He's definitely a funny dancer, and he spun me around and we were just being goofy," Ms. Linn recalled. "I realized how much fun we were having, and I thought this is ridiculous and fabulous and I love him." (Brady, 1995, p. 47)

Not everyone falls in love quite as easily as Asia. For some, the road to love is tortuous, meandering through soured relationships and fallen dreams; for others, it is a road never taken. For some, love leads to marriage and a life befitting society's storybook view of home, children, and long years together as a couple. For many, it leads to a less happy ending, prematurely concluding in divorce and custody battles.

As we noted in Chapter 9, Erik Erikson regarded young adulthood as the time of the **intimacy-versus-isolation stage**, a period focused on developing close, intimate relationships with others. Young adults' happiness stems, in part, from their relationships, and many worry about whether or not they are developing serious relationships "on time." Even those who are not interested in forming a long-term relationship typically are focused, to some extent, on connecting with others.

intimacy-versus-isolation stage
according to Erikson, the period of postadolescence into the early 30s that focuses on developing close relationships with others.

The idea of romantic love is predominately a Western concept. How do you think members of other cultures view romantic or passionate love?

Falling in Love: When Liking Turns to Loving. Whether one falls in love swiftly, as Asia did, or more slowly, most relationships develop in a fairly similar way, following a surprisingly regular progression (Burgess & Huston, 1979; Berscheid, 1985):

- Two people interact with each other more often and for longer periods of time. Furthermore, the range of settings increases.
- The two people increasingly seek out each other's company.
- They open up to each other more and more, disclosing more intimate information about themselves. They begin to share physical intimacies.
- The couple is more willing to share both positive and negative feelings, and they may offer criticism in addition to praise.
- They begin to agree on the goals they hold for the relationship.
- Their reactions to situations become more similar.
- They begin to feel that their own psychological well-being is tied to the success of the relationship, viewing it as unique, irreplaceable, and cherished.
- Finally, their definition of themselves and their behavior changes: They begin to see themselves and act as a couple, rather than as two separate individuals.

Passionate and Companionate Love: The Two Faces of Love. Is "love" just a lot of "liking"? Most developmental psychologists would answer negatively; love not only differs quantitatively from liking, it represents a qualitatively different state. For example, love, at least in its early stages, involves relatively intense physiological arousal, an all-encompassing interest in another individual, recurrent fantasies about the other individual, and rapid swings of emotion (Lamm & Wiesman, 1997). As distinct from liking, love includes elements of closeness, passion, and exclusivity (Walster & Walster, 1978; Hendrick & Hendrick, 2003).

Not all love is the same. We don't love our mothers the same way we love girlfriends or boyfriends, brothers or sisters, or lifelong friends. What distinguishes these different types of love? Some psychologists suggest that our love relationships can fall into two different categories: passionate or companionate.

Passionate (or romantic) love is a state of powerful absorption in someone. It includes intense physiological interest and arousal, and caring for another's needs. In comparison, **companionate love** is the strong affection that we have for those with whom our lives are deeply involved (Hecht, Marston, & Larkey, 1994; Lamm & Wiesman, 1997; Hendrick & Hendrick, 2003).

What is it that fuels the fires of passionate love? According to one theory, anything that produces strong emotions—even negative ones such as jealousy, anger, or fear of rejection—may be the source of deepening passionate love.

In psychologists Elaine Hatfield and Ellen Berscheid's **labeling theory of passionate love**, individuals experience romantic love when two events occur together: intense physiological arousal and situational cues indicating that "love" is the appropriate label for the feelings they are experiencing (Berscheid & Walster, 1974a; Berscheid, 2006). The physiological arousal can be produced by sexual arousal, excitement, or even negative emotions such as jealousy. Whatever the cause, if that arousal is subsequently labeled as "I must be falling in love" or "she makes my heart flutter" or "he really turns me on," then the experience is attributed to passionate love.

The theory is particularly useful in explaining why people may feel deepened love even when they experience continual rejection or hurt from their assumed lover. It suggests that such negative emotions can produce strong physiological arousal. If this arousal is interpreted as being caused by "love," then people may decide that they are even more in love than they were before they experienced the negative emotions.

But why should people label an emotional experience as "love" when there are so many possible alternatives? One answer is that in Western cultures, romantic love is seen as possible, acceptable, desirable—an experience to be sought. The virtues of passion are extolled in love ballads, commercials, television shows, and films. Consequently, young adults are primed and ready to experience love in their lives (Dion & Dion, 1988; Hatfield & Rapson, 1993; Florsheim, 2003).

It is interesting to note that this is not the way it is in every culture. For instance, in many cultures, passionate, romantic love is a foreign concept. Marriages may be arranged on the basis of economic and status considerations. Even in Western cultures, the concept of love is of

passionate (or romantic) love a state of powerful absorption in someone.

companionate love the strong affection for those with whom our lives are deeply involved.

labeling theory of passionate love the theory that individuals experience romantic love when two events occur together: intense physiological arousal and situational cues suggesting that the arousal is due to love.

relatively recent origin. For instance, the notion that couples need to be in love was not "invented" until the Middle Ages, when social philosophers first suggested that love ought to be a requirement for marriage. Their goal in making such a proposal: to provide an alternative to the raw sexual desire that had served as the primary basis for marriage before (Lewis, 1958; Xiaohe & Whyte, 1990; Haslett, 2004).

Sternberg's Triangular Theory: The Three Faces of Love. To psychologist Robert Sternberg, love is more complex than a simple division into passionate and companionate types. He suggests instead that love is made up of three components: intimacy, passion, and decision/commitment. The **intimacy component** encompasses feelings of closeness, affection, and connectedness. The **passion component** comprises the motivational drives relating to sex, physical closeness, and romance. This component is exemplified by intense, physiologically arousing feelings of attraction. Finally, the third aspect of love, the **decision/commitment component**, embodies both the initial cognition that one loves another person and the longer-term determination to maintain that love (Sternberg, 1997b, 2006).

These components can be combined to form eight different types of love depending on which of the three components is either present or missing from a relationship (see Table 12.2). For instance, *nonlove* refers to people who have only the most casual of relationships; it consists of the absence of the three components of intimacy, passion, and decision/commitment. *Liking* develops when only intimacy is present; *infatuated love* exists when only passion is felt; and *empty love* exists when only decision/commitment is present.

Other types of love involve a mix of two or more components. For instance, romantic love occurs when intimacy and passion are present, and *companionate love* when intimacy and decision/commitment occur jointly. When two people experience romantic love, they are drawn together physically and emotionally, but they do not necessarily view the relationship as lasting. Companionate love, on the other hand, may occur in long-lasting relationships in which physical passion has taken a backseat.

Fatuous love exists when passion and decision/commitment, without intimacy, are present. Fatuous love is a kind of mindless loving in which there is no emotional bond between the partners.

Finally, the eighth kind of love is *consummate love*. In consummate love, all three components of love are present. Although we might assume that consummate love represents the "ideal" love, such a view may well be mistaken. Many long-lasting and entirely satisfactory relationships are based on types of love other than consummate love. Furthermore, the type of love

intimacy component the component of love that encompasses feelings of closeness, affection, and connectedness.

passion component the component of love that comprises the motivational drives relating to sex, physical closeness, and romance.

decision/commitment component the third aspect of love that embodies both the initial cognition that one loves another person and the longer-term determination to maintain that love.

mydevelopmentlab

Log onto **MyDevelopmentLab** to watch videos of Stephanie and Ralf, two young adults searching for love, but who approach it in different ways.

TABLE 12.2 The Combinations of Love

TYPE OF LOVE	INTIMACY	PASSION	DECISION/ COMMITMENT	EXAMPLE
Nonlove	Absent	Absent	Absent	The way you might feel about the person who takes your ticket at the movies.
Liking	Present	Absent	Absent	Good friends who have lunch together at least once or twice a week.
Infatuated love	Absent	Present	Absent	A "fling" or short-term relationship based only on sexual attraction.
Empty love	Absent	Absent	Present	An arranged marriage or a couple who have decided to stay married "for the sake of the children."
Romantic love	Present	Present	Absent	A couple who have been happily dating a few months, but have not made any plans for a future together.
Companionate love	Present	Absent	Present	A couple who enjoy each other's company and their relationship, although they no longer feel much sexual interest in each other.
Fatuous love	Absent	Present	Present	A couple who decides to move in together after knowing each other for only two weeks.
Consummate love	Present	Present	Present	A loving, sexually vibrant, long-term relationship.

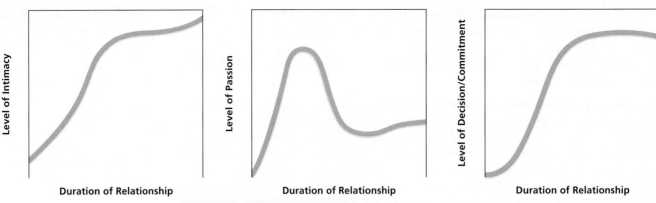

FIGURE 12.5 **The Shape of Love**
Over the course of a relationship, the three aspects of love—intimacy, passion, and decision/commitment—vary in strength. How do these change as a relationship develops?
Source: Sternberg, 1986.

that predominates in a relationship varies over time. As shown in Figure 12.5, in strong, loving relationships the level of decision/commitment peaks and remains fairly stable. By contrast, passion tends to peak early in a relationship, but then declines and levels off. Intimacy also increases fairly rapidly but can continue to grow over time.

Sternberg's triangular theory of love emphasizes both the complexity of love and its dynamic, evolving quality. As people and relationships develop and change over time, so does their love.

DEVELOPMENTAL DIVERSITY
Gay and Lesbian Relationships: Men with Men and Women with Women

Most research conducted by developmental psychologists has examined heterosexual relationships, but an increasing number of studies have looked at relationships involving gay men and those involving lesbian women. The findings suggest that gay relationships are quite similar to relationships between heterosexuals.

For example, gay men describe successful relationships in ways that are similar to heterosexual couples' descriptions. They believe that successful relationships involve greater appreciation for the partner and the couple as a whole, less conflict, and more positive feelings toward the partner. Similarly, lesbian women in a relationship show high levels of attachment, caring, intimacy, affection, and respect (Brehm, 1992; Beals, Impett, & Peplau, 2002; Kurdek, 2006).

Furthermore, the age preferences expressed in the marriage gradient for heterosexuals also extend to partner preferences for homosexual men. Like heterosexual men, homosexual men prefer partners who are the same age or younger. On the other hand, lesbians' age preferences fall somewhere between those of heterosexual women and heterosexual men (Kenrick et al., 1995; Ni Bhrolcháin, 2006; Tadinac & Hromatko, 2007).

Finally, despite the stereotype that gay males, in particular, find it difficult to form relationships and are interested in only sexual alliances, the reality is different. Most gays and lesbians seek loving, long-term, and meaningful relationships that differ little qualitatively from those desired by heterosexuals (Division 44, 2000; Diamond, 2003; Diamond & Savin-Williams, 2003).

There are virtually no scientific data regarding gay and lesbian marriage, which became a major social issue when the first legal homosexual marriages were conducted in the United States in 2004. It is clear that the question produces strong reactions, but more, it turns out, among older adults than younger ones. Although only 18 percent of those older than 65 support the legalization of gay marriage, a clear majority—61 percent—of people younger than 30 support the practice (Deakin, 2004).

Choosing a Partner: Recognizing Mr. or Ms. Right

For many young adults, the search for a partner is a major pursuit during early adulthood. Certainly society offers a great deal of advice on how to succeed in this endeavor, as a glance at the array of magazines at any supermarket check-out counter confirms. Despite all the counsel, however, the road to identifying an individual to share one's life is not always easy.

Seeking a Spouse: Is Love the Only Thing That Matters? Most people have no hesitation in stating that the major factor in choosing a husband or wife is love—most people in the United States, that is. If we ask people in other societies, love becomes a secondary consideration. For instance, consider the results of a survey in which college students were asked if they would marry someone they did not love. Hardly anyone in the United States, Japan, or Brazil would consider it. On the other hand, a goodly proportion of college students in Pakistan and India would find it acceptable to marry without love (Levine, 1993; Madathil & Benshoff, 2008).

If love is not the only important factor, what else matters? The characteristics differ considerably from one culture to another (see Table 12.3). For instance, a survey of nearly 10,000 people from around the world found that although people in the United States believed that love and mutual attraction were the primary characteristics, in China men ranked good health most important and women rated emotional stability and maturity most critical. In contrast, in South Africa men from a Zulu background rated emotional stability first, and Zulu women rated dependable character of greatest concern (Buss et al., 1990; Buss, 2003).

At the same time, there are commonalities across cultures. For instance, love and mutual attraction, even if not at the top of a specific culture's list, were relatively highly desired across all cultures. Furthermore, traits such as dependability, emotional stability, pleasing disposition, and intelligence were highly valued almost universally.

Certain gender differences in the preferred characteristics of a mate were similar across cultures—findings that have been confirmed by other surveys (e.g., Sprecher, Sullivan, & Hatfield, 1994; Buss, 2004; Schmitt, 2004). Men, more than women, prefer a potential marriage partner

What traits are valued in matters of the heart? There are both commonalities and differences across cultures in what are seen as important traits. In China, men see good health as an important consideration; Chinese women value emotional stability and maturity.

	CHINA		SOUTH AFRICA (ZULU)		UNITED STATES	
	Males	Females	Males	Females	Males	Females
Mutual attraction—love	4	8	10	5	1	1
Emotional stability and maturity	5	1	1	2	2	2
Dependable character	6	7	3	1	3	3
Pleasing disposition	13	16	4	3	4	4
Education and intelligence	8	4	6	6	5	5
Good health	1	3	5	4	6	9
Sociability	12	9	11	8	8	8
Desire for home and children	2	2	9	9	9	7
Refinement, neatness	7	10	7	10	10	12
Ambition and industriousness	10	5	8	7	11	6
Good looks	11	15	14	16	7	13
Similar education	15	12	12	12	12	10
Good financial prospects	16	14	18	13	16	11
Good cook and housekeeper	9	11	2	15	13	16
Favorable social status or rating	14	13	17	14	14	14
Similar religious background	18	18	16	11	15	15
Chastity (no prior sexual intercourse)	3	6	13	18	17	18
Similar political background	17	17	15	17	18	17

TABLE 12.3 Most Desired Characteristics in a Marriage Partner

Note: Numbers indicate rank ordering of characteristics.
Source: Buss et al., 1990.

During early adulthood the search for a partner is a major pursuit, although the road to finding an individual to share one's life is not always easy.

who is physically attractive. In contrast, women, more than men, prefer a potential spouse who is ambitious and industrious.

One explanation for cross-cultural similarities in gender differences rests on evolutionary factors. According to psychologist David Buss and colleagues (Buss, 2004), human beings, as a species, seek out certain characteristics in their mates that are likely to maximize the availability of beneficial genes. He argues that males in particular are genetically programmed to seek out mates with traits that indicate they have high reproductive capacity. Consequently, physically attractive, younger women might be more desirable since they are more capable of having children over a longer time period.

In contrast, women are genetically programmed to seek out men who have the potential to provide scarce resources in order to increase the likelihood that their offspring will survive. Consequently, they are attracted to mates who offer the highest potential of providing economic well-being (Walter, 1997; Kasser & Sharma, 1999; Li et al., 2002).

The evolutionary explanation for gender differences has come under heavy fire from critics. First, there is the problem that the explanation is untestable. Furthermore, the similarities across cultures relating to different gender preferences may simply reflect similar patterns of gender stereotyping that have nothing to do with evolution. In addition, although some of the gender differences in what men and women prefer are consistent across cultures, there are numerous inconsistencies as well.

FIGURE 12.6 Filtering Potential Marriage Partners
According to one approach, we screen potential mates through successively finer-grained filters in order to settle on an appropriate spouse.
Source: Adapted from Janda & Klenke-Hamel, 1980.

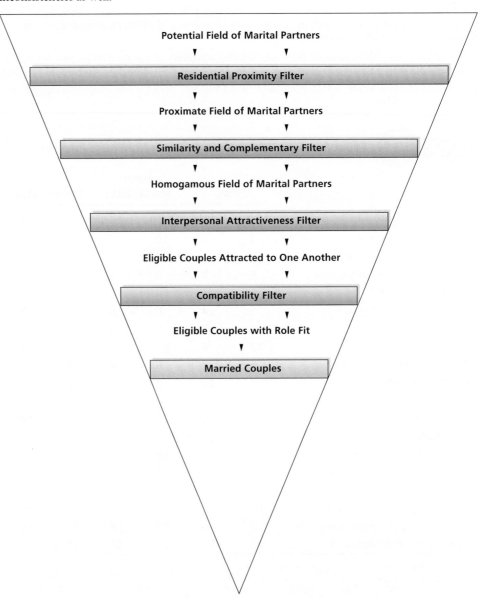

Potential Field of Marital Partners

Residential Proximity Filter

Proximate Field of Marital Partners

Similarity and Complementary Filter

Homogamous Field of Marital Partners

Interpersonal Attractiveness Filter

Eligible Couples Attracted to One Another

Compatibility Filter

Eligible Couples with Role Fit

Married Couples

Finally, some critics of the evolutionary approach suggest that finding that women prefer a partner who has good earning potential may have nothing to do with evolution and everything to do with the fact that men generally hold more power, status, and other resources fairly consistently across different cultures. Consequently, it is a rational choice for women to prefer a high-earning-potential spouse. On the other hand, because men don't need to take economic considerations into account, they can use more inconsequential criteria—like physical attractiveness—in choosing a spouse. In short, the consistencies that are found across cultures may be due to the realities of economic life that are similar throughout different cultures (Eagly & Wood, 2003).

homogamy   the tendency to marry someone who is similar in age, race, education, religion, and other basic demographic characteristics.

marriage gradient   the tendency for men to marry women who are slightly younger, smaller, and lower in status, and women to marry men who are slightly older, larger, and higher in status.

Filtering Models: Sifting Out a Spouse.   While surveys assist in identifying the characteristics that are highly valued in a potential spouse, they are less helpful in determining how a specific individual is chosen as a partner. One approach that helps explain this is the filtering model developed by psychologists Louis Janda and Karen Klenke-Hamel (1980). They suggest that people seeking a mate screen potential candidates through successively finer-grained filters, just as we sift flour in order to remove undesirable material (see Figure 12.6 on page 358).

The model assumes that people first filter for factors relating to broad determinants of attractiveness. Once these early screens have done their work, more sophisticated types of screening are used. The end result is a choice based on compatibility between the two individuals.

What determines compatibility? It is not only a matter of pleasing personality characteristics; several cultural factors also play an important role. For instance, people often marry according to the principle of homogamy. **Homogamy** is the tendency to marry someone who is similar in age, race, education, religion, and other basic demographic characteristics. Homogamy has traditionally been the dominant standard for most marriages in the United States.

The importance of homogamy is declining, however, particularly among certain ethnic groups. For example, the rate of intermarriage among African American men increased by three-quarters in the 1990s. Still, for other groups—such as Hispanic and Asian immigrants—the principle of homogamy still has considerable influence (also see Figure 12.7; Suro, 1999; Qian & Lichter, 2007).

The marriage gradient represents another societal standard that determines who marries whom. The **marriage gradient** is the tendency for men to marry women who are slightly younger, smaller, and lower in status, and women to marry men who are slightly older, larger, and higher in status (Bernard, 1982; Geary, 2006).

The marriage gradient, which has a powerful influence on marriage in the United States, has important, and unfortunate, effects on partner choice. For one thing, it limits the number of potential mates for women, especially as they age, while allowing men a wider choice of partners as their age increases. Furthermore, some men do not marry because they cannot find women of low enough status to meet the demands of the gradient, or cannot find women of the same or higher status who are willing to accept them as mates. Consequently, they are, in the words of sociologist Jessie Bernard (1982), "bottom of the barrel" men. On the other hand, some women will be unable to marry because they are higher in status or seek someone of higher status than anyone in the available pool of men—"cream of the crop" women, in Bernard's words.

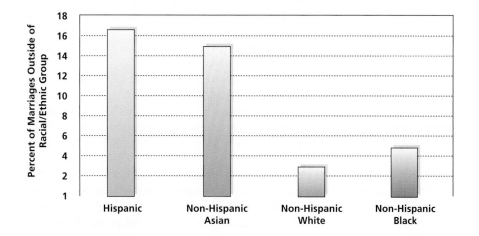

FIGURE 12.7 Marriage Outside of Racial/Ethnic Group
Although homogamy has been the standard for most marriages in the United States, the rate of marriages crossing ethnic and racial lines is substantial.
Source: Based on data from William H. Grey, Milken Institute, reported in *American Demographics*, November 1999.

POSSLQs, or persons of the opposite sex sharing living quarters, now make up about 10 percent of all couples in the United States—almost 7.5 million people.

The marriage gradient makes finding a spouse particularly difficult for well-educated African American women. Fewer African American men attend college than African American women, making the potential pool of men who are suitable—as defined by society and the marriage gradient—relatively small. Consequently, relative to women of other races, African American women are more apt to marry men who are less educated than they are—or not marry at all (Tucker & Mitchell-Kernan, 1995; Kiecolt & Fossett, 1997; Willie & Reddick, 2003).

Attachment Styles and Romantic Relationships: Do Adult Loving Styles Reflect Attachment in Infancy? "I want a girl just like the girl that married dear old Dad." So go the lyrics of an old song, suggesting that the songwriter would like to find someone who loves him as much as his mother did. Is this just a corny tune, or is there a kernel of truth in this sentiment? Put more broadly, is the kind of attachment that people experience during infancy reflected in their adult romantic relationships?

Increasing evidence suggests that it very well may be. As you may recall, attachment refers to the positive emotional bond that develops between a child and a particular individual (see Chapter 6). Most infants fall into one of three attachment categories: securely attached children, who have healthy, positive, trusting relationships with their caregivers; avoidant infants, who are relatively indifferent to caregivers and who avoid interactions with them; and ambivalent infants, who show great distress when separated from a caregiver, but who appear angry upon the caregiver's return.

According to psychologist Phillip Shaver and his colleagues, attachment styles continue into adulthood and affect the nature of romantic relationships (Tracy, Shaver, & Albino, 2003; Davis et al., 2006; Mikulincer & Shaver, 2007). For instance, consider the following statements:

1. I find it relatively easy to get close to others and am comfortable depending on them and having them depend on me. I don't often worry about being abandoned or about someone getting too close to me.

2. I am somewhat uncomfortable being close to others; I find it difficult to trust them completely, difficult to allow myself to depend on them. I am nervous when anyone gets too close, and often love partners want me to be more intimate than I feel comfortable being.

3. I find that others are reluctant to get as close as I would like. I often worry that my partner doesn't really love me or won't want to stay with me. I want to merge completely with another person, and this desire sometimes scares people away (Shaver, Hazan, & Bradshaw, 1988).

According to Shaver's research, agreement with the first statement reflects a secure attachment style. Adults who agree with this statement readily enter into relationships and feel happy and confident about the future success of their relationships. Most young adults—just over half—display the secure style of attachment (Hazan & Shaver, 1987).

In contrast, adults who agree with the second statement typically display the avoidant attachment style. These individuals, who make up about a quarter of the population, tend to be less invested in relationships, have higher break-up rates, and often feel lonely.

Finally, agreement with the third category is reflective of an ambivalent style. Adults with an ambivalent style have a tendency to become overly invested in relationships, have repeated breakups with the same partner, and have relatively low self-esteem. Around 20 percent of adults, gay and straight, fall into this category (Simpson, 1990).

Attachment style is also related to the nature of care that adults give to their romantic partners when they need assistance. For instance, secure adults tend to provide more sensitive and supportive care, being responsive to their partner's psychological needs. In comparison, anxious adults are more likely to provide compulsive, intrusive (and ultimately less helpful) aid to partners (Shaver, 1994; Feeney & Collins, 2001, 2003; Gleason, Iida, & Bolger, 2003).

It seems clear that there are continuities between infants' attachment styles and their behavior as adults. People who are having difficulty in relationships might well look back to their infancy to identify the root of their problem (Brennan & Shaver, 1995; Rholes et al., 2007). Insight into the roots of our current behavior can sometimes help us learn more adaptive skills as adults.

cohabitation couples living together without being married.

The Course of Relationships

Relationships, like the individuals who make them up, face a variety of challenges. As men and women move through early adulthood, they encounter significant changes in their lives as they work at starting and building their careers, having children, and establishing, maintaining, and sometimes ending relationships with others. One of the primary questions young adults face is whether and when to marry.

Marriage, POSSLQ, and Other Relationship Choices: Sorting out the Options of Early Adulthood.

For some people, the primary issue is not identifying a potential spouse, but whether to marry at all. Although surveys show that most heterosexuals (and a growing number of homosexuals) say they want to get married, a significant number choose some other route. For instance, the past three decades have seen both a decline in the number of married couples and a significant rise in couples living together without being married, a status known as **cohabitation** (see Figure 12.8). These people, whom the Census Bureau calls *POSSLQs, or Persons of the Opposite Sex Sharing Living Quarters*, now represent around 10 percent of all couples in the United States. In fact, married couples make up a minority of households: As of 2005, 49.7 percent of all U.S. households contained a married couple (Fields & Casper, 2001; Doyle, 2004; Roberts, 2006).

POSSLQs tend to be young: Almost a quarter of cohabiting women and over 15 percent of cohabiting men are under 25. Although most are white, African Americans are more likely to cohabit than whites. Other countries have even higher cohabitation rates, such as Sweden, where cohabitation is the norm. In Latin America, cohabitation has a long history and is widespread (Tucker & Mitchell-Kernan, 1995; Ferguson, 2007).

Why do some couples choose to cohabit rather than to marry? Some feel they are not ready to make a lifelong commitment. Others feel that cohabitation provides "practice" for marriage. Some reject the institution of marriage altogether, maintaining that marriage is outmoded and that it is unrealistic to expect a couple to spend a lifetime together (Hobart & Grigel, 1992; Cunningham & Antill, 1994; Martin, Martin, & Martin, 2001).

Those who feel that cohabiting increases their subsequent chances of a happy marriage are incorrect. On the contrary, the chances of divorce are somewhat higher for those who have previously cohabited, according to data collected in both the United States and Western Europe (Brown, 2003; Doyle, 2004; Hohmann, 2006; Rhoades, Stanley, & Markman, 2006).

Despite the prevalence of cohabitation, marriage remains the preferred alternative for most people during early adulthood. Many see marriage as the appropriate culmination of a loving relationship, while others feel it is the "right" thing to do after reaching a particular age in early adulthood. Others seek marriage because of the various roles that a spouse can fill. For instance, a spouse can play an economic role, providing security and financial well-being. Spouses also fill a sexual role, offering a means of sexual gratification and fulfillment that is fully accepted by society. Another role is therapeutic and recreational: Spouses provide a sounding board to discuss one another's problems and act as partners for activities. Marriage also offers the only means of having children that is fully accepted by all segments of society. Finally, marriage offers legal benefits and protections, such as eligibility for medical insurance under a spouse's policy and eligibility for survivor benefits like Social Security benefits (Waite, 1995; Furstenberg, 1996; DeVita, 1996; Doherty, Carroll, & Waite, 2007).

Although marriage remains important, it is not a static institution. For example, fewer U.S. citizens are now married than at any time since the late 1890s. Part of this decline in marriage is attributable to higher divorce rates (as we discussed in Chapter 10), but the decision of people to marry later in life is also a contributing factor. The median age of first marriage in the United States is now 27 for men and 25 for women—the oldest age for women since national statistics were first collected in the 1880s (see Figure 12.9; Furstenberg, 1996; U.S. Census Bureau, 2001).

In many European countries, legal alternatives to marriage are growing. For instance, France offers "Civil Solidarity Pacts," in which couples receive many of the same legal rights as

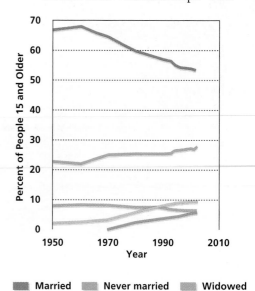

Married   **Never married**   **Widowed**

Divorced   **Cohabiting**

FIGURE 12.8 POSSLQs
The number of POSSLQs, or persons of the opposite sex sharing living quarters, has risen considerably in the last three decades. Why do you think this is the case?
Source: U.S. Bureau of the Census, 2001.

mydevelopmentlab
There are different types of marriage. Log onto **MyDevelopmentLab** to watch videos of Rati and Subaz, who are in an arranged marriage, and Scherazade and Rod who are in a typical love marriage.

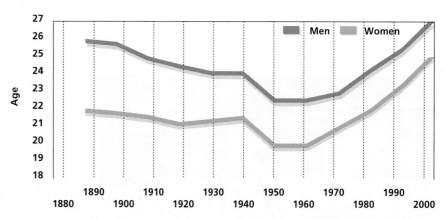

FIGURE 12.9 Postponing Marriage
The age at which women and men first marry is the highest since national statistics were first collected in the late 1800s. What factors account for this?
Source: U.S. Bureau of the Census, 2001.

married couples. What differs is that there is no legal lifetime commitment that they would be asked to make if they married; Civil Solidarity Pacts can be dissolved more easily than marriages (Lyall, 2004).

Does this mean that marriage is losing its viability as a social institution? Probably not. Most people—some 90 percent—eventually do marry, and national polls find that almost everyone endorses the notion that a good family life is important. Almost nine out of ten 18- to 29-year-olds believe that a happy marriage is an ingredient of a good life (Roper Starch Worldwide, 1997).

Why are people getting married later in life? The delay in part reflects economic concerns and the commitment to establishing a career. Choosing and starting a career presents an increasingly difficult series of decisions for young adults, and some feel that until they get a foothold on a career path and begin to earn an adequate salary, marriage plans should be put on hold (Dreman, 1997; Hall, 2006).

Staying Single: I Want to Be Alone.   For some people, neither marriage nor cohabitation is the preferred option. To them, living alone represents a good path, consciously chosen, through life. *Singlehood*, living alone without an intimate partner, has increased significantly in the last several decades, encompassing around 20 percent of women and 30 percent of men. Almost 10 percent will probably spend their entire lives in singlehood (Gerber, 2002; U.S. Bureau of the Census, 2002).

People who choose not to marry or live with a partner give several reasons for their decision. One is that they view marriage negatively. Rather than seeing marriage in the idealized terms presented in the media of the 1950s (the families in *Leave It to Beaver* or *Ozzie and Harriet*, for instance), they focus more on high divorce rates and marital strife. Ultimately, they conclude that the risks of forming a lifetime union may be too high.

Others view marriage as too restrictive. These individuals place great value on personal change and growth, which would be impeded by the stable, long-term commitment implied by marriage. Finally, some people simply do not encounter anyone with whom they wish to spend the remainder of their lives. Instead, they value their independence, autonomy, and freedom (DePaulo, 2004, 2006; also see the accompanying *From Research to Practice* box).

Despite the advantages of singlehood, there are also drawbacks. Society often stigmatizes single individuals, particularly women, holding up marriage as the idealized norm. Furthermore, there can be a lack of companionship and sexual outlets, and singles may feel that their futures are less secure financially (Byrne, 2000; Baumbusch, 2004; Pudrovska, Schieman, & Carr, 2006).

**FROM A
SOCIAL WORKER'S
PERSPECTIVE**
Why do you think society has established such a powerful norm in favor of marriage? What effects might such a norm have on a person who prefers to remain single?

The Ups and Downs of Marriage

Fifty years ago, midlife was similar for most people. Men and women who had married during early adulthood were still married to one another. One hundred years ago, when life expectancy was much shorter than it is today, people in their 40s were most likely married—but necessarily not to the same persons they had first married. Spouses often died; people might be well into their second marriage by the time of middle age.

Today the story is different and, as we said earlier, more varied. More people are single during middle adulthood, having never married. Single people may live alone or with a partner. Gay and lesbian adults, for example, may have committed relationships even though marriage is typically not an option for them. Among heterosexuals, some have divorced, lived alone, and then remarried. During middle adulthood, many people's marriages end in divorce, and many families "blend" together into new households, containing children and stepchildren from previous marriages. Other couples still spend between 40 and 50 years together, the bulk of those years during middle adulthood. Many people experience the peak of marital satisfaction during middle age.

Successful marriage involves companionship and mutual enjoyment of various activities.

What Makes Marriage Work?   Partners in successful marriages display several characteristics. They visibly show affection to one another and communicate relatively little negativity. Happily married couples

FROM RESEARCH TO PRACTICE
A Majority of American Women Are Living Without a Spouse

Besse Gardner, 24, says that she and her boyfriend met as college freshmen and started living together last April "for all the wrong reasons"—they found a great apartment on the beach in Los Angeles.

"We do not see living together as an end or even for the rest of our lives—it's just fun right now," Ms. Gardner says. "My roommate is someone I'd be thrilled to marry one day, but it just doesn't make sense right now." (Roberts, 2007, p. A1)

Besse Gardner's attitude toward marriage seems to be a growing trend among women, who are remaining unmarried for increasing stretches of their lives. A *New York Times* analysis of U.S. Census data from 2005 revealed that, for the first time, a majority of women are living without a spouse in the United States. Of 117 million women over the age of 15, 63 million are married. But more than 5 million of those married women are either legally separated or are living apart from their husbands for various reasons, leaving a minority of adult American women (49%) who are living with a spouse (Roberts, 2007).

The marriage rate for American women varies by ethnicity, ranging from a low of about 30 percent for African American women to a high of more than 60 percent for Asian women. Hispanic women (49 percent) and white women (55 percent) fall in the middle.

The census data reveal multiple factors contributing to the declining tendency for American women to marry. One reason is that women are remaining single for longer periods after a marriage ends. Women tend to outlive men, leaving many to carry on as widows. Women also remain unmarried for a longer period after a divorce than do men—and living together instead of remarrying after a divorce is becoming more common among both men and women.

But the other side of the story is that women are putting off marriage for longer periods, choosing to remain single or to just live together with their romantic partners. While 42 percent of women aged 15 to 24 were married in 1950, just 16 percent in that age bracket marry today. And even among 25- to 34-year-old women, the marriage rate has dropped markedly from 82 to 58 percent over that same time period. Experts note that women have more options today than they did 50 years ago, including careers and cohabitation. The need for the emotional and financial support of marriage is dwindling, and women seem to be approaching the commitment of marriage more cautiously. As one expert noted, "Most girls growing up today can look forward to spending more of their lives outside of a traditional marriage" (Roberts, 2007, p. A1).

- *What social changes from the 1950s to today may have contributed to the declining marriage rate among young women?*
- *Why do you think that women are less inclined to remarry after a divorce than men are?*

---

tend to perceive themselves as part of an interdependent couple rather than as one of two independent individuals. They also experience social homogamy, a similarity in leisure activity and role preferences. They hold similar interests, and they agree on a distribution of roles—such as who takes out the garbage and who takes care of the children (Gottman, Fainsilber-Katz, & Hooven, 1996; Carrere et al., 2000; Huston et al., 2001; Stutzer & Frey, 2006).

However, our awareness of the characteristics displayed by husbands and wives in successful marriages has not helped prevent what can only be called an epidemic of divorce. The statistics on divorce are grim: Only about half of all marriages in the United States remain intact. Over a million marriages end in divorce each year, and there are 4.2 divorces for every 1,000 individuals. This figure actually represents a decline from the peak in the mid-1970s of 5.3 divorces per 1,000 people, and most experts think that the rate is leveling off (National Center for Health Statistics, 2001).

As we'll see next, divorce is a problem that has its roots in early adulthood and the early years of marriage. In fact, most divorces occur during the first 10 years of marriage.

Early Marital Conflict. Conflict in marriage is not unusual. According to some statistics, nearly half of newly married couples experience a significant degree of conflict. One of the major reasons is that partners may initially idealize one another, perceiving each other through the proverbial "starry eyes." However, as the realities of day-to-day living together and interacting begin to sink in, they become more aware of flaws. In fact, perceptions of marital quality over the first 10 years of marriage on the part of both wives and husbands show a decline in the early years, followed by a period of stabilization, and then additional decline (see Figure 12.10 on page 264; Kurdek, 1999, 2002, 2003; Huston et al., 2001; Karney & Bradbury, 2005).

There are many sources of marital conflict. Husbands and wives may have difficulty making the transition from being children of their parents to autonomous adults. Others have difficulty developing an identity apart from their spouses, while some struggle to find a satisfactory

FIGURE 12.10

Perceptions of Marital Quality
At the beginning of marriage, partners see each other in a more idealized manner. But as time passes, the perception of the quality of the marriage declines.
Source: Kurdek, 1999.

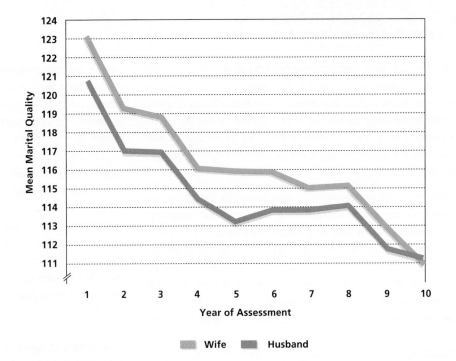

allocation of time to share with the spouse, compared with time spent with friends and other family members (Crawford, Houts, & Huston, 2002; Murray et al., 2003; Murray et al., 2006).

Most married couples, however, view the early years of marriage as deeply satisfying. For them, marriage can be a kind of extension of courtship. As they negotiate changes in their relationship and learn more about each other, many couples find themselves more deeply in love than before marriage. The newlywed period is for many couples one of the happiest of their entire married lives (Bird & Melville, 1994; Orbuch et al., 1996; McNulty & Karney, 2004).

The Course of Marital Satisfaction. Even for happily married couples, marriage has its ups and downs, with satisfaction rising and falling over the course of the marriage. In the past, most research has suggested that marital satisfaction follows the **U**-shaped configuration shown in Figure 12.11 (Figley, 1973). Specifically, marital satisfaction begins to decline just after the marriage, and it continues to fall until it reaches its lowest point following the births of the couple's children. However, at that point, satisfaction begins to grow, eventually returning to the same level that it held before the marriage (Karney & Bradbury, 1995; Noller, Feeney, & Ward, 1997; Harvey & Weber, 2002).

On the other hand, newer research is calling the U-shaped pattern into question. Several recent studies, using more sophisticated research designs, suggest that the upturn in satisfaction that occurs later in life may be illusory and that marital satisfaction continues to decline across the life span. These recent studies have employed longitudinal research, in which the marital satisfaction of the same couples is tracked over substantial time periods, and the results of these studies are painting a somewhat different picture (VanLaningham, Johnson, & Amato, 2001; Umberson et al., 2005).

One longitudinal study assessed changes in marriage quality over a period of 8 years, and another did the same over 17 years. Both studies confirmed earlier findings that marital satisfaction declines in the years just after marriage, but both also failed to find evidence of a subsequent upswing after the childbearing years. Rather, when assessed over time, marriage quality seems to continue to decline over the course of a marriage (or at best to reach a low point and level out) (Umberson et al., 2005).

It is too early to reject the U-shaped view of marital satisfaction, and it may be that individual differences in marriages account for the discrepancy in findings. What is clear is that middle-aged couples cite several sources of marital satisfaction. For instance, both men and women typically state that their spouse is "their best friend" and that they like their spouses as people. They also view marriage as a long-term commitment and agree on their aims and goals. Finally, most also feel that their spouses have grown more interesting over the course of the marriage (Levenson, Carstensen, & Gottman, 1993).

Divorce. Although the overall divorce rate has declined in the last two decades, divorce among couples during midlife is actually rising. One woman in eight who is in her first marriage will get divorced after the age of 40 (Uhlenberg, Cooney, & Boyd, 1990; Stewart et al., 1997; Enright, 2004).

Why do marriages unravel? There are many causes. One is that people in middle adulthood spend less time together than in earlier years. In individualistic Western cultures, people feel concerned with their own personal happiness. If their marriage is not satisfying, they feel that divorce may be the answer to increasing their happiness. Divorce is also more socially acceptable than in the past, and there are fewer legal impediments to divorces. In some cases—but certainly not all—the financial costs are not high. Furthermore, as the opportunities for women grow, wives may feel less dependent on their husbands, both from an emotional and an economic standpoint (Wallerstein, Lewis, & Blakeslee, 2000; Amato & Previti, 2003; Fincham, 2003).

Another reason for divorce is that, as we discussed earlier, feelings of romantic, passionate love may subside over time. Because Western culture emphasizes the importance of romance and passion, members of marriages in which passion has declined may feel that that is a sufficient reason to divorce. Finally, there is a great deal of stress in households in which both parents work, and this stress puts a strain on marriages. Much of the energy directed toward families and maintaining relationships in the past is now directed toward work and other institutions outside the home (Macionis, 2001).

Whatever the causes, divorce can be especially difficult for men and women in midlife. It can be particularly hard for women who have followed the traditional female role of staying with their children and never performing substantial work outside the home. They may face prejudice against older workers, finding that they are less likely to be hired than younger people, even in jobs with minimal requirements. Without a good deal of training and support, these divorced women, lacking recognized job skills, may remain virtually unemployable (Stewart et al., 1997; McDaniel & Coleman, 2003; Williams & Dunne-Bryant, 2006).

On the other hand, many people who divorce in midlife end up happy with the decision. Women, in particular, are apt to find that developing a new, independent self-identity is a positive outcome. Furthermore, both men and women who divorce during midlife are likely to enter new relationships, and—as we will see—they typically remarry (Enright, 2004).

Remarriage. Many of the people who divorce—some 75 to 80 percent—end up marrying again, usually within 2 to 5 years. They are most likely to marry people who have also been divorced, partly because divorced people tend to be the ones in the available pool, but also because those who have gone through divorce share similar experiences (DeWitt, 1992; de Jong Gierveld, 2004).

Although the overall rate of remarriage is high, it is far higher in some groups than in others. For instance, it is harder for women to remarry than men, particularly older women. Whereas 90 percent of women under the age of 25 remarry after divorce, less than one-third of women over the age of 40 remarry (Bumpass, Sweet, & Martin, 1990; Besharov & West, 2002).

The reason for this age difference stems from the *marriage gradient* that we discussed earlier in this module: Societal norms push men to marry women who are younger, shorter, and lower in status than themselves. As a consequence, the older a woman is, the fewer the socially acceptable men she has available to her since those men her age are likely to be looking for younger women. In addition, women have the disadvantage of societal double standards regarding physical attractiveness. Older women tend to be perceived as unattractive, while older men tend to be seen as "distinguished" and "mature" (Bernard, 1982; Buss, 2003; Doyle, 2004).

There are several reasons divorced people may find getting married again more appealing than remaining single. One motivation to remarry is to avoid the social consequences of divorce. Even in the twenty-first century, when the breakup of marriages is common, divorce carries with it a certain stigma that people may attempt to overcome by remarrying. In addition, divorced people overall report lower levels of satisfaction with life than married people (Lucas, 2005).

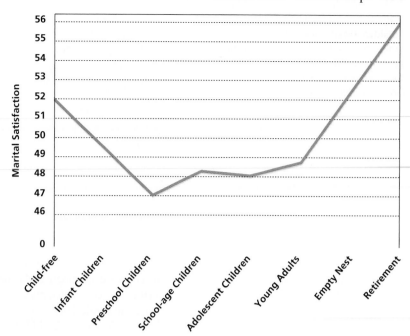

FIGURE 12.11

The Phases of Marital Satisfaction
For many couples, marital satisfaction falls and rises in a U-shaped configuration. It begins to decline after the birth of children but increases when the youngest child leaves home and eventually returns to a level of satisfaction similar to that at the start of marriage. Why do you think this pattern of satisfaction occurs?
Source: Adapted from Rollins & Cannon, 1974.

Around three-quarters of people who divorce remarry again, usually within 2 to 5 years.

FIGURE 12.12 Living Patterns of Older Americans

What, if anything, do these patterns suggest about the relative health and adjustment of older men and women?
Source: Administration on Aging, 2006.

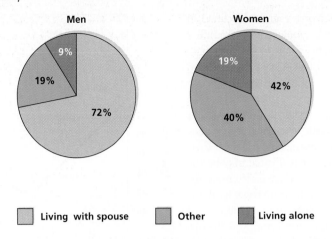

Men

Women

☐ Living with spouse ☐ Other ☐ Living alone

Divorced people miss the companionship that marriage provides. Divorced men in particular report feeling lonely and experience an increase in physical and mental health problems following divorce. Finally, marriage provides clear economic benefits, such as sharing the cost of a house and medical benefits reserved for spouses (Ross, Microwsky, & Goldsteen, 1991; Stewart et al., 1997; Thomas & Sawhill, 2005).

Second marriages are not the same as first marriages. Older couples tend to be more mature and realistic in their expectations of a partner and a marriage. They tend to look at marriage in less romantic terms than younger couples, and they are more cautious. They are also likely to show greater flexibility in terms of roles and duties; they share household chores more equitably and make decisions in a more participatory manner (Hetherington, 1999; Clarke, 2005; McCarthy & Ginsberg, 2007).

Unfortunately, though, this doesn't make second marriages more durable than first ones. In fact, the divorce rate for second marriages is slightly higher than for first marriages. Several factors explain this phenomenon. One is that second marriages may be subject to stresses that are not present in first marriages, such as the strain of blending different families. For another, having experienced and survived divorce before, partners in second marriages may be less committed to relationships and more ready to walk away from unsatisfactory ones. Finally, they may have personality and emotional characteristics that don't make them easy to live with (Cherlin, 1993; Warshak, 2000; Coleman, Ganong, & Weaver, 2001).

Despite the high divorce rate for second marriages, many people settle into remarriage quite successfully. In such cases, couples report as great a degree of satisfaction as those who were in successful first marriages (Bird & Melville, 1994; Michaels, 2006).

Marriage in the Later Years: Together, Then Alone. It's a man's world—at least when it comes to marriage after the age of 65. The proportion of men who are married at that age is far greater than that of women (see Figure 12.12). One reason for this disparity is that 70 percent of women outlive their husbands by at least a few years. Because there are fewer men available (many have died), these women are unlikely to remarry (Barer, 1994; Bourque et al., 2005).

Furthermore, the marriage gradient that we discussed earlier is still a powerful influence. Reflecting societal norms that suggest that women should marry men older than themselves, the marriage gradient works to keep women single even in the later years of life. At the same time, it makes remarriage for men much easier, since the available pool of eligible partners is much larger (Treas & Bengtson, 1987; AARP, 1990; Clements & Swenson, 2003).

The vast majority of people who are still married in later life report that they are satisfied with their marriages. Their partners provide substantial companionship and emotional support. Because at this period in life they have typically been together for a long time, they have great insight into their partners (Brubaker, 1991; Levenson, Cerstensen, & Gottman, 1993; Jose & Alfons, 2007).

At the same time, not every aspect of marriage is equally satisfying, and marriages may undergo severe stress as spouses experience changes in their lives. For instance, the retirement of one or both spouses can bring about a shift in the nature of a couple's relationship (Askham, 1994; Henry, Miller, & Giarrusso, 2005).

For some couples, the stress is so great that one spouse or the other seeks a divorce. Although the exact numbers are hard to come by, at least 2 percent of divorces in the United States involve women over the age of 60 (Uhlenberg, Cooney, & Boyd, 1990).

The reasons for divorce at such a late stage of life are varied. Often, women who divorce do so because their husbands are abusive or alcoholic. But in the more frequent case of a husband seeking a divorce from his wife, the reason is often that he has found a younger woman. Often the divorce occurs soon after retirement, when men who have been highly involved in their careers are in psychological turmoil (Cain, 1982; Solomon et al., 1998; Pudrovska et al., 2006).

Divorce so late in life is particularly difficult for women. Between the marriage gradient and the limited size of the potential pool of eligible men, it is unlikely that an older divorced woman will remarry. Divorce in late adulthood can be devastating. For many women, marriage has been their primary role and the center of their identities, and they may view divorce as a major failure. As a consequence, happiness and the quality of life for divorced women often plummet (Goldscheider, 1994; Davies & Denton, 2002).

Seeking a new relationship becomes a priority for many men and women who are divorced or whose spouses have died. As at earlier stages of life, people seeking to develop relationships use a variety of strategies to meet potential partners, such as joining singles organizations or even using the Internet to seek out companionship (Durbin, 2003).

Some people enter late adulthood having never married. For those who have remained single throughout their lives—about 5 percent of the population—late adulthood may bring fewer transitions, since the status of living alone does not change. Never-married individuals report feeling less lonely than do most people their age, and they have a greater sense of independence (Essex & Nam, 1987; Newston & Keith, 1997; Cwikel, Gramotney, & Lee, 2006).

REVIEW

▶ Dating in adolescence serves a number of functions including intimacy, entertainment, and prestige.

▶ The course of relationships typically follows a pattern of increasing interaction, intimacy, and redefinition.

▶ Types of love include passionate and companionate love. Sternberg's triangular theory identifies three basic components (intimacy, passion, and decision/commitment).

▶ According to filtering models, people apply increasingly fine filters to potential partners, eventually choosing a mate according to the principles of homogamy and the marriage gradient.

▶ In general, the values applied to relationships by heterosexual, gay, and lesbian couples are more similar than different.

▶ Cohabitation is an increasingly popular option for young adults, but most still choose marriage.

▶ Divorce is prevalent in the United States, particularly within the first 10 years of marriage.

▶ While marriages in older adulthood are generally happy, stresses due to aging can bring divorce.

APPLY

▶ In what ways do you think cognitive changes in early adulthood (e.g., the emergence of postformal thought and practical intelligence) affect how young adults deal with questions of marriage and divorce?

▶ Consider a long-term marriage with which you are familiar. Do you think the relationship involves passionate love or companionate love (or both)? What changes when a relationship moves from passionate to companionate love? From companionate to passionate love? In which direction is it more difficult for a relationship to move? Why?

Epilogue

In this chapter we examined the development of gender awareness, sexuality, and intimate relationships. We saw how preschoolers have a strong sense of being male or female, and of traditional gender roles and expectations. We discussed a range of theories that attempt to account for gender differences, including both biological and social theories. Then we considered the psychological aspects of sexual maturation in adolescence and also saw how sexual activity continues in healthy adults throughout the life span. Next, we focused on intimate relationships, beginning with the role dating plays in adolescents' lives and how love develops in young adulthood. We considered, too, the questions of whether or not to marry, and how people go about choosing a partner. In conclusion, we examined the ups and downs of marriage, and the course of marriage—and divorce—from early to late adulthood.

Turn back to the Prologue to this chapter and the late-in-life marriage of Geraldine Mooers and Dick Thomas, and answer the following questions.

1. How might choosing a marriage partner have been different for Geraldine and Dick in their 70s than it would have been 40 years earlier? What might they place greater value on now than then? What less?

2. Based on evidence in the Prologue of Geraldine and Dick's sexual activity, what might you deduce about their attitudes, health, and past relationships?

3. How does Geraldine and Dick's relationship fit the marriage gradient? How might age influence the importance—or lack of importance—of the marriage gradient in choosing a spouse?

4. Do you think gender identity plays an important role in Geraldine and Dick's relationship? Why or why not? Looking at couples you know—both young adults and older adults—do you think age affects how gender roles and expectations play out in a marriage? What effects does age have on these roles and expectations?

Looking Back

What differences are there between boys and girls in terms of behavior and treatment, and how does a sense of gender develop?

1. From the moment of birth, girls and boys are treated differently and are subject to different expectations. Mothers and fathers display different interaction patterns with their children, and the toy and play preferences of boys and girls differ and are differently encouraged by their parents. Furthermore, boys' and girls' actions are interpreted differently by parents and other adults.

2. Actual biologically based behavioral differences between boy and girl infants exist, but they are minor compared to the behavioral similarities between genders. However, as children age, gender differences become more pronounced, mostly because of environmental factors.

3. By the preschool years, gender is well established in terms of self-understanding and behavior. Preschoolers hold expectations about gender-appropriate behavior that are more rigid than at any other time during the life span, and they form ideas about the different careers that are appropriate for men and women.

4. The strong gender expectations held by preschoolers are explained in different ways by different theorists. Some point to genetic factors as evidence for a biological explanation of gender expectations. Freud's psychoanalytic theories use a framework based on the subconscious. Social learning theorists focus on environmental influences, including parents, teachers, peers, and the media, while cognitive theorists propose that children form gender schemas, cognitive frameworks that organize information that the children gather about gender.

How does sexuality develop in the adolescent years?

5. For most adolescents, masturbation is often the first step into sexuality. The age of first intercourse, which is now in the teens, has declined as the double standard has faded and the norm of permissiveness with affection has gained ground. However, as more and more adolescents have become aware of the threat of STDs and AIDS, the rate of sexual intercourse has declined.

Why are there different sexual orientations, and what determines one's orientation?

6. The most common sexual orientation among adolescents is heterosexuality, with a smaller number of adolescents having homosexual or bisexual orientations.

7. Homosexuality and heterosexuality, rather than being distinct sexual orientations, are regarded by some researchers as a continuum along which people experience their individual sexuality, which may change over time.

8. The factors that cause individuals to develop as heterosexual, homosexual, or bisexual are not completely understood, but genetic and biological factors play an important role, most likely in combination with physiological and environmental factors.

9. Gay and lesbian adolescents face challenges in a society that continues to be prejudiced against homosexuality, including the challenge of informing their parents of their orientation.

What are the functions and characteristics of dating during adolescence?

10. During adolescence, dating provides intimacy, entertainment, and prestige. Achieving psychological intimacy, difficult at first, becomes easier as adolescents mature, gain confidence, and take relationships more seriously.

How do young adults form loving relationships, and how does love change over time?

11. Young adults face Erikson's intimacy-versus-isolation stage, a period focused on developing close, intimate relationships with others.

12. According to stimulus-value-role theory, relationships pass through the consideration of surface characteristics, values, and finally the roles played by the participants.

13. Passionate love is characterized by intense physiological arousal, intimacy, and caring, while companionate love is characterized by respect, admiration, and affection.

14. Psychologist Robert Sternberg suggests that three components of love (intimacy, passion, and decision/commitment) combine to form eight types of love, through which a relationship can dynamically evolve.

How do people choose spouses, and what makes relationships work and cease working?

15. Although in Western cultures love tends to be the most important factor in selecting a partner, other cultures emphasize other factors.

16. According to filtering models, people filter potential partners initially for attractiveness and then for compatibility, generally conforming to the principle of homogamy and the marriage gradient.

17. Gays and lesbians generally seek the same qualities in relationships as heterosexual men and women: attachment, caring, intimacy, affection, and respect.

18. In young adulthood, while cohabitation is popular, marriage remains the most attractive option. The median age of first marriage is rising for both men and women.

19. Divorce is prevalent in the United States, affecting nearly half of all marriages.

What are typical patterns of marriage and divorce in middle adulthood?

20. Middle adulthood is, for most married couples, a time of satisfaction, but for many couples marital satisfaction declines steadily and divorce results.

21. Most people who divorce remarry, usually to another divorced person. Because of the marriage gradient, women over 40 find it harder to remarry than men.

22. People who marry for a second time tend to be more realistic and mature than people in first marriages, and to share roles and responsibilities more equitably. However, second marriages end in divorce even more often than first marriages.

How do marriages in late adulthood fare?

23. Marriages in later life generally remain happy, although stresses brought about by major life changes that accompany aging can cause rifts. Divorce is usually harder on the woman than the man, partly because of the continuing influence of the marriage gradient.

PEARSON mydevelopmentlab™

Find out by accessing MyVirtualChild at www.mydevelopmentlab.com and raising your own virtual child from birth to age 18.

13 Friends and Family

Prologue
Changing Relationships

Leah is dressed up and ready to go to the first real formal dance of her life. True, the smashing effect of her short beaded black dress is marred slightly by the man's shirt she insists on wearing to cover her bare shoulders. And she is in a sulk. Her boyfriend, Sean Moffitt, is four minutes late, and her mother, Linda, refuses to let her stay out all night at a coed sleepover party after the dance. . . . Leah's father, George, suggests a 2 a.m. curfew: Leah hoots incredulously. Sean pitches the all-nighter, stressing that the party will be chaperoned. Leah's mother has already talked to the host's mother, mortifying Leah with her off-hand comment that a coed sleepover seemed "weird." Rolling her eyes, Leah persists: "It's not like anybody's really going to sleep!"

(E. Graham, 1995, p. B1)

Social development is the way in which individuals' interactions with others and their social relationships grow, change, and remain stable over the course of life.

Leah's story illustrates how the social and emotional world of adolescents is considerably wider than that of younger children. As adolescents' relationships with people outside the home grow increasingly important, their interactions with their families evolve, taking on a new, and sometimes difficult, character. Lifestyles—values and modes of living—may become a bone of contention between adolescents and their parents.

In this chapter, we examine family and peer relationships throughout the life span. We begin by looking at the development of friendship and play in preschoolers and middle childhood, and then consider the importance of peers and peer groups in adolescence. We also consider the qualities people look for in friendships, and discuss the significance of the social support adult friendships offer, especially in later adulthood.

We then turn to a discussion of lifestyles, beginning with the rites of passage common to adolescents. Shifting our focus to the role work plays in determining lifestyle, we discuss how entering the workforce affects people, including the impact holding a job can have on school performance. Next, we consider the adequacy—or inadequacy—of job training secondary schools offer students. We also examine the shift in the balance between work and leisure activities that occurs in midlife. Finally, we look at the lifestyles of people in late adulthood—the paths they choose to pursue in retirement, the financial issues common to this age group, and their varied living arrangements.

The last part of the chapter explores the central societal institution in people's lives: the family. We begin with a look at the decision to have a child and the consequences of such a choice on a couple's relationship. We then consider the nature of family life and discuss how it differs from earlier eras. We look at divorce and consider a variety of family constellations. Finally, we look at the various familial ties that bind people together (or come unglued) during middle adulthood, and conclude by exploring the importance of family in late adulthood.

LOOKING AHEAD

After reading this chapter, you will be able to answer the following questions:

▶ In what sorts of social relationships and play do preschool children engage?

▶ How do gender and ethnicity affect friendships in middle childhood?

▶ What are gender, race, and ethnic relations like in adolescence?

▶ What does it mean to be popular and unpopular?

▶ How do adults choose the people who will become their friends?

▶ How does the arrival of children affect a relationship?

▶ How do today's diverse family and care arrangements affect children?

▶ What changing family situations do middle-aged adults face?

▶ What sorts of relationships are important in late adulthood?

▶ In what circumstances do older people live, and what difficulties do they face?

MODULE 13.1

Social Relationships Across the Life Span

When Juan was 3, he had his first best friend, Emilio. Juan and Emilio, who lived in the same apartment building in San Jose, were inseparable. They played incessantly with toy cars, racing them up and down the apartment hallways until some of the neighbors began to complain about the noise. They pretended to read to one another, and sometimes they slept over at each other's home—a big step for a 3-year-old. Neither boy seemed more joyful than when he was with his "best friend"—the term each used of the other.

In parallel play, children play with similar toys, in a similar manner, but don't necessarily interact with one another.

functional play play that involves simple, repetitive activities typical of 3-year-olds.

constructive play play in which children manipulate objects to produce or build something.

parallel play action in which children play with similar toys, in a similar manner, but do not interact with each other.

onlooker play action in which children simply watch others at play but do not actually participate themselves.

associative play play in which two or more children interact by sharing or borrowing toys or materials, although they do not do the same thing.

cooperative play play in which children genuinely interact with one another, taking turns, playing games, or devising contests.

Preschoolers' Friendships

An infant's family can provide nearly all the social contact he or she needs. As preschoolers, however, many children, like Juan and Emilio, begin to discover the joys of peer friendships.

Before age 3, most social activity involves simply being in the same place at the same time, without real social interaction. However, at around the age of 3, children begin to develop real friendships as peers are seen as individuals who hold special qualities and rewards. While preschoolers' relations with adults reflect children's needs for care, protection, and direction, their relations with peers are based more on the desire for companionship, play, and fun. Gradually they come to view friendship as a continuing state that offers not just immediate pleasure, but the promise of future activity (Harris, 1998, 2000; Hay, Payne, & Chadwick, 2004).

Interactions with friends change during the preschool period. For 3-year-olds, the focus of friendship is the enjoyment of doing things together and playing jointly. Older preschoolers pay more attention to trust, support, and shared interests. Throughout the entire period, however, play remains an important part of friendship (Johnson & Foster, 2005; Rotenberg, Boulton, & Fox, 2005).

Playing by the Rules: The Work of Play. In Rosie Graiff's class of 3-year-olds, Minnie bounces her doll's feet on the table as she sings softly to herself. Ben pushes his toy car across the floor, making motor noises. Sarah chases Abdul around and around the perimeter of the room.

Play is more than what children of preschool age do to pass the time. Instead, play helps preschoolers develop socially, cognitively, and physically (Roopnarine, 2002; Lindsey & Colwell, 2003; Blundon & Schaefer, 2006; Samuelsson & Johansson, 2006).

Categorizing Play. At the beginning of the preschool years, children engage in **functional play**—simple, repetitive activities typical of 3-year-olds, such as pushing cars on the floor, skipping, and jumping. Functional play involves doing something to be active rather than to create something (Rubin, Fein, & Vandenberg, 1983; Bober, Humphry, & Carswell, 2001; Kantrowitz & Evans, 2004).

By age 4, children become involved in a more sophisticated form of play. In **constructive play** children manipulate objects to produce or build something. A child who builds a house out of Legos or puts a puzzle together is involved in constructive play: He or she has an ultimate goal—to produce something. The creation need not be novel, since children may repeatedly build a house of blocks, let it fall, and then rebuild it.

Constructive play gives children a chance to practice their physical and cognitive skills and fine muscle movements. They gain experience in solving problems about the ways and the sequences in which things fit together. They also learn to cooperate with others as the social nature of play becomes more important to them (Power, 1999; Edwards, 2000; Shi, 2003).

The Social Aspects of Play. If two preschoolers sit side by side at a table, each assembling a different puzzle, are they engaged jointly in play?

According to pioneering work done by Mildred Parten (1932), the answer is "yes." She suggests that these preschoolers are engaged in **parallel play**, in which children play with similar toys, in a similar manner, but do not interact with each other. Preschoolers also engage in another form of play, a highly passive one: onlooker play. In **onlooker play,** children simply watch others at play, but do not actually participate themselves.

As they get older, however, preschool-age children engage in more sophisticated forms of social play that involve greater interaction. In **associative play** two or more children interact with one another by sharing or borrowing toys or materials, although they do not do the same thing. In **cooperative play**, children genuinely play with one another, taking turns, playing games, or devising contests.

Solitary and onlooker play continues in the later stages of the preschool period. There are simply times when children prefer to play by themselves. And when newcomers join a group, one strategy for becoming part of the group—often successful—is to engage in onlooker play, waiting for an opportunity to join the play more actively (Howes, Unger, & Seidner, 1989; Hughes, 1995; Lindsey & Colwell, 2003).

The nature of pretend, or make-believe, play also changes during the period, becoming in some ways more unrealistic—and imaginative—as preschoolers shift from using only realistic objects to using less concrete ones. Thus, at the start of the preschool period, children may pretend to listen to a radio only if they have a plastic radio on hand. Later, they may use an entirely different object, such as a large cardboard box, as a pretend radio (Bornstein et al., 1996; Japiassu, 2008).

Russian developmentalist Lev Vygotsky (1930/1978) argued that pretend play, particularly if it involves social play, is an important means for expanding preschooler's cognitive skills. Through make-believe play, children are able to "practice" activities (like pretending to use a computer or read a book) that are a part of their particular culture and broaden their understanding of the way the world functions.

One reason that children's play changes is the continuing development of preschoolers' theory of mind—their knowledge and beliefs about how the mind operates. Using their theory of mind, preschool children increasingly see the world from others' perspectives. Even children as young as 2 are able to understand that others have emotions. By age 3 or 4, preschoolers know that they can imagine something that is not physically present, such as a zebra, and that others can do the same. They can also pretend that something has happened and react as if it really had occurred, a skill that becomes part of their imaginative play (Cadinu & Kiesner, 2000; Mauritzson & Saeljoe, 2001; Andrews, Halford, & Bunch, 2003).

As preschool children get older their forms of social play become more sophisticated and show a higher level of interaction in terms of sharing, taking turns and playing games.

FROM AN
EDUCATOR'S
PERSPECTIVE

How might a preschool teacher encourage a shy child to join a group of preschoolers who are playing?

⊙ PEARSON mydevelopmentlab

To see all the types of play you have been reading about displayed in preschoolers, watch the clip "Parten's Play Categories" on **MyDevelopmentLab**.

Building Friendships in Middle Childhood

In Lunch Room Number Two, Jamillah and her new classmates chew slowly on sandwiches and sip quietly on straws from cartons of milk. . . . Boys and girls look timidly at the strange faces across the table from them, looking for someone who might play with them in the schoolyard, someone who might become a friend.

For these children, what happens in the schoolyard will be just as important as what happens in the school. And when they're out on the playground, there will be no one to protect them. No child will hold back to keep from beating them at a game, humiliating them in a test of skill, or harming them in a fight. No one will run interference or guarantee membership in a group. Out on the playground, it's sink or swim. No one automatically becomes your friend. (Kotre & Hall, 1990, pp. 112–113)

"We've done a lot of important playing here today."

Mutual trust is considered to be the centerpiece of friendship during middle childhood.

As Jamillah and her classmates demonstrate, friendship plays an increasingly important role in middle childhood. Building and maintaining friendships becomes a large part of social life and is a key developmental task for this age group.

Friends influence development in several ways. Friendships provide children with information about the world as well as themselves. Friends provide emotional support that allows children to respond more effectively to stress. Having friends makes a child a less likely target of aggression. It can teach them how to manage their emotions and help them interpret their own emotional experiences (Berndt, 2002). Friendships teach children how to communicate and interact with others. They also foster intellectual growth by increasing children's range of experiences (Harris, 1998; Nangle & Erdley, 2001; Gifford-Smith & Brownell, 2003).

Friends and other peers become increasingly influential at this stage, but parents and other family members remain significant. Most developmentalists believe that children's psychological functioning and their general development is the product of multiple factors, including peers and parents (Harris, 2000; Vandell, 2000; Parke, Simpkins, & McDowell, 2002).

Stages of Friendship: Changing Views of Friends. At this stage, a child's concept of friendship passes through three distinct stages, according to developmental psychologist William Damon (Damon & Hart, 1988).

Stage 1: Basing Friendship on Others' Behavior. In this stage, from around ages 4 to 7, children see friends as others who like them and with whom they share toys and other activities. They view the children they spend the most time with as their friends.

What children in this stage seldom do, however, is consider others' personal qualities as the basis of friendships. Instead, they use a concrete approach, primarily choosing friends for their behavior. They like those who share, shunning those who don't share, who hit, or who don't play with them. In the first stage, friends are viewed largely as presenting opportunities for pleasant interactions.

Stage 2: Basing Friendship on Trust. In the next stage, children's view of friendship becomes complicated. Lasting from around ages 8 to 10, this stage involves taking others' personal qualities and traits as well as the rewards they provide into consideration. But the centerpiece of friendship in this second stage is mutual trust. Friends are seen as those one can count on to help out when needed. Violations of trust are taken very seriously.

Stage 3: Basing Friendship on Psychological Closeness. The third stage of friendship begins toward the end of middle childhood, from ages 11 to 15, when children develop the view of friendship they will hold in adolescence. The main criteria for friendship shift toward intimacy and loyalty. Friendship becomes characterized by feelings of closeness, usually brought on by sharing personal thoughts and feelings. They are also somewhat exclusive. By the end of middle childhood, children seek friends who will be loyal, and they view friendship less in terms of shared activities than in terms of the psychological benefits it brings (Newcomb & Bagwell, 1995; Güroglu et al., 2007).

Gender and Friendships: The Sex Segregation of Middle Childhood.

Girls rule; boys drool.
Boys are idiots. Girls have cooties.
Boys go to college to get more knowledge; girls go to Jupiter to get more stupider.

Those are some of the views of elementary school boys and girls regarding members of the other sex. Avoidance of the other sex becomes quite pronounced at this age, with social networks often consisting almost entirely of same-sex groupings (Lewis & Phillipsen, 1998; McHale, Dariotis, & Kauh, 2003).

Interestingly, this segregation of friendships occurs in almost all societies. In nonindustrialized societies, same-gender segregation may result from the types of activities children engage in. For instance, in many cultures, boys are assigned one type of chore and girls another (Whiting & Edwards, 1988; Edwards et al., 2006). Participation in different activities may not wholly explain sex segregation, however: Children in more developed countries, who attend the same schools and participate in many of the same activities, still tend to avoid members of the other sex.

When boys and girls make occasional forays into the other gender's territory, the action often has romantic overtones. For instance, girls may threaten to kiss a boy, or boys might try to lure girls into chasing them. Such behavior, termed "border work," emphasizes the clear boundaries between the two sexes. In addition, it may pave the way for adolescent interactions that do involve romantic or sexual interests, when cross-sex interactions become socially endorsed (Beal, 1994; Thorne & Luria, 2003).

The lack of cross-gender interaction in middle childhood means that boys' and girls' friendships are restricted to their own sex. The nature of friendships within these two groups is quite different (Lansford & Parker, 1999; Rose, 2002).

Boys typically have larger networks of friends, and they tend to play in groups, rather than pairing off. Differences in status within the group are usually pronounced, with an acknowledged leader and a hierarchy of members. Because of the fairly rigid rankings that represent the relative social power of those in the group, known as the **dominance hierarchy**, members of higher status can safely question and oppose those lower in the hierarchy (Beal, 1994; Hawley, 2007).

Boys tend to be concerned with their place in the dominance hierarchy, and they attempt to maintain and improve their status. This makes for a style of play known as *restrictive*. In restrictive play, interactions are interrupted when a child feels his status is challenged. A boy who feels that he is unjustly challenged by a lower-status peer may attempt to end the interaction by scuffling over a toy or otherwise behaving assertively. Consequently, boys tend to play in bursts, rather than in more extended, tranquil episodes (Benenson & Apostoleris, 1993; Fry, 2005).

Friendship patterns among girls are quite different. Rather than a wide network of friends, girls focus on one or two "best friends." In contrast to boys, who seek out status differences, girls avoid differences, preferring to maintain equal-status friendships.

Conflicts among girls are usually solved through compromise, by ignoring the situation, or by giving in, rather than by seeking to make one's point of view prevail. The goal is to smooth over disagreements, making social interaction easy and nonconfrontational (Goodwin, 1990; Shute & Charlton, 2006).

Though same-sex groupings dominate middle childhood, when boys and girls do make occasional forays into each others' territory, there are often romantic overtones.

The Role of Peers in Adolescence

Teenagers' seemingly compulsive need to communicate with friends, exemplified by *Facebook* and cell phone texting, demonstrates the important role that **peers**—individuals who are about the same age or level of maturity—play in adolescence. Continuing the trend that began in middle childhood, adolescents spend increasing amounts of time with their peers, and the importance of peer relationships grows as well. There is probably no period of life in which peer relationships are as important as they are in adolescence. Even peers who are not counted as friends become extraordinarily influential in the lives of adolescents (Youniss & Haynie, 1992; Engels, Kerr, & Stattin, 2007).

Peers grow in importance in adolescence for a variety of reasons. Peers can help adolescents satisfy personal interests and can provide them with information that they feel they need for their own purposes. For instance, an interest in conservation may cause adolescents to become part of a group dedicated to stamping out pollution. Or they may join a high school Gay, Lesbian, and Bisexual Alliance not only because of their interest in supporting people with different sexual orientations, but because they themselves are questioning their sexual identity.

In addition, some groups provide prestige. Membership on a cheerleading squad or service on the School Council may be an honor in some middle schools. (In others, membership on a cheerleading squad or School Council may be a source of derision, with prestige reserved for other groups and activities.)

As we discussed earlier, peers also provide a means of social comparison, allowing teens to compare and evaluate their opinions, abilities, and even physical changes with those of others. Peers and peer groups also fill another very important need for this age group: the need to *belong*.

dominance hierarchy rankings that represent the relative social power of those in a group.

peers individuals who are about the same age or level of maturity.

The sex segregation of childhood continues during the early stages of adolescence. However, by the time of middle adolescence, this segregation decreases, and boys' and girls' cliques begin to converge.

Cliques and Crowds: Belonging to a Group. When adolescents get together, they are likely to do so in larger groups than those in which they congregated during childhood. During middle and late childhood, typical groups consisted of pairs of children, or perhaps three or four others. In contrast, adolescent groups often consist of larger collectives.

One of the consequences of the increasing cognitive sophistication of adolescents is the ability to group others in more discriminating ways. These groups are characterized by the clothing they wear, their activities, the places they frequent, and even the vocabulary they use. Even if they do not belong to the group that they use to compare themselves (*reference groups,* as we discussed earlier, present a set of *norms,* or standards, against which adolescents can judge their abilities and social success), adolescents typically are part of some identifiable group. Rather than defining people in concrete terms relating to what they do ("football players" or "musicians") as a younger school-age child might, adolescents use more abstract terms packed with greater subtleties ("jocks" or "skaters" or "stoners") (Brown, 1990; Montemayor, Adams, & Gulotta, 1994; Cillessen & Borch, 2008).

There are actually two types of groups to which adolescents tend to belong: cliques and crowds. **Cliques** are groups of 2 to 12 people whose members have frequent social interactions with one another. In contrast, **crowds** are larger, comprising individuals who share particular characteristics but who may not interact with one another. For instance, "jocks" and "nerds" are representative of crowds found in many high schools.

Membership in particular cliques and crowds is often determined by the degree of similarity with members of the group. One of the most important dimensions of similarity relates to substance use; adolescents tend to choose friends who use alcohol and other drugs to the same extent that they do. Their friends are also often similar in terms of their academic success, although this is not always true. For instance, during early adolescence, attraction to peers who are particularly well behaved seems to decrease while, at the same time, those who behave more aggressively become more attractive (Bukowski, Sippola, & Newcomb, 2000; Farmer, Estell, & Bishop, 2003; Kupersmidt & Dodge, 2004).

Membership in cliques is most obvious during the early years of adolescence. In later stages, the number of liaisons and isolates—those who are not members of a clique—actually increases. In addition, cliques eventually become less distinctive and rigid, and membership in cliques shows a fair amount of turnover. In the later stages of adolescence, cliques become less stable, and social interactions revolve around more flexible groups that are tied together by liaisons who move between members of different groups (Ennett & Bauman, 1996; Brown & Klute, 2006).

Gender Relations. As children enter adolescence from middle childhood, their groups of friends are composed almost universally of same-sex individuals. Boys hang out with boys; girls hang out with girls. Technically, this sex segregation is called the **sex cleavage**.

The situation changes as members of both sexes enter puberty. Boys and girls experience the hormonal surge that marks puberty and causes the maturation of the sex organs. At the same time, societal pressures suggest that the time is appropriate for romantic involvement. These developments lead to a change in the ways adolescents view the opposite sex. Where a 10-year-old is likely to see every member of the other sex as "annoying" and "a pain," heterosexual teenage boys and girls begin to regard each other with greater interest in terms of both personality and sexuality. (As we discussed in Chapter 12, for gays and lesbians, pairing off holds other complexities.)

As they move into puberty, boys' and girls' cliques, which previously had moved along parallel but separate tracks, begin to converge. Adolescents begin to attend boy–girl dances or parties, although mostly the boys still spend their time with boys, and the girls with girls (Richards et al., 1998).

A little later, however, adolescents increasingly spend time with members of the other sex. New cliques emerge, composed of both males and females. Not everyone participates initially: Early on, the teenagers who are leaders of the same-sex cliques and who have the highest status lead the way. Eventually, however, most adolescents find themselves in cliques that include boys and girls.

Cliques and crowds undergo yet another transformation at the end of adolescence: They become less influential and may dissolve as a result of the increased pairing off that occurs.

cliques (pronounced "kleeks") groups of 2 to 12 people whose members have frequent social interactions with one another.

crowds in contrast to cliques, crowds are larger and looser groups, comprising individuals who share particular characteristics but who may not interact with one another.

sex cleavage sex segregation in which boys interact primarily with boys and girls primarily with girls.

DEVELOPMENTAL DIVERSITY
Race Segregation: The Great Divide of Adolescence

When Philip McAdoo, a student at the University of North Carolina, stopped one day to see a friend who worked on his college campus, a receptionist asked if he would autograph a basketball for her son. Because he was African American and tall, "she just assumed that I was on the basketball team," recounted McAdoo.

Jasme Kelly, an African American sophomore at the same college, had a similar story to tell. When she went to see a friend at a fraternity house, the student who answered the door asked if she was there to apply for the job of cook.

White students, too, find racial relations difficult and in some ways forbidding. For instance, Jenny Johnson, a white 20-year-old junior, finds even the most basic conversation with African American classmates difficult. She describes a conversation in which African American friends "jump at my throat because I used the word 'black' instead of African American. There is just such a huge barrier that it's really hard. . . to have a normal discussion." (Sanoff & Minerbrook, 1993, p. 58)

The pattern of race segregation found at the University of North Carolina is repeated over and over in schools and colleges throughout the United States: Even when they attend desegregated schools with significant ethnic and racial diversity, people of different ethnicities and races interact very little. Moreover, even if they have a friend of a different ethnicity within the confines of a school, most adolescents don't interact with that friend outside of school (DuBois & Hirsch, 1990; Mouw & Entwisle, 2006).

It doesn't start out this way. During elementary school and even during early adolescence, there is a fair amount of integration among students of differing ethnicities. However, by middle and late adolescence, the amount of segregation is striking (Spencer, 1991; Ennett & Bauman, 1996; Mouw & Entwisle, 2006).

Why should racial and ethnic segregation be the rule, even in schools that have been desegregated for some time? One reason is that minority students may actively seek support from others who share their minority status (where "minority" is used in its sociological sense to indicate a subordinate group whose members lack power, compared to members of a dominant group). By associating primarily with other members of their own group, members of minority groups are able to affirm their own identity.

Members of different racial and ethnic groups may be segregated in the classroom as well. Adolescents who are members of groups that have been historically discriminated against tend to experience less school success than members of the majority group. It may be that ethnic and racial segregation in high school is based not on ethnicity itself, but on academic achievement.

If minority group members experience less academic success, they may find themselves in classes with proportionally fewer majority group members. Similarly, majority students may be in classes with few minority students. Such class assignment practices, then, may inadvertently maintain and promote racial and ethnic segregation. This pattern would be particularly prevalent in schools where rigid academic tracking is practiced, with students assigned to "low," "medium," and "high" tracks depending on their prior achievement (Lucas & Behrends, 2002).

The lack of contact among students of different racial and ethnic backgrounds in school may also reflect prejudice, both perceived and real, toward members of other groups. Students of color may feel that the white majority is prejudiced, discriminatory, and hostile, and they may prefer to stick to same-race groups. Conversely, white students may assume that minority group members are antagonistic and unfriendly. Such mutually destructive attitudes reduce the likelihood that meaningful interaction can take place (Phinney, Ferguson, & Tate, 1997; Tropp, 2003).

Is this sort of voluntary segregation along racial and ethnic lines found during adolescence inevitable? No. Adolescents who have interacted regularly and extensively with those of different races earlier in their lives are more likely to have friends of different races. Schools that actively

(continued)

Adolescents seek increasing autonomy, independence, and a sense of control over their lives.

promote contact among members of different ethnicities in classes help create an environment in which cross-race friendships can flourish (Hewstone, 2003).

Still, the task is daunting. Many societal pressures act to keep members of different races from interacting with one another. Peer pressure, too, may encourage this as some cliques may actively promote norms that discourage group members from crossing racial and ethnic lines to form new friendships.

Online Social Networks: Cyberspace Peers. Adolescents are increasingly involved in groups comprising people that they've never met in person, but with whom they are well acquainted—online. Cyberspace social networks are a growing aspect of adolescent social life, acting as virtual community centers where adolescents socialize, sometimes for hours at a time (Hempel, 2005).

One of the major sites, *Facebook*, has tens of millions of members (not only adolescents, we should note). Adolescents may flirt online with total strangers or ask a person to be their friend. They are able to keep up with the latest music and films, discussing what's hot and what's out of favor.

Using virtual social networks, adolescents can also make contact with people they know in real life, as well as finding new individuals with whom to network. Several social-networking sites, such as Facebook.com, offer the opportunity to construct an elaborate Web page, post photos and favorite songs, and list the friends each member of the network has.

It's too early to tell if Web-based social networks will simply augment or actually replace more traditional forms of peer relationships. What is clear is that they offer adolescents a major new way both to interact with existing acquaintances and to make new friends.

Changing Relations with Relations in Adolescence. When Paco Lizzagara entered junior high school, his relationship with his parents changed drastically. What had been a good relationship had become tense by the middle of seventh grade. Paco felt his parents always seemed to "be on his case." Instead of giving him more freedom, they actually seemed to be becoming more restrictive.

Paco's parents would probably see things differently. They would likely suggest that they were not the source of the tension in the household—Paco was. From their point of view, Paco, with whom they'd established what seemed to be a close, stable, loving relationship throughout much of his childhood, suddenly seemed transformed. They felt he was shutting them out of his life, and when he did speak with them, it was merely to criticize their politics, their dress, their preferences in TV shows. To his parents, Paco's behavior was upsetting and bewildering.

The Quest for Autonomy. Parents are sometimes angered, and even more frequently puzzled, by adolescents' conduct. Children who have previously accepted their parents' judgments, declarations, and guidelines begin to question—and sometimes rebel against—their parents' views of the world.

One reason for these clashes is the shift in roles that both children and parents must deal with during adolescence. Adolescents increasingly seek **autonomy**, independence, and a sense of control over their own lives. Most parents intellectually realize that this shift is a normal part of adolescence, representing one of the primary developmental tasks of the period, and in many ways they welcome it as a sign of their children's growth. However, in many cases the day-to-day realities of adolescents' increasing autonomy may prove difficult for them to deal with (Smetana, 1995). But understanding this growing independence intellectually and agreeing to allow a teen to attend a party when no parents will be present are two different things. To the adolescent, her parents' refusal indicates a lack of trust or confidence. To the parent, it's simply good sense.

In most families, teenagers' autonomy grows gradually over the course of adolescence. For instance, one study of changes in adolescents' views of their parents found that increasing autonomy led them to perceive parents less in idealized terms and more as persons in their own right. For example, rather than seeing their parents as authoritarian disciplinarians mindlessly reminding them to do their homework, they may come to see their parents' emphasis on excelling in school as evidence of parental regrets about their own lack of education and a wish to see their children have more options in life. At the same time, adolescents come to depend more on themselves and to feel more like separate individuals (see Figure 13.1).

autonomy the development and expression of independence.

generation gap a divide between adolescence and other periods of life that supposedly reflects profound differences in behavior, values, attitudes, lifestyle choices, and experiences.

The increase in adolescent autonomy changes the relationship between parents and teenagers. At the start of adolescence, the relationship tends to be asymmetrical: Parents hold most of the power and influence over the relationship. By the end of adolescence, power and influence have become more balanced, and parents and children end up in a more symmetrical, or egalitarian, relationship. Power and influence are shared, although parents typically retain the upper hand.

The Myth of the Generation Gap. Teen movies often depict adolescents and their parents with totally opposing points of view about the world. For example, the parent of an environmentalist teen might turn out to own a polluting factory. These exaggerations are often funny because we assume there is a kernel of truth in them, in that parents and teenagers often don't see things the same way. According to this argument, there is a **generation gap**, a deep divide between parents and children in attitudes, values, aspirations, and worldviews.

The reality, however, is quite different. The generation gap, when it exists, is really quite narrow. Adolescents and their parents tend to see eye to eye in a variety of domains. Republican parents generally have Republican children; members of the Christian right have children who espouse similar views; parents who advocate for abortion rights have children who are pro-abortion. On social, political, and religious issues, parents and adolescents tend to be in synch, and children's worries mirror those of their parents. Adolescents' concerns about society's problems (see Figure 13.2) are those with which most adults would probably agree (Flor & Knap, 2001; Knafo & Schwartz, 2003; Smetana, 2005).

As we've said, most adolescents and their parents get along quite well. Despite their quest for autonomy and independence, most adolescents have deep love, affection, and respect for their

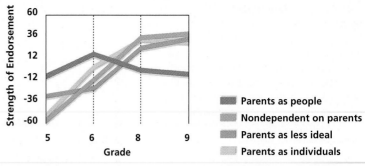

FIGURE 13.1 Changing Views of Parents
As adolescents become older, they come to perceive their parents in less idealized terms and more as individuals. What effect is this likely to have on family relations?
Source: Adapted from Steinberg & Silverberg, 1986.

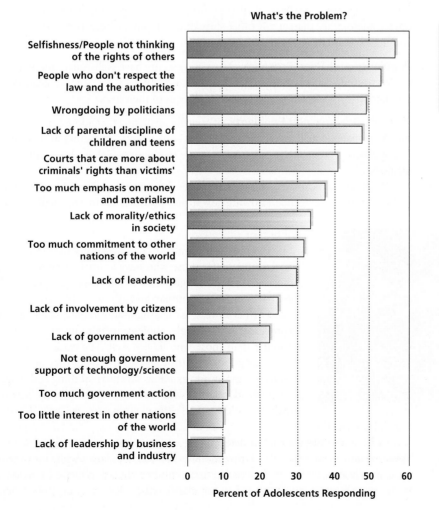

FIGURE 13.2 What's the Problem?
Adolescents' views of society's ills are ones with which their parents would be likely to agree.
Source: PRIMEDIA/Roper National Youth Survey, 1999.

mydevelopmentlab
Log onto **MyDevelopmentLab** and watch the video on adolescence to see teenagers aged 16–20 talk about making decisions, the transition to college first relationships, and their relationships with their parents.

FIGURE 13.3 **Time Spent**
by Adolescents with Parents
Despite their quest for autonomy and independence, most adolescents have deep love, affection, and respect for their parents, and the amount of time they spend alone with each parent (the lower two segments) remains remarkably stable across adolescence.
Source: Larson et al., 1996.

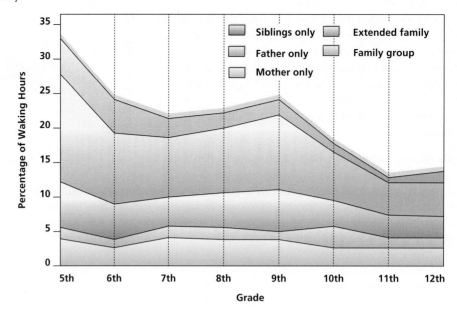

Log onto **MyDevelopmentLab** and watch a video of 18-year-old Tim and his mother talk about how peer pressure has affected Tim's life.

parents—and parents feel the same way about their children. Although some parent–adolescent relationships are seriously troubled, the majority of relationships are more positive than negative and help adolescents avoid the kind of peer pressure we'll discuss later in the chapter (Gavin & Furman, 1996; Resnick et al., 1997; Black, 2002).

Even though adolescents spend decreasing amounts of time with their families in general, the amount of time they spend alone with each parent remains remarkably stable across adolescence (see Figure 13.3). In short, there is no evidence suggesting that family problems are worse during adolescence than at any other stage of development (Steinberg, 1993; Larson et al., 1996; Granic, Hollenstein, & Dishion, 2003).

Popularity and Peer Pressure. Most adolescents have well-tuned antennae when it comes to determining who is popular and who is not. In fact, for some teenagers, concerns over popularity—or lack of it—may be a central focus of their lives.

Personal Qualities and Popularity. It's hardly surprising that adolescents' personal qualities—their personality, intelligence, and social skills—are significant factors in determining their level of popularity. Those with positive qualities are more popular than those with more disagreeable qualities.

What are the positive qualities that matter during adolescence? Popular boys and girls have high emotional intelligence, knowing how to act appropriately in a particular situation. They are enjoyable to be around—friendly, cheerful, smart, and with a good sense of humor.

But the sheer number of qualities is not the whole story. Sometimes adolescents prefer those who have at least a few negative qualities over those who are seemingly flawless. The negative aspects of their personality make them more human and approachable (Hawley, 2003).

Furthermore, some less-than-admirable qualities are associated with popularity. For example, adolescents who lie most effectively are more popular than those who lie less well. The explanation is not that lying produces popularity. Instead, effective lying may act as a kind of social skill, allowing an adolescent to say the right thing at the right moment. In contrast, adolescents who are always truthful may hurt others' feelings with their bluntness (Feldman, Tomasian, & Coats, 1999; Feldman, Forrest, & Happ, 2002).

Unpopular adolescents fall into several categories. Controversial adolescents are liked by some and disliked by others; rejected adolescents are uniformly disliked; and neglected adolescents are neither liked nor disliked.

Culture also plays a role in determining what qualities are associated with popularity. In Western cultures, for example, extroversion is related to popularity, while introverted adolescents are generally less popular. In contrast, in Asian cultures, shyness is viewed as a desirable trait, and introversion is more closely related to popularity (Chen, Rubin, & Li, 1995; Chen et al., 2002).

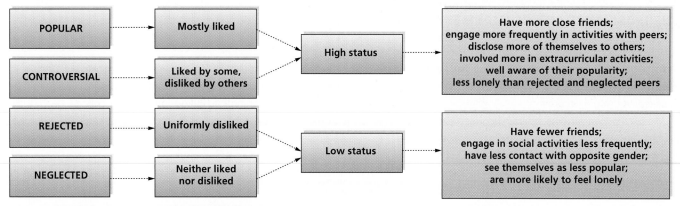

FIGURE 13.4 The Social World of Adolescence
An adolescent's popularity can fall into one of four categories, depending on the opinions of his or her peers. Popularity is related to differences in status, behavior, and adjustment.

Popularity and Rejection. Actually, the social world of adolescents is divided not only into popular and unpopular individuals; the differentiations are more complex (see Figure 13.4). For instance, some adolescents are controversial; in contrast to *popular* adolescents, who are mostly liked, **controversial adolescents** are liked by some and disliked by others. For example, a controversial adolescent may be highly popular within a particular group such as the string orchestra, but not popular among other classmates. Furthermore, there are **rejected adolescents**, who are uniformly disliked, and **neglected adolescents**, who are neither liked nor disliked. Neglected adolescents are the forgotten students—the ones whose status is so low that they are overlooked by almost everyone.

In most cases, popular and controversial adolescents tend to be similar in that their overall status is higher, while rejected and neglected adolescents share a generally lower status. Popular and controversial adolescents have more close friends, engage more frequently in activities with their peers, and disclose more about themselves to others than less popular students. They are also more involved in extracurricular school activities. In addition, they are well aware of their popularity, and they are less lonely than their less popular classmates (Englund et al., 2000; Farmer et al., 2003; Zettergren, 2004; Becker & Luthar, 2007).

In contrast, the social world of rejected and neglected adolescents is considerably less pleasant. They have fewer friends, engage in social activities less frequently, and have less contact with the opposite sex. They see themselves—accurately, it turns out—as less popular, and they are more likely to feel lonely. (To learn about another type of difficulty in maintaining friendships, see the *Neuroscience and Development* box on page 382.)

Maintaining Social Networks: The Importance of Friendship in Adulthood

Tara Daley, a widow in her 50s, joined a writing workshop after her youngest child left home and her husband died. While she enjoys the writing exercises and respects the instructor, the real reason Tara signed up for the workshop was to meet new people. "There are 20 people in the class, so I figured I could probably find at least one friend among the group," she says. Tara ended up making three new friends, all women in their 50s and 60s whose children are grown, and who have found themselves alone through widowhood or divorce. "I love to shop for antiques with Doreen, swap gardening tips with Anna, and go to concerts with Grace," Tara says. "I never have to be alone except when I want to be."

Like Tara, most of our relationships with others involve friends, and for most people, maintaining such relationships is an important part of adult life. Why? One reason is that the basic *need for belongingness* we saw in adolescents continues to lead people to establish and maintain at least a minimum number of relationships with others throughout adulthood. Most people are driven toward forming and preserving relationships that allow them to experience a sense of belonging with others (Manstead, 1997; Rice, 1999; Fiske & Yamamoto, 2005).

What Makes for Friendship in Adulthood? How do particular people end up becoming our friends? One of the most important reasons is simple proximity—people form friendships with others who live nearby and with whom they come in contact most frequently. Because of their

controversial adolescents adolescents who are liked by some and disliked by others.

rejected adolescents adolescents who are uniformly disliked.

neglected adolescents adolescents who are neither liked nor disliked.

NEUROSCIENCE AND DEVELOPMENT
A World of Faces and Facing the World

Several years ago, when Margaret Mitchell picked up her son Duncan from his Seattle school, he looked at her curiously and asked, "Are you my mommy?"

Ms. Mitchell, an attorney by training, was taken aback. When she answered, "'Yes, I'm your mommy,'" he recognized her voice and was reassured.

A short while later, Duncan, then 4 years old, was diagnosed with prosopagnosia, a selective developmental condition often referred to as "faceblindness." Although his eyesight is perfectly fine, he can't always identify people by their faces. In school, for instance, Duncan has trouble matching the faces and names of teachers and pupils.

Like many other prosopagnosics, Duncan, now 8, has a memory that functions normally in other ways. He can visually distinguish between cars and houses and toys. He knows his dog and cat and other neighborhood pets. He's a sociable child and likes being around people. But the frustration of not being able to discern faces has made everyday life from attending school to making friends unbearably difficult. (Tesoriero, 2007, p. A1)

What would your life be like if you could not remember a familiar face or recognize important people in your life? For people diagnosed with a rare condition known as faceblindness, that's an everyday experience.

Most of us, though, suffer lapses in which we are unable to remember faces due to everyday memory losses. According to new research by neuroscientist Ulrike Rimmele and colleagues (2009), it turns out that the chemical oxytocin strengthens the neuronal systems of social memory by improving the ability to recognize familiar faces.

Rimmele's research shows that after one experimental dose of an oxytocin nasal spray, adults showed improved recognition memory for faces—but not inanimate objects. In the study, participants used the spray and were shown various images. The next day, they participated in a surprise test and were shown a collection of the same and new images. Those who used the oxytocin spray more accurately recognized the faces they had seen before than those who had not used the spray. They also improved their ability to discriminate between new and familiar faces. However, the two groups did not differ in recognizing the other, nonsocial images.

These results suggest that oxytocin specifically improves social memory and strengthens the capability to correctly discriminate faces. They also demonstrate that different mechanisms exist for social and nonsocial memory as related to facial recognition.

• *What types of problems might people with faceblindness experience, and how might it be detrimental to their social lives?*

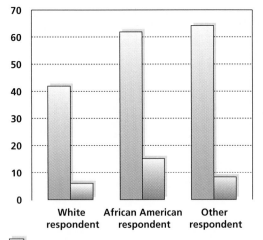

FIGURE 13.5 Rephrasing the Question
Although a relatively high percentage of whites and blacks claim to have a close friend who is a member of a different race, only a small majority actually name a person of another race or ethnicity when asked to list the names of their close friends.
Source: General Social Survey, 1998.

Legend:
☐ Percent who say they have a close friend who is black or white
☐ Percent who name a close friend who is of a different race

accessibility, people who are in close proximity can obtain rewards of friendship, such as companionship, social approval, and the occasional helping hand, at relatively little cost.

Similarity also plays an important role in friendship formation. Birds of a feather *do* flock together: People are more attracted to others who hold attitudes and values similar to their own (McCaul et al., 1995; Simpkins et al., 2006; Morry, 2007).

The importance of similarity becomes particularly evident when we consider cross-race friendships. As we noted earlier, by the time of adolescence, the number of cross-race close friendships dwindles, a pattern that continues throughout the remainder of the life span. In fact, although most adults who are surveyed claim to have a close friend of a different race, when they are queried regarding the names of close friends, few include a person of a different race (see Figure 13.5).

We also choose friends on the basis of their personal qualities. What's most important? According to results of surveys, people are most attracted to others who keep confidences and are loyal, warm, and affectionate. In addition, people like those who are supportive, frank, and have a good sense of humor (Parlee, 1979; Hartup & Stevens, 1999; Hossfeld, 2008).

The Social Networks of Later Adulthood. Elderly people enjoy friends as much as younger people do, and friendships play an important role in the lives of those in late adulthood. Time spent with friends is often valued more highly during late adulthood than time spent with family, and friends are often seen as more important providers of support than family members. Furthermore, around a third of older persons report that they made a new friend within the past year, and many older adults engage in significant interaction (see Figure 13.6; Hansson & Carpenter, 1994; Hartshorne, 1994; Ansberry, 1997).

One reason for the importance of friendship relates to the element of control. In friendship relationships, unlike family relationships, we choose whom we like and whom we dislike, meaning that we have considerable control. Because late adulthood

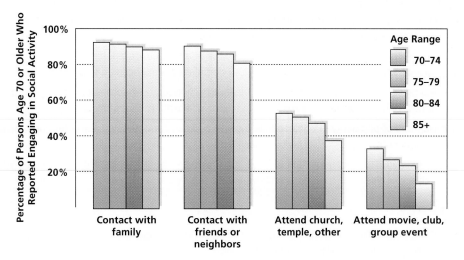

FIGURE 13.6 Social Activity in Late Adulthood
Friends and family play an important role in the social activities of the elderly.
Source: Federal Interagency Forum on Age Related Statistics, 2000.

may bring with it a gradual loss of control in other areas, such as in one's health, the ability to maintain friendships may take on more importance than in other stages of life (Krause & Borawski-Clark, 1994; Pruchno & Rosenbaum, 2003; Stevens, Martina, & Westerhof, 2006).

In addition, friendships—especially those that have developed recently—may be more flexible than family ties, given that recent friendships are not likely to have a history of obligations and past conflicts. In contrast, family ties may have a long and sometimes stormy record that can reduce the emotional sustenance they provide (Hartshorne, 1994; Magai & McFadden, 1996; Hansson, Daleiden, & Hayslip, 2004).

Another reason for the importance of friendships in late adulthood relates to the increasing likelihood, over time, that one will be without a marital partner. When a spouse dies, people typically seek out the companionship of friends to help deal with their loss and also for some of the companionship that was provided by the deceased spouse.

Of course, it isn't only spouses who die during old age; friends die too. The way adults view friendship in late adulthood determines how vulnerable they are to the death of a friend. If the friendship has been defined as irreplaceable, then the loss of the friend may be quite difficult. On the other hand, if the friendship is defined as one of many friendships, then the death of a friend may be less traumatic. In such cases, older adults are more likely to become involved subsequently with new friends (Hansson et al., 2004; Hartshorne, 1994).

Social Support: The Significance of Others. Friendships also provide one of the basic social needs: social support. **Social support** is assistance and comfort supplied by a network of caring, interested people. Such support plays a critical role in successful aging (Antonucci, 1990; Antonucci & Akiyama, 1991; Avlund, Lund, & Holstein, 2004).

The benefits of social support are considerable. For instance, people can provide emotional support by lending a sympathetic ear and providing a sounding board for one's concerns. Furthermore, social support from people who are experiencing similar problems—such as the loss of a spouse—can provide an unmatched degree of understanding and a pool of helpful suggestions for coping strategies that would be less credible coming from others.

Finally, people can furnish material support, such as helping with rides or picking up groceries. They can provide help in solving problems, such as dealing with a difficult landlord or fixing a broken appliance.

REVIEW

▶ In the preschool years, children develop friendships on the basis of personal characteristics, trust, and shared interests.

▶ The character of preschoolers' play changes over time, growing more sophisticated, interactive, and cooperative, and relying increasingly on social skills.

▶ Children's understanding of friendship changes from the sharing of enjoyable activities, through the consideration of personal traits that can meet their needs, to a focus on intimacy and loyalty.

It has been found that the benefits of social support are considerable, benefiting both the provider and receiver. What is the importance of reciprocity as a factor of social support?

social support   assistance and comfort supplied by a network of caring, interested people. Such support plays a critical role in successful aging.

▶ Peer groups are of great importance during adolescence, providing a way to meet personal interests, acquire information, and gain prestige.

▶ Cliques and crowds serve as reference groups in adolescence and offer a ready means of social comparison. Sex cleavage gradually diminishes, until boys and girls begin to pair off.

▶ Racial separation increases during adolescence, bolstered by socioeconomic status differences, different academic experiences, and mutually distrustful attitudes.

▶ Degrees of popularity in adolescence include popular, controversial, neglected, and rejected adolescents.

▶ Friendships are very important in adult life, providing social support and companionship from peers who are likely to understand the adult's feelings and problems.

APPLY

▶ Do you think TV and movie portrayals of popular and unpopular characters in high school settings are helpful or harmful to adolescents wrestling with popularity issues? Why?

▶ Does the popularity of online networking indicate a greater or lesser tendency to engage in social activities than face-to-face networking? Why?

MODULE 13.2

Family Life

Consider this quote from a spouse who just became a parent:

We had no idea what we were getting into when our first child was born. We certainly prepared for the event, reading magazine articles and books and even attending a class on child care. But when Sheanna was actually born, the sheer enormity of the task of taking care of her, her presence at every moment of the day, and the awesome responsibility of raising another human being weighed on us like nothing else we'd ever faced. Not that it was a burden. But it did make us look at the world with an entirely different perspective.

There are no rehearsals for parenthood, no one-size-fits-all blueprint for creating a family. Family life in the twenty-first century, as we shall see, is diverse, complex, and often stressful. Nevertheless, most married couples choose to have children. And with that choice, they start down a road they will travel the rest of their lives.

Parenthood Today: Choosing to Have Children

Deciding whether to have children is one of the most important decisions couples make. What makes a couple decide to have children? Childrearing certainly isn't economically advantageous: A middle-class family with two children spends around $233,000 for each child by the time the child reaches the age of 18. Add in the costs of college and the figure comes to over $300,000 per child (Lino, 2001).

Instead, young adults typically cite psychological reasons for having children. They expect to derive pleasure from watching their children grow, fulfillment from their children's accomplishments, satisfaction from seeing them become successful, and enjoyment from forging a close bond with their children. But there also may be a self-serving element in the decision to have children. For example, parents-to-be may hope that their children will provide for them in their old age, maintain a family business or farm, or simply offer companionship. Others have children because to do so is such a strong societal norm: More than 90 percent of all married couples have at least one child (Mackey, White, & Day, 1992).

For some couples, there is no decision to have children. Some children are unplanned, the result of the failure or absence of birth control methods. In some cases, the couple may have planned to have children at some point in the future, and so the pregnancy is not regarded as particularly undesirable and may even be welcomed. But in families that had actively not wanted to have children, or already had what they considered "enough" children, the pregnancy can be viewed as problematic (Leathers & Kelley, 2000; Pajulo, Helenius, & MaYes, 2006).

The couples who are most likely to have unwanted pregnancies are often the most vulnerable in society. Unplanned pregnancies occur most frequently in younger, poorer, and less educated couples. Happily, there has been a dramatic rise in the use and effectiveness of contraceptives, and the incidence of undesired pregnancies has declined in the last several decades (Centers for Disease Control and Prevention, 2003; Villarosa, 2003).

The Transition to Parenthood: Two's a Couple, Three's a Crowd? The arrival of a child alters virtually every aspect of family life, in positive and, sometimes, negative ways. The addition of a child to a household brings about a dramatic shift in the roles spouses must play. They are suddenly placed in new roles—"mother" and "father"—and these new positions may overwhelm their ability to respond in their older, though continuing, roles of "wife" and "husband." In addition, the birth of a child produces significant physical and psychological demands, including near-constant fatigue, new financial responsibilities, and an increase in household chores (Meijer & van den Wittenboer, 2007).

Furthermore, in contrast to many non-Western cultures, in which childrearing is seen as a task that involves the entire community, Western culture's emphasis on individualism makes childrearing a primarily private enterprise. Thus, mothers and fathers in Western society are largely left to forge their own paths after the birth of a child, often without significant community support (Rubin & Chung, 2006; Lamm & Keller, 2007).

Consequently, as we discussed in Chapter 12, for many couples, the strains accompanying the birth of a child produce the lowest level of marital satisfaction of any point in their marriage. This is particularly true for women, who tend to be more dissatisfied than men with their marriages after the arrival of children. The most likely reason for this gender difference is that wives often experience a greater increase in their responsibilities than husbands do, even in families in which parents seek to share childrearing chores (Levy-Shiff, 1994; Laflamme, Pomerleau, & Malcuit, 2002; Lu, 2006).

At the same time, not all couples experience a decrease in marital satisfaction upon the birth of a child. According to work by John Gottman and colleagues (Shapiro, Gottman, & Carrère, 2000; Wilson & Gottman, 2002), marital satisfaction can remain steady, and actually rise, with the birth of a child. They identified three factors that permitted couples to successfully weather the increased stress that follows the birth of a child:

- Working to build fondness and affection toward one's partner.
- Remaining aware of events in one's spouse's life and responding to those events.
- Considering problems as controllable and solvable.

In particular, those couples who were well satisfied with their marriages as newlyweds were more likely to continue to be satisfied as they raised their children. Couples who harbor realistic expectations regarding the extent of childrearing effort and other household responsibilities they face when children are born also tend to be more satisfied after they become parents. Furthermore, parents who work together as a *coparenting team,* in which they thoughtfully adopt common childrearing goals and strategies, are more apt to be satisfied with their parenting roles (Schoppe-Sullivan et al., 2006; McHale & Rotman, 2007).

In short, having children can well lead to greater marital satisfaction—at least for couples who are already satisfied with their marriage. For marriages in which satisfaction is low, having children may make a bad situation worse (Shapiro, Gottman, & Carrère, 2000; Driver, Tabares, & Shapiro, 2003).

Changing Times: Family Life in the Twenty-First Century

A look back at television shows of the 1950s (such as *Leave It to Beaver*) finds a world of families portrayed in a way that today seems oddly old-fashioned and quaint: mothers and fathers, married for years, and their good-looking children making their way in a world that seems to have few, if any, serious problems.

Even in the 1950s such a view of family life was overly romantic and unrealistic. Today, however, it is broadly inaccurate, representing only a minority of families in the United States. A quick review tells the story:

- The number of single-parent families has increased dramatically in the last two decades, as the number of two-parent households has declined. Just under one-third of all families with children are headed by single parents. Twenty-three percent of children lived with only their mothers, 5 percent lived with only their fathers, and 4 percent lived with neither of their parents. Sixty-five percent of African American children and 37 percent of Hispanic children live in single-parent households (U.S. Bureau of the Census, 1998; ChildStats.gov, 2005).

- As we shall discuss in a moment, the average size of families is shrinking. Today, on average, there are 2.6 persons per household, compared to 2.8 in 1980.

- Although the number of adolescents giving birth has declined substantially over the last five years, there are still half a million births to teenage women, the vast majority of whom are unmarried.

- Close to 50 percent of children under the age of 3 are cared for by other adults while their parents work, and more than half of mothers of infants work outside the home.

- One in three children lives in low-income households in the United States. The rates are even higher for African American and Hispanic families and for single-parent families of young children. More children under 3 live in poverty than do older children, adults, or the elderly. Furthermore, the proportion of children living in low-income families began rising in 2000, reversing a decade of decline (Federal Interagency Forum on Child and Family Statistics, 2003; National Center for Children in Poverty, 2005).

At the very least, these statistics suggest that many children are being raised in environments in which substantial stressors are present. Such stress makes it unusually difficult to raise children—never easy even under the best circumstances.

On the other hand, society is adapting to the new realities of family life in the twenty-first century. Several kinds of social support exist for the parents of infants, and society is evolving new institutions to help in their care. One example is the growing array of child-care arrangements available to help working parents that we discussed in Chapter 9.

Family Size. As we noted earlier, one of the major recent changes in family life is family size. The availability and use of effective contraceptives has dramatically decreased the number of children in the average American family. Almost 70 percent of Americans polled in the 1930s agreed that the ideal number of children was three or more, but by the 1990s the percentage had shrunk to less than 40 percent. Today, most families seek to have no more than two children—although most say that three or more is ideal if money is no object (Kate, 1998; Gallup Poll, 2004).

These preferences have been translated into changes in the actual birth rate. In 1957, the *fertility rate* reached a post–World War II peak in the United States of 3.7 children per woman and then began to decline. Today, the rate is at 2.1 children per woman, which is less than the *replacement level,* the number of children that one generation must produce to be able to replenish its numbers. In contrast, in some underdeveloped countries, the fertility rate is as high as 6.9 (World Bank, 2004).

What has produced this decline in the fertility rate? In addition to the availability of more reliable birth control methods, one reason is that increasing numbers of women have joined the workforce. The pressures of simultaneously holding a job and raising a child have convinced many women to have fewer children.

Furthermore, many women who work outside the home are choosing to have children later in their childbearing years in order to develop their careers. In fact, women between the ages of 30 and 34 are the only ones whose rate of births has actually increased over earlier decades. Still, because women who have their first children in their 30s have fewer years in which to have children, they ultimately cannot have as many children as women who begin childbearing in their 20s. In addition, research suggesting that there are health benefits for mothers in terms of spacing children further apart may lead families to ultimately have fewer children (Marcus, 2004).

As increasing numbers of women have joined the workforce, more are choosing to have fewer children and have them later.

Some of the traditional incentives for having children—such as their potential for providing economic support in old age—may also no longer be as attractive. Potential parents may view Social Security and other pensions as a more predictable means of support when they are elderly than relying on their children. There is also, as mentioned earlier, the sheer cost of raising a child, particularly the well-publicized increase in the cost of college. This, too, may act as a disincentive for bearing larger numbers of children.

Finally, some couples avoid having children because they fear they will not be good parents or simply don't want the work and responsibility involved in childrearing. Women may also fear that they will share a disproportionate amount of the effort involved in childrearing—a perception that may be an accurate reading of reality as we will discuss next.

Dual-Earner Couples. One of the major historical shifts affecting young adults that began in the last half of the twentieth century is the increase in families in which both parents work. Close to three-quarters of married women with school-aged children are employed outside the home, and more than half of mothers with children under the age of 6 are working. In the mid-1960s, only 17 percent of mothers of 1-year-olds worked full time; now, more than 50 percent do. In the majority of families, both husband and wife work (Darnton, 1990; Carnegie Task Force, 1994; Barnett & Hyde, 2001).

The income that is generated when both partners work provides economic benefits, but it also takes a toll, particularly on women. Even when both spouses work similar hours, the wife generally spends more time taking care of the children than the husband does (Huppe & Cyr, 1997; Kitterod & Pettersen, 2006). And even though men are spending more time with their children than in the past (the amount of time has increased by one-quarter in the last 20 years), wives still spend more time with their children than husbands do (Families and Work Institute, 1998).

Furthermore, the nature of husbands' and wives' contributions to the household often differ. For instance, husbands tend to carry out chores such as mowing the lawn or house repairs that are more easily scheduled in advance (or sometimes postponed), while women's household chores tend to be devoted to duties that need immediate attention, such as child care and meal preparation. As a result, wives experience greater levels of anxiety and stress (Barnett & Shen, 1997; Juster, Ono, & Stafford, 2000; Haddock & Rattenborg, 2003; Lee, Vernon-Feagans, & Vazquez, 2003; see Figure 13.7).

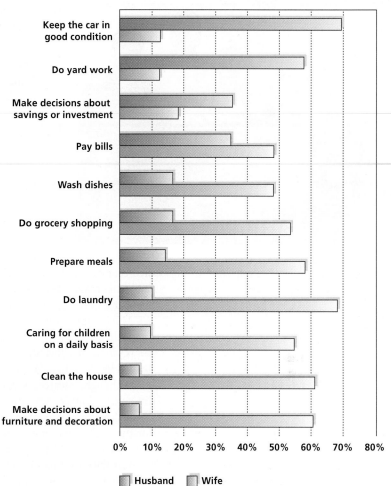

FIGURE 13.7 Division of Labor
Although husbands and wives generally work at their paying jobs a similar number of hours each week, wives are apt to spend more time than their husbands doing home chores and in childcare activities. Why do you think this pattern exists?
Source: GPSS Lifestyle Poll, 2007.

Family Constellations: The Array of Possibilities

Tamara's mother, Brenda, waited outside the door of her second-grade classroom for the end of the school day. Tamara came over to greet her mother as soon as she spotted her. "Mom, can Anna come over to play today?" Tamara demanded. Brenda had been looking forward to spending some time alone with Tamara, who had spent the last three days at her dad's house. But, Brenda reflected, Tamara hardly ever got to ask kids over after school, so she agreed to the request. Unfortunately, it turned out today wouldn't work for Anna's family, so they tried to find an alternate date. "How about Thursday?" Anna's mother suggested. Before Tamara could reply, her mother reminded her, "You'll have to ask your dad. You're at his house that night." Tamara's expectant face fell. "OK," she mumbled.

How will Tamara's adjustment be affected from dividing her time between the two homes where she lives with her divorced parents? If her mother should remarry to a man who also has children, will Tamara's life become more complicated even though there will be

Blended families occur when previously married husbands and wives with children remarry.

blended families a family consisting of remarried couples with at least one stepchild living with them.

two adults in the house? These are just a few of the questions we need to consider as we look at the ways that children's home life affects their lives.

The Impact of Divorce on Children. Having divorced parents, like Tamara, is no longer very distinctive. Only around half the children in the United States spend their entire childhoods living in the same household with both their parents. The rest will live in single-parent homes or with stepparents, grandparents, or other nonparental relatives; and some will end up in foster care (Harvey & Fine, 2004).

How do children react to divorce? The answer depends on how soon you ask the question following a divorce as well as how old the children are at the time of the divorce. Immediately after a divorce, both children and parents may show several types of psychological maladjustment for a period that may last from 6 months to 2 years. For instance, children may be anxious, experience depression, or show sleep disturbances and phobias. Even though children most often live with their mothers following a divorce, the quality of the mother–child relationship declines in the majority of cases, often because children see themselves caught in the middle between their mothers and fathers (Holyrod & Sheppard, 1997; Wallerstein, Lewis, & Blakeslee, 2000; Amato & Afifi, 2006).

During the early stage of middle childhood, children whose parents are divorcing often blame themselves for the breakup. By the age of 10, children feel pressure to choose sides, taking the position of either the mother or the father. As a result, they experience some degree of divided loyalty (Shaw, Winslow, & Flanagan, 1999).

Although researchers agree that the short-term consequences of divorce can be quite difficult, the longer-term consequences are less clear. Some studies have found that 18 months to 2 years later, most children begin to return to their predivorce state of psychological adjustment. For many children, there are minimal long-term consequences (Hetherington & Kelly, 2002; Guttmann & Rosenberg, 2003; Harvey & Fine, 2004).

On the other hand, other evidence suggests that the fallout from divorce lingers. For example, twice as many children of divorced parents enter psychological counseling as children from intact families (although sometimes counseling is mandated by a judge as part of the divorce). In addition, people who have experienced parental divorce are more at risk for experiencing divorce themselves later in life (Wallerstein et al., 2000; Amato & Booth, 2001; Wallerstein & Resnikoff, 2005; Huurre, Junkkari, & Aro, 2006).

How children react to divorce depends on several factors. One is the economic standing of the family the child is living with. In many cases, divorce brings a decline in both parents' standards of living. When this occurs, children may be thrown into poverty (Ozawa & Yoon, 2003).

In other cases, the negative consequences of divorce are less severe because the divorce reduces the hostility and anger in the home. If the household before the divorce was overwhelmed by parental strife—as is the case in around 30 percent of divorces—the greater calm of a post-divorce household may be beneficial to children. This is particularly true for children who maintain a close, positive relationship with the parent with whom they do not live (Davies et al., 2002).

For some children, then, divorce is an improvement over living with parents who have an intact but unhappy marriage, high in conflict. But in about 70 percent of divorces, the predivorce level of conflict is not high, and children in these households may have a more difficult time adjusting to divorce (Amato & Booth, 1997; Lippman & Lewis, 2008).

Living in Blended Families. For many children, the aftermath of divorce includes the subsequent remarriage of one or both parents. More than 10 million households in the United States contain at least one spouse who has remarried. More than 5 million remarried couples have at least one stepchild living with them in what have come to be called **blended families.** Overall, 17 percent of all children in the United States live in blended families (U.S. Bureau of the Census, 2001; Bengtson et al., 2004).

Living in a blended family is challenging for the children involved. There often is a fair amount of *role ambiguity,* in which roles and expectations are unclear. Children may be uncertain about their responsibilities, how to behave toward stepparents and stepsiblings, and how to make a host of decisions that have wide-ranging implications for their role in the family. For instance, a child in a blended family may have to choose which parent to spend each vacation and holiday with, or to decide between the conflicting advice coming from biological parent and stepparent (Cath & Shopper, 2001; Belcher, 2003).

In many cases, however, school-age children in blended families often do surprisingly well. In comparison to adolescents, who have more difficulties, school-age children often adjust relatively smoothly to blended arrangements, for several reasons. For one thing, the family's financial situation is often improved after a parent remarries. In addition, in a blended family there are more people to share the burden of household chores. Finally, the simple fact that the family contains more individuals increases the opportunities for social interaction (Hetherington & Clingempeel, 1992; Greene, Anderson, & Hetherington, 2003; Hetherington & Elmore, 2003).

Conversely, some children do not adjust well to life in a blended family. Some find the disruption of routine and of established networks of family relationships difficult. For instance, a child who is used to having her mother's complete attention may find it difficult to observe her mother showing interest and affection to a stepchild. The most successful blending of families occurs when the parents create an environment that supports children's self-esteem and helps all family members feel a sense of togetherness (Sage, 2003; Jeynes, 2006; Kirby, 2006).

Single-Parent Families. Almost one-quarter of all children under the age of 18 in the United States live with only one parent. If present trends continue, almost three-quarters of American children will spend some portion of their lives in a single-parent family before they are 18 years old. For minority children, the numbers are even higher: Almost 60 percent of African American children and 35 percent of Hispanic children under the age of 18 live in single-parent homes (U.S. Bureau of the Census, 2000; see Figure 13.8).

In rare cases, death is the reason for single parenthood. More frequently, either no spouse was ever present (that is, the mother never married), the spouses have divorced, or the spouse is absent. In the vast majority of cases, the single parent who is present is the mother.

What consequences are there for children living in homes with just one parent? This is a difficult question to answer. Much depends on whether a second parent was present earlier and the nature of the parents' relationship at that time. Furthermore, the economic status of the single-parent family plays a role in determining the consequences for children. Single-parent families are often less well-off financially than two-parent families, and living in relative poverty has a negative impact on children (Davis, 2003; Harvey & Fine, 2004).

In sum, the impact of living in a single-parent family is not, by itself, invariably negative or positive. Given the large number of single-parent households, the stigma that once existed toward such families has largely declined. The ultimate consequences for children depend on a variety of factors that accompany single parenthood, such as the economic status of the family, the amount of time that the parent is able to spend with the child, and the degree of stress in the household.

Multigenerational Families. Some households consist of several generations, in which children, parents, and grandparents live together. The presence of multiple generations in the same house can make for a rich living experience for children, who experience the influence both of their parents and grandparents. Multigenerational families also have the potential for conflict, with several adults acting as disciplinarians without coordinating what they do.

The prevalence of three-generation families who live together is greater among African Americans than among Caucasians. In addition, African American families, which are more likely than white families to be headed by single parents, often rely substantially on the help of grandparents in everyday child care, and cultural norms tend to be highly supportive of grandparents taking an active role (Baydar & Brooks-Gunn, 1998; Budris, 1998; Baird, John, & Hayslip, 2000; Crowther & Rodriguez, 2003).

Race and Family Life. Although there are as many types of families as there are individuals, research does find some consistencies related to race (Parke, 2004). For example, African American families often have a particularly strong sense of family. Members of African American families are frequently willing to offer welcome and support to extended family members in their homes. Because there is a relatively high level of female-headed households among African Americans, the social and economic support of extended family often is critical. In addition, there is a relatively high proportion of families headed by older adults, such as grandparents, and

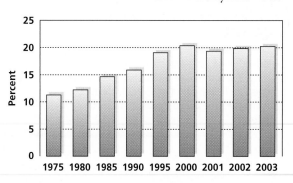

FIGURE 13.8 Increase of Single Mothers, 1975–2003
The number of mothers without spouses has increased significantly over the last two decades.
Source: U.S. Bureau of the Census, 2004.

Based on current trends almost three-quarters of American children will spend some portion of their lives in a single-parent family. What are some possible consequences for a child in a single-parent family?

Check **MyDevelopmentLab** for an Observations video on neglected children. Put yourself in the role of an educator, social worker, or health-care provider; how would you handle the issues presented in the video?

some studies find that children in grandmother-headed households are particularly well adjusted (McLoyd et al., 2000; Smith & Drew, 2002; Taylor, 2002).

Hispanic families also often stress the importance of family life, as well as community and religious organizations. Children are taught to value their ties to their families, and they come to see themselves as a central part of an extended family. Ultimately, their sense of who they are becomes tied to the family. Hispanic families also tend to be relatively larger, with an average size of 3.71, compared to 2.97 for Caucasian families and 3.31 for African American families (Cauce & Domenech-Rodriguez, 2000; U.S. Census Bureau, 2003; Halgunseth, Ispa, & Rudy, 2006).

Although relatively little research has been conducted on Asian American families, emerging findings suggest that fathers are more apt to be powerful figures, maintaining discipline. In keeping with the more collectivist orientation of Asian cultures, children tend to believe that family needs have a higher priority than personal needs, and males, in particular, are expected to care for their parents throughout their lifetimes (Ishi-Kuntz, 2000). (For another aspect of family life, see the accompanying *From Research to Practice* box.)

Poverty and Family Life

Children living in families that are economically disadvantaged face significant hardships. Poor families have fewer basic everyday resources, and there are more disruptions in children's lives. For example, parents may be forced to look for less expensive housing or may move the entire household in order to find work. The result frequently is family environments in which parents are less responsive to their children's needs and provide less social support (Evans, 2004).

The stress of difficult family environments, along with other stress in the lives of poor children—such as living in unsafe neighborhoods with high rates of violence and attending inferior schools—ultimately takes its toll. Economically disadvantaged children are at risk for

FROM RESEARCH TO PRACTICE
Families with Gay and Lesbian Parents: How Do Children Fare?

An increasing number of children have two mothers or two fathers. Estimates suggest there are between 1 and 5 million families headed by two lesbians or two gay parents in the United States, and some 6 million children have lesbian or gay parents (Patterson & Friel, 2000).

How do lesbian and gay households compare to heterosexual households? To answer the question, we first need to consider some characteristics of gay and lesbian couples without children. According to studies comparing gay, lesbian, and heterosexual couples, labor tends to be divided more evenly in homosexual households than in heterosexual households. Each partner in a homosexual relationship is more likely to carry out approximately the same number of different chores, compared with heterosexual partners. Furthermore, gay and lesbian couples cling more strongly to the ideal of an egalitarian allocation of household work than heterosexual couples do (Patterson, 1992, 1994; Kurdek, 1993, 2003; Parks, 1998).

However, as with heterosexual couples, the arrival of a child (usually through adoption or artificial insemination) changes the dynamics of household life considerably for homosexual couples. As in heterosexual unions, a specialization of roles develops. According to recent research on lesbian mothers, for instance, childrearing tends to fall more to one member of the couple, while the other spends more time in paid employment. Although both partners usually say they share household tasks and decision making equally, biological mothers are more involved in child care. Conversely, the nonbiological mother in the couple is more likely to report spending greater time in paid employment (Patterson, 1995; Ben-Ari & Livni, 2006).

Relatively little research has been done on the effects of same-sex parenting on children, and the results are not definitive. However, most studies find that the children in lesbian and gay households develop similarly to the children of heterosexual families. Their sexual orientation is unrelated to that of their parents; their behavior is no more or less gender-typed; and they seem equally well adjusted (Parke, 2004; Patterson, 2006).

Furthermore, children of lesbian and gay parents have similar relationships with their peers as children of heterosexual parents. And when they reach adolescence, their romantic relationships and sexual behavior are no different from those of adolescents living with opposite-sex parents (Patterson, 1995; Golombok et al., 2003; Wainright, Russell, & Patterson, 2004).

In short, a growing body of research suggests that there is little developmental difference between children whose parents are gay and lesbian and heterosexual parents. What is clearly different for children with same-sex parents is the possibility of discrimination and prejudice due to their parents' homosexuality. As the U.S. public engages in a highly politicized debate regarding the legality of gay and lesbian marriage, children of such unions may feel singled out because of societal discrimination.

- *What pressures do gay and lesbian families face that might be different from those of heterosexual families?*

- *How might parents in gay and lesbian households help their children in dealing with some of the unique pressures they face?*

poorer academic performance, higher rates of aggression, and conduct problems. In addition, declines in economic well-being have been linked to mental health problems (Solantaus, Leinonen, & Punamaki, 2004; Sapolsky, 2005; Morales & Guerra, 2006).

REVIEW

▶ Most couples wish to produce children, although the availability of contraception and changes in women's roles in the workplace have combined to decrease average family size.

▶ Children bring pressures to both heterosexual and homosexual relationships, causing changes in focus, roles, and responsibilities.

▶ How divorce affects children depends on such factors as financial circumstances and the comparative levels of tension in the family before and after the divorce.

▶ Children spend significantly less time with their parents in middle childhood, but parents are still the primary influence in their children's lives.

APPLY

▶ Politicians often speak of "family values." How does this term relate to the diverse family situations covered in this chapter, including divorced parents, single parents, blended families, working parents, and gay and lesbian parents?

▶ In what ways do you think parents with different parenting styles react to attempts to establish autonomy during adolescence?

MODULE 13.3

Family Ties in Middle and Late Adulthood

For Kathy and Bob, accompanying their son Jon to his college orientation was like nothing they had ever experienced in the life of their family. When Jon had been accepted at a college on the other side of the country, the reality that he would be leaving home didn't really register. It wasn't until the time came to leave him on his new campus that it hit them that their family would be changing in ways they could barely fathom. It was a wrenching experience. Not only did Kathy and Bob worry about their son in the ways that parents always worry about their children, but they felt a sense of profound loss—that, to a large extent, their job of raising their son was over. Now he was largely on his own. It was a thought that filled them with pride and anticipation for his future, but with great sadness as well. They would miss him.

Leaving their youngest child at college marks the start of a significant transition for parents, who face an "empty nest."

For members of many non-Western cultures who live in traditional extended families in which multiple generations spend their lives in the same household or village, middle adulthood is not particularly special. But in Western cultures, family dynamics undergo significant change during middle adulthood. It is in middle age that most parents experience major changes in their relationships not only with their children, but with other family members as well. It is a period of shifting role relationships that, in twenty-first-century Western cultures, encompass an increasing number of combinations and permutations.

Family Evolutions: From Full House to Empty Nest

For many parents, a major transition that typically occurs during middle adulthood is the departure of children, who may be going to college, getting married, joining the military, or taking a job far from home. Even people who become parents at relatively late ages are likely to experience this transition at some point during middle adulthood, since the period spans nearly a quarter century. As we saw in the description of Kathy and Bob, a child's departure can be a wrenching experience—so upsetting, in fact, that it has been labeled the "empty nest syndrome." The **empty nest syndrome** refers to instances in which parents experience unhappiness, worry, loneliness, and depression stemming from their children's departure from home (Lauer & Lauer, 1999; Rosen, Ackerman, & Zosky, 2002).

Many parents report that major adjustments are required. The loss can be particularly difficult for women who have stayed home to rear their children. Certainly, if traditional homemakers have little or nothing else in their lives except their children, they do indeed face a challenging period.

While coping with the feelings of loss can be difficult, some aspects of this era of middle adulthood can be quite positive for parents. Even mothers who have not worked outside the home find they have time for other outlets for their physical and psychological energies, such as community or recreational activities when the children leave. Moreover, they may feel that they now have the opportunity to get a job or to go back to school. Finally, surveys show that most people feel that being a mother is harder than it used to be, and so these mothers may now feel liberated from a comparatively difficult set of responsibilities (Heubusch, 1997; Morfei et al., 2004).

Although some feelings of loss over the departure of children are common for most people, there is little, if any, evidence to suggest that the departure of children produces anything more than temporary feelings of sadness and distress. This is especially true for women who have been working outside the home (Antonucci, 2001; Crowley, Hayslip, & Hobdy, 2003).

In fact, some discernible benefits accrue when children leave home. Married spouses have more time for one another. Married or unmarried people can throw themselves into their own work without having to worry about helping the kids with homework, carpools, and the like. The house stays neater, and the telephone rings less often.

Keep in mind that most research examining the so-called empty nest syndrome has focused on women. Because men traditionally are not as involved as women in childrearing, it was assumed that the transition when children left home would be relatively smooth for men. However, at least some research suggests that men also experience feelings of loss when their children depart, although the nature of that loss may be different from that experienced by women.

One survey of fathers whose children had left home found that although most fathers expressed either happy or neutral feelings about the departure of their children, almost a quarter felt unhappy (Lewis, Freneau, & Roberts, 1979). Those fathers tended to mention lost opportunities, regretting things that they had not done with their children. For instance, some felt that they had been too busy for their children or hadn't been sufficiently nurturing or caring.

The concept of the empty nest syndrome first arose at a time when children, after growing up, tended to leave home for good. However, times change, and the empty nest frequently becomes replenished with what have been called "boomerang children," as we discuss next.

Boomerang Children: Refilling the Empty Nest

Carole Olis doesn't know what to make of her 23-year-old son, Rob. He has been living at home since his graduation from college more than 2 years ago. Her six older children returned to the nest for just a few months and then bolted.

"I ask him, 'Why don't you move out with your friends?'" says Mrs. Olis, shaking her head. Rob has a ready answer: "They all live at home, too."

Carole Olis is not alone in being surprised and somewhat perplexed by the return of her son. There has been a significant increase in the United States in the number of young adults who come back to live in the homes of their middle-aged parents.

Known as **boomerang children**, these returning offspring typically cite economic issues as the main reason for returning. Because of a difficult economy, many young adults cannot find jobs after college, or the positions they do find pay so little that they have difficulty making ends meet. Others return home after the breakup of a marriage. Around half of all 18- to 24-year-olds live with their parents, and overall, about 14 percent of young adults live with their parents in the United States. In some European countries, the proportion is even higher (Bianchi & Casper, 2000; Lewin, 2003; Buss, 2005).

Parents' reactions to the return of their children vary, largely according to the reasons for it. If their children are unemployed, their return to the previously empty nest may be a major irritant. Fathers in particular may not grasp the realities of a difficult job market that college

empty nest syndrome   the experience that relates to parents' feelings of unhappiness, worry, loneliness, and depression resulting from their children's departure from home.

boomerang children   young adults who return, after leaving home for some period, to live in the homes of their middle-aged parents.

graduates may encounter and may be decidedly unsympathetic to their children's return. Moreover, these fathers may be affected by some subtle parent–child rivalry for the attention of the spouse (Gross, 1991; Wilcox, 1992; Mitchell, 2006).

In contrast, mothers tend to be more sympathetic to children who are unemployed. Single mothers in particular may welcome the help and security provided by returning children. Both mothers and fathers feel fairly positive about returning sons and daughters who work and contribute to the functioning of the household (Quinn, 1993; Veevers & Mitchell, 1998; Mitchell, 2006).

The Sandwich Generation: Between Children and Parents

At the same time children are leaving the nest, or perhaps even returning as boomerang children, many middle-aged adults face another challenge: growing responsibility for the care of their own aging parents. The term **sandwich generation** has come to be applied to these middle adults who feel squeezed between the needs of both their children and their aging parents (Riley & Bowen, 2005; Grundy & Henretta, 2006).

Being part of the sandwich generation is a relatively new phenomenon, produced by several converging trends. First, both men and women are marrying later and having children at an older age. At the same time, people are living longer. Consequently, the likelihood is growing that those in middle adulthood will simultaneously have children who still require a significant amount of nurturing and parents who are still alive and in need of care.

The care of aging parents can be psychologically tricky. For one thing, there is a significant degree of role reversal, with children taking on the parental role and parents in a more dependent position. Elderly people, who were previously independent, may resent and resist their children's efforts to help. They certainly do not want to be burdens on their children. For instance, almost all elderly people who live alone report that they do not wish to live with their children (CFCEPLA, 1986; Merrill, 1997).

People in middle adulthood provide a range of care for their parents. In some cases, the care is merely financial, such as helping them make ends meet on meager pensions. In other situations, it takes the form of help in managing a household, such as taking down storm windows in the spring or shoveling snow in the winter.

In more extreme cases, elderly parents may be invited to live in the home of a son or daughter. Census data reveal that multigenerational households, which include three or more generations, is the fastest-growing household arrangement of any sort. Multigenerational households increased by more than a third between 1990 and 2000, and they represent 4 percent of all households (Navarro, 2006).

Multigenerational families present a difficult situation, as parental and children's roles are renegotiated. Typically, the adult children in the middle generation—who, after all, are no longer children—are in charge of the household. Both they and their parents must adjust to the changing relationships and find some common ground in making decisions. Elderly parents may find the loss of independence particularly difficult, and this can be disturbing for their adult child as well. The youngest generation may resist the inclusion of the oldest generation.

In many cases, the burden of caring for aging parents is not shared equally, with the larger share most often taken on by women. Even in married couples where both husband and wife are in the labor force, middle-aged women tend to be more involved in the day-to-day care of aging parents, even when the parent or parents are their in-laws (Soldo, 1996; Putney & Bengtson, 2001).

Culture also influences how caregivers view their roles. For example, members of Asian cultures, which are more collectivistic, are more likely to view caregiving as a traditional and not-out-of-the-ordinary duty. In contrast, members of more individualistic cultures may perceive familial ties as less central, and caring for a member of an older generation may be experienced as more burdensome (Ho et al., 2003; Kim & Lee, 2003).

Despite the burden of being sandwiched in the middle of two generations, which can stretch the caregiving child's resources, there are also significant rewards. The psychological attachment between middle-aged children and their elderly parents can continue to grow. Both partners in the relationship can see each other more realistically. They can become closer, more accepting of

"I'm in the sandwich generation—my parents don't approve of me and my kids hate me."

⊙ mydevelopmentlab

To better understand the sandwich generation, log onto **MyDevelopmentLab** to watch a video of Amy, a woman in her mid-40s who cares for her 6-year-old son and her 82-year-old mother while balancing work and other responsibilities?

sandwich generation   adults who in middle adulthood must fulfill the needs of both their children and their aging parents.

One reason that African American grandparents are more involved with their grandchildren than white grandparents is the greater prevalence of three-generation families living together in African American households.

each other's weaknesses and more appreciative of each other's strengths (Mancini & Blieszner, 1991; Vincent, Phillipson, & Downs, 2006). As we'll discuss next, family continues to play a significant role in the lives of elderly people.

Family: The Connection of Generations

Even after the death of a spouse, most older adults are part of a larger family unit. Connections with siblings, children, grandchildren, and even great-grandchildren continue, and they may provide an important source of comfort to adults in the last years of their lives.

Siblings may provide unusually strong emotional support during late adulthood. Because they often share old, pleasant memories of childhood, and because they usually represent the oldest existing relationships a person has, siblings can provide important support. While not every memory of childhood may be pleasant, continuing interaction with brothers and sisters still provides substantial emotional support during late adulthood (Moyer 1992; Aquilino, 2006; Voorpostel & Blieszner, 2008).

Children. Even more important than siblings are children and grandchildren. Even in an age in which geographic mobility is high, most parents and children remain fairly close, both geographically and psychologically. Some 75 percent of children live within a 30-minute drive of their parents, and parents and children visit and talk with one another frequently. Daughters tend to be in more frequent contact with their parents than sons, and mothers tend to receive more communication more frequently than fathers (Field & Minkler, 1988; Krout, 1988; Ji-liang, Li-qing, & Yan, 2003).

Because the great majority of older adults have at least one child who lives fairly close by, family members still provide significant aid to one another. Moreover, parents and children tend to share similar views of how adult children should behave toward their parents (see Table 13.1). In particular, they expect children to help their parents understand their resources, provide emotional support, and talk over matters of importance such as medical issues. Furthermore, it is most often children who end up caring for their aging parents when they require assistance (Wolfson et al., 1993; Dellmann-Jenkins & Brittain, 2003; Ron, 2006).

The bonds between parents and children are sometimes asymmetrical, with parents seeking a closer relationship and children a more distant one. Parents have a greater *developmental stake*

TABLE 13.1	Parents and Children Share Similar Views of How Adult Children Should Behave Toward Their Parents	
ITEM	**CHILDREN'S RANK**	**PARENT'S RANK**
Help understand resources	1	2
Give emotional support	2	3
Discuss matters of importance	3	1
Make room in home in emergency	4	7
Sacrifice personal freedom	5	6
Care when sick	6	9
Be together on special occasions	7	5
Provide financial help	8	13
Give parents advice	9	4
Adjust family schedule to help	10	10
Feel responsible for parent	11	8
Adjust work schedule to help	12	12
Believe that parent should live with child	13	15
Visit once a week	14	11
Live close to parent	15	16
Write once a week	16	14

Source: Adapted from Hamon & Blieszner, 1990.

in close ties, since they see their children as perpetuating their beliefs, values, and standards. For their part, children are motivated to maintain their autonomy and live independently from their parents. These divergent perspectives make parents more likely to minimize conflicts they experience with their children, and children more likely to maximize them (O'Connor, 1994; Pashos & McBurney, 2008).

For parents, their children remain a source of great interest and concern. Some surveys show, for instance, that even in late adulthood parents talk about their children nearly every day, particularly if the children are having some sort of problem. At the same time, children may turn to their elderly parents for advice, information, and sometimes tangible help, such as money. And both adult generations have a stake in the next generation, as we see next (Ingersoll-Dayton, Neal, & Hammer, 2001).

Becoming a Grandparent: Who, Me?

When her eldest son and daughter-in-law had their first child, Leah couldn't believe it. At age 54, she had become a grandmother! She kept telling herself that she felt far too young to be considered anybody's grandparent.

Middle adulthood often brings one of the unmistakable symbols of aging: becoming a grandparent. For some people, becoming a grandparent has been eagerly awaited. They may miss the energy and excitement and even demands of young children, and they may see grandparenthood as the next stage in the natural progression of life. Others are less pleased with the prospect of grandparenthood, seeing it as a clear signpost of aging.

Grandparenting tends to fall into different styles. *Involved* grandparents are actively engaged in grandparenting and have influence over their grandchildren's lives. They hold clear expectations about the ways their grandchildren should behave. A retired grandmother or grandfather who takes care of a grandchild several days a week while her parents are at work is an example of an involved grandparent (Cherlin & Furstenberg, 1986; Mueller, Wilhelm, & Elder, 2002).

In contrast, *companionate* grandparents are more relaxed. Rather than taking responsibility for their grandchildren, companionate grandparents act as supporters and buddies to them. Grandparents who visit and call frequently, and perhaps occasionally take their grandchildren on vacations or invite them to visit without their parents, are practicing the companionate style of grandparenting.

Finally, the most aloof type of grandparents are *remote*. Remote grandparents are detached and distant, and they show little interest in their grandchildren. Remote grandparents, for example, would rarely make visits to see their grandchildren and might complain about their childish behavior when they did see them.

There are marked gender differences in the extent to which people enjoy grandparenthood. Generally, grandmothers are more interested and experience greater satisfaction than grandfathers, particularly when they have a high level of interaction with younger grandchildren (Smith, 1995; Smith & Drew, 2002).

African American grandparents are more apt to be involved with their grandchildren than white grandparents. The most reasonable explanation for this phenomenon is that the prevalence of three-generation families who live together is greater among African Americans than among Caucasians. In addition, African American families, which are more likely than white families to be headed by single parents, often rely substantially on the help of grandparents for everyday child care, and cultural norms tend to be highly supportive of grandparents taking an active role (Baydar & Brooks-Gunn, 1998; Baird, John, & Hayslip, 2000; Crowther & Rodriguez, 2003; Stevenson, Henderson, & Baugh, 2006).

Great-Grandchildren. Great-grandchildren play less of a role in the lives of both white and African American great-grandparents. Most great-grandparents do not have close relationships with their great-grandchildren. Close relationships tend to occur only when the great-grandparents and great-grandchildren live relatively near one another (Drew & Silverstein, 2004; Sheehan & Petrovic, 2008).

There are several explanations for the relative lack of involvement of great-grandparents with great-grandchildren. One is that by the time they reach great-grandparenthood, elderly adults are so old that they do not have much physical or psychological energy to expend on forming relationships with their great-grandchildren. Another is that there may be so many great-grandchildren that great-grandparents do not feel strong emotional ties to them. It is not uncommon for a great-grandparent who has had a large number of children to have so many

Many view a grandparent as an unmistakable sign of aging. But for others it is seen as the next stage in the natural progression of life.

great-grandchildren that they are difficult to keep track of. For example, when President John Kennedy's mother, Rose Kennedy (who had given birth to a total of nine children), died at the age of 104, she had 30 grandchildren and 41 great-grandchildren!

Yet, even though most great-grandparents may not have close relationships with their great-grandchildren, they still profit emotionally from the mere fact that they have great-grandchildren. For instance, great-grandparents may see their great-grandchildren as representing both their own and their family's continuation, as well as providing a concrete sign of their longevity (Drew & Silverstein, 2004; Sheehan & Petrovic, 2008).

Retirement

I hear all these retired folks complaining that they don't have this and they don't have that. . . . I'm not pinched. . . . My house is paid for. My car is paid for. Both my sons are grown up. I don't need many new clothes. Every time I go out and eat somewhere, I get a senior citizen's discount. This is the happiest period of my life. These are my golden years. (Gottschalk, 1983, p. 1)

This positive view of life in late adulthood was expressed by a 74-year-old retired shipping clerk. Although the story is certainly not the same for all retirees, many, if not most, find their post-worklives happy and involving. We will consider some of the ways in which people lead their lives in late adulthood.

Negotiating Retirement: Lifestyle Choices. Many people think of retirement as a time of slowing down, perhaps of withdrawing from an active lifestyle to sit out the rest of one's days in a rocking chair. But the reality is that there are many different possible approaches to retirement, including options for staying just as active while retired as in the preretirement years. Rather than the closing of a book, retirement represents the turning of a new chapter—and the story that unfolds in that new chapter has a lot to do with the retiree's expectations, goals, and preretirement plans (Dittmann, 2004; Goodman, Schlossberg, & Anderson, 2006; Nuttman-Shwartz, 2007).

Based on an extensive series of interviews, psychologist Nancy Schlossberg (2004) has identified six basic paths of retirement:

- **Continuers** use part-time or volunteer work to remain at least partially active in their preretirement work.
- **Involved spectators** take more of a back-seat role in staying connected with their previous fields.
- **Adventurers** use retirement as a time to explore entirely new pursuits, perhaps including a new field of work.
- **Searchers** are trying different activities in search of a suitable way to spend their retirement.
- **Easy gliders** don't fret about retirement much and take each day as it comes.
- **Retreaters** become depressed and withdrawn and stop searching for a meaningful pathway through retirement.

Mary and George, a couple in their 70s, have recently retired; log onto **MyDevelopmentLab** to watch them talk about how they dealt with the changes that come with retirement.

During late adulthood, the range of socioeconomic well-being mirrors that of earlier years.

The path that a person takes can change over the course of retirement, too, underscoring another fundamental point: Retirement is less of a destination than it is a journey. People who negotiate retirement most successfully are those who see it not as a time of withdrawal and stagnation but as an opportunity for development and exploration (Greer, 2004; Wang, 2007).

For many people, retirement occurs in stages as they withdraw slowly from work—perhaps by dropping to part-time work for a period before retiring altogether. Others put off retirement as long as they can; some simply enjoy their work, while others are increasingly finding that they simply do not have the financial means to retire as employers scale back pension plans and health benefits for retirees (Porter & Walsh, 2005).

Research suggests that it's just as important to prepare psychologically for retirement as it is to prepare financially. Some important considerations include the climate at work and the opportunities for future growth in one's career, relationships with family members, and community ties and activities. It's important for older adults to keep in mind that they don't just retire from work, but they also retire to a new lifestyle. Planning for what that lifestyle will be like—whether it will include part-time work, volunteer work, travel, or other activities, for example—can make a difference in adjustment to retirement (Dittmann, 2004).

Financial Issues: The Economics of Late Adulthood. People in late adulthood, like people in all other stages of life, range from one end of the socioeconomic spectrum to the other. Like the man quoted earlier in this section of the chapter, those who were relatively affluent during their working years tend to remain relatively affluent, while those who were poor at earlier stages of life tend to remain poor when they reach late adulthood.

However, the social inequities that various groups experience during their earlier lives become magnified with increasing age. At the same time, people who reach late adulthood today may experience growing economic pressure as a result of the ever-increasing human life span, which means it is more likely they will run through their savings.

Overall, 10 percent of people age 65 and older live in poverty, a proportion that is quite close to that for people under age 65. However, there are significant differences in gender and racial groups. For instance, women are almost twice as likely as men to be living in poverty. Of those elderly women living alone, around one-fourth live on incomes below the poverty line. A married woman may also slip into poverty if she becomes widowed, for she may have used up savings to pay for her husband's final illness, and the husband's pension may cease with his death (Spraggins, 2003; see Figure 13.9).

Minority women fare the worst of any category. For example, divorced black women aged 65 to 74 have a poverty rate of close to 50 percent (Rank & Hirschl, 1999; Federal Interagency Forum on Age-Related Statistics, 2000; U.S. Bureau of the Census, 2005).

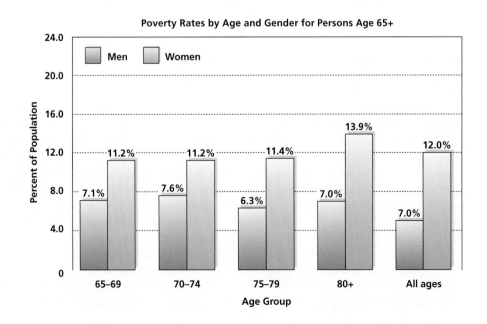

FIGURE 13.9 Poverty and the Elderly
While 10 percent of those 65 years of age and older live in poverty, women are almost twice as likely as men to be living in poverty.
Source: U.S. Bureau of the Census, 2005.

One source of financial vulnerability for people in late adulthood is their reliance on a fixed income for support. Unlike the income of a younger person, that of an elderly person, which typically comes from a combination of Social Security benefits, pensions, and savings, rarely keeps up with inflation. Consequently, as inflation drives up the price of goods such as food and clothing, income does not rise as quickly. What may have been a reasonable income at age 65 is worth much less 20 years later, as the elderly person gradually slips into poverty.

The rising cost of health care is another source of financial vulnerability in older adults. The average older person spends close to 20 percent of his or her income for health care costs. For those who require care in nursing home facilities, the financial costs can be staggering, running an average of more than $75,190 a year (MetLife Mature Market Institute, 2007).

Unless major changes are made in the way that Social Security and Medicare are financed, the costs borne by younger U.S. citizens in the workforce must rise significantly. Increasing expenditures mean that a larger proportion of younger people's pay must be taxed to fund benefits for the elderly. Such a situation is apt to lead to increasing friction and segregation between younger and older generations. Indeed, Social Security payments are one key factor in many people's decisions about how long to work.

Living Arrangements: The Places and Spaces of Their Lives

Think "old age," and if you are like most people, your thoughts soon turn to nursing homes. Popular stereotypes place most elderly people in lonely, unpleasant, institutional surroundings, under the care of strangers.

The reality is quite different. Although it is true that some people finish their lives in nursing homes, they are a tiny minority—only 5 percent. Most people live out their entire lives in home environments, typically in the company of at least one other family member.

Living at Home. A large number of older adults live alone. People over 65 represent a quarter of America's 9.6 million single-person households. Roughly two-thirds of people over the age of 65 live with other members of the family. In most cases they live with spouses. Some older adults live with their siblings, and others live in multigenerational settings with their children, grandchildren, and occasionally even great-grandchildren.

The consequences of living with a family member are quite varied, depending on the nature of the setting. For married couples, living with a spouse represents continuity with earlier life. For people who move in with their children, however, the adjustment to life in a multigenerational setting can be jarring. Not only is there a potential loss of independence and privacy, but older adults may feel uncomfortable with the way their children are raising their grandchildren. Unless there are some ground rules about the specific roles that people are to play in the household, conflicts can arise (Sussman & Sussman, 1991; Navarro, 2006).

For some groups, living in extended families is more typical than for other groups. For instance, African Americans are more likely than whites to live in multigenerational families. Furthermore, the amount of influence that family members have over one another and the interdependence of extended families are generally greater in African American, Asian American, and Hispanic families than in Caucasian families (Becker, Beyene, & Newsom, 2003).

Specialized Living Environments. For some 10 percent of those in late adulthood, home is an institution. As we'll see, there is a broad range of different types of specialized environments in which elderly people live.

One of the more recent innovations in living arrangements is the **continuing-care community**. Such communities typically offer an environment in which all the residents are of retirement age or older. Residents may need various levels of care, which is provided by the community. Residents sign contracts under which the community makes a commitment to provide care at whatever level is needed. In many such communities, people start out living in separate houses or apartments, either independently or with occasional home care. As they age and their needs increase, residents may eventually move into *assisted living,* in which people live in independent housing but are supported by medical providers to the extent required. Continuing care ultimately extends all the way to full-time nursing care, which is often provided at an on-site nursing home.

Continuing-care communities tend to be fairly homogeneous in terms of religious, racial, and ethnic backgrounds, and they are often organized by private or religious organizations. Because joining may involve a substantial initial payment, members of such communities tend to be relatively well-off financially. Increasingly, though, continuing-care communities are making efforts to

continuing-care community a community that offers an environment in which all the residents are of retirement age or older and need various levels of care.

raise the level of diversity. Furthermore, they are attempting to increase opportunities for intergenerational interaction by establishing day-care centers on the premises and developing programs that involve younger populations (Barton, 1997; Chaker, 2003; Berkman, 2006).

Several types of nursing institutions exist, ranging from those that provide part-time day care to homes that offer 24-hour-a-day, live-in care. In **adult day-care facilities**, elderly individuals receive care only during the day, but spend nights and weekends in their own homes. During the time that they are at the facility, people receive nursing care, take their meals, and participate in scheduled activities. Sometimes adult facilities are combined with infant and child day-care programs, an arrangement that allows for interaction between the old and the young (Quade, 1994; Ritchie, 2003; Tse & Howie, 2005; Gitlin et al., 2006).

Other institutional settings offer more extensive care. The most intensive institutions are **skilled-nursing facilities,** which provide full-time nursing care for people who have chronic illnesses or are recovering from a temporary medical condition. While only a small minority of those 65 and older live in nursing homes, the number increases dramatically with age. One percent of persons 65–74-years-old live in a nursing home; 5 percent for those 75–84; and 18 percent for persons 85 and older. About half of those over the age of 95 live in nursing homes. Approximately 5 percent of the elderly live in a variety of self-described senior housing that offers a number of supportive services (Administration on Aging, 2006).

The greater the extent of nursing home care, the greater the adjustment required of residents. Although some newcomers adjust relatively rapidly, the loss of independence brought about by institutional life may lead to difficulties. In addition, elderly people are as susceptible as other members of society to society's stereotypes about nursing homes, and their expectations may be particularly negative. They may see themselves as just marking time until they eventually die, forgotten and discarded by a society that venerates youth (Biedenharn & Normoyle, 1991; Baltes, 1996; Golub & Langer, 2007).

Institutionalism and Learned Helplessness. Although the fears of those in nursing homes may be exaggerated, they can lead to **institutionalism,** a psychological state in which people develop apathy, indifference, and a lack of caring about themselves. Institutionalism is brought about, in part, by a sense of *learned helplessness,* a belief that one has no control over one's environment (Butler & Lewis, 1981; Peterson & Park, 2007).

The sense of helplessness brought about by institutionalism can literally have deadly consequences. Consider, for instance, what happens when people enter nursing homes in late adulthood. One of the most conspicuous changes from their independent past is that they no longer have control over their most basic activities. They may be told when and what to eat, their sleeping schedules may be arranged by others, and even their visits to the bathroom may be regulated (Kane et al., 1997; Wolinsky, Wyrwich, & Babu, 2003).

adult day-care facilities   a facility in which elderly individuals receive care only during the day, but spend nights and weekends in their own homes.

skilled-nursing facilities   facilities that provide full-time nursing care for people who have chronic illnesses or are recovering from a temporary medical condition.

institutionalism   a psychological state in which people in nursing homes develop apathy, indifference, and a lack of caring about themselves.

FROM A
HEALTH CARE
PROFESSIONAL'S
PERSPECTIVE
What policies might a nursing home institute to minimize the chances that its residents will develop "institutionalism"? Why are such policies relatively uncommon?

BECOMING AN INFORMED CONSUMER OF DEVELOPMENT
Planning For—and Living—a Good Retirement

What makes for a good retirement? Gerontologists suggest that several factors are related to success (Kreitlow & Kreitlow, 1997; Rowe & Kahn, 1998).

- *Plan ahead financially.* Because most financial experts suggest that Social Security pensions will be inadequate in the future, personal savings are critical. Similarly, having adequate health care insurance is essential.

- *Consider tapering off from work gradually.* Sometimes it is possible to enter into retirement by shifting from full-time to part-time work. Such a transition may be helpful in preparing for eventual full-time retirement.

- *Explore your interests before you retire.* Assess what you like about your current job and think how that might be translated into leisure activities.

- *If you are married or in a long-term partnership, spend some time discussing your views of the ideal retirement with your partner.* You may find that you need to negotiate a vision that will suit you both.

- *Consider where you want to live.* Try out, temporarily, a community to which you are thinking of moving.

- *Determine the advantages and disadvantages of downsizing your current home.*

- *Plan to volunteer your time.* People who retire have an enormous wealth of skills, and these are often needed by nonprofit organizations and small businesses. Organizations such as the Retired Senior Volunteer Program or the Foster Grandparent Program can help match your skills with people who need them.

A classic experiment showed the consequences of such a loss of control. Psychologists Ellen Langer and Irving Janis (1979) divided elderly residents of a nursing home into two groups. One group of residents was encouraged to make a variety of choices about their day-to-day activities. The other group was given no choices and was encouraged to let the nursing home staff care for them. The results were clear. The participants who had choices were not only happier, they were also healthier. In fact, 18 months after the experiment began, only 15 percent of the choice group had died—compared to 30 percent of the comparison group.

In short, the loss of control over certain aspects of their daily life experienced by residents of nursing homes and other institutions can have a profound effect on their well-being. Keep in mind that not all nursing homes are the same, however. The best go out of their way to permit residents to make basic life decisions, and they attempt to give people in late adulthood a sense of control over their lives.

REVIEW

▶ Family changes in middle adulthood include the departure of children. In recent years, the phenomenon of "boomerang children" has emerged.

▶ Middle-aged adults often have increasing responsibilities for their aging parents.

▶ A further change is grandparenthood. Typically, grandparents may be involved, companionate, or remote.

▶ Family ties continue to be important throughout late adulthood. Older adults remain emotionally invested in their children.

▶ Financial issues can trouble older people, largely because their incomes are fixed, health care costs are increasing, and the life span is lengthening.

▶ Elderly people live in a variety of settings, although most live at home with a family member.

APPLY

▶ Are the phenomena of the empty nest, boomerang children, the sandwich generation, and grandparenting culturally dependent? Why might such phenomena be different in societies where multigenerational families are the norm?

▶ Why might it be desirable for older adults to move from working full time to part time at their jobs before retiring completely? How might traditional workplaces accommodate this change?

Epilogue

In this chapter, we focused on family and peer relationships across the life span and examined a variety of lifestyles. We looked at what determines popularity and the qualities children and adults seek in friends.

We then focused on the role family plays throughout our lives. We saw how the decision to have a child affects a couple's relationship, and how family life itself has changed in recent decades with the rise in divorce and the number of households where both parents work outside the home. We considered various family constellations and their effects on children.

Finally, we examined the continuing importance of family in late adulthood. We considered the lifestyles of older people as they enter retirement and examined the choices they face, the financial issues common to this age group, and their varied living arrangements.

Return for a moment to the opening Prologue, in which we looked at Leah and her parents as she prepared to attend her first formal dance. In light of what you now know about the changing roles of family and friends across the life span, consider the following questions.

1. In what ways does Leah's desire to attend a coed sleepover party exemplify the changes that occur in friendships from middle childhood to adolescence?

2. Based on the evidence in this Prologue, what can you infer about the values and behaviors of Leah's reference group? If Leah is not allowed to attend the coed sleepover, how do you think it will affect her social standing with her peers?

3. What seems to be at the heart of the conflict between Leah and her parents? Is this evidence of a deep generation gap in Leah's family? Explain.

4. In what ways is Leah exhibiting a quest for autonomy? How are the social roles Leah is expected to play in conflict here?

5. How do you think Leah's parents should resolve this disagreement? Why?

Looking Back

In what sorts of social relationships and play do preschoolers engage?

1. Preschool social relationships begin to encompass genuine friendships, which involve trust and endure over time.

2. Older preschoolers engage in more constructive play than functional play. They also engage in more associative and cooperative play than younger preschoolers, who do more parallel and onlooker playing.

How does gender affect friendships in middle childhood?

3. Boys and girls in middle childhood increasingly prefer same-gender friendships.

4. Male friendships are characterized by groups, status hierarchies, and restrictive play. Female friendships tend to involve one or two close relationships, equal status, and a reliance on cooperation.

5. Cross-race friendships become less frequent as children age. Equal-status interactions among members of different racial groups can lead to improved understanding, mutual respect and acceptance, and a decreased tendency to stereotype.

6. One of the most noticeable changes from childhood to adolescence is the greater reliance on friendships, which help adolescents define who they are.

7. In addition to friends, other peers play an influential role during adolescence as parents' supervisory role begins to diminish.

8. Peers influence one another in many ways during adolescence, providing support for academic achievement and prosocial behavior and compensation for negative school or family situations.

What are gender, race, and ethnic relations like in adolescence?

9. During adolescence, boys and girls begin to spend time together in groups and, toward the end of adolescence, to pair off.

10. In general, segregation between people of different races and ethnicities increases in middle and late adolescence, even in schools with a diverse student body.

11. Adolescents' quest for autonomy often brings confusion and tension to their relationships with their parents, but the actual "generation gap" between parents' and teenagers' attitudes is usually small.

What does it mean to be popular and unpopular?

12. Degrees of popularity during adolescence include popular and controversial adolescents (on the high end of popularity) and neglected and rejected adolescents (on the low end).

How do adults choose the people who will become their friends?

13. Proximity plays a key role in adult friendships. Most adults form friendships with people who live nearby or with whom they come into regular contact.

14. Adults tend to seek friends who share their values and attitudes. They also look for friends who are loyal, supportive, warm, trustworthy, and have a good sense of humor.

How does the arrival of children affect a relationship?

15. More than 90 percent of married couples have at least one child, but the size of the average family has decreased, due partly to birth control and partly to the changing roles of women in the workforce.

16. Children bring pressures to any marriage, shifting the focus of the marriage partners, changing their roles, and increasing their responsibilities. Gay and lesbian couples with children experience similar changes in their relationships.

How do today's diverse family and care arrangements affect children?

17. Children in families in which both parents work outside the home generally fare well.

18. Immediately after a divorce, the effects on children in the middle childhood years can be serious, depending on the financial condition of the family and the hostility level between spouses before the divorce.

19. The consequences of living in a single-parent family depend on the financial condition of the family and, if there had been two parents, the level of hostility that existed between them. Blended families present challenges to the child but can also offer opportunities for increased social interaction.

What changing family situations do middle-aged adults face?

20. The empty nest syndrome, a supposed psychological upheaval following the departure of children, is probably exaggerated. The permanent departure of children is often delayed as "boomerang" children return home for a number of years after having faced the harsh realities of economic life.

21. Adults in the middle years often face responsibilities for both their children and their aging parents. Such adults, who have been called the sandwich generation, face significant challenges.

22. Many middle-aged adults become grandparents for the first time. Researchers have identified three grandparenting styles: involved, companionate, and remote. Styles tend to differ by gender and race.

What sorts of relationships are important in late adulthood?

23. Friendships are important in later life because they offer personal control, companionship, and social support.

24. Family relationships, especially with siblings and children, provide a great deal of emotional support for people in later life.

In what circumstances do older people live, and what difficulties do they face?

25. Living arrangement options include staying at home, living with family members, participating in adult day care, residing in continuing-care communities, and living in skilled-nursing facilities.

26. Elderly people may become financially vulnerable because they must cope with rising health care and other costs on a fixed income.

PEARSON
mydevelopmentlab™

For more review plus **MyVirtualChild**, practice tests, videos, flashcards, and more, log on to **www.mydevelopmentlab.com**

14

Schooling, Culture, and Society: Living in a Multicultural World

Prologue
First Day

The night before my younger child, Will, started kindergarten, neither he nor I could sleep. Mingled with his excitement was, I imagined, concern over some of the worries that he had expressed to my husband and me: Would he be smart enough? Would he be able to read? Would there be enough time at school to play? Similar doubts haunted my own dreams like the Wild Things; I wondered whether I should have left Will in preschool for another year (with an August birthday, he would be one of the youngest in his class), whether his skills would be as advanced as the other children's, whether his teacher would appreciate his charms, tolerate his mishaps, and love him no matter what, as we do—and how I would survive without a little one at my heels.

The next morning, I helped Will get dressed in the new outfit that we had bought weeks earlier and carefully laid out the night before. To avoid last-minute panic, I'd packed his favorite lunch and his backpack the night before. After a photo session, we set off together. Although he clutched my hand on the walk to the classroom, Will lined up with his classmates as if he had been doing it for years, and trotted into the class with nary a backward glance.

(Fishel, 1993, p. 165)

Schooling marks the beginning of an intellectual and social journey that continues for many years, shaping our development in significant ways.

For both preschoolers and their parents, the experience of attending school for the first time produces a combination of apprehension, exhilaration, and anticipation. It marks the start of an intellectual as well as a social journey that will continue for many years and shape the development of children in significant ways.

In this chapter, we focus on schooling, leisure, and what it means to live in a multicultural world. We begin by examining the different types of child-care and preschool programs, and we consider what each has to offer young children. We then look at what makes children ready for school and discuss the transition from elementary to secondary school. We also consider the effectiveness of alternatives to traditional education such as home schooling and the factors that affect individual student achievement.

We then turn to looking at how people spend their leisure time. We focus on leisure during adolescence and later on in adulthood. We address the question, Does more leisure time necessarily mean a slower pace of life in the United States?

In the last part of the chapter, we look at culture and diversity. We discuss how a bicultural identity may be fostered in the schools. We examine the role that race, ethnicity, gender, and socioeconomic status play in determining culture. We also look at how members of different cultures relate to one another and how individuals develop an ethnic identity. Finally, we consider prejudice and discrimination.

LOOKING AHEAD

After reading this chapter, you'll be able to answer the following questions:

► What kinds of preschool educational programs are available in the United States, and what effects do they have?

► What factors have the most influence on school performance?

► What factors affect college attendance and performance by women and minorities?

► What do adolescents in the United States and other cultures do with their time?

► How has increased access to media and technology affected adolescents' lives?

► In what ways are individuals affected by culture and ethnicity?

► How is socioeconomic status related to race and ethnicity?

► How do prejudice, stereotypes, and discrimination work together?

MODULE 14.1

Schooling Throughout the Life Span

On a Monday morning at Judi Wyler's family child-care center, six children, ages 3 to 5, gather round an incubator. Judi, a former preschool teacher, has turned off the lights so that she can candle the eggs in the incubator. The children stare, fascinated, as the high-powered flashlight turns the eggshell transparent. "Look! The baby chick is almost as big as the egg!" shouts one of the girls. "Yes, it won't be much longer before they hatch," Judi assures the children.

The children in Judi Wyler's child-care center are having fun, but they're also learning about how a chick develops in the egg. Such hands-on lessons are increasingly a part of many preschool programs as we discuss here.

Early Childhood Education: Taking the Pre- out of the Preschool Period

The term *preschool period* is something of a misnomer: Almost three-quarters of children in the United States are enrolled in some form of care outside the home, much of which is designed either explicitly or implicitly to teach skills that will enhance intellectual as well as social abilities (see Figure 14.1). One important reason for this increase is the rise in the number of families in which both parents work outside the home. For instance, a high proportion of fathers work outside the home, and close to 60 percent of women with children under 6 are employed, most of them full time (Borden, 1998; Tamis-LeMonda & Cabrera, 2002).

However, there is another cause, one less tied to the practical considerations of child care: Developmentalists have found increasing evidence that children can benefit substantially from involvement in some form of educational activity before they enroll in formal schooling, which

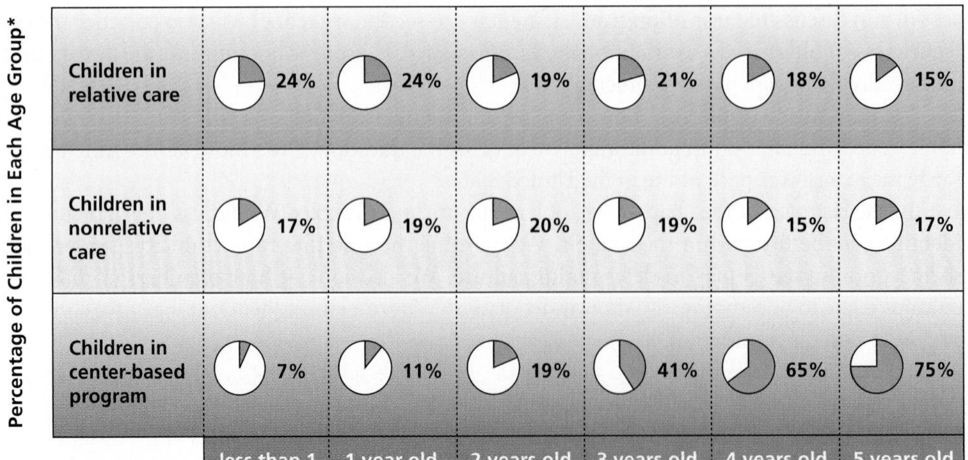

FIGURE 14.1 Care Outside the Home
Approximately 75 percent of children in the United States are enrolled in some form of care outside the home—a trend that is the result of more parents being employed full time. Evidence suggests that children can benefit from early childhood education. What role might a caregiver provide that can help the educational development of a child?
Source: U.S. Department of Education, National Center for Child Health, 2003.

	less than 1	1 year old	2 years old	3 years old	4 years old	5 years old
Children in relative care	24%	24%	19%	21%	18%	15%
Children in nonrelative care	17%	19%	20%	19%	15%	17%
Children in center-based program	7%	11%	19%	41%	65%	75%

Percentage of Children in Each Age Group*

*Columns do not add up to 100 because some children participated in more than one type of day care.

typically takes place at age 5 or 6 in the United States. When compared to children who stay at home and have no formal educational involvement, those children enrolled in *good* preschools experience clear cognitive and social benefits (Campbell, Ramey, & Pungello, 2002; Friedman, 2004; National Association for the Education of Young Children, 2005).

The Variety of Early Education. The variety of early education alternatives is vast. Some outside-the-home care for children is little more than babysitting, while other options are designed to promote intellectual and social advances. Among the major choices of the latter type are the following:

Designed to provide intellectual and social experiences, preschools vary enormously in the activities they provide.

- *Child-care centers* typically provide care for children all day, while their parents are at work. (Child-care centers were previously referred to as *day care centers.* However, because a significant number of parents work non-standard schedules and therefore require care for their children at times other than the day, the preferred label has changed to child-care centers.)

  Although many child-care centers were first established as safe, warm environments where children could be cared for and could interact with other children, today their purpose tends to be broader, aimed at providing some form of intellectual stimulation. Still, their primary purpose tends to be more social and emotional than cognitive.

- Some child care is provided in *family child-care centers*, small operations run in private homes. Because centers in some areas are unlicensed, the quality of care can be uneven, and parents should consider whether a family child-care center is licensed before enrolling their children. In contrast, providers of center-based care, which is offered in institutions such as school classrooms, community centers, and churches and synagogues, are typically licensed and regulated by governmental authorities. Because teachers in such programs are more often trained professionals than those who provide family child care, the quality of care is often higher.

- *Preschools* are explicitly designed to provide intellectual and social experiences for children. They tend to be more limited in their schedules than family care centers, typically providing care for only 3 to 5 hours per day. Because of this limitation, preschools mainly serve children from middle and higher socioeconomic levels, in cases where parents don't need to work full time.

Like child-care centers, preschools vary enormously in the activities they provide. Some emphasize social skills, while others focus on intellectual development. Some do both.

For instance, Montessori preschools, which use a method developed by Italian educator Maria Montessori, employ a carefully designed set of materials to create an environment that fosters sensory, motor, and language development through play. Children are provided with a variety of activities to choose from, with the option of moving from one to another (Gutek, 2003).

Similarly, in the Reggio Emilia preschool approach—another Italian import—children participate in what is called a negotiated curriculum that emphasizes the joint participation of children and teachers. The curriculum builds on the interests of children, promoting their cognitive development through the integration of the arts and participation in week-long projects (Hong & Trepanier-Street, 2004; Rankin, 2004).

- *School child care* is provided by some local school systems in the United States. Almost half the states in the United States fund prekindergarten programs for 4-year-olds, often aimed at disadvantaged children. Because they typically are staffed by better-trained teachers than less-regulated child-care centers, school child-care programs are often of higher quality than other early education alternatives.

The Effectiveness of Child Care. How effective are such programs? Most research suggests that preschoolers enrolled in child-care centers show intellectual development that at least matches that of children at home, and often is better. For instance, some studies find that preschoolers in child care are more verbally fluent, show memory and comprehension advantages, and even achieve higher IQ scores than at-home children. Other studies find that early and long-term participation in child care is particularly helpful for children from impoverished home environments or for children who are otherwise at risk (Campbell, Ramey, & Pungello, 2002; Clarke-Stewart & Allhusen, 2002; Vandell, 2004).

"I didn't realize how much I needed to get away from that day-care grind."

Similar advantages are found for social development. Children in high-quality programs tend to be more self-confident, independent, and knowledgeable about the social world in which they live than those who do not participate. This is not to say that all the outcomes of outside-the-home care are positive: Children in child care have been found to be less polite, less compliant, less respectful of adults, and sometimes more competitive and aggressive than their peers. Furthermore, children who spend more than 10 hours a week in preschools have a slightly higher likelihood of being disruptive in class extending through the sixth grade (Clarke-Stewart & Allhusen, 2002; NICHHD Early Child Care Research Network, 2003; Belsky et al., 2007).

Another way to consider the effectiveness of child care is to take an economic approach. For instance, one study of pre-kindergarten education in Texas found that every dollar invested in high-quality preschool programs produced $3.50 in benefits. Benefits included increased graduation rates, higher earnings, savings in juvenile crime, and reductions in child-welfare costs (Aguirre et al., 2006).

It is important to keep in mind that not all early childhood care programs are equally effective. As we observed of infant child care in Chapter 9, one key factor is program *quality*: High-quality care provides intellectual and social benefits, while low-quality care not only is unlikely to furnish benefits, but may actually may harm children (Maccoby & Lewis, 2003; Votruba-Drzal, Coley, & Chase-Lansdale, 2004; NICHD Early Child Care Research Network, 2006).

The Quality of Child Care. How can we define "high quality"? Several characteristics are important; they are analogous to those that pertain to infant child care. The major characteristics of high-quality child care include the following (Vandell, Shumow, & Posner, 2005; Layzer & Goodson, 2006; Leach et al., 2008; Rudd, Cain, & Saxon, 2008):

- The care providers are well trained.
- The child-care center has an appropriate overall size and ratio of care providers to children. Single groups should not have many more than 14 to 20 children, and there should be no more than five to ten 3-year-olds per caregiver, or seven to ten 4- or 5-year-olds per caregiver.
- The curriculum of a child-care facility is not left to chance, but is carefully planned out and coordinated among the teachers.
- The language environment is rich, with a great deal of conversation.
- The caregivers are sensitive to children's emotional and social needs, and they know when and when not to intervene.
- Materials and activities are age appropriate.
- Basic health and safety standards are followed.

No one knows how many programs in the United States can be considered "high quality," but there are many fewer than are desirable. In fact, the United States lags behind almost every other industrialized country in the quality of its child care as well as in its quantity and affordability (Zigler & Finn-Stevenson, 1995; Scarr, 1998; Muenchow & Marsland, 2007).

 DEVELOPMENTAL DIVERSITY
Preschools Around the World: Why Does the United States Lag Behind?

In France and Belgium, access to preschool is a legal right. In Sweden and Finland, the governments provide child care to preschoolers whose parents work. Russia has an extensive system of state-run *yasli-sads,* nursery schools and kindergartens, attended by 75 percent of children ages 3 to 7 in urban areas.

In contrast, the United States has no coordinated national policy on preschool education—or on the care of children in general. There are several reasons for this. For one, decisions about education have traditionally been left to the states and local school districts. For another, the

United States has no tradition of teaching preschoolers, unlike other countries in which preschool-age children have been enrolled in formal programs for decades. Finally, the status of preschools in the United States has been traditionally low. Consider, for instance, that preschool and nursery school teachers are the lowest paid of all teachers. (Teacher salaries increase as the age of students rises. Thus, college and high school teachers are paid most, while preschool and elementary school teachers are paid least.)

Preschools also differ significantly from one country to another according to the views of different societies on the purpose of early childhood education (Lamb et al., 1992; Roopnarine & Metindogan, 2006). For instance, in a cross-country comparison of preschools in China, Japan, and the United States, researchers found that parents in the three countries view the purpose of preschools very differently. Whereas parents in China tend to see preschools primarily as a way of giving children a good start academically, Japanese parents view them primarily as a way of giving children the opportunity to be members of a group. In the United States, in comparison, parents regard the primary purpose of preschools as making children more independent and self-reliant, although obtaining a good academic start and having group experience are also important (see Figure 14.2; Huntsinger et al., 1997; Johnson et al., 2003).

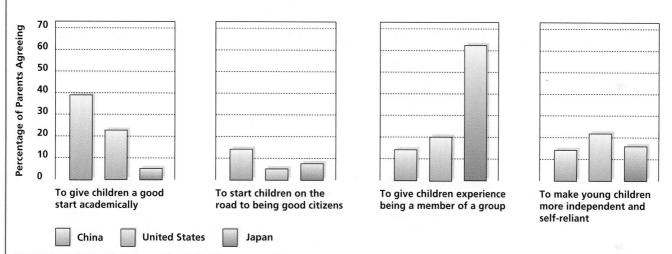

FIGURE 14.2 The Purpose of Preschool
To parents in China, Japan, and the United States, the main purpose of preschools is very different. As a preschool educator, how would you interpret these findings?
Source: Adapted from Tobin, Wu, & Davidson, 1989.

Preparing Preschoolers for Academic Pursuits: Does Head Start Truly Provide a Head Start? Although many programs designed for preschoolers focus primarily on social and emotional factors, some are geared primarily toward promoting cognitive gains and preparing preschoolers for the more formal instruction they will experience when they start kindergarten. In the United States, the best-known program designed to promote future academic success is Head Start. Born in the 1960s when the United States declared a War on Poverty, the program has served over 13 million children and their families. The program, which stresses parental involvement, was designed to serve the "whole child," including children's physical health, self-confidence, social responsibility, and social and emotional development (Zigler & Styfco, 2004; Love, Chazen-Cohen, & Raikes, 2007).

Whether or not Head Start is seen as successful depends on the lens through which one is looking. If, for instance, the program is expected to provide long-term increases in IQ scores, it is a disappointment. Although graduates of Head Start programs tend to show immediate IQ gains, these increases do not last.

On the other hand, it is clear that Head Start is meeting its goal of getting preschoolers ready for school. Preschoolers who participate in Head Start are better prepared for future schooling than those who do not. Furthermore, graduates of Head Start programs have better future school adjustment than their peers, and they are less likely to be in special education classes or to be retained in grade. Finally, some research suggests that Head Start graduates even show higher academic performance at the end of high school, although the gains are modest (Schnur & Belanger, 2000; Brooks-Gunn, 2003; Kronholz, 2003).

The most recent comprehensive evaluation of early intervention programs suggests that, taken as a group, they can provide significant benefits, and that government funds invested early in life may ultimately lead to a reduction in future costs. For instance, compared with children who did not participate in early intervention programs, participants in various programs showed gains in emotional or cognitive development, better educational outcomes, increased economic self-sufficiency, reduced levels of criminal activity, and improved health-related behaviors. Although not every program produced all these benefits, and not every child benefited to the same extent, the results of the evaluation suggested that the potential benefits of early intervention can be substantial (NICHD Early Child Care Research Network & Duncan, 2003; Love et al., 2006; Barnard, 2007; Izard et al., 2008).

Of course, traditional programs such as Head Start, which emphasize academic success brought about by traditional instruction, are not the only approach to early intervention that has proven effective. As we consider in the *From Research to Practice* box, Montessori schools, which have their own unique philosophy and approach, have also proven valuable.

From Kindergarten to High School: Preparing Students for Success

As the eyes of the six other children in his reading group turned to him, Glenn shifted uneasily in his chair. Reading had never come easily to him, and he always felt anxious when it was his turn to read aloud. But as his teacher nodded in encouragement, he plunged in, hesitantly at first, then gaining momentum as he read the story about a mother's first day on a new job. He found that he could read the passage quite nicely, and he felt a surge of happiness and pride at his accomplishment. When he was done, he broke into a broad smile as his teacher said simply, "Well done, Glenn."

Small moments such as these, repeated over and over, make—or break—a child's educational experience. Schooling marks a time when society formally attempts to transfer to new generations its accumulated body of knowledge, beliefs, values, and wisdom. The success with which this transfer is managed determines, in a very real sense, the future fortunes of the world.

What Makes Children Ready for School?   Many parents have a hard time deciding exactly when to enroll their children in school for the first time. Do children who are younger than most of the other children in their grade suffer as a result of the age difference? According to traditional wisdom, the answer is yes. Because younger children are assumed to be slightly less advanced developmentally than their peers, it has been assumed that such children would be at a competitive disadvantage. In some cases, teachers recommended that students delay entry into kindergarten in order to cope better academically and emotionally (Noel & Newman, 2008).

A massive study conducted by developmental psychologist Frederick Morrison contradicts this traditional view. He found that children who are among the youngest in first grade progress at the same rate as the oldest. Although they were slightly behind older first-graders in reading, the difference was negligible. It was also clear that parents who chose to hold their children back in kindergarten, thereby ensuring that they would be among the oldest in first grade and after, were not doing their children a favor. These older children did no better than their younger classmates (Morrison, Smith, & Dow-Ehrensberger, 1995; Vecchiotti, 2003; Morrison, Bachman, & Connor, 2005).

Other research even has identified some delayed negative reaction to delayed entry. For example, one longitudinal study examined adolescents whose entrance into kindergarten was delayed by a year. Even though many seemed to show no ill effects from the delay during elementary school, during adolescence a surprising number of these children had emotional and behavioral problems (Byrd, Weitzman, & Auinger, 1997; Stipek, 2002).

In short, delaying children's entry into school does not necessarily provide an advantage and in some cases may actually be harmful. Ultimately, age per se is not a critical indicator of when children should begin school. Instead, the start of formal schooling is more reasonably tied to overall developmental readiness, which is the product of a complex combination of factors.

FROM RESEARCH TO PRACTICE
The Montessori Approach: Is It Effective?

In immaculately ordered and naturally lit classrooms, materials play a prominent role. Children ages 3 to 6 pick their tools—a wet sponge, a textured globe, a model dinosaur skeleton—and work quietly, either alone or in groups of two or three. Down the hall, their peers do yoga on 10 mats in the library (MacDonald, 2007, p. 9D)

In the early 1900s, Dr. Maria Montessori developed an alternative to the traditional approach to educating young children in an effort to improve the poor's access to education. Montessori rejected traditional methods such as tests and grades because she felt they fostered competition and discouraged collaborative learning. Instead, she embraced self-directed exploration and discovery through hands-on, active learning. Montessori education emphasizes children's active participation in their own learning. In Montessori classrooms teachers act more as facilitators within multi-age classrooms where pupils engage in individual and small-group activities that help them learn social skills as well as academic lessons (Montessori, 1964).

Montessori argued that the traditional educational approach treated children as adults and that her method was better tailored to the distinctive ways in which children think and learn. Thousands of private schools in the United States employ the Montessori method, and Montessori programs are available at several hundred public schools.

While Montessori education is clearly a different experience from the traditional classroom, does it in fact produce better educational outcomes for children? Recent research provides compelling evidence that it does.

Researchers Angeline Lillard and Nicole Else-Quest compared two groups of 3- to 6-year-old children: One group was completing the primary level of education at a Montessori school, while the other group was completing the equivalent level at various non-Montessori schools (mainly urban public schools). These two groups were known to be equivalent before they entered their respective schools, as they had all originally applied for admission to the Montessori school, with admission being determined by a random lottery. Consequently, any differences between the groups on outcome measures could be attributed to the different educational programs (Lillard & Else-Quest, 2006).

The researchers examined a variety of cognitive/academic and social/behavioral skills that are generally important to life success. To examine differences in cognitive/academic skills, the researchers used a test that measures school readiness. The Montessori students performed significantly better than the non-Montessori group on standardized measures of reading and math skill. Moreover, the Montessori students performed better on a test of executive function that involved applying different decision rules in a card-sorting task.

The benefits weren't just academic either. The children were asked their solutions to several social problems (such as a child not sharing a playground swing). The children from the Montessori school were significantly more likely than those from the comparison school group to make appeals to justice or fairness in trying to persuade the problem child to do the right thing. On the playground, Montessori children were more likely to engage in positive shared play and less likely to engage in ambiguous rough play, such as wrestling. Finally, Montessori children were more likely to show an understanding of false beliefs, a milestone in development that we discussed in Chapter 9.

Further research is needed to determine what specific components of a Montessori education are responsible for producing these beneficial outcomes. Still, taking the Montessori approach as a whole, the advantages it produces over traditional educational programs are compelling evidence of its effectiveness.

- *Can you think of any potential drawbacks to Montessori education? Would it be appropriate for every pupil? Keep in mind that in this comparison, all of the parents originally wanted their children to attend a Montessori school. What about children whose parents aren't as supportive of the Montessori method?*

- *In what ways does the Montessori method relate to Vygotsky's view of cognitive development?*

Creating an Atmosphere That Promotes School Success. What makes children succeed in school? Although there are many factors, several practical steps can be taken to maximize children's chances of success. Among them are these:

- **Promote a "literacy environment."** Parents should read to their children and familiarize them with books and reading. Adults should provide reading models so that children see that reading is an important activity in the lives of the adults with whom they interact.

- **Talk to children.** Discuss events in the news, talk about their friends, and share hobbies. Getting children to think about and discuss the world around them is one of the best preparations for school.

- **Provide a place for children to work.** This can be a desk, a corner of a table, or an area of a room. What's important is that it be a separate, designated area.

- **Encourage children's problem-solving skills.** To solve a problem, they should learn to identify their goal, what they know, and what they don't know; to design and carry out a strategy; and finally to evaluate their result.

Homeschooling: Living Rooms as Classrooms

At 9 AM on a Wednesday, Damon Buchanan, 9 years old, sits on the couch going through one of his morning rituals: reading the horoscopes in the newspaper. In the kitchen his brothers, Jacob, age 7, and Logan, age 4, are performing one of their "experiments": dropping action figures and Fisher-Price toys into glasses of water, then freezing them. Another day of school has begun.

For students like the Buchanan brothers, there is no distinction between their living room and classroom because they are among the close to 1 million students who are homeschooled. *Homeschooling* is a major educational phenomenon in which students are taught, by their parents, in their own homes.

There are a number of reasons why parents may choose to school their children at home. Some parents feel their children will thrive with the one-to-one attention that homeschooling can bring, whereas they might get lost in a larger public school. Other parents are dissatisfied with the nature of instruction and teachers in their local public schools and feel that they can do a better job teaching their children. And some parents engage in homeschooling for religious reasons, wishing to impart a particular religious ideology (and avoid exposing their children to aspects of the popular culture and values with which they disagree) that would be impossible in a public school (Bauman, 2001; Dennis, 2004; Isenberg, 2007).

Homeschooling clearly works, in the sense that children who have been homeschooled generally do as well on standardized tests as students who have been educated traditionally. In addition, their acceptance rate into college appears to be no different from that of traditionally schooled children (Lattibeaudiere, 2000; Lauricella, 2001; Lines, 2001).

However, the apparent academic success of children schooled at home does not mean that homeschooling, per se, is effective, because their parents may be more affluent or have the kind of well-structured family situation in which children would succeed no matter what kind of schooling they had. In contrast, parents in dysfunctional and disorganized families are unlikely to have the motivation or interest to homeschool their children. For children from families like these, the demands and structure of school may be a good thing.

Critics of homeschooling argue that it has considerable drawbacks. For example, the social interaction involving groups of children that is inherent in classrooms in traditional schools is largely missing for homeschooled children. Learning in an at-home environment, while perhaps strengthening family ties, hardly provides an environment that reflects the diversity of U.S. society. Furthermore, even the best-equipped home is unlikely to have sophisticated science and technology that is available at many schools. Finally, most parents do not have the preparation of well-trained teachers, and their teaching methods may be unsophisticated. Although parents may be successful in teaching subject areas in which their child is already interested, they may have more difficulty teaching subjects that their child seeks to avoid (Cai, Reeve, & Robinson, 2002; Lois, 2006).

Because homeschooling is relatively new, few controlled experiments have been conducted examining its effectiveness. More research needs to be done to determine how and when homeschooling is an effective means to educate children.

While there are a number of reasons why parents may choose to school their children at home it has been found that homeschooled children generally do as well on standardized tests as traditionally educated students.

In Transition: Making the Move from Elementary to Secondary School. The transition from elementary school into secondary education is a normative transition, meaning it is part of the life of almost all adolescents in the United States. However, the fact that nearly everyone is doing it doesn't make it easy. The transition can be particularly difficult because of the physical, intellectual, and social changes that are occurring at about the same time.

After leaving elementary school, most students enter a *middle school*, which typically comprises grades 6 to 8 (see Figure 14.3). At the same time, most adolescents are beginning puberty and coming to grips with the changes taking place in their bodies. Furthermore, their thinking is becoming more sophisticated, and their relationships with their family and friends are becoming far more complicated than ever before.

For most adolescents, middle schools provide a very different educational structure from the one they grew accustomed to in elementary school. Rather than spending the day in a self-contained classroom, students move from one class to another. Not only must they adapt to the demands of different teachers, but their classmates in each course may be different every class period. Those classmates may be more heterogeneous and diverse than those they encountered in their elementary schools.

Furthermore, because they are the youngest and least experienced, students in middle school enter an environment in which they suddenly find themselves at the bottom of the status hierarchy. Coming from elementary schools in which they were at the top of that status hierarchy (and at which they were physically and cognitively so different from the kindergarteners and first-graders who occupied the bottom of the hierarchy), students can find the middle school experience alarming and sometimes damaging.

In addition, middle schools are typically considerably larger than elementary schools. This factor alone makes the transition to middle school more difficult. A significant amount of research demonstrates quite clearly that students do better, both academically and psychologically, in smaller, less bureaucratic educational settings (Lee & Burkam, 2003; Ready, Lee, & Welner, 2004).

School Performance in Adolescence. Do the advances that occur in metacognition, reasoning, and other cognitive abilities during adolescence translate into improvements in school performance? If we use students' grades as the measure, the answer is "yes." Grades awarded to high school students have shifted upward in the last decade. The mean grade point average for college-bound seniors was 3.3 (out of a scale of 4), compared with 3.1 a decade ago. More than 40 percent of seniors reported average grades of A+, A, or A–(College Board, 2005).

At the same time, though, independent measures of achievement, such as SAT scores, have not risen. Consequently, a more likely explanation for the higher grades is the phenomenon of grade inflation. According to this view, it is not that students have changed. Instead, instructors have become more lenient, awarding higher grades for the same performance (Cardman, 2004).

Further evidence for grade inflation comes from the relatively poor achievement of students in the United States when compared to students in other countries. For instance, students in the United States score lower on standardized math and science tests than students in other industrialized countries (see Figure 14.4 on page 412; OECD, 2005).

There is no single reason for this gap in the educational achievement of U.S. students, but a combination of factors, such as less time spent in classes and less intensive instruction, are at work. Furthermore, the broad diversity of the U.S. school population may affect performance relative to other countries, in which the population attending school is more homogeneous and affluent (Stedman, 1997; Schemo, 2001).

The poorer showing of U.S. students is also reflected in high school graduation rates. Although the United States once stood first in the percentage of the population who graduates from high school, it has dropped to 24th among industrialized countries. Only 78 percent of U.S. high school students graduate—a rate considerably lower than rates in other developed countries (OECD, 1998, 2001).

Ethnic and Racial Differences in School Achievement. Achievement differences between ethnic and racial groups are significant, and they paint a troubling picture of American education. For instance, data on school achievement indicate that, on average, African American and Hispanic students tend to perform at lower levels, receive lower grades, and score lower on

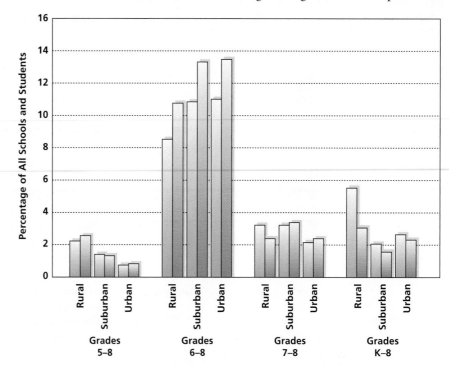

☐ % of all public elementary and secondary schools in locale

☐ % of all students enrolled in public elementary and secondary schools in locale

FIGURE 14.3
Middle School Configurations
The majority of middle schools are comprised of grades 6 to 8, particularly in suburban and urban locations.
Source: Juvonen et al., 2004.

■ Statistically different from average

■ Not statistically different from average

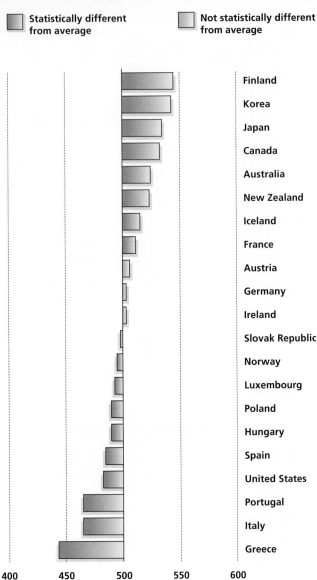

Finland	
Korea	
Japan	
Canada	
Australia	
New Zealand	
Iceland	
France	
Austria	
Germany	
Ireland	
Slovak Republic	
Norway	
Luxembourg	
Poland	
Hungary	
Spain	
United States	
Portugal	
Italy	
Greece	

400   450   500   550   600

FIGURE 14.4 Not at the Top of the Class—U.S. Math Performance Lags
When compared to the math performance of students across the world, U.S. students perform at below-average levels.
Source: Adapted from OECD, 2005.

standardized tests of achievement than Caucasian students (see Figure 14.5). In contrast, Asian American students tend to receive higher grades than Caucasian students (National Center for Educational Statistics, 2003).

What is the source of such ethnic and racial differences in academic achievement? Aside from different attributional orientations, much of the difference is due to socioeconomic factors: Because more African American and Hispanic families live in poverty, their economic disadvantage may be reflected in their school performance. When we take socioeconomic levels into account by comparing different ethnic and racial groups at the same socioeconomic level, achievement differences diminish, but they do not vanish (Meece & Kurtz-Costes, 2001; Cokley, 2003; Guerrero et al., 2006).

Anthropologist John Ogbu (1988, 1992) argues that members of certain minority groups may perceive school success as relatively unimportant. They may believe that societal prejudice in the workplace will dictate that they will not succeed, no matter how much effort they expend. The conclusion is that hard work in school will have no eventual payoff.

Ogbu suggests that members of minority groups who enter a new culture voluntarily are more likely to be successful in school than those who are brought into a new culture against their will. For instance, he notes that Korean children who are the sons and daughters of voluntary immigrants to the United States tend to be, on average, quite successful in school. On the other hand, Korean children in Japan, whose parents were forced to immigrate during World War II and work as forced laborers, tend to do relatively poorly in school. The reason for the disparity? The process of involuntary immigration apparently leaves lasting scars, reducing the motivation to succeed in subsequent generations. Ogbu suggests that in the United States, the involuntary immigration, as slaves, of the ancestors of many African American students might be related to their motivation to succeed (Ogbu, 1992; Gallagher, 1994; Ogbu, 2002; Jenkins et al., 2004).

Students' beliefs about the consequences of not doing well in school may also contribute to the racial and ethnic differences in school performance. Specifically, it may be that African American and Hispanic students tend to believe that they can succeed *despite* poor school performance. This belief may cause them to put less effort into their studies. In contrast, Asian American students tend to believe that if they do not do well in school, they are unlikely to get good jobs and be successful. Asian Americans, then, are motivated to work hard in school by a fear of the consequences of poor academic performance (Steinberg, Dornbusch, & Brown, 1992; Chong, 2007; Witkow & Fuligni, 2007).

Dropping Out of School. Although most students complete high school, nearly one out of three public high school students drop out without graduating. The consequences of dropping out are severe. High school dropouts earn 42 percent less than high school graduates, and the unemployment rate for dropouts is 50 percent.

Adolescents who leave school do so for a variety of reasons. Some leave because of pregnancy or problems with the English language. Some leave for economic reasons, needing to support themselves or their families. Others leave because they are academically or socially disengaged (Croninger & Lee, 2001; Lee & Burkam, 2003).

Dropout rates differ according to gender and ethnicity. Males are considerably more likely to drop out of school than females (see Figure 14.6). For example, in the high school class of 2003, 72 percent of girls but only 65 percent of boys earned diplomas (Greene & Winters, 2006).

In addition, although the dropout rate for all ethnicities has been declining somewhat over the last two decades, Hispanics and African American students still are more likely to leave high school before graduating than non-Hispanic white students. On the other hand, not all minority groups show higher dropout rates: Asians, for instance, drop out at a lower rate than Caucasians (National Center for Educational Statistics, 2003; Stearns & Glennie, 2006).

Poverty plays a large role in determining whether a student completes high school. Students from lower-income households are three times more likely to drop out than middle- and upper-income households. Because economic success is so dependent on education, dropping out often perpetuates a cycle of poverty (National Center for Education Statistics, 2002).

Beyond High School: The Pursuit of Higher Education and Lifelong Learning

For Enrico Vasquez, there was never any doubt: He was headed for college. Enrico, the son of a wealthy Cuban immigrant who had made a fortune in the medical supply business after fleeing Cuba 5 years before Enrico's birth, had had the importance of education constantly drummed into him by his family. In fact, the question was never whether he would go to college but what college he would be able to get into. As a consequence, Enrico found high school to be a pressure cooker: Every grade and extracurricular activity was evaluated in terms of its helping or hindering his chances of admission to a good college.

* * * *

Armando Williams's letter of acceptance to Dallas County Community College is framed on the wall of his mother's apartment. To her, the letter represents nothing short of a miracle, an answer to her prayers. Growing up in a neighborhood infamous for its drugs and drive-by shootings, Armando had always been a hard worker and a "good boy," in his mother's view. But when he was growing up, she never even entertained the possibility of his making it to college. To see him reach this stage in his education fills her with joy.

Whether a student's enrollment seems almost inevitable or signifies a triumph over the odds, attending college is a significant accomplishment. Although students already enrolled may feel that college attendance is nearly universal, this is not the case at all: Nationwide, only a minority of high school graduates enter college.

Furthermore, even for students for whom college was an inevitability, getting admitted to college may become a process that produces significant stress. Students who apply to colleges that accept only a small proportion of applicants may experience considerable anxiety as they await notification of which colleges will accept them. This stress, some of which is self-generated and some of which comes from family and peer pressure, can make the senior year of high school quite trying, as these blog excerpts suggest:

Desperately need help choosing college!!! Need advice please read!!! Can't sleep!!
Thank you O powerful (and treacherous) college gods for nothing but my current state of depression and anxiousness. (Saulny, 2006, p. 11)

We'll consider who goes to college and discuss some of the issues that relate to college attendance.

Who Goes to College? As in the U.S. population as a whole, U.S. college students are primarily white and middle class. Although nearly 69 percent of white high school graduates enter college, only 61 percent of African American and 47 percent of Hispanic graduates do so (see Figure 14.7 on page 414). Even more striking, although the absolute number of minority students enrolled in college has increased, the overall *proportion* of the minority population that does enter college has

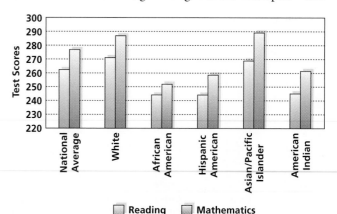

Reading   **Mathematics**

FIGURE 14.5
Achievement Test Results
Racial discrepancies between groups are apparent on a national test of reading and math achievement administered to a sample of 150,000 eighth-graders. *Source:* NAEP, 2003.

The proportion of students who enter college but never graduate is substantial, with only around 40 percent finishing four years later with a degree.

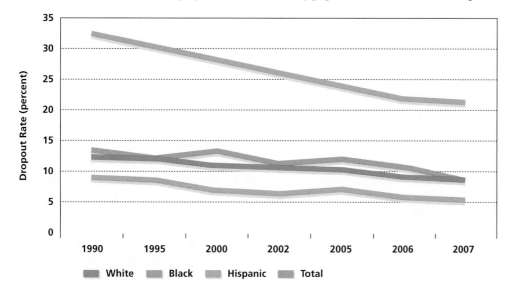

White   **Black**   **Hispanic**   **Total**

FIGURE 14.6 School Dropout Rates
Despite the fact that dropout rates have been falling for all ethnic groups, Hispanic and African American students are still more likely not to graduate. *Source:* U.S. Department of Education, National Center for Education Statistics, 2009. *The Condition of Education 2009* (NCES 2009-081), Indicator 20.

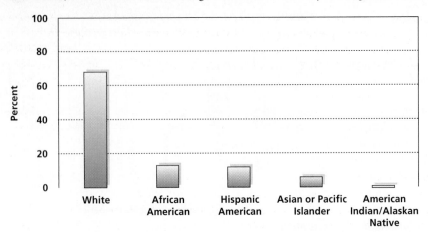

FIGURE 14.7 Who Goes to College
The proportion of African Americans and Hispanics who enter college after graduating from high school is lower than the proportion of whites.
Source: The Condition of Education 2004. National Center for Education Statistics, 2004.

FROM AN
EDUCATOR'S
PERSPECTIVE

How is the presence of older students likely to affect the college classroom, given what you know about human development? Why?

The availability of higher-paying jobs that do not require a college education is one reason why enrollment of men in college is increasing more slowly than women.

decreased over the past decade—a decline that most education experts attribute to changes in the availability of financial aid (U.S. Bureau of the Census, 1998, 2000).

Furthermore, the proportion of students who enter college but ultimately never graduate is substantial. Only around 40 percent of those who start college finish four years later with a degree. Although about half of those who don't receive a degree in four years eventually do finish, the other half never obtain a college degree. For minorities, the picture is even worse: The national dropout rate for African American college students stands at 70 percent (Minorities in Higher Education, 1995; American College Testing Program, 2001).

These observations notwithstanding, the number of students traditionally classified as "minorities" attending college is rising dramatically, and ethnic and racial minorities make up an increasingly larger proportion of the college population. Already at some colleges, such as the University of California at Berkeley, whites have shifted from the majority to the minority as diversity among the students has increased significantly. These trends, reflecting changes in the racial and ethnic composition of the United States, are significant, since higher education remains an important way for families to improve their economic well-being.

The Older, Nontraditional Student. If you picture the "average college student" as an 18- or 19-year-old, it's time to rethink. Actually, 26 percent of students taking college courses for credit in the United States are between 25 and 35. Thirty-six percent of community college students are over 30 (Dortch, 1997; U.S. Department of Education, 2005).

Why are so many older, nontraditional students taking college courses? One reason is economic. A college degree is becoming increasingly important for obtaining a job. Many employers encourage or require workers to undergo college-based training to learn new skills or update old ones.

In addition, as young adults age, they begin to feel the need to settle down with a family. This change in attitude can reduce their risk-taking behavior and make them focus more on acquiring the ability to support their family—a phenomenon that has been labeled *maturation reform*.

According to developmental psychologist Sherry Willis (1985), several broad goals underlie adults' participation in learning. First, adults sometimes seek to understand their own aging, trying to figure out what is happening to them and what to expect in the future. Second, some adults seek to understand more fully the rapid technological and cultural changes of modern life. Third, some adult learners may be seeking a practical edge in combating obsolescence on the job by acquiring new vocational skills. Finally, education may be seen as helpful in preparing for future retirement. Concerned about shifting from a work orientation to a leisure orientation, they may see education as a means of broadening their possibilities.

Gender in the Classroom.

I registered for a calculus course my first year at DePauw. Even twenty years ago I was not timid, so on the very first day I raised my hand and asked a question. I still have a vivid memory of the professor rolling his eyes, hitting his head with his hand in frustration, and announcing to everyone, "Why do they expect me to teach calculus to girls?" I never asked another question. Several weeks later I went to a football game, but I had forgotten to bring my ID. My calculus professor was at the gate checking IDs, so I went up to him and said, "I forgot my ID but you know me, I'm in your class." He looked right at me and said, "I don't remember you in my class." I couldn't believe that someone who changed my life and whom I remember to this day didn't even recognize me. (Sadker & Sadker, 1994, p. 162)

Although such incidents of blatant sexism are less likely to occur today, prejudice and discrimination directed at women are still a fact of college life. For instance, the next time you are in class, consider the gender of your classmates and the subject matter of the class. Although men and women attend college in roughly equal numbers, there is significant variation in the classes they take. Classes in education and the social sciences, for instance, typically have a larger proportion of women than men; and classes in engineering, the physical sciences, and mathematics tend to have more men than women.

The gender gap is also apparent when we look at college instructors. Although the number of female faculty members has increased, there is still evidence of apparent discrimination. For example, the more prestigious the institution, the smaller the proportion of women who have attained the highest rank. The situation is even more pronounced in the fields of math, science, and engineering, where women are significantly underrepresented (Wilson, 2004).

The persistent differences in gender distribution across subject areas likely reflect the powerful influence of gender stereotypes that operate throughout the world of education and beyond. For instance, when women in their first year of college are asked to name a likely career choice, they are much less apt to choose careers that have traditionally been dominated by men, such as engineering or computer programming, and more likely to choose professions that have traditionally been populated by women, such as nursing and social work (Glick, Zion, & Nelson, 1988; Cooperative Institutional Research Program, 1990; Avalon, 2003).

Male and female college students also have different expectations regarding their areas of competence. For instance, one survey asked first-year college students whether they were above or below average on a variety of traits and abilities. As can be seen in Figure 14.8, men were more likely than women to think of themselves as above average in overall academic and mathematical ability, competitiveness, and emotional health.

Both male and female college professors treat men and women differently in their classes, even though the different treatment is largely unintentional and often the professors are unaware of their actions. For instance, professors call on men in class more frequently than women, and they make more eye contact with men than with women. Furthermore, male students are more likely to receive extra help from their professors than women. Finally, the male students often receive more positive reinforcement for their comments than female students—exemplified by the startling illustration in Table 14.1 on page 416 (American Association of University Women, 1992; Epperson, 1988; Sadker & Sadker, 1994, 2005).

The different treatment of men and women in the classroom has led some educators to argue in favor of single-sex education for women. They point to evidence that the rate of participation and ultimately the success of women in the sciences is greater for graduates of women's colleges than for graduates of coeducational institutions. Furthermore, some research suggests that women who attend same-sex colleges may show higher self-esteem than those attending coeducational colleges, although the evidence is not entirely consistent on this count (Mael, 1998; Sax, 2005).

Why might women do better in single-sex environments? One reason is that they receive more attention than they would in coeducational settings, where professors are affected, however inadvertently, by societal biases. In addition, women's colleges tend to have more female professors than coeducational institutions, and they thereby provide more role models for women. Finally, women attending women's colleges may receive more encouragement for participation in nontraditional subjects such as mathematics and science than those in coeducational colleges (Robinson & Gillibrand, 2004).

Learning in Later Life: Never Too Late to Learn

The University of Arkansas campus is buzzing with talk of midterms and football. In a cafeteria, students are grousing about the food.

"Where are the dinner rolls?" says one. "I'm a vegetarian, and all they have is meat," complains another. Soon, though, everyone has moved on to complaining about classes.

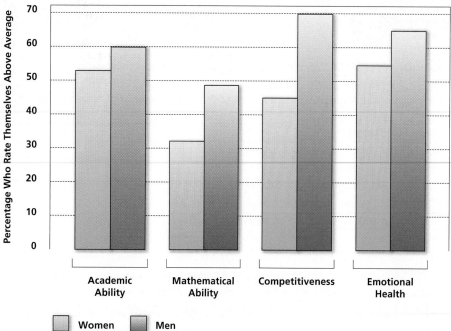

FIGURE 14.8 Self-Perception of Ability
During their first year of college, men are more likely than women to view themselves as above average in areas relevant to academic success.
Source: Sax et al., 2000.

Older adults have no trouble keeping up with demanding college courses and offer a real educational benefit by bringing their varied and substantial life experiences to the classroom.

TABLE 14.1 Gender Bias in the Classroom

The course on the U.S. Constitution is required for graduation, and more than 50 students, approximately half male and half female, file in. The professor begins by asking if there are questions on next week's midterm. Several hands go up.

BERNIE: Do you have to memorize names and dates in the book? Or will the test be more general?

PROFESSOR: You do have to know those critical dates and people. Not every one but the important ones. If I were you, Bernie, I would spend time learning them.

ELLEN: What kind of short-answer questions will there be?

PROFESSOR: All multiple choice.

ELLEN: Will we have the whole class time?

PROFESSOR: Yes, we'll have the whole class time. Anyone else?

BEN (calling out): Will there be an extra-credit question?

PROFESSOR: I hadn't planned on it. What do you think?

BEN: I really like them. They take some of the pressure off. You can also see who is doing extra work.

PROFESSOR: I'll take it under advisement. Charles?

CHARLES: How much of our final grade is this?

PROFESSOR: The midterm is 25 percent. But remember, class participation counts as well. Why don't we begin?

The professor lectures on the Constitution for 20 minutes before he asks a question about the electoral college. The electoral college is not as hot a topic as the midterm, so only four hands are raised. The professor calls on Ben.

BEN: The electoral college was created because there was a lack of faith in the people. Rather than have them vote for the president, they voted for the electors.

PROFESSOR: I like the way you think. (He smiles at Ben, and Ben smiles back.) Who could vote? (Five hands go up, five out of fifty.) Angie?

ANGIE: I don't know if this is right, but I thought only men could vote.

BEN (calling out): That was a great idea. We began going downhill when we let women vote. (Angie looks surprised but says nothing. Some of the students laugh, and so does the professor. He calls on Barbara.)

BARBARA: I think you had to be pretty wealthy, own property—

JOSH (not waiting for Barbara to finish, calls out): That's right. There was a distrust of the poor, who could upset the democracy. But if you had property, if you had something at stake, you could be trusted not to do something wild. Only property owners could be trusted.

PROFESSOR: Nice job, Josh. But why do we still have electors today? Mike?

MIKE: Tradition, I guess.

PROFESSOR: Do you think it's tradition? If you walked down the street and asked people their views of the electoral college, what would they say?

MIKE: Probably they'd be clueless. Maybe they would think that it elects the Pope. People don't know how it works.

PROFESSOR: Good, Mike. Judy, do you want to say something? (Judy's hand is at "half-mast," raised but just barely. When the professor calls her name, she looks a bit startled.)

JUDY (speaking very softly): Maybe we would need a whole new constitutional convention to change it. And once they get together to change that, they could change anything. That frightens people, doesn't it? (As Judy speaks, a number of students fidget, pass notes, and leaf through their books; a few even begin to whisper.)

Source: Sadker & Zittleman, 2009.

A typical college scene—except for all the canes, hearing aids and white hair in evidence. This is Elderhostel, a program for people 60 and older run by a Boston nonprofit organization, formed in 1975, that recruits colleges to conduct weeklong educational sessions in everything from genealogy to the archaeology of ancient Egypt. (Stern, 1994, p. A1)

More than 250,000 people enroll annually in thousands of classes organized by Elderhostel, the largest educational program for people in late adulthood. Represented on campuses across the world, the Elderhostel movement is further evidence that intellectual growth and change continue throughout people's lives. As we saw earlier, exercising cognitive skills may help older adults maintain their intellectual functioning (Sack, 1999; Simson, Wilson, & Harlow-Rosentraub, 2006).

Although not everyone can afford Elderhostel tuitions, many public colleges encourage senior citizens to enroll in classes by offering free tuition. In addition, some retirement communities are located at or near college campuses, such as the University of Michigan and Penn State University (Powell, 2004).

Although some elderly people are doubtful about their intellectual capabilities and consequently hesitate to compete with younger students in regular classes, their concern is largely misplaced. Older adults often have no trouble maintaining their standing in rigorous college classes. Furthermore, professors and other students generally find the presence of older people, with their varied and substantial life experiences, a real educational benefit (Simpson, Simon, & Wilson, 2001; Simson, Wilson, & Harlow-Rosentaub, 2006).

REVIEW

▶ A key factor in the effects of preschools are their level of quality.

▶ Montessori preschools, developed in Italy, employ a carefully designed set of materials to create an environment that fosters sensory, motor, and language development through play.

▶ Handling the transition from elementary to secondary school is especially difficult for young adolescents because of the other developmental issues that they face at around the same time.

▶ In recent years, homeschooling has emerged as a way for parents who choose it to educate their children at home while meeting district and state educational requirements.

▶ Performance in school depends on a number of factors, including socioeconomic status and race/ethnicity.

▶ African American and Hispanic high school graduates enroll in colleges in lower proportions than white high school graduates, but, overall, the number of students from minority groups attending college is on the rise and their proportions within the college population are growing.

▶ More than a quarter of all college students are 25 or older. These older, nontraditional students take college courses to learn new vocational skills, acquire technological knowledge, to achieve greater self-understanding, and to prepare for their future retirement.

APPLY

▶ In terms of the development of identity, what advantages and disadvantages would you predict for homeschooled adolescents?

MODULE 14.2

Leisure

For fun I like doing things outside, like playing sports. I played football for my high school and I also did a lot of drama classes. I was in chorus. I love acting and singing and pretty much being on stage. I love hanging out with friends and going to parties and cook-outs or camping—anything to do with a lot of people. . . . So anything fun that can make me laugh or make someone around me laugh I like. I also love going to the movies or out to eat.

The leisure time of this highly social adolescent (writing in an anonymous blog) is filled with a swirl of group activities. For others, leisure time is occupied by more solitary interests, with more hours spent in front of a computer screen than in the presence of other people. For still others, especially the many adolescents who are employed, leisure time is a rare commodity.

Almost everyone has a certain amount of leisure time at their disposal. How they carve out that time has important implications for the quality of life they enjoy. Let's examine how adolescents use leisure time, followed by a look at how older adults make choices about what to do in their spare time.

Time on Their Hands: Leisure in Adolescence

What *are* adolescents doing with their time? Surprisingly, it's a question that has been addressed systematically only recently because most adolescent specialists assumed that schooling was the predominant influence on adolescent development. But it's becoming increasingly clear that we need to better understand how adolescents spend their nonschool-related time in

As adolescents become older, they are more likely to spend a greater proportion of their time working.

FROM A
HIGH SCHOOL
ADMINISTRATOR'S
PERSPECTIVE

Are there any types of approaches that can be implemented in the school curriculum that can help students develop better uses of non–school-related time?

FIGURE 14.9 Spending Time

According to the Experience Sampling Method, suburban middle-class white adolescents differ from poor African Americans in terms of how they spend their time.

Source: Larson et al., 2001, Table 2.

order to get a complete picture of the major influences on adolescent development. To do that, adolescent scientists have used a variety of techniques designed to understand just what adolescents are doing.

Spending Time. It's not easy to know with precision what adolescents are doing. The easiest technique—simply asking them what they've been doing—is not always the most precise. Consider, for example, how you would respond if you were asked to pinpoint to the minute what you did yesterday. Although you might be able to broadly define your activities, many of the details would probably be lost. (For instance, just how often and how long did you spend checking your e-mail throughout the day?)

To overcome the problem, social scientists have devised methodologies that go beyond mere questionnaires. For example, one increasingly common technique is the *Experience Sampling Method* in which study participants wear an alarm watch that is remotely signaled to sound once every 2 hours during participants' waking hours. When the alarm sounds, participants complete a self-report form that asks what they are doing, the situation, and their emotional state. Because the Experience Sampling Method relies less on memory and more on immediate self-report, it has proven a reliable measure of how adolescents use their time (Csikszentmihalyi & Larson, 1992; Chen, 2006; Green et al., 2006).

Using the Experience Sampling Method, researchers have found that suburban, middle-class white adolescents spend, on average, almost half their time in leisure activities. Furthermore, some 29 percent is spent in "productive" activities such as school, homework, and paid work. Another quarter or so is spent on "maintenance" activities such as eating, transportation, chores and errands, and personal maintenance such as personal hygiene (Larson et al., 2001; see Figure 14.9).

Significant racial and cultural differences and individual differences have been found. For example, compared to their white suburban counterparts, poor African American adolescents living in urban areas spend somewhat less time on productive activities and somewhat more on leisure activities, especially viewing television (18 percent, compared with 13 percent of the white sample) (Larson et al., 2001).

Furthermore, adolescents fall into several broad categories in terms of time use relating to the specific activities in which they participate. More than half are quite busy, spending significant amounts of time on homework, extracurricular activities, time with friends after school and on weekends, chores, and sometimes paid work. Around a third of adolescents, however, spend time on only one or just a few activities, such as primarily engaging in paid employment, with little or no engagement in extracurricular activities. Another group spends most of their time hanging out with friends, and neither work nor participate in extracurricular activities (Shanahan & Flaherty, 2001).

In addition, some adolescents' time investments change according to their age. For instance, as they become older, they are more likely to spend a greater proportion of their time working. Individuals who were highly involved in many activities as younger adolescents usually remain busy throughout adolescence. Similarly, those who were less busy and were involved in a small number of domains continue to be involved in only a few domains. But the less busy adolescents often shift their interests over the course of adolescence (Shanahan & Flaherty, 2001).

The overall degree of time use is related to adolescent success. Busier adolescents tend to be more successful academically. They have higher grades and are better adjusted than those who are committed to fewer tasks. Busier adolescents are particularly better off than adolescents who spend minimal time in academic-related pursuits and more time in work (Shanahan & Flaherty, 2001; Mortimer, 2003).

Adolescents' use of time is not a zero-sum situation in which participation in one domain displaces participation in another domain. Instead, some adolescents are very busy, and others are not. Furthermore, some adolescents are carrying out multiple tasks simultaneously. Indeed, popular wisdom suggests that adolescents are particularly accomplished multitaskers. Is that true?

Shifting Attention: This Is Your Brain on Multitasking. When an adolescent is simultaneously texting his friends, listening to iTunes, and writing a paper for class, is there a particular part of the brain that permits him to multitask in this way? More broadly, are adolescents, more than adults, adept at multitasking?

The answer to both questions is no. No one's brain—even one belonging to the most practiced multitasking adolescent—is designed to allow for the simultaneous processing of information in multiple channels. Instead, the brain switches back and forth between different media sources, prioritizing the information that is of greatest interest and importance. Although we can do some highly routine tasks simultaneously—like chewing gum and walking—most tasks are performed sequentially. Solving calculus problems while reading a history book, or even talking on a cell phone while driving, can be challenging propositions (Rosen et al., 2003).

According to functional magnetic resonance imaging (fMRI) studies, the brain's anterior prefrontal cortex is responsible for switching attention from one task to another (see Figure 14.10). One part of the brain in particular permits adolescents (as well as the rest of us) to return to tasks that they have already started and take up where they left off. The prefrontal cortex is one of the last areas of the brain to mature, suggesting that younger adolescents may be less efficient at multitasking than older ones (Koechlin et al., 1999; Wallis, 2006).

Even the most adept multitaskers, however, are limited by the hard-wired nature of the brain in their efforts to switch among different activities. The more tasks that individuals seek to accomplish, the greater the difficulties they encounter. Not only do errors increase, but efficiency plummets. Consequently, it takes longer to complete tasks when alternating between them than when doing them sequentially (Rubenstein, Meyer, & Evans, 2001; Meyer et al., 2002; Luria & Meiran, 2005).

In short, despite popular wisdom that contemporary adolescents are particularly proficient at multitasking, there's no evidence showing that they do it better than adults. They may multitask more frequently, but they suffer from the same limitations as older people. The brain simply does not have the wiring to allow great success at multitasking.

Media and Technology Use by Adolescents.

Dominique Jones, 12, of Los Angeles, likes to IM her friends before school to find out what they plan to wear. "You'll get IMs back that say things like 'Oh, my God, I'm wearing the same shoes!' After school we talk about what happened that day, what outfits we want to wear the next day." (Wallis, 2006, p. 55)

Instant messaging and text messaging ("texting") are only some of the enormous varieties of media and technologies available to adolescents, ranging from more traditional sorts, such as radio and television, to newer forms, such as text messaging, cell phones, and MP3 players. And adolescents make use of them—to a staggering degree.

According to a comprehensive survey using a sample of boys and girls 8 to 18 years old conducted by the Kaiser Family Foundation (a well-respected think tank), young people spend an average of 6.5 hours a day with media. Furthermore, because around a quarter of the time they are using more than one form of medium simultaneously, they are actually being exposed to the equivalent of 8.5 hours per day (Rideout, Roberts, & Foehr, 2005; see Figure 14.11 on page 420).

These figures probably underestimate media use by teenagers for at least two reasons. First, the sample included preteens, many of whom likely have less opportunity and access to media than do older youth. Second, the survey was conducted in 2003 and 2004, meaning that some technologies, such as text messaging, were not as widespread as they are now. It seems reasonable, then, that media use is even more extensive than initially found in the survey.

These varied media play a number of significant functions in adolescents' lives. Not only do media provide entertainment and information, but they also help adolescents cope with the stresses of everyday life. Losing oneself in a television show or CD can be a way of escaping from one's current problems.

In addition, the media provide models and a sense of norms that are operating among other adolescents. Teenagers watching MTV's *Real World* not only are exposed to the lives of particular individuals, but they can view how people look, dress, and behave (Arnett, 1995; Head, 2005).

Clearly, the media play a number of roles in adolescents' lives. Let's look at some of the specific types of media to which teenagers are exposed and consider their consequences.

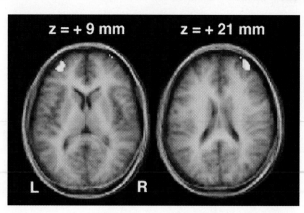

FIGURE 14.10 The Multitasking Brain
Two regions, located symmetrically in these right and left brain scans, show the switching of attention from one task to another.
Source: Koechlin et al., 1999.

Despite a growing abundance of new technologies, television viewing remains the most frequent activity among adolescents, averaging about 3 hours a day.

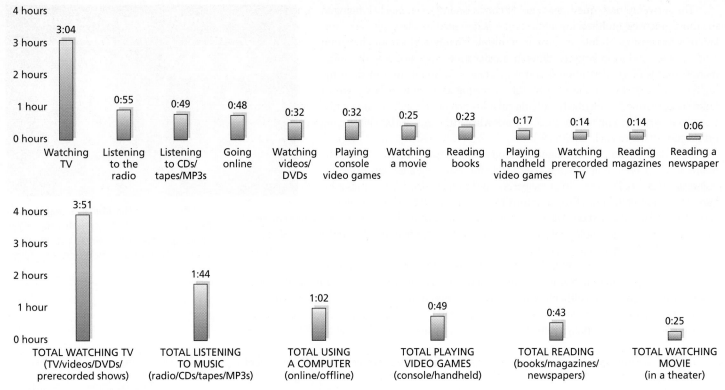

FIGURE 14.11 **Time Spent with Media in a Typical Day**
One comprehensive study by the Kaiser Family Foundation has shown that young people spend more than 6.5 hours a day interacting with various media.
Source: Rideout et al., 2005.

Viewing Television. Despite the proliferation of new technologies, television viewing remains the most frequent activity. Although figures on actual exposure to television vary significantly depending on how viewing is assessed, television use is substantial, averaging around 3 hours a day. There is some change with age, though: Older adolescents watch somewhat less television than younger adolescents, in part because older adolescents begin to have more time-consuming responsibilities, such as homework and work. In addition, older adolescents have greater mobility, permitting them to leave home to participate in other activities more easily (Roberts, Henriksen, & Foehr, 2004).

It's certainly easy for adolescents to watch television, given that two-thirds of U.S. 8- to 18-year-olds have television sets in their bedrooms. But not all of that viewing is particularly attentive. Sometimes adolescents leave the television on and only monitor what is going on, rather than paying careful attention (Comstock & Scharrer, 1999; Rideout, Roberts, & Foehr, 2005).

When they do pay attention to what they are watching, though, they are affected by their viewing in significant ways. For instance, television provides information about appropriateness of body image. In many ways, the television-based view of women's bodies is idealized in a way that barely approaches reality. Women with large breasts, small waists, and slender legs are represented as an ideal. Yet few adolescents (or anyone else) can achieve such a standard. Ultimately, the more adolescents watch television and are exposed to these idealized body images, the more negative is their own body image (Anderson et al., 2001; Clay, Vignoles, & Dittmar, 2005; Ward & Friedman, 2006).

Television also may have an impact on the physical well-being of adolescents. For instance, according to the results of one survey, teenagers with the greatest number of electronic devices were twice as likely to fall asleep in school, suggesting that the availability of the equipment reduced the number of hours the most technologically well-equipped adolescents were sleeping. In addition, obesity has been linked to the level of television viewing: More hours spent viewing are associated with higher levels of adolescent obesity—largely due to the sedentary nature of television (Hancox, Milne, & Poulton, 2004; Lawlor et al., 2005; National Sleep Foundation, 2006).

Computers and the Internet: Living in a Virtual World. Despite the fact that adolescents are spending far more time using the Internet than they did a few decades ago—when the Internet was quite new and access was limited—we still don't know a great deal about its effects on adolescent development. Surveys are only recently telling us what, at least generally, adolescents are doing when they are online.

Most of the time, adolescents are visiting websites that have to do with entertainment and sports. Older adolescents also spend more substantial amounts of time on relationship-oriented sites like *Facebook* (Roberts & Foehr, 2003).

On the other hand, although fears that cyberspace is overrun with child molesters are exaggerated, it is true that the Internet makes available material that many parents and other adults find highly objectionable. In addition, there is a growing problem with Internet gambling. High school and college students can easily bet on sports events and participate in games such as poker on the Web using credit cards (Staudenmeier, 1999; Dowling, Smith, & Thomas, 2005; Winters et al., 2005).

The growing use of computers also presents a challenge involving socioeconomic status, race, and ethnicity. Poorer adolescents and members of minority groups have less access to computers than more affluent adolescents and members of socially advantaged groups—a phenomenon known as the *digital divide*. For example, 77 percent of African American students reported using a personal computer frequently, compared with 87 percent of white students and 81 percent of Hispanic/Latino students. Asian American students had the highest rates of computer use, at 91 percent (Sax et al., 2004; Fetterman, 2005).

Differences in socioeconomic status also affect computer access across different countries. For example, adolescents in developing countries have less access to the Internet than those in industrialized countries. As computers become less expensive, however, their availability is becoming more common, opening up opportunities for cultural exchange among adolescents worldwide (Anderson, 2002, 2003).

Life Beyond Work: More Time for Leisure in Middle Adulthood

For many adults, priorities change in midlife and they now find the time to pursue dreams from early adulthood.

At 48, Marian Barnes felt the time had come to take on fewer "extra" projects at work. She was comfortable in her job and was no longer fixated on getting the next promotion. With the last of the kids off to college, Marian felt she could finally indulge in a few of the leisure activities she'd been dreaming of during the hectic years of full-time work and childrearing. She signed up for a weekly tennis group and collected the necessary signatures to run for Town Meeting, a civic activity that had always interested her.

Some of the busiest adults are young adults. As they build careers and families, they often feel as though they have little leisure time at their disposal.

For many adults priorities change in midlife. Career ambitions begin to take a back seat to social relationships and personal interests. Children leave home. Midlife adults, like Marian Barnes, may find the time has come to live some of the dreams they formulated during the too-busy years of early adulthood.

The Empty Nest: More Free Time. With the typical workweek hovering between 35 and 40 hours—and becoming shorter for most people—most middle-aged adults have some 70 waking hours per week at their disposal (Kacapyr, 1997). What do they do with their leisure time?

For one thing—just as many adolescents do—they watch television. On average, middle-aged people watch around 15 hours of television each week. But middle-aged adults do much more with their leisure time than watch television. For many people, middle adulthood represents a renewed opportunity to become involved in activities outside the home. As children leave home, parents have substantial time freed up to participate more extensively in leisure activities such as taking up sports, or civic participation such as joining town committees. Middle-aged adults in the United States spend about 6 hours each week socializing (Robinson & Godbey, 1997; Lindstrom et al., 2005).

A significant number of people find the allure of leisure so great that they take early retirement. For those who make such a choice, and who have adequate financial resources to last the dozens of years that likely remain to them, life can be quite gratifying. Early retirees tend to be in good health, and they may take up a variety of new activities (Cliff, 1991; Ransom, Sutch, & Williamson, 1991; Litwin, 2007).

A More Leisurely Pace? Although middle adulthood presents the opportunity for more leisure activities, most people report that the pace of their lives does not seem slower. Because they are involved in a variety of activities, much of their free time is scattered throughout the week in 15- and 30-minute chunks. Consequently, despite a documented increase of 5 hours of weekly leisure time since 1965, many people feel they have no more free time than they did earlier (Robinson & Godlbey, 1997).

One reason why extra leisure time may not be noticeable is that the pace of life in the United States is still considerably faster than in many countries. By measuring the length of time average pedestrians cover 60 feet, the time it takes for a customer to purchase a stamp, and the accuracy of public clocks, research has compared the tempo of living in a variety of countries. According to a composite of these measures, the United States has a quicker tempo than many other countries, particularly Latin American, Asian, Middle Eastern, and African countries. But many countries outpace the United States. For example, Western European countries and Japan operate more quickly than the United States, with Switzerland ranking first (see Table 14.2; Levine, 1997a, 1997b).

TABLE 14.2 Pace of Life Worldwide				
	OVERALL PACE	WALKING 60 FEET	POSTAL SERVICE	PUBLIC CLOCK
Switzerland	1	3	2	1
Ireland	2	1	3	11
Germany	3	5	1	8
Japan	4	7	4	6
Italy	5	10	12	2
England	6	4	9	13
Sweden	7	13	5	7
Austria	8	23	8	3
Netherlands	9	2	14	25
Hong Kong	10	14	6	14
France	11	8	18	10
Poland	12	12	15	8
Costa Rica	13	16	10	15
Taiwan	14	18	7	21
Singapore	15	25	11	4
United States	16	6	23	20
Canada	17	11	21	22
South Korea	18	20	20	16
Hungary	19	19	19	18
Czech Republic	20	21	17	23
Greece	21	14	13	29
Kenya	22	9	30	24
China	23	24	25	12
Bulgaria	24	27	22	17
Romania	25	30	29	5
Jordan	26	28	27	19
Syria	27	29	28	27
El Salvador	28	22	16	31
Brazil	29	31	24	28
Indonesia	30	26	26	30
Mexico	31	17	31	26

Rank of 31 countries for overall pace of life and for three measures: minutes downtown pedestrians take to walk 60 feet; minutes it takes a postal clerk to complete a stamp purchase transaction; and accuracy in minutes of public clocks.

Source: Adapted from Levine, 1997a.

REVIEW

▶ Adolescents spend almost half their time on leisure activities, with the rest divided between productive activities and maintenance activities.

▶ Adolescents can be categorized into two broad groups: busier and less busy, with busier adolescents tending to be more successful academically.

▶ True multitasking is no more possible for adolescents than for adults, although adolescents seem to prefer switching among a large number of activities.

▶ Adolescents have access to an enormous range of media and technologies, which can enhance entertainment and ease stress, but can also enable excessive exposure to violence and sexual content.

▶ Although people in early adulthood who are building careers and families often experience few opportunities for leisure activities, people in middle adulthood usually have more leisure time than previously. Often they use it to become more involved outside the home in recreational and community activities.

APPLY

▶ Do you think adolescents' increased access to technology and media simply continues a trend that began with radio and television, or is the abundance of new technologies likely to have significant psychological and societal effects? Why?

▶ In addition to the "digital divide" between more and less affluent adolescents, is there also a digital divide between adolescents and their parents? What effects is this likely to have?

MODULE (14.3)

Living in a Multicultural World

The students came into Room 42 after lunch today with all kinds of questions about their upcoming field trip to Boyne River. They wanted to know when they would be leaving, when they would be returning, what they should bring, whether it would be cold at Boyne River, what they would eat, where they would sleep, and so on. . . . [But when their teacher] asked for a show of hands of students from those who would be participating, I was surprised to see that many students did not put their hands up. Sahra, who was sitting directly in front of William, did not put her hand up.

"My father won't let me go," Sahra said. She explained that she could not go on field trips where they would be spending the night. Sahra's family is South Asian and her parents, especially her father, are very strict about the kinds of school activities they allow her to take part in. . . .

I asked some of the students sitting near me whether they would be going on the field trip.

"It's against my religion for girls to go out," Zeynab said.

"I can't. I need to go with my father to the hospital, to help translate for him."

"I need to pick my sister up from school and get my brother from daycare—my parents have to work."

"I work at my family's tea store, and sometimes I need to help them [i.e. my parents] with the forms." (Chan, 2006, p. 161)

For teachers in this eighth-grade classroom, composed of students whose families represent a variety of cultures, arranging a field trip is a complicated process.

As the U.S. population has become more diverse, schools have paid increased attention to issues involving student diversity and multiculturalism. And with good reason: Cultural, as well as language, differences affect both children and adults socially and educationally. The demographic makeup in the United States is undergoing an extraordinary shift. For instance, the

FIGURE 14.12 **The Changing Face of America**
Current projections of the population makeup of the United States show that by the year 2050, the proportion of non-Hispanic whites will decline as the proportion of minority group members increases. What will be some of the impacts of changing demographics on social workers?
Source: U.S. Bureau of the Census, 2001.

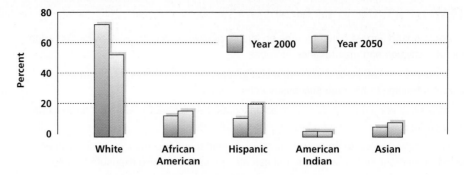

proportion of Hispanics will in all likelihood more than double in the next 50 years. Moreover, by the year 2050, non-Hispanic Caucasians will likely become a minority of the total population of the United States (U.S. Bureau of Census, 2001; see Figure 14.12).

How Culture Defines Us

An essential part of how people define themselves relates to their cultural background. Whether it involves race, ethnicity, gender, socioeconomic status, or a host of other factors, that cultural background plays a central role in determining who they are, how they view themselves, and how others treat them.

For example, because of their knowledge of their own culture, people understand what clothes are appropriate to wear, are guided in their choice of what foods to choose and what to avoid, and know which sexual practices are likely to be acceptable on a date (kissing) and which are not (forced sexual intercourse). Such knowledge reflects basic cultural beliefs and values.

We can look at culture on various levels. At the broadest level, we all belong to the human culture, sharing certain customs that are brought about by particular biological necessities (sleeping every night or eating at various times during the day rather than once every few days, for example). All humans use language, which is a defining characteristic of human culture. Furthermore, there are other cultural universals such as cooking and funeral ceremonies that, although practiced in different ways, are found in every culture.

The United States has become a more diverse culture, as we discussed earlier. Furthermore, *globalization*—the integration of cultures, social movements, and financial markets around the world—has become increasingly common across a variety of dimensions, exposing adults and children to individuals with cultural backgrounds different from their own. Ultimately, it is clear that a full understanding of human development cannot be achieved without taking culture into account.

Acculturation: When Cultures Collide. Let's begin our look at culture by considering the reactions of people when they encounter for sustained periods individuals from cultures other than their own, and how that may change them—a process called acculturation. **Acculturation** refers to the changes and adjustments that occur when groups of different people come into sustained firsthand contact.

The process of acculturation is particularly significant for people belonging to racial and ethnic minorities. They are faced with reconciling the demands of their own culture with those of the dominant culture. The issue of acculturation is particularly acute for adults and children who enter a new culture through immigration, an experience that typically involves leaving their native country and suddenly finding themselves in an entirely new culture. However, even members of racial and ethnic minorities who are raised their entire lives in the United States face pressures in reacting to their status as a subset of individuals living within a society in which they are a cultural minority.

The process of acculturation can produce one of four outcomes, depending on both the degree of identification with one's own culture and the strength of identification with the majority culture (illustrated in Figure 14.13):

- **Integration: Identifying with multiple cultures. Integration** is the process through which people maintain their own culture while simultaneously seeking to adapt and incorporate the majority culture. By embracing the dominant culture, people are able to

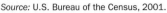
acculturation   the changes and adjustments that occur when groups of different people come into sustained firsthand contact.

integration   the process in which people maintain their own culture while simultaneously seeking to adapt and incorporate the majority culture.

feel more secure and assimilated. People who employ integration often have a *bicultural identity* in which they see themselves as part of, and comfortable with, two different cultures.

- **Assimilation: Identifying with the majority culture.** **Assimilation** occurs when a person begins to identify with the mainstream culture and rejects the minority culture. Assimilated people not only may adopt the values and beliefs of the majority, but, because they are only relatively weakly identified with their own culture, may reject the values and beliefs of their own culture (Unger et al., 2006).

- **Separation: Identifying with the minority culture and rejecting the majority culture.** **Separation** occurs when people identify with the ethnic minority culture to which they belong while rejecting or rebuffing the majority culture. Separation sometimes occurs with new immigrants, who may have difficulty integrating into their new society because they do not understand the dominant culture. Often, they eventually take on the norms and values of the dominant culture. But the process of acculturation can be slow and painful, producing anxiety and depression (Kim et al., 2005; Sawrikar & Hunt, 2006).

  Separation may also occur voluntarily, as a political act. Some people may wish to accentuate their racial or ethnic identity by actively separating themselves, both psychologically and physically, from members of the dominant culture. This strategy of separation, which can be used to bolster group identity, can have positive psychological benefits (Sue & Chu, 2003; Phinney, 2005).

- **Marginalization: Nonidentification with minority or majority cultures.** **Marginalization** occurs when people identify neither with their minority culture nor with the majority culture. Marginalized people may feel isolated from both their own cultural group and members of the majority culture, either because they have tried to connect and failed, or sometimes because they are rejected for personal reasons by others. Ultimately, they lack a clear cultural identity, and they typically feel isolated and alienated from society (Kosic, 2004; Arredondo et al., 2006).

The particular type of identification found in racial and ethnic minorities has significant implications for their well-being. Some of the outcomes—including assimilation, integration, and occasionally even separation—can produce important psychological benefits.

Strongly identifying with the majority culture, however, may be seen negatively by one's minority peers. For example, although integration of majority and minority identities would seem to bring the benefits of belonging to both cultures, this may not always be true. Thus, blacks who seek to integrate the majority culture into their lives may be derided for trying to "act white"—that is, trying to act like something they are not.

Similarly, it can be stressful for members of nondominant cultures to try to integrate themselves into the majority culture if the majority culture resists their efforts. Minority members who are prevented from fully participating in the majority culture because of prejudice and discrimination may suffer psychological harm as a result (Schwartz, Montgomery, & Briones, 2006).

For some minority-culture members, the most successful approach may be to be highly adaptive, switching back and forth between the majority and minority cultures depending on the specific situation—a process called *code switching*. For example, in some cases, minority youth are so adept at code switching that they use different vocabulary and styles of speech depending on the group with which they are interacting (Cashman, 2005).

Developing an Ethnic Identity

Think of how you would briefly describe yourself to someone who had never met you. Would you include your ethnic background? The country from which your ancestors emigrated?

If you are a member of a minority ethnic or racial group or a recent immigrant, it is very likely your description would prominently include that fact: "I'm a Korean American," "I'm Black," or "I'm a Serb." But if you are a member of a group that is dominant in society or statistically in the majority, it might not even occur to you to say, for example, "I'm white."

Identification with One's Own Culture

Identification with Majority Culture	STRONG	WEAK
STRONG	INTEGRATION	ASSIMILATION
WEAK	SEPARATION	MARGINALIZATION

FIGURE 14.13
Four Outcomes of Acculturation
Depending on both the degree of identification with one's own culture and the strength of identification with the majority culture, the process of acculturation can produce one of the four outcomes shown here.
Source: Phinney et al., 1990.

assimilation   the process in which people begin to identify with the mainstram culture and reject the minority culture.

separation   the process in which people identify with the ethnic minority culture to which they belong while rejecting or rebuffing the majority culture.

marginalization   the process that occurs when people identify neither with their minority culture nor with the majority culture.

Although the number of youth living in low-income households began to decline in the early 1990s, it has been on the rise since 2000.

The difference between the two responses reflects differences in ethnic identity and its salience in everyday life. **Ethnic identity** refers to how members of ethnic, racial, and cultural minorities view themselves, both as members of their own group and in terms of their relationships with other groups. Ethnic identity relates to the part of a person's self-concept that is derived from their awareness and knowledge that they are a member of a distinct social group (Umaña-Taylor, Bhanot, & Shin, 2006).

According to psychologist Jean Phinney, ethnic identity develops in several stages. The first stage is *unexamined ethnic identity*, which is characterized by a lack of consideration or exploration of one's ethnicity, as well as acceptance of the norms, beliefs, and attitudes of the dominant culture. In this stage, people might not even think about ethnicity or consider its impact on their lives. If they do think about their ethnicity, they may be embarrassed by it or reject it, believing that the dominant culture is superior (Phinney, 2003, 2006).

Although some people don't move beyond an unexamined ethnic identity, most reach the next stage, ethnic identity search. In *ethnic identity search,* people experience some sort of crisis that makes them become aware of ethnicity as a significant factor in their lives. It may be a shocking news event, such as a racially motivated killing, or they may be denied a job and suspect it's because of their race. In other cases, they may more gradually become aware that they are being treated differently by others because of their ethnicity.

Whatever the cause, people who enter the ethnic identity search phase become motivated to obtain a deeper understanding of their cultural identity. They may read books, attend ethnic celebrations and events, or—if their ethnic identity is tied to a religious group, such as Irish Catholics—may begin to attend religious services.

The ethnic identity search may produce resentment toward dominant groups in society. As they learn more about the consequences of prejudice and discrimination, people may come to believe that the majority should make amends for its discriminatory behavior.

Finally, the last stage of ethnic identity development is *achieved ethnic identity,* in which people fully embrace their ethnic identity. People in this stage develop a clear sense of themselves as members of an ethnic minority and realize that this has become part of the way they view themselves. Their membership is viewed with pride, and they have a sense of belonging to others who share their ethnic identity.

Whereas people earlier may have experienced resentment or hostility regarding their ethnicity, directed either toward members of majority groups, others of their own ethnicity, or even themselves, they may feel more secure and optimistic after reaching the achieved ethnic identity stage. Furthermore, earlier feelings that they had two separate identities—one that identified with the majority culture and one that identified with their ethnic culture—are replaced with a more unified ethnic identity that draws on both parts of who they are (Shih & Sanchez, 2005).

Achieving Ethnic Identity.   It's important to note that the stages of ethnic identity do not unfold according to any particular timetable. Some people may reach the achieved ethnic identity stage while still in adolescence, while for others it may occur later. Generally, the extent of identification with one's ethnicity increases with age.

Furthermore, some individuals may never enter the achieved ethnic identity stage or even the ethnic identity search stage at all. In such cases, ethnic identity is not perceived as part of the core of the individual. The danger is that a person will be treated (and sometimes discriminated against) by others due to his or her membership in an ethnic or racial group. Such treatment may be confusing at best and psychologically damaging at worst (Yasui, Dorham, & Dishion, 2004).

Ultimately, the nature and strength of a person's ethnic identity are determined both by parental socialization and by the particular experiences that an individual encounters. For example, ethnic minority parents teach their children, both explicitly and implicitly, about their own culture and about the dominant culture of the society in which they live. In addition, they may explicitly teach their children how to deal with the prejudice and discrimination that they are likely to encounter.

Finally, as we suggested earlier, ethnic identity is likely to be strongest for members of minority groups and weakest for members of the dominant societal group (which, in U.S. society, is whites). The reason: Members of the dominant group simply don't have to think as much about their ethnicity, given that they are not subject to the discrimination and prejudice experienced by

ethnic identity   how members of ethnic, racial, and cultural minorities view themselves, both as members of their own group and in terms of their relationships with other groups.

members of ethnic minority groups. In contrast, members of minority groups expend more time and effort thinking not only about their own ethnicity but about the majority group. For ethnic minority group members, ethnicity becomes more a part of who they are (Fiske, 2001; Guinote & Fiske, 2003).

The fact that whites generally have less pronounced ethnic identities does not mean that ethnicity plays no role in their lives. Being a member of a particular nonracial ethnic or religious group (Italian, Jewish, or Irish, for example) may be a significant source of pride and may be perceived as a central part of identity. Furthermore, when whites find themselves in settings in which they are in the minority, their sense of racial identity may become magnified (Roberts et al., 1999; Romero & Roberts, 2003).

The Impact of Socioeconomic Status and Poverty on Children and Adolescents

One of the greatest cultural divides between people relates to their socioeconomic status. It is not a trivial problem that affects only a small part of the population: For example, some 15 percent of adolescents in the United States are living in poverty (with income levels below $19,000/year for a family of 4), and 35 percent live in low-income households. Furthermore, although the number of youth living in low-income households began to decline in the early 1990s, it has been on the rise since 2000. The discrepancy between the rich and the poor also is growing (National Center for Children in Poverty, 2006).

Members of minority groups are proportionately more likely to be living in poverty than nonminority group members (see Figure 14.14). However, although Latino and black children and adolescents are disproportionately from low-income households, whites are the largest group of low-income individuals. More than half of the children of immigrant parents live in low-income families.

Poverty expands well beyond the stereotyped view of poor minority youth living in cities. Children and adolescents living in poverty are found throughout the United States in both urban and rural areas. According to Nobel winner Robert Solow, the cost of child poverty in the United States runs between $36 billion and $177 billion each year.

Poverty affects children and adolescents in a number of ways. In some households, there is not enough food, and children and adolescents go to school and to bed hungry. Because many poor households lack health insurance, children and adolescents living in poverty are unable to afford good medical care, and minor illnesses, left untreated, become major ones. The greater the degree of poverty, the higher the health risks.

As we've discussed in many of the previous chapters, the impact of poverty on human development is profound. It impedes children's and adolescents' ability to learn and can slow their cognitive development, making academic success less likely. In addition, poverty is associated with behavioral and emotional difficulties. Children and adolescents living in persistent poverty are less well adjusted and have more conduct problems, in part because their parents' emotional well-being is reduced, making them less successful caregivers (Maughan, 2001; Smokowski et al., 2004; Gutman, McLoyd, & Tokoyawa, 2005).

Poverty, of course, is not an insoluble problem, and solutions should be within the means of a country as affluent as the United States. However, the rate of poverty in the United States is actually higher than that in many other industrialized countries. Why? The answer has a good deal to do with aggressive antipoverty measures adopted by other nations. Compared with the United States, in other developed countries public assistance levels for poor families are often higher, health care benefits are better, and governments have more programs to help those living in poverty (Smeeding, Danziger, & Rainwater, 1995; Rainwater & Smeeding, 2007).

The lower poverty rates in countries other than the United States offer a ray of hope even to poor people in this country, suggesting that the rate can be reduced. One route is clearly educational, for the higher the parental educational level, the less the chance of a child being raised in poverty. For example, only 11 percent of children living in poverty had at least one parent who had achieved an educational level beyond high school. In contrast, an astonishing 89 percent of children whose more educated parent did not graduate from high school lived in poverty (National Center for Children in Poverty, 1996).

Another route is through improvements in government programs and benefits targeted to the poor. Although current political trends and the 1996 federal welfare reform laws have

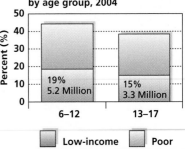

Children and adolescents living in low-income and poor families, by age group, 2004

19% 5.2 Million (6–12)
15% 3.3 Million (13–17)

Low-income   Poor

FIGURE 14.14 The Cultural Divide of Socioeconomic Status
Socioeconomic status is one of the greatest cultural divides between adolescents. According to the National Center for Children in Poverty, members of minority groups are proportionately more likely to be living in poverty than nonminority group members.
Source: National Center for Children in Poverty, 2006.

been interpreted as moving the United States further from the goal of reducing poverty, some government programs on the state and local levels have been successful in breaking the bonds of poverty. Ultimately, improvements in income levels will produce substantial benefits, not just for the poor, but for all children and for society in general (Huston, Coll, & McLoyd, 1994; Rickel & Becker, 1997; Takanishi & Hamburg, 1997; McLoyd, Aikens, & Burton, 2006).

Prejudice and Discrimination

When I was 17, I wanted to be "authentic" too. I was a white, suburban, middle class kid and I wanted to be tough, street-smart and sexy. I wanted to be cool. Part of being cool was being, well—black. And since I had no hope of changing my skin color it meant listening to black music, reading black authors, and feeling, at least, a sense of solidarity with an oppressed and talented people. But in fact I had very little contact with actual black people.

*****

Black and white kids did not play together in the schoolyard, and the black kids ate together in the cafeteria. We didn't socialize at all outside of school. This continued into high school and the only chance you might have to socialize with black people was in team sports. Even then, contact was largely limited to team activities. I did not know why this was so, and I never questioned it. It was just the way things were.

Navigating racial, ethnic, and other cultural differences is among the most difficult challenges that adolescents (and adults) face, as these anonymous blog excerpts imply. Learning how to accept and interact with individuals who are different in important ways from oneself represents an important developmental task for adolescents—a task, the success or failure of which will have consequences throughout their lives.

For some, the challenge is too great, and their prejudiced attitudes and stereotypes guide their behavior. In this final part of the chapter, we examine the basic concepts of prejudice, stereotypes, and discrimination.

Prejudice, Stereotypes, and Discrimination: The Foundations of Hate. **Prejudice** refers to the negative (or positive) evaluations or judgments of members of a group that are based primarily on group membership, and not necessarily on the particular characteristics of individuals. For example, gender prejudice occurs when a person is evaluated on the basis of being a male or female and not because of his or her own specific characteristics or abilities.

Although prejudice is generally thought of as a negative evaluation of group members, it can also be positive: As we'll see, at the same time people dislike members of groups to which they don't belong, they may also positively evaluate members of their own group. In both cases, the assessment is unrelated to qualities of particular individuals; rather, it is due simply to membership in the specific group to which the individuals belong.

The mental framework that maintains prejudice is a stereotype. A **stereotype** is a set of beliefs and expectations about members of a group that are held simply because of their membership in the group. Stereotypes are oversimplifications that people employ in an effort to make sense of the complex social environment in which they live. They determine how information is interpreted, so that even when people are exposed to evidence contrary to their stereotypes, they may interpret the information in a way that supports their prejudice (Aronson & Steele, 2005; Dovidio, Glick, & Rudman, 2005; Judd & Park, 2005).

Ultimately, prejudice and stereotypes can lead to **discrimination**, the negative (or sometimes positive) actions taken toward members of a particular group because of their membership in the group. Although prejudice and discrimination often go hand in hand, one may be present without the other.

In the most extreme case, people's biases lead them to engage in self-fulfilling prophecies. *Self-fulfilling prophecies* reflect the tendency of people to act in ways that are consistent with their expectations, beliefs, or cognitions about an event or a behavior, thereby increasing the likeli-

prejudice   the negative (or positive) evaluations or judgments of members of a group that are based primarily on group membership.

stereotype   a set of beliefs and expectations about members of a group that are held simply because of their membership in the group.

discrimination   the negative (or sometimes positive) actions taken toward members of a particular group because of their membership in the group.

hood that the event or behavior will occur. Consequently, if a person thinks that members of a certain group are lazy, he or she may act in a way that actually elicits laziness from the members of that group.

The Roots of Prejudice. Female. African American. Islamic fundamentalist. Gay. Quick: What images first come to mind when you read or hear each of these words? For most people, encountering a description of a person that includes such a label is enough to summon up a rich network of impressions, memories, and probably even predictions of how that person will behave in a given situation. The presence of such connections suggests that we are all susceptible to prejudice.

But where does prejudice originate? There are several sources.

Social Learning Explanations: The School of Stereotyping. Children are not born feeling prejudice and showing discrimination to members of different religions, ethnic groups, or races. It is something that is taught to them, in much the same way that they learn that 2 + 2 = 4.

The **social learning view**, which we encountered in Chapter 11, suggests that people develop prejudice and stereotypes about members of various groups in the same way they learn other attitudes, beliefs, and values. For instance, one important source of information for children regarding stereotypes and prejudice is the behavior and teaching of parents, other adults, and peers. Through direct reinforcement and through observation of the reinforcement given to others, people learn about members of other groups. Such learning begins at an early age: By the time they are preschoolers, children are able to distinguish between African Americans and whites, and even at that age they can possess preferential feelings for members of their own group over others (Ramsey & Myers, 1990; Cossman & Sittig, 2004).

Children are not the only ones who learn stereotypes and prejudice from others. Although significant improvements have been made in the past decade, television and other media often portray minority group members in shallow, stereotyped ways.

For instance, portrayals of African Americans perpetuate some of society's most distasteful stereotypes, with many African American males being portrayed as sexually obsessed, shiftless, and speaking primarily in jive. Other groups are stereotyped in the media in equally derogatory ways, such as Godfather-like Italian mobsters, greedy Jewish bankers, and Hispanics in criminal or menial jobs (Mok, 1998; Alexander, Brewer, & Livingston, 2005; Jost, 2005).

Social Identity Theory: The Self-Esteem of Group Membership. Think about your ethnic or religious identity for a moment. Are you proud of it? Does it make you feel good to be part of the group? Would you feel threatened if your group were criticized or attacked?

Most people feel pride in the groups to which they belong. But this pride has a downside: It can lead to prejudice and discrimination. For example, according to **social identity theory**, adolescents use group membership as a source of pride and self-worth. However, to feel such pride, they must assume that their group is, in fact, superior to others. As a result, their quest for a positive social identity leads them to inflate the positive aspects of groups to which they belong and belittle groups to which they do not belong (Abrams & Hogg, 1999; Tajfel, 2001; Tajfel & Turner, 2004).

Certainly, there is ample evidence that members of various cultural groups tend to see their own groups in more positive terms than others. For instance, one cross-cultural investigation that examined 17 different societies found that, universally, people rated the group to which they belonged as more peace-loving, virtuous, and obedient than other groups (LeVine & Campbell, 1972; Scheepers et al., 2006). Even countries in which national pride is relatively lower than that of other countries still are viewed quite positively by their citizens (see Table 14.3).

Of course, not all groups produce the same sense of self-worth as others. It is important for groups to be small enough so that people can feel somewhat unique and special. In fact, minority group membership sometimes produces stronger feelings of social identity than majority group membership. Minority group leaders of the past who used slogans such as "Black Is Beautiful" and "Gay Pride" reflected an awareness of the importance of instilling group pride. Research has supported this strategy: Ethnic group membership can be an important source of psychological support, particularly for minority group members (Mossakowski, 2003; González & Gándara, 2005).

social learning view the theory that suggests people develop prejudice and stereotypes about members of various groups in the same way they learn other attitudes, beliefs, and values.

social identity theory the theory that adolescents use group membership as a source of pride and self-worth.

TABLE 14.3	National Pride by Countries	
RANK	COUNTRY	SCORE
1	Venezuela	18.4
2	United States	17.7
3	Australia	17.5
4	Austria	17.4
5	Chile	17.1
6	Canada	17.0
7	Russia	16.7
8	The Philippines	16.7
9	New Zealand	16.6
10	Spain	16.5
11	Israel	16.2
12	Slovenia	16.1
13	South Korea	16.0
14	Japan	15.9
15	Taiwan	15.6
16	Ireland	15.3
17	Poland	15.3
18	Great Britain	15.1
19	Czech Republic	15.1
20	Norway	14.9
21	Germany-West	14.5
22	France	14.4
23	Switzerland	14.3
24	Germany-East	14.2
25	Sweden	14.0

Source: From Smith, T.W. & Seokho, K., 2006.

Overall, membership in a group provides people with a sense of personal identity and self-esteem. When a group is successful, self-esteem can rise; conversely, when self-esteem is threatened, people feel enhanced attraction to their own group and increased hostility toward members of other groups (Swann & Wyer, 1997; Branscombe, Ellemers, Spears, & Doosje, 1999; Garcia et al., 2005).

The use of group membership as a source of pride can lead to unfortunate consequences, however. For instance, in an effort to raise their own self-esteem, adolescents may come to think that their own group (known as the *ingroup*) is superior to groups to which they do not belong (the *outgroups*). Consequently, they inflate the positive aspects of the ingroup, and, at the same time, devalue outgroups and their members. Eventually they come to see members of outgroups as inferior to members of their ingroup. The ultimate result is prejudice toward members of groups of which they are not a part (Tajfel & Turner, 2004; Brown, Bradley, & Lang, 2006; Lam et al., 2006).

BECOMING AN INFORMED CONSUMER OF DEVELOPMENT
Taking a Stand Against Prejudice

Teachers and administrators can employ a number of strategies to combat prejudice in schools and create an atmosphere of respect and tolerance. But combating prejudice is everyone's responsibility, and students can do much to get actively involved in responding to hatred in their schools and communities. The Southern Poverty Law Center (2005) has put together a list of strategies for getting started:

- **Act.** The first step in combating hatred is being willing to take responsibility for doing something about it. Standing by and doing nothing sends a message to the perpetrators, the victims, and the community that prejudice is acceptable. Apathy encourages more hatred.

- **Unite.** Get others involved in direct action, too. These could be family and friends, neighbors, church and civic group members, or teachers and administrators. Ways to get others involved range from informal discussions to writing letters to the editor of a local newspaper to organizing a community rally or event.

- **Support the victims.** Being a victim of prejudice can be a traumatic experience. Victims may feel frightened, intimidated, or alienated. Giving them your support and encouragement shows them that they are valued members of the community and that they are not alone. Even a kind word or a simple gesture can make a difference.

- **Speak up.** Prejudice has a voice; tolerance needs to have a voice as well. Condemning hateful messages is a good start, but letting others know that you actively value diversity is important, too. Create an atmosphere of tolerance by communicating your values.

- **Hold leaders accountable.** Students can do a lot to combat prejudice, but people in leadership positions enjoy special influence. The way that teachers, administrators, and other people in leadership roles respond to incidents of prejudice sends a strong message to others in the community. Quick, decisive action shows that prejudice is unacceptable; slow, uninspired action—or inaction—appears to condone it. Make sure that leaders know you expect them to respond decisively.

- **Examine your own prejudices.** Even tolerant people can harbor some prejudices. Are there any social groups you disparage or just don't know much about? Do you include people who are different from you in your circle of friends and in your group activities? Be continually on the lookout for ways to learn about different cultures and ethnicities and to build bridges across racial and ethnic divides.

REVIEW

▶ Acculturation into a new culture can produce one of four outcomes: integration, assimilation, separation, or marginalization.

▶ Developing an ethnic identity, which is especially important to members of ethnic, racial, and cultural minorities, proceeds in stages from unexamined ethnic identity through ethnic identity search to achieved ethnic identity.

▶ Members of minority groups are more likely to live in poverty than members of nonminority groups, with all the disadvantages and challenges that poverty brings.

▶ Poverty rates are higher in the United States than in many other industrialized countries largely because policymakers have not supported aggressive antipoverty programs.

▶ Children and adults must deal with prejudices (judgments of members of groups), stereotypes (beliefs and expectations about members of groups), and outright discrimination (actions taken toward members of groups).

▶ The social learning view suggests that people learn prejudice the same way they learn other attitudes, beliefs, and values: from other people.

▶ According to social identity theory, adolescents use group membership as a source of pride, dividing people into the ingroup and the outgroup, which is assumed to be inferior.

APPLY

▶ What advantages do you think students who are bilingual might have in today's world? How would you design a research study to demonstrate such advantages?

▶ The United States has been called a "nation of immigrants," and yet feelings toward new immigrants are often negative. How might the phenomenon of cultural identity help to explain this?

Epilogue

In this chapter, we looked at schooling, leisure, and the ramifications of living in a multicultural world. We discussed the various options that are available in preschool education and considered their benefits to young children. We examined what makes children ready for school and how parents can increase the likelihood of academic success for their children. We also considered how race, ethnicity, gender, and socioeconomic status are related to academic performance. Then we discussed who goes to college and the increasing numbers of students over age 25 enrolled in courses. We then turned to a look at how people spend their time, both in the United States and in other cultures. Next, we discussed the increased opportunities for leisure in midlife that adults enjoy as career pressure eases off and children leave home. We addressed the question of whether increased leisure time means a slower pace of life in the United States. In the closing pages of the chapter, we looked at culture and diversity, examining how race, ethnicity, gender, and socioeconomic status shape culture. Finally, we discussed prejudice and discrimination.

Return to the Prologue, which describes Will's preparation for his first day of kindergarten, and answer the following questions.

1. What factors might Will's parents look at in deciding if he is ready to begin formal schooling? How can they help him to succeed in school in general?

2. If Will's teacher believes that children with summer birthdays should wait another year before starting kindergarten, how might this affect his or her expectations of Will? How might the teacher's expectations in this case affect Will's performance?

3. What activities do you imagine fill Will's leisure hours now? How would you expect this to change as he grows toward adolescence?

4. If Will's kindergarten is culturally diverse, how would you expect him to react initially to children from a culture different to his own? What factors in his upbringing might affect his reaction?

Looking Back

What kinds of preschool educational programs are available in the United States, and what effects do they have?

1. The United States lacks a coordinated national policy on preschool education. The major federal initiative in U.S. preschool education has been the Head Start program, which has yielded mixed, though promising, results.

2. Early childhood educational programs—center-based, school-based, or preschool—can lead to cognitive and social advances.

What factors have the most influence on school performance?

3. Many factors beyond simple ability and instructional quality influence student academic performance, including socioeconomic status (and the related factors of race and ethnicity), gender, and teacher expectations.

4. The attributions that students apply to academic success also influence school performance, especially whether the students attribute success and failure to internal, changeable factors (such as effort) or external, unchangeable factors (such as bias).

What factors affect college attendance and performance by women and minorities?

5. Despite a rise in the proportion of the college population represented by minority students, fewer African American and Hispanic high school graduates enroll in and graduate from college than white high school graduates.

6. Even though women represent a majority of the students in colleges nationwide, gender stereotyping remains a persistent problem that affects choice of classes, treatment by professors, and student expectations for success.

What do adolescents in the United States and other cultures do with their time?

7. While there are cultural, racial, and individual differences in the use of time, typical U.S. adolescents spend almost half their time in leisure activities, with the rest divided between productive and maintenance activities.

8. Adolescents can be categorized as being more or less busy, with the busier adolescents experiencing the greater amount of academic success.

9. While true multitasking is no more possible for adolescents than for adults, adolescents favor a style that involves the near-simultaneous performance of a great number of tasks and activities.

10. Cross-cultural studies reveal that adolescents in developing societies have less free time and devote more time to household labor.

How has increased access to media and technology affected adolescents' lives?

11. New technologies and media have found ready consumers in adolescents, who use media for entertainment, coping with stress, and developing a sense of the norms that apply to their age group.

In what ways are individuals affected by culture and ethnicity?

12. The demographic makeup of students in the United States is rapidly changing. By the year 2050, it is expected that non-Hispanic Caucasians will become a minority of the total population of the United States.

13. Culture helps individuals define themselves and make decisions ranging from what clothes to wear to what sexual practices are appropriate.

14. Acculturation is the process by which an individual of a different culture adjusts to a new culture and may produce integration, assimilation, separation, or marginalization.

15. It is especially important for members of minority cultures to develop an ethnic identity, a view of themselves as members of both a minority culture and a new culture.

How is socioeconomic status related to race and ethnicity?

16. Many of the problems faced by minority adolescents are more closely linked to socioeconomic status than to ethnicity or race.

17. Half of adolescents in the United States live in poverty or in low-income households, and members of minority groups are disproportionately represented in these households.

How do prejudice, stereotypes, and discrimination work together?

18. Evaluations of individuals on the basis of their membership in a group are reinforced by the existence of stereotypes, which are beliefs and expectations about group members.

19. Prejudice and stereotypes can lead to discrimination, actions taken toward group members because of their membership in the group.

How are the lives of adolescents affected by sexism and racism?

20. Adolescents use group membership as a source of pride and self-worth, but the danger is that they will conclude that their group is better than others.

21. The gender roles assigned to individuals at birth not only determine how society will regard them, but also affect how they themselves think and behave.

22. Gender stereotyping is particularly prevalent during adolescence, a time when young people are working out their own gender identity and often hold rigid views of appropriate and inappropriate behavior for males and females.

23. Because different races and ethnicities are educated in the same setting, adolescents have learned to show more positive views towards members of other races.

PEARSON
mydevelopmentlab™

**Find out by accessing MyVirtualChild at
www.mydevelopmentlab.com and raising your
own virtual child from birth to age 18.**

15 Death and Grieving: The End of Life

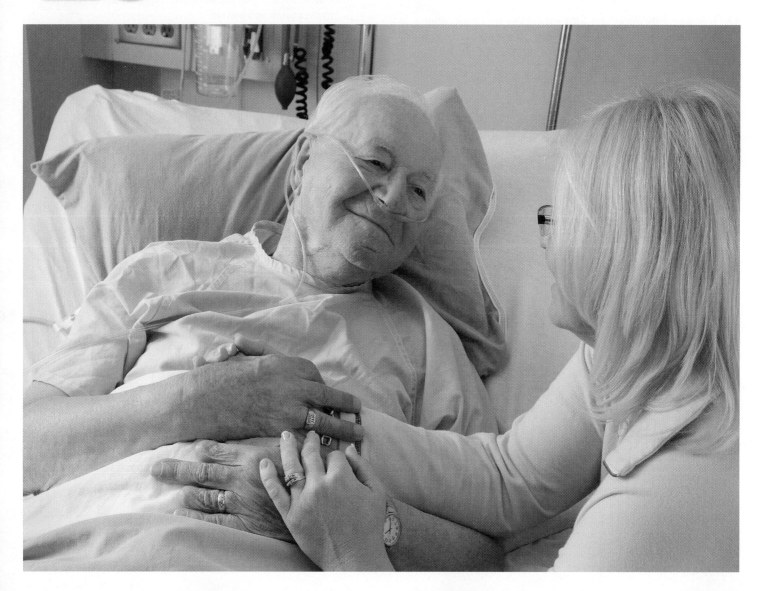

Prologue
Choosing Death

Ted Soulis knew he was about to die. He'd made his peace and said his goodbyes. His family was gathered around him, and he was not afraid. He closed his eyes and slumped over in his chair. His wife let out a gasp.

A hush fell over the room.

And then Mr. Soulis lifted his head, grinned like the devil and said, "Just a little joke."

The room erupted in laughter. It was exactly what everyone would expect of Ted Soulis, a man of great joie de vivre who lived life on his terms.

Mr. Soulis, 69, died a few hours later, with his wife and daughter at his side.

Mr. Soulis was diagnosed last month with an especially aggressive form of brain cancer.

Rather than endure the agony of chemotherapy to eke out a few more months of life, he chose to return home, surround himself with loved ones, and let the cancer run its course. The doctors gave him two weeks to live, so he bought a lot of food and a lot of wine and threw a party that drew 300 people and went on for hours.

"He went out in style," said his daughter, Shana Soulis. "I can't imagine it any differently. It was peaceful, it was beautiful, and it was on his terms." (Squatriglia, 2007, p. B7)

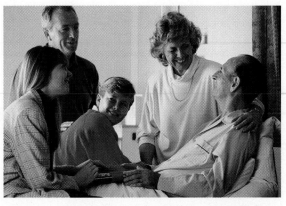

The experience of death is a milestone of life that is central to an understanding of the life span.

If ever death can be said to be good, this was a good death. After 69 years, Ted Soulis slipped away in the company of those he loved.

Death is an experience that will happen to all of us at some time, as universal to the human condition as birth. As such, it is a milestone of life that is central to an understanding of the life span.

Only in the past several decades have lifespan developmentalists given serious study to the developmental implications of dying. In this chapter we will discuss death and dying from several perspectives. We begin by considering how we define death—a determination that is more complex than it seems. We then examine how people view and react to death at different points in the life span. And we consider the very different views of death held by various societies.

Next, we look at how people confront their own deaths. We discuss one theory that people move through several stages as they come to grips with their approaching death. We also look at how people use living wills and assisted suicide.

Finally, we consider bereavement and grief. We examine the difficulties in distinguishing normal from unhealthy grief, and we discuss the consequences of a loss. We also look at mourning and funerals, discussing how people can prepare themselves for the inevitability of death.

Log onto **MyDevelopmentLab** to watch a video of Bob, who has lost both his wife and daughter, talk about his grief and the affects of the losses on him and his family.

LOOKING AHEAD

After reading this chapter, you will be able to answer the following questions:

▶ What is death, and what does it mean at different stages of the life span?

▶ In what ways do people face the prospect of their own death?

▶ How do survivors react to and cope with death?

MODULE 15.1

Death and Dying Across the Life Span

It took a major legal and political battle, but eventually Terri Schiavo's husband won the right to remove a feeding tube that had been keeping her alive for 15 years. Lying in a hospital bed all those years in what physicians called a "persistent vegetative state," Schiavo was never expected to regain consciousness after suffering brain damage due to respiratory and cardiac arrest. After a series of court battles, her husband—despite the wishes of her parents—was allowed to direct caretakers to remove the feeding tube. Schiavo died soon afterward.

Was Schiavo's husband right in seeking to remove her feeding tube? Was she already dead when it was removed? Were her constitutional rights unfairly ignored by her husband's action?

The difficulty of answering such questions illustrates the complexity of what are, literally, matters of life and death. Death is not only a biological event; it involves psychological aspects as well. We need to consider not only issues relating to the definition of death, but also the ways in which our conception of death changes across various points in the life span.

Defining Death: Determining When Life Ends

What is death? Although the question seems straightforward, defining the point at which life ceases and death occurs is surprisingly complex. Over the last few decades, medicine has advanced to the point where some people who would have been considered dead a few years ago would now be considered alive.

Functional death is defined by an absence of heartbeat and breathing. Although this definition seems unambiguous, it is not completely straightforward. For example, a person whose heart has stopped beating and whose breathing has ceased for as long as 5 minutes may be resuscitated and suffer little damage as a consequence of the experience. Does this mean that the person who is now alive was dead, as the functional definition would have it?

Because of this imprecision, heartbeat and respiration are no longer used to determine the moment of death. Medical experts now measure brain functioning. In **brain death**, all signs of brain activity, as measured by electrical brain waves, have ceased. When brain death occurs, there is no possibility of restoring brain functioning.

Some medical experts suggest that a definition of death that relies only on a lack of brain waves is too restrictive. They argue that losing the ability to think, reason, feel, and experience the world may be sufficient to declare a person dead. In this view, which takes psychological considerations into account, a person who suffers irreversible brain damage, who is in a coma, and who will never experience anything approaching a human life can be considered dead. In such a case, the argument goes, death can be judged to have arrived, even if some sort of primitive brain activity is still occurring (Ressner, 2001).

Not surprisingly, such an argument, which moves us from strictly medical criteria to moral and philosophical considerations, is controversial. As a result, the legal definition of death in most localities in the United States relies on the absence of brain functioning, although some laws still include a definition relating to the absence of respiration and heartbeat. The reality is that no matter where a death occurs, in most cases people do not bother to measure brain waves.

functional death the absence of a heartbeat and breathing.

brain death a diagnosis of death based on the cessation of all signs of brain activity, as measured by electrical brain waves.

Usually, the brain waves are closely monitored only in certain circumstances—when the time of death is significant, when organs may potentially be transplanted, or when criminal or legal issues might be involved.

The difficulty in establishing legal and medical definitions of death may reflect some of the changes in understanding and attitudes about death that occur over the course of people's lives.

Death Across the Life Span: Causes and Reactions

As the lifeguards pulled Danny's still body from the water, his friends watched in silent shock. They'd spent their summers at this lake since the third grade and Danny was a member of the varsity swim team. How could he have drowned? An autopsy would reveal that Danny had died of a rare heart complication. His heart had simply stopped in the water. The news shocked his friends even more. It had been hard enough to believe that Danny could drown, but discovering that his heart had suddenly ceased functioning—at age 16? That seemed impossible.

The most frequent causes of death during childhood are due to motor vehicle crashes, fires, and drowning. However, a substantial number of children in the United States are victims of homicide.

Death is something we associate with old age. However, for many individuals, death comes earlier. In such cases, in part because it seems "unnatural" for a younger person to die, the reactions to death are particularly extreme. In the United States today, some people believe that children should be sheltered, and it is wrong for them to know much about death. Yet people of every age can experience the death of friends—as Danny's friends did—and family members, as well as their own death. How do our reactions to death evolve as we age? We will consider several age groups.

Death in Infancy and Childhood. Despite its economic wealth, the United States has a relatively high infant mortality rate, as we discussed earlier. Although the rate has declined since the mid-1960s, the United States ranks behind 35 other countries in the proportion of infants who die during the first year of life (Centers for Disease Control, 2004).

As these statistics indicate, the number of parents who experience the death of an infant is substantial, and their reactions may be profound. The loss of a child typically brings up all the same reactions one would experience on the death of an older person, and sometimes even more severe effects as family members struggle to deal with a death at such an early age. One of the most common reactions is extreme depression (DeFrain et al., 1991; Brockington, 1992; Murphy, Johnson, & Wu, 2003).

One kind of death that is exceptionally difficult to deal with is prenatal death, or *miscarriage*, a topic touched on in the opening chapters of this book. Parents typically form psychological bonds with their unborn child, and consequently they often feel profound grief if it dies before it is born. Moreover, friends and relatives often fail to understand the emotional impact of miscarriage on parents, making parents feel their loss all the more keenly (McGreal, Evans, & Burrows, 1997; Wheeler & Austin, 2001).

Another form of death that produces extreme stress, in part because it is so unanticipated, is sudden infant death syndrome. As we discussed in Chapter 4, in cases of **sudden infant death syndrome**, or **SIDS**, a seemingly healthy baby stops breathing and dies of unexplained causes. Usually occurring between the ages of 2 and 4 months, SIDS strikes unexpectedly; a robust, hardy baby is placed into a crib at nap time or night time and never wakes up.

In cases of SIDS, parents often feel intense guilt, and acquaintances may be suspicious of the "true" cause of death. As we discussed earlier, however, there is no known cause for SIDS, which seems to strike randomly, and parents' guilt is unwarranted (Dyregrov, Nordanger, & Dyregrov, 2003; Hunt & Hauck, 2006; Krueger, 2006; Paterson et al., 2006).

During childhood, the most frequent cause of death is accidents, most of them due to motor vehicle crashes, fires, and drowning. However, a substantial number of children in the United States are victims of homicides, which have nearly tripled in number since 1960. By the early 1990s, death by homicide had become the fourth leading cause of death for children between the ages of 1 and 9 (Finkelhor, 1997; Centers for Disease Control, 2004).

For parents, the death of a child produces the most profound sense of loss and grief. There is no worse death in the eyes of most parents, including the loss of a spouse or of one's own parents. Parents' extreme reaction is partly based on the sense that the natural order of the world, in which children "should" outlive their parents, has somehow collapsed. Their reaction is often coupled with the feeling that it is their primary responsibility to protect their children from any

sudden infant death syndrome (SIDS) a disorder in which seemingly healthy infants die in their sleep.

Adolescents' views of death may be highly romanticized and dramatic.

FROM AN
EDUCATOR'S
PERSPECTIVE
Given their developmental level and understanding of death, how do you think preschool children react to the death of a parent?

harm, and they may feel that they have failed in this task when a child dies (Strength, 1999; Murphy, 2008; Rogers et al., 2008).

Parents are almost never well equipped to deal with the death of a child, and they may obsessively ask themselves afterward, over and over, why the death occurred. Because the bond between children and parents is so strong, parents sometimes feel that a part of themselves has died as well. The stress is so profound that the loss of a child significantly increases the chances of admission to a hospital for a mental disorder (Stroebe, Stroebe, & Hansson, 1993; Wayment & Vierthaler, 2002; Li et al., 2005; Mahgoub & Lantz, 2006).

Childhood Conceptions of Death. Children themselves do not really begin to develop a concept of death until around the age of 5. Although they are well aware of death before that time, they are apt to think of it as a temporary state that involves a reduction in living, rather than a cessation. For instance, a preschool-age child might say, "dead people don't get hungry—well, maybe a little" (Kastenbaum, 1985, p. 629).

Some preschool-age children think of death in terms of sleep—with the consequent possibility of waking up, just as Sleeping Beauty was awakened in the fairy tale. For children who believe this, death is not particularly fearsome; rather, it is something of a curiosity. If people merely tried hard enough—by administering medicine, providing food, or using magic—dead people might "return" (Lonetto, 1980; Andrikopoulou, 2004; Poling & Evans, 2004).

In some cases, children's misunderstanding of death can produce devastating emotional consequences. Children sometimes leap to the erroneous conclusion that they are somehow responsible for a person's death. For instance, they may assume they could have prevented the death by being better behaved. In the same way, they may think that if the person who died really wanted to, she or he could return.

Around the age of 5, children better understand the finality and irreversibility of death. In some cases, children personify death as some kind of ghostlike or devilish figure. At first, though, they do not think of death as universal, but rather as something that happens only to certain people. By about age 9, however, they come to accept the universality of death and its finality (Andrikopoulou, 2004). By middle childhood, children also learn about some of the customs involved with death, such as funerals, cremation, and cemeteries (which we will discuss later in this chapter).

Death in Adolescence. We might expect the significant advances in cognitive development that occur during adolescence to bring about a sophisticated, thoughtful, and reasoned view of death. However, in many ways, adolescents' views of death are as unrealistic as those of younger children, although along different lines.

While adolescents clearly understand the finality and irreversibility of death, they tend not to think it can happen to them, a fact that can lead to risky behavior. Many adolescents develop a *personal fable,* a set of beliefs that causes them to feel unique and special—so special that they may believe they are invulnerable and that the bad things that happen to other people won't happen to them (Elkind, 1985; Alberts, Elkind, & Ginsberg, 2007).

Many times, this risky behavior causes death in adolescence. For instance, the most frequent cause of death among adolescents is accidents, most often involving motor vehicles. Other frequent causes include homicide, suicide, cancer, and AIDS (National Center for Health Statistics, 1994).

When adolescent feelings of invulnerability confront the likelihood of death due to an illness, the results can be shattering. Adolescents who learn that they have a terminal illness often feel angry and cheated—that life has been unjust to them. Because they feel—and act—so negatively, it may be difficult for medical personnel to treat them effectively.

In contrast, some adolescents diagnosed with a terminal illness react with total denial. Feeling indestructible, they may find it impossible to accept the seriousness of their illness. If it does not interfere with their acceptance of medical treatment, some degree of denial may actually be useful, as it allows an adolescent to continue with his or her normal life as long as possible (Massimo, 2006).

Death in Young Adulthood. Young adulthood is the time when most people feel primed to begin their lives. Past the preparatory time of childhood and adolescence, they are on the threshold of making their mark on the world. Because death at such a point in life seems close to unthinkable, its occurrence is particularly difficult. Because they are actively pursuing their goals for life, they are angry and impatient with any illness that threatens their future.

In early adulthood, the leading cause of death continues to be accidents, followed by suicide, homicide, AIDS, and cancer. By the end of early adulthood, however, disease becomes a more prevalent cause of death.

For those people facing death in early adulthood, several concerns are of particular importance. One is the desire to develop intimate relationships and express sexuality, each of which are inhibited, if not completely prevented, by a terminal illness. For instance, people who test positive for the AIDS virus may find it quite difficult to start new relationships. The role of sexual activities within evolving relationships presents even more challenging issues (Rabkin, Remien, & Wilson, 1994; Remien & Rabkin, 2002).

Another particular concern during young adulthood involves future planning. At a time when most people are mapping out their careers and deciding at what point to start a family, young adults who have a terminal illness face additional burdens. Should they marry, even though it is likely that the partner will soon end up widowed? Should a couple seek to conceive a child if the child is likely to be raised by only one parent? How soon should one's employer be told about a terminal illness, when it is clear that employers sometimes discriminate against unhealthy workers? None of these questions is easily answered.

Like adolescents, young adults sometimes make poor patients. They are outraged at their plight and feel the world is unfair, and they may direct their anger at care providers and loved ones. In addition, they may make the medical staff who provide direct care—nurses and orderlies—feel particularly vulnerable, since the staff themselves are often young (Cook & Oltjenbruns, 1989; Oltjenbruns & Balk, 2007).

Death in Middle Adulthood.   For people in middle adulthood, the shock of a life-threatening disease—which is the most common cause of death in this period—is not so great. By this point, people are well aware that they are going to die sometime, and they may be able to consider the possibility of death in a fairly realistic manner.

Yet their sense of realism doesn't make the possibility of dying any easier. In fact, fears about death are often greater in middle adulthood than at any time previously—or even in later life. These fears may lead people to look at life in terms of the number of years they have remaining as opposed to their earlier orientation toward the number of years they have already lived (Levinson, 1992; Cicirelli, 2001).

The most frequent cause of death in middle adulthood is heart attack or stroke. Although the unexpectedness of such a death does not allow for preparation, in some ways it is easier than a slow and painful death from a disease such as cancer. It is certainly the kind of death that most people prefer: When asked, they say they would like an instant and painless death that does not involve loss of any body part (Taylor, 1991; Hanger et al., 2000).

Death in Late Adulthood.   By the time they reach late adulthood, people know with some certainty that their time is coming to an end. Furthermore, they face an increasing number of deaths in their environment. Spouses, siblings, and friends may have already died, a constant reminder of their own mortality.

The most likely causes of death during late adulthood are cancer, stroke, and heart disease. What would happen if these causes of death were eliminated? According to demographers' estimates, the average 70-year-old's life expectancy would increase around 7 years (see Figure 15.1; Hayward, Crimmins, & Saito, 1997).

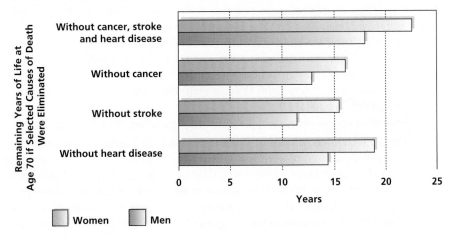

FIGURE 15.1 Adding Years
If the major causes of death were eliminated, the average 70-year-old person would live another 7 years.
Source: Hayward, Crimmins, & Saito, 1997.

The prevalence of death in the lives of elderly people makes them less anxious about dying than they were at earlier stages of life. This does not mean that people in late adulthood welcome death. Rather, it implies that they are more realistic and reflective about it. They think about death, and they may begin to make preparations for it. Some begin to pull away from the world due to diminishing physical and psychological energy (Turner & Helms, 1994; Oyebode, 2008).

Impending death is sometimes accompanied by an accelerating decline in cognitive functioning. In what is known as the *terminal decline,* a significant drop in performance in cognitive areas such as memory and reading may foreshadow death within the next few years (Small & Bäckman, 1999; Wilson, Beckett, & Bienias, 2003; Sliwinski et al., 2006; Wilson et al., 2007).

Some elderly individuals actively seek out death, turning to suicide. The suicide rate for men climbs steadily during the course of late adulthood, and no age group has a higher rate of suicide than white men over the age of 85. (Adolescents and young adults commit suicide in greater numbers, but their *rate* of suicide—the number of suicides as a proportion of the general adolescent population—is actually lower.) Suicide is often a consequence of severe depression or some form of dementia, or it can be due to the loss of a spouse. And, as we will discuss later in the chapter, some individuals, struck down with a terminal illness, seek the assistance of others in committing suicide (Blazer, 1991; De Leo, Conforti, & Carollo, 1997; Chapple et al., 2006).

One particularly important issue for older adults suffering from a terminal illness is whether their lives still have value. More than younger individuals, elderly people who are dying harbor concerns that they are burdens to their family or to society. Furthermore, they may be given the message, sometimes inadvertently, that their value to society has ended and that they have attained the status of "dying" as opposed to being "very sick" (Kastenbaum, 2000).

Do older people wish to know if death is impending? The answer, in most cases, is yes. Like younger patients, who usually state that they wish to know the true nature of an ailment, older people want the details of their illnesses. Ironically, however, candor is not something caregivers wish to provide: Physicians usually prefer to avoid telling dying patients that their illnesses are terminal (Kaufman, 1992; Goold, Williams, & Arnold, 2000; Hagerty, 2004).

At the same time, not all people wish to learn the truth about their condition or to know that they are dying. It is important to keep in mind that individuals react to death in substantially different ways. In part, their reaction is produced by personality factors. For example, people who are generally anxious are more concerned about death. In addition, there are significant cultural differences in how people view and react to death.

Can Death Education Prepare Us for the Inevitable?

"When will Mom come back from being dead?"
"Why did Barry have to die?"
"Did Grandpa die because I was bad?"

Children's questions such as these illustrate why many developmentalists, as well as **thanatologists**, people who study death and dying, have suggested that death education should be an important component of everyone's schooling. Consequently, a relatively new area of instruction, termed *death education,* has emerged. Death education encompasses programs that teach about death, dying, and grief. It is designed to help people of all ages deal better with death and dying—both others' deaths and their own personal mortality.

Death education developed in part as a response to the way we hide death, at least in most Western societies. We typically give hospitals the task of dealing with dying people, and we do not talk to children about death or allow them to go to funerals for fear of upsetting them. Even those most familiar with death, such as emergency workers and medical specialists, are uncomfortable talking about the subject. Because it is discussed so little and is so removed from everyday life, people of all ages may have little opportunity to confront their feelings about death or to gain a more realistic sense of it (Kastenbaum, 1999; McGovern & Barry, 2000; Lowton & Higginson, 2003; Wass, 2004).

Several types of death education programs exist, including the following:

- **Crisis intervention education.** When the World Trade Center was attacked, children in the area were the subjects of several kinds of crisis intervention designed to deal with their anxieties. Younger children, whose conceptions of death were shaky at best, needed explanations of the loss of life that day geared to their levels of cognitive development. Crisis intervention education is used in less extreme times as well. For example, it is common for schools to make emergency counseling available if a student is killed or commits suicide.

thanatologists people who study death and dying.

DEVELOPMENTAL DIVERSITY
Differing Conceptions of Death

In the midst of a tribal celebration, an older man waits for his oldest son to place a cord around his neck. The older man has been sick, and he is ready to relinquish his ties to this earthly world. He asks that his son lift him to his death, and the son complies.

***

To Hindus in India, death is not an ending, but rather part of a continual cycle. Because they believe in reincarnation, death is thought to be followed by rebirth into a new life. Death, then, is seen as a companion to life.

People's responses to death take many forms, particularly in different cultures. But even within Western societies, reactions to death and dying are quite diverse. For instance, consider which is better: for a man to die after a full life in which he has raised a family and been successful in his job, or for a courageous and valiant young soldier to die defending his country in wartime? Has one person died a better death than the other?

The answer depends on one's values, which are largely due to cultural and subcultural teachings, often shared through religious beliefs. For instance, some societies view death as a punishment or as a judgment about one's contributions to the world. Others see death as redemption from an earthly life of travail. Some view death as the start of an eternal life, while others believe that there is no heaven or hell and that an earthly life is all there is (Bryant, 2003).

Given that religious teachings regarding the meaning of life and death are quite diverse, it is

Differing conceptions of death lead to different rituals, as this ceremony in India illustrates.

not surprising that views of death and dying vary substantially. For instance, one study found that Christian and Jewish 10-year-olds tend to view death from a more "scientific" vantage point (in terms of the cessation of physical activity in the body) than Sunni Moslem and Druze children of the same age, who are more likely to see death in spiritual terms. We cannot be sure whether such differences are due to the different religious and cultural backgrounds of the children, or whether differences in exposure to dying people influence the rate at which the understanding of death develops. However, it is clear that members of these various groups have very different conceptions of death (Florian & Kravetz, 1985; Thorson et al., 1997; Aiken, 2000).

For members of Native American tribes, death is seen as a continuation of life. For example, Lakota parents will tell their children, "Be kind to your brother, for someday he will die." When people die, they are assumed to move to a spirit land called "Wanagi Makoce," inhabited by all people and animals. Death, then, is not viewed with anger or seen as unfair (Huang, 2004).

Members of some cultures learn about death at an earlier age than others. For instance, exposure to high levels of violence and death may lead to an awareness of death earlier in some cultures than in cultures in which violence is less a part of everyday life. Research shows that children in Northern Ireland and Israel understood the finality, irreversibility, and inevitability of death at an earlier age than children in the United States and Britain (McWhirter, Young, & Majury, 1983; Atchley, 2000; Braun, Pietsch, & Blanchette, 2000).

- **Routine death education.** Although there is relatively little curricular material on death available at the elementary school level, course work in high schools is becoming increasingly common. For instance, some high schools have specific courses on death and dying. Furthermore, colleges and universities increasingly include courses relating to death in such departments as psychology, human development, sociology, and education.

- **Death education for members of the helping professions.** Professionals who deal with death, dying, and grief as part of their careers have a special need for death education. Almost all medical and nursing schools now offer some form of death education to help their students. The most successful programs not only provide ways for providers to help patients deal with their own impending deaths and those of family members, but also allow students to explore their feelings about the topic (Downe-Wamboldt & Tamlyn, 1997; Kastenbaum, 1999; Browning, 2003).

Although no single form of death education is sufficient to demystify death, these kinds of programs may help people come to grips more effectively with what is, along with birth, the most universal—and certain—of all human experiences.

REVIEW

▶ Death has been defined as the cessation of heartbeat and respiration (functional death), the absence of electrical brain waves (brain death), and the loss of human qualities.

▶ The death of an infant or young child can be particularly difficult for parents, and for an adolescent death appears to be unthinkable.

▶ Death in young adulthood can appear unfair, while people in middle adulthood have begun to understand the reality of death.

▶ By the time they reach late adulthood, people know they will die and begin to make preparations.

▶ Cultural differences in attitudes and beliefs about death strongly influence people's reactions to it.

▶ Thanatologists recommend that death education become a normal part of learning.

APPLY

▶ Do you think people who are going to die should be told? Does your response depend on the person's age?

▶ Would it be possible to develop a basic program of death education that could be used across cultures? Why or why not?

MODULE 15.2

Understanding the Process of Dying

Helen Reynolds, 63, had undergone operations in January and April to repair and then replace a heart valve that was not permitting a smooth flow of blood. But by May her feet had turned the color of overripe eggplants, their mottled purple black an unmistakable sign of gangrene. . . . In June, she chose to have first her right leg, and then her left, amputated in hopes of stabilizing her condition. The doctors were skeptical about the surgery, but deferred to her wishes. . . .

But then Reynolds uncharacteristically began talking about her pain. On that Sunday afternoon in June, a nurse beckoned intern Dr. Randall Evans. Evans, a graduate of the University of New Mexico Medical School who planned a career in the critical-care field, was immensely popular with the nursing staff for his cordial and sympathetic manner. But, unlike the MICU nurses, he had difficulty reading Reynolds's lips (the ventilator made it impossible for her to speak aloud) and asked her to write down her request. Laboriously, she scrawled 16 words on the note pad: "I have decided to end my life as I do not want to live like this." (Begley, 1991, pp. 44–45)

Less than a week later, after the ventilator that helped her to breathe had been removed at her request, Helen Reynolds died.

Like other deaths, Reynolds's raises a myriad of difficult questions. Was her request to remove the respirator equivalent to suicide? Should the medical staff have complied with the request? Was she coping with her impending death effectively? How do people come to terms with death, and how do they react and adapt to it? Lifespan developmentalists and other specialists in death and dying have struggled to find answers to such questions.

Kübler-Ross: A Theory of Death and Dying

No individual has had a greater influence on our understanding of the way people confront death than Elisabeth Kübler-Ross. A psychiatrist, Kübler-Ross developed a theory of death and dying, built on extensive interviews with people who were dying and with those who cared for them (Kübler-Ross, 1969, 1982).

Based on her observations, Kübler-Ross initially suggested that people pass through five basic steps as they move toward death (summarized in Figure 15.2).

A hospice provides a warm and supportive environment for the dying. The emphasis is on making patients' lives as full as possible, not on squeezing out every additional moment of life at any cost. What are the advantages of hospice care to individuals and society?

Denial. "No, I can't be dying. There must be some mistake." It is typical for people to protest in such a manner on learning that they have a terminal disease. Such objections represent the first stage of dying, *denial*. In denial, people resist the idea that they are going to die. They may argue that their test results have been mixed up, that an X-ray has been read incorrectly, or that their physician does not know what he or she is talking about.

Denial comes in several forms. A patient may flatly reject the diagnosis, simply refusing to believe the news. In extreme cases, memories of weeks in the hospital are forgotten. In other forms of denial, patients fluctuate between refusing to accept the news and at other times confiding that they know they are going to die (Teutsch, 2003).

Although we might view the loss of reality implied by denial as a sign of deteriorating mental health, in fact many experts view denial in positive terms. Denial is a defense mechanism that can permit people to absorb the unwelcome news on their own terms and at their own pace. Only when they are able to acknowledge the news can they move on and eventually come to grips with the reality that they are truly going to die.

Anger. After they move beyond denial, people may be likely to express *anger*. A dying person may be angry at everyone: people who are in good health, their spouses and other family members, those who are caring for them, their children. They may lash out at others, and wonder—sometimes aloud—why *they* are dying and not someone else. They may be furious at God, reasoning that they have led good lives and that there are far worse people in the world who should be dying.

It may not be easy to be around people who are going through an anger stage. As they focus their anger on others, they may say and do things that are painful and sometimes unfathomable. Eventually, though, most patients move beyond the anger phase. This may lead to another development—bargaining.

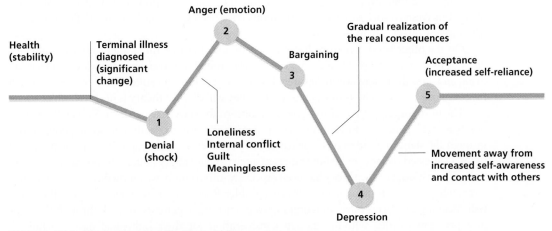

FIGURE 15.2 Moving Toward the End of Life
The steps toward death, according to Kübler-Ross (1975). Do you think there are cultural differences in the steps?

Bargaining. "If you're good, you'll be rewarded." Most people learn this equation in childhood, and many try to apply it to their impending death. In this case, "good" means promising to be a better person, and the "reward" is staying alive.

In *bargaining*, dying people try to negotiate their way out of death. They may declare that they will dedicate their lives to the poor if God saves them. They may promise that if they can just live long enough to see a son married, they will willingly accept death later.

However, the promises that are part of the bargaining process are rarely kept. If one request appears to be granted, people typically seek another, and yet another. Furthermore, they may be unable to fulfill their promises because their illnesses keep progressing and prevent them from achieving what they said they would do.

In some ways, bargaining seems to have positive consequences. Although death cannot be postponed indefinitely, having a goal of attending a particular event or living until a certain time may in fact delay death until then. For instance, death rates of Jewish people fall just before the holiday of Passover, and rise just after it. Similarly, the death rate among older Chinese women falls before and during important holidays, and rises after. It is as if the people involved have negotiated to stay alive until after the holidays have passed (Phillips & Smith, 1990; Philips, 1992).

In the end, of course, all the bargaining in the world is unable to overcome the inevitability of death. When people eventually realize that death is unavoidable, they often move into a stage of depression.

Depression. Many dying people experience phases of *depression*. Realizing that the issue is settled and they cannot bargain their way out of death, people are overwhelmed with a deep sense of loss. They know that they are losing their loved ones and that their lives really are coming to an end.

The depression they experience may be of two types. In *reactive depression*, the feelings of sadness are based on events that have already occurred: the loss of dignity that may accompany medical procedures, the end of a job, or the knowledge that one will never return from the hospital to one's home.

Dying people also experience preparatory depression. In *preparatory depression*, people feel sadness over future losses. They know that death will bring an end to their relationships with others and that they will never see future generations. The reality of death is inescapable in this stage, and it brings about profound sadness over the unalterable conclusion of one's life.

Acceptance. Kübler-Ross suggested that the final step of dying is *acceptance*. People who have developed a state of acceptance are fully aware that death is impending. Unemotional and uncommunicative, they have virtually no feelings—positive or negative—about the present or future. They have made peace with themselves, and they may wish to be left alone. For them, death holds no sting.

Evaluating Kübler-Ross's Theory. Kübler-Ross has had an enormous impact on the way we look at death. As one of the first people to observe systematically how people approach their own deaths, she is recognized as a pioneer. Kübler-Ross was almost single-handedly responsible for bringing into public awareness the phenomenon of death, which previously had languished out of sight in Western societies. Her contributions have been particularly influential among those who provide direct care to the dying.

On the other hand, her work has drawn criticism. For one thing, there are some obvious limitations to her conception of dying. It is largely limited to those who are aware that they are dying and who die in a relatively leisurely fashion. To people who suffer from diseases in which the prognosis is uncertain as to when or even if they will die, her theory is not applicable.

The most important criticisms, however, concern the stage-like nature of Kübler-Ross's theory. Not every person passes through every step on the way to death, and some people move through the steps in a different sequence. Some people even go through the same steps several times. Depressed patients may show bursts of anger, and an angry patient may bargain for more time. This criticism of the theory has been especially important news for medical and other caregivers who work with dying people. Because Kübler-Ross's stages have become so well known, well-meaning caregivers have sometimes tried to encourage patients to work through the steps in a prescribed order, without enough consideration for their individual needs (Schulz & Aderman, 1976; Kastenbaum, 1992; Meagher, 2007).

Furthermore, Kübler-Ross may have considered too limited a set of factors when she outlined her theory. For example, other researchers suggest that anxiety plays an important role

FROM A
SOCIAL WORKER'S
PERSPECTIVE
Do you think Kübler-Ross's five steps of dying might be subject to age differences? Why or why not?

throughout the process of dying. The anxiety may be about one's upcoming death, or it may relate to fear of the symptoms of the disease. A person with cancer, then, may fear death less than the uncontrollable pain that may be a future possibility (Hayslip et al., 1997; Meagher, 2007).

Finally, there are substantial differences in people's reactions to impending death. The specific cause of dying, how long the process of dying lasts, a person's age, sex, and personality, and the social support available from family and friends all influence the course of dying and people's responses to it (Stroebe, Stroebe, & Hansson, 1993; Carver & Scheier, 2002).

In short, there are significant concerns about the accuracy of Kübler-Ross's account of how people react to impending death. In response to some of these concerns, other theorists have developed some alternative ideas. Psychologist Edwin Shneidman, for example, suggests that there are "themes" in people's reactions to dying that can occur—and recur—in any order throughout the dying process. These include such feelings and thoughts as incredulity, a sense of unfairness, fear of pain or even general terror, and fantasies of being rescued (Leenaars & Shneidman, 1999).

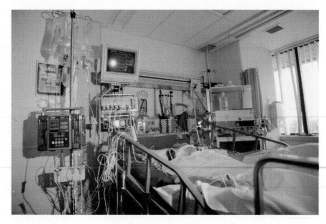

Many terminally ill patients choose "DNR," or "Do Not Resuscitate," as a way to avoid extraordinary medical interventions.

Another theorist, Charles Corr, suggests that, as in other periods of life, people who are dying face a set of psychological tasks. These include minimizing physical stress, maintaining the richness of life, continuing or deepening their relationships with other people, and fostering hope, often through spiritual searching (Corr & Doka, 2001; Corr, Nabe, & Corr, 2000, 2006).

Choosing the Nature of Death: Is DNR the Way to Go?

The letters "DNR" written on a patient's medical chart have a simple and clear meaning. Standing for "Do Not Resuscitate," DNR signifies that rather than administering any and every procedure that might possibly keep a patient alive, no extraordinary means are to be taken. For terminally ill patients, "DNR" may mean the difference between dying immediately or living additional days, months, or even years, kept alive only by the most extreme, invasive, and even painful medical procedures.

Making the Decision: How Much Control Do People Have over the Nature of Their Death? The decision to use or not to use extreme medical interventions entails several issues. One is the differentiation of "extreme" and "extraordinary" measures from those that are simply routine. There are no hard-and-fast rules; people making the decision must consider the needs of the specific patient, his or her prior medical history, and factors such as age and even religion. For instance, different standards might apply to a 12-year-old patient and an 85-year-old patient with the same medical condition. Other questions concern quality of life. How can we determine an individual's current quality of life and whether it will be improved or diminished by a particular medical intervention? Who makes such decisions—the patient, a family member, or medical personnel?

One thing is clear: Medical personnel are reluctant to carry out the wishes of the terminally ill and their families to suspend aggressive treatment. Even when it is certain that a patient is going to die, and patients determine that they do not wish further treatment, physicians often claim to be unaware of their patients' wishes. For instance, although one-third of the patients ask not to be resuscitated, less than half of these people's physicians state that they know of their patients' preference (see Table 15.1). In addition, only 49 percent of patients have their wishes entered on their medical charts. Physicians and other health care providers may be reluctant to act on DNR requests in part because they are trained to save patients, not permit them to die, and in part to avoid legal liability issues (Knaus et al., 1995; Goold, Williams, & Arnold, 2000; McArdle, 2002).

TABLE **15.1** Dying Hard: Experiences of 4,301 Patients with End-of-Life Care	
Terminal patients who did not want resuscitation	31%
Of those patients who did not want resuscitation, percentage whose physicians were aware of their preference	47%
Of those patients who did not want resuscitation, percentage whose preferences were entered on their charts	49%

Source: Knaus et al., 1995.

I,_____,
being of sound mind, make this statement as a directive to be followed if I become permanently unable to participate in decisions regarding my medical care. These instructions reflect my firm and settled commitment to decline medical treatment under the circumstances indicated below:

I direct my attending physician to withhold or withdraw treatment that merely prolongs my dying, if I should be in **an incurable or irreversible mental or physical condition** with no reasonable expectation of recovery, including but not limited to: (a) a **terminal condition;** (b) a **permanently unconscious condition;** or (c) a **minimally conscious condition in which I am permanently unable to make decisions or express my wishes.**

I direct that treatment be limited to measures to keep me comfortable and to relieve pain, including any pain that might occur by withholding or withdrawing treatment.
While I understand that I am not legally required to be specific about future treatments, **if I am in the condition(s) described above I feel especially strongly about the following treatments:**

I do not want cardiac resuscitation.
I do not want mechanical respiration.
I do not want tube feeding.
I do not want antibiotics.

However, I **do want** maximum pain relief, even if it may hasten my death.

Other directions (insert personal instructions):

These directions express my legal right to refuse treatment under federal and state law. I intend my instructions to be carried out, unless I have revoked them in a new writing or by clearly indicating that I have changed my mind.

Signed:_____ Date:_____

Address:_____

– –

Statement by Witnesses
I declare that the person who signed this document appears to be at least eighteen (18) years of age, of sound mind, and under no constraint or undue influence. The person who signed this document appeared to do so willingly and free from duress. He or she signed (or asked another to sign for him or her) this document in my presence.

Witness:_____

Address:_____

– –

Witness:_____

Address:_____

– –

FIGURE 15.3 A Living Will
What steps can people take to make sure the wishes they write into their living wills are carried out?

Living Wills. In order to gain more control over decisions regarding the nature of their death, people are increasingly signing living wills. A **living will** is a legal document that designates the medical treatments a person does or does not want if the person cannot express his or her wishes (see Figure 15.3).

Some people designate a specific person, called a *health care proxy,* to act as their representative in making health care decisions. Health care proxies are authorized either in living wills or in a legal document known as *durable power of attorney.* Health care proxies may be authorized to deal with all medical care problems (such as a coma) or only terminal illnesses.

As with DNR orders, living wills are ineffective unless people take steps to make sure their health care proxies and doctors know their wishes. Although they may be reluctant to do so in advance, people should also have frank conversations clarifying their wishes with the representatives they choose as their health care proxies.

Euthanasia and Assisted Suicide. Dr. Jack Kevorkian became well known in the 1990s for his invention and promotion of a "suicide machine," which allowed patients to push a button that releases anesthesia and a drug that stops the heart. By supplying the machine and the drugs, which patients administered themselves, Kevorkian was participating in a process known as *assisted suicide,* in which a person provides the means for a terminally ill individual to commit suicide. Kevorkian ended up spending eight years in prison after being convicted of second degree murder for his participation in an assisted suicide that was shown on the television show *60 Minutes.*

Assisted suicide continues to raise bitter conflict in the United States, and the practice is illegal in most states. The exception is the state of Oregon, which passed a "right to die law" in 1998. In the first decade that Oregon's law was in effect, less than 300 people took medication to end their own lives (Ganzini, Beer, & Brouns, 2006; Davey, 2007).

In many countries, assisted suicide is an accepted practice. For instance, in the Netherlands medical personnel may help end their patients' lives. However, several conditions must be met to make the practice permissible: At least two physicians must determine that the patient is terminally ill, there must be unbearable physical or mental suffering, the patient must give informed consent in writing, and relatives must be informed beforehand (Galbraith & Dobson, 2000; Rosenfeld et al., 2000; Naik, 2002; Kleespies, 2004).

Assisted suicide is one form of **euthanasia**, the practice of assisting terminally ill people to die more quickly. Popularly known as "mercy killing," euthanasia can take a range of forms. *Passive euthanasia* involves removing respirators or other medical equipment that may be sustaining a patient's life, to allow them to die naturally. This happens when medical staff follow a DNR order, for example. In *voluntary active euthanasia* caregivers or medical staff act to end a person's life before death would normally occur, perhaps by administering a dose of pain medication that they know will be fatal. Assisted suicide, as we have seen, lies between passive and voluntary active euthanasia. Euthanasia is an emotional and controversial—though surprisingly widespread—practice.

No one knows how widespread. However, one survey of nurses in intensive care units found that 20 percent had deliberately hastened a patient's death at least once, and other experts assert that euthanasia is far from rare (Asch, 1996; Field, 2007; Brzostek et al., 2008).

Euthanasia is highly controversial, in part because it centers on decisions about who should control life. Does the right belong solely to an individual, a person's physicians, his or her depen-

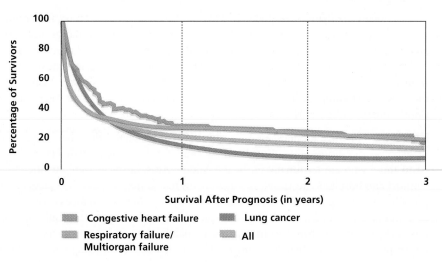

FIGURE 15.4 How Long Do "Terminal" Patients Really Live?
According to the large SUPPORT study, a significant percentage of a group of 3,693 patients given no more than a 50 percent chance of living for 6 months survived well beyond that period. Why do you think this happened?
Source: Lynn et al., 1997.

dents, the government, or some deity? Because—at least in the United States—we assume that we all have the absolute right to create lives by bringing children into the world, some people argue that we should also have the absolute right to end our lives (Solomon, 1995; Lester, 1996; Allen et al., 2006).

The Arguments Against Euthanasia.   Many opponents of euthanasia argue that the practice is morally wrong. In their view, prematurely ending someone's life, no matter how willing that person may be, is the equivalent of murder. Others point out that physicians are often inaccurate in predicting how long a person's life will last. For example, a large-scale study known as SUPPORT—the Study to Understand Prognoses and Preferences for Outcomes and Risks of Treatment—found that patients often outlive physicians' predictions of when they will die. In some cases, patients have lived for years after being given no more than a 50 percent chance of living for 6 more months (Bishop, 2006; see Figure 15.4).

Another argument against euthanasia focuses on the emotional state of the patient. Even if patients ask or sometimes beg health care providers to help them die, they may be suffering from a form of deep depression. In such cases, patients may be treated with antidepressant drugs that can alleviate the depression. Once the depression lifts, patients may change their minds about their earlier wish for death.

The debate over euthanasia is likely to continue. It is a highly personal issue, yet one that society increasingly must face as the world's elderly population increases (Becvar, 2000; Gostin, 2006).

Caring for the Terminally Ill: The Place of Death

Recall the description of Helen Reynolds's last months of life, spent in the intensive care unit of a Boston hospital. Although family members visited her frequently, Helen also faced many lonely hours watching television as her condition deteriorated.

Hospitals and Their Alternatives.   Like Reynolds, about half the people in the United States who die do so in hospitals. It need not be that way. In fact, there are several reasons why hospitals are among the least desirable locales in which to face death. Hospitals are typically impersonal, with staff rotating throughout the day. Because visiting hours are limited, people frequently die alone, without the comfort of loved ones at their bedside.

Furthermore, hospitals are designed to make people better, not to deal with the dying, and it is extraordinarily expensive to provide custodial care for dying people. Consequently, hospitals typically don't have the resources needed to deal adequately with the emotional requirements of terminally ill patients and their families.

Dying at Home.   Because of the limitations of traditional hospitals in dealing with the dying, there are now several alternatives to hospitalization. In **home care**, dying people stay in their homes and receive treatment from their families and visiting medical staff. Many dying patients prefer home care because they can spend their final days in a familiar environment, with people they love and a lifetime accumulation of treasures around them.

living wills   legal documents designating what medical treatments people want or do not want if they cannot express their wishes.

euthanasia   the practice of assisting people who are terminally ill to die more quickly.

home care   an alternative to hospitalization in which dying people stay in their homes and receive treatment from their families and visiting medical staff.

hospice care care provided for the dying in institutions devoted to those who are terminally ill.

Although the dying may prefer home care, it can be quite difficult for family members. Furnishing final care can offer family members a good deal of emotional solace because they are giving something precious to people they love. But it is extraordinarily draining, both physically and emotionally, to be on call 24 hours a day. Furthermore, because most relatives are not trained in nursing, they may provide less than optimal medical care. Many people decide they just aren't equipped to care for a dying family member at home (Perreault, Fothergill-Bourbonnais, & Fiset, 2004).

Hospices. For these families, another alternative to hospitalization that is becoming increasingly prevalent is hospice care. **Hospice care** is care for the dying provided in institutions devoted to those who are terminally ill. In the Middle Ages, hospices were facilities that provided comfort and hospitality to travelers. Drawing on that concept, today's hospices are designed to provide a warm, supportive environment for the dying. They do not focus on extending people's lives, but rather on making their final days pleasant and meaningful. Typically, people who go to hospices are removed from treatments that are painful, and no extraordinary or invasive means are employed to make their lives longer. The emphasis is on making patients' lives as full as possible, not on squeezing out every possible moment of life at any cost (Johnson, Kassner, & Kutner, 2004).

Although the research is far from conclusive, patients appear to be more satisfied with the care they receive in hospices than with the treatment received in more traditional settings. In addition, hospice care has been expanded to instances in which people wish to die at home. In such cases, trained hospice workers help care for dying individuals in their own homes, making them comfortable as they approach death. Whether it takes place at a hospice facility or at home, hospice care provides a clear alternative to traditional hospitalization for the terminally ill (Tang, Aaronson, & Forbes, 2004).

REVIEW

▶ Elisabeth Kübler-Ross has identified five steps toward dying: denial, anger, bargaining, depression, and acceptance. The stage nature of her theory has been criticized as too inflexible, and other theorists have suggested alternatives.

▶ Issues surrounding dying are highly controversial, including the degree of measures that physicians should apply to keep dying patients alive and who should make the decisions about those measures. Living wills are a way for people to take some control over the decision.

▶ Assisted suicide and, more generally, euthanasia are highly controversial and are illegal in most of the United States, although many people believe they should be legalized if they are regulated.

▶ Although most people in the United States die in hospitals, increasing numbers are choosing home care or hospice care for their final days.

APPLY

▶ Do you think assisted suicide should be permissible? Other forms of euthanasia? Why or why not?

▶ Why do you think hospice patients and their families appear to be more satisfied with the care they receive than those who receive treatment in more traditional settings?

mydevelopmentlab

You have just read about home care, now log onto **MyDevelopmentLab** to watch a video of a woman talking about the strain that bringing her husband home to die had on her.

MODULE 15.3

Grief and Bereavement

No one ever told me that grief felt so like fear. I am not afraid, but the sensation is like being afraid. The same fluttering in the stomach, the same restlessness, the yawning. I keep on swallowing.

At other times it feels like being mildly drunk, or concussed. There is a sort of invisible blanket between the world and me. I find it hard to take in what anyone says. Or perhaps, hard to want to take it in. It is so uninteresting. (Lewis, 1985, p. 394)

For something that is a universal experience, most of us are surprisingly ill prepared for the grief that follows the death of a loved one. Particularly in Western societies, where life expectancy is long and mortality rates lower than at any time in history, people are apt to view death as an atypical event rather than an expected part of life. This attitude makes grief all the more difficult to bear, particularly when we compare the present day with historical eras in which people lived shorter lives and the death rate was considerably higher. For most survivors in Western countries, the first step in grieving is some sort of funeral (Gluhoski, Leader, & Wortman, 1994; Nolen-Hoeksema & Larson, 1999; Bryant, 2003).

Because an individual's death represents an important transition, not only for loved ones but for an entire community, the rites associated with death take on an added importance. The emotional significance of death, combined with the pressure of enterprising salespersons, lead many to overspend on funerals.

Mourning and Funerals

Death is a big business in the United States. The average funeral and burial costs $7,000. The purchase of an ornate, polished coffin, transportation to and from the cemetery in a limousine, and preparation of the body for preservation and viewing are among the services that people typically purchase in planning a funeral (AARP, 2004).

In part, the relatively grandiose nature of funerals is due to the vulnerability of those planning the funeral, who are typically close survivors of the deceased. Wishing to demonstrate love and affection, the survivors are susceptible to suggestions to "provide the best" for the deceased (Culver, 2003).

But it is not only the pressure of enterprising salespersons that leads many people to spend thousands of dollars on a funeral. In large measure, the nature of funerals, like that of weddings, is determined by social norms and customs. Because an individual's death represents an important transition, not only for loved ones but for an entire community, the rites associated with death take on an added importance. In a sense, then, a funeral is not only a public acknowledgment that an individual has died, but recognition of everyone's ultimate mortality and an acceptance of the cycle of life (DeSpelder & Strickland, 1992).

In Western societies, funeral rituals follow a typical pattern, despite some surface variations. Prior to the funeral, the body is prepared in some way and is dressed in special clothing. Funerals usually include the celebration of a religious rite, the delivery of a eulogy, a procession of some sort, and some formal period, such as the wake for Irish Catholics and shivah for Jews, in which relatives and friends visit the mourning family and pay their respects. Military funerals typically include the firing of weapons and a flag draped over the coffin.

Cultural Differences in Grieving. Non-Western cultures include funeral rituals of quite different sorts. For instance, in some societies mourners shave their heads as a sign of grief, while in others they allow the hair to grow and men stop shaving for a period of time. In other cultures, mourners may be hired to wail and grieve. Sometimes noisy celebrations take place at funerals, while in other cultures silence is the norm. Even the nature of emotional displays, such as the amount and timing of crying, is determined culturally (Rosenblatt, 1988, 2001).

For example, mourners in Balinese funerals in Indonesia show little emotion because they believe they must be calm in order for the gods to hear their prayers. In contrast, mourners at African American funerals are encouraged to show their grief, and the funeral rituals are meant to allow attendees to display their feelings (Rosenblatt, 1988; Rosenblatt & Wallace, 2005; Collins & Doolittle, 2006).

Historically, some cultures have developed funeral rites that strike us as extreme. For example, in *suttee,* a traditional Hindu practice in India that is now illegal, a widow was expected to throw herself into the fire that consumed her husband's body. In ancient China, servants were sometimes buried (alive) with their masters' bodies.

Ultimately, no matter what the particular ritual, all funerals basically serve the same underlying function: They serve as a way to mark the end point for the life of the person who has died—and provide a formal forum for the feelings of the survivors, a place where they can come together and share their grief and comfort one another.

Bereavement and Grief: Adjusting to the Death of a Loved One

After the death of a loved one, a painful period of adjustment follows, involving bereavement and grief. **Bereavement** is acknowledgment of the objective fact that one has experienced a death, while **grief** is the emotional response to one's loss. Everyone's grief is different, but there are certain similarities in the ways people in Western societies adjust to the loss.

bereavement acknowledgment of the objective fact that one has experienced a death.

grief the emotional response to one's loss.

After a death, people move through a painful period of bereavement and grief. These adolescents in Bosnia mourn the loss of a friend who was killed by enemy bombardment.

FROM A
SOCIAL WORKER'S
PERSPECTIVE
Why do you think the risk of death is so high for people who have recently lost a spouse? Why might remarriage lower the risk?

Stages of Grief.   Survivors' first stage of grief typically entails shock, numbness, disbelief, or outright denial. People may avoid the reality of the situation, trying to carry on with the usual routines of their lives, although the pain may break through, causing anguish, fear, and deep sorrow and distress. If the pain is too severe, however, the person may cycle back to numbness. In some ways, such a psychological state may be beneficial because it permits the survivor to make funeral arrangements and carry out other psychologically difficult tasks. Typically, people pass through this stage in a few days or weeks, although in some cases it lasts longer.

In the next phase, people begin to confront the death and realize the extent of their loss. They fully experience their grief, and they begin to acknowledge the reality that the separation from the dead person will be permanent. In so doing, mourners may suffer deep unhappiness or even depression, a normal feeling in this situation and not one necessarily requiring treatment. They may yearn for the dead individual. Emotions can range from impatience to lethargy. However, they also begin to view their past relationship with the deceased realistically, good and bad. In so doing, they begin to free themselves from some of the bonds that tied them to their loved ones (de Vries et al., 1997; Corr & Corr, 2007).

Finally, people who have lost a loved one reach the accommodation stage. They begin to pick up the pieces of their lives and to construct new identities. For instance, rather than seeing herself as someone's widowed spouse, a woman whose husband has died may come to regard herself as a single person. Still, there are moments when intense feelings of grief occur.

Ultimately, most people are able to emerge from the grieving process and live new lives, independent from the person who has died. They form new relationships, and some even find that coping with the death has helped them to grow as individuals. They become more self-reliant and more appreciative of life.

It is important to keep in mind that not everyone passes through the stages of grief in the same manner and in the same order. People display vast individual differences, partly due to their personalities, the nature of the relationship with the deceased, and the opportunities that are available to them for continuing their lives after the loss. As with Kübler-Ross's stages of dying, the stages of grieving do not unfold in the same way for all people.

As we consider in the *From Research to Practice* box, even the strength of one's relationship with the deceased—at least in the case of longtime spouses—can have an effect on the grieving process.

Differentiating Unhealthy Grief from Normal Grief.   Although ideas abound about what separates normal grief from unhealthy grief, careful research has shown that many of the assumptions that both laypersons and clinicians hold are wrong. There is no particular timetable for grieving; particularly dubious is the common notion that grieving should be complete a year after a spouse has died. Increasing evidence suggests that for some people (but not all) grieving may take considerably longer than a year. Research also contradicts the common assumption that depression is widespread; only 15 to 30 percent of people show relatively deep depression following the loss of a loved one (Prigerson et al., 1995; Bonanno, Wortman, & Lehman, 2002; Hensley, 2006).

Similarly, it is often assumed that people who show little initial distress over a death are simply not facing up to reality and that as a consequence they are likely to have problems later. This is not the case. In fact, those who show the most intense distress immediately after a death are the most apt to have adjustment difficulties and health problems later on (Gluhoski, Leader, & Wortman, 1994; Boemer, Wortman, & Bonanno, 2005).

The Consequences of Grief and Bereavement.   In a sense, death is catching, at least in terms of survivors' mortality. Widowed people are particularly at risk of death, with the risk as much as seven times higher than normal in the first year after the death of a spouse. Particularly vulnerable are men and younger women who have been widowed. Remarriage seems to lower the risk of death for survivors. This is particularly true for men who have lost their wives, although the reasons are not clear (Martikainen & Valkonen, 1996; Aiken, 2000; Manzoli et al., 2007).

Bereavement is more likely to produce depression or other negative consequences if the person who has lost a loved one is already insecure, anxious, or fearful and therefore less able to cope effectively. Furthermore, people whose relationships were marked by ambivalence before death are more apt to suffer poor post-death outcomes than those who were secure in their relationships. Those who were highly dependent on the person who died, and who therefore feel more

FROM RESEARCH TO PRACTICE
Moving On: Surviving the Loss of a Longtime Spouse

Patty Limerick, 55, found solace in friends who surrounded her in the small hospital room the night her husband Jeff died suddenly of a stroke in 2005, and who stayed by her side in the weeks and months afterward. But she found she still needed time alone to grieve not only the death of her husband but also the end of their happy 26-year marriage. "For almost two months, I lay on the floor at night sobbing while listening to Marty Robbins sing 'At the End of a Long Lonely Day,'" she says, referring to the song played at Jeff's funeral. But as the weeks went by, the tears subsided. "It was gradual," she says, "but at some point, I realized I was listening to the song without crying." (Stitch, 2006, p. F3)

As you may well imagine, the death of a spouse is almost always a traumatic experience that is usually followed by intense grief and anguish. In the case of older couples who had been married for a very long time, losing a spouse can mean losing a lifelong companion and typically a partner's primary and sometimes sole source of emotional support. Intuition may therefore suggest that the period of grieving such a loss would be particularly prolonged for a surviving spouse who had enjoyed a close and happy marriage.

But a growing body of research suggests otherwise: It seems in fact that people who had a successful marriage are better able to work through their mourning of a lost spouse and get on with the rest of their lives than those with less successful marriages.

A recent longitudinal study of hundreds of married older adults revealed that almost half of those who reported having satisfying marriages were able to get past their grief within 6 months of the death of their spouses (Carr et al., 2000; Carr, Nesse, & Wortman, 2005; Carr & Ha, 2006).

One explanation for these findings is that people who enjoy close and happy marriages tend to have strong interpersonal skills on which to rely during their time of loss. They may be better equipped to call upon friends, family, and even a professional counselor if necessary to assist them through their grieving period. One way that others help the surviving spouse is by providing a diversion to keep him or her from dwelling on the loss and also by encouraging him or her to replace the void with new interests and activities. Strong interpersonal skills may also facilitate a positive approach to dating new people when the time is right (Carr, Nesse, & Wortman, 2005; Stitch, 2006).

Another reason for the resiliency of surviving spouses of close marriages is the knowledge that they and their departed partner had culminated what they set out to achieve: a successful and satisfying relationship. Surviving partners of strained marriages might feel more sadness over never having achieved a desired level of closeness, or they might regret not having an opportunity to resolve lingering conflicts, or they might feel guilty about not working harder to make their marriage better when they had the chance.

In contrast, surviving spouses who enjoyed a close marriage are more likely to have settled lingering issues and to have talked through what would happen after either of them died. They therefore are more likely to feel secure in knowing what their departed would have wanted for them in widowhood. Finally, spouses who have a close and secure relationship may simply have a better opportunity to say their final goodbyes as one of the partners' heath fails (Bonanno et al., 2002).

Of course, having a secure marriage is no guarantee that life as a widow or widower will be without pain. Even very resilient survivors grieve deeply in the immediate months following the death of their spouses. And indeed, it's possible to be too close to one's spouse, making the loss more difficult; men in particular may be hit hard by the loss of a wife who was their only emotional confidant. But in many cases, the final gift of a close and loving spouse is the security to move on with one's life within a reasonable time after his or her death (Boerner, Wortman, & Bonanno, 2005; Bonanno et al., 2005).

- *Do you think that these same findings would apply in the case of losing a spouse earlier in life? Why or why not?*
- *What other factors besides interpersonal closeness might affect the duration of grief after losing a longtime spouse?*

vulnerable without him or her, are apt to suffer more after the death, as are those who spend a great deal of time reflecting on a loved one's death and their feelings of grief. Bereaved people who lack social support from family, friends, or a connection to some other group, religious or otherwise, are more likely to experience feelings of loneliness and therefore are more at risk. Finally, people who are unable to make sense of the death or find meaning in it (such as a new appreciation of life) show less overall adjustment (Davis & Nolen-Hoeksema, 2001; Nolen-Hoeksema, 2001; Nolen-Hoeksema & Davis, 2002).

The suddenness of a loved one's death also appears to affect the course of grieving. People who unexpectedly lose their loved ones are less able to cope than those who were able to anticipate the death. For instance, in one study, people who experienced a sudden death still had not fully recovered 4 years later. In part, this may be because sudden, unanticipated deaths are often the result of violence, which occurs more frequently among younger individuals (Rando, 1993; Burton, Haley, & Small, 2006).

As we noted earlier in the chapter, children may need special help understanding and mourning the death of someone they love.

For information on helping children cope with death see *Becoming an Informed Consumer of Development* box on the next page.

Because of their limited understanding of death, younger children need special help in coping with grief. Among the strategies that can help are the following.

- Be honest. Don't say that a dead person is "sleeping" or "on a long trip." Use age-appropriate language to tell children the truth. Gently, but clearly, point out the irreversibility and the final and universal nature of death. For example, you might answer questions about whether Grandma will be hungry by pointing out that, "No, after a person dies, their body doesn't work anymore, so it doesn't need food."

- Encourage expressions of grief. Don't tell children not to cry or show their feelings. Instead, tell them that it is understandable to feel terrible and that they may always miss the deceased. Encourage them to draw a picture, write a letter, or express their feelings in some other way. At the same time, assure them that they will always have good memories of the person who has died.

- Reassure children that they are not to blame for the death. Children sometimes attribute a loved one's death to their own behavior—if they had not misbehaved, they mistakenly reason, the person would not have died.

- Understand that children's grief may surface in unanticipated ways. Children may show little or no grief at the time of the death, but later they may become upset for no apparent reason or revert to behaviors like sucking their thumb or wanting to sleep with their parent or parents. Keep in mind that death can be overwhelming for a child, and try to be consistently loving and supportive.

- Children may respond to books for young persons about death. One especially effective book is *When Dinosaurs Die* by Laurie Krasny Brown and Marc Brown.

REVIEW

▶ Bereavement refers to the loss of a loved one; grief refers to the emotional response to that loss.

▶ Funeral rites play a significant role in helping people acknowledge the death of a loved one, recognize their own mortality, and proceed with their lives.

▶ For many people, grief passes through denial, sorrow, and accommodation.

▶ Children need special help coping with grief.

APPLY

▶ Why do so many people in U.S. society feel reluctant to think and talk about death?

▶ What are some of the consequences of bereavement, and what sorts of approaches can be used to help deal with or overcome bereavement?

Epilogue

This final chapter of the book focused on the inevitable end of life. We discussed the complex medical, legal, and even psychological considerations that go into defining when a death has occurred. We looked at causes of death across the life span, and how children and adults at each stage of life react to death. We asked if death education can prepare people for the inevitable. We also examined the process of dying and looked at the possible stages an individual might go through as they come to terms with their own death. We also considered the controversial questions surrounding assisted suicide and euthanasia. Then we looked at the various alternatives available in caring for the terminally ill. Finally, we discussed bereavement and grieving. We covered the mourning and funeral rituals of different cultures, and examined the process of grieving and moving past grief after the death of a loved one. As we considered death and its meaning at various stages in the life span and across cultures, we saw that there are challenges to be faced and satisfaction to be drawn from a graceful departure from life whether in a hospital, hospice, or palliative or home care.

In sum, the story of the entire life span—the journey taken in this book—is one of fresh challenges and opportunities as we continuously undergo and adjust to physical and cognitive changes and learn to relate to new social situations. Development persists virtually to the point of death, and, with preparation, we can appreciate and learn from all parts of the life span.

Before you close the book, return to the chapter Prologue, about Ted Soulis's positive approach toward death. Based on your understanding of death and dying, answer the following questions.

1. To what extent do you think Soulis went through the stages described by Kübler-Ross?

2. How might Soulis have reacted differently to his impending death if he were a young man in his early 20s?

3. How might Soulis's celebratory and jocular attitude toward the ending of his life have affected the bereavement process for his family?

4. How might Soulis's final days have been different if he had elected to receive cancer treatment in the hospital? How might they have been different if he had required hospice care?

Looking Back

What is death, and what does it mean at different stages of the life span?

1. The precise point of death is difficult to define. Functional death refers to the absence of heartbeat and respiration, from which people can be resuscitated, while brain death refers to the absence of electrical activity in the brain, which is irreversible.

2. The death of an infant or a young child is among the most devastating experiences for parents, largely because it seems unnatural and entirely incomprehensible.

3. Adolescents have an unrealistic sense of invulnerability that makes them susceptible to accidental death. Denial often makes it impossible for terminally ill adolescents to accept the seriousness of their condition.

4. For young adults, death is virtually unthinkable. Young adults who are terminally ill can be difficult patients because of a strong sense of the injustice of their fate.

5. In middle adulthood, disease becomes the leading cause of death, and awareness of the reality of death can lead to a substantial fear of death.

6. People in late adulthood begin to prepare for death. Older people generally prefer to know if death is near, and the main issue they have to deal with is whether their lives continue to have value.

7. Responses to death are in part determined by culture. Death may be regarded as a release from the pains of the world, the beginning of a pleasurable afterlife, a punishment or judgment, or simply the end to life.

8. Death education can help people learn about death and consider their own mortality realistically.

In what ways do people face the prospect of their own death?

9. Elisabeth Kübler-Ross suggests that people pass through five basic stages on their way to death: denial, anger, bargaining, depression, and acceptance. The stage nature of her theory has been criticized, and other theorists have suggested alternatives.

10. A living will is a means of asserting control over decisions surrounding one's death through specification of desired medical treatments in life-threatening situations and designation of a health care proxy to enforce one's wishes.

11. Assisted suicide, a form of euthanasia, is illegal in most of the United States.

12. Although most deaths in the United States occur in hospitals, an increasing number of terminal patients are opting for either home care or a hospice.

How do survivors react to and cope with death?

13. Funeral rituals serve a dual function: acknowledging the death of a loved one and recognizing and anticipating the mortality of all who participate.

14. The death of a loved one brings a period of adjustment involving bereavement and grief. Grief may proceed through stages of shock and denial, the beginning of acceptance, and accommodation. One consequence of bereavement is an increase in the risk of death for the survivor.

15. Children need particular help in dealing with death, including honesty, encouragement of expressions of grief, reassurance that the death was not due to the child's behavior, and understanding that the child's grief may be delayed and indirect.

References

AAMR (American Association on Mental Retardation). (2002). *Mental retardation: Definition, classification, and systems of support.* Washington, DC: Author.

AARP (American Association of Retired Persons). (1990). *A profile of older Americans.* Washington, DC: Author.

AARP (American Association of Retired Persons). (1999). *A profile of older Americans.* Washington, DC: Author.

AARP. (2004, May 25). Funeral arrangements and memorial service. http://www.aarp.org/griefandloss/articles/73_a.html.

AARP. (2005, October). I can see clearly now. *AARP Bulletin*, p. 34.

AAUW (American Association of University Women). (1992). *How schools shortchange women: The A.A.U.W. report.* Washington, DC: American Association of University Women Educational Foundation.

Aber, J. L., Bishop-Josef, S. J., Jones, S. M., McLearn, K. T., & Phillips, D. A. (Eds.). (2007). *Child development, a social policy: Knowledge for action.* Washington, DC: American Psychological Association.

Abrahams, N., Jewkes, R., Laubscher, R., & Hoffman, M. (2006). Intimate partner violence: Prevalence and risk factors for men in Cape Town, South Africa. *Violence and Victims, 21*(2), 247–264.

Abrams, D., & Hogg, M. A. (Eds.). (1999). *Social identity and social cognition.* Malden, MA: Blackwell.

Abril, C., & Gault, B. (2006, March). The state of music in the elementary school: The principal's perspective. *Journal of Research in Music Education, 54,* 6–20.

Achenbach, T. A. (1992). Developmental psychopathology. In M. H. Bornstein & M. E. Lamb (Eds.), *Developmental psychology: An advanced textbook.* Hillsdale, NJ: Erlbaum.

Ackerman, B. P., & Izard, C. E. (2004). Emotion cognition in children and adolescents: Introduction to the special issue. *Journal of Experimental Child Psychology, 89,* Special Issue: Emotional cognition in Children, 271–275.

Acocella, J. (2003, August 18 & 25). Little people. *The New Yorker,* pp. 138–143.

ACOG (American College of Obstetricians and Gynecologists). (2002). *Guidelines for perinatal care.* Elk Grove, IN: Author.

Adams Hillard, P. J. (2001). Gynecologic disorders and surgery. In N. L. Stotland & D. E. Stewart (Eds.), *Psychological aspects of women's health care: The interface between psychiatry and obstetrics and gynecology* (2nd ed.). Washington, DC: American Psychiatric Publishing.

Adams, C., & Labouvie-Vief, G. (1986, November 20). *Modes of knowing and language processing: Symposium on developmental dimensions of adult adaptations. Perspectives in mind, self, and emotion.* Paper presented at the meeting of the Gerontological Association of America, Chicago.

Adams, G. R., Montemayor, R., & Gullotta, T. P. (Eds.). (1996). *Psychosocial development during adolescence.* Thousand Oaks, CA: Sage.

Adams, K. B. (2004). Changing investment in activities and interests in elders' lives: theory and measurement. *International Journal of Aging and Human Development, 58,* 87–108.

Adamson, L., & Frick, J. (2003). The still face: A history of a shared experimental paradigm. *Infancy, 4,* 451–473.

Adelmann, P. K., Antonucci, T. C., & Crohan, S. E. (1990). A causal analysis of employment and health in midlife women. *Women and Health, 16,* 5–20.

Ader, R., Felten, D., & Cohen, N. (2001). *Psychoneuroimmunology* (3rd ed.). San Diego: Academic Press.

Adler, P. A., Kless, S. J., & Adler, P. (1992). Socialization to gender roles: Popularity among elementary school boys and girls. *Sociology of Education, 65,* 169–187.

Administration on Aging (2003). *A Profile of Older Americans: 2003.* Washington, DC: U.S. Department of Health and Human Services.

Administration on Aging (2006). *Profiles of older Americans 2005: Research report.* Washington, DC: U.S. Department of Health and Human Resources.

Adolphs, R. (2002). Neural systems for recognizing emotion. *Current Opinion in Neurobiology, 12,* 169–177.

Afifi, T., Brownridge, D., Cox, B., & Sareen, J. (2006, October). Physical punishment, childhood abuse and psychiatric disorders. *Child Abuse & Neglect, 30,* 1093–1103.

Aguiar, A., & Baillargeon, R. (2002). Developments in young infants' reasoning about occluded objects. *Cognitive Psychology, 45,* 267–336.

Aguirre, G. K. (2006). Interpretation of clinical functional neuroimaging studies. In M. D'Esposisto (Ed), *Functional MRI: Applications in clinical neurology and psychiatry.* Boca Raton, FL: Informa Healthcare.

Ah-Kion, J. (2006, June). Body image and self-esteem: A study of gender differences among mid-adolescents. *Gender & Behaviour, 4,* 534–549.

Ahn, W., Gelman, S., & Amsterlaw, J. (2000). Causal status effect in children's categorization. *Cognition, 76,* B35–B43.

Aiken, L. R. (2000). *Dying, death, and bereavement* (4th ed.). Mahwah, NJ: Erlbaum.

Ainsworth, M. D. S. (1973). The development of infant-mother attachment. In B. M. Caldwell & H. N. Ricciuti (Eds.), *Review of child development research* (Vol. 3). Chicago: University of Chicago Press.

Ainsworth, M. D. S. (1993). Attachment as related to mother-infant interaction. *Advances in Infancy Research, 8,* 1–50.

Ainsworth, M. D. S., Blehar, M. C., Waters, E., & Wall, S. (1978). *Patterns of attachment: A psychological study of the strange situation.* Hillsdale, NJ: Erlbaum.

Aitken, R. J. (1995, July 7). The complexities of conception. *Science, 269,* 39–40.

Akmajian, A., Demers, R. A., & Harnish, R. M. (1984). *Linguistics.* Cambridge, MA: MIT Press.

Akshoomoff, N. (2006). Autism spectrum disorders: Introduction. *Child Neuropsychology, 12,* 245–246.

Alan Guttmacher Institute. (1993a). *Report on viral sexual diseases.* Chicago: Author.

Alan Guttmacher Institute. (1993b). *Survey of male sexuality.* Chicago: Author.

Albers, L. L. Migliaccio, L., Bedrick, E. J., Teaf, D., & Peralta, P. (2007). Does epidural analgesia affect the rate of spontaneous obstetric lacerations in normal births? *Journal of Midwifery and Women's Health, 52,* 31–36.

Albers, L. L., & Krulewitch, C. J. (1993). Electronic fetal monitoring in the United States in the 1980s. *Obstetrics & Gynecology, 82,* 8–10.

Alberts, A., Elkind, D., & Ginsberg, S. (2007). The personal fable and risk-taking in early adolescence. *Journal of Youth and Adolescence, 36,* 71–76.

Alderfer, C. (2003). The science and nonscience of psychologists' responses to the Bell Curve. *Professional Psychology: Research & Practice, 34,* 287–293.

Aldwin, C., & Gilmer, D. (2004). *Health, illness, and optimal aging: Biological and psychosocial perspectives.* Thousand Oaks, CA: Sage.

Ales, K. L., Druzin, M. L., & Santini, D. L. (1990). Impact of advanced maternal age on the outcome of pregnancy. *Surgery, Gynecology & Obstetrics, 171,* 209–216.

Alexander, M. G., Brewer, M. B., & Livingston, R. W. (2005). Putting stereotype content in context: Image theory and interethnic stereotypes. *Personality and Social Psychology Bulletin, 31,* 781–794.

Alfonso, V. C., Flanagan, D. P., & Radwan, S. (2005). The impact of the Cattell-Horn-Carroll theory on test development and interpretation of cognitive and academic abilities. In D. P. Flanagan & P. L. Harrison (Eds.), *Contemporary intellectual assessment: Theories, tests, and issues.* New York: Guilford Press.

Alisky, J. M. (2007). The coming problem of HIV-associated Alzheimer's disease. *Medical Hypotheses, 12,* 47–55.

Allan, P. (1990). Looking for work after forty: Job search experiences of older unemployed managers and professionals. *Journal of Employment Counseling, 27,* 113–121.

Allen, J., Chavez, S., DeSimone, S., Howard, D., Johnson, K., LaPierre, L., et al. (2006, June). Americans' attitudes toward euthanasia and physician-assisted suicide, 1936–2002. *Journal of Sociology & Social Welfare, 33,* 5–23.

Allen, J., Seitz, V., & Apfel, N. (2007). The sexually mature teen as a whole person: New directions in prevention and intervention for teen pregnancy and parenthood. *Child development and social policy: Knowledge for action* (pp. 185–199). Washington, DC: American Psychological Association.

Allison, B., & Schultz, J. (2001). Interpersonal identity formation during early adolescence. *Adolescence, 36,* 509–523.

Aloise-Young, P., Slater, M., & Cruickshank, C. (2006, April). Mediators and moderators of magazine advertisement effects on adolescent cigarette smoking. *Journal of Health Communication, 11,* 281–300.

Altholz, S., & Golensky, M. (2004). Counseling, support, and advocacy for clients who stutter. *Health & Social Work, 29,* 197–205.

Alvarez-Leon, E. E., Roman-Vinas, B., & Serra-Majem, L. (2006). Dairy products and health: A review of the epidemiological evidence. *British Journal of Nutrition, 96,* Supplement, S94–S99.

Alzheimer's Association. (2004, May 28). *Standard prescriptions for Alzheimer's.* Accessed at http://www.alz.org/AboutAD/Treatment/Standard.asp.

Amato, P., & Afifi, T. (2006, February). Feeling caught between parents: Adult children's relations with parents and subjective well-being. *Journal of Marriage and Family, 68,* 222–235.

Amato, P., & Booth, A. (1997). *A generation at risk.* Cambridge, MA: Harvard University Press.

Amato, P., & Previti, D. (2003). People's reasons for divorcing: Gender, social class, the life course, and adjustment. *Journal of Family Issues, 24,* 602–626.

Amato, P. R., & Booth, A. (2001). The legacy of parents' marital discord: Consequences for children's marital quality. *Journal of Personality and Social Psychology, 81,* 627–638.

American Academy of Family Physicians. (1997). *Nutritional guidelines for infants.* Leawood, KS: American Academy of Family Physicians.

American Academy of Pediatrics (1997, April 16). Press release.

American Academy of Pediatrics (2005, May 12). *AAP endorses newborn screening report from the American College of Medical Genetics.* Press release.

American Academy of Pediatrics (Committee on Psychosocial Aspects of Child and Family Health). (1998, April). Guidance for effective discipline. *Pediatrics, 101,* 723–728.

American Academy of Pediatrics (Committee on Sports Medicine and Committee on School Health). (1989). Organized athletics for preadolescent children. *Pediatrics, 84(3),* 583–584.

American Academy of Pediatrics, Dietz, W. H., (Ed.), & Stern, L. (Ed.). (1999). *American Academy of Pediatrics guide to your child's nutrition: Making peace at the table and building healthy eating habits for life.* New York: Villard.

American Academy of Pediatrics. (1997, December). Breast-feeding and the use of human milk. *Pediatrics, 100,* 1035–1039.

American Academy of Pediatrics. (2000a). *Circumcision: Information for parents.* Washington, DC: American Academy of Pediatrics.

American Academy of Pediatrics. (2004, June 3). *Sports programs.* http://www.medem.com/medlb/article_detaillb_for_printer.cfm?article_ID=ZZZD2QD5M7C&sub_cat=405.

American College of Sports Medicine. (1997, November 3). *Consensus development conference statement on physical activity and cardiovascular health.* Available: http://www.acsm.org/nhlbi.htm.

American College Testing Program. (2001). *National Dropout Rates.* Iowa City, Iowa: American College Testing Program.

American Psychological Association. (2002). *Ethical principles of psychologists and code of conduct. Updated.* Washington, DC: Author.

Amitai, Y., Haringman, M., Meiraz, H., Baram, N., & Leventhal, A. (2004). Increased awareness, knowledge and utilization of preconceptional folic acid in Israel following a national campaign. *Preventive Medicine: An International Journal Deveoted to Practice and Theory, 39,* 731–737.

Ammerman, R. T., & Patz, R. J. (1996). Determinants of child abuse potential: Contribution of parent and child factors. *Journal of Clinical Child Psychology, 25,* 300–307.

Amsterlaw, J., & Wellman, H. (2006). Theories of mind in transition: A microgenetic study of the development of false belief understanding. *Journal of Cognition and Development, 7,* 139–172.

An, J., & Cooney, T. (2006, September). Psychological well-being in mid to late life: The role of generativity development and parent-child relationships across the lifespan. *International Journal of Behavioral Development, 30,* 410–421.

Anand, K. J. S., & Hickey, P. R. (1992). Halothane-morphine compared with high-dose sufentanil for anesthesia and post-operative analgesia in neonatal cardiac surgery. *New England Journal of Medicine, 326(1),* 1–9.

Anastasi, A., & Urbina, S. (1997). *Psychological testing* (7th ed.). Englewood Cliffs, NJ: Prentice Hall.

Anderson, C. A., Funk, J. B., & Griffiths, M. D. (2004). Contemporary issues in adolescent video game playing: Brief overview and introduction to the special issue. *Journal of Adolescence, 27,* 1–3.

Anderson, C., Berkowitz, L., Donnerstein, E., Huesmann, L., Johnson, J., Linz, D., Malamuth, N., & Wartella, E. (2003). The influence of media violence on youth. *Psychological Science in the Public Interest, 4,* 81–110.

Anderson, P., & Butcher, K. (2006, March). Childhood obesity: Trends and potential causes. *The Future of Children, 16,* 19–45.

Anderson, R. W. (2002). Youth and information technology. In J. T. Mortimer & R. W. Larson (Eds.), *The changing adolescent experience: Societal trends and the transition to adulthood.* New York: Cambridge University Press.

Andreoni, J., & Petrie, R. (2008). Beauty, gender and stereotypes: Evidence from laboratory experiments. *Journal of Economic Psychology, 29,* 73–93.

Andrews, G., Halford, G., & Bunch, K. (2003). Theory of mind and relational complexity. *Child Development, 74,* 1476–1499.

Annunziato, R., & Lowe, M. (2007, April). Taking action to lose weight: Toward an understanding of individual differences. *Eating Behaviors, 8,* 185–194.

Ansberry, C. (1997, November 14). Women of Troy: For ladies on a hill, friendships are a balm in the passages of life. *Wall Street Journal,* pp. A1, A6.

Antonucci, T. C. (1990). Social supports and social relationships. In R. H. Binstock & L. K. George (Eds.), *Handbook of aging and the social sciences.* San Diego: Academic Press.

Antonucci, T. C. (2001). Social relations: An examination of social networks, social support, and sense of control. In J. E. Birren & K. W. Schaie (Eds.), *Handbook of the psychology of aging* (5th ed.). San Diego: Academic Press.

Antonucci, T. C., & Akiyama, H. (1991). Social relationships and aging well. *Generations, 15,* 39–44.

APA Reproductive Choice Working Group. (2000). *Reproductive choice and abortion: A resource packet.* Washington, DC: American Psychological Association.

Applebome, P. (1997, March 1). Dispute over Ebonics reflects a volatile mix that roils urban education. *New York Times,* p. 8.

Aquilino, W. (2006). Impact of family structure on parental attitudes toward the economic support of adult children over the transition to adulthood. *Journal of Family Issues, 26,* 143–167.

Arai, M. (2006, January). Elder abuse in Japan. *Educational Gerontology, 32,* 13–23.

Archer, S. L., & Waterman, A. S. (1994). Adolescent identity development: Contextual perspectives. In C. B. Fisher & R. M. Lerner (Eds.), *Applied developmental psychology.* New York: McGraw-Hill.

Aries, P. (1962). *Centuries of childhood.* New York: Knopf.

Arija, V., Esparo, G., Fernandez-Ballart, J., Murphy, M. M., Biarnes, E., & Canals, J. (2006). Nutritional status and performance in test of verbal and non-verbal intelligence in 6 year old children. *Intelligence, 34,* 141–149.

Arkoff, A., Meredith, G., & Dubanoski, J. (2004). Gains in well-being achieved through retrospective proactive life review by independent older women. *Journal of Humanistic Psychology, 44,* 204–214.

Arnett, J. (1995). Adolescents' uses of media for self-socialization. *Journal of Youth and Adolescence, 24,* 519–534.

Arnon, S., Shamai, S., & Ilatov, Z. (2008). Socialization agents and activities of young adolescents. *Adolescence, 43,* 373–397.

Aronson, E. (2000). *Nobody left to hate: Teaching compassion after Columbine.* New York: Freeman.

Aronson, E. (2004). *The social animal* (9th ed.). New York: Worth Publishers.

Aronson, J., & Steele, C. M. (2005). Stereotypes and the fragility of academic competence, motivation, and self-concept. In A. J. Elliot & C. S. Dweck, *Handbook of competence and motivation.* New York: Guilford Publications.

Arredondo, E., Elder, J., Ayala, G., Campbell, N., Baquero, B., & Duerksen, S. (2006, December). Is parenting style related to children's healthy eating and physical activity in Latino families? *Health Education Research, 21,* 862–871.

Arseneault, L., Moffitt, T. E., & Caspi, A. (2002). Strong genetic effects on cross-situational antisocial behavior among 5-year-old children according to mothers, teachers, examiner-observers, and twins' self-reports. *Journal of Child Psychology and Psychiatry and Allied Disciplines, 44,* 832–848.

Asch, D. A. (1996, May 23). The role of critical care nurses in euthanasia and assisted suicide. *New England Journal of Medicine, 334,* 1374–1379.

Asendorpf, J. (2002). Self-awareness, other-awareness, and secondary representation. In A. Meltzoffa & W. Prinz (Eds.), *The imitative mind: Development, evolution, and brain bases.* New York: Cambridge University Press.

Asendorpf, J. B., Warkentin, V., & Baudonniere, P. (1996). Self-awareness and other-awareness II: Mirror self-recognition, social contingency awareness, and synchronic imitation. *Developmental Psychology, 32,* 313–321.

Askham, J. (1994). Marriage relationships of older people. *Reviews in Clinical Gerontology, 4,* 261–268.

Aslin, R. N. (1987). Visual and auditory development in infancy. In J. D. Osofsky (Ed.), *Handbook of infant development* (2nd ed.). New York: Wiley.

Aspinwall, O.G., & Taylor, S.E. (1993). Effects of social comparison direction, threat, and self-esteem on affect, evaluation, and expected success. *Journal of Personality and Social Psychology, 64,* 708–722.

Atchley, R. (2003). Why most people cope well with retirement. In J. Ronch & J. Gold-field (Eds.), *Mental wellness in aging: Strengths-based approaches*. Baltimore, MD: Health Professions Press.

Atchley, R. C. (2000). *Social forces and aging* (9th ed.). Belmont, CA: Wadsworth Thomson Learning.

Atkinson, R. C., & Shiffrin, R. M. (1968). Human memory: A proposed system and its control processes. In K. W. Spence & J. T. Spence (Eds.), *The psychology of learning and motivation: Advances in research and theory* (Vol. 2, pp. 80–195). New York: Academic Press.

Attie, I., & Brooks-Gunn, J. (1989). The development of eating prblems in adolescent girls: A longitudinal study. *Developmental Psychology, 25*, 70–79.

Auestad, N., Scott, D. T., Janowsky, J. S., Jacobsen, C., Carroll, R. E., Montalto, M. B., Halter, R., Qiu, W., Jacobs, J. R., Connor, W. E. Connor, S. L., Taylor, J. A., Neuringer, M., Fitzgerald, K. M., & Hall, R. T. (2003). Visual cognitive and language assessments at 39 months: A follow-up study of children fed formulas containing long-chain polyunsaturated fatty acids to 1 year of age. *Pediatarics, 112*, e177–e183.

Aviezer, O., Sagi, A., & Resnick, G. (2002). School competence in young adolescence: Links to early attachment relationships beyond concurrent self-perceived competence and representations of relationships. *International Journal of Behavioral Development, 26*, 397–409.

Avlund, K., Lund, R., & Holstein, B. (2004). Social relations as determinant of onset of disability in aging. *Archives of Gerontology & Geriatrics, 38*, 85–99.

Axia, G., Bonichini, S., & Benini, F. (1995). Pain in infancy: Individual differences. *Perceptual and Motor Skills, 81*, 142.

Aydt, H., & Corsaro, W. (2003). Differences in children's construction of gender across culture: An interpretive approach. *American Behavioral Scientist, 46*, 1306–1325.

Aylward, G. P., & Verhulst, S. J. (2000). Predictive utility of the Bayley Infant Neurodevelopmental Screener (BINS) risk status classifications: Clinical interpretation and application. *Developmental Medicine & Child Neurology, 42*, 25–31.

Ayoub, N. C. (2005, February 25). A pleasing birth: Midwives and maternity care in the Netherlands. *Chronicle of Higher Education*, p. 9.

Bacchus, L., Mezey, G., & Bewley, S. (2006). A Qualitative exploration of the nature of domestic violence in pregnancy. *Violence Against Women, 12*, 588–604.

Baddeley, A. (1993). Working memory and conscious awareness. In A. F. Collins, S. E. Gathercole, M. A. Conway, & P. E. Morris (Eds.), *Theories of memory*. Hillsdale, NJ: Lawrence Erlbaum Associates.

Baddeley, A. (1996). Exploring the central executive. *Quarterly Journal of Experimental Psychology. A., Human Experimental Psychology, 49A*, 5–28.

Baddeley, A., & Wilson, B. (1985). Phonological coding and short-term memory in patients without speech. *Journal of Memory and Language, 24*, 490–502.

Baer, J. S., Sampson, P. D., & Barr, H. M. (2003). A 21-year longitudinal analysis of the effects of prenatal alcohol exposure on young adult drinking. *Archives of General Psychiatry, 60*, 377–385.

Bahrick, H. P., Hall, L. K., & Berger, S. A. (1996). Accuracy and distortion in memory for high school grades. *Psychological Science, 7*, 265–271.

Bailey, J. M., Kirk, K. M., Zhu, G., Dunne, M. P., & Martin, N. G. (2000). Do individual differences in sociosexuality represent genetic or environmentally contingent strategies? Evidence from the Australian twin registry. *Journal of Personality and Social Psychology, 78*, 537–545.

Baillargeon, R. (2004). Infants' physical world. *Current Directions in Psychological Science, 13*, 89–94.

Baillargeon, R. (2008). Innate ideas revisited: For a principle of persistence in infants' physical reasoning. *Perspectives on Psychological Science, 3*, 2–13.

Baird, A., John, R., & Hayslip, B., Jr. (2000). Custodial grandparenting among African Americans: A focus group perspective. In B. Hayslip, Jr. & R. Goldberg-Glen (Eds.) *Grandparents raising grandchildren: Theoretical, empirical, and clinical perspectives.* New York: Springer.

Baker, M. (2007, December). Elder mistreatment: Risk, vulnerability, and early mortality. *Journal of the American Psychiatric Nurses Association, 12*, 313–321.

Baker, T., Brandon, T., & Chassin, L. (2004). Motivational influences on cigarette smoking. *Annual Review of Psychology, 55*, 463–491.

Baker-Sennett, J., Matusov, E., & Rogoff, B. (1992). *Sociocultural processes of creative planning in children's playcrafting.* Hillsdale, NJ: Lawrence Erlbaum Associates.

Bakker, A., & Heuven, E. (2006, November). Emotional dissonance, burnout, and in-role performance among nurses and police officers. *International Journal of Stress Management, 13*, 423–440.

Ball, K., & Rebok, G. W. (1994). Evaluating the driving ability of older adults. Special Issue: Research translation in gerontology: A behavioral and social perspective. *Journal of Applied Gerontology, 13*, 20–38.

Ball, M., & Orford, J. (2002). Meaningful patterns of activity amongst the long-term inner city unemployed: A qualitative study. *Journal of Community & Applied Social Psychology, 12*, 377–396.

Baltes, M. M. (1996). *The many faces of dependency in old age.* New York: Cambridge University Press.

Baltes, M., & Carstensen, L. (2003). The process of successful aging: Selection, optimization and compensation. In U. Staudinger & U. Lindenberger (Eds.), *Understanding human development: Dialogues with lifespan psychology.* Dordrecht, Netherlands: Kluwer Academic.

Baltes, P. B. (2003). On the incomplete architecture of human ontogeny: Selection, optimization and compensation as foundation of developmental theory. In U. M. Staudinger & U. Lindenberger (Eds.), *Understanding human development: Dialogues with lifespan psychology.* Dordrecht, Netherlands: Kluwer Academic.

Baltes, P., & Freund, A. (2003a). Human strengths as the orchestration of wisdom and selective optimization with compensation. In L. Aspinwall & U. Staudinger (Eds.), *A psychology of human strengths: Fundamental questions and future directions for a positive psychology.* Washington, DC: American Psychological Association.

Baltes, P., & Freund, A. (2003b). The intermarriage of wisdom and selective optimization with compensation: Two meta-heuristics guiding the conduct of life. In C. Keyes & J. Haidt (Eds.), *Flourishing: Positive psychology and the life well-lived.* Washington, DC: American Psychological Association.

Bamshad, M. J., & Olson, S. E. (2003, December). Does race exist? *Scientific American*, 78–85.

Bamshad, M. J., et al. (2003). Human population genetic structure and inference of group membership. *American Journal of Human Genetics, 72*, 578–589.

Bandura, A. (1977). *Social learning theory.* Englewood Cliffs, NJ: Prentice-Hall.

Bandura, A. (1991). Social cognitive theory of moral thought and action. In W. M. Kurtines & J. L. Gewirtz (Eds.), *Handbook of moral behavior and development.* Hillsdale, NJ: Erlbaum.

Bandura, A. (1994). Social cognitive theory of mass communication. In J. Bryant & D. Zillmann (Eds.), *Media effects: Advances in theory and research. LEA's communication series.* Hillsdale, NJ: Erlbaum.

Bandura, A. (2002). Social cognitive theory in cultural context. *Applied Psychology: An International Review, Special Issue, 51*, 269–290.

Bandura, A. (2004). Model of causality in social learning theory. *Cognition and psychotherapy* (2nd ed.). New York: Springer Publishing Co.

Bandura, A. (2007). *Albert Bandura. A history of psychology in autobiography, Vol. IX.* Washington, DC: American Psychological Association.

Bandura, A., Grusec, J. E., & Menlove, F. L. (1967). Vicarious extinction of avoidance behavior. *Journal of Personality and Social Psychology, 5*, 16–23.

Bandura, A., Pastorelli, C., Barbaranelli, C., & Caprara, G. V. (1999). Self-efficacy pathways to childhood depression. *Journal of Personality and Social Psychology, 76*, 258–269.

Bandura, A., Ross, D., & Ross, S. (1963). Vicarious extinction of avoidance behavior. *Journal of Personality and Social Psychology, 67*, 601–607.

Banich, M. T., & Nicholas, C. D. (1998). Integration of processing between the hemispheres in word recognition. In M. Beeman & C. Chiarello (Eds.), *Right hemisphere language comprehension: Perspectives from cognitive neuroscience* (pp. 349–371). Mahwah, NJ: Erlbaum.

Barberá, E. (2003). Gender schemas: Configuration and activation processes. *Canadian Journal of Behavioural Science, 35*, 176–180.

Barer, B. M. (1994). Men and women aging differently. *International Journal of Aging and Human Development, 38*, 29–40.

Barinaga, M. (2000, June 23). A critical issue for the brain. *Science, 288*, 2116–2119.

Barker, V., Giles, H., & Noels, K. (2001). The English-only movement: A communication analysis of changing perceptions of language vitality. *Journal of Communication, 51*, 3–37.

Barkley, R. A. (1997a). *ADHD and the nature of self-control.* New York: Guilford Press.

Barkley, R. A. (1997b). Behavioral inhibition, sustained attention, and executive functions: Constructing a unifying theory of ADHD. *Psychological Bulletin, 121*, 65–94.

Barnett, R. C., & Hyde, J. S. (2001). Women, men, work, and family. *American Psychologist, 56*, 781–796.

Barnett, R. C., & Shen, Y-C. (1997). Gender, high- and low-schedule-control housework tasks, and psychological distress: A study of dual-earner couples. *Journal of Family Issues, 18*, 403–428.

Baron, J. B., & Sternberg, R. J. (1986). *Teaching thinking skills.* New York: Freeman.

Baron, R. A. (1997). Positive effects of conflict: Insights from social cognition. In C. K. W. De Dreu & E. Van de Vliert (Eds.) *Using conflict in organizations.* Thousand Oaks, CA: Sage Publications.

Baron-Cohen, S. (2003). *The essential difference: Men, women and the extreme male brain.* London: Allen Lane/Penguin.

Baron-Cohen, S. (2005). Testing the extreme male brain (EMB) theory of autism: Let the data speak for themselves. *Cognitive Neuropsychiatry, 10,* 77–81.

Barr, P., & Cacciatore, J. (2007). Problematic emotions and maternal grief. *Omega: Journal of Death and Dying, 56,* 331–348.

Barr, R., Marrott, H., & Rovee-Collier, C. (2003). The role of sensory preconditioning in memory retrieval by preverbal infants. *Learning & Behavior, 31,* 111–123.

Barr, R., Muentener, P., Garcia, A., Fujimoto, M., & Chávez, V. (2007). The effect of repetition on imitation from television during infancy. *Developmental Psychobiology, 49,* 196–207.

Barrett, D. E., & Frank, D. A. (1987). *The effects of undernutrition on children's behavior.* New York: Gordon & Breach.

Barry, C., Padilla-Walker, L., Madsen, S., & Nelson, L. (2008). The impact of maternal relationship quality on emerging adults' prosocial tendencies: Indirect effects via regulation of prosocial values. *Journal of Youth and Adolescence, 37,* 581–591.

Barton, L. J. (1997, July). A shoulder to lean on: Assisted living in the U.S. *American Demographics,* 45–51.

Basow, S. (2006). Gender role and gender identity development. *Handbook of girls' and women's psychological health: Gender and well-being across the lifespan* (pp. 242–251). New York: Oxford University Press.

Bates, J. E., Marvinney, D., Kelly, T., Dodge, K. A., Bennett, D. S., & Pettit, G. S. (1994). Child-care history and kindergarten adjustment. *Developmental Psychology, 30,* 690–700.

Bauer, P. J. (1996). What do infants recall of their lives? Memory for specific events by 1- to 2-year-olds. *American Psychologist, 51,* 29–41.

Bauer, P. J. (2004). Getting explicit memory off the ground: Steps toward construction of a neuro-developmental account of changes in the first two years of life. *Developmental Review, Special Issue: Memory development in the new millennium, 24,* 347–373.

Bauer, P. J. (2007). Recall in infancy: A neurodevelopmental account. *Current Directions in Psychological Science, 16,* 142–146.

Bauer, P. J., Wenner, J. A., Dropik, P. L., & Wewerka, S. S. (2000). Parameters of remembering and forgetting in the transition from infancy to early childhood. With commentary by Mark L. Howe. *Monographs of the Society for Research in Child Development, 65,* 4.

Baum, A. (1994). Behavioral, biological, and environmental interactions in disease processes. In S. Blumenthal, K. Matthews, & S. Weiss (Eds.), *New research frontiers in behavioral medicine: Proceedings of the National Conference.* Washington, DC: NIH Publications.

Bauman, K. J. (2001). *Home schooling in the United States: Trends and characteristics. Working paper No. 53.* Paper presented at the Annual Meeting of the Population Association of American, Washington, DC, March 29–31.

Baumbusch, J. (2004). Unclaimed treasures: Older women's reflections on lifelong singlehood. *Journal of Women & Aging, 16,* 105–121.

Baumeister, R. F. (Ed.). (1993). *Self-esteem: The puzzle of low self-regard.* New York: Plenum.

Baumeister, R. F., Bushman, B. J., & Campbell, W. K. (2000). Self-esteem, narcissism, and aggressions: Does violence result from low self-esteem or from threatened egotism? *Current Directions in Psychological Science, 9,* 26–29.

Baumeister, R. F., Campbell, J. D., Kreueger, J. I., & Vohs, K. D. (2003). Does high self-esteem cause better performance, interpersonal success, happiness, or healthier lifestyles? *Psychological Science in the Public Interest, 4,* 1–44.

Baumeister, R. F., Campbell, J. D., Kreueger, J. I., & Vohs, K. D. (2005, January). Exploding the self-esteem myth. *Scientific American,* pp. 84–91.

Baumrind, D. (1971). Current patterns of parental authority. *Developmental Psychology Monographs, 4* (1, pt. 2).

Baumrind, D. (1980). New directions in socialization research. *Psychological Bulletin, 35,* 639–652.

Baydar, N., & Brooks-Gunn, J. (1998). Profiles of grandmothers who help care for their grandchildren in the United States. *Family Relations, 47,* 385–393.

Bayley, N. (1969). *Manual for the Bayley Scales of infant development.* New York: Psychological Corporation.

Bayley, N., & Oden, M. (1955). The maintenance of intellectual ability in gifted adults. *Journal of Gerontology, 10,* 91–107.

Bayliss, D. M., Jarrold, C., Baddeley, A. D., & Gunn, D. M. (2005a). The relationship between short-term memory and working memory: Complex span made simple? *Memory, 13,* 414–421.

Bayliss, D. M., Jarrold, C., Baddeley, A. D., Gunn, D. M., & Leigh, E. (2005b). Mapping the developmental constraints on working memory span performance. *Developmental Psychology, 41,* 579–597.

Beach, B. A. (2003). Rural children's play in the natural environment. In D. E. Lytle (Ed.), *Play and educational theory and practice.* Westport, CT: Praeger Publishers/Greenwood Publishing Group.

Beal, C. R. (1994). *Boys and girls: The development of gender roles.* New York: McGraw-Hill.

Beals, K., Impett, E., & Peplau, L. (2002). Lesbians in love: Why some relationships endure and others end. *Journal of Lesbian Studies, 6,* 53–63.

Bearce, K., & Rovee-Collier, C. (2006). Repeated priming increases memory accessibility in infants. *Journal of Experimental Child Psychology, 93,* 357–376.

Bearman, P., & Bruckner, H. (2004). *Study on teenage virginity pledge.* Paper presented at meeting of the National STD Prevention Conference, Phildadelphia, PA.

Beauchaine, T. P. Taxometrics and developmental psychopathology, *Development and Psychopathology: Special Issue, 15,* 501–527.

Beaudoin, P., & Lachance, M. (2006). Determinants of adolescents' brand sensitivity to clothing. *Family & Consumer Sciences Research Journal, 34,* 312–331.

Becahy, R. (1992, August 3). AIDS epidemic. *Newsweek,* 49.

Becker, B., & Luthar, S. (2007, March). Peer-perceived admiration and social preference: contextual correlates of positive peer regard among suburban and urban adolescents. *Journal of Research on Adolescence, 17,* 117–144.

Becker, G., Beyene, Y., & Newsom, E. (2003). Creating continuity through mutual assistance: Intergenerational reciprocity in four ethnic groups. *Journals of Gerontology: Series B: Psychological Sciences & Social Sciences, 58B,* S151–S159.

Beckman, M. (2004, July 30). Neuroscience: Crime, culpability, and the adolescent brain. *Science, 305,* 596–599.

Becvar, D. S. (2000). Euthanasia decisions. In F. W. Kaslow, et al. (Eds.), *Handbook of couple and family forensics: A sourcebook for mental health and legal professionals.* New York: Wiley.

Beeger, S., Rieffe, C., & Terwogt, M. M. (2003). Theory of mind-based action in children from the autism spectrum. *Journal of Autism and Developmental Disorders, 33,* 479–487.

Begley, S. (1991, August 26). Choosing death. *Newsweek,* 43–46.

Beilin, H. (1996). Mind and meaning: Piaget and Vygotsky on causal explanation. *Human Development, 39,* 277–286.

Belcher, J. R. (2003). Stepparenting: Creating and recreating families in America today. *Journal of Nervous & Mental Disease, 191,* 837–838.

Belkin, L. (1999, July 25). Getting the girl. *New York Times Magazine,* 26–35.

Belkin, L. (2004, September 12). The lessons of Classroom 506: What happens when a boy with cerebral palsy goes to kindergarten like all the other kids. *New York Times Magazine,* 41–49.

Bellezza, F. S., Six, L. S., & Phillips, D. S. (1992). A mnemonic for remembering long strings of digits. *Bulletin of the Psychonomic Society, 30,* 271–274.

Belluck, P. (2000, October 18). New advice for parents: Saying 'That's great!' may not be. *New York Times,* p. A14.

Belluck, P. (2005, March 13). With mayhem at home, they call a parent coach. *New York Times,* pp. A1, A33.

Belsky, J. (2006). Early child care and early child development: Major findings from the NICHD Study of Early Child Care. *European Journal of Developmental Psychology, 3,* 95–110.

Belsky, J., Rovine, M., & Taylor, D. G. (1984). The Pennsylvania infant and family development project, III: The origins of individual differences in infant–mother attachment: Maternal and infant contributions. *Child Development, 55,* 718–728.

Belsky, J., Vandell, D. L., Burchinal, M., Clarke-Stewart, A. K., McCartney, K., & Owen, M. T. (2007). Are There Long-Term Effects of Early Child Care? *Child Development, 78,* 188–193.

Ben-Ari, A., & Livni, T. (2006). Motherhood is not a given thing: Experiences and constructed meanings of biological and nonbiological lesbian mothers. *Sex Roles, 54,* 521–531.

Benbow, C. P., Lubinski, D., & Hyde, J. S. (1997). Mathematics: Is biology the cause of gender differences in performance? In M. R. Walsh (Ed.), *Women men & gender: Ongoing debates* (pp. 271–287). New Haven, CT: Yale University Press.

Benedict, H. (1979). Early lexical development: Comprehension and production. *Journal of Child Language, 6,* 183–200.

Benenson, J. F., & Apostoleris, N. H. (1993, March). *Gender differences in group interaction in early childhood.* Paper presented at the biennial meeting of the Society for Research in Child Development, New Orleans.

Bengtson, V. L., Acock, A. C., Allen, K. R., & Dilworth-Anderson, P. (Eds.). (2004). *Sourcebook of family theory and research.* Thousand Oaks, CA: Sage.

Benjamin, J., Ebstein, R. P., & Belmaker, R. H. (2002). Personality genetics, 2002. *Israel Journal of Psychiatry and Related Sciences, Special Issue, 39,* 271–279.

Benjuya, N., Melzer, I., & Kaplanski, J. (2004). Aging-induced shifts from a reliance on sensory input to muscle cocontraction during balanced standing. *Journal of Gerontology, Series A: Biological Sciences and Medical Sciences, 59,* 166–171.

Benson, E. (2003, March). 'Goo, gaa, grr?' *Monitor on Psychology,* pp. 50–51.

Benson, H. (1993). The relaxation response. In D. Goleman & J. Guerin (Eds.), *Mind-body medicine: How to use your mind for better health.* Yonkers, NY: Consumer Reports Publications.

Benson, J. B., & Haith, M. M. (1995). Future-oriented processes: A foundation for planning behavior in infants and toddlers. *Infancia y Aprendizaje. No 69–70,* 127–140.

Berenbaum, S. A., & Bailey, J. M. (2003). Effects on gender identity of prenatal androgens and genital appearance: Evidence from girls with congenital adrenal hyperplasia. *Journal of Clinical Endocrinology and metabolism, 88,* 1102–1106.

Berenbaum, S. A., & Hines, M. (1992). Early androgens are related to sex-typed toy preferences. *Psychological Science, 3,* 202–206.

Berenson, P. (2005). *Understand and treat alcoholism.* New York: Basic Books.

Bergen, H., Martin, G., & Richardson, A. (2003). Sexual abuse and suicidal behavior: A model constructed from a large community sample of adolescents. *Journal of the American Academy of Child & Adolescent Psychiatry, 42,* 1301–1309.

Bergstrom, M. J., & Holmes, M. E. (2000). Lay theories of successful aging after the death of a spouse: A network text analysis of bereavement advice. *Health Communication, 12,* 377–406.

Berk, L. E., & Landau, S. (1993). Private speech of learning disabled and normally achieving children in classroom academic and laboratory contexts. *Child Development, 64,* 556–571.

Berkman, B. (Ed.) (2006). *Handbook of social work in health and aging.* New York: Oxford University Press.

Berko, J. (1958). The child's learning of English morphology. *Word, 14,* 150–177.

Berkowitz, L. (1993). *Aggression: Its causes, consequences, and control.* New York: McGraw-Hill.

Bernal, M. E. (1994, August). *Ethnic identity of Mexican-American children.* Address at the annual meeting of the American Psychological Association, Los Angeles, CA.

Bernal, M. E., & Knight, G. P. (Eds.). (2001). *Ethnic identity: Formation and transmission among Hispanics and other minorities.* Albany: State University of New York Press.

Bernard, J. (1982). *The future of marriage.* New Haven, CT: Yale University Press.

Berndt, T. J. (1999). Friends' influence on students' adjustment to school. *Educational Psychologist, 34,* 15–28.

Berndt, T. J. (2002). Friendship quality and social development. *Current Directions in Psychological Science, 11,* 7–10.

Bernstein, N. (2004, March 7). Behind fall in pregnancy, a new teenage culture of restraint. *New York Times,* 1, 20.

Berscheid, E. (1985). Interpersonal attraction. In G. Lindzey & E. Aronson (Eds.), *Handbook of social psychology* (3rd ed.). New York: Random House.

Berscheid, E. (2006). Searching for the meaning of 'love'. *The new psychology of love* (pp. 171–183). New Haven, CT: Yale University Press.

Berscheid, E., & Walster, E. (1974). Physical attractiveness. In G. Lindzey & E. Aronson (Eds.), *Handbook of social psychology* (3rd ed.). New York: Random House.

Bersoff, D. M. N., & Ogden, D. W. (1991). APA Amicus Curiae briefs: Furthering lesbian and gay male civil rights. *American Psychologist, 46,* 950–956.

Bertin, E., & Striano, T. (2006, April). The still-face response in newborn, 1.5-, and 3-month-old infants. *Infant Behavior & Development, 29,* 294–297.

Besharov, D. J., & West, A. (2002). African American marriage patterns. In A. Thernstrom & S. Thernstrom (Eds.), *Beyond the color line: New perspectives on race and ethnicity in America.* Stanford, CA: Hoover Institution Press.

Best, C. T., Tyler, M. D., Gooding T. N., Orlando, C. B., & Quann, C. A. (2009). Development of phonological constancy: Toddlers' perception of native- and Jamaican-accented words. *Psychological Science, 20,* 539–542.

Bettencourt, B. A., & Miller, N. (1996). Gender differences in aggression as a function of provocation: A meta-analysis. *Psychological Bulletin, 119,* 422–447.

Bhushan, B., & Khan, S. (2006, September). Laterality and accident proneness: A study of locomotive drivers. *Laterality: Asymmetries of Body, Brain and Cognition, 11*(5), 395–404.

Bialystok, E., McBride-Change, C., & Luk, G. (2005). Bilingualism, language proficiency, and learning to read in two writing systems. *Journal of Educational Psychology, 97,* 580–590.

Bianchi, S. M., & Casper, L. M. (2000). American Families. *Population Bulletin, 55,* No. 4.

Biedenharn, B. J., & Normoyle, J. B. (1991). Elderly community residents' reactions to the nursing home: An analysis of nursing home-related beliefs. *Gerontologist, 31,* 107–115.

Bigelow, A., & Rochat, P. (2006). Two-month-old infants' sensitivity to social contingency in mother-infant and stranger-infant interaction. *Infancy, 9,* 313–325.

Bijeljac-Babic, R., Bertoncini, J., & Mehler, J. (1993). How do 4-day-old infants categorize multisyllabic utterances? *Developmental Psychology, 29,* 711–721.

Bionna, R. (2006). Coping with stress in a changing world. New York: McGraw-Hill.

Birch, E. E., Garfield, S., Hoffman, D. R., Uauy, R., & Birch, D. G. (2000). A randomized controlled trail of early dietary supply of long-chain polyunsaturated fatty acids and mental development in term infants. *Developmental Medicine and Child Neurology, 42,* 174–181.

Bird, G., & Melville, K. (1994). *Families and intimate relationships.* New York: McGraw-Hill.

Birkhäuser. J. N. & Baker, D. (2008). The lip key. *The Observer, 21,* 14.

Biro, F., Striegel-Moore, R., Franko, D., Padgett, J., & Bean, J. (2006, October). Self-esteem in adolescent females. *Journal of Adolescent Health, 39,* 501–507.

Birsner, P. (1991). *Mid-career job hunting.* New York: Simon & Schuster.

Bishop, A. (2008). Stress and depression among older residents in religious monasteries: Do friends and God matter? *International Journal of Aging & Human Development, 67,* 1–23.

Bishop, D. V. M., & Leonard, L. B. (Eds.). (2001). *Speech and language impairments in children: Causes, characteristics, intervention and outcome.* Philadelphia, PA: Psychology Press.

Bishop, J. (2006, April). Euthanasia, efficiency, and the historical distinction between killing a patient and allowing a patient to die. *Journal of Medical Ethics, 32,* 220–224.

Bjorklund, D. F., & Ellis, B. (2005). Evolutionary psychology and child development: An emerging synthesis. In B. J. Ellis (Ed.), *Origins of the social mind: Evolutionary psychology and child development.* New York: Guilford Press.

Bjorklund, D. F., Schneider, W., Cassel, W. S., & Ashley, E. (1994). Training and extension of a memory strategy: Evidence of utilization deficiencies in the acquisition of an organizational strategy in high- and low-IQ children. *Child Development, 65,* 951–965.

Bjorklund, D. F. (1997). The role of immaturity in human development. *Psychological Bulletin, 122,* 153–169.

Black, K. (2002). Associations between adolescent-mother and adolescent-best friend interactions. *Adolescence, 37,* 235–253.

Black, M. M., & Matula, K. (1999). *Essentials of Bayley Scales of infant development II assessment.* New York: Wiley.

Blaga, O., Shaddy, D., Anderson, C., Kannass, K., Little, T., & Colombo, J. (2009). Structure and continuity of intellectual development in early childhood. *Intelligence, 37,* 106–113.

Blaine, B. E., Rodman, J., & Newman, J. M. (2007). Weight loss treatment and psychological well-being: A review and meta-analysis. *Journal of Health Psychology, 12,* 66–82.

Blair, S. N., Kohl, H. W., Paffenberger, R. S., Clark, D. G., Cooper, K. H., & Gibbons, L. W. (1989). Physical fitness and all-cause mortality: A prospective study of healthy men and women. *Journal of the American Medical Association, 262,* 2395–2401.

Blake, J., & de Boysson-Bardies, B. (1992). Patterns in babbling: A cross-linguistic study. *Journal of Child Language, 19,* 51–74.

Blakemore, J. (2003). Children's beliefs about violating gender norms: Boys shouldn't look like girls, and girls shouldn't act like boys. *Sex Roles, 48,* 411–419.

Blakeslee, S. (1995, August 29). In brain's early growth, timetable may be crucial. *New York Times,* pp. C1, C3.

Blank, M., & White, S. J. (1999). Activating the zone of proximal development in school: Obstacles and solutions. In P. Llyod & C. Fernyhough (Eds.), *Lev Vygotsky: Critical assessments: The zone of proximal development, Vol. III.* New York: Routledge.

Blanton, H., & Burkley, M. (2008). Deviance regulation theory: Applications to adolescent social influence. *Understanding peer influence in children and adolescents.* New York: Guilford Press.

Blasi, H., & Bjorklund, D. F. (2003). Evolutionary developmental psychology: A new tool for better understanding human ontogeny. *Human Development, 46,* 259–281.

Blazer, D. (1991). Suicide risk factors in the elderly: An epidemiological study. *Journal of Geriatric Psychiatry, 24,* 175–190.

Blennow, K., & Vanmechelen, E. (2003). CSF markers for pathogenic processes in Alzheimer's disease: Diagnostic implications and use in clinical neurochemistry. *Brain Research Bulletin, 61,* 235–242.

Bloom, C., & Lamkin, D. (2006). The Olympian struggle to remember the cranial nerves: Mnemonics and student success. *Teaching of Psychology, 33,* 128–129.

Bloom, L. (1993). *The transition from infancy to language: Acquiring the power of expression.* New York: Cambridge University Press.

Blount, B. G. (1982). Culture and the language of socialization: Parental speech. In D. A. Wagner & H. W. Stevenson (Eds.), *Cultural perspectives on child development.* San Francisco: Freeman.

Blum, D. (2002). *Love at Goon Park: Harry Harlow and the science of affection.* New York: Perseus Publishing.

Blundon, J., & Schaefer, C. (2006). The role of parent-child play in children's development. *Psychology and Education: An Interdisciplinary Journal, 43,* 1–10.

Blustein, D. L, & Palladino, D. E. (1991). Self and identity in late adolescence: A theoretical and empirical integration. *Journal of Adolescent Research, 6,* 437–453.

Boatella-Costa, E., Costas-Moragas, C., Botet-Mussons, F., Fornieles-Deu, A., & De Cáceres-Zurita, M. (2007). Behavioral gender differences in the neonatal period according to the Brazelton scale. *Early Human Development, 83,* 91–97.

Bober, S., Humphry, R., & Carswell, H. (2001). Toddlers' persistence in the emerging occupations of functional play and self-feeding. *American Journal of Occupational Therapy, 55,* 369–376.

Bochner, S. (1996). The learning strategies of bilingual versus monolingual students. *British Journal of Educational Psychology, 66,* 83–93.

Boehm, K. E., & Campbell, N. B. (1995). Suicide: A review of calls to an adolescent peer listening phone service. *Child Psychiatry and Human Development, 26,* 61–66.

Boerner, K., Wortman, C. B., & Bonanno, G. A. (2005). Resilient or at risk? A 4-year study of older adults who initially showed high or low distress following conjugal loss. *Journal of Gerontology, B, Psychological Sciences and Social Sciences, 60,* P67–P73.

Bohlmeijer, E., Smit, F., & Cuijpers, P. (2003). Effects of reminiscence and life review on late-life depression: A meta-analysis. *International Journal of Geriatric Psychiatry, 18,* 1088–1094.

Boivin, M., Perusse, D., Dionne, G., Saysset, V., Zoccolilo, M., Tarabulsy, G. M., Tremblay, N., & Tremblay, R. E. (2005). The genetic-environmental etiology of parents' perceptions and self-assessed behaviours toward their 5-month-old infants in a large twin and singleton sample. *Journal of Child Psychology and Psychiatry, 46,* 612–630.

Bolger, N., Foster, M., Vinokur, A. D., & Ng, R. (1996). Close relationships and adjustments to a life crisis: The case of breast cancer. *Journal of Personality and Social Psychology, 70,* 283–294.

Bonanno, G. A. (2004). Loss, trauma, and human resilience: Have we underestimated the human capacity to thrive after extremely aversive events? *American Psychologist, 59,* 20–28.

Bonanno, G. A., Moskowitz, J. T., Papa, A., & Folkman, S. (2005). Resilience to loss in bereaved spouses, bereaved parents, and bereaved gay men. *Journal of Personality and Social Psychology, 88,* 827–843.

Bonanno, G. A., Wortman, C. B., Lehman, D. R., Tweed, R. G., Haring, M., Sonnega, J., Carr, D., & Nesse, R. M. (2002). Resilience to loss and chronic grief: a prospective study from preloss to 18-months postloss. *Journal of Personality and Social Psychology, 83,* 1150–1164.

Bonanno, G., Galea, S., Bucciarelli, A., & Vlahov, D. (2006). Psychological resilience after disaster: New York City in the aftermath of the September 11th terrorist attack. *Psychological Science, 17,* 181–186.

Bonanno, G., Wortman, C., & Lehman, D. (2002). Resilience to loss and chronic grief: A prospective study from preloss to 18-months postloss. *Journal of Personality & Social Psychology, 83,* 1150–1164.

Bonke, B., Tibben, A., Lindhout, D., Clarke, A. J., & Stijnen, T. (2005). Genetic risk estimation by healthcare professionals. *Medical Journal of Autism, 182,* 116–118.

Bookheimer, S. Y., Strojwas, M. H., Cophen, M. S., Saunders, A. M., Pericak-Vance, M. A., Mazziotta, J. C., & Small, G. W. (2000, August 17). Patterns of brain activation in people at risk for Alzheimer's disease. *New England Journal of Medicine, 343,* 450–456.

Bookstein, F. L., Sampson, P. D., Streissguth, A. P., & Barr, H. M. (1996). Exploiting redundant measurement of dose and developmental outcome: New methods from the behavioral teratology of alcohol. *Developmental Psychology, 32,* 404–415.

Booth, W. (1987, October 2). Big Brother is counting your keystrokes. *Science, 238,* 17.

Borden, M. E. (1998). *Smart start: The parents' complete guide to preschool education.* New York: Facts on File.

Borland, M. V., & Howsen, R. M. (2003). An examination of the effect of elementary school size on student academic achievement. *International Review of Education, 49,* 463–474.

Bornstein, M. H. (2000). Infant into conversant: Language and nonlanguage processes in developing early communication. In N. Budwig & I. C. Uzgiris (Eds.). *Communication: An arena of development.* Westport, CT: Ablex Publishing.

Bornstein, M. H., & Lamb, M. E. (1992a). *Development in infancy: An introduction.* New York: McGraw-Hill.

Bornstein, M. H., Cote, L., & Maital, S. (2004). Cross-linguistic analysis of vocabulary in young children: Spanish, Dutch, French, Hebrew, Italian, Korean, and American English. *Child Development, 75,* 1115–1139.

Bornstein, M. H., Haynes, O. M., O'Reilly, A. W., & Painter, K. M. (1996). Solitary and collaborative pretense play in early childhood: Sources of individual variation in the development of representational competence. *Child Development, 67,* 2910–2929.

Bornstein, M. H., Putnick, D. L., Suwalsky, T. D., & Gini, M. (2006). Maternal chronological age, prenatal and perinatal history, social support, and parenting of infants. *Child Development, 77,* 875–892.

Bornstein, M., & Arterberry, M. (2003). Recognition, discrimination and categorization of smiling by 5-month-old infants. *Developmental Science, 6,* 585–599.

Bornstein, M., Putnick, D., Heslington, M., Gini, M., Suwalsky, J., Venuti, P., et al. (2008, May). Mother-child emotional availability in ecological perspective: Three countries, two regions, two genders. *Developmental Psychology, 44*(3), 666–680.

Boruch, R. F. (1998). Randomized controlled experiments for evaluation and planning. In L. Bickman & D. J. Rog (Eds.), *Handbook of applied social research methods* (pp. 161–191). Thousand Oaks, CA: Sage.

Bos, A., Muris, P., Mulkens, S., & Schaalma, H. (2006). Changing self-esteem in children and adolescents: A roadmap for future interventions. *Netherlands Journal of Psychology, 62,* 26–32.

Botvin, G. J., Epstein, J. A., Schinke, S. P., & Diaz, T. (1994). Predictors of cigarette smoking among inner-city minority youth. *Journal of Developmental and Behavioral Pediatrics, 15,* 67–73.

Bouchard, T. J., Jr. (1997, September/October). Whenever the twain shall meet. *The Sciences,* pp. 52–57.

Bouchard, T. J., Jr. (2004). Genetic influence on human psychological traits: A survey. *Current Directions in Psychological Science, 13,* 148–153.

Bouchard, T. J., Jr., & McGue, M. (1981). Familial studies of intelligence: A review. *Science, 264,* 1700–1701.

Bouchard, T. J., Jr., & Pedersen, N. (1999). Twins reared apart: Nature's double experiment. In M. C. LaBuda, E. L. Grigorenko, et al. (Eds.), *On the way to individuality: Current methodological issues in behavioral genetics.* Commack, NY: Nova.

Bouchard, T. J., Jr., Lykken, D. T., McGue, M., Segal, N. L., & Tellegen, A. (1990, October 12). Sources of human psychological differences: The Minnesota Study of twins reared apart. *Science, 250,* 223–228.

Bourne, V., & Todd, B. (2004). When left means right: An explanation of the left cradling bias in terms of right hemisphere specializations. *Developmental Science, 7,* 19–24.

Bourque, P., Pushkar, D., Bonneville, L., & Béland, F. (2005). Contextual effects on life satisfaction of older men and women. *Canadian Journal on Aging, 24,* 31–44.

Bowen, D. J., Kahl, K., Mann, S. L., & Peterson, A. V. (1991). Descriptions of early triers. *Addictive Behaviors, 16,* 95–101.

Bower, B. (1985). The left hand of math and verbal talent. *Science News, 127,* 263.

Bower, T. G. R. (1977). *A primer of infant development.* San Francisco: Freeman.

Bowers, K. E., & Thomas, P. (1995, August). Handle with care. *Harvard Health Letter,* pp. 6–7.

Bowlby, J. (1951). Maternal care and mental health. *Bulletin of the World Health Organization, 3,* 355–534.

Boyatzis, C. J., Mallis, M., & Leon, I. (1999). Effects of game type of children's gender-based peer preferences: A naturalistic observational study. *Sex Roles, 40,* 93–105.

Boyd, G. M., Howard, J., & Zucker, R. A. (Eds.) (1995). *Alcohol problems among adolescents: Current directions in prevention research.* Hillsdale, NJ: Erlbaum.

Bracken, B., & Brown, E. (2006, June). Behavioral identification and assessment of gifted and talented students. *Journal of Psychoeducational Assessment, 24,* 112–122.

Bracken, B., & Lamprecht, M. (2003). Positive self-concept: An equal opportunity construct. *School Psychology Quarterly, 18,* 103–121.

Brady, L. S. (1995, January 29). Asia Linn and Chris Applebaum. *New York Times,* p. 47.

Brainerd, C. (2003). Jean Piaget, learning research, and American education. In B. Zimmerman (Ed.), *Educational psychology: A century of contributions.* Mahwah, NJ: Lawrence Erlbaum Associates.

Brainerd, C. J., Reyna, V. F., & Brandse, E. (1995). Are children's false memories more persistent than their true memories? *Psychological Science, 6,* 359–364.

Branscombe, N. R., Ellemers, N., & Spears, R. (1999). The context and content of social identity threat. In N. Ellemers, R. Spears, & B. Doosje, *Social identity: Context, commitment, content*. Oxford, England: Blackwell Science.

Branum, A. (2006). Teen maternal age and very preterm birth of twins. *Maternal & Child Health Journal, 10*, 229–233.

Braun, K. L., Pietsch, J. H., & Blanchette, P. L. (Eds.). (2000). *Cultural issues in end-of-life decision making*. Thousand Oaks, CA: Sage Publications.

Brazelton, T. B. (1973). *The Neonatal Behavioral Assessment Scale*. Philadelphia, PA: Lippincott.

Brazelton, T. B. (1983). *Infants and mothers: Differences in development* (Rev. ed.). New York: Dell.

Brazelton, T. B. (1997). *Toilet training your child*. New York: Consumer Visions.

Brazelton, T. B., Christophersen, E. R., Frauman, A. C., Gorski, P. A., Poole, J. M., Stadtler, A. C., & Wright, C. L. (1999). Instruction, timeliness, and medical influences affecting toilet training. *Pediatrics, 103*, 1353–1358.

Brecher, E. M., & the Editors of Consumer Reports Books. (1984). *Love, sex, and aging*. Mount Vernon, New York: Consumers Union.

Breen, F., Plomin, R., & Wardle, J. (2006). Heritability of food preferences in young children. *Physiology & Behavior, 88*, 443–447.

Breheny, M., & Stephens, C. (2003). Healthy living and keeping busy: A discourse analysis of mid-aged women's attributions for menopausal experience. *Journal of Language & Social Psychology, 22*, 169–189.

Brehm, K. (2003). Lessons to be learned at the end of the day. *School Psychology Quarterly, 18*, 88–95.

Brehm, S. S. (1992). *Intimate relationships* (2nd ed.). New York: McGraw-Hill.

Bremmer, J. D. (2003). Long-term effects of childhood abuse on brain and neurobiology. *Child Adolescent Psychiatric Clinics of North America, 12*, 271292.

Bremner, G., & Fogel, A. (Eds.). (2004). *Blackwell handbook of infant development*. Malden, MA: Blackwell Publishers.

Brennan, K. A., & Shaver, P. R. (1995). Dimensions of adult attachment, affect regulation, and romantic relationship functioning. *Personality and Social Psychology Bulletin, 21*, 267–283.

Breslin, M. J., & Lewis, C. A. (2008). Theoretical models of the nature of prayer and health. *Mental Health, Religion & Culture, 11*, Special Issue, 9–21.

Bridges, J. S. (1993). Pink or blue: Gender-stereotypic perceptions of infants as conveyed by birth congratulations cards. *Psychology of Women Quarterly, 17*, 193–205.

Brockington, I. F. (1992). Disorders specific to the puerperium. *International Journal of Mental Health, 21*, 41–52.

Bromberger, J. T., & Matthews, K. A. (1994). Employment status and depressive symptoms in middle-aged women: A longitudinal investigation. *American Journal of Public Health, 84*, 202–206.

Bronfenbrenner, U. (1998). *The ecology of human development*. Cambridge, MA: Harvard University Press.

Bronfenbrenner, U. (2000). Ecological theory. In A. Kazdin (Ed.), *Encyclopedia of psychology*. Washington, DC, and New York: American Psychological Association/Oxford University Press.

Bronfenbrenner, U. (2002). Preparing a world for the infant in the twenty-first century: The research challenge. In J. Goes-Pedro, J. K. Nugent, J. G. Young, & T. B. Brazelton, *The infant and family in the twenty-first century*. New York: Brunner-Routledge.

Bronfenbrenner, U., & Morris, P. (2006). The bioecological model of human development. *Handbook of child psychology (6th ed.): Vol 1, Theoretical models of human development*. Hoboken, NJ: John Wiley & Sons Inc.

Brook, U., & Tepper, I. (1997). High school students' attitudes and knowledge of food consumption and body image: Implications for school-based education. *Patient Education & Counseling, 30*, 282–288.

Brooks-Gunn, J. (2003). Do you believe in Magic?: What we can expect from early childhood intervention programs. *Social Policy Report, 17*, 1–16.

Brooks-Gunn, J. (2003). Do you believe in Magic?: What we can expect from early childhood intervention programs. *Social Policy Report, 17*, 3–15.

Brooks-Gunn, J., & Reiter, E. (1990). The role of pubertal processes. In S. Feldman & G. Elliott (Eds.), *At the threshold: The developing adolescent*. Cambridge, MA: Harvard University Press.

Brooks-Gunn, J., Klebanov, P. K., & Duncan, G. J. (1996). Ethnic differences in children's intelligence test scores: Role of economic deprivation, home environment, and maternal characteristics. *Child Development, 67*, 396–408.

Brown, A. L., & Ferrara, R. A. (1999). Diagnosing zones of proximal development. In P. Llyod & C. Fernyhough (Eds.), *Lev Vygotsky: Critical assessments: The zone of proximal development, Vol. III*. New York: Routledge.

Brown, B. (1990). Peer groups. In S. Feldman & G. Elliott (Eds.), *At the threshold: The developing adolescent*. Cambridge, MA: Harvard University Press.

Brown, B. B., & Klute, C. (2006). Friendships, cliques, and crowds. In G. Adams & M. D. Berzonsky, *Blackwell handbook of adolescence*. Malden, MA: Blackwell Publishing.

Brown, E. L., & Bull, R. (2007). Can task modifications influence children's performance on false belief tasks? *European Journal of Developmental Psychology, 4*, 273–292.

Brown, J. D. (1998). *The self*. New York: McGraw-Hill.

Brown, J. L., & Pollitt, E. (1996, February). Malnutrition, poverty and intellectual development. *Scientific American*, 38–43.

Brown, L. M., Bradley, M. M., & Lang, P. J. (2006). Affective reactions to pictures of ingroup and outgroup members. *Biological Psychology, 71*, 303–311.

Brown, R. (1973). *A first language*. Cambridge, MA: Harvard University Press.

Brown, S. (2003). Relationship quality dynamics of cohabitating unions. *Journal of Family Issues, 24*, 583–601.

Brown, W. M., Hines, M., & Fane, B. A. (2002). Masculinzed finger length patterns in human males and females with congenital adrenal hyperplasia. *Hormones and Behavior, 42*, 380–386.

Browne, A. (1993). Violence against women by male partners: Prevalence, outcomes, and policy implications. *American Psychologist, 48*, 1077–1087.

Browne, B. A. (1998). Gender stereotypes in advertising on children's television in the 1990s: A cross-national analysis. *Journal of Advertising, 27*, 83–96.

Browne, K. (2006, March). Evolved sex differences and occupational segregation. *Journal of Organizational Behavior, 27*, 143–162.

Browning, D. (2003). Pathos, paradox, and poetics: Grounded theory and the experience of bereavement. *Smith College Studies in Social Work, 73*, 325–336.

Brownlee, S. (2002, January 21). Too heavy, too young. *Time*, 21–23.

Brubaker, T. (1991). Families in later life: A burgeoning research area. In A. Booth (Ed.), *Contemporary families*. Minneapolis, MN: National Council on Family Relations.

Bruck, M., Ceci, S. J., Francouer, E., & Renick, A. (1995). Anatomically detailed dolls do not facilitate preschoolers' reports of a pediatric examination involving genital touching. *Journal of Experimental Psychology: Applied, 1*, 95–109.

Bryant, C. D. (Ed.). (2003). *Handbook of death and dying*. Thousand Oaks, CA: Sage.

Brzostek, T., Dekkers, W., Zalewski, Z., Januszewska, A., & Górkiewicz, M. (2008). Perception of palliative care and euthanasia among recently graduated and experienced nurses. *Nursing Ethics, 15*, 761–776.

Buchanan, C. M., Eccles, J. S., & Becker, J. B. (1992). Are adolescents the victims of raging hormones? Evidence for activational effects of hormones on moods and behavior at adolescence. *Psychological Bulletin, 111*, 62–107.

Budd, K. (1999). The facts of life: everything you wanted to know about sex (after 50). *Modern Maturity, 42*, 78. (AARP/Modern Maturity Sexuality Study, August, 1999.)

Budris, J. (1998, April 26). Raising their children's children. *Boston Globe 55–Plus*, pp. 8–9, 14–15.

Bugg, J., Zook, N., DeLosh, E., Davalos, D., & Davis, H. (2006, October). Age differences in fluid intelligence: Contributions of general slowing and frontal decline. *Brain and Cognition, 62*, 9–16.

Bukowski, W. M., Sippola, L. K., & Newcomb, A. F. (2000). Variations in patterns of attraction to same- and other-sex peers during early adolescence. *Developmental Psychology, 36*, 147–154.

Bullinger, A. (1997). Sensorimotor function and its evolution. In J. Guimon (Ed.), *The body in psychotherapy* (pp. 25–29). Basil, Switzerland: Karger.

Bumpass, L., Sweet, J., & Martin, T. (1990). Changing patterns of remarriage. *Journal of Marriage and the Family, 52*, 747–756.

Burd, L., Cotsonas-Hassler, T. M., Martsolf, J. T., & Kerbeshian, J. (2003). Recognition and management of fetal alcohol syndrome. *Neurotoxicological Teratology, 25*, 681–688.

Burgess, R. L., & Huston, T. L. (Eds.). (1979). *Social exchanges in developing relationships*. New York: Academic Press.

Burgund, E., & Abernathy, A. (2008). Letter-specific processing in children and adults matched for reading level. *Acta Psychologica, 129*, 66–71.

Burke, V., Beilin, L., Durkin, K., Stritzke, W., Houghton, S., & Cameron, C. (2006, November). Television, computer use, physical activity, diet and fatness in Australian adolescents. *International Journal of Pediatric Obesity, 1*, 248–255.

Burkhammer, M. D., Anderson, G. C., & Chiu, S-H. (2004). Grief, anxiety, stillbirth, and perinatal problems: healing with kangaroo care. *Journal of Obstetrics and Gynecological Neonatal Nursing, 33*, 774–782.

Burnett, P., & Proctor, R. (2002). Elementary school students' learner self-concept, academic self-concepts and approaches to learning. *Educational Psychology in Practice, 18,* 325–333.

Burnham, M., Goodlin-Jones, B., & Gaylor, E. (2002). Nighttime sleep-wake patterns and self-soothing from birth to one year of age: A longitudinal intervention study. *Journal of Child Psychology & Psychiatry & Allied Disciplines, 43,* 713–725.

Burns, D. M. (2000). Cigarette smoking among the elderly: Disease consequences and the benefits of cessation. *American Journal of Health Promotion, 14,* 357–361.

Burrus-Bammel, L. L., & Bammel, G. (1985). Leisure and recreation. In J. E. Birren & K. W. Schaie (Eds.), *Handbook of the psychology of aging.* New York: Van Nostrand Reinhold.

Burt, V. L., & Harris, T. (1994). The third National Health and Nutrition Examination Survey: Contributing data on aging and health. *Gerontologist, 34,* 486–490.

Burton, A., Haley, W., & Small, B. (2006, May). Bereavement after caregiving or unexpected death: Effects on elderly spouses. *Aging & Mental Health, 10,* 319–326.

Bushman, B. J. (1993). Human aggression while under the influence of alcohol and other drugs: An integrative research review. *Current Directions in Psychological Science, 2,* 148–152.

Buss, D. (2005, January 23). Sure, come back to the nest. Here are the rules. *New York Times,* 8.

Buss, D. M., & Reeve, H. K. (2003). Evolutionary psychology and developmental dynamics: Comment on Lickliter and Honeycutt. *Psychological Bulletin, 129,* 848–853.

Buss, D. M. (2003). The dangerous passion: Why jealousy is a necessary as love and sex: Book review. *Archives of Sexual Behavior, 32,* 79–80.

Buss, D. M., et al. (1990). International preferences in selecting mates: A study of 37 cultures. *Journal of Cross-Cultural Psychology, 21,* 5–47.

Buss, D. M. (2003). *The evolution of desire: Strategies of human mating (Revised Edition).* New York: Basic Books.

Buss, D. M. (2004). *Evolutionary psychology: The new science of the mind, 2nd Edition.* Boston: Allyn & Bacon.

Buss, K. A., & Kiel, E. J. (2004). Comparison of sadness, anger, and fear facial expressions when toddlers look at their mothers. *Child Development, 75,* 1761–1773.

Bussey, K. (1992). Lying and truthfulness: Children's definition, standards, and evaluative reactions. *Child Development, 63,* 1236–1250.

Butler, K. G., & Silliman, E. R. (2002). *Speaking, reading, and writing in children with language learning disabilities: New paradigms in research and practice.* Mahwah, NJ: Erlbaum.

Butler, R. N. (2002). The life review. *Journal of Geriatric Psychiatry, 35,* 7–10.

Butler, R. N., & Lewis, M. I. (1981). *Aging and mental health.* St. Louis: Mosby.

Butterworth, G. (1994). Infant intelligence. In J. Khalfa (Ed.), *What is intelligence? The Darwin College lecture series* (pp. 49–71). Cambridge, England: Cambridge University Press.

Buysse, D. J. (2005). Diagnosis and assessment of sleep and circadian rhythm disorders. *Journal of Psychiatric Practice, 11,* 102–115.

Byrd, D., Katcher, M., Peppard, P., Durkin, M., & Remington, P. (2007). Infant mortality: Explaining black/white disparities in Wisconsin. *Maternal and Child Health Journal, 11,* 319–326.

Byrd, M., Nelson, E., & Manthey, L. (2006). Oral-digital habits of childhood: Thumb sucking. *Practitioner's guide to evidence-based psychotherapy.* New York: Springer Science + Business Media.

Byrd, R. S., Weitzman, M., & Auinger, P. (1997). Increased behavior problems associated with delayed school entry and delayed school progress. *Pediatrics, 100,* 654–661.

Byrne, A. (2000). Singular identities: Managing stigma, resisting voices. *Women's Studies Review, 7,* 13–24.

Byrne, B., Shankweiler, D., & Hine, D. (2008). Reading development in children at risk for dyslexia. *Brain, behavior, and learning in language and reading disorders.* New York: Guilford Press.

Cabrera, N., Shannon, J., & Tamis-LeMonda, C. (2007). Fathers' influence on their children's cognitive and emotional development: From toddlers to pre-K. *Applied Developmental Science, 11,* 208–213.

Cacciatore, J., & Bushfield, S. (2007). Stillbirth: The mother's experience and implications for improving care. *Journal of Social Work in End-of-Life & Palliative Care, 3,* 59–79.

Cadinu, M. R., & Kiesner, J. (2000). Children's development of a theory of mind. *European Journal of Psychology of Education, 15,* 93–111.

Cai, Y., Reeve, J. M., & Robinson, D. T. (2002). Home schooling and teaching style: Comparing the motivating styles of home school and public school teachers. *Journal of Educational Psychology, 94,* 372–380.

Cain, B. S. (1982, December 19). Plight of the gray divorcee. *New York Times Magazine,* pp. 89–93.

Cain, V., Johannes, C., & Avis, N. (2003). Sexual functioning and practices in a multiethnic study of midlife women: Baseline results from SWAN. *Journal of Sex Research, 40,* 266–276.

Caino, S., Kelmansky, D., Lejarraga, H., & Adamo, P. (2004). Short-term growth at adolescence in healthy girls. *Annals of Human Biology, 31,* 182–195.

Caldera, Y. M., & Sciaraffa, M. A. (1998). Parent-toddler play with feminine toys: Are all dolls the same? *Sex Roles, 39,* 657–668.

Calhoun, F., & Warren, K. (2007). Fetal alcohol syndrome: Historical perspectives. *Neuroscience & Biobehavioral Reviews, 31,* 168–171.

Calvert, S. L., Kotler, J. A., Zehnder, S., & Shockey, E. (2003). Gender stereotyping in children's reports about educational and informational television programs. *Media Psychology, 5,* 139–162.

Camarota, S. A. (2001). *Immigrants in the United States—2000: A snapshot of America's foreign-born population.* Washington, DC: Center for Immigration Studies.

Cameron, P. (2003). Domestic violence among homosexual partners. *Psychological Reports, 93,* 410–416.

Cami, J., & Farré, M., (2003). Drug addiction. *New England Journal of Medicine, 349,* 975–986.

Campbell, A., Shirley, L., & Candy, J. (2004). A longitudinal study of gender-related cognition and behaviour. *Developmental Science, 7,* 1–9.

Campbell, F., Ramey, C., & Pungello, E. (2002). Early childhood education: Young adult outcomes from the Abecedarian Project. *Applied Developmental Science, 6,* 42–57.

Campos, J. J., Langer, A., & Krowitz, A. (1970). Cardiac responses on the visual cliff in prelocomotor human infants. *Science, 170,* 196–197.

Camras, L., Meng, Z., & Ujiie, T. (2002). Observing emotion in infants: Facial expression, body behavior, and rater judgments of responses to an expectancy-violating event. *Emotion, 2,* 179–193.

Canals, J., Fernandez-Ballart, J., & Esparo, G. (2003). Evolution of Neonatal Behavior Assessment Scale scores in the first month life. *Infant Behavior & Development, 26,* 227–237.

Canfield, R., Kreher, D., & Cornwell, C. (2003). Low-level lead exposure, executive functioning, and learning in early childhood. *Child Neuropsychology, 9,* 35–53.

Canfield, R. L., & Haith, M. M. (1991). Young infants' visual expectations for symmetric and asymmetric stimulus sequences. *Developmental Psychology, 27,* 198–208.

Caplan, L. J., & Barr, R. A. (1989). On the relationship between category intensions and extensions in children. *Journal of Experimental Child Psychology, 47,* 413–429.

Cardman, M. (2004). Rising GPAs, course loads a mystery to researchers. *Education Daily, 37,* 1–7.

Carlo, G., Fabes, R. A., Laible, D., & Kupanoff, K. (1999). Early adolescence and prosocial/moral behavior II: The role of social and contextual influences. *The Journal of Early Adolescence, 19, May, 1999. Special issue: Prosocial and moral development in early adolescence, Part II,* 133–147.

Carlson, E., & Hoem, J. M. (1999). Low-weight neonatal survival paradox in the Czech Republic. *American Journal of Epidemiology, 149,* 447–453.

Carmeli, A., & Josman, Z. (2006). The relationship among emotional intelligence, task performance, and organizational citizenship behaviors. *Human Performance, 19,* 403–419.

Carmody, D. (1990, March 7). College drinking: Changes in attitude and habit. *The New York Times.*

Carnegie Task Force on Meeting the Needs of Young Children. (1994). *Starting points: Meeting the needs of our youngest children.* New York: Carnegie Corporation.

Carpendale, J. I. M. (2000). Kohlberg and Piaget on stages and moral reasoning. *Developmental Review, 20,* 181–205.

Carr, C. N., Kennedy, S. R., & Dimick, K. M. (1996). Alcohol use among high school athletes. *The Prevention Researcher, 3,* 1–3.

Carr, D., & Ha, J. (2006). *Bereavement.* New York: Oxford University Press.

Carr, D., House, J. S., Kessler, R. C., Nesse, R. M., Sonnega, J., & Wortman, C. (2000). 'Marital quality and psychological adjustment to widowhood among older adults: A longitudinal analysis': Erratum. *The Journals of Gerontology: Series B: Psychological Sciences and Social Sciences, 55B,* S374.

Carr, D., Nesse, R., & Wortman, C. (2005). *Spousal bereavement in late life.* New York: Springer.

Carr, J. (1995). *Down syndrome.* Cambridge, England: Cambridge University Press.

Carrere, S., Buehlman, K. T., Gottman, J. M., Coan, J. A., & Ruckstuhl, L. (2000). Predicting marital stability and divorce in newlywed couples. *Journal of Family Psychology, 14,* 42–58.

Carver, C., & Scheier, M. (2002). Coping processes and adjustment to chronic illness. In A. Christensen and M. Antoni (Eds.), *Chronic physical disorders: Behavioral medicine's perspective* (pp. 47–68). Malden: Blackwell Publishers.

Carver, L., & Vaccaro, B. (2007, January). 12-month-old infants allocate increased neural resources to stimuli associated with negative adult emotion. *Developmental Psychology, 43*, 54–69.

Case, R. (1991). Stages in the development of the young child's first sense of self. *Developmental Review, 11*, 210–230.

Case, R. (1992). *Neo-Piagetian theories of intellectual development.* Hillsdale, NJ: Lawrence Erlbaum Associates.

Case, R., & Okamoto, Y. (1996). The role of central conceptual structures in the development of children's thought. *Monographs of the Society for Research in Child Development, 61*, v–265.

Case, R., Demetriou, A., & Platsidou, M. (2001). Integrating concepts and tests of intelligence from the differential and developmental traditions. *Intelligence, 29*, 307–336.

Case, R., Kurland, D. M., & Goldberg, J. (1982). Operational efficiency and the growth of short-term memory span. *Journal of Experimental Child Psychology, 33*, 386–404.

Caserta, M., O'Connor, T., Wyman, P., Wang, H., Moynihan, J., Cross, W., et al. (2008). The associations between psychosocial stress and the frequency of illness, and innate and adaptive immune function in children. *Brain, Behavior, and Immunity, 22*, 933–940.

Cashman, H. R. (2005). Identities at play: Language preference and group membership in bilingual talk in interaction. *Journal of Pragmatics, 37, Special issue: Conversational Code-Switching*, 301–315.

Cassel, W. S., Roebers, C. E. M., & Bjorklund, D. F. (1996). Developmental patterns of eyewitness responses to repeated and increasingly suggestive questions. *Journal of Experimental Child Psychology, 61*, 116–133.

Cassidy, J., & Berlin, L. J. (1994). The insecure/ambivalent pattern of attachment: Theory and research. *Child Development, 65*, 971–991.

Catell, P. (2004). *Drugs & clients: What every psychotherapist needs to know.* Petaluma, CA: Solarium Press.

Catell, R. B. (1987). *Intelligence: Its structure, growth, and action.* Amsterdam: North-Holland.

Cath, S., & Shopper, M. (2001). *Stepparenting: Creating and recreating families in America today.* Hillsdale, NJ: Analytic Press.

Cauce, A., & Domenech-Rodriguez, M. (2002). Latino families: Myths and realities. In J. M. Contreras, J. K. A. Kerns, & A. M. Neal-Barnett (Eds.), *Latino children and families in the United States.* Westport, CT: Praeger.

Cavallini, A., Fazzi, E., & Viviani, V. (2002).Visual acuity in the first two years of life in healthy term newborns: An experience with the Teller Acuity Cards. *Functional Neurology: New Trends in Adaptive & Behavioral Disorders, 17*, 87–92.

Ceci, S. J. (1993). Contextual trends in intellectual development. *Developmental Review, 13, Special issue: Setting a path for the coming decade: Some goals and challenges.* 403–435.

Ceci, S. J., & Bruck, M. (1993). The suggestibility of the child witness: A historical review and synthesis. *Psychological Bulletin, 113*, 403–439.

Ceci, S. J., & Bruck, M. (1995). *Jeopardy in the courtroom.* Washington, DC: American Psychological Association.

Ceci, S. J,. & Huffman, M. L. C. (1997). How suggestible are preschool children? Cognitive and social factors. *Journal of the American Academy of Child & Adolescent Psychiatry, 36*, 948–958.

Ceci, S. J., Loftus, E. F., Leichtman, M. D., & Bruck, M. (1994). The possible role of source misattributions in the creation of false beliefs among preschoolers. Special Issue: Hypnosis and delayed recall: I. *International Journal of Clinical & Experimental Hypnosis, 42*, 304–320.

Center for Communication & Social Policy, University of California. (1998). *National television violence study, Vol. 2.* Thousand Oaks, CA: Sage.

Center for Media and Public Affairs. (1995, April 7). Adaptation analysis of violent content of broadcast and cable television stations on Thursday. Washington, DC: CMPA.

Center on Addiction and Substance Abuse. (1994). *Report on college drinking.* New York: Columbia University.

Centers for Disease Control. (1991). *Preventing lead poisoning in young children: A statement by the Centers for Disease Control.* Atlanta, GA: U.S. Department of Health and Human Services.

Centers for Disease Control (2003). Incidence-surveillance, epidemiology, and end results program, 1973–2000. Atlanta, GA: Centers for Disease Control.

Centers for Disease Control. (2004). Health behaviors of adults: United States, 1999–2001. *Vital and Health Statistics, Series 10, no. 219.* Washington, DC: U.S. Department of Health and Human Services.

Centers for Disease Control and Prevention. (1998). *1997 youth risk behavior surveillance system.* Atlanta, GA: Author.

Centers for Disease Control and Prevention. (2000). *Obesity continues to climb in 1999 among American adults.* Division of Nutrition and Physical Activity, National Center for Chronic Disease Prevention and Health Promotions. Atlanta, GA: Centers for Disease Control and Prevention.

Centers for Disease Control and Prevention (2003). Incidence-surveillance, epidemiology, and end results program, 1973–2000. Atlanta, GA: Centers for Disease Control.

Centers for Disease Control and Prevention. (2006). Physical activity and good nutrition: Essential elements to prevent chronic diseases and obesity, 2007. http://www.cdc.gov/nccdphp/publications/aag/pdf/dnpa.pdf.

Cerella, J. (1990). Aging and information-processing rate. In J. E. Birren & K. W. Schaie (Eds.), *Handbook of the psychology of aging* (3rd ed.). San Diego, CA: Academic Press.

CFCEPLA (Commonwealth Fund Commission on Elderly People Living Alone). (1986). *Problems facing elderly Americans living alone.* New York: Louis Harris & Associates.

Chadha, N., & Misra, G. (2004). Patterns of prosocial reasoning in Indian children. *Psychology and Developing Societies, 16*, 159–186.

Chaffin, M. (2006). The changing focus of child maltreatment research and practice within psychology. *Journal of Social Issues, 62*, 663–684.

Chaiklin, S. (2003). The zone of proximal development in Vygotsky's analysis of learning and instruction. In A. Kozulin and B. Gindis (Eds.), *Vygotsky's educational theory in cultural context.* New York: Cambridge University Press.

Chaker, A. M. (2003, September 23). Putting toddlers in a nursing home. *Wall Street Journal*, D1.

Chan, D. W. (1997). Self-concept and global self-worth among Chinese adolescents in Hong Kong. *Personality & Individual Differences, 22*, 511–520.

Chan, E. (2006). Teacher experiences of culture in the curriculum. *Journal of Curriculum Studies, 38*, 161.

Chao, R. K. (1994). Beyond parental control and authoritarian parenting style: Understanding Chinese parenting through the cultural notion of training. *Child Development, 65*, 1111–1119.

Chapple, A., Ziebland, S., McPherson, A., & Herxheimer, A. (2006, December). What people close to death say about euthanasia and assisted suicide: A Qualitative study. *Journal of Medical Ethics, 32*, 706–710.

Charles, S. T., Mather, M., & Carstensen, L. L. (2003). Aging and emotional memory: The forgettable nature of negative images for older adults. *Journal of Experimental Psychology: General, 132*, 237–244.

Charles, S. T., Reynolds, C. A., & Gatz, M. (2001). Age-related differences and change in positive and negative affect over 23 years. *Journal of Personality and Social Psychology, 80*, 136–151.

Chen, H. (2006). Digitization of the Experience Sampling Method: Transformation, implementation, and assessment. *Social Science Computer Review, 24*, 106–118.

Chen, J., & Gardner, H. (2005). Assessment based on multiple-intelligences theory. In D. P. Flanagan & P. L. Harrison (Eds.), *Contemporary intellectual assessment: Theories, tests, and issues.* New York: Guilford Press.

Chen, X., Liu, M., Rubin, K. H., Cen, G., Gao, X., & Li, D. (2002). Sociability and prosocial orientation as predictors of youth adjustment: A seven-year longitudinal study in a Chinese sample. *International Journal of Behavioral Development, 26*, 128–136.

Chen, X., Rubin, K. H., & Li, Z. (1995). Social functioning and adjustment in Chinese children: A longitudinal study. *Developmental Psychology, 31*, 531–539.

Cherlin, A. (1993). *Marriage, divorce, remarriage.* Cambridge, MA: Harvard University Press.

Cherlin, A., & Furstenberg, F. (1986). *The new American grandparent.* New York: Basic Books.

Cherney, I., Kelly-Vance, L., & Glover, K. (2003).The effects of stereotyped toys and gender on play assessment in children aged 18–47 months. *Educational Psychology, 23*, 95–105.

Child Health USA. (2005). *Child Health USA 2005.* Rockville, MD: U.S. Department of Health and Human Services, Maternal and Child Health Bureau.

ChildStats.gov. (2000). *America's children 2000.* Washington, DC: National Maternal and Child Health Clearinghouse.

Chisholm, J., & Ward, A. (2005). Warning signs. *Violence in schools: Cross-national and cross-cultural perspectives* (pp. 59–74). New York: Springer Science + Business Media.

Chisolm, T., Willott, J., & Lister, J. (2003). The aging auditory system: Anatomic and physiologic changes and implications for rehabilitation. *International Journal of Audiology, 42,* 2S3– 2S10.

Chiu, C., Leung, A., & Kwan, L. (2007). Language, cognition, and culture: Beyond the Whorfian hypothesis. *Handbook of cultural psychology.* New York: Guilford Press.

Choi, H. (2002). Understanding adolescent depression in ethnocultural context. *Advances in Nursing Science, 25,* 71–85.

Chomsky, N. (1968). *Language and mind.* New York: Harcourt Brace Jovanovich.

Chomsky, N. (1978). On the biological basis of language capacities. In G. A. Miller & E. Lennenberg (Eds.), *Psychology and biology of language and thought* (pp. 199–220). New York: Academic Press.

Chomsky, N. (1991). Linguistics and cognitive science: Problems and mysteries. In A. Kasher (Ed.), *The Chomskyan turn.* Cambridge, MA: Blackwell.

Chomsky, N. (1999). On the nature, use, and acquisition of language. In W. C. Ritchie & T. J. Bhatia (Eds.), *Handbook of child language acquisition.* San Diego: Academic Press.

Chomsky, N. (2005). Editorial: Universals of human nature. *Psychotherapy and Psychosomatics [serial online], 74,* 263–268.

Chong, W. (2007). The role of personal agency beliefs in academic self-regulation: An Asian perspective. *School Psychology International, 28,* 63–76.

Choy, C. M., Yeung, Q. S., Briton-Jones, C. M., Cheung, C. K., Lam, C. W., & Haines, C. J. (2002). Relationship between semen parameters and mercury concentrations in blood and in seminal fluid from subfertile males in Hong Kong. *Fertility and Sterility, 78,* 42—428

Chrisler, J., & Smith, C. (2004). Feminism and psychology. *Praeger guide to the psychology of gender.* Westport, CT: Praeger Publishers/Greenwood Publishing Group.

Christophersen, E. R., Mortweet, S. L. (2003). Disciplining your child effectively. In E. R. Christophersen & S. L. Mortweet, *Parenting that works: Building skills that last a lifetime.* Washington, DC, US: American Psychological Association.

Christova, P., Lewis, S., Tagaris, G., Ugurbil, K., & Georgopoulos, A. (2008). A voxel-by-voxel parametric fMRI study of motor mental rotation: Hemispheric specialization and gender differences in neural processing efficiency. *Experimental Brain Research, 189,* 79–90.

Chulada, P., Corey, L., Vannappagari, V., Whitehead, N., & Blackshear, P. (2006). The feasibility of creating a population-based national twin registry in the United States. *Twin Research and Human Genetics, 9,* 919–926.

Cianciolo, A. T., Matthew, C., & Sternberg, R. J. (2006). Tacit knowledge, practical intelligence, and expertise. In K. A. Ericsson, N. Charness, P. J. Feltovich, & R. R. Hoffman, *The Cambridge handbook of expertise and expert performance.* New York: Cambridge University Press.

Cicchetti, D. (2003). Neuroendocrine functioning in maltreated children. In D. Cicchetti & E. Walker (Eds.), Neurodevelopmental mechanisms in psychopathology. New York: Cambridge University Press.

Cicchetti, D., & Toth, S. L. (1998). The development of depression in children and adolescents. *American Psychologist, 53,* 221–241.

Cicirelli, V. (2001). Personal meanings of death in older adults and young adults in relation to their fears of death. *Death Studies, 25,* 663–683.

Cillessen, A., & Borch, C. (2008). Analyzing social networks in adolescence. *Modeling dyadic and interdependent data in the developmental and behavioral sciences* (pp. 61–85). New York: Routledge/Taylor & Francis Group.

Cirulli, F., Berry, A., & Alleva, E. (2003). Early disruption of the mother-infant relationship: Effects on brain plasticity and implications for psychopathology. *Neuroscience & Biobehavioral Reviews, 27,* 73–82.

Clark, E. (1983). Meanings and concepts. In J. Flavel & E. Markham (Eds.), *Handbook of child psychology: Cognitive development* (Vol. 3). New York: Wiley.

Clark, J. E., & Humphrey, J. H. (Eds.). (1985). *Motor development: Current selected research.* Princeton, NJ: Princeton Book Company.

Clark, K. B., & Clark, M. P. (1947). Racial identification and preference in Negro children. In T. M. Newcomb & E. L. Hartley (Eds.), *Readings in social psychology.* New York: Holt, Rinehart & Winston.

Clark, R., Hyde, J. S., Essex, M. J., & Klein, M. H. (1997). Length of maternity leave and quality of mother-infant interactions. *Child Development, 68,* 364–383.

Clarke, L., & Griffin, M. (2007). The body natural and the body unnatural: Beauty work and aging. *Journal of Aging Studies, 21,* 187–201.

Clarke, L. H. (2005). Remarriage in later life: Older women's negotiation of power, resources and domestic labor. *Journal of Women & Aging, 17,* 21–41.

Clarke-Stewart, A., & Friedman, S. (1987). *Child development: Infancy through adolescence.* New York: Wiley.

Clarke-Stewart, K., & Allhusen, V. Nonparental caregiving. (2002). In M. Bornstein (Ed.), *Handbook of parenting: Vol. 3: Being and becoming a parent,* 2nd ed. Mahwah, NJ: Erlbaum.

Claxton, L. J., Keen R., & McCarty, M. E. (2003). Evidence of motor planning in infant reaching behavior. *Psychological Science, 14,* 354–356.

Clay, D., Vignoles, V. L., & Dittmar, H. (2005). Body image and self-esteem among adolescent girls: Testing the influence of sociocultural factors. *Journal of Research on Adolescence, 15,* 451–477.

Clearfield, M., & Nelson, N. (2006, January). Sex differences in mothers' speech and play behavior with 6-, 9-, and 14-month-old infants. *Sex Roles, 54,* 127–137.

Clements, R., & Swensen, C. (2003). Commitment to one's spouse as a predictor of marital quality among older couples. *Love, romance, sexual interaction: Research perspectives from Current Psychology* (pp. 183–195). New Brunswick, NJ: Transaction Publishers.

Cliff, D. (1991). Negotiating a livable retirement: Further paid work and the quality of life in early retirement. *Aging and Society, 11,* 319–340.

Cnattingius, S., Berendes, H., & Forman, M. (1993). Do delayed childbearers face increased risks of adverse pregnancy outcomes after the first birth? *Obstetrics and Gynecology, 81,* 512–516.

Coats, E. J., Feldman, R. S., & Schwartzberg, S. (1994). *Critical thinking: General principles and case studies.* New York: McGraw-Hill.

Coelho, M., Ferreira, J., Dias, B., Sampaio, C., Martins, I., & Castro-Caldas, A. (2004). Assessment of time perception: The effect of aging. *Journal of the International Neuropsychological Society, 10,* 332–341.

Cohen, J. (1999, March 19). Nurture helps mold able minds. *Science, 283,* 1832–1833.

Cohen, L., & Cashon, C. (2003). Infant perception and cognition. In R. Lerner & M. Easterbrooks (Eds.), *Handbook of psychology: Developmental psychology,* Vol. 6 (pp. 267–291). New York: Wiley.

Cohen, L. B. (1972). Attention-getting and attention-holding processes of infant visual preference. *Child Development, 43,* 869–879.

Cohen, L. B., & Cashon, C. H. (2003). Infant perception and cognition. In R. M. Lerner & M. A. Easterbrooks, (Eds.), *Handbook of psychology: Developmental psychology, Vol. 6.* New York: John Wiley & Sons.

Cohen, S., Hamrick, N., Rodriguez, M. S., Feldman, P. J., Rabin B. S., & Manuck, S. B. (2002). Reactivity and vulnerability to stress-associated risk for upper respiratory illness. *Psychosomatic Medicine, 64,* 302–310.

Cohen, S., Tyrell, D. A., & Smith, A. P. (1993). Negative life events, perceived stress, negative affect, and susceptibility of the common cold. *Journal of Personality and Social Psychology, 64,* 131–140.

Cohen, S., Tyrell, D. A., & Smith, A. P. (1997). Psychological stress in humans and susceptibility to the common cold. In T. W. Miller (Ed.), *International Universities Press stress and health series, Monograph 7. Clinical disorders and stressful life events* (pp. 217–235). Madison, CT: International Universities Press.

Cohrs, J., Abele, A., & Dette, D. (2006, July). Integrating situational and dispositional determinants of job satisfaction: Findings from three samples of professionals. *Journal of Psychology: Interdisciplinary and Applied, 140,* 363–395.

Cokley, K. (2003). What do we know about the motivation of African American students? Challenging the "anti-intellectual" myth. *Harvard Educational Review, 73,* 524–558.

Colby, A., & Kohlberg, L. (1987). *The measurement of moral adjudgment* (Vols. 1–2). New York: Cambridge University Press.

Colcombe, S. J., Erickson, K. I., Scalf, P. E., Kim, J. S., Prakash, R., McAuley, E., Elavsky, S., Marquez, D. X., Hu, L., & Kramer, A. F. (2006). Aerobic exercise training increases brain volume in aging humans. *Journal of Gerontology, A. Biological Sciences and Medical Sciences, 61,* 1166–1170.

Cole, D. A., Maxwell, S. E., Martin, J. M., Peeke, L. G., Seroczynski, A. D., Tram, J. M., Joffman, K. B., Ruiz, M. D., Jacquez, F., & Maschman, T. (2001). The development of multiple domains of child and adolescent self-concept: A cohort sequential longitudinal design. *Child Development, 72,* 1723–1746.

Cole, M. (1992). Culture in development. In M. H. Bornstein & M. E. Lamb (Eds.), *Developmental psychology: An advanced textbook* (3rd ed.). Hillsdale, NJ: Erlbaum.

Cole, M. (1996). Interacting minds in a life-span perspective: A cultural-historical approach to culture and cognitive development. In P. B. Baltes & U. M. Staudinger, (Eds.), *Interactive minds: Life-span perspectives on the social foundation of cognition.* New York: Cambridge University Press.

Cole, M. (2006). Culture and cognitive development in phylogenetic, historical, and ontogenetic perspective. *Handbook of child psychology: Vol. 2, Cognition, perception, and language* (6th ed.). Hoboken, NJ: John Wiley & Sons Inc.

Cole, M., Gay, J., Glick, J. A., & Sharp, D. W. (1971). *The cultural context of learning and thinking.* New York: Basic Books.

Cole, S. A. (2005). Infants in foster care: Relational and environmental factors affecting attachment. *Journal of Reproductive & Infant Psychology, 23*, 43–61.

Coleman, M., Ganong, L., 7 Weaver, S. (2001). Relationship maintenance and enhancement in remarried families. In J. Harvey and A. Wenzel (Eds.), *Close romantic relationships: Maintenance and enhancement*. Mahwah, NJ: Erlbaum.

Coleman, P. (2005, July). Editorial: Uses of reminiscence: Functions and benefits. *Aging & Mental Health, 9*, 291–294.

Colen, C., Geronimus, A., & Phipps, M. (2006, September). Getting a piece of the pie? The economic boom of the 1990s and declining teen birth rates in the United States. *Social Science & Medicine, 63*, 1531–1545.

Coles, R., & Stokes, G. (1985). *Sex and the American teenager*. New York: Harpercollins.

Colibazzi, T., Zhu, H., Bansal, R., Schultz, R., Wang, Z., & Peterson, B. (2008). Latent volumetric structure of the human brain: Exploratory factor analysis and structural equation modeling of gray matter volumes in healthy children and adults. *Human Brain Mapping, 29*, 1302–1312.

Colino, S. (2002, February 26). Problem kid or label? *Washington Post*, HE01.

College Board (2005). 2001 College Bound Seniors Are the Largest, Most Diverse Group in History. New York: College Board.

Collett, B. R., Gimpel, G. A., Greenson, J. N., & Gunderson, T. L. (2001). Assessment of discipline styles among parents of preschool through school-age children. *Journal of Psychopathology and Behavioral Assessment, 23*, 163–170.

Collins, W. (2003). More than myth: The developmental significance of romantic relationships during adolescence. *Journal of Research on Adolescence, 13*, 1–24.

Collins, W., & Doolittle, A. (2006, December). Personal reflections of funeral rituals and spirituality in a Kentucky African American family. *Death Studies, 30*, 957–969.

Colom, R., Lluis-Font, J. M., & Andrés-Pueyo, A. (2005). The generational intelligence gains are caused by decreasing variance in the lower half of the distribution: Supporting evidence for the nutrition hypothesis. *Intelligence, 33*, 83–91.

Colpin, H., & Soenen, S. (2004). Bonding. Through an adoptive mother's eyes. *Midwifery Today with International Midwife, 70*, 30–31.

Coltrane, S., & Adams, M. (1997). Children and gender. In T. Arendell (Ed.), *Contemporary parenting: Challenges and issues. Understanding Families* (Vol. 9, pp. 219–253). Thousand Oaks, CA: Sage.

Commons, M., & Richards, F. (2003). Four postformal stages. *Handbook of adult development*. New York: Kluwer Academic/Plenum Publishers.

Compton, R., & Weissman, D. (2002). Hemispheric asymmetries in global-local perception: Effects of individual differences in neuroticism. *Laterality, 7*, 333–350.

Condit, V. (1990). Anorexia nervosa: Levels of causation. *Human Nature, 1*, 391–413.

Condry, J., & Condry, S. (1976). Sex differences: A study of the eye of the beholder. *Child Development, 47*, 812–819.

Conel, J. L. (1939/1975). *Postnatal development of the human cortex* (Vols. 1–6). Cambridge, MA: Harvard University Press.

Conklin, H. M., & Iacono, W. G. Schizophrenia: A neurodevelopmental perspective. *Current Directions in Psychological Science, 11*, 33–37.

Conn, V. S. (2003). Integrative review of physical activity intervention research with aging adults. *Journal of the American Geriatrics Society, 51*, 1159–1168.

Conner, K., & Goldston, D. (2007, March). Rates of suicide among males increase steadily from age 11 to 21: Developmental framework and outline for prevention. *Aggression and Violent Behavior, 12*(2), 193–207.

Connor, R. (1992). *Cracking the over-50 job market*. New York: Penguin Books.

Connor, T. (2008). Don't stress out your immune system—Just relax. *Brain, Behavior, and Immunity, 22*, 1128–1129.

Consedine, N., Magai, C., & King, A. (2004). Deconstructing positive affect in later life: A differential functionalist analysis of joy and interest. *International Journal of Aging & Human Development, 58*, 49–68.

Continelli, L. (2006, December 24). From boxing to books. *Buffalo News*, p. B3.

Cook, A. S., & Oltjenbruns, K. A. (1989). *Dying and grieving: Lifespan and family perspectives*. New York: Holt, Rinehart & Winston.

Cook, L. (1994). Circumcision and sexually transmitted diseases. *American Journal of Public Health, 84*, 197–201.

Cooke, L. (2007). The importance of exposure for healthy eating in childhood: A review. *Journal of Human Nutrition and Dietetics, 20*, 294–301.

Coon, K. D., Myers, A. J., Craig, D. W., Webster, J. A., Pearson, J. V., Lince, D. H., Zismann, V. L., Beach, T. G., Leung, D., Bryden, L., Halperin, R. F., Marlowe, L., Kaleem, M., Walker, D. G., Ravid, R., Heward, C. B., Rogers, J., Papassotiropoulos, A., Reiman, E. M., Hardy, J., & Stephan, D. A. (2007). A high-density whole-genome association study reveals that APOE is the major susceptibility gene for sporadic late-onset Alzheimer's disease. *Journal of Clinical Psychiatry, 68*, 613–618.

Cooper, H., & Valentine, J. (2001). Using research to answer practical questions about homework. *Educational Psychologist, 36*,143–153.

Cooperative Institutional Research Program. (1990). *The American freshman: National norms for fall 1990*. Los Angeles: American Council on Education.

Cooperstock, M. S., Bakewell, J., Herman, A., & Schramm W. F. (1998). Effects of fetal sex and race on risk of very preterm birth in twins. *American Journal of Obstetrics & Gynecology, 179*, 762–765.

Corballis, P. (2003). Visuospatial processing and the right-hemisphere interpreter. *Brain & Cognition, 53*, 171–76.

Corcoran, J., & Pillai, V. (2007, January). Effectiveness of secondary pregnancy prevention programs: A meta-analysis. *Research on Social Work Practice, 17*, 5–8.

Cordón, I. M., Pipe, M., Sayfan, L., Melinder, A., & Goodman, G. S. (2004). Memory for traumatic experiences in early childhood. *Developmental Review, 24*, 101–132.

Corliss, J. (1996, October 29). Alzheimer's in the news. *HealthNews*, pp. 1–2.

Corr, C., & Corr, D. (2007). Historical and contemporary perspectives on loss, grief, and mourning. *Handbook of thanatology: The essential body of knowledge for the study of death, dying, and bereavement* (pp. 131–142). New York, Northbrook, IL: Routledge/Taylor & Francis Group.

Corr, C., & Doka, K. (2001). Master concepts in the field of death, dying, and bereavement: Coping versus adaptive strategies. *Omega: Journal of Death & Dying, 43*, 183–199.

Corr, C., Nabe, C., & Corr, D. (2006). *Death & dying, life & living*. Belmont, CA: Thomson Wadsworth.

Corr, C., Nabe, C., & Corr, D. (2000). *Death and dying, life and living* (3rd ed.). Belmont, CA: Wadsworth/Thomson Learning.

Coscia, J., Ris, M., & Succop, P. (2003). Cognitive development of lead exposed children from ages 6 to 15 years: An application of growth curve analysis. *Child Neuropsychology, 9*, 10–21.

Cossman, J. S. (2004). Parent's heterosexism and children's attitudes toward people with AIDS. *Sociological Spectrum, 24*, 319–339.

Costa, P. T., Jr., McCrae, R. R., & Siegler, I. C. (1999). Continuity and change over the adult life cycle: Personality and personality disorders. In C. R. Cloninger, *Personality and psychopathology*. Washington, DC: American Psychiatric Association.

Costa, P., & McCrae, R. (2002). Looking backward: Changes in the mean levels of personality traits from 80 to 12. In D. Cervone & W. Mischel (Eds.), *Advances in personality science*. New York: Guilford Press.

Costello, E., Compton, S., & Keeler, G. (2003). Relationships between poverty and psychopathology: A natural experiment. *Journal of the American Medical Association, 290*, 2023–2029.

Costello, E., Sung, M., Worthman, C., & Angold, A. (2007, April). Pubertal maturation and the development of alcohol use and abuse. *Drug and Alcohol Dependence, 88*, S50–s59.

Couperus, J., & Nelson, C. (2006). Early brain development and plasticity. *Blackwell handbook of early childhood development*. Blackwell Publishing.

Courchesne, E., Carper, R., & Akshoomoff, N. (2003). Evidence of Brain Overgrowth in the First Year of Life in Autism. *Journal of the American Medical Association, 290*, 337–344.

Cowley, G. (2000, January 31). Alzheimer's : Unlocking the mystery. *Newsweek*, 46–51.

Craik, F., & Salthouse, T. A. (Eds.). (1999). *The handbook of aging and cognition* (2nd ed.). Mahwah, NJ: Erlbaum.

Craik, F. I., & Salthouse, T. A. (Eds.). (2008). *The handbook of aging and cognition* (3rd ed.). New York: Psychology Press.

Crane, E., & Morris, J. (2006). Changes in maternal age in England and Wales—Implications for Down syndrome. *Down Syndrome: Research & Practice, 10*, 41–43.

Cratty, B. (1978). *Perceptual and motor development in infants and children* (2nd ed.). Englewood Cliffs, NJ: Prentice Hall.

Cratty, B. (1986). *Perceptual and motor development in infants and children* (3rd ed.). Englewood Cliffs, NJ: Prentice-Hall.

Crawford, D., Houts, R., & Huston, T. (2002). Compatibality, leisure, and satisfaction in marital relationships. *Journal of Marriage & Family, 64*, 433–449.

Crawford, M., & Unger, R. (2004). *Women and gender: A feminist psychology* (4th ed). New York: McGraw-Hill.

Crisp, A., Gowers, S., Joughin, N., McClelland, L., Rooney, B., Nielsen, S., et al. (2006, May). Anorexia nervosa in males: Similarities and differences to anorexia nervosa in females. *European Eating Disorders Review, 14*, 163–167.

Critser, G. (2003). *Fat land: How Americans became the fattest people in the world*. Boston: Houghton Mifflin.

Crocker, J., & Knight, K. M. (2005). Contingencies of self-worth. *Current Directions in Psychological Science, 14*, 200–203.

Crocker, J., & Park, L. E. (2004). The costly pursuit of self-esteem. *Psychological Bulletin, 150*, 392–414.

Croninger, R. G., & Lee, V. E. (2001). Social capital and dropping out of high school: Benefits to at-risk students of teachers' support and guidance. *Teachers College Record*, 103, 548–581.

Crosnoe, R., & Elder, G. H., Jr. (2002). Successful adaptation in the later years: A life course approach to aging. *Social Psychology Quarterly, 65*, 309–328.

Crowley, B., Hayslip, B., & Hobdy, J. (2003). Psychological hardiness and adjustment to life events in adulthood. *Journal of Adult Development, 10*, 237–248.

Crowley, K., Callaman, M. A., Tenenbaum, H. R., & Allen, E. (2001). Parents explain more often to boys than to girls during shared scientific thinking. *Psychological Science, 12*, 258–261.

Crowther, M., & Rodriguez, R. (2003). A stress and coping model of custodial grandparenting among African Americans. In B. Hayslip and J. Patrick (Eds.), *Working with custodial grandparents*. New York: Springer Publishing.

Crutchley, A. (2003). Bilingualism in development: language, literacy and cognition. *Child Language Teaching & Therapy, 19*, 365–367.

Csikszentmihalyi, M., & Larson, R. (1984). *Being adolescent: Conflict and growth in the teenage years.* New York: Basic Books.

Csikszentmihalyi, M., & Larson, R. (1992). Validity and reliability of the Experience Sampling Method. In M. W. deVries, *The experience of psychopathology: Investigating mental disorders in their natural settings*. New York: Cambridge University Press.

Culbertson, J. L, & Gyurke, J. (1990). Assessment of cognitive and motor development in infancy and childhood. In J. H. Johnson & J. Goldman (Eds.), *Developmental assessment in clinical child psychology: A handbook* (pp. 100–131). New York: Pergamon Press.

Culver, V. (2003, August 26). Funeral expenses overwhelm survivors: $10,000-plus tab often requires aid. *Denver Post*, B2.

Cummings, E., & Henry, W. E. (1961). *Growing old.* New York: Basic Books.

Cummings, E. M., Iannotti, R. J., & Zahn-Waxler, C. (1989). Aggression between peers in early childhood: Individual continuity and developmental change. *Child Development, 60*, 887–895.

Cunningham, J. D., & Antill, J. K. (1994). Cohabitation and marriage: Retrospective and predictive comparisons. *Journal of Social and Personal Relationships, 11*, 77–93.

Cwikel, J., Gramotnev, H., & Lee, C. (2006). Never-married childless women in Australia: Health and social circumstances in older age. *Social Science & Medicine, 62*, 1991–2001.

Cyna, A. M., Andrew, M. I., & McAuliffe, G. L. (2006). Antenatal self-hypnosis for labour and childbirth: A pilot study. *Anaestheology Intensive Care, 34*, 464–4699.

da Veiga, P., & Wilder, R. (2008). Maternal smoking during pregnancy and birthweight: A propensity score matching approach. *Maternal & Child Health Journal, 12*, 194–203.

Dahl, E., & Birkelund, E. (1997). Health inequalities in later life in a social democratic welfare state. *Social Science & Medicine, 44*, 871–881.

Daley, K. C. (2004). Update on sudden infant death syndrome. *Current Opinion in Pediatrics, 16*, 227–232.

Damon, W., & Hart, D. (1988). *Self-understanding in childhood and adolescence.* New York: Cambridge University Press.

Danhauer, S., McCann, J., & Gilley, D. (2004). Do behavioral disturbances in persons with Alzheimer's disease predict caregiver depression over time? *Psychology & Aging, 19*, 198–202.

Daniels, H. (Ed.). (1996). *An introduction to Vygotsky.* New York: Routledge.

Dapretto, M., Davies, M. S., Pfeifer, J. H., Scott, A. A., Sigman, M., Bookhermer, S. Y., & Iacobon, M. (2006). Understanding emotions in others: Mirror neuron dysfunction in children with autism spectrum disorders. *Nature and Neuroscience, 9*, 28–30.

Dare, W. N., Noronha, C. C., Kusemiju, O. T., & Okanlawon, O. A. (2002). The effect of ethanol on spermatogenesis and fertility in male Sprague-Dawley rats pretreated with acetylsalicylic acid. *Nigeria Postgraduate Medical Journal, 9*, 194–198

Darnton, N. (1990, June 4). Mommy vs. Mommy. *Newsweek*, 64–67.

Dasen, P., Inhelder, B., Lavallee, M., & Retschitzki, J. (1978). *Naissance de l'intelligence chez l'enfant Baoule de Cote d'Ivoire.* Berne: Hans Huber.

Dasen, P., Ngini, L., & Lavallee, M. (1979). Cross-cultural training studies of concrete operations. In L. H. Eckenberger, W. J. Lonner, & Y. H. Poortinga (Eds.), *Cross-cultural contributions to psychology*. Amsterdam: Swets & Zeilinger.

Davey, M. (2007, June 2). Kevorkian freed after years in prison for aiding suicide. *New York Times*, p. A1.

Davey, S. G., Frankel S., & Yarnell, J. (1997). Sex and death: are they related? Findings from the Caerphilly Cohort Study. *British Medical Journal, 315*, 1–4

Davidson, J. E. (1990). Intelligence recreated. *Educational Psychologist, 25, Special issue: Intelligence and intelligence testing*, 337–354.

Davidson, J. K., Darling, C., A., & Norton, L. (1995). Religiosity and the sexuality of women: Sexual behavior and sexual satisfaction revisited. *Journal of Sex Research, 32*, 235–243.

Davidson, R. J. (2003). Affective neuroscience: A case for interdisciplinary research. In F. Kessel, & P. L. Rosenfield, Eds., *Expanding the boundaries of health and social science: Case studies in interdisciplinary innovation.* London: Oxford University Press.

Davidson, T. (1977). Wifebeating: A recurring phenomenon throughout history. In M. Roy (Ed.), *Battered women: A psychosociological study of domestic violence.* New York: Van Nostrand Reinhold.

Davies, P. T., Harold, G. T., Goeke-Morey, M. C., & Cummings, E. M. (2002). Child emotional security and interparental conflict. *Monographs of the Society for Research in Child Development, 67*.

Davies, S., & Denton, M. (2002). The economic well-being of older women who become divorced or separated in mid- or later life. *Canadian Journal on Aging, 21*, 477–493.

Davis, A. (2003). *Your divorce, your dollars: Financial planning before, during, and after divorce.* Bellingham, WA: Self-Counsel Press.

Davis, C., & Nolen-Hoeksema, S. (2001). Loss and meaning: How do people make sense of loss? *American Behavioral Scientist, 44*, 726–741.

Davis, D., Shaver, P., Widaman, K., Vernon, M., Follette, W., & Beitz, K. (2006, December). "I can't get no satisfaction": Insecure attachment, inhibited sexual communication, and sexual dissatisfaction. *Personal Relationships, 13*, 465–483.

Davis, M., & Emory, E. (1995). Sex differences in neonatal stress reactivity. *Child Development, 66*, 14–27.

Davis-Kean, P. E., & Sandler, H. M. (2001). A meta-analysis of measures of self-esteem for young children: A framework for future measures. *Child Development, 72*, 887–906.

Davison, G. C. (2005). Issues and nonissues in the gay-affirmative treatment of patients who are gay, lesbian, or bisexual. *Clinical Psychology: Science & Practice, 12*, 25–28.

Dawson-Tunik, T., Fischer, K., & Stein, Z. (2004). Do stages belong at the center of developmental theory? A commentary on Piaget's stages. *New Ideas in Psychology, 22*, 255–263.

de Anda, D., & Becerra, R. M. (2000). An overview of "Violence: Diverse populations and communities." *Journal of Multicultural Social Work, 8*, n1–2, p1–14.

de Bellis, M., Keshavan, M., Beers, S., Hall, J., Frustaci, K., Masalehdan, A., et al. (2001). Sex differences in brain maturation during childhood and adolescence. *Cerebral Cortex, 11*, 552–557.

De Gelder, B. (2000). Recognizing emotions by ear and by eye. In R. D. Lane & L. Nadel, (Eds.), et al., *Cognitive neuroscience of emotion. Series in affective science.* New York: Oxford University Press.

de Graaf-Peters, V., & Hadders-Algra, M. (2006). Ontogeny of the human central nervous system: What is happening when? *Early Human Development, 82*, 257–266.

de Jesus Moreno Moreno, M. (2003). Cognitive improvement in mild to moderate Alzheimer's dementia after treatment with the acetylcholine precursor choline alfoscerate: A multicenter, double-blind, randomized, placebo-controlled trial. *Clinical Therapeutics: The International Peer-Reviewed Journal of Drug Therapy, 25*, 178–193.

de Jong Gierveld, J. (2004). Remarriage, unmarried cohabitation, living apart together: Partner relationships following bereavement or divorce. *Journal of Marriage and Family, 66*, 236–243.

De Leo, D., Conforti, D., & Carollo, G. (1997). A century of suicide in Italy: A comparison between the old and the young. *Suicide & Life-Threatening Behavior, 27*, 239–249.

De Meersman, R., & Stein, P. (2007, February). Vagal modulation and aging. *Biological Psychology, 74*, 165–173.

de Onis, M., Garza, C., Onyango, A. W., & Borghi, E. (2007). Comparison of the WHO child growth standards and the CDC 2000 growth charts. *Journal of Nutrition, 137*, 144–148.

de Pietro, O., & Appratto, F. (2004). Advanced technologies for contents sharing, exchanging, and searching in e-learning systems. *International Journal on E-Learning, 3*, 5–12.

de Rosnay, M., Cooper, P., Tsigaras, N., & Murray, L. (2006, August). Transmission of social anxiety from mother to infant: An experimental study using a social referencing paradigm. *Behaviour Research and Therapy, 44*, 1165–1175.

De Roten, Y., Favez, N., & Drapeau, M. (2003). Two studies on autobiographical narratives about an emotional event by preschoolers: Influence of the emotions experienced and the affective closeness with the interlocutor. *Early Child Development & Care, 173,* 237–248.

de Schipper, E. J., Riksen-Walraven, J. M., & Geurts, S. A. E. (2006). Effects of child-caregiver ratio on the interactions between caregivers and children in child-care centers: An experimental study. *Child Development, 77,* 861–874.

de St. Aubin, E., & McAdams, D. P. (Eds). (2004). *The generative society: Caring for future generations.* Washington, DC: American Psychological Association.

de St. Aubin, E., McAdams, D. P., & Kim, T. C. (Eds.), (2004). *The generative society: Caring for future generations.* Washington, DC: American Psychological Association.

de Vries, B., Davis, C. G., Wortman, C. B., & Lehman, D. R. (1997). Long-term psychological and somatic consequences of later life parental bereavement. *Omega—Journal of Death & Dying, 35,* 97–117.

Deakin, M. B. (2004, May 9). The (new) parent trap. *Boston Globe Magazine,* pp. 18–21, 28–33.

Deary, I., Ferguson, K., Bastin, M., Barrow, G., Reid, L., Seckl, J., et al. (2007). Skull size and intelligence, and King Robert Bruce's IQ. *Intelligence, 35,* 519–528.

Deater-Deckard, K., & Cahill, K. (2006). Nature and nurture in early childhood. *Blackwell handbook of early childhood development* (pp. 3–21). New York: Blackwell Publishing.

Deaux, K. (2006). A nation of immigrants: living our legacy. *Journal of Social Issues, 62,* 633–651.

Deaux, K., Reind, A., Mizrahi, K., & Ethier, K. A. (1995). Parameters of social identity. *Journal of Personality and Social Psychology, 68,* 280–291.

Deb, S., & Adak, M. (2006, July). Corporal punishment of children: Attitude, practice and perception of parents. *Social Science International, 22,* 3–13.

Decarrie, T. G. (1969). A study of the mental and emotional development of the thalidomide child. In B. M. Foss (Ed.), *Determinants of infant behavior* (Vol. 4). London: Methuen.

DeCasper, A. J., & Spence, M. J. (1986). Prenatal material speech influences newborns' perception of speech sounds. *Infant Behavior and Development, 9,* 133–150.

deCastro, J. (2002). Age-related changes in the social, psychological, and temporal influences on food intake in free-living, healthy, adult humans. *Journals of Gerontology: Series A: Biological Sciences & Medical Sciences, 57A,* M368–M377.

Decety, J., & Jackson, P. L. (2006). A social-neuroscience perspective on empathy. *Current Directions in Psychological Science, 15,* 54–61.

Deforche, B., De Bourdeaudhuij, I., & Tanghe, A. (2006, May). Attitude toward physical activity in normal-weight, overweight and obese adolescents. *Journal of Adolescent Health, 38,* 560–568.

DeFrain, J., Martens, L., Stork, J., & Stork, W. (1991). The psychological effects of a stillbirth on surviving family members. *Omega—Journal of Death and Dying, 22,* 81–108.

DeFrancisco, B., & Rovee-Collier, C. (2008). The specificity of priming effects over the first year of life. *Developmental Psychobiology, 50,* 486–501.

DeGenova, M. K. (1993). Reflections of the past: New variables affecting life satisfaction in later life. *Educational Gerontology, 19,* 191–201.

Dehaene-Lambertz, G., Hertz-Pannier, L., & Dubois, J. (2006). Nature and nurture in language acquisition: Anatomical and functional brain-imaging studies in infants. *Neurosciences, 29,* Special Issue: Nature and nurture in brain development and neurological disorders, 367–373.

Dehaene-Lambertz, G., Hertz-Pannier, L., & Dubois, J. (2006). Nature and nurture in language acquisition: Anatomical and functional brain-imaging studies in infants. *Trends in Neurosciences, 29,* Special issue: Nature and nurture in **brain** development and neurological disorders. pp. 367–373—Figure 1a.

Dejin-Karlsson, E., Hanson, B. S., Oestergren, P. O., Sjoeberg, N.O., & Marsal, K. (1998). Does passive smoking in early pregnancy increase the risk of small-for-gestational age infants? *American Journal of Public Health, 88,* 1523–1527.

Delaney, C. H. (1995). Rites of passage in adolescence. *Adolescence, 30,* 891–897.

DeLisi, L., & Fleischhaker, W. (2007). Schizophrenia research in the era of the genome, 2007. *Current Opinion in Psychiatry, 20,* 109–110.

Dell, D. L., & Stewart, D. E. (2000). Menopause and mood. Is depression linked with hormone changes?. *Postgraduate Medicine, 108,* 34–36, 39–43.

Dellmann-Jenkins, M., & Brittain, L. (2003). Young adults' attitudes toward filial responsibility and actual assistance to elderly family members. *Journal of Applied Gerontology, 22,* 214–229.

Delpisheh, A., Attia, E., Drammond, S., & Brabin, B. (2006). Adolescent smoking in pregnancy and birth outcomes. *European Journal of Public Health, 16,* 168–172.

Delpit, L. (2006). What should teachers do? Ebonics and culturally responsive instruction. *Dialects, Englishes, creoles, and education.* Mahwah, NJ: Lawrence Erlbaum Associates Publishers.

Delva, J., O'Malley, P., & Johnston, L. (2006, October). Racial/ethnic and socioeconomic status differences in overweight and health-related behaviors among American students: National trends 1986–2003. *Journal of Adolescent Health, 39,* 536–545.

Demetriou, A., & Raftopoulos, A. (2004). *Cognitive developmental change: Theories, models and measurement.* New York: Cambridge University Press.

Demir, A., Ulusoy, M., & Ulusoy, M. (2003). Investigation of factors influencing burnout levels in the professional and private lives of nurses. *International Journal of Nursing Studies, 40,* 807–827.

Dempster, F. N. (1981). Memory span: Sources of individual and developmental differences. *Psychological Bulletin, 89,* 63–100.

Dempster, F. N. (1993). Resistance to interference: Developmental changes in a basic processing mechanism. In R. Pasnak & M. L. Howe (Eds.), *Emerging themes in cognitive development* (Vol. 1). New York: Springer.

Deng, C., Armstrong, P., & Rounds, J. (2007). The fit of Holland's RIASEC model to US occupations. *Journal of Vocational Behavior, 71,* 1–22.

Denizet-Lewis, B. (2004, May 30). Friends, friends with benefits and the benefits of the local mall. *New York Times Magazine,* pp. 30–35, 54–58.

Dennis, J. G. (2004). *Homeschooling high school: Planning ahead for college admission.* Cambridge, MA: Emerald Press.

Dennis, T. A., Cole, P. M., Zahn-Wexler, C., & Mizuta, I. (2002). Self in context: Autonomy and relatedness in Japanese and U.S. mother-preschooler dyads. *Child Development, 73,* 1803–1817.

Dennis, T., Cole, P., & Zahn-Waxler, C. (2002). Self in context: Autonomy and relatedness in Japanese and U.S. mother-preschooler dyads. *Child Development, 73,* 1803—817.

Dennis, W. (1966a). Age and creative productivity. *Journal of Gerontology, 21,* 1–8.

Dennis, W. (1966b). Creative productivity between the ages of 20 and 80 years. *Journal of Gerontology, 11,* 331–337.

Dennison, B., Edmunds, L., Stratton, H., & Pruzek, R. (2006). Rapid infant weight gain predicts childhood overweight. *Obesity, 14,* 491–499.

Denny, F. W., & Clyde, W. A. (1983). Acute respiratory tract infections: An overview. In W. A. Clyde & F. W. Denny (Eds.), Workshop on acute respiratory diseases among children of the world. *Pediatric Research, 17,* 1026–1029.

DePaulo, B. (2004). *The scientific study of people who are single: An annotated bibliography.* Glendale, CA: Unmarried America.

Der, G., Batty, G., & Deary, I. (2006). Effect of breast feeding on intelligence in children: Prospective study, sibling pairs analysis, and meta-analysis. *BMJ: British Medical Journal, 333,* 723–732.

Dervic, K., Friedrich, E., Oquendo, M., Voracek, M., Friedrich, M., & Sonneck, G. (2006, October). Suicide in Austrian children and young adolescents aged 14 and younger. *European Child & Adolescent Psychiatry, 15,* 427–434.

Deshields, T., Tibbs, T., Fan, M. Y., & Taylor, M. (2005, August 12). Differences in patterns of depression after treatment for breast cancer. *Psycho-Oncology,* Published Online, Wiley.

DeSpelder, L., & Strickland, A. L. (1992). *The last dance: Encountering death and dying* (3rd ed.). Palo Alto, CA: Mayfield.

Deurenberg, P., Deurenberg-Yap, M., & Guricci, S. (2002). Asians are different from Caucasians and from each other in their body mass index/body fat percent relationship. *Obesity Review, 3,* 141–146.

Deurenberg, P., Deurenberg-Yap, M., Foo, L. F., Schmidt, G., & Wang, J. (2003). Differences in body composition between Singapore Chinese, Beijing Chinese and Dutch children. *European Journal of Clinical Nutrition, 57,* 405–409.

Deveny, K. (1994, December 5). Chart of kindergarten awards. *Wall Street Journal,* p. B1.

deVilliers, P. A., & deVilliers, J. G. (1992). Language development. In M. H. Bornstein & M. E. Lamb (Eds.), *Developmental psychology: An advanced textbook.* Hillsdale, NJ: Erlbaum.

Devlin, B., Daniels, M., & Roeder, K. (1997). The heritability of IQ. *Nature, 388,* 468–471.

deVries, R. (1969). Constancy of generic identity in the years 3 to 6. *Monographs of the Society for Research in Child Development, 34,* (3, Serial No. 127).

deVries, R. (2005). *A pleasing birth.* Philadelphia, PA: Temple University Press.

DeWitt, P. M. (1992). The second time around. *American Demographics, 14,* 60–63.

Diamantopoulou, S., Rydell, A., & Henricsson, L. (2008). Can both low and high self-esteem be related to aggression in children? *Social Development, 17,* 682–698.

Diambra, L. & Menna-Barretio, L. (2004). Infradian rhythmicity in sleep/wake ratio in developing infants. *Chronobiology International, 21,* 217–227.

Diamond, L. (2003a). Love matters: Romantic relationships among sexual-minority adolescents. In P. Florsheim (Ed.), *Adolescent romantic relations and sexual behavior: Theory, research, and practical implications.* Mahwah, NJ: Erlbaum.

Diamond, L. (2003b). Was it a phase? Young women's relinquishment of lesbian/bisexual identities over a 5-year period. *Journal of Personality & Social Psychology, 84,* 352–364.

Diamond, L., & Savin-Williams, R. (2003). The intimate relationships of sexual-minority youths. In G. Adams and M. Berzonsky (Eds.), *Blackwell handbook of adolescence.* Malden, MA: Blackwell Publishers.

Dick, D., & Mustanski, B. (2006). Pubertal development and health-related behavior. *Socioemotional development and health from adolescence to adulthood* (pp. 108–125). New York: Cambridge University Press.

Dick, D. M., & Rose, R. J. (2002). Behavior genetics: What's new? What's next? *Current Directions in Psychological Science, 11,* 70–74.

Diener, E. (2000). Subjective well-being: The science of happiness and a proposal for a national index. *American Psychologist, 55,* 34–43.

Diener, E., Oishi, S., & Lucas, R. (2003). Personality, culture, and subjective well-being: Emotional and cognitive evaluations of life. *Annual Review of Psychology, 54,* 403–425.

Dietz, W. (2004). Overweight in Childhood and Adolescence. *New England Journal of Medicine, 350,* 855–57.

Dietz, W. H., & Stern, L. (Eds.). (1999). *American Academy of Pediatrics guide to your child's nutrition: Making peace at the table and building healthy eating habits for life.* New York: Villard.

DiGiovanna, A. G. (1994). *Human aging: Biological perspectives.* New York: McGraw-Hill.

DiLalla, L. F., Thompson, L. A., Plomin, R., Phillips, K., Fagan, J. F., Haith, M. M., Cyphers, L. H., & Fulker, D. W. (1990). Infant predictors of preschool and adult IQ: A study of infant twins and their parents. *Developmental Psychology, 26,* 433–440.

Dildy, G. A., et al. (1996). Very advanced maternal age: Pregnancy after 45. *American Journal of Obstetrics and gynecology, 175,* 668–674.

Dion, K. L., & Dion, K. K. (1988). Romantic love: Individual and cultural perspectives. In R. J. Sternberg & M. L. Barnes (Eds.), *The psychology of love.* New Haven, CT: Yale University Press.

Dionigi, R., & O'Flynn, G. (2007). Performance discourses and old age: What does it mean to be an older athlete? *Sociology of Sport Journal, 24,* 359–377.

DiPietro, J. A., Bornstein, M. H., & Costigan, K. A. (2002). What does fetal movement predict about behavior during the first two years of life? *Developmental Psychobiology, 40,* 358–71.

Dipietro, J. A., Costigan, K. A., & Gurewitsch, E. D. (2005). Maternal psychophysiological change during the second half of gestation. *Biological Psychology, 69,* 23–39.

Dittmann, M. (2004, November). A new face to retirement. *Monitor on Psychology, 35,* 78.

Dittmann, M. (2005). Generational differences at work. *Monitor on Psychology, 36,* 54–55.

Division 44/Committee on Lesbian, Gay, and Bisexual Concerns Joint Task Force on Guidelines for Psychotherapy with Lesbian, Gay, and Bisexual Clients. (2000). Guidelines for psychotherapy with lesbian, gay, and bisexual clients. *American Psychologist, 55,* 1440–1451.

Dixon, L., & Browne, K. (2003). The heterogeneity of spouse abuse: A review. *Aggression & Violent Behavior, 8,* 107–130.

Dixon, W. E., Jr. (2004). There's a long, long way to go. *PsycCRITIQUES.*

Dobrova-Krol, N., van IJzendoorn, M., Bakermans-Kranenburg, M., Cyr, C., & Juffer, F. (2008). Physical growth delays and stress dysregulation in stunted and non-stunted Ukrainian institution-reared children. *Infant Behavior & Development, 31,* 539–553.

Dodge, K. A., & Coie, J. D. (1987). Social information-processing factors in reactive and proactive aggression in children's peer groups. *Journal of Personality and Social Psychology, 53,* 1146–1158.

Dodge, K. A., & Crick, N. R. (1990). Social information-processing bases of aggressive behavior in children. *Personality and Social Psychology Bulletin, 16,* 8–22.

Dodgson, P. G., & Wood, J. V. (1998). Self-esteem and the cognitive accessibility of strengths and weaknesses after failure. *Journal of Personality & Social Psychology, 75,* 178–197.

Doherty, W., Carroll, J., & Waite, L. (2007). Supporting the institution of marriage: Ideological, research, and ecological perspectives. *The family in the new millennium: World voices supporting the "natural" clan Vol 2: Marriage and human dignity* (pp. 21–51). Westport, CT: Praeger Publishers/Greenwood Publishing Group.

Dolan, R. J. (2002, November 8). Emotion, cognition, and behavior. *Science, 298,* 1191–1194.

Doman, G., & Doman, J. (2002). *How to teach your baby to read.* Gentle Revolution Press.

Dombrowski, S., Noonan, K., & Martin, R. (2007). Low birth weight and cognitive outcomes: Evidence for a gradient relationship in an urban, poor, African American birth cohort. *School Psychology Quarterly, 22,* 26–43.

Domsch, H., Lohaus, A., & Thomas, H. (2009). Prediction of childhood cognitive abilities from a set of early indicators of information processing capabilities. *Infant Behavior & Development, 32,* 91–102.

Donat, D. (2006, October). Reading their way: A balanced approach that increases achievement. *Reading & Writing Quarterly: Overcoming Learning Difficulties, 22,* 305–323.

Donini, L., Savina, C., & Cannella, C. (2003). Eating habits and appetite control in the elderly: The anorexia of aging. *International Psychogeriatrics, 15,* 73–87.

Donleavy, G. (2008). No man's land: Exploring the space between Gilligan and Kohlberg. *Journal of Business Ethics, 80,* 807–822.

Donnellan, M. B., Trzesniewski, K. H., Robins, R. W., Moffitt, T. E., & Caspi, A. (2005). Low self-esteem is related to aggression, antisocial behavior, and delinquency. *Psychological Science, 16,* 328–335.

Donnerstein, E. (2005, January). *Media violence and children: What do we know, what do we do?* Paper presented at the annual National Teaching of Psychology meeting, St. Petersburg Beach, FL.

Dorer, H., & Mahoney, J. (2006). Self-actualization in the corporate hierarchy. *North American Journal of Psychology, 8,* 397–410.

Dorn, L., Susman, E., & Ponirakis, A. (2003). Pubertal timing and adolescent adjustment and behavior: Conclusions vary by rater. *Journal of Youth & Adolescence, 32,* 157–167.

Dorofaeff, T., & Denny, S. (2006, September). Sleep and adolescence. Do New Zealand teenagers get enough? *Journal of Paediatrics and Child Health, 42,* 515–520.

Dortch, S. (1997, September). Hey guys: Hit the books. *American Demographics,* pp. 4–12.

Doussard-Roosevelt, J. A., Porges, S. W., Scanlon, J. W., Alemi, B., & Scanlon, K. B. (1997). Vagal regulation of heart rate in the prediction of developmental outcome for very low birth weight preterm infants. *Child Development, 68,* 173–186.

Dovidio, J. F., Glick, P., & Rudman, L. A. (2005). *On the nature of prejudice: Fifty years after Malden.* MA: Blackwell Publishing.

Dowling, N., Smith, D., & Thomas, T. (2005). Electronic gaming machines: Are they the "crack-cocaine" of gambling? *Addiction, 100,* 33–45.

Downe-Wamboldt, B., & Tamlyn, D. (1997). An international survey of death education trends in faculties of nursing and medicine. *Death Studies. Vol. 21,* 177–188.

Doyle, L. W. Victorian Infant Collaborative Study Group. (2004). Neonatal intensive care at borderline viability—is it worth it? *Early Human Development, 80,* 103–113.

Doyle, R. (2004a, January). Living together. *Scientific American,* p. 28.

Dreman, S. (Ed.). (1997). *The family on the threshold of the 21st century.* Mahwah, NJ: Erlbaum.

Drew, L., & Silverstein, M. (2004). Inter-generational role investments of great-grandparents: Consequences for psychological well-being. *Ageing & Society, 24,* 95–111.

Drews, C. D., Murphy, C. C., Yeargin-Allsopp, M., & Decoufle, P. (1996). The relationship between idiopathic mental retardation and maternal smoking during pregnancy. *Pediatrics, 97,* 547–553.

Driedger, S. D. (1994, July 11). Cancer made me stronger. *McCleans,* p. 46.

Driver, J., Tabares, A., & Shapiro, A. (2003). Interactional patterns in marital success and failure: Gottman laboratory studies. In F. Walsh (Ed.), *Normal family processes: Growing diversity and complexity* (3rd ed.). New York: Guilford Press.

Dromi, E. (1987). *Early lexical development.* Cambridge, England: Cambridge University Press.

Dromi, E. (1993). The development of prelinguistic communication: Implications for language evaluation. In N. J. Anastasiow & S. Harel (Eds.), *At-risk infants: Interventions, families, and research* (pp. 19–26). Baltimore, MD: Brookes.

DuBois, D. L., & Hirsch, B. J. (1990). School and neighborhood friendship patterns of blacks and whites in early adolescence. *Child Development, 61,* 524–536.

DuBreuil, S. C., Garry, M., & Loftus, E. F. (1998). Tales from the crib: Age regression and the creation of unlikely memories. In S. J. Lynn, & K. M. McConkey (Eds.), *Truth in memory.* New York: Guilford Press.

Duenwald, M. (2003, July 15). After 25 years, new ideas in the prenatal test tube. *New York Times,* p. D5.

Dufresne, A., & Kobasigawa, A. (1989). Children's spontaneous allocation of study time: Differential and sufficient aspects. *Journal of Experimental Child Psychology, 47*, 274–296.

Dukes, R., & Martinez, R. (1994). The impact of gender on self-esteem among adolescents. *Adolescence, 29*, 105–115.

Dulitzki, M., Soriano, D., Schiff, E., Chetrit, A., Mashiach, S., & Seidman, D. S. (1998). Effect of very advanced maternal age on pregnancy outcome and rate of cesarean delivery. *Obstetrics and Gynecology, 92*, 935–939.

Duncan, G. J., & Brooks-Gunn, J. (2000). Family poverty, welfare reform, and child development. *Child Development, 71*, 188–196.

Duncan, G. J., Brooks-Gunn, J., & Klebanov, P. K. (1994). Economic deprivation and early childhood development. *Child Development, 65, Special issue: Children and poverty*, 296–318.

Dunham, R. M., Kidwell, J. S., & Wilson, S. M. (1986). Rites of passage at adolescence: A ritual process paradigm. *Journal of Adolescent Research, 1*, 139–153.

Dunn, E., & Laham, S. (2006). Affective forecasting: A user's guide to emotional time travel. *Affect in social thinking and behavior*. New York: Psychology Press.

Duplassie, D., & Daniluk, J. C. (2007). Sexuality: Young and middle adulthood. In A. Owens & M. Tupper (eds.), *Sexual health: Volume 1, Psychological Foundations*. Westport, CT: Praeger.

Durbin, J. (2003, October 6). Internet sex unzipped. *McCleans*, p. 18.

Durik, A. M., Hyde, J. S., & Clark, R. (2000). Sequelae of cesarean and vaginal deliveries: Psychosocial outcomes for mothers and infants. *Developmental Psychology, 36*, 251–260.

Durkin, K., & Nugent, B. (1998). Kindergarten children's gender-role expectations for television actors. *Sex Roles, 38*, 387–402.

Dutta, T., & Mandal, M. (2006, July). Hand preference and accidents in India. *Laterality: Asymmetries of Body, Brain and Cognition, 11*(4), 368–372.

Dutton, D. G. (1994). *The domestic assault of women: Psychological and criminal justice perspectives* (2nd ed.). Vancouver, BC, Canada: University of British Columbia Press.

Dutton, M. A. (1992). *Empowering and healing the battered woman: A model of assessment and intervention*. New York: Springer.

Dwairy, M., Achoui, M., Abouserie, R., & Farah, A. (2006, May). Parenting styles, individuation, and mental health of Arab adolescents: A third cross-regional research study. *Journal of Cross-Cultural Psychology, 37*, 262–272.

Dweck, C. (2002). The development of ability conceptions. In A. Wigfield Allan & J. Eccles (Eds.), *Development of achievement motivation*. San Diego: Academic Press.

Dyer, C. B., Pavlik, V. N., Murphy, K. P., & Hyman, D. J. (2000). The high prevalence of depression and dementia in elder abuse or neglect. *Journal of the American Geriatrics Society, 48*, 205–208.

Dyregrov, K., Nordanger, D., & Dyregrov, A. (2003). Predictors of psychosocial distress after suicide, SIDS and accidents. *Death Studies, 27*, 143–165.

Dyson, A. H. (2003). "Welcome to the Jam": Popular culture, school literacy and making of childhoods. *Harvard Educational Review, 73*, 328–361.

Eagly, A. H., & Wood, W. (2003). In C. B. Travis (Ed.), *Evolution, gender, and rape*. Cambridge, MA: MIT Press.

Eastman, Q. (2003, June 20). Crib death exoneration could user in new gene tests. *Science, 300*, 1858.

Eaton, W. O., & Enns, L. R. (1986). Sex differences in human motor activity level. *Psychological Bulletin, 100*, 19–28.

Ebersole, J., & Kapp, S. (2007). Stemming the tide of overrepresentation: Ensuring accurate certification of African American students in programs for the mentally retarded. *School Social Work Journal, 31*, 1–16.

Ebner, N., Freund, A., & Baltes, P. (2006, December). Developmental changes in personal goal orientation from young to late adulthood: From striving for gains to maintenance and prevention of losses. *Psychology and Aging, 21*, 664–678.

Ebstein, R. P., Novick, O., Umansky, R., Priel, B., Osher, Y., Blaine, D., Bennett, E. R., Nemanov, L., Katz, M., & Belmaker, R. H. (1996). Dopamine D4 receptor (1996) exon III polymorphism associated with the human personality trait of novelty seeking. *Nature and Genetics, 12*, 78–80.

Eccles, J., Templeton, J., & Barber, B. (2003). Adolescence and emerging adulthood: The critical passage ways to adulthood. In M. Bornstein and L. Davidson (Eds.), *Wellbeing: Positive development across the life course*. Mahwah, NJ: Erlbaum.

Eckerman, C., & Peterman, K. (2001). Peers and infant social/communicative development. In G. Bremner and A. Fogel (Eds.), *Blackwell handbook of infant development* (pp. 326–350). Malden, MA: Blackwell Publishers.

Edwards, C. P. (2000). Children's play in cross-cultural perspective: A new look at the Six Cultures study. *Cross-Cultural Research: The Journal of Comparative Social Science, 34*, 318–338.

Edwards, C., de Guzman, M., Brown, J., & Kumru, A. (2006). Children's social behaviors and peer interactions in diverse cultures. *Peer relationships in cultural context*. New York: Cambridge University Press.

Edwards, S. (2005). Constructivism does not only happen in the individual: Sociocultural theory and early childhood education. *Early Child Development & Care, 175*, 37–47.

Ehrensaft, M., Cohen, P., & Brown, J. (2003). Intergenerational transmission of partner violence: A 20-year prospective study. *Journal of Consulting & Clinical Psychology, 71*, 741–753.

Eichenbaum, H. (2004). Toward an information processing framework for memory representation by the hippocampus. In M. S. Gazzaniga (Ed.), *Cognitive neurosciences* (3rd ed., pp. 679–690). Cambridge, MA: MIT.

Eichstedt, J., Serbin, L., & Poulin-Dubois, D. (2002). Of bears and men: Infants' knowledge of conventional and metaphorical gender stereotypes. *Infant Behavior & Development, 25*, 296–310.

Einbinder, S. D. (1992). A statistical profile of children living in poverty: Children under three and children under six, 1990. Unpublished document from the National Center for Children in Poverty. New York: Columbia University, School of Public Health.

Eisbach, A. O. (2004). Children's developing awareness of diversity in people's trains of thought. *Child Development, 75*, 1694–1707.

Eisenberg, N. (2004). Another slant on moral judgment. *psycCRITQUES*, 12–15.

Eisenberg, N., & Morris, A. (2004). Moral cognitions and prosocial responding in adolescence. In R. Lerner & L. Steinberg (Eds), *Handbook of adolescent psychology*. New York: Wiley.

Eisenberg, N., & Valiente, C. (2002). Parenting and children's prosocial and moral development. In M. Bornstein (Ed), *Handbook of parenting: Vol. 5: Practical issues in parenting*. Mahwah, NJ: Erlbaum.

Eisenberg, N., & Zhou, Q. (2000). Regulation from a developmental perspective. *Psychological Inquiry, 11*, 166–172.

Eisenberg, N., & Fabes, R. A. (2006). Emotion regulation and children's socioemotional competence. In L. Baler & C. S. Tamis-LeMonda, *Child psychology: A handbook of contemporary issues*, (2nd ed.).

Eisenberg, N., Fabes, R., & Spinrad, T. (2006). Prosocial Development. *Handbook of child psychology: Vol. 3, Social, emotional, and personality development* (6th ed.). Hoboken, NJ: John Wiley & Sons Inc.

Eisenberg, N., Guthrie, I. K., Murphy, B. C., Shepard, S. A., Cumberland, A., & Carlo, G. (1999). Consistency and development of prosocial dispositions: A longitudinal study. *Child Development, 70*, 1360–1372.

Eisenberg, N., Spinrad, T. L., & Smith, C. L. (2004). Emotion-related regulation: Its conceptualization, relations to social functioning, and socialization. In P. Philippot, & R. S. Feldman, *The regulation of emotion*. Mahwah, NJ: Lawrence Erlbaum Associates.

Eisenberg, N., Spinrad, T. L., & Sadovsky, A. (2006). Empathy-related responding in children. In M. Killen, & J. G., Smetana, *Handbook of moral development*. Mahwah, NJ: Lawrence Erlbaum Associates.

Eisenberg, N., Valiente, C., & Champion, C. Empathy-related responding: Moral, social, and socialization correlates. In A. G. Miller (Ed.), *Social psychology of good and evil*. New York: Guilford Press.

Eisenbraun, K. (2007). Violence in schools: Prevalence, prediction, and prevention. *Aggression and Violent Behavior, 12*, 459–469.

Eitel, B. J. (2003). *Body image satisfaction, appearance importance, and self-esteem: A comparison of Caucasian and African-American women across the adult lifespan*. Dissertation Abstracts International: Section B: The Sciences & Engineering, 63, p. 5511.

Elder, G. A., De Gasperi, R., & Gama Sosa, M. A. (2006). Research update: neurogenesis in adult brain and neuropsychiatric disorders. *Mt. Sinai Journal of Medicine, 73*, 931–940.

Eley, T. C., Bolton, D., & O'Connor, T. G. (2003). A twin study of anxiety-related behaviours in pre-school children. *Journal of Child Psychology and Psychiatry and Allied Disciplines, 44*, 103–121.

Eley, T. C., Lichtenstein, P., & Moffitt, T. E. (2003). A longitudinal behavioral genetic analysis sof the etiology of aggressive and nonaggressive antisocial behavior. *Development and Psychopathology, 15*, 383–402.

Eley, T., Liang, H., & Plomin, R. (2004). Parental familial vulnerability, family environment, and their interactions as predictors of depressive symptoms in adolescents. *Child & Adolescent Social Work Journal, 21*, 298–306.

Elkind, D. (1978). The children's reality: Three developmental themes. In S. Coren & L. M. Ward (Eds.), *Sensation and perception*. Hillsdale, NJ: Erlbaum.

Elkind, D. (1984). *All grown up and no place to go*. Reading, MA: Addison-Wesley.

Elkind, D. (1985). Egocentrism redux. *Developmental Review, 5,* 218–226.

Elkind, D. (1996). Inhelder and Piaget on adolescence and adulthood: A postmodern appraisal. *Psychological Science, 7,* 216–220.

Elliott, K., & Urquiza, A. (2006). Ethnicity, culture, and child maltreatment. *Journal of Social Issues, 62,* 787–809.

Ellis, B. J. (2004). Timing of pubertal maturation in girls: An integrated life history approach. *Psychological Bulletin, 130,* 920–958.

Ellis, L. (2006, July). Gender differences in smiling: An evolutionary neuroandrogenic theory. *Physiology & Behavior, 88,* 303–308.

Ellis, L., & Engh, T. (2000). Handedness and age of death: New evidence on a puzzling relationship. *Journal of Health Psychology, 5,* 561–565.

Ellis, S., & Siegler, R. S. (1997). Planning and strategy choice, or why don't children plan when they should? In S. L. Friedman & E. K. Scholnick (Eds.), *Why, how, and when do we plan: The developmental psychology of planning.* Hillsdale, NJ: Lawrence Erlbaum Associates.

Ellis, W., & Zarbatany, L. (2007). Peer group status as a moderator of group influence on children's deviant, aggressive, and prosocial behavior. *Child Development, 78,* 1240–1254.

Emack, J., Kostaki, A., Walker, C., & Matthews, S. (2008). Chronic maternal stress affects growth, behaviour and hypothalamo-pituitary-adrenal function in juvenile offspring. *Hormones and Behavior, 54,* 514–520.

Emery, R. E., & Laumann-Billings, L. (1998). An overview of the nature, causes, and consequences of abusive family relationships: Toward differentiating maltreatment and violence. *American Psychologist, 53,* 121–135.

Endo, S. (1992). Infant–infant play from 7 to 12 months of age: An analysis of games in infant–peer triads. *Japanese Journal of Child and Adolescent Psychiatry, 33,* 145–162.

Endocrine Society, The (2001, March 1). *The Endocrine Society and Lawson Wilkins Pediatric Endocrine Society call for further research to define precocious puberty.* Bethesda, MD: The Endocrine Society.

Engels, R., Kerr, M., & Stattin, H. (2007). *Friends, lovers and groups: Key relationships in adolescence.* New York: John Wiley & Sons Ltd.

Englund, K., & Behne, D. (2006). Changes in infant directed speech in the first six months. *Infant and Child Development, 15*(2), 139–160.

Englund, M. M., Levy, A. K., Hyson, D. M., & Sroufe, L. A. (2000). Adolescent social competence: Effectiveness in a group setting. *Child Development, 71,* 1049–1060.

Ennett, S. T., & Bauman, K. E. (1996). Adolescent social networks: School, demographic, and longitudinal considerations. *Journal of Adolescent Research, 11,* 194–215.

Enright, E. (2004, July & August). A house divided. *AARP Magazine,* pp. 54, 57.

Ensenauer, R. E., Michels, V. V., & Reinke, S. S. (2005). Genetic testing: Practical, ethical, and counseling considerations. *Mayo Clinic Proceedings, 80,* 63–73.

Epperson, S. E. (1988, September 16). Studies link subtle sex bias in schools with women's behavior in the workplace. *Wall Street Journal,* p. 19.

Erber, J. T., Rothberg, S. T., & Szuchman, L. T. (1991). Appraisal of everyday memory failures by middle-aged adults. *Educational Gerontology, 17,* 63–72.

Erikson, E. H. (1963). *Childhood and society.* New York: Norton.

Essex, M. J., & Nam, S. (1987). Marital status and loneliness among older women: The differential importance of close family and friends. *Journal of Marriage and the Family, 49,* 92–106.

Evans, G. W. (2004). The environment of childhood poverty. *American Psychologist, 59,* 77–92.

Everson, M., & Boat, B. (2002). The utility of anatomical dolls and drawings in child forensic interviews. *Memory and suggestibility in the forensic interview.* Mahwah, NJ: Lawrence Erlbaum Associates Publishers.

Fagan, J., Holland, C., & Wheeler, K. (2007). The prediction, from infancy, of adult IQ and achievement. *Intelligence, 35,* 225–231.

Faith, M. S., Johnson, S. L., & Allison, D. B. (1997). Putting the behavior into the behavior genetics of obesity. *Behavior Genetics, 27,* 423–439.

Falck-Ytter, T., Gredeback, G., & von Hofsten, C. (2006). Infants predict other people's action goals. *Nature and Neuroscience, 9,* 878–879.

Falk, D. (2004). Prelinguistic evolution in early hominins: Whence motherese? *Behavioral and Brain Sciences 27,* 491–503.

Families and Work Institute. (1998). *Report on men spending more time with kids.* Washington, DC: Author.

Fangman, J. J., Mark, P. M., Pratt, L., Conway, K. K., Healey, M. L., Oswald, J. W., & Uden, D. L. (1994). *American Journal of Obstetrical Gynecology, 170,* 744–750.

Fantz, R. (1963). Pattern vision in newborn infants. *Science, 140,* 296–297.

Fantz, R. L. (1961). The origin of form perception. *Scientific American,* p. 72.

Farah, M., Shera, D., Savage, J., Betancourt, L., Giannetta, J., Brodsky, N., et al. (2006, September). Childhood poverty: Specific associations with neurocognitive development. *Brain Research, 1110,* 166–174.

Farmer, T. W., Estell, D. B., Bishop, J. L., O'Neal, K. K., & Cairns, B. D. (2003). Rejected bullies or popular leaders? The social relations of aggressive subtypes of rural African American early adolescents. *Developmental Psychology, 39,* 992–1004.

Farver, J. M., Welles-Nystrom, B., Frosch, D. L., & Wimbarti, S. (1997). Toy stories: Aggression in children's narratives in the United States, Sweden, Germany, and Indonesia. *Journal of Cross-Cultural Psychology, 28,* 393–420.

Faulkner, G., & Biddle, S. (2004). Exercise and depression: Considering variability and contextuality. *Journal of Sport & Exercise Psychology, 26,* 3–18.

Federal Interagency Forum on Age-Related Statistics. (2000). *Older Americans 2000: Key indicators of well-being.* Hyattsville, MD: Federal Interagency Forum on Age-Related Statistics.

Federal Interagency Forum on Child and Family Statistics. (2003). *America's Children: Key National Indicators of Well-Being, 2003.* Federal Interagency Forum on Child and Family Statistics, Washington, DC: U.S. Government Printing Office.

Feeney, B., & Collins, N. (2001). Predictors of caregiving in adult intimate relationships: An attachment theoretical perspective. *Journal of Personality & Social Psychology, 80,* 972–994.

Feinberg, A. W. (2000, October). Questions and answers. *HealthNews,* p. 10.

Feist, G., & Barron, F. (2003). Predicting creativity from early to late adulthood: Intellect, potential, and personality. *Journal of Research in Personality, 37,* 62–88.

Feldhusen, J. (2003). Precocity and acceleration. *Gifted Education International, 17,* 55–58.

Feldhusen, J. F. (2003). Lewis M. Terman: A pioneer in the development of ability tests. In B. J. Zimmerman, *Educational psychology: A century of contributions.* Mahwah, NJ: Erlbaum.

Feldhusen, J. F. (2006). The role of the knowledge base in creative thinking. In J. C. Kaufman & J. Baer, *Creativity and reason in cognitive development.* New York: Cambridge University Press.

Feldman, R. S. (Ed.). (1992). *Applications of nonverbal behavioral theories and research.* Hillsdale, NJ: Erlbaum.

Feldman, R. S., Forrest, J. A., & Happ, B.R. (2002.) Self-presentation and verbal deception: Do self-presenters lie more? *Basic and Applied Social Psychology, 24,* 163–170.

Feldman, R. S., Tomasian, J., & Coats, E. J. (1999). Adolescents' social competence and nonverbal deception abilities: Adolescents with higher social skills are better liars. *Journal of Nonverbal Behavior, 23,* 237–249.

Feldman, R., & Eidelman, A. (2003). Direct and indirect effects of breast milk on neurobehavioral and cognitive development of premature infants. *Developmental Psychobiology, 43,* 109–119.

Feldman, R., & Masalha, S. (2007). The role of culture in moderating the links between early ecological risk and young children's adaptation. *Development and Psychopathology, 19,* 1–21.

Feldman, R., Sussman, A., & Zigler, E. (2004). Parental leave and work adaptation at the transition to parenthood: Individual, marital, and social correlates. *Journal of Applied Developmental Psychology, 25,* 459–479.

Feldman, R. S. (2009). *The liar in your life.* New York: Twelve.

Fenson, L., Dale, P. S., Reznick, J. S., Bates, E., Thal, D. J., & Pethick, S. J. (1994). Variability in early communicative development. *Monographs of the Society for Research in Child Development, 59* (5, Serial No. 242).

Fenwick, K., & Morrongiello, B. (1991). Development of frequency perception in infants and children. *Journal of Speech, Language Pathology, and Audiology, 15,* 7–22.

Fenwick, K. D., & Morrongiello, B. A. (1998). Spatial co-location and infants' learning of auditory–visual associations. *Behavior & Development, 21,* 745–759.

Ferguson, S. (2007). *Shifting the center: Understanding contemporary families* (3rd ed.). New York: McGraw-Hill.

Fergusson, D. M., Horwood, L. J., & Ridder, E. M. (2006). Abortion in young women and subsequent mental health. *Journal of Child Psychology and Psychiatry, 47,* 16–24.

Fergusson, D., Horwood, L., Boden, J., & Jenkin, G. (2007, March). Childhood social disadvantage and smoking in adulthood: Results of a 25-year longitudinal study. *Addiction, 102,* 475–482.

Fernald, A. (2001). Hearing, listening, and understanding: Auditory development in infancy. In G. Bremner & A. Fogel (Eds.), *Blackwell handbook of infant development.* Malden, MA: Blackwell Publishers.

Fernald, A., & Morikawa, H. (1993). Common themes and cultural variations in Japanese and American mothers' speech to infants. *Child Development, 64,* 637–656.

Fernald, A., Taeschner, T., Dunn, J., Papousek, M., Boysson-Bardies, B., & Fukui, I. (1989). A cross-language study of prosodic modifications in mothers' and fathers' speech to preverbal infants. *Journal of Child Language, 16,* 477–501.

Fernald, A., Taeschner, T., Dunn, J., Papousek, M., Boysson-Bardies, B., & Fukui, I. (1998). A cross-language study of prosodic modifications in mothers' and fathers' speech to preverbal infants. *Journal of Child Language, 16,* 477–501.

Fernyhough, C. (1997). Vygotsky's sociocultural approach: Theoretical issues and implications for current research. In S. Hala (Ed.), *The development of social cognition* (pp. 65–92). Hove, England: Psychology Press/Erlbaum, Taylor & Francis.

Ferrario, S., Vitaliano, P., & Zotti, A. (2003). Alzheimer's disease: Usefulness of the Family Strain Questionnaire and the Screen for Caregiver Burden in the study of caregiving-related problems. *International Journal of Geriatric Psychiatry, 18,* 1110–1114.

Festinger, L. (1954). A theory of social comparison processes. *Human Relations, 7,* 117–140.

Fetterman, D. M. (1998). Ethnography. In L. Bickman & D. J. Rog (Eds.), *Handbook of applied social research methods* (pp. 473–504). Thousand Oaks, CA: Sage.

Fetterman, D. M. (2005). Empowerment evaluation: From the digital divide to academic distsress. In D. Fetterman & A. Wandersman, *Empowerment evaluation principles in practice.* New York: Guilford Press.

Fiatarone, M. S. A., & Garnett, L. R. (1997, March). Keep on keeping on. *Harvard Health Letter,* pp. 4–5.

Field, D. (2007). Death and dying. *Sociology of health and health care* (4th ed.) (pp. 181–203). Malden, MA: Blackwell Publishing.

Field, D., & Minkler, M. (1988). Continuity and change in social support between young-old and old-old or very-old age. *Journal of Gerontology, 43*(4), 100–106.

Field, M. J., & Behrman, R. E. (Eds.). (2003). *When children die.* Washington, DC: National Academies Press.

Field, T. (2001). Massage therapy facilitates weight gain in preterm infants. *Current Directions in Psychological Science, 10,* 51–54.

Field, T., Diego, M., & Hernandez-Reif, M. (2006). Prenatal depression effects on the fetus and newborn: A review. *Infant Behavior & Development, 29,* 445–455.

Fields, J., & Casper, L.M. (2001). *America's Families and Living Arrangements: March 2000.* Current Population Reports P20–537. Washington, DC: U.S Census Bureau.

Fincham, F. D. (2003). Marital conflict: Correlates, structure, and context. *Current Directions in Psychological Science, 12,* 23–27.

Fingerhut, L. A., & Kleinman, J. C. (1990). International and interstate comparisons of homicide among young males. *Journal of the American Medical Association, 263,* 3292–3295.

Fingerhut, L. A., & MaKuc, D. M. (1992). Mortality among minority populations in the United States. *American Journal of Public Health, 82,* 1168–1170.

Finkel, D., Pedersen, N., Reynolds, C., Berg, S., de Faire, U., & Svartengren, M. (2003). Genetic and environmental influences on decline in biobehavioral markers of aging. *Behavior Genetics, 33,* 107–123.

Finkelhor, D. (1997). The homicides of children and youth: A developmental perspective. In G. K. Kantor & J. L. Janinski (Ed.), *Out of the darkness: Contemporary perspectives on family violence* (pp. 17–34). Thousand Oaks, CA: Sage.

Finn, C. (2008). Neuropsychiatric aspects of genetic disorders. *Psychiatric genetics: Applications in clinical practice.* Arlington, VA: American Psychiatric Publishing, Inc.

Finnegan, L., & Kandall, S. (2008). Perinatal substance abuse. *The American Psychiatric Publishing textbook of substance abuse treatment* (4th ed.). Arlington, VA: American Psychiatric Publishing, Inc.

Fischer, K. W., & Hencke, R. W. (1996). Infants' construction of actions in context: Piaget's contributions to research on early development. *Psychological Science, 7,* 204–210.

Fischer, K. W., & Rose, S. P. (1995). Concurrent cycles in the dynamic development of brain and behavior. *Newsletter of the Society for Research in Child Development,* p. 16.

Fish, J. M. (Ed.). (2001). *Race and intelligence: Separating science from myth.* Mahwah, NJ: Erlbaum.

Fishel, E. (1993, September). Starting kindergarten. *Parents,* pp. 165–169.

Fisher, C. (2005). Deception research involving children: Ethical practices and paradoxes. *Ethics & Behavior, 15,* 271–287.

Fisher, C. B. (2003). *Decoding the ethics code: A practical guide for psychologists.* Thousand Oaks, CA: Sage Publications.

Fisher, C. B. (2004). Informed Consent and Clinical Research Involving Children and Adolescents: Implications of the Revised APA Ethics Code and HIPAA. *Journal of Clinical Child & Adolescent Psychology, 33,* 832–839.

Fiske, S. T. (2001). Effects of power on bias: Power explains and maintains individual, group, and societal disparities. In A. Y. Lee-Chai & J. A. Bargh, *Multiple perspectives on the causes of corruption.* New York: Psychology Press.

Fiske, S., & Yamamoto, M. (2005). Coping with rejection: Core social motives across cultures. *The social outcast: Ostracism, social exclusion, rejection, and bullying* (pp. 185–198). New York: Psychology Press.

Fitzgerald, D., & White, K. (2002). Linking children's social worlds: Perspective-taking in parent-child and peer contexts. *Social Behavior & Personality, 31,* 509–522.

Fivush, R., Kuebli, J., & Clubb, P. A. (1992). The structure of events and event representations: A developmental analysis. *Child Development, 63,* 188–201.

Flavell, J. H. (1994). Cognitive development: Past, present, and future. In R. D. Parke, P. A. Ornstein, J. J. Rieser, & C. Zahn-Waxler (Eds.), *A century of developmental psychology.* Washington, DC: American Psychological Association.

Flavell, J. H. (1996). Piaget's legacy. *Psychological Science, 7,* 200–203.

Flavell, J. H., Friedrichs, A. G., & Hoyt, J. D. (1970). Developmental changes in memorization processes. *Cognitive Psychology, 1,* 324–340.

Flegal, K., Tabak, C., & Ogden, C. (2006). Overweight in children: Definitions and interpretation. *Health Education Research, 21,* 755–760.

Flom, R., & Bahrick, L. (2007). The development of infant discrimination of affect in multimodal and unimodal stimulation: The role of intersensory redundancy. *Developmental Psychology, 43,* 238–252.

Flor, D. L., & Knap, N. F. (2001). Transmission and transaction: Predicting adolescents' internalization of parental religious values. *Journal of FamilyPsychology, 15,* 627–645.

Florian, V., & Kravetz, S. (1985). Children's concepts of death: A cross-cultural comparison among Muslims, Druze, Christians, and Jews in Israel. *Journal of Cross-Cultural Psychology, 16,* 174–189.

Florsheim, P. (2003). Adolescent romantic and sexual behavior: What we know and where we go from here. In P. Florsheim (Ed.), *Adolescent romantic relations and sexual behavior: Theory, research, and practical implications.* Mahwah, NJ: Erlbaum.

Flynn, E., O'Malley, C., & Wood, D. (2004). A longitudinal, microgenetic study of the emergence of false belief understanding and inhibition skills. *Developmental Science, 7,* 103–115.

Fogel, A., de Koeyer, I., & Bellagamba, F. (2002). The dialogical self in the first two years of life: Embarking on a journey of discovery. *Theory & Psychology, 12,* 191–205.

Fogel, A., Hsu, H., Shapiro, A., Nelson-Goens, G., & Secrist, C. (2006, May). Effects of normal and perturbed social play on the duration and amplitude of different types of infant smiles. *Developmental Psychology, 42,* 459–473.

Fok, M. S. M., & Tsang, W.Y.W. (2006). 'Development of an instrument measuring Chinese adolescent beliefs and attitudes towards substance use': Response to commentary. *Journal of Clinical Nursing, 15,* 1062–1063.

Folkman, S., & Lazarus, R. (1990). Coping and emotion. *Psychological and biological approaches to emotion.* Hillsdale, NJ, England: Lawrence Erlbaum Associates, Inc.

Folkman, S., & Lazarus, R. S. (1988). Coping as a mediator of emotion. *Journal of Personality and Social Psychology, 54,* 466–475.

Food and Drug Administration. (2003). Birth control guide. Retrieved April 1, 2006 from http://www.fda.gov/fdac/features/1997/babyguide2.pdf

Forrester, M. (2001). The embedding of the self in early interaction. *Infant & Child Development, 10,* 189–202.

Fowers, B. J., & Davidov, B. J. (2006). The virtue of multiculturalism: Personal transformation, character, and openness to the other. *American Psychologist, 61,* 581–594.

Fowler, C. A. (1990). Calling a mirage a mirage: Direct perception of speech produced without a tongue. *Journal of Phonetics 18,* 529–541.

Fowler, J. W., & Dell, M. L. (2006). Stages of faith from infancy through adolescence: Reflections on three decades of faith development theory. In E. C. Roehlkepartain, et al., *The handbook of spiritual development in childhood and adolescence.* Thousand Oaks, CA: Sage Publications.

Fowler, J. W., & Dell, M. L. (2006). Stages of Faith From Infancy Through Adolescence: Reflections on Three Decades of Faith Development Theory. In E. C. Roehlkepartain, P. E. King, L. Wagener, & P. L. Benson, (Eds). *The handbook of spiritual development in childhood and adolescence.* Thousand Oaks, CA: Sage Publications.

Fox, M., Pac, S., Devaney, B., & Jankowski L. (2004). Feeding infants and toddlers study: What foods are infants and toddlers eating? *Journal of the American Dietetic Association, 104,* 22–30.

Fozard, J. L., Vercruyssen, M., Reynolds, S. L., Hancock, P. A., et al. (1994). Age differences and changes in reaction time: The Baltimore Longitudinal Study of Aging. *Journal of Gerontology, 49,* 179–189.

Fraley, R. C. (2002). Attachment stability from infancy to adulthood: Meta-analysis and dynamic modeling of developmental mechanisms. *Personality and Social Psychology Review, 6,* 123–151.

Fraley, R. C., & Spieker, S. J. (2003). Are infant attachment patters continuously or categorically distributed? A taxometric analysis of Strange Situation behavior. *Developmental Psychology, 39,* 387–404.

Frankel, L. (2002). 'I've never thought about it': Contradictions and taboos surrounding American males' experiences of first ejaculation (semenarche). *The Journal of Men's Studies, 11,* 37–54.

Frankel, M., & Chapman, A. (2000). *Human inheritable genetic modifications: Assessing scientific, ethical, religious, and policy issues.* Washington, DC: American Association for the Advancement of Science.

Frankenburg, W. K., Dodds, J., Archer, P., Maschka, P., Edelman, N., & Shapiro, H. (1992). *The Denver II training manual.* Denver, CO: Denver Developmental Materials.

Franko, D., & Striegel-Moore, R. (2002). The role of body dissatisfaction as a risk factor for depression in adolescent girls: Are the differences Black and White? *Journal of Psychosomatic Research, 53,* 975–983.

Fransen, M., Meertens, R., & Schrander-Stumpel, C. (2006). Communication and risk presentation in genetic counseling: Development of a checklist. *Patient Education and Counseling, 61,* 126–133.

Frazier, L. M., Grainger, D. A., Schieve, L. A., & Toner, J. P. (2004). Follicle-stimulating hormone and estradiol levels independently predict the success of assisted reproductive technology treatment. *Fertility and Sterility, 82,* 834–840.

Fredriksen, K., Rhodes, J., Reddy, R., & Way, N. (2004). Sleepless in Chicago: Tracking the effects of adolescent sleep loss during the middle school years. *Child Development, 75,* 84–95.

Freedman, A. M., & Ellison, S. (2004, May 6). Testosterone patch for women shows promise. *Wall Street Journal,* pp. A1, B2.

Freedman, D. G. (1979, January). Ethnic differences in babies. *Human Nature,* pp. 15–20.

Freedman, D. S., Khan, L. K., Serdula, M. K., Dietz, W. H., Sriniasan, S. R., & Berenson, G. S. (2004). Inter-relationships among childhood BMI, childhood height, and adult obesity: The Bogalusa Heart Study. *International Journal of Obesity and Related Metabolic Disorders, 28,* 10–16.

Freeman, E., Sammel, M., & Liu, L. (2004). Hormones and menopausal status as predictors of depression in women in transition to menopause. *Archives of General Psychiatry, 61,* 62–70.

Freiberg P. (1998, February). President's AIDS budget wins kudos. *Newsline/People with AIDS Coalition of New York,* 23–44.

Freiberg, P. (1998 February). We know how to stop the spread of AIDS: So why can't we? *APA Monitor,* 32.

Frerking, B. (2006). I'm gonna keep that gray. *Slate.* Retrieved from http://www.slate.com/id/2147054/

Freud, S. (1920). *A general introduction to psychoanalysis.* New York: Boni & Liveright.

Freud, S. (1922/1959). *Group psychology and the analysis of the ego.* London: Hogarth.

Friborg, O., Barlaug, D., Martinussen, M., Rosenvinge, J. H., & Hjemdal, O. (2005). Resilience in relation to personality and intelligence. *International Journal of Methods in Psychiatric Research, 14,* 29–42.

Fried, P. A., & Watkinson, B. (1990). 36- and 48-month neurobehavioral follow-up of children prenatally exposed to marijuana, cigarettes, and alcohol. *Developmental and Behavioral Pediatrics, 11,* 49–58.

Friedland, R. (2003). Fish consumption and the risk of Alzheimer disease: Is it time to make dietary recommendations? *Archives of Neurology, 60,* 923–924.

Friedlander, L., Connolly, J., Pepler, D., & Craig, W. (2007). Biological, familial, and peer influences on dating in early adolescence. *Archives of Sexual Behavior, 36,* 821–830.

Friedman, D. E. (2004). *The new economics of preschool.* Washington, DC: Early Childhood Funders' Collaborative/NAEYC.

Friedman, L., Kahn, J., Middleman, A., Rosenthal, S., & Zimet, G. (2006, October). Human papillomavirus (HPV) vaccine: A position statement of the society for adolescent medicine. *Journal of Adolescent Health, 39,* 620–620.

Frishman, R. (1996, October). Hormone replacement therapy for men. *Harvard Health Letter,* pp. 6–8.

Frome, P., Alfeld, C., Eccles, J., & Barber, B. (2006, August). Why don't they want a male-dominated job? An investigation of young women who changed their occupational aspirations. *Educational Research and Evaluation, 12,* 359–372.

Fry, D. (2005). Rough-and-tumble social play in humans. *The nature of play: Great apes and humans.* New York: Guilford Press.

Fu, G., Xu, F., Cameron, C., Heyman, G., & Lee, K. (2007, March). Cross-cultural differences in children's choices, categorizations, and evaluations of truths and lies. *Developmental Psychology, 43*(2), 278–293.

Fulgini, A. J. (1998). The adjustment of children from immigrant families. *Current Directions in Psychological Science, 7,* 99–103.

Fuligni, A. J., Tseng, V., & Lam, M. (1999). Attitudes toward family obligations among American adolescents with Asian, Latin American, and European backgrounds. *Child Development, 70,* 1030–1044.

Fuligni, A., & Hardway, C. (2006, September). Daily variation in adolescents' sleep, activities, and psychological well-being. *Journal of Research on Adolescence, 16,* 353–378.

Fuligni, A., & Yoshikawa, H. (2003). Socioeconomic resources, parenting, and child development among immigrant families. In M. Bornstein & R. Bradley (Eds.), *Socioeconomic status, parenting, and child development.* Mahwah, NJ: Erlbaum.

Funk, J., Buchman, D., & Jenks, J. (2003). Playing violent video games, desensitization, and moral evaluation in children. *Journal of Applied Developmental Psychology, 24,* 413–436.

Furman, W., & Shaffer, L. (2003). The role of romantic relationships in adolescent development. In P. Florsheim (Ed), *Adolescent romantic relations and sexual behavior: Theory, research, and practical implications.* Mahwah, NJ: Erlbaum.

Furstenberg, F. F., Jr. (1996, June). The future of marriage. *American Demographics,* pp. 34–40.

Gagnon, S. G., & Nagle, R. J. (2000). Comparison of the revised and original versions of the Bayley Scales of Infant Development. *School Psychology International, 21,* 293–305.

Galambos, N., Leadbeater, B., & Barker, E. (2004). Gender differences in and risk factors for depression in adolescence: A 4-year longitudinal study. *International Journal of Behavioral Development, 28,* 16–25.

Galbraith, K. M, & Dobson, K. S. (2000). The role of the psychologist in determining competence for assisted suicide/euthanasia in the terminally ill. *Canadian Psychology, 41,* 174–183.

Galic, Z. (2007). Psychological consequences of unemployment: The moderating role of education. *Review of Psychology, 14,* 25–34.

Gallagher, J. J. (1994). Teaching and learning: New models. *Annual Review of Psychology, 45,* 171–195.

Galluccio, L., & Rovee-Collier, C. (2006). Nonuniform effects of reinstatement within the time window. *Learning and Motivation, 37,* 1–17.

Gallup Poll. (2004). How many children? *The Gallup Poll Monthly.*

Gallup, G. G., Jr. (1977). Self-recognition in primates: A comparative approach to the bidirectional properties of consciousness. *American Psychologist, 32,* 329–337.

Ganzini, L., Beer, T., & Brouns, M. (2006, September). Views on physician-assisted suicide among family members of Oregon cancer patients. *Journal of Pain and Symptom Management, 32,* 230–236.

Garcia, C., Baker, S., DeMayo, R., & Brown, G. (2005). Gestalt educational therapy. *Gestalt therapy: History, theory, and practice.* Thousand Oaks, CA: Sage Publications, Inc.

Garcia, S. D. (1998). Appearance anxiety, health practices, metaperspectives and self-perception of physical attractiveness. *Journal of Social Behavior & Personality, 13,* 307–318.

Garcia-Moreno, C., Heise, L., Jansen, H. A. F. M., Ellsberg, M., & Watts, C. (2005, November 25). Violence against women. *Science, 310,* 1282–1283.

Gardner, H. (2000). *Intelligence reframed: Multiple intelligences for the 21st century.* New York: Basic Books.

Gardner, H. (2003). Three distinct meanings of intelligence. In R. Sternberg & J. Lautrey (Eds.), *Models of intelligence: International perspectives.* Washington, DC: American Psychological Association.

Gardner, H., & Moran, S. (2006). The science of multiple intelligences theory: A response to Lynn Waterhouse. *Educational Psychologist, 41,* 227–232.

Gardner, H., & Perkins, D. (1989). *Art, mind, and education: Research from Project Zero.* Champaign, IL: University of Illinois Press.

Garlick, D. (2003). Integrating brain science research with intelligence research. *Current Directions in Psychological Science, 12,* 185–189.

Gartstein, M., Slobodskaya, H., & Kinsht, I. (2003). Cross-cultural differences in temperament in the first year of life: United States of America (US) and Russia. *International Journal of Behavioral Development, 27,* 316–328.

Gatz, M. (1997, August). *Variations of depression in later life.* Paper presented at the Annual Convention of the American Psychological Association, Chicago.

Gaulden, M. E. (1992). Maternal age effect: The enigma of Down syndrome and other trisomic conditions. *Mutation Research, 296,* 69–88.

Gauthier, Y. (2003). Infant mental health as we enter the third millennium: Can we prevent aggression? *Infant Mental Health Journal, 24,* 101–109.

Gauvain, M. (1998). Cognitive development in social and cultural context. *Current Directions in Psychological Science, 7,* 188–194.

Gavin, L. A., & Furman, W. (1996). Adolescent girls' relationships with mothers and best friends. *Child Development, 67,* 375–386.

Gavin, T., & Myers, A. (2003). Characteristics, enrollment, attendance, and dropout patterns of older adults in beginner Tai-Chi and line-dancing programs. *Journal of Aging & Physical Activity, 11,* 123–141.

Gawande, A. (2007, April 30). The way we age now. *The New Yorker,* 49–59.

Gazmararian, J. A., Petersen, R., Spitz, A. M., Goodwin, M. M., Saltzman, L. E., & Marks, J. S. (2000). Violence and reproductive health: Current knowledge and future research directions. *Mat Child Health, 4,* 79–84.

Geary, D. (2006). An evolutionary perspective on sexual and intimate relationships. *Sex and sexuality, Vol 2: Sexual function and dysfunction* (pp. 67–86). Westport, CT: Praeger Publishers/Greenwood Publishing Group.

Geary, D. C. (1998). *Male, female: The evolution of human sex differences.* Washington, DC: APA Books.

Gee, H. (2004). *Jacob's ladder: The history of the human genome.* New York: Norton.

Gelfand, M. M. (2000). Sexuality among older women. *Journal of Womens Health & Gender-Based Medicine, 9,* (Suppl 1), S-15-S-20.

Gelles, R. J. (1994). *Contemporary families.* Newbury Park, CA: Sage.

Gelman, D. (1994, April 18). The mystery of suicide. *Newsweek,* 44–49.

Gelman, R., & Gallistel, C. R. (2004, October 15). Language and the origin of numerical concepts. *Science, 306,* 441–443.

Gelman, S. A., Taylor, M. G., & Nguyen, S. (2004). Mother-child conversations about gender. *Monographs of the Society for Research in Child Development, 69.*

General Social Survey. (1998). *National Opinion Research Center.* Chicago: University of Chicago.

Genovese, J. (2006). Piaget, pedagogy, and evolutionary psychology. *Evolutionary Psychology, 4,* 127–137.

Gentilucci, M., & Corballis, M. (2006). From manual gesture to speech: A gradual transition. *Neuroscience & Biobehavioral Reviews, 30,* 949–960.

Gerard, C. M., Harris, K. A., & Thach, B. T. (2002). Spontaneous arousals in supine infants while swaddled and unswaddled during rapid eye movement and quiet sleep. *Pediatrics, 110,* 70.

Gerber, M. S. (October 9, 2002). Eighty million strong—the singles lobby. *The Hill,* p. 45.

Gerber, P., & Coffman, K. (2007). Nonaccidental head trauma in infants. *Childs Nervous System, 23,* 499–507.

Gergely, G. (2007). The social construction of the subjective self: The role of affect-mirroring, markedness, and ostensive communication in self-development. *Developmental science and psychoanalysis: Integration and innovation.* London: Karnac Books.

Gerhardt, P. (1999, August 10). Potty training: How did it get so complicated? *Daily Hampshire Gazette,* p. C1.

Gershoff, E. (2002). Corporal punishment by parents and associated child behaviors and experiences: A meta-analytic and theoretical review. *Psychological Bulletin, 128,* 539–579.

Gershoff, E. T. (2002). Parental corporal punishment and associated child behaviors and experiences: A meta-analytic and theoretical review. *Pychological Bulletin, 128,* 539–579.

Gersten, R., & Dimino, J. (2006, January). RTI (Response to Intervention): Rethinking special education for students with reading difficulties (yet again). *Reading Research Quarterly, 41,* 99–108.

Geschwind, D., & Iacoboni, M. (2007). Structural and functional asymmetries of the human frontal lobes. In B. L. Miller & J. L. Cummings (Eds.), *The human frontal lobes: Functions and disorders.* New York: Guilford Press.

Gesell, A. L. (1946). The ontogenesis of infant behavior. In L. Carmichael (Ed.), *Manual of child psychology.* New York: Harper.

Giacobbi, P., Lynn, T., & Wetherington, J. (2004). Stress and coping during the transition to university for first-year female athletes. *Sport Psychologist, 18,* 1–20.

Gibbs, N. (2002, April 15). Making time for a baby. *Time,* pp. 48–54.

Gibson, E. J., & Walk, R. D. (1960). The "visual cliff." *Scientific American, 202,* 64–71.

Gifford-Smith, M., & Brownell, C. (2003). Childhood peer relationships: Social acceptance, friendships, and peer networks. *Journal of School Psychology, 41,* 235–284.

Gilbert, D. T., Miller, A. G., & Ross, L. (1998). Speeding with Ned: A personal view of the correspondence bias. In J. M. Darley, J. Cooper et al. (Eds.), *Attribution and social interaction: The legacy of Edward E. Jones.* Washington, DC: American Psychological Association.

Gilbert, D.T., McNulty, S.E., Giuliano, T.A., & Benson, J.E. (1992). Blurry words and fuzzy deeds: The attribution of obscure behavior. *Journal of Personaltiy and Social psychology, 62,* 18–25.

Gilbert, S. (2004, March 16). New clues to women veiled in black. *New York Times,* pp. D1.

Gilbert, W. M., Nesbitt, T. S., & Danielsen, B. (1999). Childbearing beyond age 40: Pregnancy outcome in 24,032 cases. *Obstetrics and Gynecology, 93,* 9–14.

Giles-Sims, J., & Lockhart, C. (2005). Culturally shaped patterns of disciplining children. *Journal of Family Issues, 26,* 196–218.

Gillespie, N. A., Cloninger, C., R., & Heath, A. C. (2003). The genetic and environmental relationship between Cloninger's dimensions of temperament and character. *Personality and Individual Differences, 35,* 1931–1946.

Gillies, R., & Boyle, M. (2006, May). Ten Australian elementary teachers' discourse and reported pedagogical practices during cooperative learning. *Elementary School Journal, 106,* 429–451.

Gilligan, C. (1982). *In a different voice: Psychological theory and women's development.* Cambridge, MA: Harvard University Press.

Gilligan, C. (1987). Adolescent development reconsidered. In C. E. Irwin (Ed.), *Adolescent social behavior and health.* San Francisco: Jossey-Bass.

Gilligan, C., Lyons, N. P., & Hammer, T. J. (Eds.). (1990). *Making connections.* Cambridge, MA: Harvard University Press.

Gilligan, C., Ward, J. V., & Taylor, J. M. (Eds.). (1988). *Mapping the moral domain: A contribution of women's thinking to psychological theory and education.* Cambridge, MA: Harvard University Press.

Gilliland, A. L., & Verny, T. R. (1999). The effects of domestic abuse on the unborn child. *Journal of Prenatal and Perinatal Psychology and Health, Special Issue,13,* 235–246.

Gillmore, M., Gilchrist, L., Lee, J., & Oxford, M. (2006, August). Women who gave birth as unmarried adolescents: Trends in substance use from adolescence to adulthood. *Journal of Adolescent Health, 39,* 237–243.

Giordana, S. (2005). *Understanding eating disorders: Conceptual and ethical issues in the treatment of anorexia (Issues in Biomedical Ethics).* New York: Oxford University Press.

Gitlin, L., Reever, K., Dennis, M., Mathieu, E., & Hauck, W. (2006, October). Enhancing quality of life of families who use adult day services: Short- and long-term effects of the Adult Day Services Plus Program. *The Gerontologist, 46,* 630–639.

Gleason, J. B., Perlmann, R. U., Ely, R., & Evans, D. W. (1991). The babytalk register: Parents' use of diminutives. In J. L. Sokolov, & C. E. Snow (Eds.), *Handbook of research in language development using CHILDES.* Hillsdale, NJ: Erlbaum.

Gleason, J. B., Perlmann, R. U., Ely, R., & Evans, D. W. (1994). The babytalk register: Parents' use of diminutives. In J. L. Sokolov & C. E. Snow (Eds.), *Handbook of research in language development using CHILDES.* Mahwah, NJ: Erlbaum.

Gleason, J., & Ely, R. (2002). Gender differences in language development. In A. McGillicuddy-De Lisi & R. De Lisi (Eds.), *Biology, society, and behavior: The development of sex differences in cognition* (pp. 127–154). Westport, CT: Ablex Publishing.

Gleason, M., Iida, M., & Bolger, N. (2003). Daily supportive equity in close relationships. *Personality & Social Psychology Bulletin, 29,* 10361–045.

Gleitman, L., & Landau, B. (1994). *The acquisition of the lexicon.* Cambridge, MA: Bradford.

Gleitman, L., & Papafragou, A. (2005). Language and thought. *The Cambridge handbook of thinking and reasoning.* New York: Cambridge University Press.

Glick, P., Zion, C., & Nelson, C. (1988). What mediates sex discrimination in hiring decisions? *Journal of Personality and Social Psychology, 55,* 178–186.

Gluhoski, V., Leader, J., & Wortman, C. B. (1994). Grief and bereavement. In V. S. Ramachandran (Ed.), *Encyclopedia of human behavior.* San Diego: Academic Press.

Goetz, A., & Shackelford, T. (2006). Modern application of evolutionary theory to psychology: Key concepts and clarifications. *American Journal of Psychology, 119,* 567–584.

Goldberg, A. E. (2004). But do we need universal grammar? Comment on Lidz et al. *Cognition, 94,* 77–84.

Goldberg, J., Pereira, L., & Berghella, V. (2002). Pregnancy after uterine artery emoblization. *Obstetrics and Gynecology, 100,* 869–872.

Goldin-Meadow, S. (2006). Talking and thinking with our hands, *Current Directions in Psychological Science, 15,* 34–39.

Goldin-Meadow, S. (2009). Using the hands to study how children learn language. In J. Colombo, P. McCardle, & L. Freund, *Infant pathways to language: Methods, models, and research disorders.* New York: Psychology Press.

Goldman, R., (1964). *Religious thinking from childhood to adolescence.* London: Routledge & Kegan Paul.

Goldscheider, F. K. (1994). Divorce and remarriage: Effects on the elderly population. *Reviews in Clinical Gerontology, 4,* 253–259.

Goldsmith, L. T. (2000). Tracking trajectories of talent: Child prodigies growing up. In R. C. Friedman & B. M. Shore, et al. (Eds.). *Talents unfolding: Cognition and development.* Washington, DC: American Psychological Association.

Goldsmith, S. K., Pellmar, T. C., Kleinman, A. M., & Bunney, W. E. (2002). *Reducing suicide: A national imperative.* Washington, DC: National Academies Press.

Goldston, D. B. (2003). *Measuring suicidal behavior and risk in children and adolescents.* Washington, DC: American Psychological Association.

Goleman, D. (1993, July 21). Baby sees, baby does, and classmates follow. *New York Times,* p. C10.

Golinkoff, R. M. (1993). When is communication a "meeting of minds"? *Journal of Child Language, 20,* 199–207.

Golmier, I., Cehbat, J. C., & Gelinas-Chebat, C. (2007). Can cigarette warnings counterbalance effects of smoking scenes in movies? *Psychological Reports, 100,* 3–18.

Golomb, C. (2002). *Child art in context.* Washington, DC: American Psychological Association.

Golomb, C. (2003). *The child's creation of a pictorial world* (2nd ed.). Mahwah, NJ: Erlbaum.

Golombok, S., & Fivush, R. (1994). *Gender development.* Cambridge, England: Cambridge University Press.

Golombok, S., & Tasker, F. (1996). Do parents influence the sexual orientation of their children? Findings from a longitudinal study of lesbian families. *Developmental Psychology, 32,* 3–11.

Golombok, S., Golding, J., Perry, B., Burston, A., Murray, C., Mooney-Somers, J., & Stevens, M. (2003). Children with lesbian parents: A community study. *Developmental Psychology, 39,* 20–33.

Golombok, S., Murray, C., Vasanti, J., MacCallum, F., & Lycett, E. (2004). Families created through surrogacy arrangements: Parent-child relationships in the 1st year of life. *Developmental Psychology, 40,* 400–411.

Golub, S., & Langer, E. (2007). Challenging assumptions about adult development: Implications for the health of older adults. In C. M. Aldwin, C. L. Park, & A. Spiro (Eds.), *Handbook of health psychology and aging.* New York: Guilford Press.

Gondolf, E. W. (1985). Fighting for control: A clinical assessment of men who batter. *Social Casework, 66,* 48–54.

Gonnerman, M. E., Jr., Lutz, G. M., Yehieli, M., & Meisinger, B. K. (2008). Religion and health connection: A study of African American, Protestant Christians. *Journal of Health Care for the Poor and Underserved 19,* 193–199.

González, C., & Gándara, P. (2005). Why we like to call ourselves Latinas. *Journal of Hispanic Higher Education, 4,* 392–398.

Goodman, J. S., Fields, D. L., & Blum, T. C. (2003). Cracks in the glass ceiling: In what kinds of organizations do women make it to the top? *Group & Organization Management, 28,* 475–501.

Goodman, J., Schlossberg, N. K., & Anderson, M. L. (2006). *Counseling adults in transition: Linking practice with theory.* New York: Springer.

Goodstein, R., & Ponterotto, J. G. (1997). Racial and ethnic identity: Their relationship and their contribution to self-esteem. *Journal of Black Psychology, 23,* 275–292.

Goodwin, M. H. (1990). Tactical uses of stories: Participation frameworks within girls' and boys' disputes. *Discourse Processes, 13,* 33–71.

Googans, B., & Burden, D. (1987). Vulnerability of working parents: Balancing work and home roles. *Social Work, 32,* 295–300.

Goold, S. D., Williams, B., & Arnold, R. M. (2000). Conflicts regarding decisions to limit treatment: a differential diagnosis. *Journal of the American Medical Association, 283,* 909–914.

Gopnik, A., Meltzoff, A. N., & Kuhl, P. K. (2002). *The scientist in the crib: What early learning tells us about the mind.* New York: HarperCollins.

Gostin, L. (2006, April). Physician-assisted suicide A legitimate medical practice? *Journal of the American Medical Association, 295,* 1941–1943.

Goswami, U. (1998). *Cognition in children.* Philadelphia, PA: Psychology Press.

Goswami, U. (2008). *Cognitive development: The learning brain.* New York: Psychology Press.

Gottfredson, G. D., & Holland, J. L. (1990). A longitudinal test of the influence of congruence: Job satisfaction, competency utilization, and counterproductive behavior. *Journal of Counseling Psychology, 37,* 389–398.

Gottlieb, G. (2003). On making behavioral genetics truly developmental. *Human Development, 46,* 337–355.

Gottlieb, G., & Blair, C. (2004). How early experience matters in intellectual development in the case of poverty. *Preventive Science, 5,* 245–252.

Gottman, J. M., Fainsilber-Katz, L., & Hooven, C. (1996). *Meta-emotion: How families communicate emotionally.* Mahwah, NJ: Erlbaum.

Gottschalk, E. C., Jr. (1983, February 21). Older Americans: The aging man gains in the 1970s, outpacing rest of the population. *Wall Street Journal,* pp. 1, 20.

Gould, R. L. (1978). *Transformations: Growth and Change in Adult Life.* New York: Simon & Schuster.

Gould, R. L. (1980). Transformations during adult years. In R. Smelzer & E. Erickson (Eds.), *Themes of Love and Work in Adulthood,* Cambridge, MA: Harvard University Press.

Graber, J. A. (2004). Internalizing problems during adolescence. In R. M. Lerner & L. Steinberg (Eds.), *Handbook of adolescent psychology* (2nd ed.). New York: Wiley.

Grace, D., David, B., & Ryan, M. (2008). Investigating preschoolers' categorical thinking about gender through imitation, attention, and the use of self-categories. *Child Development, 79,* 1928–1941.

Grady, D. (2006, November). Management of menopausal symptoms. *New England Journal of Medicine, 355,* 2338–2347.

Graham, E. (1995, February 9). Leah: Life is all sweetness and insecurity. *Wall Street Journal,* p. B1.

Graham, I., Carroli, G., Davies, C., & Medves, J. (2005). Episiotomy rates around the world: An update. *Birth: Issues in Perinatal Care, 32,* 219–223.

Granic, I., Hollenstein, T., & Dishion, T. (2003). Longitudinal analysis of flexibility and reorganization in early adolescence: A dynamic systems study of family interactions. *Developmental Psychology, 39,* 606–617.

Grantham, T., & Ford, D. (2003). Beyond self-concept and self-esteem: Racial identity and gifted African American students. *High School Journal, 87,* 18–29.

Grantham-McGregor, S., Ani, C., & Fernald, L. (2001). The role of nutrition in intellectual development. In R. J. Sternberg & E. L. Grigorenko (Eds.), *Environmental effects on cognitive abilities.* Mahwah, NJ: Erlbaum.

Gratch, G., & Schatz, J. A. (1987). Cognitive development: The relevance of Piaget's infancy books. In J. D. Osofsky (Ed.), *Handbook of infant development* (2nd ed.). New York: Wiley.

Grattan, M. P., DeVos, E. S., Levy, J., & McClintock, M. K. (1992). Asymmetric action in the human newborn: Sex differences in patterns of organization. *Child Development, 63,* 273–289.

Gray-Little, B., & Hafdahl, A. (2000). Factors influencing racial comparisons of self-esteem: A quantitative review. *Psychological Bulletin, 126,* 26–54.

Green, A. S., Rafaeli, E., Bolger, N., Shrout, P. E., & Reis, H. T. (2006). Paper or plastic? Data equivalence in paper and electronic diaries. *Psychological Methods, 11,* 87–105.

Green, M. H. (1995). Influences of job type, job status, and gender on achievement motivation. *Current Psychology: Developmental, Learning, Personality, Social, 14,* 159–165.

Greenberg, L. (2008). Emotion and cognition in psychotherapy: The transforming power of affect. *Canadian Psychology, 49,* 49–59.

Greenberg, L., Cwikel, J., & Mirsky, J. (2007, January). Cultural correlates of eating attitudes: A comparison between native-born and immigrant university students in Israel. *International Journal of Eating Disorders, 40,* 51–58.

Greene, J. P., & Winters, M.A. (2006). *Leaving boys behind: Public high school graduation rates.* Civic Report #48. New York: Manhattan Institute for Policy Research.

Greene, S., Anderson, E., & Hetherington, E. (2003). Risk and resilience after divorce. In F. Walsh (Ed), *Normal family processes: Growing diversity and complexity.* New York: Guilford Press.

Greenfield, P. M. (1976). Cross-cultural research and Piagetian theory: Paradox and progress. In K. F. Riegel & J. A. Meacham (Eds.), *The developing individual in a changing world: Vol. 1.* The Hague, The Netherlands: Mouton.

Greenfield, P. M. (1997). You can't take it with you. Why ability assessments don't cross cultures. *American Psychologist, 52,* 1115–1124.

Greenwood, D. N., & Piertomonaco, P. R. (2004). The interplay among attachment orientation, idealized media images of women, and body dissatisfaction: A social psychological analysis. In L. J. Shrum (Ed.), *Psychology of entertainment media: Blurring the lines between entertainment and persuasion.* Mahwah, NJ: Erlbaum.

Greer, M. (2004, November). Retirement's road map. *Monitor on Psychology, 35,* 80.

Gregory, K. (2005). Update on nutrition for preterm and full-term infants. *Journal of Obstetrics and Gynecological Neonatal Nursing, 34,* 98–108.

Gregory, S. (1856). *Facts for young women.* Boston.

Greve, T. (2003). Norway: The breastfeeding top of the world. *Midwifery Today International, 67,* 57–59.

Grey, W. H. (1999). Milken Institute, reported in Suro, R. (November 1999). Mixed doubles. *American Demographics,* 57–62.

Griffith, D. R., Azuma, S. D., & Chasnoff, I. J. (1994). Three-year outcome of children exposed prenatally to drugs. *Journal of the American Academy of Child and Adolescent Psychiatry, 33,* 20–27.

Grigorenko, E. (2003). Intraindividual fluctuations in intellectual functioning: Selected links between nutrition and the mind In R. Sternberg & J. Lautrey (Eds.), *Models of intelligence: International perspectives.* Washington, DC: American Psychological Association.

Groome, L. J., Swiber, M. J., Atterbury, J. L., Bentz, L. S., & Holland, S. B. (1997). Similarities and differences in behavioral state organization during sleep periods in the perinatal infant before and after birth. *Child Development, 68,* 1–11.

Groome, L. J., Swiber, M. J., Bentz, L. S., Holland, S. B., & Atterbury, J. L. (1995). Maternal anxiety during pregnancy: Effect on fetal behavior at 38 to 40 weeks of gestation. *Developmental and Behavioral Pediatrics, 16,* 391–396.

Groopman, J. (1998 February 8). Decoding destiny. *The New Yorker,* p. 42–47.

Gross, J. (1991, June 16). More young single men hang on to apron strings. *New York Times,* pp. A1, A18.

Gross, R. T., Spiker, D., & Haynes, C. W. (Eds.). (1997). *Helping low-birthweight, premature babies: The Infant Health and Development Program.* Stanford, CA: Stanford University Press.

Grossman, K. E., Grossmann, K., & Waters, E. (Eds.). (2005). *Attachment from infancy to adulthood: The major longitudinal studies.* New York: Guilford Press.

Grunau, R. V. E., Whitfield, M. F., Petrie, J. H., & Fryer, E. L. (1994). Early pain experience, child and family factors, as precursors of somatization: A prospective study of extremely premature and fullterm children. *Pain, 56,* 353–359.

Grunbaum, J. A., Kann, L., Kinchen, S. A., Williams, B., Ross, J. G., Lowry, R., & Kolbe, L. (2002). *Youth risk behavior surveillance—United States, 2001.* Atlanta, GA: Centers for Disease Control.

Grunbaum, J. A., Lowry, R., & Kann, L. (2001). Prevalence of health-related behaviors among alternative high school students as compared with students attending regular high schools. *Journal of Adolescent Health, 29,* 337–343.

Grundy, E., & Henretta, J. (2006, September). Between elderly parents and adult children: A new look at the intergenerational care provided by the 'sandwich generation'. *Ageing & Society, 26,* 707–722.

Grusec, J. E., & Kuczynski, L. E. (Eds.). (1997). *Parenting and children's internalization of values: A handbook of contemporary theory.* New York: Wiley.

Grzywacz, J. G., Butler, A. B., & Almeida, D. M. (2008). Work, family, and health: Work-family balance as a protective factor against stresses of daily life. In A. Marcus-Newhal, et al. (Eds.) *The changing realities of work and family: A multidisciplinary approach.* New York: Wiley-Blackwell.

Guan, J. (2004). Correlates of spouse relationship with sexual attitude, interest, and activity among Chinese elderly. *Sexuality & Culture: An Interdisciplinary Quarterly, 8,* 104–131.

Guasti, M. T. (2002). *Language acquisition: The growth of grammar.* Cambridge, MA: MIT Press.

Guerrero, A., Hishinuma, E., Andrade, N., Nishimura, S., & Cunanan, V. (2006, July). Correlations among socioeconomic and family factors and academic, behavioral, and emotional difficulties in Filipino adolescents in Hawaii. *International Journal of Social Psychiatry, 52,* 343–359.

Guerrini, I., Thomson, A., & Gurling, H. (2007). The importance of alcohol misuse, malnutrition and genetic susceptibility on brain growth and plasticity. *Neuroscience & Biobehavioral Reviews, 31,* 212–220.

Guinote, A., & Fiske, S. T. (2003). Being in the outgroup territory increases stereotypic perceptions of outgroups: Situational sources of category activation. *Group Processes & Intergroup Relations, 6,* 323–331.

Gump, L. S., Baker, R. C., & Roll, S. (2000). Cultural and gender differences in moral judgment: A study of Mexican Americans and Anglo-Americans. *Hispanic Journal of Behavioral Sciences, 22,* 78–93.

Gunnarsdottir, I., & Thorsdottir, I. (2003). Relationship between growth and feeding in infancy and body mass index at the age of 6 years. *International Journal of Obesity and Metabolic Disorders, 27,* 1523–1527.

Gupta, A., & State, M. (2007). Recent advances in the genetics of autism. *Biological Psychiatry, 61,* 429–437.

Gur, R. C., Gur, R. E., Obrist, W. D., Hungerbuhler, J. P., Younkin, D., Rosen, A. D., Skilnick, B. E., & Reivich, M. (1982). Sex and handedness differences in cerebral blood flow during rest and cognitive activity. *Science, 217,* 659–661.

Güroğlu, B., van Lieshout, C. F. M., Haselager, G. J. T., & Scholte, R. H. J. (2007). Similarity and complementarity of behavioral profiles of friendship types and types of friends: Friendships and psychosocial adjustment. *Journal of Research on Adolescence, 17,* 357–386.

Gutek, G. L. (2003). Maria Montessori: Contributions to educational psychology. In B. J. Zimmerman (Ed.), *Educational psychology: A century of contributions.* Mahwah, NJ: Erlbaum.

Guterl, F. (2002, November 11). What Freud got right. *Newsweek,* 50–51.

Gutman, L. M., McLoyd, V. C., & Tokoyawa, T. (2005). Financial strain, neighborhood stress, parenting behaviors, and adolescent adjustment in urban African American families. *Journal of Research on Adolescence, 15,* 425–449.

Guttman, M. (1997, May 16–18). Are you losing your mind? *USA Weekend,* pp. 4–5.

Guttmann, J., & Rosenberg, M. (2003). Emotional intimacy and children's adjustment: A comparison between single-parent divorced and intact families. *Educational Psychology, 23,* 457–472.

Haber, D. (2006). Life review: Implementation, theory, research, and therapy. *International Journal of Aging & Human Development, 63,* 153–171.

Haberstick, B. C., Timberlake, D., Ehringer, M. A., Lessem, J. M., Hopfer, C. J., Smolen, A., & Hewitt, J. K. (2007). Can cigarette warnings counterbalance effects of smoking scenes in movies? *Addiction, 102,* 655–665.

Hack, M., Flannery, D. J., Schluchter, M., Cartar, L., Borawski, E., & Klein, N. (2002). Outcomes in young adulthood for very low birth weight infants. *New England Journal of Medicine, 346,* 149–157.

Haddock, S., & Rattenborg, K. (2003). Benefits and challenges of dual-earning: Perspectives of successful couples. *American Journal of Family Therapy, 31,* 325–344.

Hagerty, R. G., Butow, P. N., Ellis, P. A., Lobb, E. A., Pendlebury, S., Leighl, N., Goldstein, D., Lo, S. K., & Tattersall, M. H. (2004). Cancer patient preferences for communication of prognosis in the metastatic setting. *Journal of Clinical Oncology, 22,* 1721–1730.

Hahn, C-S., & DiPietro, J. A. (2001). In vitro fertilization and the family: Quality of parenting, family functioning, and child psychosocial adjustment. *Developmental Psychology, 37,* 37–48.

Haight, B. K. (1991). Psychological illness in aging. In E. M. Baines (Ed.), *Perspectives on gerontological nursing.* Newbury Park, CA: Sage.

Haight, W. L. (2002). *African-American children at church: A sociocultural perspective.* New York: Cambridge University Press.

Haines, C. (2003). Sequencing, co-ordination and rhythm ability in young children. *Child: Care, Health & Development, 29,* 395–409.

Haines, J., & Neumark-Sztainer, D. (2006, December). Prevention of obesity and eating disorders: A consideration of shared risk factors. *Health Education Research, 21,* 770–782.

Haith, M. H. (1986). Sensory and perceptual processes in early infancy. *Journal of Pediatrics, 109*(1), 158–171.

Haith, M. H. (1991, April). *Setting a path for the 90s: Some goals and challenges in infant sensory and perceptual development.* Paper presented at the biennial meeting of the Society for Research in Child Development, Seattle.

Haith, M. M. (1993). *Future-oriented processes in infancy: The case of visual expectations.* Hillsdale, NJ: Lawrence Erlbaum Associates.

Haith, M. M. (1994). *Visual expectations as the first step toward the development of future-oriented processes.* Chicago: University of Chicago Press.

Hales, K. A., Morgan, M. A., & Thurnau, G. R. (1993). Influence of labor and route of delivery on the frequency of respiratory morbidity in term neonates. *International Journal of Gynecology & Obstetrics, 43,* 35–40.

Halford, G. (2005). Development of thinking. *The Cambridge handbook of thinking and reasoning.* New York: Cambridge University Press.

Halford, G., & Andrews, G. (2006). Reasoning and problem solving. *Handbook of child psychology: Vol 2, Cognition, perception, and language (6th ed.).* Hoboken, NJ: John Wiley & Sons Inc.

Halford, G. S., Maybery, M. T., O'Hare, A. W., & Grant, P. (1994). The development of memory and processing capacity. *Child Development, 65,* 1338–1356.

Halgunseth, L. C., Ispa, J. M., & Rudy, D. (2006). Parental control in Latino families: An integrated review of the literature. *Child Development, 77,* 1282–1297.

Hall, E. G., & Lee, A. M. (1984). Sex differences in motor performance of young children: Fact or fiction? *Sex Roles, 10,* 217–230.

Hall, R. E. & Rowan, G. T. (2003). Identity development across the lifespan: Alternative model for biracial Americans. *Psychology and Education: An Interdisciplinary Journal, 40,* 3–12.

Hall, S. (2006). Marital meaning: Exploring young adults' belief systems about marriage. *Journal of Family Issues, 27,* 1437–1458.

Halliday, M. A. K. (1975). *Learning how to mean—Explorations in the development of language.* London: Edward Arnold.

Hallpike, C. (2008). The anthropology of moral development. *Social life and social knowledge: Toward a process account of development.* New York: Taylor & Francis Group/Lawrence Erlbaum Associates.

Halpern, D. F. (1996). *Thought and knowledge: An introduction to critical thinking* (3rd ed.). Mahwah, NJ: Lawrence Erlbaum Associates.

Hamberger, L., & Holtzworth-Munroe, A. (2007). Spousal abuse. *Cognitive-behavioral strategies in crisis intervention* (3rd ed., pp. 277–299). New York: Guilford Press.

Hamilton, G. (1998). Positively testing. *Families in Society, 79,* 570–576.

Hamlin, J., Hallinan, E., & Woodward, A. (2008). Do as I do: 7-month-old infants selectively reproduce others' goals. *Developmental Science, 11,* 487–494.

Hamon, R. R., & Ingoldsby, B. B. (Eds.) (2003). *Mate selection across cultures.* Thousand Oaks, CA: Sage.

Hancox, R. J., Milne, B. J., & Poulton, R. (2004). Association between child and adolescent television viewing and health: A longitudinal birth cohort study. *Lancet, 364,* 257–262.

Hane, A., Feldstein, S.,& Dernetz, V. (2003). The relation between coordinated interpersonal timing and maternal sensitivity in four-month-old infants. *Journal of Psycholinguistic Research, 32,* 525–539.

Hanger, H., Fogarty, B., Wilkinson, T., & Sainsbury, R. (2000). Stroke patients' views on stroke outcomes: Death versus disability. *Clinical Rehabilitation, 14,* 417–424.

Hankin, B. L., & Abramson, L. Y. (2001). Development of gender differences in depression: An elaborated cognitive vulnerability-transactional stress theory. *Psychological Bulletin, 127,* 773–796.

Hanson, R. F., & Spratt, E. G. (2000). Reactive attachment disorder: What we know about the disorder and implications for treatment. *Child Maltreatment, 5,* 1371–45.

Hansson, R. O., & Carpenter, B. N. (1994). *Relationship in old age: Coping with the challenge of transition.* New York: Guilford Press.

Hansson, R., & Stroebe, M. (2007). *Bereavement in late life: Coping, adaptation, and developmental influences.* Washington, DC: American Psychological Association.

Hansson, R., Daleiden, E., & Hayslip, B. (2004). Relational competence across the life span. *Growing together: Personal relationships across the lifespan* (pp. 317–340). New York: Cambridge University Press.

Hardy, L. T. (2007). Attachment theory and reactive attachment disorder: Theoretical perspectives and treatment implications. *Journal of Child and Adolescent Psychiatric Nursing, 20,* 27–39.

Harlow, H. F., & Zimmerman, R. R. (1959). Affectional responses in the infant monkey. *Science, 130,* 421–432.

Harrell, J. S., Bangdiwala, S. I., Deng, S., Webb, J. P., & Bradley, C. (1998). Smoking initiation in youth: The roles of gender, race, socioeconomics, and developmental status. *Journal of Adolescent Health, 23,* 271–279.

Harris, A., Cronkite, R., & Moos, R. (2006, July). Physical activity, exercise coping, and depression in a 10-year cohort study of depressed patients. *Journal of Affective Disorders, 93,* 79–85.

Harris, C. M. (2004). Personality and sexual orientation. *College Student Journal, 38,* 207–211.

Harris, J. (2004). *On cloning.* New York: Routledge.

Harris, J. (2006). *No two alike: Human nature and human individuality.* New York: W. W. Norton & Co.

Harris, J. F., Durso, F. T., Mergler, N. L., & Jones, S. K. (1990). Knowledge base influences on judgments of frequency of occurrence. *Cognitive Development, 5,* 223–233.

Harris, J. R. (1998). *The nurture assumption: Why children turn out the way they do.* New York: Free Press.

Harris, J. R. (2000). Socialization, personality development, and the child's environments: Comment on Vandell. *Developmental Psychology, 36,* 711–723.

Harris, J., Vernon, P., & Jang, K. (2007). Rated personality and measured intelligence in young twin children. *Personality and Individual Differences, 42,* 75–86.

Harris, P. L. (1987). The development of search. In P. Sallapatek & L. Cohen (Eds.), *Handbook of infant perception: From perception to cognition* (Vol. 2, pp. 155–207). Orlando, FL: Academic Press.

Harrison, K., & Hefner, V. (2006, April). Media exposure, current and future body ideals, and disordered eating among preadolescent girls: A longitudinal panel study. *Journal of Youth and Adolescence, 35,* 153–163.

Hart, B. (2004). What toddlers talk about. *First Language, 24,* 91–106.

Hart, B., & Risley, T. R. (1995). *Meaningful differences in the everyday experience of young American children.* Baltimore, MD: Paul Brookes.

Hart, C. H., Yang, C., Nelson, D. A., Jin, S., Bazarskaya, N., & Nelson, L. (1998). Peer contact patterns, parenting practices, and preschoolers' social competence in China, Russia, and the United States. In P. Slee & K. Rigby (Eds.), *Peer relations amongst children: Current issues and future directions.* London: Routledge.

Hart, D., Burock, D., & London, B. (2003). Prosocial tendencies, antisocial behavior, and moral development. In A. Slater & G. Bremner (Eds.), *An introduction to developmental psychology.* Malden, MA: Blackwell Publishers.

Hart, D., Hofmann, V., & Edelstein, W. (1998). The relation of childhood personality types to adolescent behavior and development: A longitudinal study of Icelandic children. *Developmental Psychology, 33,* 195–205.

Harter, S. (1990a). Identity and self-development. In S. Feldman & G. Elliott (Eds.), *At the threshold: The developing adolescent.* Cambridge, MA: Harvard University Press.

Harter, S. (1990b). Issues in the assessment of self-concept of children and adolescents. In A. LaGreca (Ed.), *Through the eyes of a child.* Boston: Allyn & Bacon.

Hartshorne, J., & Ullman, M. (2006). Why girls say 'holded' more than boys. *Developmental Science, 9,* 21–32.

Hartshorne, T. S. (1994). Friendship. In V. S. Ramachandran (Ed.), *Encyclopedia of human behavior.* San Diego: Academic Press.

Hartup, W. W., & Stevens, N. (1999). Friendships and adaptation across the life span. *Current Directions in Psychological Science, 8,* 76–79.

Harvey, A., Mullin, B., & Hinshaw, S. (2006). Sleep and circadian rhythms in children and adolescents with bipolar disorder. *Development and Psychopathology, 18,* 1147–1168.

Harvey, E. (1999). Short-term and long-term effects of early parental employment on children of the National Longitudinal Survey of Youth. *Developmental Psychology, 35,* 445–459.

Harvey, J. H., & Fine, M. A. (2004). *Children of divorce: Stories of loss and growth.* Mahwah, NJ: Lawrence Erlbaum Associates.

Harvey, J., & Weber, A. (2002). *Odyssey of the heart: Close relationships in the 21st century* (2nd ed.). Mahwah, NJ: Erlbaum.

Harwood, R. L., Schoelmerich, A., Ventura-Cook, E., Schulze, P. A., & Wilson, S. P. (1996). Culture and class influences on Anglo and Puerto Rican mothers' beliefs regarding long-term socialization goals and child behavior. *Child Development, 67,* 2446–2461.

Hasher, L., & Zacks, R. T. (1984). Automatic processing of fundamental information: The case of frequency of occurrence. *American Psychologist, 39,* 1372–1388.

Haslam, C., & Lawrence, W. (2004). Health-related behavior and beliefs of pregnant smokers. *Health Psychology, 23,* 486–491.

Haslett, A. (2004, May 31). Love supreme. *The New Yorker,* pp. 76–80.

Hatfield, E., & Rapson, R. L. (1993). Historical and cross-cultural perspectives on passionate love and sexual desire. *Annual Review of Sex Research, 4,* 67–97.

Hattery, A. (2000). *Women, work, and family: Balancing and weaving.* Thousand Oaks, CA: Sage.

Haugaard, J. J. (2000). The challenge of defining child sexual abuse. *American Psychologist, 55,* 1036–1039.

Hauser, M., Chomsky, N., & Fitch, W. (2002). The faculty of language: What is it, who has it, and how did it evolve? *Science, 298,* 1569–1579.

Hauser, S., Allen, J., & Golden, E. (2006). *Out of the woods: Tales of resilient teens.* Cambridge, MA: Harvard University Press.

Havighurst, R. J. (1973). Social roles, work, leisure, and education. In C. Eisdorfer & M. P. Lawton (Eds.), *The psychology of adult development and aging.* Washington, DC: American Psychological Association.

Hawley, P. (2007). Social dominance in childhood and adolescence: Why social competence and aggression may go hand in hand. *Aggression and adaptation: The bright side to bad behavior.* Mahwah, NJ: Lawrence Erlbaum Associates Publishers.

Hawley, P. H. (2003). Prosocial and coercive configurations of resource control in early adolescence: A case for the well-adapted Machiavellian. *Merrill-Palmer Quarterly, 4, Special issue: Aggression and Adaptive Functioning: The bright side to bad behavior,* 279–309.

Hay, D., Payne, A., & Chadwick, A. (2004). Peer relations in childhood. *Journal of Child Psychology & Psychiatry & Allied Disciplines, 45,* 84–108.

Hayashi, T., Thomas, G. M., & Huganir, R. L. (2009). Dual palmitoylation of NR2 subunits regulates NMDA receptor trafficking. *Neuron, 64,* 213–226.

Hayden, T. (1998, September 21). The brave new world of sex selection. *Newsweek,* p. 93.

Hayslip, B., Servaty, H. L., Christman, T., & Mumy, E. (1997). Levels of death anxiety in terminally ill persons: A cross validation and extension. *Omega—Journal of Death & Dying, 34,* 203–217.

Hayward, M., Crimmins, E., & Saito, Y. (1997). Cause of death and active life expectancy in the older population of the United States. *Journal of Aging and Health,* 122–131.

Hazan, C., & Shaver, P. (1987). Romantic love conceptualized as an attachment process. *Journal of Personality and Social Psychology, 52,* 511–524.

Head, D. (2005). Young people, sex and the media: The facts of life? *Journal of Family Studies, 11,* 326–327.

Healy, P. (2001, March 3). Data on suicides set off alarm. *Boston Globe,* p. B1.

Hebebrand, J., & Hinney, A. (2009). Environmental and genetic risk factors in obesity. *Child and Adolescent Psychiatric Clinics of North America, 18,* 83–94.

Hecht, M. L., Marston, P. J., & Larkey, L. K. (1994). Love ways and relationship quality in heterosexual relationships. *Journal of Social and Personal Relationships, 11,* 25–43.

Heerey, E. A., Keltner, D., & Capps, L. M. (2003). Making Sense of Self-Conscious Emotion: Linking Theory of Mind and Emotion in Children With Autism. *Emotion, 3,* 394–400.

Heimann, M. (Ed.). (2003). *Regression periods in human infancy.* Mahwah, NJ: Erlbaum.

Heimann, M., Strid, K., Smith, L., Tjus, T., Ulvund, S., & Meltzoff, A. (2006). Exploring the relation between memory, gestural communication, and the emergence of language in infancy: A longitudinal study. *Infant and Child Development, 15,* 233–249.

Heiser, S. (2007, May 23). 66-year-old woman's cross-country cycling feat tough to beat. *York Dispatch,* p. 1.

Helms, J. E., Jernigan, M., & Mascher, J. (2005). The meaning of race in psychology and how to change it: A methodological perspective. *American Psychologist, 60,* 27–36.

Helson R., & Moane, G. (1987). Personality change in women from college to midlife. *Journal of Personality and Social Psychology, 53,* 176–186.

Helson, R., & Soto, C. (2005). Up and down in middle age: Monotonic and nonmonotonic changes in roles, status, and personality. *Journal of Personality and Social Psychology, 89,* 194–204.

Helson, R., Soto, C., & Cate, R. (2006). From young adulthood through the middle ages. *Handbook of personality development.* Mahwah, NJ: Lawrence Erlbaum Associates Publishers.

Helson, R., Stewart, A. J., & Ostrove, J. (1995). Identity in three cohorts of midlife women. *Journal of Personality and Social Psychology, 69,* 544–557.

Hempel, S. (2005). Reliability. In J. Miles & P. Gilbert (Eds.) *A handbook of research methods for clinical and health psychology.* New York: Oxford University Press.

Hendrick, C., & Hendrick, S. (2003). Romantic love: Measuring cupid's arrow. In S. Lopez & C. Snyder (Eds.), *Positive psychological assessment: A handbook of models and measures.* Washington, DC: American Psychological Association.

Hendrie, H. C., Ogunniyi, A., Hall, K. S., Baiyewu, O., Unverzagt, F. W., Gureje, O., Gao, S., Evans, R. M., Ogunseyinde, A. O., Adeyinka, A. O., Musick, B., & Hui, S. L. (2001). Incidence of dementia and Alzheimer disease in 2 communities: Yoruba residing in Ibadan, Nigeria, and African Americans residing in Indianapolis, Indiana. *Journal of the American Medical Association, 285,* 739–747.

Henry, J., & McNab, W. (2003). Forever young: A health promotion focus on sexuality and aging. *Gerontology & Geriatrics Education, 23,* 57–74.

Henry, R., Miller, R., & Giarrusso, R. (2005). Difficulties, disagreements, and disappointments in late-life marriages. *International Journal of Aging & Human Development, 61,* 243–264.

Hensley, P. (2006, July). Treatment of bereavement-related depression and traumatic grief. *Journal of Affective Disorders, 92,* 117–124.

Herbert, M. R., Ziegler, D. A., Deutsch, C. K., O'Brien, L. M., Kennedy, D. N., Filipek, P. A., Bakardjiev, A. I., Hodgson, J., Takeoka, M., Makris, N., & Caviness, Jr., V. S. (2005). Brain asymmetries in autism and developmental language disorder: a nested whole-brain analysis. *Brain, 128,* 213–226.

Herdt, G. H. (Ed.). (1998). *Rituals of manhood: Male initiation in Papua New Guinea.* Somerset, NJ: Transaction Books.

Hernandez-Reif, M., Field, T., Diego, M., Vera, Y., & Pickens, J. (2006, January). Brief report: Happy faces are habituated more slowly by infants of depressed mothers. *Infant Behavior & Development, 29,* 131–135.

Herrnstein, R. J., & Murray, C. (1994). *The Bell Curve: Intelligence and class structure in American life.* New York: Free Press.

Hertel, G., & Wittchen, M. (2008). Work motivation. *An introduction to work and organizational psychology: A European perspective* (2nd ed.). Malden, MA: Blackwell Publishing.

Hertelendy, F., & Zakar, T. (2004). Prostaglandins and the mymetrium and cervix. *Prostaglandins, Leukotrienes and Essential Fatty Acids, 70,* 207–222.

Hespos, S. J., & Baillargeon, R. (2008). Young infants' actions reveal their developing knowledge of support variables: Converging evidence for violation-of-expectation findings. *Cognition, 107,* 304–316.

Heston, C. (2002, August 9). Quoted in *Charlton Heston has Alzheimer's symptoms.* http://www.cnn.com/2002/US/08/09/heston.illness. Accessed May 13, 2004.

Hetherington, E. M. (Ed.) (1999). *Coping with divorce, single parenting, and remarriage: A risk and resiliency perspective.* Mahwah, NJ: Erlbaum.

Hetherington, E. M., & Blechman, E. A. (Eds.). (1996). *Stress, coping, and resiliency in children and families.* Hillsdale, NJ: Erlbaum.

Hetherington, E. M., & Clingempeel, W. (1992). Coping with marital transitions: A family systems perspective. *Monographs of the Society for Research in Child Development, 57,* (2–3, Serial No. 227).

Hetherington, E. M., & Kelly, J. (2002). *For better or worse: Divorce reconsidered.* New York: Norton.

Hetherington, E., & Elmore, A. (2003). Risk and resilience in children coping with their parents' divorce and remarriage. In S. Luthar (Ed.), *Resilience and vulnerability: Adaptation in the context of childhood adversities.* New York: Cambridge University Press.

Heward, W. L., & Orlansky, M. D. (1988, October). The epidemiology of AIDS in the U.S. *Scientific American,* pp. 72–81.

Hewstone, M. (2003). Intergroup contact: Panacea for prejudice? *Psychologist, 16,* 352–355.

HHL (Harvard Health Letter). (1997, May). *Turning up the volume,* p. 4.

Higher Education Research Institute. (2005). *The American freshman: National norms for fall 2004.* Los Angeles: Higher Education Research Institute, UCLA.

Hightower, J. R. R. (2005). Women and depression. In A. Barnes (Ed.), *Handbook of women, psychology, and the law.* New York: Wiley.

Hildreth, K., Sweeney, B., & Rovee-Collier, C. (2003). Differential memory-preserving effects of reminders at 6 months. *Journal of Experimental Child Psychology, 84,* 41–62.

Hill, S., & Flom, R. (2007, February). 18- and 24-month-olds' discrimination of gender-consistent and inconsistent activities. *Infant Behavior & Development, 30,* 168–173.

Hillman, J. (2000). *Clinical perspectives on elderly sexuality.* Dordrecht, Netherlands: Kluwer Academic.

Hines, M., & Kaufman, F. R. (1994). Androgen and the development of human sex-typical behavior: Rough-and-tumble play and sex of preferred playmates in children with congenital adrenal hyperplasi (CAH*). Child Development, 65,* 1042–1053.

Hines, M., Golombok, S., & Rust, J. (2002). Testosterone during pregnancy and gender role behavior of preschool children: A longitudinal, population study. *Child Development, 73,* 1678–1687.

Hirsh-Pasek, K., & Michnick-Golinkoff, R. (1995). *The origins of grammar: Evidence from early language comprehension.* Cambridge, MA: MIT Press.

Hiser, E., & Kobayashi, J. (2003). Hemisphere lateralization differences: A cross-cultural study of Japanese and American students in Japan. *Journal of Asian Pacific Communication, 13,* 197–229.

Hitch, G. J., & Towse, J. N. (1995). *Working memory: What develops?* Mahwah, NJ: Lawrence Erlbaum Associates.

Hitlin, S. Brown, J. S., & Elder, G. H., Jr. (2006). Racial self-categorization in adolescence: Multiracial development and social pathways. *Child Development, 77,* 1298–1308.

Hjelmstedt, A., Widström, A., & Collins, A. (2006). Psychological correlates of prenatal attachment in women who conceived after in vitro fertilization and women Who conceived naturally. *Birth: Issues in Perinatal Care, 33,* 303–310.

HMHL (Harvard Mental Health Letter). (2005). The treatment of attention deficit disorder: New evidence. *Harvard Mental Health Letter, 21,* 6.

Ho, B., Friedland, J., Rappolt, S., & Noh, S. (2003). Caregiving for relatives with Alzheimer's disease: Feelings of Chinese-Canadian women. *Journal of Aging Studies, 17,* 301–321.

Hobart, C., & Grigel, F. (1992). Cohabitation among Canadian students at the end of the eighties. *Journal of Comparative Family Studies, 23,* 311–337.

Hocutt, A. M. (1996). Effectiveness of special education: Is placement the critical factor? *The Future of Children, 6,* 77–102.

Hoek, J., & Gendall, P. (2006). Advertising and obesity: A behavioral perspective. *Journal of Health Communication, 11,* 409–423.

Hoelterk, L., F., Axinn, W. G., & Ghimire, D. J. (2004). Social change, premarital non-family experiences, and marital dynamics. *Journal of Marriage & Family, 66,* 1131–1151.

Hofer, M. A. (2006). Psychobiological roots of early attachment. *Current Directions in Psychological Science, 15,* 84–88.

Hoffman, L. (2003). Why high schools don't change: What students and their year-books tell us. *High School Journal, 86*, 22–37.

Hoffman, M. L. (1991). Is empathy altruistic? *Psychological Inquiry, 2*, 131–133.

Hoffman, M. L. (2001). Toward a comprehensive empathy-based theory of prosocial moral development. In A. C. Bohart & D. J. Stipek, *Constructive & destructive behavior: Implications for family, school, & society*. Washington, DC: American Psychological Association.

Hogg, M. A. (2003). Social identity. In M. A. Hogg (Ed.) *Handbook of self and identity*. New York: Guilford Press.

Hohm, E., Jennen-Steinmetz, C., Schmidt, M., & Laucht, M. (2007). Language development at ten months: Predictive of language outcome and school achievement ten years later? *European Child & Adolescent Psychiatry, 16*, 149–156.

Hohmann-Marriott, B. (2006, November). Shared beliefs and the union stability of married and cohabiting couples. *Journal of Marriage and Family, 68*, 1015–1028.

Holahan, C., & Chapman, J. (2002). Longitudinal predictors of proactive goals and activity participation at age 80. *Journals of Gerontology: Series B: Psychological Sciences & Social Sciences, 57B*, P418–P425.

Holden, G. W., & Miller, P. C. (1999). Enduring and different: A meta-analysis of the similarity in parents' child rearing. *Psychological Bulletin, 125*, 223–254.

Holland, A. (1999). Syndromes, phenotypes, and genotypes: Finding the links. *The Psychologist 12*, 242–245.

Holland, J. (2008). Reading aloud with infants: The controversy, the myth, and a case study. *Early Childhood Education Journal, 35*, 383–385.

Holland, J. L. (1973). *Making vocational choices: A theory of careers*. Englewood Cliffs, NJ: Prentice-Hall.

Holland, J. L. (1987). Current status of Holland's theory of careers: Another perspective. *Career Development Quarterly, 36*, 24–30.

Holland, N. (1994, August). *Race dissonance— Implications for African American children*. Paper presented at the annual meeting of the American Psychological Association, Los Angeles.

Hollich, G. J., Hirsh-Pasek, K., Golinkoff, R. M., Brand, R. J., Brown, E. C., He, L., Hennon, E., & Rocrot, C. (2000). Breaking the language barrier: an emergentist coalition model of the origins of word learning. *Monographs of the Society for Research in Child Development, 65*, (3, Serial No. 262).

Holowaka, S., & Petitto, L. A. (2002). Left hemisphere cerebral specialization for babies while babbling. *Science, 287*, 1515.

Holyrod, R., & Sheppard, A. (1997). Parental separation: Effects on children; implications for services. *Child: Care, Health & Development, 23*, 369–378.

Holzman, L. (1997). Schools for growth: Radical alternatives to current educational models. Mahwah, NJ: Erlbaum.

Hong, S. B., & Trepanier-Street, M. (2004). Technology: A tool for knowledge construction in a Reggio Emilia inspired teacher education program. *Early Childhood Education Journal, 32*, 87–94.

Hopkins, B., & Westra, T. (1989). Maternal expectations of their infants' development: Some cultural differences. *Developmental Medicine and Child Neurology, 31*, 384–390.

Hopkins, B., & Westra, T. (1990). Motor development, maternal expectation, and the role of handling. *Infant Behavior and Development, 13*, 117–122.

Horner, K. L. (1998). Individuality in vulnerability: Influences on physical health. *Journal of Health Psychology, 3*, 71–85.

Horowitz, A. (1994). Vision impairment and functional disability among nursing home residents. *Gerontologist, 34*, 316–323.

Horwath, C. C. (1991). Nutrition goals for older adults: A review. *Gerontologist, 31*, 811–821.

Hossfeld, B. (2008). Developing friendships and peer relationships: Building social support with the Girls Circle program. *Handbook of prevention and intervention programs for adolescent girls* (pp. 42–80). Hoboken, NJ: John Wiley & Sons Inc.

Howard, A. (1992). Work and family crossroads spanning the career. In S. Zedeck (Ed.), *Work, families and organizations*. San Francisco: Jossey-Bass.

Howe, M. J. (2004). Some insights of geniuses into the causes of exceptional achievement. In L. V. Shavinina & M. Ferrari (Eds.), *Beyond knowledge: Extracognitive aspects of developing high ability*. Mahwah, NJ: Erlbaum.

Howe, M. L. (2003). Memories from the cradle. *Current Directions in Psychological Science, 12*, 62–65.

Howe, M. L., & O'Sullivan, J. T. (1990). The development of strategic memory: Coordinating knowledge, metamemory, and resources. In D. F. Bjorklund (Ed.), *Children's strategies: Contemporary view of cognitive development*. Hillsdale, NJ: Erlbaum.

Howe, M. L., Courage, M. L., & Edison, S. C. (2004). When autobiographical memory begins. In S. Algarabel, A. Pitarque, T. Bajo, S. E. Gathercole, & M. A. Conway (Eds.), *Theories of memory: Vol. 3*. New York: Psychology Press.

Howes, C., Unger, O., & Seidner, L. B. (1989). Social pretend play in toddlers: Parallels with social play and with solitary pretend. *Child Development, 60*, 77–84.

Hsu, V., & Rovee-Collier, C. (2006). Memory reactivation in the second year of life. *Infant Behavior & Development, 29*, 91–107.

Huang, J. (2004). Death: Cultural traditions. At "*On Our Own Terms: Moyers on Dying.*" Accessed May 24, 2004.

Hubbs-Tait, L., Nation, J. R., Krebs, N. F., & Bellinger, D. C. (2005). Neurotoxicants, micronutrients, and social environments: Individual and combined effects on children's development. *Journal of the American Psychological Society, 6*, 57–101.

Hubel, D. H., & Wiesel, T. N. (1979). Brain mechanisms of vision. *Scientific American, 241*, 150–162.

Hubel, D. H., & Wiesel, T. N. (2004). *Brain and visual perception: The story of a 25-year collaboration*. New York: Oxford University Press.

Hudson, J. A., Sosa, B. B., & Shapiro, L. R. (1997). Scripts and plans: The development of preschool children's event knowledge and event planning. In S. L. Friedman & E. K. Scholnick (Eds.), *The developmental psychology of planning: Why, how and when do we plan* (pp. 77–102). Mahwah, NJ: Erlbaum.

Huff, C. O. (1999). Source, recency, and degree of stress in adolescence and suicide ideation. *Adolescence, 34*, 81–89.

Hughes, F. P. (1995). *Children, play, and development* (2nd ed.). Boston: Allyn & Bacon.

Huizink, A., Mulder, E., & Buitelaar, J. (2004). Prenatal stress and risk for psychopathology: Specific effects or induction of general susceptibility? *Psychological Bulletin, 130*, 115–142.

Hulanicka, B. (1999). Acceleration of menarcheal age of girls from dysfunctional families. *Journal of Reproductive & Infant Psychology, 17*, 119–132.

Hulei, E., Zevenbergen, A., & Jacobs, S. (2006, September). Discipline behaviors of Chinese American and European American mothers. *Journal of Psychology: Interdisciplinary and Applied, 140*, 459–475.

Human Genome Program. (2003). *Genomics and its impact on science and society: A 2003 primer*. Washington, DC: U.S. Department of Energy.

Humane Genome Project. (2006). http://www.ornl.gov/sci/techresources/Human_Genome/medicine/genetest.shtm

Humphreys, J. (2003). Resilience in sheltered battered women. *Issues in Mental Health Nursing, 24*, 137–152.

Hungerford, A. (2005). The use of anatomically detailed dolls in forensic investigations: Developmental considerations. *Journal of Forensic Psychology Practice, 5*, 75–87.

Hunt, C., & Hauck, F. (2006). Sudden infant death syndrome. *Canadian Medical Association Journal, 174*, 1861–1869.

Hunt, M. (1974). *Sexual behaviors in the 1970s*. New York: Dell.

Hunt, M. (1993). *The story of psychology*. New York: Doubleday.

Hunt, P., & McDonnell, J. (2007). In S. L. Odom, et al. (Eds.) *Handbook of developmental disabilities*. New York: Guilford Press.

Hunter, J., & Mallon, G. P. (2000). Lesbian, gay, and bisexual adolescent development: Dancing with your feet tied together. In B. Greene, & G. L. Croom (Eds.), *Education, research, and practice in lesbian, gay, bisexual, and transgendered psychology: A resource manual, Vol. 5*. Thousand Oaks, CA: Sage.

Hunter, S. (2007). *Coming out and disclosures: LGBT persons across the life span*. New York: Haworth Press.

Huntsinger, C. S., Jose, P. E., Liaw, F., & Ching, W-D. (1997). Cultural differences in early mathematics learning: A comparison of Euro-American, Chinese-American, and Taiwan-Chinese families. *International Journal of Behavioral Development, 21*, 371–388.

Huppe, M., & Cyr, M. (1997). Division of household labor and marital satisfaction of dual income couples according to family life cycle. *Canadian Journal of Counseling, 31*, 145–162.

Huston, A., McLoyd, V. C., & Coll, C. G. (1997). Poverty and behavior: The case for multiple methods and levels of analysis. *Developmental Review, 17*, 36–393.

Huston, T. L., Caughlin, J. P., Houts, R. M., & Smith, S. E. (2001). The connubial crucible: Newlywed years as predictors of marital delight, distress, and divorce. *Journal of Personality and Social Psychology, 80*, 237–252.

Hutchinson, A., Whitman, R., & Abeare, C. (2003). The unification of mind: Integration of hemispheric semantic processing. *Brain & Language, 87*, 361–368.

Hutchinson, S., & Wexler, B. (2007, January). Is 'raging' good for health?: Older women's participation in the Raging Grannies. *Health Care for Women International, 28*, 88–118.

Hutton, P. H. (2004). *Phillippe Aries and the politics of French cultural history.* Amherst: University of Massachusetts Press.

Huurre, T., Junkkari, H., & Aro, H. (2006, June). Long-term psychosocial effects of parental divorce: A follow-up study from adolescence to adulthood. *European Archives of Psychiatry and Clinical Neuroscience, 256*, 256–263.

Hyde, J. S. (1994). *Understanding human sexuality* (5th ed.). New York: McGraw-Hill.

Hyde, J. S., & DeLamater, J. D. (2003). *Understanding human sexuality* (8th ed.). New York: McGraw-Hill.

Hyde, J., & DeLamater, J. (2008). *Understanding human sexuality.* (10th ed.). New York: McGraw-Hill Higher Education.

Hyde, J., & Grabe, S. (2008). Meta-analysis in the psychology of women. *Psychology of women: A handbook of issues and theories* (2nd ed.). Westport, CT: Praeger Publishers/Greenwood Publishing Group.

Hyde, J., Mezulis, A., & Abramson, L. (2008). The ABCs of depression: Integrating affective, biological, and cognitive models to explain the emergence of the gender difference in depression. *Psychological Review, 115*, 291–313.

Iglesias, J., Eriksson, J., Grize, F., Tomassini, M., & Villa, A. E. (2005). Dynamics of pruning in simulated large-scale spiking neural networks. *Biosystems, 79*, 11–20.

IJzendoorn, M., Bakermans-Kranenburg, M., & Sagi-Schwartz, A. (2006). Attachment across diverse sociocultural contexts: The limits of universality. *Parenting beliefs, behaviors, and parent-child relations: A cross-cultural perspective.* New York: Psychology Press.

Ingersoll-Dayton, B., Neal, M., & Hammer, L. (2001). Aging parents helping adult children: The experience of the sandwiched generation. *Family Relations, 50*, 263–271.

Ingersoll, E. W., & Thoman, E. B. (1999). Sleep/wake states of preterm infants: Stability, developmental change, diurnal variation, and relation with caregiving activity. *Child Development, 70*, 1–10.

Ingudomnukul, E., Baron-Cohen, S., Wheelwright, S., & Knickmeyer, R. (2007, May). Elevated rates of testosterone-related disorders in women with autism spectrum conditions. *Hormones and Behavior, 51*(5), 597–604.

Inoue, K., Tanii, H., Abe, S., Kaiya, H., Nata, M., & Fukunaga, T. (2006, December). The correlation between rates of unemployment and suicide rates in Japan between 1985 and 2002. *International Medical Journal, 13*, 261–263.

Insel, P. M., & Roth, W. T. (1991). *Core concepts in health* (6th ed.). Mountain View, CA: Mayfield.

Interlandi, J. (2007). Chemo control. *Scientific American, 296*, 30–38.

International Human Genome Sequencing Consortium. (2001). Initial sequencing and analysis of the human genome. *Nature, 409*, 860–921.

Irwin, E. G. (1993). A focused overview of anorexia nervosa and bulimia: I. Etiological issues. *Archives of Psychiatric Nursing, 7*, 342–346.

Isenberg, E. (2007). What have we learned about homeschooling? *Peabody Journal of Education, 82*(2), 387–409.

Ishi-Kuntz, M. (2000). Diversity within Asian-American families. In D. H. Demo, K. R. Allen, & M. A.Fine (Eds.), *Handbook of family diversity.* New York: Oxford University Press.

Izard, C. E. (1982). The psychology of emotion comes of age on the coattails of Darwin. *PsycCRITIQUES, 27*, 426–429.

Izard, C., King, K., Trentacosta, C., Morgan, J., Laurenceau, J., Krauthamer-Ewing, E., et al. (2008, December). Accelerating the development of emotion competence in Head Start children: Effects on adaptive and maladaptive behavior. *Development and Psychopathology, 20*(1), 369–397.

Izard, J., Haines, C., Crouch, R., Houston, S., & Neill, N. (2003). Assessing the impact of the teaching of modelling: Some implications. In S. Lamon, W. Parker, & K. Houston (Eds.), *Mathematical modelling: A way of life: ICTMA 11.* Chichester, England: Horwood Publishing.

Izawa, C., & Hayden, R. G. (1993). Race against time: Toward the principle of optimization in learning and retention. Hillside, NJ: Lawrence Erlbaum Associates.

Jackson, T. (2006, May). Relationships between perceived close social support and health practices within community samples of American women and men. *Journal of Psychology: Interdisciplinary and Applied, 140*, 229–246.

Jacobi, C., Hayward, C., de Zwaan, M., Kraemer, H. C., & Agras, W. S. (2004). Coming to terms with risk factors for eating disorders: Application of risk terminology and suggestions for a general taxonomy. *Psychological Bulletin, 130*, 19–65.

Jacobson, N., & Gottman, J. (1998). *When men batter women.* New York: Simon & Schuster.

Jacques, H., & Mash, E. (2004). A test of the tripartite model of anxiety and depression in elementary and high school boys and girls. *Journal of Abnormal Child Psychology, 32*, 13–25.

Jahoda, G. (1980). Theoretical and systematic approaches in mass-cultural psychology. In H. C. Triandis & W. W. Lambert (Eds.), *Handbook of cross-cultural psychology* (Vol. 1). Boston: Allyn & Bacon.

Jahoda, G. (1983). European "lag" in the development of an economic concept: A study in Zimbabwe. *British Journal of Developmental Psychology, 1*, 113–120.

James, W. (1890/1950). *The principles of psychology.* New York: Holt.

Janda, L. H., & Klenke-Hamel, K. E. (1980). *Human sexuality.* New York: Van Nostrand.

Jansen, B. R. J., Van der Maas, W. L, & Black J. E. (2001). Evidence for the phase transition from rule I to rule II on the balance scale task. *Developmental Review, 21*, 450–494.

Janssens, J. M. A. M., & Dekovic, M. (1997). Child rearing, prosocial moral reasoning, and prosocial behaviour. *International Journal of Behavioral Development, 20*, 509–527.

Japiassu, R. (2008). Pretend play and preschoolers. *The transformation of learning: Advances in cultural-historical activity theory.* New York: Cambridge University Press.

Javawant, S., & Parr, J. (2007). Outcome following subdural haemorrhages in infancy. *Archives of the Disabled Child, 92*, 343–347.

Jayawardena, K., & Liao, S. (2006, January). Elder abuse at end of life. *Journal of Palliative Medicine, 9*, 127–136.

Jeng, S., Yau, K. T., & Teng, R. (1998). Neurobehavioral development at term in very low-birthweight infants and normal term infants in Taiwan. *Early Human Development, 51*, 235–245.

Jenkins, A., Harburg, E., Weissberg, N., & Donnelly, T. (2004). The influence of minority group cultural models on persistence in college. *Journal of Negro Education, 73*, 69–80.

Jensen, A. (2003). Do age-group differences on mental tests imitate racial differences? *Intelligence, 31*, 107–21.

Jeynes, W. (2007). The impact of parental remarriage on children: A meta-analysis. *Marriage & Family Review, 40*, 75–102.

Ji-liang, S., Li-qing, Z., & Yan, T. (2003). The impact of intergenerational social support and filial expectation on the loneliness of elder parents. *Chinese Journal of Clinical Psychology, 11*, 167–169.

Jimenez, J., & Guzman, R. (2003). The influence of code-oriented versus meaning-oriented approaches to reading instruction on word recognition in the Spanish language. *International Journal of Psychology, 38*, 65–78.

Jimerson, S., Morrison, G., Pletcher, S., & Furlong, M. (2006). Youth engaged in antisocial and aggressive behaviors: Who are they? *Handbook of school violence and school safety: From research to practice* (pp. 3–19). Mahwah, NJ: Lawrence Erlbaum Associates Publishers.

Joe, S., & Marcus, S. (2003). Datapoints: Trends by race and gender in suicide attempts among U.S. adolescents, 1991–2001. *Psychiatric Services, 54*, 454.

Johannes, L. (2003, October 9). A better test for Down Syndrome. *Wall Street Journal*, pp. D1, D3.

Johannesen-Schmidt, M., & Eagly, A. (2002). Diminishing returns: The effects of income on the content stereotypes of wage earners. *Personality and Social Psychology Bulletin, 28*, 1538–1545.

Johnson, A. M., Wadsworth, J., Wellings, K., & Bradshaw, S. (1992). Sexual lifestyles and HIV risk. *Nature, 360*, 410–412.

Johnson, C. H., Vicary, J. R., Heist, C. L., & Corneal, D. A. (2001). Moderate alcohol and tobacco use during pregnancy and child behavior outcomes. *Journal of Primary Prevention, 21*, 367–379.

Johnson, C. L., & Barer, B. M. (1992). Patterns of engagement and disengagement among the oldest old. *Journal of Aging Studies, 6*, 351–364.

Johnson, D. C., Kassner, C. T., & Kutner, J. S. (2004). Current use of guidelines, protocols, and care pathways for symptom management in hospice. *American Journal of Hospital Palliative Care, 21*, 51–57.

Johnson, D. J., Jaeger, E., Randolph, S. M., Cauce, A. M., & Ward, J., National Institute of Child Health and Human Development: Early Child Care Research Network. (2003). Studying the effects of early child care experiences on the development of children of color in the United States: Toward a more inclusive research agenda. *Child Development, 74*, 1227–1244.

Johnson, D., & Foster, S. (2005). The relationship between relational aggression in kindergarten children and friendship stability, mutuality, and peer liking. *Early Education and Development, 16*, 141–160.

Johnson, J. L., Primas, P. J., & Coe, M. K. (1994). Factors that prevent women of low socioeconomic status from seeking prenatal care. *Journal of the American Academy of Nurse Practitioners, 6,* 105–111.

Johnson, K., & Eilers, A. (1998). Effects of knowledge and development on subordinate level categorization. *Cognitive Development, 13,* 515–545.

Johnson, M. H. (1998). The neural basis of cognitive development. In D. Kuhn & R. S. Siegler (Eds.), *Handbook of child psychology: Vol. 2: Cognition, perception, and language* (5th ed., pp. 1–49). New York: Wiley.

Johnson, N. G., Roberts, M. C., & Worell, J. (Eds.). (1999). *Beyond appearance: A new look at adolescent girls.* Washington, DC: American Psychological Association.

Johnson, S. (2009). Developmental origins of object perception. *Learning and the infant mind.* New York: Oxford University Press.

Johnson, S. L., & Birch, L. L. (1994). Parents' and children's adiposity and eating style. *Pediatrics, 94,* 653–661.

Johnston, L. D., Bachman, J. G., & O'Malley, P. M. (2008). *Monitoring the future study.* Lansing: University of Michigan.

Johnston, L. D., Bachman, J. G., & O'Malley, P. M. (2009). *Monitoring the future study.* Lansing: University of Michigan.

Jones, F., & Bright, J. (2007). Stress: Health and illness. *The Praeger handbook on stress and coping (vol.1).* Westport, CT: Praeger Publishers/Greenwood Publishing Group.

Jones, H. (2006). Drug addiction during pregnancy: Advances in maternal treatment and understanding child outcomes. *Current Directions in Psychological Science, 15,* 126–130.

Jones, S. (2006). Exploration or imitation? The effect of music on 4-week-old infants' tongue protrusions. *Infant Behavior & Development, 29,* 126–130.

Jones, S. (2007). Imitation in infancy: The development of mimicry. *Psychological Science, 18,* 593–599.

Jongudomkarn, D., & Camfield, L. (2006, September). Exploring the quality of life of people in north eastern and southern Thailand. *Social Indicators Research, 78,* 489–529.

Jorgensen, G. (2006, June). Kohlberg and Gilligan: duet or duel? *Journal of Moral Education, 35,* 179–196.

Jose, O., & Alfons, V. (2007). Do demographics affect marital satisfaction? *Journal of Sex and Marital Therapy, 33,* 73–85.

Joseph, H., Reznik, I., & Mester, R. (2003). Suicidal behavior of adolescent girls: Profile and meaning. *Israel Journal of Psychiatry & Related Sciences, 40,* 209–219.

Joseph, R. (1999). Environmental influences on neural plasticity, the limbic system, emotional development and attachment: A review. *Child Psychiatry & Human Development, 29,* 189–208.

Jost, J. T., & Hamilton, D. L. (2005). Stereotypes in our culture. In J. F. Dovidio, P. Click, & L. A. Rudman, *On the nature of prejudice: Fifty years after Allport.* Malden, MA: Blackwell Publishing.

Judd, C. M., & Park, B. (2005). Group differences and stereotype accuracy. In J. F. Dovidio, P. Click, & L. A. Rudman, *On the nature of prejudice: Fifty years after Allport.* Malden, MA: Blackwell Publishing.

Juhn, Y. J., Sauver, J. S., Katusic, S., Vargas, D., Weaver, A., & Yunginger, J. (2005). The influence of neighborhood environment on the incidence of childhood asthma: a multilevel approach. *Social Science Medicine, 60,* 2453–2464.

Juntunen, C., Wegner, K., & Matthews, L. (2002). Promoting positive career change in midlife. *Counseling across the lifespan: Prevention and treatment.* Thousand Oaks, CA: Sage Publications, Inc.

Jurimae, T., & Saar, M. (2003). Self-perceived and actual indicators of motor abilities in children and adolescents. *Perception and Motor Skills, 97,* 862–866.

Juster, F., Ono, H., and Stafford, F. (2004). *Changing times of American youth: 1981–2003.* Ann Arbor, MI: Institute for Social Research.

Juster, T., Ono, H., & Stafford, F. (2000). *Time use.* Presented at the Sloan Centers on Work and Family Conference, San Francisco.

Juvonen, J., Le, V-N., Kaganoff, T., Augustine, C. H., & Constant, L. (2004). *Focus on the wonder years: Challenges facing the American middle school.* Santa Monica, CA: Rand Corporation.

Kacapyr, E. (1997, October). Are we having fun yet? *American Demographics,* pp. 28–30.

Kagan, J. (2008). In defense of qualitative changes in development. *Child Development, 79,* 112–119.

Kagan, J., & Snidman, N. (1991). Infant predictors of inhibited and uninhibited profiles. *Psychological Science, 2,* 40–44.

Kagan, J., Arcus, D., & Snidman, N. (1993). The idea of temperament: Where do we go from here? In R. Plomin, & G. E. McClearn (Eds.), *Nature, nurture, and psychology.* Washington, DC: American Psychological Association.

Kagan, J., Kearsley, R., & Zelazo, P. R. (1978). *Infancy: Its place in human development.* Cambridge, MA: Harvard University Press.

Kahn, J. (2007, February). Maximizing the potential public health impact of HPV vaccines: A focus on parents. *Journal of Adolescent Health, 40,* 101–103.

Kahn, J., Hessling, R., & Russell, D. (2003). Social support, health, and well-being among the elderly: What is the role of negative affectivity? *Personality & Individual Differences, 35,* 5–17.

Kahn, R. L., & Rowe, J. W. (1999). *Successful aging.* New York: Dell.

Kahneman, D., Krueger, A., Schkade, D., Schwarz, N., & Stone, A. (2006, June). Would you be happier if you were richer? A focusing illusion. *Science, 312,,* 1908–1910.

Kail, R. (1991). Developmental changes in speed of processing during childhood and adolescence. *Psychological Bulletin, 109,* 490–501.

Kail, R. V. (2004). Cognitive development includes global and domain-specific processes. *Merrill-Palmer Quarterly, 50,* Special Issue: 50th Anniversary Issue: Part II, The maturing of the human development sciences: Appraising past, present, and prospective agendas, 445–455.

Kaiser, L. L., & Allen, L. American Dietetic Association. (2002). Position of the American Dietetic Association: Nutrition and lifestyle for a healthy pregnancy outcome. *Journal of the American Dietetic Association, 102,* 1479–1490.

Kalb, C. (1997, Spring/Summer). The top 10 health worries. *Newsweek Special Issue,* 42–43.

Kalb, C. (2004, January 26). Brave new babies. *Newsweek,* pp. 45–53.

Kalb, C. (2006, December 11). Peering into the future. *Newsweek,* p. 52.

Kalsi, M., Heron, G., & Charman, W. (2001). Changes in the static accommodation response with age. *Ophthalmic & Physiological Optics, 21,* 77–84.

Kaltiala-Heino, R., Kosunen, E., & Rimpela, M. (2003). Pubertal timing, sexual behaviour and self-reported depression in middle adolescence. *Journal of Adolescence, 26,* 531–545.

Kan, P., & Kohnert, K. (2008). Fast mapping by bilingual preschool children. *Journal of Child Language, 35,* 495–514.

Kane, R. A., Caplan, A. L., Urv-Wong, E. K., & Freeman, I. C. (1997). Everyday matters in the lives of nursing home residents: Wish for and perception of choice and control. *Journal of the American Geriatrics Society, 45,* 1086–1093.

Kaneda, H., Maeshima, K., Goto, N., Kobayakawa, T., Ayabe-Kanamura, S., & Saito, S. (2000). Decline in taste and odor discrimination abilities with age, and relationship between gustation and olfaction. *Chemical Senses, 25,* 331–337.

Kantrowitz, B., & Wingert, P. (1999, May 10). How well do you know your kid? (teenagers need adult attention). *Newsweek, 133*(19), 36.

Kao, G. (2000). Psychological well-being and educational achievement among immigrant youth. In D. J. Hernandez (Ed.), *Children of immigrants: Health, adjustment, and public assistance.* Washington, DC: National Academy Press.

Kao, G., & Tienda, M. (1995). Optimism and achievement: the educational performance of immigrant youth. *Social Science Quarterly, 76,* 1–19.

Kaplan, H., & Dove, H. (1987). Infant development among the Ache of Eastern Paraguay. *Developmental Psychology, 23,* 190–198.

Kaplan, R. M., Sallis, J. F., Jr., & Patterson, T. L. (1993). *Health and human behavior.* P. 254. "Age specific breast cancer annual incidence." New York: McGraw-Hill.

Kaplan, S., Heiligenstein, J., West, S., Busner, J., Harder, D., Dittmann, R., Casat, C., & Wernicke, J. F. (2004). Efficacy and safety of atomoxetine in childhood attention-deficit/hyperactivity disorder with comorbid oppositional defiant disorder. *Journal of Attention Disorders, 8,* 45–52.

Karney, B. R., & Bradbury, T. N. (1995). The longitudinal course of marital quality and stability: A review of theory, method, and research. *Psychological Bulletin, 118,* 3–34.

Karney, B. R., & Bradbury, T. N. (2005). Contextual influences on marriage. *Current Directions in Psychological Science, 14,* 171–174.

Karpov, Y. (2006). Neo-Vygotskian activity theory: Merging Vygotsky's and Piaget's theories of cognitive development. *Frontiers in: Cognitive psychology.* Hauppauge, NY: Nova Science Publishers.

Karpov, Y. V., & Haywood, H. C. (1998). Two ways to elaborate Vygotsky's concept of mediation: Implications for instruction. *American Psychologist, 53,* 27–36.

Kart, C. S. (1990). *The realities of aging* (3rd ed.). Boston: Allyn & Bacon.

Kartman, L. L. (1991). Life review: One aspect of making meaningful music for the elderly. *Activities, Adaptations, and Aging, 15,* 42–45.

Kartrowitz, E. J., & Evans, G. W. (2004). The Relation Between the Ratio of Children per Activity Area and Off-Task Behavior and Type of Play in Day Care Centers. *Environment & Behavior, 36,* 541–557.

Kasser, T., & Sharma, Y. S. (1999). Reproductive freedom, educational equality, and females' preference for resource-acquisition characteristics in mates. *Psychological Science, 10,* 374–377.

Kastenbaum, R. (1985). Dying and death: A life-span approach. In J. E. Birren & K. W. Schaie (Eds.), *Handbook of the psychology of aging.* New York: Van Nostrand Reinhold.

Kastenbaum, R. (1999). Dying and bereavement. In J. C. Cavanaugh & S. K. Whitbourne (Eds.), *Gerontology: An interdisciplinary perspective.* New York: Oxford University Press.

Kastenbaum, R. (2000). *The psychology of death* (3rd ed.). New York: Springer.

Kastenbaum, R. J. (1992). *The psychology of death.* New York: Springer-Verlag.

Kate, N. T. (1998, March). How many children? *American Demographics,* p. 35.

Kates, N., Grieff, B., & Hagen, D. (1990). *The psychosocial impact of job loss.* Washington, DC: American Psychiatric Press.

Katz, D. L. (2001). Behavior modification in primary care. The Pressure System Model. *Preventive Medicine: an International Devoted to Practice & Theory, 32,* 66–72.

Katz, L. G. (1989, December). Beginners' ethics. *Parents,* p. 213.

Katz, S., & Marshall, B. (2003). New sex for old: Lifestyle, consumerism, and the ethics of aging well. *Journal of Aging Studies, 17,* 3–16.

Kaufman, J., & Sternberg, R. (2006). *The international handbook of creativity.* New York: Cambridge University Press.

Kaufman, J. C., Kaufman, A. S., Kaufman-Singer, J., & Kaufman, N. L. (2005). The Kaufman Assessment Battery for Children—Second Edition and the Kaufman Adolescent and Adult Intelligence Test. In D. P. Flanagan & P. L. Harrison (Eds.), *Contemporary intellectual assessment: Theories, tests, and issues.* New York: Guilford Press.

Kaufman, M. T. (1992, November 28). Teaching compassion in theater of death. *New York Times,* p. B7.

Kaufmann, D., Gestert, E., Santa Lucia, R. C., Salcedo, O., Rendina-Gobioff, G., & Gadd, R. (2000). The relationship between parenting style and children's adjustment: The parents' perspective. *Journal of Child & Family Studies, 9,* 231–245.

Kavale, K. (2002). Mainstreaming to full inclusion: From orthogenesis to pathogenesis of an idea. *International Journal of Disability, Development & Education, 49,* 201–214.

Kavale, K. A., & Forness, S. R. (2000, September–October). History, rhetoric, and reality: Analysis of the inclusion debate. *Rase: Remedial & Special Education, 21,* 279–296.

Kavšek, M. (2004). Predicting later IQ from infant visual habituation and dishabituation: A meta-analysis. *Journal of Applied Developmental Psychology, 25,* 369–393.

Kaye, W. H., Devlin, B., Barbarich, N., Bulik, C. M., Thornton, L., Badanu, S. A., Fichter, M. M., Halmi, K. A., Kaplan, A. S., Strober, M., Woodside, D. B., Bergen, A. W., Crow, S., Mitchell, J., Rotondo, A. Mauri, M., Cassano, G., Keel, P., Plotnicov, K., Pollice, C., Klump, K. L., Lilenfeld, L. R., Ganjei, J. K., Quadflieg, N., Berrettini, W. H., & Kaye, W. H. (2004). Genetic analysis of bulimia nervosa: Methods and sample description. *Journal of Eating Disorders, 35,* 556–570.

Kazdin, A. E., & Benjet, C. (2003). Spanking children: Evidence and issues. *Current Directions in Psychological Science, 12,* 99–103.

Keating, D. (1980). Thinking processes in adolescence. In J. Adelson (Ed.), *Handbook of adolescent psychology.* New York: Wiley.

Keating, D. (1990). Adolescent thinking. In S.S. Feldman & G.R. Elliott (Eds.), *At the threshold.* Cambridge, MA: Harvard University Press.

Keating, D. P., & Clark, L. V. (1980). Development of physical and social reasoning in adolescence. *Developmental Psychology, 16,* 23–30.

Kecskes, I., & Papp, T. (2000). *Foreign language and mother tongue.* Mahwah, NJ: Erlbaum.

Keefer, B. L., Kraus, R. F., Parker, B. L., Elliotst, R., et al. (1991). A state university collaboration program: Residents' prespectives. Annual Meeting of the American Psychiataric Association (1990, New York). *Hospital and Community Psychiatry, 42,* 62–66.

Keel, P. K., Leon, G. R., & Fulkerson, J. A. (2001). Vulnerability to eating disorders in childhood and adolescence. In R. E. Ingram & J. M. Price (Eds.). *Vulnerability to psychopathology: Risk across the lifespan.* New York: Guilford Press.

Keller, H., Voelker, S., & Yovsi, R. D. (2005). Conceptions of Parenting in Different Cultural Communities: The case of West African Nso and Northern German Women. *Social Development, 14,* 158–180.

Keller, H., Yovsi, R., Borke, J., Kärtner, J., Henning, J., & Papaligoura, Z. (2004). Developmental consequences of early parenting experiences: Self-recognition and self-regulation in three cultural communities. *Child Development, 75,* 1745–1760.

Keller, M., & Miller, G. (2006). Resolving the paradox of common, harmful, heritable mental disorders: Which evolutionary genetic models work best? *Behavioral and Brain Sciences, 29,* 385–452.

Kellett, J. M. (2000). Older adult sexuality. In L. T. Szuchman & F. Muscarella (Eds.), *Psychological perspectives on human sexuality.* New York: Wiley.

Kellman, P., & Arterberry, M. (2006). Infant visual perception. In W. Damon & R. M. Lerner, *Handbook of child psychology:* Vol 2, *Cognition, perception, and language* (6th ed.). New York: Wiley.

Kelly, G. (2001). *Sexuality today: A human perspective* (7th ed.). New York: McGraw-Hill.

Kelly, J. (1997, January 22). The latest in take-at-home tests: IQ. *The New York Times,* p. B7.

Kemper, R. L., & Vernooy, A. R. (1994). Metalinguistic awareness in first graders: A qualitative perspective. *Journal of Psycholinguistic Research, 22,* 41–57.

Kemps, E., & Tiggemann, M. (2007). Modality-specific imagery reduces cravings for food: An application of the elaborated intrusion theory of desire to food craving. *Journal of Experimental Psychology: Applied, 13,* 95–104.

Kenrick, D. T., Keefe, R. C., Bryna, A., Barr, A., & Brown, S. (1995). Age preferences and mate choice among homosexuals and heterosexuals: A case for modular psychological mechanisms. *Journal of Personality and Social Psychology, 69,* 1166–1172.

Kiang, L., Yip, T., & Fuligni, A. J. (2008). Multiple social identities and adjustment in young adults from ethnically diverse backgrounds. *Journal of Research on Adolescence, 18,* 643–670.

Kibria, N. (2003). *Becoming Asian American: Second-generation Chinese and Korean American identities.* Baltimore, MD: Johns Hopkins University Press.

Kidwell, J. S., Dunyam, R. M., Bacho, R. A., Pastorino, E., & Portes, P. R. (1995). Adolescent identity exploration: A test of Erikson's theory of transitional crisis. *Adolescence, 30,* 785–793.

Killen, M., & Hart, D. (Eds.). (1995). *Morality in everyday life: Developmental perspectives.* New York: Cambridge University Press.

Kilner, J. M., Friston, J. J., & Frith, C. D. (2007). Predictive coding: An account of the mirror neuron system. *Cognitive Processes, 33,* 88–997.

Kim, J-S., & Lee, E-H. (2003). Cultural and noncultural predictors of health outcomes in Korean daughter and daughter-in-law caregivers. *Public Health Nursing, 20,* 111–119.

Kim, K., & Smith, P. K. (1999). Family relations in early childhood and reproductive development. *Journal of Reproductive & Infant Psychology, 17,* 133–148.

Kim, M. T., Han, H-R., Shin, H. S., Kim, K. B., & Lee, H. B. (2005). Factors associated with depression experience of immigrant populations: A study of Korean immigrants. *Archives of Psychiatric Nursing, 19,* 217–225.

Kim, S., & Park, H. (2006, January). Five years after the launch of Viagra in Korea: Changes in perceptions of erectile dysfunction treatment by physicians, patients, and the patients' spouses. *Journal of Sexual Medicine, 3,* 132–137.

Kim, Y., & Stevens, J. H. (1987). The socialization of prosocial behavior in children. *Childhood Education, 63,* 200–206.

Kim-Cohen, J. (2007). Resilience and developmental psychopathology. *Child and Adolescent Psychiatric Clinics of North America, 16,* 271–283.

Kimm, S. Y., Glynn, N. W., Kriska, A. M., Barton, B. A., Kronsberg, S. S., Daniels, S. R., Crawford, P. B., Sabry, Z. I., & Liu, K. (2003). Decline in physical activity in black girls and white girls during adolescence. *New England Journal of Medicine, 347,* 709–715.

Kimmel, D., & Sang, B. (2003). Lesbians and gay men in midlife. In L. Garnets & D. Kimmel (Eds.), *Psychological perspectives on lesbian, gay, and bisexual experiences.* New York: Columbia University Press.

King, K. (2003). Racism or sexism? Attributional ambiguity and simultaneous memberships in multiple oppressed groups. *Journal of Applied Social Psychology, 33,* 223–247.

Kinney, H. C., Randall, L. L., Sleeper, L. A., Willinger, M., Beliveau, R. A., Zec, N., Rava, L. A., Dominici, L., Iyasu, S., Randall, B., Habbe, D., Wilson, H., Mandell, F., McClain, M., & Welty, T. K. (2003). Serotonergic brainstem abnormalities in Northern Plains Indians with the sudden infant death syndrome. *Journal of Neuropathology and Experimental Neurology, 62,* 1178–1191.

Kinsey, A. C., Pomeroy, W. B., & Martin, C. E. (1948). *Sexual behavior in the human male.* Philadelphia, PA: Saunders.

Kirby, J. (2006, May). From single-parent families to stepfamilies: Is the transition associated with adolescent alcohol initiation? *Journal of Family Issues, 27,* 685–711.

Kirchengast, S., & Hartmann, B. (2003). Impact of maternal age and maternalsomatic characteristics on newborn size. *American Journal of Human Biology, 15,* 220–228.

Kitchener, R. F. (1996). The nature of the social for Piaget and Vygotsky. *Human Development, 39,* 243–249.

Kitterod, R., & Pettersen, S. (2006, September). Making up for mothers' employed working hours? Housework and childcare among Norwegian fathers. *Work, Employment and Society, 20,* 473–492.

Kitzmann, K., Gaylord, N., & Holt, A. (2003). Child witnesses to domestic violence: A meta-analytic review. *Journal of Consulting & Clinical Psychology, 71,* 339–352.

Kleespies, P. (2004). The wish to die: Assisted suicide and voluntary euthanasia. In P. Kleespies (Ed.), *Life and death decisions: Psychological and ethical considerations in end-of-life care.* Washington, DC: American Psychological Association.

Klibanoff, R., Levine, S., Huttenlocher, J., Vasilyeva, M., & Hedges, L. (2006). Preschool children's mathematical knowledge: The effect of teacher 'math talk' *Developmental Psychology, 42,* 59–69.

Klinger, J., & Artiles, A. J. (2006). English language learners struggling to learn to read: Emergent scholarship on linguistic differences and learning disabilities. *Journal of Learning Disabilities, 39,* 386–389.

Knafo, A., & Schwartz, S. H. (2003). Parenting and accuracy of perception of parental values by adolescents. *Child Development, 73,* 595–611.

Knaus, W. A., Conners, A. F., Dawson, N. V., Desbiens, N. A., Fulkerson, W. J., Jr., Goldman, L., Lynn, J., & Oye, R. K. (1995, November 22). A controlled trial to improve care for seriously ill hospitalized patients. The study to understand prognoses and preferences for outcomes and risks of treatments (SUPPORT). *Journal of the American Medical Association, 273,* 1591–1598.

Knecht, S., Deppe, M., Draeger, B., Bobe, L., Lohmann, H., Ringelstein, E. B., & Henningsen, H. (2000). Language lateralization in healthy right-handers. *Brain, 123,* 74–81.

Knickmeyer, R., & Baron-Cohen, S. (2006, December). Fetal testosterone and sex differences. *Early Human Development, 82,* 755–760.

Knight, G. P., Fabes, R. A., & Higgins, D. A. (1996). Concerns about drawing casual inferences from meta-analyses: An example in the study of gender differences in aggression. *Psychological Bulletin, 119,* 410–421.

Knight, K. (1994, March). Back to basics. *Essence,* pp. 122–138.

Knight, N., Sousa, P., Barrett, J. L., & Atran, S. (2004). Children's attributions of beliefs to humans and God: Cross-cultural evidence. *Cognitive Science: A Multidisciplinary Journal, 28,* 117–126.

Knowles, J. (2005). Birth control choices for teens. Retrieved April 1, 2006 from http://www.plannedparenthood.org/pp2/portal/files/portal/medicalinfo/birthcontrol/pub-bc-choices-teens.xml

Knutson, J. F., & Lansing, C. R. (1990). The relationship between communication problems and psychological difficulties in persons with profound acquired hearing loss. *Journal of Speech and Hearing Disorders, 55,* 656–664.

Kochanska, G. (1998). Mother–child relationship, child fearfulness, and emerging attachment: A short-term longitudinal study. *Developmental Psychology, 34,* 480–490.

Kochanska, G., & Aksan, N. (2004). Development of mutual responsiveness between parents and their young children. *Child Development, 75,* 1657–1676.

Kodl, M., & Mermelstein, R. (2004). Beyond modeling: Parenting practices, parental smoking history, and adolescent cigarette smoking. *Addictive Behaviors, 29,* 17–32.

Koechlin, E., Basso, G., Pietrini, P., Panzer, S., & Grafman, J. (1999, May 13). The role of the anterior prefrontal cortex in human cognition. *Nature, 399,* 148–51

Koenig, L. B., McGue, M., Krueger, R. F., & Bouchard, Jr., T. J. (2005). Genetic and environmental influences on religiousness: Findings for retrospective and current religiousness ratings. *Journal of Personality, 73,* 471–488.

Koh, A., & Ross, L. (2006). Mental health issues: A comparison of lesbian, bisexual and heterosexual women. *Journal of Homosexuality, 51,* 33–57.

Kohlberg, L. (1984). *The psychology of moral development: Essays on moral development* (Vol. 2). San Francisco: Harper & Row.

Kohn, A. (2006). *The homework myth: Why our kids get too much of a bad thing.* Cambridge, MA: Da Capo Press.

Koivisto, M., & Revonsuo, A. (2003). Object recognition in the cerebral hemispheres as revealed by visual field experiments. *Laterality: Asymmetries of Body, Brain & Cognition, 8,* 135–153.

Kolata, G. (1998). *Clone: The road to Dolly and the path ahead.* New York: William Morrow.

Kolata, G. (May 11, 2004). The heart's desire. *New York Times,* p. D1.

Koopmans, S., & Kooijman, A. (2006, November). Prebyopia correction and accommodative intraocular lenses. *Gerontechnology, 5,* 222–230.

Koroukian, S. M., Trisel, B., & Rimm, A. A. (1998). Estimating the proportion of unnecessary cesarean sections in Ohio using birth certificate data. *Journal of Clinical Epidemiology, 51,* 1327–1334.

Kosic, A. (2004). Acculturation strategies, coping process and acculturative stress. *Scandinavian Journal of Psychology, 45,* 269–278.

Koska, J., Ksinantova, L., Sebokova, E., Kvetnansky, R., Klimes, I., Chrousos, G., & Pacak, K. (2002). Endocrine regulation of subcutaneous fat metabolism during cold exposure in humans. *Annals of the New York Academy of Science, 967,* 500–505.

Kosmala, K., & Kloszewska, I. (2004). The burden of providing care for Alzheimer's disease patients in Poland. *International Journal of Geriatric Psychiatry, 19,* 191–193.

Koss, M. P., Goodman, L. A., Browne, A., Fitzgerald, L. F., Keita, G. P., & Russo, N. F. (1993). *No safe haven: Violence against women, at home, at work, and in the community.* Final report of the American Psychological Association Women's Programs Office Task Force on Violence Against Women. Washington, DC: American Psychological Association.

Kotre, J., & Hall, E. (1990). *Seasons of life.* Boston: Little, Brown.

Kozey, M., & Siegel, L. (2008). Definitions of learning disabilities in Canadian provinces and territories. *Canadian Psychology/Psychologie canadienne, 49,* 162–171.

Kozulin, A., (2004). Vygotsky's theory in the classroom: Introduction. *European Journal of Psychology of Education, 19,* 3–7.

Kraebel, K., & Gerhardstein, P. (2006). Three-month-old infants' object recognition across changes in viewpoint using an operant learning procedure. *Infant Behavior & Development, 29,* 11–23.

Kraemer, B., Noll, T., Delsignore, A., Milos, G., Schnyder, U., & Hepp, U. (2006). Finger length ratio (2D:4D) and dimensions of sexual orientation. *Neuropsychobiology, 53,* 210–214.

Kramer, A. F., Erickson, K. I., & Colcombe, S. J. (2006). Exercise, cognition, and the aging brain. *Journal of Applied Physiology, 101,* 1237–1242.

Krantz, S. G. (1999). Conformal mappings. *American Scientist, 87,* 144.

Krause, N. (2003a). Religious meaning and subjective well-being in late life. *Journals of Gerontology: Series B: Psychological Sciences and Social Sciences, 58B,* S160–S170.

Krause, N. (2003b). Praying for others, financial strain, and physical health status in late life. *Journal for the Scientific Study of Religion, 42,* 377–391.

Krause, N. (2008). The social foundation of religious meaning in life. *Research on Aging, 30,* 395–427.

Krause, N., & Borawski-Clark, E. (1994). Clarifying the functions of social support in later life. *Research on Aging, 16,* 251–279.

Kreitlow, B., & Kreitlow, D. (1997). *Creative planning for the second half of life.* Duluth, MN: Whole Person Associates.

Krishnamoorthy, J. S., Hart, C., & Jelalian, E, (2006). The epidemic of childhood obesity: Review of research and implications for public policy. *Social Policy Report, 19,* 3–19.

Kroger, J. (2006). *Identity development: Adolescence through adulthood.* Thousand Oaks, CA: Sage.

Krojgaard, P. (2005). Infants' search for hidden persons. *International Journal of Behavioral Development, 29,* 70–79.

Kronenfeld, J. J. (2002). *Health care policy: Issues and trends.* New York: Prager.

Kronholz, J. (2003, August 10). Trying to close the stubborn learning gap. *Wall Street Journal,* p. B1, B5.

Kronholz, J. (2003, August 19). Trying to close the stubborn learning gap. *Wall Street Journal,* B1, B5.

Krout, J. A. (1988). Rural versus urban differences in elderly parents' contact with their children. *Gerontologist, 28,* 198–203.

Krueger, G. (2006, September). Meaning-making in the aftermath of sudden infant death syndrome. *Nursing Inquiry, 13,* 163–171.

Kübler-Ross, E. (1969). *On death and dying.* New York: Macmillan.

Kübler-Ross, E. (1982). *Working it through.* New York: Macmillan.

Kübler-Ross, E. (Ed.). (1975). Death: *The final stage of growth.* Englewood Cliffs, NJ: Prentice-Hall.

Kuczaj, S. A., II, Borys, R. H., & Jones, M. (1989). On the interaction of language and thought: Some thoughts on developmental data. In A. Galletly, D. Rogers, & J. A. Sloboda (Eds.), *Cognition and the social world.* New York: Oxford University Press.

Kuczynski, L., & Kochanska, G. (1990). Development of children's noncompliance strategies from toddlerhood to age 5. *Developmental Psychology, 26,* 398–408.

Kuhl, P. K., Andruski, J. E., Chistovich, I. A., Chistovich, L. A., Kozhevnikova, E. V., Ryskina, V. L., Stolyarova, E. I., Sundberg, U., & Lacerda, F. (1997, August 1). Cross-language analysis of phentic units in language addressed to infants. *Science, 277,* 684–686.

Kuhn, D., & Franklin, S. (2006). The second decade: What develops (and how). *Handbook of child psychology: Vol 2, Cognition, perception, and language* (6th ed.). Hoboken, NJ: John Wiley & Sons Inc.

Kupersmidt, J. B., & Dodge, K. A. (Eds.). (2004). *Children's peer relations: From development to intervention.* Washington, DC: American Psychological Association.

Kurdek, L. (2002). Predicting the timing of separation and marital satisfaction: An eight-year prospective longitudinal study. *Journal of Marriage & Family, 64,* 163–179.

Kurdek, L. (2003). Differences between gay and lesbian cohabiting couples. *Journal of Social & Personal Relationships, 20,* 411–436.

Kurdek, L. (2003). Negative representations of the self/spouse and marital distress. *Personal Relationships, 10,* 511–534.

Kurdek, L. (2006, May). Differences between partners from heterosexual, gay, and lesbian cohabiting couples. *Journal of Marriage and Family, 68,* 509–528.

Kurdek, L. A. (1993). The allocation of household labor in gay, lesbian, and heterosexual married children. *Journal of Social Issues, 49,* 127–139.

Kurdek, L.A. (1999). The nature and predictors of the trajectory of change in marital quality for husbands and wives over the first 10 years of marriage. *Developmental Psychology, 35,* 1283–1296.

Kurtines, W. M., & Gewirtz, J. L. (1987). *Moral development through social interaction.* New York: Wiley.

Kuther, T. L. (2000). Moral reasoning, perceived competence, and adolescent engagement in risky activity. *Journal of Adolescence, 23,* 599–604.

Kuther, T. L., & Higgins-D'Alessandro, A. (2000). Bridging the gap between moral reasoning and adolescent engagement in risky behavior. *Journal of Adolescence, 23,* 409–422.

Kuther, T. L., & Higgins-D'Alessandro, A. (2003). Attitudinal and normative predictors of alcohol use by older adolescents and young adults. *Journal of Drug Education, 33,* 71–90.

Laas, I. (2006). Self-actualization and society: A new application for an old theory. *Journal of Humanistic Psychology, 46,* 77–91.

Labouvie-Vief, G. (1990). Modes of knowledge and the organization of development. In M. L. Commons, C. Armon, L. Kohlberg, F. A. Richards, T. A. Grotzer, & J. Sinnott (Eds.), *Adult development* (Vol. 2). *Models and methods in the study of adolescent thought.* New York: Praeger.

Lackey, C. (2003). Violent family heritage, the transition to adulthood, and later partner violence. *Journal of Family Issues, 24,* 74–98.

Laditka, S., Laditka, J., & Probst, J. (2006). Racial and ethnic disparities in potentially avoidable delivery complications among pregnant Medicaid beneficiaries in South Carolina. *Maternal & Child Health Journal, 10,* 339–350.

Laflamme, D., Pomerleau, A., & Malcuit, G. (2002). A comparison of fathers' and mothers' involvement in childcare and stimulation behaviors during free-play with their infants at 9 and 15 months. *Sex Roles, 47,* 507–518.

LaFreniere, P., Masataka, N., Butovskaya, M., Chen, Q., Dessen, M. A., Atwanger, K., Schreiner, S., Montirosso, R., & Frigerio, A. (2002). Cross-cultural analysis of social competence and behavior problems in preschoolers. *Early Education and Development, 13, Special issue: Cultural perspectives on social competence in early childhood* 201–219.

LaFromboise, T., Coleman, H. L., & Gerton, J. (1993). Psychological impact of biculturalism: Evidence and theory. *Psychological Bulletin, 114,* 395–412.

Lafuente, M. J., Grifol, R., Segarra, J., & Soriano, J. (1997). Effects of the Firstart method of prenatal stimulation on psychomotor development: The first six months. *Pre- & PeriNatal Psychology, 11,* 151–162.

Lahiri, D. K., Maloney, B., Basha, M. R., Ge, Y. W., & Zawia, N. H. (2007). How and when environmental agents and dietary factors affect the course of Alzheimer's disease: the "LEARn" model (latent early-life associated regulation) may explain the triggering of AD. *Current Alzheimer Research, 4,* 219–228.

Lam, V., & Leman, P. (2003). The influence of gender and ethnicity on children's inferences about toy choice. *Social Development, 12,* 269–287.

Lamaze, F. (1970). *Painless childbirth: The Lamaze method.* Chicago: Regnery.

Lamb, M. E., Sternberg, K. J., Hwang, C. P., & Broberg, A. G. (Eds.). (1992). *Child care in context: Cross-cultural perspectives.* Hillsdale, NJ: Erlbaum.

Lambert, W. E., & Peal, E. (1972). The relation of bilingualism to intelligence. In A. S. Dil (Ed.), *Language, psychology, and culture* (3rd ed.). New York: Wiley.

Lambert, W. W. (1971). Cross-cultural backgrounds to personality development and the socialization of aggression: Findings from the Six Culture study. In W. W. Lambert & R. Weisbrod (Eds.), *Comparative perspectives in social psychology.* Boston: Little Brown.

Lamberts, S. W. J., van den Beld, A. W., & van der Lely, A-J. (1997, October 17). The endocrinology of aging. *Science, 278,* 419–424.

Lamm, B., & Keller, H. (2007). Understanding cultural models of parenting: The role of intracultural variation and response style. *Journal of Cross-Cultural Psychology, 38,* 50–57.

Lamm, H., & Wiesmann, U. (1997). Subjective attributes of attraction: How people characterize their liking, their love, and their being in love. *Personal Relationships, 4,* 271–284.

Lamont, J. A. (1997). Sexuality. In D. E. Stewart & G. E. Robinson (Eds.), *A clinician's guide to menopause. Clinical practice* (pp. 63–75). Washington, DC: Health Press International.

Lanctot, K. L., Herrmann, N., & Mazzotta, P. (2001). Role of serotonin in the behavioral and psychological symptoms of dementia. *Journal of Neuropsychiatry & Clinical Neurosciences, 13,* 5–21.

Lancy, D. (2007). Accounting for variability in mother-child play. *American Anthropologist. Special issue: In focus: Children, childhoods, and childhood studies, 109,* 273–284.

Landström, S., Granhag, P., & Hartwig, M. (2007). Children's live and videotaped testimonies: How presentation mode affects observers' perception, assessment and memory. *Legal and Criminological Psychology, 12,* 333–347.

Landy, F., & Conte, J.M. (2004). *Work in the 21st century.* New York: McGraw-Hill.

Lane, D. M., & Pearson, D. A. (1982). The development of selective attention. *Merrill-Palmer Quarterly: Journal of Developmental Psychology, 28,* 317–337.

Lane, W. K. (1976, November). *The relationship between personality and differential academic achievement within a group of highly gifted and high achieving children.* Dissertation Abstracts International., *37*(5-A), 2746.

Langford, P. E. (1995). *Approaches to the development of moral reasoning.* Hillsdale, NJ: Erlbaum.

Lansford, J. E., & Parker, J. G. (1999). Children's interactions in triads: Behavioral profiles and effects of gender and patterns of friendships among members. *Developmental Psychology, 35,* 80–93.

Lansford, J. E., Chang, L, Dodge, K. A., Malone, P. S., Oburu, P., Palmérus, K., Bacchini, D., Pastorelli, C., Bombi, A. S. Zelli, A., Tapanya, S., Chaudhary, N., Deater-Deckard, K., Manke, B., & Quinn, N. (2005). Physical discipline and children's adjustment: Cultural normativeness as a moderator. *Child Development, 76,* 1234–1246.

LaPrairie, J. L., & Murphy, A. Z. (2009). Neonatal injury alters adult pain sensitivity by increasing opioid tone in the periaqueductal gray. *Frontiers of Behavioral Neuroscience, 3,* 31–37.

Lapsley, D. (2006). Moral stage theory. *Handbook of moral development.* Mahwah, NJ: Lawrence Erlbaum Associates Publishers.

Larsen, K. E., O'Hara, M. W., & Brewer, K. K. (2001). A prospective study of self-efficacy expectancies and labor pain. *Journal of Reproductive and Infant Psychology, 19,* 203–214.

Larson, R., & Lampman-Petraitis, C. (1989). Daily emotional states as reported by children and adolescents. *Child Development, 60,* 1250–1260.

Larson, R. W., Clore, G. L., & Wood, G. A. (1999). The emotions of romantic relationships: Do they wreak havoc on adolescents? In W. Furman, B. B. Brown, & C. Feiring (Eds.), *The development of romantic relationships in adolescence.* New York: Cambridge University Press.

Larson, R. W., Richards, M. H., Moneta, G., Holmbeck, G., & Duckett, E. (1996). Changes in adolescents' daily interactions with their families from ages 10 to 18: Disengagement and transformation. *Developmental Psychology, 32,* 744–754.

Larson, R. W., Richards, M. H., Sims, B., & Dworkin, J. (2001). How urban African American young adolescents spend their time: Time budgets for locations, activities, and companionship. *American Journal of Community Psychology, 29,* 565–597.

Lattibeaudiere, V. H. (2000). An exploratory study of the transition and adjustment of former home-schooled students to college life. *Dissertation Abstracts International Section A: Humanities & Social Sciences, 61,* p. 2211.

Lau, I., Lee, S., & Chiu, C. (2004). Language, cognition, and reality: Constructing shared meanings through communication. In M. Schaller & C. Crandall (Eds), *The psychological foundations of culture.* Mahwah, NJ: Erlbaum.

Lau, S., & Kwok, L. K. (2000). Relationship of family environment to adolescents' depression and self-concept. *Social Behavior & Personality, 28,* 41–50.

Lauer, J., & Lauer, R. (1985). Marriages made to last. *Psychology Today, 19*(6), 22–26.

Lauer, J. C., & Lauer, R. H. (1999). *How to survive and thrive in an empty nest.* Oakland, CA: New Harbinger Publications.

Laugharne, J., Janca, A., & Widiger, T. (2007). Posttraumatic stress disorder and terrorism: 5 years after 9/11. *Current Opinion in Psychiatry, 20,* 36–41.

Laumann, E. O., Paik, A., & Rosen, R. C. (1999). Sexual dysfunction in the United States: Prevalence and predictors. *Journal of the American Medical Association, 281,* 537–544.

Lauricella, T. (2001, November). The education of a home schooler. *Smart Money,* 115–121.

Lavelli, M., & Fogel, A. (2005). Developmental changes in the relationship between the infant's attention and emotion during early face-to-face communication: The 2-month transition. *Developmental Psychology [serial online],41,* 265–280.

Lavzer, J. I., & Goodson, B. D., (2006). The "quality" of early care and education settings: Definitional and measurement issues. *Evaluation Review, 30,* 556–576.

Lawlor, D. A., O'Callaghan, M. J., Mamun, A. A., Williams, G. M., Bor, W., & Najman, J. M. (2005). Socioeconomic position, cognitive function, and clustering of cardiovascular risk factors in adolescence: Findings from the Mater University study of pregnancy and its outcomes. *Psychosomatic Medicine, 67,* 862–868.

Lawton, M. P., Kleban, M. H., Moss, M., Rovine, M., & Glicksman, A. (1989). Measuring caregiving appraisal. *Journal of Gerontology: Psychological Sciences, 44,* 61–71.

Lazarus, R. S. (1968). Emotions and adaptations: Conceptual and empirical relations. In W. Arnold (Ed.), *Nebraska symposium on motivation.* Lincoln: University of Nebraska.

Lazarus, R. S. (1991). *Emotion and adaptation.* New York: Oxford University Press.

Lazarus, R. S., & Folkman, S. (1984). *Stress, appraisal, and coping.* New York: Springer.

Leach, P., Barnes, J., Malmberg, L., Sylva, K., & Stein, A. (2008). The quality of different types of child care at 10 and 18 months: A comparison between types and factors related to quality. *Early Child Development and Care, 178,* 177–209.

Leaper, C. (2002). Parenting girls and boys. In M. Bornstein (Ed), *Handbook of parenting: Vol. 1: Children and parenting.* Mahwah, NJ: Lawrence Erlbaum Associates.

Leary, W. E. (1996, November 20). U.S. rate of sexual diseases highest in developed world. *New York Times,* p. C1.

Leathers, H. D., & Foster, P. (2004). *The world food problem: Tackling causes of undernutrition in the third world.* Boulder, CO: Lynne Rienner Publishers.

Leathers, S., & Kelley, M. (2000). Unintended pregnancy and depressive symptoms among first-time mothers and fathers. *American Journal of Orthopsychiatry, 70,* 523–531.

Leavitt, L. A., & Goldson, E. (1996). Introduction to special section: Biomedicine and developmental psychology: New areas of common ground. *Developmental Psychology, 32,* 387–389.

Lee, M., Vernon-Feagans, L., & Vazquez, A. (2003). The influence of family environment and child temperament on work/family role strain for mothers and fathers. *Infant & Child Development, 12,* 421–439.

Lee, R. M. (2005). Resilience against discrimination: Ethnic identity and other-group orientation as protective factors for Korean Americans. *Journal of Counseling Psychology, 52,* 36–44.

Lee, V. E., & Burkham, D. T. (2002). *Inequality at the starting gate: Social background differences in achievement as children begin school.* Washington, DC: Economic Policy Institutes.

Leenaars, A. A., & Shneidman, E. S. (Eds.). (1999). *Lives and deaths; Selections from the works of Edwin S. Shneidman.* New York: Bruuner-Routledge.

Lefkowitz, E. S., Sigman, M., & Kit-fong Au, T. (2000). Helping mothers discuss sexuality and AIDS with adolescents. *Child Development, 71,* 1383–1394.

Legerstee, M. (1998). Mental and bodily awareness in infancy: Consciousness of self-existence. *Journal of Consciousness Studies, 5,* 627–644.

Legerstee, M., & Markova, G. (2008). Variations in 10-month-old infant imitation of people and things. *Infant Behavior & Development, 31,* 81–91.

Legerstee, M., Anderson, D., & Schaffer, A. (1998). Five- and eight-month-old infants recognize their faces and voices as familiar and social stimuli. *Child Development, 69,* 37–50.

Lehalle, H. (2006). Moral development in adolescence: How to integrate personal and social values? *Handbook of adolescent development.* New York: Psychology Press.

Lehman, D., Chiu, C., & Schaller, M. (2004). Psychology and culture. *Annual Review of Psychology, 55,* 689–714.

Leigland, L. A., Schulz, L. E., & Janowsky, J. S. (2004). Age related changes in emotional memory. *Neurobiology of Aging, 25,* 1117–1124.

Lemery, K., & Doelger, L. (2005). Genetic vulnerabilities to the development of psychopathology. *Development of psychopathology: A vulnerability-stress perspective.* Thousand Oaks, CA: Sage Publications, Inc.

Lemonick, M. D. (2000, October 30). Teens before their time. *Time, 67,* 68–74.

Leonard, C. M., Lombardino, L. J., Mercado, L. R., Browd, S. R., Breier, J. I., & Agee, O. F. (1996). Cerebral asymmetry and cognitive development in children: A magnetic resonance imaging study. *Psychological Science, 7,* 89–95.

Leonard, L. B. (1998). *Children with specific language impairment.* Cambridge, MA: MIT Press.

Leonard, T. (2005, March 22). Need parenting help? Call your coach. *Daily Telegraph (London),* 15.

Lepage, J. F., & Théret, H. (2007). The mirror neuron system: Grasping others' actions from birth? *Developmental Science, 10,* 513–523.

Lepore, S. J., Palsane, M. N., & Evans, G. W. (1991). Daily hassles and chronic strains: A hierarchy of stressors? *Social Science and Medicine, 33,* 1029–1036.

Lerner, R. M., Fisher, C. B., & Weinberg, R. A. (2000). Toward a science for and of the people: Promoting civil society through the application of developmental science. *Child Development, 71,* 11–20.

Lerner, R. M., Theokas, C., & Jelicic, H. (2005). Youth as active agents in their own positive development: A developmental systems perspective. In W. Greve, K. Rothermund, & D. Wentura (Eds.), *Adaptive self: Personal continuity and intentional self-development.* Ashland, OH: Hogrefe & Huber Publishers.

Lesik, S. (2006). Applying the regression-discontinuity design to infer causality with non-random assignment. *Review of Higher Education: Journal of the Association for the Study of Higher Education, 30,* 1–19.

Leslie, A., Knobe, J., & Cohen, A. (2006). Acting intentionally and the side-effect effect: Theory of mind and moral judgment. *Psychological Science, 17,* 421–427.

Lesner, S. (2003). Candidacy and management of assistive listening devices: Special needs of the elderly. *International Journal of Audiology, 42,* 2S68–2S76.

Lesnoff-Caravaglia, G. (2007). Age-related changes within biological systems: Integumentary, skeletal, and muscular. *Gerontechnology: Growing old in a technological society.* Springfield, IL: Charles C. Thomas Publisher.

Lester, D. (1996). Psychological issues in euthanasia, suicide, and assisted suicide. *Journal of Social Issues, 52,* 51–62.

Lester, D. (2006, December). Sexual orientation and suicidal behavior. *Psychological Reports, 99,* 923–924.

Letendre, J. (2007). 'Sugar and spice but not always nice': Gender socialization and its impact on development and maintenance of aggression in adolescent girls. *Child & Adolescent Social Work Journal, 24,* 353–368.

Leung, K. (2005). Special issue: Cross-cultural variations in distributive justice perception. *Journal of Cross-Cultural Psychology, 36,* 6–8.

Levano, K. J., Cunningham, F. G., Nelson, S., Roark, M., Williams, M. L., Guzick, D., Dowling, S., Rosenfeld, C. R., & Buckley, A. (1986). A prospective comparison of selective and universal electronic fetal monitoring in 34,995 pregnancies. *New England Journal of Medicine, 315,* 615–619.

Levay, S., & Valente, S. (2006). *Human sexuality* (2nd ed.). Sunderland, MA: Sinauer Associates.

LeVay, S., & Valente, S. M. (2003). *Human Sexuality.* Sunderland, MA: Sinauer Associates.

Leve, L. D., Kim, H. K., & Pears, K. C. (2005). Childhood temperament and family environment as predictors of internalizing and externalizing trajectories from ages 5 to 17. *Journal of Abnormal Child Psychology, 33,* 505–520.

Levenson, R. W., Carstensen, L. L., & Gottman, J. M. (1993). Long-term marriage: Age, gender, and satisfaction. *Psychology and Aging, 8,* 301–313.

Levine, R. (1994). *Child care and culture.* Cambridge: Cambridge University Press.

Levine, R. (1997a, November). The pace of life in 31 countries. *American Demographics,* pp. 20–29.

Levine, R. (1997b). *A geography of time: The temporal misadventures of a social psychologist, or how every culture keeps time just a little bit differently.* New York: HarperCollins.

LeVine, R. A., & Campble, D. T. (1972). *Ethnocentrism: Theories of conflict, ethnic attitudes, and group behavior.* Oxford, England: John Wiley & Sons.

Levine, R. V. (1993, February). Is love a luxury? *American Demographics,* pp. 29–37.

Levine, S. C., Huttenlocher, J., Taylor, A., & Langrock, A. (1999). Early sex differences in spatial skill. *Developmental Psychology, 35,* 940–949.

Levinson, D. (1992). *The seasons of a woman's life.* New York: Knopf.

Levinson, D. J. (1986). A conception of adult development. *American Psychologist, 41,* 3–13.

Levy, B. R., Slade, M. D., & Kasl, S. V. (2002). Longitudinal benefit of positive self-perceptions of aging on functioning health. *Journal of Gerontology: Psychological Sciences, 57,* 166–195.

Levy-Shiff, R. (1994). Individual and contextual correlates of marital change across the transition to parenthood. *Developmental Psychology, 30,* 591–601.

Lewin, T. (1995, May 11). Women are becoming equal providers: Half of working women bring home half the household income. *New York Times,* p. A14.

Lewin, T. (2003, December 22). For more people in their 20s and 30s, going home is easier because they never left. *New York Times,* p. A27.

Lewin, T. (2003, October 29). A growing number of video viewers watch from crib. *New York Times,* pp. A1, A22.

Lewin, T. (2005, December 15). See baby touch a screen: But does baby get it? *New York Times,* p. A1.

Lewis, B., Legato, M., & Fisch, H. (2006). Medical implications of the male biological clock. *Journal of the American Medical Association, 296,* 2369–2371.

Lewis, C. S. (1958). *The allegory of love: A study in medieval traditions.* New York: Oxford University Press.

Lewis, C. S. (1985). A grief observed. In E. S. Shneidman (Ed.), *Death: Current perspectives* (3rd ed.). Palo Alto, CA: Mayfield.

Lewis, C., & Mitchell, P. (Eds.). (1994). Children's early understanding of mind: Origins and development. Hillsdale, NJ: Erlbaum.

Lewis, M., & Ramsay, D. (2004). Development of self-recognition, personal pronoun use, and pretend play during the 2nd year. *Child Development, 75,* 1821–1831.

Lewis, M., Feiring, C., & Rosenthal, S. (2000). Attachment over time. *Child Development, 71,* 707–720.

Lewis, R., Freneau, P., & Roberts, C. (1979). Fathers and the postparental transition. *Family Coordinator, 28,* 514–520.

Lewis, T. E., & Phillipsen, L. C. (1998). Interactions on an elementary school playground: Variations by age, gender, race, group size, and playground area. *Child Study Journal, 28,* 309–320.

Lewkowicz, D. (2002). Heterogeneity and heterochrony in the development of intersensory perception. *Cognitive Brain Research, 14,* 41–63.

Leyens, J. P., Camino, L., Parke, R. D., & Berkowitz, L. (1975). Effects of movie violence on aggression in a field setting as a function of group dominance and cohesion. *Journal of Personality and Social Psychology, 32,* 346–360.

Li, C., DiGiuseppe, R., & Froh, J. (2006, September). The roles of sex, gender, and coping in adolescent depression. *Adolescence, 41,* 409–415.

Li, J., Laursen, T. M., Precht, D. H., Olsen, J., & Mortensen, P. B. (2005a). Hospitalization for mental illness among parents after the death of a child. *New England Journal of Medicine, 352,* 1190–1196.

Li, N. P., Bailey, J. M., Kenrick, D. T., & Linsenmeier, J. A. W. (2002). The necessities and luxuries of mate preferences: Testing the tradeoffs. *Journal of Personality and Social Psychology, 82,* 947–955.

Li, S. (2003). Biocultural orchestration of developmental plasticity across levels: The interplay of biology and culture in shaping the mind and behavior across the life span. *Psychological Bulletin, 129,* 171–194.

Li, Y. F., Langholz, B., Salam, M. T., & Gilliland, F. D. (2005b). Maternal and grandmaternal smoking patterns are associated with early childhood asthma. *Chest, 127,* 1232–1241.

Liao, S. (2005). The ethics of using genetic engineering for sex selection. *Journal of Medical Ethics, 31,* 116–118.

Lickliter, R., & Bahrick, L. E. (2000). The development of infant intersensory perception: Advantages of a comparative convergent-operations approach. *Psychological Bulletin, 126,* 260–280.

Lidz, J., & Gleitman, L. R. (2004). Yes, we still need Universal Grammar: Reply. *Cognition, 94,* 85–93.

Liem, D. G., & Mennella, J. A. (2002). Sweet and sour preferences during childhood: Role of early experiences. *Developmental Psychobiology, 41,* 388–95.

Lillard, A., & Else-Quest, N. (2006). Evaluating Montessori education. *Science, 313,* 1893–1894.

Lindemann, B. T., & Kadue, D. D. (2003). Age discrimination in employment law. Washington, DC: BNA Books.

Lindholm, J. A. (2006). The "interior" lives of American college students: Preliminary findings from a national study. In J .L. Heft (Ed.), *Passing on the faith: Transforming traditions for the next generation of Jews, Christians, and Muslims.* New York: Fordham University Press.

Lindsay, A., Sussner, K., Kim, J., & Gortmaker, S. (2006). The role of parents in preventing childhood obesity. *The Future of Children, 16,* 169–186.

Lindsey, B. W., & Tropepe, V. (2006). A comparative framework for understanding the biological principles of adult neurogenesis. *Progressive Neurobiology, 80,* 281–307.

Lindsey, E., & Colwell, M. (2003). Preschoolers' emotional competence: Links to pretend and physical play. *Child Study Journal, 33,* 39–52.

Lindstrom, H., Fritsch, T., Petot, G., Smyth, K., Chen, C., Debanne, S., et al. (2005, July). The relationships between television viewing in midlife and the development of Alzheimer's disease in a case-control study. *Brain and Cognition, 58,* 157–165.

Lines, P. M. (2001). Home schooling. *Eric Digest, EDO-EA-01–08,* 1–4.

Lino, M. (2001). *Expenditures on Children by Families, 2000 Annual Report.* Washington, DC: U.S. Department of Agriculture, Center for Nutrition Policy and Promotion. Miscellaneous Publication No. 1528–2000.

Lippa, R. A. (2003). Are 2D:4D finger-length rations related to sexual orientation? Yes for men, no for women. *Journal of Personality and Social Psychology, 85,* 179–188.

Lippman, J., & Lewis, P. (2008). *Divorcing with children: Expert answers to tough questions from parents and children.* Westport, CT: Praeger Publishers/Greenwood Publishing Group.

Lipsitt, L. (2003). Crib Death: A biobehavioral phenomenon? *Current Directions in Psychological Science, 12,* 164–170.

Liskin, L. (1985, November–December) Youth in the 1980s: Social and health concerns: 4. *Population Reports, 8,* No. 5.

Litrownik, A., Newton, R., & Hunter, W. (2003). Exposure to family violence in young at-risk children: A longitudinal look at the effects of victimization and witnessed physical and psychological aggression. *Journal of Family Violence, 18,* 59–73.

Litwin, H. (2007). Does early retirement lead to longer life? *Aging & Society, 27,* 739–754.

Liu, H., Kuhl, P., & Tsao, F. (2003). An association between mothers' speech clarity and infants' speech discrimination skills. *Developmental Science, 6,* F1–F10.

Livson, N., & Peskin, H. (1980). Perspectives on adolescence from longitudinal research. In J. Adelson (Ed.), *Handbook of adolescent psychology.* New York: Wiley.

Lock, R. D. (1992). *Taking charge of your career direction* (2nd ed.). Pacific Grove, CA: Brooks/Cole.

Loeb, S., Fuller, B., Kagan, S. L., & Carrol, B. (2004). Child care in poor communities: Early learning effects of type, quality and stability. *Child Development, 75,* 47–65.

Loehlin, J. C., Neiderhiser, J. M., & Reiss, D. (2005). Genetic and environmental components of adolescent adjustment and parental behavior: A multivariate analysis. *Child Development, 76,* 1104–1115.

Loftus, E. F. (1972). Nouns, adjectives, and semantic memory. *Journal of Experimental Psychology, 96,* 213–215.

Lohman, D. (2005). Reasoning abilities. *Cognition and intelligence: Identifying the mechanisms of the mind.* New York: Cambridge University Press.

Lois, J. (2006, September). Role strain, emotion management, and burnout: Homeschooling mothers' adjustment to the teacher role. *Symbolic Interaction, 29*(4), 507–530.

Lonetto, R. (1980). *Children's conception of death.* New York: Springer.

Lorenz, K. (1966). *On aggression.* New York: Harcourt Brace Jovanovich.

Lorenz, K. (1974). *Civilized man's eight deadly sins.* New York: Harcourt Brace Jovanovich.

Lorenz, K. Z. (1965). *Evolution and the modification of behavior.* Chicago: University of Chicago Press.

Loui, P., Alsop, D., & Schlaug, G. (2009). Tone deafness: A new disconnection syndrome? *The Journal of Neuroscience, 29,* 10215–10220.

Lounsbury, J. W., Hutchens, T., & Loveland, J. M. (2005). An investigation of big five personality traits and career decidedness among early and middle adolescents. *Journal of Career Assessment, 13,* 25–39.

Love, J., Chazan-Cohen, R., & Raikes, H. (2007). Forty years of research knowledge and use: From Head Start to Early Head Start and beyond. *Child development and social policy: Knowledge for action* (pp. 79–95). Washington, DC: American Psychological Association.

Love, J. M., Harrison, L., Sagi-Schwartz, A., van Ijzendoorn, M. H., Ross, C., Ungerer, J. A., Raikes, H., Brady-Smith, C., Boller, K., Brooks-Gunn, J., Constantine, J., Kisker, E. E., Paulsell, D., & Chazan-Cohen, R. (2003). Child care quality matters: How conclusions may vary with context. *Child Development, 74,* 1021–1033.

Love, J., Tarullo, L., Raikes, H., & Chazan-Cohen, R. (2006). Head Start: What do we know about its effectiveness? What do we need to know? *Blackwell handbook of early childhood development* (pp. 550–575). Malden, MA: Blackwell Publishing.

Lowe, M. R., & Timko, C. A. (2004). What a difference a diet makes: Towards an understanding of differences between restrained dieters and restrained nondieters. *Eating Behaviors, 5,* 199–208.

Lowrey, G. H. (1986). *Growth and development of children* (8th ed.). Chicago: Year Book Medical Publishers.

Lowton, K., & Higginson, I. (2003). Managing bereavement in the classroom: A conspiracy of silence? *Death Studies, 27,* 717–741.

Lu, L. (2006). The transition to parenthood: Stress, resources, and gender differences in a Chinese society. *Journal of Community Psychology, 34,* 471–488.

Lu, T., Pan, Y., Lap. S-Y., Li, C., Kohane, I., Chang, J., & Yankner, B. A. (2004, June 9). Gene regulation and DNA damage in the aging human brain. *Nature,* 1038.

Lubinski, D. (2004). Introduction to the special section on cognitive abilities: 100 years after Spearman's (1904) " 'General Intelligence,' objectively determined and measured." *Journal of Personality and Social Psychology, 86,* 96–111.

Lucas, R. E. (2005). Time does not heal all wounds: A longitudinal study of reaction and adaptation to divorce. *Psychological Science, 16,* 945–951.

Lucas, S. R., & Berends, M. (2002). Sociodemographic diversity, correlated achievement, and de facto tracking. *Sociology of Education, 75,* 328–349.

Lucas-Thompson, R., Townsend, E., Gunnar, M., Georgieff, M., Guiang, S., Ciffuentes, R., et al. (2008). Developmental changes in the responses of preterm infants to a painful stressor. *Infant Behavior & Development, 31*, 614–623.

Lucy, J. A. (1992). *Language diversity and thought: A reformulation of the linguistic relativity hypothesis.* Cambridge, England: Cambridge University Press.

Lundberg, U. (2006, July). Stress, subjective and objective health. *International Journal of Social Welfare, 15*, S41–S48.

Luo, Y., Kaufman, L., & Baillargeon, R. (2009). Young infants' reasoning about physical events involving inert and self-propelled objects. *Cognitive Psychology, 58*, 441–486.

Luria, R., & Meiran, N. (2005). Increased control demand results in serial processing: Evidence from dual-task performance. *Psychological Science, 16*, 833–840.

Lyall, S. (2004, February 15). In Europe, lovers now propose: Mary me, a little. *New York Times*, p. D2.

Lynch, M. E., Coles, C. D., & Corely, T. (2003). Examining Delinquency in Adolescents Risk Factors. *Journal of Studies on Alcohol, 64*, 678–686.

Lynn J., Teno, J. M., Phillips, R. S., Wu, A. W., Desbiens, N., Harrold J., Claessens, M. T., Wenger, N., Kreling, B., & Connors, A. F., Jr. (1997). Perceptions by family members of the dying experience of older and seriously ill patients. SUPPORT Investigators. Study to Understand Prognoses and Preferences for Outcomes and Risks of Treatments [see comments]. *Annals of Internal Medicine, 126*, 164–165.

Lynn, R. (2009). What has caused the Flynn effect? Secular increases in the Development Quotients of infants. *Intelligence, 37*, 16–24.

Lynne, S., Graber, J., Nichols, T., Brooks-Gunn, J., & Botvin, G. (2007, February). Links between pubertal timing, peer influences, and externalizing behaviors among urban students followed through middle school. *Journal of Adolescent Health, 40*, 35–44.

Lyon, G. R. (1996). Learning disabilities. *The future of children, 6*, 54–76.

Lyon, M. E., Benoit, M., O'Donnell, R. M., Getson, P. R., Silber, T., & Walsh, T. (2000). Assessing African American adolescents' risk for suicide attempts: Attachment theory. *Adolescence, 35*, 121–134.

MacArthur Foundation Research Network on Successful Midlife Development. (1999). *What age do you feel most of the time?* Vero Beach, FL: MIDMAC.

Maccoby, E. B. (1999). *The two sexes : Growing up apart, coming together.* New York: Belknap.

Maccoby, E. E., & Lewis, C. C. (2003). Less day care or different day care? *Child Development, 74*, 1069–1075.

Maccoby, E. E., & Martin, J. A. (1983). Socialization in the context of the family: Parent-child interaction. In W. Damon, & R. M. Lerner (Eds.), *Handbook of child psychology.* New York: John Wiley & Sons.

MacDonald, G. (2007, January 25). Montessori looks back—and ahead: As name marks 100 years, movement is taking stock. *USA Today*, p. 9D.

MacDonald, S., Hultsch, D., and Dixon, R. (2003). Performance variability is related to change in cognition: Evidence from the Victoria Longitudinal Study. *Psychology & Aging, 18*, 510–523.

MacDonald, W. (2003). The impact of job demands and workload stress and fatigue. *Australian Psychologist, 38*, 102–117.

MacDorman, M. F., Martin, J. A., Mathews, T. J., Hoyert, D. L., & Ventura, S. J. (2005). Explaining the 2001–02 infant mortality increase: data from the linked birth/infant death data set. *National Vital Statistics Report, 53*, 1–22.

Macionis, J. J. (2001). *Sociology.* Upper Saddle River, NJ: Prentice Hall.

Mackey, M. C. (1990). Women's preparation for the childbirth experience. *Maternal-Child Nursing Journal, 19*, 143–173.

Mackey, M. C., White, U., & Day, R. (1992). Reasons American men become fathers: Men's divulgences, women's perceptions. *Journal of Genetic Psychology, 153*, 435–445.

MacWhinney, B. (1991). Connectionism as a framework for language acquisition. In J. Miller (Ed.), *Research on child language disorders.* Austin, TX: Pro-ed.

Madathil, J., & Benshoff, J. (2008). Importance of marital characteristics and marital satisfaction: A comparison of Asian Indians in arranged marriages and Americans in marriages of choice. *The Family Journal, 16*, 222–230.

Maddi, S. R., (2006). Hardiness: The courage to grow from stresses. *Journal of Positive Psychology, 1*, 160–168.

Maddi, S., R., Harvey, R. H., Khoshaba, D. M., Lu, J. L., Persico, M., & Brow, M. (2006). The personality construct of hardiness, III: Relationships with repression, innovativeness, authoritarianism, and performance. *Journal of Personality, 74*, 575–598.

Maddox, G. L., & Campbell, R. T. (1985). Scope, concepts, and methods in the study of aging. In R. H. Binstock & E. Shanas (Eds.), *Handbook of aging and the social sciences* (2nd ed.). New York: Van Nostrand Reinhold.

Mael, F. A. (1998). Single-sex and coeducational schooling: Relationships to socioemotional and academic development. *Review of Education Research, 68*, 101–129.

Maertens de Noordhout, A., Santens, P., Gerard, J., Gonce, M., Jeanjean, A., Flamez, A., Pickut, B., Van Zandijcke, M., & Pahwa, R. (2009). Treatments for progressing Parkinson's disease: A clinical case scenario study. Parkinson's disease: From guidelines to practice in Belgium. *Acta Neurologica Belgica, 109*, 189–199.

Mahgoub, N., & Lantz, M. (2006, December). When older adults suffer the loss of a child. *Psychiatric Annals, 36*, 877–880.

Makino, M., Hashizume, M., Tsuboi, K., Yasushi, M., & Dennerstein, L. (2006, September). Comparative study of attitudes to eating between male and female students in the People's Republic of China. *Eating and Weight Disorders, 11*, 111–117.

Maller, S. (2003). Best practices in detecting bias in nonverbal tests. In R. McCallum (Ed), *Handbook of nonverbal assessment.* New York: Kluwer Academic/Plenum Publishers.

Malmberg, L., Wanner, B., & Little, T. (2008). Age and school-type differences in children's beliefs about school performance. *International Journal of Behavioral Development, 32*, 531–541.

Mancini, J. A., & Blieszner, R. (1991). Aging parents and adult children. In A. Booth (Ed.), *Contemporary families.* Minneapolis, MN: National Council on Family Relations.

Manfra, L., & Winsler, A. (2006). Preschool children's awareness of private speech. *International Journal of Behavioral Development, 30*, 537–549.

Mangan, P. A. (1997, November). *Time perception.* Paper presented at the annual meeting of the Society for Neuroscience, New Orleans.

Mangweth, B., Hausmann, A., & Walch, T. (2004). Body fat perception in eating-disordered men. *International Journal of Eating Disorders, 35*, 102–108.

Manlove, J, Franzetta, K, McKinney, K, Romano-Papillo, A, & Terry-Humen, E.(2004). *No time to waste:Programs to reduce teen pregnancy among middle school-aged youth.* Washington, DC: National Campaign to Prevent Teen Pregnancy.

Mann, C. C. (2005, March 18). Provocative study says obesity may reduce U.S. Life expectancy. *Science, 307*, 1716–1717.

Manning, M., & Hoyme, H. (2007). Fetal alcohol spectrum disorders: A practical clinical approach to diagnosis. *Neuroscience & Biobehavioral Reviews, 31*, 230–238.

Manning, W., Giordano, P., & Longmore, M. (2006, September). Hooking up: The relationship contexts of 'nonrelationship' sex. *Journal of Adolescent Research, 21*, 459–483.

Manstead, A. S. R. (1997). Situations, belongingness, attitudes, and culture: Four lessons learned from social psychology. In C. McGarty & S. A. Haslam (Eds.) et al., *The message of social psychology: Perspectives on mind in society.* Oxford, England: Blackwell Publishers.

Manzoli, L., Villari, P., Pironec, G., & Boccia, A. (2007). Marital status and mortality in the elderly: A systematic review and meta-analysis. *Social Science & Medicine, 64*, 77–94.

Mao, A., Burnham, M. M., Goodlin-Jones, B. L., Gaylor, E. E., & Anders, T. F. (2004). A comparison of the sleep-wake patterns of cosleeping and solitary-sleeping infants. *Child Psychiatry and Human Development, 35*, 95–105.

Marchant, M., Young, K. R., & West, R. P. (2004). The effects of parental teaching on compliance behavior of children. *Psychology in the Schools, 41*, 337–350.

Marcia, J. E. (1980). Identity in adolescence. In J. Adelson (Ed.), *Handbook of adolescent psychology.* New York: Wiley

Marcovitch, S., Zelazo, P., & Schmuckler, M. (2003). The effect of the number of A trials on performance on the A-not-B task. *Infancy, 3*, 519–529.

Marcus, A. D. (2004, February 3). The new math on when to have kids. *Wall Street Journal.* D1, D4.

Marczinski, C., Milliken, B., & Nelson, S. (2003). Aging and repetition effects: Separate specific and nonspecific influences. *Psychology & Aging, 18*, 780–790.

Margie, N., Killen, M., Sinno, S., & McGlothlin, H. (2005). Minority children's intergroup attitudes about peer relationships. *British Journal of Developmental Psychology, 23*, 251–269.

Markus, H. R., & Kitayama, S. (1991). Culture and the self: Implications for cognition, emotion, and motivation. *Psychological Review, 98*, 224–253.

Markward, N., Markward, M., & Peterson, C. (2009). Biological and genetic influences. *Obesity in youth: Causes, consequences, and cures.* Washington, DC: American Psychological Association.

Marschark, M., Spencer, P. E., & Newsom, C. A. (Eds.). (2003). *Oxford handbook of deaf students, language, and education.* London: Oxford University Press.

Marsh, H. W., & Ayotte, V. (2003). Do Multiple Dimensions of Self-Concept Become More Differentiated With Age? The Differential Distinctiveness Hypothesis. *International Review of Education, 49*, 463.

Marsh, H. W., & Hau, K. T. (2003). Big-fish-little-pond effect on academic self-concept. *American Psychologist, 58,* 364–376.

Marsh, H., & Hau, K. (2004). Explaining paradoxical relations between academic self-concepts and achievements: Cross-cultural generalizability of the internal/external frame of reference predictions across 26 countries. *Journal of Educational Psychology, 96,* 56–67.

Marsh, H., Ellis, L., & Craven, R. (2002). How do preschool children feel about themselves? Unraveling measurement and multidimensional self-concept structure. *Developmental Psychology, 38,* 376–393.

Marshall, E. (2000, November 17). Planned Ritalin trial for tots heads into uncharted waters. *Science, 290,* 1280–1282.

Marshall, N. L. (2004). The quality of early child care and children's development. *Current Directions in Psychological Science, 13,* 165–168.

Marshall, R., & Sutherland, P. (2008). The social relations of bereavement in the Caribbean. *Omega: Journal of Death and Dying, 57,* 21–34.

Martikainen, P., & Valkonen, T. (1996). Mortality after the death of a spouse: Rates and causes of death in a large Finnish cohort. *American Journal of Public Health, 86,* 1087–1093.

Martin, C. L. (1993). New directions for investigating children's gender knowledge. *Developmental Review, 13,* 184–204.

Martin, C. L. (2000). Cognitive theories of gender development. In T. Eckes & H. M. Trautner, (Eds.), et al. *The developmental social psychology of gender.* Mahwah, NJ: Erlbaum.

Martin, C. L., & Ruble, D. (2004). Children's search for gender cues: Cognitive perspectives on gender development. *Current Directions in Psychological Science, 13,* 67–70.

Martin, C., & Fabes, R. (2001). The stability and consequences of young children's same-sex peer interactions. *Developmental Psychology, 37,* 431–446.

Martin, C., Ruble, D., & Szkrybalo, J. (2002). Cognitive theories of early gender development. *Psychological Bulletin, 128,* 903–933.

Martin, J. A., Hamilton, B. E., Sutton, P. D., Ventura, S. J., Menacker, F., & Munson, M. L. (2005). Births: Final data for 2003. *National Vital Statistics Reports, 54,* Table J, p. 21

Martin, L., & Pullum, G. K. (1991). *The great Eskimo vocabulary hoax.* Chicago: University of Chicago Press.

Martin, P., Martin, D., & Martin, M. (2001). Adolescent premarital sexual activity, cohabitation, and attitudes toward marriage. *Adolescence, 36,* 601–609.

Martin, S., Li, Y., Casanueva, C., Harris-Britt, A., Kupper, L., & Cloutier, S. (2006). Intimate partner violence and women's depression before and during pregnancy. *Violence Against Women, 12,* 221–239.

Masataka, N. (1996). Perception of motherese in a signed language by 6–month-old deaf infants. *Developmental Psychology, 32,* 874–879.

Masataka, N. (1998). Perception of motherese in Japanese sign language by 6-month-old hearing infants. *Developmental Psychology, 34,* 241–246.

Masataka, N. (2000). The role of modality and input in the earliest stage of language acquisition: Studies of Japanese sign language. In C. Chamerlain & J. P. Morford, *Language acquisition by eye.* Mahwah, NJ: Lawrence Erlbaum Associates.

Masataka, N. (2003). *The Onset of Language.* Cambridge, England: Cambridge University Press.

Maslach, C. (1982). *Burnout—The cost of caring.* Englewood Cliffs, NJ: Prentice-Hall.

Masling, J. M., & Bornstein, R. F. (Eds.). (1996). *Psychoanalytic perspectives on developmental psychology.* Washington, DC: American Psychological Association.

Maslow, A. H. (1970). *Motivation and personality* (2nd ed.). New York: Harper & Row.

Massimo, L. (2006). Relationship between parents and sick children: Difficulties and possibilities regarding understanding. *New developments in parent-child relations* (pp. 259–267). Hauppauge, NY: Nova Science Publishers.

Masters, W. H., Johnson, V., & Kolodny, R. C. (1982). *Human sexuality.* Boston: Little, Brown.

Matlin, M. (2003). From menarche to menopause: Misconceptions about women's reproductive lives. *Psychology Science, 45,* 106–122.

Maton, K. I., Schellenbach, C. J., Leadbeater, B. J., & Solarz, A. L. (Eds.). (2004). *Investing in children, youth, families and communities.* Washington, DC: American Psychological Association.

Maton, K., Schellenbach, C., & Leadbeater, B. (2004). *Investing in children, youth, families, and communities: Strengths-based research and policy.* Washington, DC: American Psychological Association.

Matsumoto, D., & Yoo, S. H. (2006). Toward a new generation of cross-cultural research. *Perspectives on Psychological Science, 1,* 234–250.

Matthews, K. A., Wing, R. R., Kuller, L. H., Meilahn, E. N., & Owens, J. F. (2000). Menopause as a turning point in midlife. In S. B Manuck, & R. Jennings (Eds.), *Behavior, health, and aging.* Mahwah, NJ: Erlbaum.

Mattison, J., Black, A., Huck, J., Moscrip, T., Handy, A., Tilmont, E., et al. (2005). Age-related decline in caloric intake and motivation for food in rhesus monkeys. *Neurobiology of Aging, 26,* 1117–1127.

Mattson, S., Calarco, K., & Lang, A. (2006). Focused and shifting attention in children with heavy prenatal alcohol exposure. *Neuropsychology, 20,* 361–369.

Matusov, E., & Hayes, R. (2000). Sociocultural critique of Piaget and Vygotsky. *New Ideas in Psychology, 18,* 215–239.

Maughan, B. (2001). Conduct disorder in context. In J. Hill & B. Maughan, *Conduct disorders in childhood and adolescence.* New York: Cambridge University Press.

Mauritzson, U., & Saeljoe, R. (2001). Adult questions and children's responses: Coordination of perspectives in studies of children's theories of other minds. *Scandinavian Journal of Educational Research, 45,* 213–231.

Mayer, J. D., Salovey, P., & Caruso, D. R. (2000). Emotional intelligence as zeitgeist, as personality, and as a mental ability. In R. Bar-On, & J. D. A. Parker, James D. A. (Eds.), *The handbook of emotional intelligence: Theory, development, assessment, and application at home, school, and in the workplace.* San Francisco, CA: Jossey-Bass.

Mayer, J. D., Salovey, P., & Caruso, D. R. (2004). Emotional intelligence: Theory, findings, and implications. *Psychological Inquiry, 15,* 197–215.

Mayes, R., & Rafalovich, A. (2007, December). Suffer the restless children: The evolution of ADHD and paediatric stimulant use, 1900–80. *History of Psychiatry, 18*(4), 435–457.

Maynard, A. (2008). What we thought we knew and how we came to know it: Four decades of cross-cultural research from a Piagetian point of view. *Human Development, 51,* 56–65.

Maynard, A., & Greenfield, P. (2003). Implicit cognitive development in cultural tools and children: Lessons from Maya Mexico. *Cognitive Development, 18,* 489–510.

Mayo Clinic. (2000, March). Age-related macular degeneration: Who gets it and what you can do about it. *Women's Healthsource, 4,* 1–2.

Mayseless, O. (1996). Attachment patterns and their outcomes. *Human Development, 39,* 206–223.

McAdams, D., & Logan, R. (2004). What is generativity? In E. de St. Aubin and D. McAdams (Eds.), *Generative society: Caring for future generations* (pp. 15–31). Washington, DC: American Psychological Association.

McAdams, L. A., Harris, M. J., Heaton, S. C., Bailey, A., Fell, R., & Jeste, D. V. (1997). Validity of specific subscales of the positive and negative symptom scales in older schizophrenia outpatients. *Schizophrenia Research, 27,* Special issue: Schizophrenia, antipsychotics, and aging, 219–226.

McAdams, S., & Drake, C. (2002). Auditory perception and cognition. *Steven's handbook of experimental psychology (3rd ed.), Vol. 1: Sensation and perception.* Hoboken, NJ: John Wiley & Sons Inc.

McArdle, E. F. (2002). New York's Do-Not-Resuscitate law: Groundbreaking protection of patient autonomy or a physician's right to make medical futility determinations? *DePaul Journal of Health Care Law, 8,* 55–82.

McAuliffe, S. P., & Knowlton, B. J. (2001). Hemispheric differences in object identification. *Brain & Cognition, 45,* 119–128.

McCall, R. B. (1979). *Infants.* Cambridge, MA: Harvard University Press.

McCarthy, B., & Ginsberg, R. (2007). Second marriages: Challenges and risks. *The Family Journal, 15,* 119–123.

McCarthy, M. J. (1994, November 8). Hunger among elderly surges: Meal programs just can't keep up. *Wall Street Journal,* pp. A1, A11.

McCarty, M., & Ashmead, D. H. (1999). Visual control of reaching and grasping in infants. *Developmental Psychology, 35,* 620–631.

McCaul, K. D., Ployhart, R. E., Hinsz, V. B., & McCaul, H. S. (1995). Appraisals of a consistent versus a similar politician: Voter preferences and intuitive judgments. *Journal of Personality and Social Psychology, 68,* 292–299.

McCauley, K. M. (2007). Modifying women's risk for cardiovascular disease. *Journal of Obstetric and Gynecological Neonatal Nursing, 36,* 116–124.

McClelland, D. C. (1993). Intelligence is not the best predictor of job performance. *Current Directions in Psychological Research, 2,* 5–8.

McCloskey, L. A., & Bailey, J. A. (2000). The intergenerational transmission of risk for child sexual abuse. *Journal of Interpersonal Violence, 15,* 1019–1035.

McCrae R. R., Terracciano A., and 78 Members of the Personality Profiles of Cultures Project (2005). Universal features of personality traits from the observer's perspective: Data from 50 cultures. *Journal of Personality and Social Psychology, 88,* 547–561.

McCrae, R. R., & Costa, P. T., Jr. (1990). *Personality in adulthood.* New York: Guilford press.

McCrae, R. R., Costa, P. T., Jr., Ostendorf, F., Angleitner, A., Hebíková, M., Avia, M. D., Sanz, J., Sánchez-Bernardos, M. L., Kusdil, M. E., Woodfield, R., Saunders, P. R., & Smith, P. B. (2000). Nature over nurture: Temperament, personality, and life span development. *Journal of Personality and Social Psychology, 78,* 173–186.

McCrink, K., & Wynn, K. (2004). Large-number addition and subtraction by 9-month-old infants. *Psychological Science, 15,* 776–782.

McCrink, K., & Wynn, K. (2007, August). Ratio abstraction by 6-month-old infants. *Psychological Science, 18*(8), 740–745.

McCrink, K., & Wynn, K. (2009). Operational momentum in large-number addition and subtraction by 9-month-olds. *Journal of Experimental Child Psychology, 103,* 400–408.

McCullough, M., E., Tsang, J., & Brion, S. (2003). Personality traits in adolescence as predictors of religiousness in early maturity: Findings from the Terman longitudinal study. *Personality & Social Psychology Bulletin, 29,* 980–991.

McCutcheon-Rosegg, S., Ingraham, E., & Bradley, R. A. (1996). *Natural childbirth the Bradley way: Revised ed.* New York: Plume Books.

McDaniel, K. D. (1986). Pharmacologic treatment of psychiatric and neurodevelopmental disorders in children and adolescents: III. *Clinical Pediatrics, 25,* 198–204.

McDonald, K. A. (1999, June 25). Studies of women's health produce a wealth of knowledge on the biology of gender differences. *Chronicle of Higher Education, 45,* A19, A22.

McDonald, L., & Stuart-Hamilton, I. (2003). Egocentrism in older adults: Piaget's three mountains task revisited. *Educational Gerontology, 29,* 417–425.

McDonald, M. A., Sigman, M., Espinosa, M. P., & Neumann, C. G. (1994). Impact of a temporary food shortage on children and their mothers. *Child Development, 65,* 404–415.

McDonough, L. (2002). Basic-level nouns: First learned but misunderstood. *Journal of Child Language, 29,* 357–377.

McElwain, N., & Booth-LaForce, C. (2006, June). Maternal sensitivity to infant distress and nondistress as predictors of infant-mother attachment security. *Journal of Family Psychology, 20,* 247–255.

McGovern, M., & Barry, M. M. (2000). Death education: knowledge, attitudes, and perspectives of Irish parents and teachers. *Death Studies, 24,* 325–333.

McGrady, A. (2007). Relaxation and meditation. *Low-cost approaches to promote physical and mental health: Theory, research, and practice.* New York: Springer Science + Business Media.

McGreal, D., Evans, B. J., & Burrows, G. D. (1997). Gender differences in coping following loss of a child through miscarriage or stillbirth: A pilot study. *Stress Medicine, 13,* 159–165.

McGrew, K. S. (2005). The Cattell-Horn-Carroll theory of cognitive abilities: Past, present, and future. In D. P. Flanagan & P. L. Harrison (Eds.), *Contemporary intellectual assessment: Theories, tests, and issues.* New York: Guilford Press.

McGue, M., Bouchard, T., Iacono, W., & Lykken, D. (1993). Behavioral genetics of cognitive ability: A life-span perspective. In R. Plomin & G. McClearn (Eds.), *Nature, nurture and psychology* (pp. 59–76). Washington, DC: American Psychological Association.

McHale, J. P., & Rotman, T. (2007). Is seeing believing? Expectant parents' outlooks on coparenting and later coparenting solidarity. *Infant Behavior & Development, 30,* 63–81.

McHale, S., Dariotis, J., & Kauh, T. (2003). Social development and social relationships in middle childhood. In R. Lerner & M. Easterbrooks (Eds.), *Handbook of psychology: Developmental psychology, Vol. 6.* New York: Wiley.

McKee, K., Wilson, F., Chung, M., Hinchliff, S., Goudie, F., Elford, H., et al. (2005, November). Reminiscence, regrets and activity in older people in residential care: Associations with psychological health. *British Journal of Clinical Psychology, 44,* 543–561.

McKinley, N. (2006). The developmental and cultural contexts of objectified body consciousness: A longitudinal analysis of two cohorts of women. *Developmental Psychology, 42,* 679–687.

McLoyd, V., Aikens, N., & Burton, L. (2006). Childhood poverty, policy, and practice. *Handbook of child psychology, 6th ed.: Vol 4, Child psychology in practice* (pp. 700–775). Hoboken, NJ: John Wiley & Sons Inc.

McLoyd, V. C., Cauce, A. M., Takeuchi, D., & Wilson, L. (2000). Marital processes and parental socialization in families of color: a decade review of research. *Journal of Marriage and Family, 62,* 1070–1093.

McMahon, S. D., & Washburn, J. J. (2003). Violence Prevention: An Evaluation of Program Effects with Urban African-American Students. *Journal of Primary Prevention, 24,* 43–62.

McMurray, B., Aslin, R. N., & Toscano, J. C. (2009). Statistical learning of phonetic categories: Insights from a computational approach. *Developmental Science, 12,* 369–378.

McNulty, J. K., & Karney, B. R. (2004). Positive expectations in the early years of marriage: Should couples expect the bests or brace for the worst? *Journal of Personality and Social Psychology, 86,* 729–743.

McWhirter, D. P., Sanders, S., & Reinisch, J. M. (1990). *Homosexuality, heterosexuality: Concepts of sexual orientation.* New York: Oxford University Press.

McWhirter, L., Young, V., & Majury, Y. (1983). Belfast children's awareness of violent death. *British Journal of Psychology, 22,* 81–92.

Meagher, D. (2007). How we die: Theory vs. reality. *Death Studies, 31,* 266–270.

Mealey, L. (2000). *Sex differences: Developmental and evolutionary strategies.* Orlando, FL: Academic Press.

Medeiros, R., Prediger, R. D., Passos, G. F., Pandolfo, P., Duarte, F. S., Franco, J. L., Dafre, A. L., Di Giunta, G., Figueiredo, C. P., Takahashi, R. N., Campos, M. M., & Calixto, J. B. (2007). Connecting TNF-alpha signaling pathways to iNOS expression in a mouse model of Alzheimer's disease: relevance for the behavioral and synaptic deficits induced by amyloid beta protein. *Journal of Neuroscience, 16,* 5394–5404.

Medina, J. J. (1996). *The clock of ages: Why we age—How we age—Winding back the clock.* New York: Cambridge University Press.

Mednick, S. A. (1963). Research creativity in psychology graduate students. *Journal of Consulting Psychology, 27,* 265–266.

Meece, J. L., & Kurtz-Costes, B. (2001). Introduction: The schooling of ethnic minority children and youth. *Educational Psychologist, 36,* 1–7.

Meeus, W. (1996). Studies on identity development in adolescence: An overview of research and some new data. *Journal of Youth & Adolescence, 25,* 569–598.

Meeus, W. (2003). Parental and peer support, identity development and psychological well-being in adolescence. *Psychology: The Journal of the Hellenic Psychological Society, 10,* 192–201.

Mehran, K. (1997). Interferences in the move from adolescence to adulthood: The development of the male. In M. Laufer (Ed.), *Adolescent breakdown and beyond* (pp. 17–25). London, England: Karnac Books.

Meijer, A. M., & van den Wittenboer, G. L. H. (2007). Contribution of infants' sleep and crying to marital relationship of first-time parent couples in the first year after childbirth. *Journal of Family Psychology, 21,* 49–57.

Meisels, S. J., & Plunkett, J. W. (1988). Developmental consequences of preterm birth: Are there long-term deficits? In P. B. Baltes, D. L. Featherman, & R. M. Lerner (Eds.), *Lifespan development and behavior* (Vol. 9). Hillsdale, NJ: Erlbaum.

Meister, H., & von Wedel, H. (2003). Demands on hearing aid features—special signal processing for elderly users? *International Journal of Audiology, 42,* 2S58–2S62.

Meltzoff, A. N., & Moore, M. K. (1989). Imitation in newborn infants: Exploring the range of gestures imitated and the underlying mechanisms. *Developmental Psychology, 25*(6), 954–962.

Mendoza, C. (2006, September). Inside today's classrooms: Teacher voices on no child left behind and the education of gifted children. *Roeper Review, 29,* 28–31.

Meng, Z., & Jijia, Z. (2006). Effects of intonation on 6 to 10-year-old children's cognition of different types of irony. *Acta Psychologica Sinica, 38,* 197–206.

Menkens, K. (2005). Stereotyping older workers and retirement: The manager's point of view. *Canadian Journal on Aging, 24,* 353–366.

Mennella, J., Kennedy, J., & Beauchamp, G. (2006). Vegetable acceptance by infants: Effect of formula flavors. *Early Human Development, 82,* 463–468.

Mercer, J. R. (1973). *Labeling the mentally retarded.* Berkeley: University of California Press.

Merill, D. M. (1997). *Caring for elderly parents: Juggling work, family, and caregiving in middle and working class families.* Wesport, CT: Auburn House/Greenwood Publishing Group.

Merlo, L., Bowman, M., & Barnett, D. (2007). Parental nurturance promotes reading acquisition in low socioeconomic status children. *Early Education and Development, 18,* 51–69.

Merrell, K. W. (2008). *Behavioral, social, and emotional assessment of children and adolescents* (3rd ed.). Mahwah, NJ: Lawrence Erlbaum Associates Publishers.

Merriman, W., & Lipko, A. (2008). A dual criterion account of the development of linguistic judgment in early childhood. *Journal of Memory and Language, 58,* 1012–1031.

Merry, T. (2008). The actualization conundrum. *Reflections on human potential: Bridging the person-centered approach and positive psychology.* Ross-on-Wye, England: PCCS Books.

Mervis, J. (2004, June 11). Meager evaluations make it hard to find out what works. *Science, 304,* 1583.

Messer, S. B., & McWilliams, N. (2003). The impact of Sigmund Freud and The Interpretation of Dreams. In R. J. Sternberg (Ed.), *The anatomy of impact: What makes the great works of psychology great* (pp. 71–88). Washington, DC: American Psychological Association.

MetLife Mature Market Institute. (2007). *The MetLife Market Survey of Nursing Home & Home Care Costs 2006*. Westport, CT: MetLife Mature Market Institute.

Meyer, D. E., Kieras, D. E., Lauber, E., Schumacher, E. H., Glass, J., Zurbriggen, E., Gmeindl, L., & Apfelblat, D. (2002). Adaptive executive control: Flexible multiple-task performance without pervasive immutable response-selection bottlenecks. In T. A. Polk, & C. M. Seifert, Eds., *Cognitive modeling*. Cambridge, MA: MIT Press.

Meyer-Bahlburg, H. F. L., Ehrhardt, A. A., Rosen, L. R., Gruen, R. S., Veridiano, N. P., Vann, F. H., & Neuwalder, H. F. (1995). Prenatal estrogens and the development of homosexual orientation. *Developmental Psychology, 31*, 12–21.

Michael, R. T., Gagnon, J. H., Laumann, E. O., & Kolata, G. (1994). *Sex in America: A definitive survey*. Boston: Little, Brown.

Michaels, M. (2006). Factors that contribute to stepfamily success: A qualitative analysis. *Journal of Divorce & Remarriage, 44*, 53–66.

Midaeva, E., & Lyubimova, Z. (2008). Formation of language-specific characteristics of speech sounds in early ontogeny. *Human Physiology, 34*, 649–652.

Mikhail, B. (2000). Prenatal care utilization among low-income African American women. *Journal of Community Health Nursing, 17*, 235–246.

Mikulincer, M., & Shaver, P. R. (2005). Attachment security, compassion, and altruism. *Current Directions in Psychological Science, 14*, 34–38.

Mikulincer, M., & Shaver, P. R., (2007). *Attachment in adulthood: Structure, dynamics, and change*. New York: Guilford Press.

Miles, R., Cowan, F., Glover, V., Stevenson, J., & Modi, N. (2006). A controlled trial of skin-to-skin contact in extremely preterm infants. *Early Human Development, 2*(7), 447–455.

Miller, B. (1997b, March). The quest for lifelong learning. *American Demographics*, pp. 20–22.

Miller, G. A. (1956). The magical number seven, plus or minus two: Some limits on our capacity for processing information. *Psychology Review, 63*, 81–97.

Miller, G., & Cohen, S. (2001). Psychological interventions and the immune system: A meta-analytic review and critique. *Health Psychology, 20*, 47–63.

Miller, J. G. & Bersoff, D. M. (1994). Cultural influences on the moral status of reciprocity and the discounting of endogenous motivation. Special Issue: The self and the collective. *Personality and Social Psychology Bulletin, 20*, 592–602.

Miller, L., Bishop, J., Fischer, J., Geller, S., & Macmillan, C. (2008). Balancing risks: Dosing strategies for antidepressants near the end of pregnancy. *Journal of Clinical Psychiatry, 69*, 323–324.

Miller, P. A., & Jansen op de Haar, M. A. (1997). Emotional, cognitive, behavioral, and temperament characteristics of high-empathy children. *Motivation and Emotion, 21*, 109–125.

Miller, P. H., & Seier, W. L. (1994). *Strategy utilization deficiencies in children: When, where, and why*. San Diego, CA: Academic Press.

Miller, P. H., Woody-Ramsey, J., & Aloise, P. A. (1991). The role of strategy effortfulness in strategy effectiveness. *Developmental Psychology, 27*, 738–745.

Miller, R. B., Hemesath, K., & Nelson, B. (1997). Marriage in middle and later life. In T. D. Hargrave & S. M. Hanna (Eds.), *The aging family: New visions in theory, practice, and reality* (pp. 178–198). New York: Brunner/Mazel.

Miller, S. A. (1998). *Developmental research methods.* (2nd ed.). Upper Saddle River, NJ: Prentice-Hall.

Mills, J. L. (1999). Cocaine, smoking, and spontaneous abortion. *New England Journal of Medicine, 340*, 380–381.

Mimura, K., Kimoto, T., & Okada, M. (2003). Synapse efficiency diverges due to synaptic pruning following overgrowth. *Phys Rev E Stat Nonlinear Soft Matter Physics, 68*, 124–131.

Minorities in Higher Education. (1995). *Annual status report on minorities in higher education*. Washington, DC: Author.

Mischel, W. (2004). Toward an integrative science of the person. *Annual Review of Psychology, 55*, 1–22.

Mishra, R. (2001). Cognition across cultures. *The handbook of culture and psychology*. New York: Oxford University Press.

Mishra, R., & Stainthorp, R. (2007). The relationship between phonological awareness and word reading accuracy in Oriya and English: A study of Oriya-speaking fifth-graders. *Journal of Research in Reading, 30*, 23–37.

Mistry, J., & Saraswathi, T. (2003). The cultural context of child development. In R. Lerner & M. Easterbrooks (Eds.), *Handbook of psychology: Developmental psychology*, Vol. 6 (pp. 267–291). New York: Wiley.

Mitchell, B. A. (2006). *The boomerang age: Transitions to adulthood in families*. New Brunswick, NJ: AldineTransaction.

Mitchell, S. (2002). *American generations: Who they are, how they live, what they think*. Ithaca, NY: New Strategists Publications.

Mittendorf, R., Williams, M. A., Berkey, C. S., & Cotter, R. F. (1990). The length of uncomplicated human gestation. *Obstetrics and Gynecology, 75*, 73–78.

Miyamoto, R. H., Hishinuma, E. S., Nishimura, S. T., Nahulu, L. B., Andrade, N. N., & Goebert, D. A. (2000). Variation in self-esteem among adolescents in an Asian/Pacific-Islander sample. *Personality & Individual Differences, 29*, 13–25.

Mizuno, K., & Ueda, A. (2004). Antenatal olfactory learning influences infant feeding. *Early Human Development, 76*, 83–90.

Mohammed, A., Attalla, B., Bashir, F., Ahmed, F., Hassan, A., et al. (2006). Relationship of the sickle cell gene to the ethnic and geographic groups populating the Sudan. *Community Genetics, 9*, 113–120.

Moldin, S. O., & Gottesman, I. I. (1997). Genes, experience, and chance in schizophrenia—Positioning for the 21st century. *Schizophrenia Bulletin, 23*, 547–561.

Molfese, V. J., & Acheson, S. (1997). Infant and preschool mental and verbal abilities: How are infant scores related to preschool scores? *International Journal of Behavioral Development, 20*, 595–607.

Money, J., & Ehrhardt, A. A. (1972). *Man and woman, boy and girl: The differentiation and dimorphism of gender identity from conception to maturity*. Baltimore, MD: Johns Hopkins University Press.

Mongan, M. F. (2005). *HypnoBirthing: The Mongan method: A natural approach to a safe, easier, more comfortable birthing* (3rd ed.) Deerfield Beach, FL: Health Communications.

Monk, C. S., Grillon, C., Baas, J. M. P., McClure, E. B., Nelson, E. E., Zarahn, E., Charney, D. S., Ernst, M., & Pine, D. S.(2003). A neuroimaging method for the study of threat in adolescents. *Developmental Psychobiology, 43*, 359–366.

Montemayor, R., Adams, G. R., & Gulotta, T. P. (Eds.). (1994). *Personal relationships during adolescence*. Newbury Park, CA: Sage.

Montessori, M. (1964). *The Montessori method*. New York: Schocken.

Montgomery-Downs, H., & Thomas, E. B. (1998). Biological and behavioral correlates of quiet sleep respiration rates in infants. *Physiology and Behavior, 64*, 637–643.

Monthly Labor Review. (2009, November). Employment outlook: 2008–2018: Labor force projections to 2018: Older workers staying more active. *Monthly Labor Review*. Washington, DC: U.S. Department of Labor.

Montpetit, M., & Bergeman, C. (2007). Dimensions of control: Mediational analyses of the stress-health relationship. *Personality and Individual Differences, 43*, 2237–2248.

Moore, D. S. (2002, December 31). Americans' view of influence of religion settling back to pre-September 11 levels. *Gallup Poll Tuesday Briefing*.

Moore, K. L. (1974). *Before we are born: Basic embryology and birth defects*. Philadelphia: Saunders.

Moore, L., Gao, D., & Bradlee, M. (2003). Does early physical activity predict body fat change throughout childhood? *Preventive Medicine: An International Journal Devoted to Practice & Theory, 37*, 10–17.

Moore, S., & Rosenthal, D. (2006). *Sexuality in adolescence: Current trends*. New York: Routledge/Taylor & Francis Group.

Moores, D., & Meadow-Orlans, K. (1990). *Educational and developmental aspects of deafness*. Washington, DC: Gallaudet University Press.

Morales, J. R., & Guerra, N. F. (2006). Effects of multiple context and cumulative stress on urban children's adjustment in elementary school. *Child Development, 77*, 907–923.

Morange, M. (2002). *The misunderstood gene*. Cambridge, MA: Harvard University Press.

Morelli, G. A., Rogoff, B., Oppenheim, D., & Goldsmith, D. (1992). Cultural variation in infants' sleeping arrangements: Questions of independence. Special section: Cross-cultural studies of development. *Developmental Psychology, 28*, 604–613.

Moreton, C. (2007, January 14). World's first test-tube baby Louise Brown has child of her own. *The Independent*.

Morgan, R., Garavan, H., & Smith, E. (2001). Early lead exposure produces lasting changes in sustained attention, response initiation, and reactivity to errors. *Neurotoxicology & Teratology, 23*, 519–531.

Morice, A. (1998, February 27–28). Future moms, please note: Benefits vary. *Wall Street Journal*, p. 15.

Morita, Y., & Tilly, J. L. (2000). Sphingolipid regulation of female gonadal cell apoptosis. *Annals of the New York Academy of Sciences, 905*, 209–220.

Morra, S. (2008). Memory components and control processes in children's drawing. *Children's understanding and production of pictures, drawings, and art: Theoretical and empirical approaches* (pp. 53–85). Ashland, OH: Hogrefe & Huber Publishers.

Morra, S., Gobbo, C., Marini, Z., & Sheese, R. (2008). *Cognitive development: Neo-Piagetian perspectives.* New York: Taylor & Francis Group/Lawrence Erlbaum Associates.

Morris, L. B. (2001, March 21). For elderly, relief for emotional ills can be elusive. *New York Times,* p. A6.

Morris, P., & Fritz, C. (2006, October). How to improve your memory. *The Psychologist, 19,* 608–611.

Morrison, F. J., Bachman, H. J., Connor, C. M. (2005) *Improving literacy in America: Guidelines from research.* New Haven, CT: Yale University Press.

Morrison, F. J., Holmes, D. L., & Hairth, M. M. (1974). A developmental study of the effects of familiarity on short-term visual memory. *Journal of Experimental Child Psychology, 18,* 412–425.

Morrison, F. J., Smith, L., & Dow-Ehrensberger, M. (1995). Education and cognitive development: A natural experiment. *Developmental Psychology, 31,* 789–799.

Morrongiello, B., & Hogg, K. (2004). Mothers' reactions to children misbehaving in ways that can lead to injury: Implications for gender differences in children's risk taking and injuries. *Sex Roles, 50,* 103–118.

Morrongiello, B., Midgett, C., & Stanton, K. (2000). Gender biases in children's appraisals of injury risk and other children's risk-taking behaviors. *Journal of Experimental Child Psychology, 77,* 317–336.

Morry, M. (2007, February). The attraction-similarity hypothesis among cross-sex friends: Relationship satisfaction, perceived similarities, and self-serving perceptions. *Journal of Social and Personal Relationships, 24,* 117–138.

Morse, R. M., & Flavin, D. K. (1992). The definition of alcoholism. *Journal of the American Medical Association, 268,* 1012–1014.

Mortimer, J. (2003). *Working and growing up in America.* Cambridge, MA: Harvard University Press.

Mosher, C. E., & Danoff-Burg, S. (2005). Agentic and communal personality traits: Relations to attitudes toward sex and sexual experiences. *Sex Roles: A Journal of Research, 22,* 343–355.

Moshman, D., Glover, J. A., & Bruning, R. H. (1987). *Developmental psychology.* Boston: Little, Brown.

Moss, M. (1997, March 31). Golden years? For one 73-year-old, punching time clock isn't a labor of love. *Wall Street Journal,* pp. A1, A8.

Mossakowski, K. N. (2003). Coping with perceived discrimination: Does ethnic identity protect mental health? *Journal of Health and Social Behavior, 44, Special issue: Race, Ethnicity and Mental Health,* 318–331.

Motschnig, R., & Nykl, L. (2003). Toward a cognitive-emotional model of Rogers's person-centered approach. *Journal of Humanistic Psychology, 43,* 8–45.

Mouw, T., & Entwisle, B. (2006). Residential segregation and interracial friendship in schools. *American Journal of Sociology, 112,* 394–441.

Moyad, M. A. (2004). Preventing male osteoporosis: Prevalence, risks, diagnosis and imaging tests. *Urological Clinics of North America, 31,* 321–330.

Moyer, M. S. (1992). Sibling relationships among older adults. *Generations, 16,* 55–58.

Mu, Q., Bohning, D. E., Nahas, Z., Walker, J., Anderson, B., Johnson, K. A., Denslow, S., Lomarev, M., Moghadam, P., Chae, J., & George, M. S. (2004). Acute vagus nerve stimulation using different pulse widths produces varying brain effects. *Biological Psychiatry, 55,* 816–825.

Mueller, M., Wilhelm, B., & Elder, G. (2002). Variations in grandparenting. *Research on Aging, 24,* 360–388.

Muenchow, S., & Marsland, K. (2007). Beyond baby steps: Promoting the growth and development of U.S. child-care policy. *Child development and social policy: Knowledge for action* (pp. 97–112). Washington, DC: American Psychological Association.

Mumme, D., & Fernald, A. (2003). The infant as onlooker: Learning from emotional reactions observed in a television scenario. *Child Development, 74,* 221–237.

Munzar, P., Cami, J., & Farré, M. (2003). Mechanisms of Drug Addiction. *New England Journal of Medicine, 349,* 2365–2365.

Murdock, T. B., & Bolch, M. B. (2005). Risk and protective factors for poor school adjustment in lesbian, gay, and bisexual (LGB) high school youth: Variable and person-centered analyses. *Psychology in the Schools, 42,* 159–172.

Murguia, A., Peterson, R. A., & Zea, M. C. (1997, August). *Cultural health beliefs.* Paper presented at the annual meeting of the American Psychological Association, Toronto, Canada.

Murphy, C. (2008). The chemical senses and nutrition in older adults. *Journal of Nutrition for the Elderly, 27,* 247–265.

Murphy, S., Johnson, L., & Wu, L. (2003). Bereaved parents' outcomes 4 to 60 months after their children's death by accident, suicide, or homicide: A comparative study demonstrating differences. *Death Studies, 27,* 39–61.

Murray, J. (2008). Media violence: The effects are both real and strong. *American Behavioral Scientist, 51,* 1212–1230.

Murray, J. A., Terry, D. J., Vance, J. C., Battistutta, D., & Connolly, Y. (2000). Effects of a program of intervention on parental distress following infant death. *Death Studies, 4,* 275–305.

Murray, L., Cooper, P., Creswell, C., Schofield, E., & Sack, C. (2007, January). The effects of maternal social phobia on mother-infant interactions and infant social responsiveness. *Journal of Child Psychology and Psychiatry, 48,* 45–52.

Murray, S., Bellavia, G., & Rose, P. (2003). Once hurt, twice hurtful: How perceived regard regulates daily marital interactions. *Journal of Personality & Social Psychology, 84,* 126–147.

Murray, S., Griffin, D., Rose, P., & Bellavia, G. (2006). For better or worse? Self-esteem and the contingencies of acceptance in marriage. *Personality and Social Psychology Bulletin, 32,* 866–880.

Murray-Close, D., Ostrov, J., & Crick, N. (2007, December). A short-term longitudinal study of growth of relational aggression during middle childhood: Associations with gender, friendship intimacy, and internalizing problems. *Development and Psychopathology, 19,* 187–203.

Musolino, J., & Lidz, J. (2006). Why children aren't universally successful with quantification. *Linguistics, 44,* 817–852.

Mutrie, N. (1997). The therapeutic effects of exercise on the self. In K. R. Fox (Ed.), *The physical self: From motivation to well being* (pp. 287–314). Champaign, IL: Human Kinetics.

Myers, D. (2000). *A quiet world: Living with hearing loss.* New Haven, CT: Yale University Press.

Myers, N. A., Clifton, R. K., & Clarkson, M. G. (1987). When they were very young: Almost-threes remember two years ago. *Infant Behavior and Development, 10,* 123–132.

Myers, R. H. (2004). Huntington's disease genetics. *NeuroRx, 1,* 255–262.

Myklebust, B. M., & Gottlieb, G. L. (1993). Development of the stretch reflex in the newborn: Reciprocal excitation and reflex irradation. *Child Development, 64,* 1036–1045.

Nadal, K. (2004). Filipino American identity development model. *Journal of Multicultural Counseling & Development, 32,* 45–62.

Nadeau, L., Boivin, M., Tessier, R., Lefebvre, F., & Robaey, P. (2001). Mediators of behavioral problems in 7-year-old children born after 24 to 28 weeks of gestation. *Journal of Developmental & Behavioral Pediatrics, 22,* 1–10.

Nahmiash, D. (2006). *Abuse and neglect of older adults: What do we know about it and how can we identify it?* Westport, CT: Praeger Publishers/Greenwood Publishing Group.

Naik, G. (2002, November 22). The grim mission of a Swiss group: Visitor's suicides. *Wall Street Journal,* pp. A1, A6.

Nair, K. (2008). A plea for a holistic approach to aging. *Discourses on aging and dying.* New Delhi: Sage Publications India.

Nakagawa, M., Lamb, M. E., & Miyaki, K. (1992). Antecedents and correlates of the Strange Situation behavior of Japanese infants. *Journal of Cross-Cultural Psychology, 23,* 300–310.

Nanda, S., & Konnur, N. (2006, October). Adolescent drug & alcohol use in the 21st century. *Psychiatric Annals, 36,* 706–712.

Nangle, D. W., & Erdley, C. A. (Eds.). (2001). *The role of friendship in psychological adjustment.* San Francisco: Jossey-Bass.

Nathanson, A., Wilson, B., & McGee, J. (2002). Counteracting the effects of female stereotypes on television via active mediation. *Journal of Communication, 52,* 922–937.

Nation, M., & Heflinger, C. (2006). Risk factors for serious alcohol and drug use: The role of psychosocial variables in predicting the frequency of substance use among adolescents. *American Journal of Drug and Alcohol Abuse, 32,* 415–433.

National Association for the Education of Young Children. (2005). *Position statements of the NAEYC.* http://www.naeyc.org/about/positions.asp#where.

National Center for Children in Poverty. (1996). *Basic facts about low-income children – birth to age 18.* New York: National Center for Children in Poverty.

National Center for Children in Poverty. (1997). *Basic facts about low-income children – birth to age 18.* New York: National Center for Children in Poverty.

National Center for Children in Poverty. (2004). *Basic facts about low-income children – birth to age 18.* New York: National Center for Children in Poverty.

National Center for Children in Poverty. (2005). *Basic facts about low-income children in the United States.* New York: National Center for Children in Poverty.

National Center for Children in Poverty (2006). *Basic facts about low-income children in the United States.* New York: National Center for Children in Poverty.

National Center for Children in Poverty. (2007). *Basic facts about low-income children – birth to age 18.* New York: National Center for Children in Poverty.

National Center for Education Statistics. (2000). *Dropout rates in the United States: 1999.* Washington, DC: National Center for Education Statistics.

National Center for Educational Statistics. (2003). *Public High School Dropouts and Completers From the Common Core of Data: School Year 2000–01 Statistical Analysis Report.* Washington, DC: NCES.

National Center for Health Statistics (Infant and Child Health Studies Branch). (1997). *Survival rates of infants.* Washington, DC: National Center for Health Statistics.

National Center for Health Statistics. (2004). *SIDS death rate: 1980–2000.* Washington, DC: National Center for Health Statistics.

National Center for Health Statistics. (1994). *Division of vital statistics.* Washington, DC: Public Health Service.

National Center for Health Statistics. (2000). *Health United States, 2000 with adolescent health chartbook.* Hyattsville, MD.

National Center for Health Statistics. (2001). *Division of vital statistics.* Washington, DC: Public Health Service.

National Institute of Aging. (2004, May 31). *Sexuality in later life.* http://www.niapublications.org/engagepages/sexuality.asp.

National Institute of Child Health and Human Development (NICHD). (1999). Child care and mother–child interaction in the first 3 years of life. *Developmental Psychology, 35,* 1399–1413.

National Research Council. (1997). *Racial and ethnic differences in the health of older Americans.* New York: Author.

National Safety Council. (1989). *Accident facts: 1989 edition.* Chicago: National Safety Council.

National Science Foundation (NSF), Division of Science Resources Statistics. (2002). *Women, Minorities, and Persons With Disabilities in Science and Engineering: 2002.* Arlington, VA: National Science Foundation.

National Sleep Foundation. (2002). *Americans favor later high school start times, according to National Sleep Foundation Poll.* Washington, DC: National Sleep Foundation.

Navarro, M. (2006, May 25). Families add 3rd generation to households. *New York Times,* pp. A1, A22.

Nazzi, T., & Bertoncini, J. (2003). Before and after the vocabulary spurt: Two modes of word acquisition? *Developmental Science, 6,* 136–142.

NCPYP (National Campaign to Prevent Youth Pregnancy). (2003). *14 and younger: The sexual behavior of young adolescents.* Washington, DC.

Needleman, H. L., & Bellinger, D. (Eds.). (1994). *Prenatal exposure to toxicants: Developmental consequences.* Baltimore, MD: Johns Hopkins University Press.

Negy, C., Shreve, T., & Jensen, B. (2003). Ethnic identity, self-esteem, and ethnocentrism: A study of social identity versus multicultural theory of development. *Cultural Diversity & Ethnic Minority Psychology, 9,* 333–344.

Neher, A. (1991). Maslow's theory of motivation: A critique. *Journal of Humanistic Psychology, 31,* 89–112.

Neiss, M. B., Leigland, L. A., Carlson, N. E., & Janowsky, J. S. (2009). Age differences in perception and awareness of emotion. *Neurobiology of Aging, 30,* 1305–1313.

Neisser, U. (2004). Memory development: New questions and old. *Developmental Review, 24,* 154–158.

Nelson, C. A. (1987). The recognition of facial expressions in the first two years of life: Mechanisms of development. *Child Development, 58,* 889–909.

Nelson, D. A., Hart, C. H., Yang, C., Olsen, J. A., & Jin, S. (2006). Aversive parenting in China: Associations with child physical and relational aggression. *Child Development, 77,* 554–572.

Nelson, E. E., McClure, E. B., Monk, C. S., Zarahn, E., Leibenluft, E., Pine, D. S., & Ernst, M. (2003). Developmental differences in neuronal engagement during implicit encoding of emotional faces: An event-related fMRI study. *Journal of Child Psychology and Psychiatry, 44,* 1015–1024.

Nelson, K. (1996). *Language in cognitive development: Emergence of the mediated mind.* New York: Cambridge University Press.

Nelson, K., & Fivush, R. (2004). The emergence of autobiographical memory: A social cultural developmental theory. *Psychological Review, 111,* 486–511.

Nelson, L. D., Scheibel, K. E., & Ringman, J. M. (2007). An experimental approach to detecting dementia in Down syndrome: A paradigm for Alzheimer's disease. *Brain and Cognition, 64,* 92–103.

Nelson, T., & Wechsler, H. (2003). School spirits: Alcohol and collegiate sports fans. *Addictive Behaviors, 28,* 1–11.

Nesheim, S., Henderson, S., Lindsay, M., Zuberi, J., Grimes, V., Buehler, J., Lindegren, M. L., & Bulterys, M. (2004). *Prenatal HIV testing and antiretroviral prophylasix at an urban hospital—Atlanta, Georgia, 1997–2000.* Atlanta, GA: Centers for Disease Control.

Ness, J., Aronow, W., & Beck, G. (2006). Menopausal symptoms after cessation of hormone replacement therapy. *Maturitas, 53,* 356–361.

Ness, R. B., Grisso, J. A., Hirschinger, N., Markovic, N., Shaw, L. M., Day, N. L., & Kline, J. (1999). Cocaine and tobacco use and the risk of spontaneous abortion. *New England Journal of Medicine, 340,* 333–339.

Nettelbeck, T., & Rabbitt, P. M. (1992). Aging, cognitive performance, and mental speed. *Intelligence, 16,* 189–205.

Neubert, G. A., & Binko, J. B. (1992). *Inductive reasoning in the secondary classroom.* Washington, DC: National Education Association.

Newcomb, A. F., & Bagwell, C. L. (1995). Children's friendship relations: A meta-analytic review. *Psychological Bulletin, 117,* 306–347.

Newsome, W., & Kelly, M. (2006). Bullying behavior and school violence. *Fostering child & adolescent mental health in the classroom* (pp. 183–201). Thousand Oaks, CA: Sage Publications, Inc.

Newston, R. L., & Keith, P. M. (1997). Single women later in life. In J. M. Coyle (Ed.), *Handbook on women and aging* (pp. 385–399). Westport, CT: Greenwood Press.

Newton, K., Reed, S., LaCroix, A., Grothaus, L., Ehrlich, K., & Guiltinan, J. (2006). Treatment of vasomotor symptoms of menopause with black cohosh, multibotanicals, soy, hormone therapy, or placebo. *Annals of Internal Medicine, 145,* 869–879.

Ng, T., & Feldman, D. (2008). The relationship of age to ten dimensions of job performance. *Journal of Applied Psychology, 93,* 392–423.

Ni Bhrolchain, M. (2006). The age difference between partners: A matter of female choice? In C. Sauvin-Dugerdil, et al. (Eds.), *Human clocks: The bio-cultural meanings of age.* New York: Peter Lang Publishing.

NIAAA (National Institute on Alcohol Abuse and Alcoholism). (1990). *Alcohol and health.* Washington, DC: U.S. Government Printing Office.

NICHD Early Child Care Research Network. (1997). The effects of infant child care on infant–mother attachment security: Results of the NICHD study of early child care. *Child Development, 68,* 860–879.

NICHD Early Child Care Research Network. (2001). Child care and children's peer interaction at 24 and 36 months: The NICHD study of early child care. *Child Development, 72,* 1478–1500.

NICHD Early Child Care Research Network. (2001). Child-care and family predictors of preschool attachment and stability from infancy. *Developmental Psychology, 37,* 847–862.

NICHD Early Child Care Research Network. (2003a). Does quality of child care affect child outcomes at age 4 1/2? *Developmental Psychology, 39,* 451–69.

NICHD Early Child Care Research Network. (2003b). Families matter—even for kids in child care. *Journal of Developmental and Behavioral Pediatrics, 24,* 58–62.

NICHD Early Child Care Research Network. (2005). *Child care and child development: Results from the NICHD study of early child care and youth development.* New York: Guilford Press.

NICHD Early Child Care Research Network. (2006). *Child care and child development: Results from the NICHD study of early child care and youth development.* New York: Guilford Press.

NICHD. (2006) *The NICHD Study of Early Child Care and Youth Development (SECCYD): Findings for Children up to Age 4 1/2 Years.* (Figure 5, p. 20). Washington, DC: National Institute of Child Health and Human Development.

Nicolson, R., & Fawcett, A. (2008). *Dyslexia, learning, and the brain.* Cambridge, MA: MIT Press.

Niederhofer, H. (2004). A longitudinal study: Some preliminary results of association of prenatal maternal stress and fetal movements, temperament factors in early childhood and behavior at age 2 years. *Psychological Reports, 95,* 767–770.

Nielsen, M. (2006). Copying actions and copying outcomes: Social learning through the second year. *Developmental Psychology, 42,* 555–565.

Nielsen, M., Dissanayake, C., & Kashima, Y. (2003). A longitudinal investigation of self-other discrimination and the emergence of minor self-recognition. *Infant Behavior & Development, 26,* 213–226.

Nigg, J. T. (2001). Is ADHD a disinhibatory disorder? *Psychological Bulletin, 127,* 571–598.

Nihart, M. A. (1993). Growth and development of the brain. *Journal of Child and Adolescent Psychiatric and Mental Health Nursing, 6,* 39–40.

Nilsen, E., & Graham, S. (2009). The relations between children's communicative perspective-taking and executive functioning. *Cognitive Psychology, 58,* 220–249.

Nisbet, R. (1994, October 31). Blue genes. *New Republic, 211,* 15.

Nixon-Cave, K. (2001). *Influence of cultural/ethnic beliefs and behaviors and family environment on the motor development of infants 12–18 months of age in three ethnic groups: African-American, Hispanic/Latino and Anglo-European.* Unpublished doctoral dissertation, Temple University, PA.

Nobuyuki, I. (1997). Simple reaction times and timing of serial reactions of middle-aged and old men. *Perceptual & Motor Skills, 84,* 219–225.

Nockels, R., & Oakeshott, P. (1999). Awareness among young women of sexually transmitted chlamydia infection. *Family Practice, 16,* 94.

Noel, A., & Newman, J. (2008). Mothers' plans for children during the kindergarten hold-out year. *Early Child Development and Care, 178*(3), 289–303.

Nolen-Hoeksema, S. (2001). Ruminative coping and adjustment to bereavement. In M. Stroebe & R. Hansson (Eds.), *Handbook of bereavement research: Consequences, coping, and care.* Washington, DC: American Psychological Association.

Nolen-Hoeksema, S. (2003). *Women who think too much: How to break free of overthinking and reclaim your life.* New York: Henry Holt.

Nolen-Hoeksema, S., & Davis, C. (2002). Positive responses to loss: Perceiving benefits and growth. In C. Snyder & S. Lopez (Eds.), *Handbook of positive psychology.* London: Oxford University Press.

Nolen-Hoeksema, S., & Larson, J. (1999). *Coping with loss.* Mahwah, NJ: Erlbaum.

Noller, P., Feeney, J. A., & Ward, C. M. (1997). Determinants of marital quality: A partial test of Lewis and Spanier's model. *Journal of Family Studies, 3,* 226–251.

Noonan, D. (2003, September 22). When safety is the name of the game. *Newsweek,* pp. 64–66.

Noonan, D. (2003, September 29). High on testosterone. *Newsweek,* 50–52.

Nordin, S., Razani, L., & Markison, S. (2003). Age-associated increases in intensity discrimination for taste. *Experimental Aging Research, 29,* 371–381.

Norlander, T., Von Schedvin, H., & Archer, T. (2005). Thriving as a function of affective personality: Relation to personality factors, coping strategies and stress. *Anxiety, Stress & Coping: An International Journal, 18,* 105–116.

Norman, R. (2008). Reproductive changes in the female lifespan. *The active female: Health issues throughout the lifespan* (pp. 17–24). Totowa, NJ: Humana Press.

Notaro, P., Gelman, S., & Zimmerman, M. (2002). Biases in reasoning about the consequences of psychogenic bodily reactions: Domain boundaries in cognitive development. *Merrill-Palmer Quarterly, 48,* 427–449.

Nowak, M. A., Komarova, N. L., & Niyogi, P. (2001, January 5). Evolution of universal grammar. *Science, 291,* 114–116.

Nowak, M., Komarova, N., & Niyogi, P. (2002). Computational and evolutionary aspects of language. *Nature, 417,* 611–617.

NSDUH. (2004). Youth drug use continues to decline. The Substance Abuse and Mental Health Services Administration: Washington, DC.

Nugent, J. K., Lester, B. M., & Brazelton, T. B. (Eds.). (1989). *The cultural context of infancy, Vol. 1: Biology, culture, and infant development.* Norwood, NJ: Ablex.

Nuttman-Shwartz, O. (2007). Is there life without work? *International Journal of Aging & Human Development, 64,* 129–147.

O'Connor, M., & Whaley, S. (2006). Health care provider advice and risk factors associated with alcohol consumption following pregnancy recognition. *Journal of Studies on Alcohol, 67,* 22–31.

O'Connor, P. (1994). Very close parent/child relationships: The perspective of the elderly person. *Journal of Cross-Cultural Gerontology, 9,* 53–76.

O'Dea, J., & Wilson, R. (2006). Socio-cognitive and nutritional factors associated with body mass index in children and adolescents: Possibilities for childhood obesity prevention. *Health Education Research, 21,* 796–805.

O'Grady, W., & Aitchison, J. (2005). *How children learn language.* New York: Cambridge University Press.

O'Hara, R., Schroder, C., Bloss, C., Bailey, A., Alyeshmerni, A., Mumenthaler, M., Friedman, L., & Yesavage, J. (2005). Hormone replacement therapy and longitudinal cognitive performance in postmenopausal women. *American Journal of Geriatric Psychiatry, 13,* 1107–1110.

O'Toole, M. E. (2000). *The school shooter: A threat assessment perspective.* Washington, DC: Federal Bureau of Investigation.

O'Toole, M. L., Sawicki, M. A., & Artal, R. (2003). Structured diet and physical activity prevent postpartum weight retention. *Journal of Women's Health, 12,* 991–998.

Ochsner, K. N., & Gross, J. J. (2005). Putting the 'I' and the 'Me' in emotion regulation: Reply to Northoff. *Trends in Cognitive Sciences, Vol 9,* 409–410.

OECD. (1998). Education at a glance: OECD indicators, 1998. Paris: Organization for Economic Cooperation and Development.

OECD. (2001). Education at a glance: OECD indicators. Paris: Organization for Economic Cooperation and Development.

OECD. (2005). Education at a glance: OECD indicators. Paris: Organization for Economic Cooperation and Development.

Oesterdiekhoff, G. (2007). The reciprocal causation of intelligence and culture: A commentary based on a Piagetian perspective. *European Journal of Personality, 21,* 742–743.

Ogbu, J. (1992). Understanding cultural diversity and learning. *Educational Researcher, 21,* 5–14.

Ogbu, J. (2002). Cultural amplifiers of intelligence: IQ and minority status in cross-cultural perspective. *Race and intelligence: Separating science from myth* (pp. 241–278). Mahwah, NJ: Lawrence Erlbaum Associates Publishers.

Ogbu, J. U. (1988). Black education: A cultural-ecological perspective. In H. P. McAdoo (Ed.), *Black families.* Beverly Hills, CA: Sage.

Ogden, C. L., Kuczmarski, R. J., Flegal, K. M., Mei, Z., Guo, S., Wei, R., Grummer-Strawn, L. M., Curtin, L. R., Roche, A. F., & Johnson, C. L. (2002). Centers for Disease Control and Prevention 2000 growth charts for the United States: Improvements to the 1977 National Center for Health Statistics Version. *Pediatrics, 109,* 45–60.

Oğuz, V., & Akyol, A. K. (2008). Perspective-taking skills of 6-year-old children: Preschool attendance and mothers' and fathers' education and empathetic skills. *Perceptual and Motor Skills, 107,* 481–493.

Okie, S. (2005). *Winning the war against childhood obesity.* Washington, DC: Joseph Henry Publications.

Olds, T., Wake, M., Patton, G., Ridley, K., Waters, E., Williams, J., et al. (2009). How do school-day activity patterns differ with age and gender across adolescence?. *Journal of Adolescent Health, 44,* 64–72.

Olivardia, R., & Pope, H. (2002). Body image disturbance in childhood and adolescence. In D. Castle & K. Phillips (Eds.), *Disorders of body image.* Petersfield, England: Wrightson Biomedical Publishing.

Oliver, M. B., & Hyde, J. S. (1993). Gender differences in sexuality: A meta-analysis. *Psychological Bulletin, 114,* 29–51.

Oller, D. K., Eilers, R. E., Urbano, R., & Cobo-Lewis A. B. (1997). Development of precursors to speech in infants exposed to two languages. *Journal of Child Language, 24,* 407–425.

Olshansky, S. J., Passaro, D. J., Hershow, R. C., Layden, J., Carnes, B. A., Brody, J., Hayflick, L., Butler, R. N., Allison, D. B., & Ludwig, D. S. (2005, March 17). Special Report: A potential decline in life expectancy in the United States in the 21st Century. *New England Journal of Medicine, 352,* 1138–1145.

Olson, E. (2006, April 27). You're in labor, and getting Sleeeepy. *New York Time,* p. C2.

Oltjenbruns, K., & Balk, D. (2007). Life span issues and loss, grief, and mourning: Part 1: The importance of a developmental context: Childhood and adolescence as an example; Part 2: Adulthood. *Handbook of thanatology: The essential body of knowledge for the study of death, dying, and bereavement* (pp. 143–163). New York, Northbrook, IL: Routledge/Taylor & Francis Group.

Opfer, J. E., & Siegler, R. S. (2007). Representational change and children's numerical estimation. Citation. *Cognitive Psychology, 55,* 169–195.

Orbuch, T. L., House, J. S., Mero, R. P., & Webster, P. S . (1996). Marital quality over the life course. *Social Psychology Quarterly, 59,* 162–171.

Ormont, L. R. (2001). Developing emotional insulation. In L. B. Fugeri, *The technique of group treatment: The collected papers of Louis R. Ormont.* Madison, CT: Psychosocial Press.

Ortiz, S. O., & Dynda, A. M. (2005). Use of intelligence tests with culturally and linguistically diverse populations. In D. P. Flanagan, & P. L. Harrison (Eds.), *Contemporary intellectual assessment: Theories, tests, and issues.* New York: Guilford Press.

Osofsky, J. (2003). Prevalence of children's exposure to domestic violence and child maltreatment: Implications for prevention and intervention. *Clinical Child & Family Psychology Review, 6,* 161–170.

Ostrosky-Solís, F., & Oberg, G. (2006). Neuropsychological functions across the world—common and different features: From digit span to moral judgment. *International Journal of Psychology, 41,* 321–323.

Ostrov, J., Gentile, D., & Crick, N. (2006, November). Media exposure, aggression and prosocial behavior during early childhood: A longitudinal study. *Social Development, 15,* 612–627.

Outten, H., Schmitt, M., Garcia, D., & Branscombe, N. (2009). Coping options: Missing links between minority group identification and psychological well-being. *Applied Psychology: An International Review, 58,* 146–170.

Ouwehand, C., de Ridder, D. T., & Bensing, J. M. (2007). A review of successful aging models: Proposing proactive coping as an important additional strategy. *Clinical Psycholgoy Review, 43,* 101–116.

Owens, J. (2008). Socio-cultural considerations and sleep practices in the pediatric population. *Sleep Medicine Clinics, 3,* 97–107.

Owsley, C., Stalvey, B., & Phillips, J. (2003). The efficacy of an educational intervention in promoting self-regulation among high-risk older drivers. *Accident Analysis & Prevention, 35,* 393–400.

Oxford, M., Gilchrist, L., Gillmore, M., & Lohr, M. (2006, July). Predicting variation in the life course of adolescent mothers as they enter adulthood. *Journal of Adolescent Health, 39,* 20–26.

Oyebode, J. (2008). Death, dying and bereavement. *Handbook of the clinical psychology of ageing* (2nd ed., pp. 75–94). New York: John Wiley & Sons Ltd.

Oyserman, D., Kemmelmeier, M., Fryberg, S., Brosh, H., & Hart-Johnson, T. (2003). Racial ethnic self-schemas. *Social Psychology Quarterly, 66,* 333–347.

Ozawa, M., & Yoon, H. (2003). Economic impact of marital disruption on children. *Children & Youth Services Review, 25,* 611–632.

Paige, R. (2006, December). No Child Left Behind: The ongoing movement for public education reform. *Harvard Educational Review, 76,* 461–473.

Paikoff, R. L., & Brooks-Gunn, J. (1990). Physiological processes: What role do they play during the transition to adolescence? In R. Montemayor, G. R. Adams, & T. P. Gulotta (Eds.), *From childhood to adolescence: A transitional period?* Newbury Park, CA: Sage.

Paisley, T. S., Joy, E. A., & Price, R. J., Jr. (2003). Exercise during pregnancy: a practical approach. *Current Sports Medicine Reports, 2,* 325–330.

Pajkrt, E., Weisz, B., Firth, H. V., & Chitty, L. S. (2004). Fetal cardiac anomalies and genetic syndromes. *Prenatal Diagnosis, 24,* 1104–1115.

Pajulo, M., Helenius, H., & MaYes, L. (2006, May). Prenatal views of baby and parenthood: Association with sociodemographic and pregnancy factors. *Infant Mental Health Journal, 27,* 229–250.

Palan, P. R., Connell, K., Ramirez, E. Inegbenijie, C., Gavara, R. Y.l, Ouseph, J. A., & Mikhail, M. S. (2005). Effects of menopause and hormone replacement therapy on serum levels of coenzyme Q10 and other lipid-soluble antioxidants. *Biofactors, 25,* 61–66.

Palincsar, A. S., & Brown, A. L. (1984). Reciprocal teaching of comprehension-fostering and comprehension-monitoring activities. *Cognition and Instruction, 1,* 117–175.

Palincsar, A. S., Brown, A. L., & Campione, J. C. (1993). First-grade dialogues for knowledge acquisition and use. In E. Forman, N. Minick, & C. A. Stone (Eds.), *Contexts for Learning: Sociocultural Dynamics in Children's Development,* New York: Oxford University Press.

Paneth, N. S. (1995). The problem of low birth weight. *The Future of Children, 5,* 19–34.

Papaharitou, S., Nakopoulou, E., Kirana, P., Giaglis, G., Moraitou, M., & Hatzichristou, D. (2008). Factors associated with sexuality in later life: An exploratory study in a group of Greek married older adults. *Archives of Gerontology and Geriatrics, 46,* 191–201.

Papousek, H., & Papousek, M. (1991). Innate and cultural guidance of infants' integrative competencies: China, the United States, and Germany. In M. H. Borstein (Ed.), *Cultural approaches to parenting.* Hillsdale, NJ: Erlbaum.

Park, L., & Maner, J. (2009, January). Does self-threat promote social connection? The role of self-esteem and contingencies of self-worth. *Journal of Personality and Social Psychology, 96,* 203–217.

Parke, R. D. (1996). *New fatherhood.* Cambridge, MA: Harvard University Press.

Parke, R., Simpkins, S., & McDowell, D. (2002). Relative contributions of families and peers to children's social development. In P. Smith & C. Hart (Eds.), *Blackwell handbook of childhood social development.* Malden, MA: Blackwell Publishers.

Parke, R. D. (2004). Development in the family. *Annual Review of Psychology, 55,* 365–399.

Parker-Pope, T. (2003, December 9). How to give your child a longer life. *Wall Street Journal,* pp. R1, R3.

Parker-Pope, T. (2003, October 21). The case for hormone therapy. *The Wall Street Journal,* pp. R1, R3.

Parkes, C. M. (1997). Normal and abnormal responses to stress—A developmental approach. In D. Black, M. Newman, J. Harris-Hendricks, & G. Mezey (Eds.), *Psychological trauma: A developmental approach* (pp. 10–18). London, England: Gaskell/Royal College of Psychiatrists.

Parks, C. A. (1998). Lesbian parenthood: A review of the literature. *American Journal of Orthopsychiatry, 68,* 376–389.

Parks, C., Sanna, L., & Posey, D. (2003). Retrospection in social dilemmas: How thinking about the past affects future cooperation. *Journal of Personality & Social Psychology, 84,* 988–996.

Parlee, M. B. (1979, October). The friendship bond. *Psychology Today, 13,* 43–45.

Parmalee, A. H., Jr., & Sigman, M. D. (1983). Prenatal brain development and behavior. In P. H. Mussen (Ed.), *Handbook of child psychology* (Vol. 2, 4th ed.). New York: Wiley.

Parten, M. B. (1932). Social participation among preschool children. *Journal of Abnormal and Social Psychology, 27,* 243–269.

Pascalis, O., de Haan, M., & Nelson, C. A. (2002). Is face processing species-specific during the first year of life? *Science, 296,* 1321–1323.

Pascoe, J. M. (1993). Social support during labor and duration of labor: A community-based study. *Public Health Nursing, 10,* 97–99.

Pascual-Leone, J., & Johnson, J. (2005). A dialectical constructivist view of developmental intelligence. *Handbook of understanding and measuring intelligence.* Thousand Oaks, CA: Sage Publications, Inc.

Pashos, A., & McBurney, D. (2008). Kin relationships and the caregiving biases of grandparents, aunts, and uncles: A two-generational questionnaire study. *Human Nature, 19,* 311–330.

Pasqualotto, F. F., Lucon, A. M., Sobreiro, B. P., Pasqualotto, E. B., & Arap, S. (2005). Effects of medical therapy, alcohol, smoking, and endocrine disruptors on male infertility. *Revista do Hospital das Clinicas, 59,* 375–382.

Patenaude, A., F., Guttmacher, A. E., & Collins, F. S. (2002). Genetic testing and psychology: New roles, new responsibilities. *American Psychologist, 57,* 271–282.

Paterson, D. S., Trachtenberg, F. L., Thompson, E. G., Belliveau, R. A., Beggs, A. H., Darnall, R., Chadwick, A. E., Krous, H. F., & Kinney, H. C. (2006). Multiple serotonergic brainstem abnormalities in sudden infant death syndrome. *Journal of the American Medical Association, 296,* 2124–2132.

Patterson, C. (2006, October). Children of lesbian and gay parents. *Current Directions in Psychological Science, 15,* 241–244.

Patterson, C. J. (1992). Children of lesbian and gay parents. *Child Development, 63,* 1025–1042.

Patterson, C. J. (1995). Families of the baby boom: Parents' division of labor and children's adjustment. *Special Issue: Sexual orientation and human development. Developmental Psychology, 31,* 115–123.

Patterson, C., & Friel, L.V. (2000). Sexual orientation and fertility. In G.R. Bentley & N. Mascie-Taylor (Eds.), *Infertility in the modern world: Biosocial perspectives.* Cambridge, UK: Cambridge University Press.

Paul, P. (2006, January 16). Want a Brainier Baby? *Time, 167*(3), 104.

Pauli-Pott, U., Mertesacker, B., & Bade, U. (2003). Parental perceptions and infant temperament development. *Infant Behavior & Development, 26,* 27–48.

Paunonen, S. V. (2003). Big Five factors of personality and replicated predictions of behavior. *Journal of Personality and Social Psychology, 84,* 411–422.

Pavis, S., Cunningham-Burley, S., & Amos, A. (1997). Alcohol consumption and young people: Exploring meaning and social context. *Health Education Research, 12,* 311–322.

Paxton, S. J., Schutz, H. K., Wertheim, E. H., & Muir, S. L. (1999). Friendship clique and peer influences on body image concerns, dietary restraint, extreme weight-loss behaviors, and binge eating in adolescent girls. *Journal of Abnormal Psychology, 108,* 255–266.

Pear, R. (2000, March 19). Proposal to curb the use of drugs to calm the young. *New York Times,* p. 1.

Peck, R. C. (1968). Psychological developments in the second half of life. In B. L. Neugarten (Ed.), *Middle age and aging.* Chicago: University of Chicago Press.

Pedlow, R., Sanson, A., Prior, M., & Oberklaid, F. (1993). Stability of maternally reported temperament from infancy to 8 years. *Developmental Psychology, 29,* 998–1007.

Peirano, P., Algarin, C., & Uauy, R. (2003). Sleep-wake states and their regulatory mechanisms throughout early human development. *Journal of Pediatrics, 143,* Supplement, S70–S79.

Pellegrini, A. (2007). Is aggression adaptative? Yes: Some kinds are and in some ways. *Aggression and adaptation: The bright side to bad behavior.* Mahwah, NJ: Lawrence Erlbaum Associates Publishers.

Pelligrini, A. D., & Smith, P. K. (1998). Physical activity play: The nature and function of a neglected aspect of play. *Child Development, 69,* 577–598.

Peltonen, L., & McKusick, V. A. (2001, February 16). Dissecting the human disease in the postgenomic era. *Science, 291,* 1224–1229.

Peltzer, K., & Pengpid, S. (2006). Sexuality of 16- to 17- year-old South Africans in the context of HIV/AIDS. *Social Behavior and Personality, 34,* 239–256.

Penninx, B., Guralnik, J. M., Ferrucci, L., Simonsick, E. M., Deeg, D., & Wallace, R. B. (1998). Depressive symptoms and physical decline in community-dwelling older persons. *Journal of the American Medical Association, 279,* 1720–1726.

Pennisi, E. (2000, May 19). And the gene number is…? *Science, 288,* 1146–1147.

Perceptions of relational and physical aggression among college students: Effects of gender of perpetrator, target, and perceiver. *Psychology of Women Quarterly, 31,* 85–95.

Pereira, A. C., Huddleston, D. E., Brickman, A. M., Sosunov, A. A., Hen, R., McKhann, G. M., Sloan, R., Gage, F. H., Brown, T. R., & Small, S. A. (2007). An in vivo correlate of exercise-induced neurogenesis in the adult dentate gyrus. *Proceedings of the National Academy of Sciences, 104,* 5638–5643.

Peretz, I., Brattico, E., Järvenpää, M., & Tervaniemi, M. (2009). The amusic brain: In tune, out of key, and unaware. *A Journal of Neurology, 132,* 1277–1286.

Peritto, L. A., Holowka, S., & Sergio, L. E. (2004). Baby hands that move to the rhythm of language: Hearing babies acquiring sign languages babble silently on the hands. *Cognition, 93,* 43–73.

Perleth, C., Lehwald, G., & Browder, C. S. (2000). Indicators of high ability in young children. In K. A. Heller, et al. (Eds.), *International handbook of research and development of giftedness and talent.* New York: Pergamon Press.

Perlmann, R. Y., & Gleason, J. B. (1990, July). *Patterns of prohibition in mothers' speech to children.* Paper presented at the Fifth International Congress for the Study of Child Language, Budapest, Hungary.

Perozzi, J. A., & Sanchez, M. C. (1992). The effect of instruction in L1 on receptive acquisition of L2 for bilingual children with language delay. *Language, Speech, and Hearing Services in Schools, 23,* 348–352.

Perreault, A., Fothergill-Bourbonnais, F., & Fiset, V. (2004). The experience of family members caring for a dying loved one. *International Journal of Palliative Nursing, 10,* 133–143.

Perry, W. G. (1970). *Forms of intellectual and ethical development in the college years.* New York: Holt.

Perry, W. G. (1981). Cognitive and ethical growth: The making of meaning. In A. W. Chickering and Associates, *The modern American college.* San Francisco: Jossey-Bass.

Persson, A., & Musher-Eizenman, D. R. (2003). The impact of a prejudice-prevention television program on young children's ideas about race. *Early Childhood Research Quarterly, 18,* 530–546.

Persson, G. E. B. (2005). Developmental perspectives on prosocial and aggressive motives in preschoolers' peer interactions. *International Journal of Behavioral Development, 29,* 80–91.

Petersen, A. (2000). A longitudinal investigation of adolescents' changing perceptions of pubertal timing. *Developmental Psychology 36,* 37–43.

Peterson, A. C. (1988, September). Those gangly years. *Psychology Today,* pp. 28–34.

Peterson, B. (2006, June). Generativity and successful parenting: An analysis of young adult outcomes. *Journal of Personality, 74,* 847–869.

Peterson, C., & Park, N. (2007). Explanatory style and emotion regulation. In J. J. Gross, *Handbook of emotion regulation.* New York: Guilford Press.

Peterson, D. M., Marcia, J. E., & Carpendal, J. I. (2004). Identity: Does thinking make it so? In C. Lightfood, C. Lalonde, & M. Chandler (Eds.), *Changing conceptions of psychological life.* Mahwah, NJ: Erlbaum.

Peterson, L. (1994). Child injury and abuse-neglect: Common etiologies, challenges, and courses toward prevention. *Current Directions in Psychological Science, 3,* 116–120.

Peterson, M., & Wilson, J. (2004). Work Stress in America. *International Journal of Stress Management, 11,* 91–113.

Peterson, M., & Wilson, J. F. (2004). Work stress in America. *International Journal of Stress Management, 11,* 91–113.

Peterson, R. A., & Brown, S. P. (2005). On the use of beta coefficients in meta-analysis. *Journal of Applied Psychology, 90,* 175–181.

Petit, G., & Dodge, K. A. (2003). Violent children: Bridging development, intervention, and public policy. *Developmental Psychology, Special Issues: Violent Children, 39,* 187–188.

Petitto, L. A. (2000). The acquisition of natural signed languages: Lessons in the nature of human language and its biological foundations. In C. Chamerlain, J. P. Morford, & R. I. Mayberry, *Language acquisition by eye.* Mahwah, NJ: Lawrence Erlbaum Associates.

Petitto, L. A., & Marentette, P. F. (1991, March 22). Babbling in the manual mode: Evidence for the ontogeny of language. *Science, 251,* 1493–1496.

Petitto, L. A., Holowka, S., & Sergio, L. E. (2004). Baby hands that move to the rhythm of language: Hearing babies acquiring sign languages babble silently on the hands. *Cognition, 93,* 43–73.

Petrou, S. (2006). Preterm birth—What are the relevant economic issues? *Early Human Development, 82*(2), 75–76.

Pettit, G. S., Bates, J. E., & Dodge, K. A. (1997). Supportive parenting, ecological context, and children's adjustment: A seven-year longitudinal study. *Child Development, 68,* 908–923.

Pew Forum on Religion & Public Life (2008). *U.S. Religious Landscape Survey.* Washington, DC: Pew Forum on Religion & Public Life.

Philippot, P., & Feldman, R. S. (Eds.). (2005). *The regulation of emotion.* Mahwah, NJ: Lawrence Erlbaum Associates.

Phillips, D. (1992, September). Death postponement and birthday celebrations. *Psychosomatic Medicine, 26,* 12–18.

Phillips, D., & Smith, D. (1990, April 11). Postponement of death until symbolically meaningful occasions. *Journal of the American Medical Association, 269,* 27–38.

Phillips, L., & Henry, J. (2008). Adult aging and executive functioning. *Executive functions and the frontal lobes: A lifespan perspective.* Philadelphia: Taylor & Francis.

Phinney, J. (2006). Ethnic identity exploration in emerging adulthood. *Emerging adults in America: Coming of age in the 21st century.* Washington, DC: American Psychological Association.

Phinney, J. (2008). Ethnic identity exploration in emerging adulthood. *Adolescent identities: A collection of readings.* New York: The Analytic Press/Taylor & Francis Group.

Phinney, J. S. (2005). Ethnic identity in late modern times: A response to Rattansi and Phoenix. *Identity, 5,* 187–194.

Phinney, J. S., & Alipuria, L. L. (1990). Ethnic identity in college students from four ethnic groups. *Journal of Adolescence, 13,* 171–183.

Phinney, J. S., Ferguson, D. L., & Tate, J. D. (1997). Intergroup attitudes among ethnic minority adolescents: A causal model. *Child Development, 68,* 955–969.

Piaget, J. (1932). *The moral judgment of the child.* New York: Harcourt, Brace & World.

Piaget, J. (1952). *The origins of intelligence in children.* New York: International Universities Press.

Piaget, J. (1954). *The construction of reality in the child* (Margaret Cook, Trans.). New York: Basic Books.

Piaget, J. (1962). *Play, dreams and imitation in childhood.* New York: Norton.

Piaget, J. (1983). Piaget's theory. In W. Kessen (Ed.), P. H. Mussen (Series Ed.), *Handbook of child psychology: Vol 1. History, theory, and methods* (pp. 103–128). New York: Wiley.

Piaget, J., & Inhelder, B. (1958). *The growth of logical thinking from childhood to adolescence* (A. Parsons & S. Seagrin, Trans.). New York: Basic Books.

Picavet, H. S., & Hoeymans, N. (2004). Health related quality of life in multiple musculoskeletal diseases: SF-36 and EQ-5D in the DMC3 study. *Annals of the Rheumatic Diseases, 63,* 723–729.

Pingree, A. (2008). Teaching, learning, and spirituality in the college classroom. *Teaching Excellence, 19,* 1–2.

Pinker, S. (1994). *The language instinct.* New York: William Morrow.

Pinker, S. (2005). So how does the mind work? *Mind & Language, 20,* 1–24.

Planinsec, J. (2001). A comparative analysis of the relations between the motor dimensions and cognitive ability of pre-school girls and boys. *Kinesiology, 33,* 56–68.

Plante, E., Schmithorst, V., Holland, S., & Byars, A. (2006). Sex differences in the activation of language cortex during childhood. *Neuropsychologia, 44,* 1210–1221.

Plomin, R. (1994b). Nature, nurture, and social development. *Social Development, 3,* 37–53.

Plomin, R. (2005). Finding genes in child psychology and psychiatry: When are we going to be there? *Journal of Child Psychology and Psychiatry, 46,* 1030–1038.

Plomin, R. (2007). *Genetics and developmental psychology.* Detroit, MI: Wayne State University Press.

Plomin, R., & Caspi, A. (1998). DNA and personality. *European Journal of Personality, 12,* 387–407.

Plomin, R., & Rutter, M. (1998). Child development, molecular genetics, and what to do with genes once they are found. *Child Development, 69,* 1223–1242.

Plonczynski, D. J., & Plonczynski, K. J. (2007). Hormone therapy in perimenopausal and postmenopausal women: examining the evidence on cardiovascular disease risks. *Journal of Gerontological Nursing, 33,* 48–55.

Plosker, G., & Keam, S. (2006). Bimatoprost: A pharmacoeconomic review of its use in open-angle glaucoma and ocular hypertension. *PharmacoEconomics, 24,* 297–314.

Poest, C. A., Williams, J. R., Witt, D. D., & Atwood, M. E. (1990). Challenge me to move: Large muscle development in young children. *Young Children, 45,* 4–10.

Poling, D., & Evans, E. (2004). Are dinosaurs the rule or the exception? Developing concepts of death and extinction. *Cognitive Development, 19,* 363–383.

Polivy, J., & Herman, C. (2002). If at first you don't succeed: False hopes of self-change. *American Psychologist, 57,* 677–689.

Polkinghorne, D. E. (2005). Language and meaning: Data collection in qualitative research. *Journal of Counseling Psychology, 52,* Special Issue: Knowledge in context: Qualitative methods in counseling psychology research, 137–145.

Pollack, W. (1999). *Real boys: Rescuing our sons from the myths of boyhood.* Owl Books.

Pollack, W. (2006). The 'war' for boys: Hearing 'real boys" voices, healing their pain. *Professional Psychology: Research and Practice, 37,* 190–195.

Pollack, W., Shuster, T., & Trelease, J. (2001). *Real boys' voices.* New York: Penguin.

Pollak, S., Holt, L., & Wismer Fries, A. (2004). Hemispheric asymmetries in children's perception of nonlinguistic human affective sounds. *Developmental Science, 7,* 10–18.

Pollatou, E., Karadimou, K., & Gerodimos, V. (2005). Gender differences in musical aptitude, rhythmic ability and motor performance in preschool children. *Early Child Development and Care, 175,* 361–369.

Pollitt, E., Golub, M., Gorman, K., GranthamMcGregor, S., Levitsky, D., Schürch, B., Strupp, B., & Wachs, T. (1996). A reconceptualization of the effects of undernutrition on children's biological, psychosocial, and behavioral development. *Social Policy Report, 10,* 1–22.

Pomares, C. G., Schirrer, J., & Abadie, V. (2002). Analysis of the olfactory capacity of healthy children before language acquisition. *Journal of Developmental Behavior and Pediatrics, 23,* 203–207.

Ponton, L. E. (2001). *The sex lives of teenagers: Revealing the secret world of adolescent boys and girls.* New York: Penguin Putnam.

Population Council Report. (1995, May 30). The decay of families is global, studies says. *New York Times,* p. A5.

Porges, S. W., & Lipsitt, Lewis P. (1993). Neonatal responsivity to gustatory stimulation: The gustatory-vagal hypothesis. *Infant Behavior & Development, 16,* 487–494.

Porter, E., & Walsh, M. (2005, February 9). Retirement becomes a rest stop as pensions and benefits shrink. *New York Times,* p. A1.

Porter, M., van Teijlingen, E., Yip, L., & Bhattacharya, S. (2007). Satisfaction with cesarean section: Qualitative analysis of open-ended questions in a large postal survey. *Birth: Issues in Perinatal Care, 34,* 148–154.

Porter, R. H., Balogh, R. D., & Malkin, J. W. (1988). Olfactory influences on mother–infant interactions. In C. Rovee-Collier & L. Lipsitt (Eds.), *Advances in infancy research.* (Vol. 5). Norwood, NJ: Ablex.

Portes, A. (2005). English-only triumphs, but the costs are high. *Critical social issues in American education: Democracy and meaning in a globalizing world* (3rd ed.). Mahwah, NJ: Lawrence Erlbaum Associates Publishers.

Portes, A., & Rumbaut, R. (2001). *Legacies: The story of the immigrant second generation.* Los Angeles: University of California Press.

Porzelius, L. K., Dinsmore, B. D., & Staffelbach, D. (2001). Eating disorders. In M. Hersen & V. B. Van Hasselt (Eds.). *Advanced abnormal psychology* (2nd ed.). New York: Kluwer Academic/Plenum Publishers.

Posthuma, D., & de Geus, E. (2006, August). Progress in the molecular-genetic study of intelligence. *Current Directions in Psychological Science, 15,* 151–155.

Poulin-Dubois, D., Frank, I., & Graham, S. A. (1999). The role of shape similarity in toddlers' lexical extensions. *British Journal of Developmental Psychology, 17,* 21–36.

Poulin-Dubois, D., Serbin, L. A., Kenyon, B., & Derbyshire, A. (1994). Infants' intermodal knowledge about gender. *Developmental Psychology, 30,* 436–442.

Poulin-Dubois, D., Serbin, L., & Eichstedt, J. (2002). Men don't put on make-up: Toddlers' knowledge of the gender stereotyping of household activities. *Social Development, 11,* 166–181.

Powell, G. F., Brasel, J. A., & Blizzard, R. M. (1967). Emotional deprivation and growth retardation simulating idiopathic hypopituitarism: I. Clinical evaluation of the syndrome. *New England Journal of Medicine, 276,* 1272–1278.

Powell, R. (2004, June 19). Colleges construct housing for elderly: Retiree students move to campus. *Washington Post,* F13.

Power, T. G. (1999). *Play and exploration in children and animals.* Mahwah, NJ: Erlbaum.

Pratt, H., Phillips, E.,& Greydanus, D. (2003). Eating disorders in the adolescent population: Future directions. *Journal of Adolescent Research, 18,* 297–317.

Pratt, M. W., Danso, H. A., Arnold, M. L., Norris, J. E., & Filyer, R. (2001). Adult generativity and the socialization of adolescents: Relations to mothers' and fathers' parenting beliefs, styles, and practices. *Journal of Personality, 69,* 89–120.

Prechtl, H. F. R. (1982). Regressions and transformations during neurological development. In T. G. Bever (Ed.), *Regressions in mental development.* Hillsdale, NJ: Erlbaum.

Pressley, M. (1987). Are keyword method effects limited to slow presentation rates? An empirically based reply to Hall and Fuson (1986). *Journal of Educational Psychology, 79,* 333–335.

Pressley, M. (1995). *What is intellectual development about in the 1990s? Good information processing.* Mahwah, NJ: Lawrence Erlbaum Associates.

Pressley, M., & Levin, J. R. (1983). *Cognitive strategy research: Psychological foundations.* New York: Springer-Verlag.

Pressley, M., & Schneider, W. (1997). *Introduction to memory development during childhood and adolescence.* Mahwah, NJ: Lawrence Erlbaum.

Pressley, M., & VanMeter, P. (1993). Memory strategies: Natural development and use following instruction. In R. Pasnak & M. L. Howe (Eds.), *Emerging themes in cognitive development* (Vol. II). New York: Springer-Verlag.

Prezbindowski, A. K., & Lederberg, A. R. (2003). Vocabulary assessment of deaf and hard-of-hearing children from infancy through the preschool years. *Journal of Deaf Studies and Deaf Education, 8,* 383–400.

Price, D. W., & Goodman, G. S. (1990). Visiting the wizard: Children's memory for a recurring event. *Child Development, 61,* 664–680.

Price, R., & Gottesman, I. (1991). Body fat in identical twins reared apart: Roles for genes and environment. *Behavior Genetics, 21,* 1–7.

Prigerson, H. (2003). Costs to society of family caregiving for patients with end-stage Alzheimer's disease. *New England Journal of Medicine, 349,* 1891–1892.

Prigerson, H. G., Frank, E., Kasl, S. V., et al. (1995). Complicated grief and bereavement-related depression as distinct disorders: Preliminary empirical validation in elderly bereaved spouses. *American Journal of Psychiatry, 152,* 22–30.

PRIMEDIA/Roper National Youth Survey (1998). *Adolescents' view of society's ills.* Storrs, CT: Roper Center for Public Opinion Research.

Prince, M. (2000, November 13). How technology has changed the way we have babies. *Wall Street Journal,* pp. R4, R13.

Prince, R. L., Smith, M., Dick, I. M., Price, R. I., Webb, P. G., Henderson, N. K., & Harris, M. M. (1991). Prevention of postmenopausal osteoporosis. A comparative study of exercise, calcium supplementation, and hormone replacement therapy. *New England Journal of Medicine, 325,* 1189–1195.

Propper, C., & Moore, G. (2006, December). The influence of parenting on infant emotionality: A multi-level psychobiological perspective. *Developmental Review, 26,* 427–460.

Pruchno, R., & Rosenbaum, J. (2003). Social relationships in adulthood and old age. In R. Lerner and M. Easterbrooks (Eds.), *Handbook of psychology: Developmental psychology, Vol. 6.* New York: Wiley.

Pryor, J. H., Hurtado, S., Saenz, V. B., Korn, J. S., Santos, J. S., & Korn, W. S. (2006). *The American freshman: National norms for fall 2006.* Los Angeles: Higher Education Research Institute, UCLA.

Pryor, J. H., Hurtado, S., Saenz, V. B., Santos, J. L., & Korn, W. S. (2007). *The American freshman: National norms for fall 2007.* Los Angeles: Higher Education Research Institute, UCLA.

Puchalski, M., & Hummel, P. (2002). The reality of neonatal pain. *Advances in Neonatal Care, 2,* 245–247.

Pudrovska, T., Schieman, S., & Carr, D. (2006). Strains of singlehood in later life: Do race and gender matter? *Journals of Gerontology: Series B: Psychological Sciences and Social Sciences, 61B,* S315–S322.

Puntambekar, S., & Hübscher, R. (2005). Tools for Scaffolding Students in a Complex Learning Environment: What Have We Gained and What Have We Missed? *Educational Psychologist, 40,* 1–12.

Purdy, M. (1995, November 6). A kind of sexual revolution. *New York Times,* pp. B1, B6.

Putney, N. M., & Bengtson, V. L. (2001). Families, intergenerational relationships, and kinkeeping in midlife. In M. E. Lachman (Ed.), *Handbook of midlife development.* Hoboken, NJ: Wiley.

Putterman, E., & Linden, W. (2004). Appearance versus health: Does the reason for dieting affect dieting behavior? *Journal of Behavioral Medicine, 27,* 185–204.

Pyryt, M. C., & Mendaglio, S. (1994). The multidimensional self-concept: A comparison of figted and average-ability adolescents. *Journal for the Education of the Gifted, 17,* 299–305.

Qian, Z-C, & Lichter, D.T. (2007). Social Boundary and Marital Assimilation: Evaluating Trends in Racial and Ethnic Intermarriage. *American Sociological Review, 72,* 68–94.

Quade, R. (1994, July 10). Day care brightens young and old. *The New York Times,* p. B8.

Quartz, S. R. (2003). Toward a developmental evolutionary psychology: Genes, development, and the evolution of human cognitive architecture. In S. J. Scher & F. Rauscher (Eds.), *Evolutionary psychology: Alternative approaches.* Dordrecht, Netherlands: Kluwer Academic Publishers.

Quatromoni, P., Pencina, M., Cobain, M., Jacques, P., & D'Agostino, R. (2006, August). Dietary quality predicts adult weight gain: Findings from the Framingham Offspring Study. *Obesity, 14,* 1383–1391.

Quay, L. C., & Blaney, R. L. (1992). Verbal communication, nonverbal communication, and private speech in lower and middle socioeconomic status preschool children. *Journal of Genetic Psychology, 153,* 129–138.

Quinn, J. B. (1993, April 5). What's for dinner, Mom? *Newsweek,* 68.

Quinn, P. (2008). In defense of core competencies, quantitative change, and continuity. *Child Development, 79,* 1633–1638.

Quintana, C. (1998, May 17.) Riding the rails. *New York Times Magazine,* p. 66.

Raag, T. (2003). Racism, gender identities and young children: Social relations in a multi-ethnic, inner-city primary school. *Archives of Sexual Behavior, 32,* 392–393.

Rabain-Jamin, J., & Sabeau-Jouannet, E. (1997). Maternal speech to 4-month-old infants in two cultures: Wolof and French. *International Journal of Behavioral Development, 20,* 425–451.

Rabin, R. (2006, June 13). Breast-feed or else. *New York Times,* p. D1.

Rabkin, J., Remien, R., & Wilson, C. (1994). *Good doctors, good patients: Partners in HIV treatment.* New York: NCM Publishers.

Raeburn, P. (2004, October 1). Too immature for the death penalty? *New York Times Magazine,* pp. 26–29.

Rahman, Q., & Wilson, G. (2003). Born gay? The psychobiology of human sexual orientation. *Personality & Individual Differences, 34,* 1337–1382.

Rainwater, L., & Smeeding, T. (2007). Is there hope for America's low-income children? *Shifting the center: Understanding contemporary families* (3rd ed.) (pp. 770–779). New York: McGraw-Hill.

Rakison, D., & Oakes, L. (2003). *Early category and concept development: Making sense of the blooming, buzzing confusion.* London: Oxford University Press.

Raman, L., & Winer, G. (2002). Children's and adults' understanding of illness: Evidence in support of a coexistence model. *Genetic, Social, & General Psychology Monographs, 128,* 325–355.

Ramsey, P. G., & Myers, L. C. (1990). Salience of race in young children's cognitive, affective, and behavioral responses to social environments. *Journal of Applied Developmental Psychology, 11,* 49–67.

Ramsey-Rennels, J. L., & Langlois, J. H. (2006). Infants' differential processing of female and male faces. *Current Directions in Psychological Science, 15,* 59–62.

Ranade, V. (1993). Nutritional recommendations for children and adolescents. *International Journal of Clinical Pharmacology, Therapy, and Toxicology, 31,* 285–290.

Randahl, G. J. (1991). A typological analysis of the relations between measured vocational interests and abilities. *Journal of Vocational Behavior, 38,* 333–350.

Rando, T. A. (1993). *Treatment of complicated mourning.* Champaign, IL: Research Press.

Rank, M. R., & Hirschl, T. A. (1999). Estimating the proportion of Americans ever experiencing poverty during their elderly years. *Journals of Gerontology Series B-Psychological Science and Social Sciences, 54,* S184–S193.

Rankin, B. (2004). The importance of intentional socialization among children in small groups: A conversation with Loris Malaguzzi. *Early Childhood Education Journal, 32,* 81–85.

Rankin, J., Lane, D., & Gibbons, F. (2004). Adolescent self-consciousness: Longitudinal age changes and gender differences in two cohorts. *Journal of Research on Adolescence, 14,* 1–21.

Ransjö-Arvidson, A. B., Matthiesen, A. S., Lilja, G., Nissen, E., Widström, A. M., & Unväs-Moberg. (2001). Maternal analgesia during labor disturbs newborn behavior: Effects on breastfeeding, temperature, and crying. *Birth, 28,* 5–12.

Ransom, R. L., Sutch, R., & Williamson, S. H. (1991). Retirement: Past and present. In A. H. Munnell (Ed.), *Retirement and public policy: Proceedings of the Second Conference of the National Academy of Social Insurance.* Washington, DC. Dubuque, IA: Kendall/Hunt.

Rao, V. (1997). Wife-beating in rural South India: A qualitative and econometric analysis. *Social Science & Medicine, 44,* 1169–1180.

Rapkin, B. D., & Fischer, K. (1992). Personal goals of older adults: Issues in assessment and prediction. *Psychology and Aging, 7,* 127–137.

Ratanachu-Ek, S. (2003). Effects of multivitamin and folic acid supplementation in malnourished children. *Journal of the Medical Association of Thailand, 4,* 86–91.

Rattner, A., & Nathans, J. (2006, November). Macular degeneration: Recent advances and therapeutic opportunities. *Nature Reviews Neuroscience, 7,* 860–872.

Raudsepp, L., & Liblik, R. (2002). Relationship of perceived and actual motor competence in children. *Perception and Motor Skills, 94,* 1059–1070.

Ray, O. (2004). How the mind hurts and heals the body. *American Psychologist, 59,* 29–40.

Rayner, K., Foorman, B. R., Perfetti, C. A., Pesetsky, D., & Seidenberg, M. S. (2002, March). How should reading be taught? *Scientific American,* 85–91.

Raz, N., Rodrigue, K., Kennedy, K., & Acker, J. (2007, March). Vascular health and longitudinal changes in brain and cognition in middle-aged and older adults. *Neuropsychology, 21,* 149–157.

Ready, D. D., Lee, V. E., & Welner, K. G. (2004). Educational equity and school structure: School size, overcrowding, and schools-within-schools. *Teachers College Record, 106,* 1989–2014.

Redcay, E., & Courchesne, E. (2005). When is the brain enlarged in autism? A meta-analysis of all brain size reports. *Biological Psychiatry, 58,* 1–9.

Reddy, V. (1999). Prelinguistic communication. In M. Barrett (Ed,), *The development of language* (pp. 25–50). Philadelphia, PA: Psychology Press.

Ree, M., & Carretta, T. (2002). g2K. *Human Performance, 15,* 3–24.

Rego, A. (2006). The alphabetic principle, phonics, and spelling: Teaching students the code. *Reading assessment and instruction for all learners* (pp. 118–162). New York: Guilford Press.

Reifman, A. (2000). *Revisiting The Bell Curve. Psycoloquy, 11.*

Reiner, W. G., & Gearhart, J. P. (2004). Discordant sexual identity in some genetic males with cloacal exstrophy assigned to female sex at birth. *New England Journal of Medicine, 350,* 333–341.

Reis, H. T., Collins, W. A., & Berscheid, E. (2000). The relationship context of human behavior and development. *Psychological Bulletin, 126,* 844–872.

Reis, S., & Renzulli, J. (2004). Current research on the social and emotional development of gifted and talented students: good news and future possibilities. *Psychology in the Schools, 41,* 119–130.

Reiss, D., Neiderhiser, J. M., Hetherington, E. M., & Plomin, R. (2000). *The relationship code: Deciphering genetic and social influences on adolescent development.* Cambridge, MA: Harvard University Press.

Reiss, M. J. (1984). Human sociobiology. *Zygon Journal of Religion and Science, 19,* 117–140.

Remien, R., & Rabkin, J. (2002). Managing chronic disease: Individual counseling with medically ill patients. *Innovative approaches to health psychology: Prevention and treatment lessons from AIDS* (pp. 117–139). Washington, DC: American Psychological Association.

Renner, L., & Slack, K. (2006, June). Intimate partner violence and child maltreatment: Understanding intra- and intergenerational connections. *Child Abuse & Neglect, 30,* 599–617.

Reproductive Medicine Associates of New Jersey. (2002). *Older women and risks of pregnancy.* Princeton, NJ: American Society for Reproductive Medicine.

Reschly, D. J. (1996). Identification and assessment of students with disabilities. *The future of children, 6,* 40–53.

Rescorla, L., Alley, A., & Christine, J. (2001). Word frequencies in toddlers' lexicons. *Journal of Speech, Language, & Hearing Research, 44,* 598–609.

Resnick, B. (2000). A seven step approach to starting an exercise program for older adults. *Patient Education & Counseling, 39,* 243–252.

Resnick, M. D., Bearman, P. S., Blum, R. W., Bauman, K. E., Harris, M. R., Jones, L., Tabor, J., Beuhring, T., Sieving, R., Shew, M., Ireland, M., Bearinger, L. H., & Udry, J. R. (1997). Protecting adolescents from harm: Findings from the National Longitudinal Study on Adolescent Health. *Journal of the American Medical Association, 278,* 823–832.

Ressner, J. (2001, March 6). When a coma isn't one. *Time Magazine,* p. 62

Resta R., Biesecker, B. B., Bennett, R. L., Blum, S., Estabrooks, H. S., Strecker, M. N., & Williams, J. L. (2006). A new definition of genetic counseling: National Society of Genetic Counselors' Task Force Report. *Journal of Genetic Counseling, 15,* 77–83.

Reuters Health eLine. (2002, June 26). Baby's injuring points to danger of kids imitating television. *Reuters Health eLine.*

Reyna, V. F. (1997). Conceptions of memory development with implications for reasoning and decision making. In R. Vasta (Ed.), *Annals of child development: A research annual* (Vol. 12, pp. 87–118). London, England: Jessica Kingsley Publishers.

Rhoades, G., Stanley, S., & Markman, H. (2006, December). Pre-engagement cohabitation and gender asymmetry in marital commitment. *Journal of Family Psychology, 20,* 553–560.

Rholes, W., Simpson, J., Tran, S., Martin, A., & Friedman, M. (2007, March). Attachment and information seeking in romantic relationships. *Personality and Social Psychology Bulletin, 33,* 4224–38.

Rhule, D. (2005). Take care to do no harm: Harmful interventions for youth problem behavior. *Professional Psychology: Research and Practice, 36,* 618–625.

Ricciardelli, L., & McCabe, M. (2003). Sociocultural and individual influences on muscle gain and weight loss strategies among adolescent boys and girls. *Psychology in the Schools, 40,* 209–224.

Ricciardelli, L. A., & McCabe, M. P. (2004). A biopsychosocial model of disordered eating and the pursuit of muscularity in adolescent boys. *Psychological Bulletin, 130,* 179–205.

Rice, F. P. (1999). *Intimate relationships, marriages, & families* (4th ed.). Mountain View, CA: Mayfield.

Richards, J. M., & Gross, J. J. (2000). Emotion regulation and memory: The cognitive consequence of keeping one's cool. *Journal of Personality and Social Psychology, 79,* 410–424.

Richards, J. M., Butler, E. A., & Gross, J. J. (2003). Emotion regulation in romantic relationships: The cognitive consequences of concealing feelings. *Journal of Social and Personal Relationships, 20,* 599–620.

Richards, M. P. M. (1996). The childhood environment and the development of sexuality. In C. J. K. Henry & S. J. Ulijaszek (Eds.), *Long-term consequences of early environment: Growth, development and the lifespan developmental perspective.* Cambridge, England: Cambridge University Press.

Richards, M. H., Crowe, P. A., Larson, R., & Swarr, A. (1998). Developmental patterns and gender differences in the experience of peer companionship during adolescence. *Child Development, 69,* 154–163.

Richards, R., Kinney, D. K., Benet, M., & Merzel, A. P. C. (1990). Assessing everyday creativity: Characteristics of the lifetime creativity scales and validation with three large samples. *Journal of Personality and Social Psychology, 54,* 476–485.

Richardson, K., & Norgate, S. (2007). A Critical analysis of IQ studies of adopted children. *Human Development, 49,* 319–335.

Rickel, A. U., & Becker, E. (1997). *Keeping children from harm's way: How national policy affects psychological development.* Washington, DC: American Psychological Association.

Rickford, J. (2006). Linguistics, education, and the Ebonics firestorm. *Dialects, Englishes, creoles, and education.* Mahwah, NJ: Lawrence Erlbaum Associates Publishers.

Rideout V., Vandewater, E., & Wartella, E. (2003). *Zero to six: Electronic media in the lives of infants, toddlers, and preschoolers.* Menlo Park, CA: Kaiser Family Foundation.

Rideout, V., Roberts, D. F., & Foehr, U. G. (2005). *Generation M: Median in the lives of 8 to 18 year olds.* Menlo Park, CA: The Henry J. Kaiser Family Foundation.

Riebe, D., Burbank, P., & Garber, C. (2002). Setting the stage for active older adults. In P. Burbank and D. Riebe (Eds.), *Promoting exercise and behavior change in older adults: Interventions with the transtheoretical mode.* New York: Springer Publishing Co.

Riley, K. (2008). Language socialization. *The handbook of educational linguistics.* Malden. MA: Blackwell Publishing.

Riley, L., & Bowen, C. (2005, January). The Sandwich Generation: Challenges and coping strategies of multigenerational families. *The Family Journal, 13,* 52–58.

Rimer, B. K., Meissner, H., Breen, N., Legler, J. & Coyne, C. A. (2001). Social and behavioral interventions to increase breast cancer screening. In N. Schneiderman & M. A. Speers, (Eds.), *Integrating behavioral and social sciences with public health.* Washington, DC: American Psychological Association.

Rimmele, U., Hediger, K., Heinrichs, M., & Klaver, P. (2009). Oxytocin makes a face in memory familiar. *The Journal of Neuroscience, 29,* 38–42.

Ripple, C., & Zigler, E. (2003). Research, policy, and the federal role in prevention initiatives for children. *American Psychologist, 58,* 482–490.

Ritchie, L. (2003). Adult day care: Northern perspectives. *Public Health Nursing, 20,* 120–131.

Ritzen, E. M. (2003). Early puberty: What is normal and when is treatment indicated? *Hormone Research, 60,* Supplement, 31–34.

Robb, A., & Dadson, M. (2002). Eating disorders in males. *Child & Adolescent Psychiatric Clinics of North America, 11,* 399–418.

Robb, M., Richert, R., & Wartella, E. (2009). Just a talking book? Word learning from watching baby videos. *British Journal of Developmental Psychology, 27,* 27–45.

Robbins, M., Francis, L. J., & Edwards, B. (2008). Prayer, personality and happiness: A study among undergraduate students in Wales. *Mental Health, Religion & Culture, 11,* Special Issue, 93–99.

Robergeau, K., Joseph, J., & Silber, T. (2006, December). Hospitalization of children and adolescents for eating disorders in the state of New York. *Journal of Adolescent Health, 39,* 806–810.

Roberts, D., & Foehr, U. (2003). *Kids and media in America: Patterns of use at the millennium.* New York: Cambridge University Press.

Roberts, D. F., Henriksen, L., & Foehr, U. G. (2004). Adolescents and media. In R. M. Lerner & L. Steinberg (Eds.), *Handbook of adolescent psychology.* (2nd ed.). New York: John Wiley & Sons.

Roberts, R. E., Phinney, J. S., Masse, L. C., Chen, Y. R., Roberts, C. R., & Romero, A. (1999). The structure of ethnic identity of young adolescents from diverse ethnocultural groups. *Journal of Early Adolescence, 19,* 301–322.

Roberts, S. (2006, October 15). It's official: To be married means to be outnumbered. *New York Times,* p. 22.

Roberts, S. (2007, January 16). 51% of women are now living without spouse. *The New York Times,* p. A1.

Robinson, A. J., & Pascalis, O. (2004). Development of flexible visual recognition memory in human infants. *Developmental Science, 7,* 527–533.

Robinson, G. E. (2004, April 16). Beyond nature and nurture. *Science, 304,* 397–399.

Robinson, J. P., & Godbey, G. (1997). *Time for life: The surprising ways Americans use their time.* College Park: Pennsylvania State University Press.

Robinson, N. M., Zigler, E., & Gallagher, J. J. (2000). Two tails of the normal curve: Similarities and differences in the study of mental retardation and giftedness. *American Psychologist, 55,* 1413–1421.

Robinson, W. P., & Gillibrand, E. (2004, May 14). Single-sex teaching and achievement in science. *International Journal of Science Education, 26,* 659.

Rochat, P. (1999). *Early social cognition.* Hillsdale, NJ: Lawrence Erlbaum Associates.

Rochat, P. (2004). Emerging co-awareness. In G. Bremner & A. Slater (Eds.) *Theories of infant development.* Malden, MA: Blackwell Publishers.

Rodriguez, M., Iglesias, R., Regueiro, C. V., Correa, J., & Barro, S. (2007). Autonomous and fast robot learning through motivation. *Robotics and Autonomous Systems, 55,* 735–740.

Roffwarg, H. P., Muzio, J. N., & Dement, W. C. (1966). Ontogenic development of the human sleep–dream cycle. *Science, 152,* 604–619.

Rogers, C., Floyd, F., Seltzer, M., Greenberg, J., & Hong, J. (2008). Long-term effects of the death of a child on parents' adjustment in midlife. *Journal of Family Psychology, 22,* 203–211.

Roggeveen, A. B., Prime, D. J., & Ward, L. M. (2007). Lateralized readiness potentials reveal motor slowing in the aging brain. *Journal of Gerontology, B, Psychological Science and Social Science, 62,* P78–P84.

Rogoff, B. (1990). *Apprenticeship in thinking: Cognitive development in social context.* New York: Oxford University Press.

Rogoff, B., & Chavajay, P. (1995). What's become of research on the cultural basis of cognitive development? *American Psychologist, 50,* 859–877.

Rolfe, S. A. (1994). Does assessment of cognitive functioning in infancy hold the key to early detection of developmental disabilities? A review of research. *Australia & New Zealand Journal of Developmental Disabilities, 19,* 61–72.

Rolland, J., & Williams, J. (2006). Toward a psychosocial model for the new era of genetics. In S. M. Miller, S. H. McDaniel, J. S. Rolland, & S. L. Feetham (Eds.), *Individuals, families, and the new era of genetics: Biopsychosocial perspectives.* New York: W. W. Norton & Co.

Rollins, B. C., & Collins, K. L. (1974). Marital satisfaction over the family life cycle: A reevaluation. *Journal of Marriage and the Family, 36,* 271–282.

Rolls, E. (2000). Memory systems in the brain. *Annual Review of Psychology, 51,* 599–630.

Romaine, S. (1994). *Bilingualism* (2nd ed.). London: Blackwell.

Romero, A., & Roberts, R. (2003). The impact of multiple dimensions of ethnic identity on discrimination and adolescents' self-esteem. *Journal of Applied Social Psychology, 33,* 2288–2305.

Ron, P. (2006). Care giving offspring to aging parents: How it affects their marital relations, parenthood, and mental health. *Illness, Crisis, & Loss, 14,* 1–21.

Roopnarine, J. (2002). *Conceptual, social-cognitive, and contextual issues in the fields of play.* Westport, CT: Ablex Publishing.

Roopnarine, J., & Metindogan, A. (2006). Early childhood education research in cross-national perspective. *Handbook of research on the education of young children* (2nd ed.) (pp. 555–571). Mahwah, NJ: Lawrence Erlbaum Associates Publishers.

Ropar, D., Mitchell, P., & Ackroyd, K. (2003). Do children with autism find it difficult to offer alternative interpretations to ambiguous figures? *British Journal of Developmental Psychology, 21,* 387–395.

Roper Starch Worldwide. (1997, August). Romantic resurgence. *American Demographics,* p. 35.

Rosch, E. (1974). Linguistic relativity. In A. Silverstein (Ed.), *Human communication: Theoretical explorations* (pp. 95–121). New York: Halstead Press.

Rose, A. J. (2002). Co-rumination in the friendships of girls and boys. *Child Development, 73,* 1830–1843.

Rose, R. J., Viken, R. J., Dick, D.M., Bates, J. E., Pulkkinen, L., & Kaprio, J. (2003). It *does* take a village: Nonfamilial environments and children's behavior. *Psychological Science, 14,* 273–278.

Rose, S. (2008, January). Drugging unruly children is a method of social control. *Nature, 451*(7178), 521–521.

Rose, S. A., & Feldman, J. F. (1995). Prediction of IQ and specific cognitive abilities at 11 years from infancy measures. *Developmental Psychology, 31,* 685–696.

Rose, S. A., & Feldman, J. F. (1997). Memory and speed: Their role in the relation of infant information processing to later IQ. *Child Development, 68,* 630–641.

Rose, S. A., Feldman, J. F., & Jankowski, J. J. (2004). Dimensions of cognition in infancy. *Intelligence, 32,* 245–262.

Rose, S. A., Feldman, J. F., & Jenkowski, J. J. (2009). A cognitive approach to the development of early language. *Child Development, 80,* 134–150.

Rose, S. A., Feldman, J. F., & Wallace, I. F. (1992). Infant information processing in relation to six-year cognitive outcomes. *Child Development, 63,* 1126–1141.

Rose, S. A., Feldman, J. F., Wallace, I. F., & McCarton, C. (1991). Information processing at 1 year: Relation to birth status and developmental outcome during the first 5 years. *Developmental Psychology, 27,* 723–737.

Rose, S., Feldman, J., & Jankowski, J. (1999). Visual and auditory temporal processing, cross-modal transfer, and reading. *Journal of Learning Disabilities, 32,* 256–266.

Rose, S., Jankowski, J., & Feldman, J. (2002). Speed of processing and face recognition at 7 and 12 months. *Infancy, 3,* 435–455.

Roseberry, S., Hirsh-Pasek, K., Parish-Morris, J., & Golinkoff, R. M. (2009). Live action: Can young children learn verbs from video? *Child Development, 80,* 1360–1375.

Rosen, E., Ackerman, L., & Zosky, D. (2002). The sibling empty nest syndrome: The experience of sadness as siblings leave the family home. *Journal of Human Behavior in the Social Environment, 6,* 65–80.

Rosen, K. H. (1998). The family roots of aggression and violence: A life span perspective. In L. L'Abate, *Family psychopathology: The relational roots of dysfunctional behavior.* New York: Guilford Press.

Rosen, V. M., Caplan, L., Sheesley, L., Rodriguez, R., & Grafman, J. (2003). An examination of daily activities and their scripts across the adult lifespan. *Behavior Research Methods, Instruments & Computers, 35,* 32–48.

Rosenblatt, P. C. & Wallace, B. R. (2005). *African American Grief.* New York: Brunner-Routledge.

Rosenblatt, P. C. (1988). Grief: The social context of private feelings. *Journal of Social Issues, 44,* 67–78.

Rosenblatt, P. C. (2001). A social constructionist perspective on cultural differences in grief. In M. S. Stroebe, R. O. Hansson, W. Stroebe, & H. Schut (Eds.), *Handbook of bereavement research: Consequences, coping, and car.* Washington, DC: American Psychological Association Press.

Rosenfeld, B., Krivo, S., Breitbart, W., & Chochinov, H. M. (2000). Suicide, assisted suicide, and euthanasia in the terminally ill. In H. M. Chochinov & W. Breitbart (Eds.), *Handbook of psychiatry in palliative medicine.* New York: Oxford University Press.

Rosenman, R. H. (1990). Type A behavior pattern: A personal overview. *Journal of Social Behavior and Personality, 5,* 1–24.

Ross, C. E., Microwsky, J., & Goldsteen, K. (1991). The impact of the family on health. In A. Booth (Ed.), *Contemporary families.* Minneapolis, MN: National Council on Family Relations.

Ross, M., & Wilson, A. E. (2003). Autobiographical memory and conceptions of self: Getting better all the time. *Current Directions in Psychological Science, 12,* 66–69.

Rossier, J., Dahourou, D., & McCrae, R. R. (2005). Structural and mean level analyses of the Five-Factor Model and locus of control: Further evidence from Africa. *Journal of Cross-Cultural Psychology, 36,* 227–246.

Rossman, I. (1977). Anatomic and body composition changes with aging. In C. E. Finch & L. Hayflick (Eds.), *Handbook of the biology of aging.* New York: Van Nostrand Reinhold.

Rossouw, J. E., Prentice, R. L., Manson, J. E., Wu, L., Barad, D., Barnabei, V. M., Ko, M., LaCroix, A. Z., Margolis, K. L., & Stefanick, M. L. (2007). Postmenopausal hormone therapy and risk of cardiovascular disease by age and years since menopause. *Journal of the American Medical Association, 297,* 1465–1477.

Rotenberg, K., Boulton, M., & Fox, C. (2005). Cross-sectional and longitudinal relations among children's trust beliefs, psychological maladjustment and social relationships: Are very high as well as very low trusting children at risk? *Journal of Abnormal Child Psychology, 33,* 595–610.

Roth, D., Slone, M., & Dar, R. (2000). Which way cognitive development? An evaluation of the Piagetian and the domain-specific research programs. *Theory & Psychology, 10,* 353–373.

Rothbart, M. K., Ahadi, S. A., & Evans, D. E. (2000). Temperament and personality: Origins and outcomes. *Journal of Personality and Social Psychology, 78,* 122–135.

Rothbart, M., & Derryberry, D. (2002). Temperament in children. In C. von Hofsten & L. Backman (Eds.), *Psychology at the turn of the millennium,* Vol. 2: *Social, developmental, and clinical perspectives.* Florence, KY: Taylor & Frances/Routledge.

Rothbart, M. K., Derryberry, D., & Hershey, K. (2000). Stability of temperament in childhood: Laboratory infant assessment to parent report at seven years. In V. J. Molfese & D. L. Molfese (Eds.), *Temperament and personality development across the life span.* Mahwah, NJ: Erlbaum.

Rothbart, M. K., Posner, M. I., & Kieras, J. (2006). Temperament, attention, and the development of self-regulation. In K. McCartney & D. Phillips, *Blackwell handbook of early childhood development.* Malden, MA: Blackwell Publishing.

Rothbaum, F., Weisz, J., Pott, M., Miyake, K., & Morelli, G. (2000). Attachment and culture: Security in the United States and Japan. *American Psychologist, 55,* 1093–1104.

Rotheram-Borus, M., & Langabeer, K. (2001). Developmental trajectories of gay, lesbian, and bisexual youths. In A. D'Augelli & C. Patterson (Eds.), *Lesbian, gay, and bisexual identities and youth: Psychological perspectives* (pp. 97–128). New York: Oxford University Press.

Rothrauff, T., Middlemiss, W., & Jacobson, L. (2004). Comparison of American and Austrian infants' and toddlers' sleep habits: A retrospective, exploratory study. *North American Journal of Psychology, 6,* 125–144.

Rovee-Collier, C. (1993). The capacity for long-term memory in infancy. *Current Directions in Psychological Science, 2,* 130–135.

Rovee-Collier, C. (1999). The development of infant memory. *Current Directions in Psychological Science, 8,* 80–85.

Rowe, D. C. (1994). *The effects of nurture on individual natures.* New York: Guilford Press.

Rowe, J. W., & Kahn, R. L. (1997). Successful aging. *Gerontologist, 37,* 433–440.

Rowe, J. W., & Kahn, R. L. (1998). *Successful aging.* New York: Pantheon.

Rubenstein, A. J., Kalakanis, L., & Langlois, J. H. (1999). Infant preferences for attractive faces: A cognitive explanation. *Developmental Psychology, 35,* 848–855.

Rubin, D. C. (1995). Memory in oral traditions: The cognitive psychology of epic, ballads, and counting-out rhymes. New York: Oxford University Press.

Rubin, K. H. (1998). Social and emotional development from a cultural perspective. *Developmental Psychology, 34,* 611–615.

Rubin, K. H., & Chung, O. B. (Eds.) (2006). *Parenting beliefs, behaviors, and parent-child relations: A cross-cultural perspective.* New York: Psychology Press.

Rubin, K. H., Fein, G., & Vandenberg, B. (1983). In E. M. Hetherington (Ed.), *Handbook of child psychology.* Vol. 4. *Socialization, personality and social development* (pp. 693–774). New York: Wiley.

Rubinstein, J. S., Meyer, D. E., & Evans, J. E. (2001). Executive control of cognitive processes in task switching. *Journal of Experimental Psychology: Human Perception and Performance, 27,* 763–797.

Rudd, L., Cain, D., & Saxon, T. (2008). Does improving joint attention in low-quality child-care enhance language development? *Early Child Development and Care, 178*(3), 315–338.

Ruff, H. A. (1989). The infant's use of visual and haptic information in the perception and recognition of objects. *Canadian Journal of Psychology, 43,* 302–319.

Ruff, H. A., & Lawson, K. R. (1990). Development of sustained, focused attention in young children during free play. *Developmental Psychology, 26,* 85–93.

Ruffman, T., Slade, L., & Redman, J. (2005). Young infants' expectations about hidden objects. *Cognition [serial online], 97,* B35-b43.

Ruihe, H., & Guoliang, Y. (2006). Children's understanding of emotional display rules and use of strategies. *Psychological Science (China), 29,* 18–21.

Russell, S., & Consolacion, T. (2003). Adolescent romance and emotional health in the united states: Beyond binaries. *Journal of Clinical Child & Adolescent Psychology, 32,* 499–508.

Rust, J., Golombok, S., Hines, M., Johnston, K., & Golding, J.; ALSPAC Study Team. (2000). The role of brothers and sisters in the gender development of preschool children. *Journal of Experimental Child Psychology, 77,* 292–303.

Rutter, M. (2006). *Genes and behavior: Nature-nurture interplay explained.* New York: Blackwell Publishing.

Ryan, B. P. (2001). Programmed therapy for *stuttering* in children and adults. Spring, IL: Charles C. Thomas, 2001.

Ryan, C., & Rivers, I. (2003). Lesbian, gay, bisexual and transgender youth: victimization and its correlates in the USA and UK. *Culture, Health & Sexuality, 5,* 103–119.

Ryan, J. J., Sattler, J. M., & Lopez, S. J. (2000). Age effects on Wechsler Adult Intelligence Scale-III subtests. *Archives of Clinical Neuropsychology, 15,* 311–317.

Sachs, J. (2006, April 1). Will your child be fat? *Parenting, 20,* 112. Retrieved January 23, 2007 from LexisNexis Academic.

Sack, K. (1999, March 21). Older students bring new life to campuses. *New York Times,* p. WH8.

Sacks, M. H. (1993). Exercise for stress control. In D. Goleman & J. Gurin (Eds.), *Mind–body medicine.* Yonkers, NY: Consumer Reports Books.

Sadeh, A., Flint-Ofir, E., Tirosh, T., & Tikotzky, L. (2007). Infant sleep and parental sleep-related cognitions. *Journal of Family Psychology, 21,* 74–87.

Sadker, D., & Sadker, M. (2005). *Teachers, schools, and society.* New York: McGraw-Hill.

Sadker, M., & Sadker, D. (1994). *Failing at fairness: How America's schools cheat girls.* New York: Scribner's.

Sage, J. R., Anagnostaras, S. G., Mitchell, S., Bronstein, J. MJ., De Slles, A., Masterman, D., & Knowlton, B. J. (2003). Analysis of probabilistic classification learning in patients with Parkinson's disease before and after pallidotomy surgery. *Learning & Memory, 10,* 226–236.

Sales, B. D., & Folkman, S. (Eds.) (2000). *Ethics in research with human participants.* Washington, DC: American Psychological Association.

Sallis, J., & Glanz, K. (2006, March). The role of built environments in physical activity, eating, and obesity in childhood. *The Future of Children, 16,* 89–108.

Salmivalli, C., Ojanen, T., Haanpää, J., & Peets, K. (2005). 'I'm OK but you're not' and other peer-relational schemas: Explaining individual differences in children's social goals. *Developmental Psychology, 41,* 363–375.

Salthouse, T. A. (1989). Age-related changes in basic cognitive processes. In APA Master Lectures, *The adult years: Continuity and change.* Washington, DC: American Psychological Association.

Salthouse, T. A. (1994a). Aging associations: Influence of speed on adult age differences in associative learning. *Journal of Experimental Psychology: Learning, Memory, and Cognition, 20,* 1486–1503.

Salthouse, T. A. (1994b). The aging of working memory. *Neuropsychology, 8,* 535–543.

Salthouse, T. A. (2006). Mental exercise and mental aging: Evaluating the validity of the "Use it or lose it" hypothesis. *Perspectives on Psychological Science, 1,* 68–87.

Salthouse, T. A., Atkinson, T. M., & Berish, D. E. (2003). Executive functioning as a potential mediator of age-related cognitive decline in normal adults. *Journal of Experimental Psychology, General, 132,* 566–594.

Samet, J. H., Memarini, D. M., & Malling, H. V. (2004, May 14). Do airborne particles induce heritable mutations? *Science, 304,* 971.

Sampson, J., & Chason, A. (2008). Helping gifted and talented adolescents and young adults: Make informed and careful career choices. *Handbook of giftedness in children: Psychoeducational theory, research, and best practices.* New York: Springer Science + Business Media.

Samuelsson, I., & Johansson, E. (2006, January). Play and learning—inseparable dimensions in preschool practice. *Early Child Development and Care, 176,* 47–65.

Sanderson, C. A., & Cantor, N. (1995). Social dating goals in late adolescence: Implications for safer sexual activity. *Journal of Personality and Social Psychology, 68,* 1121–1134.

Sandis, E. (2000). The aging and their families: A cross-national review. In A. L. Comunian & U. P. Gielen (Eds.), *International perspectives on human development.* Lengerich, Germany: Pabst Science Publishers.

Sandler, B. (1994, January 31). First denial, then a near-suicidal plea: "Mom, I need your help." *People Weekly,* 56–58.

Sandoval, J., Frisby, Cl L., Geisinger, K. F., Scheuneman, J. D., & Grenier, J. R. (Eds.). (1998). *Test interpretation and diversity: Achieving equity in assessment.* Washington, DC: APA Books.

Sanefuji, W., Ohgami, H., & Hashiya, K. (2006). Preference for peers in infancy. *Infant Behavior & Development, 29,* 584–593.

Sanoff, A. P., & Minerbrook, S. (1993, April 19). Race on campus. *U.S. News and World Report,* pp. 52–64.

Sapolsky, R. (2005, December). Sick of poverty. *Scientific American,* 93–99.

Saravi, F. (2007). The elusive search for a 'gay gene'. *Tall tales about the mind & brain: Separating fact from fiction* (pp. 461–477). New York: Oxford University Press.

Sargent, J. D., Tanski, S. E., & Gibson, J. (2007). Exposure to movie smoking among U.S. adolescents aged 10 to 14 years: A population estimate. *Pediatrics, 119,* 1167–1176.

Sarrel, P. M. (2000). Effects of hormone replacement therapy on sexual psychophysiology and behavior in postmenopause. *Journal of Womens Health & Gender-Based Medicine, 9,* (Suppl. 1), S-25–S-32.

Sasser-Coen, J. R. (1993). Qualitative changes in creativity in the second half of life: A life-span developmental perspective. *Journal of Creative Behavior, 27,* 18–27.

Sattler, J. M. (1992). *Assessment of children: WISC—III and WPPSI—R supplement.* San Diego, CA: Jerome M. Sattler.

Saudino, K., & McManus, I. C. (1998). Handedness, footedness, eyedness, and earedness in the Colorado Adoption Project. *British Journal of Developmental Psychology, 16,* 167–174.

Saulny, S. (2006, March 3.) In baby boomlet, preschool derby is the fiercest yet. *New York Times.* C4.

Saunders, J., Davis, L., & Williams, T. (2004). Gender differences in self-perceptions and academic outcomes: A study of African American high school students. *Journal of Youth & Adolescence, 33,* 81–90.

Savage, J. (2008). The role of exposure to media violence in the etiology of violent behavior: A criminalist weighs in. *American Behavioral Scientist, 51,* 1123–1136.

Savage-Rumbaugh, E. S., Murphy, J., Sevcik, R. A., Brakke, K. E., Williams, S. L., & Rumbaugh, D. M. (1993). Language and comprehension in ape and child. *Monographs of the Society for Research in Child Development, 58,* (3–4, Serial No. 233).

Savin-Williams, R. (1998). *". . . and then I became gay." Young men's stories.* New York: Routledge.

Savin-Williams, R. (2003). Lesbian, gay, and bisexual youths' relationships with their parents. In L. Garnets and D. Kimme (Eds.), *Psychological perspectives on lesbian, gay, and bisexual experiences* (2nd ed.). New York: Columbia University Press.

Savin-Williams, R. C. (2003). Are adolescent same-sex romantic relationships on our radar screen? In P. Florsheim, *Adolescent romantic relations and sexual behavior: Theory, research, and practical implications.* Mahwah, NJ: Lawrence Erlbaum.

Savin-Williams, R. C., & Berndt, T. J. (1990). Friendship and peer relations. In S. Feldman & G. Elliott (Eds.), *At the threshold: The developing adolescent.* Cambridge, MA: Harvard University Press.

Savin-Williams, R., & Demo, D. (1983). Situational and transituational determinants of adolescent self-feelings. *Journal of Personality and Social Psychology, 44,* 824–833.

Savin-Williams, R., & Ream, G. (2003). Suicide attempts among sexual-minority male youth. *Journal of Clinical Child & Adolescent Psychology, 32,* 509–522.

Sawatzky, J., & Naimark, B. (2002). Physical activity and cardiovascular health in aging women: A health-promotion perspective. *Journal of Aging & Physical Activity, 10,* 396–412.

Sawrikar, P., & Hunt, C. J. (2005). The relationship between mental health, cultural identity and cultural values in non-English Speaking Background (NESB) Australian adolescents. *Behaviour Change, 22,* 97–113.

Sax, L., et al. (2004). *The American freshman: National norms for fall 2004.* Los Angeles: Higher Education Research Institute, UCLA.

Sax, L. (2005, March 2). The promise and peril of single-sex public education. *Education Week, 24,* 48–51.

Sax, L. J., Astin, A. W., Korn, W. S, & Mahoney, K. M. (2000). *The American freshman: National norms for fall 2000.* Los Angeles: UCLA Higher Education Research Institute.

Sax, L., & Kautz, K. J. (2003). Who first suggests the diagnosis of attention-deficit/hyperactivity disorder? *Annals of Family Medicine, 1,* 171–174.

Saywitz, K. J., & Nathanson, R. (1993). Children's testimony and their perceptions of stress in and out of the courtroom. *Child Abuse & Neglect, 17,* 613–622.

Scarr, S. (1993). Biological and cultural diversity: The legacy of Darwin for development. *Child Development, 64,* 1333–1353.

Scarr, S. (1998). American child care today. *American Psychologist, 53,* 95–108.

Scarr, S., & Carter-Saltzman, L. (1982). Genetics and intelligence. In R. J. Sternberg (Ed.), *Handbook of human intelligence* (pp. 792–896). Cambridge, England: Cambridge University Press.

Schachar, R., Ickowicz, A., Crosbie, J., Donnelly, G., Reiz, J., Miceli, P., et al. (2008). Cognitive and behavioral effects of multilayer-release methylphenidate in the treatment of children with attention-deficit/hyperactivity disorder. *Journal of Child and Adolescent Psychopharmacology, 18*(1), 11–24.

Schacter, D. L., Wagner, A. D., & Buckner, R. L. (2000). Memory systems of 1999. In E. Tulving, F. I. Craik, I. M. Fergus, et al. (Eds.), *The Oxford handbook of memory*. New York: Oxford University Press.

Schaeffer, C., Petras, H., & Ialongo, N. (2003). Modeling growth in boys' aggressive behavior across elementary school: Links to later criminal involvement, conduct disorder, and antisocial personality disorder. *Developmental Psychology, 39*, 1020–1035.

Schaie, K. W. (1977–1978). Toward a stage of adult theory of adult cognitive development. *Journal of Aging and Human Development, 8*, 129–138.

Schaie, K. W. (1991). Developmental designs revisited. In S. H. Cohen & H. W. Reese (Eds.), *Life-span developmental psychology: Methodological innovations*. Hillsdale, NJ: Erlbaum.

Schaie, K. W. (1993). The Seattle longitudinal studies of adult intelligence. *Current Directions in Psychological Science, 2*, 171–175.

Schaie, K. W. (1994). The course of adult intellectual development. *American Psychologist, 49*, 304–313.

Schaie, K. W., & Willis, S. L. (1993). Age difference patterns of psychometric intelligence in adulthood: Generalizability within and across ability domains. *Psychology and Aging, 8*, 44–55.

Schaie, K. W., & Zanjani, F. A. K. (2006). Intellectual development across adulthood. In C. Hoare, *Handbook of adult development and learning*. New York: Oxford University Press.

Schaie, K. W., Willis, S. L., & Pennak, S. (2005). An historical framework for cohort differences in intelligence. *Research in Human Development, 2*, 43–67.

Schaller, M., & Crandall, C. S. (Eds.). (2004). *The Psychological Foundations of Culture*. Mahwah, NJ: Erlbaum.

Scharfe, E. (2000). Development of emotional expression, understanding, and regulation in infants and young children. In R. Bar-On & J. Parker (Eds.), *The handbook of emotional intelligence: Theory, development, assessment, and application at home, school, and in the workplace*. San Francisco: Jossey-Bass/Pfeiffer.

Scharrer, E., Kim, D., Lin, K., & Liu, Z. (2006). Working hard or hardly working? Gender, humor, and the performance of domestic chores in television commercials. *Mass Communication and Society, 9*, 215–238.

Schatz, M. (1994). *A toddler's life*. New York: Oxford University Press.

Schaufeli, W., & Salanova, M. (2007). Efficacy or inefficacy, that's the question: Burnout and work engagement, and their relationships with efficacy beliefs. *Anxiety, Stress & Coping: An International Journal, 20*, 177–196.

Schechter, T., Finkelstein, Y., & Koren, G. (2005). Pregnant "DES daughters" and their offspring. *Canadian Family Physician, 51*, 493–494.

Scheepers, D., Spears, R., Doosje, B., & Manstead, A. (2006). The social functions of ingroup bias: Creating, confirming, or changing social reality. *European Review of Social Psychology, 17*, 359–396.

Scheiber, F. et al. (1992). Aging and the senses. In J. E. Birren, R. B. Sloane, & G. D. Cohen (Eds.), *Handbook of mental health and aging* (2nd ed.). San Diego: Harcourt Brace.

Schellenberg, E. G., & Trehub, S. E. (1996). Natural musical intervals: Evidence from infant listeners. *Psychological Science, 7*, 272–277.

Schemo, D. J. (2001, December 5). U.S. students prove middling on 32-nation test. *New York Times*, p. A21.

Schemo, D. J. (2004, March 2). Schools, facing tight budgets, leave gifted programs behind. *New York Times*, pp. A1, A18.

Scher, S. J., & Rauscher, F. (Eds.). (2003). *Evolutionary psychology: Alternative approaches*. Dordrecht, Netherlands: Kluwer Academic Publishers.

Scherf, K. S., Sweeney, J. A., & Luna, B. (2006). Brain basis of developmental change in visuospatial working memory. *Journal of Cognitive Neuroscience, 18*, 1045–1058.

Schieman, S., McBrier, D. B., & van Gundy, K. (2003). Home-to-work conflict, work qualities, and emotional distress. *Sociological Forum, 18*, 137–164.

Schkade, D. A., & Kahneman, D. (1998). Does living in California make people happy? A focusing illusion on judgments of life satisfaction. *Psychological Science, 9*, 340–346.

Schlossberg, N. (2004). *Retire smart, retire happy: Finding your true path in life*. Washington, DC: American Psychological Association.

Schmalz, D., & Kerstetter, D. (2006). Girlie girls and manly men: Chidren's stigma consciousness of gender in sports and physical activities. *Journal of Leisure Research, 38*, 536–557.

Schmidt, M., Pekow, P., Freedson, P., Markenson, G., & Chasan-Taber, L. (2006). Physical activity patterns during pregnancy in a diverse population of women. *Journal of Women's Health, 15*, 909–918.

Schmidt, P. J., & Rubinow, D. R. (1991). Menopause- related affective disorders: A justification for further study. *American Journal of Psychiatry, 148*, 844–852.

Schmitt, D. (2004). Patterns and universals of mate poaching across 53 nations: The effects of sex, culture, and personality on romantically attracting another person's partner. *Journal of Personality and Social Psychology, 86*, 560–584.

Schmitt, E. (2001, March 13). For 7 million people in census, one race category isn't enough. *New York Times*, pp. A1, A14.

Schneider, B. (1997). Psychoacoustics and aging: Implications for everyday listening. *Journal of Speech-Language Pathology & Audiology, 21*, 111–124.

Schneider, B. A., Atkinson, L., & Tardif, C. (2001). Child-parent attachment and children's peer relations: A quantitative review. *Developmental Psychology, 37*, 86–100.

Schneider, E. L. (1999, February 5). Aging in the third millennium. *Science, 283*, 796–797.

Schneider, W., & Pressley, M. (1989). *Memory between two and twenty*. New York: Springer-Verlag.

Schneider, W., & Pressley, M. (1997). *Memory development between two and twenty* (2nd ed.). Mahwah, NJ: Lawrence Erlbaum Associates.

Schnur, E., & Belanger, S. (2000). What works in Head Start. In M. P. Kluger & G. Alexander (Eds.), *What works in child welfare*. Washington, DC: Child Welfare League of America.

Schönpflug, U., & Bilz, L. (2009). The transmission process: Mechanisms and contexts. *Cultural transmission: Psychological, developmental, social, and methodological aspects*. New York: Cambridge University Press.

Schoppe-Sullivan, S., Diener, M., Mangelsdorf, S., Brown, G., McHale, J., & Frosch, C. (2006, July). Attachment and sensitivity in family context: The roles of parent and infant gender. *Infant and Child Development, 15*, 367–385.

Schoppe-Sullivan, S., Mangelsdorf, S., Brown, G., & Sokolowski, M. (2007, February). Goodness-of-fit in family context: Infant temperament, marital quality, and early coparenting behavior. *Infant Behavior & Development, 30*, 82–96.

Schore, A. (2003). *Affect regulation and the repair of the self*. New York: Norton.

Schreiber, G. B., Robins, M., Striegel-Moore, R., Obarzanek, M., Morrison, J. A., & Wright, D. J. (1996). Weight modification efforts reported by black and white preadolescent girls: National Heart, Lung, and Blood Institute Growth and Health Study. *Pediatrics, 98*, 63–70.

Schultz, R., & Curnow, C. (1988). Peak performance and age among superathletes: Track and field, swimming, baseball, tennis, and golf. *Journal of Gerontology, 43*, P113–P120.

Schulz, L. E., & Bonawitz, E. B. (2007). Serious fun: Preschoolers engage in more exploratory play when evidence is confounded. *Developmental Psychology, 43*, 1045–1050.

Schulz, R. (Ed.). (2000). *Handbook on dementia caregiving: Evidence-based interventions for family caregivers*. New York: Springer Publishing.

Schulz, R., & Aderman, D. (1976). How medical staff copes with dying patients. *Omega, 7*, 11–21.

Schumann, C. M., Barnes, C. C., Lord, C., & Courchesne, E. (2009). Amygdala enlargement in toddlers with autism related to severity of social and communication impairments. *Biological Psychiatry, 66*, 942–949.

Schuster, C. S., & Ashburn, S. S. (1986). *The process of human development* (2nd. ed.). Boston: Little, Brown.

Schutt, R. K. (2001). *Investigating the social world: The process and practice of research*. Thousand Oaks, CA: Sage.

Schutz, H., Paxton, S., & Wertheim, E. (2002). Investigation of body comparison among adolescent girls. *Journal of Applied Social Psychology, 32*, 1906–1937.

Schwartz, I. M. (1999). Sexual activity prior to coital interaction: A comparison between males and females. *Archives of Sexual Behavior, 28*, 63–69.

Schwartz, S. J., Montgomery, M. J., & Briones, E. (2006). The role of identity in acculturation among immigrant people: Theoretical propositions, empirical questions, and applied recommendations. *Human Development, 49*, 1–30.

Schwenkhagen, A. (2007). Hormonal changes in menopause and implications on sexual health. *The Journal of Sexual Medicine, 4*, Supplement, 220–226.

Scrimsher, S., & Tudge, J. (2003). The teaching/learning relationship in the first years of school: Some revolutionary implications of Vygotsky's theory. *Early Education and Development, Special Issue, 14*, 293–312.

Sears, R. R. (1977). Sources of life satisfaction of the Terman gifted men. *American Psychologist, 32*, 119–129.

Sedikides, C., Gaertner, L., & Toguchi, Y. (2003). Pancultural self-enhancement. *Journal of Personality and Social Psychology, 84*, 60–79.

Segal, B. M., & Stewart, J. C. (1996). Substance use and abuse in adolescence: An overview. *Child Psychiatry & Human Development, 26*, 193–210.

Segal, J., & Segal, Z. (1992, September). No more couch potatoes. *Parents*, p. 235.

Segal, N. L. (2000). Virtual twins: New findings on within-family environmental influences on intelligence. *Journal of Educational Psychology, 92*, 188–194.

Segal, N., McGuire, S., Havlena, J., Gill, P., & Hershberger, S. (2007). Intellectual similarity of virtual twin pairs: Developmental trends. *Personality and Individual Differences, 42*, 1209–1219.

Segall, M. H., Dasen, P. R., Berry, J. W., & Poortinga, Y. H. (1990). *Human behavior in global perspective.* Boston: Allyn & Bacon.

Segalowitz, S. J., & Rapin I. (Eds.). (2003). *Child neuropsychology, Part I.* Amsterdam, The Netherlands: Elsevier Science.

Seidman, S. (2003). The aging male: Androgens, erectile dysfunction, and depression. *Journal of Clinical Psychiatry, 64*, 31–37.

Seidman, S. N., & Rieder, R. O. (1994). A review of sexual behavior in the United States. *American Journal of Psychiatry, 151*, 330–341.

Semerci, Ç. (2006). The opinions of medicine faculty students regarding cheating in relation to Kohlberg's moral development concept. *Social Behavior and Personality, 34*, 41–50.

Senghas, A., Kita, S., & Özyürek, A. (2004, September, 17). Children creating core properties of language: Evidence from an emerging sign language in Nicaragua. *Science, 305*, 1779–1782.

Serbin, L., & Karp, J. (2004). The intergenerational transfer of psychosocial risk: Mediators of vulnerability and resilience. *Annual Review of Psychology, 55*, 333–363.

Serbin, L., Poulin-Dubois, D., & Colburne, K. (2001). Gender stereotyping in infancy: Visual preferences for and knowledge of gender-stereotyped toys in the second year. *International Journal of Behavioral Development, 25*, 7–15.

Serbin, L., Poulin-Dubois, D., & Eichstedt, J. (2002). Infants' response to gender-inconsistent events. *Infancy, 3*, 531–542.

Servin, A., Nordenström, A., Larsson, A., & Bohlin, G. (2003). Prenatal androgens and gender-typed behavior: A study of girls with mild and severe forms of congenital adrenal hyperplasia. *Developmental Psychology, 39*, 440–450.

Settersten, R. (2002). Social sources of meaning in later life. In R. Weiss & S. Bass (Eds.), *Challenges of the third age: Meaning and purpose in later life.* London: Oxford University Press.

Shanahan, M. J., & Flaherty, B. P. (2001). Biobehavioral developments, perception, and action dynamic patterns of time use in adolescence. *Child Development, 72*, 385–401.

Shapiro, A. F., Gottman, J. M. & Carrère, S. (2000). The baby and the marriage: Identifying factors that buffer against decline in marital satisfaction after the first baby arrives. *Journal of Family Psychology, 14*, 124–130.

Shapiro, L. (1997, Spring/Summer). Beyond an apple a day. *Newsweek Special Issue*, 52–56.

Sharf, R. S. (1992). *Applying career development theory to counseling.* Pacific Grove, CA: Brooks/Cole.

Shaunessy, E., Suldo, S., Hardesty, R., & Shaffer, E. (2006, December). School functioning and psychological well-being of international Baccalaureate and general education students: A preliminary examination. *Journal of Secondary Gifted Education, 17*, 76–89.

Shaver, P. (1994, August). *Attachment and care giving in adult romantic relationships.* Invited address presented at the annual meeting of the American Psychological Association, Los Angeles.

Shaver, P. R., Hazan, C., & Bradshaw, D. (1988). Love as attachment: The integration of three behavioral systems. In R. J. Sternberg & M. L. Barnes (Eds.), *The psychology of love* (pp. 68–99). New Haven, CT: Yale University Press.

Shaw, D. S., Winslow, E. B., & Flanagan, C. (1999). A prospective study of the effects of marital status and family relations on young children's adjustment among African American and European American families. *Child Development, 70*, 742–755.

Shaw, M. L. (2003). Creativity and whole language. In J. Houtz, *The educational psychology of creativity.* Cresskill, NJ: Hampton Press.

Shaywitz, B. A., Shaywitz, S.E., Blachman, B.A., Pugh, K.R., Fulbright, R.K., Skudlarski, P., Mencl, W.E., Constable, R.T., Holahan, J.M., Marchione, K.E., Fletcher, J.M., Lyon, G.R., & Gore, J.C. (2004) Development of left occipitotemporal systems for skilled reading in children after a phonologically-based intervention. *Biological Psychiatry, 55*, 926–933.

Shea, J. (2006, September). Cross-cultural comparison of women's midlife symptom-reporting: A China study. *Culture, Medicine and Psychiatry, 30*, 331–362.

Shea, J. D. (1985). Studies of cognitive development in Papua, New Guinea. *International Journal of Psychology, 20*, 33–61.

Shea, K. M., Wilcox, A. J., & Little, R. E. (1998). Postterm delivery: a challenge for epidemiologic research. *Epidemiology, 9*, 199–204.

Sheehan, N., & Petrovic, K. (2008). Grandparents and their adult grandchildren: Recurring themes from the literature. *Marriage & Family Review, 44*, 99–124.

Sheets, R. H., & Hollins, E. R. (1999). *Racial and ethnic identity in school practices.* Mahwah, NJ: Erlbaum.

Sheingold, K. (1973). Developmental differences in intake and storage of visual information. *Journal of Experimental Child Psychology, 16*, 1–11.

Sheldon, K. M., Elliot, A. J., Kim, Y., & Kasser, T. (2001). What is satisfying about satisfying events? Testing 10 candidate psychological needs. *Journal of Personality and Social Psychology, 80*, 325–339.

Sheldon, K. M., Joiner, T. E., Jr., & Pettit, J. W. (2003). Reconciling humanistic ideals and scientific clinical practice. *Clinical Psychology, 10*, 302–315.

Sheldon, S., & Wilkinson, S. (2004). Should selecting saviour siblings be banned? *Journal of Medical Ethics, 30*, 533–537.

Shellenbarger, S. (2003, January 9). Yes, that weird day-care center could scar your child, researchers say. *Wall Street Journal*, p. D1.

Sherman, E. (1991). *Reminiscence and the self in old age.* New York: Springer.

Sherwin, B. B. (1991). The psychoendocrinology of aging and female sexuality. *Annual Review of Sex Research, 2*, 181–198.

Shi, L. (2003). Facilitating constructive parent-child play: Family therapy with young children. *Journal of Family Psychotherapy, 14*, 19–31.

Shi, X., & Lu, X. (2007, October). Bilingual and bicultural development of Chinese American adolescents and young adults: A comparative study. *Howard Journal of Communications, 18*(4), 313–333.

Shih, M., & Sanchez, D. T. (2005). Perspectives and research on the positive and negative implications of having multiple racial identities. *Psychological Bulletin, 131*, 569–591.

Shimizu, M., & Pelham, B. (2004). The unconscious cost of good fortune: Implicit and explicit self-esteem, positive life events, and health. *Health Psychology, 23*, 101–105.

Shiono, P. H., & Behrman, R. E. (1995). Low birth weight: Analysis and recommendations. *The Future of Children, 5*, 4–18.

Shook, J., Vaughn, M., Litschge, C., Kolivoski, K., & Schelbe, L. (2009). The importance of friends among foster youth aging out of care: Cluster profiles of deviant peer affiliations. *Children and Youth Services Review, 31*, 284–291.

Shor, R. (2006, May). Physical punishment as perceived by parents in Russia: Implications for professionals involved in the care of children. *Early Child Development and Care, 176*, 429–439.

Shurkin, J. N. (1992). *Terman's kids: The groundbreaking study of how the gifted grow up.* Boston: Little, Brown.

Shute, R., & Charlton, K. (2006). Anger or compromise? Adolescents' conflict resolution strategies in relation to gender and type of peer relationship. *International Journal of Adolescence and Youth, 13*, 55–69.

Shweder, R. A., Much N. C., & Mahapatra, M. (1997). The 'big three' of morality (autonomy, community, divinity) and the 'big three' explanations of suffering. In A. M. Brandt & P. Rozin, *Morality and health.* Florence, KY: Taylor & Frances/Routledge.

Sieber, J. E. (1998). Planning ethically responsible research. In L. Bickman & D. J. Rog (Eds.), *Handbook of applied social research methods* (pp. 127–156). Thousand Oaks, CA: Sage.

Sieber, J. E. (2000). Planning research: Basic ethical decision-making. In B. D. Sales & S. Folkman, Eds., *Ethics in research with human participants.* Washington, DC: American Psychological Association.

Siegal, M. (2003). Cognitive development. *An introduction to developmental psychology.* Malden, MA: Blackwell Publishing.

Siegler, R. (2003). Thinking and intelligence. In M. Bornstein and L. Davidson (Eds.), *Well-being: Positive development across the life course* (pp. 311–320). Mahwah, NJ: Erlbaum.

Siegler, R. S. (1998). *Children's thinking* (3rd ed.). Upper Saddle River, NJ: Prentice Hall.

Siegler, R. S., & Ellis, S. (1996). Piaget on childhood. *Psychological Science, 7*, 211–215.

Sigman, M., Cohen, S. E., & Beckwith, L. (1997). Why does infant attention predict adolescent intelligence? *Infant Behavior & Development, 20*, 133–140.

Sigman, M., Cohen, S. E., Beckwith, L., Asarnow, R., & Parmelee, A. H. (in press). Continuity in cognitive abilities from infancy to 12 years of age. *Cognitive Development.*

Silveira, P. P., Portella A. K., Crema, L., Correa, M., Nieto, F. B., Diehl, L., Lucion, A. B, & Dalmaz, C. (2007). Both infantile stimulation and exposure to sweet food lead to an increased sweet food ingestion in adult life. *Physiological Behavior, 15,* 88–97.

Simcock, G., & Hayne, H. (2002). Breaking the barrier? Children fail to translate their preverbal memories into language. *Psychological Science, 13,* 225–231.

Simmons, R., & Blyth, D. (1987). *Moving into adolescence.* New York: Aldine de Gruyter.

Simons, L., & Conger, R. (2007, February). Linking mother-father differences in parenting to a typology of family parenting styles and adolescent outcomes. *Journal of Family Issues, 28,* 212–241.

Simons, S. H., van Dijk, M., Anand, K. S., Roofthooft, D., van Lingen, R. A., & Tibboel. D., (2003). Do we still hurt newborn babies? A prospective study of procedural pain and analgesia in neonates. *Archives of Pediatrics and Adolescence, 157,* 1058–1064.

Simonton, D. K. (1989). The swan-song phenomenon: Last-works effects for 172 classical composers. *Psychology and Aging, 4,* 42–47.

Simonton, D. K. (1997). Creative productivity: A predictive and explanatory model of career trajectories and landmarks. *Psychological Review, 104,* 66–89.

Simpkins, S., Parke, R., Flyr, M., & Wild, M. (2006, November). Similarities in children's and early adolescents? Perceptions of friendship qualities across development, gender, and friendship qualities. *Journal of Early Adolescence, 26,* 491–508.

Simpson, J. A. (1990). Influence of attachment styles on romantic relationships. *Journal of Personality & Social Psychology, 59,* 971–980.

Simpson, J., Collins, W., Tran, S., & Haydon, K. (2007, February). Attachment and the experience and expression of emotions in romantic relationships: A developmental perspective. *Journal of Personality and Social Psychology, 92,* 355–367.

Simson, S. P., Wilson, L. B., & Harlow-Rosentraub, K. (2006). Civic engagement and lifelong learning institutes: Current status and future directions. In L. Wilson & S. P. Simson, *Civic engagement and the baby boomer generation: Research, policy, and practice perspectives.* New York: Haworth Press.

Simson, S., Wilson, L., & Harlow-Rosentraub, K. (2006). *Civic engagement and lifelong learning institutes: Current status and future directions.* New York: Haworth Press.

Singer, D. G., & Singer, J. L. (Eds.). (2000). *Handbook of children and the media.* Thousand Oaks, CA: Sage.

Singer, M. S., Stacey, B. G., & Lange, C. (1993). The relative utility of expectancy-value theory and social cognitive theory in predicting psychology student course goals and career aspirations. *Journal of Social Behavior and Personality, 8,* 703–714.

Singh, G. K., & Yu, S. M. (1995). Infant mortality in the United States: Trends, differentials, and projections 1950 through 2010. *American Journal of Public Health, 85,* 957–964.

Sinnott, J. (2003). Postformal thought and adult development: Living in balance. *Handbook of adult development.* New York: Kluwer Academic/Plenum Publishers.

Sinnott, J. D. (1997). Developmental models of midlife and aging in women: Metaphors for transcendence and for individuality in community. In J. Coyle (Ed.), *Handbook on women and aging* (pp. 149–163). Westport, CT: Greenwood.

Sinnott, J. D. (1998). Career paths and creative lives: A theoretical perspective on late-life potential. In C. Adams-Price (Ed.), *Creativity and successful aging: Theoretical and empirical approaches.* New York: Springer.

Sinnott, J. D. (1998). *The development of logic in adulthood: Postformal thought and its applications.* New York: Plenum.

Sinnott-Armstrong, W. (2008). *Moral psychology, Vol 3: The neuroscience of morality: Emotion, brain disorders, and development.* Cambridge, MA: MIT Press.

Skinner, B. F. (1957). *Verbal behavior.* New York: Appleton-Century-Crofts.

Skinner, B. F. (1975). The steep and thorny road to a science of behavior. *American Psychologist, 30,* 42–49.

Skinner, J., Carruth, B., Wendy, B., & Ziegler, P. (2002). Children's food preferences: a longitudinal analysis. *Journal of the American Dietetic Association, 102,* 1638–1647.

Skinner, J. D., Ziegler, P., Pac, S., & Devaney, B. (2004). Meal and snack patterns of infants and toddlers. *Journal of the American Dietary Association, 104,* s65–s70.

Slater, A. (1995). Individual differences in infancy and later IQ. *Journal of Child Psychology and Psychiatry and Allied Disciplines, 36,* 69–112.

Slater, M., Henry, K., & Swaim, R. (2003). Violent media content and aggressiveness in adolescents: A downward spiral model. *Communication Research, 30,* 713–736.

Slavin, R. E. (1995). Enhancing intergroup relations in schools: Cooperative learning and other strategies. In W. D. Hawley & A. W. Jackson (Eds.), *Toward a common destiny: Improving race and ethnic relations in America.* San Francisco: Jossey-Bass.

Sliwinski, M., Stawski, R., Hall, C., Katz, M., Verghese, J., & Lipton, R. (2006). Distinguishing preterminal and terminal cognitive decline. *European Psychologist, 11,* 172–181.

Small, B. J., & Bäckman, L. (1999). Time to death and cognitive performance. *Current Directions in Psychological Science, 8,* 168–172.

Small, G. W., Mazziotta, J. C., Collins, M. T., et al. (1995). Apolipoprotein E. type 4 allele and cerebral glucose metabolism in relatives at risk for familial Alzheimer's disease. *Journal of the American Medical Association, 273,* 942–947.

Smedley, A., & Smedley, B. D. (2005). Race as biology is fiction, racism as a social problem is real: Anthropological and historical perspectives on the social construction of race. *American Psychologist, 60,* 16–26.

Smedley, B. D., & Syme, S. L. (Eds.). (2000). *Promoting health: Intervention strategies from social and behavioral research.* Washington, DC: National Academy of Sciences.

Smeeding, T. M. (1995). An interdisciplinary model and data requirements for studying poor children. In P. L. Chase-Lansdale & J. Brooks-Gunn (Eds.), *Escape from poverty: What makes a difference for children?* New York: Cambridge University Press.

Smetana, J. G. (2005). Adolescent-parent conflict: Resistance and subversion as developmental process. In L. Nucci, *Conflict, contradiction, and contrarian elements in moral development and education.* Mahwah, NJ: Erlbaum.

Smetana, J. G., & Turiel, E. (2003). Moral development during adolescence. In G. R. Adams & M. D. Berzonsky, *Blackwell handbook of adolescence.* Malden, MA: Blackwell Publishing.

Smith, G. C., et al. (2003). Interpregnancy interval and risk of preterm birth and neonatal death. *British Medical Journal, 327,* 313–316.

Smith, J. (2005, April 7). Coaches help mom, dad see "big picture" in parenting. *The Oregonian,* 8.

Smith, P. K. (1995). Grandparenthood. In M. H. Bornstein, *Handbook of parenting.* Hillsdale, NJ: Erlbaum.

Smith, P. K., & Drew, L.M. (2002). Grandparenthood. In M. Bornstein (Ed.), *Handbook of parenting.* Mahwah, NJ: Erlbaum.

Smith, R. (1999, March). The timing of birth. *Scientific American,* 68–75.

Smith, R. J., Bale, J. F., Jr., & White, K. R. (2005, March 2). Sensorineural hearing loss in children. *Lancet, 365,* 879–890.

Smith, S., Quandt, S., Arcury, T., Wetmore, L., Bell, R., & Vitolins, M. (2006, January). Aging and eating in the rural, southern United States: Beliefs about salt and its effect on health. *Social Science & Medicine, 62,* 189–198.

Smokowski, P. R. Mann, E., A. Reynolds, A. J., & Fraser, M. W. (2004). Childhood risk and protective factors and late adolescent adjustment in inner city minority youth. *Children and Youth Services Review, 26, Special issue: Promoting Well-Being in Children and Youth: Findings from the Chicago Longitudinal Study,* 63–91.

Smuts, A. B., & Hagen, J. W. (1985). History of the family and of child development: Introduction to Part 1. *Monographs of the Society for Research in Child Development, 50* (4–5, Serial No. 211).

Snarey, J. R. (1995). In a communitarian voice: The sociological expansion of Kohlbergian theory, research, and practice. In W. M. Kurtines & J. L. Gerwirtz (Eds.), *Moral development: An introduction.* Boston: Allyn and Bacon.

Snow, C. E. (1977). The development of conversation between mothers and babies. *Journal of Child Language, 4,* 1–22.

Snowdon, D. A., Kemper, S. J., Mortimer, J. A., Greiner, L. H., Wekstein, D. R., & Markesbery, W. R. (1996, February 21). Linguistic ability in early life and cognitive function and Alzheimer's disease in late life: Findings from the nun study. *Journal of the American Medical Association, 275,* 528–532.

Snyder, J., Cramer, A, & Afrank, J. (2005). The contributions of ineffective discipline and parental hostile attributions of child misbehavior to the development of conduct problems at home and school. *Developmental Psychology, 41,* 30–41.

Soderstrom, M. (2007). Beyond babytalk: Re-evaluating the nature and content of speech input to preverbal infants. *Developmental Review, 27,* 501–532.

Soderstrom, M., Blossom, M., Foygel, R., & Morgan, J. (2008). Acoustical cues and grammatical units in speech to two preverbal infants. *Journal of Child Language, 35,* 869–902.

Solantaus, T., Leinonen, J., & Punamäki, R-L. (2004). Children's mental health in times of economic recession: Replication and extension of the family economic stress model in Finland. *Developmental Psychology, 40,* 412–429.

Soldo, B. J. (1996). Cross-pressures on middle-aged adults: A broader view. *Journal of Gernontology: Psychological Sciences and Social Sciences, 51B,* 271–273.

Solomon, A. (1995, May 22). A death of one's own. *New Yorker,* pp. 54–69.

Solomou, W., Richards, M., Huppert, F. A., Brayne, C., & Morgan, K. (1998). Divorce, current marital status and well-being in an elderly population. *International Journal of Law, Policy and the Family, 12,* 323–344.

Somerset, W., Newport, D., Ragan, K., & Stowe, Z. (2006). Depressive Disorders in Women: From Menarche to beyond the Menopause. In L. M. Keyes & S. H. Goodman, *Women and depression: A handbook for the social, behavioral, and biomedical sciences.* New York: Cambridge University Press.

Sophian, C., Garyantes, D., & Chang, C. (1997). When three is less than two: Early developments in children's understanding of fractional quantities. *Developmental Psychology, 33,* 731–744.

Sorensen, K. (1992). Physical and mental development of adolescent males with Klinefelter syndrome. *Hormone Research, 37* (Suppl. 3), 55–61.

Sotiriou, A., & Zafiropoulou, M. (2003). Changes of children's self-concept during transition from kindergarten to primary school. *Psychology: The Journal of the Hellenic Psychological Society, 10,* 96–118.

Sotos, J. F. (1997). Overgrowth: Section IV: Genetic disorders associated with overgrowth. *Clinical Pediatrics, 36,* 37–49.

Sousa, D. L. (2005). *How the brain learns to read.* Thousand Oaks, CA: Corwin Press.

Sowell, E. R., Peterson, B. S., Thompson, P. M., Welcome, S. E., Henkenius, A. L., & Toga, A.W. (2003). Mapping cortical change across the human life span. *Nature Neuroscience, 6,* 309–315.

Sowell, E. R., Thompson, P. M., Holmes, C. J., Jerrigan, T. L., & Toga, A. W. (1999). In vivo evidence for post-adolescent brain maturation in frontal and striatal regions. *Nature Neuroscience, 10,* 859–861.

Sowell, E. R., Thompson, P. M., Tessner, K. D., & Toga, A. W. (2001). Mapping continued brain growth and gray matter density reduction in dorsal frontal cortex: Inverse relationships during postadolescent brain maturation. *Journal of Neuroscience, 21,* 8819–8829.

Spear, L. P. (2002). The adolescent brain and the college drinker: Biological basis of propensity to use and misuse alcohol. *Journal of Studies on Alcohol, Special Issue: College drinking, what it is, and what to do about it: Review of the state of the science, Suppl 14,* 71–81.

Spear, P. D. (1993). Neural bases of visual deficits during aging. *Vision Research, 33,* 2589–2609.

Spearman, C. (1927). *The abilities of man.* London: Macmillan.

Spence, S. H. (1989). Cognitive-behavior therapy in the management of chronic, occupational pain of the upper limbs. *Behaviour Research and Therapy, 27,* 435–446.

Spencer, J. (2001). How to battle school violence. http://www.msnbc.com/news/542211.asp?cp1=1#BODY.

Spencer, M. B. (1991). Identity, minority development of. In R. M. Lerner, A. C. Petersen, & J. Brooks-Gunn (Eds.), *Encyclopedia of adolescence* (Vol. 1). New York: Garland.

Spencer, N. (2001). The social patterning of teenage pregnancy. *Journal of Epidemiology & Community Health, 55,* 5.

Spiegel, D. (1993). Social support: How friends, family, and groups can help. In D. Goleman & J. Gurin (Eds.), *Mind-body medicine.* Yonkers, NY: Consumer Reports Books.

Spira, A., Bajos, N., Bejin, A., 7 Beltzer, N. (1992). AIDS and sexual behavior in France. *Nature, 360,* 407–409.

Spraggins, R. E. (2003). *Women and men in the United States: March 2002.* Washington, DC: U.S. Department of Commerce.

Sprecher, S., Sullivan, Q., & Hatfield, E. (1994). Mate selection preferences: Gender differences examined in a national sample. *Journal of Personality and Social Psychology, 66,* 1074–1080.

Springer, S. P., & Deutsch, G. (1989). *Left brain, right brain* (3rd ed.). New York: Freeman.

Squatriglia, C. (2007, February 16). Ted Soulis—charitable painter, businessman. *San Francisco Chronicle,* p. B7.

Squire, L. R., & Knowlton, B. J. (1995). Memory, hippocampus, and brain systems. In M. S. Gazzaniga, *Cognitive neurosciences.* Cambridge, MA: The MIT Press.

Sroufe, L. A. (1996). *Emotional development: The organization of emotional life in the early years.* New York: Oxford University Press.

St. Jacques, P. L., Dolcos, F., & Cabeza, R. (2009). Effects of aging on functional connectivity of the amygdala for subsequent memory of negative pictures: A network analysis of functional magnetic resonance imaging data. *Psychological Science, 20,* 74–84.

Stack, D., & Muir, D. (1992). Adult tactile stimulation during face-to-face interactions modulates five-month-olds' affect and attention. *Child Development, 63,* 1509–1525.

Stadtler, A. C., Gorski, P. A., & Brazelton, T. B. (1999). Toilet Training Methods, Clinical Interventions, and Recommendations. *Pediatrics, 103,* 1359–1361.

Stahl, S., & Nagy, W. (2006). *Teaching word meanings.* Mahwah, NJ: Lawrence Erlbaum Associates Publishers.

Staudenmeier, J. J., Jr. (1999). Children and computers. *Journal of the American Academy of Child and Adolescent Psychiatry, 38,* 5.

Staudinger, U. M., & Leipold, B. (2003). The assessment of wisdom-related performance. In C. R. Snyder (Ed.), *Positive psychological assessment: A handbook of models and measures.* Washington, DC: American Psychological Association.

Staunton, H. (2005). Mammalian sleep. *Naturwissenschaften, 35,* 15.

Stearns, E., & Glennie, E. (2006, September). When and why dropouts leave high school. *Youth & Society, 38,* 29–57.

Stedman, L. C. (1997). International achievement differences: An assessment of a new perspective. *Educational Reseaqrcher, 26,* 4–15.

Steers, R. M., & Porter, L. W. (1991). *Motivation and work behavior.* (5th ed.). New York: McGraw-Hill.

Stein, J. A., Lu, M. C., & Gelberg, L. (2000). Severity of homelessness and adverse birth outcomes. *Health Psychology, 19,* 524–534.

Stein, J. H., & Reiser, L. W. (1994). A study of white middle-class adolescent boys' responses to "semenarche" (the first ejaculation). *Journal of Youth and Adolescence, 23,* 373–384.

Stein, Z., Susser, M., Saenger, G., & Marolla, F. (1975). *Famine and human development: The Dutch hunger winter of 1944–1945.* New York: Oxford University Press.

Steinberg, L., & Silverberg, S. (1986). The vicissitudes of autonomy in early adolescence. *Child Development, 57,* 841–851.

Steinberg, L., Dornbusch, S., & Brown, B. B. (1992). Ethnic differences in adolescent achievement: An ecological perspective. *American Psychologist, 47,* 723–729.

Steinberg, L. D., & Scott, S. S. (2003). Less guilty by reason of adolescence: Developmental immaturity, diminished responsibility, and the juvenile death penalty. *American Psychologist, 58,* 1009–1018.

Steiner, J. E. (1979). Human facial expressions in response to taste and smell stimulation. *Advances in Child Development and Behavior, 13,* 257.

Steinhausen, H. C., & Spohr, H. L. (1998). Long-term outcome of children with fetal alcohol syndrome: Psychopathology, behavior, and intelligence. *Alcoholism, Clinical & Experimental Research, 22,* 334–338.

Stella, L., Verreschi, L., & Lipay, M. (2008). Chimeric hermaphroditism: An overview. *International Journal of Child and Adolescent Health, 1,* 5–9.

Stephens, C., Pachana, N., & Bristow, V. (2006). The effect of hormone replacement therapy on mood and everyday memory in younger and mid-life women. *Psychology, Health & Medicine, 11,* 461–469.

Steri, A. O., & Spelke, E. S. (1988). Haptic perception of objects in infancy. *Cognitive Psychology 20,* 1–23.

Stern, G. (1994, November, 30). Going back to college has special meaning for Mrs. McAlpin. *Wall Street Journal,* p. A1.

Sternberg, R. (2003a). A broad view of intelligence: The theory of successful intelligence. *Consulting Psychology Journal: Practice & Research, 55,* 139–154.

Sternberg, R. (2006). A duplex theory of love. *The new psychology of love* (pp. 184–199). New Haven, CT: Yale University Press.

Sternberg, R. J. (1982). Reasoning, problems solving, and intelligence. In R. J. Sternberg (Ed.), *Handbook of human intelligence* (pp. 225–307). Cambridge, England: Cambridge University Press.

Sternberg, R. J. (1986). Triangular theory of love. *Psychological Review, 93,* 119–135.

Sternberg, R. J. (1990). *Metaphors of mind: Conceptions of the nature of intelligence.* Cambridge, England: Cambridge University Press.

Sternberg, R. J. (1992). Ability tests, measurements, and markets. *Journal of Educational Psychology, 84,* 134–140.

Sternberg, R. J. (1995). For whom the Bell Curve tolls: A review of *The Bell Curve. Psychological Science, 6,* 257–261.

Sternberg, R. J. (1997). *Educating intelligence: Infusing the Triarchic Theory into school instruction.* New York: Cambridge University Press.

Sternberg, R. J. (1997b). Intelligence and lifelong learning: What's new and how can we use it? *American Psychologist, 52,* 1134–1139.

Sternberg, R. J. (2005). The triarchic theory of successful intelligence. In D. P. Flanagan & P. L. Harrison (Eds.), *Contemporary intellectual assessment: Theories, tests, and issues.* New York: Guilford Press.

Sternberg, R. J., & Grigorenko, E. L. (Eds.). (2002). *The generalfactor of intelligence: How general is it?* Mahwah, NJ: Erlbaum.

Sternberg, R. J., & Lubart, T. I. (1992). Buy low and sell high: An investment approach to creativity. *Current Directions in Psychological Science, 1,* 1–5.

Sternberg, R. J., Conway, B. E., Ketron, J. L., & Bernstein, M. (1981). Peoples' conceptions of intelligence. *Journal of Personality and Social Psychology, 41,* 37–55.

Sternberg, R. J., Kaufman, J. C., & Grigorenko, E. L. (2008). *Applied intelligence.* New York: Cambridge University Press.

Sternberg, R. J., Kaufman, J. C., & Pretz, J. E. (2002). *The creativity conundrum: A propulsion model of creative contributions.* Philadelphia, PA: Psychology Press.

Sternberg, R. J., Wagner, R. K., Williams, W. M., & Horvath, J. A. (1997). Testing common sense. In D. Russ-Eft, H. Preskill, & C. Sleezer (Eds.), *Human resource development review: Research and implications* (pp. 102–132). Thousand Oaks, CA: Sage.

Sterns, H. L., Barrett, G. V., & Alexander, R. A. (1985). Accidents and the aging individual. In J. E. Birren & K. W. Schaie (Eds.), *Handbook of the psychology of aging* (2nd ed.). New York: Van Nostrand Reinhold.

Stevens, J., Cai, J., Evenson, K. R., & Thomas, R. (2002). Fitness and fatness as predictors of mortality from all causes and from cardiovascular disease in men and women in the lipid research clinics study. *American Journal of Epidemiology, 156,* 832–841.

Stevens, N., Martina, C., & Westerhof, G. (2006, August). Meeting the need to belong: Predicting effects of a friendship enrichment program for older women. *The Gerontologist, 46,* 495–502.

Stevenson, M., Henderson, T., & Baugh, E. (2007, February). Vital defenses: Social support appraisals of black grandmothers parenting grandchildren. *Journal of Family Issues, 28,* 182–211.

Stevens-Ratchford, R. G. (1993). The effect of life review reminiscence activities on depression and self-esteem in older adults. *American Journal of Occupational Therapy, 47,* 413–420.

Stewart, A. J., & Ostrove, J. M. (1998). Women's personality in middle age: Gender, history, and midcourse corrections. *American Psychologist, 53,* 1185–1194.

Stewart, A. J., & Vandewater, E. A. (1999). "If I had it to do over again…": Midlife review, midcourse corrections, and women's well-being in midlife. *Journal of Personality and Social Psychology, 76,* 270–283.

Stewart, A. J., Copeland, A. P., Chester, N. L., Mallery, J. E., & Barenbaum, N. B. (1997). *Separating together: How divorce transforms families.* New York: Guilford Press.

Stice, E. (2003). Puberty and body image. In C. Hayward (Ed.), *Gender differences at puberty.* New York: Cambridge University Press.

Stice, E., & Shaw, H. (2004). Eating disorder prevention programs: A meta-analytic review. *Psychological Bulletin, 130,* 206–227.

Stice, E., Presnell, K., & Bearman, K. (2001). Relation of early menarche to depression, eating disorders, substance abuse, and comorbid psychopathology among adolescent girls. *Developmental Psychology, 37,* 608–619.

Stipek, D. (2002). At what age should children enter kindergarten? A question for policy makers and parents. *Social Policy Report, 16* (2), 3–16.

Stipek, D. J. (1984). Sex differences in children's attributions for success and failure on math and spelling tests. *Sex Roles, 11,* 969–981.

Stipek, D., & Kakuta, K. (2007). Strategies to ensure that no child starts from behind. In J. L. Aber, S. J. Bishop-Josef, S. M. Jones, K. T. McLean, & D. A. Phillips, *Child development and social policy.* Washington, DC: American Psychological Association.

Stitch, S. (2006, December 4). Going it alone. *Time,* p. F3.

Stock, P., Desoete, A., & Roeyers, H. (2007). Early markers for arithmetic difficulties. *Educational and Child Psychology, 24,* 28–39.

Stockdale, M. S., & Crosby, F. J. (2004). *Psychology and management of workplace diversity.* Malden, MA: Blackwell Publishers.

Stodolsky, S. S. (1974). How children find something to do in preschools. *Genetic Psychology Monographs, 90,* 245–303.

Stolberg, S. G. (1998, April 3). Rise in smoking by young Blacks erodes a success story in health. *New York Times,* p. A1.

Stolberg, S. G. (1999, August 8). Black mothers' mortality rate under scrutiny. *New York Times,* pp. 1, 18.

Stone, C. (2003). Counselors as advocates for gay, lesbian, and bisexual youth: A call for equity and action. *Journal of Multicultural Counseling & Development, 31,* 143–155.

Storfer, M. (1990). *Intelligence and giftedness: The contributions of heredity and early environment.* San Francisco: Jossey-Bass.

Straus, M. A., & Gelles, R. J. (Eds.). (1990). *Physical violence in American families.* New Brunswick, NJ: Transaction.

Straus, M. A., & Yodanis, C. L. (1996). Corporal punishment in adolescence and physical assaults on spouses in later life: What accounts for the link? *Journal of Marriage and the Family, 58,* 825–841.

Straus, M. A., Gelles, R. J., & Steinmetz, S. K. (2003). The marriage license as a hitting license. In M. Silberman (Ed.), *Violence and society: A reader.* Upper Saddle River, NJ: Prentice Hall.

Streissguth, A. (1997). *Fetal alcohol syndrome: A guide for families and communities.* Baltimore, MD: Paul H. Brookes.

Strelau, J. (1998). *Temperament: A psychological perspective.* New York: Plenum Publishers.

Strength, J. (1999). Grieving the loss of a child. *Journal of Psychology & Christianity, 18,* 338–353.

Streri, A. (2003). Intermodal relations in infancy. *Touching for knowing: Cognitive psychology of haptic manual perception.* Amsterdam, Netherlands: John Benjamins Publishing Company.

Striano, T., & Vaish, A. (2006, November). Seven- to 9-month-old infants use facial expressions to interpret others' actions. *British Journal of Developmental Psychology, 24,* 753–760.

Stroebe, M. S., Stroebe, W., & Hansson, R. O. (Eds.). (1993). *Handbook of bereavement: Theory, research, and intervention.* Cambridge, England: Cambridge University Press.

Stroebe, W. (2008). Energy balance and the genetics of body weight. *Dieting, overweight, and obesity: Self-regulation in a food-rich environment.* Washington, DC: American Psychological Association.

Stromswold, K. (2006). Why aren't identical twins linguistically identical? Genetic, prenatal and postnatal factors. *Cognition, 101,* 333–384.

Strube, M. (Ed.). (1990). Type A behavior. (Special Issue). *Journal of Social Behavior and Personality, 5.*

Stuen, C., & Fischer, M. (2007). Gerontechnology and vision. *Gerontechnology: Growing old in a technological society.* Springfield, IL: Charles C. Thomas Publisher.

Stutzer, A., & Frey, B. (2006, April). Does marriage make people happy, or do happy people get married? *Journal of Socio-Economics, 35,* 326–347.

Sue, S., & Chu, J. Y. (2003). The mental health of ethnic minority groups: Challenges posed by the supplement to the Surgeon General's report on mental health. *Culture, Medicine and Psychiatry, 27,* Special issue: The Politics of Science: Culture, race, ethnicity, and the Supplement to the Surgeon General's Report on Mental Health. pp. 447–465.

Sugarman, S. (1988). *Piaget's construction of the child's reality.* Cambridge, England: Cambridge University Press.

Suinn, R. M. (2001). The terrible twos—Anger and anxiety: Hazardous to your health. *American Psychologist, 56,* 27–36.

Sullivan, M. W., Rovee-Collier, C. K., & Tynes, D. M. (1979). A conditioning analysis of infant long-term memory. *Child Development, 50,* 152–162.

Sullivan, M., & Lewis, M. (2003). Contextual determinants of anger and other negative expressions in young infants. *Developmental Psychology, 39,* 693–705.

Suls, J., & Wallston, K. (2003). *Social psychological foundations of health and illness.* Malden, MA: Blackwell Publishers.

Suls, J., & Wills, T. A. (Eds.). (1991). *Social comparison: Contemporary theory and research.* Hillsdale, NJ: Erlbaum.

Summers, J., Schallert, D., & Ritter, P. (2003). The role of social comparison in students' perceptions of ability: An enriched view of academic motivation in middle school students. *Contemporary Educational Psychology, 28,* 510–523.

Sun, J., & Nathans, J. (2001, October). The challenge of macular degeneration. *Scientific American,* 69–75.

Super, C. M. (1976). Environmental effects on motor development: A case of African infant precocity. *Developmental Medicine and Child Neurology, 18,* 561–576.

Super, C. M., & Harkness, S. (1982). The infant's niche in rural Kenya and metropolitan America. In L. Adler (Ed.), *Issues in cross-cultural research.* New York: Academic Press.

Super, C., & Harkness, S. (1999). The environment as culture in developmental research. *Measuring environment across the life span: Emerging methods and concepts.* Washington, DC: American Psychological Association.

Suro, R. (1999, November). Mixed doubles. *American Demographics,* pp. 57–62.

Surveillance, Epidemiology, and End Results Program (SEER) Program. (www.seer.cancer.gov) SEER*Stat Database: Incidence—SEER 9 Regs Public-Use, November 2004 Sub (1973–2002), National Cancer Institute, DCCPS, Surveillance Research Program, Cancer Statistics Branch, released April 2005, based on the November 2004 submission.

Sussman, S. K., & Sussman, M. B. (Eds.). (1991). *Families: Intergenerational and generational connections.* Binghamton, NY: Haworth.

Sutherland, R., Pipe, M., & Schick, K. (2003). Knowing in advance: The impact of prior event information on memory and event knowledge. *Journal of Experimental Child Psychology, 84,* 244–263.

Sutton, J. (2002). Cognitive conceptions of language and the development of autobiographical memory. *Language & Communication, 22,* 375–390.

Swan, S., & Wyer, R. S. (1997). Gender stereotypes and social identity: How being in the minority affects judgment of self and others. *Personality and Social Psychology Bulletin, 23,* 1265–1276.

Swanson, H., Saez, L., & Gerber, M. (2004). Literacy and cognitive functioning in bilingual and nonbilingual children at or not at risk for reading disabilities. *Journal of Educational Psychology, 96,* 3–18.

Swanson, L. A., Leonard, L. B., & Gandour, J. (1992). Vowel duration in mothers' speech to young children. *Journal of Speech and Hearing Research, 35,* 617–625.

Swiatek, M. (2002). Social coping among gifted elementary school students. *Journal for the Education of the Gifted, 26,* 65–86.

Swingley, D. (2008). The roots of the early vocabulary in infants' learning from speech. *Current Directions in Psychological Science, 17,* 308–312.

Sy, T., Tram, S., & O'Hara, L. (2006, June). Relation of employee and manager emotional intelligence to job satisfaction and performance. *Journal of Vocational Behavior, 68,* 461–473.

Tadinac, M., & Hromatko, I. (2007). Own mate value and relative importance of a potential mate's qualities. *Studia Psychologica, 49,* 251–264.

Taga, K., Markey, C., & Friedman, H. (2006, June). A longitudinal investigation of associations between boys' pubertal timing and adult behavioral health and well-being. *Journal of Youth and Adolescence, 35,* 401–411.

Tajfel, H. (1982). *Social identity and intergroup relations.* London: Cambridge University Press.

Tajfel, H. (2001). Social stereotypes and social groups. In M. A. Hogg & D. Abrams (Eds.), *Intergroup relations: Essential readings.* New York: Psychology Press.

Tajfel, H., & Turner, J. C. (2004). The social identity theory of intergroup behavior. In J. T. Jost & J. Sidanius (Eds.), *Political psychology: Key readings.* New York: Psychology Press.

Takala, M. (2006, November). The effects of reciprocal teaching on reading comprehension in mainstream and special (SLI) education. *Scandinavian Journal of Educational Research, 50,* 559–576.

Takanishi, R., Hamburg, D. A., & Jacobs, K. (Eds.). (1997). *Preparing adolescents for the twenty-first century: Challenges facing Europe and the United States.* New York: Cambridge University Press.

Tallandini, M., & Scalembra, C. (2006). Kangaroo mother care and mother-premature infant dyadic interaction. *Infant Mental Health Journal, 27,* 251–275.

Tamis-LeMonda, C. (2004). Conceptualizing fathers' roles: Playmates and more. *Human Development, 47,* 220–227.

Tamis-LeMonda, C. S., & Bornstein, M. H. (1993). Antecedents of exploratory competence at one year. *Infant Behavior and Development, 16,* 423–439.

Tamis-LeMonda, C. S., & Cabrera, N. (1999). Perspectives on father involvement: Research and policy. *Social Policy Report, 13,* 1–31.

Tamis-LeMonda, C., & Cabrera, N. (2002). *Handbook of father involvement: Multidisciplinary perspectives.* Mahwah, NJ: Erlbaum.

Tan, H., Wen, S. W., Mark, W., Fung, K. F., Demissie, K., & Rhoads, G. G. (2004). The association between fetal sex and preterm birth in twin pregnancies. *Obstetrics and Gynecology, 103,* 327–332.

Tang, C., Wu, M., Liu, J., Lin, H., & Hsu, C. (2006). Delayed parenthood and the risk of cesarean delivery—Is paternal age an independent risk factor? *Birth: Issues in Perinatal Care, 33,* 18–26.

Tang, W. R., Aaronson, L. S., & Forbes, S. A. (2004). Quality of life in hospice patients with terminal illness. *Western Journal of Nursing Research, 26,* 113–128.

Tangney, J., & Dearing, R. (2002). Gender differences in morality. In R. Bornstein & J. Masling (Eds.), *The psychodynamics of gender and gender role.* Washington, DC: American Psychological Association.

Tangri, S., Thomas, V., & Mednick, M. (2003). Predictors of satisfaction among college-educated African American women in midlife. *Journal of Adult Development, 10,* 113–125.

Tanner, E., & Finn-Stevenson, M. (2002). Nutrition and brain development: Social policy implications. *American Journal of Orthopsychiatry, 72,* 182–193.

Tanner, J. (1972). Sequence, tempo, and individual variation in growth and development of boys and girls aged twelve to sixteen. In J. Kagan & R. Coles (Eds.), *Twelve to sixteen: Early adolescence.* New York: Norton.

Tanner, J. M. (1978). *Education and physical growth* (2nd ed.). New York: International Universities Press.

Tappan, M. (2006, March). Moral functioning as mediated action. *Journal of Moral Education, 35,* 118.

Tappan, M. B. (1997). Language, culture and moral development: A Vygotskian perspective. *Developmental Review, 17,* 199–212.

Tardif, T. (1996). Nouns are not always learned before verbs: Evidence from Mandarin speakers' early vocabularies. *Developmental Psychology, 32,* 492–504.

Taris, T., van Horn, J., & Schaufeli, W. (2004). Inequity, burnout and psychological withdrawal among teachers: A dynamic exchange model. *Anxiety, Stress & Coping: An International Journal, 17,* 103–122.

Tartamella, L., Herscher, E., & Woolston, C. (2005). *Generation extra large: Rescuing our children from the epidemic of obesity.* New York: Basic.

Task Force on Sudden Infant Death Syndrome (2005). The changing concept of sudden infant death syndrome: Diagnostic coding shifts, controversies regarding the sleeping environment, and new variables to consider in reducing risk. *Pediatrics, 105,* 650–656.

Tatum, Beverly. (2007). *Can we talk about race?: And other conversations in an era of school resegregation.* Boston: Beacon Press.

Tauriac, J., & Scruggs, N. (2006, January). Elder abuse among African Americans. *Educational Gerontology, 32,* 37–48.

Taveras, E., Sandora, T., Shih, M., Ross-Degnan, D., Goldmann, D., & Gillman, M. (2006, November). The association of television and video viewing with fast food intake by preschool-age children. *Obesity, 14,* 2034–2041.

Taylor, D. M. (2002). *The quest for identity: From minority groups to Generation Xers.* Westport, CT: Praeger Publishers/Greenwood Publishing.

Taylor, H. G., Klein, N., Minich, N. M., & Hack, M. (2000). Middle-school-age outcomes in children with very low birthweight. *Child Development, 71,* 1495–1511.

Taylor, L. (2005). *Introducing cognitive development.* New York: Psychology Press.

Taylor, S. E. (1991). *Health psychology* (2nd ed.). New York: McGraw-Hill.

Taylor, S., & Stanton, A. (2007). Coping resources, coping processes, and mental health. *Annual Review of Clinical Psychology, 3,* 377–401.

Teerikangas, O. M., Aronen, E. T., Martin, R. P., & Huttunen, M. O. (1998). Effects of infant temperament and early intervention on the psychiatric symptoms of adolescents. *Journal of the American Academy of Child & Adolescent Psychiatry, 37,* 1070–1076.

Tellegen, A., Lykken, D. T., Bouchard, T. J., Jr., Wilcox, K. J., Segal, N. L., & Rich, S. (1988). Personality similarity in twins reared apart and together. *Journal of Personality and Social Psychology, 54,* 1031–1039.

Tenenbaum, H. R., & Leaper, C. (1998). Gender effects on Mexican-descent parents' questions and scaffolding during toy play: A sequential analysis. *First Language, 18,* 129–147.

Tenenbaum, H., & Leaper, C. (2003). Parent-child conversations about science: The socialization of gender inequities? *Developmental Psychology, 39,* 34–47.

Terman, D. L., Larner, M. B., Stevenson, C. S., & Behrman, R. E. (1996). Special education for students with disabilities: Analysis and recommendations. *The future of children, 6,* 4–24.

Terman, L. M., & Oden, M. H. (1959). *The gifted group at mid-life: Thirty-five years follow-up of the superior child.* Stanford, CA: Stanford University Press.

Terry, D. (2000, August 11). U.S. child poverty rate fell as economy grew, but is above 1979 level. *New York Times,* p. A10.

Tesoriero, H. (July 5, 2007). Mysteries of the "faceblind" could illuminate the brain. *The Wall Street Journal,* p. A1.

Tessor, A., Felson, R. B., & Suls, J. M. (Eds.). (2000). *Psychological perspectives on self and identity.* Washington, DC: American Psychological Association.

Teutsch, C. (2003). Patient–doctor communication. *Medical Clinics of North America, 87,* 1115–1147.

Tharp, R. G. (1989). Psychocultural variables and constants: Effects on teaching and learning in schools: Special issue: Children and their development: Knowledge base, research agenda, and social policy application. *American Psychologist, 44,* 349–359.

Thatcher, S., & Greer, L. (2008). Does it really matter if you recognize who I am? The implications of identity comprehension for individuals in work teams. *Journal of Management, 34,* 5–24.

The New Yorker. (August 18 & 25, 2003). Little people. *The New Yorker,* 138–143.

Thelen, E., & Bates, E. (2003). Connectionism and dynamic systems: Are they really different? *Developmental Science, 6,* 378–391.

Thiessen, E., Hill, E., & Saffran, J. (2005). Infant-directed speech facilitates word segmentation. *Infancy [serial online], 7,* 53–71.

Thomas, A., & Chess, S. (1977). *Temperament and development.* New York: Brunner-Mazel.

Thomas, A., & Chess, S. (1980). *The dynamics of psychological development.* New York: Brunner-Mazel.

Thomas, A., & Sawhill, I. (2005). For love and money? The impact of family structure on family income. *The Future of Children, 15,* 57–74.

Thomas, A., Chess, S., & Birch, H. G. (1968). *Temperament and behavior disorders in children.* New York: New York University Press.

Thomas, P. (1994, September 6). Washington's infant mortality rate, more than twice the U.S. average, reflects urban woes. *Wall Street Journal,* p. A14.

Thomas, P., & Fenech, M. (2007). A review of genome mutation and Alzheimer's disease. *Mutagenesis, 22,* 15–33.

Thomas, P., Lalloué, F., Preux, P., Hazif-Thomas, C., Pariel, S., Inscale, R., et al. (2006, January). Dementia patients caregivers quality of life: The PIXEL study. *International Journal of Geriatric Psychiatry, 21,* 50–56.

Thomas, R. M. (2001). *Recent human development theories.* Thousand Oaks, CA: Sage.

Thompson, C., & Prottas, D. (2006, January). Relationships among organizational family support, job autonomy, perceived control, and employee well-being. *Journal of Occupational Health Psychology, 11,* 100–118.

Thompson, R. A., & Nelson, C. A. (2001). Developmental science and the media. *American Psychologist, 56,* 5–15.

Thompson, R. A., U & Nelson, C. A. (2001, January). Developmental science and the media: Early Brain Development. *American Psychologist,* 5–15.

Thompson, R., Easterbrooks, M., & Padilla-Walker, L. (2003). Social and emotional development in infancy. In R. Lerner & M. Easterbrooks (Eds.), *Handbook of psychology: Developmental psychology, Vol. 6* (pp. 91–112). New York: Wiley.

Thompson, S. M. (2000). Synaptic plasticity: Building memories to last. *Current Biology, 10,* R218–R221.

Thorne, B., & Luria, Z. (2003). Putting boundaries around the sexes: Sexuality and gender in children's daily worlds. *Down to earth sociology: Introductory readings* (12th ed.). New York: Free Press.

Thornton, J. (2004). Life-span learning: A developmental perspective. *International Journal of Aging & Human Development, 57,* 55–76.

Thorsheim, H. I., & Roberts, B. B. (1990). *Reminiscing together: Ways to help us keep mentally fit as we grow older.* Minneapolis, MN: CompCare Publishers.

Thorson, J. A., Powell, F., Abdel-Khalek, A. M., & Beshai, J. A. (1997). Constructions of religiosity and death anxiety in two cultures: The United States and Kuwait. *Journal of Psychology and Theology, 25,* 374–383.

Tincoff, R., & Jusczyk, P. W. (1999). Some beginnings of word comprehension in 6-month-olds. *Psychological Science, 10,* 172–175.

Ting, Y. (1997). Determinants of job satisfaction of federal government employees. *Public Personnel Management, 26,* 313–334.

Tinsley, B., Lees, N., & Sumartojo, E. (2004). Child and adolescent HIV risk: Familial and cultural perspectives. *Journal of Family Psychology, 18,* 208–224.

Tisserand, D., & Jolles, J. (2003). On the involvement of prefrontal networks in cognitive ageing. *Cortex, 39,* 1107–1128.

Tobin, J. J., Wu, D. Y. H., & Davidson, D. H. (1989). *Preschool in three cultures: Japan, China, and the United States.* New Haven, CT: Yale University Press.

Toch, T. (1995, January 2). Kids and marijuana: The glamour is back. *U.S. News and World Report,* p. 12.

Toga, A. W., & Thompson, P. M. (2003). Temporal dynamics of brain anatomy. *Annual Review of Biomedical Engineering, 5,* 119–145.

Tomasello, M., Carpenter, M., & Liszkowski, U. (2007). A new look at infant pointing. *Child Development, 78,* 705–722.

Tomasello, M., Carpenter, M., Call, J., Behne, T., & Moll, H. (2005). Understanding and sharing intentions: The origins of cultural cognition. *Behavioral and Brain Sciences, 28,* 675–735.

Tomblin, J. B., Hammer, C. S., & Zhang, X. (1998). The association of prenatal tobacco use and SLI. *International Journal of Language and Communication Disorders, 33,* 357–368.

Tongsong, T., Iamthongin, A., Wanapirak, C., Piyamongkol, W., Sirichotiyakul, S., Boonyanurak, P., Tatiyapornkul, T., & Neelasri, C. (2005). Accuracy of fetal heart-rate variability interpretation by obstetricians using the criteria of the National Institute of Child Health and Human Development compared with computer-aided interpretation. *Journal of Obstetric and Gynaecological Research, 31,* 68–71.

Topolnicki, D. M. (1995, January). The real immigrant story: Making it big in America. *Money,* pp. 129–138.

Torvaldsen, S., Roberts, C. L., Simpson, J. M., Thompson, J. F., & Ellwood, D. A. (2006). Intrapartum epidural analgesia and breastfeeding: A prospective cohort study. *International Breastfeeding Journal, 24,* 1–24.

Toschke, A. M., Grote, V., Koletzko, B., & von Kries, R. (2004). Identifying children at high risk for overweight at school entry by weight gain during the first 2 years. *Archives of Pediatric Adolescence, 158,* 449–452.

Tracy, J., Shaver, P., & Albino, A. (2003). Attachment styles and adolescent sexuality. In P. Florsheim (Ed.), *Adolescent romantic relations and sexual behavior: Theory, research, and practical implications.* Mahwah, NJ: Erlbaum.

Trainor, L., & Desjardins, R. (2002). Pitch characteristics of infant-directed speech affect infants' ability to discriminate vowels. *Psychonomic Bulletin & Review, 9,* 335–340.

Trautwein, U., Lüdtke, O. Kastens, C., & Köller, O. (2006). Effort on homework in grades 5–9: Development, motivational antecedents, and the association with effort on classwork. *Child Development, 77,* 1094–1111.

Treas, J., & Bengston, V. L. (1987). The family in later years. In M. B. Sussman & S. K. Steinmetz (Eds.), *Handbook of marriage and the family.* New York: Plenum.

Treasure, J., & Tiller, J. (1993). The aetiology of eating disorders: Its biological basis. *International Review of Psychiatry, 5,* 23–31.

Trehub, S. E., (2003). The developmental origins of musicality. *Nature Neuroscience, 6,* 669–673.

Trehub, S. E., Schneider, B. A., Morrongiello, B. A., & Thorpe, L. A. (1988). Auditory sensitivity in school-age children. *Journal of Experimental Child Psychology, 46,* 272–285.

Tremblay, R. E. (2001). The development of physical aggression during childhood and the prediction of later dangerousness. In G. F. Pinard & L. Pagani (Eds.), *Clinical assessment of dangerousness: Empirical contributions.* New York: Cambridge University Press.

Triandis, H. C. (1994). *Culture and social behavior.* New York: McGraw-Hill.

Trippet, S. E. (1991). Being aware: The relationship between health and social support among older women. *Journal of Women and Aging, 3,* 69–80.

Tropp, L. (2003). The psychological impact of prejudice: Implications for intergroup contact. *Group Processes & Intergroup Relations, 6,* 131–149.

Tropp, L., & Wright, S. (2003). Evaluations and perceptions of self, ingroup, and outgroup: Comparisons between Mexican-American and European-American children. *Self & Identity, 2,* 203–221.

Tryon, W. (2008). Historical and theoretical foundations. In M. Hersen & A. M. Gross (Eds.), *Handbook of clinical psychology, Vol 1: Adults.* Hoboken, NJ: John Wiley & Sons Inc.

Trzesniewski, K. H., Donnellan, M. B., & Robins, R. W. (2003). Stability of self-esteem across the life span. *Journal of Personality and Social Psychology, 84,* 205–220.

Tsao, F-M., Liu, H-M., & Kuhl, P. K. (2004). Speech perception in infancy predicts language development in the second year of life: A longitudinal study. *Child Development, 75,* 1067–1084.

Tse, T., & Howie, L. (2005, September). Adult day groups: Addressing older people's needs for activity and companionship. *Australasian Journal on Ageing, 24,* 134–140.

Tsunoda, T. (1985). *The Japanese brain: Uniqueness and universality.* Tokyo: Taishukan.

Tucker, M. B., & Mitchell-Kernan, C. (Eds.). (1995). *The decline in marriage among African Americans: Causes, consequences, and policy implications.* New York: Russell Sage.

Tudge, J., & Scrimsher, S. (2003). Lev S. Vygotsky on education: A cultural-historical, interpersonal, and individual approach to development. In B. Zimmerman (Ed.), *Educational psychology: A century of contributions.* Mahwah, NJ: Erlbaum.

Tulving, E., & Thompson, D. M. (1973). Encoding specificity and retrieval processes in episodic memory. *Psychological Review, 80,* 352–373.

Turati, C. (2008). Newborns' memory processes: A study on the effects of retroactive interference and repetition priming. *Infancy, 13,* 557–569.

Turati, C., Cassia, V. M., Simion, F., & Leo, I. (2006). Newborns' face recognition: Role of inner and outer facial features. *Child Development, 77,* 297–311.

Turiel, E. (2006). Thought, emotions, and social interactional processes in moral development. In M. Killen & J. G. Smetana, *Handbook of moral development.* Mahwah, NJ: Lawrence Erlbaum Associates.

Turkheimer, E., Haley, A., Waldreon, M., D'Onofrio, B., & Gottesman, I. I. (2003). Socioeconomic status modifies heritability of IQ in young children. *Psychological Science, 14,* 623–628.

Turner, J. C. & Onorato, R. S. (1999). Social identity, personality, and the self-concept: A self-categorizing perspective. In T. R. Tyler & R. M. Kramer (Eds.), *The psychology of the social self. Applied social research.* Mahwah, NJ: Erlbaum.

Turner, J. S., & Helms, D. B. (1994). *Contemporary adulthood* (5th ed.). Forth Worth, TX: Harcourt Brace.

Turner-Bowker, D. M. (1996). Gender stereotyped descriptors in children's picture books: Does "Curious Jane" exist in the literature? *Sex Roles, 35,* 461–488.

Twenge, J.M., & Crocker, J. (2002). Race and self-esteem: Meta-analyses comparing whites, blacks, Hispanics, Asians, and American Indians and comment on Gray-Little and Hafdahl (2000). *Psychological Bulletin, 128,* 371–408.

Twomey, J. (2006). Issues in genetic testing of children. *MCN: The American Journal of Maternal/Child Nursing, 31*, 156–163.

Tyler, K., Dillihunt, M., Boykin, A., Coleman, S., Scott, D., Tyler, C., et al. (2008). Examining cultural socialization within African American and European American households. *Cultural Diversity and Ethnic Minority Psychology, 14*, 201–204.

Tyre, P. (2006, September 11). The new first grade: Too much too soon? *Newsweek*, pp. 34–44.

Tyre, P., & McGinn, D. (2003, May 12). She works, he doesn't. *Newsweek*, pp. 45–52.

Tyre, P., & Scelfo, J. (2003, September 22). Helping kids get fit. *Newsweek*, pp. 60–62.

Uhlenberg, P., Cooney, T., & Boyd, R. (1990). Divorce for women after midlife. *Journal of Gerontology, 45*(1), S3–S11.

Umaña-Taylor, A. J., Bhanot, R., & Shin, N. (2006). Ethnic identity formation during adolescence: The critical role of families. *Journal of Family Issues, 27*, 390–414.

Umana-Taylor, A. J., Diversi, M., & Fine, M. A. (2002). Ethnic identity and self-esteem of Latino adolescents: Distinctions among the Latino populations. *Journal of Adolescent Research, 17*, 303–327.

Umana-Taylor, A., & Fine, M. (2004). Examining ethnic identity among Mexican-origin adolescents living in the United States. *Hispanic Journal of Behavioral Sciences, 26*, 36–59.

Umberson, D., Williams, K., Powers, D., Chen, M., & Campbell, A. (2005). As good as it gets? A life course perspective on marital quality. *Social Forces, 81*, 493–511.

UNAIDS & World Health Organization. (2006). *AIDS epidemic update*. Paris: World Health Organization.

Underwood, M. (2003). *Social aggression among girls*. New York: Guilford Press.

Underwood, M. (2005). Introduction to the special section: Deception and observation. *Ethics & Behavior, 15*, 233–234.

Unger, R. K. (Ed.). (2001). *Handbook of the psychology of women and gender*. New York: Wiley.

Unger, R., & Crawford, M. (1992). *Women and gender: A feminist psychology* (2nd ed.). New York: McGraw-Hill.

Unger, R., & Crawford, M. (2003, 2004). *Women and gender: A feminist psychology* (4th ed.). New York: McGraw-Hill.

UNICEF. (2005). *The state of the world's children*. New York: The United Nations Children's Fund U.S. Bureau of the Census. (2006). Women's earnings as a percentage of men's earnings: 1960–2005. Historical Income Tables-People. Table P-40. Washington, DC: U.S. Bureau of the Census.

United Nations Population Division. (2002). *World population ageing: 1950–2050*. New York: United Nations.

United Nations. (1990). *Declaration of the world summit for children*. New York: United Nations.

United Nations. (1991). *Declaration of the world summit for children*. New York: Author.

United Nations. (2002). *Building a Society for all Ages*. New York: United Nations.

University of Akron. (2006). *A longitudinal evaluation of the new curricula for the D.A.R.E. middle (7th grade) and high school (9th grade) programs: Take Charge of Your Life*. Akron: University of Akron.

Unsworth, N., & Engle, R. W. (2005). Individual differences in working memory capacity and learning: Evidence from the serial reaction time task. *Memory & Cognition, 33*, 213–220.

Updegraff, K. A., Helms, H. M., McHale, S. M., Crouter, A. C., Thayer, S. M., & Sales, L. H. (2004). Who's the Boss? Patterns of Perceived Control in Adolescents' Friendships. *Journal of Youth & Adolescence, 33*, 403–420.

Urberg, K., Luo, Q., & Pilgrim, C. (2003). A two-stage model of peer influence in adolescent substance use: Individual and relationship-specific differences in susceptibility to influence. *Addictive Behaviors, 28*, 1243–1256.

U.S. Bureau of Labor Statistics. (2003). *Wages earned by women*. Washington, DC: U.S. Bureau of Labor Statistics.

U.S. Bureau of the Census. (1990). *Studies in marriage and the family: Single parents and their children*. (Current Population Reports, Series P-23, No. 167). Washington, DC: U.S. Government Printing Office.

U.S. Bureau of the Census. (2000). *Current population reports*. Washington, DC: U.S. Government Printing Office.

U.S. Bureau of the Census (2001). *Living arrangements of children*. Washington, DC: U.S. Bureau of the Census.

U.S. Bureau of the Census. (2002). *Statistical abstract of the United States* (122nd ed.). Washington, DC: U.S. Government Printing Office.

U. S. Bureau of the Census. (2003). *Population reports*. Washington, DC: U.S. Government Printing Office.

U.S. Bureau of the Census. (2004). *Current Population Survey, 2004 Annual Social and Economic Supplement*. Washington, DC: U.S. Bureau of the Census.

U.S. Bureau of the Census. (2005). *Current population survey*. Washington, DC: U.S. Bureau of the Census.

U.S. Bureau of the Census. (2006). *Current population survey*. Washington, DC: U.S. Bureau of the Census.

U.S. Census Bureau (1998). The condition of education. *Current Population Surveys, October 2000*. Washington, DC: U.S. Census Bureau.

U. S. Census Bureau. (2001). *Population reports*. Washington, DC: GPO.

U. S. Census Bureau. (2006). *Population reports*. Washington, DC: GPO.

U. S. Center for Health Statistics. (2003). *Division of vital statistics*. Washington, DC: Public Health Service.

U.S. Department of Agriculture. (1992). *Dietary guidelines*. Washington, DC: USDA.

U.S. Department of Education (2005). 2003–2004 National Postsecondary Student Aid Study (NPSAS:04), unpublished tabulations. Washington, DC: U.S. Department of Education.

U.S. Department of Health and Human Services (USDHHS). (1990). *Health United States 1989* (DHHS Publication No. PHS 90–1232). Washington, DC: U.S. Government Printing Office.

U.S. Secret Service. (2002). *The final report and findings of the safe school initiative: Implications for the prevention of school attacks in the United States*. Washington, DC: National Threat Assessment Center.

USA Weekend. (1997, August 22–24), p. 5.

Usdansky, M. L. (1992, July 17). Wedded to the single life: Attitudes, economy delaying marriages. *USA Today*, p. A8.

Uttl, B. (2006). Age-related changes in event-cued visual and auditory prospective memory proper. *Aging, Neuropsychology, and Cognition, 13*, 141–172.

Uylings, H. (2006). Development of the human cortex and the concept of 'critical' or 'sensitive' periods. *Language Learning, 56*, 59–90.

Vaillant, G. (2003). Mental health. *American Journal of Psychiatry, 160*, 1373–1384.

Vaillant, G. E. (1977). *Adaptation to life*. Boston: Little, Brown.

Vaillant, G. E., & Vaillant, C. O. (1981). Natural history of male psychological health, X: Work as a predictor of positive mental health. *American Journal of Psychiatry, 138*, 1433–1440.

Vaillant, G. E., & Vaillant, C. O. (1990). Natural history of male psychological health, XII: A 45-year study of predictors of successful aging. *American Journal of Psychiatry, 147*(1), 31–37.

Vaish, A., Carpenter, M., & Tomasello, M. (2009). Sympathy through affective perspective taking and its relation to prosocial behavior in toddlers. *Developmental Psychology, 45*, 534–543.

Valiente, C., Eisenberg, N., & Fabes, R. A. (2004). Prediction of children's empathy-related responding from their effortful control and parents' expressivity. *Developmental Psychology, 40*, 911–926.

Van Balen, F. (2005). The choice for sons or daughters. *Journal of Psychosomatic Obstetrics & Gynecology, 26*, 229–320.

Van de Graaf, K. (2000). *Human anatomy* (5th ed., p. 339). Boston: McGraw-Hill.

Van den Berg, M., Huizink, A., van Baal, G., Tieman, W., van der Ende, J., & Verhulst, F. (2008). Genetic and environmental influences on self-reported and parent-reported behavior problems in young adult adoptees. *Genes, Brain & Behavior, 7*, 88–95.

Van Der Veer, R., & Valsiner, J. (1993). *Understanding Vygotsky*. Oxford, England: Blackwell.

Van Der Veer, R., & Valsiner, J. (Eds.). (1994). *The Vygotsky reader*. Oxford, England: Blackwell.

van Leeuwen, M., van den Berg, S., & Boomsma, D. (2008). A twin-family study of general IQ. *Learning and Individual Differences, 18*, 76–88.

Van Marle, K., & Wynn, K. (2006). Six-month-old infants use analog magnitudes to represent duration. *Developmental Science, 9*, F41–f49.

van Marle, K., & Wynn, K. (2009). Infants' auditory enumeration: Evidence for analog magnitudes in the small number range. *Cognition, 111*, 302–316.

Van Schoiack-Edstrom, L., Frey, K. S., & Beland, K. (2002). Changing adolescents' attitudes about relational and physical aggression. *School Psychology Review, 31*, 201–216.

van Strien, T., & Bazelier, F. (2007). Perceived parental control of food intake is related to external, restrained and emotional eating in 7–12-year-old boys and girls. *Appetite, 49*, 618–625.

Van Tassel-Baska, J., Olszewski-Kubilius, P., & Kulieke, M. (1994). A study of self-concept and social support in advantaged and disadvantaged seventh and eighth grade gifted students. *Roeper Review, 16,* 186–191.

van Wormer, K., & McKinney, R. (2003). What schools can do to help gay/lesbian/bisexual youth: A harm reduction approach. *Adolescence, 38,* 409–420.

van't Spijker, A., & ten Kroode, H. F. (1997). Psychological aspects of genetic counseling: A review of the experience with Huntington's disease. *Patient Education and Counseling, 32,* 33–40.

Vandell, D. L. (2000). Parents, peer groups, and other socializing influences. *Developmental Psychology, 36,* 699–710.

Vandell, D. L. (2004). Early child care: The known and the unknown. *Merrill-Palmer Quarterly, 50,* Special issue: The maturing of human developmental sciences: Appraising past, present, and prospective agendas, 387–414.

Vandell, D. L., Burchinal, M. R., Belsky, J., Owen, M. T., Friedman, S. L., Clarke-Stewart, A., McCartney, K., & Weinraub, M. (2005). *Early child care and children's development in the primary grades: Follow-up results from the NICHD Study of Early Child Care.* Paper presented at the biennial meeting of the Society for Research in Child Development, Atlanta, GA.

Vandell, D. L., Shumow, L., & Posner, J. (2005). After-school programs for low-income children: Differences in program quality. In J. L. Mahoney, R. W. Larson, & J. S. Ecccles, *Organized activities as contexts of development: Extracurricular activities, after-school and community programs.* Mahwah, NJ: Lawrence Erlbaum Associates.

Vandello, J., & Cohen, D. (2003). Male honor and female fidelity: Implicit cultural scripts that perpetuate domestic violence. *Journal of Personality & Social Psychology, 84,* 997–1010.

Vandello, J., Cohen, D., Grandon, R., & Franiuk, R. (2009). Stand by your man: Indirect prescriptions for honorable violence and feminine loyalty in Canada, Chile, and the United States. *Journal of Cross-Cultural Psychology, 40,* 81–104.

Vangelisti, A. (2006). Relationship dissolution: Antecedents, processes, and consequences. *Close relationships: Functions, forms and processes* (pp. 353–374). Hove, England: Psychology Press/Taylor & Francis (UK).

VanLaningham, J., Johnson, D., & Amato, P. (2001). Marital happiness, marital duration, and the U-shaped curve: Evidence from a five-wave panel study. *Social Forces, 78,* 1313–1341.

Vansteenkiste, M., Neyrinck, B., Niemiec, C., Soenens, B., De Witte, H., & Van den Broeck, A. (2007). On the relations among work value orientations, psychological need satisfaction and job outcomes: A self-determination theory approach. *Journal of Occupational and Organizational Psychology, 80,* 251–277.

Vecchiet, L. (2002). Muscle pain and aging. *Journal of Musculoskeletal Pain, 10,* 5–22.

Vecchiotti, S. (2003). Kindergarten: An overlooked educational policy priority. *Social Policy Report,* 3–19.

Veevers, J. E., & Mitchell, B. A. (1998). Intergenerational exchanges and perceptions of support within 'boomerang kid' family environments. *International Journal of Aging & Human Development, 46,* 91–108.

Vellutino, F. R. (1991). Introduction to three studies on reading acquisition: Convergent findings on theoretical foundations of code-oriented versus whole-language approaches to reading instruction. *Journal of Educational Psychology, 83,* 437–443.

Veneziano, R. (2003).The importance of paternal warmth. *Cross-Cultural Research: The Journal of Comparative Social Science, 37,* 265–281.

Veras, R. P., & Mattos, L. C. (2007). Audiology and aging: Literature review and current horizons. *Revista Brasileira de Otorrinolaringologia (English Edition), 73,* 122–128.

Vereijken, C. M., Riksen-Walraven, J. M., & Kondo-Ikemura, K. (1997). Maternal sensitivity and infant attachment security in Japan: A longitudinal study. *International Journal of Behavioral Development, 21,* 35–49.

Verma, J. (2004). Social values. *Psychology in India revisited: Developments in the discipline, Vol 3: Applied social and organisational psychology.* Thousand Oaks, CA: Sage Publications, Inc.

Verrity, P. (2007). *Violence and aggression around the globe.* Hauppauge, NY: Nova Science Publishers.

Vidaver, R.M. et al. (2000). Women subjects in NIH-Funded clinical research literature: Lack of progress in both representation and analysis by sex. *Journal of Women's Health Gender-Based Medicine, 9,* 495–504.

Vihman, M. M. (1991). Early syllables and the construction of phonology. In C. A. Ferguson, L. Menn, & C. Stoel-Gammon (Eds.), *Phonological development: Models, research, implications* (pp. 69–84). Hillsdale, NJ: Erlbaum.

Vilette, B. (2002). Do young children grasp the inverse relationship between addition and subtraction? Evidence against early arithmetic. *Cognitive Development, 17,* 1365–1383.

Vilhjalmsson, R., & Kristjansdottir, G. (2003). Gender differences in physical activity in older children and adolescents: The central role of organized sport. *Social Science Medicine, 56,* 363–374.

Villarosa, L. (2003, December 23). More teenagers say no to sex, and experts are sure why. *New York Times,* p. D6.

Vincent, J. A., Phillipson, C. R., & Downs, M. (2006). *The futures of old age.* Thousand Oaks, CA: Sage.

Vizmanos, B. & Marti-Henneberg, C. (2000). Puberty begins with a characteristic subcutaneous body fat mass in each sex. *European Journal of Clinical Nutrition, 54,* 203–206.

Vohs, K. D., & Heatherton, T. (2004). Ego threats elicits different social comparison process among high and low self-esteem people: Implications for interpersonal perceptions. *Social Cognition, 22,* 168–191.

Volkow, N. D., Wang, G. J., Fowler, J. S., Logan, J., Gerasimov, M., Maynard, I., Ding, Y. S., Gatley, S. J., Gifford, A., & Granceschi, D. (2001). Therapeutic doses of oral methylphenidate significantly increase extracellular dopamine in the human brain. *Journal of Neuroscience, 21,* 1–5.

Voorpostel, M., & Blieszner, R. (2008). Intergenerational solidarity and support between adult siblings. *Journal of Marriage and Family, 70,* 157–167.

Votruba-Drzal, E., Coley, R. L., & Chase-Lansdale, L. (2004). Child care and low-income children's development: Direct and moderated effects. *Child Development, 75,* 396–312.

Vurpillot, E. (1968). The development of scanning strategies and their relation to visual differentiation. *Journal of Experimental Child Psychology, 6,* 632–650.

Vyas, S. (2004). Exploring bicultural identities of Asian high school students through the analytic window of a literature club. *Journal of Adolescent & Adult Literacy, 48,* 12–18.

Vygotsky, L. S. (1926/1997). *Educational psychology.* Delray Beach, FL: St. Lucie Press.

Vygotsky, L. S. (1962). Piaget's theory of child language and thought. In L. Vygotsky, E. Hanfmann, & G. Vakar (Eds.), *Thought and language.* Cambridge, MA: MIT Press.

Vygotsky, L. S. (1979). *Mind in society: The development of higher mental processes.* Cambridge, MA: Harvard University Press. (Original works published 1930, 1933, and 1935.)

Wachs, T. (2002). Nutritional deficiencies as a biological context for development. In W. Hartup, W. Silbereisen, & K. Rainer (Eds.), *Growing points in developmental science: An introduction.* Philadelphia, PA: Psychology Press.

Wachs, T. D. (1996). Known and potential processes underlying developmental trajectories in childhood and adolescence. *Developmental Psychology, 32,* 796–801.

Wade, N. (2001, October 4). Researchers say gene is linked to language. *New York Times,* p. A1.

Wagner, D. A. (1981). Culture and memory development. In H. C. Triandis & A. Heron (Eds.), *Handbook of cross-cultural psychology: Vol. 4: Developmental psychology.* Boston: Allyn & Bacon.

Wagner, R. K. (1997). Intelligence, training, and employment. *American Psychologist, Vol 52,* Special issue: Intelligence & Lifelong Learning, 1059–1069.

Wagner, R. K., & Sternberg, R. J. (1985). Alternate conceptions of intelligence and their implications for education. *Review of Educational Research, 54,* 179–223.

Wahlin, T. (2007). To know or not to know: A review of behaviour and suicidal ideation in preclinical Huntington's disease. *Patient Education and Counseling, 65,* 279–287.

Wainwright, J. L., Russell, S. T., & Patterson, C. J. (2004). Psychosocial adjustment, school outcomes, and romantic relationships of adolescents with same-sex parents. *Child Development, 75,* 1886–1898.

Waite, H. (1995). Lesbians leaping out of the intergenerational contract: Issues of aging in Australia. In G. Sullivan & L. Leong (Eds.), *Gays and lesbians in Asia and the Pacific: Social and human services.* New York: Harrington Park Press/Haworth Press.

Wakefield, M., Reid, Y., & Roberts, L. (1998). Smoking and smoking cessation among men whose partners are pregnant: A qualitative study. *Social Science & Medicine, 47,* 657–664.

Wakschlag, L. S., Leventhal, B. L., Pine, D. S., Pickett, K. E., & Carter, A. S. (2006). Elucidating early mechanisms of developmental psychopathology: The case of prenatal smoking and disruptive behavior. *Child Development, 77,* 893–906.

Walcott, D., Pratt, H., & Patel, D. (2003). Adolescents and eating disorders: Gender, racial, ethnic, sociocultural and socioeconomic issues. *Journal of Adolescent Research, 18,* 223–243.

Walden, T., Kim, G., McCoy, C., & Karrass, J. (2007). Do you believe in magic? Infants' social looking during violations of expectations. *Developmental Science, 10,* 654–663.

Waldfogel, J. (2001). International policies toward parental leave and child care. *Caring for Infants and Toddlers, 11,* 99–111.

Walker, A. A. (1979). The development of relational concepts in three- and four-year-olds. *Journal of Educational Research, 73,* 37–40.

Walker, J., Anstey, K., & Lord, S. (2006, May). Psychological distress and visual functioning in relation to vision-related disability in older individuals with cataracts. *British Journal of Health Psychology, 11,* 303–317.

Walker, L. (1984). *The battered woman syndrome.* New York: Springer.

Walker, L. E. (1989). Psychology and violence against women. *American Psychologist, 44,* 695–702.

Walker, L. E. (1999). Psychology and domestic violence around the world. *American Psychologist, 54,* 21–29.

Walker, N. C., & O'Brien, B. (1999). The relationship between method of pain management during labor and birth outcomes. *Clinical Nursing Research, 8,* 119–134.

Walker, W. R., Skowronski, J. J., & Thompson, C. P. (2003). Life is pleasant—and memory helps to keep it that way! *Review of General Psychology, 7,* 203–210.

Wallerstein, J. S., Lewis, J. M., & Blakeslee, S. (2000). *The unexpected legacy of divorce.* New York: Hyperion.

Wallerstein, J., & Resnikoff, D. (2005). Parental divorce and developmental progression: An inquiry into their relationship. In L. Gunsberg & P. Hymowitz, *A handbook of divorce and custody: Forensic, developmental, and clinical perspectives.* Hillsdale, NJ: Analytic Press.

Wallis, C. (1994, July 18). Life in overdrive. *Time,* pp. 42–50.

Wallis, C. (2006, March 19). The multitasking generation. *Time,* 12–15.

Walster, H. E., & Walster, G. W. (1978). *Love.* Reading, MA: Addison-Wesley.

Walter, A. (1997). The evolutionary psychology of mate selection in Morocco: A multivariate analysis. *Human Nature, 8,* 113–137.

Walters, E., & Gardner, H. (1986). The theory of multiple intelligences: Some issues and answers. In R. J. Sternberg & R. K. Wagner (Eds.), *Practical intelligence.* New York: Cambridge University Press.

Wang, M. (2007). Profiling retirees in the retirement transition and adjustment process: Examining the longitudinal change patterns of retirees' psychological well-being. *Journal of Applied Psychology, 92,* 455–474.

Wang, Q. (2001). Culture effects on adults' earliest childhood recollection and self-description: Implication for the relation between memory and the self. *Journal of Personality and Social Psychology, 81,* 220–233.

Wang, Q. (2004). The emergence of cultural self-constructs: Autobiographical memory and self-description in European American and Chinese children. *Developmental Psychology, 40,* 3–15.

Wang, Q. (2006, August). Culture and the development of self-knowledge. *Current Directions in Psychological Science, 15,* 182–187.

Wang, S., & Tamis-LeMonda, C. (2003). Do child-rearing values in Taiwan and the United States reflect cultural values of collectivism and individualism? *Journal of Cross-Cultural Psychology, 34,* 629–642.

Wang, S-H., Baillargeon, R., & Paterson, S. (2005). Detecting continuity violations in infancy: A new account and new evidence from covering and tube events. *Cognition, 95,* 129–173.

Wannamethee, S. G., Shaper, A. G., Walker, M., & Ebrahim, S. (1998). Lifestyle and 15-year survival free of heart attack, stroke, and diabetes in middle-aged British men. *Archives of Internal Medicine, 158,* 2433–2440.

Ward, L. M., & Friedman, K. (2006). Using TV as a guide: Associations between television viewing and adolescents' sexual attitudes and behavior. *Journal of Research on Adolescence, 16,* 133–156.

Wardle, J., Guthrie, C., & Sanderson, S. (2001). Food and activity preferences in children of lean and obese parents. *International Journal of Obesity & Related Metabolic Disorders, 25,* 971–977.

Warin, J. (2000). The attainment of self-consistency through gender in young children. *Sex Roles, 42,* 209–231.

Warnock, F., & Sandrin, D. (2004). Comprehensive description of newborn distress behavior in response to acute pain (newborn male circumcision). *Pain, 107,* 242–255.

Warshak, R. A. (2000). Remarriage as a trigger of parental alienation syndrome. *American Journal of Family Therapy, 28,* 229–241.

Warwick, P., & Maloch, B. (2003). Scaffolding speech and writing in the primary classroom: A consideration of work with literature and science pupil groups in the USA and UK. *Reading: Literacy & Language, 37,* 54–63.

Washington Post. (2007, March 14). D.C totals for infant mortality revised. *The Washington Post,* pg. BO1.

Wass, H. (2004). A perspective on the current state of death education. *Death Studies, 28,* 289–308.

Wasserman, G., Factor-Litvak, P., & Liu, X. (2003). The relationship between blood lead, bone lead and child intelligence. *Child Neuropsychology, 9,* 22–34.

Waterhouse, J. M., & DeCoursey, P. J. (2004). Human circadian organization. In J. C. Dunlap & J. J. Loros (Eds.), *Chronobiology: Biological timekeeping.* Sunderland, MA: Sinauer Associates.

Waterland, R. A., & Jirtle, R. L. (2004). Early nutrition, epigenetic changes at transposons and imprinted genes, and enhanced susceptibility to adult chronic diseases. *Nutrition,* 63–68.

Waters, E., Merrick, S., Treboux, D., Crowell, J., & Albersheim, L. (2000). Attachment security in infancy and early adulthood: A twenty-year longitudinal study. *Child Development, 71,* 684–689.

Waters, L., & Moore, K. (2002). Predicting self-esteem during unemployment: The effect of gender financial deprivation, alternate roles and social support. *Journal of Employment Counseling, 39,* 171–189.

Watkins, D., Dong, Q., & Xia, Y. (1997). Age and gender differences in the self-esteem of Chinese children. *Journal of Social Psychology, 137,* 374–379.

Watson, J. B. (1925). *Behaviorism.* New York: Norton.

Wayment, H., & Vierthaler, J. (2002). Attachment style and bereavement reactions. *Journal of Loss & Trauma, 7,* 129–149.

Webster, J., & Haight, B. (2002). *Critical advances in reminiscence work: From theory to application.* New York: Springer Publishing Co.

Webster, R. A., Hunter, M., & Keats, J. A. (1994). Peer and parental influences on adolescents' substance use: A path analysis. *International Journal of the Addictions, 29,* 647–657.

Wechler, Issac, Grodstein, & Sellers (2000). *College binge drinking in the 1990s: a continuing problem: results of the Harvard School of Public Health 1999 College Health Alcohol Study.* Cambridge, MA: Harvard University.

Wechsler, H., Lee, J. E., Kuo, M., Seibring, M., Nelson, T. F., & Lee, H. (2002). Trends in college binge drinking during a period of increased prevention efforts: Findings from 4 Harvard School of Public Health college alcohol study surveys, 1993–2001.

Weed, K., Ryan, E. B., & Day, J. (1990). Metamemory and attributions as mediators of strategy use and recall. *Journal of Educational Psychology, 82,* 849–855.

Weichold, K., Silbereisen, R., & Schmitt-Rodermund, E. (2003). Short-term and long-term consequences of early versus late physical maturation in adolescents. In C. Hayward (Ed.), *Gender differences at puberty.* New York: Cambridge University Press.

Weijerman, M., van Furth, A., Noordegraaf, A., van Wouwe, J., Broers, C., & Gemke, R. (2008). Prevalence, neonatal characteristics, and first-year mortality of Down syndrome: A national study. *The Journal of Pediatrics, 152,* 15–19.

Weinberg, R. A. (1989). Intelligence and IQ: Landmark issues and great debates. *American Psychologist, 44*(2), 98–104.

Weinberger, D. R. (2001, March 10). A brain too young for good judgment. *New York Times,* p. D1.

Weinfield, N. S., Sroufe, L. A., & Egeland, B. (2000). Attachment from infancy to early adulthood in a high-risk sample: Continuity, discontinuity, and their correlates. *Child Development, 71,* 695–702.

Weinstock, H., Berman, S., & Cates, W., Jr. (2004). Sexually transmitted diseases among American youth: Incidence and prevalence estimates, 2000. *Perspectives on Sexual and Reproductive Health, 36,* 182–191.

Weiss, J., Cen, S., Schuster, D., Unger, J., Johnson, C., Mouttapa, M., et al. (2006, June). Longitudinal effects of pro-tobacco and anti-tobacco messages on adolescent smoking susceptibility. *Nicotine & Tobacco Research, 8,* 455–465.

Weiss, M. R., Ebbeck, V., & Horn. T. S. (1997). Children's self-perceptions and sources of physical competence information: A cluster analysis. *Journal of Sport & Exercise Psychology, 19,* 52–70.

Weiss, R. (2003, September 2). Genes' sway over IQ may vary with class. *Washington Post,* p. A1.

Weiss, R., & Raz, I. (2006, July). Focus on childhood fitness, not just fatness. *Lancet, 368,* 261–262.

Weitzman, E., Nelson, T., & Wechsler, H. (2003). Taking up binge drinking in college: The influences of person, social group, and environment. *Journal of Adolescent Health, 32,* 26–35.

Wells, G. L., Olson, E. A., & Charman, S. D. (2002). The confidence of eyewitnesses in their identifications from lineups. *Current Directions in Psychological Science, 11,* 151–154.

Werker, J. F., Pons, F., Dietrich, C., Kajikawa, S., Fais, L., & Amano, S. (2007). Infant-directed speech supports phonetic category learning in English and Japanese. *Cognition, 103,* 147–162.

Werker, J., & Fennell, C. (2009). Infant speech perception and later language acquisition: Methodological underpinnings. *Infant pathways to language: Methods, models, and research disorders.* New York: Psychology Press.

Werner, E. E. (1972). Infants around the world: Cross-cultural studies of psychomotor development from birth to two years. *Journal of Cross-Cultural Psychology, 3,* 111–134.

Werner, E. E. (2005). What can we learn about resilience from large-scale longitudinal studies? In S. Goldstein & R. B. Brooks, *Handbook of resilience in children.* New York: Kluwer Academic/Plenum Publishers.

Werner, L. (2007). Issues in human auditory development. *Journal of Communication Disorders, 40,* 275–283.

Werner, L. A., & Marean, G. C. (1996). *Human auditory development.* Boulder, CO: Westview Press.

Werner, N. E., & Crick, N. R. (2004). Maladaptive peer relationships and the development of relational and physical aggression during middle childhood. *Social Development, 13,* 495–514.

Wertsch, J. V. (1999). The zone of proximal development: Some conceptual issues. In P. Lloyd & C. Fernyhough (Eds.), *Lev Vygotsky: Critical assessments,* Vol. 3: *The zone of proximal development.* New York: Routledge.

West, J. R., & Blake, C. A. (2005). Fetal alcohol syndrome: An assessment of the field. *Experimental Biology and Medicine, 230,* 354–356.

Westerhausen, R., Kreuder, F., Sequeira Sdos, S., Walter, C., Woerner, W., Wittling, R. A., Schweiger, E., & Wittling, W. (2004). Effects of handedness and gender on macro- and microstructure of the corpus callosum and its subregions: A combined high-resolution and diffusion-tensor MRI study. *Brain Research and Cognitive Brain Research, 21,* 418–426.

Wethington, E., Cooper, H., & Holmes, C. S. (1997). Turning points in midlife. In I. H. Gotlib & B. Wheaton (Eds.), *Stress and adversity over the life course: Trajectories and turning points* (pp. 215–231). New York: Cambridge University Press.

Wexler, B. (2006). *Brain and culture: Neurobiology, ideology, and social change.* Cambridge, MA: MIT Press.

Whalen, C. K., Jamner, L. D., Henker, B., Delfino, R. J., & Lozano, J. M. (2002). The ADHD spectrum and everyday life: Experience sampling of adolescent moods, activities, smoking, and drinking. *Child Development, 73,* 209–227.

Whalen, D., Levitt, A., & Goldstein, L. (2007). VOT in the babbling of French- and English-learning infants. *Journal of Phonetics, 35,* 341–352.

Whalen, P., Davis, F. C., Oler, J. A., Kim, H., Kim, M. J., & Neta, M. (2009). Human amygdala responses to facial expressions of emotion. In P. J. Whalen & E. A. Phelps (Eds.), *The human amygdala.* New York: Guilford Press.

Whaley, B. B., & Parker, R. G. (2000). Expressing the experience of communicative disability: Metaphors of persons who stutter. *Communication Reports, 13,* 115–125.

Wheeldon, L. R. (1999). *Aspects of language production.* Philadelphia, PA: Psychology Press.

Wheeler, S., & Austin, J. (2001). The impact of early pregnancy loss. *American Journal of Maternal/Child Nursing, 26,* 154–159.

Whitaker, R. C., Wright, J. A., Pepe, M. S., Seidel, K. D., & Dietz, W. H. (1997, September 25). Predicting obesity in young adulthood from childhood and parental obesity. *New England Journal of Medicine, 337,* 869–873.

Whitbourne, S. K. (2001). *Adult development and aging: Biopsychosocial perspectives.* New York: Wiley.

Whitbourne, S. K., Zuschlag, M. K., Elliot, L. B., & Waterman, A. S. (1992). Psychosocial development in adulthood: A 22–year sequential study. *Journal of Personality and Social Psychology, 63,* 260–271.

Whitbourne, S., Jacobo, M., & Munoz-Ruiz, M. (1996). Adversity in the elderly. In R. S. Feldman (Ed.), *The psychology of adversity.* Amherst: University of Massachusetts Press.

Whiting, B. B. (1965). Sex identity conflict and physical violence: A comparative study. *American Anthropologist, 67,* 123–140.

Whiting, B. B., & Edwards, C. P. (1988). *Children of different worlds: The formation of social behavior.* Cambridge, MA: Harvard University Press.

Whorf, B. L. (1956). *Language, thought, and reality.* New York: Wiley.

Wickelgren, W. A. (1999). Webs, cell assemblies, and chunking in neural nets: Introduction. *Canadian Journal of Experimental Psychology, 53,* 118–131.

Wielgosz, A. T., & Nolan, R. P. (2000). Biobehavioral factors in the context of ischemic cardiovascular disease. *Journal of Psychosomatic Research, 48,* 339–345.

Wiggins, M., & Uwaydat, S. (2006, January). Age-related macular degeneration: Options for earlier detection and improved treatment. *Journal of Family Practice, 55,* 22–27.

Wilcox, A., Skjaerven, R., Buekens, P., & Kiely, J. (1995, March 1). Birth weight and perinatal mortality: A comparison of the United States and Norway. *Journal of the American Medical Association, 273,* 709–711.

Wilcox, H. C., Conner, K. R., & Caine, E. D. (2004). Association of alcohol and drug use disorders and completed suicide: An empirical review of cohort studies. *Drug & Alcohol Dependence, 76,* Special issue: Drug Abuse and Suicidal Behavior. pp. S11–S19.

Wilcox, M. D. (1992). Boomerang kids. *Kiplinger's Personal Finance Magazine, 46,* 83–86.

Wilcox, S., Castro, C. M., & King, A. C. (2006). Outcome expectations and physical activity participation in two samples of older women. *Journal of Health Psychology, 11,* 65–77.

Wilcox, T., Woods, R., Chapa, C., & McCurry, S. (2007). Multisensory exploration and object individuation in infancy. *Developmental Psychology, 43,* 479–495.

Wildberger, S. (2003, August). So you're having a baby. *Washingtonian,* 85–86, 88–90.

Wiley, S., Perkins, K., & Deaux, K. (2008). Through the looking glass: Ethnic and generational patterns of immigrant identity. *International Journal of Intercultural Relations, 32,* 385–398.

Wiley, T. L., Nondahl, D. M., Cruickshanks, K. J., & Tweed, T. S. (2005). Five-year changes in middle ear function for older adults. *Journal of the American Academy of Audiology, 16,* 129–139.

Williams, C., Povey, R., & White, D. (2008). Predicting women's intentions to use pain relief medication during childbirth using the Theory of Planned Behaviour and Self-Efficacy Theory. *Journal of Reproductive and Infant Psychology, 26,* 168–179.

Williams, H., & Monsma, E. (2007). Assessment of gross motor development. *Psychoeducational assessment of preschool children* (4th ed.). Mahwah, NJ: Lawrence Erlbaum Associates Publishers.

Williams, J. M., & Currie, C. (2000). Self-esteem and physical development in early adolescence: Pubertal timing and body image. *Journal of Early Adolescence, 20,* 129–149.

Williams, J., & Binnie, L. (2002). Children's concept of illness: An intervention to improve knowledge. *British Journal of Health Psychology, 7,* 129–148.

Williams, K., & Dunne-Bryant, A. (2006, December). Divorce and adult psychological well-being: Clarifying the role of gender and child age. *Journal of Marriage and Family, 68,* 1178–1196.

Willie, C., & Reddick, R. (2003). *A new look at Black families* (5th ed.). Walnut Creek, CA: AltaMira Press.

Willows, D. M., Kruk, R. S., & Corcos, E. (Eds.). (1993). *Visual processes in reading and reading disabilities.* Hillsdale, NJ: Erlbaum.

Wills, T. A., & DePaulo, B. M. (1991).) Interpersonal analysis of the help-seeking process. In C. R. Snyder & Dr. R. Forsyth (Eds.), *Handbook of social and clinical psychology: The health perspective.* New York: Pergamon Press.

Wilson, B., & Gottman, J. (2002). Marital conflict, repair, and parenting. *Handbook of parenting: Vol. 4: Social conditions and applied parenting* (2nd ed.), (pp. 227–258). Mahwah, NJ: Lawrence Erlbaum Associates Publishers.

Wilson, B., et al. (2002). Violence in children's television programming: Assessing the risks. *Journal of Communication, 52,* 5–35.

Wilson, M. N. (1989). Child development in the context of the black extended family. *American Psychologist, 44,* 380–385.

Wilson, R. (2004, December 3). Where the elite teach, it's still a man's world. *Chronicle of Higher Education, 51,* A8.

Wilson, R., Beck, T., Bienias, J., & Bennett, D. (2007, February). Terminal cognitive decline: Accelerated loss of cognition in the last years of life. *Psychosomatic Medicine, 69,* 131–137.

Wilson, R., Beckett, L., & Bienias, J. (2003). Terminal decline in cognitive function. *Neurology, 60,* 1782–1787.

Wilson-Williams, L., Stephenson, R., Juvekar, S., & Andes, K. (2008). Domestic violence and contraceptive use in a rural Indian village. *Violence Against Women, 14,* 1181–1198.

Winefield, A. (2002). The psychology of unemployment. *Psychology at the turn of the millennium, vol. 2: Social, developmental, and clinical perspectives.* Florence, KY: Taylor & Frances/Routledge.

Wines, M. (2006, August 24). Africa adds to miserable ranks for child workers. *New York Times,* p. D1.

Winger, G., & Woods, J. H. (2004). *A handbook on drug and alcohol abuse: The biomedical aspects.* Oxford, England: Oxford University Press.

Wingert, P., & Katrowitz, B. (2002, October 7). Young and depressed. *Newsweek,* pp. 53–61.

Wingert, P., & Kantrowitz, B. (2007, January 15). The new prime time. *Newsweek,* p. 38.

Wingfield, A., Tun, P. A., & McCoy, S. L. (2005). Hearing loss in older adulthood: What it is and how it interacts with cognitive performance. *Current Directions in Psychological Science, 14,* 144–147.

Winn, R. L., & Newton, N. (1982). Sexuality in aging: A study of 106 cultures. *Archives of Sexual Behavior, 11,* 283–298.

Winner, E. (1989). Development in the visual arts. In W. Damon (Ed.), *Child development today and tomorrow.* San Francisco: Jossey-Bass.

Winner, E. (2006). Development in the arts: Drawing and music. *Handbook of child psychology: Vol 2, Cognition, perception, and language* (6th ed.). Hoboken, NJ: John Wiley & Sons Inc.

Winsler, A. (2003). Introduction to special issue: Vygotskian perspectives in early childhood education. *Early Education and Development, Special Issue, 14,* 253–269.

Winstead, B. A., & Sanchez, J. (2005). Gender and psychopathology. In J. Maddux (Ed.), *Psychopathology: Foundations for a contemporary understanding.* Mahwah, NJ: Erlbaum.

Winterich, J. (2003). Sex, menopause, and culture: Sexual orientation and the meaning of menopause for women's sex lives. *Gender & Society, 17,* 627–642.

Winters, K. C., Stinchfield, R. D., & Botzet, A. (2005). Pathways for youth gambling problem severity. *Psychology of Addictive Behaviors, 19,* 104–107.

Wisborg, K., Kesmodel, U., Bech, B. H., Hedegaard, M., & Henriksen, T. B. (2003). Maternal consumption of coffee during pregnancy and still birth and infant death in first year of life: prospective study. *British Medical Journal, 326,* 420.

Wise, L., Adams-Campbell, L., Palmer, J., & Rosenberg, L. (2006, August). Leisure time physical activity in relation to depressive symptoms in the Black Women's Health Study. *Annals of Behavioral Medicine, 32,* 68–76.

Witkow, M., & Fuligni, A. (2007). Achievement goals and daily school experiences among adolescents with Asian, Latino, and European American backgrounds. *Journal of Educational Psychology, 99,* 584–596.

Witt, S. D. (1997). Parental influence on children's socialization to gender roles. *Adolescence, 32,* 253–259.

Wodrich, D. L., & Tarbox, J. (2008). Psychoeducational implications of sex chromosome anomalies. *School Psychology Quarterly, 23,* 301–311.

Woelfle, J. F., Harz, K., & Roth, C. (2007). Modulation of circulating IGF-I and IGFBP-3 levels by hormonal regulators of energy homeostasis in obese children. *Experimental and Clinical Endocrinology Diabetes, 115,* 17–23.

Wolfe, M. S. (2006, May). Shutting down Alzheimer's. *Scientific American,* 73–79.

Wolfe, W. (2007, February 24). Late life love: Older couples find that love comes when they aren't looking for it and share the stories of their late-in-life romance. *The Star Tribune* (Minneapolis, MN), p. 1E.

Wolfe, W., Olson, C., & Kendall, A. (1998). Hunger and food insecurity in the elderly: Its nature and measurement. *Journal of Aging & Health, 10,* 327–350.

Wolfner, G., Faust, D., & Dawes, R. M. (1993). The use of anatomically detailed dolls in sexual abuse evaluations: The state of the science. *Applied & Preventive Psychology, 2,* 1–11.

Wolfson, C., Handfield-Jones, R., Glass, K. C., McClaran, J., et al. (1993). Adult children's perceptions of their responsibility to provide care for dependent elderly parents. *Gerontologist, 33,* 315–323.

Wolinsky, F., Wyrwich, K., & Babu, A. (2003). Age, aging, and the sense of control among older adults: A longitudinal reconsideration. *Journals of Gerontology: Series B: Psychological Sciences & Social Sciences, 58B,* S212–S220.

Wong, B. Y. L. (1996). *The ABCs of learning disabilities.* New York: Academic Press.

Wood, A. C., Saudino, K. J., Rogers, H., Asherson, P., & Kuntsi, J. (2007). Genetic influences on mechanically-assessed activity level in children. *Journal of Child Psychology and Psychiatry, 48,* 695–702.

Wood, R. (1997). Trends in multiple births, 1938–1995. *Population Trends, 87,* 29–35.

Woolfolk, A. E. (1993). *Educational psychology* (5th ed.). Boston: Allyn & Bacon.

Workman, L., & Reader, W. (2008). *Evolutionary psychology, an introduction: Second edition.* New York: Cambridge University Press.

World Bank. (2003). *Global development finance 2003—Striving for stability in development finance.* Washington, DC: World Bank.

World Bank. (2004). *World Development Indicators 2004 (WDI).* Washington, DC: World Bank.

World Factbook, The. (2007, April 17). Estimates of infant mortality. Retrieved from https://www.cia.gov/cia/publications/factbook/rankorder/2091rank.html April 20, 2007.

World Food Programme, United Nations (2004). Retrieved: March 01, 2004, from www.wfp.org

Worrell, F., Szarko, J., & Gabelko, N. (2001). Multi-year persistence of nontraditional students in an academic talent development program. *Journal of Secondary Gifted Education, 12,* 80–89.

Wright, J. C., Huston, A. C., Truglio, R., Fitch, M., Smith, E., & Piemyat, S. (1995). Occupational portrayals on television: Children's role schemata, career aspirations, and perceptions of reality. *Child Development, 66,* 1706–1718.

Wright, R. (1995, March 13). The biology of violence. *New Yorker,* pp. 68–77.

Wright, S. C., & Taylor, D. M. (1995). Identity and the language of the classroom: Investigation of the impact of heritage versus second language instruction on personal and collective self-esteem. *Journal of Educational Psychology, 87,* 241–252.

Wrosch, C., Bauer, I., & Scheier, M. (2005, December). Regret and quality of life across the adult life span: The Influence of disengagement and available future goals. *Psychology and Aging, 20,* 657–670.

Wu, C., Zhou, D., & Chen, W. (2003). A nested case-control study of Alzheimer's disease in Linxian, northern China. *Chinese Mental Health Journal, 17,* 84–88.

Wu, P., Robinson, C., & Yang, C. (2002). Similarities and differences in mothers' parenting of preschoolers in China and the United States. *International Journal of Behavioral Development, 26,* 481–491.

Wynn, K. (1992, August 27). Addition and subtraction by human infants. *Nature, 358,* 749–750.

Wynn, K. (1995). Infants possess a system of numerical knowledge. *Current Directions in Psychological Science, 4,* 172–177.

Wynn, K. (2000). Findings of addition and subtraction in infants are robust and consistent: Reply to Wakeley, Rivera, and Langer. *Child Development, 71,* 1535–1536.

Xiaohe, X., & Whyte, M. K. (1990). Love matches and arranged marriages: A Chinese replication. *Journal of Marriage and the Family, 52,* 709–722.

Yablo, P., & Field, N. (2007). The role of culture in altruism: Thailand and the United States. *Psychologia: An International Journal of Psychology in the Orient, 50,* 236–251.

Yan, Z., & Fischer, K. (2002). Always under construction: Dynamic variations in adult cognitive microdevelopment. *Human Development, 45,* 141–160.

Yang, C. D. (2006). *The infinite gift: How children learn and unlearn the languages of the world.* New York: Scribner.

Yang, R., and Blodgett, B. (2000). Effects of race and adolescent decision-making on status attainment and self-esteem. *Journal of Ethnic & Cultural Diversity in Social Work, 9,* 135–153.

Yarrow, L. (1990, September). Does my child have a problem? *Parents,* p. 72.

Yasui, M., Dorham, C. L., & Dishion, T. J. (2004). Ethnic identity and psychological adjustment: A validity analysis for European American and African American adolescents. *Journal of Adolescent Research, 19,* 807–825.

Yee, M., & Brown, R. (1994). The development of gender differentiation in young children. *British Journal of Social Psychology, 33,* 183–196.

Yell, M. L. (1995). The least restrictive environment mandate and the courts: Judicial activism or judicial restraint? *Exceptional Children, 61,* 578–581.

Yelland, G. W., Pollard, J., & Mercuri, A. (1993). The metalinguistic benefits of limited contact with a second language. *Applied Psycholinguistics, 14,* 423–444.

Yildiz, O. (2007). Vascular smooth muscle and endothelial functions in aging. *Annals of the New York Academy of Sciences, 1100,* 353–360.

Yip, T. (2008). Everyday experiences of ethnic and racial identity among adolescents and young adults. *Handbook of race, racism, and the developing child.* Hoboken, NJ: John Wiley & Sons Inc.

Yip, T., Sellers, R. M., & Seaton, E. K. (2006). African American racial identity across the lifespan: Identity status, identity content, and depressive symptoms. *Child Development, 77,* 1504–1517.

Yoshinaga-Itano, C. (2003). From screening to early identification and intervention: Discovering predictors to successful outcomes for children with significant hearing loss. *Journal of Deaf Studies & Deaf Education, 8,* 11–30.

Young, S., Rhee, S., Stallings, M., Corley, R., & Hewitt, J. (2006, July). Genetic and environmental vulnerabilities underlying adolescent substance use and problem use: General or specific? *Behavior Genetics, 36,* 603–615.

Youniss, J., & Haynie, D. L. (1992). Friendship in adolescence. *Journal of Developmental and Behavioral Pediatrics, 13,* 59–66.

Yuill, N., & Perner, J. (1988). Intentionality and knowledge in children's judgments of actor's responsibility and recipient's emotional reaction. *Developmental Psychology, 24,* 358–365.

Zafeiriou, D. I. (2004). Primitive reflexes and postural reactions in the neurodevelopmental examination. *Pediatric Neurology, 31,* 1–8.

Zagorsky, J. (2007). Do you have to be smart to be rich? The impact of IQ on wealth, income and financial distress. *Intelligence, 35,* 489–501.

Zahn-Waxler, C., & Polanichka, N. (2004). All things interpersonal: Socialization and female aggression. *Aggression, antisocial behavior, and violence among girls: A developmental perspective* (pp. 48–68). New York: Guilford Publications.

Zahn-Waxler, C., & Radke-Yarrow, M. (1990). The origins of empathic concern. *Motivation and Emotion, 14,* 107–130.

Zahn-Waxler, C., Klimes-Dougan, B., & Slattery, M. J. (2000). Internalizing problems of childhood and adolescence: Prospects, pitfalls, and progress in understanding the development of anxiety and depression. *Development and Psychopathology, 12, Special issue: Reflecting on the past and planning for the future of developmental psychopathology,* 443–466.

Zalenski, R., & Raspa, R. (2006). Maslow's hierarchy of needs: A framework for achieving human potential in hospice. *Journal of Palliative Medicine, 9,* 1120–1127.

Zalsman, G., Oquendo, M., Greenhill, L., Goldberg, P., Kamali, M., Martin, A., et al. (2006, October). Neurobiology of depression in children and adolescents. *Child and Adolescent Psychiatric Clinics of North America, 15,* 843–868.

Zampi, C., Fagioli, I, & Salzarulo, P. (2002). Time course of EEG background activity level before spontaneous awakening in infants. *Journal of Sleep Research, 11,* 283–287.

Zaporozhets, A. V. (1965). The development of perception in the preschool child. *Monographs of the Society for Research in Child Development, 30,* 82–101.

Zaragoza, M. S., Belli, R. F., & Payment, K. E. (2007). Misinformation effects and the suggestibility of eyewitness memory. In M. Garry & H. Hayne (Eds.), *Do justice and let the sky fall: Elizabeth Loftus and her contributions to science, law, and academic freedom.* Mahwah, NJ: Erlbaum Associates Publishers.

Zauszniewski, J. A., & Martin, M. H. (1999). Developmental task achievement and learned resourcefulness in healthy older adults. *Archives of Psychiatric Nursing, 13,* 41–47.

Zehr, M. A. (2006, February 1). Advocates note need to polish 'bilingual' pitch. *Education Week, 25,* 12.

Zeidner, M., Matthews, G., & Roberts, R. D. (2004). Emotional intelligence in the workplace: A critical review. *Applied Psychology: An International Review, 53,* 371–399.

Zelazo, P. R. (1998). McGraw and the development of unaided walking. *Developmental Review, 18,* 449–471.

Zellner, D., Loaiza, S., Gonzalez, Z., Pita, J., Morales, J., Pecora, D., et al. (2006, April). Food selection changes under stress. *Physiology & Behavior, 87,* 789–793.

Zeman, J., Cassano, M., Perry-Parrish, C., & Stegall, S. (2006, April). Emotion regulation in children and adolescents. *Journal of Developmental & Behavioral Pediatrics, 27,* 155–168.

Zernike, K., & Petersen, M. (2001, August 19). Schools' backing of behavior drugs comes under fire. *New York Times,* pp. 1, 28.

Zettergren, P. (2004). School adjustment in adolescence for previously rejected, average and popular children. *British Journal of Educational Psychology, 73,* 207–221.

Zhang, Q., & Wang, Y. (2004). Trends in the association between obesity and socioeconomic status in U.S. adults: 1971 to 2000. *Obesity Research, 12,* 1622–1632.

Zhang, Q., He, X., & Zhang, J. (2007). A comparative study on the classification of basic color terms by undergraduates from Yi nationality, Bai nationality and Naxi nationality. *Acta Psychologica Sinica, 39,* 18–26.

Zhang, Y., Proenca, R., Maffel, M., Barone, M., Leopold, L., & Friedman, J. M. (1994). Positional cloning of the mouse obese gene and its human homologue. *Nature, 372,* 425–432.

Zhe, C., & Siegler, R. S. (2000). Across the Great Divide: Bridging the gap between understanding of toddlers' and older children's thinking. *Monographs of the Society for Research in Child Development, 65,* 2, Serial No. 261.

Zhou, B. F., Stamler, J., Dennis, B., Moag-Stahlberg, A., Okuda, N., Robertson, C., Zhao, L., Chan, Q., & Elliot, P., INTERMAP Research Group. (2003). Nutrient intakes of middle-aged me and women in China, Japan, United Kingdom, and United States in the late 1990s: The INTERMAP study. *Journal of Human Hypertension, 17,* 623–630.

Zhu, J., & Weiss, L. (2005). The Wechsler Scales. In D. P. Flanagan & P. L. Harrison, (Eds.), *Contemporary intellectual assessment: Theories, tests, and issues.* New York: Guilford Press.

Zigler, E. F., & Finn-Stevenson, M. (1995). The child care crisis: Implications for the growth and development of the nation's children. *Journal of Social Issues, 51,* 215–231.

Zigler, E., & Gilman, E. (1998). The legacy of Jean Piaget. In G. A. Kimble, M. Wertheimer, et al. (Eds.), *Portraits of pioneers in psychology, Vol. 3.* Mahwah, NJ: American Psychological Association.

Zigler, E., & Styfco, S. J. (1994). Head Start: Criticism in a constructive context. *American Psychologist, 49,* 127–132.

Zimmerman, B., & Schunk, D. (2003). Albert Bandura: The scholar and his contributions to educational psychology. *Educational psychology: A century of contributions.* Mahwah, NJ: Lawrence Erlbaum Associates Publishers.

Zimmerman, F., & Christakis, D. (2007). Associations between content types of early media exposure and subsequent attentional problems. *Pediatrics, 120,* 986–992.

Zimmerman, F. J., Christakis, D. A., & Meltzoff, A. N. (2007). Associations between media viewing and language development in children under age 2 years. *The Journal of Pediatrics, 151,* 364–368.

Zipke, M. (2007). The role of metalinguistic awareness in the reading comprehension of sixth and seventh graders. *Reading Psychology, 28,* 375–396.

Zito, J. (2002). Five burning questions. *Journal of Developmental & Behavioral Pediatrics, 23,* S23–S30.

Zito, J. M., Safer, D. J., dosReis, S., Gardner, J. F., Boles, M., & Lynch, F. (2000). Trends in prescribing of psychotropic medications to preschoolers. *Journal of the American Medical Association, 283,* 1025–1030.

Ziv, M., & Frye, D. (2003). The relation between desire and false belief in children's theory of mind: No satisfaction? *Developmental Psychology, 39,* 859–876.

Zuckerman, M. (2003). Biological bases of personality. In T. Millon & M. J. Lerner (Eds.), *Handbook of psychology: Personality and Social Psychology, Vol. 5.* New York: Wiley.

Glossary

abstract modeling the process in which modeling paves the way for the development of more general rules and principles (Ch. 11)

acceleration the provision of special programs that allow gifted students to move ahead at their own pace, even if this means skipping to higher grade levels (Ch. 8)

accommodation changes in existing ways of thinking that occur in response to encounters with new stimuli or events (Ch. 5)

acculturation the changes and adjustments that occur when groups of different people come into sustained firsthand contact (Ch. 14)

achievement test a test designed to determine a person's level of knowledge in a given subject area. (Ch. 8)

achieving stage the point reached by young adults in which intelligence is applied to specific situations involving the attainment of long-term goals regarding careers, family, and societal contributions (Ch. 5)

acquisitive stage according to Schaie, the first stage of cognitive development, encompassing all of childhood and adolescence, in which the main developmental task is to acquire information (Ch. 5)

activity theory the theory suggesting that successful aging occurs when people maintain the interests, activities, and social interactions with which they were involved during middle age (Ch. 9)

acute battering incident the second stage of marital aggression in which physical abuse actually occurs (Ch. 11)

addictive drugs drugs that produce a biological or psychological dependence in users, leading to increasingly powerful cravings for them (Ch. 4)

adult day-care facility a facility in which elderly individuals receive care only during the day, but spend nights and weekends in their own homes (Ch. 13)

affordances the option that a given situation or stimulus provides (Ch. 3)

agentic professions occupations that are associated with getting things accomplished (Ch. 10)

aggression intentional injury or harm to another person (Ch. 11)

Ainsworth Strange Situation a sequence of staged episodes that illustrate the strength of attachment between a child and (typically) his or her mother (Ch. 9)

alcoholics persons with alcohol problems who have learned to depend on alcohol and are unable to control their drinking (Ch. 4)

Alzheimer's disease a progressive brain disorder that produces loss of memory and confusion (Ch. 4)

ambivalent attachment pattern a style of attachment in which children display a combination of positive and negative reactions to their mothers; they show great distress when the mother leaves, but upon her return, they may simultaneously seek close contact but also hit and kick her (Ch. 9)

amniocentesis the process of identifying genetic defects by examining a small sample of fetal cells drawn by a needle inserted into the amniotic fluid surrounding the unborn fetus (Ch. 2)

androgens male hormones (Ch. 12)

anorexia nervosa a severe eating disorder in which individuals refuse to eat (Ch. 4)

applied research research meant to provide practical solutions to immediate problems (Ch. 1)

aptitude test a test designed to predict a person's ability in a particular area or line of work (Ch. 8)

artificial insemination a process of fertilization in which a man's sperm are placed directly into a woman's vagina by a physician (Ch. 2)

assimilation the process in which people understand an experience in terms of their current stage of cognitive development and way of thinking (Ch. 5, 14)

associative play play in which two or more children interact by sharing or borrowing toys or materials, although they do not do the same thing (Ch. 13)

attachment the positive emotional bond that develops between a child and a particular individual (Ch. 9)

attention information processing involving the ability to strategically choose among and sort out different stimuli in the environment. (Ch. 6)

attention-deficit/hyperactivity disorder (ADHD) a disorder marked by inattention, impulsiveness, a low tolerance for frustration, and a great deal of inappropriate activity (Ch. 6)

auditory impairment a special need that involves the loss of hearing or some aspect of hearing (Ch. 3)

authoritarian parents parents who are controlling, punitive, rigid, and cold, and whose word is law. They value strict, unquestioning obedience from their children and do not tolerate expressions of disagreement (Ch. 11)

authoritative parents parents who are firm, setting clear and consistent limits, but who try to reason with their children, giving explanations for why they should behave in a particular way (Ch. 11)

autobiographical memory memory of particular events from one's own life (Ch. 6)

autonomous cooperation stage Piaget's stage of moral development that begins at about age 10 in which children become fully aware that formal game rules can be modified if the people who play them agree (Ch. 11)

autonomy the development and expression of independence (Ch. 13)

autonomy-versus-shame-and-doubt stage the period during which, according to Erikson, toddlers (aged 18 months to 3 years) develop independence and autonomy if they are allowed the freedom to explore, or shame and self-doubt if they are restricted and overprotected (Ch. 9)

avoidant attachment pattern a style of attachment in which children do not seek proximity to the mother; after the mother has left, they seem to avoid her when she returns, as if angered by her behavior (Ch. 9)

babbling making speechlike but meaningless sounds (Ch. 7)

Bayley Scales of Infant Development a measure that evaluates an infant's development from 2 to 42 months (Ch. 8)

behavior modification a formal technique for promoting the frequency of desirable behaviors and decreasing the incidence of unwanted ones (Ch. 1)

behavioral genetics the study of the effects of heredity on behavior (Ch. 2)

behavioral perspective the approach that suggests that the keys to understanding development are observable behavior and outside stimuli in the environment (Ch. 1)

bereavement acknowledgment of the objective fact that one has experienced a death (Ch. 15)

bioecological approach the perspective suggesting that different levels of the environment simultaneously influence individuals (Ch. 1)

blended families a family consisting of remarried couples with at least one stepchild living with them (Ch. 13)

body-transcendence-versus-body-preoccupation a period in which people must learn to cope with and move beyond changes in physical capabilities as a result of aging (Ch. 9)

boomerang children young adults who return, after leaving home for some period, to live in the homes of their middle-aged parents (Ch. 13)

brain death a diagnosis of death based on the cessation of all signs of brain activity, as measured by electrical brain waves (Ch. 15)

Brazelton Neonatal Behavioral Assessment Scale (NBAS) a measure designed to determine infants' neurological and behavioral responses to their environment (Ch. 3)

bulimia an eating disorder characterized by binges on large quantities of food, followed by purges of the food through vomiting or the use of laxatives (Ch. 4)

burnout a situation that occurs when workers experience dissatisfaction, disillusionment, frustration, and weariness from their jobs (Ch. 10)

career consolidation a stage that is entered between the ages of 20 and 40, when young adults become centered on their careers (Ch. 10)

case studies studies that involve extensive, in-depth interviews with a particular individual or small group of individuals (Ch. 1)

centration the process of concentrating on one limited aspect of a stimulus and ignoring other aspects (Ch. 5)

cerebral cortex the upper layer of the brain (Ch. 3)

Cesarean delivery a birth in which the baby is surgically removed from the uterus, rather than traveling through the birth canal (sometimes known as a *c-section*) (Ch. 2)

chorionic villus sampling (CVS) a test used to find genetic defects that involves taking samples of hairlike material that surrounds the embryo (Ch. 2)

chromosomes rod-shaped portions of DNA that are organized in 23 pairs (Ch. 2)

classical conditioning   a type of learning in which an organism responds to a neutral stimulus that normally does not bring about that type of response (Ch. 1)

cliques (pronounced "kleeks")   groups of 2 to 12 people whose members have frequent social interactions with one another (Ch. 13)

cognitive development   development involving the ways that growth and change in intellectual capabilities influence a person's behavior (Ch. 1)

cognitive neuroscience approaches   approaches that examin cognitive development through the lens of brain processes (Ch. 1)

cognitive perspective   the approach that focuses on the processes that allow people to know, understand, and think about the world (Ch. 1)

cohabitation   couples living together without being married (Ch. 12)

cohort   a group of people born at around the same time in the same place (Ch. 1)

collectivistic orientation   a philosophy that promotes the notion of interdependence (Ch. 10)

communal professions   occupations that are associated with relationships (Ch. 10)

companionate love   the strong affection for those with whom our lives are deeply involved (Ch. 12)

conservation   the knowledge that quantity is unrelated to the arrangement and physical appearance of objects (Ch. 5)

constructive play   play in which children manipulate objects to produce or build something (Ch. 13)

contextual perspective   the theory that considers the relationship between individuals and their physical, cognitive, personality, and social worlds (Ch. 1)

continuing-care community   a community that offers an environment in which all the residents are of retirement age or older and need various levels of care (Ch. 13)

continuity theory   the theory suggesting that people need to maintain their desired level of involvement in society in order to maximize their sense of well-being and self-esteem (Ch. 9)

controversial adolescents   adolescents who are liked by some and disliked by others (Ch. 13)

conventional morality   Kohlberg's second level of moral reasoning in which people approach moral problems as members of society (Ch. 11)

cooperative play   play in which children genuinely interact with one another, taking turns, playing games, or devising contests (Ch. 13)

corpus callosum,   the bundle of nerves that connects the hemispheres of the brain (Ch. 12)

correlational research   research that seeks to identify whether an association or relationship between two factors exists (Ch. 1)

critical period   a specific time during development when a particular event has its greatest consequences and the presence of certain kinds of environmental stimuli is necessary for development to proceed normally (Ch. 1)

critical thinking   thinking that makes use of cognitive skills and strategies that increase the likelihood of solving problems, forming inferences, and making decisions appropriately and successfully (Ch. 6)

cross-modal transference   the ability to identify, using another sense, a stimulus that has previously been experienced only through one sense (Ch. 8)

cross-sectional research   research in which people of different ages are compared at the same point in time (Ch. 1)

crowds   in contrast to cliques, crowds are larger and looser groups, comprising individuals who share particular characteristics but who may not interact with one another (Ch. 13)

crystallized intelligence   the store of information, skills, and strategies that people have acquired through education and prior experiences and through their previous use of fluid intelligence (Ch. 8)

cycle of violence hypothesis   the theory that the abuse and neglect that children suffer predispose them as adults to abuse and neglect their own children (Ch. 11)

decision/commitment component   the third aspect of love that embodies both the initial cognition that one loves another person and the longer-term determination to maintain that love (Ch. 12)

defensive coping   unconscious strategies that distort or deny the true nature of a situation (Ch. 4)

deferred imitation   an act in which a person who is no longer present is imitated by children who have witnessed a similar act (Ch. 5)

dementia   the most common mental disorder of the elderly, it covers several diseases, each of which includes serious memory loss accompanied by declines in other mental functioning (Ch. 4)

dependent variable   the variable that researchers measure in an experiment and expect to change as a result of the experimental manipulation (Ch. 1)

developmental quotient   an overall developmental score that relates to performance in four domains: motor skills, language use, adaptive behavior, and personal and social skills (Ch. 8)

difficult babies   babies who have negative moods and are slow to adapt to new situations; when confronted with a new situation, they tend to withdraw (Ch. 9)

discontinuous change   development that occurs in distinct steps or stages, with each stage bringing about behavior that is assumed to be qualitatively different from behavior at earlier stages (Ch. 1)

discrimination   the negative (or sometimes positive) actions taken toward members of a particular group because of their membership in the group (Ch. 14)

disengagement theory   the period in late adulthood that marks a gradual withdrawal from the world on physical, psychological, and social levels (Ch. 9)

disorganized-disoriented attachment pattern   a style of attachment in which children show inconsistent, often contradictory behavior, such as approaching the mother when she returns but not looking at her (Ch. 9)

dizygotic twins   twins who are produced when two separate ova are fertilized by two separate sperm at roughly the same time (Ch. 2)

DNA (deoxyribonucleic acid) molecules   the substance that genes are composed of that determines the nature of every cell in the body and how it will function (Ch. 2)

dominance hierarchy   rankings that represent the relative social power of those in a group (Ch. 13)

dominant trait   the one trait that is expressed when two competing traits are present (Ch. 2)

double standard   the standard in which premarital sex is considered permissible for males but not for females (Ch. 12)

Down syndrome   a disorder produced by the presence of an extra chromosome on the 21st pair; once referred to as mongolism (Ch. 2, 8)

easy babies   babies who have a positive disposition; their body functions operate regularly, and they are adaptable (Ch. 9)

egocentric thought   thinking that does not take into account the viewpoints of others (Ch. 5)

ego-integrity-versus-despair stage   Erikson's final stage of life, characterized by a process of looking back over one's life, evaluating it, and coming to terms with it (Ch. 9)

ego transcendence versus ego preoccupation   the period in which elderly people must come to grips with their coming death (Ch. 9, 18)

elder abuse   the physical or psychological mistreatment or neglect of elderly individuals (Ch. 11)

embryonic stage   the period from 2 to 8 weeks following fertilization during which significant growth occurs in the major organs and body systems (Ch. 2)

emotional intelligence   the set of skills that underlies the accurate assessment, evaluation, expression, and regulation of emotions (Ch. 8)

emotional self-regulation   the capability to adjust one's emotions to a desired state and level of intensity (Ch. 9, 11)

empathy   the understanding of what another individual feels (Ch. 11)

empty nest syndrome   the experience that relates to parents' feelings of unhappiness, worry, loneliness, and depression resulting from their children's departure from home (Ch. 13)

enrichment   an approach whereby gifted students are kept at grade level but are enrolled in special programs and given individual activities to allow greater depth of study (Ch. 8)

episiotomy   an incision sometimes made to increase the size of the opening of the vagina to allow the baby to pass (Ch. 2)

Erikson's theory of psychosocial development   the theory that considers how individuals come to understand themselves and the meaning of others'—and their own—behavior (Ch. 9)

ethnic identity   how members of ethnic, racial, and cultural minorities view themselves, both as members of their own group and in terms of their relationships with other groups (Ch. 14)

euthanasia   the practice of assisting people who are terminally ill to die more quickly (Ch. 15)

evolutionary perspective   the theory that seeks to identify behavior that is a result of our genetic inheritance from our ancestors (Ch. 1)

executive stage   the period in middle adulthood when people take a broader perspective than earlier, including concerns about the world (Ch. 5)

experiment   a process in which an investigator, called an experimenter, devises two different experiences for subjects or participants (Ch. 1)

experimental research   research designed to discover causal relationships between various factors (Ch. 1)

extrinsic motivation   motivation that drives people to obtain tangible rewards, such as money and prestige (Ch. 10)

fantasy period   according to Ginzberg, the period, lasting until about age 11, when career choices are made, and discarded, without regard to skills, abilities, or available job opportunities (Ch. 10)

fast mapping   the process in which new words are associated with their meaning after a only brief encounter (Ch. 7)

female climacteric   the period that marks the transition from being able to bear children to being unable to do so (Ch. 4)

fertilization   the process by which a sperm and an ovum—the male and female gametes, respectively—join to form a single new cell (Ch. 2)

fetal alcohol effects (FAE)   a condition in which children display some, though not all, of the problems of fetal alcohol syndrome due to the mother's consumption of alcohol during pregnancy (Ch. 2)

fetal alcohol syndrome (FAS)   a disorder caused by the pregnant mother consuming substantial quantities of alcohol during pregnancy, potentially resulting in mental retardation and delayed growth in the child (Ch. 2)

fetal monitor   a device that measures the baby's heartbeat during labor (Ch. 2)

fetal stage   the stage that begins at about 8 weeks after conception and continues until birth (Ch. 2)

fetus   a developing child, from 8 weeks after conception until birth (Ch. 2)

field study   a research investigation carried out in a naturally occurring setting (Ch. 1)

fluid intelligence   is intelligence that reflects information processing capabilities, reasoning, and memory (Ch. 8)

fragile X syndrome   a disorder produced by injury to a gene on the X chromosome, producing mild to moderate mental retardation (Ch. 2)

full inclusion   the integration of all students, even those with the most severe disabilities, into regular classes and all other aspects of school and community life (Ch. 8)

functional death   the absence of a heartbeat and breathing (Ch. 15)

functional play   play that involves simple, repetitive activities typical of 3-year-olds (Ch. 13)

gender   the sense of being male or female (Ch. 12)

gender constancy   the belief that people are permanently males or females, depending on fixed, unchangeable biological factors (Ch. 12)

gender identity   the perception of oneself as male or female (Ch. 12)

gender schema   a cognitive framework that organizes information relevant to gender (Ch. 12)

generalized slowing hypothesis   the theory that processing in all parts of the nervous system, including the brain, is less efficient (Ch. 3)

generation gap   a divide between adolescence and other periods of life that supposedly reflects profound differences in behavior, values, attitudes, lifestyle choices, and experiences (Ch. 13)

generativity-versus-stagnation stage   according to Erikson, the stage during middle adulthood in which people consider their contributions to family and society (Ch. 9)

genes   the basic unit of genetic information (Ch. 2)

genetic counseling   the discipline that focuses on helping people deal with issues relating to inherited disorders (Ch. 2)

genotype   the underlying combination of genetic material present (but not outwardly visible) in an organism (Ch. 2)

germinal stage   the first—and shortest—stage of the prenatal period, which takes place during the first 2 weeks following conception (Ch. 2)

gerontologists   specialists who study aging (Ch. 3)

glaucoma   a condition in which pressure in the fluid of the eye increases, either because the fluid cannot drain properly or because too much fluid is produced (Ch. 3)

goal-directed behavior   behavior in which several schemes are combined and coordinated to generate a single act to solve a problem (Ch. 5)

goodness of fit   the notion that development is dependent on the degree of match between children's temperament and the nature and demands of the environment in which they are being raised (Ch. 9)

grammar   the system of rules that determine how our thoughts can be expressed (Ch. 7)

grief   the emotional response to one's loss (Ch. 15)

handedness   the preference of using one hand over the other (Ch. 3)

hardiness   a personality characteristic associated with a lower rate of stress-related illness (Ch. 4)

heteronomous morality   the earliest stage in Piaget's theory of moral development in which rules are seen as invariant and unchangeable (Ch. 11)

heterozygous   inheriting from parents different forms of a gene for a given trait (Ch. 2)

holophrases   one-word utterances that depend on the particular context in which they are used to determine meaning (Ch. 7)

home care   an alternative to hospitalization in which dying people stay in their homes and receive treatment from their families and visiting medical staff (Ch. 15)

homogamy   the tendency to marry someone who is similar in age, race, education, religion, and other basic demographic characteristics (Ch. 12)

homozygous   inheriting from parents similar genes for a given trait (Ch. 2)

hospice care   care provided for the dying in institutions devoted to those who are terminally ill (Ch. 15)

humanistic perspective   the theory that contends that people have a natural capacity to make decisions about their lives and control their behavior (Ch. 1)

hypothesis   a prediction stated in a way that permits it to be tested (Ch. 1)

identity achievement   the status of adolescents who commit to a particular identity following a period of crisis during which they consider various alternatives (Ch. 10)

identity diffusion   the status of adolescents who consider various identity alternatives, but never commit to one or never even consider identity options in any conscious way (Ch. 10)

identity foreclosure   the status of adolescents who prematurely commit to an identity without adequately exploring alternatives (Ch. 10)

identity-versus-identity-confusion stage   the period during which teenagers seek to determine what is unique and distinctive about themselves (Ch. 9)

immanent justice   the notion that rules that are broken earn immediate punishment (Ch. 11)

in vitro fertilization (IVF)   a procedure in which a woman's ova are removed from her ovaries, and a man's sperm are used to fertilize the ova in a laboratory (Ch. 2)

incipient cooperation stage   Piaget's stage of moral development that lasts from around age 7 to 10 in which children learn the actual formal rules of games and they play according to this shared knowledge (Ch. 11)

independent variable   the variable that researchers manipulate in an experiment (Ch. 1)

individualistic orientation   a philosophy that emphasizes personal identity and the uniqueness of the individual (Ch. 10)

industry-versus-inferiority stage   the period from age 6 to 12 characterized by a focus on efforts to attain competence in meeting the challenges presented by parents, peers, school, and the other complexities of the modern world (Ch. 9)

infant mortality   death within the first year of life (Ch. 2)

infant-directed speech   a type of speech directed toward infants that is characterized by short, simple sentences (Ch. 7)

infantile amnesia   the lack of memory for experiences that occurred prior to 3 years of age (Ch. 6)

infertility   the inability to conceive after 12 to 18 months of trying to become pregnant (Ch. 2)

information processing approaches   models that seek to identify the ways individuals take in, use, and store information (Ch. 1, 6)

initiative-versus-guilt stage   according to Erikson, the period during which children aged 3 to 6 years experience conflict between independence of action and the sometimes negative results of that action (Ch. 9)

institutionalism   a psychological state in which people in nursing homes develop apathy, indifference, and a lack of caring about themselves (Ch. 13)

instrumental aggression   aggression motivated by the desire to obtain a concrete goal, such as playing with a desirable toy that another child is playing with (Ch. 11)

integration   the process in which people maintain their own culture while simultaneously seeking to adapt and incorporate the majority culture (Ch. 14)

intelligence   the capacity to understand the world, think with rationality, and use resources effectively when faced with challenges (Ch. 8)

intelligence quotient, or **IQ**   a score that takes into account a student's mental and chronological age (Ch. 8)

intimacy component   the component of love that encompasses feelings of closeness, affection, and connectedness (Ch. 12)

intimacy-versus-isolation stage   according to Erikson, the period of postadolescence into the early 30s that focuses on developing close relationships with others (Ch. 9, 12)

intrinsic motivation   motivation that causes people to work for their own enjoyment, not for the rewards work may bring (Ch. 10)

intuitive thought   thinking that reflects preschoolers' use of primitive reasoning and their avid acquisition of knowledge about the world (Ch. 5)

Kaufman Assessment Battery for Children (KABC-II)   a children's intelligence test permitting unusual flexibility in its administration (Ch. 8)

Klinefelter's syndrome   a disorder resulting from the presence of an extra X chromosome that produces underdeveloped genitals, extreme height, and enlarged breasts (Ch. 2)

labeling theory of passionate love   the theory that individuals experience romantic love when two events occur together: intense physiological arousal and situational cues suggesting that the arousal is due to love (Ch. 12)

laboratory study   a research investigation conducted in a controlled setting explicitly designed to hold events constant (Ch. 1)

language   the systematic, meaningful arrangement of symbols, which provides the basis for communication (Ch. 7)

language-acquisition device (LAD)   a neural system of the brain hypothesized to permit understanding of language structure and provide strategies for learning the particular characteristics of a language (Ch. 7)

lateralization   the process in which certain cognitive functions are located more in one hemisphere of the brain than in the other (Ch. 3)

learning disabilities   difficulties in the acquisition and use of listening, speaking, reading, writing, reasoning, or mathematical abilities (Ch. 8)

learning theory approach   the theory that language acquisition follows the basic laws of reinforcement and conditioning (Ch. 7)

least restrictive environment   the setting most similar to that of children without special needs (Ch. 8)

lifespan development   is the field of study that examines patterns of growth, change, and stability in behavior that occurs throughout the entire life span (Ch. 1)

linguistic-relativity hypothesis   the theory that language shapes and may determine the way people of a given culture perceive and understand the world (Ch. 7)

living wills   legal documents designating what medical treatments people want or do not want if they cannot express their wishes (Ch. 15)

longitudinal research   research in which the behavior of one or more participants in a study is measured as they age (Ch. 1)

long-term memory   the memory component in which information is stored on a relatively permanent basis (Ch. 6)

loving contrition stage   the third stage of marital aggression, which occurs in some but not all cases, in which the batterer feels remorse and apologizes for his actions (Ch. 11)

low-birthweight infants   infants who weigh less than 2,500 grams (around 5 1/2 pounds) at birth (Ch. 2)

mainstreaming   an educational approach in which exceptional children are integrated as much as possible into the traditional educational system and are provided with a broad range of educational alternatives (Ch. 8)

male climacteric   the period of physical and psychological change relating to the male reproductive system that occurs during late middle age (Ch. 4)

marginalization   the process that occurs when people identify neither with their minority culture nor with the majority culture (Ch. 14)

marriage gradient   the tendency for men to marry women who are slightly younger, smaller, and lower in status, and women to marry men who are slightly older, larger, and higher in status (Ch. 12)

masturbation   sexual self-stimulation (Ch. 12)

maturation   the predetermined unfolding of genetic information (Ch. 1)

menarche   the onset of menstruation (Ch. 3)

menopause   the cessation of menstruation (Ch. 4)

mental representation   an internal image of a past event or object (Ch. 5)

mental retardation (or intellectual disability)   a state characterized by significant limitations in intellectual functioning and in adaptive behavior involving conceptual, social, and practical skills (Ch. 8)

metalinguistic awareness   an understanding of one's own use of language (Ch. 7)

metamemory   an understanding about the processes that underlie memory, which emerges and improves during middle childhood (Ch. 6)

midlife crisis   a stage of uncertainty and indecision brought about by the realization that life is finite (Ch. 9)

mild retardation   retardation with IQ scores in the range of 50 or 55 to 70 (Ch. 8)

mnemonics   formal strategies for organizing material in ways that make it more likely to be remembered (Ch. 6)

moderate retardation   retardation with IQ scores from around 35 or 40 to 50 or 55 (Ch. 8)

monozygotic twins   twins who are genetically identical (Ch. 2)

moral development   the changes in people's sense of justice and of what is right and wrong, and in their behavior related to moral issues (Ch. 11)

moratorium   the status of adolescents who may have explored various identity alternatives to some degree, but have not yet committed themselves (Ch. 10)

multifactorial transmission   the determination of traits by a combination of both genetic and environmental factors in which a genotype provides a range within which a phenotype may be expressed (Ch. 2)

multimodal approach to perception   the approach that considers how information that is collected by various individual sensory systems is integrated and coordinated (Ch. 3)

myelin   protective insulation that surrounds parts of neurons, increasing the speed of transmission of electrical impulses along brain cells (Ch. 3)

nativist approach   the theory that a genetically determined, innate mechanism directs the development of language (Ch. 7)

naturalistic observation   a type of correlational study in which some naturally occurring behavior is observed without intervention in the situation (Ch. 1)

neglect   a form of child abuse (Ch. 11)

neglected adolescents   adolescents who are neither liked nor disliked (Ch. 13)

nonorganic failure to thrive   a disorder in which infants stop growing due to a lack of stimulation and attention as the result of inadequate parenting (Ch. 4)

norms   the average performance of a large sample of children of a given age (Ch. 3)

obesity   weight greater than 20 percent above average for a given age ans height (Ch. 4)

object permanence   the realization that people and objects exist even when they cannot be seen (Ch. 5)

onlooker play   action in which children simply watch others at play but do not actually participate themselves (Ch. 13)

operant conditioning   a form of learning in which a voluntary response is strengthened or weakened by its association with positive or negative consequences (Ch. 1)

operations   organized, formal, logical mental processes (Ch. 5)

osteoporosis   a condition in which the bones become brittle, fragile, and thin, often brought about by a lack of calcium in the diet (Ch. 3, 4)

parallel play   action in which children play with similar toys, in a similar manner, but do not interact with each other (Ch. 13)

passion component   the component of love that comprises the motivational drives relating to sex, physical closeness, and romance (Ch. 12)

passionate (or romantic) love   a state of powerful absorption in someone (Ch. 12)

peers   individuals who are about the same age or level of maturity (Ch. 13)

perception   the sorting out, interpretation, analysis, and integration of stimuli involving the sense organs and brain (Ch. 3)

peripheral slowing hypothesis   the theory that suggests that overall processing speed declines in the peripheral nervous system with increasing age (Ch. 3)

permissive parents   parents who provide lax and inconsistent feedback and require little of their children (Ch. 11)

permissiveness with affection   the standard in which premarital intercourse is viewed as permissible for both men and women if it occurs in the context of a long-term, committed, or loving relationship (Ch. 12)

personality development   development involving the ways that the enduring characteristics that differentiate one person from another change over the life span (Ch. 1)

personality the sum total of the enduring characteristics that differentiate one individual from another (Ch. 9)

phenotype an observable trait; the trait that actually is seen (Ch. 2)

physical development development involving the body's physical makeup, including the brain, nervous system, muscles, and senses, and the need for food, drink, and sleep (Ch. 1)

placenta a conduit between the mother and fetus, providing nourishment and oxygen via the umbilical cord (Ch. 2)

planning the ability to allocate attentional resources on the basis of goals that one wishes to achieve (Ch. 6)

plasticity the degree to which a developing structure or behavior is modifiable due to experience (Ch. 3)

polygenic inheritance inheritance in which a combination of multiple gene pairs is responsible for the production of a particular trait (Ch. 2)

postconventional morality Kohlberg's third level of moral reasoning in which people use moral principles that are seen as broader than those of any particular society (Ch. 11)

postformal thought thinking that acknowledges that adult predicaments must sometimes be solved in relativistic terms (Ch. 5)

postmature infants infants still unborn 2 weeks after the mother's due date (Ch. 2)

practical intelligence according to Sternberg, intelligence that is learned primarily by observing others and modeling their behavior (Ch. 8)

pragmatics the aspect of language relating to communicating effectively and appropriately with others (Ch. 7)

preconventional morality Kohlberg's first level of moral reasoning in which the concrete interests of the individual are considered in terms of rewards and punishments (Ch. 11)

prejudice the negative (or positive) evaluations of judgments of members of a group that are based primarily on group membership (Ch. 14)

prelinguistic communication communication through sounds, facial expressions, gestures, imitation, and other nonlinguistic means (Ch. 7)

preoperational stage according to Piaget, the stage from approximately age 2 to age 7 in which children's use of symbolic thinking grows, mental reasoning emerges, and the use of concepts increases (Ch. 5)

presbycusis loss of the ability to hear sounds of high frequency (Ch. 3)

presbyopia a nearly universal change in eyesight during middle adulthood that results in some loss of near vision (Ch. 3)

preterm infants infants who are born prior to 38 weeks after conception (also known as premature infants) (Ch. 2)

primary aging aging that involves universal and irreversible changes that, due to genetic programming, occur as people get older (Ch. 3)

primary appraisal an individual's assessment of an event to determine whether its implications are positive, negative or neutral (Ch. 4)

primary sex characteristics characteristics associated with the development of the organs and structures of the body that directly relate to reproduction (Ch. 3)

private speech spoken language that is not intended for others, commonly used by children during the preschool years (Ch. 7)

profound retardation retardation with IQ scores below 20 or 25 (Ch. 12)

prosocial behavior helping behavior that benefits others (Ch. 11)

psychoanalytic theory the theory proposed by Freud suggesting that unconscious forces act to determine personality and behavior (Ch. 1)

psychodynamic perspective the approach that states behavior is motivated by inner forces, memories, and conflicts that are generally beyond people's awareness and control (Ch. 1)

psychoneuroimmunology (PNI) the study of the relationship among the brain, the immune system, and psychological factors (Ch. 4)

psychophysiological methods approaches that focus on the relationship between physiological processes and behavior (Ch. 1)

psychosexual development according to Freud, a series of stages that children pass through in which pleasure, or gratification, is focused on a particular biological function and body part (Ch. 1)

psychosocial development the approach that encompasses changes in our interactions with and understanding of one another, as well as in our knowledge and understanding of ourselves as members of society (Ch. 1)

psychosomatic disorders medical problems caused by the interaction of psychological, emotional, and physical difficulties (Ch. 4)

puberty the period of maturation during which the sexual organs mature (Ch. 3)

race dissonance the phenomenon in which minority children indicate preferences for majority values or people (Ch. 10)

rapid eye movement, or REM, sleep the period of sleep that is found in older children and adults and is associated with dreaming (Ch. 3)

realistic period the third stage of Ginzberg's theory, which occurs in early adulthood, when people begin to explore specific career options, either through actual experience on the job or through training for a profession, and then narrow their choices and make a commitment (Ch. 10)

recessive trait a trait within an organism that is present, but is not expressed (Ch. 2)

redefinition of self-versus-preoccupation-with-work-role the theory that those in old age must redefine themselves in ways that do not relate to their work roles or occupations (Ch. 9)

reference groups groups of people with whom one compares oneself (Ch. 10)

reflexes unlearned, organized involuntary responses that occur automatically in the presence of certain stimuli (Ch. 3)

reintegrative stage the period of late adulthood during which the focus is on tasks that have personal meaning (Ch. 5)

rejected adolescents adolescents who are uniformly disliked (Ch. 13)

relational aggression nonphysical aggression that is intended to hurt another person's feelings (Ch. 11)

reliability a quality of tests that measure consistently what they are trying to measure (Ch. 8)

responsible stage the stage where the major concerns of middle-aged adults relate to their personal situations, including protecting and nourishing their spouses, families, and careers (Ch. 5)

rhythms repetitive, cyclical patterns of behavior (Ch. 3)

sample the group of participants chosen for the experiment (Ch. 1)

sandwich generation couples who in middle adulthood must fulfill the needs of both their children and their aging parents (Ch. 13)

scaffolding the support for learning and problem solving that encourages independence and growth (Ch. 5)

scheme an organized pattern of sensorimotor functioning (Ch. 5)

scientific method the process of posing and answering questions using careful, controlled techniques that include systematic, orderly observation and the collection of data (Ch. 1)

scripts general representations in memory of a sequence or series of events (Ch. 6)

secondary aging changes in physical and cognitive functioning that are due to illness, health habits, and other individual differences, but that are not due to increased age itself and are not inevitable (Ch. 3)

secondary appraisal a person's answer to the question, "Can I handle it?," an assessment of whether the coping abilities and resources on hand are adequate (Ch. 4)

secondary sex characteristics the visible signs of sexual maturity that do not directly involve the sex organs (Ch. 3)

secure attachment pattern a style of attachment in which children use the mother as a kind of home base and are at ease when she is present; when she leaves, they become upset, and they go to her as soon as she returns (Ch. 9)

self-awareness knowledge of oneself (Ch. 10)

self-concept a person's identity, or set of beliefs about what one is like as an individual (Ch. 10)

self-esteem an individual's overall and specific positive and negative self-evaluation (Ch. 10)

senescence the natural physical decline brought about by increasing age (Ch. 3)

sensation the physical stimulation of the sense organs (Ch. 3)

sensitive period a point in development when organisms are particularly susceptible to certain kinds of stimuli in their environments, but the absence of those stimuli does not always produce irreversible consequences (Ch. 1, 3)

sensorimotor stage (of cognitive development) Piaget's initial major stage of cognitive development, which can be broken down into six substages (Ch. 5)

sensory store the initial, momentary storage of information, lasting only an instant (Ch. 6)

separation the process in which people identify with the ethnic minority culture to which they belong while rejecting or rebuffing the majority culture (Ch. 14)

separation anxiety the distress displayed by infants when a customary care provider departs (Ch. 9)

sequential studies research in which researchers examine a number of different age groups over several points in time (Ch. 1)

severe retardation retardation with IQ scores that range from around 20 or 25 to 35 or 40 (Ch. 8)

sex typically refers to sexual anatomy and sexual behavior (Ch. 12)

sex cleavage sex segregation in which boys interact primarily with boys and girls primarily with girls (Ch. 13)

sexually transmitted disease (STD) a disease that is spread through sexual contact (Ch. 4)

sexually transmitted infection (STI) a disease that is spread through sexual contact (Ch. 4)

short-term memory the short-duration, limited-capacity memory component in which selected input from the memory store is worked on (Ch. 6)

sickle-cell anemia a blood disorder that gets its name from the shape of the red blood cells in those who have it (Ch. 2)

skilled-nursing facilities facilities that provide full-time nursing care for people who have chronic illnesses or are recovering from a temporary medical condition (Ch. 13)

slow-to-warm babies babies who are inactive, showing relatively calm reactions to their environment; their moods are generally negative, and they withdraw from new situations, adapting slowly (Ch. 9)

small-for-gestational-age infants infants who, because of delayed fetal growth, weigh 90 percent (or less) of the average weight of infants of the same gestational age (Ch. 2)

social clock the culturally determined psychological timepiece providing a sense of whether we have reached the major benchmarks of life at the appropriate time in comparison to our peers (Ch. 10)

social-cognitive learning theory learning by observing the behavior of another person, called a model (Ch. 1)

social comparison the desire to evaluate one's own behavior, abilities, expertise, and opinions by comparing them to those of others (Ch. 10)

social development the way in which individuals' interactions with others and their social relationships grow, change, and remain stable over the course of life (Ch. 1)

social domain approach the concept that moral reasoning needs to be considered in the context in which judgments are being made at a given time (Ch. 11)

social identity theory the theory that adolescents use group membership as a source of pride and self-worth (Ch. 14)

social learning view the theory that suggests people develop prejudice and stereotypes about members of various groups in the same way they learn other attitudes, beliefs, and values (Ch. 14)

social referencing the intentional search for information about others' feelings to help make sense of uncertain circumstances and events (Ch. 9)

social speech speech directed toward another person and meant to be understood by that person (Ch. 7)

social support assistance and comfort supplied by a network of caring, interested people. Such support plays a critical role in successful aging (Ch. 13)

social-cognitive learning theory learning by observing the behavior of another person, called a model (Ch. 1)

sociocultural theory the approach that emphasizes how cognitive development proceeds as a result of social interactions between members of a culture (Ch. 1)

speech impairment speech that deviates so much from the speech of others that it calls attention to itself, interferes with communication, or produces maladjustment in the speaker (Ch. 3)

Stanford-Binet Intelligence Scale A test that consists of a series of items that vary according to the age of the person being tested (Ch. 8)

state degree of awareness an infant displays to both internal and external stimulation (Ch. 3)

status the evaluation of a role or person by other relevant members of a group or society (Ch. 10)

stereotype a set of beliefs and expectations about members of a group that is held simply because of their membership in the group (Ch. 14)

stillbirth the delivery of a child who is not alive, occurring in less than 1 delivery in 100 (Ch. 2)

stranger anxiety the caution and wariness displayed by infants when encountering an unfamiliar person (Ch. 9)

stuttering substantial disruption in the rhythm and fluency of speech; the most common speech impairment (Ch. 3)

sudden infant death syndrome (SIDS) a disorder in which seemingly healthy infants die in their sleep (Ch. 4, 15)

survey research a type of study in which a group of people chosen to represent some larger population are asked questions about their attitudes, behavior, or thinking on a given topic (Ch. 1)

symbolic function the ability to use a mental symbol, a word, or an object to stand for or represent something that is not physically present. (Ch. 5)

synaptic pruning the elimination of neurons as the result of nonuse or lack of stimulation (Ch. 3)

syntax the combining of words and phrases to form sentences (Ch. 7)

Tay-Sachs disease a disorder that produces blindness and muscle degeneration prior to death; there is no treatment (Ch. 2)

telegraphic speech speech in which words not critical to the message are left out (Ch. 7)

temperament patterns of arousal and emotionality that represent consistent and enduring characteristics of an individual (Ch. 2, 9)

tension building the first stage of marital aggression in which a batterer becomes upset and shows dissatisfaction initially through verbal abuse (Ch. 11)

teratogen an environmental agent such as a drug, chemical, virus, or other factor that produces a birth defect (Ch. 2)

thanatologists people who study death and dying (Ch. 15)

theoretical research research designed specifically to test some developmental explanation and expand scientific knowledge (Ch. 1)

theories explanations and predictions concerning phenomena of interest, providing a framework for understanding the relationships among an organized set of facts or principles (Ch. 1)

theories broad explanations and predictions about phenomena of interest (Ch. 1)

traits enduring dimensions of personality characteristics along which people differ (Ch. 9)

transformation the process in which one state is changed into another (Ch. 5)

triarchic theory of intelligence the belief that intelligence consists of three aspects of information processing: the componential element, the experiential element, and the contextual element (Ch. 8)

trust-versus-mistrust stage according to Erikson, the period during which infants develop a sense of trust or mistrust, largely depending on how well their needs are met by their caregivers (Ch. 9)

Type A behavior pattern behavior characterized by competitiveness, impatience, and a tendency toward frustration and hostility (Ch. 4)

Type B behavior pattern behavior characterized by noncompetitiveness, patience, and a lack of aggression (Ch. 4)

ultrasound sonography a process in which high-frequency sound waves scan the mother's womb to produce an image of the unborn baby, whose size and shape can then be assessed (Ch. 2)

uninvolved parents parents who show almost no interest in their children and indifferent, rejecting behavior (Ch. 11)

universal grammar a similar underlying structure shared by all the world's languages, according to linguist Noam Chomsky (Ch. 7)

validity a quality of tests that actually measure what they are supposed to measure (Ch. 8)

values the qualities people see as most desirable and important, affecting people's thinking and behavior (Ch. 11)

very-low-birthweight infants infants who weigh less than 1,250 grams (around 2.25 pounds) or, regardless of weight, have been in the womb less than 30 weeks (Ch. 2)

visual impairment a special need that involves significant loss of sight (Ch. 3)

Wechsler Adult Intelligence Scale-IV (WAIS-IV) A test for adults that provides separate measures of verbal and performance (nonverbal) skills, as well as a total score (Ch. 8)

Wechsler Intelligence Scale for Children-IV (WISC-IV) A test for children that provides separate measures of verbal and performance (nonverbal) skills, as well as a total score (Ch. 8)

working memory a set of temporary memory stores that actively manipulate and rehearse information. (Ch. 6)

X-linked genes genes that are considered recessive and located only on the X chromosome (Ch. 2)

zone of proximal development or ZPD according to Vygotsky, the level at which a child can *almost*, but not fully, perform a task independently, but can do so with the assistance of someone more competent (Ch. 5)

zygote the new cell formed by the process of fertilization (Ch. 2)

Photographs

COVER © Roy Morsch / CORBIS All Rights Reserved; Baby Laughing, Larry William/Corbis Edge/Corbis; Cube, Scherbet/Shutterstock Images; Teenage Friends; Smiling, Jose Luis Pelaez, Inc./Blend Images/Corbis; Happy Middle Aged Couple, Laura Doss/Fancy/Corbis.

Chapter 1 Page 2 Hank Morgan\Photo Researchers, Inc.; page 3 \AP Wide World Photos; page 7 Christiana Dittmann\Rainbow Image Library; page 11 CORBIS- NY; page 13 Courtesy of the Library of Congress; page 14 Getty Images Inc. - Hulton Archive Photos; page 15 Monty Brinton/CBS Photo\Getty Images Inc. - Hulton Archive Photos; page 16 Figure courtesy of Eric Courchesne, Director of the Autism Center of Excellence, Department of Neurosciences, UCSD; page 19 Laura Dwight\Stock Connection; page 20 © Nina Leen/Time Life Pictures/Getty Images; page 23 Bob Daemmrich\PhotoEdit Inc.; page 25 Courtesy of G. Dehaene-Lamberts INSERM/CEA; page 28 Elizabeth Crews\Elizabeth Crews Photography.

Chapter 2 Page 34 Photo Lennart Nilsson/Bonnier Alba AB, A CHILD IS BORN, Dell Publishing Company; page 35 Robert Brenner\PhotoEdit Inc.; page 37 (top left) Don W. Fawcett\Photo Researchers, Inc.; page 37 (top middle) CNRI/Science Photo Library\Photo Researchers, Inc.; page 37 (top right) Peter Menzel\Stock Boston; page 42 Bill Longcore\Photo Researchers, Inc.; page 43 Saturn Stills\Photo Researchers, Inc.; page 47 ©The New Yorker Collection 2003 Michael Shaw from cartoonbank.com. All Rights Reserved; page 48 Christopher Brown/Stock Boston, Inc.\Stock Boston; page 54 (top) Petit Format/Nestle\Photo Researchers, Inc.; page 54 (middle) Science Pictures Ltd.\Photo Researchers, Inc.; page 54 (bottom) © Petit Format/Nestle/Science Source/Photo Researchers, Inc.; page 57 © The New Yorker Collection 1998 William Hamilton from cartoonbank.com. All Rights Reserved. page 60 Chris Harvey\Getty Images Inc. - Stone Allstock; page 62 Christopher Bissell\Getty Images Inc. - Stone Allstock; page 67 National Institutes of Health; page 68 Ruth Jenkinson\MIDIRS\Photo Researchers, Inc.; page 69 Robert Holmes\CORBIS- NY.

Chapter 3 Page 72 Myrleen Ferguson\PhotoEdit Inc.; page 73 Michelle Gabel \The Image Works; page 77 Jeff Greenberg\The Image Works; page 81 (left) Ellen Senisi\The Image Works; page 81 (right) Ellen Senisi\The Image Works; page 87 Courtesy Marcus E. Raichle, M.D., Washington University Medical Center, from research based on S.E. Petersen et al., Positron emission tomographic studies of the cortical anatomy of single-word processing. *Nature* 331:585–589 (1988); page 89 The Image Works; page 90 (top left) Laura Elliott\Jupiter Images Royalty Free; page 90 (top middle) Laura Dwight\Laura Dwight Photography; page 90 (top right) Petit Format\Photo Researchers, Inc.; page 90 (bottom left) Charles Gupton\Stock Boston; page 90 (bottom right) Skjold Photographs; page 94 Steve Outram\Stock Connection; page 100 Mark Richards/PhotoEdit/Courtesy of Joe Campos & Rosanne Kermoian; page 101 (top left) Getty Images, Inc.; page 101 (top middle) Getty Images, Inc.; page 101 (top right) Getty Images, Inc.; page 105 Rex Interstock\Stock Connection; page 106 © Dylan Ellis / CORBIS All Rights Reserved; page 107 A. Ramey\PhotoEdit Inc.; page 108 Pearson Education/PH College.

Chapter 4 Page 112 JGI/Blend Images\Corbis RF; page 113 © Ariel Skelley / CORBIS All Rights Reserved; page 115 © Mats Hallgren/ CORBIS All Rights Reserved; page 118 Drew Crawford\The Image Works; page 122 AP Wide World Photos; page 123 Bob Daemmrich\The Image Works; page 124 Express Newspapers; page 125 Rouse, Dominic\Getty Images Inc. - Image Bank; page 125 Tribune Media Services TMS Reprints; page 129 Michael Newman\PhotoEdit Inc.; page 131 ©The New Yorker Collection 2003 Christopher Weyant from cartoonbank.com. All Rights Reserved; page 135 Jeff Widener\CORBIS- NY; page 139 Dr. M. Goedert/Photo Researchers, Inc.; page 140 Bookheimer, S. Y., Strojwas, M. H., Cophen, M. S., Saunders, A. M., Pericak-Vance, M. A., Mazziotta, J., C., & Small, G. W. (2000, August 17). Patterns of brain activation in people at risk for Alzheimer's disease. *New England Journal of Medicine*, 343, 450-456. Copyright 2003 Massachusetts Medical Society. All right reserved. page 142 (top) PhotoDisc/Getty Images; page 142 (bottom) Ian Hooton © Dorling Kindersley; page 145 © Doranne Jacobson/International Images.

Chapter 5 Page 150 Alain Schroeder/ONOKY/Getty Images, Inc.; page 151 Image Sourcep \Corbis RF; page 152 (top) Bill Anderson\Photo Researchers, Inc.; page 152 (bottom) David Young-Wolff\PhotoEdit Inc.; page 155 Dave King © Dorling Kindersley; page 156 LEANNE TEMME\Photolibrary.com; page 158 (top) Laura Dwight\Laura Dwight Photography; page 158 (bottom) Laura Dwight\Laura Dwight Photography; page 160 Ron Radford\SuperStock, Inc.; page 161 (top) © Mick Stevens / Conde Nast Publications / www.cartoonbank.com Published in *The New Yorker* May 29, 2000. page 161 (bottom) Brian Fitzgerald/The Tribune\AP Wide World Photos; page 163 Irven DeVore\Anthro-Photo File; page 165 Mark Gamba\CORBIS- NY; page 167 Studio M\Stock Connection; page 169 Michael Newman\PhotoEdit Inc.

Chapter 6 Page 174 LEANNE TEMME\Photolibrary.com; page 175 Chris Lowe\Photolibrary.com; page 181 © Peter Turnley / CORBIS All Rights Reserved; page 182 Laura Dwight, PhotoEdit Inc.; page 183 Jose Azel\Aurora Photos, Inc.; page 184 Carolyn Rovee-Collier; page 185 Ann Purcell\Photo Researchers, Inc.; page 188 Ron Giling/Peter Arnold, Inc.; page 189 Robert Brenner\PhotoEdit Inc.; page 192 Mikael Karlsson\Arresting Images; page 193 Shaywitz, et. al. 2004.

Chapter 7 Page 198 Leanna Rathkelly\Getty Images Inc. - Stone Allstock; page 199 Shutterstock; page 202 Laura-Ann Petitto, McGill University; page 203 Erin Moroney LaBelle/The Image Works; page 209 Courtesy of G. Dehaene-Lamberts INSERM/CEA; page 212 (left) Laura Dwight Photography; page 212 (right) Giacomo Pirozzi\Panos Pictures; page 212 (middle) Earl & Nazima Kowall\CORBIS- NY; page 216 Christina Kennedy\PhotoEdit Inc.

Chapter 8 Page 220 Stockbroker\Alamy Images Royalty Free; page 221 Lauren Shear\Photo Researchers, Inc.; page 223 Wechsler Intelligence Scale for Children−Third Edition (WISC–III). Copyright © 1990 by NCS Pearson, Inc. Reproduced with permission. All rights reserved. Photo: Laura Dwight; page 227 ©Kevin Dodge / CORBIS All Rights Reserved; page 229 Robin Nelson\PhotoEdit Inc.; page 233 Bob Abraham \Pacific Stock; page 236 Bob Daemmrich\The Image Works; page 237 Kevin R. Morris\CORBIS- NY; page 238 Zephyr Picture,\Photolibrary.com; page 242 Richard Hutchings\Photo Researchers, Inc.

Chapter 9 Page 246 Enigma\Alamy Images; page 247 ©Ellen B. Senisi\Ellen Senisi; page 248 Tony Freeman\PhotoEdit Inc.; page 249 (top) Harlow Primate Laboratory/University of Wisconsin; page 249 (bottom) Mary Ainsworth, University of Virginia. Photo by Daniel Grogan; page 250 (top) William Hamilton/Johns Hopkins University\Mary Ainsworth; page 250 (bottom left) William Hamilton/Johns Hopkins University\Mary Ainsworth; page 250 (bottom right) William Hamilton/Johns Hopkins University\Mary Ainsworth; page 251 (top) Rob Wilke\Creative Eye/MIRA.com; page 251 (bottom) © Larry Williams/CORBIS; page 253 (top left) Courtesy Dr. Carroll Izard; page 253 (top right) Carroll Izard; page 253 (bottom left) Courtesy Dr. Carroll Izard; page 253 (bottom right) Courtesy Dr. Carroll Izard; page 255 Gary Conner\Jupiter Images - FoodPix - Creatas; page 257 © Image supplied courtesy of Eric Nelson, Ph.D./National Institute of Mental Health, Mood and Anxiety Disorders Program. page 258 Peter Byron\PhotoEdit Inc.; page 259 David Young-Wolff\PhotoEdit Inc.; page 261 (left) Nathan Benn\Woodfin Camp & Associates, Inc.; page 261 (right) Chad Ehlers\Stock Connection; page 268 Hughes Martin\CORBIS- NY; page 270 Roz Chast; page 271 Ellen B. Senisi\Ellen Senisi; page 274 Krista Greco\Merrill Education.

Chapter 10 Page 278 Gordon Wiltsie/National Geographic Image Collection; page 279 Bernd Vogel\Corbis RF; page 281 Dwight, Laura\Omni-Photo Communications, Inc.; page 283 Brand X Pictures\Alamy Images; page 284 Corbis RF; page 285 (top) Marilyn Humphries\The Image Works; page 286 Altrendo Images\Getty Images - Creative Express Royalty Free; page 289 Robert Brenner\PhotoEdit Inc.; page 290 (top) Cleve Bryant\PhotoEdit Inc.; page 290 (bottom) Doonesbury © 1997 G.B. Trudeau. Reprinted with permission of Universal Press Syndicate. All rights reserved. page 291 © LWA-Dann Tardif / CORBIS All Rights Reserved; page 295 Annie Griffiths Belt\CORBIS- NY; page 296 Susan Van Etten\PhotoEdit Inc.; page 298 (top) Penny Wolin; page 299 Rhoda Sidney\The Image Works; page 301 L.D. Gordon\Getty Images Inc. - Image Bank; page 302 David Young-Wolff\PhotoEdit Inc.

Chapter 11 Page 306 © Robert Trippett/SIPA Press; page 307 David Young-Wolff\PhotoEdit Inc.; page 308 \Corbis RF; page 311 Caroline Woodham\Stock Connection; page 313 Syracuse Newspapers/Randi Anglin\The Image Works; page 316 Tony Freeman\PhotoEdit Inc.; page 318 Jose Luis Pelaez\CORBIS- NY; page 320 (bottom) Myrleen Ferguson Cate\PhotoEdit Inc.; page 321 Cary Wolinsky\Aurora Photos, Inc.; page 323 Catherine Ursillo\Photo Researchers, Inc.; page 325 (top) Albert Bandura, D. Ross & S.A. Ross, Imitation of film-mediated aggressive models. "Journal of Abnormal and Social Psychology", 1963, 66. P. 8. page 325 (bottom) Jonathan Nourok\PhotoEdit Inc.; page 328 Dwayne Newton\PhotoEdit Inc.; page 329 Michael Newman\PhotoEdit Inc.; page 331 AP Wide World Photos.

Chapter 12 Page 336 Michael Newman\PhotoEdit Inc.; page 337 Margaret Salmon and Dean Wiand; page 338 George Goodwin\George Goodwin Photography; page 339 (left) Laura Dwight\Laura Dwight Photography; page 339 (right) Ursula Markus\Photo Researchers, Inc.; page 341 (left) Corbis RF; page 341 (right) Michael Newman\PhotoEdit Inc.; page 344 David Young-Wolff\PhotoEdit Inc.; page 348 (top) Paula Lerner\Woodfin Camp & Associates, Inc.; page 348 (bottom) Jack Star \Getty Images, Inc. - PhotoDisc; page 349 Evan Johnson; page 350 Jim Cummins\Getty Images, Inc. - Taxi; page 354 Haruki Sato/HAGA\The Image Works; page 357 (top) China Tourism Press. Liu, Yang\Getty Images Inc. - Image Bank; page 358 Getty Images - Stockbyte, Royalty Free; page 360 B. Bachmann\The Image Works; page 362 (top) © The New Yorker Collection 1994 Robert Weber from cartoonbank.com. All Right Reserved; page 362 (bottom) BILL LOSH\Getty Images, Inc. - Taxi; page 365 Michael Newman\PhotoEdit Inc.

Chapter 13 Page 370 Steve Dunwell\Photolibrary.com -; page 371 David Young-Wolff\PhotoEdit Inc.; page 372 Laura Dwight\Laura Dwight Photography; page 373 (top) Jonathan Nourok\PhotoEdit Inc.; page 373 (bottom) ©The New Yorker Collection 2002 Bruce Eric Kaplan from cartoonbank.com. All Rights Reserved; page 374 Ellen Senisi; page 375 Billy Barnes\PhotoEdit Inc.; page 376 Bob Daemmrich\Stock Boston; page 378 Spencer Grant\PhotoEdit Inc.; page 380 Ron Chapple\Getty Images, Inc. - Taxi; page 383 Novastock\Stock Connection; page 386 Photolibrary.com; page 388 Getty Images, Inc.- Photodisc./Royalty Free; page 389 Donna Day\Getty Images, Inc.- Photodisc./Royalty Free; page 391 Flip Chalfant\Flip Chalfant Photography; page 393 ©The New Yorker Collection 2005 Barbara Smaller from cartoonbank.com. All Rights Reserved; page 394 Richard Lord\The Image Works; page 395 Elizabeth Crews\Elizabeth Crews Photography; page 396 (left) Jupiter Images Royalty Free; page 396 (right) Robert S. Feldman.

Chapter 14 Page 402 James Frank\Stock Connection; page 403 © C3916 Patrick van Katwijk/dpa/CORBIS All Rights Reserved; page 405 Krista Greco\Merrill Education; page 406 © 2002 The New Yorker Collection, Bruce Eric Kaplan from cartoonbank.com. All Rights Reserved. page 410 ©Ellen B. Senisi\Ellen Senisi; page 413 Getty Images - Digital Vision; page 414 Vicki

Figures and Tables

Chapter 1 Figure 1-2 p. 18 Bronfenbrenner's Approach to Development / From HANDBOOK OF CHILD PSYCHOLOGY, Volume One: Theoretical Models of Human Development, Fifth edition by W. Damon (ed.). Copyright © 1998. Reprinted by permission of John Wiley & Sons, Inc.

Chapter 2 Figure 2-7 p. 49 Genetics and IQ / From Bouchard, T. J. Jr. & McGue, M. (1981). Familial Studies of Intelligence: A Review. *Science, 212*, 1055–1059. Reprinted by permission of Professor Thomas J. Bouchard, Jr.; Figure 2-11 p. 58 Teratogen Sensitivity / From Moore, K. L. BEFORE WE ARE BORN: Basic Embryology and Birth Defects (Philadelphia: Saunders, 1974), p. 96 with permission from Elsevier.

Chapter 3 Figure 3-7 p. 85 (top) The Neuron / From HUMAN ANATOMY 5th edition by K. Van De Graaff, p. 339. Copyright © 2000 by The McGraw-Hill Companies. Reprinted by permission of the publisher; Figure 3-8 p. 85 (bottom) Neuron Networks / Reprinted by permission of the publisher from THE POSTNATAL DEVELOPMENT OF THE HUMAN CEREBRAL CORTEX, VOL I-VIII by Jesse LeRoy Conel, Cambridge, Mass.: Harvard University Press, Copyright 1939, © 1975 by the President and Fellows of Harvard College; Figure 3-10 p. 88 (top) Brain Growth Spurt / From *Newsletter of the Society for Research in Child Development*, Fisher & Rose (1995), pp. 3–16. Published by Society for Research in Child Development; Figure 3-11 p. 88 (bottom) Pruning Gray Matter / From "In Vivo Evidence for Post-Adolescent Brain Maturation in Frontal and Striatal Regions" by E. R. Sowell, P. M. Thompson, C. J. Holmes, T. L. Jernigan & A. W. Toga, *Nature Neuroscience*, (1999) 2, No. 10, p. 859. Copyright © 19991 by Macmillan Publishers Ltd. Reprinted by permission of Macmillan Publishers Ltd; Table 3-3 p. 93 Major Gross Skills in Early Childhood / From Corbin, C. A TEXTBOOK OF MOTOR DEVELOPMENT (Dubuque, IA: Brown, 1973). Reprinted by permission of McGraw-Hill; Table 3-4 p. 95 Milestones of Fine Motor Development / Adapted from "The Denver II: A Major Revision and Restandardization of the Denver Developmental Screening Test" by W. K. Frankenburg, J. Dodds, P. Archer, H. Shapiro & B. Bresnick, *Pediatrics* (1992), 89, 91–97. Copyright © 1992. Reprinted by permission of American Academy of Pediatrics.

Chapter 4 Table 4-1 p. 117 How Stressed Are You? / Test from "A Global Measure of Perceived Stress" by S. Cohen, T. Kamarck & R. Mermelstein, *Journal of Health & Social Behavior* (1983), *24*, pp. 385–396. Copyright © 1983. Reprinted by permission of Sage Publications; Table 4-2 p. 120 How to Elicit the Relaxation Response / From Dr. Herbert Benson, Mind & Body Medical Institute, MA; Figure 4-5 p. 126 Numbers of Preschool Children Taking Medication for Behavioral Problems / From "Trends in Prescribing of Psychotropic Medications to Preschoolers" by J. M. Zito, D. J. Safer, S. dosReis, J. F. Gardener, M. Boles & F. Lynch, *Journal of the American Medical Association*, (2000), *283*, 1025–1030. Copyright © 2000. Reprinted by permission of the American Medical Association; Figure 4-7 p. 127 Downward Trend / Monitoring the Future - PUBLIC DOMAIN/NR; Figure 4-8 p. 128 Binge Drinking Among College Students / From "Trends in College Binge Drinking During a Period of Increased Prevention Efforts: Findings from 4 Harvard School of Public Health College Alcohol Study Surveys: 1993–2001" by H. Wechsler, J. E. Lee, M. Kuo, M. Seibring, T.F. Nelson & H. Lee, *Journal of American College Health* (2001) 50, No.5. Copyright © 2002. Reprinted by permission of Taylor & Francis Informa UK Ltd.; Figure 4-10 p. 132 The Result of Fitness: Longevity / Adapted from "Physical Fitness and All-Cause Mortality: A Perspective Study of Healthy Men and Women" by S. N. Blair, H. W. Kohl, R.S. Paffenberger, D.G. Clark, K. H. Cooper & L. W. Gibbons, *Journal of the American Medical Association* (1989), *282*, pp. 2395–2401. Copyright © 1989. Reprinted by permission of the American Medical Association; Figure 4-11 p. 133 (Source: Jones, J. (2008, December 1). Healthcare access, cost are top health concerns. Gallup Poll, reported at http://www.gallup.com/poll/112516/healthcare-access-cost-top-health-concerns.aspx). Reprinted by permission; Figure 4-12 p. 135 Tracking Murder / Fair Use - derived from several UN publications.

Chapter 7 Table 7-2 p. 205 Growing Speech Capabilities From THE LANGUAGE INSTINCT by Steven Pinker. Copyright © 1994 by Steven Pinker. Reprinted by permission of HarperCollins Publishers; Table 7-2 p. 205 Growing Speech Capabilities / Penguin for UK rights; Figure 7-4 p. 213 Gender Differences in Language / Adapted from "The Babytalk Register: Parents' Use of Diminutives" by J. B. Gleason, R. U. Perlmann, R. Ely & D. W. Evans in HANDBOOK OF RESEARCH IN LANGUAGE DEVELOPMENT USING CHILDES by J. L. Sokolov & C. E. Snow (eds.). Copyright © 1991. Reprinted by permission of Erlbaum; Figure 7-5 p. 215 Different Language Exposure / Figure 7, p. 68 from MEANINGFUL DIFFERENCES IN THE EVERYDAY EXPERIENCES OF YOUNG AMERICAN CHILDREN by B. Hart & T. R. Risley. Copyright © 1995. Reprinted by permission of Paul H. Brookes Publishing Co., Inc., Baltimore, MD.

Chapter 8 Figure 8-3 p. 226 Sample from the Raven Progressive Matrices Test / Simulated Item similar to those in the *Raven's Progressive Matrices*. Copyright © by 1998 NCS Pearson, Inc. Reproduced with permission. All rights reserved; Figure 8-5 p. 231 Sample Items from a Test That Taps Four Domains of Intelligence / From "The Geocentric View of Intelligence and Job Performance Is Wrong" by R. J. Sternberg & R. K. Wagner, *Current Directions in Psychological Science* (1993), *2*, 105. Copyright © 1993. Reprinted by permission of John Wiley and Sons; Figure 8-6 p. 232 Creativity and Age / From "Age and Creative Productivity" by W. Dennis, *Journal of Gerontology* (1966), 21, pp. 1–8. Copyright © 1966. Reprinted by permission of The Gerontological Society of America; Table 8-2 p. 234 Sample Items from the Bayley Scales of Infant Development / *Bayley Scales of Infant Development, Second Edition (BSID-II)*. Copyright © 1993 NCS Pearson Inc. Reproduced with permission. All rights reserved; Figure 8-7 p. 239 (top) Changes in Crystalized and Fluid Intelligence / From Schaie, W. (1985). LONGITUDINAL STUDIES OF ADULT PSYCHOLOGICAL DEVELOPMENT, Guilford Press; Figure 8-8 p. 239 (bottom) Changes in Intellectual Functioning / K. Warner Schaiekws@psu.edu.

Chapter 9 Figure 9-3 p. 254 Separation Anxiety / Reprinted by permission of the publisher from INFANCY: ITS PLACE IN HUMAN DEVELOPMENT by Jerome Kagan, Richard B. Kearsley, and Philip R. Zelazo, p. 107, Cambridge, Mass.: Harvard University Press, Copyright © 1978 by the President and Fellows of Harvard College; Figure 9-5 p. 260 Adolescent Difficulties / From "Suicide: A Review of Calls to an Adolescent Peer Listening Phone Service" by K. E. Boehm in *Child Psychiatry and Human Development* (September 1, 1995), *26*. Copyright © 1995. Reprinted by permission of Springer Science & Business Media.

Chapter 10 Table 10-1 p. 285 (bottom) Marcia's Four Categories of Adolescent Development / From Marcia, J. E. (1980). "Identity in Adolescence." In J. Adelson (ed.) HANDBOOK OF ADOLESCENT PSYCHOLOGY. Wiley. Reprinted by permission of the publisher; Figure 10-3 p. 298 (bottom) Immigrants in the US, Number & Percent, / Data for 1900–2000 from Dicennial Census. For 2007, data from the March Current Population Survey. As cited in Camarota, S. A. (2007). Immigrants in the United States [emd] 2007: A profile of America's foreign-born population. Washington, DC: Center for Immigration Studies; Figure 10-4 p. 301 *Monthly Labor Review.*

Chapter 11 Figure 11-1 p. 320 (top) Objects Considered Essential or Very Important / Figure 14 from THE AMERICAN FRESHMAN: Forty Years Trends, UCLA Higher Education Research Institute. Copyright © 2008 by The Regents of the University of California. Reprinted by permission. All rights reserved; Figure 11-3 p. 326 Acts of Violence / From Center for Media & Public Affairs, 1995. Reprinted by permission; Figure 11-4 p. 327 United Nations Surveys on Crime Trends and the Operations of Criminal Justice Systems (CTS), 2000.

Chapter 12 Figure 12-1 p. 347 Adolescents and Sexual Activity / From Guttmacher Institute, "Facts on American teens' sexual and reproductive health," *In Brief*, New York: Guttmacher Institute, 2010, http://www.guttmacher.org/pubs/FB-ATSRH.pdf, accessed 04/21/2010; Table 12-3 p. 357 (bottom) Most Desired Characteristics in a Marriage Partner / From "International Preferences in Selecting Mates: A Study of 37 Cultures" by D. M. Buss, et al., *Journal of Cross-Cultural Psychology* (1990), *21*, 5–47. Copyright © 1990. Reprinted by permission of Sage Publications.

Chapter 13 Figure 13-7 p. 387 Division of Labor / Results of GPSS Lifestyle Poll, 2007: "Who is most likely to do each of the following in your household? Based on 594 adults who are currently married." Reprinted by permission of Gallup.

Chapter 14 Figure 14-3 p. 411 Middle School Configurations / From J. Juvonen, V. Le, T. Kaganoff, C. Augustine & L. Constant (2004). FOCUS ON THE WONDER YEARS: Challenges Facing the American Middle School. Rand Coproration, Santa Monica, CA. Reprinted by permission of the publisher; Table 14-1 p. 416 Gender Bias in the Classroom / From STILL FAILING AT FAIRNESS: How Gender Bias Cheats Girls and Boys in School and What We Can Do About It by David Sadker & Karen Zittleman. Copyright © 1994 by Myra Sadker and David Sadker. Copyright © 2009 by David Sadker and Karen Zittleman. Reprinted by permission by Scribner, a division of Simon & Schuster, Inc. and the authors; Table 14-1 p. 416 Gender Bias in the Classroom / Professor David Sadker/Professor Karen Zittleman; Figure 14-9 p. 418 Spending Time / From "How U.S. Children and Adolescents Spend Time: What It Does (and Doesn't) Tell Us About Their Development" by R. W. Larson, *Current Directions in Psychological Science* (2001), *10*(5), 160–164. Copyright © 2001. Reprinted by permission of John Wiley and Sons; Figure 14-13 p. 425 Four Outcomes of Acculturation / From J. Phinney, B. Lochner & R. Murphy (1990). "Ethnic Identity Development and Psychological Adjustment in Adolescence" in ADVANCES IN ADOLESCENT MENTAL HEALTH. Volume 5. Ethnic Issues by A. Stiffman & L. Davis (eds.). Copyright © 1990. Reprinted by permission of Sage Publications; Table 14-3 p. 430 National Pride by Country / From Smith, T.W. & Seokho, K. (2006). "National Pride in Cross-National and Temporal Perspective," *International Journal of Public Opinion Research, 18*, 127–136. Copyright © 2006. Reprinted by permission of Dr. Tom W. Smith/GSS Director.

Chapter 15 Figure 15-1 p. 439 Adding Years / From "Cause of Death and Active Life Expectancy in the Older Population of the United States" by M. D. Hayward, E. M. Crimmins & Y. Saito, *Journal of Aging & Health*, (1997), 122–131. Copyright © 1991. Reprinted by permission of Sage Publications; Table 15-1 p. 445 Dying Hard: Experiences of 4,301 Patients with End-of-Life Care / From "A Controlled Trial to Improve Care for Seriously Ill Hospitalized Patients. The Study to Understand Prognoses and Preferences for Outcomes and Risks of Treatment (SUPPORT)" by W. A. Knaus, A. F. Conners, N. V. Dawson, N. A. Desbitens, W. J. Fulkerson, Jr., L. Goldman, J. Lynn & R. K. Oye, *Journal of the American Medical Association* (1995, November 22) 273, pp. 1591–1598. Copyright © 1995. Reprinted by permission of the American Medical Association; Figure 15-4 p. 447 How Long do "Terminal" Patients Really Live? / From J. Lynn et al. (1997). Perceptions by Family Members of the Dying Experience of Older and Seriously Ill Patients. *Annals of Internal Medicine, 126*, 164–165.

Name Index

Subject Index

530

What's new in PSYCHOLOGY

ABNORMAL PSYCHOLOGY
Beidel, Bulik & Stanley Abnormal Psychology ©2010
9780132216128 / 0132216124

Butcher, Mineka & Hooley Abnormal Psychology: Core Concepts, 2/e ©2011
9780205765317 / 0205765319

Nevid, Rathus & Greene Abnormal Psychology in a Changing World, 8/e
©2011, 9780205773404 / 0205773400 **Due Fall 2010**

ADJUSTMENT / HUMAN RELATIONS
Duffy, Kirsh & Atwater Psychology for Living: Adjustment, Growth and
Behavior, 10/e ©2011,
9780205790364 / 0205790364

ADOLESCENT DEVELOPMENT
Arnett Adolescence and Emerging Adulthood: A Cultural Approach, 4/e ©2010
9780138144586 / 0138144583

Dolgin The Adolescent, 13e ©2011
9780205731367 / 0205731368

ADULTHOOD & AGING
Mason Adulthood and Aging ©2011
9780205433513 / 0205433510 **Due Fall 2010**

BEHAVIOR MODIFICATION
Martin & Pear Behavior Modification, 9/e ©2011
9780205792726 / 0205792723

CHILD DEVELOPMENT (Chronological Approach)
Berk Infants, Children, and Adolescents, 7/e ©2011
9780205718160 / 0205718167

Cook & Cook The World of Children, 2/e ©2010
9780205685929 / 0205685927

LIFESPAN DEVELOPMENT (Topical Approach)
Bee & Boyd The Developing Child, 12/e ©2010
9780205685936 / 0205685935

Kail Children and Their Development, 5/e ©2010
9780205654154 / 0205654150

CHILD PSYCHOPATHOLOGY
Association for Psychological Science & Dodge
Current Directions in Child Psychopathology ©2010
9780205680139 / 0205680135

CLOSE RELATIONSHIPS / INTERPERSONAL
Erber & Erber Intimate Relationships:
Issues, Theories, and Research, 2/e ©2011
9780205454464 / 0205454461

COGNITION
Ashcraft & Radvansky Cognition, 5/e ©2010
9780136050469 / 0136050468

Levitin Foundations of Cognitive Psychology ©2011
9780205711475 / 0205711472

COMMUNITY PSYCHOLOGY
Association for Psychological Science, Shinn & Thaden
Current Directions in Community Psychology ©2010
9780205680108 / 0205680100

Moritsugu, Wong, & Duffy
Community Psychology, 4/e ©2010
9780205627714 / 0205627714

CROSS-CULTURAL
MULTICULTURAL PSYCHOLOGY
White, Parham & Ajamu Psychology of Blacks, 4/e ©2011
9780131827738 / 0131827731 **Due Fall 2010**

DRUGS AND BEHAVIOR
Ettinger Psychopharmacology ©2011
9780136013068 / 0136013066 **Due Fall 2010**

HEALTH PSYCHOLOGY
Ragin Health Psychology ©2011
9780131962972 / 0131962973 **Due Fall 2010**

HUMAN SEXUALITY
Rathus, Nevid & Fichner-Rathus Human Sexuality in a
World of Diversity, 8/e ©2011
9780205786060 / 0205786065

Welch THINK Human Sexuality ©2011
9780205777716 / 0205777716

INDUSTRIAL / ORGANIZATIONAL PSYCHOLOGY
Schultz & Schultz Psychology and Work Today, 10/e ©2010
9780205683581 / 0205683584

INFANT DEVELOPMENT
Gross Infancy: From Birth to Age 3, 2/e ©2011
9780205734191 / 0205734197

INTRODUCTORY PSYCHOLOGY
Gerrig & Zimbardo Psychology and Life, 19/e ©2010
9780205685912 / 0205685919

Landrum & Davis The Psychology Major: Career Options and
Strategies for Success, 4/e ©2010
9780205684687 / 0205684688

Wade & Tavris Psychology 10/e ©2011
9780205711468 / 0205711464

Wood, Wood & Boyd The World of Psychology, 7/e ©2011
9780205763733 / 0205763731

INTRODUCTORY PSYCHOLOGY BRIEF
Baird THINK Psychology, 2/e ©2011
9780132128407 / 0132128403 **Due Fall 2010**

Ciccarelli & White Psychology: An Exploration ©2010
9780132302722 / 0132302721

Kosslyn & Rosenberg Psychology in Context, 4/e ©2011
9780205777167 / 0205777163 **Due Fall 2010**

Lilienfeld, Lynn, Namy & Woolf Psychology:
A Framework for Everyday Thinking ©2010
9780205650484 / 0205650481

Morris & Maisto Understanding Psychology 9/e (paperback) ©2010
9780205769063 / 0205769063

Morris & Maisto Understanding Psychology 9/e (casebound) ©2010
9780205769384 / 0205769381

INTRODUCTION TO COUNSELING AND PSYCHOTHERAPY

Baird The Internship, Practicum, and
Field Placement Handbook, 6/e ©2011
97802058049621 / 0205804969

LIFESPAN DEVELOPMENT (Chronological Approach)

Berk Development Through the Lifespan, 5/e ©2010
9780205687930 / 0205687938

Berk Exploring Lifespan Development, 2/e ©2011
9780205748594 / 0205748597

Craig & Dunn Understanding Human Development, 2/e ©2010
9780205753079 / 0205753078

Feldman Development Across the Life Span, 6/e ©2011
9780205805914 / 0205805914

LIFESPAN DEVELOPMENT (Topical Approach)

Feldman Life Span Development: A Topical Approach ©2011
9780205759569 / 0205759564

MORAL DEVELOPMENT

Gibbs Moral Development and Reality: Beyond the Theories of Kohlberg
and Hoffman, 2/e ©2010
9780205595242 / 0205595243

MOTIVATION

Deckers Motivation: Biological, Psychological, and Environmental, 3/e ©2010
9780205610815 / 0205610811

Association for Psychological Science & Sheldon
Current Directions in Motivation and Emotion ©2010
9780205680115 / 0205680119

PERSONALITY PSYCHOLOGY

Greene MMPI-2/MMPI: An Interpretive Manual, 3/e ©2011
9780205535859 / 0205535852 *Due Fall 2010*

Hergenhahn & Olson Theories of Personality, 8/e ©2011
9780205798780 / 0205798780

PHYSIOLOGICALBIOPSYCHOLOGY

Carlson Foundations of Behavioral Neuroscience, 8/e ©2011
9780205790357 / 0205790356

Pinel Biopsychology, 8e ©2011
9780205832569 / 0205832563

PROGRAM EVALUATION

Posavac & Carey Program Evaluation: Methods and
Case Studies, 8/e ©2011
9780205804979 / 0205804977

SENSATION PERCEPTION

Foley & Matlin Sensation and Perception, 5/e ©2010
9780205579808 / 0205579809

SOCIAL PSYCHOLOGY

Aronson, Wilson & Akert Social Psychology, 7/e ©2010
9780138144784 / 0138144788

Kenrick, Neuberg & Cialdini Social Psychology, 5/e ©2010
9780205698073 / 0205698077

STATISTICS

Aron, Aron & Coups Statistics for the Behavioral
and Social Sciences, 5/e ©2011
9780205797257 / 0205797253

George & Mallery SPSS for Windows Step by Step:
A Simple Guide and Reference, 17.0 Update, 10/e ©2010
9780205755615 / 0205755615

Salkind SPSS Quick Start ©2011
9780205735778 / 0205735770

Yockey SPSS Demystified, 2/e ©2011
9780205735822 / 0205735827 *Due Fall 2010*

THEORIES OF DEVELOPMENT

Crain Theories of Development: Concepts and
Applications, 6/e ©2011
9780205810468 / 0205810462

Green & Piel Theories of Human Development: A Comparative
Approach, 2/e ©2010
9780205665686 / 0205665683

POSITIVE PSYCHOLOGY

Baumgardner & Crothers Positive Psychology ©2009
9780131744417 / 0131744410

PSYCHOLOGICAL TESTING AND MEASUREMENT

Gregory Psychological Testing:
History, Principles and Applications, 6/e ©2011
9780205782147 / 0205782140

PSYCHOLOGY OF SEX AND GENDER

Association for Psychological Science & Goldberg
Current Directions in Gender Psychology ©2010
9780205680122 / 0205680127

Etaugh & Bridges Women's Lives:
A Psychological Exploration, 2/e ©2010
9780205594184 / 0205594182

RESEARCH METHODS EXPERIMENTAL METHODS

Christensen & Johnson Research Methods and
Design in Psychology, 11/e ©2011
9780205701650 / 0205701655

To learn more about one of these books or to order copies online, visit us at www.pearsonhighered.com